The USC Trojans
Football Encyclopedia

Also by Richard J. Shmelter

*The Los Angeles Lakers Encyclopedia* (2013)

*The Raiders Encyclopedia: All Players, Coaches, Games and More through 2009–2010* (2011)

# The USC Trojans Football Encyclopedia

RICHARD J. SHMELTER

McFarland & Company, Inc., Publishers
*Jefferson, North Carolina*

Library of Congress Cataloguing-in-Publication Data

Shmelter, Richard J., 1959–
The USC Trojans football encyclopedia / Richard J. Shmelter.
p. cm.
Includes bibliographical references and index.

**ISBN 978-0-7864-6950-5 (softcover : acid free paper) ♾**
**ISBN 978-1-4766-1511-0 (ebook)**

1. University of Southern California—Football—History.
2. Southern California Trojans (Football team)—History. I. Title.
GV958.U5857S45 2014 796.332'630979494—dc23 2014007586

British Library cataloguing data are available



On the cover: USC's Reggie Bush (5) holds off a UCLA defender in a game at the Los Angeles Memorial Coliseum on December 3, 2005 (Associated Press/Kim D. Johnson)

Printed in the United States of America

*McFarland & Company, Inc., Publishers*
*Box 611, Jefferson, North Carolina 28640*
*www.mcfarlandpub.com*

To every player, coach, and all others, past and present, who have made the University of Southern California Trojans one of the elite college football programs in the country.

And as always, to my little angel, who watches over me from above and continuously serves as a driving force in my life. You gave me the ultimate honor of being called a daddy, and that pride will never diminish, but only grow with the passing of time.

# Acknowledgments

It is often claimed that the life of an author is one of solitude. However, I find the exact opposite to be true. I have enjoyed a vast support system of family, friends, and others who may have crossed my path for only a brief instant, and kind words and encouragement have been abundant, as well as critiques that have only improved my work. To all of those who listened to my ideas, and helped to get the words onto paper, I thank you.

When one travels life's path, the journey is fulfilled when a certain special individual shares it, and deals with the good and bad of life with a writer. My wife Helen (Molly) serves as a sounding board and editor, despite being overloaded by the task on more than one occasion. Through it all she is there for me, time and time again. With her love and understanding, which is tested often, she guides me through the process of making my plans and dreams a reality. Thank you, my dear, for everything, everyday, and always.

To my mom and dad, Arlene and the late Joseph, who gave me life, a wonderful childhood, and the opportunity to share my hopes and dreams with them on countless occasions. I am proud to have had these kind and thoughtful people as my parents.

Every project has a beginning, the moment when that idea first strikes. Many times it comes up on its own over the course of one's day. Other times it comes from within a social circle, and due to a kind gesture on the part of two dear friends, this project went from conception to maturation. Jim and Cindy Hampshire initially brought the idea of a USC project to me. They then took the time to listen, encourage, proofread, and make me feel like there was nothing I could not accomplish, not only on this occasion, but future ventures as well.

Over the course of not only this project, but on previous ones, Matt Victor was there to help me work smarter instead of harder. He allowed me an opportunity to talk in great length about this project while offering excellent advice. As always, thank you, my friend!

The same can be said of Bob Martin, who allowed me to share my passion for this project and others as well. He was there to listen, proofread, and offer constant encouragement. I know that Hawaii beckons you, my friend, and may you always have the surf, sand, and sunset of that island paradise near you.

I can be proud of this work due to assistance from the archive department at the University of Southern California. If there were an All-America team for university archive departments, then USC would rule that category. University archivist Claude Zachary was indeed invaluable in my quest for information related to game results and many other items of interest. He guided me toward the university's archives, and opened up a treasure trove of information. Senior library assistant at USC Susan Hikida led me in the right direction in my quest to find missing links in the history of the football program. Tim Tessalone, the head of USC's Sports Information Office in Athletics, helped me find hard-to-obtain information that allowed me to complete this project with confidence.

And finally, to everyone I know personally or encountered briefly in Los Angeles, I appreciate your encouragement and enthusiasm constantly sparking my passion for projects involving the incredible City of Angels.

# Table of Contents


*Acknowledgments* vi

*Preface* 1

*Introduction: The City of Angels and the Land of Troy* 3

**One** The Seasons 7

**Two** All-Time Trojan Greats 193

**Three** All-Time Rosters (1888–2012) 244

**Four** All-Time Head Coaches 260

**Five** Trojan Traditions 292

**Six** Awards and Honors 308

*Chapter Notes* 321

*Bibliography* 332

*Index* 333

# Preface

Ah, the allure of endless summers on beaches named Venice, Santa Monica, and Malibu. Warm days, golden sand, bright sunshine glistening on the majestic Pacific Ocean, palm trees slightly waving, as if beckoning the masses to join in this Golden State utopia. California dreaming personified.

This nirvana gives way to a California sunset virtually unmatched in its splendor. Within hours, the sun reappears to greet another glorious day in the "Wonder City of the West." However, despite year-round sunshine, with the mercury hovering consistently in the 70-degree range, the boys of summer who occupy Los Angeles' green cathedral in Chavez Ravine hang up their Dodger caps and uniforms and are replaced by autumn's warriors. It is then in the City of Angels that the sports-minded focus travels 22 miles east of the beaches. At 3911 South Figueroa Street the perennial alpha dogs of the collegiate football ranks reside in one of the grandest structures dedicated to athletic competition, the Los Angeles Memorial Coliseum, where the legacy of the USC Trojan football team continues to be a source of pride for all those who embrace the Cardinal and Gold.

Conquest is defined as something acquired by defeating a foe. Greatness is the quality of being eminent. A conquest of greatness is therefore something many strive for, but only a select few can possess. Ever since Rutgers and Princeton played the first college football game in New Brunswick, New Jersey, in 1869, the quest for gridiron supremacy has been a driving force on campuses across the United States.

The University of Southern California is no different than any other institution of higher learning when it comes to pursuing success on the football field. What separates the USC Trojans from most of their contemporaries is that they have managed to maintain a level of excellence since their first-ever game on November 14, 1888, which ended with USC recording a 16–0 win over the Alliance Athletic Club. At times, like all mortals, they have stumbled. Unlike many, they have never truly fallen, as their heritage attests.

As of 2013, the USC football program has won 11 national championships and 38 conference titles. It has produced more than 150 All-Americans, a .702 all-time winning percentage, and seven Heisman Trophy winners. All these accolades are true testaments to the Cardinal and Gold's conquest of greatness, and this incredible saga is presented within these pages for Trojan faithful to embrace.

This encyclopedia dedicated to USC's incredible football program initially delves into the formation of the university and the city of Los Angeles, whose growth was parallel, with both becoming revered entities on a worldwide scale. Following the introduction, the first section supplies all vital information related to each season of the team's existence.

Many of the all-time greats of Troy have their achievements discussed in the second section, and an all-time roster, from 1888 through 2012, is provided in section three. A look at those men who guided the USC football program from the sidelines makes up the fourth section, which includes biographies of all the head coaches in USC history.

The fifth section is dedicated to all the traditions that complement the football program. Finally, the sixth section presents awards and honors bestowed upon players and coaches through the years.

Though I yearned with all the passion one could muster, I never had the privilege of wearing the Cardinal and Gold as a player, or attending the University of Southern California as a student. After watching a USC-UCLA football game as an adolescent, I forged a bond with the Trojans that I hoped would someday allow me to be a part of the greatness that is the Land of Troy. Thanks to the written word, and a publisher's belief in my quest, this labor of love dedicated to the USC Trojan football program allowed me the opportunity to finally be a part of this incredible university. It is an honor, as well as a humbling experience, that will never fade, much like the glorious history of the Trojans, presented within these pages.

# Introduction: The City of Angels and the Land of Troy

Anyone who has had the privilege of driving along the Pacific Coast Highway during the summertime can attest to the majestic views before their eyes. Palm trees, sunshine, and golden sandy beaches reach as far west as possible in the continental United States, and give way to the Pacific Ocean, where the sunlight striking the water resembles diamonds. It is this scenery that provided the inspiration for California music groups like the Beach Boys, Jan & Dean, and a host of others, to produce songs associated with Los Angeles' version of "Fun in the Sun."

Long before cruising along the coast was common, Portuguese explorer Juan Rodriguez Cabrillo took the ultimate trip, 420 years before songs celebrating summer were heard. In the summer of 1542, Cabrillo, sailing under the flag of Spain, became the first European to witness the beauty of what would become Los Angeles more than two hundred years later.

In 1769 Captain Gaspar de Portola and his Spanish land party set out to examine the area for sites that could be used for Franciscan friars to build missions and settlements for civilians.[1] On September 4, 1781, the official founding of Los Angeles occurred with 44 settlers gathering at San Gabriel Mission.

There is some debate among historians as to the original name given to the area. Doyce P. Nunis claimed that the Spanish dubbed the area "El Pueblo de la Reyna de los Angeles," "the Town of the Queen of the Angels." To back his claim, Nunis referred to a 1785 map that had the name on it. However, diocesan archivist Frank Weber stated that the map was incorrect. His belief was that the founders called the area "El Pueblo de Nuestra Senora de los Angeles de Porciuncula," "the Town of Our Lady of the Angeles of Porciuncula."[2] When it was all said and done, the Spanish and Mexican civilians were too busy making a life for themselves, and shortened it to "El Pueblo de los Angeles." By 1835, Mexico elevated the status of the area to a city, and in 1850, the California legislature incorporated it as the City of Los Angeles.[3]

From the time of its founding until Mexico became free of Spanish rule in 1821, Los Angeles grew in population to a few hundred. The reign of Mexico over Los Angeles lasted until war waged between the United States and Mexico from 1846 to 1848. United States forces took control of Los Angeles when they captured the city in 1847, but the bulk of the population that remained was of Mexican descent.

When gold was discovered in 1848, a rush of people from around the United States converged on the area with hopes of striking it rich. With the state of California under the control of the United States following the Mexican War, Los Angeles was far from the glamour capital of the world it grew into.

Between 1850 and 1870, Los Angeles had a reputation as a breeding ground for crime. Occupied by countless prostitutes, murderers, and thieves, many coming from other regions of the country attempting to escape arrest for previous acts of unlawfulness, Los Angeles was a rough, wide-open town, where murder happened on a daily basis, and other forms of criminal activity as well.[4]

Despite the woes suffered by Los Angeles in its early years, it rose to become one of the most renowned metropolises in the world. The amazing thing about its growth is that it started off without a natural harbor, no ample fuel source or water supply. On top of everything else, Los Angeles was totally cut off from a vast portion of the United States, with a scalding desert and massive mountains standing in the path to the city.[5]

With the odds stacked against the city, the cliché "All good things come in threes" proved true. Located some 250 miles northeast of Los Angeles is the Owens River, which solved the problem of obtaining a water supply. When Juan Rodriquez Cabrillo was on his expedition in 1542, he saw what came to be called "the Bay of Smokes," later called San Pedro Bay. This area, located about 20 miles south of what became downtown Los Angeles, was at first considered too shallow to support a wharf. Ships coming into the area could either remain far off shore and anchor their vessels and have their shipments and passengers taken to land by a ferry, or bring the ships right onto dry land. Neither of the maneuvers was popular, and if Los Angeles wanted to grow, it needed a legitimate harbor to attract the shipping industry.

Enter Phineas Banning, who became known as the "Father of Los Angeles Harbor." The Delaware native worked his way up through hard work in the staging and shipping industry, transporting people and supplies to Los Angeles. By the late 1850s, Banning, along with a group of investors, purchased 640 acres of land next to San Pedro to be used as a port.[6] Through his efforts, the shallow area was dredged, at a depth of 10 feet. The port was on its way to becoming one of the busiest in the United States starting in 1859. Banning also eased access to Los Angeles through the creation of roads, telegraph systems, and the area's first railroad, connecting San Pedro Bay to Los Angeles, which was up and running by 1869. By the time of Banning's death in 1885, his innovations were well on their way to making the Southland grow into what it became. The third good thing to go along with a water supply and port was the Southern Pacific Railroad from San Francisco, regarded as California's glamour city at this time period, into Los Angeles. When this was completed in 1876, Los Angeles had a transcontinental link that allowed masses from all over the country to come out to the beautiful surroundings that eventually would lure the masses to visit or relocate.[7]

As Los Angeles began to make great strides toward becoming a prominent and influential metropolis, Robert M. Widney arrived in 1867. Unbeknownst to the countless individuals past, present, and future, who ever earned a sheepskin from the University of Southern California, the Land of Troy was made possible two days before Christmas in 1838. For on that day, thousands of miles away from where the USC campus would stand, Robert Maclay Widney came into this world in Piqua, Ohio.

After his first 17 years in the Buckeye State, Widney set out to explore the western region of the United States in September 1855. By today's standards, traveling 1,700 miles by air to an unfamiliar place and adapting to new surroundings could be intimidating for a 17-year-old. Imagine what perseverance was needed for that same scenario in the mid–1800s. Whether by early railroad, or a stagecoach traveling twenty miles per hour with four to six horses pulling passengers, the excursion was long and arduous. There is no telling how the teenage Widney made his trek, but once he arrived out west, he existed as a hunter and trapper before finding his way to California in September 1857.[8]

Upon his arrival on the Golden Coast, Widney decided to change his life's course from working the great outdoors to cerebral exercise. He enrolled in classes at the University of the Pacific, where he studied law from 1858 to 1862. Three years later, he was accepted to the bar and relocated to Los Angeles in 1867.

From 1871 through 1874, Widney was appointed judge for both Los Angeles and San Bernardino counties, founded the Los Angeles Chamber of Commerce, and started the first rail transit company in Los Angeles, which was a horse car line from The Plaza to 6th and Pearl streets. Pearl later became Figueroa Street and helped in bringing the Southern Pacific Railroad to the city. Without a doubt, Widney applied the motto "Where vision becomes reality" from his hometown of Piqua to good use in his adopted city of Los Angeles. He then set out to establish a university in the area. The idea of creating a university was brought to the forefront in 1871 by Widney, who led the drive, and enthusiastic citizens. Over the next eight years, the dream was still just that, until reality presented itself in 308 lots of land to be used to establish Widney's vision. Widney was fortunate enough to witness the immense growth of his dream, living to the ripe old age of 90 years. By the time of his death on November 14, 1929, the University of Southern California was nearing its golden anniversary, and well on its way toward being one of the elite institutions of higher learning.

Religious affiliation had long been a source of conflict between individuals. However, in the case of Widney's dream, three men from different religions came together for the common good of future generations. In 1879, a Protestant horticulturalist, a Catholic pharmacist and businessman, and a German-Jewish banker and philanthropist presented Widney and his board of trustees a gift of 308 lots of Los Angeles real estate on which to build what would become the University of Southern California. This generous trio also provided monetarily for the building of the initial structures.

The three individuals who donated so much were Ozro W. Childs, Isaias W. Hellman and John G. Downey. The journeys that brought these three gentlemen together to help establish the university began in Sutton, Vermont; Reckendorf, Bavaria; and central Ireland.

Ozro W. Childs was born in 1824 in Sutton, Vermont, where he received his primary education. The son of a farmer, he chose to set out in the world and establish himself in other ventures rather than farm like his father. Childs initially relocated to Ohio and was a teacher. He learned to be a tinsmith while educating a future generation. When gold was discovered in California, Childs headed west along with countless other dreamers. His hopes were stymied when the fog of Northern California aggravated his asthma.[9]

Unable to continue with his pursuit of striking gold, Childs and another man boarded a ship for Southern California. His tinsmithing abilities came in handy, as he looked to set up his own business. The owner of an established hardware store sold out to Childs, and after a few years, Childs sold the business and walked away with $40,000, a small fortune in the 1850s. He then landed an opportunity to construct an addition onto the Zanja Madre, a canal system designed to bring water from the Los Angeles River into the city. His efforts were rewarded with a payment of land, which is now downtown Los Angeles. The land given to Childs ran from Sixth to Ninth streets, and Main to Figueroa. This form of payment provided Childs with the cornerstone of his solid financial future. More investments in real estate and business ventures followed, on many occasions in partnership with Isaias Hellman prior to their USC alliance. Childs' most prominent business interest was the Farmers and Merchants Bank of Los Angeles.[10]

Childs' partner in numerous business interests, Isaias W. Hellman, of German-Jewish ancestry, was born in Reckendorf, Bavaria, on October 3, 1842. Along with a brother, Hellman came to Los Angeles five months prior to his 17th birthday. For his first six years in Los Angeles, Hellman worked in a cousin's dry goods store before opening one of his own in 1865. It was while selling his wares that Hellman fell into the good fortune of becoming the city's first banker, but it was not planned. To oblige requests by his patrons, Hellman kept their gold and other valuable items in a safe. In time he purchased funds from individuals and distributed deposit books.[11]

In 1868, he founded the Hellman, Temple, and Co. with a colleague and created the second officially recognized bank in Los Angeles. Three years later, Hellman enjoyed a major success when he created the Farmers and Merchants Bank with John G. Downey. Also included in this venture was Ozro W. Childs. It was the first bank to be successful. Some of the customers who borrowed from the bank were prominent figures in Los Angeles history, including Harrison Gray Otis, Edward Doheny, and Charles Canfield. Otis used his loan to purchase the *Los Angeles Times*, and Doheny and Canfield borrowed to drill for oil.[12]

Hellman expanded his interests by investing a great deal of money into trolley lines in Los Angeles and utility companies. He also assisted in bringing the Southern Pacific Railroad to the Southland in 1876 to make the area more accessible to the masses. It only seemed right that a bell from one of the engines that powered the Southern Pacific would eventually become the Victory Bell and be presented to the winner of the annual USC-UCLA football game.

John G. Downey rounded out the trio that helped bring the University of Southern California into existence. Born in central Ireland on June 24, 1827, Downey came to America with the rest of his family in 1842, managing to escape the horrific conditions brought on by the Potato Famine. With their main food supply cut off, it was estimated that one million people died.[13]

Downey and his family made their new home in Charles County, Maryland, but financial woes prevented Downey from continuing his education past age 16. In an effort to ease his family's monetary burden, he went to work as an apprentice at an apothecary in Washington, D.C., until he was 19 years old.[14]

It was then on to the "Queen City" of Cincinnati, Ohio, to practice what he learned in the nation's capital as a druggist. However, Cincinnati would not be his final destination. Like many would-be millionaires, thoughts of vast fortune from the California gold rush lured Downey to the Golden Coast in 1849. The allure of striking it rich mining for gold wore off, but California proved to be Downey's stopping point.

Downey found employment in a San Francisco drug store and eventually migrated 400 miles south to Los Angeles, where politics became an interest. His initial experience consisted of two one-year terms in the Los Angeles Common Council in 1852 and 1856. He then held positions in the California State Assembly, and in 1859 he was elected lieutenant governor. The governor, Milton Latham, stepped down to move to the Senate and turned over the leadership of the state to Downey five days after Downey's swearing-in ceremony. He was in charge of California as of January 14, 1860. With this appointment, he became the only foreign-born governor in California history until Arnold Schwarzenegger in 2003. After his term was complete in 1862, Downey travelled back to Los Angeles, and along with Isaias W. Hellman, helped found the Farmers and Merchants Bank.

And so it came to be that these three prominent citizens of the Southland banded together in 1879 to donate the land needed for the much-needed and much-wanted university that was all but a dream for Robert Widney at the start of the decade. On what became 650 Childs Way, approximately three miles south of downtown Los Angeles, the original building of the university was constructed at a final cost of $5,060 in a mustard field. It was of Italianate design and stood two stories tall. It became known as Widney Hall, and also as Alumni House. It has been in continuous use since 1880, serving as a tribute to all that the university's founder had hoped for.[15]

On October 6, 1880, 1,000 people out of the 11,000 residents of Los Angeles came out in horse and buggy to witness the dedication and official opening of the doors to Widney Hall, thus marking in the beginning of the University of Southern California.

One day prior to the official opening, 33-year-old Marion McKinley Bovard was inaugurated as USC's first president and the next day opened the doors to Widney Hall to greet 53 students and 10 teachers.

During Bovard's time as president, from 1880 until his

death in 1891, he supervised in the formation of USC's College of Letters, Arts, and Sciences (1880), School of Music (1884), College of Medicine (1885), and School of Fine Arts (1887). He was also at the helm of the university when the football program began in 1888.[16]

Within the first year of operations, USC opened a dormitory named Hodge Hall, and in 1884, USC saw its first graduating class ready to go into the world armed with degrees. The first class consisted of three students, including Minnie Miltimore, USC's first class valedictorian.

By 1888, it was time for USC to expand again, this time into athletics. As early as 1820, a variation of football called "ballown" was played by students at Princeton University. In 1827, Harvard University held a game between freshman and sophomores, which began a tradition known as "Bloody Monday." Despite the different names, the premise was the same. Two groups of players slugging it out to advance a ball to the opponent's goal. It was a violent display, and injuries mounted, as one would expect. The violence and mob-mentality aspect of the game led to protests, which resulted in the game being banned by the early 1860s.[17]

Even though this form of athletic competition was banned from college campuses, prep schools in Boston played a very popular version known as "Boston Game." It consisted of an inflatable ball, which the players had to carry and kick. The popularity of this early form of football caught on with the public during the 1860s, and by the end of the decade, the sport once again entered the college world, this time to stay.[18]

On November 6, 1869, Rutgers University and Princeton University squared off in a combination of rugby and soccer, recognized as the first-ever intercollegiate football game. The sport grew more popular with the passing of each year, as young college students donning handlebar moustaches tested their skills against other universities.

By the time that USC opened its doors in 1880, college football was dominated by Ivy League teams from Yale, Harvard, and Princeton. Within eight years after USC began classes, football gravitated onto the Southland campus. Players gathered on a vacant lot, put up less-than-sturdy goalposts, eventually went by the moniker "the Methodists," and ushered in football at USC.

# One

# The Seasons

*In The Seasons, the following format is used: For the schedule and highlights portion of each season, games are set up as follows: Home, away, or neutral site will appear first as H, A, or N in parentheses, followed by date of game, opponent, and score, with USC's score always appearing first. If the Trojans or their opponents were nationally ranked going into a game, the team's initials will be listed below the date of the game (e.g., USC#1 ND#2). In Team Leaders section of The Seasons, all individual statistics listed contain those compiled during the regular season and in bowl game appearances. Seasonal individual statistics officially began for USC in 1925. Listed below are the years in which each individual statistic was introduced and when they first appear in the seasonal reviews: Rushing: 1925; Passing: 1937; Receiving: 1937; Scoring: 1925; Kickoff Returns: 1950; Punt Returns: 1950; Punting: 1941; Interceptions: 1950; Tackles: 1954 (from 1960 through the 1968 season, the information regarding the leader in tackles for USC was not available); Sacks: 1983. In regard to USC's conference standings, points scored, and points allowed will first appear in 1922.*

## *1888*

Head Coach: Henry H. Goddard and Frank H. Suffel
Assistant Coaches: None
Team Captain: Will Whitcomb
Record: 2–0
Finish in Conference: Independent
Finish in National Polls: No ranking

### Schedule and Highlights

**(H) Nov. 14—Alliance AC—16–0**

Unbeknownst to the participants or spectators on this day was the fact that this marked the first-ever game played in what would begin one of the greatest programs in the history of college athletics. Unfortunately, there are no records that state what player scored the first points in USC history. All that is known about this historic contest was touchdowns were worth four points, conversions two, field goals five, and like in today's game, a safety two points. However, what is known is that this incredible football program's lineage started off in stellar fashion with a shutout victory. The only known names of the players that made up the first football roster are: John Norton, Harvey Bailey, Will Whitcomb, J. Edward Young, E.E. Hall, E.E. Reed, Frank Davis, Harry Lillie, C.C. Carpenter, Arthur Carroll, Frank Lapham, and Thomas Carver.

The school colors at this time were purple and gold, but this inaugural collection of west coast gridiron pioneers came onto the field in whatever they preferred to wear due to the fact that there were no organized college teams in the region. Also, without any sanctioning body to rule over them, USC was allowed to play against any team that was willing to take the field, which meant that their early opponents consisted of high school and athletic club competition.

**(N) Jan. 19—Alliance AC—4–0**

On a vacant lot bordered by Grand, Hope, Eighth, and Ninth Streets in Los Angeles, the USC Methodists concluded their first season with a second straight shutout victory.

## *1889*

Head Coach: None
Assistant Coaches: None
Team Captains: None
Record: 2–0
Finish in Conference: Independent
Finish in National Polls: No ranking

### Schedule and Highlights

**(H) Date Not Available—St. Vincent's (Loyola)—40–0**

The Methodists continued on their winning ways with another shutout victory despite the fact that the date of this game is forever lost in history.

**(N) Nov. 28—Pasadena—26–0**

In the school's first-ever Thanksgiving Day appearance, USC played at Sportsman's Park in Pasadena, and completed their second season with a shutout, thus giving them the distinction of starting out their football program with two straight undefeated seasons. Up to this time in their illustrious history, the University of Southern California scored 86 points while given up zero. It appeared right from the start that there was something magical about football in the Southland. However, despite its successful start, the football program was disbanded for the 1890 season.

## *1891*

Head Coach: None
Assistant Coaches: None
Team Captain: Frank Lapham
Record: 1–2
Finish in Conference: Independent
Finish in National Polls: No ranking

### Schedule and Highlights

**(H) Nov. 26—Olive Club—12–16**

After not having a team in the previous season, the Methodists were once again back on the field. However, the return did not produce the success that the first two season openers did. For the first time in USC history, the football team gave up points and suffered a loss.

**(H) Jan. 23—SC Academy—34–0**

The Methodists regrouped and continued on their winning ways by recording the fifth shutout victory in team history in the span of only six games.

**(H) Feb. 22—Loyola—2–10**

With this defeat, USC endured the first losing season in their short but successful history.

## *1893*

Head Coach: None
Assistant Coaches: None
Team Captain: None
Record: 3–1
Finish in Conference: Independent
Finish in National Polls: No ranking

### Schedule and Highlights

**(H) Jan.14—Chaw-sir Club—14–2**

**(A) Nov. 18—Cal Tech—22–12**

**(A) Dec. 11—Chaffey College—6–32**

**(H) Dec. 22—Cal Tech—14–4**

In a rematch from a month earlier, the Methodists hosted Cal Tech, and the game was played in a constant rain.

## *1894*

Head Coach: None
Assistant Coaches: None
Team Captain: John A. Gray
Record: 1–0
Finish in Conference: Independent
Finish in National Polls: No ranking

### Schedule and Highlights

**(H) Cal Tech (date unknown)—12–0**

## *1895*

Head Coach: None
Assistant Coaches: None
Team Captain: Lee Bradley
Record: 0–1–1
Finish in Conference: Independent
Finish in National Polls: No ranking

### Schedule and Highlights

**(N) Nov. 18—Occidental—0–10**

This game saw USC get shut out for the first time in their history. The game was played at Athletic Park at 7th & Alameda in Los Angeles.

**(H) Dec. 7—Cal Tech—4–4**

## *1896*

Head Coach: None
Assistant Coaches: None
Team Captain: Foster Wright
Record: 0–3
Finish in Conference: Independent
Finish in National Polls: No ranking

### Schedule and Highlights

**(H) Oct. 24—Whittier Reform—0–30**

**(N) Oct. 31—Los Angeles AC—0–22**

Despite their second straight loss, the Methodists had their first recorded attendance figure climb over the 1,000 mark when a crowd of 1,500 witnessed this game at Athletic Park.

**(N) Nov. 14—Cal Tech—0–22**

The Methodists ended their worst season to date by failing to produce any points for the season. Athletic Park was the site of their third straight shutout loss, and the fourth out of their previous five games going back to 1895.

## *1897*

Head Coach: Lewis Freeman
Assistant Coaches: None
Team Captain: Harry Martin
Record: 5–1
Finish in Conference: Independent
Finish in National Polls: No ranking

### Schedule and Highlights

**(H) (date unknown)—Loyola—34–0**

**(N) Nov. 6—Los Angeles HS—10–0**
This game was played at Fiesta Park at Grand and Pico in Los Angeles.

**(N) Nov. 13—Chaffey College—38–0**

**(A) Nov. 25—Pomona—6–0**
After suffering through the previous season without scoring any points, this edition of the Methodists more than made up for it. Up to this stage of the season, they recorded their fourth straight shutout victory while making their second Thanksgiving Day appearance in school history.

**(A) Dec. 25—San Diego YMCA—0–18**
Another holiday game did not bring the Methodists good fortune this time around, as they suffered the first and only loss of this campaign.

**(A) Jan. 1—Ventura—12–0**
A third straight holiday road trip got the Methodists back into the win column, and provided them with their fourth shutout victory of the season.

## *1898*

HEAD COACH: None
ASSISTANT COACHES: None
TEAM CAPTAIN: Foster Wright
RECORD: 5–1–1
FINISH IN CONFERENCE: Independent
FINISH IN NATIONAL POLLS: No ranking

### Schedule and Highlights

**(N) Oct. 15—Los Angeles HS—0–0**
Played at Athletic Park in Los Angeles.

**(H) Oct. 22—Pasadena AC—17–0**

**(N) Nov. 19—Los Angeles HS—0–6**
Played at Fiesta Park, Los Angeles.

**(N) Nov. 24—Pomona—14–11**
Played at Fiesta Park on Thanksgiving Day.

**(N) Nov. 26—7th Regiment—34–0**
Played at Fiesta Park against California National Guard, Los Angeles.

**(N) Dec. 3—Phoenix Indian School—27–11**
Played at Fiesta Park.

**(A) Jan. 2—Santa Barbara AC—5–0**
This game was played mostly in the rain.

## *1899*

HEAD COACH: None
ASSISTANT COACHES: None
TEAM CAPTAIN: Logan Wheatley
RECORD: 2–3–1
FINISH IN CONFERENCE: Independent
FINISH IN NATIONAL POLLS: No ranking

### Schedule and Highlights

**(H) Oct. 21—Whittier Reform—11–0**

**(A) Nov. 4—Santa Ana HS—0–11**

**(H) Nov. 8—Occidental—11–0**

**(H) Nov. 15—Occidental—0–0**

**(A) Nov. 30—Pomona—0–12**
Played on Thanksgiving Day with 2,000 in attendance, this was the largest crowd to watch a USC football game up to this time.

**(A) Jan. 1—Santa Barbara AC—0–10**

## *1900*

HEAD COACH: None
ASSISTANT COACHES: None
TEAM CAPTAIN: Harry Woodard
RECORD: 1–1–1
FINISH IN CONFERENCE: Independent
FINISH IN NATIONAL POLLS: No ranking

### Schedule and Highlights

**(A) Nov. 10—Occidental—5–0**

**(N) Nov. 24—Los Angeles HS—0–0**
Played at Washington Park, Washington & Grand in Los Angeles

**(N) Nov. 29—Pomona—0–11**
Played at Washington Park on Thanksgiving Day for second year in a row against Pomona in front of 1,200 spectators. This was the first time during the season that the Methodists gave up any points.

## *1901*

HEAD COACH: Clair Tappaan
ASSISTANT COACHES: None
TEAM CAPTAIN: Logan Wheatley
RECORD: 0–1
FINISH IN CONFERENCE: Independent
FINISH IN NATIONAL POLLS: No ranking

### Schedule and Highlights

**(A) Dec. 7—Pomona—0–6**
This proved to be the latest that USC ever opened a football season.

## 1902

HEAD COACH: None
ASSISTANT COACHES: None
TEAM CAPTAIN: Dan Caley
RECORD: 2–3
FINISH IN CONFERENCE:
FINISH IN NATIONAL POLLS:

### Schedule and Highlights

**(N) Oct. 11—Loyola—5–6**
This game was played in front of 400 at Fiesta Park.

**(A) Oct. 25—Santa Ana—2–5**

**(H) Nov. 7—Santa Ana—6–0**

**(N) Nov. 15—Pomona—16–5**
Elwin Caley returned a kickoff 107 yards for a touchdown on a 110-yard playing field at Fiesta Park

**(A) Nov. 22—Sherman Institute—0–28**

## 1903

HEAD COACH: John Walker
ASSISTANT COACHES: None
TEAM CAPTAIN: Dan Caley
RECORD: 4–2
FINISH IN CONFERENCE: Independent
FINISH IN NATIONAL POLLS: No ranking

### Schedule and Highlights

**(H) Oct. 10—Cal Tech—5–0**
This game began a season that saw the Methodists play every game at home at Prager Park near Washington and Grand in Los Angeles.

**(H) Oct. 17—Los Angeles HS—10–0**
Los Angeles left the field with seven minutes left in protest over a penalty called by umpire Dean Cromwell. USC was awarded five points to make the final score 10–0.

**(H) Oct. 24—Occidental—0–5**

**(H) Oct. 31—Loyola—12–5**

**(H) Nov. 7—Orange AC—31–5**

**(H) Nov. 14—Sherman Institute—0–12**
This was a hard-fought game won by Native Americans from the Indian school in Riverside County. Two months after this game, scandal hit USC when it was learned that J.F. Seymour, Jr., the team manager, had given a check of $25 to team captain Dan Caley to play for USC. Rumors began that the amount might have been around $1,000. This placed an ominous mark on the university, due to the speculation that professionalism had found a way to tarnish the amateur ranks of athletic competition. The scandal eventually faded into history, and all the parties moved on.

## 1904

HEAD COACH: Harvey Holmes
ASSISTANT COACHES: None
TEAM CAPTAIN: Jay Bickford
RECORD: 6–1 (Southern California Intercollegiate Conference)
FINISH IN CONFERENCE: 1st
FINISH IN NATIONAL POLLS: No ranking

### Schedule and Highlights

**(N) Oct. 15—Los Angeles HS—42–0**
The Methodists started off the new season in stellar fashion by scoring the most points in their history up to this time. The game was played at Fiesta Park with a crowd of 1,600 present.

**(H) Oct. 22—Cal Tech—35–0**

**(H) Oct. 29—Occidental—36–4**

**(H) Nov. 5—Loyola—Forfeit**
USC won on forfeit after opposing coaches could not agree on a time allowed for halves. A game against USC prep students was played instead.

**(H) Nov. 5—SC Prep—26–0**
This game was played to make up for the forfeited one against Loyola.

**(N) Nov. 12—Sherman Institute—0–17**
In their first loss of the season, the Methodists played at Eagle Park in Long Beach, California. This game was called midway through the second half due to darkness.

**(A) Nov. 19—Whittier Reform—60–6**
The Methodists started off the season scoring the most points in a single game. They then ended the season with another record for most points scored in a game.

## 1905

HEAD COACH: Harvey Holmes
ASSISTANT COACHES: None
TEAM CAPTAIN: Carl Elliott
RECORD: 6–3–1 (Southern California Intercollegiate Conference)
FINISH IN CONFERENCE: Unknown
FINISH IN NATIONAL POLLS: No ranking

### Schedule and Highlights

**(H) Oct. 4—National Guard Company F—28–0**
This was third straight season that the Methodists opened their schedule with a shutout victory.

**(H) Oct. 10—Harvard School—12–0**
Because of "deficiencies" on Harvard's roster, USC's coach Harvey Holmes, and Dean Cromwell played for Harvard. This is not to be confused with Harvard University.

**(H) Oct. 16—LA Poly HS—27–0**

**(H) Oct. 18—Whittier Reform—75–0**

In a game played with 15-minute halves, the Methodists established a record for most points scored in a single game. Their old record was set a year earlier against the same school.

**(H) Nov. 1—Alumni—63–0**

Fifth straight shutout victory allowed the Methodists to set team record for longest streak without giving up a single point in one season. The combined 138 points scored over the course of two straight games set a team record.

**(A) Nov. 4—Stanford—0–16**

This was USC's first-ever game played outside of the Southern California area. It was also USC's first game against major college competition. Prior to this, USC played local colleges, high schools and athletic clubs. Following this, USC did not play another major college team for nine years.

**(A) Nov. 11—Occidental—0–10**

**(N) Nov. 25—Sherman Institute—0–15**

Played at Fiesta Park

**(H) Dec. 2—Loyola—0–0**

**(N) Dec. 9—Pomona—6–4**

After four straight losses in which the Methodists did not score, they finally ended their cold streak to finish the year with a victory.

## *1906*

HEAD COACH: Harvey Holmes
ASSISTANT COACHES: None
TEAM CAPTAIN: Oliver Best
RECORD: 2–0–2 (Southern California Intercollegiate Conference)
FINISH IN CONFERENCE: Unknown
FINISH IN NATIONAL POLLS: No ranking

### Schedule and Highlights

**(N) Oct. 6—Los Angeles HS—0–0**

Played at Fiesta Park, this game marked the fourth straight season that the Methodists were not scored on in the opener.

**(H) Oct. 13—Occidental—22–0**

With the largest crowd to date to witness a USC game, 4,000 saw the Methodists remain unbeaten or scored on.

**(A) Nov. 17—Pomona—14–0**

**(N) Nov. 29—Sherman Institute—0–0**

In front of another 4,000 spectators, this time at Fiesta Park, the Methodists finished this season on Thanksgiving Day with a spotless record of no points scored on them throughout the season. This marked the fourth time in their history that USC never gave up a single point over the course of one season.

## *1907*

HEAD COACH: Harvey Holmes
ASSISTANT COACHES: None
TEAM CAPTAIN: Charley Haigler
RECORD: 5–1 (Southern California Intercollegiate Conference)
FINISH IN CONFERENCE: Unknown
FINISH IN NATIONAL POLLS: No ranking

### Schedule and Highlights

**(N) Oct. 12—Los Angeles HS—6–0**

With a crowd of 2,000 on hand at Fiesta Park, the Methodists opened their fifth straight season with a shutout victory.

**(H) Oct. 16—Whittier Reform—57–0**

Over the previous few seasons, Whittier took an awful pounding from USC. Counting this game, the Methodists had outscored Whittier 172–6 in their last three meetings.

**(A) Oct. 26—Santa Ana HS—51–0**

**(H) Nov. 9—Whittier Reform—46–0**

**(H) Nov. 15—USS Colorado—16–4**

Eugene Shute kicked a 30-yard field goal to set a USC record.

**(N) Dec. 25—Los Angeles HS—6–16**

A Christmas Day wish for a perfect season was not to be with 2,200 in attendance at Fiesta Park, as the Methodists fell for the first time.

## *1908*

HEAD COACH: Bill Traeger
ASSISTANT COACHES: None
TEAM CAPTAIN: Stan Burek
RECORD: 3–1–1 (Southern California Intercollegiate Conference)
FINISH IN CONFERENCE: 1st
FINISH IN NATIONAL POLLS: No ranking

### Schedule and Highlights

**(N) Oct. 10—Los Angeles HS—0–12**

Los Angeles HS was becoming a nuisance for the Methodists. They ended USC's bid for a perfect season the year before, and then started the Methodists new season off with their first opening day defeat in six years. This also the first time since 1902 that USC surrendered any points in the first game of a season. This game was played at Fiesta Park in front of 2,500.

**(H) Oct. 17—Whittier Reform—15–0**

Usually the Methodists rolled over Whittier, but with rain coming down during most this game, it seemed to slow down their offensive production.

**(A) Oct. 24—Arrowhead AC—28–0**

**(H) Nov. 7—Occidental—14–0**

The largest crowd of the season came out to Bovard Field to watch the Methodists not only record a major upset, but secure USC's 50th all-time football victory as well. Occidental came into this game with experience and a weight advantage of five pounds per man. Hal Paulin kicked two field goals, and team captain Stan Burek provided the only touchdown of the day. On numerous occasions, Occidental gained good chunks of yardage, but the Methodists held them out of the end zone.[1]

**(A) Nov. 14—Pomona—6-6**

With ten minutes remaining in the game, Pomona scored the tying points.[2]

## *1909*

HEAD COACH: Dean Cromwell
ASSISTANT COACHES: None
TEAM CAPTAIN: Hal Paulin
RECORD: 3-1-2 (Southern California Intercollegiate Conference)
FINISH IN CONFERENCE: 2nd
FINISH IN NATIONAL POLLS: No ranking

### Schedule and Highlights

**(A) Oct. 9—Cal-Poly SLO—51-0**

The dawn of the Dean Cromwell coaching reign in the Southland began in stellar fashion, as the Methodists rolled to one of their biggest victories in USC history.

**(A) Oct. 16—Whittier—22-2**

**(H) Oct. 23—Loyola—6-8**

With a crowd of 1,200 on hand for USC's first home game of the season, Loyola spoiled the festivities by handing the Methodists their first only loss in the final three minutes of the game.

**(H) Oct. 30—Orange AC—51-0**

**(A) Nov. 6—Occidental—3-3**

With a capacity crowd of 3,500 on hand, the teams ended in a low-scoring deadlock. Courtney Decius set a new USC record with a 45-yard field goal. This proved to be the only field goal he ever kicked. He was the owner of that record for 64 years until Chris Limahelu broke it on January 1, 1974.

**(H) Nov. 13—Pomona—0-0**

The Methodists ended the decade the way they began it, by not allowing an opponent to score. Unfortunately, USC could not produce any points themselves, and had to settle for their second tie of the season. This proved to be the earliest that USC ever ended a season.

## *1910*

HEAD COACH: Dean Cromwell
ASSISTANT COACHES: None
TEAM CAPTAIN: Jack Malcolm
RECORD: 7-0-1 (Southern California Intercollegiate Conference)
FINISH IN CONFERENCE: Unknown
FINISH IN NATIONAL POLLS: No ranking

### Schedule and Highlights

**(H) Oct. 5—Long Beach Poly HS—22-6**

After three pre-season games that saw the Methodists' sophomores beat the freshman team 5-0, the upperclassmen battle the freshman team to a scoreless tie, and a 28-0 win over the Occidental freshmen, the regular season got underway with a convincing win over Long Beach Poly.[1]

**(H) Oct. 8—Chaffey HS—65-6**

Another convincing victory proved that the Methodists had a solid team that was capable of scoring.[2]

**(A) Oct. 15—Throop Academy—9-0**

With rain coming down for the greater part of this game, the Methodists' offense might not have rolled up as many points as in their first two games, but they still managed to remain undefeated with their first shutout of the year. Throop had a veteran backfield, but found the going tough against a determined USC defense.[3]

**(A) Oct. 22—San Diego HS—32-0**

Arthur "Babe" Hill stood out for the Methodists in another shutout victory.[4]

**(A) Oct. 29—Redlands—35-0**

The Methodists wrapped up their preliminary games in fine fashion, posting a third straight shutout, before taking on their main rivals over the next three weeks.[5]

**(H) Nov. 5—Occidental—6-0**

With the largest crowd in USC history up to this time, the Methodists remained undefeated with their fourth straight shutout, as 5,000 spectators cheered them on. This close game had 60 punts, two place-kicks, and 16 forward passes, 15 of which were credited to USC for 175 yards.[6]

**(A) Nov. 12—Whittier—11-3**

Whittier made three failed attempts to score in the first quarter, but succeeded on their fourth attempt for a 3-0 lead. Arthur "Babe" Hill scored USC's only touchdown on a fumble recovery. He also did a great job getting through blockers to stop Whittier's runners throughout the game.[7]

**(A) Nov.19—Pomona—9-9**

A crowd of 4,000 saw the home team Pomona spoil a perfect season for USC. With one minute remaining in the game, Pomona scored the tying points to send the Methodists home without their eighth victory. This was the final time in their football history that USC would have the nickname of the Methodists. Mixing speed and hard-hitting action, this was considered the best game in the Southern California area during the year.[8]

## *1911–1913*

During these three seasons, the University of Southern California stopped playing American football, deciding on rugby instead.

## *1914*

HEAD COACH: Ralph Glaze
ASSISTANT COACHES: None
TEAM CAPTAIN: Tommy Davis
RECORD: 4-3 (Played in the Southern California Intercollegiate Conference)

FINISH IN CONFERENCE: Unknown
FINISH IN NATIONAL POLLS: No ranking

## Schedule and Highlights

**(H) Sept. 26—Los Angeles AC—20–0**

At 3:15 p.m. on September 26, 1914, a new era of football began at USC. After three seasons of rugby, USC came roaring back onto the gridiron scene with a shutout victory. This game marked the first time in USC history that the new nickname of Trojans was officially applied to the football team. The first-ever touchdown scored for USC with their new nickname was by a halfback named Le Valley Lund, who ran for the score, and Gerald Craig added the conversion kick, and the Trojans lead, 7–0, at the end of the first half. Teschke returned an interception for a touchdown after LAAC got deep into USC territory. Clayton Halloway scored USC's final points of the game on a run.[1]

**(H) Oct. 10—Redlands—41–0**

The new nickname of Trojans appeared to be good for USC, as they were undefeated and were not scored upon with the moniker. The Trojans set the tone early. On USC's second play, Fred Kelly ran around the end for a 65-yard touchdown. The Trojans added one more touchdown by Clayton Halloway in the first quarter, and the second quarter saw no scoring. They pulled away in the third quarter on another touchdown run by Holloway, and two by Len Livernash. In the fourth quarter, Halloway threw a scoring strike to Tipton to complete the rout.[2]

**(H) Oct. 24—Whittier—17–14**

Jack Elmore was the standout for USC on this day. He started off the scoring with a 25-yard field goal with only five minutes expired in the first quarter. He added two conversion kicks, and consistently sent booming punts that averaged 55 yards per attempt. Tommy Davis and Len Livernash each scored a touchdown for USC, and the Trojans remained perfect on the year.[3]

**(H) Oct. 31—Occidental—13–20**

This was the first time that USC lost under the nickname of the Trojans. This was considered one of the best games involving USC during this time. It was a hard-fought affair between two rivals. This was the first time that USC lost to Occidental since 1905. Bovard Field was full of excitement as Jack Elmore kicked off to Foster, Oxy's team captain. Foster returned the ball 50 yards, and then scored on the same drive. The Tigers added another seven points, and USC cut the deficit in half by the end of the second quarter on a Fred Kelly touchdown. In the third quarter, Clayton Halloway threw a touchdown pass to Elmore, but the latter missed on the conversion, and the Trojans still trailed, 14–13. The Tigers added a third quarter touchdown, and the fourth period was a defensive struggle that remained scoreless.[4]

**(A) Nov. 7—Redlands—13–6**

It was a rematch between the Trojans and the Redlands Baptists, with the end result being another victory for USC, but with a closer final score than in their first meeting one month earlier. Coach Ralph Glaze traveled to scout USC's next opponent, Pomona, and took some of his players with him so they could observe Pomona's strengths and weaknesses. This left many second team performers to face Redlands, but a few of the Trojan stars also stayed back to help out. Jack Elmore and team captain Tommy Davis were two of the stars that played in this game, and both helped get USC on the board first. Elmore caught a long pass and made it to the Redlands 10-yard line. Davis then ran it in for a touchdown. The conversion kick was missed, but USC was on top, 6–0, and never trailed. Clayton Halloway scored the Trojans' other touchdown after catching a pass and running twenty yards to paydirt. That completed USC's scoring, all in the first half. The Baptists scored early in the second half on a fumble recovery in the USC end zone. The rest of the game was a seesaw defensive battle.[5]

**(A) Nov. 14—Pomona—6–10**

Despite the scouting trip to study Pomona, the Trojans fell victim to defeat for the second time in the season. Pomona scored a touchdown in the first quarter, and a field goal in the second, to give them their points. Hard rushes into the line were common in this game, but USC also relied on the forward pass to move the ball. It led to their only points, when Clayton Halloway threw a touchdown pass to Gerald Craig. The rest of the game became a punting duel.[6]

**(N) Nov. 26—Oregon State—6–38**

This marked the first time that USC traveled outside of California for a football game, and the first time the Trojans ever played Oregon State. Despite the historic event, the result was brutal, as the Trojans gave up the most points in a single game up to this time, and lost by the greatest margin up to this time in their history. The game was played at Tacoma Stadium in Tacoma, Washington in front of 7,000 fans, which was the most ever up to this time to witness a USC game. Oregon State's 38 points would be the most they scored on a USC team for 95 years. Jimmie James scored USC's only points, and became the only opponent to score against Oregon State all season.[7]

# *1915*

HEAD COACH: Ralph Glaze
ASSISTANT COACHES: None
TEAM CAPTAIN: Len Livernash
RECORD: 3–4
FINISH IN CONFERENCE: Independent
FINISH IN NATIONAL POLLS: No ranking

## Schedule and Highlights

**(H) Oct. 2—Los Angeles AC—21–9**

Throughout the years to come, the Trojans earned a stellar reputation for having some of the game's top offensive backfield men. This 1915 team had possibly the first star-studded one in school history. It consisted of team captain Leonard Livernash, Gerald Craig, and Frank "Rabbit" Malette, who is felt to be the first in the long and proud USC running back legacy. This trio assisted the Trojans in their opening game victory, which saw USC score all their points within a matter of twenty minutes despite a strong fight from the opposition. Livernash scored two touchdowns, and Corliss Moseley caught a 35-yard pass from Gerald Craig for USC's other touchdown that gave the Trojans a 21–0 lead in the second quarter.[1]

**(H) Oct. 16—St. Mary's—47–3**

This lopsided victory came about with an experienced USC team facing a Saints team that had trouble tackling, as the final score would testify to. On USC's fifth offensive play, Len Livernash scored and added the conversion kick. A short time later, he threw a 25-yard scoring strike to Corliss Moseley. Other USC touchdowns came on a pass from Frank Malette to Fred Kelly, a Moseley run, two Gerald Craig scoring jaunts, one of which was a 25-yard interception return, and Livernash added his second six-pointer of the day, to round out the scoring.[2]

**(A) Oct. 23—California—28–10**

With the first-ever crowd of 10,000-plus to watch USC, the Trojans remained undefeated and celebrated the victory with a parade upon their return to the Southland. At this time, USC's head coach Ralph Glaze was considered one of the top football mentors in California. Cal took a 3–0 lead in the first quarter, but that was the last time they led. Frank Malette led the Trojans downfield with some successful passes, and after Len Livernash and Corliss Moseley plowed through on the ground, Malette went back to the air with a scoring strike to Gerald Craig to give USC the advantage for good. Another highlight in this big win came when Craig threw a long touchdown pass to Moseley. The Trojan defense did an excellent job containing the Cal backfield, making many tackles behind the line of scrimmage.[3]

**(H) Nov. 8—Oregon—0–34**

This game was postponed for two days due to rain, and when the game was finally played, Oregon pounded the Trojans both on the scoreboard and physically. Willard Curry and George Marshall each suffered cracked ribs, and many other players were moving slowly following the team's first defeat of the season. The game remained a scoreless tie through the first thirty minutes. It was then that Oregon exploded, using their size to weaken the Trojan defense.[4]

**(A) Nov. 20—Utah—13–20**

Clarence "Dog" Douglas was the star of this game for the Utah Crimson. He shot through the USC line, picked off a lateral pass, and did not stop until he was in the end zone 82 yards away. He then recovered a fumble that set up a Darrell Gardner touchdown run. The Trojans managed to fight their way back to close the gap to one point, but missed on the conversion that would have tied the game. Lowell Romney then added one final six-pointer to put the game out of reach. The Trojans received their two touchdowns on a short run by Len Livernash, and on a 70-yard run by Gerald Craig.[5]

**(N) Nov. 25—California—21–23**

On Thanksgiving Day, the Trojans lost in the final minute of the game played at Washington Park in Los Angeles with a crowd of 8,000 on hand. Willis Montgomery provided the Golden Bears with a game-winning field goal as night fell upon the field. USC's scores came on a Corliss Moseley 80-yard run, and a pair of Clayton Halloway passes, with Len Livernash and Philip Murray on the receiving end of the six-pointers.[6]

**(N) Dec. 11—Whittier—2–20**

In a return to Washington Park, the Trojans fell for the fourth straight time. Whittier scored in the first and fourth quarter, while the Trojans could only muster a safety in the second quarter. This was the first time that Whittier defeated USC after five previous defeats.[7]

## *1916*

Head Coach: Dean Cromwell
Assistant Coaches: None
Team Captain: Herb Jones
Record: 5–3
Finish in Conference: Independent
Finish in National Polls: No ranking

### Schedule and Highlights

**(H) Oct. 7—Sherman Institute—14–0**

After a six-year absence, Dean Cromwell returned to guide the Trojans. His new tenure began in excellent fashion, as USC shut out their opponent in a game played in the mud. Also, all home games for USC during this season were played at Fiesta Park. The Trojans came into the 3:00 p.m. kickoff with a much heavier team, which eventually wore Sherman down. However, despite the weight difference being a factor, Sherman still played tough with solid tackling abilities. Frank "Rabbit" Malette took off on an end run, and doing what he did best as a USC's backfield star, he dodged his way through defenders on a long scoring jaunt within the first few minutes of the game for the Trojans first touchdown of the season. He also added two conversion kicks. Five minutes later, Philip Murray ran for another touchdown to complete the game's scoring.[1]

**(A) Oct. 14—Santa Fe AC—14–0**

The Trojans traveled to San Bernardino to play Santa Fe Athletic Club sporting a group of big players. Speed and finesse won out on this day, as USC ran the energy out of coach Sid Neighbor's charges. Most of the game was played in Santa Fe territory, but USC could not get in sync as a unit, otherwise the final score would have been much higher. However, the Trojans did produce two touchdowns while holding Santa Fe scoreless. On the first play of the second quarter, Harold Huyck threw a touchdown pass to Philip Murray, and Ray Clark later ran for USC's other touchdown. Huyck added both conversion kicks.[2]

**(H) Oct. 21—Utah—12–27**

Lowell Romney scored twice for Utah, and Harold Kay added another six-pointer and three conversion kicks to beat USC for the second straight time. Utah had more speed, and used it. It was claimed that they played a near perfect game. After a scoreless first quarter, Utah jumped out to a 14–0 lead before Frank Malette brought the crowd to their feet. He cut the deficit to 14–6 in the second quarter with a spectacular 90-yard touchdown run after receiving a kick. Early in the second half, Malette scored on an 80-yard run to make the Utah advantage only 14–12. However, Utah wore the Trojan defense down in the fourth quarter, scoring twice to pull away.[3]

**(H) Nov. 4—California—0–27**

A crowd of 10,000 packed Fiesta Park for this game. Andy Smith became a coaching legend at Cal during his tenure with a winning percentage of .799 over ten seasons. This was his first year leading Cal, and brought a 4–2–1 record into this game. They dropped two straight before this clash, and reversed their losing pattern with a convincing win. Despite the lopsided final score, the Trojans managed to compete on equal ground with the Golden Bears throughout the first half. Even though they were outweighed and not as experienced as Cal, the Trojans battled to a scoreless tie going into the second half. Cal then used their weight advantage and experience to produce a second half romp.[4]

**(H) Nov. 11—Los Angeles AC—34–0**

The Trojans rebounded from their second straight loss with a romp over the LAAC. They scored six points in the opening quarter, 14 in the second, and 14 in the fourth. They could have gotten more points on the board if not for numerous penalties. Harold Huyck led the Trojans with two touchdowns and three conversion kicks. He also assisted in getting USC's other points.[5]

**(H) Nov. 25—Pomona—28–3**

The Trojans avenged their loss to Pomona from two years earlier. In the second quarter, USC went on top 7–3 on a touchdown pass from Frank Malette to Philip Murray. That score held up until USC scored three touchdowns in the fourth quarter. Malette scored on a 77-yard punt return, John Sigler returned an interception 50 yards for a touchdown, and Murray added his second touchdown of the game on a 60-yard interception return. Malette added all four conversion kicks to round out the scoring.[6]

**(H) Nov. 30—Oregon State—7–16**

Oregon State snapped a two-game losing streak that saw them shut out in each defeat. This was a hard-fought game that saw the Trojans play tough throughout, especially the performance of the ends Sammy Blake and Herb Jones, who stopped Oregon State from runs to the outside. Blake later broke a bone in his hand. The Trojans received their only points on a pass from Harold Huyck to Wright Hamilton in the fourth quarter. Huyck added the conversion kick. Frank Malette was expected to once again provide an offensive spark, but a knee injury suffered in the first quarter forced him out of action.[7]

**(N) Dec. 9—Arizona—20–7**

This game was played at Phoenix Indian School, and marked the only time during the season that USC traveled outside the state of California. Harold Huyck was the star for the Trojans on this day. He threw touchdown passes to Sammy Blake and Philip Murray, and then scored the final one himself on a short run after returning an interception within close range of the Arizona goal line. He also added two conversion kicks.[8]

## *1917*

Head Coach: Dean Cromwell
Assistant Coaches: None
Team Captain: Frank Malette
Record: 4–2–1
Finish in Conference: Independent
Finish in National Polls: No ranking

### Schedule and Highlights

**(H) Oct. 20—Arizona—31–6**

Frank Malette opened the season's scoring with a field goal in the first quarter. Robert "Shorty" Miller ran three yards for USC's first touchdown, and Malette added the conversion kick to give the Trojans a 10–0 lead. Arizona cut the deficit to 10–6 in the second quarter. In the second half, it was all USC. Miller scored on his second touchdown run, and Malette kicked the conversion for a 17–6 USC advantage. In the fourth quarter, the Wildcats got deep into Trojan territory, but "Pat" Lucas ended their quest for points when he intercepted the ball. At first Lucas bobbled the ball, but secured it and ran the length of the field for a touchdown. Malette added his third conversion, and then a fourth one after Lucas scored the Trojans' last touchdown.[1]

**(H) Oct. 27—St. Mary's—0–7**

The passing game in football was a rarity at this time, but St. Mary's used it well to bring the Trojans down. USC outplayed St. Mary's throughout three quarters, but the passing attack of St. Mary's wore USC down. The result was a long touchdown pass in the fourth that allowed St. Mary's to pull this game out in the last five minutes of play. The Trojans made it into St. Mary's territory throughout most of the game, but could not cross their goal line. As usual, Frank Malette turned in a solid performance whether it was running the ball, or playing great defense.[2]

**(A) Nov. 3—21st Infantry (U S Army, San Diego, California)—3–0**

A 35-yard field goal by Frank Malette in the second quarter was all the scoring in this game played in San Diego. It also produced the lowest winning score in USC history. In addition to his field goal, Malette supplied the Trojans with numerous long runs. The Army men came out strong from the start, gaining big chunks of yardage. The USC defense, led by two freshmen linemen, Beale and Evans, held off the opposition from scoring.[3]

**(H) Nov. 10—Fort MacArthur—42–0**

The Trojans scored more points in this game than in their three previous ones. Playing with a broken right hand, Frank Malette started the scoring off early. Within five minutes after the opening kickoff, Malette scored on a 15-yard run around the end and added the first of his three conversion kicks. Dan McMillan blocked a punt and it was recovered by Wright Hamilton, who took it in for a touchdown to make it 14–0. George Oertley threw a 40-yard touchdown pass to Malette to give USC a commanding 21–0 lead. After this game, Oertley left the team when he received his call to report for military duty. "Pat" Lucas scored two touchdowns in the third quarter, and Evans added a pair of conversion kicks to give USC a 35–0 lead heading into the fourth quarter. The only points scored in the final quarter were on a one-yard run by freshman Charley Dean. Evans then closed out the scoring with his third conversion kick.[4]

**(A) Nov. 17—Utah—51–0**

The Trojans continued to make up for lost time in the point production department. For the second straight week, they rang up a huge total. After losing to Utah two straight times, the Trojans left nothing to chance. Frank "Rabbit" Malette took command of the field by running for long gains and throwing passes. Malette scored two touchdowns and added three extra points in the rout. Wright Hamilton and Herbert Hunter each scored three touchdowns. A new mascot was introduced by USC in the form of a white female rat named "May," who the players felt was responsible for their good luck against Utah.[5]

**(N) Nov. 24—Mare Island—0–34**

The Mare Island team was considered one of the best teams assembled. It was an All-Star Marine team captained by University of Oregon tackle Johnny Beckett, who was a second team All-American performer. Played at Washington Park in Los Angeles, the Trojans were outweighed and totally out outplayed. Frank Malette received a bad cut above his eye, but still fought on. He almost broke free on a kickoff after USC was trailing 34–0, but after getting 40 yards upfield, he was stopped by the last player that had a chance to get him.[6]

**(H) Nov. 29—California—0–0**

Played on Thanksgiving Day in front of a crowd numbering 10,000, the Trojans were outweighed and did not have the same level of experience as the Golden Bears had. However, they fought hard in what became a punting duel. With three minutes left, Cal got to the USC two-yard line. They then fumbled, lost six yards, and the game ended right after that.[7]

## *1918*

HEAD COACH: Dean Cromwell
ASSISTANT COACHES: None
TEAM CAPTAINS: Harold Galloway and Herbert Hunter
RECORD: 2–2–2
FINISH IN CONFERENCE: Independent
FINISH IN NATIONAL POLLS: No ranking

### Schedule and Highlights

**(N) Nov. 23—Stanford—25–8**

Twelve days before USC kicked off their 1918 campaign, at 11:01 on the morning of November 11, 1918, the armistice was signed by the Germans to end World War I. After getting prepared for the regular season with pre-season games against Poly High School and the Naval Reserve, the Trojans traveled to Tournament Park in Pasadena, California, to play Stanford. The Trojans displayed great teamwork, especially when throwing the ball, and it overwhelmed Stanford.[1]

**(A) Nov. 30—Whittier Reform—13–13**

Coach Chamberlain's cadets from Whittier showed their toughness against a more experienced team, and came away with a deadlock at the end of the game. USC team captains Harold Galloway and Herbert Hunter stood out for the Trojans, while Maxwell gave Whittier something to cheer about by scoring on a 95-yard run.[2]

**(A) Dec. 7—Pomona—0–0**

This game was played for the most part with rain coming down. In USC's second straight tie game, neither team was able to get closer than 10 yards away from the other's end zone. The game eventually became a punting duel between USC's Harold Galloway and Nisbet of Pomona. Trojan players that stood out were Hunter, Beale, and Leadingham.[3]

**(H) Dec. 14—California—7–33**

This game marked the latest that USC ever played a home opener. Andy Smith's Cal Golden Bears invaded Bovard Field with a 6–2 record, and three straight shutout victories. The Trojans were able to perform on equal ground with Cal in the first quarter, but then the Bears just pounded away at the Trojans, who were not capable of keeping up with the onslaught.[4]

**(H) Dec. 21—Occidental—6–7**

This was considered the most exciting game of the season. The Trojans appeared to be in control of the game until the Tigers recovered a fumble in the third quarter, and that led to Occidental recording their second straight win over USC, with the last one coming in 1914.[5]

**(H) Dec. 25—Redlands—10–0**

This was the final time that USC ever played Redlands, and kept their record perfect against them at 4–0. Wright Hamilton and George Oertly starred for USC in this season-ending victory. This was also the final football game ever coached at USC by Dean "the Maker of Champions" Cromwell.[6]

## *1919*

HEAD COACH: Elmer Henderson
ASSISTANT COACHES: None
TEAM CAPTAIN: John Fox
RECORD: 4–1
FINISH IN CONFERENCE: Independent
FINISH IN NATIONAL POLLS: No ranking

### Schedule and Highlights

**(H) Oct. 25—Pomona—6–0**

A new era in USC football dawned with the arrival of head coach Elmer "Gloomy Gus" Henderson. He would eventually take the Trojans to the verge of the national prominence that they continue to enjoy since the 1920's. In his first game as head coach, Henderson's Trojans outplayed their rivals from Pomona in every phase of the game. In the middle of the first half, the Trojans began driving toward what would be the game's only points. After a balanced attack of runs and passes, John Leadingham threw a touchdown pass to Dan McMillan. The remainder of the game consisted mostly of a punting duel, with Leadingham doing the kicking for USC. The defense limited Pomona to only one first down. Charley Dean might have saved the game for USC in the closing seconds when he intercepted a pass that might have had a good chance of leading to a touchdown.[1]

**(H) Nov. 1—Occidental—27–0**

The Tigers of Occidental entered this game after the loss of their mascot, but looked to find some solace in beating the

Trojans for a third straight time. That did not happen, as the Trojans jumped out to an early lead within the first five minutes of the game. Jimmy Smith got the honors of scoring USC's first touchdown of the game after he picked up an Occidental fumble and took it over the goal line. Charley Dean added two touchdown runs to make the score 20–0. With the game well in hand, Henderson sent his second-string players in for some work during the second half. Holmes Packer ran for USC's final touchdown, and the Trojans remained undefeated and unscored upon during the early stages of the Elmer Henderson tenure.[2]

**(H) Nov. 8—California—13–14**

The California Bears were emerging as the football powerhouse of the west coast at this time under coach Andy Smith. When they came to Bovard Field for this game, they had a 4–1–1 record, and by the slimmest of margins, handed Elmer Henderson his first loss as coach of the Trojans. With 9,000 fans watching the action, the Trojans, who were supposed to lose this game by at least 30 points, fooled all the doubters by playing a tough game against a much bigger opponent. In the latter stages of the first quarter, the Trojans got on the board first when Eddie Simpson returned an interception 50 yards for a touchdown. Roy Evans added the conversion kick and USC shocked Cal by leading 7–0. The Trojans expanded their lead to 13–0 in the second quarter after Cal's fullback fumbled on the USC 30-yard line. Charley Dean picked the loose ball up and ran it all the way for six points. In the second half, Cal displayed their might by scoring on a pass from Rowe to Cline in the third quarter. Another touchdown pass in the third quarter tied the game, but Cline added what turned out to be the winning points on a conversion kick. The fourth quarter never saw neither team threaten to score.[3]

**(H) Nov. 15—Utah—28–7**

With sweltering temperatures hovering about Los Angeles, the Trojans won for the second straight time over Utah. USC led by a 7–0 count at the end of the first half, and then added two more touchdowns in the third quarter and one in the fourth to win convincingly over a physically drained Utah team that could not adapt to the heat. John Leadingham scored USC's first touchdown on a 15-yard fumble recovery. Eddie Simpson blocked a punt and Bill Isenhouer recovered the ball in the end zone for another defensive touchdown. The Trojan offense scored the team's final two touchdown on a pass from Charley Dean to James Woodward, and on a Holmes Packer run right before the end of the game.[4]

**(H) Nov. 27—Stanford—13–0**

This game was played on Thanksgiving Day in the mud, but despite the elements, the Trojans ended the decade of the 1910's on a positive note. Charley Dean continually plowed his way through a big Stanford line, and his other backfield mates also stunned Stanford with long gains. John Leadingham scored USC's first touchdown in the second quarter to give the Trojans a 6–0 halftime advantage. The Trojans might have gotten another touchdown in the first half, but time ran out with them on the Stanford one-yard line. Charley Dean ran for USC's other touchdown, and Roy Evans added the conversion kick for USC's final point of the decade.[5]

## *1920*

HEAD COACH: Elmer Henderson
ASSISTANT COACHES: None
TEAM CAPTAIN: Roy Evans
RECORD: 6–0
FINISH IN CONFERENCE: Independent
FINISH IN NATIONAL POLLS: No ranking

### Schedule and Highlights

**(H) Oct. 9—Cal Tech—46–7**

"Gloomy Gus" Henderson's charges began the Roaring Twenties in convincing fashion. This game was first scheduled as a practice game, but went into the record books as the official season opener with 5,000 in attendance. Despite some fumbling woes, the Trojans romped their way to victory. Charley Dean provided solid running, as did Ed Leahy, who used his speed to avoid many defenders. By the second half, Henderson sent in mostly all new players to finish off what turned into a 40-point victory.[1]

**(H) Oct. 16—Stanford—10–0**

This was one of the hardest-fought games from USC's early history. Stanford never seriously threatened to pull out the win, but the second half was a scoreless slugfest played predominately near midfield. John Leadingham scored on a run in the first quarter, and Roy Evans added a 35-yard field goal in the second quarter to complete the scoring. USC's backfield star Charley Dean was carried off the field in the third quarter with a severely sprained ankle.[2]

**(H) Oct. 23—Occidental—48–7**

Playing without Charley Dean due to his injured ankle, the Trojans used other offensive weapons to easily dispose of the Occidental Tigers. James Woodward, Andy Toolen, and Clarence Butterfield, all scored touchdowns to give USC a 21–7 halftime advantage. The Trojans then scored four more six-pointers in the second half. Butterfield scored again, this time on a fumble recovery in the end zone, Paul Greene had one touchdown, and the swift Ed Leahy had a pair of long scoring runs. At the end of this dominant win, the Trojans outgained the Tigers 303 yards to 13.[3]

**(A) Oct. 30—Pomona—7–0**

Following their easy win over Occidental seven days earlier, the Trojans had a struggle on their hands with Pomona. Each team battled for control of the line of scrimmage, holding off every scoring threat but one. The Trojans were able to penetrate the Pomona goal line for the lone score. In the first quarter, Pomona made it to the USC 25 before a Leo Calland interception ended the threat. Paul Beale later blocked a kick, and recovered the ball, just shy of the goal line. James Woodward scored, and Roy Evans added the conversion. In the latter stages of the game, Pomona made a serious charge at the USC end zone, but an incredible goal line stand with three minutes left secured the win to keep the Cardinal & Gold undefeated.[4]

**(H) Nov. 13—Nevada—38–7**

Throughout the history of USC's great running backs, there was always one signature game that stood out from all the rest.

For Charley Dean, the Nevada game of 1920 proved to be his greatest performance. For the first time since the Stanford game, Dean was physically healthy, which was good news for Trojan fans. He pounded the ball up the middle, ran around the ends, and when the game was over, Dean set a single-game USC record with four touchdowns. Ed Leahy once again used his speed to dazzle the opposition, and scored a pair of touchdowns.[5]

**(N) Nov. 25—Oregon—21–0**

The Trojans blanked their final opponent on the way to a perfect season with a record crowd of 20,000 looking on. With Tournament Park serving as the venue, USC gained 324 yards while holding Oregon to a mere 47. Going into the fourth quarter, the Trojans held a narrow 7–0 margin complements of a Charley Dean touchdown. Dean added another touchdown run, but had to leave the game after that due to a leg injury. John Leadingham threw a scoring strike to James Smith for USC's final six-pointer of the season with close to ten minutes remaining. Roy Evans connected on all three extra point kicks to round out the Trojan scoring. The Trojan defense allowed no forward passes to be completed, an occurrence that would happen 14 other times in USC history. Another record established in this game was allowing no first downs.[6]

## *1921*

HEAD COACH: Elmer Henderson
ASSISTANT COACHES: None
TEAM CAPTAIN: Charley Dean
RECORD: 10–1
FINISH IN CONFERENCE: Independent
FINISH IN NATIONAL POLLS: No ranking

### Schedule and Highlights

**(H) Oct. 1—USS Arizona—62–0**

This game was part of a doubleheader to open the new season. Bovard Field was reduced to a mud bath, but the Trojans managed to make their way through the mess for a convincing victory. USC opened up a 20–0 lead at the end of the first quarter, and continued to pile up the points. Phillip Tiernan led the onslaught with four touchdowns. Gordon Campbell added a pair of six-pointers, and Amor Galloway, Howard "Hobo" Kincaid, and the fleet-footed Ed Leahy, each added one touchdown apiece.[1]

**(H) Oct. 1—USS New York—35–0**

In the other game of a doubleheader, the Trojans once again prevailed by way of a shutout. In this game, the players from the USS New York put up a tough showing, battling the Trojans to a scoreless tie at the end of the first quarter. "Gloomy Gus" Henderson's charges then exploded for 14 points in each of the next two quarters to put the game away. Charley Dean and John Leadingham each scored two touchdowns to lead the Trojans.[2]

**(H) Oct. 8—Cal Tech—70–0**

Despite the quarters in the second half being cut to ten minutes each, the Trojans still managed to run up a single-game scoring record, and set another team record with 10 extra points. The Cal Tech Engineers never had a chance in this massacre at Bovard Field. Team Captain Charley Dean, Leo Calland, and Amor Galloway, each scored two touchdowns, while Leadingham, Kincaid, Dolley, and Hunter, all had one to help the Trojans set a single-game scoring record. The other team record of ten extra points was established thanks to the kicking abilities of Roy Evans, who connected on six, and Andy Toolen on four.[3]

**(H) Oct. 12—Sub Base—34–0**

This game, just like the doubleheader played on October 1st, was a practice, but the result was the same. The Trojans were proving to be a hard team to score against, as they posted their fourth straight shutout, and fifth over two seasons.[4]

**(A) Oct. 15—Occidental—42–0**

The opponent was different, but the result was the same. The Trojans piled up the points while limiting the opposition to very little. In the case of Occidental, they were allowed no points to give USC their sixth straight shutout, and seventh over two seasons. Frank Lockett and Andy Toolen each scored two touchdowns to pace the victors.[5]

**(A) Oct. 19—Sub Base—28–0**

With a crowd of 10,000 sailors in attendance, the Sub Base team from San Pedro, once again got blanked by the Trojans in a practice game. This game allowed many of the previously injured Trojans an opportunity to test out their limbs, and it appeared that they achieved their goal.[6]

**(H) Oct. 29—Pomona—35–7**

The year before, USC had a struggle against Pomona, winning by a 7–0 margin. This time out, it was Pomona that scored seven points. However, the Trojans compiled 35 for another easy win. The Trojans scored in the first quarter, and held a slim 7–0 advantage until the second half. They then added seven points in the third quarter, and put the game away in the fourth with 21 points. Pomona became the first team to score on USC in seven straight games going back to the previous season, but their lone touchdown came with USC well in control and using reserve players by that time. James Woodward scored a pair of touchdowns, while John Leadingham, Howard Kincaid, and Charley Dean, all added their names to the scoring column one time.[7]

**(A) Nov. 5—California—7–38**

The Golden Bears of Cal under head coach Andy Smith were the kings of the west coast during this time, while the Trojans were a few years away from taking over Cal's spot as the region's consistent alpha dogs. With a capacity crowd of 25,000 looking on, USC suffered their first loss of the decade at the hands of Cal's "Wonder Team" and star Brick Muller. The Trojans were able to hang tough with their foes from Northern California for a while, trailing by only a 14–7 count at the end of the first half. The Golden Bears then added major distance between themselves and the Trojans over the course of the second half. Cal shocked USC with a passing attack that was similar to using the modern day screen pass, and USC head coach "Gloomy Gus" Henderson had a hard time adjusting to it. Following this game, USC alum started to complain about Henderson's coaching ability despite his great success throughout his time as head coach.[8]

**(H) Nov. 19—Whittier—14-0**

After their lone loss of the season, the Trojans regrouped and went back to the business of winning. With touchdowns from Gordon Campbell and Howard Kincaid, the Cardinal & Gold were supreme rulers of the Southern California region. They scored in the first three minutes on a fumble recovery in the end zone by Campbell, who suffered a cracked collarbone during the game. His touchdown remained the only one until the fourth quarter.[9]

**(N) Nov. 26—Oregon State—7-0**

Played at Tournament Park in Pasadena, California, the Trojans showed the 17,500 in attendance that they were a solid team once again. Oregon State looked to be invincible over the first half of the season, scoring 221 points while allowing only 10. They then went on a three-game losing streak heading into this matchup, and could muster a mere 10 points in those losses. The USC line played like a concrete wall, not letting much get past them. In this low-scoring affair, the punting skills of John Leadingham kept Oregon State pinned deep in their own territory.[10]

**(N) Dec. 3—Washington State—28-7**

Once again played at Pasadena's Tournament Park, the Trojans were deemed as underdogs to the 4-1-1 Cougars, whose only loss came at the hands of the powerful Cal Golden Bears. With 12 members of the Trojans playing in their final college game, they set out to leave the Cardinal & Gold fold in excellent fashion. With only eight minutes expired in the first quarter, John Leadingham scored on a one-yard run to give USC a lead they never relinquished. Team Captain Charley Dean was one of the players seeing action for the last time as a Trojan. Throughout his final game as a member of the USC football program, Dean continually pounded the ball through the Washington State defense to claim his place among the all-time great backfield stars in Trojan history.[11]

# *1922*

HEAD COACH: Elmer Henderson
ASSISTANT COACHES: None
TEAM CAPTAIN: Leo Calland
RECORD: 10-1 overall (3-1 in Pacific Coast Conference)
(Ranked 9th best record in college football out of 109 teams)
FINISH IN CONFERENCE: 4th place
FINISH IN NATIONAL POLLS: No ranking
POINTS SCORED PER GAME: 21.5 to rank 28th out of 109 teams
POINTS ALLOWED PER GAME: 2.8 to rank 6th

## Schedule and Highlights

**(H) Sept. 30—USS Mississippi—20-0**

This game was part of a doubleheader, and the Trojans started off another season with a solid performance in this shutout win over USS Mississippi.[1]

**(H) Sept. 30—Alumni—20-0**

Charley Dean and Frank Malette were two of the earliest backfield stars in the long lineage of outstanding ball carriers in USC history. Their time as active members of the varsity was behind them by the 1922 season. However, along with other former players, Dean and Malette suited up to face the current edition of the Cardinal & Gold in the alumni game. No member of the alumni squad was able to penetrate into the varsity's end zone, and the result was a convincing shutout victory. Roy "Bullet" Baker scored for the varsity, and his performance impressed head coach "Gloomy Gus" Henderson into realizing that Baker was the next backfield star for the Trojans. This game was part of a doubleheader played by the Trojans, and also proved to be their 100th victory in USC history.[2]

**(A) Oct. 7—Pomona—54-13**

In the opening minutes of this game, Winchell Boice grabbed a fumble and ran 70 yards to open the scoring. Roy Baker ran for two touchdowns, and the Trojans opened up a 20-6 advantage by the end of the first quarter and were never challenged.[3]

**(H) Oct. 14—Arizona—15-0**

The Wildcats gave the Trojans a tough fight throughout much of the game. The only points up to the fourth quarter came on a John Milton field goal in the opening stanza. Gordon Campbell provided the Trojans with excellent running ability on punt returns and breakaway jaunts into the Arizona defense. He added a touchdown to his solid performance in the game's closing minutes. Hal Galloway also scored a touchdown, Leo Calland and Lowell Lindley provided excellent blocking skills, and the defense outdueled Arizona to shut out the Wildcats.[4]

**(H) Oct. 21—Nevada—6-0**

The Trojans were involved in another struggle, but once again, they prevailed, securing this victory with nine minutes left to play.[5]

**(N) Oct. 28—California—0-12**

This was the first football game played at the Rose Bowl in Pasadena, California. It also marked the first-ever game conference game played in USC history. The PCC opener saw the Trojans go against the Cal Golden Bears, who were still the kings of the western region. They were the only team to defeat the Trojans up to this time of the 1920s, doing it twice, including this time out. Cal scored every way possible. A field goal, touchdown, and safety, all added up to a victory for coach Andy Smith's "Wonder Team." Despite the loss, the Trojans gave Cal one of their toughest games during this time of dominance.[6]

**(H) Nov. 4—Occidental—46-0**

With many of his starters recovering from the tough game against Cal, coach Henderson wanted to rest them in preparation for Stanford. With 10,000 in attendance at Bovard Field, the hometown Trojans rolled to an easy win, scoring seven touchdowns in the process.[7]

**(A) Nov. 11—Stanford—6-0**

Under rainy conditions, the Trojans' 400-mile trek to Palo Alto proved to be worthwhile. Great defense and punting were the order of the day, as USC excelled in both departments to record their second straight shutout and first-ever win for the Trojans in the Pacific Coast Conference. Otto Anderson kept Stanford pinned down with booming punts that averaged fifty yards. Chet Dolley scored the game's only points on a one-yard run. This win, coupled with Cal's refusal to play in the Rose Bowl game, gave USC a chance to possibly play in their first bowl game.[8]

**(N) Nov. 18—Idaho—14–0**

This game, played at the Rose Bowl, had a major effect on who would play Penn State in the 1923 Rose Bowl Game. The Trojans provided their faithful with a splendid game on both sides of the ball. The defense did their job containing the Vandals, and recorded USC's third straight shutout. On offense, the Trojans displayed a well-balanced attack. Roy Baker, Phillip Tiernan, and Howard Kincaid, all handled the running duties, and Hal Galloway threw for two touchdowns, with Hayden Phythian on the receiving end of both scoring strikes.[9]

**(N) Nov. 30—Washington State—41–3**

Once again playing at the Rose Bowl, The Trojans wrapped up their first season playing in the PCC with a convincing win on Thanksgiving Day. Six times the Cardinal & Gold crossed the goal line while holding an eighth opponent from scoring a touchdown during the season. Roy "Bullet" Baker shot through the defense for three touchdowns, while John Riddle, Otto Anderson, and Gordon Campbell, all scored one touchdown apiece with 20,000 in attendance. It was now time for the Trojans to embark on their first exposure to post-season action, an occurrence that would become commonplace in the years to come.[10]

**Rose Bowl, (N) Jan. 1—Penn State—14–3**

"The Granddaddy of Them All." To college football fans, those five words can only refer to the Rose Bowl Game, a New Years Day tradition unlike any other since the first-ever clash in 1902. This post-season classic also became like a second home for the Trojans in the future. However, on the first day of 1923, this proved to be USC's initial experience in a bowl game, and the first Rose Bowl game played in the structure still in use well into the new millennium. This also marked the first time Penn State appeared in a post-season bowl game.

At this time period in the early 1920s, the California Golden Bears were the dominant power on the west coast's college football scene. They declined the invitation to represent the Pacific Coast Conference, so USC, in their first season of PCC membership, were the substitutes. Cal's loss was USC's gain, and Penn State's misery.

Penn State's woes began even before kickoff, as they were stuck in a traffic jam that made the team 45 minutes late getting to the stadium. When they finally did get to the Rose Bowl, the scheduled kickoff set for 2:15 p.m. was already running 10 minutes behind schedule. Penn State head coach Hugo Bezdek requested, and received, extra time to allow his players the opportunity to go through warm-up drills. The additional time was appreciated by the Nittany Lions, but lacked the same enthusiasm from USC's side. Dismay was so great that USC's mentor, Elmer "Gloomy Gus" Henderson, and Bezdek came close to waging a prizefight against each other over the issue.

The game started an hour late, and at first, the extra time allotted Penn State seemed to pay off. Henderson's "Gloomy Gus" moniker had to be apparent when the Nittany Lions took a 3–0 lead in the first quarter on a 20-yard field goal by Mike Palm. However, after that initial score, none of the additional time needed to warm up helped the representatives from the Keystone State. They were held to five first downs and 104 yards of total offense. Meanwhile, the Trojans first taste of bowl competition was christened with two touchdowns in the second and third quarters.

Halfback Gordon Campbell's name became the subject of USC trivia experts by being the first to score a touchdown in the school's illustrious bowl history. His one-yard blast into the end zone was followed by John Hawkins' conversion kick. Prior to Campbell's historic tally, Harold Galloway made one of the greatest plays up to that time in college football. On fourth down at the Penn State 10-yard line, Galloway made a spectacular diving catch of a poorly thrown ball from Campbell that helped set up USC's first score. He was knocked out when he landed on the two-yard line, and had to sit out the remainder of the quarter. Roy "Bullet" Baker scored USC's other touchdown in the third quarter on a one-yard run, and once again Hawkins added the extra point. For the day, Baker ran the ball 29 times for 123 yards.

This game not only provided milestones for the Trojans as a team, but it also marked the beginning of Giles Pellerin's passion for the Cardinal & Gold. This was the first time Pellerin saw the Trojans play, and starting three years later, he began an incredible streak of being in attendance for 797 consecutive USC football games. Ironically, his streak ended in 1998 at the Rose Bowl Stadium, the same site in which he saw his first USC game.[11]

## *1923*

HEAD COACH: Elmer Henderson
ASSISTANT COACHES: None
TEAM CAPTAIN: Chet Dolley
RECORD: 6–2 overall (2–2 in Pacific Coast Conference)
(Ranked 26th best record in college football out of 109 teams)
FINISH IN CONFERENCE: Tied for 3rd
FINISH IN NATIONAL POLLS: No ranking
POINTS SCORED PER GAME: 21.6 to rank 23rd out of 109 teams
POINTS ALLOWED PER GAME: 7.8 to rank 58th

### Schedule and Highlights

**(H) Sept. 29—Cal Tech—18–7**

This was the final game ever played on the USC campus, as the Trojans moved into the LA Coliseum the following week. The action was slow moving for the Trojans, as they attempted to get their rhythm going. During this adjustment period, Cal-Tech held the powerful Trojans scoreless throughout the first half with 10,000 in attendance for the final game at Bovard Field. The second half was a different story, as the Cardinal & Gold got a pair of touchdowns from Gordon Campbell and one from Otto Anderson, who earned his place in USC football history by being the last player to score a touchdown at Bovard Field.[1]

**(H) Oct. 6—Pomona—23–7**

This marked the first varsity football game played at the newly constructed Los Angeles Memorial Coliseum. The attendance for this historic event was 12,863. The Trojans received their first-ever Coliseum touchdown, complements of end Gene Dorsey in the first five minutes of the game. The Hollywood High School product scooped up a Pomona fumble and dashed 25 yards for the six-pointer and into USC trivia lore. The Trojans added 10 points in the second quarter on a John Riddle touchdown run, and a John Hawkins' field goal. Hawkins also added two conversion kicks. John Loustalot ran for USC's final points on this historic day in the third quarter. The starting lineup for USC in this first-ever game played at the Los Angeles Memorial Coliseum was: Hayden Phythian (LE), Fay Thomas (LT), John Hawkins (LG), Carleton Rice (C), Raymond Earle (RG), Ralph Cummings (RT), Gene Dorsey (RE), Chet Dolley (QB), John Riddle (LH), Wallace Newman (RH), Gordon Campbell (HB).[2]

**(H) Oct. 13—Nevada—33-0**

Nevada earned the distinction of being the first team to suffer a shutout loss to the Trojans at the LA Coliseum. John Hawkins opened the scoring by catching a touchdown pass from Wallace Newman. Hawkins also added two conversion kicks. Chet Dolley scored two touchdowns, and Otto Anderson and Henry Lefebvre each scored once.[3]

**(A) Oct. 20—Washington—0-22**

After three straight wins against non-conference foes, the Trojans opened their PCC schedule with a loss. This was one of the worst defeats up to this time period. Speed and power were common for Washington, and the combination allowed the Huskies to prevail in a major upset. Washington also displayed physical skills, as they sent Trojan players to the bench with a broken nose, cracked shoulder blade, and a wrenched knee.[4]

**(A) Oct. 27—Stanford—14-7**

Stanford came into the game with a 4-0 record, and had outscored the opposition 208 to six. It was assumed by many football insiders that Stanford would continue on with their winning ways against USC, especially after the Trojans were embarrassed by Washington one week earlier. However, the Trojans used that upset loss as a rallying cry. They then traveled up to Palo Alto and handed Stanford their first loss of the year. Stanford opened the scoring at the beginning of the second quarter. It was then that Holly Adams became a hero in the Land of Troy. Four times during this game, Stanford's great all-around performer, Ernie Nevers, had four punts blocked. On two of those occasions, Adams produced USC's touchdowns. In the second quarter, Harold Adams blocked a Nevers' punt and the ball bounced into the awaiting hands of Holly Adams, who scored USC's first touchdown. John Hawkins then tied the game at 7-7 with a conversion kick. That score remained the same until the fourth quarter when "Swede" Anderson blocked a punt, and once again, Holly Adams scored after recovering the loose ball, this time for the game-winner. This was the fifth straight time that USC sent Stanford down in defeat.[5]

**(H) Nov. 10—California—7-13**

A crowd of 72,000 came out to the Coliseum to see if the Trojans could repel another tough opponent from Northern California. The Golden Bears were unstoppable during their first seven games leading up to this matchup, as they prevented every opponent from scoring. They almost achieved another shutout, but the passing of Wallace Newman, coupled with the receiving skills of Gene Dorsey allowed the Trojans to make it down to the Cal one-yard line with 10 seconds remaining. Chet Dorsey then scored from six inches away as time expired. He became the only player to score on Cal all season. John Hawkins added a conversion kick to give the Trojans a moral victory over such a dominant opponent.[6]

**(H) Nov. 17—Arizona—69-6**

The Trojans severely tamed the Arizona Wildcats in one of the most-lopsided victories at the LA Coliseum. The Trojans led by a 17-0 count at the end of the first half, and then exploded for 51 points over the next two quarters. The 10-touchdown barrage was led by John Riddle's three scoring jaunts. Also scoring multiple touchdowns for USC were Henry Lefebvre and Otto Anderson, both of whom scored twice.[7]

**(H) Nov. 24—Idaho—9-0**

The Trojans finished their PCC schedule with back-to-back wins to even their conference record at 2-2. This was also the first season in USC history that the team saw the attendance for each game go well over the five digit mark. Chet Dolley finished the season by running well against the Vandals, and scored the game's only touchdown after catching a pass and making his way through four defenders on his way to the end zone. The Trojans finished with 264 yards of total offense, and nine out of 17 pass attempts.[8]

## *1924*

HEAD COACH: Elmer Henderson
ASSISTANT COACHES: None
TEAM CAPTAIN: John Hawkins
RECORD: 9-2 overall (2-1 in Pacific Coast Conference)
(Ranked 10th best record in college football out of 111 teams)
FINISH IN CONFERENCE: Tied for 4th
FINISH IN NATIONAL POLLS: No ranking
POINTS SCORED PER GAME: 24.5 to rank 10th out of 111 teams
POINTS ALLOWED PER GAME: 4.0 to rank 13th

### Schedule and Highlights

**(H) Sept. 27—Cal Tech—78-6**

This proved to be a great way to open a season. The Trojans set a team record with 12 touchdowns, and Ed Green set a school record with a 98-yard kickoff return. It was a record that held up for fifty years until Anthony Davis broke it. This 1924 team was considered to be Elmer Henderson's best during his tenure at USC. The Trojans scored their first touchdown five minutes after the opening kickoff, and built a 38-0 halftime lead. Helping USC establish a record for most touchdowns in a single game were Ray Earle with three six-pointers, followed by two from both Mort Kaer and L.V. "Babe" Weddle, one from Hank Lefebvre, Bob lee, Hobbs Adams, Newton Stark, and Manuel Laraneta.[1]

**(H) Oct. 4—Pomona—14-0**

Eugene Nixon took his Pomona charges into this clash with "Gloomy Gus" Henderson, and the experienced Pomona line contained runs both to the inside and on sweeps. The Trojan defense also refused to yield, and in the end, the Cardinal & Gold prevailed with a shutout victory. Team captain John Hawkins led by example, scoring both touchdowns and also connecting on the conversion kicks. This marked the 20th time these teams faced each other, and this extended USC's unbeaten streak against Pomona to eight games.[2]

**(H) Oct. 11—Arizona—29–0**

The opponent was different, but the results were the same. The Arizona Wildcats came into the Coliseum and left as USC's second straight shutout victim. Bill Cook got into his first game of the season, and was personally responsible for getting USC a pair of touchdowns. After a scoreless first quarter, Ray Earle scored the game's initial touchdown in the second stanza. The Trojans recorded a safety to give them a 9–0 lead at the end of the first half. Cook ran for a touchdown to make it 15–0, and then he threw a pass to John Hawkins that got the ball down to the one-yard line. John Riddle scored from there to make it 22–0, and Burt Heiser then added a final six-pointer with 18,000 in attendance. This win allowed USC to remain a perfect 6–0 against Arizona since the first meeting in 1916.[3]

**(N) Oct. 18—Oregon State—17–3**

On a mere four days rest, the Trojans were back on the field with Oregon State as the opponent. They kept a streak of not allowing a touchdown since the opener alive with 15,000 looking on at Multnomah Field in Portland, Oregon. The game started off as a punting duel, but then the Trojans pulled away on touchdowns from Ray Earle and John Riddle, and a 40-yard field goal by Norm Anderson.[4]

**(H) Oct. 25—Nevada—21–7**

Nevada came into the Coliseum looking for their first win over the Trojans since this series began in 1920. They appeared headed in the right direction by scoring the game's first points on a touchdown. This was the first touchdown allowed by USC in a month. The Trojans came back in the second quarter with the help of a solid passing attack. John Hawkins jumped high to catch a pass from Wallace Newman and found his way into the end zone with defenders all around him. Hawkins added the conversion, and the score was deadlocked at 7–7 going into the second half. The Trojans took the lead for good in the third quarter on a Ray Earle touchdown run. Five minutes later, Hawkins returned a punt 43 yards for the game's final six points.[5]

**(A) Nov. 1—California—0–7**

This was a matchup between two undefeated teams, as Henderson met Andy Smith's Bears before 60,000 in USC's first appearance in Memorial Stadium in Berkeley. Jim Dixon scored the game's lone touchdown on a 12-yard run in the second quarter. This pushed USC's record against Cal to 1–8–1, and started the demise of Henderson, who could only beat USC's main rival once during his tenure.[6]

**(H) Nov.8—St. Mary's—10–14**

Stanford was originally scheduled for this date, but "Slip" Madigan's St. Mary's Gaels served as a replacement. In one of the biggest upsets on the west coast in 1924, the Trojans came as close as they could to winning, but lost out in the end. They had the ball right on the Gaels' goal line when time ran out. The Trojans started off great, as Henry Lefebvre ran for an 80-yard touchdown on the game's first play from scrimmage. John Hawkins added a field goal a few minutes before the end of the first half, and the Trojans were up, 10–7. Two long pass completions assisted the Gaels in getting downfield, and they scored what were the winning points early in the second half.[7]

**(H) Nov. 15—Whittier—51–0**

The Poets of Whittier usually provided USC with a victory. In seven previous encounters, the Trojans prevailed six times. In this game, however, the Poets played tough during the first half. A Bob Lee touchdown in the second quarter was responsible for the only points of the first half. The Trojans then exploded for 45 points in the second half to defeat Whittier by the greatest margin up to this time in their series against them. Mort Kaer scored three touchdowns, Lee added his second of the day, and Henry Lefebvre, John Riddle, and John Hawkins all scored once. Hawkins also added three conversion kicks to his total.[8]

**(H) Nov. 22—Idaho—13–0**

This marked the third time these teams played each other, and USC won all of them by shutout. Idaho's defense gave the Trojans a battle by stopping them just shy of the end zone on three occasions. After a scoreless first half, the Trojans got close enough for John Hawkins to kick a pair of field goals, and the game's only touchdown came on a pass from Ed Green to Hayden Pythian.[9]

**(H) Dec. 6—Syracuse—16–0**

This was a game of firsts for USC. It marked their first-ever homecoming game, and the first time they played Syracuse, who came into the game with an 8–1–1 record. Syracuse was regarded as one of the top teams in the east. Hobbs Adams stood out in this shutout victory. With the game in its early stages, Adams blocked a kick, which was recovered by teammates Ted Gorrell and Fay Thomas at the Syracuse 11-yard line. Hobbs then kicked a 13-yard field goal to open the scoring with only three minutes expired in the first quarter. Four minutes later, Adams returned a punt 45 yards for a touchdown. The score remained 9–0 until the fourth quarter when Ed Green threw a 45-yard touchdown pass to John Hawkins. Hawkins added the conversion kick, and the game came to an end a short time later. This victory allowed the Trojans to gain attention and receive their first real bit of national recognition.[10]

**Christmas Festival Bowl, (H) Dec. 25—Missouri—20–7**

Head coach Gwinn Henry and his Missouri Tigers spent Christmas Day among the beautiful surroundings that Southern California offers. They earned a trip to Los Angeles for the Christmas Festival Bowl after recording a 7–1 regular season that included six shutouts, with three straight as they headed into this game.

The game remained a scoreless tie going into the third quarter, as both defenses played stellar football. The Trojans then broke through the tough Missouri defense, scoring all their points in the third quarter. With 47,000 in attendance at the Coliseum, USC received touchdowns by Henry Lefebvre, Red Badgro, and Hayden Pythian. It was the final appearance for Elmer "Gloomy Gus" Henderson as USC's head coach.[11]

# *1925*

HEAD COACH: Howard Jones
ASSISTANT COACHES: Aubrey Devine, Cliff Herd
TEAM CAPTAIN: Hobbs Adams
RECORD: 11–2 overall (3–2 in Pacific Coast Conference)
(Ranked 12th best record in college football out of 104 teams)
FINISH IN CONFERENCE: Tied for 3rd
FINISH IN NATIONAL POLLS:
POINTS SCORED PER GAME: 35.1 to rank 3rd out of 104 teams
POINTS ALLOWED PER GAME: 4.2 to rank 15th

## Schedule and Highlights

**(H) Sept. 26—Whittier—74–0**

The Whittier Poets came into this game with former Trojan captain Leo Calland as the coach. However, USC's Howard Jones won on this day in his coaching debut with the Cardinal & Gold. This was the worst defeat Whittier suffered from the Trojans. Mort Kaer opened the scoring in the first quarter, and added a second touchdown on a 40-yard run later. Kaer also threw the ball very well, as did Howard Elliott, who scored one touchdown. Morley Drury and Bill Cook each scored twice, and Bob Lee and Henry "the Flying Frenchman" Lefebvre got their names in the scoring column as well.[1]

**(H) Sept. 26—Cal Tech—32–0**

This game was part of a very successful doubleheader, as the Trojans manhandled two opponents on the same day by a commanding 106–0 margin. Morris Badgro caught a touchdown pass from Mort Kaer, and Howard Elliott ran for another score to give the Trojans a 12–0 halftime advantage. The Trojans added a touchdown in the third quarter, and then Kaer and Charles Galindo finished off the scoring with touchdowns in the final stanza.[2]

**(H) Oct. 3—Pomona—80–0**

The Trojan gridiron machine appeared to be headed toward unbelievable heights, as they rolled to their greatest margin of victory. Howard Elliott tied a USC record with four rushing touchdowns. The Trojans also tied a team record with 12 touchdowns scored in a single game, and set a team and conference record with 978 yards of total offense. Getting in on the scoring were Mort Kaer, who had three touchdowns, Bob Lee, Bill Cook, Morley Drury, Morris Badgro, and Manuel Laraneta. This was the final time that USC played Pomona. This series began in 1897, and over the course of 21 meetings, the Trojans posted a 13–4–4 record against the Sagehens.[3]

**(H) Oct. 10—Utah—28–2**

The powerful Trojans won, but were held to 28 points after scoring an incredible amount of 186 points in their first three games. Utah held USC to one touchdown in the first half, and forced them to punt from their own goal line on three occasions throughout the first half. The second half provided the Trojan faithful with more excitement. USC powered their way for three touchdowns, and Morley Drury added conversion kicks after all four Trojan touchdowns. Howard Elliott threw touchdown passes to Morris Badgro and Newton Stark, and ran for one himself. Mort Kaer scored the other Trojan touchdown on this day.[4]

**(H) Oct. 17—Stanford—9–13**

Glenn "Pop" Warner's boys proved too much for the Howard Jones' charges in their PCC opener. A crowd of 72,000 filled the Coliseum for the largest attendance figure of the season. This was a very tough, physical game that saw the Trojans get to the Stanford one-yard line early in the game, only to be stopped short of the end zone. Stanford's star all-around player Ernie Nevers scored the game's first touchdown, but the conversion was missed, and Stanford held a 6–0 lead. Michael Murphy scored Stanford's other touchdown in the second quarter to make it a 13–0 game. The Trojans received their only touchdown on a pass from Morley Drury to Howard Elliott. Drury added the conversion. The Trojans got two more points when Newton Stark blocked a Nevers' kick near the goal line. The ball rolled into the end zone and was recovered by a Stanford player for a safety.[5]

**(H) Oct. 24—Arizona—56–0**

The Trojans came back strong from their first defeat in Howard Jones' coaching reign. In their second straight shutout over Arizona, the Trojans scored eight touchdowns. Bill Cook scored three touchdowns, Howard Elliott scored twice and threw a touchdown pass to Morley Drury, Henry Lefebvre added one six-pointer, and a blocked punt by Brice Taylor led to another touchdown.[6]

**(A) Oct. 30—Idaho—51–7**

The Trojans evened their PCC record at 1–1 with another impressive scoring barrage. Wind and wet conditions made the field slippery, but the powerful Trojan offensive attack still managed to score over 50 points for the fourth time this season. This was the first time that the Trojans played on the road with Howard Jones as coach. Brice Taylor and Jeff Cravath anchored a line that blew open holes for the "Thundering Herd" to run through with fantastic results. Morley Drury ran for two touchdowns and caught a touchdown pass from Mort Kaer. Kaer scored three touchdowns himself, Ray Earle returned a fumble recovery for a touchdown, and Manuel Laraneta scored on a 48-yard interception return. This was the first time in four games against the Trojans that Idaho was able to score any points.[7]

**(H) Nov. 7—Santa Clara—29–9**

The "Thundering Herd" tamed the Broncos of Santa Clara with Morley Drury leading the attack. He did everything for USC on this day, whether it was passing, running, catching, or kicking, he did it all very well. Drury scored three touchdowns, and added four conversion kicks, to give him 22 points for the game. He also set up a touchdown with a 38-yard run down to the Santa Clara 12-yard line. Bill Cook scored three plays later.[8]

**(H) Nov. 14—Montana—27–7**

The Montana Grizzlies came into the Coliseum with a lighter team, and the power of USC's "Thundering Herd" proved too much for them. The Trojans gained yards with ease, and within the first three minutes of the game, Manuel Laraneta threw a touchdown pass to Mort Kaer. Kaer scored two more touchdowns, and Laraneta added one. In the second half, the Grizzlies managed to play USC a bit tougher and got their only points during that time.[9]

**(H) Nov. 21—Iowa—18–0**

The Iowa Hawkeyes were considered one of the top teams in the Big Ten Conference, but the Trojans showed that the west was best, securing their fifth shutout of the season in USC's homecoming game. Manuel Laraneta was the main weapon for the Trojans on this day. He scored two touchdowns and had an interception that stopped an Iowa scoring threat. The Trojans were up by a 12–0 score at the end of the first half due to Laraneta's six-pointers, and then added a third touchdown in the fourth quarter when Mort Kaer ran off tackle to paydirt.[10]

**(H) Nov. 28—Washington St.—12–17**

Washington State came into this game with a 1–3–1 record, and unable to score any points in three straight games. They apparently saved their best for the Trojans, who entered this contest with a 9–1 record. Washington State's Roy Meeker ran the opening kickoff back to midfield. Meeker was also the Cougars' quarterback, and caught USC off guard when he threw a pass that gave Washington State a quick six points after one minute of play. Manuel Laraneta got USC on the board with a touchdown in the first half, and then the Trojans took a 12–10 lead on a Howard Elliott touchdown run in the second half. The Trojans were driving for another score when Meeker intercepted a pass. Near the end of the game, the Cougars scored the winning points on a long pass. Manuel Laraneta scored USC's other touchdown. This loss caused the Trojans to fall to 2–2 in the PCC. Despite the loss, some of the Trojans were recognized for their exceptional play. Guard Brice Taylor was bestowed with All-American honors, and All-Coast selection went to Jeff Cravath (center), Hobbs Adams (end), and Morley Drury (halfback).[11]

**(H) Dec. 5—Oregon State—28–0**

The Trojans rebounded from their loss to Washington State, and finished their PCC schedule off in winning fashion. This was a true testament of Howard Jones' famed "Thundering Herd" style of power. Mort Kaer scored three touchdowns, and Howard Elliott returned an interception 36 yards for the Trojans' other touchdown. Jeff Cravath helped shut out a sixth opponent by stopping drives with three interceptions.[12]

**(H) Dec. 12—St. Mary's—12–0**

This seventh shutout of the season brought an end to Howard Jones' first year as head coach of the Trojans. Mort Kaer ran for one touchdown and threw to Field Thompson for USC's other score. Jeff Cravath played an exceptional game on the line, whether it was blocking for backs on offense, or making stops on opposing ball carriers on defense. Following this game, Cravath was elected team captain for the following season by a unanimous vote.[13]

### Team Leaders

Rushing: Mort Kaer—576 yards on 105 carries
Scoring: Mort Kaer—114 points on 19 touchdowns

## *1926*

Head Coach: Howard Jones
Assistant Coaches: Aubrey Devine, Cliff Herd
Team Captain: Jeff Cravath
Record: 8–2 overall (5–1 in Pacific Coast Conference)
(Ranked 21st best record in college football out of 96 teams)
Finish in Conference: 2nd
Finish in National Polls: No ranking
Points Scored Per Game: 31.7 to rank 2nd out of 96 teams
Points Allowed Per Game: 5.2 to rank 24th

### Schedule and Highlights

**(H) Sept. 25—Whittier—74–0**

Speed and power are two ingredients needed to produce stellar results on a football team. The 1926 Trojans were one of those teams that possessed both, and made the most of their opportunities. On offense, USC packed an incredible punch, and on the defensive side, they dished out a great deal of punishment. They then went out in their season opener and lived up to their reputation by dismantling the Whittier Poets in resounding fashion, 74–0. The "Red Bluff Terror," Mort Kaer, accounted for four six-pointers, and quarterback Don Williams lit up the scoreboard with three more touchdowns. Williams also threw a touchdown pass to Morris Badgro.[1]

**(H) Oct. 2—Santa Clara—42–0**

Santa Clara was the next victim rolled over by the USC juggernaut. This time the Trojans won, 42–0, thanks to a ground pounding running attack and passing game that left the Broncos battered and bruised. Running back Morley Drury led the assault with 118 yards rushing on 21 carries and two touchdowns, and added three conversion kicks. Manuel Laraneta broke a scoreless tie in the second quarter with a long touchdown run, and later threw a scoring strike to Gene Dorsey. Lloyd Thomas intercepted a pass, and on the following play, caught a touchdown pass from Howard Elliott, and Max Thomas added a touchdown.[2]

**(H) Oct. 9—Washington State—16–7**

The Trojans rebounded from the previous season loss to Washington State in their Pacific Coast Conference opener to remain undefeated. This time out, the Trojans were faced with a challenging afternoon, as their powerful offense was prevented from piercing the goal line on three separate occasions, from inside the Washington State five-yard line in the second quarter. The Trojans led by a mere 2–0 count at the half, but then relied on an aerial attack by Mort Kaer's touchdown passes to Morley Drury and Morris "Red" Badgro. When not throwing touchdown passes, Kaer managed to run for 113 yards on 30 carries against a tough defense.[3]

**(H) Oct. 16—Occidental—28–6**

The Occidental Tigers came into this game with a 1–1–1 record, and received their first win of the season one week earlier by shutting out Redlands, 27–0. Their confidence was high as they traveled to USC. They managed to stop the powerful Trojans from crossing the goal line four times after getting inside the 10-yard line, but the feisty band of Tigers still did not have enough fight in them to hold back a USC ground attack, ranked third in the nation that produced three 100-yard rushers. Manual Laraneta led the Trojans with 177 yards on 25 carries, Mort Kaer added 164 yards on 12 carries and three touchdowns, and Howard Elliott carried the ball 12 times for 113 yards and one touchdown.[4]

**(A) Oct. 23—California—27–0**

The Golden Bears of Cal awaited the Trojans next. Cal's coach, Clarence Price, attempted to downplay the scoring prowess of their rivals by calling USC the "Doddering Herd," which was a slam on the mightier-sounding "Thundering Herd." Price appeared to be trying anything to pump up his team after two straight losses left them at 2–2 coming into this game. However, the negative comment from Price did little to stop the Trojans from showing Cal that they were indeed a "Thundering Herd." They rolled up 608 yards of offense, and Mort Kaer established a new single-game USC rushing record with 183 yards, and scored two touchdowns. Manual Laraneta recorded 130 yards for his second straight 100-yard performance, and threw a touchdown pass to Don Williams. Williams added a touchdown pass of his own to Field Thompson. Team Captain Jeff Cravath showed his grit as one of the best centers in the nation. Despite playing with a leg injury, Cravath managed to perform brilliantly, whether it was by opening holes for runners, recovering fumbles, or stopping opposing runners when on defense. California did not complete one pass.[5]

**(H) Oct. 30—Stanford—12–13**

Glenn "Pop" Warner once again got the best of Howard Jones by the narrowest of margins to knock the Trojans from the unbeaten ranks. With a crowd of 78, 500 on hand at the Los Angeles Memorial Coliseum, the battle of unbeatens clashed in a classic battle. The Trojans drew first blood in the first quarter when Mort Kaer capped off a 60-yard drive with a short yardage touchdown. Lloyd Thomas then expanded the Trojan advantage to 12–0 when he took a fumble recovery 50 yards for the score. Manual Laraneta missed both extra point attempts, and that eventually led to USC's downfall. Stanford came back to cut the lead to 12–6 at the half, and then produced the tying touchdown on a Bill Hoffman to Dick Hyland pass that covered 50 yards. The winning point was then added when George Bogue connected on the conversion kick.[6]

**(N) Nov. 11—Oregon State—17–7**

The Trojans rebounded on a trip to Multnomah Stadium in Portland, Oregon. In a game that saw the USC ground forces slowed by a wet and muddy field, Mort Kaer still churned out 114 yards on 31 carries to power USC to victory. Kaer also threw a touchdown pass to Manuel Laraneta, and then scored the clinching six-pointer in the final stanza. Brice Taylor added a field goal for USC's first points of the game in the opening quarter. Oregon scored in the final minute when the game was already out of reach.[7]

**(H) Nov. 20—Idaho—28–6**

With Mort Kaer nursing a leg injury, Howard Elliott paced the attack by scoring three touchdowns, and had an additional four points on conversion kicks. He also threw a touchdown pass to Morris Badgro to help the Trojans with a solid win over Idaho.[8]

**(H) Nov. 25—Montana—61–0**

Coach Howard Jones announced that he was going to keep Mort Kaer out of this game due to his leg injury. The loss of their All-American did not hamper the Trojans, as they wrapped up their PCC schedule with a blowout victory on Thanksgiving Day. Manuel Laraneta and Howard Elliott both scored three touchdowns apiece and Don Williams added a pair.[9]

**(H) Dec. 4—Notre Dame—12–13**

This homecoming game marked the dawn of one of college's sports greatest rivalries. It was Knute Rockne's Fighting Irish that spoiled USC's homecoming with a narrow victory. The Fighting Irish came into the Coliseum for their first-ever meeting with the Trojans in foul moods. Their chance at an unbeaten season was spoiled one week earlier in a 19–0 loss to Carnegie Tech.[10] The Trojans won the coin toss and elected to kick off. Brice Taylor was then responsible for starting off this classic rivalry by sending the opening kickoff into the end zone. An offsides penalty forced the Trojans to re-kick, and this time Taylor's kick was fielded by John Niemiec on his 15 and returned to the Notre Dame 33. Notre Dame drew first blood in the second quarter when Charlie Riley scored on a 16-yard run around the left end. Mort Kaer produced USC's first touchdown in this long-running series on a 1-yard run. Taylor's extra point attempt was blocked, and the Trojans trailed by a slim 7–6 margin at the half. The Trojans took the lead on a nine-yard run by Don Williams, who was the workhorse on an 11-play drive that saw him carry the ball 10 times. On the conversion attempt, Morley Drury's kick hit an upright and came back onto the field. The score remained 12–7 until Notre Dame began their winning drive in the latter stages of the fourth quarter. In the closing two minutes, the Fighting Irish were faced with a third-and–13 situation, and the Coliseum crowd of 74,378 seemed to be feeling that victory was close for their beloved Trojans. However, an Art Parisien to John Niemiec pass in the closing seconds from 23 yards out, proved to be the game-winner in what legendary Notre Dame coach Knute Rockne claimed to be the best game he ever witnessed.[11]

### Team Leaders

RUSHING: Mort Kaer—852 yards on 155 carries
SCORING: Mort Kaer—72 points on 12 touchdowns

## *1927*

HEAD COACH: Howard Jones
ASSISTANT COACHES: Jeff Cravath, Aubrey Devine, Cliff Herd
TEAM CAPTAIN: Morley Drury
RECORD: 8–1–1 overall (4–0–1 in Pacific Coast Conference)
(Ranked 16th best record in college football out of 99 teams)
FINISH IN CONFERENCE: Tied Stanford for 1stplace
FINISH IN NATIONAL POLLS: No ranking
POINTS SCORED PER GAME: 28.7 to rank 8th out of 99 teams
POINTS ALLOWED PER GAME: 6.4 to rank 28th

### Schedule and Highlights

**(H) Sept. 24—Occidental—33–0**

On September 20, 1927, a crowd of 60,000 came out to the LA Coliseum to pay homage to Charles Lindbergh, who became the first aviator to fly solo across the Atlantic Ocean. Four days later, Morley Drury had a crowd of 20,000 witness "the Noblest Trojan of Them All" attack the Occidental team on land, rushing for 100 yards on 22 carries and two touchdowns in this lopsided victory. Adding touchdowns in this opening day romp were Harry Edelson, Don Williams, and Howard Elliott[1]

**(H) Oct. 1—Santa Clara—52–12**

In another convincing win, Morley Drury ran for 107 yards on 13 carries and scored twice. The Trojans' "Thundering Herd" exploded for three scores in the second quarter to take a 25–0 lead into the second half. The second quarter point explosion saw Don Williams score once, and Howard Elliott accounted for two touchdowns by running for one and throwing to Francis Tappaan for another one. Drury added an exciting 57-yard run after taking a lateral pass from Harry Edelson. Elliott scored again on a 40-yard interception return, Lloyd Thomas ran back a kickoff 89 yards, and Rocky Kemp threw to Karl Kreiger for USC's final touchdown[2]

**(H) Oct. 8—Oregon State—13–12**

After two easy victories, the Trojans found themselves in a struggle in their PCC opener. The Trojans won it in the final five minutes, in a game that was considered one of the best played in the Coliseum up to this time. Orile Robbins of Oregon State set a conference record by scoring from 76 yards out with a blocked punt. Howard Elliott scored USC's first touchdown on an eight-yard run. Oregon State then came back later in the first half to score on a blocked punt by Morley Drury deep in USC territory. Drury got off some long runs in the third quarter, but on some of those occasions, the gains were negated by penalties or fumbles. Oregon State added their second touchdown of the game on a 70-yard fumble recovery, and the Trojans were facing the possibility of losing for the first time. However, a big break with four minutes left in the game allowed USC to remain undefeated. Oregon State fumbled on their four-yard line and Elliott recovered. He then scored his second touchdown of the game to pull out the victory.[3]

**(A) Oct. 15—Stanford—13–13**

Morley Drury was living up to his legend as "the Noblest Trojan" by pounding the ball inside the tackles or around the ends. When he was finished, Drury carried the ball 39 times for 140 yards, and one touchdown. He also had three interceptions that stopped Stanford advances. Russ Saunders provided the Trojans with their other touchdown.[4]

**(H) Oct. 22—Cal Tech—51–0**

The Trojans scored eight touchdowns in this blowout victory. The Trojans were so dominant that for the majority of the first half, the game was almost exclusively played in Cal Tech territory. USC led 18–0 at the end of the first half, and then the second team came in to continue on with exceptional play. The game was virtually over by the end of the third quarter, with the Trojans up, 32–0. Don Williams scored two of USC's eight touchdowns. Also adding touchdowns were Howard Elliott, Don Moses, Mahlon Chambers, and Karl Kreiger.[5]

**(H) Oct. 29—California—13–0**

With 85,000 in attendance at the Coliseum, the Trojans were set to face Cal's "Wonder Team." The Golden Bears came into this game with a 5–0 record, and only allowed six points scored on them in the first game of the season. They were on four-game streak of shutout victories as they took the field against the Cardinal & Gold. None of that mattered, however, as the "Thundering Herd" ran hard and the defense could not be penetrated. In this true team effort, Morley Drury was amazing. He ran for 203 yards on 42 carries to establish a new USC single-game rushing record. The old record was 183 yards set in 1926 by Mort Kaer. Don Williams ran for one touchdown, and threw a scoring strike to Lawrence McCaslin[6]

**(H) Nov. 12—Colorado—46–7**

Jeff Cravath served as head coach for this game while Howard Jones scouted the Washington-Cal matchup. The former team captain, and current assistant, did a great job in a substitute role. Helping make Cravath look good was the exceptional talent of Morley Drury, who scored three touchdowns, including an exciting 42-yard run. With the score at 13–0, Cravath sent in the second team, and they continued on toward an easy victory. Howard Elliott ran for one score and threw to Tony Steponovich for another one. Don Moses added one six-pointer, and Rocky Kemp bolted through the Colorado defense for a 53-yard scoring jaunt to complete the rout.[7]

**(H) Nov. 19—Washington State—27–0**

Don Williams ran for 150 yards on 20 carries, with one of those on an exciting 73-yard touchdown run. Rocky Kemp also added a long-distance scoring run from 53 yards out to spark the Trojans. The Trojans took the lead in the first seven minutes on a Don Moses run, and Howard Elliott scored USC's other touchdown on an 11-yard run.[8]

**(N) Nov. 26—Notre Dame—6–7**

An incredible crowd of 120,000 jammed into Soldier Field in Chicago to witness this game between the 7–0–1 Trojans and the 6–1–1 Fighting Irish. Not only was this the largest crowd to ever see the Trojans play in person, but one of the largest in the history of college football. Among the massive crowd were many of Chicago's famous bootleggers, but thankfully no problems arose, considering that the Windy City was ranked the most notorious metropolis in the nation during the height of Prohibition.

Both teams gave the fans their money's worth with a nail-biting struggle. The Trojans scored first when team captain Morley Drury tossed a 15-yard scoring strike to Russ Saunders, but Drury's conversion kick missed its mark. A few series later, Notre Dame tied the game on a 25-yard pass from Charley Riley to Ray Dahman. Dahman then booted what proved to be the winning point when he split the uprights with his conversion kick. All the scoring occurred in the first 10 minutes of the game, and from there it was a tough ground battle, with Drury running for 102 yards on 29 carries and Notre Dame's Christy Flanagan pounding out 124.

The game had a touch of controversy that added to the drama of this classic rivalry. Drury threw a pass in the direction of Lawrence McCaslin on fourth down, but Charley Riley intercepted it at the Notre Dame three-yard line. He looked to advance the ball and was hit hard by Saunders, causing Riley to fumble. The loose ball went out of the end zone and was originally ruled a safety, giving the Trojans an 8–7 lead. However, umpire John Schommer changed the ruling by claiming Riley never had possession, and it went into the stat book as an incomplete pass. Notre Dame took over on downs from that point, and despite much protest by USC players and coaches, Schommer's ruling stood up and the Trojans lost a heartbreaker.[9]

**(H) Dec. 3—Washington—33–13**

On USC's homecoming weekend, Morley Drury performed for the final time as a Trojan, and left the Coliseum in outstanding fashion. He ran for 183 yards on 17 carries, scored three touchdowns, and added an extra point to give him 19 points for the game. One of his scoring runs covered 76 yards. As he left the Coliseum after scoring his third and final touchdown, the crowd of 60,000 rose up from their seats to give the "Noblest Trojan of them all" a standing ovation. Don Moses also topped the century mark on the ground with 112 yards on 23 carries and one touchdown.[10]

TEAM LEADERS

RUSHING: Morley Drury—1,163 yards on 223 carries
SCORING: Morley Drury—76 points on 11 touchdowns and 10 extra points

## *1928*

HEAD COACH: Howard Jones
ASSISTANT COACHES: Jeff Cravath, Aubrey Devine, Cliff Herd
TEAM CAPTAIN: Jesse Hibbs
RECORD: 9–0–1 overall (4–0–1 in Pacific Coast Conference)
(Ranked 3rd best record in college football out of 100 teams)
FINISH IN CONFERENCE: 1st—1928 PCC Champions
FINISH IN NATIONAL POLLS: 1928 National Champions
POINTS SCORED PER GAME: 26.7 to rank 8th out of 100 teams
POINTS ALLOWED PER GAME: 5.9 to rank 30th

### Schedule and Highlights

**(H) Sept. 29—Utah State—40–12**

The Trojans opened against the swift and experienced Aggies. However, the Cardinal & Gold were far too powerful, and rolled up a 21–0 halftime lead. Don Williams led the attack with 111 yards rushing on 14 carries and two touchdowns. Frank Anthony opened the scoring for the Trojans by recovering a loose ball that touched a Utah State player on a punt return. The ball rolled into the end zone and Anthony pounced on it for six points. Russ Saunders ran for a touchdown, and Marger Apsit and Lloyd Thomas both returned interceptions for touchdowns, and the Trojans started off the new season in excellent fashion.[1]

**(H) Oct. 6—Oregon State—19–0**

Don Williams topped the century mark on the ground for the second straight week by running for 104 yards on 23 carries and two touchdowns. USC's other touchdown came when Lawrence McCaslin blocked a kick and Clark Galloway recovered the ball in the end zone. Oregon State came into the Coliseum with backfield star Howard Maple, who was considered the best runner in the Great Northwest, but the Trojans kept him out of the end zone all day.[2]

**(H) Oct. 13—St. Mary's—19–6**

For the third straight week, Don Williams ran for over 100 yards, this time compiling 149 yards on 33 carries to help keep the Trojans undefeated. The St. Mary Gaels played tough, and the game was tied at 6–6 late in the third quarter. Williams broke the tie with a seven-yard touchdown reception from Lloyd Thomas, and Herschel Bonham added an insurance touchdown run that allowed USC to pull away at the end.[3]

**(A) Oct. 20—California—0–0**

This was matchup of two undefeated teams, and in the end, neither one could get an advantage on the other. The field conditions at Berkeley were awful, as the playing surface lacked grass, was covered with a thin layer of sand, and was wet. With 75,000 in attendance, Cal focused their attention on stopping USC's talented back, Don Williams. They succeeded, and inflicted punishment on him throughout the game. The Trojans were favored, but the Golden Bears rose up to the challenge defensively.[4]

**(H) Oct. 27—Occidental—19–0**

Another struggle was waged, as the Trojans found themselves in a tough game against Occidental, a team they were supposed to dominate. It remained close throughout he first half, but then USC got rolling and took control. A bad snap from center sent the ball sailing toward the Occidental goal line early in the third quarter. Lawrence McCaslin got to the ball, scooped it up, and raced 15 yards for a touchdown. Still in the third quarter, Francis Tappaan ran untouched for a 12-yard touchdown on a sweep. Marshall Duffield completed the scoring with a one-yard run on the first play of the fourth quarter.[5]

**(H) Nov. 3—Stanford—10–0**

Howard Jones had not beaten Pop Warner in three tries until his "Thundering Herd" did it before 80,000 at the Coliseum. Warner felt this Stanford team was his best, but they lost five turnovers to USC. Stanford had a 10-pound per man weight advantage over the Trojans, but it was offset by USC's "quick-mix" defense and a speedy backfield of Don Williams, Russ Saunders and Marshall Duffield. This was a landmark game, as it signaled USC's rise to powerhouse status among colleges on the west coast. From this game on, Jones never went down in defeat to Warner again. Russ Saunders scored the game's only touchdown.[6]

**(H) Nov. 10—Arizona—78–7**

Marshall Duffield ran for 110 yards on 18 carries and scored four touchdowns in this romp. Everett Brown also topped the century rushing mark with 101 yards on 15 carries and scored two touchdowns. Bert Ritchey also scored a pair of touchdowns, while Jess Hill, Harry Edelson, Russ Saunders, and Jess Mortensen, each scored one, and the Trojans tied a team record with 12 touchdowns in a single game.[7]

**(H) Nov. 17—Washington State—27–13**

Howard Jones considered this to be one of his team's toughest challenges to the season as game day approached. Washington State had a 7–1 record, and recorded three straight shutouts leading up to this game at the Coliseum. The game proved to be a tough affair, but the loss of five fumbles hurt Washington State. The Trojans held a slight 13–6 halftime advantage due to a Lloyd Thomas to Russ Saunders 10-yard pass and a 75-yard run by Marshall Duffield. Washington State came back at the start of the second half when Ted Rohwer returned a kickoff 95 yards. Francis Tappaan then recovered and returned a fumble 37 yards for six points, and later caught a six-yard touchdown pass from Saunders.[8]

**(H) Nov. 24—Idaho—28–7**

The Trojans were held scoreless in the first half, but then got going. Don Williams ran for two touchdowns, as did Jess Hill, with one of his coming on a run that covered 60 yards. Russ Saunders ran for 122 yards on 27 carries, and with this victory, the Trojans clinched the Pacific Coast Conference championship.[9]

**(H) Dec. 1—Notre Dame—27–14**

On what was their homecoming weekend, the Trojans came into this game favored for the first time against Notre Dame. The Trojans lived up to being favorites by getting a big play when Jesse Hibbs blocked a punt and Don Williams recovered on the USC 36 late in the first quarter. That led to the game's first points on a Russ Saunders three-yard run, but Hibbs missed the conversion kick. The Trojans struck again in the second quarter when Williams connected with Marger Apsit for a 19-yard touchdown. The USC defense got into the act when end Tony Steponovich picked off a John Niemiec pass and ran it back for a touchdown. Hibbs added the extra point, and USC was up by a comfortable 20–0 margin. The Trojans added one more six-pointer on a short pass from Williams to Lowrey McCaslin, and USC won their first-ever contest against Notre Dame on the way to the program's first national championship.[10]

TEAM LEADERS

RUSHING: Don Williams—681 yards on 173 carries
SCORING: Don Williams—47 points on 7 touchdowns and 5 extra points

## *1929*

HEAD COACH: Howard Jones
ASSISTANT COACHES: Sam Barry, Aubrey Devine, Cliff Herd
TEAM CAPTAIN: Nate Barragar
RECORD: 10–2 overall (6–1 in Pacific Coast Conference)
(Ranked 11th best record in college football out of 100 teams)
FINISH IN CONFERENCE: 1st—1929 PCC Champions
FINISH IN NATIONAL POLLS: No ranking
POINTS SCORED PER GAME: 41.0 to rank 1st out of 100 teams
POINTS ALLOWED PER GAME: 5.8 to rank 19th

### Schedule and Highlights

**(H) Sept. 28—UCLA—76–0**

In time, UCLA would rise to the ranks of being on equal ground with the Trojans. However, when this classic cross-town rivalry began, it was USC's Thundering Herd against UCLA's pathetic sheep following the herd. The Bruins had only 74 games worth of experience compiled over ten seasons coming into this game. The Trojans, on the other hand, had 36 years and 226 games to their credit. On this day, experience won out in big fashion.

With 35,000 on hand to witness the start of what would one day become a classic rivalry, Russ Saunders ran for 50 yards late in the first quarter to begin the massacre. Erny Pinckert, Jess Hill, and Gus Shaver all added touchdowns in the first half to give the Trojans a 32–0 halftime advantage. In the second half, USC's head coach Howard Jones eased up on the battered Bruins by replacing his All-Americans, but that still did not slow up the Trojans.

In the end, records were shattered. Russ Saunders ran for 234 yards on just 14 carries to set a new USC single-game rushing record previously held by Morley Drury since 1927. Jess Hill chipped in with 152 yards rushing on 14 carries, and as a team, the Trojans gained 753 yards on the ground to establish a USC single-game and conference record. They also tied a team record with 12 touchdowns in one game.[1]

**(H) Oct. 5—Oregon State—21–7**

The Trojans scored all their points in the second quarter. Jim Musick ran for one, and Ernie Pinckert threw two scoring strikes to Garrett Arbelbide.[2]

**(A) Oct. 12—Washington—48–0**

This was the worst beating Washington had taken from USC up to this time in their history. The "Thundering Herd" galloped over and around the Huskies for seven touchdowns, with Jess Hill leading the way. He ran for 110 yards on only nine carries and scored two touchdowns, as did Jim Musick.[3]

**(H) Oct. 19—Occidental—64–0**

In another offensive explosion, the mighty "Thundering Herd" pounded Occidental into the ground with a powerful running attack that saw three USC backs go over the century mark and produce 10 touchdowns. Marshall Duffield led the charge with 122 yards on a mere nine carries, and scored three touchdowns. Gus Shaver had 110 yards on 11 carries and two touchdowns, and Harold Hammack 105 yards on only five carries and scored one touchdown. Rocky Kemp scored a pair of touchdowns, while Jess Hill and Charles Willingham each accounted for one touchdown apiece in this scoring fest.[4]

**(A) Oct. 26—Stanford—7–0**

Two days before this game, the stock market crashed on what became known as "Black Thursday," and it sent the United States into a crippling financial depth of despair that was the Great Depression. On this first weekend of sports following the crash, Marshall Duffield led the Trojans' offensive machine with 104 yards rushing on 25 carries. Duffield also threw a touchdown pass covering 24 yards to Francis Tappaan on the third play of the second quarter for the game's lone six-pointer with a crowd of 80,000 looking on.[5]

**(H) Nov. 2—California—7–15**

The Trojans took the field ranked number one by the Dickinson System, which was considered the elite authority on college football at the time. They were also riding a 16-game unbeaten streak. However, with 79,000 on hand to watch the Trojans continue on their path toward another national title, the Golden Bears shattered the dream. The Trojans did not help themselves in their quest to remain on top of the national polls by fumbling at crucial times and displaying a weak pass defense. Benny Lom stood out for Cal, and his 83-yard touchdown run was the top highlight of the game.[6]

**(H) Nov. 9—Nevada—66–0**

The Trojans rebounded easily from their first loss of the season by recording their fifth shutout in seven games. Leading the way was Gus Shaver, who ran for 106 yards on 26 carries. Tony Jurich led the scoring parade with three touchdowns. This was the final time that USC and Nevada played, with the Trojans winning each of the five meetings.[7]

**(N) Nov. 16—Notre Dame—12–13**

With a capacity crowd of 112,912 on hand inside Chicago's Soldier Field, the Fighting Irish came out to face the Trojans as the country's number one ranked team after USC fell to Cal two weeks prior to this clash. Notre Dame's coach Knute Rockne was battling a life-threatening case of phlebitis, a condition where blood clots form in the veins of a person's legs. They can travel to the lungs and be fatal. Rockne suffered pain with the ailment, and had his leg wrapped heavily with bandages. In order to take pressure off the leg, he was confined to a wheelchair during this game.

The Trojans struck paydirt first in the first quarter. After stopping each other's advance on the game's opening drives, USC took possession on their own 48. Two plays later, from the Notre Dame 48, Marger Aspit caught a Marshall Duffield pass at the 25 and raced untouched for a touchdown. Duffield missed the conversion, and USC led, 6–0. Notre Dame tied the game up before the end of the first half on a 53-yard pass from John Elder to two-time All-American Frank Carideo, who then missed on the extra point attempt, and the teams went into the locker room for halftime tied at 6–6.

Joe Savoldi gave Notre Dame their first lead of the game with a one-yard touchdown run, and Carideo was good on the ever-important conversion kick that gave the Irish a 13–6 advantage. On the ensuing kickoff, Russ Saunders received the ball on his four, and then went the distance to record a 96-yard touchdown that brought the Trojans to within one point of another deadlock. Unfortunately, Jim Musick missed the conversion, and the Trojans went down in defeat by the slimmest of margins.[8]

**(H) Nov. 23—Idaho—72–0**

The Trojans scored two touchdowns in the first five minutes, and the rout was on. Gus Shaver ran for 100 yards on 12 carries, and Russ Saunders established a single-game school record with 190 yards passing. He also threw for three touchdowns.[9]

**(H) Nov. 30—Washington State—27–7**

Washington State was on the way to posting their first season of 10 or more victories in the 35-year history of the program. They came into this game with an 8–1 record and two straight shutouts. The Trojans, however, were still the alpha dogs of the PCC, and showed it with this convincing win. Russ Saunders led the offensive attack with131 yards on 30 carries.[10]

**(H) Dec. 14—Carnegie Tech—45–13**

The Trojans sent 65,000 fans home happy with a resounding victory on homecoming weekend. Russ Saunders ran for 126 yards on 24 carries, and as a team, the Trojans set a record for most rushing yards compiled over a season with 3,954.[11]

**Rose Bowl, (N) Jan. 1—Pittsburgh—47–14**

Seven years to the day had passed before the Trojans got back to the Rose Bowl. They made up for lost time by totally dismantling the Pitt Panthers, and handing their coach, Jock Sutherland, one of the worst defeats throughout a long and successful career. It was the most points given up by Pitt since 1903.

On the opposite side of the spectrum, this was Howard Jones' first experience in the New Year's Day classic, and his players presented him with a lopsided victory led by quarterback Russ Saunders, whose performance earned him MVP honors. Saunders lived up to his nickname of "Racehorse," as he possessed the abilities of a championship thoroughbred on the first day of the new decade. He threw for three touchdowns, and ran for 67 yards and another score (16 yards). Harry Edelson was on the receiving end of two scoring strikes (55 and 39 yards), and Erny Pinckert hauled in the one more from 25 yards out. Marshall Duffield also turned in a solid performance for USC by scoring on two touchdown runs, each from one yard out, and throwing for another, with Thomas Wilcox on the receiving end of a 57-yarder to complete the scoring on this day.[12]

### Team Leaders

Rushing: Russ Saunders—972 yards on 185 carries
Scoring: Russ Saunders—84 points on 14 touchdowns

## *1930*

Head Coach: Howard Jones
Assistant Coaches: Sam Barry, Aubrey Devine, Cliff Herd
Team Captain: Marshall Duffield
Record: 8–2 overall (5–1 in Pacific Coast Conference)
(Ranked 20th best record in college football out of 106 teams)
Finish in Conference: 2nd
Finish in National Polls: No ranking
Points Scored Per Game: 38.2 to rank 3rd out of 106 teams
Points Allowed Per Game: 6.6 to rank 36th

### Schedule and Highlights

**(A) Sept. 27—UCLA—52–0**

Once again, the Bruins failed to score against their crosstown adversaries. Orv Mohler carried the ball 18 times for 179 yards, and team captain Marshall Duffield added 89 yards and three touchdowns for the Trojans. As a team, USC totaled 421 rushing yards to a mere 31 for UCLA. Following this game, the series was cancelled to allow UCLA the opportunity to get stronger and more competitive against the powerful Trojans.[1]

**(H) Oct. 4—Oregon State—27–7**

This edition of the Oregon State Beavers under head coach Paul Schissler was regarded as having a top-ranked defense. In their first two games, they shut out their opponents, and five others over the course of the season. However, the Trojans rang up the most points against Oregon State during the year, with Orv Mohler leading the charge by running for 192 yards on 26 carries. The Trojan defense managed to hold off the Beavers on multiple scoring opportunities after they were well into USC territory.[2]

**(A) Oct. 11—Washington State—6–7**

Washington State head coach O.E. "Babe" Hollingberry and the Cougars came into this game with two straight wins. In his four years at Washington State, Hollingberry had not suffered a defeat while coaching at Rogers Field. His streak stayed perfect, as the Cougars got by the Trojans by the slimmest of margins. However, the Trojans almost pulled the game out in the final minutes. An Orv Mohler to Marger Apsit scoring strike provided USC with their lone points, but the extra point was missed. They then recovered a fumble near midfield and were closing in on the Washington State end zone when time ran out.[3]

**(H) Oct. 18—Utah State—65–0**

The Trojans got a pair of 100-yard rushers in this blowout win. Gus Shaver led the "Thundering Herd" ground attack with 151 yards on 16 carries, and Orv Mohler tallied 138 yards on 17 carries. They both added a pair of touchdowns to their day's work. Blanchard Beatty led the Trojans with three touchdowns in this convincing win. Bill Hunter served as head coach for this game while Howard Jones was out scouting USC's next opponent Stanford.[4]

**(A) Oct. 25—Stanford—41–12**

A capacity crowd of 89,000 came out to witness this clash between these two powerhouse teams. The legendary Glenn "Pop" Warner was in his seventh season as Stanford's head coach, and he built a juggernaut over that time. This season was no exception, and the only blemish on an unbeaten season was this loss to the Trojans. Marshall Duffield led the men of Troy by running for 119 yards on 17 carries. The Trojans scored four touchdowns in the first half, and finished the game with 481 yards of offense while limiting Stanford to 141.[5]

**(H) Nov. 1—Denver—33–13**

Once again, a pair of Trojan backfield men topped the century mark on the ground. This time, it was Blanchard Beatty with 136 yards on 31 carries and Al Maloney with 133 yards on 24 carries. Denver was coached by former Trojan Jeff Cravath, and displayed a toughness that allowed them to be deadlocked at 6–6 going into the second half. USC head coach Howard Jones substituted frequently, using 40 players to wear down the determined Denver team. The Trojans took control less than five minutes into the second half when Orv Mohler scored a pair of touchdowns.[6]

**(H) Nov. 8—California—74–0**

With this resounding victory, USC was able to beat both Cal and Stanford in the same season for the first time in their history. Erny Pinckert only needed seven carries to gain 101 yards and score one touchdown, in an easy victory. Orv Mohler led the scoring onslaught with four touchdowns, and Jim Musick added three six-pointers. Marshall Duffield, Gus Shaver, and Ralph Wilcox, all scored one touchdown apiece. The Trojans finished with 763 yards of total offense, with 474 yards gained on the ground and 289 through the air. The Trojans were up by a close 8–0 count at the end of the first quarter. It was then that they exploded to complete one of their greatest victories in school history. They score 20 points in the second quarter, 33 in the third, and 13 in the final stanza. With five minutes remaining in the game, both coaches agreed to stop play, and the game ended at that time.[7]

**(H) Nov. 15—Hawaii—52–0**

Another easy victory was the result of this contest, as the Trojans rang up 126 points in two games while allowing zero to be scored against them. Howard Jones used a mixture of his famous "Thundering Herd" running at the defense, and then incorporated a passing attack to add balance to his explosive offense. This plan proved too much for the Roaring Rainbows of Hawaii to deal with. Orv Mohler added two more touchdowns to his season statistics, giving him six over the last two games. By the second half, Jones used reserve players to finish out the game.[8]

**(H) Nov. 27—Washington—32–0**

Played in the mud, the elements did nothing to stop the powerful Trojans. For the third straight game, they recorded a shutout, and over that time, scored a total of 158 points. Despite the convincing victory, the Trojans lost five players to injuries. Star running back Erny Pinckert hurt his back while attempting to knock down a Washington pass. His replacement, Harold Hammack, came in and played well. Orv Mohler picked up the slack for his injured teammates by getting away from defenders for big gains. The Trojans finished the game with 373 yards of total offense.[9]

**(H) Dec. 6—Notre Dame—0–27**

Notre Dame came into this game at 9–0 and ranked #1 in the nation. Their toughest game of the year was a week prior to this clash when they narrowly beat Army, 7–6. Amazingly, the Trojans were listed as slight favorites, and the Fighting Irish came out to Los Angeles to prove that they were still the alpha dogs of the college football world. A crowd of 73,967 was on hand for USC's homecoming game, and the Irish gave the Trojan little to cheer about. Paul O'Connor rushed for 118 yards on 10 carries, and Notre Dame outrushed USC 331 yards to 89, and held a huge 428 to 146 yard advantage in total offense. This proved to be Knute Rockne's final game as coach of the Fighting Irish. On March 31, 1931, while en route to Los Angeles, the airplane he was aboard crashed near Bazaar, Kansas, killing everyone on the flight.[10]

### Team Leaders

Rushing: Orv Mohler—983 yards on 145 carries
Scoring: Orv Mohler—102 points on 17 touchdowns

## *1931*

Head Coach: Howard Jones
Assistant Coaches: Sam Barry, Aubrey Devine, Cliff Herd
Team Captain: Stan Williamson
Record: 10–1 overall (7–0 in Pacific Coast Conference)
(Ranked 3rd best record in college football out of 110 teams)
Finish in Conference: 1st—1931 PCC Champions
Finish in National Polls: 1931 National Champions
Points Scored Per Game: 33.0 to rank 3rd out of 110 teams
points allowed per game: 4.7 to rank 24th

### Schedule and Highlights

**(H) Sept. 26—St. Mary's—7–13**

With 75,000 in the LA Coliseum, the heavily favored Trojans held a 7–0 lead going into the third quarter, complements of a Gus Shaver run from the one-foot line in the first quarter. Johnny Baker added the conversion. The underdog Galloping Gaels then came back on scores from halfback Bud Toscani with a 44-yard reception and end George Canrinus with a 30-yard reception, to hand Howard Jones his first-ever opening day defeat in six previous seasons. This was also the first time since 1908 that the Trojans lost their first game of the season.[1]

**(H) Oct. 3—Oregon State—30–0**

The Trojans got even following their defeat a week earlier by pounding Oregon State at Olympic Stadium. The Trojans scored one touchdown in each quarter, with Gus Shaver running for three six-pointers in the overwhelming win. Orv Mohler scored USC's other touchdown, and Ernie Smith kicked a field goal.[2]

**(H) Oct. 10—Washington State—38–6**

Back at the Coliseum, USC left nothing to chance in front of their home crowd. Orv Mohler had a huge day running the ball. He gained 176 yards on 18 carries, and tied a school record by scoring four rushing touchdowns. On one of his record-setting scoring runs, he tore through an overwhelmed Washington State defense for an exciting 65-yard jaunt.[3]

**(H) Oct. 17—Oregon—53–0**

Two weeks earlier, the Trojans prevented Oregon State from scoring. Fourteen days later, the other delegates from "the Beaver State," the Ducks, were mauled and also shut out by the powerful Trojans. Gus Shaver led the attack with 114 yards on 21 carries, and two touchdowns. Joining in a scoring barrage that saw USC ring up eight six-pointers were Orv Mohler with two touchdowns, and Erny Pinckert, Ford Palmer, Blanchard Beatty, and Willard Brouse, with one apiece. This was Oregon's first loss of the season.[4]

**(A) Oct. 24—California—6–0**

After three straight lopsided victories, the Trojans managed to squeak out a 6–0 win in a game that saw both teams combine for zero passing yards. Cal was very under rated, but played tough against the most dominant team from the west coast, in what was looked at as one of the most exciting clashes played at Berkeley over the previous few seasons. With two minutes left in the second quarter, the running of Raymond Sparling, Gus Shaver, and Orv Mohler got the ball downfield. Sparling got the honors by scoring the game's lone six-pointer on a run.[5]

**(H) Nov. 7—Stanford—19–0**

With 95,000 packed into the Coliseum, the Trojans recorded their fourth shutout of the season. This was USC's fourth straight win over Pop Warner's Stanford Cardinal, and it was also the first time this season that Stanford lost. The Trojans held an advantage throughout the game, allowing Stanford only two legitimate chances at getting deep into USC territory. Gus Shaver, who ran for 147 yards on 21 carries, opened the scoring with a 4-yard run in the opening stanza. Orv Mohler added two scoring runs to cap off USC's big win.[6]

**(H) Nov. 14—Montana—69–0**

The Montana Grizzlies were completely outclassed in the Coliseum by the Trojans, who scored a point for every minute of play, plus added nine extra points for good measure. Without using many of his starters, Howard Jones' charges got two scoring jaunts from Gus Shaver and Orv Mohler, three from Homer Griffith, and one apiece from Kenneth Fay, James Musick, and Richard Barber. The mauling was so great that Erny Pinckert was able to run for 110 yards on a mere three carries.[7]

**(A) Nov. 21—Notre Dame—16–14**

With the first capacity crowd on hand at Notre Dame Stadium, the Fighting Irish lost for the first time in 26 games. The Trojans trailed by 14 points at the beginning of the fourth quarter, and then came back strong on the running of Gus Shaver and the passing of Orv Mohler. Shaver got USC on the board with a one-yard run, but Johnny Baker's conversion attempt was blocked. Shaver added a second touchdown to his day's work, and this time, Baker was true with the conversion kick to bring USC to within one point at 14–13. It was then, with one minute left in the game, that Johnny Baker rose to the top of USC lore, becoming a legend, thanks to his kicking prowess. From 33 yards away, Baker looked to attempt a field goal that would give USC their first lead of the game. The snap from center was perfect, as was the hold, and Baker then sent the ball airborne. The end result was the ball splitting the uprights to give the Trojans the lead. A Gordon Clark interception then killed any hopes that the Fighting Irish might have had regarding a comeback, and USC had their first win in South Bend. Upon their return to Los Angeles, a crowd of 300,000 was on hand to welcome home their conquering heroes.[8]

**(H) Dec. 5—Washington—44–7**

USC clinched the Pacific Coast Conference title with this homecoming victory. Orv Mohler ran for 110 yards on 13 carries and scored three touchdowns. Gus Shaver added three of his own touchdowns as well, and Garrett Arbelbide scored USC's other touchdown.[9]

**(H) Dec. 12—Georgia—60–0**

Ray Sparling exploded for 129 yards on just six carries, and Gus Shaver tallied 115 yards on 14 carries, as the Trojans pounded Georgia. This was the first true rout of Georgia in a long time, and the Trojans began the mauling early on by scoring their first touchdown with the game just three minutes old. Sparling, Shaver, and Richard Barber all had three touchdowns, and Orv Mohler, Gordon Clark, and Harold Hammack, all recorded one each.[10]

**Rose Bowl, (N) Jan. 1—Tulane—21–12**

The waves from the majestic Pacific Ocean pound the shores of Southern California beaches, creating an awesome display at Mother Nature at her finest. New Year's Day, a different type of wave decided to attempt the same feat. The Green Wave of Tulane had good reason to feel as powerful as the Pacific Ocean when they rolled into the Southland on the first day of 1932. They posted a spotless regular season record of 11–0 that included eight shutout victories. However, the mighty Thundering Herd of USC was there to greet them with six All-Americans on the roster, and the results were anything but majestic for Tulane.

The Trojans scored first on a six-yard run by Ray Sparling to take a 7–0 advantage into the second half. Erny Pinckert, who went on to receive the MVP award for this game, scored two touchdowns in the third quarter from 28 and 23 yards out to give USC a solid 21–0 lead. Head coach Bernie Bierman's charges attempted to stage a comeback on the passing arm of Don Zimmerman, and the running of "Wop" Glover, but fell short. This victory gave the Trojans a perfect 4–0 slate in post-season play, and more importantly, secured their second national championship in the past four seasons.[11]

TEAM LEADERS

RUSHING: Gus Shaver—936 yards on 199 carries
SCORING: Gus Shaver—100 points on 16 touchdowns and 4 extra points

## *1932*

HEAD COACH: Howard Jones
ASSISTANT COACHES: Sam Barry, Aubrey Devine, Cliff Herd
TEAM CAPTAIN: Tay Brown
RECORD: 10–0 overall (6–0 in Pacific Coast Conference)
(Ranked 1st best record in college football out of 109 teams)
FINISH IN CONFERENCE: 1st—1932 PCC champions
FINISH IN NATIONAL POLLS: 1932 National Champions
POINTS SCORED PER GAME: 20.1 to rank 23rd out of 120 teams
POINTS ALLOWED PER GAME: 1.3 to rank 2nd

### Schedule and Highlights

**(H) Sept. 24—Utah—35–0**

After dropping their previous opening game, the Trojans left no doubt as to whom the alpha dog would be at the start of the 1932 season. In what turned out to be the worst loss for an Ike Armstrong–coached team, with the exception of a 26-point to USC in 1925, the charges from Utah saw Orv Mohler score twice, and Richard Barber, Homer Griffith, and John Seixas all added one touchdown apiece for the Trojans.[1]

**(H) Oct. 1—Washington State—20–0**

Once again the Trojans' defense flexed its muscle, recording a second straight shutout. Ford Palmer, Homer Griffith, and Cotton Warburton each had touchdowns, and Gus Shaver ran for 137 yards on 27 carries for the mighty USC powerhouse.[2]

**(H) Oct. 8—Oregon State—10–0**

For the third consecutive week, the Trojans did not show any hospitality to an opposing offense. The Beavers of Oregon State came to the City of Angels, and left on the losing side of a shutout. With 40,000 looking on, Orv Mohler ran for 108 yards on 15 carries, and threw a 40-yard scoring strike to Ford Palmer for the game's only touchdown. Ernie Smith nailed a 14-yard field goal in the final stanza to finish out the scoring.[3]

**(H) Oct. 15—Loyola—6–0**

In a classic defensive battle, the undefeated and unscored upon Trojans hosted Loyola. For 55 minutes, neither team was able to produce any points. It was then that Cotton Warburton kept USC's record spotless by scoring the game's lone points.[4]

**(A) Oct. 22—Stanford—13–0**

The defending national champion Trojans continued to live up to that honor, and looked to add another such crown to their illustrious legacy with a trip to Palo Alto for a game that pitted the tough USC defense, against the stellar passing attack of coaching legend Pop Warner. When this rivalry game was complete, it was Howard Jones' charges that thwarted Warner's aerial show with their fifth shutout in as many outings. A Bob McNeish to Ford Palmer scoring toss broke the scoreless affair in the second quarter. Homer Griffith added a touchdown in the third quarter, and Ernie Smith booted the conversion.[5]

**(H) Nov. 5—California—27–7**

For the first time all season, the mighty Trojan defense allowed points to be scored against them. In the fourth quarter, the University of California produced the first points against USC when Dave Meek caught a 35-yard scoring strike. However, the Trojans already had the game well under control, thanks to a solid running game that recorded 163 yards. Homer Griffith scored three touchdowns, Cotton Warburton one, and Ernie Smith added three conversion kicks.[6]

**(H) Nov. 12—Oregon—33–0**

Cotton Warburton ran for 122 yards on 20 carries, the Trojan defense held Oregon to zero completed passes, and the mighty men of Troy reverted back to their ways of producing another shutout. With 35,000 looking on, the hometown Trojans delighted their fans with touchdowns coming from Homer Griffith, Gordon Clark, Cotton Warburton, and Robert Erskine. The dominant USC defense prohibited the Oregon offense from not only completing a pass, but the unit also kept the Ducks from getting within their 38-yard line throughout the entire game.[7]

**(A) Nov. 24—Washington—9–6**

In their closest game of the year, the Trojans rang up their eighth victory, and a second straight PCC title, on Thanksgiving Day with a muddy field serving as the backdrop. Substitute halfback Cal Clemens broke a scoreless tie in the second quarter with a 19-yard field goal, and Cotton Warburton added a touchdown early in the fourth quarter to give USC their points. Washington closed the gap late in the game to make this the closest margin of victory for the Trojans in 1932. This marked USC's 17th straight win over two seasons.[8]

**(H) Dec. 10—Notre Dame—13–0**

This series was turning into a classic after only five years, and saw the winner emerge as national champion since 1928. This time was no exception, as the Trojans fans among the 100,000 spectators jammed into the Coliseum were happy after this homecoming day shutout. This game was a battle of two tough defenses that refused to give up much. Throughout the year, USC only allowed two touchdowns and 13 points, while Notre Dame gave up three touchdowns and 18 points. The Trojans got their points in this game on a 21-yard pass from Homer Griffith to Rupert McNeish, and then Griffith ran for USC's other touchdown from two yards out.[9]

**Rose Bowl, (N) Jan. 2—Pittsburgh—35–0**

Three years earlier, Jock Sutherland brought his unbeaten Pitt Panthers into Pasadena and left with one of the worst defeats in his coaching career. In this edition of the Rose Bowl, the old adage of "history repeating itself" held up, as the Trojans once again handed Sutherland's team a major beat down.

Pitt came into this game at 8–0–2, and for the first two quarters, they were able to hold back a Trojan onslaught. USC scored first in the opening stanza on a 35-yard pass from Homer Griffith to Ford Palmer that was followed up by Ernie Smith's conversion kick. That score held up until Griffith was on the receiving end of a 2-yard touchdown toss from Kenneth Bright in the third quarter. Smith's extra point kick made it a 14–0 game heading into the fourth quarter.

The Trojans then put serious distance between themselves and their opponents from the Keystone State, complements of touchdown runs from one and 10 yards out by Cotton Warburton, who led all ball carriers with 87 rushing yards. Richard Barber finished off the fourth quarter scoring barrage with a two-yard touchdown run. When it was finally over, the Trojans clinched back-to-back national championships, and sent the Panthers back east with their worst loss to date in school history.[10]

TEAM LEADERS

RUSHING: Cotton Warburton—420 yards on 115 carries
SCORING: Homer Griffith—48 points on 8 touchdowns

## *1933*

HEAD COACH: Howard Jones
ASSISTANT COACHES: Sam Barry, Jeff Cravath, Aubrey Devine, Cliff Herd
TEAM CAPTAIN: Ford Palmer
RECORD: 10–1–1 overall (4–1–1 in Pacific Coast Conference) (Ranked 11th best record in college football out of 126 teams)
FINISH IN CONFERENCE: 3rd place
FINISH IN NATIONAL POLLS: No ranking
POINTS SCORED PER GAME: 21.4 to rank 7th out of 126 teams
POINTS ALLOWED PER GAME: 2.5 to rank 8th

### Schedule and Highlights

**(H) Sept. 23—Occidental—39–0**
The players set to start for USC throughout the season did not play in this first game of a doubleheader, and the second half was shortened to approximately 14 minutes. Bill Howard scored three touchdowns, and the Trojans outgained Occidental, 359 yards to 46.[1]

**(H) Sept. 23—Whittier—51–0**
The second game of the doubleheader saw the starters for USC play most of the game, and they compiled 304 yards while allowing just 48. Backfield star Cotton Warburton broke his nose and had to wear a protective mask throughout most of the season.[2]

**(H) Sept. 30—Loyola—18–0**
USC recorded the football program's 200th victory with a third straight shutout. Loyola came into the Coliseum with a strong defense, and the Trojans were also very efficient at keeping opponents out of their end zone. The result was a scoreless tie after the first half came to an end. The Trojans finally broke through in the third quarter when Homer Griffith scored on a short yardage run. Griffith then threw a 47-yard touchdown pass to Gordon Clark, and Bill Howard scored USC's last six-pointer.[3]

**(H) Oct. 7—Washington State—33–0**
Cotton Warburton gained 221 yards on 14 carries in USC's conference opener, and once again the Trojans reigned victorious by way of a shutout. Warburton scored three touchdowns, two of which came from 75 and 80 yards out. Bill Howard and Calvin Clemens, Jr., also scored.[4]

**(H) Oct. 14—St. Mary's—14–7**
Homer Griffith ran for 101 yards on 20 carries and one touchdown. A crowd of 85,000 was at the Coliseum to witness USC get revenge over the Gaels for their 1931 win over the Trojans that prevented them from going undefeated. Following that season opening loss to the Gaels two years earlier, the Trojans rolled to 25 straight wins, including this one, but St. Mary's did not make it easy. Inky Wotkyns opened the scoring for USC in the first quarter with a one-yard run. The Gaels came back to tie the game in the second quarter, and in doing so, became the first team in 1933 to score on the mighty Trojan defense. Griffith then scored what proved to be the game winner, 14 plays after St. Mary's tied the game.[5]

**(N) Oct. 21—Oregon State—0–0**
This game was played at Multnomah Field in Portland, Oregon. The tough 11 "Iron Men" of Oregon State lived up to their moniker by playing the entire game with no substitutions. Their toughness and stamina allowed Oregon State to end USC's 25-game winning streak.[6]

**(A) Oct. 28—California—6–3**
With eight minutes left to play, Cal held a 3–0 lead on a rainy, foggy day in Northern California. Cotton Warburton then kept the Trojans unbeaten by running over the right side of the field for 59 yards and the winning touchdown. His brilliant game-winner was obscured from most fans by fog.[7]

**(H) Nov. 11—Stanford—7–13**
Stanford's "Vow Boys" ended USC's 27-game unbeaten streak, and in dong so, handed the Trojans their only loss of the season. This loss ended any hopes for USC claiming a third straight national championship. Cotton Warburton scored USC's only touchdown on a 43-yard run.[8]

**(H) Nov. 18—Oregon—26–0**
The Trojans used power and finesse to bring down the only previously unbeaten team on the west coast. Cliff Propst scored on a run to give the Trojans a 6–0 lead at the end of the first half. USC then blew a close game open in the second half, as Inky Wotkyns, Bill Howard, and Cotton Warburton, all scored. Warburton's touchdown came on an exciting 53-yard reception.[9]

**(A) Nov. 25—Notre Dame—19–0**
Notre Dame came into this game treading in unchartered territory. They were 2–4–1, and suffered four shutout losses in the process. The Trojans overpowered this pathetic edition of the Fighting Irish in every offensive category. Cotton Warburton led the charge with 100 yards rushing on 19 carries and two touchdowns. The Trojans received their other touchdown on a three-yard pass from Bob McNeish to Homer Griffith. The vic-

tory allowed the Trojans to pull even at 3–3 with Notre Dame in the all-time series.[10]

**(H) Dec. 2—Georgia—31–0**

The Trojans averaged 65 yards per possession on their five scoring drives. Cotton Warburton threw two touchdown passes to Julius Bescos and scored one himself. Homer Griffith powered the ground attack with 110 yards on 16 carries.[11]

**(H) Dec. 9—Washington—13–7**

The Trojans were looking to gain a share of another PCC title on their homecoming weekend. However, the Huskies did not make it easy for them. Washington stopped two potential USC touchdowns early in the game. Bill Smith made a great catch and then outran Cliff Propst to give Washington a 7–0 lead. In the opening minutes of the second half, Cotton Warburton had a pass intercepted, but the officials called interference on Washington, and the infraction placed the ball on the five-yard line. Three plays later, Warburton ran for a touchdown, but the conversion attempt was blocked. Aaron Rosenberg recovered a fumble on the ensuing kickoff and Warburton scored again a few plays later on a pass from Calvin Clemens for what proved to be the game winner.[12]

TEAM LEADERS

RUSHING: Cotton Warburton—885 yards on 149 carries
SCORING: Cotton Warburton—72 points on 12 touchdowns

## *1934*

HEAD COACH: Howard Jones
ASSISTANT COACHES: Sam Barry, Jeff Cravath, Aubrey Devine, Cliff Herd
TEAM CAPTAIN: Julie Bescos
RECORD: 4–6–1 overall (1–4–1 in Pacific Coast Conference)
(Ranked 92nd best record in college football out of 124 teams)
FINISH IN CONFERENCE: 7th place
FINISH IN NATIONAL POLLS: No ranking
POINTS SCORED PER GAME: 10.9 to rank 75th out of 124 teams
POINTS ALLOWED PER GAME: 10.0 to rank 76th

### Schedule and Highlights

**(H) Sept. 22—Occidental—20–0**

The Trojans opened up another season with a pair of convincing wins. In the first game of a doubleheader, Bill Howard scored twice and Garland Matthews added USC's other six-pointer, in this shutout victory. The Trojans overpowered Occidental by gaining 343 yards while allowing 81.[1]

**(H) Sept. 22—Whittier—40–14**

Playing in a doubleheader did nothing to slow the Trojan express down. USC gained 331 yards of offense, 320 of which was on the ground. Bill Howard and Inky Wotkyns had two touchdowns apiece, and Cotton Warburton added the other Trojan touchdown. On the day, Howard led the Trojan attack with 146 yards rushing on 23 carries, Wotkyns had 107 yards on 18 carries, and Warburton 59 yards on 13 attempts.[2]

**(H) Sept. 29—College of Pacific—6–0**

The Trojans had a struggle after a pair of easy wins one week earlier. This game remained scoreless until the third quarter, and it took the bounce of the ball in the right direction to give USC a break. In the third quarter, a punt sailed to the Pacific 15-yard line, and the ball hit the ground. It then hit a Pacific player on the foot, making it was a live ball. USC's Gerald Ostling quickly grabbed the ball at the Pacific 15 to give the Trojans renewed life. Inky Wotkyns wasted no time taking advantage of the opportunity given the Trojans, as he ran for a touchdown on the following play.[3]

**(H) Oct. 6—Washington State—0–19**

Long punts and the backfield of Ted Christofferson and Ed Brett kept the Cougars on the move and eventually led to USC's defeat by shutout in their conference opener. Punts that carried as far as 72 yards kept the Trojans pinned down, while the Cougars were able to put points on the board after a scoreless first half. Christofferson broke the deadlock with a 39-yard run in the third quarter, and Washington State added 12 more points in the fourth period to win by a comfortable margin.[4]

**(A) Oct. 13—Pittsburgh—6–20**

Pitt got revenge for a pair of Rose Bowl defeats against the Trojans following the 1929 and 1931 seasons. The backfield of Weinstock and Wiesenbaugh ran well to keep the Trojans reeling on defense. Both scored touchdowns for the Panthers, while a pass from Cotton Warburton to Calvin Clemens accounted for USC's only touchdown.[5]

**(H) Oct. 20—Oregon State—6–6**

The Trojans proved to be unstoppable early in this game, and went on a scoring drive that made the "Thundering Herd" legendary. Cliff Propst capped the drive off with a touchdown, and that was all the scoring USC did. Oregon State then tied the game with 1:42 remaining, but missed on what could have been the game-winning conversion kick.[6]

**(A) Oct. 27—Stanford—0–16**

Stanford's freshman class of 1932 made a promise not to go down in defeat to USC during their time in Palo Alto. They achieved their goal in 1933, handing USC their only loss of the season. In 1934, the Trojans were in a rut coming into this game. Since their opening game, USC had trouble scoring, producing only 18 points in the next four games. Problems continued for USC, and that group of determined Stanford players kept the vow to never lose to the Cardinal & Gold. For close to half the game, the Trojans held Stanford without any points. They then went on a 10-play drive that started on their 34-yard line, with a Bobby Grayson touchdown capping the march. Grayson added another touchdown to his day's achievements, and the Indians sent USC back home with another defeat. This tied the record for most points Stanford ever scored against USC, with the first time coming in 1905, when Stanford won by the exact same score. This also proved to be the first time since 1926 that a conference opponent was able to beat USC on two straight occasions.[7]

**(H) Nov. 10—California—2–7**

Cal scored early, but the USC defense held tough after that, allowing the Golden Bears zero pass completions. The Trojans got close to scoring three times, making it to the Cal 16, eight, and right on the goal line, but they failed to capitalize on those deep drives.[8]

**(H) Nov. 17—Oregon—33-0**

Played mostly in the rain and mud, the conditions did not stop Inky Wotkyns from running for 132 yards on 22 carries and two touchdowns. This was USC's first conference win of the season, and the first game played at the Coliseum in wet conditions since Howard Jones took over as head coach in 1925. After a scoreless opening quarter, the Trojans got 14 points in the second quarter, seven in the third, and 12 in the fourth. Cal Clemens had a solid game for USC. His blocking opened big holes for the backs to run through, and his 47-yard interception return set up the first score, a run by Wotkyns from the one-foot line. Clemens also kicked three conversions. Cotton Warburton threw a touchdown pass to Ward Browning, Dave Davis broke loose for a 75-yard scoring jaunt, Wotkyns added an eight-yard run for six points, and Alvin Coughlin returned an interception for another touchdown, in USC's best game in two months.[9]

**(H) Dec. 1—Washington—7-14**

The Huskies scored 14 points in the second quarter. At the start of the second half, the Trojans received their only touchdown when Hueston Harper broke through the Washington line, blocked a punt, and recovered it in the end zone.[10]

**(H) Dec. 8—Notre Dame—0-14**

USC's homecoming weekend marked the first time in this series that the Trojans came into their game with Notre Dame sporting a losing record. Mike Layden, brother of head coach Elmer Layden, scored a pair of touchdowns that provided Notre Dame's points on this day. The Fighting Irish dominated the statistics, and the Trojans suffered their first losing season since 1915.[11]

TEAM LEADERS

RUSHING: Inky Wotkyns—588 yards on 133 carries
SCORING: Inky Wotkyns—30 points on 5 touchdowns

## *1935*

HEAD COACH: Howard Jones
ASSISTANT COACHES: Sam Barry, Jeff Cravath, Aubrey Devine, Cliff Herd
TEAM CAPTAINS: Art Dittberner, Cliff Propst
RECORD: 5-7 overall (2-4 in Pacific Coast Conference)
(Ranked 96th best record in college football out of 128 teams)
FINISH IN CONFERENCE: 8th place
FINISH IN NATIONAL POLLS: No ranking
POINTS SCORED PER GAME: 12.9 to rank 61st out of 128 teams
POINTS ALLOWED PER GAME: 10.3 to rank 81st

### Schedule and Highlights

**(H) Sept. 28—Montana—9-0**

The Grizzlies played tough, but in the end, the Trojans won their opening game by shutout for the 27th time in their history. Max Belko kicked a 40-yard field goal for USC's first points of the season, and Cliff Propst scored a touchdown in the second quarter. The second half remained scoreless, and Montana was held to zero pass completions throughout the game.[1]

**(H) Oct. 5—College of Pacific—19-7**

USC needed a fourth quarter rally to beat Amos Alonzo Stagg's team. The first quarter was controlled by Pacific, as USC had trouble adjusting to Stagg's passing attack. The result was a 7-0 Pacific lead until the Trojans got going with a passing attack of their own. Quarterback Nick Pappas got the Trojans to within one point of a tie with a touchdown pass to Bill Gaisford. The conversion failed, but Pappas gave the Trojans the lead for good in the third quarter by running for a touchdown. He finished the game with 90 of USC's 165 rushing yards. The Trojans scored an insurance touchdown when Gaisford hauled in his second touchdown from Rodney Cameron.[2]

**(H) Oct. 12—Illinois—0-19**

Illinois came into the Coliseum with a play called "the Flying Trapeze," and it helped them shut the Trojans out on their home turf. Quarterback Wib Henry scored two touchdowns, and a blocked punt was returned 50 yards for another score.[3]

**(H) Oct. 19—Oregon State—7-13**

Oregon State got their points, and then USC started to get going. Unfortunately, a chance to tie or win fell a few yards shy. After Nick Pappas was forced from the game with a sprained ankle, the USC offense relied on "the Oceanside Thunderbolt," Glen Thompson, to rally them. Thompson, with his arm in a brace to help his sore elbow, guided the Trojans to a touchdown with solid runs. He was leading the Trojans for another score when the game ended.[4]

**(A) Oct. 26—California—7-21**

The California Golden Bears awaited the Trojans with a spotless 5-0 record, which saw them give up zero points under first-year head coach Leonard "Stub" Allison. Cal remained perfect, but the Trojans fought hard against their Northern California rivals. Cal scored a pair of touchdowns through the air, and one on the ground. The Trojans became the first team up to this stage of the season to score on Cal when Leavitt Thurlow blocked a kick and Art Dittberner fell on the loose ball in the end zone for six points.[5]

**(H) Nov. 9—Stanford—0-3**

Another tough opponent from Northern California was up next for USC. Stanford came into this game with a 4-1 record, and allowed only 13 points to be scored on them throughout those games. Great punting by both teams kept the opposition pinned down in their own territory, until Stanford was able to get close enough to produce the game's only points. With one minute remaining in the game, Stanford's "Monk" Moscrip kicked a field goal to produce the lowest winning score ever recorded against USC up to this time.[6]

**(H) Nov. 16—Washington State—20-10**

The 5-2 Cougars came to the Coliseum, and for three quarters, they were in control, leading 10-0. The Trojans were looking to end a four-game losing streak with 45,000 of their fans in attendance. In less than eight minutes during the fourth quarter, the Trojans rallied. David Davis set up the first USC score with a pass to Gene Hibbs that got the ball to the Washington State two-yard line. On the next play, Davis ran for a touchdown. A few minutes later, Davis threw the go-ahead touchdown to

Homer Beatty from 25 yards out to make it a 14–10 USC advantage. Davis then added his second touchdown run of the game following a Hibbs fumble recovery.[7]

**(A) Nov. 23—Notre Dame—13–20**

Played in cold conditions in South Bend, Indiana, the Fighting Irish made it two straight against USC. The Trojans made things interesting by scoring on the their second offensive series, with David Davis running for a six-yard touchdown. Max Belko's extra point attempt was then blocked by Bill Shakespeare, and USC led, 6–0. The Irish came back to take the lead in the third quarter on a Shakespeare to Wally Fromhart pass that covered 25 yards. Fromhart added the extra point, and Notre Dame was up, 7–6, and never relinquished the lead. Fromhart threw a 43-yard scoring strike to Wayne Millner, and then kicked the conversion to give Notre Dame a 14–6 advantage. The Trojans closed to within one early in the fourth quarter on a Glenn Thompson one-yard run, and Homer Beatty's extra point kick made it a 14–13 ballgame. Late in the game, from the Notre Dame 38, Thompson went for it all with a long pass, but Fromhart intercepted it at the 10, and returned the ball 82 yards down to the USC eight-yard line. On first down, Shakespeare scored on a sweep to put the game away.[8]

**(H) Dec. 7—Washington—2–6**

On USC's homecoming weekend, the Trojans got out to a quick 2–0 lead when Washington halfback Byron Haines was tackled in end zone on the opening kickoff. Haines made up for the error by scoring the game's only touchdown in the second quarter. The Trojans got close to scoring on three occasions, but each time they were stopped short of their objective. Despite the loss, David Davis ran for 101 yards on 26 carries.[9]

**(H) Dec. 14—Pittsburgh—7–12**

For the second straight season, the Pitt Panthers defeated the Trojans. The Panthers received their points in the first and third quarters on touchdowns from Frank Patrick and Herbert Randour. The Trojans had two major drives deep into Pitt territory stopped by stellar defensive stands. They finally scored in the last few minutes of the game on a pass from David Davis to Bill Gaisford.[10]

**(A) Dec. 25—Kamehameha HS Alumni—33–7**

The Trojans managed to put together a solid game in the island paradise of Hawaii on Christmas Day. The Trojans struck quickly in this game, scoring their first points with nine minutes off the clock in the opening quarter. Bill Howard capped a 91-yard drive with a run into the end zone from one yard out. David Davis added a touchdown run, and later in the game, George McNeish blocked a punt and Art Dittberner picked up the ball and scored. The defense also got into the scoring column when Chuck Williams intercepted a pass, and then lateralled the ball to Bob Sanders before he was brought down. Sanders continued on the trek downfield until he completed a 55-yard touchdown run.[11]

**Poi Bowl, (A) Jan. 1—Hawaii—38–6**

A trip to Hawaii is on the wish list of many individuals. The warm, beautiful surroundings have long called to the masses, and on the first day of 1936, the University of Southern California football team was among the many who answered the call.

The Poi Bowl was designed to invite football programs from the Pacific Coast Conference, with the exception being in 1937, to come a play against the University of Hawaii. There were five editions of this contest, and the Trojans gained the honor of playing in the first one. This game was considered a College Division/Minor Bowl Game, and recognized as just a regular season contest by both the NCAA and USC.

Honolulu Stadium played host to the Trojans, and Howard Jones and his men of Troy were not kind guests. The Hawaii Rainbows were successful under head coach Otto Klum, and had star running back Thomas Kaulukukui on their roster at the time of USC's invasion. However, neither Klum's coaching expertise or Kaulukukui's running abilities could counterbalance the onslaught USC provided.

Jones used two teams to help his players conserve energy in the sweltering heat. However, it did not matter what group of Trojans were on the field at the time, or what the weather conditions were, USC rolled. David Davis got the scoring festivities going in the first quarter with a short yardage scoring strike to James Sutherland. Sutherland then added the extra point kick. Davis struck again with his passing ability, this time on a 74-yard touchdown toss to Bill Gaisford. The conversion failed, but the Trojans were in control with a 13–0 lead.

Davis decided to score a touchdown with his legs, and added USC's third six-pointer of the day on a one-yard run. Max Belko kicked the extra point, and USC was up, 20–0. Bill Gaisford recovered a Hawaii fumble, and Nick Pappas turned the error into a touchdown run after eluding six tacklers. The extra point was missed, but at this stage, it did not matter, as the Trojans were up, 26–0. Pappas added a short yardage touchdown run to his day's work, and the Trojans eventually coasted to the victory in what was the only appearance for USC in the Poi Bowl.[12]

### Team Leaders

Rushing: Nick Pappas—414 yards on 102 carries
Scoring: Bill Gaisford—18 points on 3 touchdowns
Davie Davis—18 points on 3 touchdowns

## *1936*

Head Coach: Howard Jones
Assistant Coaches: Sam Barry, Jeff Cravath, Aubrey Devine, Cliff Herd
Team Captain: Gil Kuhn
Record: 4–2–3 overall (3–2–2 in Pacific Coast Conference)
(Ranked 55th best record in college football out of 131 teams)
Finish in Conference: Tied for 3rd place
Finish in National Polls: This season marked the beginning of the still-used Associated Press ranking system of the Top 25 teams in Division 1-A. USC did not secure a place among the Top 25 at the end of the season.
Points Scored Per Game: 14.3 to rank 51st out of 131 teams
Points Allowed Per Game: 7.2 to rank 36th

### Schedule and Highlights

**(H) Sept. 26—Oregon State—38–7**

The Trojans started off the '36 season with a solid win over Oregon State. Led at the beginning by USC's much-talked about

"Sophomore Eleven," the group of underclassmen started the game and led the Trojans to their first two touchdowns to give USC a 12–0 halftime lead. The sophomores scored the season's first points after 11 minutes expired in the game before giving way to the senior starters. Ambrose Schindler threw a touchdown pass to Ralph Stanley, and USC never relinquished the lead. Schindler threw another scoring strike later to Jim Henderson. David Davis scored two touchdowns, and Richard Berryman had one, as the Trojans amassed 279 yards passing in this season opening romp.[1]

**(H) Oct. 3—Oregon—26–0**

Oregon came into the Coliseum with its strongest team to face the Trojans since 1915. For the first half of the game, they kept a stagnant USC team under control, going into the second half with a 0–0 tie. The second half was a different story, as the Trojan offense began clicking. Sparked by David Davis' two touchdowns runs, the Trojans won with ease, improving their PCC and regular season record to 2–0. For the game, Davis ran for 109 yards on 22 carries, and the defense held Oregon to zero pass completions.[2]

**(A) Oct. 10—Illinois—24–6**

David Davis made it two straight weeks of topping the century mark by rushing for 101 yards on 26 carries in another convincing win for the Trojans. Davis was the main weapon for USC, as he mixed passes with runs to bring the Trojans their first intersectional win since 1933. Davis threw two touchdown passes, with Ralph Stanley and Gene Hibbs on the receiving end of the scoring strikes. Jimmy Jones added a 10-yard touchdown run, and Hibbs recorded two safeties. The first came when he blocked a punt out of the end zone, and the other came when he tackled the Illinois quarterback in the end zone.[3]

**(H) Oct. 17—Washington State—0–0**

In this scoreless tie, which pitted the PCC's top two teams tied for first place with 2–0 records in the conference, Nick Pappas stood out for the Trojans with 111 rushing yards on 24 carries. Pappas took over for David Davis at quarterback after Davis suffered a chest injury. The Trojans had three opportunities to score after driving deep into Washington State territory, but two penalties and an interception thwarted those chances.[4]

**(A) Oct. 24—Stanford—14–7**

USC came in ranked sixth in the AP poll, and left the game still unbeaten. David Davis returned at quarterback after suffering a chest injury the previous week. His mobility was hampered due to wearing a heavy rib protector. He was replaced by sophomore signal caller Ambrose Schindler, who threw a touchdown pass to Ray Wehba that gave USC a 7–0 halftime lead. Coye Dunn provided the Trojans with their other touchdown on a 33-yard interception return that put USC up, 14–0. This win gave the Trojans a 3–0–1 record in the PCC race, right behind Washington (4–0) and Washington State (4–0–1).[5]

**(H) Nov. 7—California—7–13**

USC# 11

The Cal Golden Bears came into the Coliseum with a 3–4 record, and on a three-game losing streak in the PCC. Out of the race for a conference title, Cal had nothing to lose, and earned the opportunity to hand a long-time rival an upset defeat. Cal took a 6–0 lead, and then David Davis scored the tying touchdown on a plunge from the one-foot line. Jim Henderson's conversion kick gave the Trojans a very brief 7–6 advantage. Within 35 seconds after Davis' touchdown, Cal was back on top, this time for good. From the USC 45yard line, two straight passes got them the game-winning touchdown.[6]

**(A) Nov. 14—Washington—0–12**

USC#15th

The Trojans came into this PCC showdown with the tenth ranked Washington Huskies, who were on top of the conference with a 4–0–1 record while USC was second at 3–1–1. With close to 24,000 in attendance on Washington's homecoming weekend, the Huskies took a major step in clinching the PCC championship. Jimmy Cain was the backfield star for Washington, and he scored the game's first touchdown in the second quarter. The Huskies also added their other touchdown in the second quarter. The Trojans never got closer to the end zone than the Washington 18-yard line.[7]

**(H) Nov. 26—UCLA—7–7**

After a six-year hiatus, the series was resumed with 85,000 in attendance, and the Bruins were finally able to compete on level ground against their mighty neighbors. Fullback Billy Bob Williams earned the honor of being the first-ever UCLA player to score points against USC in this series. The historic moment occurred after USC's quarterback Ambrose Schindler got hit hard and fumbled. UCLA's Sherman Chavoor, who suffered a severe injury to his elbow, but refused to leave the field, pounced on the loose ball at the USC 40. Ten plays later, Williams ran into the end zone from two yards out. Jimmy Jones evened things up for the Trojans in the third quarter with a four-yard run. Despite fumbling five times and throwing three interceptions, the Trojans were lucky to escape this meeting with a tie, and finished the PCC race in third place.[8]

**(H) Dec. 5—Notre Dame—13–13**

Notre Dame dominated the Trojans statistically in this edition of the "Glamour Game." The Irish had major advantages in total plays (94 to 36), first downs (18 to one), total yards (406 to 53), and pounded out a ground attack that outgained the Trojans 157 yards to 19. However, winning the battle of stats does not always mean victory, and this game proved it.

With 71,201 in attendance for USC's homecoming game, the Irish took the field as the #9 ranked team in the country. They then proved their status by scoring on their opening possession. Bob Wilke, who started the game off with a 22-yard kickoff return, finished the drive on the 11th play with a three-yard run. James Henderson blocked the extra point attempt and Notre Dame had an early 6–0 lead.

Late in the second quarter, the Irish faced a fourth-and-five from the USC 32. Gill Kuhn halted the Notre Dame advance with an interception at the 10, and he returned it to the USC 25. After a loss of one yard, the Trojans got their fans to their feet with a Flea-flicker play. Ambrose Schindler gained 11 yards before he was meet by defenders. He spun around and tossed the ball back to Dick Berryman, but the ball fell to the ground. It took one bounce and Berryman grabbed it and ran for the touchdown to complete the 76-yard play, 65 of which were covered by Berryman. The Trojans opportunity to take the tie was stymied when Henderson missed on the extra point attempt.

With four minutes left in the first half, Notre Dame got to the USC nine within seven plays. On first and goal, Wilke dropped back and threw toward the left side of the field. Laurence Langley of USC was right there to intercept the pass at the four, and took it the distance for six points. It set a school record for longest return of an interception, and tied Russ Saunders 96-yard kickoff return in 1929 for the longest scoring play in this series. Henderson added the extra point with 47 seconds remaining in the first to give the Trojans a 13–6 lead. The Irish then sent the game into the history books as a tie when Larry Danbom threw to Nevin McCormick for a 15-yard touchdown and Andy Puplis' extra point kick knotted the game at 13.[9]

TEAM LEADERS

RUSHING: Davie Davis—501 yards on 141 carries
SCORING: Davie Davis—30 points on 5 touchdowns

## *1937*

HEAD COACH: Howard Jones
ASSISTANT COACHES: Sam Barry, Julius Bescos, Jeff Cravath, Robert McNeish
TEAM CAPTAIN: Chuck Williams
RECORD: 4–4–2 overall (2–3–2 in Pacific Coast Conference)
(Ranked 69th best record in college football out of 126 teams)
FINISH IN CONFERENCE: 7th place
FINISH IN NATIONAL POLLS: No ranking in Top 25
POINTS SCORED PER GAME: 13.6 to rank 48th out of 126 teams
POINTS ALLOWED PER GAME: 9.8 to rank 79th

### Schedule and Highlights

**(H) Sept. 25—College of Pacific—40–0**

Ambrose Schindler set the tone early in this game by running for a 64-yard touchdown in the first few minutes of play, and added a four-yard scoring run a short time later. Schindler suffered a leg injury that forced him from the game early in the third quarter, but his replacement, Grenville Lansdell, kept the onslaught going. Lansdell mixed passing and running abilities to torment the Pacific defense. He threw two touchdown passes, with Bill Fisk and Chuck Williams scoring on Lansdell's tosses. Oliver Day scored on a two-yard run and Mickey Anderson caught a touchdown pass from Doyle Nave. The Trojans prevented Pacific from getting one first down the entire game en route to their biggest margin of victory since 1933. This was also USC's 28th shutout win on opening day.[1]

**(H) Oct. 2—Washington—0–7**

The Trojans took the momentum created by their convincing victory in the opener into this game against the defending PCC champion Huskies. Unfortunately, just like in the previous season's matchup with Washington, USC lost and failed to produce any points. This time it was four fumbles that hampered the Trojans' chances. Jimmy Johnson provided the Huskies with the only points they needed on this day when he ran for a one-yard touchdown, and Al Cruver added the conversion kick.[2]

**(H) Oct. 9—Ohio State—13–12**

USC scored the winning points with nine minutes remaining, and Ambrose Schindler ran for 101 yards on 28 carries. The Trojans got out to a 6–0 halftime advantage on a one-yard run by Schindler, but the conversion attempt was missed. Schindler was forced to the sideline with painful leg cramps early in the third quarter, and while he rested his sore limb, the Buckeyes took a 12–6 lead. Schindler returned to action in the fourth quarter, and rallied the Trojans to victory with a touchdown pass to Mickey Anderson. Ralph Stanley then added the game-winning conversion kick.[3]

**(H) Oct. 16—Oregon—34–14**

Amby Schindler topped the century mark for the second straight week. This time he gained 133 yards on 16 carries, and tied a USC single-game record with four rushing touchdowns, as the Trojans evened their PCC record to 1–1. Each time Schindler carried the ball, he averaged eight yards. All his scoring jaunts came in the first half before he was forced from the game in the second half due to leg cramps. This victory was the 100th in Howard Jones' USC coaching career.[4]

**(A) Oct. 23—California—6–20**
USC#11 Cal#1

The top-ranked Golden Bears coached by Stub Allison awaited the Trojans next. Cal totally overwhelmed USC with powerful runs by the backfield. Running back Vic Bottari scored two touchdowns to force a tie for the PCC scoring lead with USC's Ambrose Schindler at 42 points apiece. Grenville Lansdell, who replaced an injured Schindler, led the Trojans on a 66-yard drive for their only points in the third quarter after Cal had built a 20–0 led at the end of the first half.[5]

**(A) Oct. 30—Washington State—0–0**

Almost this entire game was played in fog so heavy at times that the players were not visible from the sidelines. To add to this problem, the playing surface was wet and slick, and temperatures were near zero. All this made for a bad day running the ball, and led to Howard Jones proclaiming that these were the worst weather conditions he had witnessed in his 25-year coaching career. Despite the elements, the Trojans still managed to gain 235 offensive yards and 13 first downs. Ambrose Schindler continued to perform well, finishing this scoreless deadlock with 99 rushing yards on 34 carries.[6]

**(H) Nov. 6—Stanford—6–7**

Amby Schindler ran for 110 yards on 23 carries and USC's only touchdown. This marked the third time in 12 years that Stanford beat the Trojans by the margin of three points or less. In 1926, they won, 13–12, and in 1935, it was a field goal that gave them a 3–0 victory. Pete Fay caught a touchdown pass from Jimmy Groves, and Doc Luckett connected on the conversion kick to send the Trojans down in defeat for the second time in three games.[7]

**(H) Nov. 13—Oregon State—12–12**

Grenny Lansdell broke the century mark in rushing for the first time in what would become an illustrious USC career. He finished with 117 yards on 19 carries and one touchdown. The Trojans opened the scoring in the first quarter on a touchdown run by Ambrose Schindler. That six-pointer allowed Schindler to tie Cal's Vic Bottari for the PCC scoring lead with 54 points each. Lansdell added USC's other touchdown in the second quarter on a one-yard run. Oregon State's Joe Gray put on a solid display by completing 10 out of 12 pass completions, and threw two scoring strikes, with both going to Joe Wendlick.[8]

**(A) Nov. 27—Notre Dame—6–13**

This season marked the Notre Dame football program's golden anniversary, and they came into this annual clash as the #9 ranked team in the country. The Trojans, however, came into the game as 20-point underdogs. They shocked the college football world by jumping out to a 6–0 lead in the second quarter on a seven-yard pass from Grenville Lansdell to Gene Hibbs. That was how the first half ended, as Irish fans everywhere were stunned by the results.

The Trojans were still hanging on to their lead late in the third quarter when the Irish decided to wake up the echoes and shake down the thunder. Andy Puplis dropped into punt formation for Notre Dame, and decided to run instead of kick the ball back to USC. His decision was a good one, as he recorded a 58-yard touchdown run to tie the game. The score remained 6–6 when Charles Williams blocked the conversion kick.

In the fourth quarter, USC drove down to the Notre Dame 22, and then Puplis once again haunted the Trojans, this time with an interception at the 12. With time running out, and the Irish facing a third-and-five from their own 17, halfback Mario Tonnelli earned his place in the history of this series. He broke loose for a run of 70 yards before he was stopped on the USC 13. A penalty on USC moved the ball to the eight, and Tonnelli finished off the drive, and the Trojans in the process, with a run through a huge hole created by his linemen with 1:45 left in the game. Puplis then kicked the conversion to give the Irish the win. This game completed Notre Dame's 50th season as they posted a dominant record of 293–65–24 for a .798 winning percentage.[9]

**(A) Dec. 4—UCLA—19–13**

The Trojans looked to be cruising to an easy victory on the day of their homecoming, but the Bruins wanted to spoil the festivities, and almost accomplished it. The Trojans took a 19–0 lead with nine minutes left to play, and were looking to be in complete control. They allowed the Bruins a mere 25 yards on the ground, and only 46 through the air for 51 minutes of action. Things then got interesting. It all started with a poor snap from USC's Don McNeil. The ball sailed off the head of fullback Roy Engle and was recovered by UCLA tackle Larry Murdock at the USC 44. A few plays later, Kenny Washington fired a pass to Hal Hirshon on the USC 10. Hirshon outdueled USC's Joe Shell for the ball and scored. A short time later, as night was blanketing the Los Angeles area, Washington dropped back to pass, and let fly with a rocket toss from his own 15. The ball sailed 61 yards in the air and into the hands of Hirshon deep in USC territory. He scored easily and following another conversion kick, the Bruins closed to within five points. With time running out, the Bruins got to the USC 14, but on fourth-and-16, with just over a minute left on the clock, Washington's pass fell in and out of a receiver's hands to end what could have been one of the best comebacks in UCLA's history.[10]

Team Leaders

Rushing: Amby Schindler—599 yards on 134 carries
Passing: Grenny Lansdell—28 out of 63 attempts for 310 yards and 4 touchdowns
Receiving: Bill Sangster—10 catches for 125 yards
Scoring: Amby Schindler—54 points on 9 touchdowns

# *1938*

Head Coach: Howard Jones
Assistant Coaches: Sam Barry, Julius Bescos, Jeff Cravath, Robert McNeish
Team Captain: Don McNeil
Record: 9–2 overall (6–1 in Pacific Coast Conference)
(Ranked 14th best record in college football out of 122 teams)
Finish in Conference: Tied California for 1st place
Finish in National Polls: 7th place in AP
Points Scored Per Game: 15.6 to rank 41st out of 122 teams
Points Allowed Per Game: 5.9 to rank 30th

## Schedule and Highlights

**(H) Sept. 24—Alabama—7–19**

The Alabama Crimson Tide used a pounding running attack featuring George Zivich, and pinpoint scoring strikes from Herky Mosley, to prevail over a sluggish USC squad that was considered a strong contender for the Pacific Coast Conference title. Ollie Day scored for the Trojans in the fourth quarter to prevent a shutout in front of 65,000 in the Coliseum.[1]

**(H) Oct. 1—Oregon State—7–0**

The Trojans redeemed themselves by opening their Pacific Coast Conference schedule with a narrow 7–0 win over the Oregon State Beavers. The Trojans gained 271 yards of total offense while limiting Oregon State to only 19, and holding them to zero first downs. Ollie Day broke a scoreless tie in the third quarter with a touchdown run, and Phil Gaspar added the extra point.[2]

**(A) Oct. 8—Ohio State—14–7**

In USC's first trip away from Los Angeles, they continued on with their winning ways. The Trojans took a quick advantage with only 1:04 expired from the clock following the opening kickoff. Grenville Lansdell provided the excitement for the Trojans by taking a punt on the USC 18, and racing 82 yards for a touchdown. The Buckeyes tied the game up following a blocked punt on a Jim Langhurst run in the second quarter. Ollie Day then threw a scoring strike to Al Krueger in the third quarter for what turned out to be the game winner.[3]

**(H) Oct. 15—Washington State—19–6**

The Trojans remained undefeated in the Pacific Coast Conference with a hard fought victory over the Washington State Cougars with 45,000 on hand at the Coliseum. The Cougars were looking for their first win, and first touchdown, in three previous outings. Despite their dismal record coming into this game, they stayed close with the heavily favored Trojans, going into the final stanza knotted tie at 6–6. A pass from Ollie Day to John Stonebraker provided the Trojans with their first touchdown. Tackle George Hubert then gave the Cougars their first six-pointer of the season after blocking a punt and returning it 30 yards to paydirt in the third quarter. Boyd Morgan broke the deadlock with a 35-yard punt return, and then Doyle Nave scored the game's final touchdown to give USC some breathing room. The Trojans had 11 first downs in the game while holding Washington State to two. They also outrushed the Cougars 134 yards to 29, and outpassed them 126 yards to eight.[4]

**(A) Oct. 22—Stanford—13–2**

The Trojans made it a perfect 3–0 slate in the PCC race with this victory over their long-time rivals, but it was another battle. Stanford took a 2–0 lead three minutes into the game on a safety. It then became a defensive struggle for these two unbeaten teams throughout the first half. A Grenville Lansdell pass to fullback Bill Sangster from just inside the Stanford 20-yard line produced a touchdown, and put the Trojans on top to stay in the third quarter. Mickey Anderson added an insurance touchdown in the fourth quarter to keep USC on top of the conference standings.[5]

**(N) Oct. 29—Oregon—31–7**

USC #19

The Trojans finally had an easy win, as they rang up their first convincing victory of the season. Played on muddy field conditions at Multnomah Stadium in Portland, Oregon, the Trojans got touchdowns from Boyd Morgan, Grenville Lansdell, John Stonebraker, Jack Banta, and Doyle Nave. This impressive win allowed USC to remain undefeated in the PCC, and set up a showdown with the unbeaten California Golden Bears.[6]

**(H) Nov. 5—California—13–7**

USC #13 Cal #3

With their largest crowd in six years watching this conference showdown, the Trojans scored a 13–7 upset victory. Cal came into this matchup riding an 18-game wining streak, and waged a fierce scoreless battle with USC up to the end of the first half. Grenville Lansdell then put USC on top in the third quarter with a six-yard sweep around the left side, much to the approval of 95,000 in attendance at the Coliseum. They expanded their lead to 13–0 on a Jack Banta one-yard run in the fourth quarter. The USC defense played exceptionally well, holding the powerful Cal team to a mere two first downs.[7]

**(A) Nov. 12—Washington—6–7**

USC #9

In the rain at Washington, the Huskies scored an upset of the conference leaders. The Trojans reign as sole possessors of first place in the PCC ended by the narrowest of margins on a trip to Seattle against the 1–4–1 Huskies. All the scoring occurred in the first half, with Washington's Jimmy Johnston getting an opening quarter six-pointer on a 52-yard run. Don Jones then added what proved to be the game-winning point by sending the conversion kick through the uprights. The Trojans' tally came on a 72-yard punt return by USC's star offensive weapon Grenville Lansdell. However, Phil Gaspar's attempt to tie the game ended on a sour note, as his kick was low and wide of the uprights. The Huskies got 10 first downs to only three for USC, and outgained them on the ground 167 yards to 77. Through the air, Washington was able to gain 45 yards, while the Trojans never completed a pass.[8]

**(H) Nov. 24—UCLA—42–7**

This lopsided victory allowed the Trojans to tie Cal for the PCC championship, and because they beat the Golden Bears in head-to-head competition, USC earned the right to play in the Rose Bowl. This marked the final game for UCLA coach Bill Spaulding, and his last quest at beating a Howard Jones-led team.

At first, it appeared that Spaulding might have a chance this time out, as the Trojans committed two fumbles, with one leading to a ten-yard touchdown pass from Kenny Washington to Woody Strode. The Bruins led by a 7–0 count until halfway through the second quarter. Howard Jones tolerated no nonsense from his team, and replaced nine of his starters with backups, and they came through. Jimmy Jones set up a Jack Banta two-yard touchdown run with a 50-yard completion. Al Krueger then picked off a Kenny Washington pass and returned it 52 yards for a score that gave the Trojans a 13–7 lead going into the third quarter. The Trojans continued to pour it on, adding 29 points in the second half to win with ease.[9]

**(H) Dec. 3—Notre Dame—13–0**

USC #8 ND #1

After a few down years, this series was returned to the grand spectacle that it was. With both teams back in the upper echelon of the national rankings, USC scored an upset of Notre Dame as 97,146 watched from the stands at the Coliseum. The first quarter was lethargic as only one first down was achieved. The second quarter began much like the first. The Trojans missed a close range field goal with three minutes remaining just before halftime. Notre Dame then took over on their own 20, but soon after faced a fourth-and–22 situation with under one minute left. Opting to run out of punt formation, Bob Saggau's quest at a first down fell 14 yards shy at the Notre Dame 39. A few plays later, Ollie Day connected with Al Krueger on a 36-yard touchdown pass with a mere five seconds left in the half. The extra point was missed, but the Trojans held a 6–0 lead going into the second half. After a scoreless third quarter, Milton Piepul fumbled and USC's James Jones recovered at the Notre Dame 35. The Trojans then went on a 10-play drive that was capped by Bill Anderson scoring on a three-yard run. Phil Gaspar added the extra point, and the Trojans were on their way to crushing Notre Dame's hope of winning a national championship. The Fighting Irish tried to come back, but an interception by James Jones at the goal line killed the drive and secured the shutout.[10]

**Rose Bowl, (N) Jan. 2—Duke—7–3**

USC #7 Duke #3

The silver anniversary of the Rose Bowl saw the perfect Duke Blue Devils come to Pasadena looking to end USC's spotless 5–0 bowl record. Not only did Duke win all their nine regular season games, but did so by never relinquishing a single point all year. This game went down as an all-time bowl classic, and a true underdog success story. Doyle Nave went from a fourth-string quarterback to a hero within four plays. After amassing a mere 28 ½ minutes of playing time all season, Nave was pressed into action on one of the grandest stages in college football.

Throughout three quarters, the game remained scoreless until Tony Ruffa split the uprights with a 23-yard field goal to give the Blue Devils a slim 3–0 advantage. With the game winding down, and Duke's famed defensive front, "the Seven Iron Dukes" controlling Howard Jones' charges, it appeared that the Blue Devils would clinch a perfect season without giving up a single point.

It was then that Doyle Nave was sent into the game against incredible odds, and emerged as a main focal point in Trojan lore. It had all the making of a Hollywood feel good film attached to it, with Nave and end "Antelope" Al Krueger in the starring roles. With the clock working against the Trojans, and their running game not getting anywhere against the stubborn defense, Jones conjured up a different plan of attack after USC reached just inside the Duke 39-yard line. He sent Nave into the game who was regarded as a solid passer. There was a wild tale spun for many years that a USC assistant coach on the sideline made up a story that he received a call from his fellow assistants perched up high in the press box, insisting to put Nave into the game. This tall tale was proven wrong by USC assistant Julie Bescos, who claimed that it was himself and fellow assistant Robert McNeish who saw a weakness in the almost invincible Duke defense, and called assistant Sam Barry down on the sideline, relaying to him that this would be an excellent time to use Nave's passing talents. Barry informed Jones, and Nave went into the game, and down in USC history.

With two minutes left, Nave hooked up with Krueger for a gain of 13 yards. Another pass to Krueger got the ball to the Duke 17. On the following play, Krueger was once again on the receiving end, but lost two yards after making the catch. In the huddle, with time away, the play "27 down and out" was called, meaning that Krueger was once again the focal point of Nave's pass attempt. Nave dropped back and waited for his receiver to get past defender Eric Tipton. Krueger lived up to his moniker of "Antelope," by swiftly getting an advantage on Tipton. Nave delivered a pinpoint pass toward Krueger in the corner of the end zone for a 19-yard touchdown, and the first points allowed by Duke all year. What no other team could do all year took Nave and Krueger one minute and twenty seconds to accomplish. Phil Gaspar added the extra point, and the Trojans went on to a stunning victory. Nave and Krueger shared the MVP award, and Nave became an instant hero, getting an outpouring of fan mail from across the country. One touch of irony was that Nave had not even logged enough playing time throughout the season to qualify for a varsity letter, but Jones disregarded that piece of information and presented him with one.[11]

TEAM LEADERS

RUSHING: Grenny Lansdell—462 yards on 118 carries
PASSING: Grenny Lansdell—44 out of 112 attempts for 458 yards and 2 touchdowns
RECEIVING: Bob Hoffman—11 catches for 112 yards
SCORING: Grenny Lansdell—31 points on 5 touchdowns and 1 extra point

## *1939*

HEAD COACH: Howard Jones
ASSISTANT COACHES: Sam Barry, Julius Bescos, Jeff Cravath, Robert McNeish
TEAM CAPTAIN: Joe Shell

RECORD: 8–0–2 overall (5–0–2 in Pacific Coast Conference) (Ranked 6th best record in college football out of 124 teams)
FINISH IN CONFERENCE: 1st place
FINISH IN NATIONAL POLLS: 3rd place in AP
1939 National Champions in Dickinson System
POINTS SCORED PER GAME: 18.1 to rank 21st out of 124 teams
POINTS ALLOWED PER GAME: 3.3 to rank 6th

### Schedule and Highlights

**(H) Sept. 30—Oregon—7–7**

Oregon gave the defending PCC co-champions a tough go of it in the conference opener for both teams. The Ducks scored their lone six-pointer in the second quarter to lead 7–0 at the end of the first half. The Trojans tried to attack Oregon throughout the game with a steady stream of fresh players, but each time they were held out of the end zone. With time ticking away, and an upset in the works, the Trojans got on the board when Doyle Nave threw an 11-yard touchdown pass to Robert Peoples. Peoples set the USC record single-game receiving record with eight catches. Phil Gaspar then added the all-important conversion kick that deadlocked the game with seven minutes remaining.[1]

**(H) Oct. 7—Washington—27–0**

This time out with Washington, the Trojans left nothing to chance. They controlled this game from the start, and easily won their second straight PCC contest. The Trojans scored their first touchdown midway through the first quarter, and never looked back. Grenny Lansdell led the USC offensive attack with 113 yards on the ground in 15 carries and scored two touchdowns.[2]

**(H) Oct. 14—Illinois—26–0**

For the second straight week, the mighty Trojans proved too much for the opposition. For the first time in the season, they played outside the conference, and did not show their foes from the Midwest much hospitality. With 60,000 looking on inside the Coliseum, the Trojans dominated Illinois on the ground and in the air. They rushed for 207 yards, while holding Illinois to 23 yards. When passing, USC gained 116 yards, and allowed only 23. On a 90-degree day, Amby Schindler led the Trojans with a pair of touchdowns, one coming on a 66-yard punt return. Doyle Nave and Grenny Lansdell scored USC's other touchdowns.[3]

**(A) Oct. 28—California—26–0**

USC #8

After a tie in the season opener, the powerful Trojans rolled over three straight opponents, including this long-time rival. The Golden Bears played tough in front of 50,000 home fans, but then the Trojans pulled away quickly in the third quarter with 20 points. Grenny Lansdell threw a 15-yard pass to Bob Winslow to open the scoring. Bob Peoples added an 11-yard run, and then Lansdell ran for the third six-pointer of the quarter. Ambrose Schindler threw a 41-yard pass to John Stonebraker for USC's final tally in what was the most lopsided win in this series since 1926.[4]

**(N) Nov. 4—Oregon State—19–7**

USC #7 OSU #11

In a showdown of conference unbeatens, the Trojans overpowered Oregon State on the ground and through the air. With a packed stadium of 32,611 in Portland, Oregon, USC took a major step in clinching another PCC championship, and a shot at the national title. After a scoreless first quarter, Doyle Nave threw a 12-yard touchdown pass to Jim Slatter. The Trojans struck again through the air in the second quarter, this time on a 19-yard pass from Ambrose Schindler to Al Krueger that gave USC a 13–0 halftime advantage. Grenny Lansdell scored on a short-yardage run in the third quarter to end the Trojans' point production.[5]

**(H) Nov. 11—Stanford—33–0**

USC #4

Grenny Lansdell ran for 100 yards on 14 carries, and the Trojans handed Stanford the worst beating in this series since it began in 1905. Lansdell attacked the defense with passes and his running ability, and scored two touchdowns. USC scored one touchdown in the opening quarter, and then exploded for 20 points in the second quarter to put the game away by halftime with a commanding 27–0 advantage.[6]

**(A) Nov. 25—Notre Dame—20–12**

USC #4 ND #7

Two months earlier, the dawn of world conflict that came to be known as World War II began when Germany invaded Poland. The United States was still two years away from being brought into the fight, and the world of sports continued to be a major topic of interest. Notre Dame Stadium was filled with 55,000 fans on a wet and breezy day to watch the Fighting Irish take the field for the 400th game in their illustrious history.

The Trojans wasted little time attempting to spoil the festivities by lighting up the scoreboard on this dreary day. On their first possession, Grenville Lansdell gained 24 yards on six carries, and Robert Peoples darted for 21 yards on three attempts. Lansdell then capped the 12-play, 67-yard drive off with a touchdown run from the two to give USC a quick 6–0 lead, but Phil Gaspar missed the extra point try. For the game Lansdell gained 101 yards on 24 carries.

USC quickly got the ball back after Robert Hoffman intercepted a pass on the Notre Dame 42. However, nothing materialized, and the game became a punting duel. The Trojans did get close to paydirt midway through the second quarter. They got the ball to the Notre Dame one, but Doyle Nave fumbled into the end zone for a touchback, and the score was 6–0 at the end of the first half.

Milton Piepul got the Irish knotted up at 6–6 early in the fourth quarter on a short yardage touchdown run, but he then missed on the extra point try. Grenville Lansdell added his second six-pointer of the game when he swept the right side of the line on fourth-and-two from the Notre Dame five-yard line. His touchdown, coupled with Robert Jones' conversion kick, gave USC a 13–6 lead.

On Notre Dame's next series, Benny Sheridan broke through the line and was off to the end zone after covering 60 yards. John Kelleher failed on the conversion, and the Trojans clung to a slim one-point lead. With four minutes left in the game, Notre Dame failed to complete a pass on fourth-and-11 at their own 39. After taking over on downs, the Trojans scored on their second play when Ambrose Schindler attacked the middle of the field, and won out by completing a 39-yard jaunt to six points to give the Trojans a nice cushion. With Jones' extra point, USC was up, 20–12. The Irish got to the USC 11 to make things interesting down the stretch, but time ran out on them.[7]

**(H) Dec. 2—Washington—9–7**

USC #1

Washington started off the season with four straight losses. They then turned the season around with four consecutive victories that brought them into the Coliseum with a 4–4 record. They were also looking to continue a streak of beating USC for the sixth straight year. With a crowd of 50,000 in attendance for USC's homecoming, Washington scored a touchdown in the first quarter, and then played a solid game in an attempt to hold off the powerful Trojans. For the first 58 minutes, the plan worked, as their seven-point lead held up. The Trojans got their first points on a fluke. Washington's Ernie Steele intercepted a Doyle Nave on the goal line, but then fell backward into the end zone for a safety. The Trojans then pulled out the win with 1:45 remaining when Grenny Lansdell threw a 16-yard scoring strike to John Stonebraker.[8]

**(A) Dec. 9—UCLA—0–0**

USC #3 UCLA #9

Grenny Lansdell ran 15 times for 101 yards and Bobby Robertson knocked down Ned Matthews' 4-yd pass in the end zone with less than five minutes left to preserve the tie and send USC to the Rose Bowl. This was the first time in this rivalry series that both teams were ranked going into the game. It was also the first time that the Rose Bowl was at stake. Ending in a 0–0 tie, it was also the first time for this as well. Witnessed by a huge crowd of 103,303 and by virtue of the tiebreaker, USC went to the Rose Bowl.[9]

**Rose Bowl, (N) Jan. 1—Tennessee—14–0**

Once again an undefeated team from the Land of Dixie invaded Pasadena on New Year's Day. This time it was the 10–0 Tennessee Volunteers under head coach Robert Neyland. Just like Duke the year before, the Volunteers were not only unbeaten, but never relinquished a single point all season long. They were also riding a 23-game winning streak.

The Trojans were no strangers to this scenario, and went about their business of bowl dominance accordingly, regardless of the tough opposition that awaited them. The Trojans had long been known for their solid backfield tradition, and Grenny Lansdell and Ambrose Schindler helped add to that legacy against this seemingly invincible defense from the "Volunteer State." Schindler ran for 81 yards, Lansdell 51, and as a team, the Trojan ground forces gained 229 yards of Rose Bowl real estate.

After a scoreless first quarter, Schindler scored on a one-yard run, and then connected with Al Krueger for a one-yard scoring strike in the fourth quarter. Despite looking unbeatable coming into the game, Tennessee was completely out-performed by USC. The Trojans possessed three of the most important things a team can have, size, strength, and speed. These ingredients were used in this game, and the Trojans came away victors and possessors of a fourth national championship under Howard Jones, and a perfect 7–0 bowl game record.[10]

TEAM LEADERS

RUSHING: Grenny Lansdell—742 yards on 154 carries
PASSING: Grenny Lansdell—42 out of 85 attempts for 479 yards and 2 touchdowns
RECEIVING: Bob Peoples—16 catches for 128 yards and 1 touchdown
SCORING: Grenny Lansdell—54 points on 9 touchdowns

## *1940*

HEAD COACH: Howard Jones
ASSISTANT COACHES: Sam Barry, Julius Bescos, Jeff Cravath, Robert McNeish, Gaius Shaver
TEAM CAPTAIN: Ed Dempsey
RECORD: 3–4–2 overall (2–3–2 in Pacific Coast Conference)
(Ranked 75th best record in college football out of 121 teams)
FINISH IN CONFERENCE: 7th place
FINISH IN NATIONAL POLLS: No ranking in Top 25
POINTS SCORED PER GAME: 9.8 to rank 98th out of 121 teams
POINTS ALLOWED PER GAME: 10.9 to rank 53rd

### Schedule and Highlights

**(H) Sept. 28—Washington State—14–14**

Bob Robertson opened the scoring for the Trojans' new season early in the first quarter on an eight-yard run. The Cougars came back to tie it in the second quarter. The Trojans then went back on top on a four-yard pass from Bob Peoples to Jack Banta. The Cougars refused to fold, and on a long scoring pass and conversion kick, they tied the game with 8:40 remaining.[1]

**(H) Oct. 5—Oregon State—0–0**

In a tough game, both teams went up and down the field, but each time was stopped. On two occasions, Oregon State threatened, but a Jack Banta interception and a penalty took away those opportunities. The Trojans were inside the Oregon State 10-yard line in the closing seconds, but a field goal attempt went wide.[2]

**(A) Oct. 12—Illinois—13–7**

Illinois had a seven-point lead, and Bob Peoples got the Trojans started by returning the second half kickoff back 45 yards. Bob Robertson scored on four-yard run to bring USC to within one point. A bad punt then gave USC the ball on the Illinois 23. Five plays later, the Trojans had their first win of the new decade, complements of Robertson's second scoring jaunt of the game. Bob de Lauer added the conversion to round out the scoring.[3]

**(H) Oct. 19—Oregon—13–0**

USC #17

The Trojans once again finished with 13 points and another victory. The passing arm of Bob Peoples provided USC with both touchdowns. He first connected with Joe Davis on a two-yard scoring strike, and then added an insurance touchdown on a pass to Al Krueger. The Trojans doubled the final yardage figures by gaining 222 while holding Oregon to 101.[4]

**(A) Oct. 26—Stanford—7–21**

USC #17, Stanford #9

The Trojans were unbeaten in their first four games of the new decade. However, long-time rival Stanford received the honor of sending USC into the loss column. The game was tied until Stanford's Norm Standlee scored on a short-yardage run to put Stanford up for good with three minutes left in the game. The Trojans received their touchdown on a one-yard run by Jack Banta.[5]

**(H) Nov. 9—California—7–20**

By virtually the same score, another long-time foe, the Golden bears, knocked the Trojans down to a record of 2–2–2. Bob Robertson ran for 104 yards on 24 carries and a touchdown in a losing effort. The main highlight of this game came from Cal's Jim Jurkovich, who entered the NCAA record books with an interception return of 100 yards.[6]

**(A) Nov. 16—Washington—0–14**

Washington #17

This loss placed the Trojans below the .500 mark for the first time this late in the season since 1937. They did manage to get to the Washington two-yard line on one occasion, but a penalty pushed them back and out of scoring opportunity.[7]

**(H) Nov. 30—UCLA—28–12**

This game saw both teams come into it with losing records. The Trojans were on a three-game losing streak, and the Bruins only had one victory in nine previous outings. However, bragging rights for control over the City of Angels was the prize, and Bob Robertson helped USC's cause by running for 179 yards on 33 carries and a touchdown. The Trojans received their other three touchdowns from Bob Peoples, Bob Berryman, and Jack Banta, on a day where they failed to complete one pass in four attempts, but amassed a staggering 407 yards on the ground.[8]

**(H) Dec. 7—Notre Dame—6–10**

The Trojans definitely suffered from a reversal of fortune coming into this clash with the Irish. They fell from national champion status to 3–3–2, while Notre Dame entered the game at 6–2. The 85,808 fans inside the LA Coliseum were quickly treated to a steady scoring clip, with the teams combining for 16 points in the first 17 minutes of the game. With the California sun shining down on the Southland, the Trojans struck back quickly after surrendering a short yardage field goal from the foot of Notre Dame team captain Milt Piepul. Bobby Peoples gave USC a 6–3 advantage with an exciting 53-yard scoring run. Unfortunately, conversion kicks were not USC's forte against the Irish during this time period, as they missed their 16th conversion attempt out of 27 previous attempts up to this time in the series.

The Trojans came right back by driving to the Notre Dame five before facing a fourth down situation from the three as time expired in the opening stanza. They tried a field goal, but the snap from center was fumbled away at the 15. The Irish then went on an 85-yard march, with Piepul scoring from the three, and then added the extra point for what turned out to be the game's final point. Despite the loss, Bob Robertson rushed for 121 yards. This game also saw the final link to the conception of the series come to an end. This classic series began with two of the game's greatest coaches in Knute Rockne and Howard Jones. In 1931, the world lost Rockne in a plane crash, and this turned out to be the final game that Jones would lead the Trojans. Prior to the beginning of summer drills in preparation for the upcoming season, Howard Jones fell victim to a fatal heart attack on July 27, 1941 at age 55.[9]

### TEAM LEADERS

RUSHING: Bobby Robertson—667 yards on 146 carries
PASSING: Bob Peoples—21 out of 63 attempts for 479 yards and 2 touchdowns
RECEIVING: Al Krueger—9 catches for 98 yards and 1 touchdown
SCORING: Bob Robertson—30 points on 5 touchdowns

## *1941*

HEAD COACH: Sam Barry
ASSISTANT COACHES: Julius Bescos, Raymond Brown, Shelby Calhoun, Robert McNeish, Gaius Shaver
TEAM CAPTAIN: Bob de Lauer
RECORD: 2–6–1 overall (2–4–1 in Pacific Coast Conference)
(Ranked 105th best record in college football out of 119 teams)
FINISH IN CONFERENCE: 8th place
FINISH IN NATIONAL POLLS: No ranking in Top 25
POINTS SCORED PER GAME: 7.1 to rank 107th out of 119 teams
POINTS ALLOWED PER GAME: 14.9 to rank 80th

### Schedule and Highlights

**(H) Sept. 27—Oregon State—13–7**
Doug Essick caught a Ray Woods pass from six yards out to provide the game-winning points with 13 seconds remaining in Sam Barry's debut as USC's head coach over the eventual PCC champion Beavers. This win was the crowning glory in an otherwise dismal season.[1]

**(H) Oct. 4—Ohio State—0–33**
The entire Ohio State team got to see action in this blowout victory. The Buckeyes got out to a quick two-touchdown lead, and were never threatened. Jack Graf stood out for Ohio State by scoring the game's first touchdown and threw for another.[2]

**(H) Oct. 11—Oregon—6–20**
Oregon defeated the Trojans for the first time since 1915. The lone bright spot for USC in this game was a 70-yard touchdown pass from Bob Robertson to Bob Jones.[3]

**(H) Oct. 18—Washington State—7–6**
Paul Taylor scored on a two-yard run, and Bob Jones provided the Trojans with the game-winning conversion kick. Bob Robertson played a solid game on defense, and averaged 4.1 yards per carry on offense.[4]

**(A) Oct. 25—California—0–14**
The Golden Bears recorded a shutout with much of the credit going to the punt return unit. That unit prevented the Trojans from gaining any yards on returns, which never allowed them to set themselves up with better field position.[5]

**(H) Nov. 8—Stanford—0–13**
Stanford #9
The Trojans set a team record with two straight games of being held scoreless with 86,305 on hand at the Coliseum. This also marked the second straight season in which the Trojans fell to both Stanford and Cal in the same year.[6]

**(A) Nov. 22—Notre Dame—18–20**
ND #4
The winds of war were quickly sweeping toward the United States. Two weeks following this game, the thought of world conflict coming to America's doorstep became a reality when Japanese air forces attacked military installations at Pearl Harbor in Hawaii.

This matchup between these two schools was the first in the 15-year history of the series that two new head coaches would be on both sidelines. Frank Leahy, a former Notre Dame player under Knute Rockne was now leading the Fighting Irish, while Sam Barry took over the Trojans following the untimely death of Howard Jones in July.

Barry's forces opened the scoring during the first quarter. Facing a fourth down from the Notre Dame 20, Bob Robertson threw to Ralph Heywood in the end zone. Heywood jumped high and out-dueled a defender for the ball, with the result being a touchdown. The extra point attempt was blocked, and the Trojans had a 6–0 lead.

USC regained possession quickly on an interception by Robertson, who returned his theft 45 yards to the Notre Dame 19. The Irish then stopped the Trojans from getting into the end zone, and a field goal attempt was missed. Quarterback Bob Hargrave then got the Irish on the scoreboard with a short yardage run, and Steve Juzwik added the extra point to give Notre Dame a 7–6 advantage. Juzwik then scored on a four-yard run to up the Notre Dame lead to 13–6.

The Trojans took the ensuing kickoff, and from their own 35, drove to the Irish nine before Bill Musick threw to Bill Bledsoe for a touchdown. The extra point attempt was blocked, and the Trojans trailed, 13–12, at the end of the first half. In the third quarter, the Irish got to the USC 17. Angelo Bertelli then threw a short pass to Owen Evans, who avoided a trio of defenders en route to a six-pointer. Juzwik's conversion kick then upped the Irish advantage to 20–12.

The Trojans fought on, getting to the Notre Dame 25 before a penalty halted their advance. As the third quarter was coming to a close, USC once again got deep into Notre Dame territory, but were stopped on downs at the three. They finally did score one final time, with Robertson running for an eight-yard touchdown with six minutes remaining in the game. A two-point conversion pass that could have tied the game was missed when a Bob Jones pass to Douglas Essick missed its mark.[7]

**(H) Nov. 29—Washington—13–14**
This game was played under rainy conditions, and the Trojans gave a good effort. A 20-yard touchdown run by Bob Robertson provided the top highlight for USC.[8]

**(A) Dec. 6—UCLA—7–7**
The Trojans were lethargic at best coming into their finale. They lost six of their previous eight games, but looked to give their 4–5 rivals a tough fight. In an attempt to confuse the Trojans, UCLA's head coach Edwin Horrell switched from a T-Formation to a Sing Wing. The move worked, as USC had a hard time adjusting to the change. The Bruins then went on a 60-yard driver that ended with Vic Smith scoring from the eight. Bob Robertson answered back for USC with a plunge from the ½-yard line.

This game came down to one exciting play that added to the lore of this classic series. The Trojans had marched down to the UCLA 10 in the final seconds of the fourth quarter. On the final play of the game, Bob Musick threw to Ralph Heywood on the one, but UCLA's Ted Forbes intercepted the pass. Forbes' momentum then carried him into the end zone. While attempting to get out of the end zone, he fumbled, and the ball rolled to the back of the end zone where a Bruins' player fell on it. If the fumble had not occurred, USC would have won on a safety.

With the conclusion of this game, the Trojans produced only 64 points, which was the lowest point production in team history. They also produced the lowest amount of touchdowns in a season with 10, and had the fewest combined yards rushing and passing with 1,795. One day after this game went into the record books, Pearl Harbor was attacked by Japanese forces, which took the United States into World War II.[9]

### TEAM LEADERS

RUSHING: Bobby Robertson—483 yards on 120 carries
PASSING: Bobby Robertson—33 out of 73 attempts for 530 yards and 3 touchdowns
RECEIVING: Paul Taylor—10 catches for 149 yards
SCORING: Bob Robertson—18 points on 3 touchdowns
PUNTING: Ralph Heywood—49 for 1,839 yards (37.5 avg.)

## *1942*

HEAD COACH: Jeff Cravath
ASSISTANT COACHES: Shelby Calhoun, Gaius Shaver
TEAM CAPTAIN: Don Willer was elected team captain at the end of the 1941, and remained the official team captain despite his enlistment in the United States Navy. During his time in the military, Willer played football for St. Mary's Pre-Flight team.
RECORD: 5–5–1 overall (4–2–1 in Pacific Coast Conference)
(Ranked 73rd best record in college football out of 121 teams)
FINISH IN CONFERENCE: 4th place
FINISH IN NATIONAL POLLS: No ranking in Top 25
POINTS SCORED PER GAME: 16.7 to rank 46th out of 121 teams
POINTS ALLOWED PER GAME: 11.6 to rank 62nd

### Schedule and Highlights

**(H) Sept. 26—Tulane—13–27**

Tulane scored four touchdowns in the first three quarters, and then held off a Trojan rally that produced two touchdowns.[1]

**(A) Oct. 3—Washington—0–0**

The Trojans repelled five attempts by Washington after they got inside the USC 20-yard line. The Trojans had two failed scoring attempts in the first and fourth quarters.[2]

**(A) Oct. 10—Ohio State—12–28**

Ohio State was on the way to a national championship when they kept the Trojans winless. USC scored first on a long pass from Mickey McCardle to Jack Trout. McCardle also connected on another scoring strike later, this time going to Doug Essick for the six points.[3]

**(H) Oct. 17—Washington State—26–12**

Washington State #10

This victory snapped a USC team record of eight straight games without a win dating back to the previous year. Mickey McCardle had some crowd-pleasing broken field runs, and he scored two touchdowns for USC. This proved to be Washington State's only conference loss of the season.[4]

**(N) Oct. 24—Stanford—6–14**

Played at San Francisco's Kezar Stadium, an early score and a turnover in the third quarter helped Stanford beat USC for the third straight time. The Trojans got their points in the final minute when Paul Taylor passed to Walt Jacobsmeyer.[5]

**(H) Nov. 7—California—21–7**

Mickey McCardle ran for 113 yards on 12 carries and scored two touchdowns over a favored Cal team. This win allowed the Trojans to remain in the PCC race.[6]

**(H) Nov. 14—Oregon—40–0**

Four first half touchdowns allowed USC to coast through the second half. In the end, USC outgained Oregon 432 yards to 120. Head coach Jeff Cravath let his reserves play after the Trojans built a 34–0 halftime lead. This proved to be USC's largest margin of victory in PCC competition since 1933. It also gave the Trojans a 3–1–1 record in the conference, and a shot at the championship.[7]

**(H) Nov. 28—Notre Dame—0–13**

USC #14 #8 ND

The nation's headlines were big, bold, and bewildering, as the Axis powers continued to dominate in both the European and Pacific campaigns. Despite the ominous presence hovering about the United States, the Notre Dame-USC game offered a brief sixty minutes of diversion.

A crowd of 90,000 filled the LA Coliseum on USC's homecoming weekend to witness these two top-ranked teams square off. This edition of the "Glamour Game" was nothing like its moniker, as five players were ejected, and 17 penalties were called that amounted to 145 yards in losses. There were also some infractions that the teams refused to accept, or simply were not called by the officials.

Notre Dame quarterback Angelo Bertelli threw for a pair of touchdowns to account for the game's scoring. Late in the second quarter, Bill Livingstone set up the Irish nicely at the USC 49 after returning a punt 17 yards. Two plays later, Bertelli threw to Creighton Miller over the middle for a 48-yard touchdown. The extra point attempt was missed, and the Irish led, 6–0.

As halftime approached, the Irish scored the final points of the game. From the USC nine-yard line, Bertelli connected with Livingstone on a touchdown pass, and John Creevey was true on the extra point kick to make it a 13–0 Irish advantage with three minutes remaining in the first half.

The second half was a scoreless affair with a great deal of rougher-than-usual play. Tempers were so hot by the end of the game that players from both sides engaged in fighting, and some fans even joined in on the action. Due to travel restrictions enforced to limit fuel consumption for the remainder of World War II, this classic rivalry was suspended for the next three years.[8]

**(H) Dec. 5—Montana—38–0**

This marked USC's 250th football victory and Vincent Porter ran for 108 yards on a mere five carries. As a team, the

Trojans compiled 508 yards of offense while limiting Montana to only 35. This was part of a double-header that saw UCLA beat Idaho in the first game, and then USC romp to give the Southland a sweep on the day.[9]

**(H) Dec. 12—UCLA—7–14**
UCLA #13

Up to this time in the brief history of this classic rivalry, the Trojans had five wins and three ties against the Bruins. With the PCC championship on the line, a crowd of 87,000 was on hand to see UCLA's star T-Formation quarterback Bob Waterfield attempt to lead his Bruins to victory over Jeff Cravath's Trojans in his first-ever USC-UCLA clash as head coach. The Bruins took an early lead on a two-yard run by Ken Snelling, and Waterfield extended the UCLA advantage to 14–0 in the fourth quarter when he tossed a 42-yard scoring strike to Burr Baldwin. The Trojans looked to rally in an attempt to remain unbeaten against UCLA when Mickey McCardle scored on a 10-yard run to help cut the deficit in half. However, it was not meant to be, as the Bruins won for the first time in their history over the Trojans, clinched their first Rose Bowl berth, and earned the right to possess the Victory Bell, which began its reign as the trophy presented to the winner of this annual meeting.[10]

**(H) Dec. 19—St. Mary's Pre-Flight—21–13**

The USC connection to St. Mary's saw former players Larry Stevens, Ray George, Roy Engle, and Bob de Lauer, all start for St. Mary's. The Trojans' head coach in 1941, Sam Barry, served as athletic director for the Airdevils. This also marked the smallest crowd to witness a USC game at the Los Angeles Memorial Coliseum (6,643).[11]

TEAM LEADERS

RUSHING: Mickey McCardle—413 yards on 96 carries
PASSING: Mickey McCardle—24 out of 55 attempts for 395 yards and 5 touchdowns
RECEIVING: Ralph Heywood—12 catches for 205 yards and 2 touchdowns
SCORING: Mickey McCardle—31 points on 5 touchdowns and 1 extra point
Jim Hardy—31 points on 5 touchdowns and 1 extra point
PUNTING: Ralph Heywood—58 for 2,195 yards (37.8 avg.)

## *1943*

HEAD COACH: Jeff Cravath
ASSISTANT COACHES: Shelby Calhoun, Gaius Shaver, Bob Winslow
TEAM CAPTAIN: Ralph Heywood
RECORD: 8–2 overall (5–0 in Pacific Coast Conference)
(Ranked 16th best record in college football out of 76 teams)
FINISH IN CONFERENCE: 1st place
FINISH IN NATIONAL POLLS: No ranking in Top 25
POINTS SCORED PER GAME: 15.5 to rank 43rd out of 76 teams
POINTS ALLOWED PER GAME: 5.8 to rank 5th

### Schedule and Highlights

**(A) Sept. 25—UCLA—20–0**

Travel restrictions due to World War II made USC and UCLA play each other twice over the next three seasons. This marked the first time the Trojans incorporated the T-Formation, and a piece of USC was that Jim Hardy became the first Trojan signal caller to use the formation. The T-Formation appeared to work wonders, as the Trojans played a great game made up of solid line play and a good ground attack. Eddie Saenz rambled for 108 yards on just eight carries, with a huge chunk of his total coming on an 86-yard touchdown run. Also scoring for the Trojans were George Callanan and Duane Whitehead.[1]

**(A) Oct. 2—California—7–0**

The Trojans scored in the first quarter, and then held to keep them perfect. With solid running from Eddie Saenz, Duane Whitehead, and Mickey McCardle, the Trojans got the ball to the California seven. Howard Callanan then scored what turned out to be the winning points from the seven. Dick Jamison then added the extra point. California played a good game themselves, gaining good yardage, but the Trojan defense held them from getting past midfield on numerous occasions.[2]

**(H) Oct. 9—St. Mary's Pre-Flight—13–0**
USC# 10

St. Mary's came to the Coliseum armed with the 1941 Heisman Trophy winner from Minnesota, Bruce Smith. Smith did not disappoint the crowd, and showcased his talent with sweeping runs, emerging from this game as the best back on the field. However, the Trojans still prevented the Pre-Flighters from reaching the end zone with a strong defensive effort. The backs from USC also put on a fine showing, with Howard and George Callanan, and Eddie Saenz, displaying blazing speed that counter balanced Bruce Smith's running and passing prowess. The Trojans got their touchdowns on a 61-yard lateral from Jim Hardy to Ralph Heywood, who finished the game with four catches for 101 yards, and on a nine-yard run by George Callanan. Heywood's receiving yardage total set a USC record for most in one game.[3]

**(A) Oct. 16—San Francisco—34–0**
USC # 8

The Trojans remained unbeaten with an easy win on the road in front of a small crowd of 6,000. This was the only time that USC and San Francisco ever faced each other. Eight players got into the scoring column for USC, and they rolled to 450 yards of offense. The scoring jaunts that stood out were runs by Mickey McCardle (55 yards), and Eddie Saenz (43 yards), and on a 26-yard run out of punt formation by Ralph Heywood.[4]

**(H) Oct. 23—College of Pacific—6–0**
USC# 7 Pacific #6

In a battle of undefeated teams, the Trojans emerged victorious thanks to a fourth quarter touchdown pass from George Callanan to his brother Howard. Pacific was led by legendary coach Amos Alonzo Stagg, who at 81 years old, was still able to put together a solid squad. Stagg assembled a tough line that managed to contain USC's swift running game, holding them to 121 yards.[5]

**(H) Oct. 30—California—13–0**
USC#5 California #20

This game saw USC to set a team record with their sixth straight shutout win. Freshman Gordon Gray scored on a 51-

yard pass from quarterback Jim Hardy. George Callanan added the other touchdown after first intercepting a pass and returning it to midfield. Seven plays later, he swept the left side of the line to score from the California 12.[6]

**(A) Nov. 6—San Diego Navy—7–10**

USC# 4

The Trojans finally succumbed to the bitter taste of defeat despite outgaining their opponent on the ground 209 yards to 120. San Diego Navy scored the first six-pointer allowed by USC all season in the first quarter on a pass from Glenn Lee to Earl Platt. The Trojans tied the game in the second quarter when Jim Hardy lateralled to center Bill Gray, who ran 40 yards for the score. The winning points came on an Ed Nelson field goal from short range in the third quarter.[7]

**(H) Nov. 13—March Field—0–35**

USC#9 March #15

The rankings were misleading, as March totally destroyed the Trojans on this day. March Field was a team assembled by the 4th Air Force, and they set records by scoring the most touchdowns against USC in one quarter (four), and the most points in one quarter (28).[8]

**(H) Nov. 27—UCLA—26–13**

With a mere 35,000 in attendance for USC's homecoming, the Trojans won a poorly played contest that saw 14 fumbles, eight of which were by USC, blocked kicks, and an intercepted lateral. The Trojans scored first when Gordon Gray picked up a blocked punt and ran it in for six points. The Bruins then went on top, 13–7, at the end of the first half, by scoring on a blocked kick and on an 84-yard interception return of a lateral. The Trojans started off the second half with Ted Ossowski recovering a fumble on the UCLA 20. Two plays later, George Callanan scored on a 13-yard run. With the score knotted up at 13-all in the fourth quarter, USC climaxed their regular season with a pair of touchdowns that sealed their second victory over UCLA in the season. Earle Parsons broke the tie with a short yardage run from inside the UCLA ten, and then Eddie Saenz scored on a 40-yard punt return.[9]

**Rose Bowl, (N) Jan. 1—Washington—29–0**

This 30th edition of the Rose Bowl was the first and only time that the game was not inter-sectional. With the United States in the midst of World War II, travel restrictions were in effect. For this reason, the 1944 Rose Bowl would pit USC against the favored #12 ranked Washington Huskies under head coach Ralph Welch. The Huskies only played four games during the year, but won them all. However, none of their opponents were from the Pacific Coast Conference, and this Rose Bowl would be the game to decide the PCC champion for 1943.

This game marked the first Rose Bowl to be broadcast overseas on the radio so that American soldiers in Western Europe could listen. If any were USC fans, then they enjoyed what transpired thousands of miles away from the fighting going on in Europe. The Trojans took a 7–0 lead in the second quarter and never looked back. Quarterback Jim Hardy led the way by throwing three touchdown passes. George Callanan caught two from 11 and 10 yards out, and Gordon Gray hauled in Hardy's other scoring strike from 21 yards away. Gray also scored on another reception in the fourth quarter, this time on a 36-yard pass from Joseph Bell. The Trojans added two more points to their total on a safety in the fourth quarter. This marked the fourth straight Rose Bowl Game in which the Trojans did not allow a touchdown.[10]

### TEAM LEADERS

RUSHING: Eddie Saenz—445 yards on 71 carries
PASSING: Jim Hardy—33 out of 71 attempts for 516 yards and 6 touchdowns
RECEIVING: Ralph Heywood—11 catches for 196 yards and 2 touchdowns
SCORING: George Callanan—36 points on 6 touchdowns
PUNTING: Jim Hardy—32 for 1,097 yards (34.2 avg.)

## *1944*

HEAD COACH: Jeff Cravath
ASSISTANT COACHES: Shelby Calhoun, Gaius Shaver, Bob Winslow
TEAM CAPTAIN: Jim Hardy
RECORD: 8–0–2 overall (3–0–2 in Pacific Coast Conference)
(Ranked 7th best record in college football out of 95 teams)
FINISH IN CONFERENCE: 1st place
FINISH IN NATIONAL POLLS: 7th place in AP
POINTS SCORED PER GAME: 24.0 to rank 23rd out of 95 teams
POINTS ALLOWED PER GAME: 7.3 to rank 11th

### Schedule and Highlights

**(H) Sept. 23—UCLA—13–13**

This proved to be one of the greatest regular season football games ever played at the Coliseum. With the temperature hovering at 100-degrees, the Trojans took a 13–0 lead at the half on a Gordon Gray run that opened the scoring. A few minutes later, Don Burnside intercepted a Bob Waterfield pass and ran it back 38 yards to the UCLA two-yard line. Two plays later, Burnside ran the ball in for the score.

UCLA's Johnny Roesch then found his way into Bruins history. The 160-pound halfback scored two touchdowns in the final three minutes to help his team gain a tie. The first six-pointer came when he scored to cap off a six-play, 49-yard drive. His second touchdown was one for the ages. With time running out, Roesch gathered in a punt on his 20. He turned on the speed, racing down the sidelines until he began to stumble at the USC 20. He then regained his balance to complete the trek into the end zone as the game ended. Trailing 13–12 with no time left, the Bruins looked to send this one into the record books as a tie. Bob Waterfield positioned himself to attempt the conversion kick. His kick hit the crossbar and went over as hoards of fans looked to converge onto the field. It took the officials one minute to make a decision as to whether the kick was good or not. After signaling a good kick, the field was swarmed with fans.[1]

**(H) Sept. 30—College of Pacific—18–6**

Gordon Gray ran for 103 yards on 12 carries and two touchdowns against a Pacific team coached by the "grand old man of football," 82-year old Amos Alonzo Stagg. Despite being undermanned, Stagg's team put up a struggle, and was never completely out of the game. Milford Dreblow scored USC's other touchdown.[2]

**(H) Oct. 7—California—6–6**

The Trojans scored on a 31-yard pass from Jim Hardy to Gordon Gray in the second quarter to take the lead. Cal then recovered a fumble on the USC 35, and drove downfield, with Jim Muir scoring from the one to produce the tie.[3]

**(N) Oct. 14—St. Mary's Pre-Flight—6–0**

This game was played at Ratcliffe Stadium in Fresno, California. It marked the first time that a USC varsity home game was played outside of the LA Coliseum since 1923, and it was also the team's first night game. Gordon Gray scored the game's only points in the second quarter.[4]

**(H) Oct. 23—Washington—38–7**

USC#15

Nine days earlier, the Trojans played in their first-ever night game. On this date, they played their first night game at the LA Coliseum. It proved to be a big success despite USC's long-standing policy of playing on Saturday afternoons due to scheduling conflicts. The attendance of 62,865 was USC's largest for a home game that year, and as a result, the night game became a regular part of the USC schedule. Playing under the lights also seemed to be good for the team, as they crushed the Huskies. Gordon Gray became the first Trojan to score a touchdown in a night game at the Coliseum by returning a punt for six points in the opening quarter. Jim Hardy, Don Burnside, George Callanan, and Pat West all scored for the Trojans.[5]

**(H) Oct. 28—St. Mary's—34–7**

St. Mary's brought a team of young and inexperienced players into this clash, and the results were not good for the Gaels. They hung tough by stopping two drives by the Trojans, but then the might of the Cardinal & Gold proved too much. With the game turning into a rout, the Trojans used mostly second and third string players for a good portion of the game. Robert Morris scored two touchdowns to pace the Trojan attack.[6]

**(H) Nov. 4—San Diego Navy—28–21**

USC# 13

Don Burnside (Doll), ran for 137 yards on 16 carries, and scored two touchdowns. His first was a two-yard run in the second quarter that helped tie the game at 7–7. The Trojans then led by a 21–7 count in the third quarter, only to have San Diego Navy come back to tie it at 21–21 in the fourth quarter. Burnside provided the heroics when he scored on an 11-yard run for what turned out to be the winning points with four minutes remaining in the game. San Diego Navy's Gus White added some excitement for the opposition when he returned a kickoff 100 yards.[7]

**(A) Nov. 18—California—32–0**

USC # 12

The Trojans ran out of the T-Formation, which was starting to take over as the premier offensive attack in football, and the results were a convincing victory over their long-time rivals from Northern California. They opened the scoring with five minutes expired in the first quarter, and never looked back. George Callanan provided USC's offensive spark with 134 yards rushing on 14 carries.[8]

**(A) Nov. 25—UCLA—40–13**

USC #8

This time out, the Trojans left nothing to chance in their homecoming game against their cross-town rivals with 77,203 in attendance at the LA Coliseum. Bob Morris ran for 105 yards on 12 carries thanks to great line play that blew open holes to run through. Morris gave an outstanding performance in place of George Callanan, who left the game early with a knee injury. The Trojans scored in every quarter, outrushed UCLA 329 yards to 27, finished the regular season undefeated, and clinched a Rose Bowl berth.

With just three minutes expired in the first quarter, Duane Whitehead opened the scoring with a one-yard run. In the second quarter, Whitehead added his second six-pointer of the game on a two-yard run, and Jim Hardy scored from the one, to make the USC advantage 20–0 at the end of the first half. Hardy scored with 10 minutes to go in the third quarter to give the Trojans a 27–0 lead, and by this time, they were on their way to a perfect season. Don Garlin, who replaced an injured Don Burnside, swept the left side of the line to add another touchdown to USC's day. Garlin's touchdown run made it 34–0 at the end of the third quarter, and George Murphy then finished off USC's scoring with eight minutes remaining in the game on a quarterback sneak from one yard out.[9]

**Rose Bowl, (N) Jan. 1—Tennessee—25–0**

USC# 7 Tennessee #12

This bowl victory was USC's ninth straight post-season victory, and it established a team and conference record. This was also their third straight shutout win, and fourth in five previous Rose Bowl games. The Tennessee Volunteers, with a team predominantly consisting of freshmen, came into the game with a 7–0–1 record under third year head coach John Barnhill, who put together an impressive 25–3–2 record during that time.

The Trojans did not want to add a 26th victory to Barnhill's stats at Tennessee, and set the tempo early. John Ferraro blocked a punt in the opening minutes of the game, and it led to a 30-yard touchdown run by Jim Callanan. Jim Hardy added two touchdown passes and ran one himself from nine yards out to complete the scoring. Paul Salata (22 yards) and Scott MacLachlen (49 yards) were on the receiving end of Hardy's touchdown passes. Don Burnside led the ground attack for the Trojans with 114 yards on 13 carries.[10]

### TEAM LEADERS

RUSHING: Don Burnside (Doll)—428 yards on 70 carries
PASSING: Jim Hardy—58 out of 117 attempts for 739 yards and 10 touchdowns
RECEIVING: Gordon Gray—12 catches for 181 yards and 3 touchdowns
SCORING: Gordon Gray—42 points on 7 touchdowns
PUNTING: Jim Hardy—42 for 1,533 yards (36.5 avg.)

## *1945*

HEAD COACH: Jeff Cravath
ASSISTANT COACHES: Sam Barry, Julius Bescos, Robert NcNeish, Gaius Shaver, Bob Winslow
TEAM CAPTAIN: Jim Callanan
RECORD: 7–4 overall (5–1 in Pacific Coast Conference)

(Ranked 32nd best record in college football out of 101 teams)
FINISH IN CONFERENCE: 1st place
FINISH IN NATIONAL POLLS: 11th place in AP
POINTS SCORED PER GAME: 18.6 to rank 43rd out of 101 teams
POINTS ALLOWED PER GAME: 13.6 to rank 46th

## Schedule and Highlights

**(A) Sept. 21—UCLA—13–6**

A huge throng of 90,000 was on hand at the Coliseum just three weeks after World War II officially ended with the signing of Japan's surrender aboard the USS *Missouri.* After a scoreless first quarter, the Bruins capped a 79-yard drive in the second quarter on a touchdown run by Skip Rowland. That was all for the Bruins on this day. The Trojans, who outweighed the Bruins by 22 pounds per man, answered back with touchdowns coming on a Verl Lillywhite pass to Bob Morris, and a Ted Tannehill run.[1]

**(A) Sept. 29—California—13–2**

In their second straight PCC victory, the Trojans scored in the first two quarters, and then held off Cal the rest of the way. Halfback Bob Morris scored both USC touchdowns on a nine-yard run and on a 24-yard reception from Verl Lillywhite. A shutout was spoiled when quarterback Jim Peterson was tackled in the end zone for a safety in the third quarter.[2]

**(H) Oct. 6—St. Mary's Pre-Flight—26–14**

The Trojans remained perfect thanks to a pair of blocked punts in the third quarter that were turned into points, and helped put the game away for the Cardinal & Gold. Robert Morris and Jim Callanan sparked an injury-riddled USC team. Morris scored two touchdowns, and Callanan blocked a kick that led to points. John Pehar also blocked a kick that helped USC gain points.[3]

**(A) Oct. 13—San Diego Navy—6–33**

USC #6

In a major upset, San Diego Navy sent the Trojans down in defeat for the first time since March Field beat them in 1943. Leading the way for San Diego Navy was Mel "Tommy Gun" Tommervik, whose passing and running skills proved too much for USC on this day. He was involved in four out of the five scores for San Diego Navy. The Trojans trailed, 20–0, at the end of the first quarter, and USC was saved from being shut out when Jim Callanan blocked a punt and Doug Gee recovered it and ran for a touchdown.[4]

**(H) Oct. 20—College of Pacific—52–0**

USC #14

Without throwing one pass throughout the entire game, the Trojans were able to pound the ball at will against a Pacific team that consisted of only 17 players. Pacific was coached by the legendary Amos Alonzo Stagg, but not even his long and illustrious career could prevent his outnumbered team from giving up more than 50 points for the fourth time during the season. Jeff Cravath only used his starters for a short time, and USC rolled to 356 yards while limiting Pacific to 61. Third-string halfback George Crum scored three touchdowns, and Jim Peterson and Joe Bradford each returned an interception for six-pointers. Other Trojans who entered the scoring column were Blake Headley, Roy Cole, and Doug Gee.[5]

**(A) Oct. 27—Washington—7–13**

USC# 20

This was USC's first PCC loss since UCLA beat them in 1942. The Trojans were up, 7–6, late in the game until a fake field goal did them in. Instead of going for the three points, Wally Dash threw to Gordon Hungar for a touchdown with eight minutes left. Ted Tannehill ran for 120 yards on 22 carries for USC, and scored their only touchdown on a run from inches away.[6]

**(H) Nov. 3—St. Mary's—0–26**

St. Mary's #8

With 80,000 looking on at the LA Coliseum, the Gaels of St. Mary's trounced the Trojans. The Gaels were led by Hawaiian backfield stars Herman Wedemeyer, who ran for the opening score after setting it up with a 51-yard pass, and Chuck Cordiero.[7]

**(H) Nov. 10—California—14–0**

After Oregon State upset Washington, this shutout victory took the Trojans to the top of the PCC standings. They dominated the Golden Bears on the ground, rushing for 182 yards while holding Cal to a mere four. The mighty Trojan defense also intercepted four passes. Roy Cole and Verl Lillywhite scored USC's touchdowns.[8]

**(H) Nov. 24—Oregon State—34–7**

Ted Tannehill ran for 112 yards on 10 carries and three touchdowns to pace a ground attack that amassed 318 yards as a team. The Trojans trailed by a 7–6 count, and then scored the go-ahead points and never looked back against the same team that helped USC get back in the PCC race two weeks earlier by beating the Washington Huskies.[9]

**(H) Dec. 1—UCLA—26–15**

USC#16

With 103,000 in the stands at the Coliseum, Ted Tannehill ran for 107 yards on 10 carries and scored two touchdowns. The Trojans ran up a 19–0 lead at the half during their homecoming game, and the defense held UCLA to only 50 yards rushing. This victory clinched another Rose Bowl berth for the Trojans.[10]

**Rose Bowl, (N) Jan. 1—Alabama—14–34**

All good things must come to an end, and the Alabama Crimson Tide made that old adage hold true by becoming the first program to defeat the Trojans in bowl competition. Alabama rolled to a 20–0 halftime lead, and completely smothered the USC offense. Alabama held USC to six rushing yards and 35 through the air, while compiling 351 yards of total offense. Quarterback Harry Gilmer was known for his throwing arm, but against USC, he used his legs. He did throw for one touchdown, and but ran for 116 yards on 16 carries and one six-pointer. Gilmer's feats made him the game's MVP. The Trojans avoided the shutout by scoring twice in the fourth quarter when Harry Adelman caught a 26-yard pass from Verl Lillywhite, and Chick Clark returned a blocked kick for USC's other touchdown.[11]

### TEAM LEADERS

RUSHING: Ted Tannehill—574 yards on 99 carries
PASSING: Jerry Bowman—29 out of 64 attempts for 401 yards and 2 touchdowns
RECEIVING: Harry Adelman—12 catches for 127 yards and 2 touchdowns

SCORING: Ted Tannehill—42 points on 7 touchdowns
PUNTING: Jerry Bowman—28 for 1,091 yards (39.0 avg.)

## *1946*

HEAD COACH: Jeff Cravath
ASSISTANT COACHES: Roy Baker, Sam Barry, Roy Engle, Raymond George, Jess T. Hill, Norm Verry, Bob Winslow
TEAM CAPTAIN: Doug Essick
RECORD: 6–4 overall (5–2 in Pacific Coast Conference)
(Ranked 46th best record in college football out of 120 teams)
FINISH IN CONFERENCE: 3rd place
FINISH IN NATIONAL POLLS: No ranking in Top 25
POINTS SCORED PER GAME: 15.8 to rank 56th out of 120 teams
POINTS ALLOWED PER GAME: 10.6 to rank 34th

### Schedule and Highlights

**(H) Sept. 27—Washington State—13–7**

The Trojans opened the season in exciting fashion. They went on a 78-yard drive that resulted in Ted Tannehill running for a short yardage touchdown in the final five seconds to pull out the victory. He fumbled while crossing over the goal line, but teammate Bob Hendren pounced on the loose ball to preserve the victory. Tannehill also scored USC's first touchdown.[1]

**(H) Oct. 5—Ohio State—0–21**

With the country's largest crowd of the weekend (80,047) inside the Coliseum, Ohio State fullback Joe Whisler ran for 70 yards and scored all three Buckeye touchdowns to hand USC their first loss.[2]

**(N) Oct. 12—Oregon State—0–6**

This game was played at Multnomah Stadium in Portland, Oregon. The Trojans set countless positive records throughout their illustrious football history, but in this one, they tied a dismal one with by being shutout for two straight games. The injuries were also mounting for USC. With Ted Tannehill already out for the season, quarterback Mickey McCardle suffered a serious injury to his kneecap after crashing into the Oregon state bench. The lone score of this game came on a run by halfback Lee Gustafson.[3]

**(H) Oct. 19—Washington—28–0**

The Trojans returned the favor after losing by two straight shutouts. They led 14–0 at the end of the first quarter, and 28–0 at the beginning of the fourth stanza. Don Garlin scored two touchdowns, and Terry Ragan and John Rossetto added USC's other six-pointers. As a team, the Trojans rushed for 357 yards while holding the Huskies to 42.[4]

**(A) Oct. 26—Stanford—28–20**

The Trojans came from behind in the fourth quarter to win their second straight game. The victory gave them a 3–1 record in the PCC behind UCLA (4–0) and Oregon (3–0–1). Bob Musick scored two touchdowns, and combined with backfield mate Johnny Naumu for 144 rushing yards. Naumu ran for a touchdown, and gave the Trojans their first lead of the game at 21–20 in the fourth quarter with a conversion kick after Doug Essick recovered a Musick fumble in the end zone for the tying points.[5]

**(H) Nov. 2—Oregon—43–0**

This win kept the Trojans' hopes alive for the PCC title while making Oregon's a bit harder. USC ran for 422 yards as a team, and held Oregon to 30. Art Battle led the ground attack with 86 yards on 10 carries, and scored two touchdowns. Verl Lillywhite, Mickey McCardle, Mike Garzoni, Johnny Rossetto, and Hubie Kerns, all joined Battle in the scoring department. Kerns was the college quarter-mile champions in 1943, and used his talents by producing the longest scoring jaunt of the game from 59 yards out.[6]

**(H) Nov. 9—California—14–0**

USC # 14

After a scoreless first half, Mickey McCardle scored a pair of touchdowns to pace the Trojans to back-to-back shutout victories. As a team, the Trojans dominated the rushing statistics, 215 yards to 64.[7]

**(A) Nov. 23—UCLA—6–13**

USC # 10 UCLA # 4

Since beating the Trojans for the first time in their history back in 1942, the Bruins were a combined 0–5–1 against them coming into this contest. By kickoff of this game, the state of California had recorded its wettest November in 50 years, and the Coliseum resembled a mud bath. The Bruins came into this game with a spotless 8–0 record under second-year head coach Bert LaBrucherie. The Bruins struck first in USC's homecoming game when Bill Chambers blocked a kick by Verl Lillywhite. The loose ball was scooped up by UCLA's Don Malmberg at the USC 16 and taken in for a touchdown. The Trojans countered with a four-yard scoring run from Don Burnside to tie the game at 6–6.

Throughout this game, the Bruins had a plan to punt often regardless of the down in an attempt to catch a break due to the slippery and wet conditions. When trying to handle a wet ball, mishaps can occur often, and that was what the Bruins were hoping for. They used this plan of attack four times in the first and second quarters, and eight times in the third. On one of those occasions late in the third quarter, their persistence paid off. USC's Mickey McCardle was hit hard while fielding a punt deep in his territory. He fumbled and the ball was recovered by UCLA on the Trojans' five. Ernie Case scored the go-ahead touchdown, and the Bruins snapped their losing streak to the Trojans despite being held to zero pass completions.

The meeting marked the first time that the date of this annual clash was set for the third weekend in November. This tradition will last until 2004, with the exception being in 1975, when it was played on the Friday following Thanksgiving.[8]

**(A) Nov. 30—Notre Dame—6–26**

USC#16 ND#2

Notre Dame's ground attack churned out 517 rushing yards, and 623 yards of total offense, both amounts the most ever given up by USC. This was the way the "Glamour Game" was renewed since the teams last met in 1942. With World War II now over, the college football world once again had top-of-the-line talent instead of players not yet old enough for the military draft, or unable to meet the physical requirements set forth by the armed services.

The Fighting Irish were one of the programs that flourished following the war, and this period of the late 1940's proved to be one of the greatest in Notre Dame history. The 1946 squad came into this matchup with a 7–0–1 record, and mauled the opposition by a 28-point-per-game average. With a crowd of over 50,000 on hand to watch this renewal, the Irish never allowed the Trojans to get close. Despite being called back by a penalty, the opening kickoff was returned 80 yards for a score, complements of Coy McGee. Even though it was null and void, the return sent the message that Notre Dame was powerful and ready to reclaim their position as college football's top team.

In the second quarter, McGee scored again, this time on a 78-yard run, and it was not called back. For the game, McGee rushed for 146 yards on just six carries. Later in the same quarter, George Ratterman threw a 22-yard touchdown pass to Leon Hart, and Fred Earley kicked the conversion to make it 13–0.

The Trojans recorded their lone tally in the third quarter to come within seven points of the lead. Bob Musick recovered his second fumble of the game at the Notre Dame 45. It was then converted into six points after a pass interference penalty placed the ball on the Notre Dame one. On second down, Johnny Naumu scored, but he then missed on the conversion to make it a 13–6 ballgame. The score remained the same until the fourth quarter. McGee added his second six-pointer of the game on an eight-yard run, and Gerry Cowhig later ran one in from the same distance to finish out the scoring. This marked the fourth straight time Notre Dame emerged victorious over the Trojans, and they eventually finished the season as the national champions.[9]

**(A) Dec. 21—Tulane—20–13**

Over the course of the season, the Trojans recorded only one touchdown coming by throwing the ball. This would be the fewest ever in the history of the program. The lone scoring strike came in this game on USC's first offensive series of the game. Mickey McCardle threw to team captain Doug Essick for the score, and the Trojans were on their way. Tulane tied the game at 6–6, but a Johnny Rossetto one-yard run, plus a conversion kick, gave USC a 13–6 halftime advantage. Bob Musick added USC's final touchdown of the season in the second half.[10]

### TEAM LEADERS

RUSHING: Art Battle—296 yards on 69 carries
PASSING: Mickey McCardle—39 out of 74 attempts for 490 yards and 1 touchdown
RECEIVING: Gordon Gray—13 catches for 168 yards
SCORING: John Naumu—20 points on 2 touchdowns and 8 extra points
PUNTING: Verl Lillywhite—20 for 777 yards (38.8 avg.)

## *1947*

HEAD COACH: Jeff Cravath
ASSISTANT COACHES: Roy Baker, Sam Barry, Roy Engle, Raymond George, Jess T. Hill, Norm Verry
TEAM CAPTAIN: Don Clark
RECORD: 7–2–1 overall (6–0 in Pacific Coast Conference)
(Ranked 18th best record in college football out of 120 teams)
FINISH IN CONFERENCE: 1st place
FINISH IN NATIONAL POLLS: 8th place in AP
POINTS SCORED PER GAME: 19.3 to rank 39th out of 120 teams
POINTS ALLOWED PER GAME: 11.4 to rank 44th

### Schedule and Highlights

**(H) Sept. 27—Washington State—21–0**

The Trojans sent a message that they were ready to regain the PCC crown with a solid performance against the Cougars. Johnny Naumu, Jim Powers, and Jay Roundy all scored six-pointers for the victors.[1]

**(H) Oct. 4—Rice—7–7**

The Trojans failed to score on three occasions early in the game, but managed to cross the goal line with 2:10 left to bring the game to a tie at the end. Gordon Gray caught a pass from Jim Powers on the Rice 15 to keep an 81-yard drive going. Four plays later, Verl Lillywhite capped the drive off with a six-yard run. Tommy Walker added the all-important extra point.[2]

**(A) Oct. 11—Ohio State—32–0**

USC#20

The Trojans reverted back to the "Thundering Herd" days of Howard Jones by pounding the opposition with speed and power. The Trojans received their five touchdowns from Don Doll, Gordon Gray, Jim Powers, Edsel Curry, and George Davis.[3]

**(H) Oct. 18—Oregon State—48–6**

USC#11

The Trojans continued on with their parade of touchdowns, this time recording seven in a rout of Oregon State. This was the worst beating handed out to Oregon State by USC since the teams started playing each other in 1915. A crowd of 61,301 saw the Trojans use speed and hard-hitting line play to completely destroy Oregon State. USC ran for 331 yards as a team compared to 74 for the Beavers. The Trojans' scoring fest came on touchdowns from Don Doll, Paul Cleary, Verl Lillywhite, Mickey McCardle, Gordon Gray, Jack Kirby, and Lou Futrell.[4]

**(A) Oct. 25—California—39–14**

USC#10 Cal#4

The Trojans shot up seven positions in the national rankings, and lived up to that status with another dominant victory. They scored two touchdowns in the first quarter, one each in the next two, and finished up with two in the final stanza. Don Doll provided an extra dose of excitement by taking the second half kickoff back 95 yards for a touchdown that completely demoralized the Golden Bears, who were only trailing by six points at the end of the first half. Doll's return was the first time since 1929 that USC scored on a kickoff return when Russ Saunders accomplished the feat against Notre Dame.[5]

**(A) Nov. 1—Washington—19–0**

USC#5

This game was played mostly in rain, but the soggy conditions did nothing to slow down the Trojans' juggernaut. This was USC's first win in Seattle in fifteen years, but they had to work for it. The game was close throughout the first three quarters, as USC clung to a slim 6–0 lead. They then added a pair of touchdowns in the fourth quarter to pull away at the end. Mickey McCardle scored USC's first six-pointer on an 11-yard pass from George Murphy. Verl Lillywhite and Dean Dill rounded out USC's scoring for the day.[6]

**(H) Nov. 8—Stanford—14–0**
USC#5

The Trojans took a giant step toward the PCC title and a Rose Bowl invitation by blanking their second straight opponent. Don Doll scored in the first quarter on a one-yard run, and the game remained that way until the fourth quarter, when George Murphy ran for a 10-yard touchdown to clinch a hard-fought victory against a winless Stanford team.[7]

**(H) Nov. 22—UCLA—6–0**
USC#4 UCLA#18

With a huge crowd of 102,050 on hand, the Trojans scored the game's only points on a 32-yard pass from Jim Powers to Jack Kirby in the second quarter. They them spent the remainder of the game holding off UCLA's advances. The Bruins managed to get to the USC four in the closing minutes. With 55 seconds remaining, and facing a fourth-and-two situation, the Bruins attempted a pass, but Gordon Gray became the hero for USC by intercepting in the end zone to kill the final threat.[8]

**(H) Dec. 6—Notre Dame—7–38**
USC#3 ND#1

With the defending champs coming into this game at 8–0, and the host Trojans perched at 7–0–1, a crowd of 104,953 came out to produce the largest crowd to ever witness a football game at the LA Coliseum. In addition to the legitimate ticket holders, a few hundred others charged through a gate on the south side of the Coliseum to get in. In the frenzied attempt to gain entrance into the Southland's massive sports venue, the throng stampeded two police officers in the process. More police came upon the scene to prevent any additional occurrences from happening.

Despite the passionate feelings of those Trojan backers packed inside the Coliseum, this much-anticipated clash turned into a rout by the juggernaut from South Bend, Indiana.

Just like in the previous year's game, the Trojans were able to hang with the Irish for a time, as they only trailed, 10–7, going into the second half.

Notre Dame got on the board first in the opening quarter. Verl Lillywhite coughed up the ball for USC on the Trojans' first play following the opening kickoff, and the ball was recovered by Charles Conner at the USC 33. The Irish advanced the ball 21 yards before the Trojans held firm, but they were able to salvage the drive with a 12-yard field goal from Fred Earley for a 3–0 lead. With time running out in the opening stanza, the Irish struck paydirt on a one-yard run by Emil Sitko. Earley booted the extra point attempt through the uprights for a 10–0 advantage.

Jimmy Powers allowed the Trojans to get on the scoreboard right before halftime. He intercepted a pass, and then proved instrumental in getting USC across the goal line. He ripped off a run of 12 yards, and then threw an 18-yard pass to Jack Kirby. Kirby then capped the nine-play, 4-yard drive off with a run of eight yards. Tom Walker's conversion made it a close one at the half.

The Irish appeared tired of toying with the Trojans, and looked to put some distance between themselves and their foes from the City of Angels. After Bob Livingstone brought the second half kickoff out to his 24, Emil Sitko blasted through the USC defense for a 76-yard touchdown jaunt, which made it 17–7 following the conversion. Coming on the heels of Sitko's long run, a Johnny Lujack interception was turned into another touchdown, this one coming on a short run by John Panelli. Early's conversion then upped Notre Dame's lead to 24–7, and victory loomed apparent. However, the Irish were not through. After the Trojans were stopped on downs at the Notre Dame eight, the following play was one for the record books. On first down, Bob Livingstone took a handoff, and did not stop until he crossed the goal line 92 yards away. This went down in history as the longest run from scrimmage against USC. With the score now at 31–7, the Irish looked to add an exclamation point to the festivities, and did so when Alfred Zmijewski returned an interception 28 yards for the game's final touchdown. This win allowed Notre Dame to double their victories over the Trojans by a 12 to six margin, plus one tie, and they went on to win their second straight national championship.[9]

**Rose Bowl, (N) Jan. 1—Michigan—0–49**
USC# 8 Michigan #2

This proved to be USC's worst bowl game defeat in their history. The mighty Michigan Wolverines were 9–0, ranked second in the country, and led by head coach Fritz Crisler. They were dubbed "the Mad Magicians," and were strong on both sides of the ball.

They proved their might by amassing 491 yards of total offense, with halfback and this game's MVP, All-American Bob Chappuis, leading the way. Chappuis ran for 91 yards and connected on 14 of 24 pass attempts for 139 yards and two touchdowns. Jack Weisenburger ran for 91 yards and scored three touchdowns. Jim Brieske kicked the most conversion kicks against USC in their history with seven, and as a team, the Wolverines threw for four touchdowns, which were the most against USC in their history.[10]

### Team Leaders

RUSHING: Don Doll—246 yards on 57 carries
PASSING: Jim Powers—50 out of 94 attempts for 603 yards and 5 touchdowns
RECEIVING: Mickey McCardle—17 catches for 115 yards and 1 touchdown
SCORING: Jack Kirby—30 points on 5 touchdowns
PUNTING: Verl Lillywhite—26 for 1,020 yards (39.8 avg.)

## *1948*

HEAD COACH: Jeff Cravath
ASSISTANT COACHES: Roy Baker, Sam Barry, Roy Engle, Raymond George, Jess T. Hill, Bob Snyder, Norm Verry, Bob Winslow
TEAM CAPTAIN: Bob Bastian
RECORD: 6–3–1 overall (4–2 in Pacific Coast Conference)
(Ranked 43rd best record in college football out of 117 teams)
FINISH IN CONFERENCE: 3rd place
FINISH IN NATIONAL POLLS: No ranking in Top 25
POINTS SCORED PER GAME: 14.2 to rank 79th out of 117 teams
POINTS ALLOWED PER GAME: 8.7 to rank 9th

## Schedule and Highlights

**(H) Sept. 17—Utah—27–0**

The defending PCC champions started off the new season in excellent fashion under the lights at the Coliseum. This game also allowed the Trojans the opportunity to boast of never losing a night game in their history. The Trojans scored early in the first quarter on a Dean Dill four-yard run, and that proved to be all the go-ahead points USC needed on this evening.[1]

**(H) Sept. 24—Oregon State—21–6**

The Trojans opened defense of their PCC title by beating Oregon State in a night game at the Coliseum. Don Doll provided the Trojans with their first score of the game on a three-yard run in the opening quarter. A Jim Powers to Jay Roundy pass gave USC a 14–6 halftime advantage, and Dean Dill threw to Jack Kirby for USC's final touchdown of the game. Dill also added three conversion kicks to his night's accomplishments. Despite their 15-point victory, the Trojans were stopped from scoring by three goal line stands.[2]

**(A) Oct. 2—Ohio State—0–20**

Fumbles at critical times, coupled with missed signals, led to a poor showing in Columbus, Ohio. Ohio State's Bob Dorsey recovered a Trojan fumble early in the game, and the turnover was converted into a Joe Whisler touchdown run. The Buckeyes never looked back from that point on, and held the USC running attack to only 51 yards.[3]

**(H) Oct. 9—Rice—7–0**

The Trojans only scored one touchdown, but it was enough to record their third straight win of the season. They turned back five Rice scoring threats after the Owls came close to the USC end zone. The Trojans' points came on a 19-play, 80-yard drive in the middle of the first half, with Don Doll finishing it off with a 28-yard run. Dean Dill then added the extra point.[4]

**(N) Oct. 16—Oregon—7–8**

This time one touchdown was not enough for the men of Troy. The Oregon Ducks bettered them by one point. USC received their touchdown on a Don Doll run in the second half. Three times after this scoring drive, the Trojans got into Oregon territory, but were stopped. With seconds left in the game, Jim Powers threw a long pass to Bill Jessup, and pass interference was called. This gave USC one final chance from the Oregon 25. Unfortunately, a field goal attempt went wide and with it, the Trojans hopes of victory were crushed. This game played at Multnomah Stadium in Portland, Oregon, was the first time that USC traveled by airplane.[5]

**(A) Oct. 23—Stanford—7–6**

The Trojans finished another game with seven points, and this time, they won by a single point in what was referred to as one of the most exciting games of the season. Near the end of the first half, Jim Powers connected on a scoring strike to Bill Jessup, and Dean Dill added the extra point, which proved to be the game-winner. Stanford scored with 10 minutes left, but failed on the conversion attempt. They then recovered a fumble on their own one-yard line, and almost went the length of the field until Don Doll intercepted a pass on the USC five to end the threat.[6]

**(H) Oct. 30—California—7–13**

Cal#4

For the fourth straight game, the Trojans scored just seven points. Unfortunately, the Golden Bears had 13 at the end, to remain undefeated on the year. This loss gave USC a 2–2 record in those seven-point games. The Trojans hung tough against their Northern California foes, as they turned back two scoring threats, and only trailed by a 6–0 count at the end of the first half. In the second half, the Trojans went 56 yards, but fumbled just shy of a possible touchdown. Cal then went 87 yards for their second touchdown. Jack Kirby provided the Trojans with their touchdown on a one-yard run.[7]

**(H) Nov. 13—Washington—32–7**

In this game, it was the Huskies that produced seven points, and the Trojans totaled 25 more to win with ease. This was the most points USC scored all season. The Trojans displayed a punishing ground attack that saw six backs averaged more than four yards per carry and account for 220 yards of offense. With 10 minutes expired in the game, USC went 66 yards to paydirt, with Art Battle getting the scoring honors. On the ensuing kickoff, Washington fumbled and USC recovered on the four. Don Doll scored, and the Trojans had a 13–0 first quarter advantage. Doll added another touchdown on a 16-yard run, and Bill Bertz and Bill Martin also scored six-pointers for USC.[8]

**(A) Nov. 20—UCLA—20–13**

This game was the first one in this series to be broadcast on television. Station KLAC-TV had the honors of bringing this game into homes lucky enough to have television sets throughout the Los Angeles area. The Bruins came into the game with only three wins on the year, and were heavy 14-point underdogs. However, despite records, a rivalry game always brings out the best in the participants, as UCLA put up a tough fight.

In the first quarter, a fumble and clipping penalty gave UCLA two scoring chances, but the Trojans dug in and stopped them. After having trouble getting the offense on track until late in the second quarter, the Trojans, behind a solid running attack and a stellar defensive effort, took a 14–6 lead. A Jim Powers pass to Jack Kirby gained 25 yards, and then Jay Roundy and Powers ran to get the ball to the UCLA two-yard line. Kirby scored the touchdown, and Dean Dill kicked the extra point to give USC a 7–0 lead. The Bruins came back with a quick touchdown, but Jack Nix blocked the conversion attempt. The Trojans received their second touchdown on a 60-yard pass from Dill to Kirby with two seconds left in the first half. The Bruins never had a chance to come close after that. The Trojans opened the second half with a 66-yard drive that was capped off with Doll scoring a touchdown. The Bruins then closed out the game's scoring with an 80-yard drive.[9]

**(H) Dec. 4—Notre Dame—14–14**

ND#2

The Fighting Irish were once again near the top of the college football world. They came into this annual battle riding a 27-game unbeaten streak, a 21-game winning streak, and defeating the opposition by a 25-point-per-game average.

This marked the second straight year that the Trojans hosted the game, and another whopping crowd filled the LA Coliseum, this time reaching 100,571 for USC's homecoming weekend. The powerful Irish were favored by as many as 24 points against the 6–3 Trojans, but despite the incredible odds facing them, USC played tough and in the end, this edition of the "Glamour Game" went down in history as one of the best in the series.

There was no scoring throughout the opening quarter, and then Notre Dame drew first blood in the early stages of the second quarter. One of college football's preeminent performers during this time was Notre Dame's big end Leon Hart, who was one year away from claiming the Heisman Trophy. He lived up to his reputation as a force to be reckoned with by catching a pass from Frank Tripucka. The play started at the USC 46, and Tripucka hit Hart with the pass at the 39. He then used his massive 6–4, 245-pound frame to power his way through the defense en route to paydirt. Steve Oracko added the extra point, and the Irish were up, 7–0, which was the score at halftime.

The Trojans got even in the latter part of the third quarter. Jack Kirby started things off by intercepting a pass at the Notre Dame 42. A short time later, the drive was capped off with Bill Martin scoring from the two. Dean Dill added the extra point to make it knotted up at 7-all.

With nine minutes left in the game, the Trojans and their fans could feel the makings of an upset. They were hitting hard, and pounced on their sixth fumble recovery of the game at midfield. Despite not scoring after this opportunity, they seemed to be sending a message that Notre Dame was in a struggle. They held the Irish on their next possession, and Notre Dame was forced to punt. From the Notre Dame 47, Jack Kirby got things going with a 16-yard run. Dill then threw to Ernie Tolman at the 18 with four minutes to play. Within a few plays, Bill Martin cracked into the end zone from the four with 2:30 showing on the clock. Dill converted on the extra point attempt to give the Trojans a 14–7 lead.

The Irish got a big boost on the ensuing kickoff, as Bill Gay bolted for 86 yards before being stopped at the USC 13. Notre Dame caught another break following a failed pass on third-and-five from the eight-yard line. Instead of facing a fourth down, the Irish were awarded a first down at the one-yard line due to a pass interference penalty against the Trojans. On second down, battering ram-like running back Emil Sitko took his 5–9, 180-pound body on a short thrust into the end zone with 35 seconds remaining. Steve Oracko then sent the important extra point attempt through the uprights to preserve Notre Dame's unbeaten streak.[10]

### Team Leaders

Rushing: Don Doll—265 yards on 67 carries
Passing: Jim Powers—49 out of 106 attempts for 511 yards and 2 touchdowns
Receiving: Don Doll—15 catches for 157 yards
Scoring: Don Doll—36 points on 6 touchdowns
Punting: Jim Powers—29 for 1,016 yards (35.0 avg.)

## *1949*

Head Coach: Jeff Cravath
Assistant Coaches: Roy Baker, Sam Barry, Bill Fisk, Raymond George, Walter G. Hargesheimer, Harry Smith
Team Captain: Jim Bird
Record: 5–3–1 overall (4–2 in Pacific Coast Conference)
(Ranked 43rd best record in college football out of 119 teams)
Finish in Conference: Tied for 3rd place
Finish in National Polls: No ranking in Top 25
Points Scored Per Game: 23.8 to rank 35th out of 119 teams
Points Allowed Per Game: 18.9 to rank 64th

### Schedule and Highlights

**(H) Sept. 24—Navy—42–20**

With only eight minutes expired in the first quarter, Jay Roundy returned a punt 67 yards for a touchdown. He then hauled in a 27-yard pass from Jim Powers for another six points. The Trojans added a pair of touchdowns in the second quarter, complements of Bill Martin (16-yard run) and Ralph Pucci (one-yard run). Martin added a second touchdown to his day's work from one-yard out. Bill Jessup caught a 59-yard scoring strike from Powers for USC's other touchdown. Frank Gifford kicked six straight conversions to equal a Coliseum record.[1]

**(H) Oct. 1—Washington State—35–7**

The Trojans came back from an early deficit to win their PCC opener over the Cougars. After Washington State took the opening kickoff and drove 71 yards for a touchdown, the Trojans tied the game at 7–7 late in the second quarter on a one-yard run by Bill Bowers. That score was set up by a Bill Martin fumble recovery. USC opened the second half with a 59-yard drive that was capped off by a one-yard run from Bill Martin. An interception by George Davis set up USC's third touchdown, which came on a 39-yard pass from Jim Powers Bowers. Powers threw for another touchdown, this time to Dan Zimmerman (26 yards), and Al Cantor ran for a two-yard score to account for USC's touchdowns. The Trojans had 18 first downs and 407 yards of offense in this convincing victory.[2]

**(H) Oct. 8—Ohio State—13–13**

USC#8 OSU#11

This battle of top-ranked teams ended without a decision. However, despite playing without two regular running backs and three linemen, the Trojans won a moral victory with this tie. The Buckeyes scored first, but then the Trojans came right back on a one-yard run by Bill Martin, but the extra point was missed, and USC trailed, 7–6, at the end of the first half. Ohio State extended its lead to 13–6 on a long run by Fred Morrison after he caught a short pass, but the conversion attempt was blocked. Bill Martin entered the scoring column for the second time in the game, this time on a two-yard run, and Frank Gifford tied it up with the conversion kick.[3]

**(A) Oct. 15—California—10–16**

USC#12 CAL#9

Frank Gifford's 22-yard field goal in the fourth quarter was USC's first since Max Belko's field goal in the 1935 opener against Montana. Cal's Frank Brunk provided excitement for the home crowd by returning a kickoff 100 yards. After trailing 7–0 at the half, the Trojans went 61 yards to score on a one-yard run by Bill Martin. Gifford then kicked his field goal to give USC a 10–6 lead. However, the Trojan advantage was short-lived, as Brunk's incredible kickoff return provided the Golden Bears with their go-ahead points.[4]

**(H) Oct. 22—Oregon—40–13**

USC#19

The Trojans rallied from being down in the first half to prevail by a wide margin. Oregon held a 6–0 lead going into the second half on a pair of field goals, but the second half proved to be a different story. On the strength of an excellent passing attack, USC put six touchdowns on the board while holding Oregon to a mere seven points. Jim Powers passing abilities allowed him to enter the USC record books with three touchdown tosses in a single game. Those three touchdown passes tied Powers with former Trojans Russ Saunders, Davie Davis, and Jim Hardy. On the receiving end of Powers' record-tying tosses were Bill Jessup (30 yards), Al Cantor (21 yards), and Dan Zimmerman (28 yards). Bill Martin scored from three yards out, Johnny Williams returned a punt 72 yards, and Dean Schneider scored on a 45-yard interception return.[5]

**(A) Oct. 29—Washington—40–28**
USC#15

Jim Powers once again found his way into the USC record books. This time he set a new school record with 293 passing yards, and also threw for three touchdowns. The previous single-game passing record was set by Russ Saunders on November 23, 1929. The Trojans wasted little time getting on the board, as they scored within five plays after receiving the opening kickoff. Jim Powers began his big day with a five-yard run. He then threw an 81-yard touchdown pass to Al Cantor, which was the longest scoring strike up to this time in USC history. Bill Martin added USC's third touchdown of the game on a two-yard run. He also scored on another two-yard run in the second half. Pat Duff caught a 12-yard pass from Powers, and Bill Jessup was on the receiving end of Powers' third scoring strike from 26 yards out.[6]

**(H) Nov. 5—Stanford—13–34**
USC#12

Despite losing their homecoming game, Jim Powers provided a solid performance with 290 passing yards and a pair of touchdowns to give him 12 on the season. The Trojans were seven-and-a-half-point favorites over the 4–2–1 Stanford Indians. However, like in so many clashes between rivals, records do not mean much. Stanford proved that by handing USC their second PCC defeat. Hal Hatfield and Bill Bowers were on the receiving end of Powers' two touchdown throws.[7]

**(H) Nov. 19—UCLA—21–7**

This season christened in the era at UCLA of Henry "Red" Sanders, who regarded as one of the greatest coaches in that school's history. Sanders had the Bruins at 6–2 coming into this game against a USC team suffering from injuries. They had to do without quarterback Jim Powers, who was nursing an injured hip, and some of the backups were also hurt. This left the fate of the Trojans' offense in the hands of sophomore Dean Schneider, a quarterback that never saw action at USC until this game. Despite being so nervous in the huddle that he had trouble calling plays in the first half, Schneider seemed to shake off any inexperience he might have had by opening the scoring with a nine-yard pass to Bill Jessup. The Bruins responded with a 12-yard pass from Ernie Johnson to Bob Wilkinson that helped tie the game at 7–7 in the third quarter. Schneider brought the Trojans back by driving the offense down the field, capping the march off with a 10-yard scoring strike to Johnny Williams on fourth-and-four for what became the winning points. Fullback Don Burke added a third USC touchdown on the ground to give the Trojans some extra breathing room.[8]

**(A) Nov. 26—Notre Dame—0–32**
USC #17 ND#1

After a year's absence away from another national title, the Fighting Irish once again were perched on top of the rankings, and ready to claim their third national championship in four seasons. Coming on the heels of one of the most exciting games in the history of this series, this 1949 edition proved just the opposite.

Played in the cold climes in November in the Midwest, the Trojans got off to a good start by recovering a fumble in the first few seconds of the game. Unfortunately, they could not capitalize on the turnover. They then tried to trick the Irish on fourth down in the opening quarter when Dean Schneider attempted to throw out of punt formation. However, Don Stillwell could not hang on to the ball, and Notre Dame took over on downs at the USC 40. From this point on, it was all over for the Trojans.

Notre Dame took advantage of the Trojans' botched pass on fourth down. They moved down the field swiftly like the championship-caliber team they were. On the second play of the possession, Bob Williams threw a 36-yard touchdown pass to Leon Hart, who would be announced as the Heisman Trophy winner three days following this game. The Irish increased their lead to 13–0 a short time later when John Petitbon returned an interception 43 yards for a touchdown.

The Trojans had a chance to get on the board in the early stages of the second quarter. However, after making their way to the Notre Dame 18 after a Don Rogers interception at the 27 set them up well, they failed to convert on fourth-and-one. Another mistake proved costly for USC when Jay Roundy dropped a punt that was recovered by the Irish at the USC 24. Three plays later, Emil Sitko scored on a five-yard run to make it a 19–0 affair. Sitko added his name to the trivia surrounding this series by being the first to ever score four touchdowns in this history of this classic rivalry. He achieved the feat in the time span of 1947 to 1949. Frank Spaniel added a two-yard run in the third quarter, and Bill Barrett ended the rout with a one-yard scoring run in the fourth quarter. This victory not only helped the Fighting Irish claim another national championship, but allowed them to reach 38 straight games without a loss following a win over SMU one week after this game with USC.[9]

### TEAM LEADERS

RUSHING: Bill Martin—357 yards on 128 carries
PASSING: Jim Powers—87 out of 148 attempts for 1,215 yards and 12 touchdowns
RECEIVING: Pat Duff—21 catches for 183 yards and 1 touchdown
SCORING: Bill Martin—54 points on 9 touchdowns
PUNTING: Jim Powers—48 for 1,910 yards (39.8 avg.)

## *1950*

HEAD COACH: Jeff Cravath
ASSISTANT COACHES: Roy Baker, Bill Fisk, Raymond George, Walter G. Hargesheimer, Mike Milligan, Walter S. Milligan, Harry Smith
TEAM CAPTAINS: Paul McMurtry, Volney Peters
RECORD: 2–5–2 overall (1–3–2 in Pacific Coast Conference)
(Ranked 91st best record in college football out of 120 teams)

FINISH IN CONFERENCE: 7th place
FINISH IN NATIONAL POLLS: No ranking in Top 25
POINTS SCORED PER GAME: 12.7 to rank 100th out of 120 teams
POINTS ALLOWED PER GAME: 20.2 to rank 78th

## Schedule and Highlights

**(H) Sept. 29—Iowa—14–20**
USC#12

This was USC's first night game loss in their history. Underdog Iowa won the game with ten minutes left. After trailing by a 7–0 count, the Trojans came alive near the end of the first half and at the start of the second half. They took a 14–7 lead with Wilbur Robertson pacing the surge. He scored on a quarterback sneak, and then threw a touchdown pass to Hal Hatfield. Iowa then came back in the final two quarters. The Hawkeyes' main weapon was Jerry Faske, who scored two touchdowns and set up the third.[1]

**(A) Oct. 7—Washington State—20–20**

After their loss to Iowa, USC dropped out of the national rankings. They managed to tie this game with 1:20 left in their PCC opener despite being held to zero pass completions. The Trojans came back from a 20–0 deficit on one of the best rallies in USC history. Frank Gifford scored two touchdowns on runs covering 15 and two yards, and kicked two conversions, including the one that tied the game. Johnny Williams provided the Trojans with their other points on a 75-yard punt return.[2]

**(H) Oct. 14—California—7–13**
CAL#7

The Trojans were headed to another exciting fantastic finish, only to come up one yard shy of the Cal end zone in the final 30 seconds. Jim Sears scored on a three-yard run in the fourth quarter to tie the game at 6–6. Frank Gifford's conversion kick temporarily gave USC a 7–6 advantage. Cal then scored what turned out to be the winning points with 7:30 left.[3]

**(N) Oct. 21—Navy—14–27**

The Trojans traveled to Memorial Stadium in Baltimore, Maryland, in an attempt to gain their first victory of the new decade against a winless Navy team. Jim Sears scored on a 24-yard run in the fourth quarter, and Wilbur Robertson ran one in from six yards out to help USC close the gap to 20–14. Navy then secured their first win with a 66-yard scoring drive.[4]

**(H) Oct. 28—Oregon—30–21**

It was inevitable that a powerhouse program like USC had for many years would come around and secure a victory after the worst start in team history up to this time. Wilbur Robertson scored two touchdowns, Johnny Fouch ran for a 20-yard score, Cosimo Cutri ran for a 51-yard touchdown on his first carry of the season, and Dick Genther kicked a 14-yard field goal. Al Carmichael led the ground assault with 161 yards on 14 carries.[5]

**(A) Nov. 4—Stanford—7–7**

What was first looked at by pre-season predictions to be the top game in the PCC, was reduced to a low-scoring affair by a pair of sub-par teams. Stanford started off the season with four straight wins, but dropped the next two before facing USC. The Trojans scored early after Johnny Williams took a handoff and then threw a touchdown pass to Jim Sears, who was alone in the end zone. Frank Gifford added the conversion to give USC their final point of the game. After holding Stanford on seven plays from inside USC 10-yard line late in the fourth quarter, Stanford scored and added the tying conversion kick.[6]

**(H) Nov. 18—Washington—13–28**
WASH#19

The Trojans were nearing the end of a rare dismal season when Washington came to Los Angeles. Played on a rain-drenched field, the Huskies and Trojans ran up some big numbers considering the weather conditions. USC finished with 427 yards to Washington's 342, with the backfield of Jim Sears and Al Carmichael leading the Trojans. Sears ran for 116 yards on only eight carries, and Carmichael scored one of USC's touchdowns. Sol Naumu scored USC's first touchdown that put them in the lead. The Trojans battled all the way to the fourth quarter, and only one point separated the teams. Washington then took control with a scoring drive, and an interception return for a touchdown secured the victory.[7]

**(A) Nov. 25—UCLA—0–39**

When the season began, UCLA running back Ted Narleski was fourth on the depth chart. However, by this game he went from sub to hero by running for 138 yards and three touchdowns, and helped the Bruins hand USC the worst defeat up to this time in the series. This was the third time that UCLA beat the Trojans in 20 attempts, and their first win over the Cardinal & Gold since 1946.[8]

**(H) Dec. 2—Notre Dame—9–7**

All things must come to an end, and the Fighting Irish saw those words hold true after a loss to Purdue in their second game of the season brought the curtain down on Notre Dame's 39-game unbeaten streak. The rest of the season was a tough one for the Irish, as they came into the LA Coliseum with a not very Notre Dame–like record of 4–3–1. The Irish would also be without their exceptional coach Frank Leahy, who was in a hospital fighting the effects of the flu back in Michigan.

Despite the Trojans' poor 1–5–2 record, it was their homecoming weekend, and a very healthy crowd of 70,000 came out to see the 22nd edition of the "Glamour Game." This was not a wild shootout that kept the scoreboard operator extremely busy. In fact, the Trojans only produced one first down throughout the entire game, but in the end, all that mattered was they finally beat the Fighting Irish for the first time since 1939. In the process of doing that, the Trojans recorded their 300th football victory.

Notre Dame scored first, on the final play of the opening stanza when quarterback Bob Williams scored from the one-yard line. Vincent Meschivitz added the Irish's last point of the day with the conversion to make it a 7–0 game.

The joy of having the lead was very short-lived. On the ensuing kickoff, Jim Sears raced 94 yards for a touchdown, and Frank Gifford's conversion knotted the game at 7–7. The score remained deadlocked until the third quarter was five minutes old. On fourth down from the Notre Dame 20, Bob Williams went back to punt, but Paul McMurtry broke through the line to block the kick. The ball then found its way out of the end zone for a safety, which proved to be the first one recorded in this series. It also proved to be the game winner for the Trojans.

As the final seconds ticked of the clock, the Trojans hoisted their head coach, Jeff Cravath, up on their shoulders for one final victory ride as mentor of the Cardinal & Gold. He served as team captain on the first USC squad to face Notre Dame back in 1926, and was relieved of his duties as coach 18 days after this game.[9]

### TEAM LEADERS

RUSHING: Al Carmichael—514 yards on 103 carries
PASSING: Wilbur Robertson—50 out of 106 attempts for 481 yards and 1 touchdown
RECEIVING: Hal Hatfield—22 catches for 192 yards and 1 touchdown
SCORING: Frank Gifford—25 points on 2 touchdowns and 13 extra points
KICKOFF RETURNS: Jim Sears—6 for 198 yards (33.0 avg.)
PUNT RETURNS: John Williams—35 for 325 yards (9.3 avg.)
PUNTING: Sol Naumu—27 for 985 yards (36.4 avg.)
INTERCEPTIONS: John Williams—3 for 63 yards
Frank Gifford—3 for 19 yards

## *1951*

HEAD COACH: Jess Hill
ASSISTANT COACHES: Don Clark, Bill Fisk, Walter G. Hargesheimer, Mel Hein, Jesse Mortensen
TEAM CAPTAINS: Pat Cannamela, Dean Schneider
RECORD: 7–3 overall (4–2 in Pacific Coast Conference)
(Ranked 21st best record in college football out of 116 teams)
FINISH IN CONFERENCE: 4th place
FINISH IN NATIONAL POLLS: No ranking in Top 25
POINTS SCORED PER GAME: 22.4 to rank 35th out of 116 teams
POINTS ALLOWED PER GAME: 16.8 to rank 49th

### Schedule and Highlights

**(H) Sept. 22—Washington State—31–21**

Despite some opening day jitters and five fumbles, the Trojans won the first game of the season, which was also the PCC opener. A Johnny Williams fumble on the USC eighth quickly produced the game's first touchdown, with the Cougars taking advantage of the costly turnover. Williams redeemed himself on the ensuing kickoff by returning it 90 yards without ever being touched to tie the game. In the second quarter, Frank Gifford kicked a 24-yard field goal, Al Carmichael ran for a 35-yard touchdown, and Jim Sears threw a 15-yard scoring strike to Don Stillwell, as the Trojans dominated. In the second half, Washington State came back to score a pair of touchdowns after taking advantage of two USC fumbles. Pat Duff then scored on a four-yard run in the game's final minutes to secure the victory for USC.[1]

**(H) Sept. 29—San Diego Navy—41–7**

This was the second game of a double-header. In the first game, USC reserve players lost to the Marines of Camp Pendleton, 27–17. Against the Bluejackets of San Diego Navy, USC coach Jess Hill played his starters, and the result was a lopsided Trojan victory. Frank Gifford ran for 129 yards on 20 carries, scored two touchdowns, and kicked five conversions. The second half saw USC score four touchdowns. Scoring on the ground were Al Carmichael (eight yards) and George Bozanic (55 yards), and Rudy Bukich threw two touchdown passes to Jim Sears (65 yards) and Ron Miller (14 yards).[2]

**(A) Oct. 6—Washington—20–13**
WASH#12

The Trojans remained perfect, securing their third victory of the season with 5:54 left. The Trojans got going with power plays in the first half, scoring on a one-yard run from Leon Sellers. Jim Sears also scored on a one-yard run to break a tie with seconds remaining before halftime. Rudy Bukich connected on three key passes to get the ball to the Washington two, and then scored himself from there to provide USC with their final points. The Trojan defense took over, and constantly pounded the Huskies. One of the unit's key moments was a goal line stand that kept Washington out of the end zone after they came within inches of the USC end zone. One of the highlights of this game came from Washington's Hugh McElhenny, who was regarded as one of the most exciting college players of all time. He added to his legendary career by returning a punt 100 yards to tie an NCAA record.[3]

**(H) Oct. 13—Oregon State—16–14**
USC#14 OSU#18

The Beavers came out quick, scoring two touchdowns in the first quarter after a penalty and fumble assisted them. However, despite their early difficulties, the Trojans rallied back to remain undefeated. USC started out on the comeback trail in the second quarter after a Dick Nunis interception gave USC the ball on the Oregon State 20. Rudy Bukich connected with Cosimo Cutri on a pass from five yards out to get the Trojans on the board. Frank Gifford then threw a touchdown pass to Bob Buckley, and kicked a 13-yard field goal in the third quarter from what proved to be the game-winner. Two interceptions by Dan Zimmerman in the fourth quarter stopped any hopes that Oregon State had of coming back.[4]

**(A) Oct. 20—California—21–14**
USC#11 CAL#1

The Trojans came in to this game as underdogs and left the field as world-beaters. Frank Gifford ran for 135 yards on 18 carries, and Leon Sellers scored on a two-yard run with 2:44 remaining in the game to snap Cal's 38-game regular season undefeated streak. With 81,490 in attendance, fumbles and penalties hampered the USC offense in the first half while Cal scored a pair of touchdowns. Gifford provided the Cardinal & Gold with something exciting early in the third quarter that got momentum to swing their way. He took the ball and ran a sweep around the right end, and with great blocking leading him, went all the way to the end zone to complete a 69-yard scoring jaunt. Leon Sellers later broke a tie by scoring a short yardage touchdown that gave USC a perfect 5–0 record.[5]

**(H) Oct. 27—Texas Christian—28–26**
USC#6

The Trojans rose up five spots in the national polls, and lived up to that status with their sixth straight win. Frank Gifford scored two touchdowns, with the second one giving USC a 21–20 lead, and they never relinquished it. Al Carmichael and Pat Duff also scored on touchdown runs for USC. Despite the loss, TCU quarterback Ray McKown was outstanding. He set two opponent records against USC with most yards passing (270 yards), and total offense (340 yards). As a team, TCU threw for 289 yards to set another opponent record.[6]

**(N) Nov. 3—Army—28–6**

USC #6

On a cold day in Yankee Stadium, the Trojans held Army to zero first downs, and Frank Gifford assisted the offensive attack by running for 138 yards on 26 carries and passed for an additional 50 yards. Army took an early lead following a USC fumble, but then it was all Trojans. Pat Duff, Cosimo Cutri, and Harold Han, all accounted for touchdown runs, and Johnny Williams returned a punt for the final USC score. The Trojans amassed 446 yards of offense and 23 first downs.[7]

**(H) Nov. 10—Stanford—20–27**

USC#6 Stanford #7

Taking a perfect 7–0 record into their homecoming game, the Trojans left the field as seven-point losers to seventh ranked Stanford. With the largest crowd (96,130) to ever watch these two teams play each other, it was a wild fourth quarter that gave Stanford the win and erased USC's chances of a PCC title. Stanford took an early 7–0 lead, but the Trojans rallied back with a 75-yard drive that Frank Gifford capped off with an 18-yard run. An Al Carmichael touchdown gave USC the lead, but Bob Mathias answered back for Stanford with a 96-yard kickoff return. A 48-yard run by Carmichael gave USC excellent field position, but the Trojans lost the ball six inches away from the end zone. Two plays later, Charlie Ane recovered a Stanford fumble in the end zone to give USC another six points. Stanford came back to tie, as two penalties on USC helped the drive along. With the score tied at 20–20, an interception gave Stanford the ball on the USC 11, and a Harry Hugasian touchdown run provided the game-winner. Al Carmichael stood out for the Trojans with 112 rushing yards on only six carries.[8]

**(H) Nov. 24—UCLA—7–21**

USC#11 UCLA #18

UCLA's sophomore tailback Paul Cameron needed 41 yards to set a new school record for total offense. The old record was 1,394 yards, and he had no problem placing his name first in the record book. He ran for 40 yards and passed for 88 to help pace the Bruins to their second straight win over USC, which was the first time in this series that UCLA accomplished that feat. This proved to be the worst game for USC against Red Sanders' Westwood charges. With 71,738 at the Coliseum, the Bruins sizzled while the Trojans fizzled. Their loss to Stanford cost USC the PCC crown, and it seemed to dampen their spirits. The exciting USC offense was held to 33 yards on the ground by UCLA's defense.

The Trojans recovered a fumble early in the first quarter, but could not cash in, only getting as far as the UCLA 27. A fumble by the Trojans on their 42 was turned into seven points, and they were down by a 21–0 count and all but out of the game by then.[9]

**(H) Dec. 1—Notre Dame—12–19**

With weather conditions around the Southland providing a bleak mixture of mist and smog, the turnout was only 55,783 for this edition of the "Glamour Game." The visibility became so bad that the Coliseum lights were turned on in the second half, and those up in the press box had a difficult time making out the players down on the field.

This game also showcased a bit of history for USC, as it was the first time they appeared on a national television telecast. This series had produced many exciting moments, and this 23rd meeting would end with a team winning by a touchdown or less for the 12th time.

The Trojans scored first early in the second quarter on an eight-yard run by Frank Gifford, who then missed the extra point try. At this stage, Notre Dame head coach sent in freshman quarterback Ralph Guglielmi, and the 18-year old responded to the challenge set by his legendary mentor. By completing key passes that kept the drive going, Guglielmi got the Irish deep into USC territory. John Lattner then scored a short time later on a run from inside the five-yard line. Dan Zimmerman blocked the extra point try, so the score remained tied at 6–6.

USC broke the deadlock in the third quarter on a five-yard run by Jim Sears, but once again, Gifford missed on the conversion to kept it a six-point advantage for USC at 12–6. That was all the scoring for USC on this day. The Irish clawed their way back, starting with a Eugene Carrabine interception that provided a spark for the offense. His theft came as after the Trojans made it to the Irish 33. He intercepted on the 27, and seven running plays followed that got the ball to the USC 39. Neil Worden then rambled for a touchdown that tied the game at 12–12, but for the 41st time out of 88 touchdowns scored up to this point in the series, the extra point was missed. Notre Dame then broke the tie, and secured the win, in the fourth quarter. John Petitbon scored on a sweep from inside the 10-yard line, and Bob Joseph converted on the only extra point attempt of the game to finish off the scoring. Despite the loss to their rivals, the Trojans made great strides to get back past glory. They improved by five wins over the previous year, and prevented an opposing player to gain over 100 yards against them.[10]

### Team Leaders

Rushing: Frank Gifford—841 yards on 195 carries
Passing: Dean Schneider—48 out of 106 attempts for 606 yards
Receiving: Dean Schneider—13 catches for 161 yards and 1 touchdown
Scoring: Frank Gifford—74 points on 7 touchdowns, 26 extra points, and 2 field goals
Kickoff Returns: John Williams—15 for 408 yards (27.2 avg.)
Punt Returns: John Williams—39 for 438 yards (11.3 avg.)
Punting: Des Koch—33 for 1,430 yards (43.3 avg.)
Interceptions: Dick Nunis—6 for 84 yards

## *1952*

Head Coach: Jess Hill
Assistant Coaches: Don Clark, Bill Fisk, Walter G. Hargesheimer, Mel Hein, Jesse Mortensen
Team Captains: Bob Van Doren, Lou Welsh
Record: 10–1 overall (6–0 in Pacific Coast Conference)
(Ranked 3rd best record in college football out of 113 teams)
Finish in Conference: 1st place
Finish in National Polls: 5th place AP, tied for 4th place with Oklahoma in the UPI poll. This was the first time that USC appeared on

the United Press International poll since the UPI began ranking the Division 1-A teams in 1950.
POINTS SCORED PER GAME: 23.1 to rank 26th out of 113 teams
POINTS ALLOWED PER GAME: 4.3 to rank 1st

## Schedule and Highlights

**(H) Sept. 19—Washington State—35–7**
USC#16

Under the lights at the Coliseum, the Trojans started off the '52 season in excellent fashion. Running out of a single-wing formation, the Trojans incorporated the talents of three tailbacks, Rudy Bukich, Jim Sears, and Al Carmichael, in this commanding PCC opening game victory. In this 1950's version of USC's famed "Thundering Herd," the Trojans opened the scoring with 25 seconds left in the first quarter when Leon Sellers scored on a two-yard run. With only 30 seconds left in the first half, USC struck again on a nine-yard pass from Rudy Bukich to Don Stillwell. Defensive back Jim Psaltis, who had three interceptions in the game, provided a record-setting performance by returning two interceptions for touchdowns (55 and 33 yards). Jim Sears added USC's other touchdown on a 77-yard punt return.[1]

**(H) Sept. 26—Northwestern—31–0**
USC#16

In another night game at the Coliseum, the Trojans continued on with another dominate performance. After holding a slight 3–0 lead going into the fourth quarter, the Trojans then exploded for 28 points to win convincingly. Quarterback Rudy Bukich ran and passed his way to an excellent game. He scored one touchdown himself, and passed to Linden Crow for another six-pointer. Crow also ran for a 60-yard touchdown. George Timberlake finished off the USC touchdown parade by returning an interception 35 yards to paydirt.[2]

**(H) Oct. 4—Army—22–0**
USC#7

Jim Sears starred for the undefeated Trojans by throwing for two touchdowns and running for another. Just like in their previous game, the Trojans held a slight edge going into the second half. The lone score throughout the first half occurred when USC end Bill Hattig blocked a punt and it rolled out of the end zone for a safety that gave USC a modest 2–0 advantage. Sears connected with Ron Miller for the game's first touchdown in the third quarter. Sears added another scoring strike in the fourth quarter, this time to Aramis Dandoy, and ran for a score himself to close out the scoring and give the Trojans a second straight shutout victory.[3]

**(H) Oct. 10—San Diego Navy—20–6**
USC# 7

Once again under the lights at the LA Coliseum, the Trojans stayed among the ranks of the undefeated. Jim Sears set the tempo for the evening off right by returning a punt 66 yards for the game's opening points. Al Carmichael added a touchdown for the offense, and the defense got into the scoring act when Bill Hattig returned an interception 32 yards for a touchdown.[4]

**(N) Oct. 18—Oregon State—28–6**
USC#7

The Trojans took their unbeaten team on the road to Multnomah Stadium in Portland, Oregon. They left the Great Northwest with a fifth straight victory in a performance that saw the USC defense hold the Beavers to only 43 yards of total offense. Jim Sears threw for two touchdowns, with George Bozanic (51 yards), and Jim Miller (10 yards) and the receiving end of the scoring tosses. Sears also scored a touchdown, and Al Carmichael added USC's other six-pointer.[5]

**(H) Oct. 25—California—10–0**
USC#7 CAL#4

In their homecoming game, the Trojans scored all the game's points in the first quarter, and then played excellent defense to record the team's third shutout of the season. Jim Sears scored the lone touchdown on a 69-yard punt return, and Sam Tsagalakis kicked a 14-yard field goal.[6]

**(A) Nov. 8—Stanford—54–7**
USC#6

The Trojans blasted the 5–2 Stanford team in Palo Alto with a crowd of 50,000 watching the dismantling of their home team. USC ran and passed their way to a combined 508 yards of total offense while giving up 193. Six of the eight touchdowns scored came on passes, with Tom Nickoloff leading the way with a school-record of three. Also catching scoring strikes for the Trojans were George Bozanic, Linden Crow, and Ron Miller. Harold Han ran for a touchdown, and Marv Goux returned an interception 31 yards for the other USC six-pointer. Desmond Koch had a busy game by connecting on six conversion kicks.[7]

**(H) Nov. 15—Washington—33–0**
USC#5 WASH #17

Rain hit the Southland for this game, but it did nothing to stop the Trojans from remaining perfect on the year, and recording a fourth shutout victory. This was the first time in 44 games that Washington fell victim of a shutout. The Trojan defense completely shut down one of college football's best quarterbacks in Don Heinrich, who was held to two completions out of 18 pass attempts for 14 yards. He was also intercepted five times, with two returned for touchdowns.[8]

**(A) Nov. 22—UCLA—14–12**
USC#4 UCLA#3

This game was one for the ages in regards to this series. A crowd of 96,869 was on hand to see this battle of unbeatens slug it out with the PCC championship and a Rose Bowl berth on the line. The Bruins drew first blood when Pete Dailey kicked a 22-yard field goal for a 3–0 lead. This marked the first time in this series that a field goal accounted for any scoring. The Trojans countered on an Al Carmichael pitch to Jim Sears that the latter took 65 yards to paydirt. The Bruins closed the gap to 7–5 when they tackled Harold Han in the end zone for a safety. Bill Stits then finished off a short 30-yard drive by plowing over from the one to give UCLA a 12–7 lead. All of UCLA's points came on the four ways a team can score, a touchdown, field goal, safety, and conversion.

The Bruins then mounted a drive in the third quarter that could have put the game in jeopardy for USC. They made it all the way to the Trojan 18, and then Paul Cameron looked to connect with Ernie Stockert. However, as Cameron let go of the ball, he was hit and Stockert was knocked to the ground at the line of scrimmage. That left the ball just floating in the air in a very vulnerable state for UCLA. It was then that All-American Elmer Willhoite became a Trojan hero. He intercepted the pass and rambled down to the UCLA eight. On fourth down, Sears connected with Carmichael for what turned out to be the winning touchdown.[9]

**(A) Nov. 29—Notre Dame—0–9**
USC#2 ND#7

The Trojans were rolling as they headed to South Bend to play in cold weather conditions against the underdog Fighting Irish. USC came in to this game at 9–0, and one spot away from assuming the leadership of the college football rankings. They crushed their previous opponents by an average of 23 points a game, and were on the way to finishing the year with a team record 31 interceptions and most punt return yards (827), which set a conference record.

The juggernaut from the Los Angeles was ready to go after the national championship as the ball left the kicking tee to begin the 24th meeting of these two storied programs. A crowd of 58,394 braved the frigid weather that glazed the field over with ice, which was not a good thing for the swift runners on the USC team.

For the fifth straight time against the Irish, USC received a break on the opening kickoff. This time, Notre Dame's Joe Heap, while attempting to get a grip on the ball, fumbled it out of bounds on the six. Pinned deep, the Irish were unable to advance the ball far enough and had to punt. Unfortunately, nothing positive happened for the Trojans on this opportunity or any other during this edition of the "Glamour Game."

The Irish got a break of their own in the second quarter and capitalized on it. Jim Sears fielded a punt, and looked to lateral it to Al Carmichael, who was not near the action. Menil Mavraides recovered the ball for Notre Dame on the USC 19, and a short time later, Johnny Lattner ran for a one-yard touchdown with 8:35 remaining in the first half. The conversion attempt failed, but on this day, it would not prove to be a factor in the game's outcome. The Irish added a 17-yard field goal by Bob Arrix in the third quarter to complete the scoring to hand the Trojans their only loss of the season.[10]

**Rose Bowl, (N) Jan. 1—Wisconsin—7–0**
USC#5 WIS#11

This 39th edition of the Rose Bowl pitted a successful veteran of bowl experience against a team that was in its first trip to post-season play. The Trojans entered this game with a record of 9–2 in bowl game competition. After winning their first nine bowl games, they fell victim to two straight defeats in 1946 and 1948.

This was not only the first bowl game appearance for the Big-Ten Co-Champion Wisconsin Badgers, but the first time meeting between these colleges. With the great Mel Allen broadcasting across the airways on NBC Radio, and 101,500 in the stands on a sunny California day, Wisconsin showed no signs of novice jitters. They controlled the game statistically, but when it was over, they did not dominate the most important part of the game, with that being the end result on the scoreboard.

The Badgers' tough running back, Alan "the Horse" Ameche, powered a ground attack that allowed Wisconsin to outgain USC, 211 yards to a mere 48. Ameche ran for 133 yards, and compiled a major chunk of his total with a 54-yard gain early in the third quarter that got Wisconsin to the USC 21 yard line. Roy Burks then fumbled and USC end Bob Hooks pounced on the ball at the 27. USC quarterback Rudy Bukich then guided the Trojans down the field on a nine-play drive that included five passes. The final one proved to be the game winner when he threw a 22-yard scoring strike to Al Carmichael, who was all by himself at the goal line. Sam Tsagalakis kicked the extra point and the Trojans hung on from there for not only their 10th bowl victory, but the first win for the Pacific Coast Conference in the Rose Bowl against a Big Ten foe since the two conferences began playing each other exclusively in the game since 1947. This win also allowed USC coach Jess Hill to become the only person to win a Rose Bowl game as a player and later as a head coach. A key element in this history was the exceptional kicking of Bukich and the nation's top punter, Des Koch. This dynamic duo kept the Badgers pinned deep by averaging over 51 yards a kick, with Koch getting off a booming, Rose Bowl record punt of 72 yards. With his arm and foot leading the Trojans on this day, Rudy Bukich was selected as the game's MVP.[11]

TEAM LEADERS

RUSHING: Leon Sellers—386 yards on 103 carries
PASSING: Jim Sears—48 out of 102 attempts for 712 yards and 8 touchdowns
RECEIVING: Tom Nickoloff—25 catches for 372 yards and 3 touchdowns
SCORING: Jim Sears—36 points on 6 touchdowns
KICKOFF RETURNS: Al Carmichael—9 for 161 yards (17.9 avg.)
PUNT RETURNS: Jim Sears—30 for 478 yards (15.9 avg.)
PUNTING: Des Koch—55 for 2,435 yards (44.2 avg.)
INTERCEPTIONS: Jim Psaltis—9 for 113 yards and 2 touchdowns

## *1953*

HEAD COACH: Jess Hill
ASSISTANT COACHES: George Ceithami, Don Clark, Bill Fisk, Mel Hein, Jesse Mortensen, Nick Pappas
TEAM CAPTAINS: George Bozanic, Tom Nickoloff
RECORD: 6–3–1 overall (4–2–1 in Pacific Coast Conference)
(Ranked 30th best record in college football out of 110 teams)
FINISH IN CONFERENCE: 3rd place
FINISH IN NATIONAL POLLS: No ranking in Top 25
POINTS SCORED PER GAME: 19.9 to rank 34th out of 110 teams
POINTS ALLOWED PER GAME: 16.1 to rank 57th

### Schedule and Highlights

**(A) Sept. 19—Washington State—29–13**
USC#8

Starting on their own 16-yard line, the Trojans went the distance in 12 plays, the drive climaxed by Harold Han's scoring strike to Ron Miller. That started USC on the way to an opening day victory over one of their PCC foes. Aramis Dandoy was the offensive powerhouse for USC on this day. He ran for 169 yards on 19 carries for an 8.1 average per carry and scored two touchdowns covering 90 and three yards. His 90-yard scoring jaunt was a new school record. He also completed three out of seven pass attempts for 53 yards to finish the game with 222 yards of total offense, while the entire Cougar team could gain only 49.[1]

**(H) Sept. 26—Minnesota—17–7**
USC#8

Aramis Dandoy once again had a solid performance for USC. The "Torrance Tornado" carried the ball 10 times for 64 yards, completed four of nine pass attempts for 40 yards, and threw a 15-yard touchdown pass to George Bozanic to open the scoring. Harold Han scored USC's other touchdown, and Sam Tsagalakis kicked a 20-yard field goal for the Trojans, who ran up a 17–0 halftime lead.[2]

**(H) Oct. 2—Indiana—27–14**
USC#7

A back-to-back meeting with another Big Ten opponent allowed the Trojans to boost their record to 3–0. Indiana got out to a 7–0 first quarter lead, but USC went on a 60-yard drive to tie the game, and a 7–7 deadlock was how the teams went into the second half. Aramas Dandoy's six-yard touchdown run gave USC their first lead of the game, and the Trojans were up, 14–7 Leon Sellers threw a scoring strike to Al Baldock to make it 20–7. With the score at 20–14, George Bozanic returned an interception 35 yards for USC's fourth touchdown.[3]

**(A) Oct. 10—Washington—13–13**
USC#7

The Trojans were back to PCC action by week four, and made a trip to tangle with the Huskies in a game played mostly in the rain. USC was a much stronger team, but Washington had something to prove after a 50–0 beating by Michigan. They jumped out to a 13–0 halftime lead before the Trojans rallied to tie it with 12:52 left in the game. Early in the second half, Aramis Dandoy sparked the team by returning a punt 70 yards for a touchdown, but the extra point was missed. The fourth quarter was a few minutes old when Linden Crow intercepted a pass a raced 79 yards for six points. Sam Tsagalakis kicked the conversion to tie the game.[4]

**(H) Oct. 17—Oregon State—37–0**
USC#13

After a tough game with Washington, USC returned to the Coliseum and made easy work of Oregon State. Backfield star Aramis Dandoy was out with injuries, but Jim Decker and Desmond Koch stepped up to fill the void. Decker scored in the first quarter, and Koch scored twice in the second quarter, to give the Trojans a 21–0 halftime lead. Team co-captain George Bozanic passed to Tom Nickoloff for a touchdown in the third quarter, and Harold Han ran for a nine-yard score to make it 35–0. The Trojans added a safety to complete the scoring.[5]

**(A) Oct. 24—California—32–20**
USC#11

The game started off with both teams feeling the other out with no scoring. The Golden Bears then began fumbling, and the Trojans took advantage, scoring four times off those turnovers. Near the end of the first quarter, Harold Han broke the scoreless tie with a six-yard run. A few minutes lapsed before the Trojans capitalized on another fumble, this time with Landon Exley scoring on a quarterback sneak from the one-yard line. Han then scored his second touchdown from five yards out, and George Bozanic added six more points to the scoreboard for USC on a quarterback sneak to make it 25–14 at halftime. Ron Miller scored USC's final touchdown, and the Trojans now had a 3–0–1 record in the PCC.[6]

**(N) Oct. 31—Oregon—7–13**
USC#7

In a hard fought game, the underdog Ducks knocked USC out of the ranks of the unbeaten. Oregon broke a scoreless tie with 45 seconds left in the first half. An Aramis Dandoy touchdown capped off a 77-yard drive in the early stages of the third quarter, and the conversion tied the game at 7–7. Oregon came back to reclaim the lead with 13:38 left in the fourth. The Trojans tried to come back, but a clipping penalty led to them bogging down.[7]

**(H) Nov. 7—Stanford—23–20**
USC#17 STAN #11

USC won their homecoming game with 14 seconds left on a 38-yard field goal by Sam Tsagalakis. An Aramis Dandoy touchdown and a Tsagalakis conversion kick tied the game at 7–7 eight minutes into the second quarter. The Trojans then took the lead on a 48-yard pass from George Bozanic to Linden Crow to make it 13–7. A pair of touchdown passes gave Stanford a 20–13 lead, and then Bozanic threw to Tom Nickoloff from 26 yards out, and the conversion kick knotted the score at 20–20. Ron Miller intercepted a pass at midfield and returned it to the Stanford 20 with time running out. It was then that Tsagalakis sent the winning field goal through the uprights.[8]

**(H) Nov. 21—UCLA—0–13**
USC#9 UCLA#5

With a national television audience and 85,366 in attendance, the Bruins scored touchdowns on runs by Bob Davenport and Paul Cameron. This win propelled UCLA into the Rose Bowl, and they accomplished this goal with -2 yards passing. However, they pounded out 250 yards on the ground while USC helped their rivals' cause by fumbling and throwing interceptions.

With the PCC title up for grabs, USC had a chance to tie for the conference lead. UCLA had to win, and Cal had to beat or tie Stanford, then the Bruins would own the PCC championship and gain a Rose Bowl berth. The first quarter of the "Battle of Los Angeles" ended in a scoreless tie, and the Bruins scored midway through the second quarter to go into halftime up, 7–0. The second half looked to be just as much a tussle, as each team failed to sustain a drive. Halfway through the third quarter, the Trojans received a big loss when Aramis Dandoy suffered a head injury that forced him to leave the game. The Bruins added insurance points, and with Cal tying Stanford, 21–21, UCLA was Pasadena bound.[9]

**(H) Nov. 28—Notre Dame—14–48**
USC#20 ND#2

The Fighting Irish were ranked second in the national polls, and played like they were made of championship caliber on the 25th anniversary of this series. With slightly under 98,000 inside the LA Coliseum, Notre Dame's Johnny Lattner set a record against USC by scoring 24 points himself. He also set series records with 157 yards rushing and four touchdowns. In his three games against USC from 1951 to 1953, Lattner scored six touchdowns. Three days following this game, it was announced that Lattner won the Heisman Trophy.

The Irish dominated this game from start to finish. Joe Heap put Notre Dame up early with a 94-yard punt return for a score, and the Irish never looked back. On their following possession, Notre Dame made it 13–0 with Lattner scored on a nine-yard run. Ralph Guglielmi kicked the first of what would amount to five extra points on the day.

The Trojans fought back to make it close temporarily in the second quarter on a five-yard run by Des Koch. Sam Tsagalakis pulled USC to within six points with the conversion kick to make it 13–7. It only took the Irish four plays to get the six points back. Neil Worden ran for 55 yards to eat up the majority of the real estate on the drive, and then capped it off with a two-yard touchdown run to run the score up to 20–7.

The Trojans fumbled on a punt return early in the second half, and the Irish recovered on the USC 15. Two plays later, Lattner scored on a 10-yard run to up the Irish advantage to 27–7. The Trojans then received their final points of the game when Aramis Dandoy scored from 12 yards out, and Tsagalakis added the extra point to make it 27–14. It was then time for Lattner to add two more six-pointers to his day's work. He struck on Notre dame's next possession following USC's final touchdown with a one-yard run to make it 34–14. Guard Pat Bisceglia recovered what was ruled a lateral in the end zone for another third quarter score for Notre Dame to make it 41–14. By this time, most of the Trojan fans had departed, but Lattner added another scoring jaunt for those still in attendance to complete the blowout victory. This USC–Notre Dame clash marked the final one for coaching legend Frank Leahy, who had to retire for health reasons. He left the coaching profession with an outstanding 107–13–9 record, including seven undefeated teams, and four national championships. Against the Trojans, Leahy posted an 8–1–1 record.[10]

### Team Leaders

Rushing: Aramis Dandoy—578 yards and 113 carries
Passing: Aramis Dandoy—24 out of 55 attempts for 2442 yards and 1 touchdown
Receiving: Tom Nickoloff—16 catches for 214 yards and 2 touchdowns
Scoring: Aramis Dandoy—42 points on 7 touchdowns
Kickoff Returns: Aramis Dandoy—7 for 148 yards (21.1 avg.)
Punt Returns: Aramis Dandoy—14 for 222 yards and 1 touchdown (16.6 avg.)
Punting: Des Koch—22 for 981 yards (44.6 avg.)
Interceptions: Aramis Dandoy—3 for 47 yards

## *1954*

Head Coach: Jess Hill
Assistant Coaches: George Ceithami, Don Clark, Bill Fisk, Mel Hein, Joe Margucci, Jesse Mortensen, Nick Pappas
Team Captains: Ed Fouch, Lindon Crow
Record: 8–4 overall (6–1 in Pacific Coast Conference)
(Ranked 33rd best record in college football out of 111 teams)
Finish in Conference: 2nd place. USC gained a Rose Bowl berth by finishing in second place due to the PCC's "no-repeat" rule. UCLA won the PCC, but was ineligible to go to Rose Bowl because of it.
Finish in National Polls: 17th place in AP and 11th place in UPI
Points Scored Per Game: 21.5 to rank 33rd out of 111 teams
Points Allowed Per Game: 13.2 to rank 35th

### Schedule and Highlights

**(H) Sept. 17—Washington State—39–0**
USC#17

Quarterback Jim Contratto started the year off under the lights of the Coliseum by throwing three touchdown passes against PCC rival Washington State. Co-captain Linden Crow had the honor of scoring the first touchdown of the season, which came on a pass from Contratto. Jon Arnett gathered in Contratto's other two scoring strikes. Frank Hall threw a touchdown pass to Bing Bordier, and Wayne Kurlak and Ron Calabria ran for six-pointers in the rout of the Cougars.[1]

**(H) Sept. 24—Pittsburgh—27–7**
USC# 15

In a night game at the LA Coliseum, Lindon Crow had three receptions for 133 yards and one touchdown. His yardage gained receiving established a new USC single-game record originally set by Ralph Heywood in 1943. Jon Arnett added three rushing touchdowns for USC.[2]

**(A) Oct. 2—Northwestern—12–7**
USC#9

Northwestern had never lost to a PCC opponent until this game. A Bing Bordier hit on the Wildcat quarterback caused a fumble that Ed Fouch grabbed out of the air and returned 68 yards for a touchdown. The men of Troy were then on their way to a third straight victory. An eight-yard pass from Jim Contratto to Chuck Greenwood accounted for USC's other points in the second quarter.[3]

**(H) Oct. 8—Texas Christian—7–20**
USC#9

Under the lights at the Coliseum, USC lost to underdog Texas Christian. In the loss, Leon Clarke had a big day with four receptions for 114 yards and one touchdown. With a brief moment of continued success in the first quarter, the Trojans' offense never had the chance to get going against a very determined TCU team. Chuck Leimbach caught a Jim Contratto touchdown pass and Sam Tsagalakis added the extra point to provide USC's points.[4]

**(N) Oct. 16—Oregon—24–14**

This game was played at Multnomah Stadium in Portland, Oregon, and it marked the first time during the season that USC was not ranked among the top 20 teams in the country. Jon Arnett turned in a solid performance with 179 rushing yards on 18 carries and three touchdowns. Arnett set up his third touchdown by returning an interception 36 yards to the Oregon four. He also completed four out of five pass attempts.[5]

**(H) Oct. 23—California—29–27**
USC#17

Lindon Crow recovered a Cal fumble on the opening kickoff and scored on a three-yard run ten plays later to start USC on their way to a narrow two-point victory. Crow added another fumble recovery to his day's work, and also scored a second touchdown on a pass from Jim Contratto. Contratto also threw a touchdown pass to Chuck Leimbach. With USC up, 21–20, Crow ran for his third touchdown of the game, and took away six points from Cal by recovering a fumble in the Trojan end zone. The Trojans received their other points on a safety.[6]

**(H) Oct. 30—Oregon State—34–0**
USC#10

Aramis Dandoy had 103 yards rushing on 14 carries and two touchdowns. Both of his touchdowns came on turnovers after Ed Fouch recovered two fumbles. Also scoring for USC in this blowout were Jim Contratto (51-yard run), Ron Calabria (five-yard run), and Ron Brown (19-yard run).[7]

**(A) Nov. 6—Stanford—21–7**
USC#10

The Trojans clinched a trip to the Rose Bowl with this win. Jim Contratto accounted for a pair of touchdowns on a one-yard run and by throwing a 19-yard pass to Aramis Dandoy. Ron Brown scored USC's other touchdown on a 15-yard run.[8]

**(H) Nov. 13—Washington—41–0**
USC#8

USC won big on their homecoming weekend, and Gordon Duvall ran for 112 yards on only four carries, one of which was a 77-yard touchdown jaunt. Aramis Dandoy set the tone early for USC by returning the opening kickoff 95 yards for a touchdown. A short time later, Leon Clarke blocked a punt, and two plays later, Jim Contratto scored. Dandoy added another touchdown, and the rout was on. Jon Arnett (15-yard run), and Linden Crow (12-yard run), accounted for USC's other touchdowns.[9]

**(A) Nov. 20—UCLA—0–34**
USC#7 UCLA#2

UCLA tied a record first set by March Field in 1943 by scoring four touchdowns in one quarter against USC. The Bruins also tied a record for most touchdown passes against USC with four. The game was a close one for three quarters, with the Bruins holding a narrow 7–0 advantage. Both teams battled it out in the trenches over that time, with temperatures reaching 110-degrees on the field. The win gave UCLA a perfect 9–0 record, their second straight PCC championship, and a share of the national title. With 102,548 on hand at the Coliseum, it produced the largest attendance figure in the country to watch a football game throughout the 1954 season.[10]

**(A) Nov. 27—Notre Dame—17–23**
USC#17 ND#4

The Trojans had emerged victorious only once since 1939 against the Irish, and this edition of the "Glamour Game" did nothing to change that ominous streak. With head coach, and former Notre Dame player Terry Brennan, leading the Irish charges, they continued on their winning ways against their Southland foes.

With the weather ugly at best, the teams took to the field at Notre Dame Stadium with 56,438 braving the wet and cold conditions. The Irish came into the game as 14-point favorites, but it was the Trojans that looked to shock the college football world with an upset. They started off on the right path when Jim Contratto scored on a three-yard run, and Sam Tsagalakis kicked the extra point for a first quarter USC advantage. This marked the first time since 1941 that the Trojans were able to score on the Irish in the opening quarter. Jim Heap threw a 12-yard pass to Jim Morse for a touchdown, and Don Schaefer's extra point knotted the game at 7–7 going into the second half.

Five minutes into the third quarter, USC broke the deadlock with a short-range field goal by Tsagalakis to make it 10–7. Schaefer scored one a two-yard run to give Notre Dame its first lead of the game, and he then added the conversion kick to make it a 14–10 Irish advantage. Schaefer's touchdown also produced a piece of history, as it was the 100th touchdown scored in this series.

The Trojans fought back to once again take the lead. A nine-play, 72-yard drive was highlighted by Jim Contratto connecting on five passes, with the final one going for 21 yards and a touchdown to Chuck Griffith. Ed Fouch added the extra point, and USC led, 17–14, with 10:30 remaining in the game.

The Irish defense flexed its muscle, and prevented the Trojans from mounting another scoring opportunity. The Notre Dame offense appreciated the defense's stellar work, and responded with the game winning points. With 5:57 left, Jim Morse caught a 72-yard touchdown pass from Ralph Guglielmi, which turned out to be the winning points. Schaefer added the extra point, and the Irish led, 21–17. Notre Dame scored the game's final two points on a safety 70 seconds after Morse dazzled the home crowd with his spectacular catch and run. The Trojans were pinned back at their own 14, and a bad snap from center went into the end zone. USC's Frank Clayton gave chase, but could not get a grip on the ball. He then swatted it out of the end zone to give the Irish a safety.[11]

**Rose Bowl, (N) Jan. 1—Ohio State—7–20**
USC#17 OSU#1

Ohio State and USC staged some classic Rose Bowl moments through the years, with many of the matchups having national championship implications. In 1955, the Buckeyes and Trojans met for the first time in Pasadena, and a share of the national title was on the line. Unfortunately, it was not the Trojans, but Ohio State, that was playing for a piece of the ultimate prize.

With Ohio State's legendary football coach Woody Hayes patrolling the sidelines for the first time in the Rose Bowl, the Buckeyes achieved their goal by beating USC to secure the first-ever split national championship in college football. The split occurred when the Associated Press bestowed their crown on Ohio State, while the Coaches Poll favored UCLA.

Leading the Buckeyes to a share of a national title was quarterback Dave Leggett, who completed six of 11 pass attempts for one touchdown, and also ran one in himself. Running Back Howard "Hopalong" Cassady chipped in with 92 rushing yards in a game that saw Ohio State compile 304 yards on the ground and 360 in total offense. The Trojans' lone touchdown came on an 86-yard punt return by Aramis Dandoy in the second quarter.[12]

## TEAM LEADERS

RUSHING: Jon Arnett—601 yards on 96 carries
PASSING: Jim Contratto—32 out of 79 attempts for 702 yards and 9 touchdowns
RECEIVING: Leon Clarke—13 catches for 232 yards
SCORING: Jon Arnett—55 points on 9 touchdowns and 1 extra point
KICKOFF RETURNS: Aramis Dandoy—5 for 192 yards (38.4 avg.)
PUNT RETURNS: Jon Arnett—11 for 129 yards (11.7 avg.)
PUNTING: Jim Contratto—36 for 1,382 yards (38.4 avg.)

INTERCEPTIONS: Jon Arnett—3 for 54 yards
Marv Goux—3 for 45 yards
TACKLES: Marv Goux—110

## *1955*

HEAD COACH: Jess Hill
ASSISTANT COACHES: George Ceithami, Don Clark, Bill Fisk, Mel Hein, Joe Margucci, Jesse Mortensen, Nick Pappas
TEAM CAPTAINS: George Galli, Marv Goux
RECORD: 6–4 overall (3–3 in Pacific Coast Conference)
(Ranked 43rd best record in college football out of 110 teams)
FINISH IN CONFERENCE: 6th place
FINISH IN NATIONAL POLLS: 13th place in AP and 12th place in UPI
POINTS SCORED PER GAME: 26.5 to rank 8th out of 110 teams
POINTS ALLOWED PER GAME: 15.8 to rank 62nd

### Schedule and Highlights

**(H) Sept. 17—Washington State—50–12**
USC#13

This marked USC's 75th anniversary as a university, and the Trojans celebrated the historic achievement with a convincing victory. Washington State scored early in the game, but USC then poured it on. Helping to maul the Cougars were Jon Arnett, who scored two touchdowns, George Belotti returned a punt for a 35-yard touchdown, and C.R. Roberts scored a touchdown on a 24-yard interception.[1]

**(H) Sept. 23—Oregon—42–15**
USC#9

The Trojans improved to 2–0 in the PCC standings with this win over the Ducks. Oregon scored early in the first quarter, but on the second play of the following quarter, the Trojans took the lead and never trailed again. Jon Arnett scored 28 points to set a new team and PCC single-game scoring record.[2]

**(H) Sept. 30—Texas—19–7**
USC#9

This was the first west coast appearance by the Texas Longhorns, and they went back to the Lone Star State on the short end of the score. Running back Gordon Duvall scored on two receptions, and C.R. Roberts added a third touchdown that was wedged between Duvall's pair of six-pointers. This victory allowed USC to remain perfect and average 37 points a game.[3]

**(A) Oct. 8—Washington—0–7**
USC#10 WASH#18

The USC scoring machine that produced three straight wins bogged down in the rainy conditions of the Great Northwest. The Huskies had not beaten USC in four years, but a touchdown in the final six minutes proved to be all they needed to send the men of Troy down in defeat for the first time. The game was an offensive struggle for both teams, with USC threatening once in the first half. After Washington's touchdown, the Trojans tried to attack through the air, but the rain shut down that phase of their game plan.[4]

**(H) Oct. 14—Wisconsin—33–21**
USC#16 WIS#6

With the lights shining down on the LA Coliseum turf, Jon Arnett ran for 134 yards on 13 carries and scored on a 55-yard run on USC's first possession. C.R. Roberts also traveled a good distance of 30 yards for another score in this upset victory.[5]

**(A) Oct. 22—California—33–6**
USC#10

The Trojans gained 297 yards on the ground, with Jon Arnett averaging 5.8 yards per carry and scoring three touchdowns. Gordon Duvall averaged nine yards per rushing attempt, and scored on a 58-yard run. This win gave the Trojans a 3–1 record in the PCC.[6]

**(A) Oct. 29—Minnesota—19–25**
USC#10 USC

The Trojans went into Big Ten country, and were forced to play in terrible weather conditions. With snow coming down, the Gophers treated their homecoming crowd to a 14-point victory over the highly ranked Trojans. Despite the bad weather, USC was able to produce some exciting moments. Gordon Duvall returned a kickoff 73 yards to start the second half, Ernie Merk returned a punt 93 yards, Jon Arnett took a punt 72 yards upfield, and the defense held Minnesota to zero pass completions. Unfortunately, these great efforts could not help the USC offense capitalize on them.[7]

**(H) Nov. 5—Stanford—20–28**
USC#16

USC's homecoming crowd of 63,265 saw the Trojans fall for the second straight week. Stanford quarterback John Brodie was the PCC's top passer, and he lived up to his ranking against the Trojans. He completed 14 passes for 216 yards and two touchdowns to assist Stanford in winning its first PCC game of the season.[8]

**(H) Nov. 19—UCLA—7–17**
UCLA#5

"Jaguar Jon" Arnett was an explosive star for the Trojans at this time. He proved his reputation by taking the opening kickoff 97 yards for a touchdown that shocked the highly ranked Bruins in front of 95,878 spectators and a national television audience. Unfortunately, the exciting play was erased by an offside penalty, and all it did was spark the mighty Bruins. It was then time for a running back from UCLA to take the stage, and his name was Sam Brown, a 173-pounder from Oakland. He tore through the Trojan defense for 150 yards on 27 carries and one touchdown. The Bruins scored the clincher on a 59-yard, 13-play drive capped off on a run by hard-charging fullback Bob Davenport. The Trojans got their points on a Jim Contratto run in the fourth quarter that narrowed the gap to 10–7. This was the first time since 1952 that the Trojans scored on the Bruins. This game also marked UCLA's third straight win over USC, which was the first time that the Bruins achieved that feat.[9]

**(H) Nov. 26—Notre Dame—42–20**
ND#5

The Trojans were finally able to secure their first win over the Irish since 1950, and only the second one since 1939. They also achieved this much-awaited victory in fine fashion, scoring a major upset in the process. This edition of the "Glamour Game" showcased the talents of Notre Dame's Golden Boy Paul Hornung and USC's "Jaguar" Jon Arnett. This tandem of offensive weaponry did not disappoint the 95,000 that came out to the Coliseum. Hornung and Arnett combined to produce 37 points and a whopping 546 yards. Hornung scored two touchdowns, added a pair of extra point kicks, and rang up 354 yards of total offense. Arnett answered with three touchdowns, five extra point kicks, and amassed 192 yards running, catching, and on kick returns.

The Trojans wasted little time lighting up the scoreboard. They took the opening kickoff on a 68-yard drive in 11 plays, capping it off when quarterback Elsworth Kissinger scored on a run from the one. Arnett added the extra point, and USC was up, 7–0. In almost a mirrored fashion, the Irish mounted a 67-yard drive in 11 plays that resulted in a Hornung eight-yard run on fourth-and-seven. He shook off two tacklers, and entered the end zone with a pair of USC defenders hanging on him. Hornung then booted the game-tying extra point.

The Trojans broke the tie on the first play of the second quarter when C.R. Roberts ran 15 yards to paydirt to give USC a 14–7 lead. They extended it to 21–7 after Notre Dame fumbled the ensuing kickoff and George Galli pounced on the ball at the Irish 21. Arnett scored a few plays later on an 11-yard run. With two minutes left in the first half, the Irish combination of Hornung and Jim Morse got Notre Dame back in the game. On first down from the Notre Dame 22, Hornung threw a long pass that Morse hauled in for a 78-yard touchdown. Hornung's conversion attempt sailed wide of the goal posts, but the Irish had a dose a momentum going into halftime down by only a 21–13 count.

The third quarter went in to the books without producing any points, but then the drama started to unfold with 11:58 left in the game. Hornung teamed up with Morse once again, this time for a gain of 60 yards down to the USC six. Hornung finished the drive off himself with a touchdown run from the one. He then added the extra point, and the Irish had closed the gap to 21–20. The Trojans refused to let this one get away from them, and exploded for 21 points to get the upset victory over their South Bend tormentors. On third-and six from the USC 36, Jim Contratto shook of two defenders and threw a pass to Arnett. Arnett caught the ball on the Notre Dame 26 and took it to the end zone to complete the 64-yard scoring jaunt. He then kicked the extra point to give the Trojans a little breathing room with a 28–20 advantage.

On Notre Dame's next offensive series, USC's Laird Willot batted a Hornung pass attempt, and Bing Bordier intercepted the deflected ball at midfield. Ron Brown ran for 36 yards on first down, and on the following play, from the Notre Dame 12, Contratto threw a touchdown pass to Don McFarland. Arnett's extra point kick made it 35–20, to give the Trojans their largest margin against Notre Dame since 1933. With just under three minutes left, it was safe to assume that USC was on the verge of victory. Just for good measure, the Trojans added one final six-pointer. Don McFarland intercepted a Hornung pass at the Notre Dame 23, and Arnett capped the final USC scoring drive with a seven-yard run. He then booted the conversion through the uprights to send the Trojan faithful home happy after suffering four straight losses to the Irish.[10]

### TEAM LEADERS

RUSHING: Jon Arnett—672 yards on 141 carries
PASSING: Jim Contratto—22 out of 52 attempts for 406 yards and 5 touchdowns
RECEIVING: Leon Clarke—15 catches for 215 yards and 2 touchdowns
SCORING: Jon Arnett—108 points on 15 touchdowns and 18 extra points
KICKOFF RETURNS: Jon Arnett—15 for 418 yards (27.9 avg.)
PUNT RETURNS: Jon Arnett—16 for 282 yards and 1 touchdown (17.6 avg.)
PUNTING: Jim Contratto—28 for 807 yards (35.1 avg.)
INTERCEPTIONS: Jim Contratto—3 for 29 yards
TACKLES: Orlando Ferrante—103

## *1956*

HEAD COACH: Jess Hill
ASSISTANT COACHES: George Ceithami, Don Clark, Bill Fisk, Mel Hein, Joe Margucci, Nick Pappas
TEAM CAPTAINS: Jon Arnett, Ellsworth Kissinger
RECORD: 8–2 overall (5–2 in Pacific Coast Conference)
(Ranked 13th best record in college football out of 111 teams)
FINISH IN CONFERENCE: Tied for 2nd place
USC was banned from Rose Bowl eligibility due to PCC penalty. It was discovered that some USC football players received monthly cash allowances from outside sources. This resulted in a two-year probation period, and two-year television ban, and a one-year ban on postseason participation.
FINISH IN NATIONAL POLLS: 18th place in AP and 15th place in UPI
POINTS SCORED PER GAME: 21.8 to rank 26th out of 111 teams
POINTS ALLOWED PER GAME: 12.6 to rank 43rd

### Schedule and Highlights

**(A) Sept. 22—Texas—44–20**
USC#15

In their first-ever night game outside of California, the Trojans were paced by a record-setting performance from C. R. Roberts, who set a new USC single-game rushing mark with 251 yards on 12 carries. Russ Saunders previously set the record in 1929. Included in Roberts' great evening were runs of 73, 50, and 74 yards respectively.[1]

**(H) Sept. 28—Oregon State—21–13**
USC#6

Jon Arnett scored twice, and quarterback Frank Hall once, to lead USC to a 21–7 halftime lead. The Beavers fought back in the second half, but fumbles proved costly for them.[2]

**(A) Oct. 6—Wisconsin—13–6**
USC#10

Jon Arnett ran for 182 yards on 25 carries and one touchdown. Ernie Zampese set a school record for the longest punt, which covered 85 yards. The other USC touchdown came on a 35-yard pass from Frank Hall to Bob Rosendahl.[3]

**(H) Oct. 20—Washington—35–7**
USC#9

The backfield tandem of Jon Arnett and C.R. Roberts tore through the Washington defense. Arnett finished with 157 yards on 22 carries, and Roberts had 152 yards on 17 carries to help keep USC perfect on the season. Due to penalties brought on by USC players receiving cash allowances, those linked to the scandal were allowed to play in only five games throughout the 1956 season. Due to the penalty, this was Arnett's final home game as a Trojan.[4]

**(A) Oct. 27—Stanford—19–27**
USC#6

Jon Arnett recorded his third straight 100-yard rushing performance with 117 yards on 25 carries. Arnett's performance ended his Trojan career behind only Orv Mohler in total yards gained rushing. Also playing in their final USC games due to the penalty against the football program were Frank Hall, George Belotti, Fabian Abram, Chuck Leimbach, Fred Pierce, and Bob Isaacson.[5]

**(A) Nov. 3—Washington State—28–12**
USC#20

After trailing 12–7 at the end of the first half, C.R. Roberts broke the game open by returning the second half kickoff 96 yards for a touchdown. Ernie Zampese scored his second touchdown of the game, and Elis Kissinger rounded out USC's scoring with a quarterback sneak.[6]

**(H) Nov. 10—California—20–7**
USC# 16

In their homecoming game, the Trojans got off to a slow start, but then the offense came around late in the third quarter. Mike Henry blocked a punt on the Cal 39, and C.R. Roberts picked the ball up on the seven and scored. Ernie Zampese intercepted a pass on the Cal, returned it to the five, and scored four plays later. Zampese also threw a touchdown pass to Tony Ortega for USC's final six points.[7]

**(N) Nov. 17—Oregon—0–7**
USC#14

In a low-scoring affair at Multnomah Stadium in Portland, Oregon, USC held Oregon to zero pass completions. Oregon scored the game's only points on their third possession, covering 50 yards in 10 plays, and outgained the Trojans in the game 215 yards to 154. Jim Conroy replaced injured quarterback Elis Kissinger in the third quarter and ran for 89 yards on eight carries for USC.[8]

**(A) Nov. 24—UCLA—10–7**

This was the first time since 1952 that the Trojans came away as conquerors of Los Angeles. C. R. Roberts gained 102 yards on 23 carries, and as a team, the Trojans ran for 314 yards while allowing a mere 23. The difference in this game was a 22-yard field goal by Ellsworth Kissinger, who prior to this game had never made a successful field goal in high school or college. It was also the first time USC recorded points on a field goal against UCLA. The Trojans broke a scoreless tie in the third quarter with a 14-yard pass from C.R. Roberts to Hillard Hill that capped a 67-yard drive. Kissinger's kick came in the middle of the fourth quarter. The Trojans had a shutout going until the final 50 seconds of the game when Stu Farber's one-yard run spoiled the bid.[9]

**(H) Dec. 1—Notre Dame—28–20**
USC#17

After beating Notre Dame only twice since 1939, the Trojans were in need of adding another victory over their foes from South Bend. Not since 1938 and 1939 had the Trojans defeated the Irish twice in a row, until this matchup. Ernie Zampese rushed for 125 yards on 20 carries, and the Trojans prevented the Irish, and every other team they faced in 1956, from having a player gain 100 yards on the ground against them. This was also the only time that USC went through an entire season without playing a ranked team.

Notre Dame fell on a rough path after a solid run that produced three national championships over the previous 13 years, and only 11 losses from 1941 through 1953. This edition of the fighting Irish came into the Coliseum with a 2–7 record. However, star offensive weapon Paul Hornung was back, and he produced the only true bright spots for Notre Dame faithful. He finished the season ranked second in the nation in total offense, and was responsible for over half of the Irish's total offensive production. He made All-American, and became the first and only player in history to win the Heisman Trophy from a losing team.

The announcement of Hornung winning the Heisman was three days away as the teams took the field on a warm day in Los Angeles with 64,538 looking on. Hornung had to move over from his quarterback position to halfback due to injuries on both thumbs. This seemed like history would repeat itself, as both teams lit up the scoreboard on their initial offensive series for the second straight year. Jim Conroy did the honors for USC with a scoring run from 10 yards out, and Ellsworth Kissinger added the extra point for a 7–0 USC lead. The Irish then went 76 yards on 10 plays, with quarterback Bob Williams scoring from the six. Hornung missed on the opportunity to tie the game with a failed conversion attempt, so the Trojans still had the lead at 7–6.

The Trojans got the touchdown back on their next possession when C.R. Roberts threw a 15-yard touchdown pass to Hillard Hill. Rex Johnson kicked the extra point, and the Trojans were up, 14–6. With 6:36 remaining in the first half, the Irish scored on a 10-yard pass from Williams to Bob Wetoska. This time Hornung connected on the extra point kick, and the Trojans clung to a slim 14–13 half-time lead.

The Trojans gave themselves some distance in the third quarter when Conroy threw a 15-yard scoring strike to Don Voyne. Kissinger kicked the extra point, and USC was up, 21–13. Hornung lived up to hype as Notre Dame's ultimate offensive threat on the ensuing kickoff. He received the kick on his five, and within seconds, made his way 95 yards to the USC end zone. His legs were not that tied out for the conversion attempt, and he split the uprights to bring the Irish to within one point at 21–20 going into the fourth quarter. Ernie Zampese delivered the clincher for USC early in the fourth quarter. With the Trojans looking at a fourth-and-one from the Notre Dame 38, Zampese took the handoff and headed toward the line off tackle. He got the necessary yardage for a first down, and then some. He completed his run by crossed the goal line, and Kissinger added the extra point to bring the scoring to a climax with 14 minutes left in the game. This victory was a sweet sendoff for USC head coach Jess Hill, who left the coaching ranks to serve as athletic director.[10]

## TEAM LEADERS

RUSHING: C.R. Roberts—775 yards on 140 carries
PASSING: Frank Hall—10 out of 23 attempts for 196 yards and 2 touchdowns

RECEIVING: Tony Ortega—7 catches for 223 yards and 1 touchdown
SCORING: Jon Arnett—43 points on 6 touchdowns and 7 extra points
KICKOFF RETURNS: C.R. Roberts—9 for 234 yards (26.0 avg.)
PUNT RETURNS: Ernie Zampese—10 for 91 yards (9.1 avg.)
PUNTING: Ernie Zampese—27 for 1,112 yards (41.2 avg.)
INTERCEPTIONS: Ernie Zampese—6 for 98 yards
TACKLES: C.R. Roberts—67

## *1957*

HEAD COACH: Don Clark
ASSISTANT COACHES: Al Davis, George C. Dickson, Don Doll, Marv Goux, Mel Hein, Joe Margucci
TEAM CAPTAINS: Jim Conroy, Mike Henry
RECORD: 1–9 overall (1–6 in Pacific Coast Conference)
(Ranked 106th best record in college football out of 112 teams)
FINISH IN CONFERENCE: Tied for 7th place
USC was banned from Rose Bowl eligibility due to PCC penalty
FINISH IN NATIONAL POLLS: No ranking in Top 25
POINTS SCORED PER GAME: 8.6 to rank 101st out of 112 teams
POINTS ALLOWED PER GAME: 20.4 to rank 93rd

### Schedule and Highlights

**(N) Sept. 21—Oregon State—0–20**
USC#19 OSU#13

For the second straight year, the Trojans were shut out while playing at Multnomah Stadium in Portland, Oregon. The Beavers took over after a scoreless first quarter, recording points in each of the remaining quarters. Fullback Clarence Beamer starred for Oregon State by carrying the ball 20 times and averaging 6.5 yards per rushing attempt. This proved to be the start of the worst season in USC's long and proud football history with eight seniors not able to play due to sanctions placed on the program from the PCC.[1]

**(H) Sept. 28—Michigan—6–16**
MICH#10

Michigan was regarded as one of the country's most powerful teams, but the Trojans still put up a fight to earn much respect from the media. Billy Howard scored USC's touchdown after taking a lateral from Rex Johnston close to the goal line.[2]

**(H) Oct. 4—Pittsburgh—14–20**

This night game at the Coliseum witnessed a flare up of tempers and 254 yards lost due to penalties. USC's touchdowns came from Rex Johnston on a 10-yard run, and Willie Wood threw a 40-yard pass to Don Voyne.[3]

**(A) Oct. 19—California—0–12**

USC's six-year dominance over Cal ended with a shut out. This was another game that saw its share of penalties, as the teams combined for losses of 250 yards.[4]

**(H) Oct. 26—Washington State—12–13**

The Trojans came close to winning their first game of the season. This was the first time in 23 years that Washington State beat USC, and the first time that the Trojans lost in the Coliseum against a team from the Northwest since 1950. Willie Wood and Rex Johnston scored for USC, and in the closing seconds, Wood missed on what would have been a winning field goal.[5]

**(A) Nov. 2—Washington—19–12**

USC finally put one in the win column, and prevailed with 6:30 left in the game for their only victory of the season. Phil Debovsky blocked a punt and Rod Humenik picked the ball up and scored from 12 yards out. Rex Johnston scored on an 18-yard run, and Tony Ortega finished off a 91-yard drive with a short yardage touchdown to secure the game for USC.[6]

**(H) Nov. 9—Stanford—7–35**

Unlike on many previous homecoming weekends when USC reigned supreme, this one saw anything but that for the Trojans. Stanford got out to a 21–7 halftime lead and was never threatened. USC's only score came on a 20-yard pass from Willie Wood to Don Voyne.[7]

**(H) Nov. 16—Oregon—7–16**
Oregon#16

Oregon's Jack Morris had 212 yards of offensive production to help the Ducks get by the hapless Trojans. USC did show some signs of life near the end of the third quarter. They got on the board in the fourth quarter on a 48-yard drive that was capped off by Don Buford's seven-yard run. He then added the extra point kick.[8]

**(H) Nov. 23—UCLA—9–20**

The Trojans were suffering hard times coming into this game. In their first five games, they surrendered 81 points, and coming into this game, they had fumbled 37 times. The Bruins on the other hand were 7–2 and looking to add another win onto their season. At first, the Trojans came on strong, driving to the UCLA 28 after the opening kickoff. Unfortunately, the fumble woes that plagued USC throughout the year once again haunted them to kill the drive. UCLA's junior tailback, Don Long, then took control of the game, and emerged as a star. Getting an opportunity to play due to injuries, Long did not disappoint. He threw for 181 yards and three touchdowns, scored another one himself, intercepted a pass, and caused a safety. The Trojans received their points when Ed Isherwood tackled Long in the end zone for a safety, and on a Tom Maudlin one-yard run. This game proved to be the final one of Red Sanders career. The legendary UCLA coach died of a heart attack on August 14, 1958.[9]

**(A) Nov. 30—Notre Dame—12–40**
ND#12

The Fighting Irish rebounded from their dismal 1956 season, and had a 5–3 record as they readied themselves to play host to the Trojans. In a reversal of fortune, this time it was USC that suffered through the worst season in the program's history, coming into this game at 1–8. At the end of sixty minutes going against Notre Dame, the Trojans recorded their ninth loss in one season, which set the all-time school mark for defeats in one year.

To make matters worse for the Trojans was the fact that they had to leave the warm climate of Los Angeles and head to South Bend, where 20-degree temperatures greeted them. It marked the coldest weather conditions in the history of the "Glamour Game." Despite the frigid conditions, 54,793 huddled together to watch the Irish pound the Trojans into submission.

Notre Dame struck quickly, and set the tempo of the game

early. Bob Williams intercepted a pass and ran 28 yards down to the USC 29. Six plays later, Ron Toth ran for a three-yard touchdown. The Trojans then fumbled on their third play following the ensuing kickoff, and the Irish recovered on the USC 27. Five plays later, Williams threw a 17-yard scoring strike to Monty Stickles, who added the extra point that gave Norte Dame a 13–0 lead. The Trojans closed to within seven points on a 10-yard run by Rex Johnston to make it 13–6. The Irish wasted little time in getting those points back, as Pat Doyle returned the ensuing kickoff back 92 yards for a touchdown to give Notre Dame a 19–6 edge.

The Irish added another seven points after taking the second half kickoff. They went on a 10-play, 66-yard drive that Jim Cotty capped off with a run from two yards out. Stickles added the extra point for a commanding 26–6 lead. Late in the third quarter, Tom Maudlin scored on a one-yard run for USC to make the score 26–12. Notre Dame added two more touchdowns in the fourth quarter on a seven-yard pass from Williams to Stickles, and an eight-yard pass from George Izo to Dick Prendergast.[10]

### Team Leaders

RUSHING: Rex Johnston—304 yards on 74 carries
PASSING: Tom Maudlin—48 out of 100 attempts for 552 yards
RECEIVING: Larry Boies—14 catches for 144 yards
SCORING: Rex Johnston—25 points on 4 touchdowns and 1 extra point
KICKOFF RETURNS: Don Buford—10 for 161 yards (16.1 avg.)
PUNT RETURNS: Willie Wood—5 for 137 yards (27.4 avg.)
PUNTING: Jim Conroy—31 for 1,171 yards (37.9 avg.)
INTERCEPTIONS: Rex Johnston—1 for 15 yards
Don Douglas—1 for 3 yards
Monte Clark—1 for 2 yards
Ron Mix—1 for 0 yards
Tony Ortega—1 for 0 yards
Gary Finneran—1 for 0 yards
TACKLES: Ken Antle—79

## *1958*

HEAD COACH: Don Clark
ASSISTANT COACHES: Al Davis, Don Doll, Raymond George, Marv Goux, Mel Hein, Joe Margucci
TEAM CAPTAINS: Ken Antle, Monte Clark
RECORD: 4–5–1 overall (4–2–1 in Pacific Coast Conference)
(Ranked 61st best record in college football out of 112 teams)
FINISH IN CONFERENCE: 3rd place
FINISH IN NATIONAL POLLS: No ranking in Top 25
POINTS SCORED PER GAME: 15.1 to rank 59th out of 112 teams
POINTS ALLOWED PER GAME: 12.0 to rank 35th

### Schedule and Highlights

**(H) Sept. 19—Oregon State—21–0**
OSU#12

Signs of improvement were apparent, as the Trojans got revenge on Oregon State for their defeat by shutout in the previous season opener. This time, the Trojans returned the favor by nearly the exact same score. The USC defense made the going difficult for Oregon State's much-publicized running back Nub Beamer, while the Trojan offense finished ahead of the Beavers in total offensive production. The game was less than nine minutes old when Rex Johnston ran for the first points of the season from two feet away. Willie Wood threw a 38-yard pass to Hillard Hill, and Marlin McKeever hauled in a 35-yard scoring strike from Tom Maudlin, to give USC their points.[1]

**(A) Sept. 27—Michigan—19–20**

The Trojans were down 20–7 at the beginning of the fourth quarter, but rallied for two touchdowns to close to within a point of Michigan. With slightly over seven minutes expired in the fourth quarter, Rex Johnston ran 66 yards for a touchdown, but the conversion attempt went wide. With five minutes left, Tom Maudlin connected with Hillard Hill on a 36-yard pass for a score, but two straight penalties on the extra point attempt prevented USC from tying the game.[2]

**(H) Oct. 3—North Carolina—7–8**

Another one point defeat prevented the Trojans from having a perfect record. This time the culprits were from the Land of Dixie. USC scored first in the opening quarter after a pass interference penalty gave them the ball on the North Carolina one-yard line. Tom Maudlin scored and Rex Johnston kicked the conversion. The Tarheels struck back in the second quarter on a 27-yard run by halfback Wade Smith. Fullback Don Coker then provided what turned out to be the game-winning point when he plowed off tackle for the two-point conversion.[3]

**(N) Oct. 11—Oregon—0–25**
ORE#15

The defending PCC champion Ducks did not need a nail-biting finish against the Trojans. After two straight one-point losses, the men of Troy were handed a convincing defeat. This game was played at Multnomah Stadium in Portland, Oregon, which was getting to be a house of horrors for the Cardinal & Gold, as they dropped their third straight game there by a shutout. With quarterback Willie Wood out with an injury from the Michigan game, the Trojans were limited offensively, and were hampered by four fumbles. Oregon wasted little time setting the tone for the game, as halfback Willie West ran for a 66-yard touchdown on the fourth play of the game.[4]

**(H) Oct. 18—California—12–14**

Cal was on their way to claiming a Rose Bowl berth when they came to the Coliseum for USC's homecoming weekend. The Golden Bears jumped out to a 14–0 lead, and held off a USC resurgence. The Trojans rolled to 351 yards of offense, with Angelo Coia turning in a solid performance with 86 rushing yards, and averaging 12 yards per carry.[5]

**(N) Oct. 25—Washington State—14–6**

Another trip to the Great Northwest saw the Trojans play at Spokane Memorial Stadium in Spokane, Washington. This trip, however, resulted in USC winning the game. Quarterback Willie Wood returned to action after missing a month with an injury. Washington State scored first, but the Trojans came back to tie the game on a Jerry Traynham scoring run. Wood then celebrated his return by leading the Trojans to victory in the final 95 seconds. He achieved this by throwing a 77-yard pass to Hillard Hill.[6]

**(A) Nov. 1—Stanford—29–6**

Head coach Don Clark rotated two lines that allowed the Trojans to take control of the trenches and contain Stanford's offense. Hillard Hill scored a pair of touchdowns for USC, while

Angelo Coia and Don Buford added one apiece. The Trojans compiled 312 yards of offense while limiting Stanford to 67.[7]

**(H) Nov. 8—Washington—21–6**

The Trojans won their third straight game to even their record at 4–4. Tom Maudlin and Don Buford helped the Trojans backfield gain 224 yards, while the USC defense held Washington's star running back, Luther Carr, to three yards on five carries. Clark Holden, George Van Vliet, and Jerry Persinger, all scored for USC.[8]

**(A) Nov. 22—UCLA—15–15**

After a scoreless game at the half, both teams came to life in the second half. This tough fought game saw UCLA leading 15–7 in the fourth quarter. Tom Maudlin scored USC's first points on a one-yard run. He then threw an interception that was returned for a touchdown to put the Bruins up by eight points. Luther Hayes then took the ensuing kickoff back for a 74-yard touchdown with 6:50 left in the game, and Maudlin ran for the two-point conversion to tie the game. Don Buford ran for 101 yards on 14 carries to help the Trojans outgain the Bruins 359 yards to 148. This proved to be the final game for USC in the Pacific Coast Conference.[9]

**(H) Nov. 29—Notre Dame—13–20**

ND#18

The Irish came into the Coliseum for their 30th meeting with USC sporting a 5–4 record, and were favored by 11 points. With 67,000 in attendance, the teams gave the spectators a wild offensive display over the first 34 minutes. The Trojans received the opening kickoff, but a Bob Sholtz interception ended that possession. Sholtz's theft set the Irish up at the USC 42, and a short time later, Nick Pietrosante scored on a one-yard run, but the extra point attempt was missed.

The Trojans made up for their costly turnover by taking a one-point lead following the ensuing kickoff. Don Buford returned the kick to the USC 48, and five plays after that, from the Notre Dame 41, he threw a touchdown pass to Hillard Hill. Don Zachik broke the tie with the conversion kick that gave the Trojans a 7–6 lead. On the first play of the second quarter, Buford intercepted a pass, and returned it 44 yards to the Notre Dame 24. The Trojans capitalized on the turnover when Jerry Traynham scored on a three-yard run. A pass attempt for a two-point conversion failed, and the Trojans held a 13–6 lead. Bob Williams closed the gap to 13–12 by halftime when he scored a Notre Dame touchdown on a six-yard run. The opportunity to send the game into the second half tied failed due to a bad snap from center.

The Irish took the second half kickoff, and used their running attack to advance to the USC 21. From there, Bob Williams threw to Norm Odyniec for way would be the winning points. Williams then tossed a pass to Jim Cotty for the two-point conversion to make it 20–13. Notre Dame managed to hold off USC with a tremendous goal line stand to preserve the win. After going 77 yards, the Trojans had a fourth-and-goal about one foot from the end zone. Clark Holden attempted to run on first down, but he fumbled, and luckily, teammate Tom Maudlin jumped on the ball at the one to keep the possession alive for USC. On second down, Maudlin tried to sweep to the outside, but he was stopped for a loss of one. He tried another run on third down, but was taken down for no gain. Finally, on fourth-and-two, Don Buford gave his team one last chance to score on this drive, but was tackled by Myron Pottios short of the end zone.[10]

### TEAM LEADERS

RUSHING: Don Buford—306 yards on 64 carries
PASSING: Tom Maudlin—41 out of 95 attempts for 535 yards and 4 touchdowns
RECEIVING: Hillard Hill—11 catches for 319 yards and 5 touchdowns
SCORING: Hillard Hill—36 points on 6 touchdowns
KICKOFF RETURNS: Don Buford—6 for 210 yards (35.0 avg.)
PUNT RETURNS: Don Buford—12 for 84 yards (7.0 avg.)
PUNTING: Marlin McKeever—19 for 670 yards (35.3 avg.)
INTERCEPTIONS: Don Buford—3 for 73 yards
Tom Maudlin—3 for 20 yards
TACKLES: Mike McKeever—92

## *1959*

HEAD COACH: Don Clark
ASSISTANT COACHES: Al Davis, Raymond George, Marv Goux, Mel Hein, Joe Margucci, John McKay, Jim Sears
TEAM CAPTAINS: Ron Mix, Willie Wood
RECORD: 8–2 overall (3–1 in Athletic Association of Western Universities)
(Ranked 15th best record in college football out of 112 teams)
FINISH IN CONFERENCE: Tied for 1st place with Washington
USC was banned from post-season bowl games due to NCAA penalty. This infraction stemmed from football players receiving air transportation over the limit allowed by NCAA rules. The penalty was a two-year probation, two-year television ban, and a one-year ban from postseason play.
FINISH IN NATIONAL POLLS: 14th place in AP and 12th place in UPI
POINTS SCORED PER GAME: 19.5 to rank 28th out of 112 teams
POINTS ALLOWED PER GAME: 9.0 to rank 13th

### Schedule and Highlights

**(N) Sept. 19—Oregon State—27–6**

After three straight trips to Multnomah Stadium in Portland, Oregon, the Trojans were finally able to win in that venue following three straight shutout losses. Played mostly in the rain at night, the Trojans showed why they were the pre-season pick to rule the western region of the country. The sophomore running tandem of Lynn Gaskill and Alan Shields gave the Trojans a pair of fast runners with the ability to breakaway for long gains every time they touched the ball. Both accounted for two touchdowns.[1]

**(H) Sept. 25—Pittsburgh—23–0**

USC#11 PITT#14

The defensive line play of Mike and Marlin McKeever, Ron Mix, and George van Vliet, tormented the Pitt quarterback on a consistent basis. The offensive backfield of Lynn Gaskill, Alan Shields, and Jim Maples, combined for 158 rushing yards, and Maples scored on a 50-yard reception and a five-yard run. This was the first time in 20 years that Pitt was shut out.[2]

**(H) Oct. 2—Ohio State—17–0**

USC#11 OSU#14

The Trojans recorded a second straight shutout victory while playing in Ohio State's first-ever night game. USC quarterback Ben Charles passed and ran the Trojans to victory. Charles' passing set up a field goal, and then he tossed a 38-yard scoring strike to Luther Hayes. He also ran for a four-yard touchdown.[3]

**(A) Oct. 17—Washington—22–15**
USC#7 WASH#18

USC scored the winning points with 6:34 left in the game. This was USC's first-ever game in the AAWU, and they worked hard to emerge victorious. Trailing, 15–14, the Trojans went on an eight-play, 80-yard drive to win it on a Willie Wood six-yard run. Dave Morgan killed any hopes that Washington had of coming back when he intercepted a pass on the game's final play. Jerry Traynham led the USC ground attack with 157 yards on 23 carries.[4]

**(H) Oct. 24—Stanford—30–28**
USC#5

Clark Holden had a day to remember by running for 125 yards on 22 carries, and tied a school record with four rushing touchdowns. Stanford led, 21–12, at the half due to the passing skills of the nation's top quarterback, Dick Norman. He completed 11 of 19 attempts for 163 yards and two touchdowns in the first half. After that, however, the Trojan defense clamped down on Norman with a consistent pass rush. Holden then scored three of his touchdowns to give USC their fifth straight win in as many games. As a team, the Trojans rushed for 375 yards.[5]

**(A) Oct. 31—California—14–7**
USC#6

Trailing 7–6, USC scored winning points with 12:13 left to remain undefeated. Willie Wood starred in what turned out to be the winning drive. He first returned a kickoff 30 yards to the USC 48, and eventually capped the drive off himself with a seven-yard run. Angelo Coia then scored the two-point conversion.[6]

**(H) Nov. 7—West Virginia—36–0**
USC#6

It took USC three quarters to get untracked, but they then scored three times in the fourth to pull away from the Mountaineers. Willie Wood connected on key passes to get the Trojans into scoring position, and Alan Shields, Angelo Coia, and Warren Stephenson, all capped off drives off with touchdowns. The Trojans compiled 398 yards of total offense, and Bob Levingston ran for 110 yards on only eight carries for an incredible 13.7 yards every time he touched the ball.[7]

**(H) Nov. 14—Baylor—17–8**
USC#4

A 28-yard Don Zachik field goal gave the Trojans a slim 3–0 lead going into the fourth quarter. They then opened up a close contest after Ron Mix recovered a fumble at the Baylor 16. Clark Holden produced a nine-yard touchdown run following the turnover, and Jim Conroy added a one-yard scoring run to give USC a little breathing room down the stretch. Led by the McKeever brothers, Mike and Marlin, the defense dominated Baylor's running attack by allowing it only three yards for the entire game.[8]

**(H) Nov. 21—UCLA—3–10**
USC #4

The Trojans bid for an undefeated season ended on the Coliseum turf with 83,917 looking on. It appeared that USC had everything going for them. It was their homecoming game, they outweighed the 3–3–1 Bruins by 20 pounds, and UCLA's starting quarterback Bill Kilmer was out of action in the first half with a bruised ankle. However, when two fierce rivals take to the field, anything can happen despite odds stacked against one of the teams. That was the case for the Bruins on this day. The Trojans clung to a slim 3–0 lead on a Don Zachik field goal. The Bruins then came back to tie the game in the fourth quarter on an Ivory Jones field goal. Kilmer, sore ankle and all, brought the Bruins back on an 87-yard drive that was aided by a pass interference penalty. The infraction moved the ball 46 yards upfield, giving the Bruins excellent field position at the USC seven. Fullback Ray Smith then plowed over for the winning points with 8:06 remaining in the game.[9]

**(A) Nov. 28—Notre Dame—6–16**
USC#7

Two weeks earlier, the Trojans were undefeated and once again near the top of the national rankings. Fourteen days later, they suffered a second straight loss that knocked them out of the running for a national title. This was another loss to an underdog, this time in the cold of South Bend, Indiana.

The Irish came into this game with a 4–5 record, but were still only a one-point underdog to the 8–1 Trojans. The weather was brutal, with freezing conditions making the going extremely difficult for USC. The elements affected the Trojans so much that USC athletic director Jess Hill suggested that their road games with Notre Dame be switched to October, but the game would remain on the schedule for November when the Irish traveled to Los Angeles. Hill's proposal was accepted, and the scheduling for the "Glamour Game" has remained the same since this time.

With only 48,684 frigid spectators in the stands on this bleak day, the attendance figure was the lowest for this series since 1937. Gerry Gray put Notre Dame on the board first with a two-yard run in the first quarter, and Monty Stickles added the extra point to produce all the scoring in the first half. With the third quarter at the halfway mark, the Irish recorded another seven points when Gray scored from the one and Stickles kicked the extra point to make it 14–0. Gray added two more points to the Irish's total on the ensuing kickoff when he tackled Angelo Coia in the end zone for a safety. Coia redeemed himself in the fourth quarter by preventing a shutout when he caught a 13-yard touchdown pass from Ben Charles. The Trojans attempted a two-point conversion pass, but it failed.

The bright spots for the Trojans were that they prevented an opposing player from running for 100 yards throughout the season, and they achieved a three-way tie for the AAWU championship with UCLA and Washington.[10]

### Team Leaders

Rushing: Jerry Traynham—583 yards on 123 carries
Passing: Ben Charles—20 out of 46 attempts for 348 yards and 4 touchdowns
Receiving: Luther Hayes—9 catches for 179 yards and 2 touchdowns

Marlin McKeever—9 catches for 107 yards
SCORING: Clark Holden—30 points on 5 touchdowns
KICKOFF RETURNS: Jerry Traynham—5 for 105 yards (21.0 avg.)
PUNT RETURNS: Alan Shields—5 for 86 yards and 1 touchdown (17.2 avg.)
PUNTING: Clark Holden—26 for 955 yards (36.7 avg.)
INTERCEPTIONS: Willie Wood—5 for 105 yards
TACKLES: Mike McKeever—107

## *1960*

HEAD COACH: John McKay
ASSISTANT COACHES: Don Coryell, Raymond George, Marv Goux, Mel Hein, Dave Levy, Joe Margucci, Norm Pollom
TEAM CAPTAINS: Mike McKeever, George Van Vliet
RECORD: 4–6 overall (3–1 in Athletic Association of Western Universities)
(Ranked 70th best record in college football out of 113 teams)
FINISH IN CONFERENCE: 2nd place
FINISH IN NATIONAL POLLS: No ranking in Top 25
POINTS SCORED PER GAME: 9.5 to rank 99th out of 113 teams
POINTS ALLOWED PER GAME: 15.2 to rank 66th

### Schedule and Highlights

**(H) Sept. 16—Oregon State—0–14**
USC#6

This marked the beginning of the John McKay coaching era at USC. His debut saw the Trojans go into this game as at least a three-touchdown favorite, but Oregon State had other ideas with 32,928 in the Coliseum. With the running tandem of Don Kasso and Terry Baker starring for Oregon State, the Beavers stunned the crowd, winning for the first time in Los Angeles since 1935.[1]

**(H) Sept. 24—Texas Christian—6–7**

The Trojans got closer to giving John McKay his first win as coach, but a missed extra point proved to be the deciding factor over the Horned Frogs. Running back Bob Levingston scored on a five-yard run to give the Trojans their first points of the John McKay era.[2]

**(A) Oct. 1—Ohio State—0–20**
OSU#9

The Buckeyes' trip to Los Angeles the previous season resulted in a shutout loss. This time out, they returned the favor as the Trojans made a trip to Columbus, Ohio. Ohio State took the lead on their second possession, with powerful 217-pound fullback Bob Ferguson scoring on a 74-yard run. Ferguson added two more touchdowns to his day's work after interceptions helped set Ohio State up. Ferguson finished with 157 yards on 20 carries, and as a team, the Buckeyes outgained USC 274 yards to 69.[3]

**(H) Oct. 7—Georgia—10–3**

This was the last time that USC wore their white road jerseys at the LA Coliseum due to Georgia only having red jerseys at the time. Prior to this, USC wore white jerseys at home frequently during the 1930's. The change seemed to work some magic, as the Trojans finally presented John McKay with his first win as head coach. Sophomore quarterback Bill Nelsen led USC in total offense with 47 yards on the ground and 26 through the air. The stats might not have been eye-popping, but they got the job done. Nelsen also scored the game's only touchdown from one yard out. Nelsen's touchdown was set up by a Dave Morgan interception off Fran Tarkenton, and it assisted the Trojans in snapping a five-game losing streak dating back to the previous year.[4]

**(H) Oct. 15—California—27–10**

Hal Tobin ran for 145 yards on 17 carries to help the Trojans record their second straight victory. This was USC's conference opener, and the winless Golden Bears made them work for the victory. Down, 10–7, in the third quarter, Tobin gained much of his rushing total on a 63-yard jaunt to paydirt after breaking away from three defenders. His touchdown run provided the Trojans with the momentum that carried them to a win.[5]

**(A) Oct. 29—Stanford—21–10**

The Trojans were on a roll, evening out their record to 3–3 with a third straight victory. Assisting USC to remain perfect in the AAWU standings was Jerry Traynham, who intercepted a pass on the fourth play of the game, and returned in 35 yards for a touchdown. Hal Tobin and Ben Wilson also added touchdowns for the Trojans. Halfback Ken Del Conte did not score, but he had a solid performance by averaging 13.6 yards each time he carried the ball.[6]

**(H) Nov. 5—Washington—0–34**
WASH#7

The Trojans fell back to the ranks of the defeated, and the Huskies clinched a Rose Bowl berth with this convincing win. Played mostly in rain with 43,475 in attendance at the Coliseum, Washington took control early after recovering a fumble on the opening kickoff. Two minutes later, they scored a touchdown. The Trojans did manage to get as far as the Washington five-yard line, but another fumble stopped the advance.[7]

**(A) Nov. 12—Baylor—14–35**

Baylor's Ronnie Bull ran for 86 yards and scored three touchdowns to down the Trojans for the second straight week. Despite getting 357 yards of offensive production, and a solid performance by quarterback Bill Nelsen, who passed for 239 yards and two touchdowns, USC fumbled six times. Nelsen's two scoring strikes in the closing minutes of the game helped the Trojans avoid a shutout.[8]

**(A) Nov. 19—UCLA—17-6**
UCLA#11

The previous year, the Trojans were favored to win this rivalry game, but the Bruins rose up to shock them. This time around, the Trojans were underdogs and returned the favor in John McKay's first USC-UCLA game as head coach. UCLA was 5–1–1 coming into this game with three straight shutouts and ranked number 11 in the country. The Trojans struck for two touchdowns in the first two quarters, and added a field goal in the fourth quarter for insurance on their homecoming weekend. Scoring for USC were Marlin McKeever on a 21-yard pass from Bill Nelsen, Hal Tobin on a two-yard run, and Don Zachik on a 10-yard field goal. The three-touchdown underdog Trojans then gave their new head coach a victory ride at the conclusion of the game.[9]

**(H) Nov. 26—Notre Dame—0–17**

This was a day that did not display the greatest of the Trojans, the much-envied Southern California weather, or the reputation of this series dubbed, 'the Glamour Game." Without a doubt, this rivalry is in the upper echelon among college football, and through years past, and those that followed, this clash saw national championships won or lost due to the outcome.

In the first meeting of the 1960s, however, nothing was farther from the truth. The Trojans came into this game under new head coach John McKay with a 4–5 record, while the Irish, after winning their opening game, lost eight straight coming into this contest. The dismal records of these two usual titans matched the weather, as Los Angeles was rainy and miserable. The weather, coupled with poor records by the teams, resulted in a crowd of only 28,297 in the vast LA Coliseum, which was the second lowest gathering to watch a USC–Notre Dame game.

Another black mark on this game was the fact that a California native did most of the damage for the Fighting Irish on this day. Whether it was throwing, running, playing defense, or punting, sophomore Daryle Lamonica did it all for Notre Dame on this dreary November day in the Southland.

Following the opening kickoff, Notre Dame started from their own 29, and with Lamonica guiding the team, the Irish climaxed the drive with a 31-yard field goal by Joe Perkowski for a 3–0 lead. The Trojans did not have possession for very long after the ensuing kickoff. Lamonica intercepted a Bill Nelsen pass, and returned it 19 yards to the USC 45. Lamonica then threw a pass covering 18 yards to Dennis Murphy, and a few plays later, Lamonica scored from the one, and Perkowski's extra point made it 10–0. The Irish capped off the game's scoring late in the second quarter on a nine-yard run by Bob Scarpitto, and Perkowski added the extra point.

The Trojans had opportunities to score, but on the last play of the first half, Lamonica tackled Marlin McKeever after he reached the Notre Dame 10 with a pass thrown by Nelsen. At the end of the game, Ben Charles threw to Jim Maples, but he dropped the ball just as he was on the goal line, which sent the Trojans down in defeat to Notre Dame by way of a shutout for the sixth time on the history of this series up to this time.[10]

TEAM LEADERS

RUSHING: Hal Tobin—318 yards on 61 carries
PASSING: Bill Nelsen—29 out of 72 attempts for 446 yards and 3 touchdowns
RECEIVING: Marlin McKeever—15 catches for 218 yards and 1 touchdown
SCORING: Hal Tobin—18 points on 3 touchdowns
KICKOFF RETURNS: Jerry Traynham—5 for 83 yards (16.6 avg.)
PUNT RETURNS: Carl Skvarna—4 for 52 yards (13.0 avg.)
PUNTING: Marlin McKeever—39 for 1,444 yards (37.0 avg.)
INTERCEPTIONS: Al Prukop—3 for 23 yards
TACKLES: Not available

## *1961*

HEAD COACH: John McKay
ASSISTANT COACHES: Raymond George, Mike Giddings, Marv Goux, Mel Hein, Dave Levy, Joe Margucci
TEAM CAPTAIN: Britt Williams
RECORD: 4–5–1 overall (2–1–1 in Athletic Association of Western Universities)
(Ranked 67th best record in college football out of 111 teams)
FINISH IN CONFERENCE: Tied for 2nd place
FINISH IN NATIONAL POLLS: No ranking in Top 25
POINTS SCORED PER GAME: 15.0 to rank 61st out of 111 teams
POINTS ALLOWED PER GAME: 16.7 to rank 70th

### Schedule and Highlights

**(H) Sept. 22—Georgia Tech—7–27**

The Georgia Tech Bulldogs won this game in the trenches, as their line play dominated the Trojans. Despite the lopsided loss, Willie Brown starred for the Trojans. He tied a USC record with eight receptions in one game, gaining 87 yards on those catches. The record was originally set on September 30, 1939, by Robert Peoples. Quarterback Pete Beathard scored USC's only touchdown.[1]

**(H) Sept. 29—Southern Methodist—21–16**

Willie Brown ran for 183 yards on 13 carries, and set a USC record for the longest run from scrimmage (93 yards), breaking the old record of 90 yards set by Aramis Dandoy in 1953. Quarterback Bill Nelsen accounted for USC's other touchdowns on a pair one-yard runs.[2]

**(H) Oct. 7—Iowa—34–35**

IOWA#1

USC trailed by 21–0, but came back with 34 points and lost with just inside a minute left in the game against the number one ranked team in the country. With a crowd of 30,263 at the Coliseum, and millions of others watching on television, the Trojans scored on a five-yard pass from Bill Nelsen to Hal Bedsole with 48 seconds remaining to bring USC to within one point of the Hawkeyes. Nelsen then attempted a two-point conversion pass to Bedsole for the lead, but the ball was bobbled and dropped. The Trojans totaled 220 rushing yards with the I-Formation, which was the first time in USC history that it proved its effectiveness. This was the first season that USC used John McKay's version of the formation, and it was dubbed by many negative nicknames from the press corps until the results proved the critics wrong. This marked the dawn of the success enjoyed by the Trojans with the I-Formation.[3]

**(A) Oct. 14—Notre Dame—0–30**

ND#8

History repeated itself on two occasions in this 33rd edition of the USC–Notre Dame game. The weather was once again dreary with rain, and the Fighting Irish beat the Trojans via a shutout, which prevented a John McKay-led USC team to score against Notre Dame in two attempts.

The Irish came into this game with a perfect 2–0 record, and looked to keep the streak going. They established their position in this game early in the first quarter when Daryle Lamonica ran for a 12-yard touchdown to complete a 10-play, 55-yard drive. That would be the only score Notre Dame needed on this day, but they continued to light up the scoreboard for 23 more points with the majority of the 50,427 in attendance enjoying the rout.

Lamonica threw a 19-yard touchdown pass to Jim Kelly, Joe Rutkowski ran for 12 yards, but Joe Perkowski missed on the extra point, and the Irish were up, 20–0, at that stage. They added their final ten points on a one-yard run by Lamonica in the third quarter, and Perkowski connected on a 49-yard field goal in the fourth quarter.[4]

**(A) Oct. 21—California—28–14**

The Trojans rebounded from the beating they took in South Bend the previous week. Pete Beathard got the start at quarterback, and responded by throwing a pair of touchdown passes to Hal Bedsole, who finished with seven receptions for 124 yards. Beathard also ran for a touchdown. The USC line played a great game that saw them continually open holes for the backs to run through.[5]

**(H) Oct. 28—Illinois—14–10**

Pete Beathard completed 12 of 16 pass attempts for 157 yards, and threw for USC's first points of the game on a 29-yard scoring strike to Hal Bedsole. Illinois came back to take a 10–6 halftime lead, but Ben Wilson scored the go-ahead points on a two-yard run in the third quarter. For the game, Wilson ran for 134 yards on 20 carries. Illinois made things exciting near the end, as they were on the USC eight-yard line when the game ended.[6]

**(A) Nov. 4—Washington—0–0**

This game saw both teams fairly even on not only the scoreboard, but in the final statistics category as well. The defenses clamped down on the passing attacks, with USC allowing 49 yards and Washington 63. On the ground, the Trojans ran for 223 yards and Washington 239. Ben Wilson rushed for 93 yards on 24 carries, and Pete Beathard gained 85 on nine carries. The Huskies did score a touchdown in the third quarter, but it was called back due to a holding penalty, and both teams missed on field goal opportunities. Beathard looked to get points on the board with 1:22 remaining, but an interception stopped the advance.[7]

**(H) Nov. 11—Stanford—30–15**

On USC's homecoming weekend, Pete Beathard ran for 124 yards on just nine carries. On the Trojans' first offensive series, Beathard gained over half of his rushing total on a 69-yard touchdown run. After two Stanford fumbles, USC scored again on a Ben Wilson run. The Trojans then expanded on a 12–7 halftime lead to win easily. Wilson added another touchdown to his day's work, and Bill Nelsen and Hal Tobin each scored once.[8]

**(A) Nov. 18—Pittsburgh—9–10**

The Trojans could not capitalize on numerous breaks in the first half, and had to settle for a field goal by Carl Skvarna for their only points in the first thirty minutes. The second half proved to be a tough one for USC, as they fumbled three times inside the Pitt 20-yard line. With 4:22 remaining in the game, Warren Stephenson recovered a fumble for USC, and the Trojans took advantage of the turnover by scoring on a pass from Bill Nelsen to Hal Bedsole. Instead of going for the tie, the Trojans gambled on the two-conversion for the win, but a pass attempt to Willie Brown was batted down to secure the victory for Pitt.[9]

**(H) Nov. 25—UCLA—7–10**

For the first time in nine years, this classic rivalry had something other bragging rights on the line. Both were in position to gain a Rose Bowl berth with a win, and the battle for that opportunity had to be waged on a muddy field due to rain making for a bleak day in the Southland. The bruins came into this game with the conference's total offense leader in Bobby Smith and the rushing leader in Mike Haffner. Smith lived up to his credentials, and became the hero of Westwood by running for what became the winning touchdown that propelled UCLA into the Rose Bowl. Smith first gave the Bruins a 3–0 lead on a 31-yard field goal. The Trojans came back to claim a 7–3 halftime lead on a 52-yard punt return by Pete Beathard. In the third quarter, UCLA lineman Joe Bauwens intercepted a pass and ran it back to the USC 32. Seven running plays later, Smith scored the game winner from six yards out. The Trojans had an opportunity to possibly get out of this game with a tie, but a 38-yard field goal attempt by Carl Skvarna hit the crossbar of the goal post and bounced back. The USC offense only crossed midfield six times in this game, and never got closer than the Bruins' 33.[10]

### TEAM LEADERS

RUSHING: Ben Wilson—619 yards on 139 carries
PASSING: Bill Nelsen—39 out of 86 attempts for 683 yards and 4 touchdowns
RECEIVING: Hal Bedsole—27 catches for 525 yards and 6 touchdowns
SCORING: Hal Bedsole—38 points on 6 touchdowns and a 2-point conversion
KICKOFF RETURNS: Ben Wilson—8 for 164 yards (20.5 avg.)
PUNT RETURNS: Jim Maples—6 for 62 yards (10.3 avg.)
PUNTING: Ernie Jones—38 for 1,504 yards (39.6 avg.)
INTERCEPTIONS: Bill Nelsen—3 for 67 yards
Dave Morgan—3 for 53 yards
TACKLES: Not available

## *1962*

HEAD COACH: John McKay
ASSISTANT COACHES: Raymond George, Mike Giddings, Marv Goux, Mel Hein, Dave Levy, Joe Margucci
TEAM CAPTAINS: Marv Marinovich, Ben Wilson
RECORD: 11–0 overall (4–0 in Athletic Association of Western Universities)
(Ranked 1stfor the best record in college football out of 120 teams)
FINISH IN CONFERENCE: 1st place
FINISH IN NATIONAL POLLS: 1st place in AP and 1st place in UPI—1962 National Champions
POINTS SCORED PER GAME: 23.7 to rank 16th out of 120 teams
POINTS ALLOWED PER GAME: 8.4 to rank 13th

### Schedule and Highlights

**(H) Sept. 22—Duke—14–7**
DUKE#8

USC started the season as an underdog to Duke, but emerged victorious on their way to a perfect record. After Duke scored first, the Trojans first tied the game on a four-yard pass from Pete Beathard to Willie Brown. The Trojans moved ahead to stay on a 51-yard scoring strike from Bill Nelsen to Hal Bedsole with under two minutes left in the first half. This marked the first time that coach John McKay won a season opener at USC.[1]

**(A) Sept. 29—Southern Methodist—33–3**
USC#9

Willie (the Wisp) Brown set the tone early by returning a kickoff 92 yards for a touchdown. The Trojans put the game away in the second half on two scoring strikes from Bill Nelsen to Hal Bedsole, who had four receptions for 112 yards.[2]

**(A) Oct. 6—Iowa—7–0**
USC#6

The Trojans turned an Iowa fumble into the game's only touchdown. This was only the second time in 10 years that Iowa was held scoreless. Ron Heller provided USC with their touchdown on a 19-yard run following a Loran Hunt fumble recovery on the Iowa 24. In all, Iowa lost five fumbles and had two interceptions.[3]

**(H) Oct. 20—California—32–6**
USC#3

This conference opener saw 26 penalties called, with the Trojans losing 120 yards and Cal 92. After a scoreless first quarter, USC got a pair of touchdowns on Bill Nelsen scoring strikes to Hal Bedsole and Jay Clark. USC's quarterbacking duo of Nelsen and Pete Beathard combined for 17 out of 29 pass completions for a then-school record of 329 yards through the air. The same two players gained a good portion of the Trojans' 128 rushing yards on option plays. For the game, Bedsole had six receptions for 201 yards and two touchdowns. His yardage gained receiving set a new USC single-game record previously held by Linden Crow in 1954.[4]

**(A) Oct. 27—Illinois—28–16**
USC#4

Willie Brown ran for 111 yards on 12 carries, and Hal Bedsole caught three passes for 111 yards and two touchdowns. With 45 seconds left in the first half, Pete Beathard threw a 73-yard touchdown to Bedsole that opened up a tight 8–7 game. Willie Brown then gave the Trojans extra breathing room with a 73-yard touchdown run in the third quarter to make it 21–8 in favor of USC.[5]

**(H) Nov. 3—Washington—14–0**
USC#3 WASH# 9

In this battle of unbeatens, the Trojans won their homecoming game via a shutout. Willie Brown ran for 99 yards on 14 carries, and Pete Beathard threw a touchdown pass to Hal Bedsole, and ran for a four-yard score to complete the scoring. The USC defense did a tremendous job stopping the Huskies' dangerous running game, while allowing only 24 yards through the air, and they also intercepted three passes.[6]

**(A) Nov. 10—Stanford—39–14**
USC#2

With a balanced offensive attack that produced 216 rushing yards and 201 through the air, the Trojans built a 25–0 lead in the third quarter. Stanford had a huge line from tackle to tackle, and it was able to handle USC's offensive barrages early on. However, the Trojans took a 10–0 halftime lead on a Tom Lupo field goal and a four-yard run by Pete Beathard. He added another touchdown run from one yard out. Bill Nelsen threw a pair of touchdown passes, and Craig Fertig ran for USC's other six-pointer.[7]

**(H) Nov. 17—Navy—13–6**
USC#2

Willie Brown ran for 143 yards on eight carries, but Navy fought hard and made USC work for this victory. Navy took an early 6–0 lead on a Roger Staubach run before the Trojans scored the go-ahead points in the second quarter when Pete Beathard threw a seven-yard touchdown pass to Hal Bedsole. Tom Lupo then put the Trojans in front for good with the conversion kick. Willie Brown added USC's other six-pointer in the third quarter on a 56-yard run. Navy made it interesting down the stretch, but a fumble into the end zone was recovered by USC's Gary Potter to keep the Trojans' perfect season going strong.[8]

**(A) Nov. 24—UCLA—14–3**
USC#1

The Trojans remained undefeated, but had to work hard to keep their bid at perfection going. A UCLA field goal in the second quarter was all the scoring up to the fourth quarter, and then USC came alive. Held scoreless for 50 minutes, the Trojans made up for lost time thanks to Willie Brown. With a crowd of 86,740 looking on, Bill Nelsen threw a pass to Brown on fourth-and eight from the UCLA 26. Brown leaped into the air and came down with a spectacular reception at the two. Ben Wilson then scored the go-ahead points and Tom Lupo added the extra point. The Bruins fought back hard, but Pete Beathard intercepted a pass to halt the advance. He then took the Trojans on an 82-yard drive, which he capped off with a one-yard run that added insurance points.[9]

**(H) Dec. 1—Notre Dame—25–0**
USC#1

USC's head coach John McKay had suffered through two straight shutouts in his tenure at USC. However, this season his charges were able to return the favor. This shutout victory concluded the best improvement in USC's football history, as the Trojans went from four wins the previous season to 11 and were on the verge of capturing the first national championship of the McKay coaching reign.

The bold headline of the *Los Angeles Times* sports section said it best. Perfect Ending: Trojans, 25; Irish, 0. The 81,676 inside the LA Coliseum felt the same, as the USC faithful watched the Trojans get out to an early 7–0 lead on their first possession, and never looked back.

After kicking off to Notre Dame to start the game, the Trojans quickly shut the Irish down and forced a punt. Running back Willie Brown went into action by catching a short pass from Pete Beathard and picked up five yards. After adding three yards on the run, Brown once again caught a short pass and made his way from midfield to the Notre Dame 18 before being stopped. The drive ended happily for USC a few plays later when Ben Wilson scored from the one to give the Trojans their first points against Notre Dame since John McKay took over the program two years earlier. Tom Lupo kicked the extra point, and USC was on the way to a spotless regular season record.

The Irish got to the USC 28 before Joe Farrell fumbled and Hal Bedsole recovered the loose ball for USC on the 22. The Trojan offense then traveled 78 yards, with big gains coming on runs by Beathard (28 yards) and Brown (21 yards). Ben Wilson once again got the call from the one, and scored his second six-pointer of the game, but Lupo conversion was unsuccessful, and the Trojans led, 13–0, at the half.

The third quarter was scoreless, and the Trojans added two more touchdowns in the fourth quarter. Bill Nelsen threw a 14-

yard pass to Fred Hill, Craig Fertig capped off the day's scoring with a six-yard run. Both attempts at two-point conversions failed, but on this day, it did not matter. The Trojans ended a five-game losing streak to the Fighting Irish, and were ready to finish their quest for a perfect season and a national championship in the Rose Bowl.[10]

**Rose Bowl, (N) Jan. 1—Wisconsin—42–37**
USC#1 WIS#2

Exactly ten years to the day after staging a defensive duel, the same two teams met again. This time, however, USC and Wisconsin produced one of the most classic displays of offensive firepower ever witnessed up to this time. This game also proved to be the first time that the top two ranked teams in the country would face each other in a bowl game.

The Trojans looked like they were going to cruise to an easy win in coach John McKay's first Rose Bowl experience at the helm. After a 7–7 tie at the end of the opening stanza, the Trojans opened up a barrage that ended with USC up, 42–14, going into the fourth quarter. The men of Troy received their points from four Pete Beathard scoring tosses and two touchdown runs, one by Ben Wilson (1 yard) and the other by Ron Heller (25 yards). On the receiving end of Beathard's touchdown passes were Ron Butcher (13 Yards), Hal Bedsole (57 and 23 yards), and Fred Hill (13 yards). Beathard connected on eight of 12 pass attempts for the game, and Willie Brown and Bedsole both topped the century mark in receiving yards. Brown had 108 yards on three receptions, and Bedsole 101 on four catches.

As the final 15 minutes got underway, it appeared that the Trojans would easily bring home their first national championship since 1939. However, the Badgers had made a long trip to Pasadena, and looked to go down fighting. What transpired in that final quarter allowed this Rose Bowl to become one for the ages.

Wisconsin quarterback Ron Vander Kelen successfully staged drives that produced 23 unanswered points before time ran out and 11 Rose Bowl records were set. Vander Kelen passed for two touchdowns during this attempted comeback, and for the game, lit the California skies up for 401 yards on 33 of 48 pass attempts. His late game heroics were rewarded when he shared co-MVP honors with Pete Beathard.[11]

### TEAM LEADERS

RUSHING: Willie Brown—574 yards on 88 carries
PASSING: Pete Beathard—54 out of 107 attempts for 948 yards and 10 touchdowns
RECEIVING: Hal Bedsole—33 catches for 827 yards and 11 touchdowns
SCORING: Hal Bedsole—68 points on 11 touchdowns and a 2-point conversion
KICKOFF RETURNS: Willie Brown—9 for 303 yards and 1 touchdown (33.7 avg.)
PUNT RETURNS: Willie Brown—9 for 88 yards (9.8 avg.)
PUNTING: Ernie Jones—63 for 2,498 yards (39.7 avg.)
INTERCEPTIONS: Willie Brown—5 for 47 yards
TACKLES: Not available

## *1963*

HEAD COACH: John McKay
ASSISTANT COACHES: Raymond George, Mike Giddings, Marv Goux, Mel Hein, Dave Levy, Joe Margucci
TEAM CAPTAINS: Pete Beathard, Willie Brown
RECORD: 7–3 overall (3–1 in Athletic Association of Western Universities)
(Ranked 25th best record in college football out of 120 teams)
FINISH IN CONFERENCE: 2nd place
FINISH IN NATIONAL POLLS: 16th place in UPI
POINTS SCORED PER GAME: 20.7 to rank 21st out of 120 teams
POINTS ALLOWED PER GAME: 11.4 to rank 32nd

### Schedule and Highlights

**(A) Sept. 21—Colorado—14–0**
USC#1

The defending national champs started off the new season in excellent fashion. Playing in the rain and mud of Folsom Field, the Trojans held Colorado to zero pass completions. Pete Beathard completed five of 16 pass attempts for USC, and scored both touchdowns on short runs.[1]

**(H) Sept. 28—Oklahoma—12–17**
USC#1 OK#3

After 12 straight wins, the number one team in the country was toppled in their home opener with temperatures hovering at 120 degrees on the Coliseum turf. Oklahoma ran 89 plays to USC's 50, and pounded out 307 of their 360 yards of total offense on the ground, with running backs Joe Don Looney and Jim Grisham doing the damage. The Trojans attempted to rally from a 17–6 deficit, and closed the gap to five points with a one-yard run by Willie Brown in the fourth quarter.[2]

**(H) Oct. 4—Michigan State—13–10**
USC#8

In a night game at the Coliseum, the Trojans rallied back from a 10–0 deficit. The winning touchdown came with 8:03 to go in the fourth quarter when Hal Bedsole made a diving catch in the end zone on a 16-yard pass from Pete Beathard.[3]

**(A) Oct. 12—Notre Dame—14–17**
USC#7

For the first time in the 1960s, this rivalry game did not end with a shutout. Instead, the underdog Fighting Irish upset the defending national champions in a close finish to keep the Trojans looking for their first win against Notre Dame in Indiana since 1939. With warm temperatures on an Indiana day, the Irish and Trojans took the field with 59,135 ready to enjoy the 35th edition of the "Glamour Game."

The Trojans took the first step toward momentum halfway through the first quarter. Mike Garrett recovered a fumble on the Irish 46, but within a few plays, Pete Beathard threw an interception that Tom McDonald returned 62 yards for a touchdown. Ken Ivan's extra point made it a 7–0 Notre Dame advantage.

The Trojans shook off the costly turnover by going 74 yards in nine plays to tie the game. Making up for his interception, Beathard logged key gains of nine and 16 yards before he finished off with a three-yard run. Dick Brownell's extra point knotted the game in the second quarter. The Irish stormed back in five plays after the ensuing kickoff. Bill Wolski provided a workhorse-like effort with the Irish starting on their own 37. He carried for five yards, and two plays later, ran for a big gain of 36 yards down to the USC eight. Once again, two plays later, Wolski finished the drive off successfully with a touchdown run covering six yards. Ivan added the extra point, and Notre Dame led, 14–7.

After Notre Dame recovered a Willie Brown fumble and marched down to the seven-yard line, looked to be on the verge of taking total control of the game. Instead, the Trojan defense held, and Ivan's attempted field goal was blocked by tackle Gary Kirner. The Trojans then took their newfound momentum and went 93 yards in 10 plays, with a 12-yard Beathard to Garrett touchdown toss bringing USC to within one point of the Irish. Brownell assisted USC in gaining a tie by connecting on the conversion kick to knot the game at 14–14 going in to the half-time festivities.

The game remained deadlocked going in the fourth quarter, and then Ken Ivan kicked a 33-yard field goal with 6:28 left in the game to put Notre Dame in front for good. The Trojans could not get a drive going after the ensuing kickoff, and the Irish ate up the final four minutes to preserve their 24-year winning streak over USC in Indiana.[4]

**(H) Oct. 19—Ohio State—32–3**

OSU#4

A crowd of 61,883 saw the Trojans beat the undefeated Buckeyes behind Pete Beathard's passing and running. He threw for 159 yards and a touchdown, and ran for 31 yards on eight carries and scored a touchdown. The Trojans rolled to 407 yards of total offense, while allowing the Buckeyes only 119 yards on the ground and 59 through the air. The Trojan defense also intercepted four passes.[5]

**(A) Oct. 26—California—36–6**

The Trojans had 5,000 fans make the trek up to Northern California to support the Cardinal & Gold against one of their longest-standing rivals. They were disappointed, as the Trojans gained 389 yards of total offense and had the game under control by halftime with a 28–0 lead. Trojan quarterbacks combined for 242 yards through the air, and Willie Brown sparked the offense with punt returns that covered 43 and 36 yards. Brown finished off one of the drives with a touchdown reception from Pete Beathard.[6]

**(A) Nov. 2—Washington—7–22**

The Trojans' hopes for another trip to the Rose Bowl were halted in the mud up in Washington. Back in 1926, the Trojans beat Washington to prevent them from going to the Rose Bowl. Thirty-seven years later, the Huskies got revenge on the men of Troy. Washington blocked a punt early in the first quarter, and recovered the ball in the end zone for a touchdown less than two minutes into the game. They never looked back after that. The Trojans received their points on a 24-yard pass from Craig Fertig to John Thomas in the second quarter. USC's other quarterback, Pete Beathard, was forced to leave the game in the fourth quarter with a back injury.[7]

**(H) Nov. 9—Stanford—25–11**

The Trojans bounced back from their defeat with a homecoming victory over long-time rival Stanford. Craig Fertig filled in as quarterback for an injured Pete Beathard, and after a shaky start, he did a good job leading the team. Stanford led, 11–8, early in the fourth quarter, and then a pair of touchdown catches by Willie Brown helped to bring the Trojans back. The USC backfield of Mike Garrett, Willie Brown, and Ron Heller, combined for 132 yards, which outgained the entire Stanford team, who finished with 131.[8]

**(H) Nov. 15—Oregon State—28–22**

Under the Coliseum lights, the running ability of Mike Garrett shined upon the USC faithful, as he totaled 159 yards on 26 carries. His backfield mate, Willie Brown, chipped in with 94 yards on 13 carries, and had an exciting scoring jaunt of 54 yards that helped break the game open for USC in the third quarter to give them a 22–14 lead. Garrett and Brown combined for 253 yards of offense, which was more than Oregon State could muster both running and passing.[9]

**(H) Nov. 30—UCLA—26–6**

This game was originally scheduled for November 23, but was postponed after the assassination of President Kennedy in Dallas, Texas. The Trojans came into this matchup as 13 ½-point favorites, and lived up to that status with this convincing victory. They ran for 322 yards as a team, with Mike Garrett leading the way with 119 yards on 12 carries. They also threw for 208 yards. Scoring for the Trojans were Hal Bedsole (six-yard pass from Pete Beathard), Beathard (two-yard run), Willie Brown (two-yard run), and Rich McMahon (one-yard run). With the completion of this game, the USC defense did not allow any 100-yard runners all season.[10]

### Team Leaders

Rushing: Mike Garrett—833 yards on 128 carries
Passing: Pete Beathard—66 out of 140 attempts for 944 yards and 5 touchdowns
Receiving: Willie Brown—34 catches for 448 yards and 3 touchdowns
Scoring: Willie Brown—44 points on 7 touchdowns and a 2-point conversion
Kickoff Returns: Mike Garrett—15 for 352 yards (23.5 avg.)
Punt Returns: Willie Brown—13 for 129 yards (9.9 avg.)
Punting: Ernie Jones—43 for 1,690 yards (39.3 avg.)
Interceptions: Tom Lupo—3 for 59 yards and 1 touchdown
Willie Brown—3 for 17 yards
Tackles: Not available

## *1964*

Head Coach: John McKay
Assistant Coaches: Raymond George, Mike Giddings, Marv Goux, Mel Hein, Dave Levy, Joe Margucci
Team Captains: Craig Fertig, Bill Fisk
Record: 7–3 overall (3–1 in Athletic Association of Western Universities)
(Ranked 22nd best record in college football out of 120 teams)
Finish in Conference: Tied for 1st place with Oregon State
Oregon State was selected to represent the AAWU in the Rose Bowl.
Finish in National Polls: 10th place in both the AP and UPI
Points Scored Per Game: 20.7 to rank 21st out of 120 teams
Points Allowed Per Game: 13.0 to rank 45th

### Schedule and Highlights

**(H) Sept. 18—Colorado—21–0**

In a night game at the Coliseum, Mike Garrett ran for 127 yards on 24 carries and scored all three USC touchdowns, plus a two-point conversion. For the first time in his career, Garrett was tackled for a loss from scrimmage. In the second quarter, he lost two yards, but more than made up for it with a spectacular performance. Ron Heller helped the cause by running for 82 yards.[1]

**(A) Sept. 26—Oklahoma—40–14**

OK#2

Craig Fertig completed 16 out of 28 pass attempts for 212 yards and one touchdown. He also ran for two touchdowns to produce one of the best performances from a USC quarterback up to this time in their history. Rod Sherman was Fertig's main target, and he turned in a good showing with seven receptions for 101 yards in this convincing win over the Sooners.[2]

**(A) Oct. 3—Michigan State—7–17**

USC#2

The Trojans went into East Lansing, Michigan, ranked number two in the nation, and were shocked by the Spartans. The Michigan State used five defensive backs to shut down USC's passing attack, and that group was led by Don Japinga, who intercepted a Fertig pass with eight minutes left to kill off one drive. He also broke up a pass to prevent another Trojan advance. Mike Garrett led the USC offense on this day with 94 rushing yards on 26 carries, and he scored USC's only touchdown.[3]

**(H) Oct. 10—Texas A&M—31–7**

Mike Garrett was USC's main offensive weapon, as he ran for 121 yards on 24 carries, returned five punts for 79 yards, one kickoff for 37 yards, and scored a pair of touchdowns in this romp over Texas A&M. The Trojan defense did an outstanding job by limiting the Aggies to 136 yards of total offense.[4]

**(A) Oct. 17—Ohio State—0–17**

OSU#2

Another visit to Big Ten country proved to be a disappointment. With the "Three yards and a cloud of dust" philosophy of legendary Ohio State coach Woody Hayes working to perfection, the Buckeyes pounded out yardage on the ground, eating up valuable time on the clock. Fullback Willard Sander delivered the most damage to the Trojan defense by rushing for 120 yards. This was the first time since 1961 that the Trojans failed to score any points.[5]

**(H) Oct. 24—California—26–21**

The Trojans were down by a point when Craig Fertig threw a 22-yard touchdown pass to Rod Sherman with 50 seconds left to finish off a 95-yard drive. Fertig set a new school record with 371 passing yards. The old record was by Jim Powers on October 29, 1949. Fertig also threw for four touchdowns. Mike Garrett was known as an excellent tailback, but on this day, he proved to be a great receiver as well by catching six passes for 122 yards and one touchdown.[6]

**(H) Oct. 31—Washington—13–14**

Despite Mike Garrett's 122 yards rushing on 26 carries, and Fred Hill's 11 receptions for 112 yards, the Trojans lost their homecoming game when Washington scored the go-ahead points with 4:49 left to play. Hill's 11 catches set a new USC single-game record that Willie Brown owned for three years.[7]

**(A) Nov. 7—Stanford—15–10**

The Trojans had possession of the ball for 46 plays throughout the first half, and Mike Garrett scored two touchdowns to add to his conference scoring leadership. It appeared that USC was in control of the game, but two penalties in the third quarter allowed Stanford to keep control of the ball for most of the quarter. This gave Stanford the opportunity to rally back to challenge the Trojans in the second half, but a 33-yard field goal by Dick Brownell helped USC hold on for the win.[8]

**(A) Nov. 21—UCLA—34–13**

Mike Garrett exploded for 180 yards on 28 carries to help the Trojans amass 339 yards on the ground in another rout of their cross-town rivals. The Bruins closed the deficit to 14–7 early in the second half, but then the Trojans took control to produce the largest score in this series since 1944. Craig Fertig threw three scoring strikes, with Dave Morton on the receiving end of two (31 yards and nine yards), and Rod Sherman (49 yards). Sherman also ran for a 38-yard touchdown, and Ron Heller had a two-yard run go for a score.[9]

**(H) Nov. 28—Notre Dame—20–17**

ND#1

A funny thing happened to the undefeated and number one ranked Fighting Irish on their way to a national title. They stopped off at the LA Coliseum and left in shock after the Trojans knocked them off the college football throne. Up to the second half of this game, it appeared that Notre Dame was well on its way to victory, and new head coach Ara Parseghian would remain perfect at the helm in South Bend.

With 83,840 watching, the powerful Irish, favored by two touchdowns over USC, and their newly crowned Heisman Trophy winning quarterback, John Huarte, got out to a 17–0 halftime lead. A USC fumble assisted the Irish in getting on the board in the first quarter. Ken Ivan turned the USC mishap into three points with a 25-yard field goal. A 73-yard drive in the second quarter resulted in a 22-yard touchdown pass from Huarte to Jack Snow. Ivan's extra point made it 10–0. Bill Wolski capped off the Irish touchdown production on this day with a five-yard run, and Ivan connected on the conversion kick.

During halftime, the Trojans had a never-say-die attitude, and coach McKay told his team to take the second half kickoff and drive the length of the field and they would be right back in the game. McKay's words were encouraging, and the Trojans followed their mentor's orders to perfection. Starting on the USC 34, the Trojans went the distance on a 10-play, 66-yard drive that was finished off by Mike Garrett running for a one-yard touchdown. Dick Brownell added the extra point, and the Trojans cut the deficit to 10, and momentum was quickly swinging their way.

The Irish looked to get the touchdown back, and got down to the USC nine before a fumble caused loss of possession. On another occasion in the fourth quarter, Joe Kantor scored for Notre Dame from one yard out, but a holding penalty wiped the six-pointer off the board. Huarte then saw three straight pass attempts fall incomplete, and USC took over control of the ball.

With time running out, the Trojans looked to capitalize on Notre Dame's inabilities to score when close to the goal line. Starting from their own 12 following Kantor's touchdown that was nullified, the Trojans covered 88 yards of Coliseum real estate in 10 plays. Craig Fertig threw a 23-yard touchdown toss to Fred Hill, who was all by himself in the end zone to record the score. The extra point kick was missed, but the lead was cut to four points with enough time left for a comeback.

The Trojans stopped Notre Dame on three downs, and Jack Snow punted the ball away from deep in his own territory. Mike Garrett took the ball back to the Notre Dame 40 before fumbling. As is customary when a fumble occurs, a mad scramble takes place to pounce on the loose ball. Guard Frank Lopez was the hero for USC, as he got to the ball first to save his team's chances of rallying down the stretch.

With 1:30 remaining on the clock, Fertig and Rod Sherman made sure that Lopez's effort did not go to waste. Fertig dropped back, and watched Sherman get past safety Tony Carey. Fertig then sent a pass toward his receiver, and Sherman made an over-the-shoulder catch to complete a 15-yard touchdown pass. Brownell's extra point sailed through the uprights, and headlines from coast to coast proclaimed how USC knocked off the number one team in the country. For the game, Sherman had seven receptions for 109 yards.[10]

### TEAM LEADERS

RUSHING: Mike Garrett—948 yards on 217 carries
PASSING: Craig Fertig—109 out of 209 attempts for 1,671 yards and 11 touchdowns
RECEIVING: Fred Hill—33 catches for 436 yards and 2 touchdowns
SCORING: Mike Garrett—62 points on 10 touchdowns and a 2-point conversion
KICKOFF RETURNS: Mike Garrett—10 for 253 yards (23.7 avg.)
PUNT RETURNS: Mike Garrett—17 for 173 yards (10.2 avg.)
PUNTING: Craig Fertig—44 for 1,647 yards (37.4 avg.)
INTERCEPTIONS: Nate Shaw—3 for 40 yards
Mike Giers—3 for 32 yards
TACKLES: Not available

## *1965*

HEAD COACH: John McKay
ASSISTANT COACHES: Craig Fertig, Mike Giddings, Marv Goux, Charlie Hall, Mel Hein, Dave Levy, Jim Strangeland
TEAM CAPTAINS: Chuck Arrobio, Mike Garrett
RECORD: 7–2–1 overall (4–1 in Athletic Association of Western Universities)
(Ranked 17th best record in college football out of 120 teams)
FINISH IN CONFERENCE: 2nd place
FINISH IN NATIONAL POLLS: 10th place in AP, and 9th place in UPI
POINTS SCORED PER GAME: 26.2 to rank 12th out of 120 teams
POINTS ALLOWED PER GAME: 9.2 to rank 10th

### Schedule and Highlights

**(H) Sept. 17—Minnesota—20–20**
USC#7

This was regarded as one of USC's toughest schedules, and that theory held true in this season opening night game from the LA Coliseum. With one of the country's best offensive lines blocking for him, Heisman Trophy candidate Mike Garrett ran for 146 yards on 33 carries. He scored a pair of touchdowns in the first half to help the Trojans gain a 14–13 halftime advantage. His second six-pointer that gave USC the lead with three seconds left in the half. Minnesota came back to regain the lead, but then the Trojans tied it up with 6:24 left on a one-yard run by quarterback Troy Winslow. Rod Sherman missed the extra point attempt, and Tim Rossovich missed on a 47-yard field goal try with 16 seconds left that more than likely would have given the Trojans a win.[1]

**(A) Sept. 25—Wisconsin—26–6**

The Trojans left in doubt about who would emerge victorious in this matchup with another Big Ten opponent. Mike Garrett ran for 154 yards on 24 carries and two touchdowns, and threw for another six-pointer, as the Trojans gained 300 rushing yards while holding Wisconsin to 11. Garrett also assumed the top spot on USC's all-time rushing list during this game, surpassing Orv Mohler's three-season mark set from 1930 through 1932.[2]

**(H) Oct. 2—Oregon State—26–12**

In USC's conference opener, Mike Garrett ran for 172 yards on 31 carries and three touchdowns to help the Trojans remain unbeaten.[3]

**(A) Oct. 9—Washington—34–0**
USC#8

Mike Garrett ran for 175 yards on 31 carries, and quarterback Troy Winslow set a school record, and tied a conference record, with the highest percentage of pass completions with a minimum of 10 attempts. He was perfect on all 11 passes that he threw. Two of Winslow's completions went for touchdowns, and he ran for another one. In what head coach John McKay felt was the best the Trojans played under his leadership up to this time, the Cardinal & Gold gained 340 of their 445 yards of total offense on the ground while the defense limited the Huskies to a mere 11 rushing yards.[4]

**(H) Oct. 16—Stanford—14–0**
USC#6

Stanford brought a 3–0–1 record, and hopes of a Rose Bowl berth into the Coliseum. For three-and-a-half quarters, they played the Trojans tough. Mike Garrett then took control of the festivities. On third-and-seven from the USC 24-yard line, Garrett, who was nursing a sore foot during the game, showed no signs of being hampered, as he bolted through the defense for a 76-yard touchdown run. By the end of the game, "Iron Mike" rambled for 205 yards on 31 carries. In the final two minutes of the game, Rod Sherman scored USC's other touchdown on a 25-yard run one play after Ed King intercepted a Stanford pass. This win placed the Trojans on top of the AAWU standing with a perfect 3–0 record.[5]

**(A) Oct. 23—Notre Dame—7–28**
USC#4 ND#7

The 37th renewal of this classic matchup once again saw a Heisman Trophy winner on the field. Even though Mike Garrett was still one month away from officially being crowned as the new Heisman recipient, he was well on his way to college football's ultimate individual award when he took the field with 59,235 fans in attendance at South Bend. Unfortunately, just like in the previous USC–Notre Dame matchup, the team with the Heisman winner lost. Despite all of Garrett's accomplishments, it was a fullback donned in the gold and blue of the Fighting Irish that stole the show on this date.

Larry Conjar's #32 jersey was the focal point for Irish faithful on this rainy day, as he carried the ball 25 times for 116 and four touchdowns. His 24 points tied a record for most points scored by one individual against USC in a single game. The Irish built a solid 21–0 halftime lead, but unlike in the previous meeting with USC, where they lost after being up by 17 points at the half, they held the Trojans in check over the game's final 30 minutes.

The hard-charging Conjar scored his first two touchdowns in the first quarter on runs of two and three yards. He added a one-yard blast in the second quarter, and capped off his big day with another one-yard run on the initial drive of the second half. Ken Ivan kicked four extra points to round out the Irish scoring. The Trojans avoided the shutout by conducting a 76-yard drive in the fourth quarter with heavy rain coming down. Troy Winslow connected with John Thomas on an eight-yard pass to get the Trojans on the board, and Tim Rossovich kicked the extra point to complete the scoring.[6]

**(A) Nov. 6—California—35–0**
USC#6

Mike Garrett was used primarily as a decoy on offense, rushing for 67 yards on 11 carries. However, he still showed his brilliant talent by setting school records with 162 yards on punt returns, and two touchdowns on punt returns. His two returns for touchdowns also tied a conference record, and came from 74 and 87 yards. The Trojan defense clamped down on Cal, preventing them from never getting inside the USC 32-yard line throughout the first three quarters, and limited the Golden Bears to 171 yards of total offense.[7]

**(H) Nov. 13—Pittsburgh—28–0**
USC#6

The Trojans recorded their fourth shutout victory of the year behind a great performance from Mike Garrett, who ran for 156 yards on 26 carries and three touchdowns. He topped the 1,000-yard rushing mark for the season, becoming the fifth player in conference history up to this time to achieve that distinction. Don McCall scored USC's other touchdown on a three-yard run.[8]

**(H) Nov. 20—UCLA—16–20**
USC#6 UCLA#7

After three straight losses to USC, with the previous two coming in convincing fashion, the Bruins rallied from a 16–6 fourth quarter deficit to pull out the win. Up to the fourth quarter, the Trojans appeared to be in control of the annual clash with their neighborhood rivals. After spotting the Bruins a 6–0 first quarter advantage, the Trojans came back in the second quarter to take a 7–6 lead on a 10-yard pass from Troy Winslow to Mickey Upton. Winslow added another scoring strike to his stats in the fourth quarter when he connected with Rod Sherman from ten yards out. Tim Rossovich padded USC's lead to ten with a 20-yard field goal, soon-to-be-named winner of the Heisman Trophy, Mike Garrett, tore through the UCLA defense for 210 yards on 40 carries, and the Trojans looked to be headed for their fourth straight victory over the Bruins.

The Bruins' sophomore quarterback Gary Beban then awoke his team, and led UCLA to what was dubbed "the 81 second explosion." He first threw a 34-yard touchdown to Dick Witcher following a fumble recovery on the USC 34. For the game, the Trojans suffered five fumbles and did not recover any of them. Beban then tossed a two-point conversion to Byron Nelson to cut the USC lead to 16–14. The Bruins successfully recovered an on-side kick, and facing a third-and–24 situation from the UCLA 48, everyone knew that a pass was coming, but it could not be stopped. Kurt Altenberg hauled in a Beban pass, scored the winning touchdown, and the Bruins were on their way to the Rose Bowl.[9]

**(H) Nov. 27—Wyoming—56–6**
USC#8

Four days before his final game in a USC uniform, Mike Garrett was named the winner of the Heisman Trophy. With 39,233 at the Coliseum to watch Garrett for the last time as a college player, the star tailback did not disappoint. He ran for 112 yards on 24 carries and three touchdowns. Weeks before this game, Garrett became USC's all-time leading rusher. Against Wyoming, he conquered the entire college football world in that category by surpassing Ollie Matson from the University of San Francisco as the NCAA's all-time rusher. Matson's 15-year record fell to Garrett on the first play of the second quarter, at which time he received a standing ovation from the Coliseum crowd. Garrett was bestowed with two more ovations during this game. The second one came when he came off the field with 2:40 left in the game, and the final ovation was given at the conclusion of the game.

The Trojans also had other offensive stars in this romp over Wyoming. Troy Winslow threw for 320 yards and four touchdowns, David Morton caught five passes for 181 yards and three touchdowns, Rod Sherman had seven receptions for 105 yards and one touchdown, and Tim Rossovich kicked eight extra points.[10]

### Team Leaders

Rushing: Mike Garrett—1,440 yards on 267 carries
Passing: Troy Winslow—78 out of 127 attempts for 1,019 yards and 11 touchdowns
Receiving: Dave Moton—29 catches for 493 yards and 5 touchdowns
Scoring: Mike Garrett—96 points on 16 touchdowns
Kickoff Returns: Mike Hunter—8 for 162 yards (20.3 avg.)
Punt Returns: Mike Garrett—13 for 235 yards and 2 touchdowns (18.1 avg.)
Punting: Gary Fite—37 for 1,369 yards (37.0 avg.)
Interceptions: Phil Lee—4 for 14 yards
Mike Hunter—4 for 2 yards
Tackles: Not available

## *1966*

Head Coach: John McKay
Assistant Coaches: Dick Coury, Craig Fertig, Marv Goux, Rod Humenuik, Phil Krueger, Dave Levy, Joe Margucci, Bill Snyder, Jim Strangeland
Team Captains: Nate Shaw, Rod Sherman
Record: 7–4 overall (4–1 in Athletic Association of Western Universities)
(Ranked 40th best record in college football out of 119 teams)
Finish in Conference: 1st place

FINISH IN NATIONAL POLLS: 18th in UPI
POINTS SCORED PER GAME: 18.1 to rank 50th out of 119 teams
POINTS ALLOWED PER GAME: 11.6 to rank 23rd

## Schedule and Highlights

**(A) Sept. 17—Texas—10–6**
USC#9

The Trojans scored all their points in the first half, and then used a consistent ground attack to take time off the clock in the game's closing minutes to preserve the win. Tim Rossovich scored USC's first points of the new season on a 23-yard field goal, and Troy Winslow ran for a nine-yard touchdown to account for the Trojans' points.[1]

**(H) Sept. 24—Wisconsin—38–3**
USC#5

This night game at the Coliseum marked USC's 400th football victory, and Don McCall ran for 104 yards on 18 carries in this lopsided conquest over the Badgers. The Trojans only held a slim 6–3 lead in the first half on a touchdown pass from Troy Winslow to Ray Cahill. The 12-yard reception was Cahill's first touchdown as member of the USC varsity. A pair of touchdowns by halfback Rod Sherman provided the spark for USC in the third quarter en route to an easy win.[2]

**(N) Oct. 1—Oregon State—21–0**
USC#5

The Trojans remained perfect with Portland's Multnomah Stadium serving as the venue for USC's conference opener. On a rain-drenched field, the Trojan defense allowed only six first downs, and the offense was sparked by Ron Drake's eight receptions for 104 yards. Rod Sherman broke a scoreless tie in the second quarter with an exciting 76-yard scoring jaunt, and he finished the game with 111 yards on the ground. Don McCall ran for 90 yards and a pair of second half touchdowns (two and one yard), and fullback Mike Hull added 82 rushing yards to USC's total.[3]

**(H) Oct. 8—Washington—17–14**
USC#6

Starting quarterback Troy Winslow was injured in the first quarter and replaced with sophomore Steve Sogge. Sogge then took the Trojans on a touchdown drive that was capped off on a 10-yard run by Don McCall, who finished the game with 116 yards on 25 carries. The Huskies battled back to tie the score at 7–7 with 18 seconds left in the first half. With Toby Page now in at quarterback, the Trojans took a 10–7 lead on a 30-yard field goal by Pat Cashman. Washington came right back to take a 14–10 lead. This seesaw struggle had USC regain the lead for good on the second play of the fourth quarter when Page threw a scoring strike from five yards out to Ron Drake. Nate Shaw then secured the victory by intercepting a pass in the end zone with 1:23 remaining.[4]

**(A) Oct. 15—Stanford—21–7**
USC#5

A trip to Palo Alto continued the Trojans on the path to perfection, as they won for the fifth straight time in 1966, and their ninth in a row over Stanford. The Trojan defense pounded Stanford quarterback Chuck Williams, dumping him for 63 yards in losses. The unit also shut down Stanford's running game, allowing it a mere 34 yards on 37 attempts. The Trojans once again had the services of starting quarterback Troy Winslow, and he responded by getting USC into the end zone on the team's opening possession with a touchdown pass to Rod Sherman. The second time USC had possession, they added another six-pointer, this time on a run by Don McCall. They scored their final points in the second quarter after an Ed King interception set the offense up in excellent shape at the Stanford 18. Winslow then tossed his second touchdown pass of the day, on this occasion the scoring honors went to Ron Drake.[5]

**(H) Oct. 22—Clemson—30–0**
USC#5

The Trojans had to do without the services of their leading ground gainer Don McCall, who suffered strained ligaments in the win over Stanford. Rod Sherman provided USC with a solid effort out of the backfield. Not only did Sherman do much of the running, but he also caught five passes for 70 yards, and helped USC compile an incredible 449 yards of offensive production. Mike Battle got things going for USC with a 74-yard punt return in the first quarter. The Trojans' received two more first half touchdowns on runs by Troy Winslow (four yards) and Toby Page (eight yards), to give them an 18–0 halftime advantage. In the second half, Rod Sherman scored on a one-yard run, and Page connected with Bob Klein on a 16-yard scoring strike. The USC defense once again was brilliant, as it prevented Clemson from never getting closer than the Trojan 45.[6]

**(A) Oct. 28—Miami, Fla.—7–10**
USC#5

Perfection for the Trojans was halted after a trip to the "Sunshine State." The fifth-ranked Miami defense clamped down on the Trojans in this tightly contested game. Ray Harris gave the Hurricanes a 3–0 lead on an 18-yard field goal in the second quarter. The Trojans came back to take their only lead of the game when Rod Sherman, who got swarmed by defenders while attempting to run, quickly threw to Ron Drake for a six-yard touchdown. Drake had 10 receptions in the game, and a total of 43 on the year, which set a then-USC single-season record. Pat Cashman's extra point then gave the Trojans a 7–3 halftime advantage. Miami's defense then prevented USC from any more point production. However, the Hurricanes were able to get one final tally against the tough USC defense. Doug McGee ran for a four-yard touchdown on the first play of the fourth quarter to put Miami in the lead for good.[7]

**(H) Nov. 5—California—35–9**
USC#9

The Trojans shook off the effects of their first defeat against the Golden Bears on USC's homecoming weekend. This lopsided victory, coupled with Washington's upset over UCLA, clinched the AAWU championship for the Trojans. Despite the convincing final score, Cal hung close to USC halfway through the third quarter, trailing by only a 14–9 deficit. With injuries to running backs Don McCall and Steve Grady, the Trojans had to move Jim Lawrence from flanker to halfback, and he responded in true Trojan fashion. Lawrence ran for 89 yards on 18 carries, and fullback Mike Hull finished with 94 yards and two touchdown runs. The Trojans scored twice in the first quarter on an eight-yard pass from Troy Winslow to Lawrence, and then Winslow dove over a mass of players from the one. Cal got their lone first half points on a safety, but then a USC fumble and a pass interference penalty gave the Golden Bears the ball on the Trojan four. Duane Mayfield then caught a touchdown pass to pull Cal to within five points off the lead. Lawrence then rambled for a gain of 35 yards to set up a one-yard touchdown run by Hull, and the rout was on. Hull officially secured the victory with a 68-yard scoring run in the early stages of the fourth quarter. Hull's run gave USC a 28–9 lead, and with one second remaining in the game, Wilson Bowie scored the game's final touchdown on a one-yard run.[8]

**(A) Nov. 19—UCLA—7–14**

USC#7 UCLA# 8

Many substitute players have been called upon to rally a team when a star performer is injured. On this occasion, it was quarterback Norm Dow, with virtually no varsity experience that filled in for Gary Beban. The first half was scoreless, with USC controlling the game statistics-wise. Dow was obviously nervous, but by the end of the game, he was the king of Los Angeles. The Bruins scored early in the third quarter when Dow swept the right end behind excellent blocking to complete a seven-play, 42-yard drive with a touchdown from five yards out. The Trojans countered with a one-yard touchdown run from Dan Scott. The game-winner came in the fourth quarter when Cornell Champion scored on a 21-yard run. For the game, Dow ran for 82 yards on 19 carries in what he considered the greatest 60 minutes of his life. In the losing effort, Mike Hull had 148 yards on 14 carries.[9]

**(H) Nov. 26—Notre Dame—0–51**

USC#10 ND#1

No Heisman winners in this year's matchup after Huarte and Garrett, but one common occurrence happened. For the fourth time in the decade, a shutout was recorded, and not in a good way for the Trojans. This was the largest margin of victory ever against USC, and it hurt even worse going through the blowout at home.

The Fighting Irish came into Los Angeles as the number one ranked team in the nation, and proved that status by a 51-point margin of victory. Quarterback Coley O'Brien, who replaced the injured Terry Hanratty, threw for 255 yards on 21 out of 31 pass attempts and three touchdowns. Right from their opening possession, the Irish dominated. They went from their own 20 to paydirt in 16 plays, with Larry Conjar, the star of last year's USC–Notre Dame game, scoring on a two-yard run. Tom Schoen then intercepted a Toby Page pass and went 66 yards to score in the first quarter. Joe Azzaro added both extra points, plus a 38-yard field goal, to make it 17–0. O'Brien then threw two scoring strikes to Jim Seymour from 13 and 39 yards out. Azzaro kicked both extra points, and the Irish were in complete control at the half with a 31–0 lead.

In the third quarter, O'Brien threw his final touchdown pass, this one covering 22 yards to Dan Harshman. Azzaro's conversion upped the score to 38–0, and then Nick Eddy added a run for a nine-yard touchdown to give Notre Dame a 44–0 lead going into the fourth quarter. The slaughter ended with Dave Martin intercepting a pass and returning it 33 yards for Notre Dame's final touchdown. Azzaro converted on the extra point to end the scoring. The Irish went on to finish the year at 9–0–1, and claimed the 1966 national championship, while the Trojans had to wait eleven months for the possibility of redemption.[10]

**Rose Bowl, (N) Jan. 2—Purdue—13–14**

USC #11—Purdue #7

Four years removed from their first national championship under John McKay, the Trojans once again made the 15-mile trek north of the USC campus to the Rose Bowl on New Year's Day. However, unlike four years earlier, when they were ranked #1 and their opponent #2, the Trojans found themselves in what was dubbed "the Runner-up Bowl."

Jack Mollenkopf brought his Purdue Boilermakers to the program's first Rose Bowl after posting an 8–2 overall record and they were 6–1 in the Big Ten. At this time, the Big Ten Conference had a rule that prohibited a team from playing in back-to-back Rose Bowls. Michigan State had won the 1966 Big Ten title with a spotless 7–0 conference record, but could not return to Pasadena because they went the previous season.

USC was also sent to Pasadena under controversial circumstances. Due to a glitch in scheduling, the Trojans played an extra conference game than UCLA. Despite UCLA being 9–1 overall, including a victory over USC, they were 3–1 in the final AAWU standings. The Trojans, however, finished their conference games at 4–1, and were awarded the Rose Bowl berth after a vote by the AAWU's Athletic Directors. It was felt that voting USC into this Rose Bowl was a way to make up for a snub in 1964 when they tied Oregon State for the AAWU title and the Beavers were awarded a berth to the Rose Bowl.

Whatever the reason on how the Trojans and Boilermakers got to Pasadena, they staged an exciting, defensive struggle. There was no scoring in the first quarter, and then both teams got on the board in the second quarter to send the game into halftime deadlocked at 7–7. Purdue, a two-touchdown favorite coming into this game, drew first blood when fullback Perry Williams capped a 16-play, 57-yard drive with a touchdown run covering one yard. Hard-charging halfback Don McCall gave the Trojans their first points of the game on a blast up the middle from one yard out. Williams added his second touchdown run of the game in the third quarter, this one coming from two yards out. Bob Griese added his second conversion kick of the game, and Purdue was up, 14–7, going into the fourth quarter. With 101,455 jammed in to the famed Rose Bowl stadium, the Trojans mounted a drive that ended with Troy Winslow connecting with Rod Sherman from 19 yards out for the touchdown. With 2:28 left, and his team trailing by one, coach John McKay decided to try for the win by going for the two-point conversion instead of kicking the extra point that could have tied it up. Winslow threw a pass in the direction of Jim Lawrence, but Purdue Co-Captain, George Catavolos, came up quickly from his defensive back position to intercept the ball to preserve Purdue's first taste of victory at the Rose Bowl.[11]

### TEAM LEADERS

RUSHING: Don McCall—560 yards on 127 carries

PASSING: Troy Winslow—82 out of 138 attempts for 1,023 yards and 6 touchdowns

RECEIVING: Ron Drake—52 catches for 607 yards and 4 touchdowns

SCORING: Rod Sherman—38 points on 6 touchdowns and a 2-point conversion

KICKOFF RETURNS: Jim Lawrence—15 for 303 yards (25.7 avg.)
PUNT RETURNS: Mike Battle—22 for 219 yards and 1 touchdown (9.8 avg.)
PUNTING: Rich Leon—26 for 991 yards (38.4 avg.)
INTERCEPTIONS: Nate Shaw—5 for 97 yards
TACKLES: Not available

## *1967*

HEAD COACH: John McKay
ASSISTANT COACHES: Dick Coury, Craig Fertig, Marv Goux, Rod Humenuik, Phil Krueger, Dave Levy, Jim Strangeland
TEAM CAPTAINS: Tim Rossovich, Adrian Young
RECORD: 10–1 overall (6–1 in Athletic Association of Western Universities)
(Ranked 1st for best record in college football out of 118 teams)
FINISH IN CONFERENCE: 1st place
FINISH IN NATIONAL POLLS: 1st place in AP and 1st place in UPI
1967 National Champions
POINTS SCORED PER GAME: 23.5 to rank 27th out of 118 teams
POINTS ALLOWED PER GAME: 7.9 to rank 2nd

### Schedule and Highlights

**(H) Sept. 15—Washington State—49–0**
USC#7

The Trojans opened what was described as their toughest schedule with a conference foe, and they quickly established themselves as the team to beat in the AAWU. Fullback Dan Scott scored three touchdowns, Jim Lawrence scored on a 26-yard reverse, Sandy Durko on a 43-yard interception, and Mike Battle returned a punt 32 yards to give the Trojans touchdowns from the offense, defense, and special teams. Earl McCullouch had five receptions for 145 yards, and O.J. Simpson ran for 94 yards on 17 carries in his debut as USC tailback.[1]

**(H) Sept. 23—Texas—17–13**
USC# 4 TEX#5

The Trojans' next opponent was not as easy as their previous one. In this battle with the Longhorns, the Trojans had to come back from a 7–0 first quarter deficit. O.J. Simpson ran for 158 yards on 30 carries, and scored USC's first points of the game on a two-yard run. This was also Simpson's first-ever touchdown for the Trojans. Steve Sogge connected with Bob Miller from seven yards out in the third quarter to give the Trojans control of the game, and Rikki Aldridge added a 30-yard field goal in the fourth quarter to round out USC's point production.[2]

**(A) Sept. 30—Michigan State—21–17**
USC#2

O.J. Simpson ran for 190 yards on 31 carries, and Jim Lawrence caught five passes for 100 yards and scored the go-ahead touchdown in USC's come-from-behind victory. The Trojans got on the board in the first quarter when Simpson scored on an eight-yard run. A fumbled punt by the Trojans was recovered at the USC one and Dwight Lee's touchdown allowed the Spartans to tie the game at 7–7. A one-yard run by Simpson put the Trojans back on top, but Michigan State scored 10 points in the latter stages of the second quarter to take a 17–14 lead in the locker room at halftime. The Trojans received what turned out to be the winning points on an 11-play, 74-yard drive that was capped off with Simpson throwing a seven-yard scoring strike to Lawrence. This win elevated USC into the number one ranking in the nation.[3]

**(H) Oct. 7—Stanford—30–0**
USC#1

With the number one ranking in the nation, the Trojans set out to prove their high standing. O.J. Simpson ran for 160 yards on 29 carries and Earl McCullouch caught seven passes for 122 yards and two touchdowns to spark the offense. Steve Sogge came into this game as the top passer in the AAWU, and continued to impress by connecting on 10 out of 19 pass attempts for 176 and a pair of touchdowns. Mike Battle came through for the defense by getting two interceptions. Fullback Mike Hull was lost for the rest of the season after suffering a knee injury.[4]

**(A) Oct. 14—Notre Dame—24–7**
USC#1 ND#5

After the previous season's blowout loss to Notre Dame, the Trojans were not the favorites coming into the game despite their number one ranking. The odds makers were also concerned about the fact that USC had not won in South Bend since 1939.

With 59,075 on hand for Notre Dame's homecoming festivities, the Trojans exploded for 24 second half points to win in convincing fashion. O.J. Simpson led the offensive attack with 150 yards on 38 carries, and linebacker Adrian Young sparked the defensive unit with a single-game school record four interceptions. His four thefts also tied a conference record, and as a unit, USC intercepted seven passes.

After a scoreless first quarter, Notre Dame was sparked by an interception of their own, deep in USC territory. Steve Sogge had a pass picked off by Jim Smithberger on the USC 19 and returned to the three. On first down, Irish quarterback Terry Hanratty swept around the right side of the line to score. Joe Azzaro added the extra point, and Notre Dame held a slim 7–0 halftime advantage.

During halftime, USC's John McKay made some adjustments that were just what his charges needed. Realizing that the Trojans were having problems throwing against Notre Dame, as well as running the ball between the tackles, McKay called for wider runs. The idea worked, and the Trojans were on their way to victory.

On the kickoff to begin the second half, Notre Dame's Chuck Landolfi fumbled, and Steve Swanson recovered for USC on the 18. Following a run by Steve Sogge, O.J. Simpson carried the ball on six straight plays, with the final one producing a one-yard touchdown. Rikki Aldridge kicked the game-tying extra point, and the Trojans never looked back.

An interception by defensive back Bill Jaroncyk of a Hanratty pass gave the Trojans possession at the Notre Dame 42. Simpson carried for seven yards, and then finished off the drive off on the following play. After taking a pitchout from Sogge, Simpson swept around the left side, and within seconds, was in the end zone to complete a 35-yard touchdown run. Aldridge added the extra point, and the Trojans were in the lead to stay on this sunny Indiana day. The Trojans added three more points in the third quarter on a 22-yard field goal by Aldridge to take USC into the final 15 minutes on top, 17–7.

Defensive back Mike Battle intercepted a Hanratty pass on the USC 47, and returned it to the Notre Dame 17. In all, Hanratty suffered five interceptions, and had a mild concussion in the fourth quarter, which forced him to the sidelines. His replacement, Coley O'Brien, threw an additional two interceptions. After Battle's interception return set the Trojans up nicely, the offense took advantage of the generous gift by scored four plays later on Simpson's third touchdown of the game, this time coming on a one-yard run. Aldridge added the extra point, and for the first time since 1939, the Trojans headed back to the Southland from South Bend victorious.[5]

**(A) Oct. 21—Washington—23–6**

USC#1

The Trojans had to overcome rainy weather conditions and the loss of four fumbles to prevail. They trailed, 7–6, going into the fourth quarter, and then scored 16 points to remain the top-ranked team in the country. O. J. Simpson helped the cause by running for 235 yards on 30 carries and two touchdowns. His first came on an 86-yard run in the opening quarter, and he scored the second six-pointer on the first play of the fourth quarter from 11 yards out. Simpson also threw for USC's final touchdown, a 16-yarder to Earl McCullouch.[6]

**(H) Oct. 28—Oregon—28–6**

USC#1

On USC's homecoming weekend, Steve Grady ran for 108 yards on 18 carries. He also scored his first-ever touchdown as a Trojan on an 11-yard run up the middle. Grady got the call to fill in for O.J. Simpson, who left the game early in the third quarter with an ankle injury. The Trojans received their other touchdowns from Bob Klein (seven-yard pass from Steve Sogge), Dan Scott (one-yard run), and Toby Page (seven-yard run). The Trojan defense played a great game, allowing Oregon only 25 yards and one first down throughout the first half. The unit was so solid that the Ducks were stopped from crossing into USC territory all but one time through three quarters.[7]

**(A) Nov. 4—California—31–12**

USC#1

Steve Grady filled in for O. J. Simpson, who was still nursing a tender ankle. Just like in the previous game, Grady responded with a solid performance by running for 103 yards on 31 carries. Quarterback Steve Sogge threw for three touchdowns, with Earl McCullouch catching two of the scoring strikes. Cal hung tough with the powerful Trojans, only trailing by five points at the start of the fourth quarter. It was then that McCullouch's two touchdown receptions blew the game open.[8]

**(A) Nov. 11—Oregon State—0–3**

USC#1

Played in the rain, O.J. Simpson was not hampered by the elements or a recently injured ankle, as he ran for 188 yards on 33 carries. Unfortunately, the rest of the team could not get going, and Oregon State tied a record with Stanford first set in 1935 as the only two teams to beat the Trojans with the lowest score ever. The lone points in this game came on a Mike Haggard 30-yard field goal with 5:05 remaining in the first half.[9]

**(H) Nov. 18—UCLA—21–20**

USC#4 UCLA# 1

A huge crowd of 90,772 came out to witness what was being called the game of the century. In the end, it truly lived up to its billing. This was also the battle of the arm vs. the legs. Quarterback Gary Beban was the headline grabber for UCLA, while the swift and powerful legs of O.J. Simpson kept the scribes in Los Angeles busy as well. Both were Heisman Trophy hopefuls, and each carried their teams to the brink of a conference title, a Rose Bowl berth, and the possibility of a national championship. All these things were riding on the outcome of this game as kickoff approached.

The Bruins hit paydirt first on a Greg Jones 12-yard run. The Trojans countered their Westwood foes when Pat Cashman intercepted a Beban pass on the USC 45 and returned it for a touchdown. Rikki Aldridge added the extra point to tie the game at 7–7 at the end of the first quarter. Simpson then put the Trojans on top with a run up the middle that covered 13 yards as two defenders hung on him. This showed the true testament of the USC tailback, which was a mixture of speed and power. Simpson's scoring jaunt was set up by Earl McCullough's 52-yard run. Following the conversion kick, USC was up, 14–7, at the end of the first half.

Gary Beban, who would win the Heisman Trophy over Simpson ten days after this game, helped his cause by getting the Bruins even at 14–14 early in the third quarter with a 53-yard pass to George Farmer. Beban then gave UCLA their first lead since the opening quarter when he threw his second scoring strike of the game, this time to Dave Nuttall from 20 yards out. Zenon Andrusyshyn then attempted to add the extra point, but 6'8" defensive end Bill Hayhoe had other ideas. Hayhoe jumped high in the air and blocked the kick, which would prove to play an important role in this game's outcome.

The Bruins only had one minute to enjoy holding a 20–14 lead. From the USC 36, facing a third-and-seven situation, with 10:38 left in the fourth quarter, Simpson took a handoff and ran around the left side of the line. His sprinter's speed allowed him to break free, and he cut back to the middle of the field at about the UCLA 40. With Earl McCullough warding off potential defenders, Simpson made his way to paydirt untouched. This 64-yard dash to the end zone quickly became one of the most famous runs in college football history, and tied the game at 20–20. Rikki Aldridge then sent the ball over the crossbar to give the Trojans what proved to be the game-winning point. For the game, Simpson ran for 177 yards on 30 carries. Following Simpson's run to immortality, the Trojan defense took over, stopping Bruins three times in the closing minutes, and they also blocked two field goal attempts.[10]

**Rose Bowl, (N) Jan. 1—Indiana—14–3**

The previous Rose Bowl was considered a runner-up bowl, but one year later, the Trojans left no doubt that they belonged in the 1968 edition of the "Granddaddy of Them All." Ranked #1 in both the AP and Coaches Poll, a victory in this game would assure USC of their second national championship in five years. They would be facing the 9–1 Indiana Hoosiers under head coach John Pont, in what would prove to be the team's only trip to the Rose Bowl.

After halting Indiana on the game's opening series, the Trojans established their presence early by scoring the first time the offense had possession. Covering 84 yards in 13 plays, college football's leading ground gainer in 1967, O.J. Simpson, capped the drive off with a two-yard run. The Hoosiers got on the board for the only time in the second quarter on a Dave Kornowa 27-yard field goal to make it a close 7–3 USC advantage at the half. Indiana was playing tough despite being a two-touchdown underdog coming into this game. However, in the end, the Trojans had O.J. Simpson to pound the defense, and he accomplished just that, eventually wearing Indiana down. He carried the ball 25 times for 128 yards, and added another touchdown run that covered eight yards in the third quarter. For his efforts, Simpson was selected as the game's MVP, and the Trojans were crowned 1967 national champions.[11]

### Team Leaders

RUSHING: O.J. Simpson—1,543 yards on 291 carries
PASSING: Steve Sogge—75 out of 151 attempts for 1,032 yards and 7 touchdowns
RECEIVING: Earl McCullouch—30 catches for 540 yards and 5 touchdowns
SCORING: O.J. Simpson—78 points on 13 touchdowns
KICKOFF RETURNS: O.J. Simpson—8 for 204 yards (25.5 avg.)
PUNT RETURNS: Mike Battle—49 for 608 yards and 2 touchdowns (12.4 avg.)
PUNTING: Rikki Aldridge—54 for 1,858 yards (34.4 avg.)
INTERCEPTIONS: Mike Battle—5 for 87 yards
TACKLES: Not available

## *1968*

HEAD COACH: John McKay
ASSISTANT COACHES: Willie F. Brown, Dick Coury, Craig Fertig, Marv Goux, Rod Humenuik, Phil Krueger, Dave Levy
TEAM CAPTAINS: O.J. Simpson, Steve Sogge
RECORD: 9–1–1 overall (6–0 in Pacific–8 Conference)
(Ranked 7th best record in college football out of 119 teams)
FINISH IN CONFERENCE: 1st place
FINISH IN NATIONAL POLLS: 4th place in AP and 2nd place in UPI
POINTS SCORED PER GAME: 23.5 to rank 43rd out of 119 teams
POINTS ALLOWED PER GAME: 15.3 to rank 22nd

### Schedule and Highlights

**(A) Sept. 21—Minnesota—29–20**
USC#2 Minn#16

The Trojans scored two touchdowns in the last four minutes to pull out the win. O.J. Simpson ran for 236 yards on 39 carries, and tied a school record with four rushing touchdowns. Two his four six-pointers came in USC's fourth quarter rally. Simpson also caught six passes for 57 yards, and had three kickoff returns for 72 yards to give him an incredible total of 365 yards of offense. This performance secured Simpson's top spot in the 1968 Heisman Trophy race. Minnesota got out to a 10–0 lead in the first quarter, but the defending national champion Trojans rallied back to tie the game at 13–13 by halftime. They once again trailed, this time by a 20–13 count with eight minutes left. It was then that Simpson added two of his four six-pointers and Ron Ayala kicked a field goal to pull out this season opening victory.[1]

**(A) Sept. 28—Northwestern—24–7**
USC#3

O.J. Simpson ran for 189 yards on 34 carries and scored three touchdowns, giving him seven after only two games. Even though the young Trojan defense gave up 393 yards of offense, the unit got tough whenever Northwestern threatened to score. The only time the Wildcats were able to cross the goal line came in the fourth quarter with USC in control at 17–0.[2]

**(H) Oct. 5—Miami, Fla.—28–3**
USC#2 MIA#13

This was supposed to be a classic showdown between Miami's All-American linebacker Ted Hendricks and USC's All-American runner. However, the epic clash never came to be, as O.J. Simpson ran for 163 yards on 38 carries, outgaining the entire Miami offense in the process. He scored a pair of touchdowns on runs covering one and three yards. Steve Sogge, who completed 11 of 17 pass attempts for 136 yards, threw USC's first scoring strike of the season, a 28-yarder to Jim Lawrence. This was also the first Trojan six-pointer not scored by Simpson. A four-yard pass from Mike Holmgren to Bob Chandler completed the scoring for USC. The Trojan defense played strong as a unit, allowing just 116 yards of total offense.[3]

**(A) Oct. 12—Stanford—27–24**
USC#2 STAN#18

USC won its first-ever PAC-8 game with 11:51 left. Stanford, in an effort to downplay the incredible talent of their rival, painted "Squeeze O.J." and "O.J. Who?" on their helmets. The intimidation effect did nothing to stop O.J. Simpson, as he ran for 220 yards on 47 carries and three touchdowns. Steve Sogge threw for 153 yards, with Jim Lawrence gaining 121 of those yards on four receptions to help USC's cause. Ron Ayala added a pair of field goals to round out the Trojans' scoring.[4]

**(H) Oct. 19—Washington—14–7**
USC#1

O.J. Simpson ran for 172 yards on 33 carries, and scored the go-ahead touchdown in the fourth quarter. On the winning drive, Simpson was the workhorse, carrying the ball seven times for 57 yards. Bob Klein chipped in on the winning drive with two receptions that gained 14 and 23 yards. Late in the game, Washington drove down to the goal line, but was stopped from getting in for the score. The Trojans then mounted an 11-play drive to victory, with Simpson scoring from nine yards out. He also scored USC's other touchdown.[5]

**(A) Nov. 2—Oregon—20–13**
USC#1

The Trojans played this one in the rain of the Great Northwest, and had to go the distance to pull out a victory that kept their top spot in the national ranking intact. The Ducks came into this game on a three-game winning streak after dropping their first three. They were looking to finally get over the .500 mark, and performed very well in an attempt to achieve that goal. They limited O.J. Simpson to 67 yards on 25 carries for his worst day running the ball as a Trojan. The Ducks also outgained USC in total offensive yards by a 359 to 196 margin.

On this occasion, the heroics went to quarterback Steve Sogge, who guided the Trojans 62 yards in the closing minutes to pull out the win. With 1:12 left on the clock, Sogge threw a three-yard touchdown pass to Bob Klein for the game-winner. The Trojans got out to a 13–0 lead by the third quarter. Steve Sogge connected with his favorite receiver, Jim Lawrence, on a nine-yard scoring strike in the first quarter, and O.J. Simpson added his 15th touchdown of the season in the third quarter on a one-yard run. Lawrence later suffered a broken clavicle. Oregon then stormed back to tie after taking advantage of an interception and a fumbled kickoff return by the Trojans. It was then that Sogge directed USC to their winning points. On the defensive side of the ball, the Trojans had a big game from lineman Bill Redding, who got in on 16 tackles.[6]

**(H) Nov. 9—California—35–17**

USC#1 CAL#11

With 80,871 looking on at the Coliseum on homecoming weekend, the Trojans turned in a well-balanced offensive attack that gained 430 total yards, and no late game heroics were needed to pull out the win. O.J. Simpson ran for 164 yards on 31 carries and two touchdowns, Steve Sogge threw three touchdown passes, and Bob Chandler caught eight passes for 115 yards and one touchdown against the 5–1–1 Golden Bears. Simpson scored on runs of 39 and seven yards for his 16th and 17th six-pointers of the season. Sogge's scoring strikes went to Bob Klein (four yards), Sam Dickerson (28 yards), and to the sophomore Bob Chandler (10 yards), who played a great game in place of the injured Jim Lawrence.[7]

**(H) Nov. 16—Oregon State—17–13**

USC#1 OSU#13

The Trojans play in a town where the film industry has produced its share of dramatic motion pictures. The 1968 version of the Trojans lived up to Hollywood's dramatic standards by once again pulling out another close victory to earn the moniker of the Cardiac Kids. O.J. Simpson ran for 238 yards on 47 carries, and set a school record with 20 carries in one quarter, with them coming in the fourth quarter. All of USC's points were scored in the fourth quarter, and this come-from-behind win clinched the Pac-8 championship for USC.

The Trojans trailed, 7–0, at the end of the third quarter, and then a Gerry Shaw interception gave USC the ball at the Oregon State 29, and this proved to be the spark the Cardinal & Gold needed. A few plays later, Steve Sogge threw a 22-yard scoring strike to Terry DeKraai that tied the game. Ron Ayala then kicked a 17-yard field goal to give the Trojans a 10–7 lead. A Sandy Durko interception gave the ball back to USC, and Simpson carried four straight times, with the final carry going for a 40-yard touchdown with 1:20 remaining.[8]

**(A) Nov. 23—UCLA—28–16**

USC#1

Within three days after this game, O.J. Simpson became the newly crowned Heisman Trophy winner. His performance against UCLA left no doubt that the coveted prize was presented to the correct player. En route to breaking the single-season NCAA rushing record, Simpson hauled the ball 40 times through Bruin defenders for 205 yards and three touchdowns on a day that combined smog and fog in the air.

Despite Simpson's great day, the Trojans had a struggle on their hands late in the game. Holding on to a slim 21–16 lead in the fourth quarter, the Bruins drove from their own 25 to the USC one-yard line with time ticking down. With thoughts of upsetting the top-ranked team in the country, UCLA definitely had the nation's attention as quarterback Jim Nader looked to the end zone with a pass attempt. However, the wet turf caused him to slip and he was downed at the three. Finally, on fourth down, USC linebacker Bob Jensen batted a pass attempt away from a potential receiver and the Trojans took over on downs. It was then Simpson's time to eat up the clock and Coliseum real estate on his way to victory and the Heisman. He got the call on virtually every play, and made the most of his chances, tearing up big chunks of yardage until he capped the possession off with a four-yard touchdown burst to put another classic USC-UCLA clash into the history books.[9]

**(H) Nov. 30—Notre Dame—21–21**

USC#2 ND#9

Two years earlier, Notre dame came in to the Coliseum and destroyed USC, handing them a 51–0 beat down that was the worst defeat in the program's history. It seemed that the Irish were looking to spoil the day for their hosts from the Southland, but not before the Trojans struck first.

With just 40 seconds expired in the opening quarter, Joe Theismann had a pass intercepted by defensive back Sandy Durko and returned it 21 yards for the game's initial points. Vic Ayala's conversion was good, and USC was quickly up, 7–0. The Fighting Irish then roared back with 21 straight points to claim a 21–7 halftime advantage. They accomplished this by first tying the game on a three-yard run by Ron Dushney, and a Scott Hempel conversion. They then took the lead on a swift four-play, 77-yard drive that was capped off by Bob Gladieux's 57-yard run and Hempel's extra point. The third Notre Dame score was set up after the Irish got good field position on a punt from the end zone. Starting on the USC 45, the Irish were in the end zone six plays later thanks to a trick play. From the USC 13, Theismann tossed a pitchout to Coley O'Brien. The swift halfback then faked a run to the right, and threw the ball back to Theismann. The sophomore quarterback turned receiver for this play, and caught the ball on the run for a touchdown with 30 seconds left in the first half. Hempel's extra point sent the teams into the locker room for the halftime festivities with the visitors up, 21–7. During that first half, the Irish rolled up a whopping 324 yards of offense while holding USC's star tailback O.J. Simpson to a mere 23 rushing yards.

The Trojans began the climb back after taking the second half kickoff out to their 35-yard line. On the 14th play of the drive, Simpson bolted into the end zone from one yard out, and Ayala's extra point brought the defending national champion Trojans to within seven points of a tie heading into the final quarter. With 10:14 remaining on the clock, Steve Sogge connected on a 40-yard scoring strike to Sam Dickerson, and Ayala's all-important conversion kick sailed through the uprights to bring the first game in this series to end in a tie to a climax. The Irish did have a chance to pull a win out, but Hempel sent a 33-yard field goal wide with 33 seconds left.[10]

**Rose Bowl, (N) Jan. 1—Ohio State—16–27**

The Trojans came into this game attempting to be the first team to win unanimous back-to-back national championships since the Oklahoma Sooners in 1955 and 1956. The Alabama Crimson Tide won in 1964, and then split the championship with Michigan State in 1965. This game was also the second time that the #1 team in the country (Ohio State) faced #2 in the Rose Bowl for the right to claim college football's grand prize. One final piece of trivia regarding this matchup was it marked the first time since the Big Ten/PCC-AAWU-Pac-8 Rose Bowl alliance that both teams came in unbeaten.

The Buckeyes under legendary head coach Woody Hayes were a spotless 9–0 with a group of talented players called "the Super Sophomores." This group consisted of John Brockington, Leo Hayden, Jim Otis, Jim Stillwagon, and Jack Tatum. They would be opposing the defending national champions led by Heisman Trophy winner O.J. Simpson. The Trojans were the #1 ranked team in the country since October 19, but their tie with Notre Dame allowed Ohio State to top them.

This great matchup kicked off college football's 100th anniversary. It first appeared that USC was going to kick off college football's anniversary in fine fashion, as they jumped out to a 10–0 lead in the second quarter. With a crowd of 102,063 in the stands, and Curt Gowdy and Kyle Rote calling the action for a national television audience, Ron Ayala sent a 21-yard field goal through the uprights to break a scoreless tie in the second quarter. Simpson, who finished the day with 171 yards on 28 carries, then electrified the Trojan faithful by tearing through the Buckeye defense for an 80-yard touchdown run. He also caught eight passes for an additional 85 yards.

The Buckeyes remained focused, and removed the zero next to their name when punishing fullback Jim Otis plunged over from one yard out to help cut the USC deficit to 10–7. The Scarlet & Gray then knotted the game at 10–10 with three seconds left in the first half on a 26-yard field by Jim Roman. The teams remained deadlocked until Roman kicked a 25-yard field with 1:40 left in the third quarter to give the Buckeyes their first lead of the game. The opening minutes of the fourth quarter saw Ohio State expand their lead to ten points when Rex Kern threw a four-yard touchdown to Leo Hayden. Ohio State then took total control of the game when Kern threw his second scoring strike of the game, this time to Ray Gillian from 16 yards out. This made the score 27–10 with ten minutes left, but the Trojans suffered through numerous costly turnovers during the game, and could not gain any ground on a determined Ohio State team. The Trojans managed to cut the Buckeyes' advantage to 27–16 on a Steve Sogge to Sam Dickerson 19-yard pass, but it came with only 45 seconds remaining.[11]

### TEAM LEADERS

RUSHING: O.J. Simpson—1,880 yards on 383 carries
PASSING: Steve Sogge—122 out of 207 attempts for 1,454 yards and 9 touchdowns
RECEIVING: Jim Lawrence—26 catches for 386 yards and 2 touchdowns
O. J. Simpson—26 catches for 211 yards
SCORING: O.J. Simpson—138 points on 23 touchdowns
KICKOFF RETURNS: Bob Chandler—12 for 234 yards (19.5 avg.)
PUNT RETURNS: Mike Battle—32 for 230 yards (7.2 avg.)
PUNTING: John Young—39 for 1,500 yards (38.4 avg.)
INTERCEPTIONS: Gerry Shaw—6 for 37 yards
TACKLES: Not available

## *1969*

HEAD COACH: John McKay
ASSISTANT COACHES: Willie F. Brown, Larry Bryan, Craig Fertig, Joe Gibbs, Marv Goux, Rod Humenuik, Phil Krueger, Dave Levy
TEAM CAPTAINS: Jim Gunn, Bob Jensen
RECORD: 10–0–1 overall (6–0 in Pacific–8 Conference)
(Ranked 5th best record in college football out of 122 teams)
FINISH IN CONFERENCE: 1st place
FINISH IN NATIONAL POLLS: 3rd place in AP and 4th place in UPI
POINTS SCORED PER GAME: 23.7 to rank 42nd out of 122 teams
POINTS ALLOWED PER GAME: 11.6 to rank 13th

### Schedule and Highlights

**(A) Sept. 20—Nebraska—31–21**
USC#5

Led by sophomore quarterback Jimmy Jones, and junior tailback Clarence Davis, the Trojans started off the final season of the decade in good shape. Jones threw for two touchdowns, and Davis ran for 114 yards on 27 carries, to take a commanding 28–7 led into the fourth quarter. Mike Berry scored a pair of touchdowns, and Charlie Evans (four yards) and Bob Chandler (45 yards), were on the receiving end of Jones' touchdown passes. Nebraska attempted a comeback in the final six minutes, but a John Young interception thwarted any hopes of that. Following the turnover, Ron Ayala put the game out of reach with a 34-yard field goal. In addition to Young's interception, USC's "Wild Bunch" defense got big games from Greg Slough and Tyrone Hudson, who each made seven tackles, and All-American Jimmy Gunn recorded three tackles behind the line of scrimmage. This marked the beginning of college football's 100th season, and the 10th for the coaching reign of John McKay at USC.[1]

**(H) Sept. 27—Northwestern—48–6**
USC#5

Clarence Davis ran for 165 yards on 21 carries, and the Trojans finished with 462 yards of total offense in this romp over Northwestern in USC's home opener. Davis set the tone early on by running 73 yards for a touchdown on USC's first play from scrimmage. He also added a 10-yard scoring jaunt to his day's work. Jimmy Jones threw an 11-yard touchdown pass to Bob Chandler to give the Trojans a 20–0 halftime lead. Jones left the game in the third quarter with a minor arm injury after completing six of 16 pass attempts for 81 yards. Jim Fassel replaced Jones, and on his first-ever pass for USC, he connected with Sam Dickerson for a 27-yard touchdown. Fassel threw a second touchdown pass, this time an eight-yarder to Terry DeKraai. Lou Harris scored on a 25-yard run, and for the game, the USC backfield of Davis, Harris, and Mike Berry, amassed 287 rushing yards.[2]

**(A) Oct. 4—Oregon State—31–7**
USC#5

The Trojans opened their Pac-8 schedule with another convincing win. They trailed by a 7–0 score early on, and clung to a 10–7 lead at the half. After the Beavers' lone points were scored, the "Wild Bunch" defense shut the offense down, limiting it to only two drives that crossed midfield for the rest of the game. Linebacker Bob Jensen provided the spark for the defense with seven tackles. The Trojans' offense took advantage of the tough defense applied by the "Wild Bunch," and then exploded for three touchdowns in the second half to win easily. Clarence Davis led the offensive attack with 181 yards on 29 carries and one touchdown. The trio of Davis, Lou Harris, and

Mike Berry, once again ran over the opposition, this time for 247 yards. Jimmy Jones was back at the helm of the offense, and threw for three touchdowns. On the receiving end of Jones' scoring strikes were Terry DeKraai (12 yards), Sam Dickerson (27 yards), and Gary Orcutt (18 yards). Ron Ayala added a 21-yard field goal to USC's point production.[3]

**(H) Oct. 11—Stanford—26–24**
USC#4 STAN#16

Under the lights at the Coliseum, the Trojans had to battle to the end to remain perfect on the year. Trailing by one point, Ron Ayala sent a 34-yard field goal through the uprights with no time left in the game to secure this thrilling victory for USC. Clarence Davis was once again the offensive star, as the junior tailback ran for 198 yards on 39 carries.

Stanford, led by quarterback Jim Plunkett, who threw for 296 yards against the "Wild Bunch" defense, jumped out to a 12–0 lead. The Trojans rallied back to take a 13–12 lead on a Mike Berry four-yard run, and a 57-yard interception return by Tyrone Hudson. The lead then changed hands six times. A Ron Ayala 30-yard field goal gave USC a 23–21 lead until Steve Horowitz connected on a three-pointer with 66 seconds left to play to give Stanford a 24–23 lead. The Trojans then had 85 yards to go with only 55 seconds left. On fourth down, Davis kept the drive alive with a gain of seven. Jimmy Jones then threw to Gerry Mullins for 28 yards, Sam Dickerson for 17, and once again to Mullins at the 17. Mullins did not get out of bounds to stop the clock, but he did get a first down, at which time the clock is stopped to move the down markers. It was then that Ayala came on the field with five seconds left, and kicked the game-winning field goal that kept USC undefeated.[4]

**(A) Oct. 18—Notre Dame—14–14**
USC#3 ND#11

It took 40 meetings between these teams to produce the first-ever tie one year earlier. It only took 11 months to duplicate the feat. In their previous meeting, it was USC that forced a tie in the fourth quarter. This time out, Notre Dame returned the favor with 6:51 left.

The first half was a defensive struggle, and ended in a scoreless tie. The Trojans had three serious opportunities to score in the first half. They got deep into Notre Dame, only to fumble on the seven-yard line, Ron Ayala missed a 35-yard field goal, and a Clarence Davis touchdown run was taken away due a holding penalty. On the other side, USC's famed Wild Bunch defense smothered the Irish offensive attack, allowing them a mere 35 yards and two first downs.

The Irish managed to get going against the Wild Bunch by getting on the scoreboard first. An 11-play, 74-yard drive ended when Bill Barz ran for a one-yard touchdown and Scott Hempel kicked the extra point. The Trojans evened the count in the third quarter after traveling 75 yards in 11 plays. A Jimmy Jones pass covering 19 yards was caught by Terry DeKraai for the six-pointer, and Ayala's conversion brought the game to a 7–7 deadlock.

The Trojans got a big turnover when Tyrone Hudson intercepted a Joe Theismann pass in the fourth quarter. He picked it off at the Notre Dame 40, and made his way to the 15 before being stopped. Jones then added his second touchdown pass of the game, this time from 14 yards out to Sam Dickerson, and Ayala's extra point gave USC a 14–7 advantage. The Irish came back with a turnover that led to the tying points with eight minutes left in the game. Mike McCoy blocked a punt and Walt Patulski recovered on the USC seven. On fourth down, Denny Allan scored from the one, and Hempel kicked the all-important extra point that ended the game in the series' second straight tie.[5]

**(H) Oct. 25—Georgia Tech—29–18**
USC#7

The Trojans made their homecoming game a thrilling affair by coming back with two late touchdowns to remain undefeated. Trailing, 18–15, in the fourth quarter, USC scored the go-ahead touchdown on a 55-yard pass from Jimmy Jones to Sam Dickerson. The Trojans recovered a fumble on the ensuing kickoff, and converted it into an insurance touchdown when Clarence Davis ran it in from nine yards out with three minutes left to play.[6]

**(A) Nov. 1—California—14–9**
USC#6

In another nail-biting finish, the Trojans overcame a 6–0 deficit going into the fourth quarter. A fumble recovery on a punt return sparked USC, and they converted the turnover into six points on a four-yard run by Mike Berry. Ron Ayala then added the go-ahead point with the conversion kick. With 6:47 remaining, Cal reclaimed the lead on a 30-yard field goal from Randy Wersching. The Trojans then pulled the win out with 57 seconds left on a one-yard run by Clarence Davis, who finished the game with 132 yards on 34 carries.[7]

**(H) Nov. 8—Washington State—28–7**
USC#6

The Trojans blew open a tight game that saw them hold a 14–7 lead going into the second half. Quarterback Jimmy Jones then ran for two touchdowns in the second half to give the Trojans an easy win and send Washington State down in defeat for the seventh straight time in the season. Clarence Davis powered the offensive attack with 196 yards rushing on 34 carries and one touchdown.[8]

**(A) Nov. 15—Washington—16–7**
USC#6

The Huskies were looking for their first win of the year, and played a very inspired brand of defense that contained the highly respected USC ground game. The game was tied at 7–7 in the fourth quarter. Ron Ayala broke the deadlocked with a 31-yard field goal that was set up when the Trojan defense recovered a fumble. Clarence Davis added a three-yard touchdown run later in the quarter to give USC some insurance.[9]

**(H) Nov. 22—UCLA—14–12**
USC#5 UCLA#6

Once again this rivalry would not only provide bragging rights in Los Angeles, but crown the conference champion as well. Both teams entered the game highly ranked and at 8–0–1, and it became another classic in this great series.

With a crowd of 90,814 packed into the Coliseum, the Bruins struck first in the opening minutes of the first quarter. After taking a handoff from Dennis Dummit, halfback Greg Jones threw an option pass to George Farmer that covered 41 yards and a touchdown. A two-point conversion pass failed, and

UCLA was up, 6–0. The Trojans came back to tie it on a 13-yard scoring run by Clarence Davis, and Ron Ayala's extra point kick put USC up by the slimmest of margins, 7–6, at the end of the first half.

That score held up until the fourth quarter. Throughout this game, UCLA quarterback Dennis Dummit was consistently hounded and pounded by USC's famed Wild Bunch defense. Dummit was a gifted quarterback ranked in the upper echelon among college football's signal callers during the season. Despite immense pressure from the Wild Bunch, which as a unit sacked him ten times, he still managed to throw for 253 yards. Even though battered and weary from a long afternoon of attempted escapes from such a tenacious defense, Dummit led the Bruins to the go-ahead touchdown with three minutes left in the game. He finished the drive off with a seven-yard toss to Gwen Cooper that gave UCLA a 12–7 advantage, but a second attempt at a two-point conversion failed, and the Trojans looked to capitalize on their rivals' misfortune.

Jimmy Jones, Dummit's adversary, was having a tough time completing passes. At one point in the game, he completed one pass out of 14 attempts for one yard. Despite his lethargic showing, he did not want to succumb to defeat at the hands of his cross-town rival. He connected for three first downs that got the ball to the UCLA 43, but the Trojans soon failed on fourth down to keep the drive alive. It appeared that the conference crown was going to reside in Westwood within a short time. However, a penalty flag was thrown and it changed everything. The Bruins were called for pass interference on USC receiver Sam Dickerson as he was hit from behind while attempting to catch a pass. The ball was advanced to the UCLA 32 after the penalty yardage was tacked on, and the Trojans had a new set of downs.

Jones struck quickly after the Trojans' good fortune. He called for a 64-X Post Corner, which was a successful play throughout the year to Dickerson. Dickerson ran the corner route, and Jones let the ball fly while a pass rush was converging on him. The result was a 32-yard scoring strike with 1:32 remaining in the game that gave the Trojans the lead, and eventually another conference title.[10]

**Rose Bowl, (N) Jan. 1—Michigan—10–3**

USC#5 MICH#7

Like Fielding Yost and Fritz Crisler, Bo Schembechler's name is forever linked to the legends that patrolled the sidelines for the Michigan Wolverines. Schembechler made an immediate statement en route to his legacy by becoming the first head coach since Bennie Oosterbaan in 1948 to guide the Maize and Blue to a conference championship in his first season at the helm. However, Schembechler never got to patrol the sidelines in this Rose Bowl because he suffered a heart attack the night prior to the game, thus leaving the coaching responsibilities in the hands of defensive coordinator Jim Young. The Wolverines also suffered a blow when their leading rusher, Glenn Doughty, damaged his knee while practicing for the game and had to have surgery.

On the other side, the Trojans and the Rose Bowl were becoming old friends, as the Cardinal & Gold made their fourth straight trip to Pasadena to do battle with a Big Ten foe on New Year's Day. The Trojans got on the board first with a 25-yard field goal by Ron Ayala in the opening quarter. Michigan, despite their problems before the game, managed to stay close to USC, and tied the game at 3–3 by halftime on a Tim Killian 20-yard field goal.

The famed "Wild Bunch" defensive unit of USC took over, and lived up to their moniker as a tough unit that did not allow much real estate to be taken from them. The defensive front, consisting of Jimmy Gunn, Tody Smith, Charlie Weaver, and Al Cowlings, made this trip to Pasadena a miserable experience for Michigan's offense. They hounded and punished the Wolverines throughout the tightly contested game, and came up with a big play that eventually led to a USC victory. Defensive back Sandy Durko intercepted a pass, and that allowed the Trojans to score what became the winning points. On the drive following Durko's theft, quarterback Jimmy Jones connected with receiver Bob Chandler on third-and six from the Michigan 33. Chandler caught the ball on the 20, and after breaking multiple tackles, made his way into the end zone. Ayala added the extra point, and the famed USC defense did the rest to preserve another Rose Bowl success story for the Land of Troy.

The Wolverines were stopped on three drives after getting into USC territory in fourth quarter, and when the clock struck 0:00, they went back to Michigan with their first bowl game defeat in the history of the program. Bob Chandler was chosen the game's MVP after catching three passes for 78 yards, including the only touchdown scored in this contest. Clarence Davis led the Trojan ground attack, and all ball carriers, with 76 yards on 15 carries.[11]

### TEAM LEADERS

RUSHING: Clarence Davis—1,351 yards on 297 carries
PASSING: Jimmy Jones—88 out of 209 attempts for 1,220 yards and 13 touchdowns
RECEIVING: Sam Dickerson—24 catches for 473 yards and 6 touchdowns
SCORING: Clarence Davis—54 points on 9 touchdowns
KICKOFF RETURNS: Lou Harris—11 for 230 yards (20.9 avg.)
PUNT RETURNS: Sandy Durko—31 for 251 yards (8.1 avg.)
PUNTING: John Young—42 for 1,625 yards (38.7 avg.)
INTERCEPTIONS: Tyrone Hudson—6 for 129 yards and 1 touchdown
TACKLES: Greg Slough—93

## *1970*

HEAD COACH: John McKay
ASSISTANT COACHES: Willie F. Brown, Craig Fertig, Joe Gibbs, Marv Goux, Hudson Houck, Rod Humenuik, Phil Krueger, Dave Levy, Al Saunders, Pete Yoder
TEAM CAPTAINS: Charlie Weaver, Bob Chandler
RECORD: 6–4–1 overall (3–4 in Pacific–8 Conference)
(Ranked 48th best record in college football out of 123 teams)
FINISH IN CONFERENCE: Tied for 6th
FINISH IN NATIONAL POLLS: 15th place in AP and 19th in UPI
POINTS SCORED PER GAME: 31.2 to rank 11th out of 123 teams
POINTS ALLOWED PER GAME: 21.2 to rank 59th

### Schedule and Highlights

**(N) Sept. 12—Alabama—42–21**

USC#3 ALA#16

In a night game played at Legion Field in Birmingham, Alabama, this was regarded for more than just another USC victory. It was played with the Trojans sporting numerous African-American players against an all-white Alabama team, deep in the heart of Dixie. With Sam Cunningham, Clarence Davis, and Jimmy Jones standing out in the victory, it convinced Alabama coaching icon Paul "Bear" Bryant that recruiting African-Americans could only improve his team, and also give many players an opportunity to obtain a scholarship and get an education. Cunningham ran for 135 yards on just 12 carries and two touchdowns. Bryant was so impressed with Cunningham's performance that he invited the sophomore powerhouse runner into the Alabama locker room following the game. He then introduced Cunningham to his players by stating that this is what a football player looks like.[1]

**(H) Sept. 19—Nebraska—21–21**
USC#3 NEB#9

Under the lights at the Coliseum, the Trojans tied up the game up with 6:44 left. Clarence Davis led the USC ground attack with 116 yards on 27 carries.[2]

**(A) Sept. 26—Iowa—48–0**
USC#7

Clarence Davis ran for 151 yards on 17 carries in less than one half. Sam Cunningham added 87 yards on seven carries, and Lou Harris ran for 80 yards on eight carries, as the Trojans compiled a whopping 660 yards of offense. Jimmy Jones completed eight of 12 pass attempts for 91 yards, threw for one score and ran for two more. The Trojans got out to a 7–0 lead in the first quarter, and then scored all four times they had the ball in the second quarter to put the game away.[3]

**(H) Oct. 3—Oregon State—45–13**
USC#5

In USC's conference opener, Jimmy Jones lit up the night skies of Los Angeles with 304 yards passing and three touchdowns. He also ran for one score. The Trojan backfield as a unit ran for 207 yards, and the "Wrecking Crew" defense held the Beavers to an average of three yards per play, and only 17 yards on the ground.[4]

**(A) Oct. 10—Stanford—14–24**
USC#4 STAN#12

Stanford handed the Trojans their first defeat of the season despite some great individual performances by USC players. Clarence Davis ran for 131 yards on 34 carries, Jimmy Jones passed for 277 yards and one touchdown, and Bob Chandler had eight receptions for 106 yards and one touchdown.[5]

**(H) Oct. 17—Washington—28–25**
USC#11

With a minimum of six kickoff returns required, the Trojans set a team and NCAA record by averaging 46.2 yards per return. Bob Chandler had six receptions for 124 yards.[6]

**(A) Oct. 24—Oregon—7–10**
USC#10

On a rainy day, the underdog Ducks beat USC with 13:05 remaining in the game. The Trojans took the opening kickoff and went 59 yards in 14 plays, 13 of which were on the ground. They scored a touchdown and that was all the point production for USC on this day.[7]

**(H) Oct. 31—California—10–13**
USC#18

Cal spoiled USC's homecoming by scoring the winning points with 4:59 left. A 46-yard field goal by Randy Wersching proved to be the deciding factor. Jimmy Jones had 208 yards through the air and one touchdown in the defeat. Clarence Davis scored USC's lone touchdown after taking a short pass from Jones and running 76 yards to paydirt. On two other occasions, the Trojans got to the Cal one-yard line but could not score. The Trojan defense intercepted five passes, with Ron Ayala accounting for two of the thefts.[8]

**(N) Nov. 7—Washington State—70–33**

Played at Joe Albi Stadium in Spokane, Washington, the Trojan tandem of Clarence Davis and Rod McNeill helped in the dismantling of Washington State, who went down in defeat for the seventh straight time in the season. Davis ran for 118 yards on nine carries, and McNeill had 113 yards on 11 carries. Offense was the fashion of the day, as USC finished with 603 yards, 429 of which were on the ground, and the Cougars ended up with 530 yards.[9]

**(A) Nov. 21—UCLA—20–45**

After losing the three previous meetings with USC, the Bruins came out fast and furious. They ripped off 24 points in the first quarter on a pair of Dennis Dummit touchdown tosses, a Marv Kendricks run, and a Cayton Record field goal. The Trojans kept it close in the opening stanza on a Jimmy Jones to Sam Dickerson touchdown pass that covered 51 yards, and a one-yard run by Clarence Davis. For the game, Dickerson had four receptions for 134 yards. Jones added a six-yard run in the third quarter to finish out USC's scoring, and threw for 219 yards on the day. His counterpart, Dummit, who completed 19 of 30 pass attempts for 272 yards, added his third scoring strike of the game in the second quarter, and a Randy Tyler one-yard run virtually had the game won for the Bruins at the half, as they were up by a commanding 38–14 advantage. Dummit also broke Gary Beban's school passing records for both season and career. Marv Kendricks added a 20-yard touchdown run to complete UCLA's scoring barrage, and he also established a new single-game school record with 182 rushing yards. As a team, the Bruins tied a record with 32 first downs, which was the most recorded against a USC squad. This was also the most points scored by the Bruins against the Trojans up to this time in this series' history.[10]

**(H) Nov. 28—Notre Dame—38–28**
ND#4

Notre Dame, and their senior All-American quarterback Joe Theismann, set records against the Trojans, but failed to win the biggest prize, the game itself. Theismann passed for 526 yards, which was the most ever given up by the Trojans through the air. His 502 yards running and passing combined also set a record for most given up by a USC team. His counterpart, USC signal caller Jimmy Jones, passed for 226 yards and one touchdown in this wild shootout at the LA Coliseum. Jones also established two new USC career-passing records in this game, with 209 completions and 1,877 yards through the air.

The Irish came into this game with a spotless 9–0 record and loaded with returning lettermen ready to try for a national championship. With 64,694 in the standings on a rainy day, Notre Dame took their first step toward continuing on their rise to the top of the national polls. Early in the opening quarter, Theismann used his golden arm to get the Irish into USC territory. He then let his legs take over, and ran for a 25-yard touchdown to cap off a 12-play, 80-yard drive. Scott Hempel added the extra point, and Notre Dame was in control, or so they thought.

Over the course of the next eight minutes, USC exploded for three touchdowns that gave them a 21–7 lead at the end of the first quarter. Charles Evans scored on a three-yard run, and Ron Ayala tied the game at 7–7 with the extra point. Clarence Davis broke the tie with a five-yard run, but Ayala's extra point try went wide. Sam Dickerson then hauled in a 45-yard touchdown pass from Jimmy Jones to give USC a 19–7 lead. Jones connected with Bob Chandler on a two-point conversion pass to climax the Trojans' offensive explosion.

Notre Dame was in a strange position, as they had never fallen behind by 14 points during the season. They managed to close the gap to seven points halfway through the second quarter when Theismann threw a nine-yard scoring toss to John Cieszkowski and Hempel added the extra point. The Trojans got three of those points back on a 19-yard Ayala field goal to make the score 24–14 at the end of the first half.

The Trojans set out to put the game away in the third quarter, and they took great strides toward that goal by scoring 14 points over five minutes. Willie Hall got things going for the Trojans when he caused a fumble by Darryll Dewan after applying a hit to the Notre Dame runner. Kent Carter recovered the loose ball on the Notre Dame 17-yard line. The drive was capped off when offensive tackle Pete Adams fell on a Mike Berry fumble in the end zone for a touchdown. Adams' rare chance to score a six-pointer was followed by Ayala's conversion. Willie Hall was once again the force behind USC's next score as well. This time he hit Theismann in the end zone, causing the signal caller to fumble the ball, and defensive tackle John Vella jumped on the ball for a USC touchdown. Ayala added another extra point, and the Trojans were in control. The odds of two linemen scoring in the same game is very unusual, and for this reason, Pete Adams and John Vella shared the joy of their scores in the locker room following the upset victory by calling themselves "the Touchdown Twins."

The Irish scored two touchdowns in the third and fourth quarters. The first came on a 46-yard pass from Theismann to Larry Parker, and then Theismann scored from one yard out. The deficit was cut to 10 points with close to 14 minutes still remaining in the game, but USC shut down one of the top teams in the country the rest of the way to secure one of the greatest upsets in this famed series.[11]

### Team Leaders

Rushing: Clarence Davis—972 yards on 214 carries
Passing: Jimmy Jones—121 out of 234 attempts for 1,877 yards and 10 touchdowns
Receiving: Bob Chandler—41 catches for 590 yards and 3 touchdowns
Scoring: Clarence Davis—66 points on 11 touchdowns
Kickoff Returns: Clarence Davis—14 for 444 yards and 1 touchdown (31.8 avg.)
Punt Returns: Tyrone Hudson—26 for 191 yards (7.3 avg.)
Punting: Ron Ayala—50 for 1,716 yards (34.3 avg.)
Interceptions: Ron Ayala—8 for 113 yards
Tackles: Greg Slough—112

## *1971*

Head Coach: John McKay
Assistant Coaches: Willie F. Brown, Craig Fertig, Wayne Fontes, Marv Goux, Hudson Houck, Skip Husbands, Dave Levy, Don Lindsay, Al Saunders, Pete Yoder
Team Captains: John Vella, Willie Hall
Record: 6–4–1 overall (3–2–1 in Pacific–8 Conference)
(Ranked 46th best record in college football out of 128 teams)
Finish in Conference: 2nd place
Finish in National Polls: 20th place in AP
Points Scored Per Game: 20.8 to rank 52nd out of 128 teams
Points Allowed Per Game: 14.9 to rank 24th

### Schedule and Highlights

**(H) Sept. 10—Alabama—10–17**
USC#5 ALA#16

The Trojans gave up 340 yards with a newly built young defense, and coaching legend Paul "Bear" Bryant won his 200th game. One bright spot for USC was the running of Lou Harris, who gained 116 yards on 16 carries.[1]

**(A) Sept. 18—Rice—24–0**
USC#17

A pair of touchdown runs by Charles Hinton (20 yards), and Lou Harris (five yards), gave USC a 14–0 advantage and they never looked back. Mike Rae added a 22-yard field goal, and Edesel Garrison caught a 36-yard pass to complete the scoring. Garrison was a standout sprinter, and this was his first-ever college touchdown.[2]

**(H) Sept. 25—Illinois—28–0**
USC#16

Under the lights of the LA Coliseum, the Trojans recorded their second straight shutout. The young defensive unit was able to put together 10 straight quarters in which they prevented the opposition from scoring. The unit also had four interceptions. Despite seven fumbles, and the loss of five of them, the offensive backfield ran for 254 yards. Sam Cunningham and Charles Hinton each scored a touchdown, and Jimmy Jones completed 14 out of 20 pass attempts for 182 yards and one touchdown. He added an additional 52 yards rushing on eight carries to his day's work.[3]

**(A) Oct. 2—Oklahoma—20–33**
USC#17 OK#8

Sam Cunningham ran for 123 yards on 26 carries, and the USC defense held Oklahoma to zero pass completions despite suffering their second loss of the season.[4]

**(H) Oct. 9—Oregon—23–28**

Sam Cunningham ran for 187 yards on 23 carries, but Oregon scored the winning points with 7:43 left. It appeared that the Trojans were in control of this game, as they were up, 23–14 on touchdown runs by Sam Cunningham (65 yards) and

Jimmy Jones (23 yards). Jones added a touchdown pass to Charles Young (nine yards), and Mike Rae kicked a 20-yard field goal. The Ducks then cut the deficit to 23–21 at the start of the fourth quarter. Fumbles were beginning to haunt the Trojans during the season, and one in this game gave them nightmares. Cunningham had a spectacular game, but a fumble on the USC 48 led to an Oregon win. The Trojans rallied back with 25 seconds left on a 77-yard pass from Jones to Edesel Garrison, but the touchdown was called back due to an ineligible receiver downfield penalty. This loss gave USC a 2–3 record.[5]

**(H) Oct. 16—Stanford—18–33**
STAN#15

Played at night and in the rain, Stanford went 63 yards to score the first time they had the ball, and they never looked back, knocking USC down to a 2–4 record. Poor field position hurt the Trojans throughout the first half, but Mike Rae came in at quarterback in the fourth quarter to attempt a rally. He completed seven of 12 pass attempts for 164 yards and two touchdowns.[6]

**(A) Oct. 23—Notre Dame—28–14**
ND#6

It appeared that USC was having a good time spoiling Notre Dame's unbeaten seasons. In the previous matchup, the Irish came into the game at 9–0, only to have their quest for a perfect season and possible national championship thwarted by the Trojans. This time, on their own field, the Irish met the same fate. Notre Dame was rolling leading up to USC's arrival in South Bend. They were 5–0, had just shut out two straight opponents, and allowed only 16 points before the Trojans took the field to change all that, despite coming into this game on the downslide.

At 2–4, and in the midst of a three-game losing streak, the Trojans were badly in need of an uplifting showing. With 59,075 looking on from the stands, and rain-filled clouds looming overhead, the Trojans set out to upset their long-time rivals. Halfway through the first quarter, Bruce Dyer intercepted a pass on the USC 24, and returned it to the Notre Dame 48. Three plays later, the Trojans were in the end zone thanks to a 31-yard pass from Jimmy Jones to Edesel Garrison. Mike Rae added the extra point, and USC took a lead they would never relinquish.

A 66-yard return of the ensuing kickoff by Gary Diminick set the Irish up very well at the USC 34. Seven plays followed, and the end result was a one-yard run by Andy Huff, and Robert Thomas' extra point tied the game at 7–7. The Trojans then let loose with a 21-point barrage that put the game away. Charles Hinton started the onslaught with a 65-yard return of the ensuing kickoff, setting USC up at the Notre Dame 35. On the four play of that possession, Garrison scored his second touchdown of the game, this time on a 24-yard pass from Rae, who then added the extra point to give USC a 14–7 lead at the end of the opening stanza.

Edesel Garrison was quickly becoming a major problem for Notre Dame, and finished the game with five receptions for 127 yards and two touchdowns. In the second quarter, he hauled in a 42-yard pass from Jones that got the Trojans down to the Irish four. Powerful running back Sam "the Bam" Cunningham, then capped the drive off with a one-yard run on fourth down. Rae added the extra point for a 21–7 USC advantage. The defense joined in on the scoring fest, as Bruce Dyer intercepted another pass, and on this theft, he took it the distance, covering 53 yards for six points. Rae concluded USC's scoring for the game with his fourth conversion kick to make it a comfortable 28–7 Trojan lead.

With Notre Dame getting overwhelmed on the field, tempers boiled, and a fight broke out between Greg Marx and USC's John Vella. Over the course of the next few minutes, what started off as a boxing match in cleats, quickly escalated into a full-blown, bench-clearing riot. Even USC head coach John McKay got into the act by pushing Marx. Luckily, the massive 250-pound Marx did not hit McKay, which might have caused serious injury to the USC mentor.

The halftime break came at the right time to allow the teams to calm down. The second half came and went without incident, and the lone points throughout the final thirty minutes came on a four-yard run by John Cieszkowski, and the conversion kick was added by Thomas to bring this edition of the "Glamour Game" to a climax with a final score of 28–14. A newspaper headline in Los Angeles read, "How Sweet It Is," referring to USC's upset victory. It also seemed like a prequel for the rest of the season, as the Trojans rallied following their win over Notre Dame to salvage the year.[7]

**(A) Oct. 30—California—28–0**
USC#20

The Trojans evened their record at 4–4. Known for most of John McKay's coaching tenure as a running team, the Trojans looked to pass more, and in this game, it worked out very well. Lynn Swann and Charles Young combined for nine catches, and Edesel Garrison had five receptions for 69 yards. Swann scored two touchdowns, and Young one. Jimmy Jones completed 13 of 17 pass attempts for 144 yards and threw for two touchdowns and ran for another one. Mike Rae alternated with Jones at quarterback on every other series, and guided the Trojans on an 11-play, 75-yard drive in which he completed five passes in a row and capped the drive off with a 13-yard scoring strike to Swann. Despite this lopsided defeat, Cal committed no penalties.[8]

**(H) Nov. 6—Washington State—30–20**
USC#17

The Trojans shifted back to using a running attack as the focal point of the game plan on homecoming weekend. The backfield ran for 322 yards, with Lou Harris leading the way to victory with 158 yards on 29 carries and three touchdowns. He also ran back a kickoff 84 yards for another touchdown. The Trojan defense got five turnovers (two fumbles and three interceptions), and held the Pac-8 rushing leader Bernard Jackson to 56 yards, which was his lowest total of the year.[9]

**(A) Nov. 13—Washington—13–12**
USC#15 WASH#19

The Trojans won it with 2:08 left, and Lou Harris ran for 126 yards on 24 carries, giving him back-to-back games of topping the century rushing mark. He gained 95 of his rushing total in the first half alone. Plagued by two interceptions and three fumbles, USC allowed the Huskies to stay close, and eventually take a 12–10 lead. Washington's Sonny Sixkiller not only had a great name, but he was considered to be the best quarterback on the west coast. However, in this game, Sixkiller threw three interceptions in the second half, with one going to Skip Thomas that led to a game-winning 28-yard field goal by Mike Rae.[10]

**(H) Nov. 20—UCLA—7–7**
USC#15

The Bruins came into this game at 2–7, but against a fierce rival, records do not mean much. Playing well above what anyone expected out of them, the Bruins got out the Coliseum with a 7–7 tie. UCLA head coach Pepper Rodgers left the field proud of what his team accomplished, while John McKay was less than pleased.

The Trojans got on the board first. After a scoreless first quarter, Lou Harris took the ball over the goal line from one-yard out, and Mike Rae added the extra point kick to take USC into the second half up, 7–0. For the game, Harris had 118 yards on 29 carries. Marv Kendricks scored UCLA's lone six-pointer in the third quarter on a seven-yard run, and Efren Herrera split the uprights with the all-important extra point kick that knotted the game at 7.

In this tough defensive struggle, which saw USC prevent the Bruins from completing a single pass, both teams had opportunities to score. The Trojans almost pulled it out with three seconds left. From the UCLA 37, Jimmy Jones threw a pass intended for Lynn Swann, but the ball went over Swann's head and into the end zone.[11]

TEAM LEADERS

RUSHING: Lou Harris—801 yards on 167 carries
PASSING: Jimmy Jones—89 out of 161 attempts for 995 yards and 7 touchdowns
RECEIVING: Lynn Swann—27 catches for 305 yards and 2 touchdowns
SCORING: Mike Rae—37 points on 22 extra points and 5 field goals
KICKOFF RETURNS: Charles Hinton—11 for 271 yards (24.6 avg.)
PUNT RETURNS: Lynn Swann—11 for 157 yards (14.3 avg.)
PUNTING: Dave Boulware—68 for 2,588 yards (38.1 avg.)
INTERCEPTIONS: Bruce Dyer—6 for 131 yards and 1 touchdown
Artimus Parker—6 for 61 yards
Steve Fate—6 for 50 yards
TACKLES: Mike McGirr—104

## *1972*

HEAD COACH: John McKay
ASSISTANT COACHES: Willie F. Brown, Craig Fertig, Wayne Fontes, Raymond George, Marv Goux, Skip Husbands, Dave Levy, Don Lindsay, John Robinson
TEAM CAPTAINS: Sam Cunningham, John Grant
RECORD: 12–0 overall (7–0 in Pacific–8 Conference)
(Ranked 1st for best in college football out of 127 teams)
FINISH IN CONFERENCE: 1st place
FINISH IN NATIONAL POLLS: 1st place in both the AP and UPI
1972 National Champions
POINTS SCORED PER GAME: 38.9 to rank 3rd out of 127 teams
POINTS ALLOWED PER GAME: 11.2 to rank 8th

### Schedule and Highlights

**(N) Sept. 9—Arkansas—31–10**
USC#8 ARK#4

Viewed by many to be the greatest Trojan football team of all time, began their quest toward that honor, with an easy victory over Arkansas. After serving two years as a backup, Mike Rae took control of USC's quarterbacking duties for the first time and gave an outstanding performance. He connected on 18 of 24 pass attempts for 269 yards, and set up two touchdowns with long completions and broke a 3–3 halftime deadlock in the third quarter with a five-yard touchdown run. Rae also got the Trojans on the board in the second quarter with a 26-yard field goal. Rod McNeill led the Trojan ground attack with 117 yards on 28 carries and a pair of touchdowns. Sophomore linebacker Richard Wood made an immediate impact on the defense by recording 18 individual tackles and one interception.[1]

**(H) Sept. 16—Oregon State—51–6**
USC#1

USC head coach John McKay felt that this Trojan team was the quickest he ever had, and they went out and proved the words of praise did not go unnoticed. They rang up 663 yards of total offense, and Rod McNeill paced the ground attack with 111 yards on 18 carries and three touchdowns, while Mike Rae threw for 248 yards and one touchdown.[2]

**(A) Sept. 23—Illinois—55–20**
USC#1

After dismantling teams from the SEC and the Pac-8, the Trojans set their sites on prey from the Big-Ten Conference. Illinois provided the next victim for the USC juggernaut, and once again, the game proved to be a no-contest affair. Illinois played the Trojans close throughout the first half, only trailing, 20–14. The Trojans then ripped Illinois in the second half, scoring 15 in the third quarter and 20 in the final stanza. Sophomore tailback Anthony Davis scored three touchdowns, J.K. McKay added two, and in all, the Trojans tallied nine six-pointers before the game was finished.[3]

**(H) Sept. 30—Michigan State—51–6**
USC#1

For the third straight week, the Trojans overpowered an opponent with 50 or more points, and after just four games, the Trojans had 188 points. This was the worst defeat for Michigan State since 1947. The defense came into its own by recording four sacks, seven fumbles, and three interceptions. Offensively, Lynn Swann stood out with a 92-yard punt return and he caught a 30-yard touchdown pass from Pat Haden in the fourth quarter, in which the Trojans scored 27 of their points.[4]

**(A) Oct. 7—Stanford—30–21**
USC#1 STAN#15

The two-time defending Pac-8 champion Stanford Cardinal looked to make things difficult on the new conference alpha dogs. They had the game tied at 13–13 in the first half until a bad snap from center allowed the Trojans to break out. The snap from center went over Stanford punter Bill Reid's head with 1:31 left in the second quarter. Reid chased after the loose ball, with USC's James Sims in hot pursuit. The punter recovered the ball at the Stanford five, but Sims was there to tackle him. Three plays later, sophomore tailback Anthony Davis blasted into the end zone from the one to break the tie. Mike Rae added a 37-yard field goal, and Lynn Swann caught a four-yard pass from Pat Haden to extend USC's lead to 30–13 in the fourth quarter.[5]

**(H) Oct. 14—California—42–14**
USC#1

The Trojans were back to their dominant ways with an excellent display of power against another long-time foe from Northern California. Mike Rae and Sam Cunningham ran for two touchdowns apiece, and Charles Young caught two touchdown passes from Pat Haden to assist the Trojans in this romp.[6]

**(H) Oct. 21—Washington—34–7**
USC#1 WASH#18

On USC's homecoming weekend, the Trojans won easily against a Washington team that dropped their second straight game after starting out the season 5–0. This was also the eighth straight time the Huskies lost to USC. Tailback Anthony Davis carried the ball 16 times for 92 yards and two touchdowns, one of which was a sideline hugging 44-yarder. The USC defense dominated the Huskies, holding them to minus seven yards in the first half.[7]

**(A) Oct. 28—Oregon—18–0**
USC#1

The Oregon Ducks were 2–5 coming into this game with the Trojan juggernaut, but played the Southland powerhouse tough for almost 40 minutes. Playing on a rain-soaked artificial turf surface in Eugene, Oregon, the elements hampered the explosive USC offensive attack. They lost six fumbles, and the game remained scoreless until tailback Anthony Davis busted loose in the third quarter. With 6:06 left in the third quarter, Davis scored on a 48-yard run, and close to two minutes later, he dashed for a 55-yard touchdown. When the game was over, Davis ran 206 yards on 25 carries to help the Trojans remain perfect on the year.[8]

**(N) Nov. 4—Washington State—44–3**
USC#1

Rain, wind, and gray skies were the dismal weather conditions faced by the Trojans on a trip to Washington State. However, the weather had no bearing on the Trojans, as they once again turned in a dominant performance led by sophomore tailback Anthony Davis. He ran for 195 yards on 31 carries and three touchdowns. For the game, he compiled 291 yards of total offense. The Pac-8's top-ranked defense against the run held the Cougars to 116 yards on the ground, which was 84 yards below their average until they ran into the tough USC defense.[9]

**(A) Nov. 18—UCLA—24–7**
USC#1 UCLA# 14

In his varsity experience against the UCLA football team, 5'-9" sophomore tailback Anthony Davis made headlines by ripping off 178 yards on 25 carries for the top-ranked Trojans. He assisted USC in remaining perfect on the year by scoring on a 23-yard run that gave the Trojans a 10–0 first quarter lead. Mike Rae opened the scoring with a 32-yard field goal. The Bruins closed the gap to 10–7 when James McAlister ran off tackle from two yards out. Efren Herrera missed on a 33-yard field goal that would have tied the game in the second quarter, and that was as close as UCLA got to the lead for the rest of the game. Anthony Davis took charge on an 80-yard drive following Herrera's field goal attempt. He ran the ball seven times for 47 yards before Rod McNeill scored from the one and Rae added the extra point to extend the USC advantage to 17–7 at the half. The USC defense then shut down UCLA's "Wishbone T" running attack. Rae scored the second half's lone points on a seven-yard run, and then added the extra point to clinch USC's fifth Pac-8 title in seven years, while the Bruins season ended at 8–3.[10]

**(H) Dec. 2—Notre Dame—45–23**
USC#1 ND#10

In the two previous encounters with USC, Notre Dame came into the game undefeated, only to have the Trojans spoil the quest for perfection. This time it was USC that was sporting a spotless record, and the Irish looked to return the favor. However, it was not meant to be, all thanks to a sophomore tailback sensation name Anthony Davis.

Depending on what side of the spectrum one is on, the name Anthony Davis conjures up a wealth of emotions. On one side, Cardinal and Gold faithful instantly break into wide grins. However, those donning the Navy and Gold of Notre Dame can only muster up a stoic expression at best. " Notre Dame Killer" is a moniker that Anthony Davis has worn as a badge of honor since his incredible performance in this game. The sophomore tailback rose to the top of Troy's long legacy in their series against Notre Dame by single-handedly destroying the Golden Domers.

The Trojans only took a mere 13 seconds to establish themselves as the alpha dog in this fight. Anthony Davis took the opening kickoff on his three-yard line, and took off to the left after solid blocking opened up daylight for him. He then completed a 97-yard kickoff return by crossing the goal line to establish a school record for longest kickoff return. Mike Rae's extra point attempt failed, and USC had a quick 6–0 lead before many of the 75,243 at Coliseum were even in their seats.

Undaunted by the swift scoring attack from their west coast foes, the Fighting Irish went on an 82-yard drive that was capped off in nine plays with a 45-yard field goal by Bob Thomas to cut the USC lead in half. The Trojans came right back with a six-play, 53-yard drive that was helped by a 40-yard pass interference penalty against Notre Dame's Reggie Barnett. The penalty placed the ball on the one, Davis scored from there, and Rae added the extra point to give USC a 13–3 advantage. With the opening quarter winding down, the Irish were deep in their own territory when Eric Penick fumbled on the nine. Dale Mitchell recovered the loose ball for USC, and three plays later, it was Anthony Davis who once again found himself in the Notre Dame end zone, this time after a five-yard run. The extra point attempt failed, and at the end of the game's first 15 minutes, the Trojans were in command, 19–3.

The explosiveness of the first quarter was not duplicated in the second stanza, as it turned out to be primarily a defensive struggle. The Irish put the only points on the board during the quarter on a five-yard pass from Tom Clements to Willie Townsend. Bob Thomas' conversion kick took the teams into the second half with a 19–10 USC advantage.

Charles Hinton intercepted a pass for the Trojans in the third quarter, and the turnover led to a 41-yard drive that Davis' finished off with his fourth six-pointer of the game, this one coming on a four-yard run. Once again, the extra point was missed, but USC was now up, 25–10.

Despite being down by 15 points at this stage, Notre Dame

was able to move the ball well, and the Trojans were not able to get a great deal of pressure on the quarterback. These two elements allowed the Irish to make things interesting for their faithful, and a bit uneasy for USC fans. Notre Dame's Mike Townsend rose up to help his fellow Irish teammates by intercepting a pair of passes that were each turned into touchdowns. Tom Clements capitalized on the turnovers with two touchdown passes, the first going to Gary Diminick (11 yards), and the second to Mike Creaney (10 yards). Bob Thomas added a conversion kick following Diminick's score, but USC's Steve Fate knocked away a Clements pass on a two-point conversion attempt that would have tied the game. However, the damage of Townsend's interceptions resulted in Notre Dame closing to within two points at 25–23.

The momentum created by their comeback was short-lived for the Fighting Irish, all thanks to Anthony Davis. On the ensuing kickoff, Davis received the ball on his four, and this time he used the right sideline as his route to paydirt. Following the 96-yard kickoff return, Rae added the extra point, and USC was up, 32–23, going into the fourth quarter. An Artimus Parker interception return of 19 yards placed the ball on the Notre Dame 26, and allowed Davis the opportunity to try for a sixth touchdown. The sophomore tailback made his teammate's interception not go to waste, as he ran for an eight-yard touchdown. With Rae's extra point, USC was now in control once again at 39–23, and Anthony Davis was well on his way to legendary status in the annals of USC football history. He also was the owner of several new school and conference records. He tied a USC record with four rushing touchdowns, and owned outright the school records for most touchdowns in a single game (six), most points scored in a single game (36), all-purpose yards in one game (368), most yards gained on kickoff returns (218), and most kickoff returns for touchdowns (two), which also tied an NCAA record. His 36 points and six touchdowns tied Pac-8 records.

In addition to his 268 yards on kickoff returns, Davis rushed for 99 yards and had 51 yards receiving. His 99 yards on the ground allowed Davis the opportunity to finish the regular season with 1,034 yards, to become only the fourth USC back to top the 1,000-yard barrier. Prior to Davis, the other Trojans to reach that rushing plateau were Morley Drury, Mike Garrett, O.J. Simpson, and Clarence Davis. Sam "the Bam" Cunningham provided the Trojans with their other touchdown on a one-yard run with 2:44 remaining in the game.[11]

**Rose Bowl, (N) Jan. 1—Ohio State—42–17**

USC#1 OSU#3

The long and illustrious history of college football has been graced with teams that rose to the top of the ranks to the status of all-time greats. Yale and Harvard in the late 1880's to early 1900's come to mind, as do the Notre Dame powerhouse teams under Knute Rockne and Frank Leahy, and the almost invincible Army teams of the 1940's. These incredible teams were prequels to the saga that transpired in the Land of Troy throughout the 1972 season.

With a perfectly balanced attack on both sides of the ball, the '72 Trojans are considered one of the greatest college football teams of all-time. Legendary announcer Keith Jackson, who witnessed some of the greatest moments in college football history, felt that this edition of the Trojans was the best he had ever seen, and many other experts felt the same.

So it was, that on January 1, 1973, this Cardinal & Gold juggernaut took the field in Pasadena for the 59th Rose Bowl game with the 9–1 Ohio State Buckeyes standing in their way of a third national championship in ten years and a place among the immortal teams of the past.

The #3 ranked Buckeyes under head coach Woody Hayes were not that intimidated at first by their stellar opponents. Throughout the first half, with 106,869 in attendance on a 58-degree day, the Buckeyes went head-to-head with the mighty Trojans, and emerged from a tough defensive struggle tied at 7–7 going into the second half. Following a Buckeye fumble, the Trojans opened the scoring four plays later when Mike Rae connected with Lynn Swann from 10 yards out. Rae then added the extra point kick. Both Swann and Rae went on to have big days for USC. Swann led all receivers with six receptions for 108 yards, and Rae completed 18 of 25 pass attempts for 229 yards. The Buckeyes countered on a one-yard run by Randal Keith to even things up at the end of the first half.

The third quarter proved to the world that the Trojans were as good as their hype. They exploded for 21 points to basically put the game's outcome, and any doubt surrounding their exceptional prowess, to rest. Sam "the Bam" Cunningham, the Trojans' powerhouse fullback, blasted his way into the end zone twice, with the first coming from two yards out, and the other from one. In between Cunningham's scoring bursts, Anthony Davis, the sophomore sensation tailback, took off on a 20-yard touchdown run that helped USC go into the fourth quarter up, 28–10. For the game, Davis led all ball carriers with 157 yards on 23 carries. Throughout the regular season, the Trojan defense did not allow an opposing running back to gain 100-plus yards, and they continued on with that streak in this game, although Archie Griffin came close, running for 95 yards on 20 carries.

The Trojans were not finished pouring on just yet. In the fourth quarter, Cunningham added a pair of one-yard touchdown runs to his day's effort, and in the process, set a Rose Bowl record by scoring four touchdowns in a single game, and was awarded the game's MVP award. Another record set was a combined total of 45 points scored in one half, which was later surpassed by USC and Texas in 2006. Helping to set the new record were scores from Ohio State on a 21-yard field goal from Blair Conway in the third quarter, and a five-yard run from John Bledsoe in the fourth.[12]

### Team Leaders

Rushing: Anthony Davis—1,191 yards on 207 carries
Passing: Mike Rae—114 out of 199 attempts for 1,754 yards and 5 touchdowns
Receiving: Charles Young—29 catches for 470 yards and 3 touchdowns
Scoring: Anthony Davis—114 points on 19 touchdowns
Kickoff Returns: Anthony Davis—12 for 468 yards and 2 touchdowns (39.0 avg.)
Punt Returns: Lynn Swann—19 for 253 yards and 1 touchdown (13.3 avg.)
Punting: Dave Boulware—49 for 1,761 yards (36.1 avg.)
Interceptions: Artimus Parker—6 for 107 yards
Tackles: Richard Wood—129

# *1973*

HEAD COACH: John McKay
ASSISTANT COACHES: Willie F. Brown, Craig Fertig, Wayne Fontes, Raymond George, Marv Goux, Skip Husbands, Dave Levy, Don Lindsay, John Robinson
TEAM CAPTAINS: Lynn Swann, Artimus Parker
RECORD: 9–2–1 overall (7–0 in Pacific–8 Conference)
(Ranked 17th best record in college football out of 129 teams)
FINISH IN CONFERENCE: 1st place
FINISH IN NATIONAL POLLS: 8th place in AP and 7th place in UPI
POINTS SCORED PER GAME: 26.8 to rank 27th out of 129 teams
POINTS ALLOWED PER GAME: 16.8 to rank 41st

## Schedule and Highlights

**(H) Sept. 15—Arkansas—17–0**
USC#1

Despite 10 penalties, two of which erased long touchdown runs by Lynn Swann, the defending national champs opened the season with a shutout victory. This was the first time in 73 games that Arkansas failed to score any points. Anthony Davis provided the Trojans with their first points on a touchdown run with just seconds remaining in the first half. Quarterback Pat Haden, who completed 12 of 20 pass attempts for 143 yards, added another touchdown with a 14-yard run, and soccer-style kicker Chris Limahelu connected on a 22-yard field goal to round out USC's point production on this day.[1]

**(A) Sept. 22—Georgia Tech—23–6**
USC#1

In USC's 14th straight victory, Lynn Swann scored two first half touchdowns to spark the Trojans. His first six-pointer came on a 48-yard punt return, and his second was on a 15-yard pass from Pat Haden. Haden added another scoring strike in the fourth quarter, this time to J,K. McKay from 15 yards out. Anthony Davis, one of the top Heisman Trophy candidates, was held to 24 yards on 12 carries by a tough defense in the first half. He did manage to shake free in the second half, and finished the game with 71 yards on 24 carries.[2]

**(H) Sept. 29—Oklahoma—7–7**
USC#1 OK#8

A crowd of 84,016 was on hand at the Coliseum to witness a battle of two top-ranked teams. The Trojans were only able to generate 161 yards of total offense, and with this tie, their winning streak was halted at 14 games. This tie also knocked the Trojans from the top spot in the national polls. Following a fumbled punt by Oklahoma in the second quarter, the Trojans were able to score their lone six-pointer on a 15-yard pass from Pat Haden to J.K. McKay. The Sooners tied the game in the third quarter on a two-yard run by quarterback Steve Davis, which was followed by the all-important extra point kick that sent this game into the history books deadlocked 7–7.[3]

**(A) Oct. 6—Oregon State—21–7**
USC#4

Anthony Davis ran for 106 yards on 36 carries and two touchdowns. Oregon State cut the deficit to 14–7 late in the third quarter, which was only the second touchdown given up by the USC defense in four games. Davis' one-yard touchdown run in the fourth quarter allowed the Trojans a bit of insurance down the stretch.[4]

**(H) Oct. 13—Washington State—46–35**
USC#4

Anthony Davis ran for 102 yards on 21 carries, Pat Haden threw for 245 yards and four touchdowns, and Lynn Swann had 10 receptions for 148 yards and two touchdowns, as the Trojans rallied to beat the Cougars. Washington State held a 21–17 halftime advantage. Anthony Davis then scored on a 14-yard run to put the Trojans in the lead for good in the third quarter. They then added 23 points in the fourth quarter to pull away at the end.[5]

**(H) Oct. 20—Oregon—31–10**
USC#6

On USC's homecoming weekend, Pat Haden threw for 240 yards and two touchdowns, and Lynn Swann had five receptions for 122 yards and one touchdown. The Trojans scored their first two touchdowns in a span of 18 seconds in the opening stanza. After Pat Haden connected with J.K. McKay on a 35-yard touchdown pass, Danny Reese returned an interception 30 yards for a touchdown. This victory enabled the Trojans to extend their unbeaten streak to 23 games.[6]

**(A) Oct. 27—Notre Dame—14–23**
USC#6 ND#8

For the fourth straight year, at least one of these teams came into the matchup undefeated. This time out, both were undefeated, with USC's only blemish being a tie one month earlier. This was another classic showdown in the "Glamour Game," and this time out, the clash lived up to its moniker. The Trojans were defending national champs, with a good chance to repeat. The Irish were 5–0, and ready to fight their way to capturing the throne.

The damage caused by Anthony Davis' six touchdowns against the Irish the previous year, left Notre Dame faithful suffering close to eleven months of agony. In an attempt to exonerate the nightmare, a stuffed dummy wearing Davis' #28 USC jersey was hung in effigy on the Notre Dame campus leading up to the Trojans' visit to South Bend.

The Irish got on the scoreboard at the halfway point of the first quarter shortly after USC's Jim Lucas had a punt partially blocked by Tim Rudnick. Lucas was only able to get off a 15-yard kick, and the Irish had excellent field position as a result. On the sixth play following the punt, Bob Thomas kicked a 32-yard field goal to give Notre Dame a 3–0 lead. The Trojans came back to claim the top spot on the scoreboard at the end of the first quarter. They accomplished this on a nine-play, 65-yard drive that ended when Anthony Davis scored on a one-yard run. On that scoring drive, Davis was the workhorse, as he carried the ball six times for 22 yards. Following this scoring drive, the Irish clamped down on Davis, allowing him only an additional 43 yards on 13 carries. Chris Limahelu kicked the extra point, and USC went into the second quarter up, 7–3, which would be their final lead of the game.

With the running attack eating up most of the 14-play, 59-yard drive, Notre Dame closed to within one point of the lead on a 33-yard field goal by Thomas in the second quarter. The Irish took advantage of another short punt by Lucas, this time a 22-yarder, to score their first touchdown of the game. An 11-

play, 47-yard drive resulted in a one-yard run by quarterback Tom Clements, and Thomas' extra point gave Notre Dame a 13–7 halftime bulge.

Notre Dame struck quickly in the second half. With the third quarter not even four minutes old, Eric Penick shot through the line off tackle, and with solid blocking opening up daylight, the junior running back was off on an 85-yard touchdown jaunt. Thomas kicked the conversion to give Notre Dame a comfortable 20–7 lead. USC's Lynn Swann was one of the most exciting receivers throughout his playing days, both as a college and professional athlete. His acrobatic leaps to secure a pass were legendary, and in this game, he made one of them on a 27-yard touchdown reception from Pat Haden that cut the deficit to 20–14 after Limahelu's extra point kick.

Bob Thomas added a 32-yard field goal to get back three points for Notre Dame, and that was the way the scoring ended, as the fourth quarter remained scoreless. The Irish finished the season at 11–0, and won the national championship.[7]

**(A) Nov. 3—California—50–14**

USC#9

Anthony Davis ran for 106 yards on 26 carries, and tied a school record with four rushing touchdowns. He scored on runs from six, 15, 20, and one yard, and added a fifth touchdown to his day's work by returning a free kick 80 yards to finish off the game's scoring in the fourth quarter, in which USC totaled 29 of their points. Rod McNeill joined Davis in the 100-yard rushing club, as he ran for 164 yards on 24 carries. As a team, the Trojans compiled 392 rushing yards to just 43 for the Golden Bears.[8]

**(H) Nov. 10—Stanford—27–26**

USC#8

Stanford's Rod Garcia set a record for the longest field goal ever kicked against USC with a 59-yard boot. He also added three additional field goals to his day's work from 42, 52, and 25 yards out. However, Garcia's great kicking performance was far outweighed by his counterpart Chris Limahelu. Limahelu kicked a 27-yard field goal in the first quarter to tie the game, and then, with three seconds remaining and the Trojans trailing by two points, he connected on a game winning 34-yarder. This last second victory allowed USC to remain perfect in the Pac-8 with a 5–0 record and tied with UCLA for the top spot in the conference.[9]

**(A) Nov. 17—Washington—42–19**

USC#9

The Trojans broke open a close game in the fourth quarter to register a rout at the end. With USC holding a slim 21–19 advantage heading into the fourth quarter, Anthony Davis scored on a four-yard run, and then eight seconds later, Ray Rodriguez recovered a fumble for another touchdown. The Trojans totaled 290 rushing yards for the game, and Anthony Davis led the way with 122 yards on 26 carries, and Rod McNeill chipped in with115 yards on 20 carries.[10]

**(H) Nov. 24—UCLA—23–13**

USC#9 UCLA#8

Crossing the century mark running against UCLA seemed like old times for Anthony Davis. A year earlier, he dashed for 178 yards, and this time out, the star tailback rambled for 145 yards on 27 carries, scored on a four-yard run, and set up a field goal in this edition of the "Battle of Los Angeles." Davis' efforts in this game also allowed him to become only the second running back in USC history to surpass the 1,000-yard mark in two straight seasons.

The Bruins closed to within 7–3 on a 42-yard Efren Herrera field goal before the Trojans upped their advantage to eleven points on a 16-yard pass from Pat Haden to J.K. McKay with 4:30 expired in the second quarter. UCLA then drove 84 yards in nine plays to make it 14–10 on a Kermit Johnson three-yard run. Chris Limahelu added a 35-yard field goal to give the Trojans a 17–10 halftime lead. The second half became a battle of kickers, as Limahelu added two (32 and 28 yards), and Herrera one from 27 yards to complete the scoring.

Coming into this game, the Bruins possessed the nation's highest scoring rushing team, but it was not enough to overthrow the Trojans. Four turnovers in the second half also hampered UCLA's chances.[11]

**Rose Bowl, (N) Jan. 1—Ohio State—21–42**

USC#7 OSU#4

Woody Hayes and his Buckeyes had one full year to stew over the blowout defeat handing them by the Trojans in the previous Rose Bowl. This time out, Hayes brought his 9–0–1 Ohio State charges into Pasadena looking to even the score on a cool 55-degree and cloudy day with 105,267 in attendance. He succeeded in his mission, and almost by the exact score that the Trojans beat the Buckeyes by in the 1973 game.

The Buckeyes were known for having a strong running game, led by sophomore running back sensation Archie Griffin. He lived up his reputation as a gifted running back by dashing through the Trojan defense for 149 yards on 22 carries, including a 47-yard touchdown run that capped off the game's scoring in the fourth quarter. In addition to Griffin's solid performance, quarterback Cornelius Greene kept the offense moving by completing six of eight passes for 129 yards and running for 45 yards on seven carries and one touchdown. His efforts allowed Greene to take home the game's MVP award. Another key performer for the Buckeyes was fullback Pete Johnson, who ran for 94 yards and three touchdowns.

The Trojans kept the game close for the first half, as the teams went into halftime deadlocked at 14–14. Chris Limahelu kicked two long-range field goals from 47, which set a USC record for longest field goal, and 42 yards, and Pat Haden connected with his favorite receiver John McKay, the coach's son, on a 10-yard strike. This duo then teamed up again on a two-point conversion pass to give USC a brief 14–7 advantage in the second quarter. Despite the loss, Haden and McKay turned in fine showings for the Trojans. Haden completed 21 of 39 pass attempts for 229 yards, while McKay hauled in six receptions for 83 yards. Chris Limahelu also had a good day kicking in the cool weather. His first field goal, which opened the game's scoring in the first quarter from 47 yards out, was the longest in team history.

The Trojans broke the tie on their second possession of the third quarter on an Anthony Davis one-yard touchdown. Davis was USC's leading ground gainer in this game, rushing for 74 yards on 16 carries. Following Davis' short yardage touchdown, the Buckeyes exploded for 28 points while holding the Trojans to none.[12]

### TEAM LEADERS

RUSHING: Anthony Davis—1,112 yards on 276 carries
PASSING: Pat Haden—137 out of 247 attempts for 1,832 yards and 13 touchdowns
RECEIVING: Lynn Swann—42 catches for 714 yards and 6 touchdowns
SCORING: Anthony Davis—90 points on 15 touchdowns
KICKOFF RETURNS: Anthony Davis—16 for 409 yards and 1 touchdown (25.6 avg.)
PUNT RETURNS: Lynn Swann—19 for 189 yards and 1 touchdown (10.0 avg.)
PUNTING: Dave Boulware—18 for 653 yards (36.3 avg.)
INTERCEPTIONS: Danny Reece—8 for 101 yards and 1 touchdown
Artimus Parker—8 for 100 yards
TACKLES: Richard Wood—117

## *1974*

HEAD COACH: John McKay
ASSISTANT COACHES: Foster Andersen, Willie F. Brown, Wayne Fontes, Raymond George, Marv Goux, Skip Husbands, Dave Levy, Don Lindsay, John Robinson, Bruce Snyder, Ed. C. Sowash
TEAM CAPTAINS: Pat Haden, Richard Wood
RECORD: 10–1–1 overall (6–0–1 in Pacific–8 Conference)
(Ranked 6th best record in college football out of 129 teams)
FINISH IN CONFERENCE: 1st place
FINISH IN NATIONAL POLLS: 2nd place in AP and 1st place in UPI
1974 UPI National Champions
POINTS SCORED PER GAME: 30.2 to rank 9th out of 129 teams
POINTS ALLOWED PER GAME: 11.8 to rank 11th

### Schedule and Highlights

**(N) Sept. 14—Arkansas—7–22**
USC#5 ARK#20

The Razorbacks came into this game as 14-point underdogs, but an incredible defensive effort lifted them to a stunning victory at War Memorial Stadium in Little Rock, Arkansas. USC's Pat Haden found the going extremely difficult, as he did not complete a pass until the last play of the third quarter. Prior to that, he threw 13 passes, with three of them going for interceptions. Leading the way was Floyd Hogan, who picked off two of USC's four interceptions. His thefts resulted in 10 points for Arkansas on their way to a win. Anthony Davis prevented a shutout when he returned a first quarter kickoff 106 yards for the Trojans lone touchdown.[1]

**(A) Sept. 28—Pittsburgh—16–7**
USC#18 PITT#8

The Trojans fell 13 spots in the national polls following their opening day loss, but rallied back from a 7–3 third quarter deficit to even their record at 1–1. Pat Haden continued to have trouble moving the team, and then suffered a concussion. Sophomore Vince Evans replaced Haden, and he managed to ignite the offense with the Trojans down by four points. Despite fumbling three times in Pitt territory in the second half, Evans scored an insurance touchdown on a 13-yard run with 1:06 remaining in the game. Anthony Davis was the main offensive weapon for the Trojans. He ran for 149 yards on 33 carries, and scored USC's go-ahead touchdown in the fourth quarter on a two-yard run. The Trojans received their other points on a Chris Limahelu 25-yard field goal in the first quarter. The Pitt Panthers had some history made in this game when sophomore running back Tony Dorsett became the school's all-time rushing leader in just his 15th varsity outing.[2]

**(H) Oct. 5—Iowa—41–3**
USC#9

Senior defensive back Charles Phillips had a busy, and very successful, day while donning the Cardinal & Gold. He set a USC and Pac-8 record with 181 yards on interception returns. He also tied a school record with two interception returns for scores. In the second quarter, with the Trojans up by 11 points, he grabbed his first theft, and raced 83 yards to paydirt. In the third quarter, he struck again, this time rambling 98 yards to the end zone. The Trojans received their other points on an Anthony Davis 80-yard kickoff return to open USC's scoring barrage after trailing 3–0 in the first quarter. Pat Haden ran for one score (11 yards), and threw for another that covered 17 yards to J.K. McKay. Vince Evans tossed a 14-yard scoring strike to John Cantwell in the fourth quarter to complete the rout.[3]

**(N) Oct. 12—Washington State—54–7**
USC# 7

A trip to Joe Albi Stadium in Spokane, Washington, brought the Trojans another lopsided victory. The star of the game was tailback Anthony Davis, who ran for 194 yards on 26 carries and two touchdowns in only one half of work. This was Davis' best game up to this point of the season. As a team, the Trojans rolled to 462 yards on the ground in the Pac-8 opener.[4]

**(A) Oct. 19—Oregon—16–7**
USC#6

Three field goals by Chris Limahelu (21, 25, and 37 yards) proved to be the difference in this game that kept the Trojans undefeated in the Pac-8 race. Anthony Davis scored USC's lone touchdown on a one-yard run, and finished the game with 160 yards rushing on 38 carries.[5]

**(H) Oct. 26—Oregon State—31–10**
USC#6

On homecoming weekend, Anthony Davis added his name to the Pac-8 record books when he scored the 41st touchdown of his college career. The record setting six-pointer came in the second quarter on a 13-yard run to erase the old mark set by Duke Morrison of Cal from 1920 through 1922. He added another touchdown in the fourth quarter from 11 yards out, and finished the game with143 yards on 26 carries. Pat Haden teamed up with Jim Obradovich (eight yards) and J.K. McKay (38 yards), who had six receptions for 100 yards, to account for USC's other touchdowns. Chris Limahelu added a field goal from 30 yards out to round out the Trojans' scoring.[6]

**(H) Nov. 2—California—15–15**
USC#6

Chris Limahelu missed on a 38-yard field goal with 49 seconds left, and Cal's Jim Breech failed on a 34-yarder with seven seconds to bring this game to a tie. This was prior to playing tiebreakers during regular season games. The Trojans were favored to win by at least three touchdowns, but had to work for the tie. The Golden Bears led throughout the game until Pat Haden scored on a one-yard run, and then connected with Jim Obradovich on a two-point conversion pass that tied the score late in the third quarter. Anthony Davis scored USC's other touchdown on a one-yard run, and finished the game with 119 yards on 39 carries. Teammate Allen Carter also rushed for 119 yards on 20 carries.[7]

**(A) Nov. 9—Stanford—34–10**

USC#11

The Trojans came into this game tied for first place in the Pac-8, but emerged as the team to beat for the conference crown. Helping to get the Trojans to 4–0–1 in the Pac-8 was Anthony Davis, who ran for 119 yards on 22 carries and two touchdowns from one yard and 21 yards. He also threw for a six-pointer to J.K. McKay that covered nine yards. With his 119 yards on the ground, Davis moved into second place on USC's all-time rushing list with 3,267, only trailing O.J. Simpson for the school's career record. Freshman Dwight Ford added a touchdown run from three yards out, and Chris Limahelu connected on a pair of field goals, both from 22 yards away, to complete USC's scoring.[8]

**(H) Nov. 16—Washington—42–11**

USC#8

Anthony Davis continued on his impressive trek by running for 147 yards on 29 carries, and scored two touchdowns. His first was on a seven-yard pass from Pat Haden, and the other was on a one-yard run. Haden also connected with Shelton Diggs for a touchdown that covered 36 yards and opened the scoring in the first quarter. Other Trojans that lit up the scoreboard were Allen Carter (one-yard run), Vince Evans (three-yard run), and Dwight Ford (36-yard run). This victory put USC at 5–0–1, and created a Pac-8 showdown with UCLA, who was a 4–1–1 following their game.[9]

**(A) Nov. 23—UCLA—34–9**

USC#8

Anthony Davis was one of the premier running backs that the college ranks produced in the early 1970's. The 5'9" future All-American's prowess was a true testament to what the USC tailback tradition was all about. He was explosive, and did much damage to many defenses throughout his illustrious career donning the Cardinal & Gold. However, he seemed to save a little something extra for USC's top rivals. This game was no exception, as he rambled for 195 yards on 31 carries, and scored on an eight-yard run to assist in the mauling of UCLA. Along the way to helping USC clinch a third straight Pac-8 championship, Davis broke O.J. Simpson's USC and Pac-8 rushing records on his first carry of the game with a gain of 16 yards. He finished the game with a career mark of 3,609 yards compared to Simpson's 3,423.

The Trojans scored on their first possession by going 70 yards in nine plays. Pat Haden capped the drive off with an eight-yard run. Haden also connected with J.K. McKay from 17 yards out for another score, and Chris Limahelu added a 30-yard field goal to extend the Trojans' advantage to 17–9 at the end of the first half. Another USC record fell in this game, and that honor went to Limahelu, who blasted a record setting 50-yard field goal in the third quarter that broke his old mark set in the previous Rose Bowl. He also added a 30-yard field goal in the second quarter, and Dennis Thurman ended the beating of USC's cross-town rival with an 84-yard touchdown after recovering a fumble.[10]

**(H) Nov. 30—Notre Dame—55–24**

USC#6 ND#5

This game marked the end of the Ara Parseghian era at Notre Dame. For 11 seasons, he guided the Fighting Irish to a record of 95–17–4 for an impressive .836 winning percentage. Losses are a common factor in coaching, even as minimal as they were for Parseghian. However, of his previous 16 defeats leading up to this clash, none were as shocking.

On the other side of the spectrum, there was never a more stunning comeback in USC history, or in all of college football history. The Fighting Irish were defending national champions, and came into this showdown with the number one ranked defense and a 9–1 record. Notre Dame came out strong in this clash at the Coliseum, ringing up a 24–0 lead late in the second quarter. The Trojans' hopes of contending for a national title seemed bleak at best as halftime approached. However, with only 10 seconds left before heading off to the locker room, Anthony Davis caught a seven-yard touchdown pass from Pat Haden that gave USC supporters a slight reason to smile despite the fact that the extra point attempt was blocked.

The Trojans came out for the second half trailing 24–6, and the incredible occurrences that transpired over the course of the second half will never fade from USC lore. Davis, the "Notre Dame Killer," once again lived up to his moniker that was established two years earlier. He took the second half kickoff and raced 102 yards for a touchdown. A two-point conversion run failed, but the deficit was now cut in half. By the time the third quarter reached its climax, the Trojans exploded for 35 points. In addition to his tremendous kickoff return, Davis adding two more scoring runs from six and four yards, and Pat Haden hooked up with J.K. McKay on scoring strikes from 18 and 45 yards. Haden added another touchdown pass to his day's work in the fourth quarter, with that one going to Shelton Diggs from 16 yards out. For the day, Haden threw for 225 yards and four touchdowns, and J.K. McKay had four receptions for 110 yards and two touchdowns. Charles Phillips then added one final six-pointer to the barrage when he intercepted a pass and raced 58 yards for USC's final tally. In all, the Trojans scored 55 points in under 17 minutes.[11]

**Rose Bowl, (N) Jan. 1—Ohio State—18–17**

USC#5 OSU#3

For the third straight year, the Trojans and Buckeyes faced each other on New Year's Day. In the first two meetings, the results were one-sided, but in this, the final chapter in the trilogy, the best was saved for last. The Buckeyes came into this game at 10–1 with the newly crowned Heisman Trophy winner, Archie Griffin. Besides the exciting abilities of running back Griffin, the Buckeyes were solid at other positions, and were favored in this game by five-and-a-half points.

A massive crowd of 106,721 filled the Rose Bowl in anticipation of a running back duel between Griffin and Heisman Trophy runner-up Anthony Davis. The hope of a great show between these two great college runners would not materialize. Unfortunately, Davis injured his ribs in the second quarter and did not return. Before he left, Davis carried the ball 13 times for 67 yards.

The Trojans struck first on a Chris Limahelu field goal from 30 yards out in the opening quarter. The Buckeyes took a 7–3 lead into the locker room at the end of the first half on a Champ Henson two-yard run and a Tom Klaban conversion kick. After a scoreless third quarter, the Trojans moved back on top, 10–7, when tight end Jim Obradovich caught a nine-yard scoring strike from Pat Haden, and Limahelu added the extra point. Ohio State then took a 17–10 lead on a three-yard run from Cornelius Greene, and a 32-yard field goal from Klaban. With six minutes to go, the Trojans took possession on their own 17. With Davis watching from the sidelines, nursing painful ribs, his backup, Allen Carter, lived up to the proud USC tailback tradition by blasting through the Ohio State defense for a gain of 30 yards. For the game, Carter tied Archie Griffin for game-high rushing honors with 75 yards. Griffin had an NCAA record of 22 straight 100-yard performances coming into this matchup, and the Trojan defense did their part to make sure the streak did not continue. Fullbacks Dave Farmer and Ricky Bell picked up vital yards to keep the drive going, and the Trojans now were at the Ohio State 38. On first-and-ten, quarterback Pat Haden teamed up with his long-time friend J.K. McKay for one of USC's all-time classic scoring strikes. McKay was able to get behind defender Steve Luke in the right corner of the end zone. The result was a six-pointer that cut the Buckeye lead to one point.

After head coach John McKay saw his son and Haden connect for the touchdown, he had no doubt in his mind what he wanted next. He decided to gamble on a two-point conversion attempt, and put the game into the trusting hands of his quarterback Pat Haden. Haden rolled out and passed to Shelton Diggs, who made a spectacular diving catch while on his knees. The score was now 18–17 with a little more than two minutes remaining in the game. The Buckeyes had enough time to pull out a victory, and got close to the USC 45. It was from there that Tom Skladany attempted a 62-yard field goal. It sailed straight, but fell five yards short as time ran out, and the Trojans went on to clinch a share of the national championship. Pat Haden completed 12 of 22 pass attempts for 181 yards, and was awarded the game's Co-MVP along with receiver J.K. McKay, who hauled in five receptions for 104 yards. It also gave USC's head coach John McKay his fifth Rose Bowl victory, which tied him with another USC coaching legend, Howard Jones.[12]

### TEAM LEADERS

RUSHING: Anthony Davis—1,421 yards on 301 carries
PASSING: Pat Haden—70 out of 149 attempts for 988 yards and 13 touchdowns
RECEIVING: Johnny McKay—34 catches for 550 yards and 8 touchdowns
SCORING: Anthony Davis—110 points on 18 touchdowns and a 2-point conversion
KICKOFF RETURNS: Anthony Davis—12 for 484 yards and 3 touchdowns (40.3 avg.)
PUNT RETURNS: Marvin Cobb—12 for 116 yards (9.7 avg.)
PUNTING: Jim Lucas—43 for 1,632 yards (38.0 avg.)
INTERCEPTIONS: Charles Phillips—7 for 302 yards and 3 touchdowns
TACKLES: Kevin Bruce—99

## *1975*

HEAD COACH: John McKay
ASSISTANT COACHES: Foster Andersen, Willie F. Brown, Craig Fertig, Wayne Fontes, Marv Goux, Skip Husbands, Dave Levy, Don Lindsay, Bruce Snyder, Ed C. Sowash
TEAM CAPTAINS: Kevin Bruce, Danny Reece
RECORD: 8–4 overall (3–4 in Pacific-8 Conference)
(Ranked 36th best record in college football out of 137 teams)
FINISH IN CONFERENCE: 5th place
FINISH IN NATIONAL POLLS: 17th place in AP and 19th place in UPI
POINTS SCORED PER GAME: 20.6 to rank 61st out of 137 teams
POINTS ALLOWED PER GAME: 11.7 to rank 15th

### Schedule and Highlights

**(H) Sept. 12—Duke—35–7**
USC#4

The defending national champions came into this season without many key players. However, a new Trojan superstar emerged by the name of Ricky Bell. He carried the ball 34 times for 256 yards, to set a new USC single-game rushing record previously set by C. R. Roberts in 1956. Ironically, Roberts was among the 56,727 in attendance at the Coliseum. Bell also tied a USC single-game record with four rushing touchdowns.[1]

**(H) Sept. 19—Oregon State—24–7**
USC#4

In their Pac-8 opener, the Trojans gained 414 yards of total offense, with Ricky Bell leading the way. Bell ran for 215 yards on 28 carries to give him a nation-leading 471 rushing yards. Two of his runs were for long touchdowns from 53 and 25 yards out. Ted Roberson, starting his first game of the season at cornerback, provided the Trojans with their other touchdown on a 29-yard interception return. Despite the win, the Trojans lost the services of starting fullback Dave Farmer due to a broken leg.[2]

**(H) Sept. 27—Purdue—19–6**

Danny Reece was the star of the game for the Trojans against the Boilermakers of the Big Ten Conference. He returned four punts 150 yards, with his 47 and 68-yarders setting up touchdowns. Vince Evans (12 yards), and Ricky Bell (one yard), scored on runs set up by Reece. Bell's touchdown gave the Trojans a 19–0 lead and total control of the game. Reece came up just 13 yards shy of breaking the Pac-8 single-game punt return yardage mark of 162 yards set by USC's Mike Garrett in 1965.[3]

**(A) Oct. 4—Iowa—27–16**
USC# 3

Two fumbles early in the game were turned into ten points for Iowa with less than seven minutes expired in the first quarter. The Trojans then settled down and came out victorious. Rob Hertel was subbing at quarterback for an injured Vince Evans, and he rallied USC with two touchdown runs (three and six yards), and a 10-yard scoring strike to Randy Simmrin. Ricky Bell led the ground attack with 163 yards on 26 carries, while the Trojan defense held the Hawkeyes to only 71 rushing yards. Larry Nunnally assisted in the cause with eight unassisted tackles.[4]

**(H) Oct. 11—Washington State—28–10**
USC#3

Washington State got out to a 3–0 lead in the first quarter only to see the Trojans then explode for 28 straight points. Ricky

Bell was his usual splendid self, rushing for 217 yards on 38 carries, and scored his eighth touchdown of the year on a three-yard run. Rob Hertel gave the Trojans the lead for go with a two-yard run, and Danny Reece had five punt returns for 125 yards, one of with went for 64 yards and a touchdown. This win extended USC's Pac-8 unbeaten streak to 27 games, and it was their 24th consecutive win at the LA Coliseum.[5]

**(H) Oct. 18—Oregon—17–3**
USC#3

Despite some sloppy play and penalties, the Trojans remained perfect in the Pac-8 race with a 6–0 record on homecoming weekend. However, they lost quarterback Bob Hertel with a broken leg, but Vince Evans was able to return after injuring his thumb three weeks earlier. Ricky Bell ran for 128 yards on 26 carries and one touchdown (three-yard run). With his rushing total in this game, Bell was able to go over the 1,000-yard mark with five games still remaining. Doug Hogan returned an interception 61 yards for USC's other touchdown, and Glen Walker kicked a 45-yard field goal. This victory tied John McKay with Howard Jones for most victories as head coach of Trojans. This loss kept Oregon winless on the year, and extended their losing streak to 14 straight.[6]

**(A) Oct. 25—Notre Dame—24–17**
USC#3 ND#14

USC's hard-charging running back Ricky Bell was tearing up the college football landscape, and considered a top Heisman Trophy candidate coming into this game. The day before USC was set to take the field against the Fighting Irish, chants of "Ring Ricky's Bell" rang out loud and strong. However, it was Bell that quieted the crowd by running for 165 yards on 40 carries to help head coach John McKay pass Howard Jones as USC's all-time leader in football wins with 122.

This game, between the two programs that claimed national championships for three straight seasons, began with Notre Dame scoring on their first offensive series. A two-play, 57-yard drive was capped off when Al Hunter took a reverse and ran 52 yards for a touchdown. Kevin Bruce blocked Dave Reeve's conversion kick, and Notre Dame was up, 6–0. The Trojans struck back after David Lewis recovered a fumble. The turnover resulted in an eight-play, 55-yard drive that produced a 21-yard touchdown toss from Vince Evans to Shelton Diggs. Glen Walker added the go-ahead extra point, and USC was up, 7–6.

The Irish took a 14–7 halftime lead after Luther Bradley blocked a punt and Tom Lopienski scooped the ball up and ran a 13-yard touchdown. Kris Haines caught a pass from Hunter for a two-point conversion.

USC came out for the second half using a ground attack that ate up 35 yards, and ended with Ricky Bell scoring from two yards out. Walker's extra point tied the game at 14–14. Dave Reeve got Notre Dame back on top with a 27-yard field goal, and that was the last time the Irish could boast of having the lead in this game.

From the own 29, Bell punished the Notre Dame defense with runs of 19, 12, and 11 yards, and the drive was finished off when Vince Evans ran into the end zone from two yards out. Walker's conversion kick made the score 21–17, and he later added a 35-yard field goal to complete the scoring.[7]

**(A) Nov. 1—California—14–28**
USC#4

The long-time rivalry between USC and Cal has created some memorable moments for both programs. On this day, the glory belonged to the Golden Bears. Led by the running of Chuck Muncie, the passing of Joe Roth, and the receiving of Steve Rivera, Cal snapped the Trojans' 28-game unbeaten streak in the Pac-8. Muncie ran for 143 yards and caught five passes for 62 yards. Roth threw for 244 yards, and Rivera caught nine passes for 131 yards to spark Cal. On defense, Phil Heck had 12 unassisted tackles, and led a defense that limited USC to 196 yards of total offense. Despite the tough going, Ricky Bell still managed to produce, as he gained most of USC's offensive production with 121 yards rushing on 27 carries and one touchdown. Vince Evans scored USC's other touchdown on a 29-yard run.[8]

**(H) Nov. 8—Stanford—10–13**
USC#9

Stanford all but knocked the Trojans out of the Rose Bowl for the first time in four years with a last second victory. Stanford scored first on a Mike Langford's 55-yard field goal late in the first quarter. That booming field goal was the second longest in Pac-8 history, missing the record by four yards. The Trojans' only touchdown came on a 68-yard pass from Vince Evans to Junior Lee. A Ron Ingle five-yard run gave Stanford a 10–7 lead at the end of the first half before Glen Walker tied the game at 10–10 by the end of the third quarter with a 38-yard field goal. Stanford then won the game after an interception placed the ball on the USC 38 with little time remaining. Mike Langford then won it by kicking a 37-yard field goal with no time left on the clock. This was the first time since Stanford beat them in 1971 that the Trojans lost at the Coliseum, and the first time since 1971 that they lost two straight conference games. Once again, despite the loss, Ricky Bell rang up impressive rushing numbers, this time gaining 195 yards on 35 carries.[9]

**(A) Nov. 15—Washington—7–8**
USC#13

The rain came down in the Great Northwest, and with it, the Trojans' hope of snapping a two-game losing streak was washed away with the rain. USC lost four out of six fumbles, and the Huskies managed to win by the slimmest of margins. Mosi Tatupu scored USC's only touchdown on a one-yard run in the first quarter. Ricky Bell was the envy of college running backs across the nation in 1975, and he once again provided the bulk of the offensive production for USC. He ran for 190 yards on 42 carries, and in the process, broke O.J. Simpson's Pac-8 single-season record of 1,709 yards set in 1968.[10]

**(H) Nov. 28—UCLA—22–25**
UCLA#14

Running out of a Veer attack that tore off 414 yards of total offense against a tough USC defense, the Bruins clinched a trip to the Rose Bowl and a share of the Pac-8 title with Cal. The Bruins battled through a conference record 11 fumbles, with eight lost, to prevail. They were led by a powerful ground force that featured Wendell Tyler running for 130 yards, which allowed him to become UCLA's top single-season rushing leader with 1,216 yards. Eddie Ayers came in second with 98 yards, and quarterback John Sciarra added 85 on the ground and passed for 86 more and threw for two touchdowns.

The Trojans struck first with four minutes expired in the opening quarter when the nation's top rushing leader, Ricky Bell, scored on a one-yard run, and following the extra kick, USC was up, 7–0. The Bruins countered with a five-yard run by Eddie Ayers as t he final 30 seconds were about to tick off the end of the first quarter. The extra point kick was missed, and USC clung to a slim one-point lead.

The Trojans extended their lead to 14–6 early in the second quarter on a Vince Evans four-yard run. Then UCLA struck like lightning, and by the end of the first half, were up, 18–14. A short time after Evans' six-pointer, Wendell Tyler brought the Bruin boosters to their feet with a 57-yard touchdown jaunt that closed the USC advantage to two points. John Sciarra and tight end Don Pederson then hooked up on an 18-yard scoring strike to give UCLA their first lead of the game with 5:39 left in the half.

The final 30 minutes began with a slight touch of mayhem after UCLA's Wally Henry returned the second half kickoff 80 yards to the USC 20. One play after that exciting return, Wendell Tyler fumbled and Kevin Bruce recovered for the Trojans. The ball was then turned back over to the Bruins when fullback Mosi Tatupu fumbled and Harold Hardin recovered. After this rendition of pigskin hot potato, Sciarra wasted no time connecting with Pederson once again for a six-pointer on the first play following the Tatupu fumble. The scoring strike came from 19 yards out, and the Bruins were successful for the first time in the game on their conversion to up their advantage to 25–14 in the third quarter. The Trojans made it close when Ricky Bell ran three yards for a score on the first play of the fourth quarter. He then ran for the two-point conversion to finish out the scoring. On the day, Bell had 136 yards on 36 carries.[11]

**Liberty Bowl, (N) Dec. 22—Texas A & M—20–0**

For the first time since 1924, the Trojans found themselves playing in a different post-season bowl game other than the Rose Bowl. The defending national champion Trojans took the field on a cold 30-degree day at Liberty Bowl Memorial Stadium in Memphis, Tennessee, looking to give head coach John McKay a victorious sendoff in what would be the final time he patrolled the sidelines in the college ranks after 16 seasons at USC.

McKay's charges did not disappoint their legendary mentor, as they handed Texas A&M their first shutout loss in 52 games with 52,129 in attendance. Behind the passing of Vince Evans, and the running of the nation's top rusher Ricky Bell, the Trojans' offense gained 315 yards against the top-rated defense in the country. Bell ran for 82 yards on 28 carries, and caught a 76-yard touchdown pass from Evans. His efforts gained Bell the game's MVP Award. Evans completed six of 13 pass attempts for 174 yards, and Randy Simmrin had three receptions for 82 yards. One of his receptions went for 65 yards, and set up a Mosi Tatupu one-yard touchdown run in the early in the second quarter. Glen Walker added two field goals from 45 and 40 yards to complete the scoring. This was USC's 15th victory in 21 bowl appearances.[12]

TEAM LEADERS

RUSHING: Ricky Bell—1,957 yards on 385 carries
PASSING: Vince Evans—35 out of 112 attempts for 695 yards and 3 touchdowns
RECEIVING: Randy Simmrin—26 catches for 478 yards and 1 touchdown
SCORING: Ricky Bell—88 points on 14 touchdowns and two 2-point conversions
KICKOFF RETURNS: Mike Robinson—4 for 101 yards (25.3 avg.)
PUNT RETURNS: Danny Reece—28 for 418 yards and 1 touchdown (14.9 avg.)
PUNTING: Glen Walker—61 for 2,397 yards (39.3 avg.)
INTERCEPTIONS: Clint Strozier—5 for 22 yards
TACKLES: David Lewis—90

## *1976*

HEAD COACH: John Robinson
ASSISTANT COACHES: Foster Andersen, Marv Goux, Paul Hackett, Mike Haluchak, Hudson Houck, Skip Husbands, Don Lindsay, Pat Morris, Bob Toledo, Norv Turner
TEAM CAPTAINS: Ricky Bell, Vince Evans, Eric Williams
RECORD: 11–1 overall (7–0 in Pacific-8 Conference)
(Ranked 3rd best record in college football out of 137 teams)
FINISH IN CONFERENCE: 1st place
FINISH IN NATIONAL POLLS: 2nd place in both AP and UPI
POINTS SCORED PER GAME: 32.2 to rank 5th out of 137 teams
POINTS ALLOWED PER GAME: 11.6 to rank 12th

### Schedule and Highlights

**(H) Sept. 11—Missouri—25–46**
USC#8

This game marked the beginning of the John Robinson era at USC, but it did not end the way Trojan faithful had hoped. Everything fell apart for the Trojans, as they had three fumbles, seven penalties, gave up 315 rushing yards throughout the game, and surrendered four touchdowns in the first half. With stitches in his hand, Missouri quarterback Steve Pisarkiewicz still managed to complete nine of 16 pass attempts for 171 yards and three touchdowns. Running back Curtis Brown added a great performance with 101 yards rushing on 20 carries, caught a touchdown pass, and returned a kickoff for another six-pointer. The lone bright spot for the Trojans was the running of Ricky Bell, who gained 172 yards on 29 carries.[1]

**(A) Sept. 18—Oregon—53–0**

This game helped the Trojans erase their bitter opening day loss. Ricky Bell was the headline grabber in this one, as he ran for 193 yards on 32 carries, and tied a school record with four rushing touchdowns. He outgained a bewildered Oregon team, who as a team could only muster 49 yards on the ground. The Ducks committed ten turnovers.[2]

**(A) Sept. 25—Purdue—31–13**
USC#19

Ricky Bell rushed for 177 yards, and scored on a five-yard run to break a 7–7 tie in the third quarter. The Trojans then exploded for 17 additional points to win convincingly. Fullback Mosi Tatupu ran for two touchdowns (one and 27 yards), Vince Evans threw to Randy Simmrin for another (four yards), and Glen Walker finished out the scoring with a 44-yard field goal.[3]

**(H) Oct. 2—Iowa—55–0**
USC#13

The Iowa Hawkeyes came in to this game with the Big Ten's top-rated defense, but the Trojans proved too much to handle.

Ricky Bell and freshman Charles White tore up the Iowa defense, with White running for 120 yards and Bell 119 yards. Vince Evans connected with Shelton Diggs on a 17-yard touchdown pass with only two-and-a-half minutes expired in the game, and the onslaught continued. For the game, Diggs had six receptions for 106 yards and a pair of touchdowns. Backup quarterback Rob Hertel came in with USC up by a 21–0 count, and added two scoring strikes. The Trojans so dominated that Iowa produced the fewest passing yards against a USC team with minus 11.[4]

**(N) Oct. 9—Washington State—23–14**

USC#11

This game was played inside the Seattle Kingdome, and marked the first time USC played in a dome. Ricky Bell proved that inside or out, he was a force to be reckoned with. He ran for 347 yards to set a new USC single-game rushing record that he set in 1975. His 51 carries also set a school and Pac-8 record for most carries in a single game. Washington State fought back to tie the game at 14–14 early in the fourth quarter thanks to the passing of Jack Thompson, who threw for 340 yards against the Trojan defense. The game was then turned over to Bell, who pounded away at the Cougar defense, coming up just four yards shy of the all-time NCAA single-game rushing record.[5]

**(H) Oct. 23—Oregon State—56–0**

USC#7

In this homecoming game, the Trojans not only battered Oregon State on the scoreboard, but also physically as five players were forced from the game. The Trojans also suffered a major loss when Ricky Bell was forced from the game with a hip injury after gaining 68 yards on just six carries in the first quarter. Freshman Charles White came to the rescue, and carried on the proud USC tailback tradition by rushing for 107 yards on 18 attempts. The Trojans as a team rang up 526 yards to gain the top spot in the nation with a 491.7 total yards per game average.[6]

**(H) Oct. 30—California—20–6**

USC#4

Charles White once again came in when Ricky Bell was forced out of the game in the second half. He gained 91 yards on 14 carries, and quarterback Vince Evans added 54 yards on the ground and a touchdown in addition to passing for 120 more yards. Cal was enable to get a steady flow going on offense, and the Trojan defense allowed them minus four yards rushing and passing combined. This proved to be the lowest amount ever against a USC team, and also set a conference record. With this victory, the Trojans were locked in a first place tie for Pac-8 leadership at 4–0 with UCLA.[7]

**(A) Nov. 6—Stanford—48–24**

USC#4

The Trojan offensive machine continued to roll, as Charles White gained 136 yards on 23 carries, and Shelton Diggs had three receptions for 100 yards, and tied a school record with three touchdown receptions in one game. The old record was also set against Stanford back in 1952. The defense intercepted four passes, with cornerback Ricky Odom's three thefts leading the way.[8]

**(H) Nov. 13—Washington—20–3**

USC#3

The good news was that Ricky Bell's hip no longer hampered him. Unfortunately, he had a tender left ankle that stymied his ability to run like he was accustomed to. He could only muster 21 yards on 12 carries, but on a positive note, he was able to take over O.J. Simpson's number two spot on the Pac-8's all-time rushing list with 3,431 yards. Shelton Diggs had back-to-back games of 100-plus receiving yards, this time hauling in four passes for 118 yards and a touchdown. The Trojans had a scare when quarterback Vince Evans was knocked unconscious, but he proved to be all right and ready for the conference showdown with UCLA.[9]

**(A) Nov. 20—UCLA—24–14**

USC#3 UCLA#2

With both John McKay and Dick Vermeil starting tenures in the NFL, this rivalry was left in the hands of first-year head coaches, John Robinson and Terry Donahue. However, both men proved they were capable of success by coming into this "Battle of Los Angeles" with impressive records. The Trojans came in with the nation's top-ranked offense, and the Bruins possessed the third best offensive attack and a 9–0–1 record. With such offensive firepower, a high-scoring affair loomed with a crowd of 90,519 inside the LA Coliseum. However, the opposite occurred, as USC's defense stymied the UCLA offense over the first 53 minutes of play.

For over ninety percent of this game, the Bruins could only cross midfield on a few occasions, while USC was in total control, ahead by a convincing 24–0 margin. Initially, even the Trojans had trouble driving down the field throughout the first half. They did manage to produce a 7–0 lead going into the second half, but it was the defense that lit the scoreboard up. While carrying the ball for a gain of three yards, UCLA's Theotis Brown got his elbow hit by one of his blockers, and the ball shot out for anyone to grab. Defensive back Dennis Thurman came up with the valuable commodity as the ball was hanging in the air. He then raced 47 yards for the game's first score.

Glen Walker extended USC's lead to 10–0 in the third quarter with a 42-yard field goal. In the fourth quarter, Ricky Bell, who finished the game with 167 yards on 36 carries, scored the first offensive touchdown of the day on a one-yard run. Vince Evans then ran 36 yards to finish off the Trojans' point production. It was then that the Bruins attempted to make things interesting. Theotis Brown scored on a nine-yard run with 3:59 left, and Jeff Dankworth added a second UCLA tally on a one-yard run with 2:56 to go. This was the sixth straight time that USC beat UCLA with the conference title at stake. The other times were in 1967, 1969, 1972, 1973, and 1974.[10]

**(H) Nov. 27—Notre Dame—17–13**

USC#3 ND#13

The Trojan steamroller continued on its path of destruction, and this game against their other top rival allowed them to win for the 10th straight time. After a scoreless first quarter, the Fighting Irish squandered three opportunities to score in the second quarter. Two fumbles and a failed attempt on fourth-and-one, spurred the Trojans to gain momentum.

With senior quarterback Vince Evans not at his best, coach John Robinson replaced him with backup Rob Hertel. Hertel proved Robinson's faith in him by connecting on six of seven pass attempts in a 67-yard drive that was capped with a six-yard scoring toss to Shelton Diggs just seconds away from halftime.

The Trojans came out now with a full dose of momentum, and started the second half off with a four-play, 80-yard drive that ended with Evans throwing a 63-yard touchdown pass to Randy Simmrin, who finished the game with six receptions for 121 yards. Notre Dame looked to copy USC's swift scoring march by producing one of their own in the opening seconds of the fourth quarter. On three straight passes, the Irish went 68 yards, with Vagas Ferguson scoring on a 17-yard reception from Rusty Lisch. The Trojans then extended their lead to 17–7 on a Glen Walker 46-yard field goal before Notre Dame stormed back to close the gap to four points. The Irish were aided by a pass interference call on defensive back Ricky Odom that placed the ball on the USC one. Lisch then scored from there, but an attempt at a two-point conversion run failed, and that was the way another chapter in this classic series went into the record books.[11]

**Rose Bowl, (N) Jan. 1—Michigan—14–6**
USC#2 MICH#3

After watching their ultimate rival, the Ohio State Buckeyes, make four straight trips to Pasadena as Big Ten representatives in the Rose Bowl, the Michigan Wolverines looked to end that streak. They handed the Buckeyes a 22–0 loss in the final regular season game to finish at 10–1, and lead the nation in total offense (448.1 yards per game), and point production on both offense (38.7 per game) and defense (7.2 per game). As for the Trojans, besides their incredible running attack, the special team unit shined, allowing a mere five yards on 11 punt returns to set a school and conference record.

This was a matchup of the #2 ranked Trojans against #3 Michigan, and both teams were loaded with quality players. The first quarter was a scoreless tug-of-war, but then Michigan broke the tie on a Rob Lytle one-yard run halfway trough the second quarter. Bob Wood's conversion kick was blocked, and the Wolverines led, 6–0. The Trojans struck back quickly on their next possession. Vince Evans capped an 80-yard drive with a one-yard run, and Glen Walker scored the go-ahead point with his conversion kick to give USC a slim 7–6 lead with 1:28 left in the first half.

The third quarter saw the teams revert back to solid defense that prohibited neither offense crossing the opposing goal line. During this time, Michigan was only able to get four first downs, and the Trojans used a powerful ground assault to eat up the clock in the fourth quarter. Freshman Charles White, who finished with a game-high 114 yards on 32 carries, scored on a seven-yard run with three minutes remaining to give the Trojans more of a cushion. Walker added the extra point, and that completed the scoring at 14–6. White was pressed into full time duty when Ricky Bell suffered a head injury in the first quarter after carrying the ball four times for 16 yards. This win allowed John Robinson to become the only coach in USC history to record 11 victories in his first season as coach of USC.[12]

TEAM LEADERS

RUSHING: Ricky Bell—1,433 yards on 280 carries
PASSING: Vince Evans—95 out of 177 attempts for 1,440 yards and 10 touchdowns
RECEIVING: Shelton Diggs—37 catches for 655 yards and 8 touchdowns
SCORING: Ricky Bell—86 points on 14 touchdowns and a 2-point conversion
KICKOFF RETURNS: Charles White—14 for 295 yards (21.1 avg.)
PUNT RETURNS: Dennis Thurman—17 for 68 yards (4.0 avg.)
PUNTING: Glen Walker—57 for 2,139 yards (37.5 avg.)
INTERCEPTIONS: Dennis Thurman—8 for 170 yards and 1 touchdown
TACKLES: Eric Williams—126

## *1977*

HEAD COACH: John Robinson
ASSISTANT COACHES: Marv Goux, Paul Hackett, Mike Haluchak, Hudson Houck, Don Lindsay, John Marshall, Pat Morris, Rich Olson, Mike Sanford, Bob Toledo, Norv Turner
TEAM CAPTAINS: Rob Hertel, Clay Matthews
RECORD: 8–4 overall (5–2 in Pacific–8 Conference)
(Ranked 38th best record in college football out of 145 teams)
FINISH IN CONFERENCE: Tied for 2nd place
FINISH IN NATIONAL POLLS: 13th place in AP and 12th place in UPI
POINTS SCORED PER GAME: 29.8 to rank 16th out of 145 teams
POINTS ALLOWED PER GAME: 17.7 to rank 57th

### Schedule and Highlights

**(A) Sept. 10—Missouri—27–10**
USC#4

The only team to beat USC during John Robinson's tenure as head coach was the Missouri Tigers. After that defeat in the previous season opener, the Trojans ran off 11 straight wins. Despite fumbles and penalties, the Trojans got revenge over Robinson's lone loss with 65,298 looking on at Faurot Field. The Trojans had a 14–0 lead by the end of the first half, but the Tigers came back to close to 14–10 early in the fourth quarter. Rob Hertel then took USC on a 73-yard drive that was capped with him throwing a touchdown pass to Bill Gay. Hertel later put the game away for good with a 10-yard touchdown. For the game, he completed 12 of 20 pass attempts for 203 yards and three touchdowns. Sophomore Charles White lived up to the proud USC tailback tradition by running for 155 yards on 35 carries and scored the Trojans' first touchdown on an 18-yard run. Receiver Randy Simmrin continued on with his solid college career by catching five passes for 107 yards and one touchdown.[1]

**(A) Sept. 17—Oregon State—17–10**
USC#2

USC's Pac-8 opener saw them hampered by fumbles, penalties, and interceptions. Six times they got to inside the Oregon State 40, but missed out on scoring chances. However, in a week of major college football upsets, the Trojans managed to avoid that mishap, even though the Beavers had tied the game at 10–10 in the second half. Rob Hertel and Randy Simmrin then saved the day for USC by teaming up on a 50-yard game-winning touchdown pass with 11:48 left on the clock. The Trojans amassed 415 yards of total offense. Charles White provided the bulk of yardage with a workhorse-like performance that saw him carry the ball 38 times for 188 yards.[2]

**(H) Sept. 24—Texas Christian—51–0**
USC#2

It took 17 years for the Trojans to get even with TCU, but they accomplished their revenge in a big way. This win kept

USC's record on the year perfect, while TCU remained winless. Frank Jordan tied a school record with three field goals in one game, and connected on all of them in the first half. His kicks came from 49, 28, and 45 yards out. Charles White, the second-leading rusher in the nation, saw limited action in this convincing victory, but still gained 81 yards and scored one touchdown. Other Trojan running backs also had very productive days. Lynn Cain ran for 87 yards, while Rod Conners led the USC ground attack with 124 yards on 13 carries, and Dwight Ford had 117 yards on only nine carries and two touchdowns, one coming from 70 yards out. Garry Cobb scored on a 30-yard interception return, Calvin Sweeney on a seven-yard pass from Rob Hertel, and Kevin Williams one for a six-pointer from 18 yards out. Randy Simmrin caught four passes for 63 yards to extend his streak of catching at least one pass per game to 27 straight, which was an on going school record.[3]

**(H) Sept. 30—Washington State—41–7**
USC#2

With 61,809 inside the Coliseum, the Trojans extended their winning streak to 15 straight, and also recorded the football program's 500th victory. Charles White ran for 128 yards on 27 carries and two touchdowns, while Dwight Ford had his second straight 100-yard rushing performance. This time he ran for 118 yards on 13 carries, and scored on runs covering 14 and 52 yards. Ford averaged nine yards per carry, caught two passes for 17 yards, and returned a pair of kickoffs back for a combined 49 yards. Rob Hertel connected on 11 of 18 pass attempts for 182 yards, and Randy Simmrin caught a 48-yard scoring strike.[4]

**(H) Oct. 8—Alabama—20–21**
USC#1 ALA#7

The Trojans came into this game with the Crimson Tide riding the nation's longest current winning streak of 15 straight, and with the number one ranking on the line. Unfortunately, both came to an end on the Coliseum turf to Paul "Bear" Bryant's charges by the slimmest of margins. The Trojans rallied back after being down, 21–6, on two long scoring drives conducted by quarterback Rob Hertel. Before that, Frank Jordan supplied USC with points on two field goals. In an attempt to bring the Trojans back, Hertel threw a 10-yard touchdown pass to Calvin Sweeney, and followed up with a pass to Mosi Tatupu for a two-point conversion to make the score 21–14. The Trojans got the ball back, and with 35 seconds left, Lynn Cain scored to close the gap to one point. John Robinson decided to go for the win, but Hertel's two-point pass attempt intended once again for Tatupu was intercepted by Barry Krauss to seal the victory. For the game, Hertel completed 18 of 30 pass attempts for 239 yards and one touchdown. Randy Simmrin caught six passes for 120 yards to extend his consecutive game streak of getting at least one reception to 29. The Trojans came into this game averaging 315.5 rushing yards, but Alabama allowed them only 120, with Charles White being held to 63 yards on 15 carries. USC also was hampered by 10 penalties that cost them 124 yards. This was only the second loss as head coach of the Trojans for John Robinson up to this time.[5]

**(H) Oct. 15—Oregon—33–15**
USC#6

Despite dropping in the ranking, the Trojans rebounded from their first loss with an easy victory over the Ducks on homecoming weekend. The Trojans were favored by five touchdowns to win, and were up by a 33–0 count halfway through the third quarter when John Robinson let his backup players get some playing time. Rob Hertel set the tone for the game early by throwing a 51-yard scoring strike to Randy Simmrin in the first quarter. Hertel only played in the first half, and completed nine out of 18 pass attempts for 171 yards and two touchdowns. He then gave way to sophomore Paul McDonald, who hit on four of eight attempts for 47 yards. The win gave USC a 3–0 record in the Pac-8 race.[6]

**(A) Oct. 22—Notre Dame—19–49**
USC#5 ND#11

Charles White turned in a fine rushing performance with 135 yards on 25 carries, and Calvin Sweeney caught five passes for 114 yards and one touchdown, but Irish eyes were all definitely smiling, to coin a classic song, on this day. While going through pre-game warm-ups wearing their blue jerseys, Notre Dame head coach Dan Devine had a dose of inspiration in mind for his charges. A few months prior to this game, Devine ordered green jerseys to represent the traditional color of Irish nationalism since the 17th century. He revealed his idea to the four Notre Dame captains, but not to any others. When he unleashed the brand new green jerseys before kickoff of the USC game, the locker room erupted, and the emotion followed the team onto the field, with the end result a resounding thrashing of the Trojans.

With 59,075 fans on hand to witness the green-clad Golden Domers with a warm afternoon serving as nature's backdrop, quarterback Joe Montana led the Fighting Irish on an 11-play, 80-yard drive in the first quarter that was capped by Dave Mitchell's four-yard run. Dave Reeve connected on the extra point, and the Irish were on their way to victory.

The Trojans momentarily made things interesting when Tyrone Sperling put a vicious hit on Terry Eurick, which caused the ball to go flying. USC linebacker Mario Celotto snagged the loose ball out of the air on the Notre Dame five-yard line, and went into the end zone. Frank Jordan's extra point kick tied the game at 7–7. Another USC linebacker came up with a big play a few minutes later, but it never materialized into anything positive for the Trojans. Ed Gutierrez recovered a fumble on the USC 10, however, the Irish got the ball right back on the following play when Charles White fumbled and Bobby Leopold recovered for Notre Dame on the USC 14. Six plays later, Joe Montana scored from the one. On the extra point attempt, the snap from center was not solid, but Ted Burgmeier picked the ball up and threw to Tom Domin for the two-point conversion to make the score 15–7.

Then it was downhill for the Trojans. The play that broke the game open came after Luther Bradley intercepted a pass and gave Notre Dame possession on the USC 37. The Trojan defense held on three plays, and on fourth down, Reeve came on to attempt a long-range field goal. Instead, the play was a fake. Reeve's holder, Ted Burgmeier, jumped up after taking the snap from center and ran for a first down to the USC 13. Montana then connected on a 13-yard pass to All-American tight end Ken MacAfee for the score. Reeve added the extra point, and the rout was on.

In the third quarter, the Irish ran up the score to 35–7. Bob Golic blocked a Marty King punt, and Jay Case picked up the ball and ran 30 yards for a touchdown. Reeve added the extra point. Montana and MacAfee teamed up again, this time on a one-yard scoring toss, but the extra point attempt was missed.

The Trojans added two more touchdowns, but to little fanfare. Lynn Cain scored on a four-yard run, and Rob Hertel threw a 14-yard pass to Calvin Sweeney for USC's other six-pointer. Both attempts on two-point conversions failed. The blowout victory carried Notre Dame through the rest of the season, and eventually to earning their second national title of the decade.[7]

**(A) Oct. 29—California—14–17**
USC#10

A pair of interceptions cost the Trojans in their third loss out of the past four games. The first one was returned to the USC three, and the second came with 1:04 left and the Trojans needing a field goal to tie or a touchdown to win. The Trojans scored their first points four minutes into the second half on a four-yard run by Lynn Cain that tied the game at 7–7. Their final score of the game came on a 31-yard pass from Rob Hertel to Calvin Sweeney. Randy Simmrin's 35 yards receiving allowed him to become USC's all-time leader in receiving yardage. Charles White ran for 154 yards on 32 carries, and Dwight Ford had 93 yards on nine carries.[8]

**(H) Nov. 5—Stanford—49–0**
USC#16

This win gave the Trojans a 4–1 conference record, and put them into a three-way tie with UCLA and Washington for the Pac-8 lead. The Trojans outgained Stanford in running the ball by a 453 to 42-yard margin, on a day that saw USC compile 592 yards of total offense. Charles White led the ground attack with 126 yards on 16 carries and two touchdowns. He also caught a 22-yard touchdown pass from Rob Hertel. His rushing total in this game allowed White to move into seventh place all-time among USC rushers. His 1,972 career yards surpassed Gus Shaver and Jon Arnett. At the conclusion of this game, White had 1,114 yards, which broke Anthony Davis' Pac-8 sophomore record of 1,034 yards set in 1972. Dwight Ford ran for 124 yards on 11 carries and one touchdown, with his scoring jaunt covering 63 yards. "The Mowin' Samoan," Mosi Tatupu, had his best day running the ball as a Trojan, gaining 101 yards on 13 carries. This trio of Trojan runners helped USC set a team record of 27 first downs achieved by running the ball. Randy Simmrin extended his catch-per-game streak to 33 straight, and the Trojan defense came up with four interceptions.[9]

**(A) Nov. 12—Washington—10–28**
USC#14

Three fumbles and three second half interceptions proved to be costly for the Trojans, as their hopes for another trip to the Rose Bowl ended on a cold, rainy day in the Great Northwest. The Huskies performed just the opposite, committing no turnovers. A USC fumble led to Washington's first touchdown, but the Trojans came back to trail by only a 7–3 margin at the end of the first half. A roughing-the-kicker penalty on USC in the third quarter led to another Washington touchdown, and by the time it was 21–3, the game was all but over. The Trojans got as close as 21–10 on a one-yard touchdown run by Charles White, who finished with 101 yards rushing on 22 carries. The Trojans were ranked third in the nation in total offense, and despite the many turnovers, still managed to outgain Washington, 337 yards to 273.[10]

**(H) Nov. 25—UCLA—29–27**
UCLA#17

As this series neared the 50th anniversary of the first clash in 1929, it produced many heart-stopping moments and fantastic finishes. This 1977 edition was one of those that became a classic, as a Frank Jordan field goal split the uprights from 38 yards out in the final two seconds to give USC a narrow victory with 86,168 on hand at the LA Coliseum. This USC victory also prevented the Bruins from going to the Rose Bowl.

The Bruins made a solid statement at the beginning of the game that they were ready to head to the Rose Bowl by getting out to a 10–0 lead in the first quarter. Frank Corral kicked a 52-yard field goal to start things off, and then a Charles White on the USC three-yard line was turned into a Theotis Brown touchdown from the one, four plays later.

It was at this time that Rob Hertel started on his way to leading the Trojans back. For the game he completed 15 of 24 pass attempts for 254 yards and three touchdowns. This gave Hertel 15 touchdown passes on the season, which set a new school record. He began by conducting a 71-yard drive that included three solid gains through the air, and resulted in a Frank Jordan 25-yard field goal to get the Trojans on the board. Hertel then connected on two touchdown passes, with the first going to Bill Gay from 20 yards out. The extra point was missed, and the Trojans trailed, 10–9. They then took their first lead of the game when Hertel connected with Kevin Williams on a 40-yard scoring strike. Hertel then threw to Gay for a two-point conversion, which gave USC a 17–10 advantage at the end of the first half.

Using excellent pass protection to his benefit, Hertel led the Trojans to nine more points in the third quarter. He threw another touchdown pass to Williams (27 yards), and set up a 36-yard Jordan field goal with a 25-yard pass to Randy Simmrin, who finished the game with six receptions for 108 yards. UCLA quarterback Rick Bashore threw a 32-yard pass to James Owens for a touchdown that made the score 26–17 going into the final stanza.

It appeared that the Trojans were in control going into the fourth quarter, but a Brian Baggott interception led to a Corral three-pointer from 20 yards to cut the USC advantage to 26–20 with only 1:39 expired in the fourth quarter. The Trojans were unable to generate a scoring drive, but the Bruins did not. An 80-yard march concluded on the 16th play when tight end Don Pederson caught a one-yard pass from Bashore to tie the game with 2:51 left. Corral then gave the Bruins their first lead since the second quarter when he kicked the extra point that put UCLA up, 27–26.

It was then that the Trojans' offense came alive for one final chance at victory, and the timing could not have been better. On the winning 13-play, 63-yard drive, major contributions came from Charles White, who gained 17 yards on two carries, and Hertel connected with Dwight Ford for nine yards, and Randy Simmrin for 17. The Trojans also got assistance when Johnny Lynn was called for pass interference against receiver Kevin Williams on third-and10, with the ball at midfield and one minute remaining. The penalty moved the ball to the UCLA 40, and allowed the Trojans to continue on their march to victory. With this heart-stopping win, the Trojans knocked UCLA out of Rose Bowl contention and helped Washington earn a trip to Pasadena on New Years Day.[11]

**Bluebonnet Bowl, (N) Dec. 31—Texas A & M—47–28**
USC#20 TEX#17

For the third straight year, the Trojans were playing in a different bowl game. However, despite the venue, the results were the same for the Cardinal & Gold, as they emerged victorious in a wild shootout inside the Houston Astrodome. Leading the charge for USC were quarterback Rob Hertel, and running backs, Charles White and Dwight Ford. Hertel connected on 11 of 15 pass attempts for 246 yards and four touchdowns. Two of his scoring strikes went to Calvin Sweeney (29 and 40 yards), with the other ones going to Randy Simmrin (14 yards) and Charles White (25 yards). Hertel's four touchdown passes tied a school single-game record, and earned him the game's outstanding back award. The running tandem of White and Ford tore up the Aggies' defense. White ran for 186 yards on 21 carries, and Ford 157 on 14 carries. On one of his carries, Ford ran for a 94-yard touchdown, which set a school single-game record for longest run from scrimmage. Another individual school record fell, when Simmrin caught his 99th career pass to move past Lynn Swann's 95 for first place on the all-time list. For the game, a combined 45 Bluebonnet Bowl records were either broken or tied. USC set a total offense record (624 yards), and the teams combined to produce 1,153 yards of total offense. Also scoring for the Trojans were Mosi Tatupu (eight-yard run) and Frank Jordan (22 and 29-yard field goals). Those two field goals gave Jordan 14 on the season, tying him with Chris Limahelu for an all-time single-season school record. The 8–4 Aggies came out fast in this game, scoring the first 14 points in the opening quarter. The Trojans then answered with 34 straight points from the late first quarter through the third to take control of the game.[12]

TEAM LEADERS

RUSHING: Charles White—1,478 yards on 285 carries
PASSING: Rob Hertel—132 out of 245 attempts for 2,145 yards and 19 touchdowns
RECEIVING: Randy Simmrin—41 catches for 840 yards and 5 touchdowns
SCORING: Frank Jordan—68 points on 26 extra points and 14 field goals
KICKOFF RETURNS: Dwight Ford—16 for 319 yards (19.9 avg.)
PUNT RETURNS: Lynn Cain—31 for 216 yards (7.0 avg.)
PUNTING: Marty King—49 for 1,953 yards (39.9 avg.)
INTERCEPTIONS: Ricky Odom—5 for 15 yards
TACKLES: Dennis Johnson—105

## *1978*

HEAD COACH: John Robinson
ASSISTANT COACHES: Jerry Attaway, Marv Goux, Paul Hackett, Gil Haskell, Hudson Houck, Don Lindsay, John Marshall, Bob Toledo, Norv Turner
TEAM CAPTAINS: Lynn Cain, Rich Dimler
RECORD: 12–1 overall (6–1 in Pacific–10 Conference)
(Ranked 1st for best record in college football out of 138 teams)
FINISH IN CONFERENCE: 1st place
FINISH IN NATIONAL POLLS: 2nd place in AP and 1st place in UPI
1978 UPI National Champions
POINTS SCORED PER GAME: 24.5 to rank 33rd out of 138 teams
POINTS ALLOWED PER GAME: 11.8 to rank 10th

### Schedule and Highlights

**(H) Sept. 9—Texas Tech—17–9**
USC#9

The Trojans had earned a reputation as a team that struggled in their season openers over the past few years. This game was no exception. The Red Raiders of Texas Tech came into the Coliseum as 19-point underdogs with a roster consisting of 22 freshman or sophomores on a 44-player roster, and held a 9–0 halftime advantage on the Trojans. Despite nine fumbles, five of them lost, and five penalties, the Trojans managed to regroup and completely destroy Texas Tech in the second half. They rolled to 304 yards in the second half while limiting the Red Raiders to only seven. A pair of one-yard touchdown runs by Lynn Cain and Charles White in the third quarter supplied points necessary to overthrow their scrappy opponent. Frank Jordan completed USC's scoring in the fourth quarter with a 34-yard field goal. Charles White started off the year right with 156 yards rushing on 30 carries. His one-yard touchdown run 18 seconds left in the third quarter gave USC the lead for good.[1]

**(A) Sept. 16—Oregon—37–10**
USC#8

The Trojans came into Eugene, Oregon, for their Pac-10 opener with a simple game plan that had been commonplace for decades. Run the ball, and that they did. Charles White rambled through the Oregon defense for 173 yards on 32 carries and a pair of touchdowns. As a team, the Trojans ran the ball 50 times for 213 yards. After spotting Oregon a 3–0 lead in the first quarter, The Trojans took a 7–3 lead three minutes later on a Lynn Cain nine-yard run and were never challenged again. The Trojan defense accounted for five interceptions, with Herb Ward taking his 64 yards to paydirt in the fourth quarter. The unit also held Oregon to 57 yards rushing on 39 attempts.[2]

**(N) Sept. 23—Alabama—24–14**
USC#7 ALA#1

Once again using their time-honored tradition of a brilliant running attack as the main offensive weapon, the Trojans went into Alabama with 77,000 looking on, and got revenge over the Crimson Tide for a one-point loss the previous season. Running behind what many considered the nation's best offensive line, Heisman Trophy candidate Charles White gained 199 yards on 29 carries, and Lynn Cain had 97 yards on 18 carries. White scored on a 40-yard run to give the 10 1/2-point underdog Trojans a lead they never relinquished. As a team, the Trojans ran the ball 65 times for 309 yards. When not handing the ball off, quarterback Paul McDonald managed to throw a pair of touchdown passes to Kevin Williams from six and 40 yards out.[3]

**(H) Sept. 29—Michigan State—30–9**
USC#3

The Trojans rose up four places in the national rankings after knocking off number one Alabama, and continued on with their winning ways against Big Ten foe Michigan State. The Trojan defense did a great job containing Ed Smith, one of the top quarterbacks in the college ranks. They allowed him only 141 yards through the air, and had three interceptions. Lynn Cain led the USC ground attack with 96 yards rushing, and Charles White added 82 yards on 20 carries and a pair of touchdowns (one and two yards). Paul McDonald threw two touchdown passes to James Hunter for 13 yards and Calvin Sweeney for 50 yards.[4]

**(A) Oct. 14—Arizona State—7–20**
USC#2

The second-ranked Trojans traveled to Tempe, Arizona, to play one of the new additions to the conference. The Sun Devils did not show much hospitality, as they handed USC their first loss of the year. The ASU defense clamped down on the highly-respected USC running game, limiting it to only 70 yards on 39 carries, and holding tailback par-excellence, Charles White, to 59 yards on 18 carries. The unit also blitzed quarterback Paul McDonald often, forcing him to throw before he was ready. The 13-point favorite Trojans could muster up their lone score with 23 seconds left in the game on a 31-yard pass from McDonald to Dan Garcia.[5]

**(H) Oct. 21—Oregon State—38–7**
USC#7

The Trojans rebounded from their loss to Arizona State in fine fashion with a convincing homecoming game win over the Beavers. Charles White ran for 154 yards on 22 carries and two touchdowns from 41 and 13 yards out to lead a backfield that piled up 350 yards on the ground in 64 attempts. Freshman running back Marcus Allen mixed speed and flashy moves to gain 68 yards on 15 carries and scored on a four-yard run. Paul McDonald was smooth at quarterback, completing 10 out of 16 pass attempts for 138 yards and two touchdowns. The Trojan defense made life tough on Oregon State signal caller Steve Smith by sacking him nine times.[6]

**(H) Oct. 28—California—42–17**
USC#6

Teams from Los Angeles were not kind to the California Golden Bears. One week earlier, UCLA won over them, 45–0, and then the Trojans won in convincing fashion over the team from Northern California. Charles White ran for 187 yards on 31 carries to lead a backfield that amassed 386 rushing yards. Lynn Cain added 133 yards on 13 carries and two touchdowns. Paul McDonald was also brilliant at quarterback. He completed 10 of 17 pass attempts for 175 yards and four touchdowns. Kevin Williams was on the receiving end of three McDonald scoring strikes, which tied a school record for most in a single game. Cal took a 3–0 lead into the second quarter, but the Trojans then scored 28 straight points in the second stanza to pull away.[7]

**(A) Nov. 4—Stanford—13–7**
USC#6

The Trojans' other rivals from Northern California made the game a lot closer, but the result was the same, as the Cardinal & Gold prevailed to improve to 4–1 in the Pac-10 race to the Rose Bowl. UCLA was on top of the conference at 6–0, followed by 5–1 Washington. The Trojans compiled 420 yards of total offense, with Charles White gaining almost half of that himself. He ran for 201 yards on 38 carries and scored USC's go-ahead touchdown on a one-yard run in the second quarter. This was White's best game yardage-wise in his three-year Trojan career, and it gave him 3,547 rushing yards, which allowed him to move past O.J. Simpson into third place on the Pac-10's all-time rushing list. Frank Jordan supplied USC with their other points on field goals coming from 34 and 38 yards.[8]

**(H) Nov. 11—Washington—28–10**
USC#5 WASH#19

The Trojans had two major roadblocks on their path to a Rose Bowl berth. They conquered the first hurdle by beating the Huskies by the exact same score that Washington defeated them by one year earlier. With the Washington defense keying on Charles White, the junior tailback found the going tough. He also had a hard time running on a rain-drenched field. These two elements produced only 47 yards for White on 21 carries, and took him out of the Heisman Trophy race. Despite fumbling three times, and losing two of them, White scored a pair of touchdowns. His first, a 10-yard reception from Paul McDonald, gave USC a 7–3 lead, and sparked a 21-point second quarter for USC. His second six-pointer came early in the fourth quarter on an eight-yard run. Lynn Cain provided the Trojans with stellar running on this day, as he carried the ball 25 times for 128 yards. Paul McDonald was very consistent yet again, this time completing 12 of 16 pass attempts for 192 yards and two touchdowns. This victory now set up a Pac-10 showdown between the 5–1 Trojans and 6–1 UCLA Bruins.[9]

**(A) Nov. 18—UCLA—17–10**
USC#5 UCLA#14

The Trojans were once again kings of the Pac-10 after a two-year absence from the throne. It did not take them long to establish who the conference alpha dog was going to be, as the Trojans scored on their first possession of the game and never relinquished the lead. With only 3:53 expired in the first quarter, USC capped an eight-play, 63-yard drive off when Frank Jordan split the uprights from 21 yards out to give the Trojans a 3–0 lead.

Junior quarterback Paul McDonald completed seven of 10 pass attempts on the day for 97 yards and two touchdowns. His first scoring strike came early in the second quarter to Calvin Sweeney from 36 yards out. With Jordan's extra point kick, the Trojans were now up, 10–0. A few minutes later, McDonald threw to Kevin Williams for a 10-yard touchdown, and Jordan gave the Trojans their final point of the game.

The Bruins got on the board for the first time late in the third quarter on a 22-yard Peter Boermeester field goal. With 5:10 left in the game, the Bruins hit paydirt on an 81-yard bomb from Rick Bashore to Severn Reece. The Trojans famed running attack then took over and ran the clock out.

In regards to the USC running attack, Charles White, ran for 145 yards on 33 carries, and owned a piece of conference history in the process. On third and six from the USC 47, with 1:11 left on the clock, White picked up 11 yards, which gave the Trojans a first down and ended any hope that the Bruins had of pulling this one out in the closing seconds. When White dashed for the game-clinching yardage, he became the Pac-10's all-time leading rusher. He added five more yards on the next play, which gave him a career total of 3,739 yards, surpassing former Trojan great Anthony Davis.[10]

**(H) Nov. 25—Notre Dame—27–25**

USC#3 ND#8

After the blowout loss to Notre Dame in the previous "Glamour Game," the Trojans came back strong. Charles White ran for 205 yards on 37 carries, and Paul McDonald passed for 281 yards. However, it all came down to Frank Jordan connecting on a 37-yard field goal with two seconds left in the game that gave USC a victory over the defending national champion Fighting Irish.

The Trojans opened the scoring in the first quarter when McDonald capped a five-play, 55-yard drive with a scoring toss to Kevin Williams that covered 30 yards. Jordan missed on the extra point kick, and USC led, 6–0. The Irish, on a quest to win their 600th football victory, cut the deficit in half with a 47-yard field goal by Joe Unis near the end of the first quarter.

With Charles White supplying the ground attack, McDonald hitting on passes, Calvin Sweeney making five catches for 105 yards, and the defense clamping down, the Trojans outscored Notre Dame, 11–0, in the second quarter. McDonald extended USC's lead to 14–3 with a 35-yard touchdown pass to Dan Garcia, and then threw for a two-point conversion to James Hunter. Jordan added a 39-yard field goal to give USC a 17–3 halftime advantage.

The Irish came alive in the second half. With quarterback Joe Montana connecting on 17 pass completions during that time, the Irish took a late lead and almost pulled off a classic comeback. Instead, it would be Frank Jordan's name that rose to the forefront in the legacy of this great series.

In the third quarter, the Trojans still appeared in total control. After a Joe Unis field goal from 26 yards out narrowed the gap to 17–6, Charles White scored on a one-yard run, and Jordan's extra point made it 24–6 going into the fourth quarter. It was then that Montana and company struck fear into the Land of Troy.

With 12:26 left in the game, Montana connected with Kris Haines on a 57-yard pass that capped off a quick two-play, 80-yard drive. An attempt at a two-point conversion failed, and Notre Dame had now cut USC's lead in half, 24–12. Things started to get serious among the USC faithful when Montana connected on numerous passes that ate up big gains. With 3:01 left, Pete Buchanan scored on a one-yard run to finish off a 14-play, 98-yard drive. Unis added the extra point, and Notre Dame was only down by six points. The fired up Notre Dame defense held USC on their next possession, and took over on their own 43 following a punt.

With the clock ticking down, the Irish went 57 yards in seven plays to take their first lead of the game with a mere 46 seconds remaining. Montana threw a two-yard pass to Pete Holohan for the touchdown, but Montana missed on a two-point conversion pass to Haines.

The score was now 25–24 in favor of Notre Dame, as USC began one final drive to victory. Paul DiLulo took the kickoff back 30 yards, and five plays later, Jordan lined up for what would be his game-winning 37-yard field goal with two seconds left. Paul McDonald did a yeoman's effort to get the Trojans into position for the winning three-pointer. With a sprained ankle, he first connected with Vic Rakhshani on a ten-yard pass. The Trojans then dodged a bullet when McDonald had the ball come out of his hand and into the grasp of a Notre Dame player. The Irish thought it was a fumble recovery, but the officials ruled it an incomplete pass. Only 19 seconds left, the Trojans had new life, and made the most out of it. McDonald connected with Calvin Sweeney for a huge gain of 35 yards, and White carried for a pickup of four. This was when Jordan came onto the field, and within a few seconds, he sent Notre Dame home on the short end of the score in the 50th edition of this series. The Trojans went on to claim a piece of the national championship in the Rose Bowl five weeks later, which was the seventh time in 13 years that either Notre Dame or USC won a national title.[11]

**(A) Dec. 2—Hawaii—21–5**

The Trojans committed errors and penalties against Hawaii that allowed the charges from the "Aloha State" the opportunity to stage an upset. Halfway through the fourth quarter, USC held a narrow 7–5 lead before pulling away. The Trojan defense, accounted for two touchdowns on a Ronnie Lott interception and a Dennis Johnson fumble recovery, but both were negated by penalties. Charles White provided the spark for USC on their trip to the island paradise by rushing for 152 yards on 31 carries.[12]

**Rose Bowl, (N) Jan. 1—Michigan—17–10**

USC#3 MICH#5

This game was a matchup of two top-ranked teams and legendary Michigan coach Bo Schembechler came out to Pasadena for the fifth time in the decade, still in search of his first Rose Bowl victory.

The game was a showcase for defensive football, as both offenses found the going tough. The Trojans used a defensive effort to produce their initial points of the game. On Michigan's first offensive series of the game, Rick Leach had a pass intercepted by Ronnie Lott. The Trojans' great defensive back then covered 33 yards of Rose Bowl real estate before being stopped at the Michigan 16. Three plays later, Paul McDonald rolled to his left and connected with his tight end Hoby Brenner for a nine-yard touchdown. Frank Jordan added the conversion kick, and the Trojans were quickly on top, 7–0.

It was then Michigan's turn to put points on the board following a turnover early in the second quarter. A Paul McDonald fumble was recovered by Gene Bell, and four plays later, Gregg Willner kicked a 36-yard field goal to make it a 7–3 game. In addition to this fumble, McDonald was hounded by the Michigan's defense, causing him to lose another fumble and suffer five sacks for a loss of 47 yards.

The stage was then set for one of the most-talked about incidents in Rose Bowl history. Halfway through the second quarter, Charles White got the call to carry the ball on the Trojans' seventh play of a 50-yard drive. From the three-yard line, White took possession of the ball following the handoff and headed for the sky. While jumping over those battling it out in the trenches, he had the ball stripped by linebacker Ron Simpkins, and Michigan recovered the fumble on the one-yard line. White showed his reaction to what just happened by pounding his fist to the turf in disappointment. It was then that White went down in history as the recipient of the "Phantom Touchdown." It became apparent that two views of the same occurrence could bring about different results. No truer case of this happened when line judge Gilbert Marchman raised his hands over his head to signal a USC touchdown while it was obvious to all that White had fumbled before crossing the goal line. As Marchman signaled touchdown, umpire Don Mason ruled it a fumble and Michigan's ball. A discussion followed, and after a brief meeting, referee Paul Kamanski signaled touchdown. The six-pointer was awarded to White on Marchman's feelings that he broke the plane, and the line judge is the one who watches for forward progress. Marchman held true to what he felt was the correct call, and the play went into the history as a three-yard touchdown run by White that gave the Trojans a 14–3 lead following Jordan's extra point kick.

The Trojans' defense struck once again late in the second quarter. Michigan quarterback Rick Leach was the possessor of an NCAA record for most touchdowns produced (81), but during the first half of this game, his prowess was not appreciated by the USC defense. He threw his second interception of the game, this time to Dennis Smith, who returned his theft 31 yards. Two plays after Smith's interception, Jordan converted on a 35-yard field goal as time expired in the first half to give the Trojans a convincing 17–3 halftime bulge.

Despite Leach's poor first half, in which he connected on only two of 10 pass attempts for 28 yards, he rallied in the second half to finish the game strong. His final stats showed 10 completions out of 21 attempts for 137. He also added a touchdown toss to his day's work, connecting with Roosevelt Smith from 44 yards out at the 7:57 mark of the third quarter to make it a 17–10, which was the way it ended.

The defenses took over from there, and the Trojans would go on to claim a share of the 1978 national championship, while Bo Schembechler's quest for his first Rose Bowl victory as Michigan's mentor was once again denied. Charles White rushed for 99 yards on 32 carries, and his efforts allowed him the privilege of being named the Rose Bowl Co-MVP along with Michigan's Rick Leach.[13]

### TEAM LEADERS

RUSHING: Charles White—1,859 yards on 374 carries
PASSING: Paul McDonald—115 out of 203 attempts for 1,690 yards and 19 touchdowns
RECEIVING: Calvin Sweeney—32 catches for 644 yards and 2 touchdowns
SCORING: Charles White—86 points on 14 touchdowns and a 2-point conversion
KICKOFF RETURNS: Raymond Butler—21 for 438 yards (20.9 avg.)
PUNT RETURNS: Raymond Butler—26 for 171 yards (6.6 avg.)
PUNTING: Marty King—70 for 2,921 yards (41.7 avg.)
INTERCEPTIONS: Dennis Smith—7 for 77 yards
TACKLES: Dennis Johnson—124

## *1979*

HEAD COACH: John Robinson
ASSISTANT COACHES: Jerry Attaway, Artie Gigantino, Marv Goux, Paul Hackett, Gil Haskell, Hudson Houck, Don Lindsay, John Marshall, Norv Turner
TEAM CAPTAINS: Dennis Johnson, Charles White
RECORD: 11–0–1 overall (6–0–1 in Pacific–10 Conference) (Ranked 2nd best record in college football out of 140 teams)
FINISH IN CONFERENCE: 1st place
FINISH IN NATIONAL POLLS: 2nd place in both the AP and UPI
POINTS SCORED PER GAME: 32.4 to rank 6th out of 140 teams
POINTS ALLOWED PER GAME: 14.2 to rank 29th

### Schedule and Highlights

**(A) Sept. 8—Texas Tech—21–7**
USC#1

The defending national champions started the new season off with many star players getting injuries. The injury list included Heisman Trophy candidate Charles White (shoulder), center Chris Foote (ankle), tackle Anthony Munoz (knee), and Ronnie Lott (shoulder). Without many key players, the Trojans seemed ready to go down in defeat. However, backup performers came in and the Trojans pulled out their first win of the year. One player that rose to the challenge was Marcus Allen, who in his first starting role as a Trojan, ran for 105 yards on 20 carries in place of Charles White. Allen's impact was swift. Three plays after White came off the field, Allen scored USC's first touchdown of the year on a one-yard run. Michael Hayes added 84 yards on 19 carries, and Paul McDonald threw two touchdown passes to lead the offense. The Trojan defense had three interceptions.[1]

**(A) Sept. 15—Oregon State—42–5**
USC#1

The top-ranked Trojans once again took to the road, this time for their Pac-10 opener with the Beavers. Mike Harper led the USC ground game with 126 yards on 20 carries, and Marcus Allen scored two touchdowns in the first quarter (two and five yards) to set the tone. The Trojans went out to a 35–3 halftime advantage when Paul McDonald threw two scoring strikes to Kevin Williams (10 and 23 yards), and Harper scored on a one-yard run. Harper added a five-yard touchdown run in the third quarter to complete USC's scoring for the day.[2]

**(H) Sept. 22—Minnesota—48–14**
USC#1

The Trojans were finally able to play in front of their fans in the home opener. Charles White returned to his starting tailback spot after a shoulder injury hampered him since the season opener. He ran for 153 yards on 10 carries, and scored on jaunts from 68 and 10 yards. Marcus Allen ran for a four-yard touchdown, Paul McDonald threw a 17-yard touchdown pass to Hoby Brenner, and Ray Butler returned a punt 67 yards for a fifth touchdown in the first half, and USC had a 35–0 halftime lead. With only five minutes expired in the second quarter, USC head coach John Robinson began taking his starters out, allowing the reserves to get some playing time.[3]

**(A) Sept. 29—LSU—17–12**
USC#1 LSU#20

The Trojans took their number one ranking into LSU's "Death Valley" for the first-ever meeting with the Tigers. Both teams gave everything they had, and with 32 seconds remaining, it was USC that scored what proved to be the winning points. Eric Hipp gave the Trojans a 3–0 advantage going into the second quarter on a 32-yard field goal. The Tigers then came back to hold a 12–3 lead in the fourth quarter. Charles White then scored on a four-yard run with 9:54 remaining in the game to bring USC to within two points of a tie. Then, with 32 seconds remaining, Paul McDonald threw the game-winner to Kevin Williams from eight yards out. McDonald extended his streak to eight games with a touchdown pass, and USC won for the 12th straight time. Charles White placed himself back in contention for the Heisman Trophy by running for 185 yards on 31 carries. The Trojan defense played a solid game by tackling LSU runners for losses on ten occasions, and defensive back Jeff Fisher led the team with nine tackles.[4]

**(H) Oct. 6—Washington State—50–21**
USC#1

Charles White ran for 142 yards on 17 carries and two touchdowns, and Paul McDonald completed 16 of 23 pass attempts for 212 yards and two touchdowns to help get the Trojans to a 43–14 halftime advantage. Marcus Allen added 72 yards rushing on five carries, and scored on runs of 11 and one yard. The Trojans took to the air 24 times in the first half, and scored 27 of their points in the second quarter. They also ran the ball 45 times for 318 yards as a team.[5]

**(H) Oct. 13—Stanford—21–21**
USC#1

On homecoming weekend, the Trojans built a 21–0 halftime lead on two runs by Charles White (seven and one yard), and Marcus Allen (15 yards). The second half was a completely different story, as Stanford rallied to score 21 points in the final 20 minutes to snap USC's 13-game winning streak, and knock them out of the top spot in the national polls. Also ended was Paul McDonald's streak of throwing at least one touchdown pass in nine straight games. With three seconds left, Eric Hipp attempted to pull out a USC victory, but his 39-yard field goal try was blocked. Charles White kept rising in the Heisman Trophy rating with an incredible rushing performance of 221 yards on 32 carries.[6]

**(A) Oct. 20—Notre Dame—42–23**
USC#4 ND#9

Charles White and Paul McDonald said their farewells to the "Glamour Game" in stellar fashion. White ran for 261 yards on 44 carries, and tied a USC record with four rushing touchdowns. McDonald completed 21 out of 32 pass attempts for 311 yards and two touchdowns.

In the final 21 minutes of this game, the teams combined for eight scores, and totaled 1,126 yards of offense. However, prior to the offensive explosion, this game was a very low scoring affair. The first quarter saw no points produced, and at halftime, the scored was knotted at 7–7. Finally, the Trojans broke the deadlock only 23 seconds into the second quarter. The drive was a lengthy one, starting at the USC one. The Trojans received the ball deep in their own territory after stopping the Irish on downs. They then traveled 99 yards in 13 plays, with a 12-yard pass from McDonald to Dan Garcia, who finished the game with eight receptions for 149 yards. Eric Hipp kicked the extra point. Garcia was the game's top receiver with eight catches for 149 yards, but he could not remember much of his great accomplishment. Late in the game, he was knocked unconscious for a few minutes, and could only remember that he scored a touchdown.

Notre Dame scored some five minutes later as Vagas Ferguson, the nation's seventh leading rusher, scored on a one-yard run, and Chuck Male sent the game into the second half tied at 7–7. The first half proved to be a physical battle for dominance, but then the teams decided to just light up the scoreboard by outdueling each other offensively.

Halfway through the third quarter, Charles White finished off a six-play drive with a three-yard run, and Hipp connected on the extra point for a 14–7 USC lead. White provided 31 yards rushing on two carries during the drive, and McDonald hit on three key passes to keep the chains moving. Four minutes later, White added his second six-pointer of the game, this time on a one-yard run. Hipp once again added the extra point, and the Trojans had some breathing room at 21–7. The Irish managed to close to within 21–14 in the final 21 seconds of the third quarter on a 22-yard run by Ferguson, who finished the day with 185 yards on 25 carries.

Over the final fifteen minutes of this game, the Trojans put 21 points on the scoreboard to equal the amount they had throughout the game. Kevin Williams caught a 12-yard scoring toss from McDonald, and Hipp's extra point made it 28–14. The Irish struck back on a Jim Stone two-yard run with 12 minutes remaining. The extra point attempt was missed, but Notre Dame closed to within eight with plenty of time left.

The Trojans then pulled away two minutes later on a one-yard run by White, and Hipp's fourth conversion kick gave USC a 35–20 lead. Chuck Male kicked a 42-yard field goal for Notre Dame, but then White ended officially ended any hopes of a comeback with a one-yard run in the final 28 seconds. Hipp's conversion was the final point scored by USC on Notre Dame in the decade of the 1970's.[7]

**(A) Oct. 27—California—24–14**
USC#3

Charles White once again tore through the opposition, this time for 198 yards rushing on 44 carries and two touchdowns. His touchdown runs of two and five yards came in the fourth quarter to help the Trojans open up a close game that was tied at 7–7 going into the final stanza. Eric Hipp gave USC a 17–14 lead with 2:46 remaining, and then White added his second touchdown run of the game with two seconds left on the clock. Paul McDonald threw for 212 yards and one touchdown, the Trojans rolled up 466 yards of offense, and on top of the Pac-10 standings with a 3–0–1 record.[8]

**(H) Nov. 3—Arizona—34–7**
USC#3

The Trojans continued on their quest to repeat as Pac-10 champions with Charles White and Paul McDonald leading the offensive attack. White ran for 167 yards on 32 carries and one touchdown, and Paul McDonald set a school passing yardage record with 380 yards. The old record was established by Craig Fertig on October 24,1964. McDonald's record came by completing 25 of 35 pass attempts, and he threw for three touchdowns. Dan Garcia had six receptions for 101 yards, and Kevin Williams had five for 110 yards and two touchdowns.[9]

**(A) Nov. 10—Washington—24–17**
USC#4 WASH#15

Charles White was quickly closing in on the coveted Heisman Trophy by running for 243 yards on 38 carries. As a team, the Trojans clinched the Pac-10 championship and a back-to-back Rose Bowl berth. This was USC's 10th conference title, and 10th Rose Bowl appearance, over the previous 14 years. They came into this game at 4–0–1 in the conference, with Washington right behind them at 4–1. After spotting the Huskies a 3–0 lead at the end of the first quarter, the Trojans came back to take a 17–3 lead by the third quarter on two Paul McDonald touchdown passes and an Eric Hipp field goal. The Huskies rallied to tie the game at 17–17 in the fourth quarter. Charles White then took over, running for gains of 29 and 27 yards on two straight plays, to help get the Trojans to the Washington 11-yard line. From there, Marcus Allen scored what proved to be the game-winner, and the USC defense took over from there to secure a trip to Pasadena on New Year's Day.[10]

**(H) Nov. 24—UCLA—49–14**
USC#4

Charles White's swan song at the LA Coliseum, while donning the famed Cardinal & Gold with #12 on it, could not have climaxed a magnificent career any better. He carried the ball 35 times for 194 yards, and tied a school record with four rushing touchdowns. If there was any doubt about his exceptional talent, it was laid to rest nine days after this game when he was officially crowned the winner of the 1979 Heisman Trophy.

The Bruins came into this game as 15-point underdogs, with a 5–5 record. In many cases, records are cast aside when rivals clash, and sometimes, the underdog emerges victorious. However, this 1979 edition of the "Battle for Los Angeles" did not follow the script where the underdog prevails in the end. Reminiscent of the first USC-UCLA game fifty years earlier, the Trojans rolled over the Bruins early and often. In that initial game back in 1929, USC built a 32–0 lead, and fifty years later, they added three points to that, setting a series record for most points in a half with 35. The record-setting point barrage began with White capping of a 14-play, 78-yard drive with a touchdown run from two yards out late in the first quarter. Defensive back Ronnie Lott then struck with a 30-yard interception for a touchdown shortly after White's run to paydirt. White then dominated the second quarter scoring with three touchdown runs from one, 26, and two yards, respectively.

Paul McDonald, who connected on 17 of 23 pass attempts for 199 yards, hit Vic Rakhshani on a five-yard scoring toss in the third quarter. He also suffered a rare occurrence by throwing an interception. Prior to the interception in the third quarter, McDonald had a Pac-10 record of 143 straight passes without being intercepted. Backup tailback Michael Hayes finished off the Trojan point explosion with a 54-yard run late in the fourth quarter. The Bruins received their points on two Rick Bashore to JoJo Townsell passes from 79 and five yards out.[11]

**Rose Bowl, (N) Jan. 1—Ohio State—17–16**
USC#3 OSU#1

After four consecutive trips to the Rose Bowl in the early 1970s, Ohio State suffered a three-year absence from the "Granddaddy of Them All." However, when the final season of the decade came to a conclusion, the Buckeyes left no doubt as to whom the Big Ten representatives in Pasadena were going to be. They ran the table, taking on all comers, and emerged victorious each time en route to being the top team in the country.

The one constant since the 1950's regarding the Scarlett & Gray was coaching icon Woody Hayes. In the previous season's Gator Bowl, Hayes punched Clemson linebacker Charlie Bauman, after he intercepted a pass that killed an Ohio State drive. Hayes was fired the following day after compiling a 238–72–10 lifetime coaching record. It was such a dramatic way for such a revered mentor to exit the gridiron, but time rolled on in Columbus regardless, and a new coach had to be found.

Ohio State hired 48-year old Earl Bruce, a long-time coach on both the high school and college levels since the 1950s, to replace Hayes. He served as an assistant to Woody Hayes from 1966 through 1971, and with star sophomore quarterback Art Schlichter as his field general, Bruce had Ohio State on the verge of a national championship in his first outing as head coach of the Buckeyes. All Ohio State had to do was walk off the Rose Bowl turf victorious, and they would be the alpha dogs of the college football world.

Awaiting the Buckeyes were their old Rose Bowl rivals from the early part of the decade. The Trojans were not going to sit idly by and let the Buckeyes wrap up a spotless record on them, and began their quest to stymie Ohio State's victory celebration in their neighborhood. The Trojans jumped out to a 10–0 lead on an Eric Hipp 41-yard field goal in the opening stanza, and a 53-yard pass from Paul McDonald to Kevin Williams, who put his blazing speed to work on the game's initial touchdown jaunt.

The Buckeyes came back to tie the game by halftime the same way USC jumped out to their 10-point advantage. Kicker Vlade Janakievski got Ohio State's first points on a 35-yard field goal late in the second quarter. As halftime was nearing, Charles White fumbled and Jim Laughlin recovered for Ohio State. Schlichter wasted little time getting the Buckeyes to paydirt. Three plays after starting from his own 20, with time ticking away in the second quarter, Schlichter let a bomb fly, and Gary Williams caught it and scored to complete the 67-yard touchdown with 21 seconds left in the first half. Janakievski then added the extra point to knot the game at 10-all going in to the second half.

Until the closing minute-and-half of the second half, Janakievski provided the only scoring on two field goals from 37 and 24 yards away to give the Buckeyes a 16–10 lead. With 5:21 remaining in the game, the Trojans' offense came out onto the field ready to take possession of the ball possibly for the final time of the season. It was make or break time, and the Trojans chose the former.

With record-breaking Heisman Trophy winner Charles White lined up in USC's famed I-Formation for his final drive in Cardinal & Gold, the Trojans were perched on not only victory, but on the verge of adding to their already spectacular legacy as one of the greatest football programs of all-time. Starting from their own 17-yard line with 5:21 left to play, and a crowd of 105,526 looking on, the Trojans reverted back to the days of a ground pounding attack that would have made the "Thundering Herd" from USC's glory days of the 1920's and 30's proud.

On first down, White took the ball and darted 32 yards off the right guard spot. He then ran for 28 yards on the next play on a sweep around the right end in a classic display of USC's Student Body Right formation. White then came to the sideline to take a brief rest. In his absence, tailback Michael Hayes ran for a gain of seven, and Marcus Allen added five more yards on the next play to give the Trojans a new set of downs at the Ohio State 11. White returned to the action with the crowd cheering at his presence. After acknowledging the frenzied throng with a wave, White took his place in the huddle with a piece of tape across the bridge of his nose that protected a cut, and with blood, dirt, and grass stains covering his uniform. Showing definite signs of being in a classic gridiron battle, White looked to end his illustrious USC career in exquisite fashion. He gained three more yards, then five and another two, which got the ball just shy of the goal line with a new set of downs. It seemed apparent to all witnessing this fantastic finish the identity of who would get the ball next. What remained uncertain was if those in scarlet and gray uniforms could stop the Trojan juggernaut in cleats. The mystery was quickly solved, as White got the call. He took the ball, went airborne, and climaxed the drive by landing the end zone for the touchdown with 1:32 left to tie the score. In this eight-play, 83-yard drive, White carried the ball seven times for 71 yards. Hipp then came in and kicked the Trojans to victory by being true with the conversion. The Buckeyes still had time for one final run at the national championship. From his own 20, Schlichter attempted four straight passes, but they all fell incomplete. The Trojans then took over possession, and just let the clock run out.

This exciting 17–16 win capped off a career that was nothing short of amazing for Charles White. For the game, he carried the ball 39 times for 247 yards, breaking Rose Bowl records in the process. His 247 rushing yards broke the old mark of 194 set by Iowa's Bob Jeter in 1959, and his 39 carries erased the long-standing records of Stanford's Ernie Nevers in 1925, and Vic Bottarei of Cal in 1938, who previously shared the mark with 34. There was no debating the fact that White should receive the game's MVP award, which was the second straight time he received the honor. Also having a solid game in his USC swan song was quarterback Paul McDonald, who completed his college career by connecting on 11 of 24 attempts for 234 yards and a touchdown.[12]

### TEAM LEADERS

RUSHING: Charles White—2,050 yards on 332 carries
PASSING: Paul McDonald—164 out of 264 attempts for 2,223 yards and 18 touchdowns
RECEIVING: Danny Garcia—29 catches for 492 yards and 3 touchdowns
SCORING: Charles White—114 points on 19 touchdowns
KICKOFF RETURNS: Raymond Butler—16 for 285 yards (17.8 avg.)
PUNT RETURNS: Raymond Butler—22 for 303 yards and 1 touchdown (13.8 avg.)
PUNTING: Dave Pryor—42 for 1,542 yards (36.7 avg.)
INTERCEPTIONS: Dennis Smith—3 for 96 yards
Ronnie Lott—3 for 76 yards and 1 touchdown
Herb Ward—3 for 47 yards and 1 touchdown
TACKLES: Dennis Johnson—114

## *1980*

HEAD COACH: John Robinson
ASSISTANT COACHES: Jerry Attaway, Artie Gigantino, Marv Goux, Paul Hackett, Gil Haskell, Hudson Houck, Don Lindsay, Nate Shaw, Norv Turner
TEAM CAPTAINS: Ronnie Lott, Keith Van Horne
RECORD: 8–2–1 overall (4–2–1 in Pacific–10 Conference)
(Ranked 18th best record in college football out of 138 teams)
FINISH IN CONFERENCE: 3rd place
USC was banned from bowl game eligibility due to Pacific–10 penalty
FINISH IN NATIONAL POLLS: 11th place in AP and 12th place in UPI
POINTS SCORED PER GAME: 24.1 to rank 38th out of 138 teams
POINTS ALLOWED PER GAME: 12.2 to rank 12th

### Schedule and Highlights

**(A) Sept. 13—Tennessee—20–17**
USC#5

The Trojans took their 20-game unbeaten streak into Tennessee looking to extend it. They got out to a 10–0 halftime lead, but the Volunteers came back to tie the score at 17–17 with four minutes left. Defensive back Jeff Fisher intercepted a pass and returned it to the Tennessee 44-yard line. Assisted by several pass completions, the Trojans got to within striking distance, and Eric Hipp kicked a winning field goal from 47 yards out with no time left to secure an opening day victory for the Trojans. Marcus Allen continued on with the proud tailback tradition at USC by running for 132 yards on 39 carries and one touchdown.[1]

**(H) Sept. 20—South Carolina—23–13**
USC#4 SOUTH CAROLINA#20

The Trojans opened their home schedule against South Carolina and future Heisman Trophy winner George Rogers. The Gamecocks came into this game with two straight shutouts in which they outscored their opponents 110–0. However, USC ended that streak with less than four minutes expired in the first quarter. They capitalized on a Rogers fumble, and went 30 yards in six plays with Marcus Allen scoring on a one-yard run. Allen added a nine-yard touchdown run later in the game, and finished with 107 yards on 31 carries. Eric Hipp kicked a 47-yard field goal, and a Gordon Adams to Kevin Williams scoring strike amount to 23 points for USC, which was enough to keep them unbeaten in 21 straight games.[2]

**(A) Sept. 27—Minnesota—24–7**
USC#5

Marcus Allen continued his assault on the century mark, as he ran for 216 yards on 42 carries and two touchdowns. The Trojans never trailed, but Minnesota kept things close, as USC only held a slim 10–7 lead with 3:30 remaining in the game. Just like in their previous game, the Trojans added two touchdowns to expand their lead to win by a comfortable margin.[3]

**(H) Oct. 4—Arizona State—23–21**
USC#4

Marcus Allen ran for 132 yards on 36 carries and one touchdown. He also caught five passes for 42 yards, and Gordon Adams completed 20 of 29 pass attempts for 226 yards and one touchdown on USC's homecoming weekend. The Sun Devils were the last team to send the Trojans down in defeat, and they looked to end USC's 22-game unbeaten streak on the university's 100th anniversary celebration. With a tough defensive effort, Arizona State gave the Trojans a rough go of it, especially Marcus Allen, who was limited to four yards rushing and fumbled once in the early stages of the game. The Trojans then took to the air, and Gordon Adams lit up the Los Angeles sky. Hoby Brenner caught seven passes for 87 yards, and Eric Hipp tied a USC record with three field goals in one game. Arizona State gave it one last effort with a 72-yard field goal attempt that fell short, and USC's unbeaten streak went to 23 games.[4]

**(A) Oct. 11—Arizona—27–10**
USC#2

The Trojans took on the Pac-10's other representative from the Grand Canyon State, with the same results as in their previous game. Once again it was Marcus Allen and quarterback Gordon Adams that provided the Trojans with offensive punch. Allen ran for 201 yards on 41 carries and three touchdowns. His 41 carries set an Arizona Stadium record. Adams passed for 209 yards and one six-pointer. After leading, 13–0, at the end of the first half, USC had an interception and blocked punt lead to Arizona getting 10 points that cut the deficit to three points. The Trojans steadied themselves, scored two more touchdowns, and won with ease. This was the ninth time that USC played Arizona since 1916, and the Trojans remained a perfect 9–0 against the Wildcats.[5]

**(A) Oct. 18—Oregon—7–7**
USC#2

In the past two trips to Oregon in 1976 and 1978, the Trojans left with easy wins, compiling a score of 90–10 in those games. However, the new decade saw the Trojans struggle with the Ducks, and got out of Eugene, Oregon, with a 7–7 tie. Oregon was 2–2–1 at the time, but proved to be the Pac-10's version of spoilers in 1980. The Trojans received their only points halfway through the second quarter on a 38-yard pass from Gordon Adams to Jeff Simmons. Penalties and fumbles hurt USC from getting more points. Despite the low score, Marcus Allen was quickly securing his place as the alpha dog of college runners, rushing for 159 yards on 35 carries.[6]

**(H) Nov. 1—California—60–7**
USC#7

This game saw opposite sides of the spectrum for running backs. While Marcus Allen tore through the Cal defense for 133 yards on 29 carries and two touchdowns, the Golden Bears recorded the fewest rushing yards ever gained against USC with minus 28. After their previous opponents kept the games close, Cal did not present any such threat. The Trojans gained 555 yards of offense, and exploded for 39 points in the second half, and extended their unbeaten streak to 27 games.[7]

**(A) Nov. 8—Stanford—34–9**
USC#4

Marcus Allen was living up to the great tradition that was the USC tailback by running for 195 yards on 34 carries and scored USC's first two touchdowns on short runs. This was the 28th straight game that the Trojans emerged unbeaten, breaking the school record for longest unbeaten streak set from 1931 to 1933. The defense played an excellent game. The Stanford offense, led by quarterback John Elway, was considered one of the elite in the country. They came into this game averaging 452.2 yards of offense per game, but the Trojan defense held them to 247 total offensive yards, including only 13 by rushing.[8]

**(H) Nov. 15—Washington—10–20**
USC#2

This loss ended USC's 28-game unbeaten streak, but even in defeat, Marcus Allen was able to excite the Trojan faithful with his exceptional running abilities. He finished the game with 216 yards on 30 carries. The Trojans committed eight turnovers, but they still managed to keep the score close, especially in the first half, when the teams were deadlocked at 3–3 after the first thirty minutes. Washington struck with two touchdowns at the beginning of the second half. Allen then threw a 36-yard scoring strike to Jeff Simmons before the Huskies added a field goal and held off the Trojans to end their unbeaten streak and secure a Rose Bowl berth.[9]

**(A) Nov. 22—UCLA—17–20**
USC#12 UCLA#18

The Bruins came into this game at 7–2, and left it with their first victory over the Trojans in five years. Like in previous years, this classic rivalry came down to one exciting play that pulled out a win, and allowed another player to become part of the lore that surrounded this great series.

This time it was UCLA's Freeman McNeill that will forever be part of the legacy because of his heroics late in the game. With the fourth quarter still in its early stages, the Bruins trailed, 17–14, with possession of the ball at their own 42-yard line. Regular starting quarterback Tom Ramsey proved ineffective in the first quarter, and UCLA head coach Terry Donahue replaced him with sophomore Jay Schroeder.

Schroeder rose to the challenge by connecting on nine of 11 pass attempts for 165 yards and two touchdowns. However, it was his second scoring toss that made history. Schroeder let a pass go down the left sideline. USC defensive back Jeff Fisher deflected the ball. In most cases with a deflected pass, the ball will either be intercepted or fall harmlessly to the ground. This was one of those rare times when neither scenario occurred. McNeill was in the area at the right moment, and caught the deflection, got past Trojan defender Dennis Smith, and completed the 58-yard jaunt to paydirt with 2:07 remaining in the game. McNeill not only secured the win, but gave his coach Terry Donahue his first victory over USC after four years of coming up short.

The Trojans struck first with a 3–0 lead at the end of the opening stanza on an Eric Hipp 32-yard field goal. McNeill then gave the Bruins a 7–3 halftime advantage with a six-yard run. The third quarter saw USC briefly regain the lead on a Scott Tinsley scoring toss to Jeff Simmons that covered 12 yards. Schroeder then threw to Michael Brant for 25 yards to give the Bruins a 14–10 lead at the end of the third quarter.

Marcus Allen, USC's star tailback, and the nation's rushing leader with a 165-yard per game average, was held in check by a UCLA defense that used an eight-man front in an attempt to stop Allen. It worked, as Allen only gained 72 yards on 37 carries for a paltry 1.95 yards per carry. He did, however, manage to crack into the end zone on a one-yard run to give the Trojans a

17–14 lead before McNeill's spectacular play later in the closing minutes.[10]

**(H) Dec. 6—Notre Dame—20–3**
USC#17 ND#2

Notre Dame came into the LA Coliseum looking for their first win there since 1966. This time they appeared to be in good position to end the streak. They were 9–0–1, and one spot away from the top of the college football rankings. However, the Trojans refused to allow the streak to end.

Both defenses held firm in the opening quarter, as neither team lit up the scoreboard. The Trojans then made up for lost time in the second quarter. Defensive back Dennis Smith recovered a Phil Carter fumble on the Notre Dame 31, and six plays later, Michael Harper scored on a six-yard run. Eric Hipp added the extra point, and then accounted for a 22-yard field goal that gave USC a 10–0 halftime lead.

With freshman quarterback Blair Kiel unable to produce any points, Notre Dame head coach Dan Devine replaced him with senior Mike Courey. The switch did little to spark the offense. The Irish did score with Courey at quarterback, but the points came after a turnover gave Notre Dame excellent field position. Scott Zettek recovered a Michael Harper fumble close to the USC goal line, but after Courey was sacked for a 12-yard loss, the Irish had to settle for a 30-yard field goal from the foot of Harry Oliver.

In the fourth quarter, linebacker Chip Banks raced 49 yards down to the Notre Dame one after intercepting a Courey pass. The Irish prevented the Trojans from getting into the end zone, but the drive was salvaged when Hipp connected on a 17-yard field goal to increase USC's lead to 13–3. The Trojans added one final touchdown to their day's work on Harper's second scoring run of the game, this time on a 10-yard run. This was USC head coach John Robinson's 50th win with the program, and the game also marked the final time Dan Devine roamed the sidelines for Notre Dame.[11]

### Team Leaders

Rushing: Marcus Allen—1,563 yards on 354 carries
Passing: Gordon Adams—104 out of 179 attempts for 1,237 yards and 7 touchdowns
Receiving: Marcus Allen—30 catches for 231 yards
Scoring: Marcus Allen—84 points on 14 touchdowns
Kickoff Returns: Michael Harper—6 for 153 yards (25.5 avg.)
Punt Returns: Timmy White—14 for 77 yards (5.5 avg.)
Punting: Dave Pryor—48 for 1,911 yards (39.8 avg.)
Interceptions: Ronnie Lott—8 for 166 yards and 1 touchdown
Tackles: Chip Banks—107

## *1981*

Head Coach: John Robinson
Assistant Coaches: Foster Andersen, Jerry Attaway, Artie Gigantino, Marv Goux, Gil Haskell, Hudson Houck, Walt Ransom, Nate Shaw, R.C. Slocum, Norv Turner
Team Captains: Marcus Allen, Chip Banks
Record: 9–3 overall (5–2 in Pacific–10 Conference)
(Ranked 19th best record in college football out of 137 teams)
Finish in Conference: Tied for 2nd place
Finish in National Polls: 14th place in AP and 13th place in UPI
Points Scored Per Game: 24.5 to rank 32nd out of 137 teams
Points Allowed Per Game: 14.2 to rank 26th

### Schedule and Highlights

**(H) Sept. 12—Tennessee—43–7**
USC#5

The Trojans had 62,147 in attendance at the Coliseum for their home opener under the lights. They got out to a 26–0 halftime advantage, added 17 more points in the second half, and compiled 532 yards of offense. The defense limited Tennessee to 159 total yards. Marcus Allen ran for 210 yards on 22 carries and tied a school record with four rushing touchdowns.[1]

**(A) Sept. 19—Indiana—21–0**
USC#2

The Trojans continued on with their winning ways, this time by posting a shutout. Marcus Allen was the main weapon for USC, as he ran for 274 yards on 40 carries and two touchdowns. As a unit, the offense gained 465 yards, while the defense held Indiana to 190 yards of total offense.[2]

**(H) Sept. 26—Oklahoma—28–24**
USC#1 OK#2

In this battle of the two top-ranked teams, Marcus Allen continued to amaze the college football community by running for 208 yards on 39 carries and two touchdowns. Allen's first touchdown tied the game in the opening quarter. His second, a three-yard run in the fourth quarter, cut Oklahoma's lead to 24–21. Fred Cornwell then caught a seven-yard touchdown pass from John Mazur with two seconds left to allow the Trojans to remain the top-ranked team in the nation.[3]

**(A) Oct. 3—Oregon State—56–22**
USC#1

Marcus Allen ran for 233 yards on 35 carries and three touchdowns. Along the way to another incredible performance, Allen set two NCAA records in the process. He became the first college player in history to rush for more than 200 yards in four straight games, and his 925 yards on the ground in the opening games overtook Greg Pruitt's old record of 905 set as an Oklahoma Sooner one decade earlier. The USC running attack led by Allen was so powerful, that it accounted for 407 of the team's 541 total yards.[4]

**(H) Oct. 10—Arizona—10–13**
USC#1

The Trojans opened up a 10–0 lead after less than eight minutes and appeared on the way to another easy win. Marcus Allen scored USC's lone touchdown on a 74-yard run, and finished the game with 211 yards on 26 carries. He also extended his NCAA record to five straight games of 200 or more rushing yards. Steve Jordan added a 21-yard field goal for the Trojans. The Wildcats then cut the deficit to 10–6 by the third quarter on a pair of Brett Weber field goals. The game winner was provided when Tom Tunnicliffe threw a 13-yard touchdown pass to Vance Johnson. This marked the first time in their history that Arizona defeated the Trojans.[5]

**(H) Oct. 17—Stanford—25–17**
USC#7

In USC's homecoming game, Marcus Allen continued on with his incredible season running the football. In this game

Allen ran for 153 yards on 40 carries and one touchdown. This was the first time all season that he was held under 200 rushing yards. Freshman kicker Steve Jordan added his name to the USC record book by hitting on a 52-yard field goal that surpassed Chris Limahelu's old mark of 50 yards set in 1974. He added two more field goals to become the fifth Trojan to kick three field goals in one game, tying a record that his brother Frank Jordan also owned a piece of. The Trojans came out fast in this game, gaining 262 of their 346 total yards in the first half. Quarterback John Mazur threw for 175 of those yards in the first half. With the Trojans at a 25–3 advantage, Stanford quarterback John Elway attempted to rally his team by throwing for 199 yards in the second half. The USC defense did their part by recording eight sacks, four of which came from tackle Harvey Edwards.[6]

**(A) Oct. 24—Notre Dame—14–7**
USC#5

The Fighting Irish were on their way to the first losing season since 1963 when the Trojans came into South Bend to play on a cold Midwest October day. The Trojans had the pleasure of having ten players from USC's 1931 team on hand to cheer for the present team. They were there to honor their great Notre Dame coach Knute Rockne on the 50th anniversary of his untimely death in a plane crash.

Neither team was able to get on the board throughout the first half, despite many opportunities to do so. Notre Dame missed a short-range field goal, and crossed into USC territory three times before giving up possession. The Trojans also got across midfield three times, reaching as far as the Irish 28. Finally, near the halfway mark of the third quarter, the tie was broken when Marcus Allen ran the final 14 yards on a five-play, 69-yard drive. Freshman kicker Steve Jordan then booted the extra point to make it a 7–0 affair. Allen continued to tear up the opposition with his running. On this occasion, he ran for 147 yards on 33 carries, and by game's end, he walked off the field victorious all four times he played against Notre Dame.

As the third quarter was winding down, the Irish tied the game on a five-yard run by Phil Carter. The Trojans then went on to victory after Joey Browner returned a punt six yards to the Notre Dame 44. Within three plays, the Trojans secured the win. Allen started the winning drive off with run of 21 yards down the sideline. He was then dumped for a loss of three yards by All-American linebacker Bob Crable. That set up second down and 13 to go from the Notre Dame 26. Todd Spencer got the call, and bolted through a big hole opened for him by Bruce Matthews, a few seconds later, he crossed the goal line with 4:52 remaining. Jordan then added the game's final point.[7]

**(H) Oct. 31—Washington State—41–17**
USC#4 WASH#14

On a warm Southern California day, the Trojans romped over the Cougars by dominating every quarter. Marcus Allen led the onslaught by running for 289 yards on 44 carries. He scored four out of the five USC touchdowns, and set an NCAA record with 200 or more rushing yards in a season with six. As a unit, the Trojan offense gained a whopping 543 yards, with Allen getting over half that amount all by himself. Chip Banks provided the defense with a solid showing by finishing with 15 tackles.[8]

**(A) Nov. 7—California—21–3**
USC#3

The Trojans clung to a 7–0 lead in the first half on Marcus Allen's 19th touchdown of the season. In the third quarter, the Trojans stayed on the ground, gaining 135 yards and getting another touchdown from Allen. He later added a third touchdown. In addition to his three-touchdown performance, Allen also overtook Tony Dorsett of Pitt as the all-time single-season rushing record holder with 1,968 yards. He set the record in the fourth quarter, and finished the game with 243 yards on 46 carries.[9]

**(A) Nov. 14—Washington—3–13**
USC#3

The Huskies became the first team in 10 years to beat the Trojans two straight times. Marcus Allen was held under 200 rushing yards, but still finished with an impressive 155 yards on 38 carries. Allen was the top yardage gainer for the Trojans, as his rushing total accounted for almost all of the team's 182 total yards. Hurting the Trojans on this day were 11 penalties and 83 yards in losses caused by those infractions. This tough loss killed USC's hopes of a Rose Bowl berth.[10]

**(H) Nov. 21—UCLA—22–21**
USC#10 UCLA#15

Through the history of this cross-town series, many names were immortalized for their performance. More often than not, players who touched the ball on a frequent basis were the ones that garnered headlines and lore. However, in this game, a player not used to holding the ball was the star, as his possession of the ball only took a split second, but the result would remain one of the key moments in the "Battle of Los Angeles."

With four seconds remaining, and USC holding a slim one point lead, nose guard George Achica blocked Norm Johnson's 46-yard field goal attempt to preserve the win and knock UCLA out of Rose Bowl contention.

The Trojans opened the scoring on a Steve Jordan 38-yard field goal, but Kevin Nelson put the Bruins in the lead with an 11-yard run. The Trojans then went back on top by a 12–9 count in the second quarter on another Jordan field goal, this time from 44 yards out, and on a Marcus Allen seven-yard run. A 23-yard touchdown pass from Tom Ramsey to Ricky Coffman, and a Norm Johnson 32-yard field goal with 49 seconds left in the first half gave the Bruins an 18–12 lead.

The Bruins scored the only points of the third quarter on a Johnson 28-yard field goal to increase their advantage to 21–12 going into the fourth quarter. Jordan cut the deficit to 21–15 early in the fourth quarter with a 22-yard field goal. The Trojans got possession back when Troy West intercepted a pass at the UCLA 39. The Trojans then went to their famed ground attack to wear the defense down. With Allen and Todd Spencer running the ball, the offense got to the UCLA five-yard line. Allen then ran through a huge hole on the left side created by his linemen to tie the game at 21–21 with 2:14 left to play. On the day, Allen turned in another incredible performance en route to the Heisman Trophy. He carried the ball 40 times for 219 yards, followed by his backfield mate Spencer's 86 yards on 12 carries. Following Allen's game-tying six-pointer, Jordan added the all-important conversion kick, and the Trojans were up by one.

It appeared that the Trojans had the game wrapped up for good with 1:19 left when Joe Turner intercepted a Ramsey pass. However, linebacker August Curley was penalized for roughing the passer, and the Bruins were awarded 15 yards and a first down at the USC 44. UCLA then got to the 29 before calling on Johnson with seconds remaining for an attempt at a game winning field goal. It was then that George Achica's block ended the Bruins' hopes of victory.[11]

**Fiesta Bowl, (N) Jan. 1—Penn State—10–26**
USC#8 PENN#7

These teams might have been close in the national polls, but in this game, played at Sun Devil Stadium in Tempe, Arizona, the Nittany Lions were far superior. This was supposed to feature record-setting Heisman Trophy winner Marcus Allen against the always-threatening talents of Penn State running back Curt Warner. The clash of west coast, east coast runners never played out, as Warner dominated the matchup with 145 yards on 26 carries, and two touchdowns. He earned Offensive Player of the Game honors, while Marcus Allen was hounded throughout the game by a tenacious Penn State defense. It appeared that it was going to be a rough outing for Allen from the beginning, as he fumbled on the first play of the game. Penn State's Roger Jackson recovered the fumble, and Warner scored two plays later on a 17-yard run. For the game, Allen carried the ball 30 times for 85 yards, which was well below his season average of 212.9 rushing yards per game. It also marked only the second time in Allen's tenure as a USC tailback that he was held under the century mark. The first time came in 1980 against UCLA.

USC linebacker Chip Banks got the Trojans on the board in the first quarter after returning an interception 20 yards for a touchdown. Steve Jordan then tied the game at 7–7 with the conversion kick. From there it was all Penn State, as they lit the scoreboard up with 17 straight points to take command in the third quarter with a 24–7 advantage. Penn State received their scores on a 52-yard pass from Todd Blackledge to Gregg Garrity, a Brian Franco 21-yard field goal, and Warner scored his second six-pointer of the game, this time from 21 yards, to put this Fiesta Bowl away. Jordan added USC's final points of the day on a 37-yard field goal, and Penn State closed out the festivities by recording a safety on a blocked punt that went out of the end zone. The win allowed Penn State to finish #3 in the national polls, and gave them a spotless 3–0 mark in Fiesta Bowl competition.[12]

### TEAM LEADERS

RUSHING: Marcus Allen—2,427 yards on 433 carries
PASSING: John Mazur—93 out of 194 attempts for 1,128 yards and 7 touchdowns
RECEIVING: Marcus Allen—34 catches for 256 yards and 1 touchdown
SCORING: Marcus Allen—138 points on 23 touchdowns
KICKOFF RETURNS: Fred Crutcher—16 for 316 yards (19.8 avg.)
PUNT RETURNS: Joey Browner—17 for 136 yards (8.0 avg.)
PUNTING: Dave Pryor—51 for 2,097 yards (41.1 avg.)
INTERCEPTIONS: Chip Banks—4 for 27 yards and 1 touchdown
TACKLES: Chip Banks—137

## *1982*

HEAD COACH: John Robinson
ASSISTANT COACHES: Foster Andersen, Jerry Attaway, Artie Gigantino, Marv Goux, Gil Haskell, Hudson Houck, Russ Purnell, Walt Ransom, Nate Shaw, Ted Tollner, Norv Turner
TEAM CAPTAINS: George Achica, Joey Browner, Bruce Matthews
RECORD: 8–3 overall (5–2 in Pacific–10 Conference)
(Ranked 19th best record in college football out of 113 teams)
FINISH IN CONFERENCE: Tied for 3rd place
USC was banned from bowl game eligibility due to an NCAA penalty. This infraction occurred over money being given to players over tickets sales. Also included in this investigation were charges of academic fraud, improper employment and eligibility. These charges brought with them a three-year probation, a two-year postseason ban, a two-year television ban, and recruiting limitations.
FINISH IN NATIONAL POLLS: 15th place in AP and 14th in *USA Today*. The *USA Today* newspaper began its poll of Division 1-A teams in 1982.
POINTS SCORED PER GAME: 27.5 to rank 27th out of 113 teams
POINTS ALLOWED PER GAME: 13.0 to rank 9th

### Schedule and Highlights

**(A) Sept. 11—Florida—9–17**
USC#10 FLA#11

The program renowned as Tailback U crumbled on this day, as USC gained only 84 yards on the ground in front of a record crowd of 73,230 at Florida Field. Florida linebacker Wilbur Marshall led a tough Florida defense with 13 tackles. Quarterback Sean Salisbury and receiver Jeff Simmons performed well for USC despite the loss. Salisbury threw for 222 yards and one touchdown, a 19-yard pass to tight end Pat McCool. Simmons had five receptions for 103 yards.[1]

**(H) Sept. 18—Indiana—28–7**
USC#19

Tailback U came around as Fred Crutcher ran for 123 yards on 28 carries. The Trojans scored the first four times they had possession, with Sean Salisbury directly involved in three of the four six-pointers USC produced. He scored on a quarterback sneak, and threw two touchdown passes to Todd Spencer and Todd Dellutri. Dellutri's reception was his first-ever at USC. Joey Browner scored USC's other touchdown on a 54-yard punt return.[2]

**(A) Sept. 25—Oklahoma—12–0**
USC#18

This was the first time in 181 games that Oklahoma was shut out. The Trojans received one of their touchdowns on an exciting play. First, Sean Salisbury handed off to Fred Crutcher, who then pitched the ball to receiver Timmie Ware. Ware then threw for a 67-yard touchdown to Jeff Simmons. Salisbury threw a one-yard pass to John Kamana for USC's other touchdown. Riki Gray and Joey Browner led the Trojan defense with 13 and 10 tackles, respectively.[3]

**(H) Oct. 2—Oregon—38–7**
USC#16

The USC defense once again prevented an opponent from scoring. Oregon's only touchdown came on a blocked punt in the second quarter. With tailbacks Michael Harper and Fred

Crutcher out with injuries, fullback Todd Spencer moved over to tailback and did not disappoint. He carried the ball 29 times for 149 yards, scored three touchdowns, and had three receptions for 48 yards.[4]

**(A) Oct. 16—Stanford—41–21**
USC#14

The Trojans continued on with a nation-best streak of scoring in 171 straight games. Despite losing 14 players to injuries from the start of the season, USC improved to 4–1. Helping to fill the void created by injuries was fourth-string tailback Anthony Gibson, who became the third USC tailback in the season to top the 100-yard barrier. Filling in for the injured Todd Spencer, Gibson ran for 120 yards on 19 carries and scored three touchdowns. Before his injury, Spencer gained 99 yards on 14 carries. Also assisting the Trojans was Sean Salisbury, who passed for 210 yards.[5]

**(H) Oct. 23—Oregon State—38–0**
USC#12

The USC defense had a goal line stand and 17 tackles for losses to assist the Trojans on homecoming weekend. The offense was sparked by the passing ability of Sean Salisbury, who completed 10 of 14 attempts for 130 yards in the first half. During the second half, a great deal of reserve players received playing time. Scoring for USC in their second shutout victory of the season were Anthony Gibson (on a pair of one-yard runs), Todd Spencer (one-yard run), Andrew Jackson (six-yard run), Timmie Ware (13-yard pass from Salisbury), and Steve Jordan (22-yard field goal).[6]

**(A) Oct. 30—Arizona State—10–17**
USC#12 ASU#7

Jeff Simmons tied a USC single-game record with 11 receptions first set by Fred Hill in 1964. Simmons gained 173 yards and scored one touchdown in USC's first loss since opening day. In a battle between the Pac-10's top two defenses, quarterback Sean Salisbury suffered a serious injury to his right knee ligaments in the third quarter. Scott Tinsley replaced him, and threw for 99 yards in an attempt to rally the Trojans.[7]

**(H) Nov. 6—California—42–0**
USC#16

The Trojans were back in the win column after their third shutout of the season. Todd Spencer ran for 69 yards and three touchdowns before an ankle sprain took him out of action. Scott Tinsley, Sean Salisbury's replacement at quarterback, completed six of 11 pass attempts, and USC gained 299 yards of total offense. The Trojan defense intercepted a team record eight passes, with two going for touchdowns. Tackle Byron Darby and cornerback Darrel Hopper each scored after their interceptions, and Keith Browner's set up a touchdown. In addition to their interceptions, the defense held Cal to a mere 23 rushing yards.[8]

**(A) Nov. 13—Arizona—48–41**
USC#16

The Trojans set a team and NCAA record by returning three interceptions for touchdowns. The defenders who returned their interceptions for touchdowns were Joey Browner (53 yards on the last play of the first half), Troy West (27 yards), and Darrel Hopper (59 yards). Scott Tinsley and Jeff Simmons starred for the offense. Tinsley threw for 209 yards and three touchdowns, and Simmons had six receptions for 105 yards and two touchdowns.[9]

**(A) Nov. 20—UCLA—19–20**
USC#15 UCLA#11

One year earlier, it was a swat that ended UCLA's hopes of victory against USC. This time out, it was a sack that delivered doom, but it the Bruins that proved the old adage of what comes around goes around to be true. With a damaged right knee that was in need of surgery, UCLA's nose guard Karl Morgan came up huge when he preserved a win by sacking quarterback Scott Tinsley on an attempted two-point conversion pass, after the Trojans had scored with no time remaining in the game.

The Bruins took an early lead, scoring on their first possession of the game. Tom Ramsey capped off an 80-yard drive with a scoring strike covering nine yards to tight end Harper Howell. Steve Jordan then got the Trojans on the board with a 44-yard field goal before a 23-yard run by Danny Andrews gave the Bruins a 14–3 lead at the end of the first quarter.

A Don Rogers interception returned possession over to the Bruins at the USC 36 in the second quarter, and John Lee kicked a 45-yard field goal to extend UCLA's advantage to 17–3. The Trojans were able to cut the deficit to 17–10 by halftime, after safety Tony Brewer recovered a Kevin Nelson fumble. Five plays later, Todd Spencer scored on a three-yard run in the closing minutes of the second quarter.

The only points scored in the third quarter came with 2:22 expired from the clock. Scott Tinsley fumbled, and UCLA defensive tackle Mark Walen recovered the ball on the USC 29. Three plays later, Lee kicked a 42-yard field goal that gave the Bruins a 20–10 lead going into the fourth quarter.

The UCLA defense played tough and kept the Trojans clamped down. Early in the fourth quarter, the Bruins continued on with their defensive prowess after the Trojans drove from the USC 41 to the UCLA 16. The defense allowed some big ground gains, but tightened up from there. Over the next seven plays, USC could only get to the six yard line. Facing a fourth-and-goal, Steve Jordan salvaged the drive with a 21-yard field goal to bring the Trojans to within seven points of the lead, at 20–13.

The USC defense was also performing well, especially in the second half. They held the Bruins to a mere one first down throughout the second half. A punting duel was the fashion during the second half, but then the Trojans decided to make things interesting down the stretch. After forcing UCLA to punt with 5:28 left, Scott Tinsley went to work against the Bruins' pass defense. He connected with Jeff Simmons for 17 yards, and to Timmy White for 15. The Bruins once again began to tighten up their defensive stand the closer USC got to the end zone. The Trojans were on the UCLA 15 with slightly over two minutes remaining. Seven plays later, Tinsley broke through the defense with a one-yard scoring toss to tight end Mark Boyer with three seconds remaining on the clock. Trailing by one point, the Trojans went for the win instead of a tie, as 95,763 looked on from the confines of the Rose Bowl. It was then that Karl Morgan earned his place among the players of lore in the history of the "Battle for Los Angeles."[10]

**(H) Nov. 27—Notre Dame—17–13**
USC#17

This victory secured a team record for most consecutive winning seasons at USC with 21. It also tied a Pac-10 record. Scott Tinsley threw for 243 yards, and the defense prevented not one single opposing runner to gain over 100 yards all season. This was also John Robinson's final game of his first tenure as USC's head coach.

Notre Dame got out to a 10–0 second quarter lead on a Larry Moriarty two-yard run and a 40-yard field goal by Mike Johnston. The Trojans were able to get points on the board when Steve Jordan kicked a 35-yard field goal with five seconds remaining in the first half.

The Trojan running game had its share of trouble against the Irish defense. In the second half, the plan of attack was to go through the air, and Scott Tinsley directed the offense to a pair of six-pointers that proved to be the game winners. However, prior to Tinsley filling the Southland sky with passes, the Irish extended their lead to ten points on a 47-yard Mike Johnston field goal for a 13–3 lead. Receiver Jeff Simmons had a big day for the Trojans by catching 11 passes for 149 yards. His reception total tied his single-game mark set one month earlier against Arizona State.

Tinsley then went to work on the Notre Dame secondary. The Trojans got their first touchdown on a seven-play, 70-yard drive, which saw Tinsley throw for 52 yards to four different receivers. Also helping the USC cause was a pass interference penalty on Chris Brown. Michael Harper finished the drive off with a six-pointer from the five-yard line to close the gap to 13–10.

With the game ticking away and three minutes left in the fourth quarter, The Trojans started what turned out to be the winning drive from their own 40. Tinsley once again used his arm and receivers to account for 36 yards of real estate. Chris Brown was flagged for another pass inference penalty, and the infraction placed the ball on the one. Harper got the call, but fumbled as he dove over the goal line. However, the ruling on the field was that he fumbled after crossing the goal line, therefore the touchdown counted with 48 seconds left. It proved to be one of the most controversial rulings in the series' history. The Irish had one final attempt at victory. They made it down to the USC 32 and had time for one chance at the end zone. Blair Kiel threw to Tony Hunter in the end zone. Joey Browner and Darrel Hopper converged to break the pass up before Hunter could haul it in for the game winner. With victory sealed, the Trojans then gave head coach John Robinson one last victory ride on their shoulders.[11]

### Team Leaders

Rushing: Todd Spencer—596 yards on 141 carries
Passing: Sean Salisbury—82 out of 142 attempts for 1,062 yards and 6 touchdowns
Receiving: Jeff Simmons—56 catches for 973 yards and 5 touchdowns
Scoring: Steve Jordan—68 points on 35 extra points and 11 field goals
Kickoff Returns: Joey Browner—6 for 134 yards (22.3 avg.)
Punt Returns: Joey Browner—29 for 273 yards and 1 touchdown (9.4 avg.)
Punting: Dave Pryor—64 for 2,741 yards (42.8 avg.)
Interceptions: Troy West—5 for 62 yards and 1 touchdown
Tackles: Riki Gray—131

## *1983*

Head Coach: Ted Tollner
Assistant Coaches: Foster Andersen, Frank Flaks, Artie Gigantino, Darren Moon, Pat Morris, Russ Purnell, Donnie Rea, Nate Shaw, Jerry Simmons, Norv Turner, Dave Wannstedt
Team Captains: Tony Brewer, Jeff Brown, Keith Browner, Fred Cornwell, Tony Slaton
Record: 4–6–1 overall (4–3 in Pacific–10 Conference)
(Ranked 70th best record in college football out of 112 teams)
Finish in Conference: 4th place
USC was banned from bowl game eligibility due to an NCAA penalty
Finish in National Polls: No ranking in Top 25
Points Scored Per Game: 19.1 to rank 74th out of 112 teams
Points Allowed Per Game: 21.6 to rank 60th

### Schedule and Highlights

**(H) Sept. 10—Florida—19–19**
USC#9 FLA#18 USC

With seven seconds left, USC had a pass intercepted, but Florida was penalized on the play for having 12 men on the field. The Trojans were awarded 15 yards and had renewed hope. They took advantage of the opportunity given to them by scoring on a 25-yard pass from Salisbury to Timmie Ware with no time left on the clock. Unfortunately, a botched snap on what would have been the winning extra point kick ended the game in a tie. Salisbury threw for 229 yards and two touchdowns, and Ware finished with four receptions for 117 yards in Ted Tollner's coaching debut at USC.[1]

**(A) Sept. 17—Oregon State—33–10**
USC#14

Fred Crutcher ran for 111 yards on 17 carries, and as a team, the Trojans amassed 289 yards on the ground for the most since 1981. The defense forced six turnovers, three of which set up touchdowns, and the end result was the first coaching victory at USC for Ted Tollner.[2]

**(H) Sept. 24—Kansas—20–26**
USC#10

In the first three games of the season, the Trojans experienced a tie, a win, and then defeat, with the latter coming at the hands of the Jayhawks. Kansas rolled to 483 total offensive yards, but USC finished with an impressive 362. This was the most offensive yardage allowed by a USC defense since the 1979 Notre Dame game. Sean Salisbury produced a solid game for USC with 233 passing yards and one touchdown.[3]

**(A) Oct. 1—South Carolina—13–38**

This was the first-ever game between two college football teams with the initials of USC. Fumbles and errors led the Trojans to their second straight defeat for the first time in three years.[4]

**(H) Oct. 8—Washington State—38–17**

After a pair of losses to non-conference opponents, the Trojans returned to Pac-10 action, and came away with a spotless 2–0 record within the conference after this convincing victory. Fred Crutcher ran for 106 yards on 25 carries, Sean Salisbury threw for 256 yards and three touchdowns, and the offense totaled 486 yards of offense. USC turnovers allowed the Cougars to tie the game at 17–17 going in to the second half, but the Trojan defense then shut Washington State down while the offense rang up 21 points. This was the 13th straight time that USC won over Washington State.[5]

**(H) Oct. 15—Arizona State—14–34**

ASU#18

The Trojans went down in defeat for the first time in Pac-10 competition on homecoming weekend. The Sun Devils got out to a 34–0 lead before the Trojans managed to score two touchdowns in the second half.[6]

**(A) Oct. 22—Notre Dame—6–27**

The controversial ending to the previous matchup with the Trojans remained in the minds of the Irish as USC's arrival in South Bend approached. Despite being seven-point underdogs, the Irish looked to the past for inspiration and received it in the form of green jerseys. Six years to the day, the Irish changed from their blue jerseys to green and crushed the Trojans en route to the 1977 national championship. Following the season, they returned to blue until this game. The jerseys used in 1983 did have blue trim to stay with the proud tradition of Notre Dame, but the end result was the same.

With 59,075 looking on, the Irish took a 7–0 lead late in the first quarter on an Allen Pinkett run that covered 11 yards. He added a nine-yard touchdown run in the second quarter, and a Mike Johnston field goal from 30 yards out made it a 17–0 Notre Dame advantage at the half.

In the third quarter, Pinkett added his third touchdown run of the game, with this one coming from 11 yards out, and it gave the Irish a convincing 24–0 lead. Trojans were able to erase the zero next to their name when Michael Harper capped off USC's lone scoring drive with a one-yard run. The attempt at a two-point conversion failed, and Johnston added a 39-yard field goal for Notre Dame to complete the scoring.[7]

**(A) Oct. 29—California—19–9**

Michael Harper ran for 100 yards on 27 carries and scored one touchdown to provide spark to the offense. Linebacker Jack Del Rio recorded four sacks, and as a unit, the defense intercepted three passes. On special teams, the star was kicker Steve Jordan, who entered the USC record books by kicking four field goals in one game.[8]

**(H) Nov. 5—Stanford—30–7**

The Trojans evened their record at 4–4–1 with solid efforts on both sides of the ball. Sean Salisbury threw for 207 yards and one touchdown, and Timmie Ware had four receptions for 118 yards and one touchdown, to spark the offense to 454 yards of total offense. The defensive unit recorded seven sacks for 50 yards in losses, with one of those sacks going for a safety. Safety Jerome Tyler had an interception that he returned 20 yards for a touchdown.[9]

**(A) Nov. 12—Washington—0–24**

WASH#18

This was the first time in 187 games that USC was shut out. Five turnovers did not help the Trojans, and the only bright spots for USC on this day were the plays of defenders Duane Bickett, Jack Del Rio, and Tommy Haynes, who finished with a combined 42 tackles.[10]

**(H) Nov. 19—UCLA—17–27**

The Bruins had to be chanting the classic holiday tune, "I'll Be Home For Christmas," after they clinched the Pac-10 championship and a Rose Bowl berth just a short ride up the road from their Westwood campus.

Despite the Trojans sub-par season, they played tough in the first half of the game, holding a 10–6 advantage at halftime. After spotting the Bruins a 6–0 lead on a pair of John Lee field goals (25 and 20 yards), the Trojans went on top, 7–6, capping off a 70-yard drive with a Todd Spencer run from one yard out. Steve Jordan added the go-ahead extra point. The big play of the scoring drive came when tight end Joe Cormier caught a short pass from Sean Salisbury and gained 32 yards down to the one yard line. Two plays later, Spencer scored. Cormier led all receivers with nine receptions for 87 yards, and Salisbury hit on 19 of 25 pass attempts for 218 yards.

USC got the ball back quickly when UCLA quarterback Rick Neuheisel rushed a pass while being blitzed. The end result was an interception by safety Tony Brewer, who returned the ball from midfield to the UCLA 32, before being stopped and setting the Trojans up with excellent field position. Four plays later, with 16 seconds left in the first half, Jordan kicked a 30-yard field goal for a 10–6 USC lead.

The Bruins seized the lead once again with ten minutes left in the third quarter. The 11-play, 80-yard drive was finished off on a seven-yard pass from Neuheisel to Karl Dorrell. Lee's conversion made it 13–10, and UCLA never looked back. Lupe Sanchez returned a punt 39 yards to the USC 21, and Kevin Nelson scored on a 12-yard sweep two plays later to help boost UCLA's lead to 20–10. The Bruins delivered the back breaker a few minutes later. USC tailback Michael Harper, who ran for 120 yards on 27 carries, fumbled a pitchout that Jeff Chaffin recovered for UCLA at the Trojan 26. On third down from the 17, Bryan Wiley carried the ball up the middle, and ran for the Bruins' 21st point of the third quarter. Lee's third extra point kick made it 27–10.

Early in the fourth quarter, Todd Spencer scored his second touchdown of the game for USC, this time from seven yards out to cut the deficit to 10 points with 10:35 remaining in the game. The Bruins then controlled the ball, and time eventually ran out on the Trojans.[11]

### TEAM LEADERS

RUSHING: Michael Harper—685 yards on 151 carries
PASSING: Sean Salisbury—142 out of 248 attempts for 1,882 yards and 10 touchdowns
RECEIVING: Hank Norman—31 catches for 407 yards and 1 touchdown
SCORING: Steve Jordan—56 points on 20 extra points and 12 field goals
KICKOFF RETURNS: Michael Harper—8 for 126 yards (15.8 avg.)
PUNT RETURNS: Tommy Haynes—21 for 130 yards (6.2 avg.)
PUNTING: Troy Richardson—57 for 2,372 yards (41.6 avg.)
INTERCEPTIONS: Jerome Tyler—4 for 55 yards and 1 touchdown
TACKLES: Jeff Brown—152
SACKS: Jack Del Rio—13

## *1984*

HEAD COACH: Ted Tollner
ASSISTANT COACHES: Foster Andersen, Frank Falks, Artie Gigantino,

Darren Moon, Pat Morris, Chuck Pagano, Russ Purnell, Donnie Rea, Nate Shaw, Jerry Simmons, Norv Turner, Craig VerSteeg, Dave Wannstedt

TEAM CAPTAINS: Neil Hope, Ken Ruettgers

RECORD: 9–3 overall (7–1 in Pacific-10 Conference)

(Ranked 13th best record in college football out of 110 teams)

FINISH IN CONFERENCE: 1st place

FINISH IN NATIONAL POLLS: 10th place in AP, 9th place in UPI, and 11th place in *USA Today*

POINTS SCORED PER GAME: 18.3 to rank 77th out of 110 teams

POINTS ALLOWED PER GAME: 14.4 to rank 13th

## Schedule and Highlights

**(H) Sept. 8—Utah State—42–7**

After two seasons of being ineligible from post-season play, the Trojans were off probation and ready to get back to bowl game competition. Zeph Lee rushed for 161 yards on 11 carries. Included in his carries was a 94-yard touchdown run that equaled a school record for longest touchdown run from scrimmage. Sean Salisbury had a good game by completing 12 of 20 pass attempts for 171 yards.[1]

**(A) Sept. 22—Arizona State—6–3**

USC#17

After never leaving Tempe, Arizona with a win in two failed attempts, the Trojans finally achieved their goal with temperatures hovering in the sweltering 90-degree range, and despite three fumbles. However, in their quest for victory, they lost quarterback Sean Salisbury with torn cartilage in his right knee. In 1982 he was also injured against the Sun Devils. The Trojans received their points on two Steve Jordan field goals, both coming from 50 yards out. The Sun Devils got to the USC 10-yard line with 59 seconds left, but a 27-yard field goal attempt by All-American kicker Luis Zendejas hooked to the left.[2]

**(H) Sept. 29—LSU—3–23**

USC#15

Once again USC's total point production came by way of a field goal. However, unlike against Arizona State, the Trojans gave up 23 points to lose for the first time in 1984. With redshirt freshman quarterback Kevin McLean filling in for the injured Sean Salisbury, the USC offense could only gain 157 yards through the air and 112 on the ground. The Trojans suffered three interceptions and two lost fumbles. The USC defense played well, holding LSU to under 100 yards below their average of total offensive production.[3]

**(A) Oct. 6—Washington State—29–27**

This was USC's first trip to Pullman, Washington, in 28 years. Fred Crutcher ran for 171 yards on 37 carries. Steve Jordan beat out his old record for longest field goal by one yard, when he booted a 53-yarder to erase his old mark set two years earlier. Jordan also set a school record with his 93rd career conversion kick. Defensive back Tim McDonald had three interceptions, and the Trojans built a 20–0 lead by the early third quarter. The Cougars then closed to the gap to 20–13 before freshman running back Ryan Knight scored on a 47-yard run to give the Trojans some breathing room with 5:32 left in the game. Washington State quarterback Mark Rypien set a record for most touchdown passes against a USC defense with four, and led the Cougars back to within two points. An attempt at a two-point conversion pass was intercepted by Jerome Tyler to clinch the game.[4]

**(A) Oct. 13—Oregon—19–9**

The Trojans stayed perfect in the Pac-10 with a 3–0 record after a trip to Eugene, Oregon. The Trojans got out to a 10–0 lead by the end of the first quarter, and 13–6 by halftime. The defense then came through with sacks and pass deflections to shut down Oregon. Fred Crutcher provided the offense with much of its spark by running for 135 yards on 24 carries.[5]

**(H) Oct. 20—Arizona—17–14**

A perfect 4–0 record was USC's reward after this homecoming victory. The defense held Arizona to 58 yards rushing after the Wildcats were averaging 148.3 yards per game. A fumble recovery by linebacker Sam Anno led to what became the game-winning points on a Steve Jordan 31-yard field goal. Tim Green helped the cause by throwing for 212 yards and one touchdown.[6]

**(H) Oct. 27—California—31–7**

USC#20

The Trojans took another step toward the Pac-10 championship against long-time rival, the Cal Golden Bears. Tailback Fred Crutcher suffered a shoulder injury, but his replacement, Ryan Knight, filled in with a 122-yard rushing performance on 22 carries that included two touchdowns, both coming from one yard out. Knight became the third USC freshman tailback to gain 100 yards or more in a game. The others were Charles White (1976), and Darrell Harper (1979). The defense recorded three sacks, just as many turnovers, and made it tough for Cal to have any effectiveness running or passing the ball.[7]

**(A) Nov. 3—Stanford—20–11**

USC#18

The Trojan defense rose up to produce one of its best performances of the season. It held Stanford to 65 rushing yards, had a pair of interceptions that were turned into points, and sacked the quarterback three times. The unit also came through with a goal line stand early in the second half that proved to be the turning point of the game. The offense had Fred Crutcher come through by running for 146 yards on 41 carries, and he scored two touchdowns that gave USC a 20–3 advantage in the second half.[8]

**(H) Nov. 10—Washington—16–7**

USC#12 WASH#1

Fred Crutcher helped the Trojans knock off the top-ranked Huskies by running for 116 yards on 35 carries. The Huskies took a 7–6 lead in the first half, with USC getting two field goals from Steve Jordan (51 and 47 yards). Jordan added another field goal from 46 yards away in the fourth quarter with 10:36 left. Washington finished with a 330 to 311-yard advantage in total offense, but the Trojans held them to 85 yards on the ground. Much of Washington's yardage came while they were attempting to make a comeback. This victory gave USC the Pac-10 championship and a Rose Bowl berth.[9]

**(A) Nov. 17—UCLA—10–29**

USC#7

The Trojans had already clinched a Rose Bowl berth before facing the two time defending Pac-10 champion Bruins. In a bittersweet finale, the Trojans had the Rose Bowl in their future, but were outclassed against their cross-town rivals. This marked the first time since 1955 that the Bruins defeated USC on three straight occasions, as 90,096 looked on with sunny skies engulfing the area.

UCLA kicker John Lee was one of the best at his craft, and against the Trojans, he lived up to his reputation. Lee kicked five field goals to give him 29 on the season, which established a new NCAA record. It was also the most field goals kicked in one game against USC. Lee's first three-pointer of the game came halfway through the opening quarter from 46 yards, and UCLA never relinquished the lead. He added three more field goals in the first half from 29, 43, and 37 yards. Steve Bono passed to Mike Sherrard for a five-yard touchdown in the closing seconds of the first half to produce the game's lone six-pointer up to this stage, and give UCLA a 19–3 halftime advantage. Steve Jordan supplied USC with their first half points on a 45-yard field goal.

The Bruins blew the game wide open when Dennis Price returned an interception 63 yards to expand the lead to 26–3 with 5:50 left in the third quarter. USC quarterback Tim Green then added a two-yard run, and Jordan's extra point made it 26–10. Lee connected on his fifth field goal, a 49-yarder, to complete the scoring with 9:07 left in the game.

In addition to Lee's outstanding performance, this game also showcased the running abilities of two freshmen. UCLA's Gaston Green ran for 134 yards, which was the only time all season that an opposing running back crossed the century mark against the Trojan defense. USC's freshman, Ryan Knight, ran for 100 yards on 25 carries.[10]

**(H) Nov. 24—Notre Dame—7–19**
USC#14

Eight times the Fighting Irish came into the LA Coliseum, and left just as many times beaten. Not since crushing the Trojans into the Coliseum turf in 1966 had the Irish won against USC in Los Angeles. All that changed on a dismal, cold, rainy November afternoon in the Southland. USC had problems running plays around the corners in the sloppy conditions, but the Irish embraced the elements cast before them. While the Trojans were accustomed to sunshine and mild conditions, the Fighting Irish felt right at home, seeing that the weather was similar to a November day back in South Bend, Indiana. The Trojans fumbled the ball eight times, with six going to Notre Dame, and were outgained in total offense 346 yards to 242.

The first quarter went into the history books as a scoreless affair, but then the Trojans struck paydirt for their only points of the game. The drive covered 67 yards of sloppy real estate, and climaxed on a three-yard run by freshman Ryan Knight. Steve Jordan then kicked the extra point, and the Trojans were finished for the day. The Irish came back to take a 13–7 halftime lead on an 11-yard pass from Steve Beuerlein to Tim Brown, and a three-yard run by Allen Pinkett. The conversion was missed after the snap from center was off its mark. Kicker John Carney picked the ball up and attempted to throw for two points, but the pass fell incomplete.

Notre Dame capitalized on two fumble recoveries in the third quarter, and Carney turned the USC mishaps into six points on a pair of 45-yard field goals to finish the scoring. The Trojans had opportunities to get points on the board, but three drives into Notre Dame territory in the second half ended with fumbles. The only positive thing for USC was the fact that they owned another Pac-10 championship, and were headed off to the Rose Bowl on New Year's Day.[11]

**Rose Bowl, (N) Jan. 1—Ohio State—20–17**
USC#18 OSU#6

This was a rekindling of a classic post-season rivalry. Not since 1980 had these two powers met in the Rose Bowl, and in the end, the Trojans once again prevailed over the Buckeyes in a close contest, reminiscent of the tough defensive clashes witnessed in the 1940's and 50's. Since the Rose Bowl became an exclusive matchup between the Big Ten and Pac-10 back in 1947, the series was knotted at 19–19 coming into this edition of the "Granddaddy of Them All." With their victory in this game, USC put the Pac-10 one win up, and gave the conference its 13th win out of the previous 15 Rose Bowls.

The quest for their 18th Rose Bowl victory did not start off well for the Trojans. Ohio State's powerful 6–2, 240-pound running back, and runner-up for the Heisman Trophy, Keith Byars, tore through the USC defense on his first carry of the game for a gain of 50 yards. The star runner averaged 150.5 yards per game during the season, and was well on his way to shattering that. However, the USC defense clamped down on Byars with a swarming defense, limiting him to 59 more yards on 22 carries the rest of the way. After the defense led by Jack Del Rio, Duane Bickett, and the rest of the unit shut down Ohio State's running attack, the Buckeyes were forced to go to the air. Quarterback Mike Tomczak threw for 290 yards, but the Trojans intercepted him three times, turning two of those thefts into touchdowns.

The Buckeyes got on the board first after Byars covered 50 yards on his first carry. With only 2:52 expired in the first quarter, Rich Spangler kicked a 21-yard field goal to give Ohio State their only lead of the game. Steve Jordan was one of college football's most reliable kickers, and possibly the owner of the shortest tenure for a record. Still in the first quarter, the Trojans went on a nine-play, 46-yard drive that Jordan salvaged with a 51-yard field goal, which set the new record for longest in Rose Bowl history. His kick also tied the game at 3–3. Linebacker Neil Hope then started what turned into the go-ahead points for USC. He intercepted Tomczak, and eight plays later, the Trojans covered 45 yards, with the final three producing a touchdown pass from Tim Green to tight end Joe Cormier with 1:54 left in the first quarter. Jordan added the extra point to give USC a 10–3 lead going in to the second quarter.

Defensive back Tommy Haynes intercepted Tomczak, and the turnover quickly produced seven points. Two plays after Haynes gave possession back to USC, Green connected with Timmie Ware on a 19-yard touchdown with only 22 seconds off the clock in the second quarter. Jordan's conversion then gave USC a 17–3 lead. The rest of the quarter remained scoreless until Spangler split the uprights from 46 yards away with no time left in the first half to make the score 17–6.

Spangler once again connected on a three-pointer with 8:37 left in the third quarter. His kick narrowed the gap to 17–9, and also set a Rose Bowl record with a distance of 52 yards, breaking the old mark by one yard set in the first quarter by Jordan. Jordan then came back four minutes later to boot another 51-yarder to give the Trojans a 20–9 lead going in to the fourth quarter. Cris Carter then scored Ohio State's only six-pointer of the game at the midway portion of the fourth quarter. Tomczak fired a low pass that made its way through the USC secondary and into Carter's hands to complete an 18-yard touchdown. Tomczak then ran for the two-point conversion to close to within 20–17. Besides scoring a touchdown, Carter also claimed a Rose Bowl record with 172 yards receiving, breaking the old mark of 164 by Don Hutson in 1935. Carter amassed that total on nine catches.

The Buckeyes made one final try for a victory, as Tomczak drove the team from the Ohio State 35 to the USC 38 with 1:13 left in the game. Facing a third-and-five, Tomczak looked to pass, but defensive tackle Brent Moore came up with a huge play by stripping the ball from Tomczak's hands. Tomczak was able to recover his own fumble, but fell on it for a nine-yard loss. On fourth and long, he threw an incomplete pass, and the Trojans were able to celebrate another Rose Bowl success story. Tim Green received the MVP award on offense after completing 13 of 24 pass attempts for 128 yards and two touchdowns. Linebacker Jack Del Rio was awarded the MVP on defense.[12]

### Team Leaders

Rushing: Fred Crutcher—1,155 yards on 307 carries
Passing: Tim Green—116 out of 224 attempts for 1,448 yards and 5 touchdowns
Receiving: Hank Norman—39 catches for 643 yards and 2 touchdowns
Scoring: Steve Jordan—73 points on 22 extra points and 17 field goals
Kickoff Returns: Elbert Watts—16 for 301 yards (18.8 avg.)
Punt Returns: Darrel Hopper—23 for 165 yards (7.2 avg.)
Punting: Troy Richardson—65 for 2,566 yards (39.5 avg.)
Interceptions: Tommy Haynes—5 for 8 yards
Tackles: Neil Hope—160
Sacks: Jack Del Rio—7

## *1985*

Head Coach: Ted Tollner
Assistant Coaches: Foster Andersen, Frank Falks, Artie Gigantino, Dave Holden, Darren Moon, Pat Morris, Chuck Pagano, Donnie Rea, Nate Shaw, Jerry Simmons, Ron Turner, Craig VerSteeg, Dave Wannstedt
Team Captains: Matt Koart, Hank Norman
Record: 6–6 overall (5–3 in Pacific–10 Conference)
(Ranked 48th best record in college football out of 110 teams)
Finish in Conference: Tied for 4th place
Finish in National Polls: No ranking in Top 25
Points Scored Per Game: 18.6 to rank 79th out of 110 teams
Points Allowed Per Game: 15.6 to rank 22nd

### Schedule and Highlights

**(A) Sept. 7—Illinois—20–10**
USC#6 ILL#11

The USC defense presented a big question mark after the unit lost many members to graduation. However, all doubt was cast away when the unit had four interceptions, two by Junior Thurman, and they held Illinois to 10 yards rushing on 21 attempts. Sam Anno did his part by registering 14 tackles. On offense, the Trojans scored on two of their first three possessions, and were led by the running tandem of Ryan Knight and Fred Crutcher, who combined for 172 yards. Knight had 89 yards and Crutcher 83. Sean Salisbury threw for two touchdowns in the first half to give USC a 17–0 halftime lead, and Randy Tanner had four receptions for 119 yards and one touchdown as they beat Illinois, 20–10.[1]

**(H) Sept. 21—Baylor—13–20**
USC#3

Baylor shocked the Trojans in their home opener. Costly turnovers hurt USC, including an interception at the goal line, which killed one drive and a fumble of an intercepted pass led to a field goal for Baylor. Baylor also ran for 203 yards on 50 carries, while USC totaled 153 on 48. A late defensive stand by Baylor stopped USC on four straight downs, as USC could get no closer than the three. Despite the loss, Sean Salisbury threw for 235 yards and two touchdowns, and Hank Norman had 10 receptions for 132 yards and one touchdown.[2]

**(A) Sept. 28—Arizona State—0–24**
USC#18

The Trojans opened their Pac-10 championship in poor defensive fashion. Five fumbles and one interception proved costly, as USC fell 15 spots in the national polls after this shutout defeat, and they dropped to a 1–2 record. Following a Fred Crutcher fumble on the ASU two-yard line, with the Trojans only down by seven points at the time, Aaron Cox scored on a 95-yard pass from Jeff Van Raaphorst, to set the record for longest pass play against USC. The only optimistic thing Trojan faithful was able to take from this loss was the performance of freshman tailback Aaron Emanuel, who ran for 76 yards on 14 carries in his Trojan debut.[3]

**(H) Oct. 5—Oregon State—63–0**

The Trojans evened their record at 2–2 with a huge win on homecoming weekend, and won by a shutout for the first time in three years. As a team, the Trojans rushed for 276 yards, totaled 431 yards of offense, scored the most points in one single game since 1970, and posted the largest margin of victory since 1930. USC held Oregon State to minus three yards rushing, and 143 yards of total offense, which was the fewest since Washington's 120 in 1981. Fred Crutcher led the Trojan ground attack with 80 yards on 12 carries and two touchdowns. Aaron Emanuel made his Coliseum debut at tailback, and ran for 78 yards and one touchdown. Sean Salisbury threw for two touchdowns, and Erik McKee, Gene Arrington, and Al Washington, all scored their first touchdowns as Trojans.[4]

**(H) Oct. 19—Stanford—30–6**

Stanford's quarterback history is an impressive one, with the Heisman Trophy and All-American status gracing the program at that position. The Trojans' most famous position is at tailback, which is also filled with Heisman winners and All-Americans. On this day, it was the Trojans' heritage that won out. Aaron Emanuel ran for 122 yards on 21 carries, and Fred Crutcher had 105 yards on 22 carries and three touchdowns. Hank Norman added a big game in the receiving department with two receptions for 113 yards.[5]

**(A) Oct. 26—Notre Dame—3–37**

The previous meeting between these teams ended with Notre Dame winning for the first time in the LA Coliseum since 1966. In this 57th edition of the "Glamour Game," the Irish revisited 1966 once again, as they beat the Trojans by the largest margin since blasting them by 51 points in '66. On a beautiful autumn day in South Bend, Indiana, that had temperatures in the low 70's, Notre Dame wasted very little time establishing who would rule the day. With just 11 seconds off the clock following the opening kickoff, USC's Randy Tanner was hit on his 15-yard line and fumbled. Troy Wilson recovered for Notre Dame on the USC two, and Allen Pinkett ran it in from there on the game's first offensive play.

Quarterback Steve Beuerlein scored the Irish's second touchdown on a six-yard run, and John Carney booted a 26-yard field goal early in the second quarter to up the advantage to 17–0. After stopping USC's Aaron Emanuel on fourth-and-one just inside Notre Dame territory, the Irish scored once again. On the seventh play of the drive, Frank Stams shook off a pair of tackles and found his way into the end zone to complete a five-yard run that gave Notre Dame a convincing 24–0 lead. They added three more points before the end of the first half on a 33-yard field goal from John Carney.

Twelve years earlier, the Trojans rallied back from a 24-point deficit against the Irish, but this time, things were different. The Trojans were able to put a minor dent into the deficit after an eight-play, 43-drive resulted in a 39-yard field goal from Don Shafer to make it 27–3. Carney got the three points back with a 43-yard field goal, and then Terry Andrysiak threw an eight-yard pass to Joel Williams and Carney's extra point finished off the scoring in this Irish mauling of the Trojans.[6]

**(H) Nov. 2—Washington State—31–13**

After their 34-point loss to Notre Dame, the Trojans rebounded with a dominant showing against the Cougars. On offense, the Trojans had 413 total yards, with 178 of those yards coming on the ground. Fred Crutcher ran for 93 yards and Ryan Knight had 85. Washington State's highly publicized RPM backfield of quarterback Mark Rypien, and running backs Kerry Porter and Rueben Mayes, were all being toted as All-American prospects. The WSU offense came into this game averaging nearly 460 yards a game to rank seventh in the nation in that category, and scored an average of 26.9 points per game. The Trojan defense rose up to allow the Cougars 296 yards of offense, which was the fourth time during this season that the unit prevented an opponent from getting 300 yards.[7]

**(A) Nov. 9—California—6–14**

USC's first trip to Berkeley, California, in eight years had the Trojans perched at 3–1 in the Pac-10 and looking to repeat as conference champions. However, the Cardinal & Gold had an offense that went stagnant, and a pair of field goals was all that they would produce. Individually, the Trojans received solid performances from linebacker Marcus Cotton with 15 tackles, and Ryan Knight had 62 yards rushing on 14 carries.[8]

**(A) Nov. 16—Washington—17–20**

The Trojans were up by four points with under four minutes left, and had the ball at the Washington one with a first-and-goal situation. Things then went south, as quarterback Rodney Peete and tailback Ryan Knight, both starting for the first time at the college level, were unsuccessful on a handoff. The result was a fumble that the Huskies took 98 yards, with the drive capped off by the winning touchdown with 56 seconds remaining. Peete was brought into the starting quarterback role in an attempt to help out a stagnant offense. Despite the fumble toward the end of the game, Peete gave hope that he was an up-and-coming star signal caller. He completed 12 out of 17 pass attempts for 175 yards and one touchdown. He also ran for 50 yards, which provided the offense with an added dimension. Like Peete, Ryan Knight turned in a solid performance, rushing for 135 yards on 44 carries, and Hank Norman had five receptions for 124 yards.[9]

**(H) Nov. 23—UCLA—17–13**

UCLA#8

Victory and defeat were strange bedfellows in this edition of the USC-UCLA annual clash. The Bruins lost their rivalry game, but got a helping hand in gaining access to a Rose Bowl berth when Arizona upset Arizona State, who needed to win or tie to represent the Pac-10 in Pasadena.

Throughout this game, the Trojans found themselves either briefly tied or trailing until the final 1:13 of the fourth quarter. The six-and-a-half-point favorite Bruins took the opening kickoff and coupled with the passing of David Norrie, and the running of Gaston Green, UCLA got to the USC 20 before a fumble stopped the advance. On their next series, the Bruins made up for the earlier mishap with a nine-play, 63-yard drive that Eric Ball finished off with a one-yard run. John Lee added the extra point, and the Bruins were up, 7–0. Rodney Peete and Joe Cormier teamed up on a 34-yard scoring pass, and Don Shafer added the extra point to end the first quarter in a 7–7 tie. For the game, Cormier gained 101 yards on eight receptions.

Early in the second quarter, the Bruins made it down to the USC six-yard line, and needed only a foot to get a first down. Instead of testing the USC defense, UCLA head coach Terry Donahue opted for his reliable kicker John Lee to break the tie. Lee responded with a 22-yard field goal to give the Bruins a 10–7 lead. He added a 34-yard field goal later in the quarter to put the Bruins up by a 13–7 count at the end of the first half.

The Trojans scored the only points of the third quarter on a Shafer field goal from 38 yards out midway through the quarter. The Bruins had the chance to all but clinch the game early in the fourth quarter with a 13–10 lead. They drove down to the USC one, but when tailback Eric Ball jumped in the air on second down trying to cross the goal line, the ball came out of his grasp. Linebacker Marcus Cotton snatched the ball out of the air, and made his way to the USC 12 to give the Trojans new life.

In the game's closing minutes, with 90,064 watching the action inside the LA Coliseum, a 19-year old Rodney Peete became a star for the Trojans. He took USC on a 14-play, 56-yard drive that resulted in the winning points. Ryan Knight got the drive going in fine fashion by ripping off a gain of 21 yards, and added another one that covered 11 more. For the game, he ran for 147 yards on 32 carries. Peete also gained 11 yards on a quarterback draw, and then ran for three yards on a crucial fourth-and-two situation from the UCLA six. Then, with 1:13 left on the clock, Peete scored on a quarterback sneak, and Shafer's conversion gave the Trojans the win.[10]

**(N) Nov. 30—Oregon—20–6**

The Mirage Bowl was a game played at Tokyo Memorial Stadium in Tokyo, Japan. In the 1985 edition, USC and Oregon were selected to perform on the international stage, and the Trojans came out on top in a season that was filled with highs and lows. The defense held Oregon to 187 offensive yards, with linebacker Marcus Cotton leading the way with 15 tackles and three sacks. The Trojans received their points from Ryan Knight with a one-yard run, Hank Norman scored on a four-yard pass from Rodney Peete, and Don Shafer kicked a 33-yard field goal.[11]

**Aloha Bowl, (N) Dec. 28—Alabama—3–24**

ALA#15

The unranked Trojans' only solace after this game was the fact that they had an opportunity to visit the island paradise of Hawaii. This game marked the second time in school history that USC played Alabama in the post season. The first time was in the 1946 Rose Bowl, and the Crimson Tide rolled over the Trojans by 20 points. Thirty-nine years later, with the setting at Aloha Stadium in Honolulu, Hawaii, with 35,183 looking on from the stands, Alabama added an extra point onto their margin of victory.

The addition of the Aloha Bowl saw the two top bowl teams of all-time square off, as USC produced the most post-season wins with 21, while Alabama led all other programs with the most bowl game appearances at 38. The Crimson Tide came into the game with an 8–2–1 record, and on the power of a solid second half, they easily earned their ninth victory of the year.

Alabama scored first on a 48-yard field goal by Van Tiffin in the first quarter, and Don Shafer tied the game with a 24-yard field goal in the second quarter. This defensive struggle then turned in Alabama's favor. They still kept the pressure on USC defensively, allowing the Trojans only 61 yards on the ground throughout the game. Craig Turner put the Crimson Tide in front for good with a one-yard run in the third quarter, and following Van Tiffin's extra point, they were up, 10–3. Alabama scored two more touchdowns, both coming in the fourth quarter. Mike Shula threw a 24-yard touchdown pass to Clay Whitehurst, and Al Bell ran for 14 yards for the Tide's final touchdown. Van Tiffin added both extra points. Alabama rang up 317 yards of total offense, with 205 coming on the ground. Gene Jelks won the offensive MVP award, and Cornelius Bennett earned defensive MVP honors.[12]

### TEAM LEADERS

RUSHING: Ryan Knight—732 yards on 195 carries
PASSING: Sean Salisbury—98 out of 172 attempts for 1,180 yards and 6 touchdowns
RECEIVING: Joe Cormier—44 catches for 409 yards and 2 touchdowns
SCORING: Don Shafer—71 points on 23 extra points and 16 field goals
KICKOFF RETURNS: Lonnie White—10 for 193 yards (19.3 avg.)
PUNT RETURNS: Al Washington—20 for 130 yards (6.5 avg.)
PUNTING: Chris Sperle—46 for 1,753 yards (38.1 avg.)
INTERCEPTIONS: Junior Thurman—4 for 48 yards and 1 touchdown
Tim McDonald—4 for 13 yards
TACKLES: Keith Davis—128
SACKS: Marcus Cotton—10

# *1986*

HEAD COACH: Ted Tollner
ASSISTANT COACHES: Michael Ackerley, Foster Andersen, Frank Falks, Artie Gigantino, Dave Holden, Steve Mariucci, Pat Morris, Donnie Rea, Nate Shaw, Jerry Simmons, Ron Turner
TEAM CAPTAINS: Jeff Bregel, Tim McDonald
RECORD: 7–5 overall (5–3 in Pacific–10 Conference)
(Ranked 34th best record in college football out of 105 teams)
FINISH IN CONFERENCE: Tied for 4th place
The football program was found guilty of NCAA fractions stemming from improper distribution of complimentary tickets, recruiting contact, minor recruiting incentives, and out-of-season practice and tryout sessions. The NCAA gave the Trojans a two-year probation, scholarship reductions, and recruiting limitations for coaches.
FINISH IN NATIONAL POLLS: No ranking in Top 25
POINTS SCORED PER GAME: 22.0 to rank 58th out of 105 teams
POINTS ALLOWED PER GAME: 19.9 to rank 46th

## Schedule and Highlights

**(H) Sept. 13—Illinois—31–16**

The Trojans christened a more balanced offensive attack than in previous seasons. Rodney Peete threw for 197 yards and one touchdown, and ran for a 32-yard score. Aaron Emanuel ran for 78 yards and a touchdown, while Ryan Knight had 60 yards rushing. Ken Henry caught four passes for 98 yards and a pair of touchdowns. His first came on a 26-yard pass from Peete, and the other came after Randy Tanner took a lateral from Peete and threw to Henry for a 30-yard scoring strike.[1]

**(A) Sept. 20—Baylor—17–14**

BAY#9

The Trojans won this game with no time left on a 32-yard field goal by Don Shafer in a driving rainstorm that soaked the field during the final six minutes of the game. The defense came up big on multiple occasions. They stopped Baylor on four straight plays, which in turn led to the winning field goal, and defensive back Tim McDonald set the school record with the longest fumble recovery of 99 yards. The offense sputtered somewhat until midway through the fourth quarter. Their breakout points came on a 12-yard pass from Rodney Peete to Ken Henry. The Trojan offense compiled 197 total yards and did not earn a first down until the fourth quarter.[2]

**(H) Sept. 27—Washington—20–10**

USC#12 WASH#6

The Trojans remained perfect, defeating a second straight opponent that was ranked in the top 10 coming into the game. Down 10–3 in the third quarter, Rodney Peete gave the ball to Randy Tanner behind the line of scrimmage. Ken Henry streaked down the field, and Tanner threw a pass that resulted in a 67-yard touchdown to Henry that led to a 10–10 tie. Peete and Henry connected on a 13-yard scoring strike in the fourth quarter for what turned out to be the game-winning points. Washington came into this game with 90 points scored in their previous two games, but the Trojan defense did an excellent job shutting down the high-scoring Huskies.[3]

**(H) Oct. 4—Oregon—35–21**

USC#9

With a balanced offensive attack, USC scored all their points in the first half while compiling 389 yards of offense.

Aaron Emanuel ran for 144 yards on 17 carries and two touchdowns, and Rodney Peete threw for 258 yards and one touchdown. In the second half, the Trojans lost five fumbles, which allowed the Ducks to make the final score closer.[4]

**(A) Oct. 11—Washington State—14–34**
USC#9

The only bright spots for the Trojans in their first loss of the season were Rodney Peete and Ken Henry. Despite turning the ball over on two interceptions and a fumble, Peete threw for 253 yards and one touchdown, and Henry had seven receptions for 148 yards and one touchdown. In all, the Trojans had five turnovers, and Washington State scored the game's first 17 points. The Cougar defense did an excellent job stuffing the Trojan runners, limiting the ground attack to 75 yards while WSU ran for 309 yards.[5]

**(H) Oct. 18—Arizona State—20–29**
USC#15 ASU#10

On homecoming weekend, the festivities were dampened as fumbles once again haunted the Trojans. The Sun Devils were then able to produce 17 of their 29 points after starting possessions inside USC territory.[6]

**(A) Oct. 25—Stanford—10–0**
STAN#19

The Trojans got back into the win column thanks to a defensive effort that saw USC limit Stanford's main offensive weapons to minimal yards. They held quarterback John Paye to 122 yards through the air, running back Brad Muster to 64 yards of offense, and receiver Jeff Davis only caught two passes for 19 yards. The Trojans got their points on an 18-yard pass from Rodney Peete to Erik Affholter, and on a 22-yard field goal by Don Shafer.[7]

**(A) Nov. 1—Arizona—20–13**
USC#18 ARI#14

The Trojans prevailed against Arizona despite six fumbles. The Trojan defense did their part by forcing five turnovers to help their cause. Linebacker Marcus Cotton led the unit with seven tackles and two sacks. Greg Coauette forced two fumbles, and Tim McDonald stopped an Arizona scoring threat by intercepting a pass on the goal line. The Trojans were up by a 13–6 count when a 43-yard pass from Rodney Peete to Ken Henry put the game away.[8]

**(H) Nov. 15—California—28–3**
USC#13

This game turned out to be the Ryan Knight Show. Out of USC's 80 offensive plays, Knight ran the ball on 36 of them in his first game as a starter since week four, and he pressed into service due to injuries to Aaron Emanuel and Steve Webster. Knight responded to the prestigious role of being a USC tailback by running for 204 yards and tying a school record with four rushing touchdowns.[9]

**(A) Nov. 22—UCLA—25–45**
USC#10 UCLA#18

Tailback Gaston Green led the offensive attack that gave the Trojans their third worst beating in the series against UCLA with a sellout crowd of 98,370 jammed into the Rose Bowl. Green's performance of 224 rushing yards and four touchdowns helped the Bruins build an invincible 38–0 third quarter lead. Green tied a record for most points scored against USC on an individual basis with 24, and owned a new record outright of having the most individual rushing attempts against USC with 39.

With 6:55 left in the first quarter, Green exploded for a 46-yard touchdown run to cap at five-play, 58-yard drive, and the rout was on. With 27 seconds left in the opening quarter, Green ran for another six-pointer, this time from 27 yards. In the second quarter, David Franey kicked a 23-yard field goal before Green scored his third touchdown of the game. His two-yard run helped extend the UCLA advantage to 24–0, and Matt Stevens expanded the distance between the teams to 31 points he threw a 39-yard touchdown pass to Karl Dorrell to close out the first half scoring.

Green added his final touchdown run of the game early in the third quarter on a one-yard run to help make it 38–0. The Trojans finally got on the scoreboard with 9:28 remaining in the third quarter on a one-yard run by Ryan Knight. Following a three-yard scoring strike from Stevens to Marcus Greenwood, that put the Bruins up, 45–7, Knight added his second one-yard touchdown run. The Trojans added two final touchdowns to their total on a pair of touchdown passes from Rodney Peete to Randy Tanner from 13 and 15 yards out. When the mauling was over, the Bruins rolled up 512 yards of offense, which was the most given up by the Trojans all season.[10]

**(H) Nov. 29—Notre Dame—37–38**
USC#17

This time around, it was the Trojans that jumped out to a solid halftime lead, but in the end, a fantastic finish was responsible for giving Notre Dame their fourth straight win over USC. Notre Dame rallied from a 20–9 halftime deficit, and with no time left on the clock, John Carney successfully completed the second half surge with a 19-yard field goal to win by the slimmest of margins. Notre Dame quarterback Steve Beuerlein was instrumental in the comeback, as he threw four touchdown passes, which tied a record for most ever posted against a USC defense. USC's Don Shafer also placed his name in the record books by kicking the longest field goal in school history from a distance of 60 yards.

The Trojans got on the board first after taking the opening kickoff 40 yards in eight plays. Don Shafer capped the drive with a 48-yard field goal to give USC a 3–0 lead. The Irish came back to claim the lead on a short yardage pass from Steve Beuerlein to Andy Heck, but the extra point attempt was blocked by Tim McDonald. The Trojans got the lead back in the second quarter, complements of a 58-yard interception return for a touchdown by Lou Brock. Shafer added the extra point, and USC was up by a 10–6 count.

Following his costly interception, Beuerlein was replaced at quarterback by Terry Andrysiak. However, Andrysiak's first chance to get the Irish some points was thwarted when Notre Dame was stopped at the USC 36. Rodney Peete quickly went to work to get more points for his Trojans. He connected on a long pass to Lonnie White that covered 53 yards, and Leroy Holt finished the drive off with a three-yard run to expand USC's advantage to 17–6 after Shafer's conversion.

Beuerlein was once again back at the controls of the Irish offense following the ensuing kickoff, and responded by taking Notre Dame into range for a successful 33-yard goal by John Carney to cut the deficit to 17–9. The Trojans had time to set up for some more points with the clock winding down in the first half. Peete connected with Randy Tanner on a 22-yard pass with time working against them. There was only time for a long-range field goal attempt of 60 yards, and Shafer drilled it through the uprights to set a school and conference record, in addition to giving USC a 20–9 halftime lead.

The Trojans added three points to their total early in the third quarter after Pernell Taylor fumbled for the Irish on the first play from scrimmage to start the second half. Shafer then kicked a 23-yard field goal to give USC a 23–9 lead. John Carney got the three points back on a 32-yard three-pointer. With the help of a roughing-the-kicker penalty against Skip Holtz, the son of Notre Dame head coach Lou Holtz, the Trojans were able to continue on with their quest down the field. The 15-play, 70-yard drive was capped off when Todd Steele scored on a one-yard run, and Shafer's extra point gave the Trojans a commanding 30–12 advantage.

There was still plenty of time to come back from this deficit, and Notre Dame did rally to produce one of the greatest finishes in this long and storied series. Tim Brown was one of the most explosive players in the history of Notre Dame football. He exhibited his talents on the ensuing kickoff with his team down by 18 points. He took the kickoff back 57 yards, and that sparked the Irish. Beuerlein ended the drive by hitting Braxston Banks with a 22-yard scoring strike, and followed that up with a two-point conversion pass to Milt Jackson that cut the USC lead to 30–20.

The Trojans answered back with an 11-play, 67-yard drive that Peete completed with a one-yard run. Shafer's conversion then made it a 37–20 ballgame with 12:26 remaining in the fourth quarter. It was time for the Irish to sink or swim, as the saying goes, and they decided on the latter. In just three plays, Notre Dame covered 69 yards, with the payoff coming on a 42-yard touchdown pass from Beuerlein to Jackson. Carney's extra point narrowed the gap to 37–27.

USC looked to hold of the Irish onslaught, and marched down to the Notre Dame five, before being stopped. Facing a fourth down situation, the Trojans' coaching staff decided to go for the first down instead of an easy field goal attempt. The plan failed, as Peete was stopped short of his objective. Peete thought he made the necessary yardage, and expressed his opinion to the officials, who did not approve of the argument, and flagged the USC quarterback 15 yards for unsportsmanlike conduct.

With renewed momentum, the Irish went 80 yards in eight plays. Beuerlein first connected with Tim Brown on a 49-yard pass that ate up a huge chunk of real estate. He then threw his second touchdown pass to Banks, this time from five yards out. Beuerlein then threw a successful two-point conversion pass to Andy Heck to make the score 37–35. With time not a friend to the Irish at this point, they had to get the ball back without allowing USC to pad their lead. The Notre Dame defensive unit accomplished just that, and forced the Trojans to punt on fourth down. Tim Brown took the punt on his 28-yard line, and tore through the USC defenders for a gain of 56 yards before he was stopped on the 12. The Irish stayed on the ground for five plays, getting to the one with two seconds left on the clock. Carney then completed the comeback with a 19-yard field goal as time ran out. This victory allowed Steve Beuerlein to become the only Notre Dame quarterback to defeat USC four times. He passed for 285 yards and four touchdowns, which set a Notre Dame record.[11]

**Citrus Bowl, (N) Jan. 1—Auburn—7–16**
AU#10

One year after visiting Hawaii for a post-season appearance, the Trojans found themselves in another often traveled to destination, Orlando, Florida, with the mission of taking on the Auburn Tigers in the Citrus Bowl at Orlando Stadium. Unfortunately, just like in their previous bowl game, the Trojans left the field with a loss. This defeat was the third straight suffered by the Trojans, and head coach Ted Tollner's final game leading the program.

The Trojans got out to 7–0 lead in the first quarter when linebacker Marcus Cotton returned an interception 24 yards for USC's only kick. The Tigers tied the game in the second quarter on a Jeff Burger pass to tight end Walter Reeves that covered three yards. Auburn then took the lead for good after 6'-6," 230-pound linebacker touchdown, which was followed by Don Shafer's extra point Aundray Bruce forced Rodney Peete to fumble. Tailback Brent Fullwood, college football's top runner during the season, converted USC's turnover into six points with a four-yard run, to give the Tigers a 14–7 halftime lead. Fullwood led the Auburn attack with 152 rushing yards. The second half was a defensive struggle, with the lone points coming on a safety when Peete was called for intentionally grounding. This proved to be a rough outing for Peete. After becoming the first sophomore to ever pass for over 2,000 yards over the course of a single season, he was sacked five times and intercepted on four occasions. For the game, he managed to complete only 12 of 30 pass attempts for 113 yards. The USC ground game did not fare much better, as Auburn's defense allowed only 44 yards on 30 carries, and 157 yards of total offense.

The Trojans made the climax of this game interesting, as Louis Brock blocked a punt late in the fourth quarter, and USC got to within inches of the goal line. However, on fourth-and-inches, Leroy Holt was stopped shy of the end zone to preserve Auburn's 500th all-time victory.[12]

### TEAM LEADERS

RUSHING: Ryan Knight—536 yards on 148 carries
PASSING: Rodney Peete—160 out of 305 attempts for 2,138 yards and 10 touchdowns
RECEIVING: Ken Henry—43 catches for 807 yards and 7 touchdowns
SCORING: Don Shafer—65 points on 30 extra points and 12 field goals
KICKOFF RETURNS: Lonnie White—29 for 716 yards (24.7 avg.)
PUNT RETURNS: Randy Tanner—23 for 103 yards (4.5 avg.)
PUNTING: Chris Sperle—49 for 1,926 yards (39.3 avg.)
INTERCEPTIONS: Louis Brock—4 for 99 yards and 1 touchdown
TACKLES: Rex Moore—206
SACKS: Marcus Cotton—10

## *1987*

HEAD COACH: Larry Smith
ASSISTANT COACHES: Bobby April, Gary Bernardi, Harry Hiestand, John Matsko, Tom Roggeman, Clarence Shelmon, Jerry Simmons, Charles Stobart, Ron Turner, Kevin Wolthausen

TEAM CAPTAINS: Dave Cadigan, Greg Coauette
RECORD: 8–4 overall (7–1 in Pacific–10 Conference)
(Ranked 22nd best record in college football out of 104 teams)
FINISH IN CONFERENCE: Tied for 1st place with UCLA
FINISH IN NATIONAL POLLS: 18th place in AP and 17th place in both the UPI and *USA Today*
POINTS SCORED PER GAME: 26.8 to rank 30th out of 104 teams
POINTS ALLOWED PER GAME: 19.1 to rank 32nd

## Schedule and Highlights

**(A) Sept. 7—Michigan State—13–27**
USC#19 MSU#17

With 14 starters returning, hopes for a great season were plentiful throughout the Southland. However, Michigan State had other plans, as they snapped USC's 17-game winning streak over Big Ten opponents. Prior to this defeat, the Trojans had not lost to a Big Ten team since the 1974 Rose Bowl. In the first-ever night game at Spartan Stadium, the Trojans committed five turnovers, and MSU running back Lorenzo White ran for 111 yards and two touchdowns. The Trojans received solid performances from Rodney Peete who had 229 yards passing and Randy Tanner caught eight receptions for 107 yards and one touchdown.[1]

**(H) Sept. 19—Boston College—23–17**

This was Larry Smith's first victory as USC's head coach, and it snapped Boston College's 10-game winning streak, which was the second longest in the country at the time. Steven Webster ran for 119 yards on 24 carries, Rodney Peete threw for 248 yards and two touchdowns, and Ken Henry had six receptions for 120 yards and one touchdown, to lead the Trojans to their first win of the new season.[2]

**(A) Sept. 26—California—31–14**

After trailing, 7–0, the Trojans exploded for 31 straight points to easily defeat the Golden Bears. Strong safety Cleveland Colter provided excitement by returning an interception 94 yards for a touchdown, coming up just five yards shy of the USC record set by Bud Langley in 1936. Steven Webster had his second straight 100-yard game, this time gaining 109 yards on 25 carries and scoring one touchdown. Rodney Peete threw for 235 yards and one touchdown. Cal's punter Scott Tabor produced a conference record for recording a 55.6 punting average against USC in this game.[3]

**(H) Oct. 3—Oregon State—48–14**

The Trojans gained 582 net yards, which was the most since the Notre Dame game in 1979. USC earned their scores with long-distant drives, the least being 63 yards. Rodney Peete completed 15 of 18 pass attempts for 249 yards and two touchdowns. He also ran for a pair of six-pointers. Steven Webster recorded his third straight 100-yard game. He ran for 132 yards on 26 carries and one touchdown. As a team, the Trojans rushed for 322 yards while Oregon State only could muster up 37 yards on the ground. Linebacker Marcus Cotton set a school record with four sacks in one game.[4]

**(A) Oct. 10—Oregon—27–34**

Oregon stayed perfect in the Pac-10 with a ball controlled passing attack by Bill Musgrave. The Ducks got out to a 21–0 halftime lead, and were up by as many as 20 points early in the fourth quarter. Rodney Peete threw for 279 yards and three touchdowns, and Erik Affholter had eight receptions for 147 yards and two touchdowns for the Trojans.[5]

**(A) Oct. 17—Washington—37–23**

The Trojans stayed alive in the Pac-10 race and lifted their overall record to 4–2. The Trojans came into this game was the Pac-10 leader in total offense, averaging 457.2 yards per game. They finished this game with 442 yards, 319 gained on the ground. Leading the ground attack was Steven Webster, who ran for 182 yards on 40 carries and two touchdowns. The game was close, tied at 23–23, halfway through the fourth quarter until Rodney Peete threw a nine-yard scoring strike to Paul Green.[6]

**(A) Oct. 24—Notre Dame—15–26**
ND#10

This was the first time Larry Smith led USC out onto the field as head coach for the "Glamour Game." From the start, it looked like the experience would be a good one, as the Trojans covered 70 yards on six plays on their opening possession. The quick drive was capped when Rodney Peete threw for a nine-yard touchdown to John Jackson and Quin Rodriguez added the extra point for an early 7–0 lead. Unfortunately, that was the last time the Trojans held an advantage on this trip to South Bend. After smooth sailing on their initial offensive series, the Trojans could not put together another serious threat for some time.

The Fighting Irish proved to be on the other side of the spectrum. They jumped out to a 20–7 lead and never looked back. Two Ted Gradel field goals from 26 and 32 yards out, coupled with runs from Tony Rice (26 yards), and Tim Brown (five yards), provided the 13-point Irish bulge. USC got a break early in the third quarter when they recovered a fumble, but a Peete interception by Ned Bolcar at the Notre Dame 27, ended that threat. The Irish later added six more points on an 11-yard run from Mark Green. An attempt at a two-point conversion run failed, but Notre Dame was up by a commanding 26–7 count. Peete moved the Trojans downfield with key passes totaling 47 of his 275 yards on the day, and the 10-play, 89-yard drive was completed when Scott Lockwood ran it in from the five. Peete then connected with Randy Tanner on a two-point conversion pass to finish off the scoring. Erik Affholter turned in a solid performance for the Trojans despite the outcome by catching eight passes for 102 yards.[7]

**(H) Oct. 31—Washington State—42–7**

A heavy rainstorm made the Coliseum look like a swamp. Because of the poor weather, only 24,834 showed up to create the smallest crowd to attend a USC home game since 1950. Despite the condition of the field, the Trojans still managed to gain a whopping 538 yards of offense, with 374 coming on the ground. Once again, Steven Webster was the top ground gainer, this time producing 157 yards on 23 carries and he scored two touchdowns. Webster also caught three passes for 51 yards. This victory gave the Trojans a 4–1 record in the Pac-10 race.[8]

**(H) Nov. 7—Stanford—39–24**

On this homecoming weekend, it was Rodney Peete who stood out most for the Trojans. He passed for 273 yards and five touchdowns, which set a school record for most in a single game. In doing so, Peete overtook seven other Trojan quarterbacks, who were all tied with four apiece. Peete's 17 completions also allowed him to become USC's all-time leader in that category with 355, surpassing Sean Salisbury's 346. John Jackson was on the receiving end of three Peete scoring strikes, which allowed him to tie a school record for most touchdown receptions in a single game.[9]

**(H) Nov. 14—Arizona—12–10**

In a hard-fought game, the Trojans drove 86 yards late in the game to produce the game winner. With 1:11 left on the clock, Quin Rodriguez kicked an 18-yard field goal to give USC a 6–1 record in the Pac-10 going into the final conference game against UCLA. That game-winning field goal was Rodriguez's fourth three-pointer of the game, which tied a school record for most in one game with Steve Jordan in 1983–84. Steven Webster ran for 161 yards on 34 carries, and he became the 17th all-time Trojan running back to top 1,000 yards in a season.[10]

**(H) Nov. 21—UCLA—17–13**

This was the 19th time that a Rose Bowl berth awaited the winner of this game. USC came into this game with a 7–3 record, and 6–1 in the Pac-10, while UCLA sported a 9–1 slate and a 7–0 conference record. When it was over, the Trojans improved their record over the Bruins to 13–5–1 when the Rose Bowl was the prize to the victor of the "Battle for Los Angeles."

Throughout a good portion of the game, the Trojans performed like eight-and-a-half-point underdogs. They had three touchdowns taken away due to penalties, and trailed after three quarters by a 13–3 count. They then saved their best for last, and in dramatic fashion, which was commonplace in this series, the Trojans placed their 32nd all-time win over UCLA into the history books.

The Bruins scored first when the hero of the previous USC-UCLA game, Gaston Green, capped off an 11-play, 72-yard drive with a six-yard run with 8:25 left in the first quarter. Green had another great day against the Trojans, as he led all ball carriers with 138 yards on 30 attempts.

The Trojans tried to get even on the scoreboard with the Bruins, but penalties stymied their hopes early in the second quarter. A 21-yard pass from Rodney Peete to John Jackson got the ball to the UCLA 18, but a holding penalty took that away. On the same possession, Peete threw a 34-yard pass to Ken Henry for a touchdown, only to have it taken away by a delay-of-game penalty. The Bruins also had a touchdown called back due to a holding penalty. However, one play after the penalty negated six points, kicker Alfredo Velasco salvaged three points for UCLA with a 32-yard field goal to give the Bruins a 10–0 halftime lead.

The Bruins looked to be in control of the game early in the third quarter after taking over possession on the USC 27, following a poor punt by Chris Sperle that went only 18 yards. Four plays later, Velasco added his second 32-yard field goal of the day to extend UCLA's advantage to 13–0 with 12:02 left in the third quarter.

The Trojans finally got points on the board midway through the third quarter when Quin Rodriguez finished off a 10-play, 62-yard drive with a 26-yard field goal. The Trojans almost closed the gap even more near the end of the quarter. Ricky Ervins fumbled at the UCLA 23, but Rodney Peete reacted quickly by picking the ball up and throwing a touchdown pass to Randy Tanner. Unfortunately, the Trojans once again fell victim to a penalty flag, this time for having an illegal receiver downfield.

After coming close on multiple occasions to get a touchdown, the Trojans finally got into the end zone without a penalty flag being thrown. On the same drive, just 51 seconds into the fourth quarter, Tanner caught a six-yard pass from Peete, and Rodriguez added the extra point to make it a 13–10 UCLA lead.

With eight minutes remaining in the game, the Trojans went ahead for the first time, and held the lead to the end. Free safety Mark Carrier started the Trojans off on their winning drive by intercepting a Troy Aikman pass that he returned for a 72-yard touchdown. However, USC's old nemesis, the penalty flag, once again took away the touchdown. An illegal block on Carrier's return took away the six points, but still allowed USC to keep possession. They began the drive on the UCLA 42-yard line, and Carrier was credited with a return of 29 yards after the penalty was called.

Six plays after Carrier's interception, Peete found Erik Affholter in the corner of the end zone for a 33-yard touchdown after the receiver made a juggling catch to secure the ball and the victory. The Bruins tried for a comeback from their own 19-yard line with 67 seconds remaining. It was then that Carrier rose up for the Trojans by intercepting his second pass to end UCLA's hopes.

Rodney Peete had one of his best days as a college quarterback. He completed 23 out of 35 pass attempts for 304 yards and two touchdowns. Erik Affholter, who earned a place among the all-time USC heroes of this classic series with UCLA, led all receivers with nine receptions for 151 yards, caught the winning six-pointer, and helped the Trojans obtain another trip to the Rose Bowl Game.[11]

**Rose Bowl, (N) Jan. 1—Michigan State—17–20**

USC#16 MSU#8

This marked the fifth time throughout the lengthy history of the Rose Bowl that teams that had squared off in the regular season found their way for an encore in Pasadena on New Year's Day. In the season opener, the Trojans lost by 14 points to the Spartans, and four months later, they cut the margin to three, but the result was the same.

The Spartans came into the 74th Rose Bowl with an 8–2–1 record, and ranked eighth in both the AP and Coaches polls. This was Michigan State's first Rose Bowl appearance since 1966, and they made up for lost time by getting out to a 14–3 halftime lead on a pair of Lorenzo White touchdowns with 103,847 in attendance. The Trojans got on the board first with Quin Rodriguez hitting on a 34-yard field goal. White then ran for touchdowns covering five and three yards respectively to give the Spartans their 11-point lead at the end of the first half.

Rodney Peete teamed up with receiver Ken Henry on a pair of touchdowns from 33 and 22 yards out that allowed the Trojans to tie the game at 17–17 at the midway point of the fourth quarter. The first one closed the Michigan State advantage to 14–10, and following a John Langeloh 40-yard field goal that upped the Spartans' lead to seven points, Peete fired his second scoring strike to Henry. For the game, Peete completed 22 of 41 pass attempts for 249 yards.

The game did not remain deadlocked for long, as the Spartans moved down the field for what turned out to be the game-winning field goal from Langeloh that covered 36 yards with four minutes remaining in the game. The key play in the winning drive came when quarterback Bobby McAllister was close to getting sacked. He ran out of trouble and managed to get a 36-yard pass into the hands of receiver Andre Rison to keep the drive going.

The Trojans were plagued by five turnovers throughout this game, and the final one put an end to any hopes of coming back. USC got down to the Michigan State 29 with two minutes left, but Peete mishandled the snap from center and the Spartans recovered the ball. Now, with only 1:37 left, all Michigan State did was run out the clock, and the sweet smell of roses followed them back to their East Lansing campus. Linebacker Percy Snow was awarded the MVP after a monster of a game, in which he recorded 17 unassisted tackles. Lorenzo White was the workhorse for the Spartans on offense by carrying the ball 35 times for 113 yards and two scores. With this win, the Spartans helped the Big Ten snap a six-game losing streak at the Rose Bowl. As for the Trojans, despite rolling up 410 yards of total offense, they lost their third straight bowl game.[12]

### TEAM LEADERS

RUSHING: Steven Webster—1,109 yards on 239 carries
PASSING: Rodney Peete—197 out of 332 attempts for 2,709 yards and 21 touchdowns
RECEIVING: Erik Affholter—44 catches for 649 yards and 4 touchdowns
SCORING: Quin Rodriguez—74 points on 35 extra points and 13 field goals
KICKOFF RETURNS: Cleveland Colter—15 for 291 yards (19.4 avg.)
PUNT RETURNS: Randy Tanner—31 for 273 yards (8.8 avg.)
PUNTING: Chris Sperle—55 for 1,979 yards (36.0 avg.)
INTERCEPTIONS: Cleveland Colter—6 for 114 yards and 1 touchdown
TACKLES: Keith Davis—158
SACKS: Marcus Cotton—12

## *1988*

HEAD COACH: Larry Smith
ASSISTANT COACHES: Bobby April, Gary Bernardi, Ray Dorr, John Matsko, Tom Roggeman, Clarence Shelmon, Charles Stobart, Kevin Wolthausen
TEAM CAPTAIN: Rodney Peete
RECORD: 10–2 overall (8–0 in Pacific–10 Conference)
(Ranked 7th best record in college football out of 105 teams)
FINISH IN CONFERENCE: 1st place
FINISH IN NATIONAL POLLS: 7th place in both AP and *USA Today* and 9th place in UPI
POINTS SCORED PER GAME: 30.8 to rank 18th out of 105 teams
POINTS ALLOWED PER GAME: 15.3 to rank 11th

### Schedule and Highlights

**(A) Sept. 1—Boston College—34–7**
USC#8

USC kicked off their centennial athletic season in fine fashion. With key players out with injuries, it looked like things might be tough going for the Trojans. However, USC physically blasted Boston College, and won with ease. With Steven Webster recovering from knee surgery, the Trojans were without the previous season's Pac-10 rushing champion. Fullback Leroy Holt stepped up to fill the void by leading the ground attack with 86 yards on 18 carries and one touchdown. Rodney Peete completed 21 of 33 pass attempts for 271 yards and one touchdown, and the Trojans gained 502 yards on 87 offensive plays.[1]

**(A) Sept. 10—Stanford—24–20**
USC#6

In their Pac-10 opener, the defending conference champions came back from a 13–0 second quarter deficit to win with 1:19 left in the game, on a 10-yard pass from Rodney Peete to John Jackson. The Trojans kept the streak alive of not having lost at Stanford Stadium since 1970. Aaron Emanuel ran for 121 yards on 17 carries and scored two touchdowns. Quin Rodriguez added USC's other points with a 20-yard field goal.[2]

**(H) Sept. 24—Oklahoma—23–7**
USC#4 OK#3

A crowd of 86,124 turned out for USC's home opener. The attendance was the largest non-UCLA game crowd at the Coliseum since Notre Dame came to town in 1966. Oklahoma suffered bad field position throughout most of the game, and never made it a close game. The Trojan defense held the Sooners to only 222 yards of total offense, half of what they were accustomed to gaining. Of those yards allowed, 89 were given up on the ground. The Trojans compiled 366 yards of offense, with 199 gained rushing. This defeat kept Oklahoma coach Barry Switzer winless against the Trojans in four tries. Rodney Peete added another record to his accomplishments. With his 238 yards of total offense in this game, he had a career amount of 6,462 yards, which surpassed the previous record of 6,240 set by Charles White in the late 1970's. The Trojans received their points on two Aaron Emanuel runs, and three Quin Rodriguez field goals.[3]

**(A) Oct. 1—Arizona—38–15**
USC#3

On a warm night in the desert, USC head coach Larry Smith made his first appearance against his former team. With a well-balanced offensive attack, the Trojans rolled to 451 yards with some impressive individual accomplishments happening in the process. Ricky Ervins, filling in for Aaron Emanuel, who was out with an ankle injury, ran for 135 yards on 26 carries and one touchdown, Rodney Peete threw for 219 yards and three touchdowns, and Erik Affholter had nine receptions for 126 yards. Affholter tied a school single-game record by catching three touchdown passes.[4]

**(H) Oct. 8—Oregon—42–14**
USC#3 ORE#18

Offensive firepower kept the Trojans rolling along. This homecoming game saw a crowd of 63,452 inside the Coliseum to produce the largest attendance figure for an Oregon-USC game. Four Oregon turnovers led to three USC touchdowns. Rodney Peete threw for 270 yards and two touchdowns, and John Jackson had seven receptions for 155 yards and two touchdowns.[5]

**(H) Oct. 15—Washington—28–27**
USC#3 WASH#16

The Trojans remained perfect at 6–0 overall and 4–0 in the Pac-10, but what looked to be an easy win turned out to be a nail-biter. The Trojans took control early on touchdown runs from Leroy Holt for one yard and Rodney Peete for eight yards, appeared to be pulling away with a 21–7 lead in the third quarter. The Huskies closed to within seven points before Scott Lockwood's four-yard run extended the USC advantage to 28–14. Lockwood was pressed into carrying the burden of the backfield because of injuries to Aaron Emanuel, Steven Webster, and Ricky Ervins. Lockwood handled the burden well by rushing for 133 yards on 27 carries. The Huskies came back with two touchdowns in the fourth quarter to close to within one point, but failed on a two-point conversion attempt with 1:39 remaining in the game. In addition to his touchdown run, Rodney Peete also threw a scoring strike and completed 16 of 22 pass attempts for 186 yards.[6]

**(A) Oct. 29—Oregon State—41–20**
USC#3

The Trojans gained 523 yards of offense, with 280 coming on the ground. The result was another victory that kept them perfect on the season and in the hunt for a national championship. They were holding a six-point lead early in the fourth before exploding for 21 points to win with ease. Leroy Holt was the backfield star for the Trojans by rushing for 102 yards on 14 carries. Erik Affholter scored three receiving touchdowns on seven receptions for 135 yards, and Rodney Peete threw for 243 yards and three touchdowns. Oregon State quarterback Erik Wilhelm tied a conference record with 37 pass completions against USC, which was also the most ever given up by a Trojan defense.[7]

**(H) Nov. 5—California—35–3**
USC#2

This was USC's best start to a season since 1972. Rodney Peete led the way on offense to keep the Trojans perfect. He completed 22 of 29 pass attempts for 305 yards and three touchdowns. This was the third time that Peete threw three scoring strikes in one game during the season. His touchdown passes went to Scott Galbraith for 42 yards, John Jackson for 11 yards, and Leroy Holt for eight yards. Erik Affholter caught five passes, which gave him a career total of 102, and moved him into fourth place in the USC record books. The Trojans received their other touchdowns by Ricky Ervins on a two-yard run, and by defensive back Cleveland Colter, who returned an interception 29 yards for six points. One year earlier, Colter scored on an interception against Cal, covering 94 yards.[8]

**(A) Nov. 12—Arizona State—50–0**
USC#2

The Trojans had lost four out of five previous games at Sun Devil Stadium, but partially made up for those defeats with a resounding win. This was Arizona State's worst defeat since losing to Nevada Reno, 74–2, in 1946. It was also their worst home loss, and their worst in Pac-10 competition. The Trojans amassed an incredible 691 yards of offense, and scored on drives ranging from 54 to 91 yards, plus on a 47-yard field goal by Quin Rodriguez. Rodney Peete continued on his campaign as a serious Heisman Trophy contender by throwing for 361 yards and three touchdowns. He also ran for a two-yard touchdown. Erik Affholter had eight receptions for 135 yards and one touchdown, and Gary Wellman caught four passes for 115 yards and one touchdown. Adding touchdowns to USC's point barrage on this day were John Jackson with a five-yard pass from Peete, Leroy Holt with a four-yard run, Calvin Holmes had a two-yard run, and Aaron Emanuel with a one-yard run.[9]

**(A) Nov. 19—UCLA—31–22**
USC#2 UCLA#6

With this victory, the Trojans clinched the Pac-10 championship, and their 26th trip to the Rose Bowl Game. Aaron Emanuel ran for 113 yards on 27 carries to help spark the Trojans to become the first team in conference history to win eight conference games in one season.

The Bruins came into this game with a 9–1 record, and they got on the board first with 9:44 left in the first quarter. Capping off a 10-play, 42-yard drive was Alfredo Velasco with a 46-yard field goal. The Trojans came back to claim a 7–3 lead at the end of the first quarter on a four-yard run by Emanuel. Quin Rodriguez added the extra point.

With the second quarter just three minutes old, Erik Affholter caught a third down pass from Rodney Peete that covered 29 yards and a touchdown. Rodriguez kicked the extra point and the Trojans were up, 14–3. The Bruins came back with a drive that got them down to the USC nine before stalling. On fourth down, Velasco kicked his second three-pointer, this one coming from 27 yards out to cut the Trojan lead to 14–6. UCLA once again got deep into USC territory, but the Trojan defense kept them out of the end zone. Velasco added his third field goal of the first half, a 25-yarder with six minutes left before halftime, to make it 14–9.

Ricky Ervins sparked the Trojans by returning the ensuing kickoff 60 yards. The offense took advantage of Ervins' effort by scoring after an eight-play, 39-yard drive. Peete capped the short drive with a one-yard touchdown run, and Rodriguez extended the USC bulge to 21–9 with 5:25 left in the first half. With 32 seconds left in the half, Troy Aikman finished off a seven-play, 70-yard drive with a 10-yard scoring strike to Reggie Moore. Velasco kicked the extra point, and UCLA had cut the deficit to 21–16.

Emanuel recorded his second six-pointer of the game with 8:16 left in the third quarter on a three-yard run. Rodriquez's extra point made it 28–16 heading into the fourth quarter. The final quarter went along scoreless until the last few minutes. With 2:50 left, Rodriguez kicked a 21-yard field goal, and Aikman threw a 26-yard touchdown pass to Brendan McCracken with 1:41 remaining.[10]

**(H) Nov. 26—Notre Dame—10–27**
USC#2 ND#1

This was the reason why the clash between these two powers was called the "Glamour Game." Surprisingly, despite all the great games waged in this series, never until this 60th edition had the teams come into the annual matchup ranked one and two in the nation. It was truly a classic waiting to happen, with the winner more-than-likely headed off to play for the national championship. In the end, the Fighting Irish did prevail over West Virginia in the Fiesta Bowl to claim their first national crown since 1977 with a spotless 12–0 record.

Notre Dame set the tone for this game on their first play from scrimmage. From his own two-yard line, quarterback Tony Rice dropped back into the end zone and unleashed a long pass that was caught for 55 yards by Raghib "Rocket" Ismail. Even though the drive produced no points, it did send a message that the Irish were willing to take chances. On Notre Dame's next possession, Rice had no need to throw deep. This time he let his legs send a message to USC, as he ran for a 65-yard touchdown. Reggie Ho added the extra point, and the Irish never gave up the lead.

Still in the opening quarter, Notre Dame expanded its lead to 14–0 after Frank Stams recovered an Aaron Emanuel fumble on the USC 19-yard line. Five plays later, Mark Green scored on a run from the two, and Ho kicked the conversion. In the second quarter, the Trojans a solid opportunity to add some points on the board, but Ricky Ervins fumbled on the Notre Dame 19 to kill the drive. The Trojans were able to prevent the Irish from scoring after that turnover, and took over possession following a punt. It was then that USC put together their lone touchdown drive of the game. Covering 66 yards in 11 plays, Scott Lockwood ran the ball in from the one. Quin Rodriguez's extra point kick cut the Irish advantage in half, at 14–7. The Trojans looked to get even closer, but a Peete pass intended for John Jackson, was intercepted by defensive back Stan Smagala and returned 64 yards for a touchdown. The extra point attempt was not made, but it appeared that Smagala's touchdown was the turning point of this game.

The Trojans managed once again to cut the deficit in half, this time on a 26-yard Rodriguez field goal, to take USC in the fourth quarter trailing, 20–10. The Irish were still in control of this game, and there was no miracle to be had by the Trojans this time. As insurance, Notre Dame added seven final points to their day's work on a one-yard run by Mark Green, and a conversion kick by Ho.[11]

**Rose Bowl, (N) Jan. 2—Michigan—14–22**

USC#5 MICH#11

The 75th anniversary of the Rose Bowl saw two teams that met four previous times in the New Years Day classic, with USC holding a 3–1 advantage prior to this meeting. Coming into this edition of the Rose Bowl, Michigan head coach Bo Schembechler had the most victories of any active coach in the college ranks, and led the Wolverines to eight previous Rose Bowl appearances during his tenure. Unfortunately, since his first trip in 1970, the legendary mentor found the going rough at the Rose Bowl, coming into this game with the Trojans at 1–7.

Kicker Mike Gillette gave his coach a slight edge en route to his second overall Rose Bowl when he kicked a 49-yard field goal to put the Wolverines up, 3–0, at the end of the first quarter. The Trojans came back to claim a 14–3 halftime advantage on two Rodney Peete runs covering one and four yards. Quin Rodriguez connected on both extra point kicks.

It was then that the Trojans found the going tough, failing to make one single first down throughout the third quarter. Momentum had definitely swung the Wolverines way in the second half, and they took advantage of it. At the start of the second half, Michigan marched 70 yards to their first touchdown. Demetrius Brown capped the drive off with a six-yard pass to Chris Calloway, but a two-point conversion run failed. That score cut Michigan's deficit to 14–9 heading into the fourth quarter. The Wolverines took the lead for good with only four seconds expired in the fourth quarter. The drive ate up 92 yards, and was sparked by a Leroy Hoard run of 32 yards. Hoard then scored from the one to put Michigan up, 15–14. Once again, an attempt at a two-point conversion failed.

The Trojans showed some signs of life offensively in the fourth quarter after a lethargic third quarter. Peete ran for 24 yards on two carries, and then fired a pass to tight end Scott Galbraith for 11 yards. Peete had guided the Trojans to the Michigan 30 before stalling. Rodriguez then tried a 47-yard field goal, but the kick sailed wide right with 5:28 left to play.

Leroy Hoard stepped up to seal the victory for the Wolverines on a first down carry from the Michigan 30. He bolted up the middle, and the powerful 220-pound sophomore covered 61 yards before being stopped by defensive back Chris Hale on the USC nine yard line. A five-yard penalty moved the ball back to the 14, but all it did was slow down the inevitable. Hoard carried the ball to the five, and then the Trojans were called for a personal foul that moved the ball half the distance to the goal line. With the ball now at the two, the Wolverines took three cracks at the end zone before Hoard found a slight patch of daylight to get through from one yard out. Gillette added the extra point, and the Wolverines were up, 22–14, with two minutes left to play.

Peete gave it his all to lead the Trojans on the comeback trail, and got the offense to the Michigan 27-yard line with 66 seconds left on the clock. USC was then hit with a five-yard offside penalty. Ricky Ervins dropped a pass, and then linebacker John Milligan came up with an interception to seal USC's fate. Hoard was selected as the game's MVP after running for 142 yards on 19 carries. It was the first time during the 1988 season that an opposing running back topped the 100-yard mark against the Trojans. Prior to this game, USC was ranked second in defense against the run, having given up an average of 76.6 yards per game on the ground. This was USC's fourth straight bowl defeat, and they became the first Pac-10 representative to lose back-to-back Rose Bowls since 1964 and 1965, when Washington and Oregon State earned the initial dubious honor.[12]

## TEAM LEADERS

RUSHING: Aaron Emanuel—545 yards on 108 carries
PASSING: Rodney Peete—223 out of 359 attempts for 2,812 yards and 18 touchdowns
RECEIVING: Erik Affholter—68 catches for 952 yards and 8 touchdowns
SCORING: Quin Rodriguez—76 points on 34 extra points and 14 field goals
KICKOFF RETURNS: Calvin Holmes—13 for 240 yards (18.5 avg.)
PUNT RETURNS: Cleveland Colter—13 for 52 yards (4.0 avg.)
PUNTING: Chris Sperle—43 for 1,696 yards (39.4 avg.)
INTERCEPTIONS: Chris Hale—4 for 47 yards
TACKLES: Scott Ross—137
SACKS: Craig Hartsuyker—8
Dan Owens—8

# *1989*

HEAD COACH: Larry Smith
ASSISTANT COACHES: Bobby April, Gary Bernardi, Ray Dorr, John Matsko, Tom Roggeman, Mike Sanford, Clarence Shelmon, Kevin Wolthausen
TEAM CAPTAINS: Leroy Holt, Tim Ryan
RECORD: 9–2–1 overall (6–0–1 in Pacific–10 Conference)
(Ranked 16th best record in college football out of 106 teams)
FINISH IN CONFERENCE: 1st place
FINISH IN NATIONAL POLLS: 8th place in AP, 9th place in UPI, and 7th place in *USA Today*
POINTS SCORED PER GAME: 28.0 to rank 34th out of 106 teams
POINTS ALLOWED PER GAME: 11.0 to rank 3rd

## Schedule and Highlights

**(H) Sept. 4—Illinois—13–14**
USC#5 ILL#22

This game was scheduled to be played in Moscow, USSR, and dubbed the Glasnost Bowl, but was changed to Los Angeles due to contract difficulties with game organizers. The Trojans were up, 13–0, through three quarters, but then Illinois quarterback Jeff George threw two touchdown passes in the fourth quarter. The game winner came with 2:19 left on a pass from George to Steve Williams. This was only the third time in 13 years that the Trojans lost a season opener. This marked the quarterbacking debut of Todd Marinovich, but the offense had trouble throughout the game. Marinovich completed 14 of 27 pass attempts for 120 yards, and the running game was almost nonexistent. The Trojans only rushed for 79 yards, with Aaron Emanuel leading the team with 32 yards on 15 carries. USC's only touchdown came when Marcus Hopkins blocked a punt, then picked it up on the Illinois 37 and went untouched for the touchdown. This was the first time in 32 years that a Trojan player scored on a blocked punt. The last to do it was Rod Humenuik. In Larry Smith's three years as head coach of the Trojans, his record against Big Ten teams was 0–4.[1]

**(H) Sept. 16—Utah State—66–10**
USC#13

After a stagnant offensive performance in their opener, the Trojans more than made up for it with a blowout victory. USC scored the most points since putting up 70 against Washington State in 1970. This was also the fourth time that the Trojans mauled Utah State. The other beatings came in 1928, 1930, and 1984. USC gained 654 yards of offense, with 491 of those yards coming on the ground on 49 carries. That gave the Trojans a 10.02 yards-per-carry average. Ricky Ervins led the ground attack with 180 yards on 15 carries and two touchdowns. Also scoring rushing touchdowns for USC were Aaron Emanuel, Leroy Holt, and backup quarterback Shane Foley, who also threw for a touchdown. Todd Marinovich completed 10 of 18 pass attempts for 92 yards and two touchdowns. His first touchdown pass as a Trojan came near the end of the first half, going to Frank Griffin from four yards out. Freshman receiver Larry Wallace never caught a pass for USC until this game, and hauled in two for touchdowns. Grant Runnerstrum kicked a 45-yard field goal, and Ernest Spears returned an interception 38 yards for a touchdown.[2]

**(H) Sept. 23—Ohio State—42–3**
USC#12

After four unsuccessful attempts to beat a team from the Big Ten as coach of the Trojans, Larry Smith finally won his first, and in convincing fashion. This was Ohio State's worst loss since Michigan beat them 58–6 in 1946. The Trojans gained 491 yards, and were led on offense by freshman quarterback Todd Marinovich, who finally was able to showcase his talents. He completed 14 out of 22 pass attempts for 246 yards and four touchdowns while nursing a sprained wrist on his throwing hand. John Jackson had two receptions for 108 yards and one touchdown, which was from 87 yards out, and set a new USC record for longest scoring strike in team history. Gary Wellman caught two of Marinovich's touchdown passes (19 and 17 yards), and Scott Galbraith hauled in the other from 11 yards out. Galbraith also caught a three-yard touchdown pass from Shane Foley. Mazio Royster scored on a one-yard run for the only touchdown coming on the ground. Ricky Ervins led the rushing attack with 117 yards on 21 carries.[3]

**(A) Sept. 30—Washington State—18–17**
USC#11 WASH#19

The Trojans won this game with four seconds left. Todd Marinovich guided USC 91 yards in 18 plays, with the end result being a two-yard touchdown pass to Ricky Ervins. Marinovich then threw to Gary Wellman for the winning two-point conversion. The drive took three-and-a-half minutes, and Marinovich completed 11 out of 17 pass attempts on the march toward victory. For the game, he was 27 out of 41 for 268 yards. His 27 completions broke USC's old single-game record of 25 set by Paul McDonald in 1979. In addition to scoring that last second touchdown, Ricky Ervins ran for 132 yards on 22 carries, and John Jackson had 11 receptions for 102 yards and one touchdown. This win gave the Trojans a 4–1 record, and snapped a nine-game winning streak dating back to the previous year for Washington State.[4]

**(H) Oct. 7—Washington—24–16**
USC#9

This game provided a big milestone in the program's history, as it was USC's 600th football victory. Todd Marinovich was virtually unstoppable in the first half, completing 16 of 17 pass attempts for 170 yards. He finished the game with 23 completions out of 35 attempts for 284 yards and one touchdown. John Jackson caught a 29-yard pass in the third quarter, which allowed him to become USC's all-time career leader with 124, surpassing Erik Affholter in the record books. He finished the game with seven receptions for 95 yards. This was USC's 15th straight Pac-10 victory, and their conference streak since the Trojans won 17 in a row between 1972 and 1974.[5]

**(A) Oct. 14—California—31–15**
USC#10

With their 16th straight Pac-10 win, the Trojans took over sole possession of first place in the conference. This was USC's fourth straight win over Cal, the 11th out of 12 previous meetings, and their 26th out of the last 31. The Trojans built a 24–7 halftime lead, and gained 499 yards for the game. For the first time since the Stanford game in 1985, the Trojans had a pair of running backs top the century mark. Leroy Holt finished with 160 yards on 21 carries, and Ricky Ervins ran for 124 yards on 31 carries. Todd Marinovich threw for 206 yards and one touchdown, and also ran for one himself. This game featured fights and penalties, and USC was hit with 12 penalties for 137 yards in losses.[6]

**(A) Oct. 21—Notre Dame—24–28**
USC#9 ND#1

For the second year in a row, Notre Dame entered their game against the Trojans as the top team in the country. The defending national champions then rallied to continue on their quest at a second straight title. This marked Notre Dame's 19th win in a row, and their seventh consecutive victory over the Trojans, which was the longest winning streak against USC by any team. Todd Marinovich was exceptional in this game as he set a school record with 55 pass attempts, completing 33 for 333 yards and three touchdowns.

This game started off rough, as an all out brawl occurred when Notre Dame players would not let USC get on the field from the tunnel. After order was restored, Marinovich led the Trojans to a 17–7 lead at the end of the first half. USC got going early when Notre Dame's "Rocket" Ismail fumbled on the opening kickoff after getting out to his 41-yard line. Ismail was hit by David Webb, and Brian Tuliau recovered for USC at the Irish 40. With only 2:08 off the clock, Marinovich capped off a scoring drive on the eighth play with a 12-yard pass to Larry Wallace for a 7–0 USC lead.

In order to make good on his earlier mishap, Ismail took the ensuing kickoff back 58 yards to the USC 38. Seven plays later, quarterback Tony Rice ran the ball across the goal line from seven yards out to even the count at 7–7. Ismail then gave the Trojans another gift when he fumbled a punt at the Notre Dame 15 that Junior Seau recovered. Marinovich had the Trojans back on top two plays later on a 15-yard scoring strike to John Jackson for a 14–7 lead. For the game, Jackson had 14 receptions for 200 yards. His reception total set a new USC single-game record previously held by Fred Hill (1964), and Jeff Simmons (1982). Quin Rodriguez added a 28-yard field goal to pad the Trojan lead to 17–7 at the end of the first half.

The Irish then fought back all the way to victory, starting on their first possession of the second half. Ricky Watters scored on a two-yard run to bring the Irish to within three points of the lead at 17–14. They then took their first lead of the game in the fourth quarter on a 35-yard run by Anthony Johnson that made the score 21–17. Undaunted, Marinovich guided USC back on top with a 16-yard touchdown pass to Gary Wellman to make the score 24–21.

With 9:01 left in the game, Rice took the Irish 80 yards, and scored the go-ahead points himself on a 16-yard run with 5:18 left. For the game, Rice led all ball carriers with 99 yards on 18 carries. Notre Dame's defense held after Rice's touchdown, and a final Hail Mary pass by Marinovich was knocked down to bring the curtain down on another "Glamour Game."[7]

**(H) Oct. 28—Stanford—19–0**
USC#10

This was USC's 17th straight Pac-10 victory, which tied a school record, and gave them the fourth longest win streak in conference history. The Trojan defense was one of the best in the nation at stopping the run, and they proved it in this game, allowing Stanford minus six yards on the ground, and a total of 134 offensive yards. The Trojan offense compiled 487 yards on homecoming weekend. Leading the way for USC was Ricky Ervins, who ran for 100 yards on 27 carries and one touchdown, Todd Marinovich, who completed 22 of 32 pass attempts for 303 yards, and John Jackson, who had seven receptions for 110 yards. Leroy Holt scored on a five-yard run, and Quin Rodriguez kicked two field goals from 28 and 25 yards out.[8]

**(H) Nov. 4—Oregon State—48–6**
USC#9

With this victory, the Trojans ran their winning streak against conference opponents to 18, which set a new school record, and gave them the third-longest win streak in conference history. This was the 18th straight time the Trojans beat Oregon State, and Larry Smith upped his all-time record against Oregon State to 10–0, included in that statistic was his time as coach at Arizona. Ricky Ervins ran for 110 yards on 20 carries, and Todd Marinovich completed 14 out of 18 pass attempts for 226 yards and three touchdowns, to lead the offense. The Trojan defense was the top-ranked unit against the run, and showed that status by holding Oregon State to minus 13 yards on the ground. The defense also recorded eight sacks, with linebacker Junior Seau tying a school record with four sacks in one game. Seau also became USC's single-season sack record holder, surpassing Jack Del Rio's mark of 13 set in 1983, which was the first year that sacks were included in the statistics.[9]

**(A) Nov. 11—Arizona—24–3**
USC#9 ARI#25

The Trojans clinched a third consecutive Rose Bowl berth with their 19th straight Pac-10 victory. That streak tied the UCLA teams from 1953–56 for the second longest in conference history. The record of 22 straight belonged to Cal from 1947 to 1950. Out of the past 16 meetings between these programs, the Trojans came away victorious 15 times. The only time that the Wildcats beat USC during that stretch was in 1981 with Larry Smith as coach of Arizona. Todd Marinovich completed 11 of 19 pass attempts for 168 yards, and ran for one touchdown. Ricky Ervins recorded his seventh 100-yard game by gaining 151 yards on 21 carries. This was the most 100-yard games by one individual in a single season for USC, since Marcus Allen had 11 in 1981. For the year, Ervins had 1,096 yards, making him the 18th Trojan to break the 1,000-yard rushing barrier.[10]

**(H) Nov. 18—UCLA—10–10**
USC#8

The Bruins held a slight edge on the Trojans throughout the decade. Coming into this matchup, UCLA had a 5–4 record in the 1980's against USC, and the men of Troy looked to even things out as the decade was nearing its end. However, neither team could boast of claiming the crown of "King of Los Angeles," as the game ended in a tie for the first time since 1971.

For the Trojans, Ricky Ervins ran for 173 yards on 28 carries, and Tim Ryan tied a school record with four sacks in one game. The Bruins, who came into this game with a 3–7 record, fell inches short of an upset when Alfredo Velasco's 54-yard field goal attempt hit the crossbar and bounced away with two seconds remaining.

The host Trojans were back near the top of the national rankings, and led all of college football with the least amount of yards allowed against the run. The 17-point favorite Trojans looked like a top-ranked team in their opening scoring drive with 86,672 looking on inside the Coliseum. On his play from scrimmage, quarterback Todd Marinovich threw to Gary Wellman for a gain of 39 yards. He teamed up with Wellman on the final play of the drive, which was a 13-yard scoring strike. Quin Rodriguez added the extra point, and USC was up, 7–0. During that nine-play, 79-yard drive, Marinovich threw for 73 yards, and looked to be on pace for a big game. Unfortunately, he only was able to connect for 81 more yards throughout the rest of the game, and was victim to three interceptions. As a team, the Trojans also lost three of six fumbles that they had, and were penalized nine times for 80 yards. The Bruins did not fare much better. They were hit with seven penalties for 79 yards in losses, had 151 yards through the air, and rushed for 51 net yards as a team.

The Bruins produced their lone touchdown in the second quarter after Eric Turner intercepted a pass, which gave UCLA the ball at midfield. They went on a seven-play, 49-yard drive that ended with Kevin Williams sweeping the right side from three yards out. Velasco's extra point tied the game 5:24 to go in the first half. The Trojans then scored their final points of the game at the end of the first half when Rodriguez connected on a 40-yard field goal to give USC a 10–7 lead.

The third quarter went into the record books with no point production. The Bruins then tied the game with only 1:17 expired from the clock in the fourth quarter on a 49-yard field goal by Velasco. Despite the lethargic display of offensive firepower throughout the game, exciting drama began to unfold as the clock ticked off the final minutes. The Trojans had gotten deep into UCLA territory, but Leroy Holt fumbled, and UCLA's Rocen Keeton recovered the loose ball at the 12 with 2:02 left on the clock. Quarterback Bret Johnson immediately went to work against the clock and 11 defenders. He connected with Scott Miller for a gain of 52 yards down to the USC 36. Shawn Wills gained a yard as the clock showed 53 seconds left, and Johnson added one more yard to bring up a third down situation. The Bruins' goal was to get to the 32-yard line to give Velasco a chance at a field goal from 49 yards out. Wills was then tackled by Cleveland Colter at the 37 for a three-yard loss. It would now be a field goal attempt from 54 yards that Velasco had to make to pull out a fantastic finish. When the ball left the kicker's foot, it appeared to be heading the right direction, and UCLA players were beginning to cheer their approval. The celebration that could have been at the Westwood campus quickly was put on hold when the ball smacked into the crossbar, and drifted away to preserve the tie.[11]

**Rose Bowl, (N) Jan. 1—Michigan—17–10**

USC#12 MICH#3

Bo Schembechler was ready to sit down as Michigan's head coach after an illustrious 20 years as mentor of the maize and blue. In a head-coaching career that began in 1963 at Miami University of Ohio, Schembechler compiled a 234–65–8 record. While at Michigan since 1969, he won or shared 13 Big Ten titles, and looked to improve his Rose Bowl record to 3–7 with a victory over the Trojans. This game would also serve as a reunion between Schembechler and USC coach Larry Smith, who served under Bo as an assistant for six years.

The Wolverines came in to this game at 10–1 still with hopes of claiming a national championship. The chance to give Schembechler one final victory ride started off slow, as the defenses dug in to produce a scoreless opening quarter. The Trojans then broke the deadlock early in the second quarter. Dan Owens blocked a Michigan punt to get things jump-started, and Todd Marinovich cracked the goal line six plays later from the one. Quin Rodriguez added the extra point, and USC was on top, 7–0. J.D. Carlson got the Wolverines on the board with a 19-yard field goal, and Rodriguez put the Trojans back up by seven at halftime, complements of a 34-yard three-pointer.

Tailback Allen Jefferson scored on a two-yard run, and Carlson's conversion tied the game at 10–10 in the third quarter. It was then that another classic Rose Bowl moment was provided by the Trojans. With just under six minutes to play in the game, Michigan had a successful fake punt called back due to a holding penalty, and the infraction gave the Trojans possession on the 25. It took 11 plays and 75 yards to accomplish a fantastic finish. Tailback Ricky Ervins, who made his home five minutes away from the Rose Bowl, and was employed there a few years earlier as a parking lot attendant, became the hero for USC. He ran for a game-clinching 14-yard touchdown with 1:10 to play, and Rodriguez added the extra point for a 17–10 victory, which snapped USC's bowl game losing streak at four. Ervins, who gained 126 yards on 30 carries, and caught five passes for an additional 44 yards, earned MVP honors. His counterpart, Michigan's Leroy Hoard, also topped the century mark on the ground. This was the second year in a row that Hoard was the only running back to rush for over 100 yards against USC.[12]

### TEAM LEADERS

RUSHING: Ricky Ervins—1,395 yards on 269 carries
PASSING: Todd Marinovich—219 out of 352 attempts for 2,578 yards and 16 touchdowns
RECEIVING: John Jackson—62 catches for 964 yards and 5 touchdowns
SCORING: Quin Rodriguez—73 points on 40 extra points and 11 field goals
KICKOFF RETURNS: Travis Hannah—5 for 116 yards (23.2 avg.)
PUNT RETURNS: Larry Wallace—26 for 183 yards (7.0 avg.)
PUNTING: Ron Dale—33 for 1,284 yards (38.9 avg.)
INTERCEPTIONS: Mark Carrier—7 for 58 yards
TACKLES: Delmar Chesley—124
SACKS: Tim Ryan—20

## *1990*

HEAD COACH: Larry Smith
ASSISTANT COACHES: Bobby April, Gary Bernardi, Ray Dorr, John Matsko, Tom Roggeman, Mike Sanford, Clarence Shelmon, Kevin Wolthausen
TEAM CAPTAIN: Don Gibson
RECORD: 8–4–1 overall (5–2–1 in Pacific–10 Conference)
(Ranked 34th best record in college football out of 107 teams)
FINISH IN CONFERENCE: 2nd place

Finish in National Polls: 20th place in AP and 22nd place in both the UPI and *USA Today*
Points Scored Per Game: 26.8 to rank 35th out of 107 teams
Points Allowed Per Game: 21.1 to rank 39th

## Schedule and Highlights

**(N) Aug. 31—Syracuse—34–16**
USC#9

The Trojans traveled to Giants Stadium in East Rutherford, New Jersey, for the Kickoff Classic VIII with the youngest USC team in 25 years, consisting of only seven returning starters. The inexperience apparently did not have an effect of the Trojans, as Todd Marinovich started the season off right by throwing for 337 yards and three touchdowns. Gary Wellman also earned status as a top-notch receiver by catching nine passes for 109 yards and one touchdown.[1]

**(H) Sept. 15—Penn State—19–14**
USC#6

The duo of Todd Marinovich and Gary Wellman once again helped USC earn a victory. In the Trojans' home opener, Marinovich threw for 240 yards and one touchdown, while Wellman finished with nine receptions for 121 yards. On his touchdown pass to Frank Griffin, Marinovich became the sixth Trojan quarterback to surpass 3,000 yards passing in a career. The defending Pac-10 rushing champion, Ricky Ervins, scored on a one-yard run for USC.[2]

**(A) Sept. 22—Washington—0–31**
USC#3 WASH#21

On the hottest September 22nd in Seattle history, the Trojans suffered their worst conference defeat since a 34–0 loss to Washington in 1960. This ended USC's 20-game conference winning streak two victories shy of the all-time record. The Huskies totally shut the USC offense down, as Todd Marinovich was only able to complete seven out of 16 pass attempts for 80 yards and threw two interceptions. The running attack of Scott Lockwood and Ricky Ervins did not fare any better, as they gained a mere 11 yards between them.[3]

**(A) Sept. 29—Ohio State—35–26**
USC#18 OSU#12

The Trojans traveled to Columbus, Ohio, to go against long-time Rose Bowl foe, the Ohio State Buckeyes. The second half of the game was played in heavy rain and with thunder and lightning. The weather conditions were bad enough that officials were forced to suspend the game with 2:36 to play after USC recovered an onside kick. At the time the game was called, USC running back Ricky Ervins struck the Ohio State defense like thunder and lightning, as he amassed 199 yards on 28 carries and two touchdowns. USC cornerback Zuri Hector ran for a touchdown after recovering a blocked punt to set the tone only a few minutes into the game.[4]

**(H) Oct. 6—Washington State—30–17**
USC#15

The running tandem of Mazio Royster and Scott Lockwood was so dominant in this game that Royster exploded for 203 yards on 34 carries and three touchdowns, while Lockwood had 102 yards on 20 carries. This dominant display of running the football it surely allowed USC to live up to its moniker of "Tailback U." This was Royster's first start, and his performance was better than that of the four USC Heisman Trophy-winning running backs in their initial game as a Trojan.[5]

**(A) Oct. 13—Stanford—37–22**
USC#16

Mazio Royster topped the century mark on the ground for a second straight week with 112 rushing yards on 22 carries. When Royster wasn't tearing up the turf, Todd Marinovich was sending passes through the air, and he finished with an impressive 338 yards and three touchdowns. He also caught a nine-yard touchdown pass from Curtis Conway on an option play. Marinovich's main target was Gary Wellman, who had nine receptions for 174 yards and two touchdowns. The Stanford passing attack looked unstoppable from the start, as quarterback Jason Palumbis threw for 260 yards early in the game. The Trojan defense then adjusted and shut the air attack down. They also clamped down on Stanford's running game by limiting it to only four yards.[6]

**(H) Oct. 20—Arizona—26–35**
USC#15

On USC's homecoming weekend, Scott Lockwood gained 124 yards on 16 carries despite the loss. The Trojans held a 17–7 lead at halftime, but then the offense slowed down to a halt in the third quarter. Meanwhile, the Arizona offense starting heating up, and scored 21 points to help them prevail. Ronald Veal ran for three Arizona touchdowns, and as a team, the Wildcats finished with 252 rushing yards.[7]

**(A) Oct. 27—Arizona State—13–6**
USC#21

Head coach Larry Smith suspended starting quarterback Todd Marinovich after reports that he was missing classes. In his place, Smith went with Shane Foley, who made the first start of his college career. Foley responded by connecting on his first five passes, and finished the game with 12 completions out of 19 attempts for 125 yards. He also ran for 67 yards. As a team, the Trojans ran for 296 yards and earned 30 first downs.[8]

**(H) Nov. 3—California—31–31**
USC#21

The Trojans had solid offensive showing from the trio of Mazio Royster, Todd Marinovich, and Gary Wellman. Royster ran for 175 yards on 24 carries, Marinovich threw for 291 and two touchdowns, and Wellman had nine receptions for 142 yards. Cal tied the game with 1:22 remaining, but missed the opportunity to win after Robbie Keen missed a 43-yard field goal with four seconds left.[9]

**(A) Nov. 10—Oregon State—56–7**
USC#23

This marked a major milestone for USC's "Super Fan" Giles Pellerin, who was in attendance for his this 700th consecutive Trojan football game. The Trojans gave Pellerin a very nice thank you gift by mauling Oregon State. Mazio Royster ran for 125 yards on 26 carries and one touchdown, and Travis Hannah had six receptions for 102 yards and two touchdowns to pace the onslaught. Backup quarterback Shane Foley chipped in with 115 yards passing and threw a pair of touchdowns, and the defense only allowed 157 yards to be gained against it. This gave Larry Smith his 100th win as head coach of the Trojans.[10]

**(A) Nov. 17—UCLA—45–42**
USC#19

The old west was filled with stories of monumental shootouts that became legend and recreated on many occasions in motion pictures. USC and UCLA share the same neighborhood with that of the Hollywood dream factories, and for the course of sixty minutes of mayhem, the Trojans and Bruins put on a football version of a Wild West shootout. This 60th edition of "the Battle for Los Angeles" was possibly the greatest contest staged between these two programs, and when it was over, they combined for 87 points with gunslinger quarterbacks sophomore Todd Marinovich and freshman Tommy Maddox pulling the triggers that sparked this offensive onslaught. Marinovich threw for 215 yards and two touchdowns on 16 out of 25 attempts. Maddox showed no signs of freshman jitters in such a big game, as he amassed 409 yards and three touchdowns.

The scoring fest started early and did not stop until the final 16 seconds. In addition to Maddox's three touchdown tosses, he also threw as many interceptions. The first one occurred in the opening seconds when defensive back Stephon Pace picked off Maddox after he hurried a pass in an attempt to avoid a rush by defensive lineman Don Gibson. Pace intercepted at the UCLA 27 and returned it for a touchdown with only 52 seconds off the clock. This was the earliest six-pointer ever scored in the history of this series. An attempt at a two-point conversion following a bad snap from center on the extra point try, resulted in an incomplete pass, and the Trojans held a 6–0 lead.

Five minutes later, Maddox redeemed himself by running nine yards for the tying touchdown. The Bruins then took their first lead of the game on Brad Daluiso's extra point kick. With 3:22 remaining in the quarter, Marinovich took the Trojans 84 yards on 12 plays to reclaim the lead. He hit on two key passes totaling 29 yards, and the drive was helped along when UCLA defensive back Eric Turner was penalized 14 yards for a personal foul that put the ball at the Bruins' 14. Mazio Royster capped the drive off with a seven-yard run, and Marinovich threw to Scott Lockwood for a two-point conversion, that made gave the Trojans a 14–7 lead going into the second quarter.

The Trojans held their seven-point advantage until halfway through the second quarter. The Bruins then went 76 yards in six plays to even things up. Maddox threw a 47-yard scoring strike to Sean LaChapelle, and Daluiso tied the game at 14-all with the extra point kick. Marinovich put the Trojans back on top a few minutes before the first half ended when he scored on a one-yard quarterback sneak and Quin Rodriguez added the conversion kick to make it a USC advantage of 21–14 going into the second half. That tie-breaking, five-play, 29-yard scoring drive, was set up by a Don Gibson fumble recovery.

The third quarter was the lowest scoring 15 minutes of this game, but it was the calm before the storm that became a point barrage over the final quarter of play. A Rodriguez 20-yard field goal was all the Trojans mustered up in the third quarter, and the Bruins scored a touchdown on a Brian Brown five-yard run to send the game into the wild fourth quarter with USC up, 24–21.

In the opening minutes of the fourth quarter, Maddox once again fell victim to an interception return for a touchdown. His pass intended for Reggie Moore was tipped in the air by USC defensive back Stephon Pace and grabbed by fellow Trojan defender Jason Oliver. A few seconds later, Oliver was in the end zone to complete a 34-yard interception return. Rodriguez kicked the extra point, and USC was up by a 31–21 count.

UCLA receiver Scott Miller had a big day by catching eight passes for 175 yards. Two of his receptions went for touchdowns in the fourth quarter that gave the Bruins a 35–31 lead with 9:17 left in the game. His scoring grabs came from 29 and 38 yards out. Marinovich struck back with 3:19 left when he threw a 21-yard touchdown to Johnnie Morton that capped off an eight-play, 47-yard drive. Rodriguez's conversion kick made it 38–35, but UCLA had one final rally left in their arsenal. Maddox led UCLA on a seven-play, 75-yard drive, hitting on two key passes to Miller and Moore, and running for an 11-yard gain himself. Fullback Kevin Smith scored on a one-yard run to finish the drive off with 1:19 left on the clock. Daluiso added the extra point, and the Bruin backers among the 98,088 inside the Rose Bowl felt the game was theirs, as UCLA was up, 42–38.

This series has produced some classic fantastic finishes, and the Trojans created one this time out. From the USC 26-yard line, Marinovich kept the Trojans moving. On a third down play, he connected on a pass to Gary Wellman that covered 27 yards, getting the Trojans inside UCLA territory at their 45. The tandem teamed up again for a gain of 22 yards that put the ball on the UCLA 23 with 26 seconds remaining. Marinovich went to the air once again, this time hitting Morton in the corner of the end zone. Morton jumped for and brought down the pass for a 23-yard score that completed the drive on its fifth play. Rodriguez added the final point of the game with a conversion kick that clinched a 45–42 USC victory with 16 seconds left in the game.[11]

**(H) Nov. 24—Notre Dame—6–10**
USC#18 ND#7

Todd Marinovich passed for 273 yards, and Gary Wellman had nine receptions for 101 yards to lead the Trojans. Unfortunately, it was not enough to hold off defeat at the hands of the Irish for the eighth straight time. This was the longest streak for either team since this series began in 1926. This loss gave the Trojans a 2–2–1 record at the Coliseum, which was the most in the historic venue by USC since 1971.

The Trojans started off in good shape, moving the ball 73 yards on 13 plays in their opening series and eating up 6:38 off the clock. The end result was a 22-yard field goal by Quin Rodriguez. On that drive, Marinovich completed his first four pass attempts for 52 yards, and tailback Mazio Royster carried the ball six times for 27 yards.

Notre Dame's first offensive series came and went quickly, as they failed to get a first down within three plays. Marinovich took over again, and completed four straight pass attempts for 37 yards, and the Trojans were on the Notre Dame 38. Linebacker Mike Stonebreaker then sacked Marinovich for a loss of nine yards, and after he ran for a gain of ten, Marinovich's third down pass was incomplete, and the Trojans had to punt on fourth down.

The Irish then got down to the USC 12, and after running back Ricky Watters lost three yards, Notre Dame was penalized for a personal foul, and the ball was moved back to the USC 30. This was the only penalty called throughout the entire first half. Craig Hentrich salvaged the drive with a 30-yard field goal with 8:55 remaining in the first half. This was the way the first half ended, with these two storied programs locked up at 3–3. The first quarter was dominated by USC, as a massive crowd of 91,639 saw the Trojans compile 133 yards while holding Notre Dame to 46. The Irish returned the favor in the second quarter when they gained 125 yards to USC's 21.

The Trojans followed the same pattern from their opening series of the game. They scored on their first offensive series of the second half when Rodriguez kicked a 30-yard field goal to give USC a 6–3 lead. The Irish scored the game's final points in the third quarter when Tony Brooks took a pitchout from quarterback Rick Mirer and went into the end zone from one yard out to complete a 15-play, 69-yard drive with 3:14 left in the quarter. Hentrich's conversion made it 10–6.

The Trojans made one last effort to win with 91 seconds left and the ball resting on the Notre Dame 46. Marinovich threw a pass to fullback Scott Lockwood for 11 yards, but the gain was nullified due to a holding penalty. What started off good, soon ended very poorly for the Cardinal & Gold. Facing a fourth-and-11 situation, Marinovich connected with Gary Wellman on a sideline pass, but the receiver was pushed out of bounds just shy of a first down. Wellman was sure he had the necessary yardage needed to move the chains, but the officials saw things differently. Wellman and Marinovich got into an argument with the officials over the spot of the ball, but all it got the Trojans was a 15-yard penalty.[12]

**John Hancock Bowl, (N) Dec. 31—Michigan State—16–17**
USC#21 MSU#22

This marked the eighth different bowl game in which USC played in, and it was the 900th game in the program's history. With the Sun Bowl in El Paso, Texas, serving as the backdrop, the Trojans scored the only points of the first quarter with 54 seconds left. A seven-yard pass from Todd Marinovich to Gary Wellman, with a Quin Rodriquez extra point gave the Trojans a 7–0 lead.

Up to the middle of the second quarter, the Trojans had contained the Spartans very well, limiting them to only a pair of first downs. It seemed that USC was in control of this game at this stage, as Marinovich had the Trojans on the doorstep of the end zone once again. However, the dynamics of the game changed when Marinovich lost control of the ball on fourth-and-one at the Michigan Stater one. It was then that the Spartans found renewed life, and made the most of the opportunity.

Quarterback Dan Enos took Michigan State 80 yards downfield, with three pass completions totaling 38 yards pacing the attack. Tailback Hyland Hickson finished the drive off with an 18-yard run. John Langeloh then tied the game at 7–7 with the extra point, and that was how the first half went into the history books.

The Trojans came out for the second half with a great ball control attack, which ate up the first nine minutes of the third quarter. Unfortunately, the lengthy drive stalled at the Michigan State seven, but Rodriguez salvaged it with a 20-yard field goal to give USC their final lead of the game at 10–7. It was after this that the Spartans rallied for good. Facing a third-and-13 from his own 26, Enos sent a long pass over the middle to Courtney Hawkins. The receiver was caught between two defenders, but somehow found a way to haul the pass in. Enos then teamed up with Hawkins again for the go-ahead touchdown with 2:53 left in the third quarter. Hawkins' 21-yard touchdown reception, and Langeloh's extra point, made it a 14–10 game. This was the first touchdown reception by a Michigan State receiver all season. Marinovich was intercepted for the second time, and the Spartans got three points off the turnover on a 52-yard field goal from Langeloh to head into the fourth quarter with a 17–10 lead.

In the early stages of the fourth quarter, Rodriguez booted a career-best 54-yard field goal to make the score 17–13 with 13:07 left. Marinovich then suffered his third interception of the game after a pass intended for Wellman was tipped by linebacker Chuck Bullough and intercepted by free safety Mike Iaquaniello. The Trojans got the ball back the same way they gave it up. Stephon Pace intercepted an Enos pass, and the Trojans had new life with the ball at midfield and 9:01 remaining.

It was at this time that USC head coach Larry Smith pulled Marinovich out of the game, and replaced him with Shane Foley. The relationship between Smith and Marinovich was a volatile one at best. The benching prompted Marinovich to begin a ranting session against his coach with a national television audience looking on. Despite the problems brewing on the USC sideline, Foley managed to drive the Trojans 41 yards in nine plays to the 17. From there the drive stalled when Foley muffed a pitchout to Mazio Royster. The ball went wide of Royster's grasp, but the sophomore tailback managed to keep possession of the ball for the Trojans after jumping on it at the 26. Unfortunately, the botched play took the Trojans from a third-and-short situation, to that of a third-and-11. With 3:07 left, Rodriguez connected on a 43-yard field goal to make the score 17–16. Smith opted to try the field goal instead of going for a first down on the notion that the USC defense would hold the Spartans and the Trojans could regain possession and squeak out a last-second victory. Sometimes the best of plans do not work out. Such was the case in this game. Michigan State was able to run out the clock and secure the win.

Courtney Hawkins was awarded as the game's MVP after catching six passes for 106 yards. USC outside linebacker took home the Most Valuable Lineman award after recording two sacks and forcing a fumble. Mazio Royster produced a solid performance despite the loss with 125 rushing yards on 32 carries.[13] As for the saga of Todd Marinovich, he never played another game for the Trojans. In a season that began with Heisman Trophy hopes, it ended with his arrest for cocaine possession one month after this game. He then entered the NFL draft instead to returning to USC.[14]

## TEAM LEADERS

RUSHING: Mazio Royster—1,168 yards on 235 carries
PASSING: Todd Marinovich—196 out of 322 attempts for 2,423 yards and 13 touchdowns

RECEIVING: Gary Wellman—66 catches for 1,015 yards and 5 touchdowns
SCORING: Quin Rodriguez—94 points on 37 extra points and 19 field goals
KICKOFF RETURNS: Curtis Conway—26 for 555 yards (21.4 avg.)
PUNT RETURNS: Curtis Conway—12 for 161 yards and 1 touchdown (13.4 avg.)
Scott Lockwood—11 for 161 yards (14.6 avg.)
PUNTING: Ron Dale—59 for 2,413 yards (40.9 avg.)
INTERCEPTIONS: Stephon Pace—4 for 43 yards and 1 touchdown
Mike Salmon—4 for 27 yards
TACKLES: Kurt Barber—84
SACKS: Craig Hartsuyker—9

## *1991*

HEAD COACH: Larry Smith
ASSISTANT COACHES: Gary Bernardi, Bob Cope, Ray Dorr, John Matsko, Wayne Nunnely, Tom Roggeman, Mike Sanford, Kevin Wolthausen
TEAM CAPTAIN: Matt Gee
RECORD: 3–8 overall (2–6 in Pacific–10 Conference)
Ranked 83rd best record in college football out of 107 teams)
FINISH IN CONFERENCE: 8th place
FINISH IN NATIONAL POLLS: No ranking in Top 25
POINTS SCORED PER GAME: 20.8 to rank 62nd out of 107 teams
POINTS ALLOWED PER GAME: 25.1 to rank 73rd

### Schedule and Highlights

**(H) Sept. 2—Memphis State—10–24**
USC#16

The season opened with a surprising defeat. In the first half, Reggie Perry ran for a touchdown, and Cole Ford added a field goal, to give the Trojans a 10–3 lead. The second half was a different story, as the Trojan defense crumbled and the offense could not get any more points on the board. Curtis Conway's 100-yard touchdown on a kickoff return sparked USC, but it was nullified by a holding penalty.[1]

**(H) Sept. 14—Penn State—21–10**
PSU#5

A Mike Hinz's quarterback snap on the opening drive sparked the Trojans, and the offense continued the momentum. With only 6:40 off the clock, Reggie Perry threw a touchdown pass to Yonnie Jackson to put USC into the lead. Penn State came back to tie it up in the second quarter until a Matt Gee fumble resulted in a Deon Strother one-yard run gave USC a 14–7 lead. Reggie Perry finished off the Trojans' scoring with a two-yard run.[2]

**(H) Sept. 21—Arizona State—25–32**
USC#22

The Sun Devils took a 25–10 halftime lead, with USC's points coming on a 12-yard run by Curtis Conway and a 22-yard field goal by Cole Ford. In the second half, the Trojans rallied on two Mazio Royster touchdown runs, but they could only get as close as seven points off the lead.[3]

**(A) Sept. 28—Oregon—30–14**

The Trojans took to the road after posting a 1–2 record at the Coliseum. The first half was tight and low scoring. Two Cole Ford field goals (31 and 37 yards) were enough to allow USC to be deadlocked at 6–6 going into the second half. The Trojan offense then came to life, with Mazio Royster running for a touchdown and another Cole Ford field foal made it 16–6 after three quarters. Royster added his second touchdown of the game, and finished the game with 132 yard on 29 carries. An interception return for a touchdown by Jason Uhl allowed USC to prevail by a comfortable margin and even out their record at 2–2.[4]

**(A) Oct. 12—Washington State—34–27**

This marked the 70th game in which these two teams faced off. Over the course of time leading up to this matchup, the Trojans only lost five times to the Cougars. They kept their dominance intact on a second half comeback. Sophomore tailback Deon Strother ran for a team-high 122 yards on 22 carries, scored on a three-yard run, and threw a 28-yard touchdown pass to Larry Wallace that gave USC a 24–21 third quarter lead. Mazio Royster chipped in with 114 yards on 23 carries to top the 100-yard rushing mark for the second straight week.[5]

**(H) Oct. 19—Stanford—21–24**

In this, their homecoming game, USC went ahead 21–17 with 3:37 left. However, Stanford rallied back to win on a 12-yard pass from Steve Stenstrom to Chris Walsh with 1:11 left to play. USC's Chris Ford attempted to tie the game, and just missed on a 45-yard field goal attempt with no time left. Despite the loss, Curtis Conway and Reggie Perry came away with solid individual efforts. Conway returned a kickoff 82 yards, and Perry completed 19 of 27 pass attempts for 189 yards in the second half. He finished the game with 201 yards through the air.[6]

**(A) Oct. 26—Notre Dame—20–24**
ND#5

The luck of the Irish continued in the Land of Troy, as Notre Dame sent the Trojans down in defeat. With 59,075 in attendance at Notre Dame Stadium, the Trojans battled back from two 14-point deficits, only to fall short by four points in the end. Notre Dame fullback Jerome Bettis opened the scoring early on a 53-yard run with 13:08 left in the first quarter. Bettis had a great day, rushing for 178 yards on 24 carries, and he scored another touchdown in this game.

With just over eight minutes left in the game, Notre Dame was up, 21–7, despite a controversial call that went the Irish's way. Tony Brooks caught a short pass from Rick Mirer and ran down the sideline and dove for the end zone. It was ruled a 12-yard touchdown, but replay showed that Brooks fumbled on the one-yard line and the ball was recovered in the end zone by USC linebacker Gidion Murrell for what should have been a touchback. Unfortunately, the touchdown stood. The Trojans came back when linebacker Kurt Barber, who had a team high 14 tackles, sacked quarterback Rick Mirer, causing a fumble in the process. Terry McDaniels recovered the ball for USC at the Irish 20, and two plays later, Mazio Royster ran up the middle for a 14-yard touchdown to help get the Trojans to within seven points. Notre Dame came back with a field goal to make it a 24–14 game with 4:50 remaining.

The Trojans then went 73 yards in 12 plays, capping the drive with a four-yard touchdown run by Raoul Spears to cut the Irish advantage to four points. Reggie Perry looked to Johnnie Morton on a two-point conversion pass, but he overthrew him even though Morton was wide open. Cole Ford then attempted an onside kick with 1:50 left. The kick went the required 10 yards, and a mad dash for the ball occurred. USC cornerback Marvin Pollard appeared to have recovered the ball, seeing that he came out of the pileup with possession. However, the officials claimed that Notre Dame's Irv Smith recovered the ball. This sparked a 15-yard unsportsmanlike penalty on USC's head coach Larry Smith, who for good reason, erupted when he heard the call and took off running across the field toward the officials. The game, and USC's hopes of victory, ended soon after.[7]

**(A) Nov. 2—California—30–52**
CAL#10

Even though the Trojans gave up 52 points, the USC offense got solid performances from Deon Strother's 153 yards and Johnnie Morton's eight receptions for 135 yards. Up to this time in their history, this was the most points allowed by USC.[8]

**(H) Nov. 9—Washington—3–14**
WASH#2

The Trojans came out strong, driving down to the Washington 14-yard line on their first possession. Unfortunately, that initial show of offensive might came to an end with a missed field goal, and that was all the excitement generated by USC. The Huskies answered with two scores, and that was it for the Trojans. With the offense going stagnant, it was decided upon to replace sophomore quarterback Reggie Perry with freshman Rob Johnson. The move allowed USC to get their only points of the game, as Johnson led the team downfield and close enough for J.J. Dudum to kick a field goal.[9]

**(A) Nov. 16—Arizona—14–31**

The Wildcats jumped out to 10–0 lead, and held off a surge by USC that closed the gap to 17–14 early in the third quarter. With the passing game having problems, the Trojans looked to the ground attack to carry them. Estrus Crayton answered the challenge by running for 185 yards on 27 carries and two touchdowns.[10]

**(H) Nov. 23—UCLA—21–24**
UCLA#25

On some occasions, despite the many incidents that can alter a game, the outcome is determined by one key play by one individual. Throughout the history of the USC-UCLA series, there were individuals that came up with a game-clinching play, and in 1991, it was UCLA linebacker Arnold Ale.

The events leading up to Ale's heroics began with UCLA scoring on their second offensive series. Midway through the opening quarter, Louis Perez kicked a 49-yard field goal to give the Bruins a 3–0 lead. With 2:20 left in the first quarter, the Bruins struck quickly when tailback Kevin Williams scored on a 72-yard run on the first play of a drive. Perez kicked the conversion, and the Bruins were up, 10–0, at the end of the opening quarter.

The Bruins expanded their bulge to 17 points with 2:52 remaining in the first half. On third-and-goal from the USC one, Maury Toy got the call, but fumbled before getting into the end zone. Tight end Brian Allen was there to recover the ball in the end zone for six points, and Perez added the conversion kick. It seemed that the Trojans were about to go down for the sixth straight time without much of a fight. However, the Trojans reared up and made things interesting. USC quarterback Reggie Perry led the Cardinal & Gold on a seven-play, 67-yard scoring drive by connecting with Larry Wallace on a key third down pass that gained 30 yards. With 46 seconds left in the first half, Perry threw a 13-yard touchdown pass to Curtis Conway, and J.J. Dudum added the extra point to close the deficit to ten at the start of the third quarter.

On the Trojans' second possession of the third quarter, they closed the gap to three points when Perry scored on a one-yard run with 6:10 expired off the clock. Dudum's conversion kick then made it 17–14. Looking to take away USC's momentum, Bruins' quarterback Tommy Maddox connected on five of six pass attempts for 68 yards. He finished the 11-play, 73-yard drive by throwing a scoring strike to Maury Toy from 17 yards out. Perez kicked the extra point that gave UCLA a 24–14 lead heading into the fourth quarter.

The Trojans loaded up again and came back to once again close to within three points of the lead. With only four seconds expired from the clock in the fourth quarter, Perry threw his second touchdown pass of the game, this time a six-yarder to tight end Yonnie Jackson. Dudum kicked the conversion, and with virtually the entire fourth quarter still remaining, the Trojans had an opportunity to rally back from a 17-point deficit.

The Trojans had many late game-winning drives with little time left on the clock. They looked to add to that lore in this neighborhood rivalry. Starting from the USC four, Estrus Crayton ran for ten yards and a first down at the 14. For the game, Crayton had 126 yards on 21 carries. Perry then connected with Yonnie Jackson for a gain of nine. Four plays later, facing a third-and16 from the 35, Perry threw to Travis Hannah for a pickup of 23 yards, and it got the Trojans into UCLA territory at the 42. Two minutes were all that remained, and 84,623 inside the Coliseum were getting their money's worth on this day. Perry went to the air on first down, and almost threw an interception, but linebacker Randy Cole could not hold onto the ball. Crayton carried for five yards total on the next two plays, and USC now faced a fourth-and-five situation with 1:19 left. Following a timeout, Perry took the snap from center, and looked for an open receiver to keep the drive alive. Johnnie Morton tore up the right sideline and had the defender beat on the route to the end zone. At that same moment, linebacker Arnold Ale came in without opposition and blasted Perry. The jolt knocked off Perry's helmet and dislodged the ball from his grasp. The loose ball was then recovered by UCLA's Mike Chalenski to clinch the victory for the Bruins. This win snapped a four-game losing streak to the Trojans, and gave USC a school record of six straight losses. This was only the third time in 30 years that USC finished a football season with a losing record.[11]

### Team Leaders

Rushing: Deon Strother—614 yards on 129 carries
Passing: Reggie Perry—131 out of 255 attempts for 1,574 yards and 3 touchdowns
Receiving: Johnnie Morton—49 catches for 662 yards
Scoring: Cole Ford—42 points on 21 extra points and 7 field goals
Deon Strother—42 points on 7 touchdowns
Mazio Royster—42 points on 7 touchdowns

KICKOFF RETURNS: Curtis Conway—20 for 493 yards (24.7 avg.)
PUNT RETURNS: Curtis Conway—24 for 172 yards (7.2 avg.)
PUNTING: Ron Dale—65 for 2,628 yards (40.4 avg.)
INTERCEPTIONS: Jason Oliver—5 for 11 yards
TACKLES: Matt Gee—97
SACKS: Kurt Barber—4

## *1992*

HEAD COACH: Larry Smith
ASSISTANT COACHES: Gary Bernardi, Bob Cope, Ray Dorr, Ricky Hunley, Wayne Nunnely, Bob Palcic, Clancy Pendergast, Tom Roggeman, Mike Sanford, Kevin Wolthausen
TEAM CAPTAIN: Stephon Pace
RECORD: 6–5–1 overall (5–3 in Pacific–10 Conference)
(Ranked 49th best record in college football out of 107 teams)
FINISH IN CONFERENCE: Tied for 3rd place
FINISH IN NATIONAL POLLS: No ranking in Top 25
POINTS SCORED PER GAME: 22.0 to rank 59th out of 107 teams
POINTS ALLOWED PER GAME: 20.8 to rank 43rd

### Schedule and Highlights

**(A) Sept. 5—San Diego State—31–31**

This appearance in the Ralph's Holiday Classic kicked off the Trojans' 100th all-time football team. Rob Johnson threw for 278 yards and four touchdowns, and Johnnie Morton tied a USC record with three touchdown receptions. San Diego State came close to pulling out a victory, but Andy Trakas missed two field goal attempts in the last minute of the game from 30 and 55 yards.[1]

**(A) Sept. 19—Oklahoma—20–10**
OK#13

The Trojans scored all their points in the fourth quarter to prevail over the Sooners. Rob Johnson threw for 201 yards and one touchdown, and Curtis Conway had nine receptions for 115 yards and one touchdown. This victory snapped a seven-game winless streak for the Trojans.[2]

**(A) Oct. 3—Washington—10–17**
USC#20 WASH#1

The Trojans got to the Washington 28-yard line when time ran out to give USC a 1–1–1 record. This marked the first time in team history that the Trojans started a season off with three road games. Estrus Crayton ran for 105 yards on 25 carries, and Curtis Conway had five receptions for 112 yards and one touchdown.[3]

**(H) Oct. 10—Oregon—32–10**
USC#20

This impressive win snapped a four-game losing streak at home, and it was USC's first victory in seven games against a Pac-10 opponent. Johnnie Morton once again tied a school record with three touchdown receptions. For the game, Morton had eight receptions for 114 yards. Rob Johnson completed 11 out of 16 pass attempts, and threw three touchdown passes, all going to Morton. Curtis Conway also got into the USC record book with a 96-yard punt return, which was the longest in team history. The old record of 93 yards was set by Ernie Merk, 38 years earlier. The defense recorded 13 sacks, with linebackers Willie McGinest and Jeff Kopp leading the way with three apiece.[4]

**(H) Oct. 17—California—27–24**
USC#18

The Trojans were down, 24–13, before Estrus Crayton scored twice in the final 5:45 on runs of two and one yard respectively. His second six-pointer came with 2:27 left to give USC the win. Brain William then sealed the win with an interception as the clock showed only 2:19 remaining.[5]

**(H) Oct. 24—Washington State—31–21**
USC#15 WASH#13

The Cougars came into the Coliseum for USC's homecoming game sporting a perfect 6–0 record. They scored first late in the opening quarter, and then it was all USC. The Trojans poured it on, scoring 24 straight points two touchdowns from Curtis Conway, a one-yard run by Estrus Crayton, and a 27-yard field goal from Cole Ford. Fullback Wes Bender added an eight-yard touchdown run for USC's final points. Washington State rallied back in the fourth quarter to close the deficit to 24–21 on a 34-yard pass from Drew Bledsoe to Deron Pointer with 3:19 remaining. Those were the first points allowed by the Trojan defense in the fourth quarter up to this time in the season.[6]

**(A) Oct. 31—Arizona State—23–13**
USC#13

After a scoreless first quarter, the Trojans went up, 14–10, until the Sun Devils scored ten points in 82 seconds at the end of the third quarter. Curtis Conway then gave the Trojans some insurance points by returning a kickoff 95 yards to make it 21–10. This was USC's first kickoff return for a touchdown since Anthony Davis did it against Notre Dame on November 30, 1974.[7]

**(A) Nov. 7—Stanford—9–23**
USC#11 STAN#21

Interceptions hurt the Trojans on this day, but they did manage to close the deficit to seven points with a Cole Ford field goal and a Dwight McFadden run. Johnnie Morton once again turned in a solid performance with five receptions for 113 yards.[8]

**(H) Nov. 14—Arizona—14–7**
USC#18 ARI#9

The Trojans pulled out this win with 6:35 left. Rob Johnson threw for 213 yards, and Johnnie Morton had four receptions for 108 yards. One of Morton's catches was good for 65 yards and set up the winning touchdown. The go-ahead points came on a trick play. Tailback Deon Strother ran to his right and threw a cross-field pass to Rob Johnson, who made a leaping catch in the end zone for a 12–7 USC lead. Estrus Crayton ran for USC's other touchdown, and it was the first time all season that Arizona surrendered a touchdown in the first half of any previous game. As a unit, the defense gave up only 68 rushing yards after Arizona averaged 182.9 yards on the ground coming into this game. Linebacker Jeff Kemp led the defense with 11 tackles.[9]

**(A) Nov. 21—UCLA—37–38**
USC#15

The Rose Bowl in Pasadena, one of college football's most cherished cathedrals, became the home of the UCLA Bruins ten years earlier when not serving as the setting for a New Year's Day tradition. There were many illustrious moments staged by USC and UCLA in the Rose Bowl stadium, and this 62nd edition of the "Battle for Los Angeles" was one of them. Estrus Crayton ran for 140 yards on 28 carries for the Trojans, and UCLA's J.J. Stokes gained 263 yards on just six receptions to produce the most yardage allowed by a receiver against a USC defense.

This wild game saw the teams deadlocked at 17–17 at the end of the first half. The Bruins then overcame a 14-point deficit at the beginning of the fourth quarter to pull out a nail-biting victory. USC got on the board in the game's first six minutes on a Cole Ford 36-yard field goal. The Bruins took a 7–3 lead five minutes later on an 18-yard run by Kevin Williams and a Louis Perez extra point. Perez then extended UCLA's advantage to 10–3 with a personal-best 47-yard field goal as the clock showed 2:47 remaining in the opening stanza. The Trojans sent the game into the second quarter tied at 10 on a trick play. Quarterback Rob Johnson is usually the one tossing touchdown passes, but on this occasion, he was the receiver. Switching roles with receiver Curtis Conway, Johnson caught a 36-yard pass that pulled USC to within one point on the Bruins. Ford's conversion kick then knotted the score. With his touchdown pass, Conway had the opportunity to score to a six-pointer by throwing, running, receiving, and returning a punt and kickoff during his days as a Trojan.

UCLA's John Barnes threw for 385 yards, and three touchdowns in this game. His first scoring strike came midway through the second quarter, with J.J. Stokes on the receiving end of a 57-yard pass. Perez added the extra point, and the Bruins had a 17–10 lead. Four minutes expired from the clock before the Trojans knotted the game at 17–17 on a Rob Johnson one-yard run and a Ford conversion kick.

The Trojans got the upper hand in the third quarter, scoring 14 points while holding UCLA to none. USC took their first lead of the game since the opening quarter when Bruce Luzzi recovered a blocked punt in the end zone that teammate Zuri Hector got his hands on with 8:50 remaining in the quarter. Toward the end of the third quarter, Estrus Crayton broke free on a 32-yard scoring jaunt, and Ford added his second conversion kick of the quarter to give the Trojans what appeared to be a comfortable lead heading into the final 15 minutes.

For the first two minutes of the fourth quarter, USC still looked like they were on their way to victory, but the final 12:49 of the game provided a different ending. Barnes and Stokes teamed up on a 29-yard pass and catch that cut the USC advantage to seven points following Perez's conversion. The Barnes-to-Stokes act struck again a few minutes later, with the result being a gain of 59 yards that got the ball down to the USC seven. Kevin Williams then carried the ball on the next two plays, scoring his second touchdown run of the game, this time from the one. With Perez's extra point, the game was deadlocked again with 7:06 left. Barnes and Stokes saved the best for last. On third-and-four from the UCLA 10, Barnes connected with Stokes on a pass that the receiver took all the way to paydirt. The 90-yard go-ahead touchdown occurred with 3:08 left, and Perez's extra point gave the Bruins a 38–31 lead.

Rob Johnson looked to add his name to the list of all-time heroes in this series by leading the Trojans on an 11-play, 69-yard scoring drive. He kept the drive alive by hitting on two fourth down passes to Yonnie Jackson and Johnnie Morton. With 41 seconds left, Johnson finished the drive off himself with a one-yard run. The Trojans needed a win to obtain a share of the Pac-10 championship with Washington. For that reason, there was no question they would attempt a two-point conversion. Johnson threw to Yonnie Jackson in the left corner of the end zone, but linebacker Nkosi Littleton batted the ball away, and with it, USC's hopes of victory and a piece of the conference title.[10]

**(H) Nov. 28—Notre Dame—23–31**
USC#19 ND#5

For Notre Dame, their tenth straight win over USC was referred to as a decade of dominance. In the Land of Troy, however, it was a decade of despair. Notre Dame tailback Reggie Brooks provided the offensive firepower, as he carried the ball 19 times for 227 yards of the Irish's 330 total rushing yards. He scored three touchdowns on runs covering 12, 55, and 44 yards.

Like in their previous matchup with the Irish, the Trojans came close, and the game's final outcome was determined in the final seconds when cornerback Tom Carter's intercepted a Rob Johnson pass in the end zone. The Irish brought an 8–1–1 record into this game, and took a 7–3 lead on their first possession of the opening quarter. After Cole Ford gave USC a 3–0 lead with a field goal, Reggie Brooks scored his first touchdown on a 12-yard run that capped a seven-play, 74-yard drive.

The Trojans came right back with key Rob Johnson throwing key passes to Curtis Conway and Johnnie Morton. The 71-yard drive was finished of with a one-yard touchdown run by Deon Strother. In the second quarter, Craig Hentrich kicked a 37-yard field goal to give the Irish a 10–10. Cole Ford booted his second three-pointer, this time from 38 yards out to give USC a 13–10 advantage.

This scoring seesaw was put to an end when Brooks shot through the line and ran 55 yards to give Notre Dame a 17–13 lead with 1:19 left in the first half. The Trojans did manage to close to 17–16 as the first half ended on a 32-yard field goal by Ford after the Trojans recovered a fumbled punt by Notre Dame's Charles Stafford.

Brooks extended Notre Dame's lead to 24–16 with his third score of the game, this one from 44 yards out, in the third quarter. Rob Johnson, who finished with 302 yards through the air, brought the Trojans back with an 18-yard scoring strike to Estrus Crayton that made it a 24–22 Notre Dame lead with 3:05 to go in the third quarter. USC coach Larry Smith contemplated going for a two-point conversion to tie, but felt there was still enough time left in the game. Ford was called on to kick the extra point, and it was now a 24–23 ballgame. Midway through the fourth quarter, Brooks took off on a 42-yard run down to the USC 19. That run helped the Irish get one more touchdown. Jerome Bettis then carried the ball on four straight plays, with the final one ending on an eight-yard touchdown. The Trojans made it an interesting finish. Down, 31–23, a 41-yard pass from Johnson to Travis Hannah got the ball to the Notre Dame five-yard line. On first down, Johnson was sacked for a loss of seven yards, and then his pass intended for Morton was intercepted by Carter to preserve the win for the Irish.[11]

**Freedom Bowl, (N) Dec. 29—Fresno State—7–24**
USC#23

The Trojans only had to go 30 miles south to play in their 35th bowl game. Anaheim Stadium played host to the ninth Freedom Bowl, and the Trojans came in as eight-point favorites in their first-ever meting with Fresno State. The Bulldogs came into this game with an 8–4 record, which consisted of a five-game winning streak and a share of the Western Athletic Conference championship. They possessed the nation's top-ranked scoring offense (40.5), but the defense was ranked 98thout of 107 teams. However, in the end, the offense might have finished this Freedom Bowl below their points-per-game average, but the defense played well above expectation.

This game was claimed to be the biggest in Fresno State history, and half of the 50,745 in attendance were Bulldog backers that traveled from the San Joaquin Valley in 600 buses to watch the game in person.

The first quarter ended in a scoreless tie. The Trojans then got on the board with 12:31 left in the second quarter after Curtis Conway set USC nicely with a 22-yard punt return that put the ball on the Fresno State 49. Conway would be lost for the second half after he sprained his right knee. Due to his injury, his 23-game streak of catching at least one pass came to an end. Eight plays after Conway's punt return, Deon Strother scored from the one on his only carry of the game. Cole Ford added the extra point, and USC was done scoring.

The Bulldogs, however, were just getting started, and responded on their next possession. Fullback Lorenzo Neal capped off an 11-play, 70-yard drive with a touchdown run from the one, and Derek Mahoney tied the game at 7–7, and that was how the first half scoring ended.

Mahoney broke the tie in the third quarter with a 43-yard field goal to take Fresno State into the fourth quarter up by a 10–7 count. The Bulldogs were forced to punt on their next series, but Estrus Crayton fumbled the punt after being hit. Chris Williams recovered for Fresno State at the USC 38, but gave up the ball on downs. Another USC turnover, this time an interception at the goal line on the first play of the fourth quarter, killed an opportunity for the Trojans. Anthony Daigle added a touchdown run of two yards, and Ron Rivers scored on a run that covered five yards to put the game late. Rivers finished with a game-high 104 yards on the ground, and Freedom Bowl MVP Lorenzo Neal recorded 75 yards. Rivers' six-pointer was set up after James Burton intercepted a Rob Johnson pass, and Mahoney added both conversion kicks following the touchdowns. For the Trojans, this was one of their worst bowl appearances ever. Against an alleged weak defense, they were only able to gain 183 yards of total offense, which was the lowest of the season. It also proved to be the final game of the Larry Smith's tenure as head coach.[12]

### TEAM LEADERS

RUSHING: Estrus Crayton—700 yards on 183 carries
PASSING: Rob Johnson—163 out of 285 attempts for 2,118 yards and 12 touchdowns
RECEIVING: Curtis Conway—49 catches for 764 yards and 5 touchdowns
Johnnie Morton—49 catches for 756 yards and 6 touchdowns
SCORING: Cole Ford—58 points on 25 extra points and 11 field goals
KICKOFF RETURNS: Curtis Conway—27 for 675 yards and 1 touchdown (25.0 avg.)
PUNT RETURNS: Curtis Conway—31 for 346 yards and 1 touchdown (11.2 avg.)
PUNTING: John Stonehouse—80 for 3,099 yards (38.7 avg.)
INTERCEPTIONS: Jason Sehorn—3 for 22 yards
Stephon Pace—3 for 7 yards
TACKLES: Brian Williams—91
SACKS: Willie McGinest—16

## *1993*

HEAD COACH: John Robinson
ASSISTANT COACHES: Ricky Hunley, Don Lindsay, Mike Riley, Mike Sanford, Dennis Thurman, Charles White
TEAM CAPTAINS: Craig Gibson, Willie McGinest, Deon Strother
RECORD: 8–5 overall (6–2 in Pacific–10 Conference)
(Ranked 36th best record in college football out of 106 teams)
FINISH IN CONFERENCE: Tied for 1st place with Arizona and UCLA
UCLA received a Rose Bowl bid due to victories over both USC and Arizona.
FINISH IN NATIONAL POLLS: 25th place in UPI and *USA Today*/Hall of Fame
POINTS SCORED PER GAME: 26.8 to rank 36th out of 106 teams
POINTS ALLOWED PER GAME: 19.4 to rank 30th

### Schedule and Highlights

**(N) Aug. 29—North Carolina—9–31**
USC#19 NC#20

This was USC's first-ever Sunday game, and they played in the "Disneyland Pigskin Classic," in Anaheim Stadium. This marked the return of USC coaching legend John Robinson, who came back into the Cardinal & Gold fold after eleven years. Using an option formation, North Carolina rushed for 291 yards, and in the process, handed USC their worst opening day defeat since 1961. To add to USC's woes, starting tailback Dwight McFadden broke his ankle. The Trojans' lone touchdown came on a five-yard pass from Rob Johnson to Tyler Cashman late in the game.[1]

**(H) Sept. 4—Houston—49–7**

This was the first football game played in the renovated LA Coliseum, and the first time these two teams faced each other. Johnnie Morton christened the event by setting a school record with 15 receptions, erasing the old record set by John Jackson in 1989 against Notre Dame. Morton gained 186 yards on his big day, and also tied a school record with three touchdown catches. Rob Johnson chipped in with a solid performance consisting of 25 completions out of 33 attempts for 279 passing yards and four touchdowns. Freshman tailback Shawn Walters also had a good game, rushing for 82 yards on eight carries and one touchdown.[2]

**(A) Sept. 11—Penn State—20–21**
PS#15

The Trojans rallied back from a 21–7 halftime deficit. They scored a touchdown with 37 seconds left, but missed on a two-point conversion pass Rob Johnson to Johnny McWilliams, which proved to be the deciding factor. For the game, Johnson threw for 291 yards and a pair of touchdowns, and Johnnie Morton had six receptions for 109 yards.[3]

**(H) Sept. 25—Washington State—34–3**

Rob Johnson set a new school record with 392 passing yards in the Pac-10 opener. He also threw for three scores. Johnson's new record broke the one set by Paul McDonald in 1979. Johnnie

Morton assisted Johnson in setting his record, and in the process, established one himself. He caught eight passes for 229 yards and one touchdown. His 229 receiving yards set the single-game record previously held by Hal Bedsole in 1962. As a team, the Trojans set a record for most passing yards in a single-game. At the beginning of the fourth quarter, Kyle Wachholtz replaced Johnson, and with his passing yards included in Johnson's, the Trojans compiled a new record of 413 yards through the air. The old record was 397 against Arizona State in 1988.[4]

**(A) Oct. 2—Arizona—7–38**

ARI#12

Arizona's "Desert Swarm" defense held USC to 47 rushing yards, and sacked Rob Johnson six times. A great deal of USC's problems stemmed from having an offensive line weakened by injuries. To make a bad situation worse, All-American lineman Tony Boselli was another casualty to USC's wall of protection when he hurt his knee.[5]

**(A) Oct. 9—Oregon—24–13**

Rob Johnson and Johnnie Morton continued to deliver excellent showings as the year progressed. Johnson threw for 307 yards and three scores, while completing a career-high 28 pass attempts. Morton caught seven passes for 113 yards and two touchdowns. He came into this game 89 yards away from USC's all-time receiving yardage record held by John Jackson. With 11:50 left in the third quarter, Morton caught a four-yard pass for the record.[6]

**(H) Oct. 16—Oregon State—34–9**

In USC's homecoming game, Johnnie Morton once again tied a school record with three touchdown receptions, and also set another one. He had seven receptions for 157 yards. Those catches gave Morton a career total of 167, which broke John Jackson's school record of 163 receptions set from 1986 to 1989. He added a Pac-10 record to his impressive resume when his career receiving yardage reached 2,560 yards, breaking Stanford's Ken Margerum's total of 2,517. Oregon State came in to this game with a wishbone offensive attack that gained a compiled 1,086 rushing yards in their two previous games. The Trojan defense turned in a great performance by holding the Beavers to 223 rushing yards and zero pass completions. USC had 498 yards of total offense, and Deon Strother scored the Trojans' first rushing touchdown in 11 quarters.[7]

**(A) Oct. 23—Notre Dame—13–31**

ND#2

Despite losing ten straight to Notre Dame coming into this game, the Trojans managed to keep the score close in the last four encounters with the Irish. However, this time, Notre Dame jumped out to an early lead, were never threatened, and improved to 8–0 on the year.

With no clouds and 63-degree temperatures engulfing South Bend, Indiana, Lee Becton got the Irish on the board quickly. On the second play of the game, Becton ran through the right side of USC's defense, and within seconds, was in the end zone to complete a 70-yard touchdown run. Becton finished the game with 177 yards on 20 carries.

After stopping the Trojans on their first possession, Notre Dame struck again. This time they ate up seven minutes and 49 seconds off the clock on a drive that started on their own 33. This time consuming drive saw a "bounce pass" incorporated into it, which got the ball to the USC two-yard line. From USC's 10-yard line, quarterback Paul Failla pitched the ball to Becton, but it fell short. Becton then short-hopped the ball, which was considered a fumble recovery, and he ran it to the two. On the following play, fullback Marc Edwards ended the marathon drive with a run that put the Irish on top, 14–0. Jeff Burris scored on a four-yard run to complete an 80-yard drive to make the score 21–0.

The Trojans got on the board in the second quarter when Rob Johnson took them 80 yards in 13 plays. During this scoring march, Johnson connected on 12 straight pass attempts. His final pass of the drive was good for a 13-yard pass over the middle to fullback Deon Strother with 2:19 remaining in the first half. The Irish did not allow the Trojans to gain momentum from their scoring drive, and posted one of their own before halftime. They traveled 60 yards, with Ray Zellars scoring on a 29-yard pass from Failla with 46 seconds left in the half to give Notre Dame a commanding 28–7 lead, and easily on their way to their 38th all-time victory over USC.

The Trojans got deeper in a hole in the third quarter by not being able to get a first down in their first three possessions. Three bad punts that only sailed 20, 30, and 11 yards did not help. Kevin Pendergast added a 43-yard field goal to Notre Dame's total to give them a 31–7 advantage in the third quarter. The Trojans staged one final scoring drive in the fourth quarter to make the game appear closer on paper than it did on the field. With 6:04 remaining in the game, Johnson threw an eight-yard touchdown pass to tight end Johnny McWilliams. Johnson finished the game with 269 yards through the air and two touchdowns. Johnnie Morton provided the Trojans with a solid performance, as he caught six passes for 109 yards.[8]

**(A) Oct. 30—California—42–14**

The Trojans came into Memorial Stadium and played what head coach John Robinson felt was his team's best performance of the year. Rob Johnson threw for 369 yards and two touchdowns, and Johnnie Morton had seven receptions for 118 yards, one touchdown, set a new USC record with 1,106 receiving yards in one season, and became the Pac-10's all-time career leader in receptions with 180.[9]

**(H) Nov. 6—Stanford—45–20**

This was a day of rewriting the USC football record book for Rob Johnson and Johnnie Morton. Johnson threw for 349 yards and three touchdowns, and set two school records. His 231 completions set a single-season record previously owned by Rodney Peete (223 in 1988). He also surpassed Peete with 23 touchdown passes in a single-season, breaking Peete's mark of 21 set in 1987. Johnnie Morton had four receptions for 127 yards and two touchdowns en route to setting new school and conference records. His two touchdown receptions gave him 12 on the year, breaking Hal Bedsole's record of 11 set in 1962. His four catches pushed his season total to 71, breaking Erik Affholter's 1988 record of 68. Finally, Morton's 1,233 receiving yards in one season set a new Pac-10 record previously held by Mike Levenseller in 1976.

Deon Strother chipped in with a balanced offensive showing by rushing for 58 yards on five carries, and catching four passes for 76 yards. The Trojan defense held Stanford to 11 points under their season average, and with this victory, USC was 5–1 in the Pac-10 race.[10]

**(A) Nov. 13—Washington—22–17**

WASH#25

The Trojans ended Washington's 17-game home winning streak with Shawn Walters and Rob Johnson pacing the attack. Walters ran for 116 yards on 25 carries and two touchdowns. This was the first time during the season that a USC player gained 100 yards in a game. Johnson completed 24 out of 37 pass attempts for 252 yards and one touchdown. For the year, Johnson threw for 2,978 yards to set a record for most yards gained passing, breaking the old mark set by Rodney Peete in 1988. On defense the standout was sophomore strong safety Micah Phillips. Filling in for the injured Mike Salmon, Phillips had 13 tackles, deflected three passes, and recovered a Washington fumble. Coming into this game, the Trojans were in a three-way tie for first place in the Pac-10 with UCLA and Arizona. Following this big win, they were at the top of the standings by themselves with one game standing between them and another conference championship.[11]

**(H) Nov. 20—UCLA—21–27**

USC#22 UCLA#16

An interception in the final minute allowed the Bruins to extend their winning streak over the Trojans to three games. More importantly, this victory gave UCLA their first Rose Bowl appearance in eight years.

Throughout the history of this great series, standout individual performances were plentiful. This 1993 edition proved to be no exception, as UCLA strong safety Marvin Goodwin added his name to the list of heroes to emerge from the "Battle for Los Angeles." With 50 seconds remaining, Goodwin intercepted a Rob Johnson pass in the end zone to not only preserve the win, but it earned the Bruins a trip to the Rose Bowl.

With a sellout crowd of 93,458 at the Coliseum, the Bruins dominated the line of scrimmage, and that resulted in two successful drives in the first quarter. With 5:22 expired in the opening stanza, quarterback Wayne Cook scored on a five-yard run to give the Bruins a lead they would never give up. With slightly over two minutes to go in the first quarter, Skip Hicks ran four yards to put UCLA up, 14–0. The Bruins added a 47-yard field goal by Bjorn Merten as the first half came to an end to extend the lead to 17–0. After thirty minutes of play, the Bruins were dominating the Trojans with 151 rushing yards to minus one.

The Trojans came to life in the third quarter, cutting the deficit to three points with just over eleven minutes left in the quarter. A 52-yard pass from Rob Johnson to Ken Grace got the ball to the one, and Shawn Walters scored from there for USC's first points of the game. Grace turned in a solid showing for USC with four receptions for 106 yards. Cole Ford added the extra point and the game was now a 17–7 affair. The Trojans got another seven points two minutes later as a result of an Erroll Small fumble recovery at the UCLA 11. Three plays later, Johnson connected with tight end Johnny McWilliams on a nine-yard scoring strike. Ford's conversion then made it 17–14.

The Bruins looked to stop USC's momentum, and two sacks on Johnson during the Trojans' next possession did just that and forced a punt. Bryan Adams made up for his earlier fumbled punt return by taking this one 32 yards to the USC 36-yard line. Four plays later, Cook threw to J.J. Stokes from 17 yards out to give the Bruins a 24–14 advantage heading into the fourth quarter. That touchdown reception was Stokes' 17th of the season, allowing him to tie the Pac-10 record held by Mario Bailey of Washington since 1991.

The Trojans came back early in the fourth quarter to once again close to within three points. With 13:33 left, Johnson threw a six-yard touchdown pass to Brad Banta, and Ford's extra point made it 24–21. Johnson finished with 23 completions out of 36 pass attempts for 307 yards. The Bruins closed out the scoring with a 20-yard field goal from Merten with 6:12 left.

It was now time for the Trojans to make one final chance at victory and a trip to the Rose Bowl. Johnson gave it his best effort, as he took USC 79 yards to the Bruins' two-yard line with 1:16 left. Two runs by Shawn Walters did little to help, and then Johnson went to the air. Looking for tight end Tyler Cashman, he threw into a group of three defenders, one of which was Marvin Goodwin, who came up with the interception. Quarterback Wayne Cook then took three snaps from center to run out the clock, as well as USC's Pasadena dreams.[12]

**Freedom Bowl, (N) Dec. 30—Utah—28–21**

The Trojans were able to redeem themselves following a poor showing at the previous Freedom Bowl. This marked the Trojans' 36th bowl appearance, and the third time in 14 games that they played in this venue. With 43,150 in attendance at Anaheim Stadium, the Trojans exploded for a 28–0 lead in the first 17 minutes of the game. Johnnie Morton got the festivities going with a 31-yard touchdown reception from Rob Johnson after using his 6'-4" frame to out jump three defenders for the ball. Cole Ford added the extra point. On USC's next possession, it was once again a Johnson to Morton pass, this time from nine yards out, which produced a six-pointer. Ford's conversion made it 14–0. Behind the blocking of Tony Boselli, tailback David Dotson capped a six-play, 43-yard drive with a two-yard scoring run to give the Trojans a commanding 20–0 lead at the end of the first quarter.

In the first minute-and-a-half of the second quarter, the Trojans struck again, this time on Johnson's third touchdown pass of the day. He found tight end Johnny McWilliams from five yards out, and a Johnson to Brad Banta two-point conversion pass gave the Trojans a 28–0 lead gong into the second half.

Utah then began a comeback surge by scoring on three of their first five possessions in the second half. A 59-yard pass from Mike McCoy to Henry Lusk started the comeback attempt. That was followed by scoring runs from Jamal Anderson (34 yards), and Keith Williams (one yard), which pulled Utah to with seven points of the lead with 3:56 remaining in the fourth quarter. The Trojans then held off the onslaught by holding possession until the final eight seconds. One last ditch came when McCoy threw a pass, hoping for either a receiver to catch it, or a pass interference penalty on USC. Neither happened, but cornerback John Herpin came up with his second interception of the game to end Utah's late rally, and USC's two-game bowl losing streak. Johnnie Morton was named the game's MVP, as he led all receivers with a Freedom Bowl record 10 receptions for 147 yards and two touchdowns, which tied a Freedom Bowl record. Rob Johnson also had a huge game for the Trojans. He completed 30 of 44 pass attempts for 345 yards and three touchdowns. His 30 completions helped the Trojans establish a new team record of 327 on the year.[13]

### TEAM LEADERS

RUSHING: Shawn Walters—711 yards on 156 carries
PASSING: Rob Johnson—308 out of 449 attempts for 3,630 yards and 29 touchdowns
RECEIVING: Johnnie Morton—88 catches for 1,520 yards and 14 touchdowns
SCORING: Johnnie Morton—86 points on 14 touchdowns and a 2-point conversion
KICKOFF RETURNS: Ken Grace—19 for 428 yards (22.5 avg.)
PUNT RETURNS: Jason Sehorn—30 for 225 yards (7.5 avg.)
PUNTING: John Stonehouse—68 for 2,607 yards (38.3 avg.)
INTERCEPTIONS: Jason Sehorn—7 for 45 yards
TACKLES: Jeff Kopp—83
SACKS: Willie McGinest—6

## *1994*

HEAD COACH: John Robinson
ASSISTANT COACHES: Don Lindsay, Mike Riley, Mike Sanford, Dennis Thurman, Charles White
TEAM CAPTAINS: Tony Boselli, Jeff Kopp, Brian Williams
RECORD: 8–3–1 overall (6–2 in Pacific–10 Conference)
(Ranked 19th best record in college football out of 107 teams)
FINISH IN CONFERENCE: Tied for 2nd place
FINISH IN NATIONAL POLLS: 13th place in both the AP and UPI, and 14th place in *USA Today*/Hall of Fame
POINTS SCORED PER GAME: 29.7 to rank 28th out of 107 teams
POINTS ALLOWED PER GAME: 20.2 to rank 27th

### Schedule and Highlights

**(H) Sept. 3—Washington—24–17**
USC#13 WASH#23

This was the earliest the Trojans ever opened a season against a conference opponent. This game also marked the first football game played in the post–Northridge earthquake in the renovated LA Coliseum. In this season-opening victory, USC's Tailback U. tradition returned, as freshman Delon Washington ran for 109 yards on 10 carries, and sophomore Shawn Walters scored two touchdowns. On defense, cornerback John Herpin had two interceptions.[1]

**(A) Sept. 10—Penn State—14–38**
USC#14 PS#8

Penn State jumped out to a 21–0 lead with a powerful offense and tough defense. Despite being sacked six times, Rob Johnson threw for 221 yards, and that proved to be one of the only highlights for USC on this day.[2]

**(H) Sept. 24—Baylor—37–27**
USC#19 BAY#24

The Trojans rebounded from their first loss of the season with a trio of stars pacing an attack that gained 600 yards of total offense. Shawn Walters ran for 207 yards on 31 carries and three touchdowns. This was the most yards gained rushing by a Trojan since Marcus Allen in 1981. Rob Johnson threw for 364 yards and one touchdown, and Keyshawn Johnson caught four passes for 105 yards.[3]

**(H) Oct. 1—Oregon—7–22**
USC#19

Rob Johnson passed for 237 yards and USC's only touchdown, but injured his ankle in the third quarter, and was replaced by sophomore Brad Otton. Ken Grace had six receptions for 107 yards. This was Oregon's second win over USC in the past 23 years.[4]

**(A) Oct. 8—Oregon State—27–19**

The Trojans came back from a 13–2 deficit, and by the third quarter, were in the lead. USC had a well-balanced offensive attack led by tailbacks Rodney Sermons and Shawn Walters, and quarterback Brad Otton. Sermons ran for 74 yards on 23 carries, Walters 68 yards on 16 attempts, and Otton, filling in for the injured Rob Johnson, completed 13 out of 21 pass attempts for 208 yards and two touchdowns. Keyshawn Johnson had six receptions for 139 yards, and Micah Phillips scored USC's first-ever defensive extra point.[5]

**(A) Oct. 15—Stanford—27–20**

Shawn Walters topped the 200-yard rushing barrier for the second time in one month. He ran for 234 yards on 31 carries and two touchdowns. Keyshawn Johnson chipped in on the victory over a long-standing foe with seven receptions for 146 yards and one touchdown. This was USC's 15th win over Stanford out of 17 previous encounters.[6]

**(H) Oct. 22—California—61–0**

In 1991, Cal scored the most points on USC (52). That apparently did not sit well with the Trojans. Over the next three matchups with Cal, the Trojans outscored the Bears, 130 to 38. Included in that total was this blowout on USC's homecoming weekend. This was USC's first shutout since Stanford in 1989. Brad Otton, once again starting at quarterback for the injured Rob Johnson, threw for 196 yards and two touchdowns. Backup signal caller Matt Koffler also added a pair of touchdown tosses. Other highlights from this lopsided victory included Keyshawn Johnson's four receptions for 110 yards, Ken Grace's 75-yard punt return, Jerald Henry's 60-yard touchdown on a recovery of a blocked kick, and two touchdowns apiece from Shawn Walters and Terry Barnum. The only excitement anyone from Cal generated was when a fan of the Bears spit on a police officer and was removed from the Coliseum.[7]

**(A) Nov. 5—Washington State—23–10**
USC#22 WS#16

The Trojans got back into the national rankings for this game, and Keyshawn Johnson helped them stay there by catching eight passes for 145 yards and a USC record-tying three touchdowns. Rob Johnson threw for 327 yards and three scores. The Cougars came into this game with the nation's second-ranked defense, but it was the Trojan defense that shined, holding Washington State to 50 yards rushing. Linebacker Jeff Kopp's eight tackles and two quarterback sacks paced the defense. After this win, the Trojans were tied for the Pac-10 lead with Oregon and Arizona.[8]

**(H) Nov. 12—Arizona—45–28**
USC#17 ARI#13

Arizona came into this game was one of the leaders in the Pac-10 race, and their "Desert Swarm" defense, was considered one of the toughest to go against. However, the Trojans' offense proved too much to handle. Rob Johnson threw for 390 yards and three touchdowns, Keyshawn Johnson had five receptions for 109 yards, and Edward Hervey also caught five passes, gaining 120 yards and scoring one touchdown after getting the ball in his hands. Brad Otton added 44 yards through the air to give USC a new school record of 434 passing yards in a single game.[9]

**(A) Nov. 19—UCLA—19–31**
USC#13

Rob Johnson threw for 246 yards and one touchdown. Keyshawn Johnson caught 11 passes for 175 yards and a touchdown, but those great performances were once again not enough to remove the UCLA albatross from the Cardinal & Gold. Just like in their previous meetings, the Trojans saw opportunities for victory vanish in the second half due to a UCLA surge. This time it was a 21-point third quarter that eventually sent the Trojans down in defeat for the fourth straight time against their cross-town rivals.

The Trojans got on the board first with 8:08 left in the first quarter. With a key pass on third-and 11 from Rob Johnson to Keyshawn Johnson keeping the drive alive, the Trojans eventually got within field goal range. The 14-play, 60-yard drive was capped off by a 37-yard field goal from Cole Ford that produced the only score in the opening stanza.

The Bruins' Bjorn Merten tied the game at 3–3 with two seconds expired in the second quarter on an 18-yard field goal. Ford split the uprights with a 29-yard field goal four minutes later to give USC a 6–3 lead. The game's first touchdown came with just over three minutes left in the second quarter. One play after a UCLA fumble, Rob Johnson threw a 29-yard scoring strike to Keyshawn Johnson, but an attempt at a two-point conversion run failed. It still gave the Trojans a 12–3 lead at the end of the first half, but all that changed in the infamous third quarter.

The Bruins struck quickly on their first possession of the second half. With only two minutes off the clock in the third quarter, the Bruins traveled 65 yards in six plays for their first touchdown, a 10-yard pass from Wayne Cook to J.J. Stokes. Following Merten's extra point, the Bruins cut the deficit to two points and were ready to pounce on the Trojans.

The Bruins made the going rough for Rob Johnson. Despite his 246 yards passing, Johnson was also sacked six times, he fumbled once, and was intercepted twice. One of those interceptions was a diving grab by Abdul McCullough at the USC 33-yard line. Three plays later, Sharmon Shah ran for a five-yard touchdown, and UCLA never trailed again. Shah went on to lead all ball carriers with 135 yards on 25 attempts. Merten's conversion then made it a 17–12 score. On USC's next possession, Johnson was sacked twice to hamper the drive, and the Bruins' offense struck again. With just under three minutes left in the third quarter, Cook threw his second touchdown pass of the game, this time a 30-yarder to Jim McElroy, and Merten's extra point gave UCLA a 24–12 lead heading in to the fourth quarter.

The Trojans came back with a 74-yard drive that Leonard Green finished off with a four-yard run in the opening seconds of the fourth quarter. Ford's conversion made it a 24–19 game, but that was as far as USC would get to the lead. With 8:22 left, Cook scored on a one-yard run, and Merten's extra point finished off the scoring at 31–19. Rob Johnson attempted to bring the Trojans back, but an interception by cornerback Teddy Lawrence ended those hopes with 3:11 remaining on the clock.[10]

**(H) Nov. 26—Notre Dame—17–17**
USC#17

The Trojans finally ended Notre Dame's winning streak at 11. Since the game ended in a tie, it allowed Notre Dame to have a 12-game unbeaten streak against USC.

Temperatures at 48-degrees, and a cold wind was coming in between 20 to 25 m.p.h, greeted the teams as the ball left the tee to begin this 66th edition of the "Glamour Game." The Irish scored on their first possession, going 68 yards in 12 plays, with Stefan Schroffner kicking a 29-yard field goal to give the Irish an early 3–0 advantage. The Trojans came right back to claim the lead in the second quarter after a short punt gave them excellent field position at the Notre Dame 34. Five plays later, Rob Johnson connected on a five-yard scoring strike to Johnny McWilliams. This was Johnson's 55th career touchdown pass. Cole Ford added the conversion, and USC was up, 7–3.

The ensuing kickoff was carried out of the end zone by the wild wind whipping through the Los Angeles area. Lee Becton then gave the Irish good field position on the first play of the drive on a run gaining 28 yards. Ron Powlus then threw to Derrick Mayes for 18 yards, and Becton's six-yard burst up the middle, gave the Irish the ball at the USC 22. The drive was capped off when Powlus threw an 11-yard touchdown pass to Ray Zellars with 1:01 remaining in the first half. Schroffner's extra point then sent the Irish into the second half with a 10–7 lead.

With four minutes expired in the third quarter, Ford tied the game at 10–10 with a 23-yard field goal. The Irish came back to reclaim the lead five minutes later on a one-yard run by Powlus and a conversion kick by Schroffner. Trailing by a score 17–10 with 6:43 left in the game, the Trojans came up with a huge play that led to the tying points. The Irish had lined up for a 37-yard field goal attempt by Schroffner. If successful, this would have given USC a 10-point deficit to dig out of with time running out. However, linebacker Israel Ifeanyi and safety Sammy Knight prevented that from happening. The 6-foot-6 Ifeanyi used his height advantage to jump up and block the field goal. Knight then recovered the loose ball and ran 56 yards to the Notre Dame 16. Tailback Shawn Walters had a cracked right thumb, but the injury did not get in the way of him crossing the goal line. He carried the ball four times on the short drive, with the final one coming from the one-foot line and resulting in a touchdown. Ford then sent the game into the record books as a 17–17 tie after connecting on the conversion kick with 4:53 left in the game. Keyshawn Johnson had six receptions for 114 yards for his eighth game over the century mark, and the seventh in a row. This was also the 750th consecutive game viewed by Trojan super fan Giles Pellerin.[11]

**Cotton Bowl, (N) Jan. 2—Texas Tech—55–14**
USC#21

It is claimed that everything is bigger in Texas, and the Trojans definitely proved it by the most points in any of their 37 bowl appearances. This blowout victory was the program's 24 bowl win, and USC's first time playing at the Cotton Bowl in Dallas, Texas. This convincing win was USC's 17th out of 19 previous meetings against the Southwest Conference. On an individual basis, this game also helped Rob Johnson and Keyshawn Johnson add their names to the USC record books. Johnson threw for 289 yards on 16 of 21 attempts, and his yardage gave him 8,472 yards over his USC career, which allowed him to move past Rodney Peete as the all-time leader in school history. He also threw three touchdown passes against Texas Tech to give him a record 58 for his career, and his career pass completion rating of 64.6 percent set a Pac-10 record. Keyshawn Johnson was selected the game's Outstanding Offensive Player after catching eight passes for a Cotton Bowl record 222 yards, and came up just seven yards off the all-time USC record. His three touchdown receptions set another Cotton Bowl record, and tied the USC all-time mark. Kicker Cole Ford got into the Cotton Bowl record setting act by connecting on seven conversion kicks. As a team, the Trojans set Cotton Bowl records for most points in a game, and most points in a quarter (28).

With 70,218 in attendance, on a day that saw a Southwestern Conference team play host of the Cotton Bowl for the final time after 59 years, the Trojans scored three touchdowns in one minute and 16 seconds starting on their second possession. Shawn Walters got the scoring barrage going with an 11-yard run. Texas Tech then fumbled on the ensuing kickoff. From the Texas Tech 19, Rob Johnson threw a scoring strike to Terry Barnum on the first play of the series. On Texas Tech's next series, John Herpin intercepted on the third play, and returned it 26 yards for a touchdown that made the score 21–0. On USC's next possession, Johnson fired a 12-yard touchdown toss to Keyshawn Johnson to end the first quarter with USC up, 28–0.

When not busy kicking conversions, Cole Ford found the time to add a pair of field goals from 39 and 42 yards out to give the Trojans a 34–0 halftime advantage, and all but claim victory despite having 30 minutes left to play.

Rob Johnson threw his third touchdown pass of the day, and Keyshawn Johnson was on the receiving end of his second, this time from 22 yards out to make the score 41–0. Keyshawn then caught his record-setting third touchdown pass from Brad Otton, who replaced Rob Johnson in the third quarter. Otton's touchdown pass to Keyshawn covered 86 yards, and now had the Trojans up, 48–0. Texas Tech finally got on the board with 2:14 left in the third quarter on a Zebbie Lethridge eight-yard run. Otton threw a two-yard pass to tight end Jeff Diltz to end the touchdown explosion for the Trojans. Texas Tech then scored the game's final six-pointer on a 45-yard pass from Sone Cavazos to Stacy Mitchell with no time left on the clock.[12]

### TEAM LEADERS

RUSHING: Shawn Walters—976 yards on 193 carries
PASSING: Rob Johnson—186 out of 276 attempts for 2,499 yards and 15 touchdowns
RECEIVING: Keyshawn Johnson—66 catches for 1,362 yards and 9 touchdowns
SCORING: Cole Ford—82 points on 40 extra points and 14 field goals
KICKOFF RETURNS: Ken Grace—25 for 480 yards (19.2 avg.)
PUNT RETURNS: Ken Grace—24 for 186 yards (7.8 avg.)
PUNTING: John Stonehouse—65 for 2,865 yards (44.1 avg.)
INTERCEPTIONS: John Herpin—7 for 70 yards and 1 touchdown
TACKLES: Jeff Kopp—102
SACKS: Erroll Small—5

## *1995*

HEAD COACH: John Robinson
ASSISTANT COACHES: DelVaughn Alexander, Joe Barry, Rod Marinelli, Mike Riley, Mike Sanford, Dennis Thurman, Charles White
TEAM CAPTAINS: Terry Barnum, Errick Herrin
RECORD: 9–2–1 overall (6–1–1 in Pacific-10 Conference)
(Ranked 13th best record in college football out of 108 teams)
FINISH IN CONFERENCE: Tied for first place with Washington
USC received Rose Bowl bid based on having a better overall record than Washington
FINISH IN NATIONAL POLLS: 12th place in AP and 11th place in both the UPI and *USA Today*/Hall of Fame. This was the final season that United Press International had a football poll.
POINTS SCORED PER GAME: 29.6 to rank 25th out of 108 teams
POINTS ALLOWED PER GAME: 17.7 to rank 16th

### Schedule and Highlights

**(H) Sept. 9—San Jose State—45–7**
USC#7

With many starters returning, the Trojans came into this game tabbed by some experts to contend for a national championship. In this convincing season opener, the Trojans more than lived up to the hype. Keyshawn Johnson had eight receptions for 124 yards to lead an offensive attack that gained 462 total yards. Brad Otton completed 14 of 20 pass attempts for 182 yards and one touchdown. Otton also ran for one touchdown, and Shawn Walters scored twice.[1]

**(H) Sept. 16—Houston—45–10**
USC#6

Brad Otton threw a 57-yard touchdown pass to Keyshawn Johnson on the Trojans' first offensive play in yet another convincing victory. For the game, Otton threw for 223 yards and a school record-tying four touchdowns. Keyshawn Johnson had eight receptions for 176 yards and two touchdowns, and Shawn Walters led a ground assault with 76 yards on eight carries and one touchdown. As a team, the Trojans amassed 534 yards of offense. For the second straight game, the Trojan defense allowed only one touchdown, and tackle Matt Keneley had 10 tackles and two sacks.[2]

**(A) Sept. 23—Arizona—31–10**
USC#5 ARI#25

After dominating non-conference opponents, the Trojans set their sights on Pac-10 foes, and the convincing wins continued for the Cardinal & Gold. Arizona's "Desert Swarm" defense held the Trojans scoreless in the first quarter, but then the USC offense came to life. They scored 21 points, all on drives covering 70 yards or more over the next two quarters, to take a 21–0 lead into the fourth quarter. Keyshawn Johnson had nine receptions for 112 yards and one touchdown. This was Johnson's 11th straight game of going over the 100-yard mark, which tied an NCAA record. Kyle Wachholtz threw for three touchdowns, and the running game gained 172 yards on 33 carries.[3]

**(H) Sept. 30—Arizona State—31–0**
USC#5

The Trojans recorded a second straight 31-point performance against an opponent from Arizona. This time it was the Sun Devils that were victimized by the passing tandem of Kyle Wachholtz and Brad Otton, who combined for 305 yards and two touchdowns. Wachholtz and Otton were ranked as the top two quarterbacks statistically in the Pac-10, and neither one had thrown an interception up to this time of the season. The Trojans gained 517 yards of total offense. Delon Washington ran for 118 yards on 25 carries, and Keyshawn Johnson continued to amaze. He caught 13 passes for 171 yards and one touchdown, and set an NCAA record with his 12th straight game of 100 or more yards receiving.[4]

**(A) Oct. 7—California—26–16**
USC#5

In their previous meeting with Cal, the Trojans totally dominated the game, winning by a 61–0 count. This time, the Bears put up a fight against one of the nation's elite teams. Cal held the Trojans scoreless until halfway through the second quarter. A 19-yard pass from Kyle Wachholtz to John Allred put USC up, 6–0. Cal then did something that no team up to this time of the '95 season was able to, with that being to take a lead on USC. The excitement of leading, 7–6, was short-lived, however, as Wachholtz threw his second scoring strike, this time to Tyler Cashman, that gave USC a 12–7 halftime advantage. They never trailed after that. A pair of touchdown runs from LaVale Woods helped the Trojans in the second half on their way to remaining perfect on the year. Delon Washington led the ground game with 135 yards on 29 carries.[5]

**(H) Oct. 14—Washington State—26–14**
USC#5

The '95 season was proving to be reminiscent of the great ones enjoyed over decades in the Southland. The Trojans jumped out to a 19–0 halftime lead, and the defense did their part by finishing the game allowing a mere 43 yards on the ground. Tackle Darrell Russell led the unit with six unassisted tackles, five of which went for lost yardage.[6]

**(A) Oct. 21—Notre Dame—10–38**
USC#5 ND#17

Notre Dame came close to seeing their lengthy unbeaten streak against the Trojans come to an end the previous year. In this 67th edition of the "Glamour Game," the Irish left in doubt that their unbeaten streak would extend to 13-games over USC. Running behind an offensive line that averaged 6–6" and 285 pounds, the backfield tandem of Autrey Denson and Marc Edwards, pounded away at the Trojan defense. Denson finished the game with 95 yards on 27 carries and one touchdown, while Edwards had 82 yards on 17 carries and three touchdowns.

Edwards gave the Irish a lead they only gave up briefly with a nine-yard run in the first quarter to give Notre Dame a 6–0 advantage after the opening stanza. A 17-yard pass from Kyle Wachholtz to Keyshawn Johnson tied the game in the second quarter, and then Adam Rendon gave the Trojans their only lead by connecting on the conversion kick. Johnson finished with six receptions for 122 yards. Then it was all Notre Dame. Quarterback Ron Powlus guided the Irish on a 13-play, 60-yard drive that consisted of 11 straight running plays. The drive was capped off on an Edwards' two-yard run. Edwards then threw a two-point conversion pass to Powlus that made the score 14–7.

The Trojans lost the ball on downs at the Notre Dame 41, and with Powlus throwing five passes out of nine plays, Denson finished it off with a seven-yard run up the middle to extend the Irish lead to 21–7 at the end of the first half. Rendon kicked a 25-yard field goal for the only points of the third quarter, and that cut the Notre Dame lead to 21–10. The Trojan offense then failed to score on their last six possessions, while the Irish got two touchdowns and a safety to complete a dominant victory that all but knocked USC out of national championship contention. Notre Dame received their 17 fourth quarter points on a safety by Kory Minor, who sacked Wachholtz in the end zone, a two-yard pass from Powlus to Pete Chryplewicz, and a one-yard run by Edwards.[7]

**(A) Oct. 28—Washington—21–21**
USC#13 WASH#17

The Trojans returned to Pac-10 action following their crushing first defeat. The effects of that loss appeared to linger, as USC was trailing 21–0, before scoring 21 points in the fourth quarter to tie it up with 33 seconds left. Brad Otton threw a two-yard pass to Johnny McWilliams, and then Adam Rendon's conversion kick tied it, allowing the Trojans to keep up with their race to the conference championship. After using a two-quarterback system during this season, head coach John Robinson decided to go with Otton was the full-time starter, and he finished the game with 251 yards and a pair of touchdown tosses. Keyshawn Johnson, continuing on with his brilliant career, had eight receptions for 111 yards.[8]

**(H) Nov. 4—Stanford—31–30**
USC#14

On homecoming weekend, the Trojans were involved in another nail-biter, this time winning it with 39 seconds left. After trailing in the second quarter, 16–0, the Trojans rallied back on touchdowns from Delon Washington (eight-yard run) and Rodney Sermons (one-yard run), and a 36-yard field goal by Adam Rendon. Washington finished with 144 rushing yards on 22 carries. The game-winner came with 39 seconds to play on an eight-yard pass from Kyle Wachholtz pass to Keyshawn Johnson, who then came in as a safety on defense and knocked down a Hail Mary pass at the goal line at the final gun. Wachholtz got the majority of playing time at quarterback after Brad Otton left the game in the first quarter with a slight concussion.[9]

**(A) Nov. 11—Oregon State—28–10**
USC#12

John Robinson was brought in to restore the glory days of Trojan football, much of which he was responsible for in the 1970's. In the third year of his second tenure, he did just that, as the Trojans secured the Pac-10 championship and a Rose Bowl berth for the first time since 1989. On a cold, rainy night in Corvallis, Oregon, Kyle Wachholtz received his first start at quarterback during the season, and completed 16 of 26 pass attempts for 154 yards and two touchdowns. Delon Washington led the ground attack with 158 yards on 28 carries and two touchdowns.[10]

**(H) Nov. 18—UCLA—20–24**

USC#11

Since the football left the tee to begin the first meeting back in 1929, this series has been a steppingstone of everlasting lore for those individuals that rose to the challenge during the 60 minutes of mayhem created by the "Battle for Los Angeles." At the conclusion of this edition, an 18-year old freshman quarterback named Cade McNown became one of those lucky players to rise up to stardom. He had a steady blend of running and passing that kept the chains moving, which eventually led to another Bruin victory. He connected on eight of 17 pass attempts for 131 yards, and ran for 36 yards on seven carries.

With 91,363 at the Coliseum, the Bruins broke open a scoreless first quarter ten minutes into the game. The 11-play, 70-yard drive was kept alive when McNown gained 29 yards on key passes, with the final one getting the ball to the one-yard line. James Milliner scored from there, and Bjorn Merten added the extra point. Two minutes later, McNown led the Bruins 68 yards in five plays to their second touchdown. The big gainer of this short drive was a 59-yard pass from McNown to Jim McElroy that got the ball to the one. Cheyane Caldwell took it over the goal line, and Merten's conversion made it 14–0 at the end of the first quarter.

Jim McElroy set up UCLA's second touchdown with a 59-yard reception, and then threw for the Bruins' next six-pointer. Early in the second quarter, McElroy took a reverse and instead of running, he threw a 35-yard pass to Kevin Jordan for the touchdown. Merten's extra point gave the Bruins a commanding 21–0 lead.

The Trojans began to rally after Daylon McCutcheon returned an interception 59 yards to the UCLA 19. Four plays later, Brad Otton threw a five-yard touchdown pass to Johnny McWilliams. Adam Abrams kicked the extra point and the Trojans cut the deficit to 21–7 going into the second half.

The third quarter remained scoreless, but then Delon Washington scored on a two-yard run just 21 seconds into the fourth quarter. With Abrams' conversion, the Trojans were now only down, 21–14. For the game, Washington finished with 152 yards rushing on 30 carries, and became the first USC running back to break the 1,000-yard barrier in a season since 1990. In addition to Washington's performance, the Trojans also got a big game out of Keyshawn Johnson, who caught 12 passes for 116 yards.

The Bruins struck quickly to stop USC's momentum. Derek Ayers returned the ensuing kickoff 39 yards to the UCLA 43, and then Milliner ran for a 29-yard gain. The five-play, 36-yard drive was finished off with a 36-yard field goal from Greg Andrasick to give the Bruins a 24–14 lead. The Trojans ate up nine minutes on a 20-play, 82-yard drive that ended with Otton throwing a one-yard scoring strike to Tyler Cashman with 3:30 left in the game. A two-point conversion pass failed, and the Trojans ran out of time.[11]

**Rose Bowl, (N) Jan. 1—Northwestern—41–32**

USC#17 NW#3

The story of Cinderella has been told since Charles Perrault's work first found its way to the masses in 1697. Since then, the rags-to-riches saga has been applied to a plethora of real life situations. On many occasions, its usage has been used in the world of sports, much to the excitement of a public yearning to root for an underdog.

In 1995, the Cinderella label was given to the Northwestern Wildcats, and for good reason. From 1972 through 1994, the football program was absolutely terrible. It began with a 2–9 finish in 1972, and continued to get worse, with the 1980's proving to set the benchmark for futility. In a three-year span from 1979 to 1982, the Wildcats lost 34 straight games, and still struggled even after "the Streak" ended on September 25, 1982. From 1982 through 1994, the team's best record was a 4–7 finish in 1986. It seemed like a never-ending slide into the ranks to despair each and every season.

In 1992, another coach came on the scene at Northwestern in the person of 46-year old Gary Barnett, who came to the Wildcats with 12 years of coaching experience behind him. He made a bold statement to the student body upon his hiring that he would take the Wildcats to the Rose Bowl. At first the statement seemed like typical jargon spun by a new coach to keep interest in the program going. In Barnett's first three seasons, he compiled a total of eight wins, and the Wildcats were not close to going to Pasadena on New Year's Day without buying a ticket to the stadium.

In 1995, Barnett's words from a few years earlier were suddenly starting to pan out. "Expect Victory" was the motto around Northwestern, and after going into their season opener as 28-point underdogs to Notre Dame, and emerging from that encounter as winners, the Wildcats were on their way. They finished the regular season at 10–1 and ranked third in the national polls. They won their first Big Ten title since 1936, which was the longest stretch in the conference between titles, and earned a trip to only their second bowl game, with the first being the 1949 Rose Bowl.

The Trojans were old acquaintances to Pasadena, and John Robinson was looking to keep his spotless Rose Bowl record intact. Coming into this game, Robinson was 3–0 in Pasadena, and with a 24–7 lead in the second quarter, it appeared that his streak would easily continue.

Using a two-minute, no-huddle offense in their first two series, the Trojans got on the board quickly. After the opening kickoff, the Trojans capped off an 83-yard drive with LaVale Woods scoring from the one, and Adam Abrams extra point made it 7–0. The Wildcats did not seemed fazed by USC's quick-hitting offensive attack, and remained steadfast in their opening possession. They drove 68 yards, with Darnell Autry running the final three yards, and with Brian Gowins conversion, the game was knotted at 7–7 after each team successfully completed their opening drives.

The Trojans then struck back with 17 straight points in the second quarter, with each unit getting in on the scoring fest. Brad Otton got things going with a 21-yard scoring toss to Terry Barnum to break the tie. Abrams then kicked a 30-yard field goal, and cornerback Daylon McCutcheon scored a six-pointer for the defense by returning a fumble recovery 53 yards to paydirt. Abrams added both extra points following the touchdowns, and the Trojans were up, 24–7. Northwestern capitalized on a USC fumble, as Gowins kicked a 29-yard field goal with two seconds remaining in the first half to make it a 24–10 ballgame.

Northwestern came out ready for a comeback, and scored

on their first four possessions of the second half. They began with a 28-yard field by Gowins, and following a successful on-side kick, Autry scored on a nine-yard run to close the gap to 24–19. The Trojans then expanded their lead to 31–19 on a 56-yard pass from Otton to Keyshawn Johnson, coupled with an extra point kick from Abrams. Quarterback Steve Schnur added a one-yard run for Northwestern, and Gowins' conversion narrowed the Wildcats' deficit to 31–26 going into the fourth quarter.

Northwestern had chipped away at USC's commanding lead, and finally overtook the Trojans with a two-yard run by Autry to give the Wildcats a 32–31 lead following a missed conversion. Abrams then returned the lead back to the Trojans for good with 9:09 left to play. He achieved this with a career-long field goal from 46 yards out that capped a 12-play, 39-yard drive, and gave USC a 34–32 advantage.

The Wildcats tried to reclaim the lead, but their Cinderella season hit a roadblock when Schnur had a pass intercepted by Jesse Davis, who covered 41 yards on the return before being stopped at the Northwestern 31 with 6:42 remaining. Eight plays later, Delon Washington scored the game-clincher from two yards out, and Abrams added the extra point to make the score 41–32 with 2:55 to go.

Keyshawn Johnson was crowned the game's MVP after catching 12 passes for a Rose Bowl record 216 yards. Brad Otton completed 29 of 44 pass attempts for 391 yards, which was the third highest total in Rose Bowl history. This game also marked the 50th Anniversary of the PAC-10/Big Ten Rose Bowl agreement.[12]

### Team Leaders

RUSHING: Delon Washington—1,109 yards on 236 carries
PASSING: Brad Otton—159 out of 256 attempts for 1,923 yards and 14 touchdowns
RECEIVING: Keyshawn Johnson—102 catches for 1,434 yards and 7 touchdowns
SCORING: Keyshawn Johnson—42 points on 7 touchdowns
KICKOFF RETURNS: Chris Miller—12 for 286 yards (23.8 avg.)
PUNT RETURNS: Larry Parker—29 for 266 yards (9.2 avg.)
PUNTING: John Stonehouse—46 for 2,007 yards (43.6 avg.)
INTERCEPTIONS: Jesse Davis—5 for 62 yards
TACKLES: Sammy Knight—89
SACKS: Israel Ifeanyi—5

## *1996*

HEAD COACH: John Robinson
ASSISTANT COACHES: DelVaughn Alexander, Mark Banker, Mike Riley, Mike Sanford, Dennis Thurman, Charles White
TEAM CAPTAINS: John Allred, Sammy Knight
RECORD: 6–6 overall (3–5 in Pacific–10 Conference)
(Ranked 52nd best record in college football out of 111 teams)
FINISH IN CONFERENCE: Tied for 5th place
FINISH IN NATIONAL POLLS: No ranking in Top 25
POINTS SCORED PER GAME: 27.1 to rank 48th out of 111 teams
POINTS ALLOWED PER GAME: 22.2 to rank 43rd

### Schedule and Highlights

**(N) Aug. 25—Penn State—7–24**
USC#7 PSU#11

The Kickoff Classic XIV from Giants Stadium in East Rutherford, New Jersey, marked the earliest that USC kicked off a football season. Penn State's Curtis Enis ran for 241 yards, which was the most rushing yards ever gained by an individual against a Trojan defense. Enis also scored three touchdowns. The Trojan offense appeared to be totally out of sync. Brad Otton only completed 11 of 28 pass attempts for 144 yards, and the running game could only muster 138 yards on 34 carries. USC received their points late in the fourth quarter when linebacker Chris Claiborne recovered a fumble in the end zone.[1]

**(A) Sept. 7—Illinois—55–3**
USC#19

What the Trojans lacked in their opening day defeat, they more than made up for in this romp over Illinois. They jumped out to a 24–3 halftime lead, and then added 31 more points in the second half, to finish the game with 582 yards of total offense. Brad Otton connected on 12 of 18 pass attempts for 301 yards and two touchdowns, Chris Miller had three receptions for 155 yards and one touchdown, and LaVale Woods ran for a pair of six-pointers. With the game well in control, the Trojans still created excitement in the fourth quarter when backup quarterback Matt Koffler threw a 97-yard touchdown pass to R. Jay Soward, which set a record for the longest pass play in USC history.[2]

**(H) Sept. 14—Oregon State—46–17**
USC#16

The Trojan offense continued on a tear for the second straight week, as the unit gained a whopping 621 yards. On the ground, they gained 314 yards on 22 carries, and were led by the tandem of Chad Morton and LaVale Woods. Morton ran for 143 yards on 13 carries and one touchdown, while Woods ran for 122 yards on 12 carries and one touchdown. Woods also added his name to the USC record book for having the longest run from scrimmage (96 yards). Brad Otton completed 17 of 29 pass attempts for 254 yards and a pair of touchdowns, and Chris Miller had seven receptions for 116 yards.[3]

**(A) Sept. 21—Houston—26–9**
USC#15

The Trojans had beaten the Cougars twice in the last three years, and once against handed them a defeat. Houston came into this game with a 3–0 record and one of the nation's most exciting offenses, scoring 119 points in those three wins. The Trojan defense became the only unit to hold the Cougars to single-digit scoring all season, allowing them 131 yards on the ground and 150 through the air. They also stopped Houston from getting into the end zone, as all their points came on field goals. As for the Trojan offense, they kept up a steady pace of excitement. Brad Otton completed 24 of 37 pass attempts for 290 yards and two touchdowns. Receiver Billy Miller caught both of Otton's touchdown passes for the first two of his college career. John Allred set a school record by catching 10 passes, which was the most for a USC tight end, and gained 103 yards. With this victory, the Trojans raised their record to 3–0 in games played inside domed stadiums.[4]

**(H) Oct. 5—California—15–22**
USC#17

After three straight wins by convincing margins, it took a long-time rival to bring the Trojans back down. The Bears were led by first-year head coach Steve Mariucci, and came into the Coliseum with a 4–0 record and scoring an average of 42 points a game. They took control of the game, and led, 19–0, in the fourth quarter. Leading the Cal attack was quarterback Pat Barnes, who threw for 229 yards and two touchdowns, and tailback Brandon Willis, who ran for 150 yards. In all, the Bears gained 415 yards of total offense. The Trojans had trouble getting started offensively, and the running game was only able to produce 102 yards on 28 carries. Brad Otton threw touchdown passes to LaVale Woods and Rodney Sermons to make the game appear closer than it was. This was Cal's first win at the LA Coliseum since 1970.[5]

**(H) Oct. 12—Arizona—14–7**

The Wildcats came into this game on a three-game losing streak to USC. They then left town with it extended to four straight in a close Trojan victory. Brad Otton completed 23 of 41 pass attempts for 220 yards despite being sacked seven times. LaVale Woods led the team with 76 yards rushing, and ran for a pair of one-yard touchdowns.[6]

**(A) Oct. 19—Arizona State—35–48**
ASU#4

The Trojans looked to make it a sweep over Arizona-based teams, and almost pulled it off. The Sun Devils came into this game with a perfect 7–0 record, but the Trojans threatened to send them down in defeat with an early first quarter surge. With 10:23 still remaining in the first quarter, USC jumped out to a 14–0 lead on a 15-yard pass from Brad Otton to John Allred, and a 13-yard run by LaVale Woods. Helping the cause was the fact that ASU quarterback Jake Plummer threw three interceptions in the first half after throwing that many all season. Arizona State rallied back to tie the game at 14–14 by halftime on two touchdown runs by Terry Battle. After a scoreless third quarter, the teams exchanged touchdowns in the fourth quarter. Otton gave USC a 21–14 advantage with a 29-yard pass to Chris Miller before ASU came back to tie it once again. R. Jay Soward then returned a kickoff back 98 yards to put USC back on top, 28–21. Battle then sent the game into overtime by scoring his third six-pointer of the game with 1:30 left in regulation.

This was the first time both teams went into overtime in their histories. In the first overtime, Otton threw an 11-yard pass to Rodney Sermons that put USC up, 35–28. Plummer then forced a second overtime period when he threw a six-yard pass to Keith Poole to deadlock the game at 35–35. The Sun Devils got the ball first in the second overtime, and on the first play, Battle ran for a 25-yard touchdown to give ASU a 42–35 lead. For the game, Battle ran for 184 yards on 30 carries, and set a record by scoring the most points by one individual against a USC defense with 24. A few plays later, a controversy occurred that ended USC's hopes of an upset and their chances of repeating as Pac-10 champions. On third-and-six from the ASU 21-yard line, Otton was going down due to a pass rush, he threw a shovel pass toward LaVale Woods, but the ball hit the ground. The Trojans thought the pass was incomplete and went to try for at least one more play. Cornerback Courtney Jackson saw it differently, thinking it was still a live ball, and raced 85 yards for a touchdown. The officials saw things the same way as Jackson, awarded ASU the six points and the game was over. Despite the heart-breaking loss, linebacker Chris Claiborne turned in an unbelievable game consisting of 20 tackles and one interception.[7]

**(A) Oct. 26—Washington State—29–24**

The Cougars came into this game with a 5–2 record and riding a two-game winning streak. They were looking good in an attempt to keep the winning times rolling by taking a 10–7 halftime lead. R. Jay Soward then deadlocked the game nine seconds into the second half with a 78-yard kickoff return. The game was tied at 17–17 in the fourth quarter when Shawn Walters gave the Trojans their first lead of the game with a one-yard run. The conversion kick was blocked, and USC led. 23–17. With 8:45 remaining, the Cougars reclaimed the lead at 24–23, but Delon Washington saved the day for USC. Washington finished with 99 yards on the ground, and with 2:05 left in regulation, he scored on a 17-yard run that proved to be the game-winner. The Cougars attempted to rally, and got top the USC 11-yard line with 39 seconds remaining until a fumble recovered by Sammy Knight halted the drive and preserved the win for USC. This started a four-game losing streak for Washington State.[8]

**(H) Nov. 2—Washington—10–21**
WASH#21

On homecoming weekend, the Trojans hosted the team they shared the Pac-10 championship with one year earlier. The Trojans did not play like defending champs, as their offensive output consisted of 124 yards. The running game finished with a horrific minus-14 yards on 30 attempts, and Brad Otton completed 13 out of 29 pass attempts for 138 yards. Despite their lethargic showing, the Trojans actually held a 10–3 halftime advantage on an 11-yard pass from Otton to Rodney Sermons and a 27-yard field goal from Adam Abrams. Tailback Corey Dillon led the Washington attack with 128 yards and 37 carries and two touchdowns.[9]

**(A) Nov. 9—Stanford—20–24**

The Trojans looked to be headed to an easy win over Stanford in Palo Alto. They held a 20–7 halftime advantage, but the game of football is divided into two halves, and in this case, it proved to be USC's demise. Stanford came into this game ranked 110th out of 111 teams in rushing yards with a 77.4 yards-per-game-average. In the first half, the Trojan defense held them to 32 yards on the ground, but then running back Mike Mitchell exploded, eating up yard after yard. In the first half, Mitchell had gained one yard, then ran for 148 in the second half. As a team, Stanford ran for 163 yards in the second half to win by four points. Stanford's defense completely shut USC's offense down in the second half, allowing it 19 rushing yards and intercepted three passes. This was the fifth time during the season that the Trojan defense allowed an opposing running back to gain over 120 yards. Brad Otton passed for 277 yards and two touchdowns for USC.[10]

**(A) Nov. 23—UCLA—41–48**

This was another tale of two halves. The first thirty minutes belonged to the Trojans, and after building a 24–7 halftime advantage, it appeared that they would finally end their five-game losing streak against UCLA. However, the final thirty minutes saw the Bruins come all the way back and tie the game to force overtime, which eventually led them to a sixth straight victory over USC.

In the previous matchup between these teams, Cade McNown starred as a freshman quarterback. This time around, it was a freshman receiver for USC by the name of R. Jay Soward that earned his place in the lore of this cross-town rivalry. Soward caught six passes for a school record 260 yards and three touchdowns, also a school record shared with seven other players up to this time. The 260 receiving yards broke Johnnie Morton's record of 229 yards set against Washington State in 1993. Not only did Soward now own the USC record, but he also laid claim to the NCAA freshman record of 243 yards set in 1991 by Darnay Scott of San Diego State.

The Trojans got out to a 10–0 first quarter lead on a 27-yard field goal by Adam Abrams and a 19-yard pass from Brad Otton to Soward, which was followed by an Abrams conversion kick. Sammy Knight extended the USC advantage to 17–0 with 9:19 left in the first half on a 74-yard interception return plus Abrams extra point kick. Cade McNown scored UCLA's first points of the game with 4:10 remaining in the half on a three-yard run. Bjorn Merten's conversion then brought the Bruins to within ten points of the Trojans. One minute later, the Trojans got those points back on a quick three-play, 67-yard drive capped off with Otton throwing a 60-yard touchdown pass to Soward. Abrams conversion then sent USC into the second half with a commanding 24–7 lead.

The 80,644 in attendance at the Rose Bowl had to collectively feel that the Trojans were in an excellent position to snap their losing streak to UCLA at the conclusion of the remaining thirty minutes of action. The Bruins had other ideas, and staged one the greatest comeback in their history. With only 2:06 expired in the third quarter, the Bruins went on a four-play, 74-yard drive that ended with a 52-yard pass from McNown to Danny Farmer for a touchdown. Merten's extra point once again cut the deficit to ten points. With 5:19 left in the third quarter, Otton threw his third touchdown pass of the game, this time a 12-yarder to Chris Miller, and Abrams conversion kick put the Trojans up, 31–14. The Bruins finished off the third quarter scoring with 12 seconds remaining on a 10-yard run by McNown and a Merten conversion kick to send the game into the fourth quarter with USC in the lead by a score of 31–21.

Brad Otton, who threw for 273 yards and three touchdowns, had to leave the game after he was blasted in the ribs by UCLA defender Weldon Forde. Matt Koffler replaced Otton and threw for USC's final touchdown of the game, a 78-yard pass to Soward. Abrams added the extra point, and the Trojans had a 38–21 lead early in the fourth quarter. It was then that the Bruins staged a legendary comeback that consisted of scoring 17 points in the 6:12 of regulation. A 47-yard field goal from Merten started the onslaught, which was followed by a Keith Brown one-yard run, and with Merten's conversion, the Bruins were only down, 38–31, wit 2:49 left in the fourth quarter.

The Trojans then gave up the ball on a fumble that Kusanti Abdul-Salaam recovered and ran 11 yards to the UCLA 44. With the clock ticking down, McNown drove the Bruins 56 yards on six plays, throwing key passes to Jim McElroy, Jamal Clark, and Rodney Lee, all totaling 45 yards of real estate. Skip Hicks then ran up the middle for an 11-yard touchdown with 39 seconds remaining. Merten then kicked the all-important extra point, and the game was sent into overtime tied at 38.

The Bruins chose to let the Trojans get the ball first in overtime. Abrams then sent a 25-yard field goal through t he uprights to give USC a 41–38 lead. Merten then kicked a 40-yard field goal to force a second overtime. In the second overtime, the Bruins had possession first, and it took them only one play to score. Hicks scored on a 25-yard run to finish of a day, which saw him rush for a game-high 116 yards and score a pair of crucial touchdowns. Merten kicked the extra point, and the Bruins had their only lead of the game, at 48–41. The Trojans had one final possession to either tie or win it with a touchdown and a two-point conversion. However, there was no need for that type of strategy. Matt Koffler's fourth down pass was intercepted by Anthony Cobb in the end zone, to clinch the win for UCLA.[11]

**(H) Nov. 30—Notre Dame—27–20**
ND#10

United States presidents Ronald Reagan, George H. Bush, and Bill Clinton, all served in the nation's office since USC had last beaten Notre Dame in football. Since 1983, the Irish walked off the field victorious, while the Trojans only solace was the classic sports rallying cry of "wait 'til next year."

Next year finally came in this 68th edition of the "Glamour Game," as the Trojans finally broke free from the navy and gold albatross from South Bend, Indiana. However, late in the fourth quarter, the possibility of victory for the Cardinal & Gold looked bleak, as they trailed by eight points with time running out against the 8–2 Fighting Irish.

With 90,296 inside the LA Coliseum, quarterback Brad Otton was set to play in his final college game with a flak jacket on to protect a bruised breastbone he suffered against UCLA seven days earlier. Unfortunately, his exit was quicker than he had anticipated. On the game's sixth play, Otton was slammed to the ground by Kory Minor and forced to leave the game. After spending time in the locker room, Otton returned to action and ended his USC career by completing 13 of 25 passes for 183 yards and two touchdowns. His leadership was definitely needed on a day when the USC ground attack could muster only 92 yards. On the defensive side, linebacker Sammy Knight had an exceptional performance that included 14 tackles, one sack, and two fumble recoveries.

The Trojans took a 6–0 lead in the first quarter on a pair of Adam Abrams field goals. The first came from 30 yards out with only two minutes expired from the clock. Eight minutes later, he added a 38-yarder. With 37 seconds off the clock in the second quarter, Jamie Spencer tied the game with a one-yard run, and Jim Sanson added the extra point to put Notre Dame into a 7–6. That score remained the same throughout the rest of the first half.

The Irish expanded their lead to 14–6 on the only score of the third quarter when Ron Powlus threw a 25-yard touchdown pass to Cikai Champion. Sanson added the conversion kick to put Notre Dame up by eight points with 15 remaining in regulation. The Trojans fought back to close the deficit to two points when Brad Otton threw a five-yard touchdown pass to Chris Miller with 8:21 left in the fourth quarter. An attempt at a two-point conversion pass failed, and USC trailed, 14–12. The Irish once again got their lead back up to eight points with four minutes left on a nine-yard run by Autry Denson, but Sanson missed on the conversion attempt.

With time now a major factor, the Trojans trailed by a 20–12 count. Otton, injured breastbone and all, led USC on a 67-yard drive that was capped off on a 15-yard run up the middle by Delon Washington with 1:50 left in regulation. Washington then ran for a two-point conversion, barely getting the ball over the goal line, to tie the game at 20–20 and send it into USC's first-ever overtime game at the LA Coliseum.

Starting on the 25-yard line to begin the overtime period, Otton completed passes for gains of 14 yards to Rodney Sermons and seven yards to John Allred. He returned to Sermons, who scored on a five-yard pass. Abrams added the extra point and USC was up, 27–20. The Irish had one final opportunity to send the game into another overtime. Powlus started the drive with a pass for six yards to Pete Chryplewicz. Denson was then gang tackled for a loss of five yards, and a pass attempt on third down fell incomplete. It all came down to one play, and linebacker Mark Cusano got his hand on a pass to defect it, and the game was over, giving the Trojans the opportunity to not only end Notre Dame's 13-game unbeaten streak against them, but finish the season at 6–6. This also was USC's first overtime win in three tries during the season. This was the final game Lou Holtz coached at Notre Dame and the first time he lost to USC.[12]

### TEAM LEADERS

RUSHING: LaVale Woods—601 yards on 119 carries
PASSING: Brad Otton—196 out of 370 attempts for 2,649 yards and 20 touchdowns
RECEIVING: Chris Miller—43 catches for 793 yards and 5 touchdowns
SCORING: Adam Abrams—72 points on 33 extra points and 13 field goals
KICKOFF RETURNS: R. Jay Soward—14 for 440 yards and 2 touchdowns (31.4 avg.)
PUNT RETURNS: Chad Morton—16 for 149 yards (9.3 avg.)
PUNTING: Jim Wren—66 for 3,006 yards (45.6 avg.)
INTERCEPTIONS: Sammy Knight—5 for 74 yards and 1 touchdown
TACKLES: Sammy Knight—121
SACKS: Darrell Russell—9

## *1997*

HEAD COACH: John Robinson
ASSISTANT COACHES: DelVaughn Alexander, Hue Jackson, Dennis Thurman, Charles White, Mike Wilson
TEAM CAPTAINS: Jonathan Himebauch, Brian Kelly
RECORD: 6–5 overall (4–4 in Pacific-10 Conference)
(Ranked 48th best record in college football out of 112 teams)
FINISH IN CONFERENCE: Tied for 5th place
FINISH IN NATIONAL POLLS: No ranking in Top 25
POINTS SCORED PER GAME: 21.2 to rank 79th out of 112 teams
POINTS ALLOWED PER GAME: 21.2 to rank 38th

### Schedule and Highlights

**(H) Sept. 6—Florida State—7–14**
USC#23 FSU#5

New starting quarterback John Fox ran for a two-yard touchdown to help the Trojans gain a 7–7 tie from the second quarter until the fourth. Florida State then went on a 97-yard drive in nine plays to win it on a three-yard run by Dee Feaster.[1]

**(H) Sept. 13—Washington State—21–28**
USC#23

The loss to Florida State did not affect USC in the national rankings, as they remained at number 23. However, this loss completely knocked the Trojans out of the polls. Not since USC's dismal 1–9 record in 1957 had the Cougars defeated the Trojans at the LA Coliseum. Kevin McKenzie made a great one-handed grab of a 51-yard pass from Ryan Leaf that provided Washington State with a touchdown with 4:18 left to play. Leaf completed 21 of 40 pass attempts for 355 yards and three touchdowns to lead the Cougars to victory. Despite this loss, the Trojans had some solid performances of their own. R. Jay Soward returned a kickoff 95 yards for a touchdown, John Fox passed for 229 yards, and Billy Miller had 10 receptions for 138 yards.[2]

**(A) Sept. 27—California—27–17**

The once great tradition of USC being "Tailback U" was in jeopardy of being obsolete as the Trojans geared up for this clash with their long-time rivals. They were ranked 112th and dead last in the nation in rushing. During the week of practice, the offensive line and running backs worked extra hard to reverse that horrible ranking. It seemed to work, as LaVale Woods ran for 129 yards on 32 carries and two touchdowns. His output more than doubled that of the entire USC backfield over their first two games. Assisting in recording USC's first victory of the year were John Fox, who threw for 250 yards and two touchdowns, and R. Jay Soward, who had seven receptions for 148 yards and two touchdowns.[3]

**(H) Oct. 4—UNLV (University of Nevada, Las Vegas)—35–21**

The Trojans were trailing, 21–14, with 12:03 remaining in the fourth quarter before rallying with 21 points to even their record at 2–2. R. Jay Soward caught two touchdown passes (44 and 78 yards), and Malaefou MacKenzie ran for an 11-yard touchdown to bring the Trojans the win. Soward finished the game with five receptions for 167 yards, and MacKenzie ran for 104 yards on 19 carries and two touchdowns to become only the fifth freshman running back in USC history to go over 100 yards in a game. John Fox threw for 355 yards and two touchdowns, and Billy Miller had eight receptions for 112 yards in a game that produced the 100th win of John Robinson's college coaching career.[4]

**(A) Oct. 11—Arizona State—7–35**

The Trojans returned to being pitiful, and the Sun Devils walked all over them, gaining 528 yards of total offense in the process. John Fox was only able to complete eight of 23 pass attempts for 70 yards while Arizona State's freshman quarterback Ryan Kealy threw for 281 yards and three touchdowns. The Sun Devils only held a slim 13–7 halftime lead before exploding for 22 straight points in the second half.[5]

**(A) Oct. 18—Notre Dame—20–17**

Notre Dame and USC are two of the most successful football programs in the nation. Each lineage is filled with some of the greatest moments in history, and their long-standing rivalry is regarded as one of the best. At times throughout this intense series, the teams had below average records coming into the matchup, but that never diminished the excitement generated over sixty minutes of action. This 1997 clash was one of those rare occasions when both the Irish and the Trojans were below the .500 mark. Notre Dame was 2–4, while USC came in at 2–3, and those records reflected a game filled with missed field goals, bobbled footballs, and numerous penalty flags. The teams had a combined loss of 231 yards due to penalties, with USC getting flagged 15 times for 156 yards.

The Irish got off to a good start when Allen Rossum returned the opening kickoff 56 yards, and then scored on their first two offensive series. With only 2:18 expired in the first quarter, Autry Denson scored on a two-yard run, and Jim Sanson added the extra point to give the Irish a 7–0 lead. Six minutes later Delon Washington scored on a three-yard run, and Adam Abrams tied the game at 7–7 with the conversion kick. With 1:29 remaining in the first quarter, Tony Driver ran for a one-yard touchdown, and Sanson added the extra point to give Notre Dame a 14–7 lead heading into the second quarter.

Like the Irish, the Trojans also scored on their first two possessions. R. Jay Soward got the honors for USC when his eight-yard touchdown reception from John Fox brought the Trojans to within one point of the Irish, and then Abrams tied the score at 14–14 with 12:11 left in the first half. The game remained deadlocked until 37 seconds were left in the first half. It was then that Sanson gave Notre Dame a 17–14 advantage at halftime with a 27-yard field goal.

Abrams scored the only points of the third quarter on a 42-yard field goal that sent the game into the final stanza tied at 17–17. The year before, USC linebacker Mark Cusano batted away a Ron Powlus pass to clinch the victory. This time, he once again came through in the clutch for the Trojans. The Irish were at midfield and on the move. Powlus threw a pass intended for Bobby Brown, but the ball was tipped by Cusano and then found its way into his hands for the interception. He returned the ball 27 yards to the Notre Dame 29 with two-and-a-half minutes remaining in regulation. Four plays later, Abrams gave the Trojans their second straight win over Notre Dame with a 37-yard field goal as the clock showed 1:05 left to be played. The 20–17 victory gave USC a 3–3 record, while the Irish fell to 2–5. This was USC's first win in South Bend since 1981.[6]

**(H) Oct. 25—Oregon—24–22**

On USC's homecoming weekend, the Trojans got out to a 21–3 halftime lead on a pair of Rodney Sermons touchdowns and one from R. Jay Soward. Adam Abrams added a 25-yard field goal in the third quarter before Oregon came back with 12 points in the fourth quarter to make things interesting down the stretch. Marc Matock partially deflected Joshua Smith's 36-yd field goal attempt, causing it to fall short with eight seconds left to preserve the win. Delon Washington had 130 rushing yards on 25 carries, and Billy Miller caught nine passes for 105 yards to assist the Trojans.[7]

**(A) Nov. 1—Washington—0–27**

WASH#7

The state of Washington made a clean sweep of the Trojans in convincing fashion. This marked the first time in eight years that USC was shut out, with the last time also being to Washington but by a 31–0 count. The Trojans' offense could only generate 86 yards through the air, and 71 on the ground. They were also hampered by 11 penalties for a loss of 75 yards. Jerome Pathon ran for 120 yards and one touchdown for Washington.[8]

**(H) Nov. 8—Stanford—45–21**

This win evened USC's Pac-10 record to 3–3, and the Trojans rolled up 511 yards of total offense, with 309 coming on the ground. They limited Stanford to 75 yards through the air in the first half, and had a 31–7 lead going into the fourth quarter. This was a major improvement from the poor showing displayed a week earlier against Washington. Chad Morton ran for 109 yards on just seven carries, and R. Jay Soward caught eight passes for 81 yards and two touchdowns.[9]

**(A) Nov. 15—Oregon State—23–0**

Adam Abrams kicked three field goals from 46, 23, and 32 yards out, R. J. Soward caught a 31-yard touchdown pass, Billy Miller had five receptions for 80 yards, including one for a 45-yard touchdown, and John Fox threw for 228 yards and a pair of six-pointers. All this added up to a shutout and gave USC a 4–3 record in the Pac-10. This game also ended USC's streak of 111 consecutive live football telecasts.[10]

**(H) Nov. 22—UCLA—24–31**

UCLA#7

The first half of this game resembled a boxing match where the combatants stood toe-to-toe and slugged it out, matching punches with no clear-cut winner emerging. The Bruins came into this game on an eight-game winning streak, and got on the board first. Cade McNown threw a nine-yard scoring strike to Mike Grieb within the first three minutes of the game. Chris Sailer added the extra point, and UCLA was up, 7–0. The Trojans wasted very little time tying the game. Only 17 seconds after UCLA lit up the scoreboard, the Trojans did the same on their first play from scrimmage when John Fox threw an 80-yard pass to R. Jay Soward. Adam Abrams then tied the game at 7–7. Fox finished the game with 258 yards passing, and Soward had eight receptions for 181 yards. Skip Hicks capped an 80-yard drive with a touchdown run from 16 yards out, and Sailer's conversion make it 14–7. Anthony Volsan recovered a fumbled punt on the UCLA 24-yard line, and three plays later, Fox threw his second touchdown pass of the game, this time covering 17 to Mike Bastianelli. Abrams' conversion kick made it 14–14 at the end of the first quarter.

With the help of a facemask penalty on a third-and-six situation, the Trojans were able to continue on with what was a four-play, 68-yard scoring drive. Chad Morton gave the Trojans their first and only lead of the game with a 49-yard touchdown run. Abrams added the extra point, and USC was up, 21–14. The first half ended in a 21–21 deadlock when McNown threw a nine-yard scoring strike to Jim McElroy and Sailer kicked the extra point.

The Bruins held USC scoreless in the third quarter, but they added ten points on a 38-yard pass from McNown to Grieb and a 32-yard field goal by Sailer. The Trojans cut the deficit to 31–24 on a 36-yard field goal by Abrams with 3:10 remaining in the game. They then recovered their onside kick near midfield to give them an opportunity to pull this one out. The UCLA defense tightened up, and held the Trojans to negative yardage on the next three downs. Facing a fourth-and-20 situation, Fox heaved a pass downfield that was intercepted by Wasswa Serwanga with 1:15 left on the clock. The Bruins ran out the clock and ran their winning streak over USC to seven straight with 91,350 looking on at the Coliseum.[11]

TEAM LEADERS

RUSHING: Delon Washington—444 yards on 125 carries
PASSING: John Fox—153 out of 280 attempts for 1,940 yards and 12 touchdowns
RECEIVING: Billy Miller—56 catches for 649 yards and 2 touchdowns
SCORING: R. Jay Soward—66 points on 11 touchdowns
KICKOFF RETURNS: R. Jay Soward—15 for 394 yards and 1 touchdown (26.3 avg.)
PUNT RETURNS: Chad Morton—21 for 168 yards (8.0 avg.)
PUNTING: Jim Wren—76 for 3,216 yards (42.3 avg.)
INTERCEPTIONS: Rashard Cook—3 for 22 yards
TACKLES: Rashard Cook—79
SACKS: Chris Claiborne—7
Sultan Abdul-Malik—7

# *1998*

HEAD COACH: Paul Hackett
ASSISTANT COACHES: Jason Gelber, Steve Greatwood, Hue Jackson, Ed Orgeron, Shawn Slocum, Dennis Thurman, Mike Wilson, William L. Young
TEAM CAPTAINS: Adam Abrams, Chris Claiborne, Billy Miller, Chad Morton
RECORD: 8–5 overall (5–3 in Pacific-10 Conference)
(Ranked 38th best record in college football out of 112 teams)
FINISH IN CONFERENCE: Tied for 3rd place
FINISH IN NATIONAL POLLS: No ranking in Top 25
POINTS SCORED PER GAME: 26.6 to rank 46th out of 112 teams
POINTS ALLOWED PER GAME: 18.5 to rank 18th

## Schedule and Highlights

**(H) Aug. 30—Purdue—27–17**

This marked the ninth edition of the Pigskin Classic. It was played with 118-degree temperatures hovering around the field, on what was the 75th anniversary season of USC playing at the LA Coliseum. Freshman quarterback Carson Palmer came off the bench to lead the Trojans to 17 points in the second half to pull out the win. Chad Morton scored what proved to be the game-winner on a 13-yard run with 3:02 remaining on the clock. This victory for Paul Hackett, in his coaching debut with USC, was the first time since Jess Hill in 1951, that a coach won the first game of his tenure with the Trojans.[1]

**(H) Sept. 12—San Diego State—35–6**

USC#22

Ted Tollner returned to the Coliseum as head coach of San Diego State after coaching the Trojans back in the 1980's. His return was not a pleasant one, as the Trojans rolled over the winless Aztecs. R. Jay Soward was the main offensive weapon for USC by accounting for 256 yards on only nine attempts. He caught two touchdown passes, and returned a punt 74 yards for another score. Chad Morton chipped in with 110 rushing yards on 23 carries and one touchdown.[2]

**(H) Sept. 19—Oregon State—40–20**

USC#18

The Trojans remained perfect under Hackett's leadership, beating Oregon State for the 24th straight time. Chad Morton ran for 123 yards on 23 carries and scored a touchdown. Adam Abrams kicked four field goals, and linebacker Chris Claiborne capped the day off by returning an interception 40 yards for a touchdown in the final 59 seconds of the game.[3]

**(A) Sept. 26—Florida State—10–30**

USC#18 FSU#10

Despite heavy rain, a sellout crowd watched the Seminoles defeat the Trojans for the first time in the season. Quarterback Chris Weinke threw for 228 yards and two touchdowns, Sebastian Janikowski kicked three field goals, and the Florida State defense caused the Trojans to turn the ball over five times, and limited them to a mere 23 yards through the air and a convincing 257 to 71 advantage in total yardage.[4]

**(H) Oct. 3—Arizona State—35–24**

USC#21

After trailing, 17–7, at the half, the Trojans outscored the Sun Devils 22–0 in the fourth quarter to snap a two-game losing streak to ASU. A blocked punt by Antuan Simmons was picked up and returned for a 14-yard touchdown by Ifeanyi Ohalete with 13:16 left in the fourth quarter, which put the Trojans ahead to stay. Larry Parker helped the Trojan offense with five receptions for 105 yards. The Sun Devils got a tremendous performance from J.R. Redmond, who set a school record with 350 all-purpose yards.[5]

**(H) Oct. 10—California—31–32**

USC#19

One week earlier, the Trojans rallied for 22 points in the fourth quarter to win. This time, they saw the Golden Bears do the same to them. Cal scored 22 points in the final 19 minutes to pull out their first win at the Coliseum since 1970. Petros Papadakis ran for 118 yards on 13 carries, and R. Jay Soward caught four passes for 105 yards and a touchdown for the Trojans.[6]

**(A) Oct. 17—Washington State—42–14**

The Cougars were looking to win back-to-back games against the Trojans for the first time in their history, but R. Jay Soward scored two touchdowns, and Chris Claiborne had two interceptions to help the Trojans prevent it from happening. The Trojans only held a 21–14 lead at halftime, and the Cougars still had a chance. The Trojan defense then slammed the door on any chance Washington State had. In the Cougars' second half possessions, the Trojans forced four punts, intercepted four passes, and limited them to 93 total yards. Meanwhile, the USC offense scored 21 points and finished the game with 456 yards of total offense.[7]

**(A) Oct. 24—Oregon—13–17**

ORE#12

Chad Morton ran for 104 yards on 20 carries, caught three passes for 79 yards, and Larry Parker had four receptions for 106 yards, but the Trojans lost out in what came to be a tough defensive game. Oregon scored 14 second half points and then held off a USC comeback attempt. Oregon quarterback broke a 10–

10 tie in the fourth quarter when he ran untouched for a 62-yard touchdown that proved to be the game-winner. The loss dropped the Trojans to 3–2 in the Pac-10, and out of contention for a trip to the Rose Bowl.[8]

**(H) Oct. 31—Washington—33–10**

On USC's homecoming weekend, Chad Morton topped the century mark with 110 rushing yards on 13 carries, Carson Palmer threw for 279 yards, and Billy Miller caught five passes for 109 yards to lead the offense. On the defensive side, Antuan Simmons got his name in the USC record book by tying a school record with two interception returns for touchdowns. Both his interceptions came in the fourth quarter, and covered 29 and 90 yards, respectively. As a unit, the Trojan defense had five interceptions throughout the game. Washington established a conference record with 68 pass attempts, which was the most ever against a USC defense.[9]

**(A) Nov. 7—Stanford—34–9**

Stanford came into this game ranked eighth in the nation in passing, averaging 343 yards through the air per game. However, USC clamped down on the explosive air attack with their fourth-ranked defense against the pass, allowing Stanford 166 passing yards. The Trojans forced four turnovers, and sent Stanford down in defeat for the sixth straight time in the season. This marked the first time that Stanford lost that many games in a row since 1983. Safety Rashard Cook recorded 13 tackles, and linebacker Zeke Moreno had 11 stops.[10]

**(A) Nov. 21—UCLA—17–34**

UCLA#3

For the eighth straight time, the Trojans suffered defeat at the hands of their rivals from Westwood. With this convincing victory, the Bruins were able to continue on with their 20-game winning streak, which was the longest in the nation.

Freshman running back DeShaun Foster's first experience in this classic rivalry was nothing short of spectacular. He ran for 109 yards on 15 carries, and tied a school record with four touchdowns. Foster's 24 points also tied a record for most points scored against USC on an individual basis. USC's Chad Morton topped the century mark with 120 yards on 19 carries, and R. Jay Soward turned in a solid performance for the Trojans as well with seven receptions for 124 yards.

The Trojans scored first on an Adam Abrams 36-yard field goal, and that was the extent of the excitement for USC faithful. The Trojans did not help themselves by losing four fumbles in the game's first 22 ½ minutes, which led to 13 of UCLA's points. Following Abrams three-pointer, Foster caught a four-yard touchdown pass from Cade McNown that capped a 77-yard drive, and the Bruins' lead was never challenged after that. Foster then added a one-yard run to paydirt to up the UCLA advantage to 14–3.

USC attempted to make a game of it early in the second quarter after linebacker Chris Claiborne returned an interception 66 yards down to the UCLA four. Two plays later, freshman signal caller Carson Palmer connected with Antoine Harris on a four-yard scoring toss that made it a 14–10 ballgame. Foster struck again quickly after USC's tally on a 65-yard scoring jaunt that put UCLA up, 21–10. Chris Sailer added field goals from 38 and 26 yards out following two fumble recoveries, and the Bruins were in total control with a 27–10 lead.

Midway through the third quarter, USC added a six-pointer to the scoreboard with a one-yard run by Petros Papadakis that cut the deficit to 27–17. However, that was all the scoring for the Trojans on this day. Foster added his final touchdown of the day on a one-yard run with 13:09 remaining in the game.

This edition of the USC-UCLA rivalry also marked a sad end to the longest record ever produced in affiliation with the Land of Troy. USC's "Super Fan," Giles Pellerin, who was viewing his 797th consecutive Trojan game, died of cardiac arrest at halftime in the Rose Bowl parking lot.[11]

**(H) Nov. 28—Notre Dame—10–0**

ND#9

The Trojans took out their frustration of getting soundly beaten by UCLA the previous week on the Fighting Irish. The Trojans stacked the defense with nine players up front, as both safeties were brought up close to clamp down on Notre Dame's I-Formation. Also hampering the Irish was the loss of starting quarterback Jarious Jackson, who had to miss this game due to a knee injury suffered a week earlier. His replacements, Arnaz Battle and Eric Chappell combined for a paltry 94 yards through the air on seven completions out of 22 attempts and four interceptions. The stellar defensive effort by the Trojans prevented Notre Dame from completing a pass until the end of the third quarter, and also held star runner Autry Denson to only 46 yards on 19 carries.

A crowd of 90,069 witnessed USC shutout Notre Dame for the first time since 1962, and win for the third straight time against their rival. This was the first time since 1987 that Notre Dame was shut out, and after falling to 9–2 following the loss, was knocked out of national championship contention.

On a day that saw the Southland engulfed with rain prior to kickoff, the game remained scoreless throughout the first half. The Trojans hit paydirt on their second offensive series of the third quarter when freshman quarterback Carson Palmer took the ball across the goal line from two yards out to complete a five-play, 64-yard march. Adam Abrams added USC's other points on a 23-yard field goal. Chad Morton ran for 128 yards on 27 carries, with 100 of those yards coming in the second half, and R. Jay Soward caught seven passes for 124 yards for the Trojans.[12]

**Sun Bowl, (N) Dec. 31—TCU—19–28**

First year head coach Dennis Franchione achieved what no other mentor at Texas Christian University was able to accomplish in four decades. Led by tailback Basil Mitchell's 185 yards and two touchdowns, and a defense that limited the Trojans' offense to a Sun Bowl record-low of -23 yards, the Horned Frogs won their first bowl game since 1957. TCU used an option offense that rolled up 314 yards on the ground, and played solid defense, to produce a commanding 28–3 lead in the early stages of the second half with 46,612 on hand in El Paso, Texas. Not only did the 16-point underdog Horned Frogs dominant the Trojans on the field in the first half, but did the same in time of possession, holding onto the ball for an incredible 20 minutes and 15 seconds. After TCU had a 21–0 lead, Adam Abrams gave the Trojans their lone points of the first half on a 34-yard field goal.

Down by 25 points made the Trojans take to the air, and despite being put in a predictable situation, they managed to rally with 16 straight points to cut the TCU advantage to 28–20. Carson Palmer threw to Billy Miller for a 23-yard touchdown to begin the attempted comeback. Abrams added the extra point, and then Petros Papadakis scored on a one-yard run with 1:34 left in the third quarter. The Trojans tried for the two-point conversion, but the pass failed. Abrams then closed out the scoring with a 46-yard field goal early in the fourth quarter.[13]

TEAM LEADERS

RUSHING: Chad Morton—985 yards on 199 carries
PASSING: Carson Palmer—130 out of 235 attempts for 1,755 yards and 7 touchdowns
RECEIVING: Billy Miller—49 catches for 623 yards and 3 touchdowns
SCORING: Adam Abrams—86 points on 38 extra points and 16 field goals
KICKOFF RETURNS: R. Jay Soward—16 for 344 yards (21.5 avg.)
PUNT RETURNS: R. Jay Soward—7 for 202 yards and 2 touchdowns (28.9 avg.)
PUNTING: Mike MacGillivray—87 for 3,284 yards (37.7 avg.)
INTERCEPTIONS: Chris Claiborne—6 for 159 yards and 2 touchdowns
TACKLES: Chris Claiborne—120
SACKS: Sultan Abdul-Malik—8

## *1999*

HEAD COACH: Paul Hackett
ASSISTANT COACHES: Steve Greatwood, Hue Jackson, Steve Morton, Ed Orgeron, Rocky Seto, Shawn Slocum, Dennis Thurman, Mike Wilson, William L. Young
TEAM CAPTAINS: David Gibson, Chad Morton, Ifeanyi Ohalete
RECORD: 6–6 overall (3–5 in Pacific-10 Conference)
(Ranked 55th best record in college football out of 114 teams)
FINISH IN CONFERENCE: Tied for 6th place
FINISH IN NATIONAL POLLS: No ranking in Top 25
POINTS SCORED PER GAME: 29.0 to rank 33rd out of 114 teams
POINTS ALLOWED PER GAME: 23.2 to rank 41st

### Schedule and Highlights

**(A) Sept. 4—Hawaii—62–7**
USC#21

The Trojans scored the first six times they had the ball, and the game was over by the end of the first half. Carson Palmer hit on 14 of 16 pass attempts for 167 yards and one touchdown, Malaefou MacKenzie scored three rushing touchdowns, Kareem Kelly had five receptions for 104 yards, and Chad Morton ran for 95 yards on 19 carries. This lose gave Hawaii their 19th straight loss, which was the longest in the country at the time.[1]

**(H) Sept. 18—San Diego State—24–21**
USC#17

The 23-point favorite Trojans built up a 17–0 lead, but almost lost when a Carson Palmer interception was returned for a touchdown in the closing minutes. That cut the Trojans' lead to three points, but the defense stopped the Aztecs on a fourth-and six from the USC 44 to pull out the victory. San Diego State's rally fell short, and gave them their 26th straight non-conference road loss going back to 1981.[2]

**(A) Sept. 25—Oregon—30–33**
USC#16

This game went into three overtimes before Oregon's third-string kicker Josh Frankel ended it with a 27-yard field goal. This was the longest game in USC history, and the Trojans set a team record and tied a Pac-10 record with 21 penalties. Oregon received eight first downs after penalties to establish the most against a USC team, and it also set a conference record. R. Jay Soward turned in a solid showing for USC with 12 receptions for 148 yards and one touchdown.[3]

**(H) Oct. 2—Oregon State—37–29**

This was the 1,000th football game in USC history, and the Trojans went out and redeemed themselves from their triple overtime defeat from the previous week. Chad Morton ran for 153 yards and two touchdowns on 27 carries, R. Jay Soward returned a punt 85 yards for a touchdown, and linebacker Zeke Moreno scored on a 17-yard fumble recovery and a 71-yard interception return. In addition to his two six-pointers, Moreno had 11 tackles and a sack to lead in what was the Trojans 26th straight win over Oregon State.[4]

**(A) Oct. 9—Arizona—24–31**
USC#22

Arizona got great performances out of Trung Canidate (194 yards rushing), and Dennis Northcutt (eight receptions for 121 yards), to spark the Wildcats offense. The Arizona defense did their part by recording seven sacks and holding the Trojans to minus 20 yards rushing. Despite the loss, Mike Van Raaphorst threw for 291 yards and two touchdowns, Kareem Kelly had six receptions for 100 yards, and Windrell Hayes had nine receptions for 115 yards and a touchdown.[5]

**(A) Oct. 16—Notre Dame—24–25**

What goes around comes around is a commonly used phrase. In regards to the USC–Notre Dame series, the Fighting Irish returned the favor to the Trojans 25 years after USC rallied from a 24–0 deficit to pull out one of college football's greatest comebacks. A quarter century came and went before Notre Dame could boast of the same type of rally against their long-time foes from the City of Angels.

With wind and rain serving as the backdrop, the Irish came back from a 24–3 disadvantage that faced them in the early stages of the third quarter. The Trojans helped Notre Dame out by imploding due to costly penalties and mistakes, which are detrimental to a team's success.

USC's Ifeanyi Ohalete was flagged for a personal foul, and that infraction allowed the Irish to keep marching down the field for what started their comeback. Quarterback Jarious Jackson completed the drive with a seven-yard touchdown toss to tight end Dan O'Leary, and momentum took over from there.

Mike Van Raaphorst turned in a solid performance for the Trojans, as he completed 23 of 41 pass attempts for 298 yards and two touchdowns. However, his fumble on USC's next possession following O'Leary's touchdown, caused another Notre Dame score. R. Jay Soward also had a great game for the Trojans with 10 catches for 101 yards and one touchdown, and Windrell Hayes had eight receptions for 107 yards and a touchdown. With rain coming down hard, Jackson led the offense, and then Tony

Driver scored on a two-yard run. The extra point was missed, but Notre Dame had now closed the gap to 24–16 with 13:30 left in the game.

The Trojans once again hurt themselves with a penalty, this time for holding on third-and-eight. The Irish converted that mistake into three points on a 33-yard field goal by David Miller to make it a 24–19 ballgame with 8:07 remaining. The game-winning drive started for Notre Dame on their own 26 with 6:30 showing on the clock. Tony Fisher caught a Jackson pass down the sideline for a gain of 28 yards, and the Irish eventually got to the USC 18. Jackson then looked to pass, but decided to run instead. He shot up the middle and got to the one-yard line before fumbling into the end zone. Teammate Jabari Holloway pounced on the ball in the end zone to finish off the comeback with 2:40 remaining in the game, and instantly sealed his legacy among the Irish faithful.[6]

**(H) Oct. 23—Stanford—31–35**

Things looked great for USC early on, as they led 21–0 in the first quarter. For the game, Chad Morton ran for 151 yards on 22 carries for his 10th game rushing over the century mark, and also scored one touchdown. Kareem Kelly caught eight passes for 129 yards to give him a new USC freshman receiving record of 34 receptions for 632 yards. Mike van Raaphorst set a new school passing yardage record with 415 yards and threw for three touchdowns. The old passing record was set by Rob Johnson on September 25,1993. Both teams combined for 1,043 yards of offense, but it was Stanford that came away with the win. They fought back to score three straight touchdowns from the end of the second quarter and into the early part of the third, which allowed them to get their first lead of the game. This marked the fourth time during this season that USC gave up a second half lead. This was Stanford's first win at the LA Coliseum since 1991, and gave them a 5–0 record in the Pac-10.[7]

**(A) Oct. 30—California—7–17**

Things continued to get worse for USC, as they fell to defeat for the fourth straight week despite a fine performance by Kareem Kelly, who had nine receptions for 170 yards and one touchdown. Led by Deltha O'Neal, the Cal defense put a beating on the Trojans that included nine sacks and four turnovers. O'Neal returned an interception 67 yards for a score, and set up a field goal with a 60-yard punt return.[8]

**(H) Nov. 6—Arizona State—16–26**

USC's homecoming weekend was hampered with the team's fifth straight loss, which was the longest losing streak for the Trojans in eight years. J.R. Redmond led an Arizona State ground attack with 148 yards and ran for three touchdowns. Tight end Todd Heap caught seven passes for 100 yards and a touchdown, and Ryan Kealy passed for 223 yards against the hapless Trojans.[9]

**(A) Nov. 13—Washington State—31–28**

Chad Morton ran for 117 yards on 29 carries and three touchdowns, and the Trojans were able to stop their five-game losing streak by beating a team they dominated for many decades. Since 1921, including this game, the Trojans compiled a 50–6–4 record against the Cougars.[10]

**(H) Nov. 20—UCLA—17–7**

Streaks, like records, were made to be broken. The Trojans finally snapped UCLA's eight-game winning streak over them. Running back Chad Morton had proclaimed months earlier that USC would finally end the Bruins' reign. He then went out and backed up his words by rushing for 143 yards on 36 carries.

Both teams came into this annual tussle with losing records for the first time since 1941. They then lived up to their sub-par seasons by committing 25 penalties, in addition to botched tackling and failure to hold onto passes. After losing his starting quarterback job two years earlier, John Fox came back to his old position after a stint on defense. This was his third straight game back at quarterback, and he did a solid job by completing 17 passes out of 34 attempts for 216 yards and two touchdowns. Kareem Kelly was on the receiving end of Fox's scoring strikes from 22 and five yards out. David Newbury added USC's other points on a 22-yard field in the first quarter to open the scoring.[11]

**(H) Nov. 26—Louisiana Tech—45–19**

LT#25

The Trojans finished the season with the most penalties in team history (128). Louisiana Tech's Tim Rattay attempted 68 passes, which tied him for the most ever against a USC defense. The Washington Huskies attempted the same amount against USC in 1998. The Trojans ran for 309 yards, and Chad Morton gained 85 yards and scored three touchdowns in his final game as a Trojan. This third straight win allowed USC to rally and finish the season with a respectable 6–6 record. Louisiana Tech and its high-powered offense lost for the first time in eight games, and ended their final season of the millennium at 8–3.[12]

### Team Leaders

Rushing: Chad Morton—1,141 yards on 262 carries
Passing: Mike Van Raaphorst—139 out of 258 attempts for 1,758 yards and 8 touchdowns
Receiving: Windrell Hayes—55 catches for 720 yards and 4 touchdowns
Scoring: Chad Morton—90 points on 15 touchdowns
Kickoff Returns: Chad Morton—19 for 341 yards (17.9 avg.)
Punt Returns: R. Jay Soward—18 for 218 yards and 1 touchdown (12.1 avg.)
Punting: Mike MacGillivray—74 for 3,067 yards (41.4 avg.)
Interceptions: Kris Richard—6 for 63 yards and 2 touchdowns
Tackles: Zeke Moreno—108
sacks: Matt Childers—5
Lonnie Ford—5
Ennis Davis—5

## *2000*

Head Coach: Paul Hackett
Assistant Coaches: Andy Christoff, Dan Ferrigno, Hue Jackson, Steve Morton, Ed Orgeron, Kennedy Pola, Brian Schottenheimer, Dennis Thurman, William L. Young
Team Captains: Ennis Davis, Eric Demmon, Zeke Moreno, Petros Papadakis
Record: 5–7 overall (2–6 in Pacific-10 Conference)
(Ranked 74th best record in college football out of 116 teams)
Finish in Conference: Tied for 8th place
This marked the first time that USC finished in last place in conference play throughout their football history.

FINISH IN NATIONAL POLLS: No ranking in Top 25
POINTS SCORED PER GAME: 25.8 to rank 59th out of 116 teams
POINTS ALLOWED PER GAME: 28.1 to rank 79th

## Schedule and Highlights

**(N) Aug. 27—Penn State—29–5**
**USC#15 PSU#22**

The Kickoff Classic XVIII from Giants Stadium, East Rutherford, New Jersey, saw the Trojans start off the new millennium in fine fashion. Sophomore tailback Sultan McCullough ran for 128 yards on 29 carries, and the Trojans outrushed Penn State by a dominating margin of 164 to six. This marked the lowest rushing total by a Penn State team under the coaching reign of Joe Paterno.[1]

**(H) Sept. 9—Colorado—17–14**
USC#11

The Trojans remained perfect thanks to a David Newbury field goal from 24 yards out with 13 seconds left in the game. Carson Palmer threw for 275 yards and one touchdown, Kareem Kelly had 10 receptions for 145 yards, and Sultan McCullough added 91 yards on the ground.[2]

**(H) Sept. 23—San Jose State—34–24**
USC#9

This marked USC's 500th game in the LA Coliseum. Trailing 24–12 to the 23-point underdog San Jose State, the Trojans scored 22 unanswered points in final the 8:07 of the fourth quarter to remain undefeated. Petros Papadakis scored three touchdowns, Sultan McCullough ran for 136 yards on 21 carries, Kareem Kelly caught seven passes for 106 yards, and Carson Palmer completed 22 of 38 pass attempts for 338 yards and two touchdowns.[3]

**(A) Sept. 30—Oregon State—21–31**
USC#8

This loss ended USC's Pac-10 record 26-game winning streak over Oregon State. Leading the way for the Beavers was running back Ken Simonton, who ran for 234 yards and three touchdowns, to help OSU remain undefeated at 4–0. Carson Palmer threw for 282 yards and two touchdowns for USC, but also threw three interceptions.[4]

**(H) Oct. 7—Arizona—15–31**
USC#18

The Wildcats' defense smothered the Trojans with five sacks, five turnovers, and limited USC to a mere 10 yards rushing. USC also missed on two field goal attempts, and had two extra point kicks blocked. Freshman Clarence Farmer ran for 134 yards, and Ortege Jenkins ran for a pair of touchdowns and threw for another one in this total team effort for Arizona. Carson Palmer, once again the victim of three interceptions, threw for 321 yards, and Keary Colbert caught six passes for 113 yards for the Trojans.[5]

**(H) Oct. 14—Oregon—17–28**
ORE#9

The Trojans fell to 3–3 thanks to Oregon quarterback Joey Harrington's great performance. He threw for 382 yards and four touchdowns, which tied a record for most touchdown passes against a USC defense. The win kept Oregon perfect in the Pac-10 race at 3–0. Sophomore tailback Sultan McCullough ran for 152 yards on 23 carries for the Trojans.[6]

**(A) Oct. 21—Stanford—30–32**

The Trojans dropped their fourth straight game, and fell below the .500 mark after Stanford scored 12 points in the final 5:22 to pull out the win. Backup quarterback Chris Lewis threw a 20-yard touchdown pass to Jamien McCullum on fourth-and-goal as time expired to give Stanford their third victory of the year. Prior to Stanford's comeback, the Trojans scored 22 straight points in the second half, only to see it all vanish. Kerry Carter tied a record for most points scored on a USC defense with 24, as he rushed for four touchdowns, and DeRonnie Pitts caught 13 passes for 176 yards. Despite the defeat, Sultan McCullough continued to be a steady performer at tailback, running for 130 yards on 11 carries.[7]

**(H) Oct. 28—California—16–28**

Things continued on a downward spiral for USC, as homecoming weekend was dampened by a fifth straight loss. Jemeel Powell did major damage with an 83-yard punt return for a touchdown, and then intercepted a pass later on. The Cal defense recorded seven sacks, Kyle Boller threw two touchdown passes, and the Golden Bears beat the Trojans for the fourth time in their last five matchups. The was the first time in their history that USC started off conference play at 0–4, and the first time since 1991 that they lost five straight games.[8]

**(A) Nov. 4—Arizona State—44–38**

The Trojans came out and opened up a 35–6 third quarter lead. However, the Sun Devils fought back by scoring four touchdowns in the last 15:46 of regulation to force overtime. This marked an NCAA Division 1-A record third straight overtime game for Arizona State. Chad Pierson scored the game-winner in the second overtime on a two-yard run to break USC's five-game losing streak. Sultan Abdul-Malik helped the Trojans by forcing a fumble on ASU's final play of the game, and Matt Childers recovered to secure the win. Sultan McCullough once again had a solid performance running the ball, this time gaining 176 yards on 23 carries.[9]

**(H) Nov. 11—Washington State—27–33**

Washington State's quarterback Matt Kegel used his first start to showcase his talent. He threw for 242 yards against USC after starter Jason Gesser broke his leg the previous week. The Cougars took a 7–0 lead and never relinquished it on their way to Washington State's fourth win of the year. The loss dropped the Trojans into last place in the Pac-10 with a 1–6 record. Kareem Kelly had a good game for the Trojans with seven receptions for 114 yards and one touchdown.[10]

**(A) Nov. 18—UCLA—38–35**

The Victory Bell, the symbol of conquest in this great series, has resided in Westwood since 1991. In 1999, the Trojans changed the address card for the cherished trophy, and liked having it around so much that they decided to hold onto it for at least another, year thanks to down-to-the-wire 38–35 win.

Kicker David Bell, USC's third-string kicker at the start of season, hit a game winning field goal from 36 yards out with nine seconds to play. It was only his second three-pointer in six career attempts. In addition to Bell's heroics, Carson Palmer had an excellent game, completing 26 of 37 pass attempts for 350 yards and four touchdowns. Sultan McCullough gave the Trojans a balanced attack by running for a game-high 105 yards on 26 carries and one touchdown.

The Bruins got out to a quick 7–0 lead following the opening kickoff. Frank Strong fielded the ball for USC, and returned the kickoff to the Trojan 32. Two penalties then sent USC back to their three-yard line. On the first play from scrimmage, Chad Pierson had the ball forced from him by Tony White, and Marques Anderson jumped on the loose pigskin in the end zone with only 20 seconds knocked off the clock.

The Trojans came back to tie things up four minutes later when Palmer fired his first scoring toss of the game. Antoine Harris was on the receiving end of the pass that covered eight yards to cap off an 11-play, 80-yard drive. Freddie Mitchell then passed to Brian Poli-Dixon from 45 yards out to give the Bruins the lead once again shortly after USC tied the game, and the first quarter ended with UCLA up, 14–7.

McCullough scored on a six-yard run and Bell added the extra point early in the second quarter to tie the game at 14. The gridiron tug of war continued, as the Bruins lit the scoreboard up with 2:01 left in the first half on a four-yard pass from Cory Paus to Ed Ieremia-Stansbury, and Griffith's conversion made it 21–14 UCLA. The Trojans had one final drive before halftime, and made the most out of it. With 24 seconds left, Palmer threw his second touchdown pass of the game, this time a 39-yarder to Kareem Kelly, and Bell's extra point sent the teams into the locker room deadlocked at 21–21.

Once again neither team refused to bend, and the third quarter ended in a tie. Closing in on the midway point of the quarter, Mitchell caught a four-yard pass from Paus, and Griffith added the conversion. With slightly under three minutes to go, the Trojans hit paydirt on Palmer's third scoring strike. Keary Colbert capped a 10-play, 71-yard drive by hauling in Palmer's pass from 12 yards out. Bell's extra point took the teams into the fourth quarter again knotted up at 28–28.

Early in the fourth, Palmer added one final touchdown pass to his day's work, with it covering 57 yards, and going to Steve Stevenson. Bell then kicked his fifth extra point of the game, and the Trojans had their first lead all day. Just to add more drama to the festivities, the Bruins came back to tie it at 35–35 with 1:05 left on a nine-play, 75-yard drive. UCLA was facing a fourth-and-goal from the one, and a Paus to Mitchell pass temporarily gave the Westwood faithful something to cheer about. Griffith then booted his fifth conversion kick of the game.

It was then that the stage was set for Bell to take his rightful place in USC lore. The Trojans began the march to victory from their 35-yard line following the ensuing kickoff. They got the ball close to field goal range on a 13-yard run by Malaefou MacKenzie, a 12-yard pass to Kareem Kelly, and a five-yard pass to Antoine Harris. The Trojans were then helped out by a holding penalty that added 10 yards to their advance. MacKenzie then ran for seven yards to set USC up for Bell's game-winning 36-yard field goal. This was one of the most exciting games in this series, and produced 557 total yards of offense for USC, and 328 for the Bruins.[11]

**(H) Nov. 25—Notre Dame—21–38**
ND#11

Notre Dame freshman quarterback Matt LoVecchio ran for a pair of six-pointers, and threw for 142 yards to assist the Fighting Irish in winning at the LA Coliseum against USC for the first time since 1992. LoVecchio's performance, along with that of fellow Irish teammates, sealed the fate of USC's head coach Paul Hackett, who was relieved of his duties two days after this game.

The Irish got off to a 7–0 lead on a one-yard run by Terrance Howard, and USC countered the six-pointer with one of their own. Carson Palmer finished off a 65-yard drive with a three-yard run, and that was as close as the Trojans would get. Early in the second quarter, Notre Dame scored two touchdowns within four minutes to move out to a 21–7 lead. A blocked punt led to a four-play, 50-yard drive that was capped off by a LoVecchio one-yard run to put the Irish in front for good. Three plays later, an interception by Tony Driver was returned 43 yards to the USC 19. Tony Fisher punched the ball over the goal line from the one to make it a 21–7 Notre dame advantage. The Trojans cut the deficit to 21–14 by halftime on a 59-yard pass from Palmer to Kareem Kelly.

A Glenn Earl interception was turned into seven points within five plays, as LoVecchio added his second touchdown run of the game to up Notre Dame's lead to 28–21. The Trojans rallied on a 10-yard pass from Palmer to Antoine Harris on the first play of the fourth quarter to make the score 28–21. The Irish then pulled away down the stretch on a 39-yard field goal from Nick Setta, and a two-yard run by Julius Jones ended the scoring with just under three remaining in the game.[12]

### Team Leaders

Rushing: Sultan McCullough—1,163 yards on 227 carries
Passing: Carson Palmer—228 out of 415 attempts for 2,914 yards and 16 touchdowns
Receiving: Kareem Kelly—55 catches for 796 yards and 4 touchdowns
Scoring: Petros Papadakis—48 points on 8 touchdowns
Kickoff Returns: Frank Strong—25 for 540 yards (21.6 avg.)
Punt Returns: Kris Richard—13 for 98 yards (7.5 avg.)
Punting: Mike MacGillivray—58 for 2,267 yards (39.1 avg.)
Interceptions: Troy Polamalu—2 for 43 yards and 1 touchdown
DeShaun Hill—2 for 12 yards
Chris Cash—2 for 9 yards
Tackles: Zeke Moreno—103
sacks: Ennis Davis—6

## *2001*

Head Coach: Pete Carroll
Assistant Coaches: Aaron Ausmus, Chris Carlisle, Norm Chow, Nick Holt, Lane Kiffin, Wayne Moses, Ed Orgeron, Kennedy Pola, Steve Sarkisian, Rocky Seto, Keith Uperesa, DeWayne Walker, Kirby Wilson
Team Captains: Charlie Landrigan, Troy Polamalu, Antuan Simmons
Record: 6–6 overall (5–3 in Pacific–10 Conference)
(Ranked 62nd best record in college football out of 117 teams)
Finish in Conference: 5th place
The football program was penalized by the NCAA on charges stemming from tutors committing academic fraud by writing term papers for players. The penalty for this was a two-year probation and scholarship reductions.

FINISH IN NATIONAL POLLS: No ranking in Top 25
POINTS SCORED PER GAME: 24.8 to rank 72nd out of 117 teams
POINTS ALLOWED PER GAME: 17.2 to rank 9th

## Schedule and Highlights

**(H) Sept. 1—San Jose State—21–10**

The Pete Carroll era kicked off in fine fashion with Sultan McCullough leading the charge. Using his blazing speed, McCullough ran for 167 yards and all three of USC's touchdowns.[1]

**(H) Sept. 8—Kansas State—6–10**

KS#12

The Trojans were a part of history, but not the type they wanted. Kansas State coach Bill Snyder was able to obtain the 100th victory of his career against the Trojans, and hand Pete Carroll his first-ever loss leading the Cardinal & Gold. Josh Scobey ran for 165 yards, but it was guard Nick Leckey that helped the most when he recovered a fumble in the end zone for Kansas State's lone six-pointer. This marked Kansas State's 29th straight regular season victory over teams outside of their conference.[2]

**(A) Sept. 22—Oregon—22–24**

ORE#7

The Trojans fell for the second straight game by the slightest of margins. Oregon drove 61 yards in seven plays in the final minute of the game, and Jared Siegel kicked the game-winning field goal from 32 yards out with 12 seconds left. This marked the eighth time that quarterback Joey Harrington conducted a comeback, and the Ducks posted their 23 straight home victory. For the Trojans, Kareem Kelly had four catches for 165 yards, and Carson Palmer had a huge day despite coming up two points short of the win. He completed 25 of 40 pass attempts for 411 yards, but was sacked five times and suffered three interceptions by Steve Smith.[3]

**(H) Sept. 29—Stanford—16–21**

Quarterback Randy Fasani threw for 194 yards and a pair of touchdowns to lead Stanford to its first 3–0 start since 1986. Meanwhile, the Trojans slipped to 1–3 overall, and remained winless in the Pac-10 race. Carson Palmer threw for 240 yards for the Trojans.[4]

**(A) Oct. 6—Washington—24–27**

WASH# 11

Washington had the reputation for coming back to win in the fourth quarter three times during the season. The Huskies were led by backup quarterback Taylor Barton, who replaced Cody Pickett in the second quarter, after he suffered a separated shoulder. Barton threw for 197 yards and two touchdowns. It was John Anderson who received the top headlines when he kicked a 32-yard field goal with no time left to secure the Huskies' 12th straight win. The Trojans, still looking for their first Pac-10 victory under Pete Carroll, were led by Sultan McCullough's 132 rushing yards on 32 carries.[5]

**(H) Oct. 13—Arizona State—48–17**

The Trojans finally got Pete Carroll his first-ever Pac-10 victory as head coach with a resounding blowout victory over an Arizona State team that was ranked second in the nation in scoring with a 45.2 points-per-game average. The Trojans were held to minus 13 yards in the first quarter, and then exploded for three touchdowns on their way to the win. Carson Palmer threw for 295 yards and three touchdowns, as the Trojans were able to snap a four-game losing streak.[6]

**(A) Oct. 20—Notre Dame—16–27**

This edition of the "Glamour Game" marked the 75th anniversary of this classic series, and just like in the first meeting back in 1926, Notre Dame emerged victorious. After starting off the season with three straight losses, the Fighting Irish rebounded quite well. Against the Trojans, they had to overcome a double-digit deficit, but accomplished the task behind the leadership of quarterback Carlyle Holiday. Making his fourth start, Holiday guided the Irish to a 3–3 record coming into the USC contest, and he ran for 98 yards, and completed nine of 12 pass attempts for 133 yards to produce a balanced offensive attack.

The Trojans started out well, getting out to a 13–3 lead on a pair of Carson Palmer touchdown passes. On the receiv-ing end of Palmer's scoring tosses were Chad Pierson (54 yards) and Keary Colbert (20 yards). The balance of power then shifted toward the Irish in the second quarter, and they outscored the Trojans, 24–3, the rest of the way. In the latter stages of the quarter, the Trojans attempted a fake punt, but punter Mike MacGillivray was stopped for no gain. On the fourth play following the failed fake punt, the Irish were in the end zone, complements of a four-yard run by Terrance Howard.

The Trojans added three points to their total early in the third quarter following a fumble by Carlyle Holiday. An 18-yard field goal by David Davis gave the Trojans a 16–10 lead, and it also the final ones scored by the Cardinal & Gold on this day. Holiday scored on a 35-yard run, and the Irish clinched the game on a five-yard run by Julius Jones with 1:21 left on the clock.[7]

**(A) Oct. 27—Arizona—41–34**

Arizona battled back from a 21-point deficit in the second quarter, but it was not enough for them to win their first conference game in over a year. The Trojans won this one thanks to Kris Richard's 58-yard interception return for a touchdown with 1:50 left on the clock. Carson Palmer threw for 248 yards and two touchdowns.[8]

**(H) Nov. 3—Oregon State—16–13**

The Trojans evened their conference record at 3–3 with this exciting overtime game on homecoming weekend. Carson Palmer ran in the game-winner from four yards out in the first overtime period. The Trojans were able to dodge two failed field goal attempts by Oregon State's Ryan Cesca late in the fourth quarter. This win gave the Trojans their 18th straight over Oregon State at the LA Coliseum, who left Los Angeles with their last victory over USC in 1960.[9]

**(A) Nov. 10—California—55–14**

The Trojans posted their fourth straight Pac-10 victory with a romp over winless Cal. Chris Howard ran for a pair of touchdowns, and Carson Palmer passed for 235 yards for USC on a wet and dreary day in Northern California. This marked the first time since 1959 that the Golden Bears lost every one of their home games in one season.[10]

**(H) Nov. 17—UCLA—27-0**
UCLA#20

This win ended a season that saw USC lose five games by five points or less, and the first season it lost twice in the final 12 seconds. However, against their cross-town rivals, the Trojans left nothing to chance by winning in convincing fashion. Carson Palmer connected on 14 of 23 pass attempts for 180 yards and a touchdown, which went to Keary Colbert from four yards out. David Davis added two 20-yard field goals, and Chris Howard scored on a 34-yard run. The defensive unit, which turned in a spectacular effort, accounted for USC's other six-pointer on an Antuan Simmons interception return. Safety Troy Polamalu chipped in with a great performance that saw him block a punt, which was turned into a field goal, and an interception that helped set up the USC offense for a touchdown.[11]

**Las Vegas Bowl, (N) Dec. 25—Utah—6-10**

The first bowl game of the Pete Carroll regime ended up in the gambling capital of America with 22,385 on hand at Sam Boyd Stadium in Las Vegas, Nevada. The attendance figure produced the smallest to watch USC in a bowl game. This marked the 10th edition of the Las Vagas Bowl, and the 16 combined points was the lowest in the game's history. This came as no surprise because both teams possessed top-ranked defenses. In addition to losing their second straight bowl game, the Trojans had a four-game winning streak end, and this loss gave back-to-back losing seasons for the 13th time in their history. It also marked the first time since 1916 that Utah defeated the Trojans.

Utah had the opportunity to use up time due to the tough ground-pounding running attack of Adam Tate and 1,000-yard rusher Dameon Hunter. Tate accounted for a game-high 103 yards on 23 carries, Hunter added 94 yards on 17 carries, and took home Utah's MVP of the game honors.

Utah opened the scoring late in the first quarter when Tate ran for three yards to complete a seven-play, 48-yard drive on the Utes' second offensive series of the game. The Trojans attempted to get on the scoreboard with a 47-yard field goal, but David Davis, the Pac-10's most reliable kicker during the regular season missed, which ended his streak of 12 consecutive three-pointers. Utah then added a field goal of their own with 29 seconds left in the first half on a 26-yarder from Ryan Kaneshiro.

Down by 10 at the start of the third quarter, the Trojans avoided a shutout after receiving the kickoff that started the second half. USC marched 80 yards in 12 plays with fullback Sunny Byrd scoring on a two-yard run. Davis' woes continued, as he missed the extra point kick. Troy Polamalu was the major standout for the Trojans, as he lived up to his All-American status by making a Las Vegas Bowl record 20 tackles, 12 of which were solo stops, and also a game record. He easily was selected USC's MVP of the game.[12]

### TEAM LEADERS

RUSHING: Sultan McCullough—410 yards on 115 carries
PASSING: Carson Palmer—221 out of 377 attempts for 2,717 yards and 13 touchdowns
RECEIVING: Kareem Kelly—49 catches for 801 yards and 3 touchdowns
SCORING: David Davis—82 points on 1 touchdown, 31 extra points and 15 field goals
KICKOFF RETURNS: Darrell Rideaux—19 for 362 yards (19.1 avg.)
PUNT RETURNS: Kevin Arbet—25 for 225 yards (9.0 avg.)
PUNTING: Mike MacGillivray—79 for 3,082 yards (39.0 avg.)
INTERCEPTIONS: Troy Polamalu—3 for 116 yards and 2 touchdowns
Kevin Arbet—3 for 90 yards and 1 touchdown
TACKLES: Troy Polamalu—118
SACKS: Lonnie Ford—7

## *2002*

HEAD COACH: Pete Carroll
ASSISTANT COACHES: Aaron Ausmus, Greg Burns, Chris Carlisle, Brennan Carroll, Norm Chow, Tim Davis, Nick Holt, Lane Kiffin, Ed Orgeron, Kennedy Pola, Steve Sarkisian, Rocky Seto, Keith Uperesa
TEAM CAPTAINS: Carson Palmer, Troy Polamalu
RECORD: 11-2 overall (7-1 in Pacific-10 Conference)
(Ranked 6th best record in college football out of 117 teams)
FINISH IN CONFERENCE: Tied for 1st place with Washington State
Washington State gained a Rose Bowl berth by beating USC in head-to-head competition.
FINISH IN NATIONAL POLLS: 4th place in both the AP and *USA Today*
POINTS SCORED PER GAME: 35.8 to rank 9th out of 117 teams
POINTS ALLOWED PER GAME: 18.5 to rank 17th

### Schedule and Highlights

**(H) Sept. 2—Auburn—24-17**
USC#18

USC players wore a gold football-shaped decal on their helmets reading "Goux" in memory of legendary assistant coach Marv Goux, who passed away in July 2002. This season also saw the unveiling of new jerseys, similar to those worn from 1958 to 1969. Carson Palmer hit on almost 72 percent of his passes for 302 yards and one touchdown. He then used his legs to pull out the win with a one-yard quarterback sneak with 1:26 left to play in regulation. Tailback Malaefou MacKenzie had six receptions for 117 yards to become the first USC running back to go over the century mark in receiving yards in a single game since Mike Garrett in 1964.[1]

**(A) Sept. 14—Colorado—40-3**
USC#17 COL#18

A smothering defense and a balanced offensive attack in football usually will bring a victory. Such was the case for the Trojans, who incorporated both in this lopsided win. The defense allowed only 61 yards of total offense, the lowest given up by a USC defense since 1952 against Oregon. Sultan McCullough ran for 110 yards on 15 carries and one touchdown. Carson Palmer threw for 244 yards and one touchdown, and ran for another one. On defense, safety Troy Polamalu had 11 tackles, which earned him Pac-10 defensive Player of the Week honors.[2]

**(A) Sept. 21—Kansas State—20-27**
USC#11 KS#25

A trip to Manhattan, Kansas, saw the Trojans struggle for three quarters, producing only 129 total yards. They were down, 27-6, until 10 minutes were left in the game. Two fourth quarter touchdowns got USC to within seven points, but one final chance at a win or tie ended after they reached the Kansas State 33. From there they failed to convert on fourth down with 30 seconds left in regulation, and they suffered their first defeat of the season. This game also saw Terrence Newman score the first-ever defensive extra point against USC when he returned a blocked extra point attempt in the second quarter. This was USC's first trip to the state of Kansas, and the first time that Kansas State beat a ranked non-conference team at home. This also was Kansas State's 38th straight win over a non-conference team at home, and their 36th straight home victory during the month of September.[3]

**(H) Sept. 28—Oregon State—22–0**
USC#18 ORE#23

The Trojans dropped off seven positions in the national rankings, but got back on their winning ways with this shutout victory in the Pac-10 opener for both schools. This was the first time since 1976 that USC won their conference opener via a shutout, and the 19th straight loss for Oregon State at the LA Coliseum. Ryan Killeen kicked three field goals, Mike Williams caught two touchdown passes, and Carson Palmer threw for 231 yards to power the Trojans.[4]

**(A) Oct. 5—Washington State—27–30**
USC#18 WS#17

This was the 300th time the Trojans were on live television, but it was Washington State that celebrated the honor. The game went into overtime, and Drew Dunning connected on 35-yard field goal to win it. Prior to his game-winner, Dunning forced overtime with another 35-yard field goal with 1:50 remaining in regulation. The loss overshadowed outstanding performances from Carson Palmer (381 yards passing) and Mike Williams (six receptions for 112 yards). The loss ended USC's six-game Pac-10 winning streak, and gave them only their third loss in Pullman, Washington.[5]

**(H) Oct. 12—California—30–28**
USC#20

The Trojans came back strong after trailing, 21–3, in their 90th all-time game with Cal, at the LA Coliseum. They then scored 27 straight points to pull out the win. This victory also broke a three-game winning streak enjoyed by Cal at the LA Coliseum. Ryan Killeen kicked three field goals, Sultan McCullough ran for 176 yards on 39 carries and one touchdown, and Carson Palmer connected on 25 of 39 pass attempts for 289 yards and a pair of touchdowns. Mike Williams led all receivers in the game with 103 receiving yards on six catches, and caught one of Palmer's scoring strikes.[6]

**(H) Oct. 19—Washington—41–21**
USC#19 WASH#22

The game was deadlocked at 7–7 before the Trojans exploded for 27 straight points during the second and third quarters to pull away from the Huskies. Their 41 points were the most USC scored on Washington since 1974. Carson Palmer was showing the nation why he was a frontrunner for the Heisman Trophy by completing 21 of 34 pass attempts for 348 yards and four touchdowns. Mike Williams was Palmer's primary receiver, catching nine passes for 159 yards and three touchdowns, which tied a school single-game record for most receiving touchdowns by one individual. Another record was set, but this one was by Washington's Braxton Cleman, who had 15 receptions, which was the most ever caught against a USC defense.[7]

**(A) Oct. 26—Oregon—44–33**
USC#15 ORE#14

The Trojans trailed by five points at the end of the first half, and then scored 30 straight points to snap a four-game losing streak to Oregon. With the largest crowd (56,754) to ever see a football game in the state of Oregon, Carson Palmer delivered a record-setting performance. He set a USC record with 448 passing yards, breaking the old mark set by Mike Van Raaphorst on October 23, 1999. He also tied a school record with five touchdown passes. Mike Williams got into the record-setting act by hauling in13 receptions to establish the most by a USC freshman in one game. Williams compiled 226 yards on those catches, and scored two touchdowns. Justin Fargas ran for 139 yards on 27 carries to lead all ball carriers.[8]

**(A) Nov. 9—Stanford—49–17**
USC#10

Carson Palmer continued on with his golden arm. He threw for 317 yards on 22 out of 32 attempts, and four touchdowns to help USC break a three-game losing streak to Stanford. With those four scoring strikes, Palmer became USC's career record holder for touchdown passes.[9]

**(H) Nov. 16—Arizona State—34–13**
USC#8

USC's homecoming was made a lot brighter thanks to a convincing win of the Sun Devils. This was USC's fifth straight win, their fifth straight 30-plus point game, and their eighth straight victory at the Coliseum. Carson Palmer threw for 214 yards and two touchdowns, Justin Fargas ran for 125 yards on 26 carries, and Keary Colbert led all receivers with seven catches for 98 yards.[10]

**(A) Nov. 23—UCLA—52–21**
USC#7 UCLA#25

Pete Carroll remained perfect over UCLA, and in his second outing against the Westwood foes, he left no doubt about the outcome. From the time the ball left the tee to start the game, until the clock struck zero to end this 72nd meeting between these schools, the Trojans dominated, rolling up 468 total yards of offense in the process. This was the second time in the series that USC won four straight, and produced the most points against a Bruins' team since scoring 52 back in 1930. This also was the first time since 1993 that both teams were ranked coming into the game.

The Trojans wasted little time lighting up the scoreboard. With just 16 seconds expired in the first quarter, Carson Palmer connected on a 34-yard touchdown pass to Kareem Kelly. The quick scoring strike was set up when Grant Mattos recovered a UCLA fumble on the opening kickoff. Palmer then took advantage of the turnover by teaming up with Kelly on USC's first offensive play of the game. Then following a UCLA punt, Palmer once again struck quickly, getting the Trojans on the board within five plays. This time he threw a 51-yard touchdown pass to Keary Colbert.

Palmer connected on his first seven pass attempts of the game, and finished the rout of UCLA with 19 completions out of 32 attempts for 254 yards. He also added two more scoring strikes to his day's work. He threw a two-yard pass to Malaefou

MacKenzie in the second quarter, and then tight end Gregg Guenther hauled in Palmer's fourth scoring strike from three yards away in the third quarter.

The USC ground attack also produced three touchdowns, first with Justin Fargas scoring on a one-yard run in the opening quarter to help give the Trojans a commanding 28–7 lead by halftime. In the second half, USC hit paydirt on a pair of long runs by Colbert (34 yards) and Hershel Dennis (38 yards). Ryan Killeen booted a 27-yard fields goal in the fourth quarter, and accounted for seven more points on conversion kicks. The USC defense did an excellent job by getting five sacks and just as many turnovers.[11]

**(H) Nov. 30—Notre Dame—44–13**

USC#6 ND#7

The Trojans kept the offense on high octane, as they mauled Notre Dame after spotting them a 13–10 lead in the second quarter. In consecutive weeks, USC rang up a combined 96 points on their two top rivals. With 91,432 inside the LA Coliseum, Carson Palmer made his final statement to the Heisman voting community by hitting on 32 of 46 pass attempts for 425 yards and four touchdowns. Palmer's yardage through the air and touchdown passes, were the most ever allowed by a Notre Dame team. Another record set against Notre Dame was USC's 610 yards of total offense, which produced the most ever rolled up on an Irish team. Not since 1974 had USC scored this amount of points on Notre Dame, and this victory snapped a three-game losing streak for USC against them. In addition to Palmer's great performance, other stellar efforts were produced by tailback Justin Fargas, who had a game-high 120 rushing yards, and receiver Mike Williams, who hauled in ten passes for 169 yards.

Notre Dame got out to a 6–0 lead at the end of the first quarter on a pair of Nick Setta field goals from 34 and 32 yards. Palmer then threw his first scoring strike of the game, a six-yarder, to Mike Williams. Ryan Killeen added the go-ahead extra point, and then a 22-yard field goal, to give the Trojans a 10–6 lead in the second quarter. The Irish came back to take their final lead of the game on a Carlos Pierre-Antoine return of a blocked punt that covered 27 yards.

The Trojans then responded with 34 straight points to put the game safely away by the end of the third quarter. The onslaught began with Palmer once again teaming up with Williams in the second quarter, this time on a 19-yard scoring strike. The third quarter produced a 15-yard Palmer to Malaefou MacKenzie touchdown pass, and two Killeen field goals from 27 and 29 yards. The final quarter saw USC add the game's final points on a Sultan McCullough 11-yard run, and a 10-yard pass from Palmer to MacKenzie.

This season marked the first time in USC history that the Trojans scored at least 30 points in its last eight games. They also faced nine AP-ranked teams, which was the most USC ever faced in a season.[12]

**Orange Bowl, (N) Jan. 2—Iowa—38–17**

USC#5 IOWA#3

The Trojans completed their season of resurgence back to the upper echelon of the college football world with a convincing victory at Pro Players Stadium in Miami, Florida. This proved to be USC's first win in the state of Florida in five tries, and the program's first-ever Bowl Championship Series (BCS) opportunity.

Led by the newly crowned Heisman Trophy winner, Carson Palmer, the Trojans amassed 550 yards of total offense en route to their first 11-win season since 1979, when another Heisman Trophy winner, Charles White, was the focal point of the offense. Palmer completed 21 of 31 pass attempts for 303 yards and a touchdown to earn MVP of the game honors. Other standout performances by members of the victorious Trojans came from Justin Fargas with 122 rushing yards on 20 carries and two touchdowns, and Mike Williams with six receptions for 99 yards and one touchdown.

The Trojans trailed 10–7 at the end of the first quarter, and then exploded for 31 straight points to easily put the game away down the stretch. The Hawkeyes came out to claim the lead immediately, as C.J. Jones took the opening kickoff back 100 yards. Fargas then scored USC's first points in the opening stanza on a four-yard run, and Ryan Killeen added the first of his five extra point kicks. Killeen also started the 31-point avalanche in the second quarter with a 35-yard field goal to tie the game at 10-all going into the second half.

It was then all USC from that point on. Palmer threw an 18-yard touchdown pass to Williams to give the Trojans their go-ahead points, and the rout was on. Fargas finished off the third quarter scoring with a 50-yard scoring jaunt. Sultan McCullough ran for a five-yard score, and Sunny Byrd capped off the assault with a six-yard run. This game saw the Trojans compile 400 yards or better for the ninth straight time, and they set a single-season team record with 186 first downs coming on passes. The defense also came through by capping off the season without allowing an opposing runner to top the century mark.[13]

### Team Leaders

Rushing: Sultan McCullough—814 yards on 179 carries
Passing: Carson Palmer—309 out of 489 attempts for 3,942 yards and 33 touchdowns
Receiving: Mike Williams—81 catches for 1,265 yards and 14 touchdowns
Scoring: Ryan Killeen—95 points on 47 extra points and 16 field goals
Kickoff Returns: Hershel Dennis—9 for 151 yards (16.8 avg.)
Punt Returns: Greig Carlson—27 for 177 yards (6.6 avg.)
Punting: Tom Malone—62 for 2,609 yards (42.1 avg.)
Interceptions: Jason Leach—4 for 52 yards
Tackles: Matt Grootegoed—81
sacks: Matt Grootegoed—8

## *2003*

Head Coach: Pete Carroll
Assistant Coaches: Aaron Ausmus, Greg Burns, Chris Carlisle, Brennan Carroll, Norm Chow, Tim Davis, Nick Holt, Lane Kiffin, Ed Orgeron, Kennedy Pola, Steve Sarkisian, Rocky Seto
Team Captains: Keary Colbert, Melvin Simmons
Record: 12–1 overall (7–1 in Pacific–10 Conference)
(Ranked 4th best record in college football out of 117 teams)
Finish in Conference: 1st place
Finish in National Polls: 1st place in AP and 2nd place in *USA Today*
2003 Associated Press National Champions

POINTS SCORED PER GAME: 41.1 to rank 5th out of 117 teams
POINTS ALLOWED PER GAME: 18.4 to rank 17th

## Schedule and Highlights

NOTE: During the season, the USC players wore a football-shaped sticker on their helmets with "54" inside in gold lettering in memory of Drean Rucker, an incoming freshman linebacker who drowned in July of 2003.

**(A) Aug. 30—Auburn—23–0**
USC#8 AU#6

Since the Auburn football program began in 1892, this was the worst opening game loss in their history. It was also the Trojans 36th shutout victory in a season opener, their first since 1973, their first road opener won by a shutout since 1963, and their first shutout of a top 10 team since 1982. They dominated the game from the start, as Darnell Bing picked off a pass on third play of game, and Matt Leinart, starting in his first game as a Trojan, connected with Mike Williams three plays later from five yards out. Ryan Killeen kicked three field goals (28, 42, 35 yards), and Hershel Dennis added a 14-yard touchdown run to finish out the scoring. On the defensive side of the ball, the Trojans allowed only 43 rushing yards and never let Auburn get inside the USC 33.[1]

**(H) Sept. 6—Brigham Young University—35–18**
USC#4

The Trojans opened up a big 21–0 first quarter lead in their first-ever meeting with BYU. Matt Leinart threw two touchdown passes (Mike Williams 1-yard and Keary Colbert 48 yards), and defensive end Omar Nazel returned an interception 16 yards to produce the 21-point advantage. Brigham Young nearly came back after that, closing the gap to 21–18 in the fourth quarter. USC then added touchdowns on a Leinart-to-Williams 18-yard pass, and on a Hershel Dennis 11-yard run, to pull away at the end. Punter Tom Malone was named the Pac-10 Special Teams Player of the Week after averaging 52 yards on six punts. This was USC's 10th win a row and 10th straight in the Coliseum. A crowd of 75,315 was the most to watch a USC home opener since 1988.[2]

**(H) Sept. 13—Hawaii—61–32**
USC#4

Hawaii completed the most passes against a USC defense with 40, but they still offered no threat to USC, improving to 3–0 on the season. It was the most points USC had scored at home since against Cal in 1994, and the most in a game since scoring 62 at Hawaii in 1999. This was USC's 11th straight win (longest streak since 1979–80), and their 11th in row at the Coliseum (longest streak there since 1977–79).[3]

**(A) Sept. 27—California—31–34**
USC#3

It took three overtime periods to give Cal their first win over a Top 5 team since 1975. The Trojans forced overtime when Ryan Killeen connected on a 33-yard field goal with 16 seconds left in regulation to tie the game at 24–24. Both teams failed to score in the first overtime, and after Cal got a touchdown on a 20-yard pass from Reggie Robertson to Jonathan Makonnen, Matt Leinart threw a six-pointer to Keary Colbert from 10 yards out. Killeen sent the game into the third overtime by connecting on the extra point. Tyler Fredrickson, who had two previous field goal attempts blocked, connected on a 38-yarder to give the Golden Bears the win that snapped USC's 11-game winning streak.[4]

**(A) Oct. 4—Arizona State—37–17**
USC#10

Trailing 17–10 just after halftime, the Trojans scored 27 unanswered points to win convincingly over the Sun Devils. LenDale White's 140 rushing yards set a school record for the most by a true freshman. White had two of his carries go for touchdowns, Matt Leinart threw for 289 yards and a pair of touchdowns, Ryan Killeen added three field goals, Mike Williams caught five passes for 108 yards, as did Keary Colbert, for 100 yards and a touchdown, to help the Trojans get back on their winning ways.[5]

**(H) Oct. 11—Stanford—44–21**
USC#9

This was USC's 700th victory, and Mike Williams tied a school record with three touchdown receptions. He finished the game with seven catches for 129 yards. LenDale White set a record by becoming the first freshman in USC history to have back-to-back 100-yard plus rushing performances, this time getting 108 yards on 23 carries and a touchdown. The Trojans overpowered Stanford so much, that they compiled 413 yards of offense by the end of the first half, while allowing only 91.[6]

**(A) Oct. 18—Notre Dame—45–14**
USC#5

With a sold-out crowd of 80,795 packed into Notre Dame Stadium for the 75th edition of the "Glamour Game," the Trojans came out and dominated the Irish for the second straight year. After a close first quarter that saw the teams combine for 35 points, USC shut Notre Dame out the rest of the way. The Trojans added 24 more points to the 21 they scored in the first quarter. This allowed them the opportunity to record the most points scored on the Irish in their stadium since 1960. It also tied for the greatest margin of victory against Notre Dame.

The Trojans opened the scoring in the first few minutes of the opening quarter on an 18-yard pass from Matt Leinart to Keary Colbert. Ryan Killeen kicked the first of six extra points to give USC a lead they would never lose. Notre Dame answered USC's challenge on a 22-yard scoring jaunt from Julius Jones, and D.J. Fitzpatrick tied it up at 7–7 with the conversion kick. Reggie Bush quickly gave the Trojans the lead back on USC's next possession. On the fourth play of the drive, Bush exploded into the Irish defense, and 58 yards later, was in the end zone to make the score 14–7. Freshman quarterback Brady Quinn then threw a two-yard touchdown pass to tight end Anthony Fasano, and Fitzpatrick's extra point got Notre Dame back on even ground at 14–14. The wild first quarter scoring fest ended with Mike Williams on the receiving end of a seven-yard scoring strike from Leinart, to give the Trojans a 21–14 lead. That touchdown also sparked a 31-point scoring barrage for USC. After the incredible scoring spree in the first quarter, the lone points of the second stanza came when Hershel Dennis caught a three-yard pass from Leinart to give the Trojans a 28–14 halftime advantage.

In the third quarter, Leinart tossed his fourth touchdown

pass of the game, this time to tight end Gregg Guenther from seven yards out. Killeen kicked a 29-yard field goal, and USC was in total control of the game with a 38–14 lead going in to the fourth quarter. Dennis finished off the 31-point assault on Notre Dame with a two-yard run.

Leinart threw for 351 yards and four touchdowns, which tied him for the most six-pointers against Notre Dame in a single game. Mike Williams caught a game-high nine passes for 112 yards, and Keary Colbert hauled in eight for 120 yards. Reggie Bush led the ground attack with 89 yards on six carries, and linebacker Melvin Simmons led the team with 13 tackles.[7]

**(A) Oct. 25—Washington—43–23**
USC#5

Matt Leinart threw for 351 yards and four touchdowns to assist the Trojans in front of a sold-out crowd of 72,015 in Seattle, Washington. This marked the first time USC won in Seattle in ten years, and their 43 points were the third highest total in the history of the series with the Huskies. Reggie Bush caught five passes for 132 yards and two touchdowns, while Hershel Dennis led the game with 98 rushing yards on 14 carries.[8]

**(H) Nov. 1—Washington State—43–16**
USC#3

The crowd of 82,478 was the most to ever attend a USC–Washington State clash, and they were treated to a convincing Trojan victory on homecoming weekend. This win ended the Cougars' six-game winning streak, and put the Trojans into a tie for the top spot in the Pac-10 race. LenDale White ran for 149 yards on 12 carries and one touchdown to lead the offense. The defense produced a yeoman's effort by holding Washington State to 17 points below their average. They had four turnovers, which produced 26 points, recorded five sacks, and held the Cougars to minus 25 yards on the ground, which set a new school record.[9]

**(A) Nov. 15—Arizona—45–0**
USC#2

This marked the first time in 146 games that Arizona was shut out, all thanks to a magnificent, well-balanced team effort by the Trojans. Matt Leinart threw for 296 yards and four touchdowns. Mike Williams caught 11 passes for 157 yards, and tied a school record with three touchdown receptions. LenDale White led the ground forces with 90 yards on 15 carries and a pair of touchdowns. The Trojans were able to build a 35–0 halftime advantage, and they produced a season-best of 587 total offensive yards. The defense turned in another stellar performance by limiting the Wildcats to 195 yards of offense, and only 50 on running plays.[10]

**(H) Nov. 22—UCLA—47–22**
USC#2

With the largest crowd in ten years witnessing the "Battle of Los Angeles," the Trojans treated their faithful among the 93,172 in attendance to another high-powered scoring fest. This fifth straight victory of their neighborhood rivals saw USC light up the scoreboard on offense, defense, and special teams. This convincing win also allowed the Trojans to record the second time that they beat UCLA and Notre Dame consecutively in the same season since 1978 and 1979.

USC jumped out to a 14–0 first quarter lead and were never threatened. In the early stages of the opening quarter, Mike Williams was on the receiving end of a 21-yard Matt Leinart pass, and Ryan Killeen kicked the extra point. On USC's next series, LenDale White ran the ball into the end zone from one yard out, and Killeen added another extra point to his career total.

The Trojans then added another 19 points in the second quarter to give them a 33–2 halftime lead. Scoring for USC in the second quarter were Williams (four-yard pass from Leinart), two Killeen field goals (38 and 32 yards plus one extra point kick), and defensive end Kenechi Udeze on a fumble recovery in the end zone. The Bruins received their only points of the first half when cornerback Matt Clark blocked Killeen's extra point attempt following Udeze's touchdown. Clark then returned his block for a safety.

The USC defense scored their second touchdown in the third quarter when defensive tackle Mike Patterson scooped up a fumble and returned it 52 yards. The two fumble recoveries for touchdowns set a team record and tied an NCAA mark. Following Killeen's extra point, the Trojans were up, 40–2. UCLA quarterback Drew Olson threw a 17-yard touchdown pass to tight end Marcedes Lewis toward the end of the third quarter before Reggie Bush got the points back on a 96-yard kickoff return. After Killeen's extra point, the Trojans were up, 47–9, going into the fourth quarter.

Following Bush's kickoff return, UCLA's Maurice Drew did the same thing, taking the ensuing kick 99 yards. The two-point conversion failed, and then Olson threw to Joe Cowan for the final touchdown of the day. This victory gave the Trojans a share of the Pac-10 championship after Washington State lost to Washington. The win also secured USC a Rose Bowl berth. Leinart threw for 289 yards, and Mike Williams caught 11 passes for 181 yards to lead the Trojans.[11]

**(H) Dec. 6—Oregon State—52–28**
USC#2

Matt Leinart tied a school record with five touchdown passes, finishing the game with 278 yards on 22 of 38 attempts. Mike Williams and Reggie Bush each caught two of Leinart's scoring strikes, and Steve Smith hauled in the other one. Cornerback Will Poole had a good day with two interceptions, one of which he returned for a touchdown. The Trojans clinched outright possession of the Pac-10 championship, and set team and conference records on two occasions by scoring 40 or more points for seven straight games, and getting 39 of their touchdowns through passing. They also set the Pac-10 season average of 77,804 for home game attendance.[12]

**Rose Bowl, (N) Jan. 1—Michigan—28–14**
USC#1 MICH#4

What was once old is new again, as the Trojans were back in the Rose Bowl against a common New Years Day foe, the Michigan Wolverines. Back in the 1979 Rose Bowl, the Trojans claimed a national championship after defeating Michigan. A quarter of a century came and went while USC sought another coveted piece of national championship hardware. Finally, on January 4, 2004, they were perched at the doorstep of another national crown, with the Wolverines being the last roadblock on their path to the summit of the college football world.

With 93,849 in the stands, the Trojans took it to Michigan

early, leaving nothing to chance. They built a 21–0 lead by the third quarter, and the final result was never in doubt. Defensive tackle Shaun Cody got the momentum going in USC's direction early in the first quarter when he blocked a field goal attempt. The USC offense then took quick advantage of Cody's effort, and four plays into their first possession of the game, they were up, 7–0. Keary Colbert was on the receiving end of a Matt Leinart pass that covered 25 yards. Colbert made a great catch over his shoulder, and Ryan Killeen converted on the first of four extra point kicks in the game. With time running out in the first half, linebacker Lofa Tatupu intercepted a pass and returned 26 yards before being stopped just shy of the goal line. Leinart then threw to LenDale White for a six-yard touchdown to give the Trojans a 14–0 lead going into the second half.

Keary Colbert made another incredible reception on USC's first drive of the second half, this time coming from 47 yards out, and the Trojans were in control, 21–0. The Wolverines finally got on track on their next offensive possession. They ate up eight minutes of the clock, and capped the time-consuming drive off with John Navarre throwing to his tight end Tim Massaquoi from the USC five-yard line. Garrett Rivas added the extra point, and the Wolverines cut their deficit to 21–7.

After throwing for three touchdowns, Matt Leinart decided to see what it was like to catch one. On a trick play, Leinart hauled in a 15-yard scoring strike from receiver Mike Williams, who took the ball on a reverse. Michigan cut the USC lead in half early in the fourth quarter on a two-yard run by Chris Perry and a conversion kick from Rivas. With the score at 28–14, the Wolverines had a chance at a comeback, but were only able to control the ball for four minutes the rest of the way.

Matt Leinart threw for 327 yards on 23 out of 34 attempts, and was selected as the Rose Bowl MVP. Keary Colbert caught six passes for 149 yards to lead the Trojans in that category. With this, their 21st Rose Bowl win, the Trojans locked up the Associated Press national championship, and gave them their first 12-win season since the last time they laid claim to a national title in 1978.[13]

### TEAM LEADERS

RUSHING: LenDale White—754 yards on 141 carries
PASSING: Matt Leinart—255 out of 402 attempts for 3,556 yards and 38 touchdowns
RECEIVING: Mike Williams—95 catches for 1,314 yards and 16 touchdowns
SCORING: Ryan Killeen—122 points on 65 extra points and 19 field goals
KICKOFF RETURNS: Reggie Bush—18 for 492 yards and 1 touchdown (27.3 avg.)
PUNT RETURNS: Greig Carlson—21 for 188 yards (9.0 avg.)
PUNTING: Tom Malone—42 for 2,060 yards (49.0 avg.)
INTERCEPTIONS: Will Poole—7 for 70 yards and 1 touchdown
TACKLES: Lofa Tatupu—98
SACKS: Kenechi Udeze—16.5

## *2004*

HEAD COACH: Pete Carroll
ASSISTANT COACHES: Greg Burns, Chris Carlisle, Brennan Carroll, Norm Chow, Tim Davis, Lane Kiffin, Todd McNair, Ken Norton, Ed Orgeron, Rocky Seto, Carl Smith
TEAM CAPTAINS: Shaun Cody, Matt Grootegoed, Matt Leinart
RECORD: 13–0 overall (8–0 in Pacific-10 Conference)
(Ranked 1st for best record in college football out of 120 teams)
FINISH IN CONFERENCE: 1st place
FINISH IN NATIONAL POLLS: 1st place in both the AP and *USA Today*
2004 National Champions
POINTS SCORED PER GAME: 38.2 to rank 6th out of 120 teams
POINTS ALLOWED PER GAME: 13.0 to rank 3rd

### Schedule and Highlights

**(N) Aug. 28—Virginia Tech—24–13**
USC#1

The Trojans set out to prove they rightfully ranked as the top team in the country with 91,665 in attendance at FedEx Field in Landover, Maryland, for the Black Coaches Association Football Classic.

However, Virginia Tech hung tough in this first-ever matchup between these two teams, taking a 10–7 lead into the locker room at the end of the first half. The Trojans then clamped down and only allowed three points by Virginia Tech in the second half, while adding 17 to come out on top. Reggie Bush was the offensive star for USC. He caught five passes for 127 yards, and tied a school record with three receiving touchdowns. In all, Bush had 258 all-purpose yards.[1]

**(H) Sept. 11—Colorado State—49–0**
USC#1

The Trojans opened their home schedule with 85,521 on hand at the Coliseum. This was the first time the Trojans came into a home opener ranked as the top team in the country since 1981, and it was also the first matchup between these teams. Another milestone achieved by USC was their first shutout victory in a home opener since 1973, and the first time Colorado State did not score in 85 games.

It was LenDale White's day to shine in the Land of Troy, as the powerful running back gained 123 yards on 14 carries and scored three rushing touchdowns. Reggie Bush added 84 yards on 12 carries and scored a touchdown. Matt Leinart threw for 231 yards and a pair of six-pointers. On the day when the Trojans unveiled their 2003 national championship banner, they amassed 553 yards of total offense, with 322 of them coming on the ground. Five of USC's scores were thanks to the defense creating six turnovers.[2]

**(A) Sept. 18—Brigham Young University—42–10**
USC#1

The Trojan juggernaut rolled into Provo, Utah, and steamrolled the Brigham Young Cougars. For the second straight game, USC gained over 500 yards of total offense. Helping the offense gain 514 yards were the "Thunder and Lighting" tandem of Reggie Bush and LenDale White. Bush topped the century mark on the ground for the first time in his USC career with 124 yards on 14 carries and one touchdown. White powered his way to 110 yards on 17 carries and one touchdown to give the Trojans their first double 100-yard rushing performance since 1996. This was the second straight game in which White gained over 100 yards. When the team was not tearing up the turf with their stellar running game, Matt Leinart balanced the offensive attack by throwing for 236 yards and two touchdowns.[3]

**(A) Sept. 25—Stanford—31–28**
USC#1

The Trojans opened their conference schedule against long-time rival Stanford. Ryan Killeen got USC on the board first with a 23-yard field goal, and Matt Leinart connected with Steve Smith from two yards out to give the Trojans a 10–0 first quarter lead. Stanford had the reputation for spoiling some of USC's seasons, and looked to add to that part of their history by scoring on four straight possessions to take a 28–17 lead at the end of the first half.

The Trojan defense then clamped down, shutting Stanford out in the second half. The offense then did their part by gaining 224 of their 383 yards of total offense in the second half. Matt Leinart, who completed 23 of 30 pass attempts for 284 yards and one touchdown, used his legs to score on a one-yard run to close the Stanford advantage to 28–24 going into the fourth quarter. Reggie Bush then ignited USC in a drive for the winning points with a 33-yard punt return that led to LenDale White scoring from two yards out with just over six minutes remaining in the game. For the game, Bush had 240 all-purpose yards with a team-high 95 yards rushing, and Steve Smith led all receivers with seven receptions for 129 yards.[4]

**(H) Oct. 9—California—23–17**
USC#1 CAL#7

Another rival from Northern California was up next for USC on ESPN's first-ever visit to the LA Coliseum with its "College Game Day" pre-game show. With 90,008 looking on inside the Coliseum, the Trojans never trailed, but they needed a late goal line stand to hold off the Golden Bears, who were the last team to beat USC in their 26 previous games dating back to October 12, 2002, against Cal. Despite the win, Cal dominated in total offense by a 424 to 205-yard margin, and quarterback Aaron Rodgers tied an NCAA single-game record with 23 straight pass completions, and set the NCAA mark of 26 straight with work from his previous game. However, when Cal needed it most, Rodgers could not maneuver against the Trojan defense down the stretch. After taking Cal down to the USC nine with 1:47 left in the fourth quarter, Rodgers was sacked by defensive tackle Manuel Wright, and then threw three straight incompletions to clinch the victory for USC. This marked the first time since 1968 that both USC and Cal were ranked coming into their matchup.[5]

**(H) Oct. 16—Arizona State—45–7**
USC#1 ASU#15

This game was highlighted by the 50 millionth fan, Jim Farrell of Long Beach, to pass through the turnstiles to see a USC football game, home or away. Farrell and the rest of the 90,211 on hand at the Coliseum were treated to a great offensive display that saw USC roll up 446 yards of total offense, and Dwayne Jarrett tie a school record with 3 touchdown receptions. Jarrett led the Trojans with five receptions for 139 yards, and Matt Leinart passed for 224 yards on 13 of 24 attempts and four touchdowns.[6]

**(H) Oct. 23—Washington—38–0**
USC#1

The Trojans once again had a great showing on both sides of the ball. The defense allowed a mere 165 yards, including minus nine rushing, and ended Washington's national-best active streak of consecutive games without being shut out at 271. The Trojans rolled to 453 yards of total offense in their largest margin of victory over Washington since 1954, and their first shutout of them since 1965. The defense allowed only 63 yards through the air and six first downs. LenDale White ran for a game-high 94 yards on 17 carries and two touchdowns, while Matt Leinart completed 24 of 43 pass attempts for 217 yards and two touchdowns in three quarters of work.[7]

**(A) Oct. 30—Washington State—42–12**
USC#1

With temperatures hovering in the 30's, and wet conditions engulfing the field, the Trojans supplied the heat with a talented running tandem and a gifted quarterback. In their first time going into Martin Stadium in Pullman, Washington, as the number one ranked team, USC got two-touchdown performances from Reggie Bush, LenDale White, and Matt Leinart. Bush and White scoring with their running talents, while Leinart went airborne for his. White had a game-high 77 yards rushing on 16 carries, and Leinart connected on 23 out of 28 pass attempts for 235 yards. The Trojans amassed 289 yards of offense in the first half to take a 35–0 lead.[8]

**(A) Nov. 6—Oregon State—28–20**
USC#1

On a foggy and cold night in Corvallis, Oregon, the Trojans overcame a 13–0 second quarter deficit by scoring 28 straight points. This was the first time since 1937 that USC played with fog hovering around the field. Tight end Dominique Byrd led the team in receptions with seven for 85 yards, and scored two touchdowns. Matt Leinart threw for 205 yards and two touchdown passes to Byrd, and LenDale White ran for a game-high 116 yards on 25 carries and a touchdown. Reggie Bush did his part by rushing for 88 yards, and scored on a 65-yard punt return. The offensive attack was very balanced, as the Trojans ran for 210 yards and passed for 205. The defense came through with great performance against the run, limiting the Beavers to 34 yards on the ground.[9]

**(H) Nov. 13—Arizona—49–9**
USC#1

In USC's final game before back-to-back rivalry games with Notre Dame and UCLA, the Trojans set a Pac-10 record with their 15th consecutive conference home victory on homecoming weekend. After spotting Arizona a 3–0 lead at the end of the opening quarter, the Trojans exploded for 49 points over the course of the following three quarters to secure a third straight Pac-10 title. Helping USC compile a season-high of 585 yards of offense, LenDale White ran for 119 yards on 16 carries and three touchdowns, Matt Leinart threw for 280 yards and three touchdowns, and Dwayne Jarrett, who caught two of Leinart's scoring strikes, led the game with six receptions for 144 yards.[10]

**(H) Nov. 27—Notre Dame—41–10**
USC#1

Matt Leinart was on his way to becoming USC's sixth Heisman Trophy winner when he took the field against Notre Dame in front of 92,611 at the LA Coliseum. When he left the field following the game, he had all but sealed up the chance of bringing another Heisman back to USC. He completed 24 of 34 pass attempts for 400 yards and five touchdowns. His five scoring strikes tied a USC single-game record, and also equaled the most ever thrown against Notre Dame by any opponent. The top-ranked Trojans also dominated the Irish for the third straight year by 31 or more points.

USC began the quest of winning their 21st straight home game amid cold and wet weather conditions. The Irish looked to be competitive, giving USC a tough go of it into the second quarter. They scored first on a one-yard pass from Brady Quinn to Billy Palmer, and added a 28-yard field goal from D.J. Fitzpatrick to take a 10–3 advantage. USC's lone points up to this stage of the game came on a 39-yard field goal from Ryan Killeen in the first quarter.

The Trojans then exploded for 38 straight points. The offensive barrage began with a 12-yard pass from Leinart to Dwayne Jarrett, and Killeen's extra point tied the game at 10–10. The Leinart and Jarrett combination scored again before the end of the first half, this time on a 57-yard pass and catch to make it 17–10 going into the third quarter. For the game, Jarrett led all receivers with six receptions for 102 yards.

USC put the game out of reach when they scored on their first four series of the second half. Killeen started it off with a 42-yard field goal, and then Reggie Bush caught a 69-yard touchdown pass from Leinart to end the third quarter with USC on top, 27–10. Leinart added his fourth and fifth touchdown tosses in the final quarter. Steve Smith hauled one in from 35 yards out, and Jason Mitchell entered the scoring column with a 23-yarder.[11]

**(A) Dec. 4—UCLA—29–24**

USC#1

After three straight convincing losses to USC, the Bruins made things a bit more interesting in this 75th anniversary matchup of these cross-town rivals. The deciding factor for the Trojans was kicker Ryan Killeen, who set a school record with five field goals. Also playing a major role in this five-point victory was Reggie Bush, who ran for 204 yards, and two long scoring jaunts, on 15 carries. Counting his yards gained on kick returns and receiving, Bush compiled a career-high of 335 all-purpose yards. Matt Leinart chipped in with a solid showing by completing 24 of 34 pass attempts for 242 yards.

The Trojans got out to a 10–0 first quarter advantage on a 65-yard run by Bush, and a 37-yard field goal by Killeen. The Bruins cut the deficit to three points when Craig Bragg scored on a UCLA-record setting punt return of 96 yards. The Bruins looked to tie the game a short time later, but missed on a field goal attempt. Two plays later, Bush scored on an 81-yard run to give USC a 17–7 lead. The rest of the first half belonged to the kickers, as UCLA's Justin Medlock connected on a 43-yard field goal, and Killeen connected on a 42-yarder in the closing seconds of the half to give USC a 20–10 advantage. Up to this point, USC was overwhelming the Bruins with 268 yards of offensive production compared to UCLA's 72.

With the third quarter at the halfway mark, Killeen kicked a 34-yard field goal. The Bruins responded with a nine-yard touchdown run from Manuel White that narrowed the gap to 23–17 at the start of the fourth quarter. Killeen then extended USC's lead to 29–17 with field goals from 36 and 34 yards. The Bruins made it close at the end on a Drew Olson four-yard pass to Marcedes Lewis.

The Trojans piled up 477 yards, and clinched the Pac-10 championship plus the right to play in the BCS Championship Game. This was USC's sixth straight win over UCLA, which was their longest in the series, allowed them to sweep both UCLA and Notre Dame in the same season for the third straight time to establish a school record, and to post their first 12–0 record since 1972.[12]

**Orange Bowl, (N) Jan. 4—Oklahoma—55–19**

USC#1 OK#2

The Trojans made the most out of their first experience in a BCS Championship Game. With Pro Player Stadium in Miami, Florida, serving as the venue for this championship game, USC equaled their school record for most points scored in a bowl game. The Oklahoma Sooners never had a chance in this game, as the Trojan juggernaut, led by quarterback Matt Leinart, proved to be too much for any team to handle. This game also marked the first time that a pair of Heisman Trophy winners played against each other. Jason White was the winner of the 2003 award, and Leinart the heir apparent in 2004.

It looked like Oklahoma was ready to give the powerful Trojans a run for the title in the early going. They traveled 92 yards halfway through the first quarter to score the game's initial points. The honor of capping the drive went to Travis Wilson, who caught a five-yard pass from Jason White, and Garrett Hartley added the extra point, to give the Sooners a 7–0 lead.

That proved to be the last time Oklahoma embraced the lead in this game, as USC rolled to a 38–10 halftime advantage, and all but sealed up the national championship. Matt Leinart tied a USC record with five touchdown passes, and began on his quest at the record books with a 33-yard toss to tight end Dominique Byrd. Ryan Killeen added the first of his seven extra points to tie the game at 7–7. Killeen also got into the USC record book during this game for compiling a single-season scoring amount of 329 points. The Trojans were set up to take the lead for good in this game when safety Josh Pinkard recovered a mishandled Oklahoma punt return. On the following play, LenDale White ran for a six-yard touchdown, and Killeen's conversion gave USC a 14–7 lead at the end of the first quarter.

Over the course of the next 15 minutes of play, the Sooners did not know what hit them. Dwayne Jarrett started a 28-point second quarter point barrage off with a 54-yard touchdown reception from Leinart following a Jason Leach interception. An Eric Wright interception on Oklahoma's next possession was turned into another USC six-pointer three plays later. This time, Leinart connected with Steve Smith from five yards out. A Garrett Hartley 29-yard field goal gave Oklahoma three points in the quarter before USC added two more touchdowns. The Leinart-Smith combination struck again, this time on a 33-yard scoring strike, and Killeen kicked a 44-yard field goal to bring the first half point production to a climax.

The USC offensive attack continued to pour it on at the beginning of the second half. On their first two possessions, they scored 10 more points to push their lead to 48–10 going into the fourth quarter. Leinart teamed up with Smith one final time on a four-yard pass, and Killeen kicked a 42-yard field goal. The

Trojans received their final points of the romp on an eight-yard run by LenDale White. That final six-pointer was set up when linebacker Matt Grootegoed intercepted a pass early in the fourth quarter. Five plays later, White was in the end zone. The Sooners added a safety and a Jason White-to-Travis Wilson pass from eight yards out to complete the scoring.

Matt Leinart followed up his Heisman Trophy presentation from one month earlier by having a great game. He completed 18 of 35 pass attempts for 332 yards. His five touchdown passes tied a school record, and he was selected as the BCS Championship Game MVP. Steve Smith caught seven passes for 113 yards, and tied a school record with three touchdown receptions in a single game. Dwayne Jarrett hauled in five passes for 115 yards, and LenDale White led all ball carriers with 118 rushing yards on 15 attempts.[13]

### Team Leaders

Rushing: LenDale White—1,103 yards on 203 carries
Passing: Matt Leinart—269 out of 412 attempts for 3,322 yards and 33 touchdowns
Receiving: Dwayne Jarrett—55 catches for 849 yards and 13 touchdowns
Scoring: Ryan Killeen—112 points on 64 extra points and 16 field goals
Kickoff Returns: Reggie Bush—21 for 537 yards (25.6 avg.)
Punt Returns: Reggie Bush—24 for 376 yards and 2 touchdowns (15.7 avg.)
Punting: Tom Malone—49 for 2,144 yards (43.8 avg.)
Interceptions: Matt Grootegoed—5 for 107 yards
Tackles: Lofa Tatupu—104
sacks: Shaun Cody—10

## *2005*

Head Coach: Pete Carroll
Assistant Coaches: Greg Burns, Chris Carlisle, Brennan Carroll, Jethro Franklin, Lane Kiffin, Todd McNair, Ken Norton, Yogi Roth, Pat Ruel, Steve Sarkisian, Rocky Seto
Team Captains: Darnell Bing, Reggie Bush, Matt Leinart, Dallas Sartz
Record: 12–1 overall (8–0 in Pacific-10 Conference)
(Ranked 2nd best record in college football out of 119 teams)
Finish in Conference: 1st place
Finish in National Polls: 2nd place in both the AP and *USA Today*
Points Scored Per Game: 49.1 to rank 2nd out of 119 teams.
Points Allowed Per Game: 22.8 to rank 35th

### Schedule and Highlights

**(A) Sept. 3—Hawaii—63–17**
USC#1

The Trojans began their attempts at claiming a third straight national title in a very convincing manner. With a sold out crowd of 50,000 in Aloha Stadium on a beautiful Hawaiian day, USC ran their record to 6–0 against Hawaii, and scored 60 or more points against them for the third straight time. This was the largest amount of points USC scored in an opening game since 1929 against UCLA. Matt Leinart passed for 332 yards, Reggie Bush had 158 all-purpose yards, Dwayne Jarrett tied a school record with three touchdown receptions, Mario Danelo tied a school record with nine extra points, and the Trojans amassed 518 yards of total offense.[1]

**(H) Sept. 17—Arkansas—70–17**
USC#1

The Trojans continued to roll with a home opener crowd of 90,411 jammed into the Coliseum, and school records fell by the plenty. The Trojans scored the most points in the history of their home openers, the most points since 1970 against Washington State, and the most points in the Coliseum since 1930 over Cal. Mario Danelo set a school record with 10 extra point kicks, and the team's 188 points scored in three consecutive games, going back to 2005 Orange Bowl, set a team record for most points scored in three straight games. The Trojans also set records for Arkansas, but not in a positive way. Their 736 yards of total offense was the most allowed by Arkansas since 1918. Reggie Bush ran for 125 yards on eight carries and two touchdowns, LenDale White added a pair of six-pointers, and Matt Leinart passed for 381 yards in a game that saw the Trojans score on their first six possessions.[2]

**(A) Sept. 24—Oregon—45–13**
USC#1 ORE#24

The most prolific offensive machine of the decade continued to pound the opposition. After trailing 13–0 late in first half, USC ran off 45 straight points. This gave them 233 points in four straight games, which set a team record for most points scored in that amount of games. Reggie Bush compiled 267 all-purpose yards and two touchdowns, including 122 rushing yards on 20 carries. LenDale White ran for 111 yards on 15 carries and two touchdowns, Matt Leinart passed for 315 yards and three touchdowns, and Dwayne Jarrett had eight receptions for 94 yards and a pair of six-pointers. In all, the Trojans rolled up 593 yards, with 278 come on the ground against a defense that was allowing only 81 yards rushing per game up to this time.[3]

**(A) Oct. 1—Arizona State—38–28**
USC#1 ASU#14

For the second straight week, the Trojans found themselves down at the half, this time by a convincing 21–3 margin. The high-powered USC offensive machine did not seem too alarmed, as they outscored the Sun Devils in the second half 35–7. They produced 409 of their 631 total yards in the second half, and gained 373 rushing yards throughout the game, which was the most since they ran for 491 against Utah State in 1989. The tailback tandem of Reggie Bush and LenDale White continued to make headlines. White ran for 197 yards on 19 carries and one touchdown, while Bush rang up 158 yards on 17 carries and two touchdowns.[4]

**(H) Oct. 8—Arizona—42–21**
USC#1

The Trojans once again had a close score at the end of the first half, as they led, 14–7. It was then business as usual for the Cardinal & Gold. They entertained the 90,221 inside the Coliseum by scoring 28 points in the second half to win easily at the end. LenDale White powered the ground attack with 179 yards on 24 carries, and scored four touchdowns, tying a school record for most rushing touchdowns in a single game. Reggie Bush added 110 yards on 14 carries, to give the Trojans a new school record for their third straight game with two runners topping the century mark. Matt Leinart threw for 360 yards and a pair of touchdowns to Dwayne Jarrett, who led the receiving corps with nine catches for 116 yards. Steve Smith caught seven passes for 135 yards, and it was great way to complete USC's Festival 125 that was a celebration of the university's 125th anniversary.[5]

**(A) Oct. 15—Notre Dame—34–31**
USC#1 ND#9

Notre Dame looked to add some luck of the Irish in this edition of "the Glamour Game" by wearing green jerseys. Coming into this annual clash, Notre Dame had lost four straight to USC when the Trojans were the top-ranked team in the nation. It appeared that the green jerseys were working their magic by the end of the first half, as the Irish were up, 21–14. The game was knotted at 21 going into the fourth quarter, and four lead changes occurred in the final 15 minutes, until what went down in history as "the Bush Push" clinched the victory for USC.

This exciting matchup began with Reggie Bush scoring on a 36-yard run halfway through the first quarter. Mario Danelo added the extra point to give USC a 7–0 lead. The Irish came right back to tie on a Travis Thomas 16-yard run and D.J. Fitzpatrick's extra point. LenDale White gave the Trojans the lead back near the end of the first quarter on a three-yard run. Danelo's extra point kick took USC into the second quarter up by a 14–7 count. The Irish then held the powerful Trojans scoreless in the second quarter while they added 14 points on a 32-yard pass from Brady Quinn to Jeff Smardzija and a 60-yard punt return from Tom Zbikowski. Fitzpatrick converted on both extra point kicks to give Notre Dame a seven-point advantage going in to the second half.

Bush ran for a 45-yard touchdown two plays after he returned a punt 20 yards, and Danelo added a conversion kick, to produce the only points of the third quarter. The Irish were able to get into USC territory following Bush's score, but Darnell Bing knocked the ball out of tight end Anthony Fasano's grasp and Keith Rivers recovered the fumble at the USC 27 to end the threat.

Notre Dame did break the tie early in the fourth quarter on a 32-yard field goal by Fitzpatrick, to give the Irish a 24–21 lead. With the clock down to five minutes left on it, Bush capped off an 80-yard drive with a nine-yard run, and Danelo's extra point made it 28–24, in favor of the Trojans. On Notre Dame's next possession, Quinn directed a drive that consisted of him connecting on four passes for 53 yards, and Darius Walker picked up 29 yards on a run. Quinn then finished the drive off with a five-yard run, followed by Fitzpatrick's extra point, and the Irish were up, 31–28, with slightly over two minutes left in regulation.

The Trojans got to the Notre Dame two-yard line after a daring call got them into Notre Dame territory. Facing a fourth-and nine from the USC 26, Leinart called an audible that resulted in a 61-yard reception by Dwayne Jarrett. Four plays later, the Trojans were knocking on the door of the end zone at the two. Matt Leinart then ran toward the sideline, and linebacker Corey Mays caused Leinart to fumble the ball out of bounds with seven seconds remaining at the one. Even though the time was stopped on the field, the stadium timekeeper allowed time to run off the scoreboard, causing the Notre Dame faithful to run out onto the field in triumphant celebration. However, the joy was short-lived, as seven seconds were tacked back on the clock. After the field was cleared, the Trojans looked to turn Notre Dame's joy into that of despair. On second-and-goal from the one, Pete Carroll signaled to Leinart to spike the ball to stop the clock, but it was a fake attempt to throw the Irish off. Instead, Carroll had wanted Leinart to go for six points and the win. Leinart carried the ball, but was met by a hoard of defenders. Bush then helped his quarterback by pushing him into the end zone for the winning touchdown. The thrust gave Leinart more momentum, which allowed him to cross the goal line with three seconds left to complete the 75-yard drive, and gave this illustrious series another chapter with "the Bush Push." Danelo's extra point attempt was missed, but the Trojans did not need it, as their number one ranking and quest for another perfect season remained intact. The Trojans also set a school record with their 13th straight road win.

Bush finished the game with 160 yards rushing on 15 carries and three touchdowns, Leinart completed 17 of 32 pass attempts for 301 yards, and Jarrett hauled in four receptions for 101 yards, to lead the Trojans.[6]

**(A) Oct. 22—Washington**
USC#1

As what was becoming the norm to Trojan faithful, the Cardinal & Gold rolled again, this time dismantling Washington up in the Great Northwest. They scored on their first four possessions, and the game was virtually over by the end of the first half. Matt Leinart completed 20 of 26 pass attempts for 201 yards and four touchdowns while only playing for three quarters. Leinart hit a milestone in this game by becoming the Pac-10's all-time career leader in touchdown passes. When his USC career was complete, Leinart's all-time total grew to 87. Dwayne Jarrett caught three of Leinart's scoring strikes to tie a school record for most in one game. The Trojans gained 390 yards of total offense, and the defense posted five sacks and held Washington to only 59 rushing yards.[7]

**(H) Oct. 29—Washington State—55–13**
USC#1

This homecoming game marked several milestones. It was USC's school record 20th consecutive PAC-10 win, Pete Carroll's 50th victory as head coach of the Trojans, and the first time in the program's history that 400 yards were compiled through the air and 300 more were added on the ground. LenDale White ran for 157 yards on 20 carries and one touchdown, while Reggie Bush added 97 yards on 17 carries to help the Trojans amass 312 rushing yards. Matt Leinart threw for 364 yards and three touchdowns, and John David Booty had 69, to allow USC to crack the 400-yard barrier in that category. The end result was the most total yards (745) ever allowed by Washington State. On the defensive side, the Trojans held the Cougars to a season low of 284 total yards of offense after they were averaging 518.6 up to this game.[8]

**(H) Nov. 5—Stanford—51–21**
USC#1

Another sellout crowd of 90,212 saw the Trojans put this one away by the end of the first quarter. It was 24–0 at the end of the opening stanza, and 44–7 by halftime. The end result of

51 points was the most USC ever scored against Stanford at home, and the most points ever allowed by Stanford since 54 were run up on them in 1952. This was also a school-record fifth straight game of scoring 50-plus points a game over the course of one season. Matt Leinart threw four touchdown passes in the first half, and had 22 completions out of 28 attempts for 259 yards. Reggie Bush led the game in rushing with 113 yards on 12 carries and one touchdown, while Dwayne Jarrett led the team with eight receptions for 101 yards and one touchdown.[9]

**(A) Nov. 12—California—35–10**

USC#1

Since last losing to Cal in triple-overtime in 2003, the Trojans rolled to 31 straight victories, including 21 in a row over Pac-10 foes. This time, a trip to Northern California this time saw no need for overtime. They got out to a commanding 21–3 halftime lead, and coasted on to their 32nd consecutive win, and a record-tying 22 straight Pac-10 victories, which temporarily allowed them to share the all-time top spot in conference play with the 1947–50 California Golden Bears. LenDale White ran for three touchdowns and a game-high 90 yards on 16 carries. With his rushing total from this game, White became the first Trojan running back since Marcus Allen (1980–81), to gain 1,000 yards on the ground in two straight seasons. Reggie Bush ran for 82 yards on 17 carries, and he also topped the 1,000-yard barrier to give USC the program's first tandem to crack that amount of yardage in the same season. The Trojans also became the first team in NCAA history to produce a quarterback with over 3,000 yards passing, two runners over 1,000 yards, and a receiver that gained 1,000 yards all in the same season. Matt Leinart threw for 246 yards, and ran for a pair of six-pointers. This was the third straight year he passed for over 3,000 yards. His achievement set a school record and tied a conference record. Dwayne Jarrett went over 1,000 yards receiving for the year by catching five passes for 69 yards.[10]

**(H) Nov. 19—Fresno State—50–42**

USC#1 FRE#16

In a college football version of a Wild West shootout, the Trojans rallied from an eight-point halftime deficit to win by that margin of points thanks to a 28-point explosion in the third quarter. Reggie Bush produced one of the greatest single-game offensive showings in college football history. He set a USC record of 513 all-purpose yards, with 294 rushing yards on 23 carries and one touchdown, 68 on three receptions, 135 on kickoff returns, and 16 on punt returns. His incredible performance also set a Pac-10 record. His all-purpose yardage total was the second best in NCAA history. Fresno State's Paul Pinegar tied a record with four touchdown passes in one game, which was the most against a USC defense. Fresno State tied UCLA's record set in 1990 for the most points scored against USC in a losing effort.[11]

**(H) Dec. 3—UCLA—66–19**

USC#1 UCLA# 11

The LA Coliseum has been the site of many exciting individual performances in many athletic endeavors. On this date, it was Reggie Bush that earned his place among those who turned in a performance for the ages. He carried the ball 24 times for an incredible 260 yards rushing and a pair of touchdowns for 13 and 10 yards, respectively. This performance solidified Bush's chances of securing the Heisman Trophy. This gave Bush two 200-plus rushing days against the Bruins, which was the first time that a Trojan runner was able to achieve such a feat.

With 92,000 watching Bush's talents from the stands inside the Coliseum, the Trojans produced the most points against UCLA since their first-ever meeting in 1929. This lopsided victory allowed USC to set several records. It was their 34th straight victory, their 23rd straight PAC-10 win, 27th consecutive home win, and an NCAA record 16th win in a row over an AP Top 25 team. In addition, the Trojans also set team records by scoring 383 points against conference opponents and for scoring 50 or more points in a game seven times during the season.

Besides Bush's great game, LenDale White rushed for 154 yards on 14 carries and a pair of touchdowns (19 and eight yards). He also caught a 24-yard scoring strike from Matt Leinart, who completed 21 out of 40 pass attempts for 233 yards. In addition to his touchdown pass to White, Leinart connected on two others, with Dwayne Jarrett (eight yards) and Fred Davis (15 yards), getting the honors. Cornerback Justin Wyatt scored on a 38-yard fumble return, David Kirtman on a two-yard run, and Mario Danelo added a 35-yard field goal, to assist the Trojans in this romp over their cross-town rivals.[12]

**Rose Bowl, (N) Jan. 4—Texas—38–41**

USC#1 TEX#2

In their bid for a second straight BCS championship, and third national title overall, the Trojans faced the Texas Longhorns in their home away from home, the Rose Bowl. This cherished venue served as the site for the 2006 BCS Championship Game, and had the USC juggernaut sporting two Heisman Trophy winners in Matt Leinart and Reggie Bush. This tandem, along with all the deep talent on the USC roster, had to get past Texas' explosive offensive weapon, quarterback Vince Young, for the privilege to hoist another piece of championship hardware at the end of the game.

The Trojans started off their defense of the national championship with a four-yard touchdown run by LenDale White that was made possible when linebacker Kaluka Maiava recovered a fumble on a punt return. Mario Danelo added the extra point, and USC was on top, 7–0, at the end of the first quarter. Texas answered USC's seven points with 16 of their own in the second quarter on three straight possessions. David Pino got Texas on the board with a 46-yard field goal, followed by a 12-yard run by tailback Selvin Young, and climaxed when Ramonce Taylor ran 30 yards to paydirt. Pino missed the extra point after Young's six-pointer, but made up for after Taylor's jaunt. Danelo got three points back for the Trojans on a career-long 43-yard field goal with two seconds remaining in the second quarter to make the score 16–10 at halftime.

The second half resembled a classic Wild West shootout, as the teams combined for 53 points, which was the most ever scored in one half at the Rose Bowl. LenDale White tied the game in the early stages of the third quarter on a three-yard run, and Danelo gave the Trojans a one-point lead with the conversion kick. Vince Young brought Texas back with a 14-yard run, and Pino's extra point made it 23–17. The Trojans came right back on White's third touchdown run of the game, this one coming from 12 yards out. Danelo once again converted on the extra point attempt, and USC went into the fourth quarter clinging to a 24–23 lead.

On the first play of the fourth quarter, Pino missed on a field goal attempt, and USC went 80 yards for a touchdown, with Reggie Bush covering the final 26 on a run to the end zone. Danelo's conversion put the Trojans up, 31–23. On Texas' next possession, Pino made up for his earlier miss by nailing a 34-yard field goal to allow the Longhorns to close the gap to 31–26 with 8:46 remaining in regulation. Leinart connected with Dwayne Jarrett on a 22-yard scoring strike, and Danelo's extra point appeared to give USC a comfortable 38–26 advantage with 6:42 to go in the fourth quarter. Jarrett's touchdown reception was his 16th of the season, which tied a USC single-season record.

Vince Young then strapped the Longhorns to his back, and with his arm and legs, took Texas to their first national championship since 1970. In eight plays, Young guided Texas into the end zone, finishing the drive himself with a 17-yard run. Pino's extra point then made it a 38–33 USC advantage with 4:03 left. The Trojans could have virtually clinched the game after getting to midfield on their next possession, if only they converted on a fourth-and-two situation. After the Longhorns prevented the powerful Trojan offense from gaining a first down at midfield with 2:09 left, Vince Young worked one final touch of magic. On the 11th play of their next possession, Young scored the winning points on an eight-yard run, and then ran for a two-point conversion to bring the curtain down on USC's chance at another national title. This marked the first time in five matchups with Texas that USC went down in defeat, and the loss also ended the Trojans' 34-game winning streak.

Vince Young, who finished in second place behind Reggie Bush in the Heisman Trophy voting, took a backseat to no one in this game. He was a one-man wrecking machine that produced one of the greatest individual performances in college football history. He rushed for 200 yards on 19 carries, and three touchdowns, and also completed 30 of 40 pass attempts for 267 yards in the 20th straight win for Texas. He was an easy choice for the game's MVP.

The Trojans also had some great performance in this action-packed offensive showcase. LenDale White ran for 124 yards on 20 carries, and scored three touchdowns. Reggie Bush added 82 yards on the ground in 13 carries and one six-pointer. He also caught six passes for 95 yards. Dwayne Jarrett led all receivers with 121 yards on 10 receptions, and Matt Leinart connected on 29 out of 40 pass attempts for 365 yards and one touchdown.

At the end of the year, the explosive Trojans set a team with 4,157 passing yards. Team and Pac-10 records also were set with 87 touchdowns scored over the season, most yards running and passing combined (7,537), most first downs (376) and highest yards per game average (579.8).[13]

### TEAM LEADERS

RUSHING: Reggie Bush—1,740 yards on 200 carries
PASSING: Matt Leinart—283 out of 431 attempts for 3,815 yards and 28 touchdowns
RECEIVING: Dwayne Jarrett—91 catches for 1,274 yards and 16 touchdowns
SCORING: LenDale White—156 points on 26 touchdowns
KICKOFF RETURNS: Reggie Bush—28 for 493 yards (17.6 avg.)
PUNT RETURNS: Reggie Bush—18 for 179 yards and 1 touchdown (9.9 avg.)
PUNTING: Tom Malone—32 for 1,335 yards (41.7 avg.)
INTERCEPTIONS: Darnell Bing—4 for 119 yards and 1 touchdown
TACKLES: Oscar Lua—66
SACKS: Lawrence Jackson—10

## *2006*

HEAD COACH: Pete Carroll
ASSISTANT COACHES: Chris Carlisle, Brennan Carroll, Nick Holt, Lane Kiffin, Todd McNair, Ken Norton, Yogi Roth, Pat Ruel, Steve Sarkisian, Rocky Seto
TEAM CAPTAINS: John David Booty, Ryan Kalil, Oscar Lua, Dallas Sartz
RECORD: 11–2 overall (7–2 in Pacific-10 Conference)
(Ranked 6th best record in college football out of 119 teams)
FINISH IN CONFERENCE: Tied for 1st place with California
USC gained a Rose Bowl berth by beating California in head-to-head competition.
FINISH IN NATIONAL POLLS: 4th place in both the AP and *USA Today*
POINTS SCORED PER GAME: 30.5 to rank 18th out of 119 teams
POINTS ALLOWED PER GAME: 15.2 to rank 11th

### Schedule and Highlights

**(A) Sept. 2—Arkansas—50–14**
USC#6

The Trojans started off their new season in fine fashion with a new quarterback and a trio of freshman tailbacks. John David Booty took over as USC's signal caller when Matt Leinart's career was completed. In his debut, Booty did an excellent job by completing 24 of 35 pass attempts for 261 yards and three touchdowns. His scoring strikes went to Patrick Turner (14 yards), Fred Davis (nine yards), and Ryan Powdrell (one yard). C.J. Gable, Emmanuel Moody, and Allen Bradford, were all freshmen performing at tailback, and all gave stellar efforts. Gable ran for 51 yards and a touchdown (three-yard run), Moody led all ball carriers with 58 yards and scored on a nine-yard run, and Bradford chipped in with a one-yard scoring run. Mario Danelo added two field goals from 35 and 38 yards out to complete USC's scoring. Their 50 points were the most scored on an Arkansas team in Fayetteville since 1919.[1]

**(H) Sept. 16—Nebraska—28–10**
USC#4 NEB#19

John David Booty continued to perform well in his first year as a starting quarterback at USC. He completed 25 of 36 pass attempts for 257 yards, and connected on three touchdown passes. Dwayne Jarrett was his main target, and the star receiver hauled in 11 catches for 136 yards and two touchdowns (12 and five yards), and became USC's all-time career touchdown reception leader. Booty's other touchdown pass went to Steve Smith from three yards out. Tailback Chauncey Washington added USC's other touchdown with a seven-yard run. Emmanuel Moody made Trojan history by becoming the first true freshman to start in two straight games. He also had a game-high 70 yards rushing. On the defensive side, linebacker Rey Maualuga led the way with 11 tackles. This game ended USC's streak of scoring at least 30 points per game at 15 in a row.[2]

**(A) Sept. 23—Arizona—20-3**
USC#3

Thanks to a tough defensive effort, and an offensive attack that produced 381 yards, with 256 of them coming in the second half, the Trojans were able to keep some streaks alive. They recorded their 24th straight Pac-10 victory, 17th straight road win, and kept their NCAA record of 55 straight 20-plus point games going. The amazing thing about this era in USC football was the fact that this was the lowest point production for them in 52 games. The Wildcats made it tough for USC throughout the first half, as the Trojans clung to a slim 3–0 lead thanks, to a Mario Danelo field goal of 35 yards. In the second half, Danelo added another field goal for 33 yards and John David Booty connected with Dwayne Jarrett on a three-yard scoring strike. Emmanuel Moody, who rushed for a game-high 130 yards, added a nine-yard scoring run to his day's work.[3]

**(A) Sept. 30—Washington State—28-22**
USC#3

John David Booty had another great day in this young season, as he connected on 23 of 32 pass attempts for 269 yards and three touchdowns. Steve Smith was his primary receiver on this day, hauling in 11 receptions for 186 yards and two touchdowns (seven and 11 yards). Chris McFoy caught Booty's other touchdown toss from seven yards out. Tailback Chauncey Washington scored USC's other six-pointer on a three-yard run, and led all ball carriers with 73 yards on the ground. This game was an all-out offensive show, as Washington State rolled up 418 yards, and USC 404.[4]

**(H) Oct. 7—Washington—26-20**
USC#3

The schools from the Great Northwest had played the Trojans tough, but in the end, the men of Troy once again prevailed by six points. The Trojans used a trick play on their first possession to get things going. While lined up for a field goal attempt, backup quarterback Michael McDonald, who was the holder for the field goal, got up and tossed a 20-yard touchdown pass to Steve Smith. John David Booty and Patrick Turner teamed up from 17 yards out for USC's other six-pointer. For the game, Booty connected on 23 of 40 pass attempts for 243 yards, and Turner led USC receivers with 12 receptions for 116 yards. The game was then turned over to kicker Mario Danelo, who added a career best four field goals from 34, 25, 32, and 21 yards out, to preserve the victory. Washington gave it their best effort to upset the Trojans, and got to the USC 39-yard line before an interception on the game's final play ended their hopes. Linebacker Keith Rivers had a great game that consisted of 12 tackles and two pass deflections. Once again this was a wild offensive show, as the Trojans rang up 411 yards and Washington 379.[5]

**(H) Oct. 14—Arizona State—28-21**
USC#3

Chauncey Washington was the hero of this game, as his two-yard run with 4:29 to go provided the clinching points, and handed Arizona State their seventh straight loss to USC. Washington was the workhorse on the winning drive, carrying the ball 10 times for 64 yards. For the game, he led all ball carriers with 108 yards on 22 carries. The Trojans built a 21–0 first half lead on two John David Booty passes and a two-yard run from C.J. Gable. Allen Bradford caught a 17-yard pass to open the scoring, and Dwayne Jarrett hauled in Booty's other touchdown pass from 14 yards out. The Sun Devils then made things a little uneasy for the 91,126 Trojan fans in the Coliseum when they rallied back to tie the game late in the third quarter. This marked USC's 30th straight home win, 27th straight Pac-10 victory, and 21st consecutive Pac-10 home win. It was also the 58th straight game that USC scored at least 20 points. This marked only the second time since 1968 that USC won three straight games by a touchdown or less, and the first time since 2001 that the Trojans emerged victorious five straight times by scoring fewer than 30 games in those games.[6]

**(A) Oct. 28—Oregon State—31-33**
USC#3

It had to happen eventually, and another trip to the Great Northwest served as the setting for USC's first loss in 38 regular season games, dating back to a defeat on September 27, 2003. This snapped USC's PAC-10 record for consecutive PAC-10 wins (27) and school records for consecutive road (18) and PAC-10 road (13) wins and consecutive sellouts (12). This also marked the most points that Oregon State scored on USC since 1914.

After being hurt by four turnovers, the Trojans tried their best to rally back after being down, 33–10, in the late stages of the third quarter. Up to this time, the Trojans received their points on a Chauncey Washington two-yard run, and a 29-yard field goal by Mario Danelo. John David Booty started the USC rally by connecting with his tight end Fred Davis on a four-yard pass with 23 seconds left in the third quarter. Booty then found Steve Smith for a pair of touchdowns for 37 and two yards in the fourth quarter. After Smith's final touchdown reception cut the deficit to two, Booty tried to work his magic one final time, but a potential game-tying two-point conversion pass intended for Dwayne Jarrett with seven seconds to go was knocked down by Jeff Van Orsow to preserve the upset victory for Oregon State.[7]

**(A) Nov. 4—Stanford—42-0**
USC#9

The Trojans took out their frustration over the previous week on Stanford. In their first shutout over Stanford since 1989, and the largest margin of victory over them since 1977, John David Booty provided the spark with three second quarter touchdown tosses. On the day, Booty hit on 12 of 21 pass attempts for 203 yards, and his scoring strikes went to Dwayne Jarrett (21 yards), Steve Smith (seven yards), and Fred Davis (two yards). Jarrett led all receivers with 118 yards on five catches. Chauncey Washington, who led all ball carriers with 74 rushing yards, scored the game's opening points on a 15-yard run, Terrell Thomas returned a blocked field goal 71 yards for a score, and backup signal caller Mark Sanchez rounded out the Trojan scoring fest with a four-yard run in the fourth quarter. USC limited Stanford to only 30 yards rushing, while they rang up 355 yards of total offense. This was the eighth consecutive time that the Trojans followed up a loss with a victory, and it also allowed them to add to their NCAA record of 60 straight games of scoring at least 20 points.[8]

**(H) Nov. 11—Oregon—35–10**
USC#7 ORE#21

On their homecoming weekend, the Trojans looked to not be beaten again by a team from Oregon. With 92,000 plus in attendance, they made sure that the game was in control from the second quarter on. After a scoreless first quarter, C.J. Gable accounted for USC's first points with a two-yard run. Chauncey Washington then scored the next three touchdowns for USC on runs covering five, three, and 43 yards. Washington also led all ball carriers with 119 yards on 15 carries. Dwayne Jarrett, who led the receivers with seven catches for 91 yards, teamed up with John David Booty for a 12-yard touchdown to close out the scoring. The defense did an excellent job clamping down on a highly explosive Oregon offense that came into this game averaging 456.2 yards per game. USC limited them to 358 total yards, and only 102 on the ground. This proved to be Oregon's lowest point total since 2004, and the least amount scored against USC since 1992. Leading the way on defense was defensive end Lawrence Jackson, who had 10 tackles and three sacks. Cary Harris and Keith Rivers also chipped in with 10 tackles apiece.[9]

**(H) Nov. 18—California—23–9**
USC#4 CAL#17

After all the years of these two teams playing each other, surprisingly, this marked the first time that they ever faced each other in a night game. Regardless of the time it was played, the Trojans were ready, and John David Booty's two touchdown passes in the fourth quarter broke open a game that was knotted at 9–9 going into the fourth quarter. On the day, Booty connected on 18 of 31 pass attempts for 238 yards, and threw his touchdown strikes to Dwayne Jarrett (25 yards) and Steve Smith (37 yards) on back-to-back possessions. The Trojans received their other points on three first half field goals. Mario Danelo had two (19 and 32 yards), and David Buehler hit on 49-yarder that tied the game in the third quarter. Buehler's kick was the longest field goal since 1998. Once again the tough USC defense held a high-powered offense at bay. Cal came into this game averaging 431.3 yards per game and 34.7 points. When the Trojans were finished with them, the Golden Bears were limited to a season-low of 275 yards, and only 99 on the ground. This victory allowed the Trojans to clinch a fifth straight Pac-10 championship and make their 31st trip to the Rose Bowl. On the other side, the loss prevented Cal from clinching their first Rose Bowl appearance since 1958.[10]

**(H) Nov. 25—Notre Dame—44–24**
USC#3 ND#6

It was 80 years since the first USC–Notre Dame clash, and over the course of this classic series, many stars have emerged. This edition proved to be no different, as Dwayne Jarrett added his name to the long list of players that earned everlasting recognition from their exploits in this game. He caught seven passes for 132 yards, and tied a USC record with three touchdown receptions. He teamed up with quarterback John David Booty on the first two scores of the game, coming from nine and five yards out. He then tied the school record with a 43-yarder in the fourth quarter. The Trojans got out to quick 21–3 lead by scoring the first three times they had possession. In addition to Jarrett's two touchdowns receptions, Booty scored on a one-yard run in the second quarter. USC received their other points from Chauncey Washington (two-yard run), Mario Danelo (34-yard field goal), and Brian Cushing (42-yard kickoff return). Besides Jarrett's outstanding performance, other Trojans that chipped in with stellar outings were Booty, who completed 17 of 28 pass attempts for 265 yards, C.J. Gable, who led all ball carriers with 107 rushing yards, and linebacker Dallas Sartz, who led the team with eight tackles. This lifted the Trojans' NCAA record of 20-plus point games to 63, and this was also the first time since 1988 that both teams were ranked high in the AP polls at the same time.[11]

**(A) Dec. 2—UCLA—9–13**
USC#2

There is nothing like preventing a fierce rival from succeeding. The Trojans came into this game with a serious opportunity to secure a spot in the BCS Championship Game. The Bruins came into this game with two straight victories after dropping four consecutive games, and were 6–5 heading into this annual clash with their cross-town rivals. What then transpired over the course of sixty minutes on the field gave the Bruins one of their greatest upsets against the Trojans. In the process, this loss snapped USC's NCAA-record streak of 63 consecutive 20-point plus games, and knocked them out of BCS Championship Game contention.

With 90,622 in attendance at the Rose Bowl, the Bruins got on the board first late in the opening quarter. Quarterback Patrick Cowan scored on a one-yard run, and Justin Medlock added the extra point to give UCLA a 7–0 lead. The 12-play, 91-yard scoring drive was the longest by UCLA throughout the year, and also the longest given up by the Trojans in 2006. The Trojans came back to grab a 9–7 halftime lead. Their first points of the game occurred when the Bruins were called for holding in the end zone, which gave USC a safety. C.J. Gable then gave USC their only lead of the game on a one-yard run, followed by a Mario Danelo conversion kick. Gable led the Trojans with 52 yards rushing on 19 carries. In all, the inspired UCLA defense held the Trojan running game to 55 net rushing yards, and applied constant pressure on John David Booty. Despite the pressure, Booty managed to complete 23 of 39 pass attempts for 274 yards.

The Bruins also held the Trojans scoreless throughout the second half. UCLA did not get into the end zone in the second half, but Justin Medlock's foot was all they needed to prevail. He hit on a 22-yard field goal in the third quarter for the go-ahead points, and added a 31-yarder in the fourth quarter to finish off the scoring. The Trojans made it interesting down the stretch. They got to the UCLA 18-yard line before linebacker Eric McNeal intercepted a John David Booty pass to preserve the victory with 1:10 left on the clock. Even in defeat, the Trojans were able to clinch their 31st trip to the Rose Bowl Game on New Year's Day.[12]

**Rose Bowl, (N) Jan. 1—Michigan—32–18**
USC#8 MICH#3

A chance to play in an unprecedented third straight BCS Championship Game was thwarted one month earlier at the Rose Bowl against UCLA. The loss to the Bruins knocked USC out of contention for another national title, but they still laid claim to another PAC-10 championship. This was the third time over a one-year span that Rose Bowl Stadium served as the site for a significant game for USC. The previous January, the Trojans played there for the BCS championship after the game's planners selected the Rose Bowl for the site of the 2006 matchup between USC and Texas. The UCLA game was a regular season affair, and on January 1, 2007, the historic stadium was back to being used for what it started out as, the revered Rose Bowl Game, a New Years Day tradition for the ages.

Despite UCLA using the Rose Bowl as their home field during the regular season, the Trojans were able to call the stadium their second home, seeing that they appeared in so many Rose Bowl games. In this, their 31st trip to the Rose Bowl Game, the Trojans faced Michigan for the eighth time in this classic venue. With 93,853 in the stands, this total gave USC a record 11th sellout crowd over the course of the season.

Toward the end of first quarter, a 26-yard field goal by Mario Danelo gave USC a lead they never relinquished. On Michigan's next offensive series, they tied the game at 3–3 on a Garrett Rivas 43-yard field goal, and that was all the scoring for the first half. Neither team exhibited much offensive excitement, as USC gained 122 yards of total offense, while Michigan mustered 79. Both running attacks were almost non-existent. The Trojans tallied just 20 yards, and the Wolverines minus nine.

The second half saw the emergence of the Trojans. Defensive end Lawrence Jackson got things going in the right direction of USC early in the third quarter. He intercepted a Chad Henne pass close to midfield, and within four plays, the Trojans were on top for good. John David Booty threw a two-yard touchdown pass to Chris McFoy, and Danelo's conversion made it a 10–3 ballgame.

Michigan came into this game with the best defense against the run, so USC attacked the unit through the air, which was an area that the Wolverines were considered vulnerable. Over the course of the following 29 plays, all but two were passes, and the Trojans rolled up 22 points. With the third quarter winding down, Booty threw his second touchdown pass of the game, this time to Dwayne Jarrett from 22 yards out. Danelo missed the extra point kick, but USC was slowly pulling away with a 16–3 lead. The third quarter scoring ended with Danelo connecting on a 26-yard field goal that gave the Trojans a 19–3 advantage heading into the fourth quarter. The field goal was made possibly after quarterback Chad Henne fumbled while being sacked by linebacker Brian Cushing. Lawrence Jackson, who got USC jumpstarted with an interception early in the quarter, pounced on the loose ball to give the Trojans possession.

Michigan came back to narrow the gap to 19–11 when Henne connected on an 11-yard touchdown pass to Adrian Arrington, and that was followed by Mike Hart running for a two-point conversion. Booty then threw his third and fourth touchdown passes to put the game away. Jarrett was on the receiving end of a 62-yarder, and Steve Smith hauled in the other Booty scoring strike from seven yards out. Danelo missed on the extra point try after Jarrett's touchdown, but connected after Smith's score to make it a 32–11 USC advantage with less than seven minutes left to play. Henne made the final score closer with a 41-yard touchdown pass from Henne to Steve Breaston, and Rivas added the game's last point.

Dwayne Jarrett was named the game's Offensive MVP after catching 11 passes for 205 yards and two touchdowns. Steve Smith had seven receptions for 108 yards and a touchdown, and John David Booty threw for 391 yards on 27 completions out of 45 attempts and four touchdowns.[13]

### Team Leaders

Rushing: Chauncey Washington—744 yards on 157 carries
Passing: John David Booty—269 out of 436 attempts for 3,347 yards and 29 touchdowns
Receiving: Steve Smith—71 catches for 1,083 yards and 9 touchdowns
Scoring: Mario Danelo—89 points on 44 extra points and 15 field goals
Kickoff Returns: C.J. Gable—16 for 432 yards (27.0 avg.)
Punt Returns: Desmond Reed—20 for 109 yards (5.4 avg.)
Punting: Greg Woidneck—48 for 1,838 yards (38.3 avg.)
Interceptions: Taylor Mays—3 for 40 yards
Tackles: Keith Rivers—85
sacks: Dallas Sartz—7

## *2007*

Head Coach: Pete Carroll
Assistant Coaches: Chris Carlisle, Brennan Carroll, Nick Holt, Demetrice Martin,Todd McNair, John Morton, Ken Norton, Yogi Roth, Pat Ruel, Steve Sarkisian, Rocky Seto
Team Captains: Sam Baker, John David Booty, Lawrence Jackson, Keith Rivers
Record: 11–2 overall (7–2 in Pacific–10 Conference)
(Ranked 5th best record in college football out of 120 teams)
Finish in Conference: Tied for 1st place with Arizona State
USC gained a Rose Bowl berth by beating Arizona State in head-to-head competition.
Finish in National Polls: 3rd place in AP and 2nd place in *USA Today*
Points Scored Per Game: 32.6 to rank to rank 35th out of 120 teams
Points Allowed Per Game: 16.0 to rank 2nd

### Schedule and Highlights

**(H) Sept. 1—Idaho—38–10**
USC#1

USC honored late kicker Mario Danelo, who died on January 6, 2007 after falling off a 120-foot cliff, by lining up just 10 men, without a placekicker, for an extra point attempt following USC's first touchdown on a Stafon Johnson four-yard run. The Trojans got out to 21–0 lead early in the second quarter by scoring on their first three offensive series, and were never challenged. With this win, the Trojans were a perfect 8–0 against Idaho, and it was the first time since 1929 that these two teams played each other. John David Booty threw for 206 yards and three touchdowns, with C.J Gable (eight yards), Vidal Hazelton (one yard), and Stanley Havili (three yards), on the receiving ends. Johnson added another touchdown run from one yard out, and David Buehler kicked a 36-yard field goal to round out USC's point production.[1]

**(A) Sept. 15—Nebraska—49–31**
USC#1 NEB#14

With Stafon Johnson running for 144 yards on 11 carries and one touchdown, the Trojans gave head coach Pete Carroll a fine birthday present. This was the most points allowed at home by Nebraska since 1945. This was USC's first trip to Lincoln, Nebraska since 1969, and they were also the first top-ranked team to play at Memorial Stadium since 1978. John David Booty threw a pair of touchdown passes to Stanley Havili, who also ran for a two-yard score, and Anthony McCoy. Chauncey Washington scored two rushing touchdowns, both from one yard out, and Allen Bradford ran for a six-yard score to complete the USC point barrage.[2]

**(H) Sept. 22—Washington State—47–14**
USC#1

The Cougars made a game of it in the first quarter after tying the score at 7–7. The Trojans then exploded for 27 straight points to easily win at home in front of 86,876 Trojan faithful. John David Booty threw for 289 yards and four touchdowns in USC's 35th straight home win and 24th consecutive Pac-10 home victory, both of which helped the Trojans extend conference records. Tight end Fred Davis caught two of Booty's scoring strikes (six and 14 yards), while Allen Bradford (four yards) and Vidal Hazelton (20 yards), were on the receiving end of the other two. Stanley Havili scored on a one-yard run, Chauncey Washington on a seven-yard run, and David Buehler added two field goals (23 and 29 yards) for USC.[3]

**(A) Sept. 29—Washington—27–24**
USC#1

This was USC's first night game against Washington in Seattle, and it provided the closest finish for the Trojans up to this time in the season. The Huskies were nearly 20-point underdogs, but the Trojans had 16 penalties for 161 yards in losses, three turnovers, and suffered injuries to three starting players. However, through all their mishaps, the running tandem of Stafon Johnson and Chauncey Washington led a ground attack that gained 224 of USC's 460 total offensive yards. Johnson ran for 122 yards on 14 carries and one touchdown, while Washington added 106 yards on 21 carries and one six-pointer. John David Booty threw for 236 yards and a touchdown to Patrick Turner (23 yards), and David Buehler kicked two field goals from 22 and 33 yards out.[4]

**(H) Oct. 6—Stanford—23–24**
USC#2

The inevitable happened, and it took a 41-point underdog to end an incredible streak. Stanford came into the LA Coliseum with a 1–3 record, and with 49 seconds remaining, Tavita Pritchard threw a game-winning 10-yard pass to Mark Bradford on fourth down. Derek Belch then added the conversion kick to give Stanford a one-point victory. This loss snapped USC's 35-game home winning streak and 24-game Pac-10 home winning, both of which were conference records. The Trojans outgained Stanford 459 yards to 235, but they also had five turnovers, gave up four sacks, had eight penalties, four interceptions, and were only able to convert on seven of 19 third down attempts. John David Booty had 364 yards passing and threw a pair of touchdowns to Fred Davis (63 yards) and Ronald Johnson (47 yards). Chauncey Washington scored on a one-yard run, and David Buehler kicked a 34-yard field goal for USC.[5]

**(H) Oct. 13—Arizona—20–13**
USC#10

The Trojans fell hard in the national polls, dropping eight spots following their shocking loss a week earlier. They managed to rebound with a close win against the Wildcats. The game was tied at 10–10 at the end of the first half, and then Arizona took a 13–10 lead into the fourth quarter. The Trojans then rallied behind the performances of two underclassmen in sophomore quarterback Mark Sanchez and freshman tailback Joe McKnight. McKnight returned a punt 45 yards, and that set the Trojans up for Sanchez to connect with tight end Fred Davis on a 25-yard scoring strike that gave USC their go-aheads points. David Buehler added a 23-yard field goal with 57 seconds left for insurance. Sanchez was filling in for John David Booty, who was sidelined with a broken finger. A Chauncey Washington 18-yard run, and a 27-yard field goal by Buehler, gave the Trojans a 10–0 lead before Arizona came back to take a three-point lead.[6]

**(A) Oct. 20—Notre Dame—38–0**
USC#13

This proved to be USC's most convincing win in the 81-year history of this classic series. It was also the first time since 1933 that the Trojans shut out the Irish in South Bend, and Notre Dame's worst loss at home since 1956.

Mark Sanchez was called upon to start at quarterback in place of the injured John David Booty, and the sophomore signal caller rose to the challenge. He threw for 235 yards on 21 of 38 pass attempts and four touchdowns. Sanchez began his quest to add his name to the long list of great performances in this series by throwing a 10-yard scoring strike to tight end Fred Davis to start the scoring in the first quarter. Allen Bradford was on the receiving end of Sanchez's second touchdown toss from eight yards out in the second quarter, and David Buehler kicked a 30-yard field goal to give the Trojans a 17–0 halftime advantage.

In the third quarter, Sanchez threw his final two touchdown passes to Stanley Havili (five yards) and Vidal Hazelton (48 yards). Joe McKnight finished off the scoring in this dominant showing with a 51-yard run in the fourth quarter. The Fighting Irish dropped to 1–7 with this loss for their worst start in a season since 1960. This also marked the Trojans sixth straight victory over Notre Dame.[7]

**(A) Oct. 27—Oregon—17–24**
USC#9 ORE#5

The good news was that the highly ranked USC defense held the explosive Oregon spread offense to their lowest yardage amount of the year. The Ducks were averaging 46.6 points and 550.9 total offensive yards per game. The Trojans allowed 339, but they also had three turnovers in the second half that led to 14 Oregon points. On a cool afternoon at Autzen Stadium, with a stadium and state record crowd of 59,277 on hand, Oregon tailback Jonathan Stewart ran for a game-high 103 yards and two touchdowns. The Trojans received their points from David Buehler (30-yard field goal), and on two Mark Sanchez touchdown passes, which went to Patrick Turner (nine yards) and David Ausberry (14 yards). The win kept Oregon's national title hopes alive, while USC's were thwarted.[8]

**(H) Nov. 3—Oregon State—24–3**
USC#13

This marked USC's 750th win with the largest crowd (85,713) to ever see a USC–Oregon State game. This convincing homecoming game victory saw all the scoring done in the first half, and was USC's 21st straight win over Oregon State at the LA Coliseum going back to 1963. The Trojan defense allowed the Beavers just 50 yards of total offense by the end of the first half, and 176 for the game. John David Booty returned at quarterback after missing three games due to a broken finger. He completed 19 out of 33 pass attempts for 157 yards and a pair of touchdowns. Chauncey Washington caught one of Booty's scoring strikes from 26 yards out, and also ran for a one-yard touchdown. Patrick Turner hauled in Booty's other touchdown pass (13 yards), and David Buehler kicked a 47-yard field goal for USC.[9]

**(A) Nov. 10—California—24–17**
USC#12 CAL#24

This was USC's first night game in Berkeley, California, and they marked the historic event by bringing home a victory. It marked USC's fourth straight win over Cal, and their sixth out of seven previous games. Tailback Chauncey Washington ran for a career-high 220 yards on 29 carries and one touchdown (36 yards). John David Booty threw a five-yard touchdown pass to Stanley Havili, David Buehler kicked a 28-yard field goal, and Stafon Johnson scored what proved to be the game-winner on a three-yard run with 7:38 left on a rainy evening in Northern California.[10]

**(A) Nov. 22—Arizona State—44–24**
USC#11 ASU#7

John David Booty starred for the offense, and Lawrence Jackson excelled on the defensive side of the ball. Booty threw for 375 yards on 26 out of 39 pass attempts and four touchdowns. He also ran for a one-yard touchdown. Vidal Hazelton (four yards), Stanley Havili (five yards), Joe McKnight (seven yards), and Fred Davis (34 yards), were on the receiving end of Booty's scoring tosses, and David Buehler added three field goals for USC. Davis led the Trojans' receiving corps with five catches for 119 yards. Defensive end Lawrence Jackson had eight tackles, and tied a school record with four sacks, and set another one with his 5.5 tackles for lost yardage. This was USC's 20th appearance on Thanksgiving Day, and their first since 1938.[11]

**(H) Dec. 1—UCLA—24–7**
USC#8

The historic Trojan running game lived up to its reputation by compiling 231 yards on the ground. Joe McKnight ran for a game-high 89 yards, and ran for the opening score from five yards out. Chauncey Washington added 73 yards and USC's second touchdown on a 10-yard run to extend the Trojan advantage to 14–0 in the second quarter. David Buehler kicked a 46-yard field goal to extend USC's lead to 17–0 before the Bruins got on the in the final seven seconds of the first half. Tight end Dominique Johnson made a great one-handed leaping catch to complete a nine-yard scoring toss from Pat Cowan to make it a 17–7 score going into the second half. The third quarter remained scoreless, and then USC scored the game's final points on a 12-yard pass from John David Booty to Fred Davis, who became USC's all-time reception leader among tight ends. The Trojans' final score was set up by a Terrell Thomas interception. The Trojan defense held UCLA to only 12 rushing yards and 168 yards of total offense.[12]

**Rose Bowl, (N) Jan. 1—Illinois—49–17**
USC#6 ILL#13

Victory was never in doubt, as the Trojans scored on their opening drive, and ran up a 21–0 lead in the first half, to all but end the game after thirty minutes of action. Not including the 2005 BCS Championship Game, when the Rose Bowl was used as the site for the national title contest, this 49-point performance tied a USC record for most points scored in a Rose Bowl game. It was the largest margin of victory in the Rose Bowl since 1984, and the win gave the Trojans an NCAA record of six straight 11-win seasons.

The Trojans started the mauling of Illinois by scoring on their opening possession of the game when John David Booty threw an eight-yard pass to Chauncey Washington. David Buehler then kicked the first of seven extra points. Linebacker Rey Maualuga quickly returned possession back over to USC with an interception. On the first play after the interception, from the Illinois 34-yard line, Garrett Green, after taking a lateral, threw to Desmond Reed for a touchdown that gave USC a 14–0 lead at the end of the first quarter. Washington added his second touchdown of the game late in the second quarter on a three-yard run, and a 28-yard Jason Reda field goal with 38 seconds left in the first half got Illinois on the board to make the score 21–3 going into the third quarter.

The Illini looked to start a comeback on their first series of the second half. Rashard Mendenhall ran for a 79-yard touchdown, which was the longest run against the Trojans' defense since 2004. Reda's extra point kick narrowed the gap to 21–10, but then USC answered with four straight scoring drives to produce a commanding lead of 49–10 in the fourth quarter. USC's first six-pointer of the second half was the result of a turnover. Illinois was driving for another touchdown that could have easily swung momentum over to their side, as Jacob Willis had the ball knocked out of his hands by linebacker Kaluka Maiava on the Trojans' one-yard line. Fellow linebacker Brian Cushing jumped on the ball in the end zone, and USC was awarded a touchback. Starting from their own 20, the Trojans drove down to the Illinois two-yard line, where a Booty pass to tight end Fred Davis capped off the series.

USC once again took advantage of turnovers by adding two more touchdowns. Cornerback Cary Harris, who led the Trojans with 10 tackles throughout the game, intercepted a pass, and later the defense recovered a fumble. The results of those turnovers were touchdowns from Joe McKnight on a six-yard run and a 15-yard pass from Booty to David Ausberry. With the game nearing its end, the Trojans added their final touchdown on a three-yard run by Hershel Dennis. Illinois scored the game's final touchdown on a 56-yard pass from Eddie McGee to Arrelious Benn.

The Trojans set a new Rose Bowl record with 633 yards of total offense, and the teams rolled up a combined 1,078 yards. John David Booty was awarded the game's Offensive MVP trophy after connecting on 25 out of 37 pass attempts for 255 yards and three touchdowns. Tight end Fred Davis led all receivers with seven catches for 87 yards, and the USC ground assault was powered by Joe McKnight's 125 yards on only 10 carries. Stafon Johnson added 104 yards on nine carries, and Chauncey Washington finished with 75 yards on 12 carries. Linebacker

Rey Maualuga was honored with the Defensive MVP Award after finishing with three sacks, an interception, and causing a fumble. In a losing effort, Illinois' Rashard Mendenhall led all ball carriers with 155 yards on 17 carries, and quarterback Juice Williams threw for 245 yards.[13]

### TEAM LEADERS

RUSHING: Chauncey Washington—969 yards on 195 carries
PASSING: John David Booty—215 out of 340 attempts for 2,361 yards and 23 touchdowns
RECEIVING: Fred Davis—62 catches for 881 yards and 8 touchdowns
SCORING: David Buehler—100 points on 52 extra points and 16 field goals
KICKOFF RETURNS: Ronald Johnson—25 for 620 yards (24.8 avg.)
PUNT RETURNS: Joe McKnight—19 for 160 yards (8.4 avg.)
PUNTING: Greg Woidneck—60 for 2,274 yards (37.9 avg.)
INTERCEPTIONS: Terrell Thomas—4 for 44 yards
TACKLES: Rey Maualuga—79
SACKS: Lawrence Jackson—10.5

## *2008*

HEAD COACH: Pete Carroll
ASSISTANT COACHES: Chris Carlisle, Brennan Carroll, Nick Holt, Demetrice Martin, Todd McNair, John Morton, Ken Norton, Kris Richard, Yogi Roth, Pat Ruel, Steve Sarkisian, Rocky Seto
TEAM CAPTAINS: Jeff Byers, Brian Cushing, Kevin Ellison, Mark Sanchez
RECORD: 12–1 overall (8–1 in Pacific–10 Conference)
(Ranked 3rd best record in college football out of 120 teams)
FINISH IN CONFERENCE: 1st place
FINISH IN NATIONAL POLLS: 3rd place in AP and 2nd place in *USA Today*
POINTS SCORED PER GAME: 37.5 to rank 14th out of 120 teams
POINTS ALLOWED PER GAME: 9.0 to rank 1st

### Schedule and Highlights

**(A) Aug. 30—Virginia—52–7**
USC#3

A cross-country trip to Charlottesville, Virginia, did not have any ill effects on the Trojans. Suffering no signs of jet lag, the Cardinal & Gold rolled to their 11th straight victory in the season opener. In their first-ever game against Virginia, the defense allowed only 32 rushing yards and forced four turnovers. Mark Sanchez threw for 338 yards and three touchdowns, while the running attack lived up to the status of Tailback U, as five different USC tailbacks scored. Stafon Johnson (two yards), C.J. Gable (33 yards), and Allen Bradford (two yards), all scored on the ground. Joe McKnight caught a 10-yard touchdown pass from Sanchez, and the final tailback to score, Marc Tyler, caught a 10-yard pass from Mitch Mustain. Patrick Turner (20 yards) and Ronald Johnson (49 yards), were on the receiving end of Sanchez's other two scoring strikes, and David Buehler added a 20-yard field goal, in USC's dominant win.[1]

**(H) Sept. 13—Ohio State—35–3**
USC#1 OSU#5

There were many classic moments produced by these two teams when they met in Rose Bowl competition through the years. In this regular season matchup, the only joy expressed by this game's outcome was from Trojan faithful. With a national television audience, and 93,607 in attendance at the Coliseum, the top-ranked Trojans handed the Buckeyes their worst defeat since 1994, and it was the first time in 12 years that Ohio State failed to score a touchdown. Mark Sanchez completed 17 of 28 pass attempts for 172 yards and four touchdowns. His scoring strikes went to Stanley Havili (35 yards), Blake Ayles (one yard), and Damian Williams (24 and 17 yards). Linebacker Rey Maualuga added USC's other touchdown with a 48-yard interception return. Joe McKnight ran for a game-high 105 yards on 12 carries, and the Trojans compiled 348 yards of total offense against one of college football's top-rated defenses.[2]

**(A) Sept. 25—Oregon State—21–27**
USC#1

In this Pac-10 opener, 25-point underdog Oregon State shocked USC, and ended the Trojans' 15-game winning streak in the month of September. This was the second time in their history that Oregon State upset a top-ranked USC team since the first occurrence in 1967. This also was the second straight time that USC lost in Corvallis, Oregon. Freshman tailback Jacquizz Rodgers ran for 186 yards and two touchdowns for the Beavers, while the Trojans running attack was held to 86 yards.[3]

**(H) Oct. 4—Oregon—44–10**
USC#9 ORE#23

The Trojans fell eight spots in the national rankings, and took out their frustration on the Oregon Ducks. With a strong second quarter that produced 24 points, the Trojans easily won their 26th straight home night game. Mark Sanchez completed 19 out of 28 pass attempts for 332 yards and three touchdowns, and David Buehler kicked three field goals, to help USC get back on the winning track. Sanchez spread out his passes, throwing to nine different receivers. Joe McKnight and Patrick Turner shared top receiving honors with five catches each. All of Sanchez's touchdown passes came in the 24-point second quarter, with Turner (11 yards), Damian Williams (34 yards), and Ronald Johnson (63 yards) on the receiving end of those scoring strikes. For his efforts, Sanchez earned Pac-10 Offensive Player of the Week honors. As a team, the Trojans compiled 598 yards of total offense, while holding an Oregon team that averaged 308.6 rushing yards per game, to a mere 60.[4]

**(H) Oct. 11—Arizona State—28–0**
USC#8

This shutout victory over the Sun Devils was USC's 400th win at the LA Coliseum. The USC defense was once again outstanding, as they allowed only 75 yards on the ground and forced four turnovers. Joe McKnight ran for 143 yards on 11 carries, and Mark Sanchez ran for one touchdown (one yard), and threw for another, a four-yarder to Damian Williams. Stafon Johnson ran for a two-yard score, and cornerback Kevin Thomas returned an interception 46 yards for USC's other six points.[5]

**(A) Oct. 18—Washington State—69–0**
USC#6

In the last two weeks, the location did not matter to the Trojans. Whether in the LA Coliseum, or in Pullman, Washington, the result was the same, as the Cardinal & Gold posted a second straight shutout victory. This was the Trojans first back-to-back shutout since 1971, and their most decisive shutout since 1931. This also marked USC's 400th Pac-10 victory. In regards to Washington State, this was the most decisive loss ever in their history, and it snapped their 280-game scoring streak. Mark Sanchez threw for 253 yards, and tied a school record with five touchdown passes, with all of them coming in the first half. Patrick Turner caught two of Sanchez's touchdown tosses (23 and 14 yards), Ronald Johnson had two as well (three and 16 yards), and Anthony McCoy caught the final scoring strike from 21 yards out. When not filling the skies with passes, the Trojans used a powerful ground attack that compiled 362 yards and produced three 100-yard rushers. Broderick Green led the Trojans with 121 yards on 18 carries and scored two touchdowns. Stafon Johnson ran for 112 yards on 11 carries, and C.J. Gable had 109 yards on 16 carries and three touchdowns.[6]

**(A) Oct. 25—Arizona—17–10**
USC#6

Arizona's second quarter field goal snapped USC's streak of scoreless quarters at 11, but the Trojans used a tough defense that allowed only 184 yards against it to prevail in a hard-fought win. Coming into this game, the Wildcats averaged 40.4 points per game, and were ranked ninth in the nation in that category. David Buehler kicked a 43-yard field goal in the first quarter, and the Trojans never trailed after that. Stafon Johnson, who had a game-high 83 rushing yards, scored on a two-yard run to give USC a 10–3 halftime advantage. The Wildcats, despite being stymied by a tough defensive effort, managed to tie the game in the third quarter. The Trojans then took the lead for good on a 30-yard pass from Mark Sanchez to Stanley Havili to clinch USC's seventh straight win over Arizona.[7]

**(H) Nov. 1—Washington—56–0**
USC#7

The Trojans made it a clean sweep of opponents from the state of Washington. Two weeks earlier, they blanked the Cougars of Washington State, and then did the same to the Huskies on homecoming weekend. This proved to be USC's highest point production, and largest margin of victory ever against Washington. The Trojans had 485 yards of total offense, and scored on their first six possessions to hold a commanding 42–0 halftime advantage. Patrick Turner, who had six receptions for 100 yards, caught both of Mark Sanchez's touchdown passes from four and 32 yards out to start the scoring fest. Sanchez later ran for a one-yard touchdown. C.J. Gable ran for a game-high 108 yards on 10 carries, and scored a pair of touchdowns (nine and six yards). Three other tailbacks also got into the scoring column. Stafon Johnson scored on a one-yard run, Broderick Green from five yards, and Marc Tyler finished off USC's onslaught with a six-yard run in the fourth quarter.[8]

**(H) Nov. 8—California—17–3**
USC#7 CAL#21

With 88,523 in attendance, the Trojans continued on with their winning ways, this time over their adversaries from Northern California. The Trojan defense once again proved their worth by holding the Golden Bears, who averaged 36.4 points per game coming into this matchup, to 27 rushing yards and 138 through the air. This marked the fifth time during the season that USC held an opponent from scoring a touchdown. Mark Sanchez threw for 238 yards and both of USC's touchdowns. Patrick Turner (19 yards) and Ronald Johnson (six yards), caught Sanchez's scoring strikes, and David Buehler started the scoring off in the first quarter with a 27-yard field goal.[9]

**(A) Nov. 15—Stanford—45–23**
USC#6

In front of the first capacity crowd at new Stanford Stadium (50,425), the Trojans beat their other long-time foes from the northern region of California. This was also Stanford's first home defeat of the season. After spotting Stanford a 10–3 first quarter lead, the Trojans tied the game at 17, going into the second half. From that point on, it was all Trojans, as they outscored Stanford, 28–6, in the second half to present Pete Carroll with his 100th win as head coach of the Trojans. Stafon Johnson ran for 115 yards on 14 carries, and scored a pair touchdowns on runs of seven and three yards. C.J. Gable ran for 85 yards, and scored on a brilliant 93-yard kickoff return in the second quarter. Mark Sanchez threw touchdown passes to Damian Williams (five yards) and Stanley Havili (50 yards), and David Buehler added a 37-yard field goal for USC.[10]

**(H) Nov. 29—Notre Dame—38–3**
USC#5

A well-balanced offensive attack, coupled with a smothering defensive performance, led the Trojans to an overwhelming victory in the 80th edition of "the Glamour Game." This was USC's seventh straight victory over the Irish, which was their longest in the history of the series. It also was the 28th consecutive win in a home night game for USC.

The Trojans took command late in the first quarter on a two-yard run by Stafon Johnson, and then scored on three consecutive possessions to take a 24–0 halftime lead. Joe McKnight ran for a 55-yard touchdown, Damian Williams caught a 12-yard pass from Mark Sanchez, and David Buehler kicked a 35-yard field goal to give USC their convincing halftime edge. C.J. Gable scored on a one-yard run in the third quarter, and Brandon Walker finally got the Irish on the board with a 41-yard field goal early in the fourth quarter. Sanchez threw a 17-yard touchdown pass to Patrick Turner after that to complete the blowout victory.

For the game, Sanchez completed 22 of 31 pass attempts for 267 yards, Damian Williams caught seven passes for 86 yards, Patrick Turner six for 83 yards, and McKnight led the game with 63 rushing yards. The defense prevented Notre Dame from getting a first down until the final play of the third quarter, and held them to 91 yards of total offense while the USC offense rolled up 449 yards.[11]

**(A) Dec. 6—UCLA—28–7**
USC#5

Another balanced offensive attack, and a tough defensive effort, gave USC another dominant victory over a storied rival. This time it was "the Battle of Los Angeles" that showcased the talents of the Trojans on both sides of the ball. This game saw both teams sporting home jerseys for the first time since 1982. Per an NCAA football rule, because USC was not in its white road jerseys, they were charged with a time out at the opening kickoff. UCLA responded by calling a time out immediately after to even things up. This matchup finished off the conference schedule, and gave the Trojans a team and conference record of seven straight Pac-10 championships. This win also allowed the Trojans to record their 11th victory of the season for a seventh straight time to set a team and NCAA record. It win also gave head coach Pete Carroll a perfect 28–0 record in November games.

The Trojans did not start off well on their first posses-sion. A fumble led to the Bruins taking a 7–0 lead on a 21-yard pass from Dominique Johnson to Kahlil Bell. However, that was the last time UCLA would get close to the lead, and only made it into USC territory one more time. On their last two possessions of the first quarter, the Trojans tied the game, and then took the lead for good. Joe McKnight scored on a 12-yard run, and David Buehler tied the score with the conversion kick. Mark Sanchez connected with Damian Williams on a 12-yard pass, and Buehler added his second extra point to give USC a 14–7 lead at the end of the first quarter. The Trojans added another touchdown before the end of the first half when Stafon Johnson capped off a 16-play drive with a run of two yards. Buehler's extra point sent USC into the third quarter with a 21–7 advantage. The game's final points came in the third quarter on a Sanchez-to-Patrick Turner pass that covered 18 yards. Buehler added his fourth extra point, and the Trojans were on their way to another Rose Bowl. Mark Sanchez threw for 269 yards, Joe McKnight ran for 99 yards, and Turner had a game-high five receptions for 81 yards.[12]

**Rose Bowl, (N) Jan. 1—Penn State—38–24**
USC#5 PSU#6

The first Rose Bowl game to be played at the current stadium was in 1923. It pitted the Trojans, in their first-ever bowl appearance, against Penn State. Eighty-six years later, the same two teams squared off in the New Year's Day classic.

The Trojans started off this rematch of the '23 game with a 27-yard touchdown reception from Mark Sanchez to Damian Williams late in the first quarter. Penn State answered with a nine-yard run by quarterback Daryll Clark, and Kevin Kelly's extra point kick tied the game at 7–7 at the end of the opening stanza.

Like many times in their recent history, the Trojans caught fire and pulled away from the opposition. This game was one in which history repeated itself, as the Trojans scored 24 straight points on to build a commanding 31–7 halftime advantage. Sanchez started the scoring spree with a six-yard run, and then David Buehler kicked a 30-yard field goal. Sanchez then rifled a 19-yard pass to Ronald Johnson. The Trojans' final points of the first half came after safety Will Harris recovered a Penn State fumble. Sanchez converted the turnover into a 20-yard touchdown pass to C.J. Gable 36 seconds before halftime.

Defense won out in a scoreless third quarter, but the fourth quarter saw Penn State get a 17–7 advantage on USC. However, the Trojans did too much damage throughout the first half to be in danger of losing. The Nittany Lions got their points on two Daryll Clark passes to Derrick Williams (two yards) and Jordan Norwood (nine yards), plus a 25-yard field goal by Kevin Kelly. The Trojans added one final six-pointer on a Sanchez-to-Ronald Johnson 45-yard pass.

Sanchez was honored as the Rose Bowl Offensive MVP after connecting on 28 of 35 pass attempts for 413 yards and four touchdowns. Linebacker Kaluka Maiava received the Defensive MVP award by making four tackles and deflecting two passes. Damian Williams led all receivers with 10 receptions for 162 yards, and tailback Stafon Johnson led all runners with 63 yards on 15 carries. USC became the first team to win three straight Rose Bowls, and they set an NCAA record with seven straight BCS bowl appearances.[13]

### TEAM LEADERS

RUSHING: Stafon Johnson—705 yards on 138 carries
PASSING: Mark Sanchez—241 out of 366 attempts for 3,207 yards and 34 touchdowns
RECEIVING: Damian Williams—58 catches for 869 yards and 9 touchdowns
SCORING: David Buehler—92 points on 65 extra points and 9 field goals
KICKOFF RETURNS: Ronald Johnson—14 for 380 yards (27.1 avg.)
PUNT RETURNS: Stafon Johnson—33 for 305 yards (9.2 avg.)
PUNTING: Greg Woidneck—47 for 1,733 yards (36.9 avg.)
INTERCEPTIONS: Kevin Thomas—3 for 53 yards and 1 touchdown
Drew McAllister—3 for 37 yards
Cary Harris—3 for 0 yards
TACKLES: Rey Maualuga—79
SACKS: Kyle Moore—5

## *2009*

HEAD COACH: Pete Carroll
ASSISTANT COACHES: Jeremy Bates, Chris Carlisle, Brennan Carroll, Jethro Franklin, Todd McNair, Justin Mesa, John Morton, Ken Norton, Kris Richard, Pat Ruel, Brian Schneider, Rocky Seto
TEAM CAPTAINS: Jeff Byers, Taylor Mays, Josh Pinkard, Damian Williams
RECORD: 9–4 overall (5–4 in Pacific-10 Conference)
(Ranked 22nd best record out of 120 teams)
FINISH IN CONFERENCE: Tied for 5th place
FINISH IN NATIONAL POLLS: 22nd place in AP and 20th place in *USA Today*
POINTS SCORED PER GAME: 26.5 to rank 64th out of 120 teams
POINTS ALLOWED PER GAME: 19.8 to rank 22nd

### Schedule and Highlights

**(H) Sept. 5—San Jose State—56–3**
USC#4

Matt Barkley's debut as quarterback of the Trojans followed a lineage of All-Americans and Heisman Trophy winners. The freshman signal caller's first four series were not of legendary status, as they ended with a pair of fumbles and two punts. However, after San Jose took a 3–0 lead, Barkley shook off the jitters and threw for 233 yards and one touchdown. The proud tradition of USC tailbacks also provided a heavy dose of offensive punch, as they ran for six touchdowns in this blowout victory. The Trojans scored on six straight possessions starting in the second quarter, and rolled up 343 rushing yards. Stafon Johnson and Joe McKnight each scored two touchdowns, and Marc Tyler and Allen Bradford were the other tailbacks that scored for USC.[1]

**(A) Sept. 12—Ohio State—18–15**
USC#3 OSU#8

The Trojans history is long and proud, filled with countless tales of spectacular drives down the field, with one of them coming at Ohio Stadium with a record crowd of 106,033 on hand. It was a 14-play, 86-yard trek across a swatch of Columbus real estate led by Matt Barkley, Joe McKnight, and Stafon Johnson. McKnight ran for 11 yards, and then picked up 21 more yards on a pass from Barkley on a third-and-eight. Barkley then threw to Anthony McCoy over the middle for 26 yards to the Ohio State 37. Barkley kept another set of downs going with a quarterback sneak on fourth-and-short. McKnight carried three straight times to get the Trojans inside the Buckeye 10. Barkley then did another quarterback sneak that got the Trojans a first-and-goal. Stafon Johnson then took his turn carrying the ball. He swept the right side of the line and went into the end zone untouched for a game-winning two-yard touchdown with 1:05 remaining. This gave USC their 10th straight victory over Big Ten opponents.[2]

**(A) Sept. 19—Washington—13–16**
USC#3

After their thrilling win over Ohio State, the Trojans traveled to the Great Northwest for their Pac-10 opener against Washington. The Trojans came into the matchup close to 20-point favorites, while the Huskies were on a record 15-game losing streak in Pac-10 competition. Unfortunately, for the fourth straight year, the Trojans fell victim to an unranked team. With three seconds left, Nick Folk kicked a 22-yard field goal to secure the win for the underdog Huskies. The Trojans had their lowest point production in three years. Joe McKnight had 100 yards rushing and one touchdown for USC, and Matt Barkley was out of action with a shoulder injury. His replacement, Aaron Corp, completed 13 out of 22 pass attempts for 110 yards.[3]

**(H) Sept. 26—Washington State—27–6**
USC#12

The Trojans fell nine spots in the national rankings after their shocking loss to the Huskies. Back at home for their other foes from Washington, the Trojans scored three touchdowns in the first 12 minutes, and beat the Cougars easily. Matt Barkley's shoulder was healthy enough for him to complete 13 of 22 pass attempts for 247 yards and a pair of touchdowns. Damian Williams was Barkley's top receiver with five catches for 100 yards and one touchdown. This was USC's 11th straight win at the Coliseum.[4]

**(A) Oct. 3—California—30–3**
USC#7 CAL#24

For the first time since 1998, the Cal Golden Bears were held without a touchdown at home. While the Trojan defense was keeping Cal out of the end zone, the USC offense had no trouble finding it. Joe McKnight rushed for 119 yards and two touchdowns, Matt Barkley completed 20 of 35 pass attempts for 283 yards, Damian Williams caught eight passes for 101 yards, and Jordan Congdon kicked three field goals.[5]

**(A) Oct. 17—Notre Dame—34–27**
USC#6 ND#25

The Trojans made it eight straight against Notre Dame, but it was close at the end. The Trojans led, 34–14, in the fourth quarter before the Irish closed the gap to seven. Anthony McCoy added his name to the long list of Trojan heroes to emerge from this series with Notre Dame. He accomplished this by setting a school record with 153 yards receiving, which was the most by a USC tight end. Two of his receptions helped set up touchdowns, and another one assisted in the Trojans getting a field goal. Matt Barkley played a great game in his first exposure to this classic series by completing 19 of 29 pass attempts for 380 yards and a pair of touchdowns. Both of Barkley's scoring strikes went to Damian Williams from 20 and 41 yards out.

Barkley's 20-yard touchdown pass to Williams opened the scoring in the first quarter to complete a five-play, 88-yard drive, and Jordan Congdon added the extra point. The Irish got even near the end of the first quarter on a two-yard run by Robert Hughes, and Nick Tausch's extra point took the game into the second quarter tied at 7–7. Two Congdon field goals from 24 and 37 yards out were all the scoring in the second quarter, and they gave the Trojans a 13–7 halftime advantage.

The Trojans extended their lead to 27–14 at the end of the third quarter on Barkley's 41-yard touchdown pass to Williams and a three-yard run by Allen Bradford. Congdon added both conversion kicks. The Irish received their points in the third quarter on a 45-yard pass from Jimmy Clausen to Golden Tate and a Tausch conversion kick. The Trojans looked to take command of the game in the early stages of the fourth quarter when Joe McKnight scored on a one-yard run and Congdon's extra point gave USC a 34–14 advantage.

Under partly sunny skies, and temperatures near 50-degrees, the Trojans appeared to be headed off into the sunset as easy victors over their South Bend rivals. It was then that the mood in Notre Dame Stadium went from doom to temporary excitement, as the Irish attempted a rally that almost pulled the game out. Clausen started the rally with a two-yard run, but Tausch had his conversion kick blocked to make it 34–20. The Irish then cut the deficit even more four minutes later when Clausen connected with Tate from 15 yards out, and Tausch's extra point brought Notre Dame to within seven at 34–27. Clausen tried to get the Irish even closer in the final seconds, but three incomplete passes into the end zone allowed USC to win in South Bend. This victory gave USC the opportunity to join Michigan and Michigan State as the only schools to beat Notre Dame eight consecutive times.[6]

**(H) Oct. 24—Oregon State—42–36**
USC#4

With the largest crowd (89,718) to see a USC–Oregon State game, the Beavers recorded their most points against USC since 1914. In their previous encounters with Oregon State, the Trojans lost by six points for their only defeat of the year. Revenge is sweet, and this time, USC won by six points. Leading the way offensively was Allen Bradford, who ran for a career-best 147 yards and two touchdowns. The Beavers rang up 482 yards of total offense, and cut the USC deficit to six points with 5:41 left in regulation. The Trojans were then successful on two third down plays to run out the clock and secure the win.[7]

**(A) Oct. 31—Oregon—20–47**
USC#4 ORE#10

This was Oregon's highest point production against USC, as a record crowd of 59,592 looked on at Autzen Stadium. The

Ducks made a statement that they were the new alpha dogs of the Pac-10 by handing the Trojans their worst defeat in 12 years. This win kept Oregon perfect in the Pac-10 with a 5–0 record. Jeremiah Masoli threw for 222 yards, and he ran for an additional 164 yards. LaMichael James ran for 184 yards, and Oregon compiled 391 yards on the ground.[8]

**(A) Nov. 7—Arizona State—14–9**
USC#12

This was USC's 100th consecutive game ranked in the AP Top 25, and their 10th straight win over Arizona State. However, the Sun Devils made the Trojans work for this one. With a sputtering offense, and nine penalties accounting for 98 yards in losses, the Trojans turned to the defense to help secure this win. Never in the Pete Carroll era at USC did the Trojans lose two straight, and a Matt Barkley pass to Damian Williams covering 75 yards produced what turned out to be the winning points that prevented back-to-back defeats. The USC defense did their part by holding off Arizona State on their final four possessions. Will Harris came up big for the Trojans by intercepting a Hail Mary pass in the end zone on the game's final play.[9]

**(H) Nov. 14—Stanford—21–55**
USC#11 STAN#25

Tony Gerhart ran for 178 yards and three touchdowns, Andrew Luck threw two touchdown passes, and in the end, Stanford scored the most points ever against USC. This game also saw the most touchdowns ever scored against the Trojans. Stanford also tied a record for most touchdowns (four) scored against USC in one quarter in what became USC's worst homecoming loss. With a crowd of 90,071 looking on in horror Stanford's Nate Whitaker kicked seven conversion kicks to tie Jim Brieske's mark of seven set in the 1948 Rose Bowl as the most against the Trojans in their history.[10]

**(H) Nov. 28—UCLA—28–7**
USC#24

This was USC's 600th conference game, and with a 7 p.m. start, it was the second latest in the series behind 1945's 8 p.m. start. This game saw the Trojans win their third straight over the Bruins, giving up just 21 points in those games against their cross-town rivals.

A crowd of 85,713 at the Coliseum witnessed one of the lowest-scoring games between these two teams. The only points of the first half came on a Malcolm Smith 62-yard interception return with 6:31 left in the first quarter. This was the fewest first half points in a USC-UCLA game since 1976, and the Trojans held a slight 140–138 edge in total yards.

The second half saw a greater point production, as Allen Bradford ran for a pair of touchdowns, including one with 1:30 remaining. The Bruins got their only points when fullback Chane Moline took a direct snap and ran for a two-yard touchdown with 5:41 left. This game saw the most excitement in the final 44 seconds. With the Trojans up, 21–7, the Bruins looked to prevent the Trojans from running out the clock. They called timeout, and looked to use up their remaining two in an attempt to get the Trojans to punt. Matt Barkley then was told to run a play-action pass with Pete Carroll's approval. Barkley followed orders to perfection, with the result being a 48-yard touchdown pass to Damian Williams. The Trojans began to celebrate, and the Bruins felt that they were being taunted. Players from both sides rushed in, but tempers were cooled down enough to finish out the game.[11]

**(H) Dec. 5—Arizona—17–21**
USC#20

What started out as a season with championship dreams, ended with USC's fourth loss. Arizona quarterback Nick Foles threw a 36-yard touchdown pass to Juron Criner with 3:14 to play for what turned out to be the winning points. This victory gave the Wildcats their best season in a decade. The Trojans took the lead with 7:13 left on a 37-yard field goal by Jordan Congdon. The Wildcats then converted on three consecutive third downs on the game-winning drive. With clouds hovering over the Coliseum, and tens of thousands of empty seats, the Trojans ended their least successful regular season since 2001. The Trojans ended the game with Barkley getting sacked with seven seconds left. Allen Bradford led USC with 66 rushing yards, and scored the tying touchdown in the third quarter. Ronald Johnson accounted for USC's other touchdown on a pass from Barkley.[12]

**Emerald Bowl, (N) Dec. 26—Boston College—24–13**

USC wrapped up the first decade of the new millennium by playing at AT&T Park in San Francisco, California. This was USC's first game in San Francisco since 1943, and the first time they faced Boston College since 1988. This game was unique in the fact that both teams had to share the same sideline due to the field's layout as a baseball stadium.

The Trojans took control early with freshman quarterback Matt Barkley leading the way. He guided USC into the end zone on their first two possessions, capping each drive with a touchdown pass. Barkley's target on both touchdown tosses was Stanley Havili, who scored from 53 and five yards out, respectively. Jordan Congdon kicked a pair of extra points, and USC was up, 14–0, in the second quarter. Boston College made a run at the Trojans, and closed to within one point by the end of the first half. Running back Montel Harris got the Eagles on the board at the 9:54 mark of the second quarter with a seven-yard jaunt. Steve Aponavicius missed the extra point kick to make the score 14–6. Following an interception, Dave Shinskie threw a 61-yard touchdown pass to Rich Gunnell, and this time Aponavicius' extra point attempt split the uprights to cut the Eagles' deficit to 14–13 by halftime. Gunnell's 61-yard reception was the longest on a USC defense since 2004.

In the second half, the Trojans seized the momentum from Boston College, and clamped down to secure their 16th straight non-conference win, and 32nd bowl game victory. They accomplished those impressive milestones with a solid defensive effort that limited the Eagles to 91 yards of total offense in the second half, and only a mere 19 throughout the third quarter. The USC defense also assisted the offense by returning possession back over to them following two turnovers that resulted in 10 points. Defensive tackle Jurrell Casey recovered a fumble, and that resulted in a 38-yard field goal from Jordan Congdon to give the Trojans a 17–13 lead going into the fourth quarter. An interception by cornerback Shareece

Wright paved the way for a one-yard touchdown run by Matt Barkley. Congdon added the extra point to complete the scoring.

Receiver Damian Williams was selected as the game's Offensive MVP after catching 12 passes for 189 yards, and two of those receptions set the Trojans up for a pair of touchdowns. Stanley Havili had six receptions for 83 yards and two touchdowns, and tailback Allen Bradford led the USC ground attack with 72 yards on 17 carries. As for the freshman field general, Matt Barkley, he responded to the challenge of leading the Trojans to victory by completing 27 of 37 pass attempts for 350 yards and two touchdowns. He also ran for one touchdown. This game also marked the end of one of USC's greatest coaching reigns. After leading the Trojans back to the upper echelon of college football for nine seasons, Pete Carroll left the Southland for the Great Northwest to coach the NFL's Seattle Seahawks.[13]

### Team Leaders

Rushing: Joe McKnight—1,014 yards on 164 carries
Passing: Matt Barkley—211 out of 352 attempts for 2,735 yards and 15 touchdowns
Receiving: Damian Williams—70 catches for 1,010 yards and 6 touchdowns
Scoring: Jordan Congdon—77 points on 41 extra points and 12 field goals
Kickoff Returns: C.J. Gable—19 for 348 yards (18.3 avg.)
Punt Returns: Damian Williams—24 for 340 yards and 2 touchdowns (14.2 avg.)
Punting: Jacob Harfman—48 for 1,909 yards (39.8 avg.)
Interceptions: Will Harris—4 for 62 yards and 1 touchdown
Tackles: Taylor Mays—96
sacks: Nick Perry—8
Everson Griffen—8

## *2010*

Head Coach: Lane Kiffin
Assistant Coaches: Keary Colbert, Sammy Knight, Aaron Ausmus, Joe Barry, John Baxter, James Cregg, Willie Mack Garza, Clay Helton, Monte Kiffin, John Morton, Kennedy Pola, Ed Orgeron
Team Captains: Matt Barkley, Stanley Havili, Michael Morgan, Malcolm Smith, Shareece Wright
Record: 8–5 overall (5–4 in Pacific–10 Conference)
(Ranked 35th best record in college football out of 120 teams)
Finish in Conference: Tied for 3rd place
USC was banned from bowl game eligibility due to an NCAA penalty. The allegations related to this investigation stemmed from reports that Reggie Bush received improper funds from outside sources while still a student/athlete at USC. The penalty for this charge was a four-year probation period, a two-year bowl ban, a loss of 30 scholarships over a three-year period, and the football program was forced to vacate the final two games of the 2004 season, and the entire 2005 season.
Finish in National Polls: No ranking in Top 25
Points Scored Per Game: 31.0 to rank 37th out of 120 teams
Points Allowed Per Game: 26.7 to rank 63rd

### Schedule and Highlights

**(A) Sept. 2—Hawaii—49–36**
USC#14

The names changed through the opening decade of the new millennium, but the result was a constant winning tradition. From Palmer to Leinart, Booty to Sanchez, the quarterback position at USC produced Heisman winners and All-Americans. The passing of the torch went to Matt Barkley the previous year, and the freshman carried on admirably while serving as field general. Proving that the sophomore jinx was non-existent to him, Barkley started off his second year at USC with an incredible showing. He completed 18 of 23 pass attempts for 257 yards and five touchdowns, which tied a school record. Receiver Ronald Johnson also tied a school record with three touchdown receptions. Marc Tyler lived up to the tailback reputation at USC by rushing for 154 yards on 17 carries and one touchdown. This was the seventh time in as many games that USC defeated Hawaii, and it gave the Trojans their 13th straight opening game victory, and Lane Kiffin's first as head coach.[1]

**(H) Sept. 11—Virginia—17–14**
USC#16

The Trojans went from the tropical paradise of Hawaii to the Golden Coast of California for their home opener. With 81,375 inside the Coliseum, the Trojans held on to prevail for their 32nd straight victory in a home night game. Matt Barkley completed 20 of 35 pass attempts for 202 yards and two touchdowns. The Trojans held off scoring threats by Virginia when T.J. McDonald intercepted a pass in the end zone, and Shareece Wright blocked a field goal attempt.[2]

**(A) Sept. 18—Minnesota—32–21**
USC#20

Robert Woods ignited USC with a 97-yard kickoff return for a touchdown in the third quarter after the Trojans were trailing, 14–13. David Ausberry caught a 21-yard pass from Matt Barkley, and Allen Bradford ran for 56 yards for two more touchdowns that allowed USC to take a 32–14 fourth quarter lead. After two straight games of being outgained in total yards, the Trojans came out on top with 408 yards to 307. Bradford ran for 131 yards on 12 carries, and Barkley threw for 192 yards and two touchdowns to give him nine on the year. This was the first time in 30 years that these teams faced each other.[3]

**(A) Sept. 25—Washington State—50–16**
USC#20

USC fullback Stanley Havili rang up 187 yards, with 80 on the ground in just four carries, and 107 more on five receptions, to lead the Trojans offense to a big win in their conference opener. Havili scored on a 22-yard pass from Mitch Mustain, and ran for a 59-yarder to give the Trojans their first points of the game. Matt Barkley also had a solid performance by connecting on 16 out of 25 pass attempts for 290 yards and three touchdowns.[4]

**(H) Oct. 2—Washington—31–32**
USC#18

Washington kicker Erik Folk was the least popular individual in the Land of Troy. For the second straight year, Folk took the Trojans out of the undefeated ranks when the Huskies went 61 yards in 10 plays to set up Folk's game-winning kick from 32 yards out with no time left. This loss snapped USC's 32-game winning streak of home night games, and Washington's point total was the most they scored against USC since 1960. In this battle of former USC assistants (Kiffin and Steve Sarkisian), the teams combined for over 1,000 yards of offensive production. Washington amassed 537 and USC 484 in a game that saw seven lead changes. Tailback Allen Bradford ran for 223 yards on 21 carries and two touchdowns for USC. Matt Barkley threw for 186 yards, but no touchdowns, which snapped his streak of 12 straight games of throwing at least one scoring strike.[5]

**(A) Oct. 9—Stanford—35–37**
STAN#16

A one-point heart-breaking loss a week earlier was followed by another defeat on the final play of the game. This time Nate Whitaker connected on a 30-yard field goal to lift Stanford to a slim victory after USC took a 35–34 lead with 1:08 left on a three-yard run by Allen Bradford. Stanford then went 62 yards to set up the winning kick with a record crowd of 51,607 in renovated Stanford Stadium. This was the first season in USC history that the Trojans lost twice on game's final play of regulation. This game also saw the USC football program set a school record with their 112th consecutive game on live television. Robert Woods was the star for USC when he caught 12 passes for 224 yards, and tied a school record with three touchdown receptions. He added 86 yards on kickoff returns to give him 310 yards of total offense. Matt Barkley also had a big game, as he completed 28 of 45 pass attempts for 390 yards and three touchdowns.[6]

**(H) Oct. 16—California—48–14**

The Trojans got back on track by not allowing Cal to get close. They got out to a 42–0 halftime lead, and then coasted to an easy victory. Matt Barkley threw for 352 yards on 25 out of 37 attempts and five touchdowns, with them all coming in the first half. Barkley's brilliant performance allowed him to once again tie a school record for most touchdown passes in a single game. In their seventh straight win over Cal, the Trojans rolled up 602 yards of total offense against one of the top-ranked defenses in the nation. The Trojan defense held Cal to a season-low of 245 yards, and only 52 on the ground. Robert Woods had seven receptions for 116 yards and two touchdowns. Ronald Johnson also caught a pair of touchdown passes, and David Ausberry hauled in Barkley's other six-pointer. The Trojans also had a well-balanced running attack with Marc Tyler gaining 79 yards and one touchdown, and C.J. Gable with 72 yards.[7]

**(H) Oct. 30—Oregon—32–53**
USC#24 ORE#1

The top-ranked Oregon Ducks slugged it out with the Trojans in an offensive display on USC's homecoming weekend that saw them produce 599 yards and USC 377. Oregon scored the game's final 24 points, and recorded the most points they ever scored against USC in Los Angeles. Oregon quarterback Darron Thomas tied a record with four touchdown passes against a USC defense, and is one of five to hold the record, including ex–Oregon quarterback Joey Harrington, who added his name to the list in 2000. LaMichael James also had a big day for Oregon by rushing for 239 yards and three touchdowns. For the Trojans, Matt Barkley threw for 264 yards on 26 out of 49 attempts and one touchdown. He also ran for a touchdown.[8]

**(H) Nov. 6—Arizona State—34–33**

The Trojans managed to squeeze by the Sun Devils for their 11th straight win over them thanks to a Joe Houston 29-yard field goal. Houston connected on the game-winner with 3:06 left in the fourth quarter following a nine-play, 68-yard drive after the Sun Devils took their first lead of the game. Arizona State then moved downfield for Thomas Weber to attempt a 42-yard field goal with 1:34 left, but he missed it to preserve the win for USC. Marc Tyler ran for a game-high 119 yards on 12 carries, and caught five passes for an additional 32 yards and one touchdown. Matt Barkley threw for 215 yards on 26 out of 37 pass attempts and three touchdowns. Rounding out the top performances for the Trojans was safety T.J. McDonald, who had 13 tackles and a blocked punt to his credit.[9]

**(A) Nov. 13—Arizona—24–21**
ARI#18

Once again a battle with a team from the Grand Canyon State resulted in another close margin of victory. This was the first season in which five USC games were decided by three points or less. The Trojans scored on three straight possessions in the first half to open up a 21–7 lead. From there, Arizona held USC to a 30-yard field goal by Joe Houston while they amassed 14 points to make things interesting down the stretch. The Wildcats scored a touchdown with 1:01 left, but USC recovered an onside kick to secure the win. Marc Tyler provided the biggest offensive punch for the Trojans with 161 yards rushing on 31 carries and one touchdown. Matt Barkley completed 21 of 35 pass attempts for 170 yards and one touchdown to tight end Rhett Ellison. Barkley also ran for a touchdown.[10]

**(A) Nov. 20—Oregon State—7–36**
USC#20

On a cold evening in Corvallis, Oregon, the Beavers warmed up their fans with a convincing victory. This was USC's third straight loss in Corvallis, and the fourth in five previous games. This was Oregon State's second highest point total scored against USC since the 38 they produced in 1914. The seven points USC scored was the lowest they had against Oregon State since 1967. C.J. gable provided the Trojans with their only touchdown on a 13-yard run in the third quarter. The Trojans suffered injuries to Matt Barkley, Marc Tyler, offensive tackle Tyron Smith, and linebacker Chris Galippo. Oregon State got a solid performance from tailback Jacquizz Rodgers, who ran for 128 yards on 26 carries and one touchdown. He also caught seven passes.[11]

**(H) Nov. 27—Notre Dame—16–20**

For the first time since 1941, both USC and Notre Dame had new head coaches at the helm of both programs at the same time. This was also only the ninth time in the history of this series that both teams were not ranked at the time of their game with each other.

With Mitch Mustain making his first start at quarterback filling in for an injured Matt Barkley, the Trojans got on the board first. Linebacker Chris Galippo intercepted a pass on Notre Dame's second offensive series. The Trojans took advantage of the turnover by converting on a 45-yard field goal by Joe Houston to give USC a 3–0 lead going into the second quarter.

The Irish then took a 13–3 lead in the second quarter on a pair of touchdown passes. The first one came on a one-yard toss from Tommy Rees to Michael Floyd that capped a 16-play, 79-

yard drive with 2:39 left in the first half. Rees added his second scoring strike, also from one yard out, to Duval Kamara with seven seconds remaining in the first half. David Ruffer converted on a conversion kick after Notre Dame's first touchdown, but missed on the second.

A steady rain hit the Los Angeles area near the end of the halftime intermission, and on a wet surface, the Trojans tied the game at 13–13 heading into the fourth quarter. Linebacker Devon Kennard intercepted a pass early in the third quarter, and it led to a 23-yard Joe Houston field goal. Defensive end Nick Perry then stripped the ball and recovered a fumble that led to a one-yard quarterback sneak by Mitch Mustain late in the quarter. Houston's conversion tied the score. Mustain's touchdown run was the first offensive six-pointer surrendered by Notre Dame after 13 quarters and 227 plays.

The Trojans took their first lead of the game since the first quarter on a 37-yard field goal by Houston with 6:25 remaining in the fourth quarter. The three-pointer was set up by an interception from safety Marshall Jones. With the night getting colder and wetter, the 85,417 in attendance saw Robert Hughes add his name to the lore of this famed series by scoring on a five-yard run with 2:23 left to give Notre Dame and new head coach Brian Kelly the victory. The winning drive consisted of nine plays and 46 yards, and Ruffer's conversion gave the Irish their final point of the game. The Trojans attempted to rally, but Mustain had a pass intercepted at the one-yard line by safety Harrison Smith with 36 seconds left.

This win snapped Notre Dame's eight-game losing streak to USC, and also ended USC"s 19-game non-conference game winning streak, and 15-game none-league home game winning streak. In Mustain's first starting role, he completed 21 out of 38 pass attempts for 183 yards, and Robert Woods was his favorite receiver with a team-high nine receptions for 87 yards.[12]

**(A) Dec. 4—UCLA—28–14**

Allen Bradford lived up to the USC tailback tradition by running for 212 yards on 28 carries and a pair of long scoring jaunts in the 80th all-time meeting of these cross-town rivals. This was the first time since 2000 that neither team was ranked coming into this neighborhood clash.

The Trojans struck first with 71,105 looking on at the Rose Bowl. It marked the lowest attendance for a USC-UCLA game since 1971 (68,426). Tailback Dillon Baxter threw a five-yard pass to tight end Rhett Ellison out of the Wildcat Formation, and Joe Houston added the extra point for a 7–0 lead. This was the first time since Reggie Bush in 2004 that USC had a player other than a quarterback throw for a touchdown. The Bruins countered quickly to tie the game up at 7–7 going into the second quarter. Two plays after the Trojans lit up the scoreboard, UCLA tailback Johnathan Franklin ran for a 59-yard touchdown. Kai Forbath kicked the tying extra point.

The Trojans went into the halftime intermission with a 14–7 lead thanks to the defensive tandem of linebackers Chris Galippo and Malcolm Smith. Galippo stripped the ball from Johnathan Franklin's grasp, and Smith picked it up and ran 68 yards to give USC a lead they would never relinquish. Houston added the extra point.

The third quarter remained scoreless, and then Allen Bradford took control of the USC offensive production in the final stanza. He finished off a 97-yard drive after taking a short pass from Matt Barkley and going 47 yards for a touchdown. With Houston's extra point, the Trojans were in control at 21–7. On USC's next offensive series, Bradford sprinted 73 yards for the Trojans' final six points of the game, and with Houston's extra point, they were up, 28–7, late in the game. The Bruins managed to cut the deficit in half with 23 seconds left on a 10-yard pass from quarterback Richard Brehaut to tight end Joseph Fauria. Forbath connected on the conversion kick to complete the scoring. The Trojans finished the season with the most kickoff returns (51), and yards gained on kickoff returns (1,248), in team history.[13]

### TEAM LEADERS

RUSHING: Marc Tyler—913 yards on 171 carries
PASSING: Matt Barkley—236 out of 377 attempts for 2,791 yards and 26 touchdowns
RECEIVING: Robert Woods—65 catches for 792 yards and 6 touchdowns
SCORING: Joe Houston—73 points on 43 extra points and 10 field goals
KICKOFF RETURNS: Robert Woods—38 for 971 yards and 1 touchdown (25.6 avg.)
PUNT RETURNS: Ronald Johnson—22 for 312 yards and 1 touchdown (14.2 avg.)
PUNTING: Jacob Harfman—44 for 1,810 yards (41.1 avg.)
INTERCEPTIONS: Nickell Robey—4 for 33 yards and 1 touchdown
TACKLES: T.J. McDonald—89
SACKS: Jurrell Casey—4.5

## *2011*

HEAD COACH: Lane Kiffin
ASSISTANT COACHES: Aaron Ausmus, Joe Barry, John Baxter, James Cregg,Ted Gilmore, Clay Helton, Shawn Howe, Monte Kiffin, Sammy Knight, Justin Mesa, Kennedy Polamalu, Ed Orgeron
TEAM CAPTAINS: Matt Barkley, Rhett Ellison, TJ McDonald, Christian Tupou
RECORD: 10–2 overall (7–2 in Pacific–12 Conference)
(Ranked 13th best record in college football out of 120 teams)
FINISH IN CONFERENCE: 1st place in South Division of Pac-12 Conference. Due to an NCAA ban, USC could not claim the division title, participate in the conference championship game, or any other bowl games. The South Division title went to UCLA, who finished second to USC.
FINISH IN NATIONAL POLLS: 6th place in AP and was ineligible for ranking in any other polls.
POINTS SCORED PER GAME: 35.8 to rank 16th out of 120 teams
POINTS ALLOWED PER GAME: 23.6 to rank 45th

### Schedule and Highlights

**(H) Sept. 3—Minnesota—19–17**

A 40-foot by 150-foot high-definition video board on the west rim of the Coliseum had its debut in this game. The second largest of its kind in college football, the video board made its debut at an excellent time, being able to showcase the extreme talent of offensive sensation Robert Woods, and the junior quarterback Matt Barkley. Woods' performance as a Trojan marked one of the greatest in college football history. He caught 17 passes for 177 yards and three touchdowns. He broke the USC single-game reception record by two, which was owned by

Johnnie Morton since 1993, and his three receiving touchdowns tied a school record. He also had three kickoff returns for 73 yards. Matt Barkley completed a school record 34 pass attempts to break Todd Marinovich's mark of 33 set in 1989. He connected on 16 straight passes at one stretch during the game, had 304 yards and three touchdowns. His scoring strikes to Woods came from seven, 43, and two yards, respectively. This was USC's 14th straight opening day victory, their 12th consecutive win over a Big Ten team, and fifth straight over Minnesota.[1]

**(H) Sept. 10—Utah—23–14**

Utah's debut into the Pac-12 was not a successful one, but it did allow the Trojans to remain perfect on the season. In Utah's first appearance against USC at the LA Coliseum since 1948, tailback Marc Tyler ran for 113 yards on 24 carries as well as one touchdown on a six-yard run, and the Trojans amassed 416 yards of total offense. Robert Woods continued to be a sensation, as he caught eight passes for 102 yards, and Matt Barkley completed 20 of 32 pass attempts for 264 yards and one touchdown. With time running out, Utah attempted a 41-yard field goal that would have tied the game at 17. Matt Kalil blocked the attempt, and cornerback Torin Harris picked up the loose ball and ran 68 yards for a touchdown as time ran out. Andre Heidari kicked a 47-yard field goal, and Xavier Grimble caught Barkley's touchdown pass from nine yards out, for USC's other points.[2]

**(H) Sept. 17—Syracuse—38–17**

Matt Barkley lit up the skies above Los Angeles by completing 26 of 39 pass attempts for 324 yards and a school record-tying five touchdowns. As a team, the Trojans finished with 501 yards of total offense. This was the third time in Barkley's college career that he threw five touchdown passes in a single game. His scoring strikes went to Rhett Ellison (five yards), Robert Woods (31 yards), Randall Telfer (44 yards), Marqise Lee (43 yards), and Xavier Grimble (nine yards). This was the third time USC played Syracuse, and the first time since 1924 that the Orangemen visited the LA Coliseum.[3]

**(A) Sept. 24—Arizona State—22–43**

The Trojans rallied back from a 21–9 halftime deficit to take a 22–21 lead late in the third quarter. A 24-yard pass from Matt Barkley to Marqise Lee and a 10-yard run by Marc Tyler gave the Trojans that one-point lead. Tyler finished with a game-high 149 rushing yards on 22 carries. The Sun Devils then came back with three touchdowns in the final 20 minutes of the game to win with ease. Cameron Marshall, who ran for 141 yards, scored his second and third touchdowns of the game during that spurt to assist Arizona State. On this hot evening that saw temperatures hit 98 degrees by kickoff, Barkley completed 21 of 33 pass attempts for 227 yards, and Robert Woods caught eight passes for 131 yards. This victory snapped Arizona State's 11-game losing streak to USC, and the Trojans' five-game winning streak in Tempe, Arizona.[4]

**(H) Oct. 1—Arizona—48–41**

The Trojans and Wildcats added extra heat to an already warm Southern California day by combining for 1,136 yards of total offense. It the most combined yards of total offense in a USC game since the 1977 Bluebonnet Bowl against Texas A&M, in which the teams produced 1,139 yards. Matt Barkley was a passing wizard, completing 32 out of 39 attempts for a school record of 468 yards and four touchdowns. His 470 yards of total offense also set a school record, and he ran for a one-yard touchdown to complete one of the greatest quarterback performances in USC history. Both of the records Barkley broke previously belonged to Carson Palmer. Robert Woods caught 14 passes for 255 yards, which was five yards off the school record, and two touchdowns. Marqise Lee had eight receptions for 144 yards and one touchdown, and Xavier Grimble caught Barkley's other scoring strike. Safety T.J. McDonald chipped in with two interceptions that led to points. The Trojans scored on their first six possessions to build a 17–0 lead at the end of the first quarter. The passing arm of Nick Foles accounted for 425 yards, and got the Wildcats going. Three touchdowns from Ka' Deem Carey also added to this game being exciting and interesting down the stretch. This was the Trojans ninth win over the Wildcats in the last 10 matchups.[5]

**(A) Oct. 13—California—30–9**

Two interceptions by Dion Bailey helped the Trojan defense get five turnovers, Matt Barkley threw a pair of scoring strikes, and Andre Heidari kicked three field goals, to assist the Trojans in this eighth straight win over Cal. The Trojans were never threatened in this one, as they jumped out to a 20–0 halftime advantage on two Heidari field goals and two touchdown passes from Barkley to Marqise Lee (39 yards) and Brandon Carswell (seven yards). Tailback Curtis McNeal led all ball carriers with 86 yards, and scored USC's final touchdown on a two-yard run.[6]

**(A) Oct. 22—Notre Dame—31–17**

With a sold-out crowd of 80,795 in South Bend, Indiana, gathered on a cool evening, and with a national television audience looking on, the 83rd edition of the "Glamour Game" got underway. The Trojans left this game with their ninth time in the previous ten meetings with the Irish, their fifth straight win in South Bend, and a school record of 14 consecutive non-conference road wins. This was the first time in the history of this iconic series that the Trojans played Notre Dame in South Bend at night, and the latest kickoff in series history (7:30 p.m.).

The 10-point underdog Trojans struck fast, scoring on three of their first four offensive series. On USC's initial drive, Matt Barkley connected with tight end Randall Telfer on a two-yard scoring strike, and Andre Heidari added the extra point. Barkley then struck again through the air, this time to Robert Woods on a three-yard pass. Heidari kicked the extra point to give the Trojans a 14–0 lead at the end of the first quarter. Heidari then extended the USC advantage to 17–0 late in the second quarter with a 25-yard field goal. The Irish then closed the gap to 17–10 by the end of the first half on a 96-yard kickoff return by George Atkinson III, and a 25-yard field by David Ruffer with 21 seconds left.

The Trojans stalled on their opening drive of the second half. The Irish had a possession that started on their own nine-yard line, and after 19 plays, reached the USC one late in the third quarter. On third-and-goal, quarterback Dayne Crist fumbled the snap from center and safety Jawanza Starling picked the loose ball up and ran 80 yards for a touchdown. Heidari added the extra point and USC led, 24–10, going into the fourth quarter.

The Irish shook off the effects of the turnover and scored

early in the fourth quarter on a 25-yard run by running back Jonas Gray, and Ruffer's conversion made it 24–17. Turnovers once again got the best of Notre Dame, as they had a fumble and an interception on their next two series that allowed the Trojans to seal the victory. The Trojans converted a fumble recovery by linebacker Chris Galippo into a 14-yard touchdown pass from Barkley to Robert Woods. Heidari's extra point finished out the scoring with USC up, 31–17. The interception by cornerback Nickell Robey allowed the Trojans to run the clock out.

Matt Barkley continued to perform at a Heisman-Trophy worthy level by completing 24 of 35 pass attempts for 224 yards and three touchdowns. Robert Woods had 12 receptions for 119 yards and one touchdown, and tailback Curtis McNeal ran for 118 yards on 24 carries. This win gave Lane Kiffin the distinction of being the first USC head coach to win on the road against Notre Dame in his first season at the helm of the Trojans.[7]

**(H) Oct. 29—Stanford—48–56**

Despite the loss, this was one of the most exciting games in USC history. It was without a doubt one of the top matchups in their long history against Stanford. The 93,607 at the Coliseum, and a national television audience, definitely got the most out of this one, which saw a new USC record set for most combined points in one game (104). Stanford's 56 points were the most ever scored against USC up to this time in their history. This was also Stanford's third straight win over the Trojans, and the second consecutive time that the outcome of this matchup came down to the final play. With this win, Stanford continued on with the nation's longest winning streak of 16 in a row. Running back Stepfan Taylor's two-yard run with 38 seconds left in regulation, coupled with Eric Whitaker's conversion kick, sent the game into overtime tied at 34–34.

The teams then scored two touchdowns apiece to force a third overtime period. Taylor forced the game into overtime with a touchdown run, and then ended it with a five-yard run. Andrew Luck then threw a two-point conversion pass to Coby Fleener. This battle between the northern and southern regions of California did not lack outstanding offensive performances. The Trojans rang up 432 yards, and were led by Matt Barkley's 284 passing yards and three touchdowns, with two of them coming in overtime. Barkley spread the wealth around on his scoring strikes, connecting with three different receivers. Marqise Lee (28 yards), Robert Woods (15 yards), and Randall Telfer (12 yards), were on the receiving end of Barkley's touchdown passes. Curtis McNeal ran for a game-high 145 yards on 20 carries, and scored on two runs covering 61 and 25 yards. For Stanford, quarterback Andrew Luck showed why he was one of the top college players in the nation, leading his team to 516 yards of total offense. He completed 29 out of 40 pass attempts for 330 yards and three touchdowns. He also ran for a touchdown.[8]

**(A) Nov. 4—Colorado—42–17**

On a chilly Colorado evening, the Trojans won in convincing fashion against one of the Pac-12's new members. Matt Barkley threw for a school record six touchdowns, and USC beat Colorado for the sixth time in as many meetings. After Colorado scored on the game's opening possession, Barkley and the offense ran off 28 straight points to take control of the game by halftime. For the game, Barkley completed 25 out of 39 pass attempts for 318 yards. Robert Woods had nine receptions for 130 yards, and caught two of Barkley's touchdown tosses. Marqise Lee also caught nine passes for 124 yards and two touchdowns. Xavier Grimble and Amir Carlisle were on the receiving end of Barkley's other two touchdown passes. Carlisle also ran for a game-high 90 yards. This game marked the first time that the Trojans had three freshman linebackers starting at the same time in Lamar Dawson, Tre Madden, and Hayes Pullard.[9]

**(H) Nov. 12—Washington—40–17**

By almost the identical score, the Trojans beat another Pac-12 opponent. In doing so, USC broke a two-game losing streak to Washington by opening up a 221–3 halftime advantage, and the Huskies never came close to threatening. This was the 50th time in the history of their series with Washington that USC emerged victorious. Tailback Curtis McNeal ran for 148 yards that included a 79-yard touchdown. As a team, the Trojans compiled 252 rushing yards. Marqise Lee scored a pair of touchdowns on a nine-yard reception and an 88-yard kickoff return. The Trojans had 426 yards of total offense, while the defense held the nation's seventh ranked runner, tailback Chris Polk, to 36 yards.[10]

**(A) Nov. 19—Oregon—38–35**

With a sold out crowd of 59,933 ravenous Oregon fans, cold temperatures in the mid–30's, and the number fourth ranked team in the nation facing them, the Trojans prevailed. In doing so, they knocked Oregon out of any chance at playing for the national championship. The two-touchdown underdog Trojans were led by Matt Barkley, who continued on with his spectacular junior season. He completed 26 out of 34 pass attempts for 323 yards and four touchdowns. Marqise Lee caught eight passes for 187 yards and hauled in Barkley's first touchdown pass of the game from 59 yards out. Robert Woods had a pair of touchdown receptions (12 and four yards), and tight end Randall Telfer caught a five-yard pass from Barkley for USC's final six points, which gave the Trojans a 38–14 lead late in the third quarter. The Ducks then rallied with 21 straight points before a 37-yard field goal with no time left, which would have forced overtime, missed its mark. The loss ended Oregon's 21-game home winning streak (longest in the nation at the time), along with their streaks of 19 straight conference victories and nine straight during the season.[11]

**(H) Nov. 26—UCLA—50–0**

This classic series had its share of heart-stopping finishes. However, this was not one of those times, as the Trojans racked up their largest margin of victory over the Bruins since beating them 52–0 in 1930. With 93,607 in attendance at the Coliseum, the Trojans scored on their first four offensive series. On the game's fourth play, Barkley connected on a 42-yard pass to Marqise Lee for USC's first points. Andre Heidari then connected on the first of his six conversion kicks. The Bruins came right back with a march to the USC goal line on their ensuing possession. A goal line stand stymied UCLA's scoring opportunity, and the Trojans responded with a quick five-play, 98-yard scoring drive. Curtis McNeal made the drive end fast with a 73-yard touchdown run that helped give the Trojans a 14–0 lead at the end of the first quarter.

The Trojans went 92 yards for a score the next time they had the ball. Barkley threw a one-yard pass to tight end Randall

Telfer for a touchdown, and then connected with Xavier Grimble on a two-point conversion pass that made it 22–0 early in the second quarter. On their following series, the Trojans got creative. They faked a field goal, and the result was a three-yard touchdown pass from Barkley to tight end Rhett Ellison that made the score 29–0. Before the first half ended, the Bruins tried to get something going, and reached the USC seven-yard line. The hope of getting any points on this drive ended when safety T.J. McDonald intercepted a pass in the end zone.

The Trojans did not rest on their laurels at the beginning of the second half, scoring on their first three possessions. Lee caught his second touchdown pass of the game, this time from 52 yards out, to start off the second half scoring spree. Roberts Woods capped off a 93-yard drive by catching a Barkley touchdown pass from four yards out to end the third quarter with USC up, 43–0. The Trojans then hit the half-century mark in point production early in the fourth quarter when Barkley and Woods teamed up again on a touchdown, this time covering 41 yards. The Bruins tried to avoid being shut out, and got deep into USC territory late in the game, but lost the ball on downs.

For the game, the Trojans gained 572 yards of offense. Matt Barkley completed 35 of 42 pass attempts for 423 yards and tied a school record that he already owned with six touchdown passes. Marqise Lee had 13 receptions for 224 yards, and Robert Woods caught 12 passes for 113 yards. Curtis McNeal led the USC ground attack with a game-high 124 yards on 12 carries to help him get over the 1,000-yard mark for the season. This was USC's fifth straight win over UCLA, and their seventh straight against them at the Coliseum. It gave the Trojans first place in the Pac-12 South Division, but unfortunately, they could not play for the Pac-12 championship due to being in the final year of an NCAA ban that prohibited them from post-season games. Even though UCLA finished two games behind the Trojans in the South Division, they got the chance to play for the Pac-12 championship instead.[12]

### TEAM LEADERS

RUSHING: Curtis McNeal—1,005 yards on 145 carries
PASSING: Matt Barkley—308 out of 446 attempts for 3,528 yards and 39 touchdowns
RECEIVING: Robert Woods—111 catches for 1,292 yards and 15 touchdowns
SCORING: Andre Heidari—95 points on 50 extra points and 15 field goals
KICKOFF RETURNS: Robert Woods—17 for 393 yards (23.1 avg.)
PUNT RETURNS: Robert Woods—13 for 118 yards (9.1 avg.)
Nickell Robey—12 for 132 yards (11.0 avg.)
PUNTING: Kyle Negrete—39 for 1,562 yards (40.1 avg.)
INTERCEPTIONS: T.J. McDonald—3 for 37 yards
TACKLES: Dion Bailey—81
Hayes Pullard—81
SACKS: Nick Perry—9.5

## *2012*

HEAD COACH: Lane Kiffin
ASSISTANT COACHES: Aaron Ausmus, John Baxter, James Cregg, Scottie Hazelton, Clay Helton, Shawn Howe, Monte Kiffin, Tee Martin, Justin Mesa, Ed Orgeron, Kennedy Polamalu, Marvin Sanders
TEAM CAPTAINS: Matt Barkley, Khaled Holmes, T.J. McDonald, Nickell Robey
RECORD: 7–6 overall (5–4 in Pac-12 Conference)
(Ranked 58th best record in college football out of 124 teams)
FINISH IN CONFERENCE: 2nd place in South Division of Pac-12 Conference
FINISH IN NATIONAL POLLS: No ranking in Top 25
POINTS SCORED PER GAME: 32.1 to rank 40th out of 124 teams
POINTS ALLOWED PER GAME: 24.3 to rank 40th

### Schedule and Highlights

**(H) Sept. 1—Hawaii—49–10**
USC#1

The Trojans wasted little time proving that their number one ranking was no fluke. On the first offensive play of the game, Matt Barkley threw to Marqise Lee for a 75-yard touchdown with 93,607 looking on at the Los Angeles Memorial Coliseum. That opened the scoring floodgates for USC, who came into the contest with their first number one ranking since 2008. The score was 35–0 by the half, and the Trojans never let the Warriors remotely get close in a convincing 49–10 affair. Heisman Trophy frontrunner Barkley staked his claim on college's football's coveted prize by completing 23 of 38 pass attempts for 347 yards and four touchdowns. His other scoring strikes went to Robert Woods (20 and 2 yards), and Randall Telfer (11 yards). The Trojans also got six-pointers from Hayes Pullard on a 27-yard interception return, a 31-yard run by Silas Redd, a 28-yard field goal from Andre Heidari, and an exciting 100-yard kickoff return by Lee. Lee became only the second player in USC history to cover that many yards on a kickoff return. His incredible return just added to what was a brilliant performance turned in by the Trojan receiver, who hauled in 10 receptions for 187 yards and a touchdown. With this victory, USC remained a perfect 8–0 against the University of Hawaii dating back to 1930.[1]

**(A) Sept. 8—Syracuse—42–29**
USC#2

Matt Barkley and his receiving dynamic duo of Marqise Lee and Robert Woods once again amazed the masses with their abilities. When it was all said and done in East Rutherford, New Jersey, the number two ranked Trojans dismantled Syracuse, 42–29. Barkley completed 23 of 30 passes for 187 yards and a school record six touchdown passes. Lee finished with 11 receptions for 66 yards and three six-pointers, while Woods caught 10 passes for 93 yards and two touchdowns. Woods also amassed 200 yards of all-purpose yards. Xavier Grimble was on the receiving end of Barkley's other touchdown toss. Tailback Silas Redd led the USC ground attack with a game-high 107 yards on 15 carries. This was the fourth time that USC played Syracuse, and the Trojans prevailed each time.[2]

**(A) Sept. 15—Stanford—14–21**
USC#2—STAN#21

A trip to rival Stanford ended with one team emerging unbeaten. Unfortunately for Trojan fans, the Stanford Cardinal remained undefeated with a 21–14 victory over the number two-ranked team in the country. Stepfan Taylor ran for 153 yards and two scores, and a Josh Nunes to Zach Ertz 37-yard touchdown pass proved to be the game winner for Stanford. This marked the fourth straight time that Stanford came out victorious against USC. In this heart-breaking loss that stymied USC's national championship hopes, Matt Barkley threw for 254 yards on 20 of 41 pass completions, but suffered two interceptions in front of a sold out Stanford Stadium crowd that broke out into a frenzy at the conclusion of the game, rushing the field to celebrate the Cardinal starting off their third straight season at 3–0. Despite the loss, Marqise Lee had eight receptions for 100 yards, and led the Trojans with 178 all-purpose yards.[3]

**(H) Sept. 22—California—27–9**
USC#13

This marked the 100th time that USC faced California, and this victory gave the Trojans their 65th in the series that began in 1915. This also was the Trojans ninth straight win over the Bears. Cal came into the matchup averaging 34 points a game, but was limited to only three field goals, and just 77 yards on the ground. The defense recorded nine sacks, with defensive end Morgan Breslin leading the way with 3.5. Meanwhile, the Trojans compiled 488 total yards, and received two touchdowns from Marqise Lee on 11 and three-yard scoring strikes from Matt Barkley. Tailback Silas Redd ran for a 33-yard touchdown, and Andre Heidari kicked two field goals after missing two games with a knee injury. Barkley completed 22 out of 34 pass attempts for 192 yards, Lee had 11 receptions for 94 yards, and Redd ran for a game-high 158 yards on 21 carries. Curtis McNeal also topped the century mark in rushing, gaining 115 yards on 10 carries.[4]

**(A) Oct. 4—Utah—38–28**
USC#13

This was USC's first visit to Salt Lake City, Utah, since 1917, but they had to harder a bit harder on this trip than on the previous one, when they easily beat Utah 51–0. Utah got out to a 14–0 lead with just three minutes expired in the first quarter, and held a 21–10 advantage in the second quarter. The Trojans then ran off 28 straight points by the fourth quarter. Matt Barkley completed 76.7 percent of his passes by connecting on 23 of 30 attempts for 303 yards and three touchdowns. Marqise Lee had 12 receptions for 192 yards, covering 83 of those yards on a touchdown catch. Randall Telfer (23 yards) and Robert Woods (six yards), caught Barkley's other touchdown tosses. Silas Redd ran for a game-high 77 yards, and opened USC's scoring in the first quarter with a three-yard run. Cornerback Nickell Robey returned an interception 38 yards for USC's final touchdown, and Andre Heidari kicked a 32-yard field goal plus five extra points. This was USC's 186th straight game in which they scored, and it tied a school record.[5]

**(A) Oct. 13—Washington—24–14**
USC#11

When Andre Heidari kicked a 23-yard field goal on their first possession of the game, it marked the 187th straight game that the Trojans scored, setting a new school record in the process. The Trojans also received points from Silas Redd (11-yard run), Xavier Grimble (18-yard pass from Matt Barkley), and Anthony Brown (21-yard return of a blocked punt). Redd was USC's offensive star with 155 yards rushing on a mere six carries, to easily earn game-high honors in that category.[6]

**(H) Oct. 20—Colorado—50–6**
USC#11

In the gambling Mecca of Las Vegas, Nevada, "Lucky Seven" is a very popular brand of slot machine. However, in the Land of Troy, that number is also lucky when dealing with the Colorado Buffaloes. This was the seventh time in their history that USC played Colorado, and following this game, they remained a perfect 7–0 against them. This was also the greatest margin of victory posted by the Trojans in those seven games. With 83,274 inside the Coliseum, Matt Barkley was virtually unstoppable when throwing the ball. He completed a Pac-12 single-game accuracy rating record of 95.0 percent by connecting on 19 of 20 attempts. That record was based on a minimum of 20 pass attempts. He just missed the NCAA record by .8 percent. Barkley threw for 298 yards and tied his own school record of six touchdown passes in one game, five of which came in the first half to tie another school record for most scoring strikes in one half. As if that were not enough for him on this day, Barkley set a new Pac-12 record with 102 career touchdown passes, breaking the old mark of 99 set by former Trojan quarterback Matt Leinart. Robert Woods was Barkley's main target, catching eight passes for 132 yards and four touchdowns (39, 29, 17, and three yards). For his efforts, Woods also broke records. His four touchdown receptions set a new single-game school record, and tied the Pac-12 mark. Through this game, Woods had 220 career receptions, which made him USC's new all-time record holder in that category, surpassing Dwayne Jarrett's mark of 216. Marqise Lee had six receptions for 103 yards, including a 55-yard touchdown grab from Barkley. Barkley's other scoring strikes went to Xavier Grimble from eight yards out. Barkley's backup, Max Wittek, got an opportunity to throw his first touchdown pass as a Trojan to tailback D.J. Morgan, for the first six-pointer of his college career as well. Wittek's touchdown pass gave USC seven for the game, which set a new school record for most in one game. This game set another milestone, as it marked the 300th win for USC in the month of October.[7]

**(A) Oct. 27—Arizona—36–39**
USC#10

After being down 10–0 at the end of the first quarter, the Trojans came back to take a 28–13 lead in the third quarter. The Wildcats, led by quarterback Matt Scott, rallied from a 15-point deficit from that stage on, scoring 26 straight points in the process, en route to their eighth all-time victory over the Trojans. This loss ended USC's five-game winning streak in Tucson, Arizona, and it was the sixth consecutive time that an Arizona-USC game was won by a touchdown or less. Scott completed 27 of 50 pass attempts for 369 yards and three touchdowns. He added 100 yards rushing and one touchdown, in one of the best individual games ever against the Trojans. Despite the close defeat, the Trojans also had some incredible performances in this wild west showdown that USC compile 618 yards of offense and Arizona 588. Marqise Lee was simply amazing, as he caught 16 passes for 345 yards and two touchdowns. His 345 receiving yards set new school and Pac-12 records, and gave him the fifth highest total in NCAA history. He gained 123 yards on three kickoff returns and rushed for one yard to give him 469 all-purpose yards, which was the second highest total in NCAA history. Robert Woods joined Lee in the record books after catching nine passes for 93 yards. This devastating receiving tandem set a new USC record for most receiving yards by two players in one game (438), and tied another school record for most receptions by two players combined (25). Matt Barkley got into the record book yet again, this time by setting a new single-game mark with 493 passing yards. His 497 total yards set another USC record, his third 400-yard passing game tied a school record, and he broke a Pac-12 record for most touchdowns passing and rushing combined (111).[8]

**(H) Nov. 3—Oregon—51–62**
USC#18—ORE#2

The best way to sum up this scoring fest is WOW!!! The combined 113 points set a new USC record, Oregon posted the most points ever allowed by the Trojans, and USC's 51 points were the most ever scored by them in a losing effort. This marked Oregon's 12th straight win after losing to USC the year before. It was also their 13th consecutive road win, and 22nd straight of scoring 30 or more points. The teams combined for 1,345 yards of offensive production, and Oregon's 730 yards set a school record and a 66-year old USC opponent record. Other opponent records that fell in this game were most touchdowns scored (nine), points after touchdowns (eight), and first downs (37). The Trojans surrendered 426 rushing yards, which was the most by an opponent since Texas A&M in the 1977 Bluebonnet Bowl. On an individual basis, Oregon running back Kenjon Barner set USC individual opponent records with most rushing yards (321), most touchdowns (five), and most points scored (30). Freshman quarterback Marcus Mariota tied a USC opponent record for most touchdown passes against USC with four. Kicker Rob Beard's eight conversion kicks set the record for most points after touchdown by one player.

On the Trojans' side, records also fell. Marqise Lee's 251 yards on kickoff returns set a Pac-12 record, his eight kickoff returns set a school record, and his 408 all-purpose yards ranked him 16th all-time on the NCAA list. He also had 12 receptions for 157 yards and two touchdowns. Matt Barkley tied a school record with 35 pass completions. He threw 54 passes, gained 484 yards, and finished with five touchdowns. When his big day was over, Barkley was the new Pac-12 career record holder for completions, total offense, and became the first player in Pac-12 history to have 2,500 or more yards of total offense for four seasons. Nelson Agholor chipped in with six receptions for 162 yards and a touchdown, Robert Woods had six catches for 71 yards and one touchdown, and Silas Redd rushed for a team-high 92 yards on 18 carries and two touchdowns. A three-yard pass from Barkley to Randall Telfer, and a 39-yard field goal and six conversion kicks by Andre Heidari, accounted for USC's other points.[9]

**(H) Nov. 10—Arizona State—38–17**
USC#21

The Trojans avenged their previous loss to the Sun Devils after blowing open a close game in the third and fourth quarters. Curtis McNeal lived up to the proud tailback tradition established generations earlier at USC by rushing for 163 yards on 31 carries. With the Trojans trailing by three points in the third quarter, McNeal exploded for two touchdown runs covering five and 27 yards, and caught a 22-yard pass from Matt Barkley, to help USC pull away at the end. Barkley completed 20 of 33 pass attempts for 222 yards and three touchdowns. Beside the one to McNeal, Barkley's other scoring strikes went to Marqise Lee (80 yards), who finished with 10 receptions for 161 yards, and Xavier Grimble (four yards). Andre Heidari scored USC's other points on a 26-yard field goal and five conversion kicks. The USC defense recorded seven sacks, and linebacker Lamar Dawson had a team-high 11 tackles and one interception.[10]

**(A) Nov. 17—UCLA—28–38**
USC#21—UCLA#17

This marked the 82nd time these teams faced each other in football, with USC winning 46 times, including the last five in a row, and 12 out of the previous 13 games. As in many previous years, this clash determined a conference champion. In this edition of the "Battle of Los Angeles," the winner would secure the South Division title of the Pac-12, and head to the conference championship game. The Bruins did not forget the awful pounding they took one year earlier at the hands of the Trojans, and set out to break the dominance displayed by USC over them in recent meetings.

The Bruins made their presence felt early by intercepting a pass on the game's first play. They quickly capitalized on the turnover when quarterback Brett Hundley scored on a one-yard run. Ka'imi Fairbairn added the extra point and UCLA had a 7–0 lead. Fairbairn extended UCLA's lead to 10–0 on the Bruins' next possession when he capped an 84-yard drive with a 23-yard field goal. The Trojans continued to dig themselves deeper into despair when they lost a fumble on the third play of their ensuing possession in their own territory. That turnover resulted in a 17-yard touchdown pass from Hundley to tight end Joseph Fauria late in the first quarter. Fairbairn's extra point kick sent the Bruins into the second quarter with a commanding 17–0 lead.

The Bruins were not through just yet. On their next offensive series, they went 74 yards, and it was capped off by a 16-yard run from tailback Johnathan Franklin with 7:38 left in the first half. Fairbairn's conversion then gave UCLA what appeared to be an insurmountable lead of 24–0. However, in the history of this series, comebacks were commonplace.

In an attempt to create another great comeback, the Trojans rallied for 14 points on their next two possessions. Matt Barkley got USC on the board with a 33-yard pass to Nelson Agholor, and Andre Heidari kicked the extra point. On the following drive, it was Barkley's arm that once again lit up the scoreboard, this time on a two-yard pass to tight end Randall Telfer. With Heidari's conversion, the first half ended with the Bruins' lead cut to 24–14, and momentum on USC's side.

The Trojans got even closer to coming all the way back just three plays into the third quarter. Defensive tackle George Uko got the scoring honors when he recovered a UCLA fumble in the end zone. Heidari missed the extra point attempt, but the Trojans had cut what appeared to be a massive deficit to 24–20.

The Bruins stopped the 20-point surge of their opponent by partially blocking a punt, and used that to their advantage. Hundley ended that drive with his second touchdown run of the game, this time from three yards out. With Fairbairn's conversion, the Bruins were up, 31–20, at the end of the third quarter.

The Trojans made one final assault on the end zone that got them to within three points midway through the fourth quarter. Barkley threw his third touchdown pass of the game, with Marqise Lee on the receiving end of this one from 14 yards out. Robert Woods then caught a two-point conversion pass to make the score 31–28. The Bruins then locked the game down with an 83-yard drive that ended with Franklin running 29 yards for a touchdown. With Fairbairn's extra point, UCLA had the game under control with a 38–28 lead and 4:02 remaining in the fourth quarter. It appeared that Los Angeles' weather history was on UCLA's side. During the second half, the game was played mostly with rain coming down. On two other occasions when it rained during a USC-UCLA game (1946, 1961), the Bruins also prevailed.

This game was an offensive showcase that saw USC gain 513 yards and UCLA 406. The Bruins had solid performances from Johnathan Franklin, who rushed for a game-high 171 yards, Brett Hundley completed 22 of 30 pass attempts for 234 yards, and Shaquelle Evans had eight receptions for 114 yards. For the Trojans, Barkley completed 20 of 38 pass attempts for 301 yards and three touchdowns before a shoulder injury late in the game forced him to the sidelines. Curtis McNeal ran for 161 yards on 21 carries, and Marqise Lee had nine receptions for 158 yards and one touchdown.[11]

**(H) Nov. 24—Notre Dame—13–22**

ND#1

Five field goals and two goal line stands in the fourth quarter prevented the Trojans from beating the top-ranked team in the country in the 84th edition of the "Glamour Game" with a sold-out crowd of 93,607 in the Coliseum. This marked the first time that the Irish came into this game ranked number one since 1989, and the first time they came in undefeated against USC since 1993.

Notre Dame's Kyle Brindza tied a USC opponent record with five field goals. His first came on a 27-yarder in the first quarter on Notre Dame's opening series to give the Irish a lead they would not relinquish. Notre Dame's only touchdown of the game came late in the first quarter on a nine-yard run by Theo Riddick, who finished the game with 146 yards on 20 carries. Brindza's extra point gave the Irish a 10–0 lead going into the second quarter.

Max Wittek got the call at quarterback for USC in place of the injured Matt Barkley. He responded to the challenge by getting the Trojans on the board in the second quarter. He threw an 11-yard touchdown pass to Robert Woods, and Andre Heidari's extra point cut the deficit to 10–7. The remainder of the game became a kicking duel, as Brindza kicked a pair of field goals from 29 and 52 yards out, while Heidari had a 39-yarder, to make it a 16–10 Notre Dame advantage at the end of the first half.

The only points produced in the third quarter came on a 33-yard Brindza field goal, to send the Irish in to the fourth quarter with a 19–10 lead. Heidari got the Trojans their final points of the regular season on a 21-yard field goal, and then Brindza added his fifth field goal of the game from 19 yards out to complete the scoring at 22–13. The Trojans did threaten twice in the fourth quarter, getting inside the Notre Dame five-yard line. The first time they salvaged the drive with Heidari's 21-yard three-pointer, but the second attempt to get into the end zone was stopped after four attempts at first-and-goal from the one with under three minutes remaining.

The Irish finished the game with 439 total yards compared to USC's 281. Wittek's starting role as USC quarterback saw him complete 14 out of 23 pass attempts for 186 yards. Playing in his final regular season game as a Trojan, receiver Robert Woods caught seven passes for 92 and USC's only touchdown.[12]

**Sun Bowl, (N) Dec. 31—Georgia Tech—7–21**

The season began as a Hollywood feel good movie, with the Trojans ranked number one and led by an All-American-type Heisman Trophy candidate at quarterback. However, on the final day of the year, quarterback Matt Barkley was reduced to watching the game from the sideline due to a shoulder injury suffered in the UCLA game. As a team, the Trojans finished well out of the race for any national recognition after a 21–7 loss to the Yellow Jackets ended USC's season at 7–6.

With a crowd of 47,922 in attendance at Sun Bowl Stadium in El Paso, Texas, Georgia Tech's Tevin Washington threw for a touchdown and ran for another to lead his team to a victory that allowed the Yellow Jackets to finish at 7–7 and end a seven game losing streak in bowl contests. Redshirt freshman Max Wittek, who replaced Barkley, threw a touchdown and three interceptions in his bowl game debut. Silas Reed caught Wittek's lone scoring strike from nine yards out, and also ran for 88 yards on 17 carries.[13]

### TEAM LEADERS

RUSHING: Silas Redd—905 yards on 167 carries
PASSING: Matt Barkley—246 out of 387 attempts for 3,273 yards and 36 touchdowns
RECEIVING: Marqise Lee—118 catches for 1,721 yards and 14 touchdowns
SCORING: Marqise Lee—90 points on 15 touchdowns
KICKOFF RETURNS: Marqise Lee—30 for 856 yards and 1 touchdown (28.5 avg.)
PUNT RETURNS: Robert Woods—16 for 61 yards (3.8 avg.)
PUNTING: Kyle Negrete—44 for 1,879 yards (42.7 avg.)
INTERCEPTIONS: Dion Bailey—4 for 4 yards
TACKLES: T.J. McDonald—112
SACKS: Morgan Breslin—13

*Two*

# All-Time Trojan Greats

## *Marcus Allen*

Abraham Lincoln High School in San Diego was originally built in 1949 and torn down in 2003 to make way for a new one. Despite the change, the memories of Marcus Allen's scholastic career carried over when the new Lincoln opened in 2007.

The sports legacy of Marcus Allen began when he was 10 years old in southeast San Diego. At that age, Allen decided that he wanted to play baseball, and then it was on to the gridiron where a star was born, and eventually led to him becoming one of the most revered athletes to come out of the San Diego area. At Lincoln High School, Allen's presence, donning the green and white of the Hornets, drew countless praise from all those fortunate enough to play with him, but extremely unfortunate for those opposing him.

At the beginning of his scholastic career in the mid–1970s, Allen was placed at safety, where he once made 30 unassisted tackles in one game. Lincoln coach, Vic Player, placed the offense into Allen's capable hands when he added quarterback responsibilities to his duties at the start of his junior season. The addition proved to be a sensational move, as Allen emerged as one of the top schoolboy stars by his senior season of 1977. He passed for 1,900 yards, ran for 1,198 more, and led Lincoln to the 1977 San Diego County championship. In the 34–6 victory over Kearney High School in the title game, Allen scored every one of Lincoln's touchdowns. He ran for touchdowns that covered 85, 30, 20, and 10 yards, and also scored on an interception return of 60 yards.

After the football seasons were over, Allen's talents were taken indoors, where he earned All-CIF accolades as a guard on the basketball team. During his time at Lincoln, Allen earned three letters each in football and basketball, and was selected as the winner of the 1977–78 California High School Athlete of the Year Award. He also was selected to the high school All-America Team.

Needless to say, the talents that Allen possessed attracted much attention from college recruiters. However, the final decision was an easy one, as he wanted to become a USC Trojan, like his boyhood idol O.J. Simpson. At first, the coaching staff wanted Allen as a defensive back, but just four days into his freshman year, he was switched to tailback, where he served as a backup. As a sophomore, he was moved over to fullback to block for tailback Charles White. In his first day of practice as a fullback, Allen broke his nose, but remained steadfast in his task. By the end of the 1979 season, he had helped clear the way for White on runs that earned him the Heisman Trophy.[1]

With White's departure for the NFL after the '79 season, the USC tailback tradition was about to be presented to Marcus Allen, and he not only accepted it, but established records that made him a collegiate legend. Throughout the 1980 season, Allen piled up enough rushing yards to finish as the nation's second-leading ground gainer with 1,563 yards, but the best was yet to come.

John Robinson was USC's head coach during Allen's stay on campus, and had proclaimed that Allen was the greatest player he ever witnessed. This sterling comment by a man who had seen many excellent players cross his path, was cemented in what transpired throughout the 1981 season. When the final play of the final game of USC's '81 season was recorded for posterity, Allen had turned in the greatest single-season rushing performance in NCAA Division I history. He became the first to break the 2,000-yard rushing barrier, finishing with 2,342 yards. He averaged 219.9 yards rushing per game, and had eight games during the year in which he topped the 200-yard mark. He led the nation in scoring with 12.5 points per game, and was an obvious runaway winner when it came to deciding on who the 1981 Heisman Trophy recipient should be. He also brought home All-American honors, his second All-Pac-10 selection, and other top player of the year awards such as the Maxwell Trophy and the Walter Camp Foundation Player of Year. He was so impressive, that the university retired his #33 in honor of his accomplishments.

Up to this point in his football career, Allen had conquered all levels. It was then time for him to take on the ultimate level of competition, the National Football League, where the Los Angeles Raiders chose Allen in the first round of the 1982 college draft. He quickly proved that his success on the high school and college levels was no fluke, as he won the 1982 NFL Rookie of the Year Award. Over the course of an illustrious professional career that ended in 1997, Allen became the only player in history in be awarded the Heisman Trophy, NFL Rookie of the Year, NFL Player of the Year, Super Bowl Most Valuable Player, and to be enshrined in both the College and Pro Football Halls of Fame.[2]

His versatility as a runner gave Allen the opportunity to conform to whatever the offense needed at the time. He had the great ability to switch from being a finesse runner to a power back, and had the instincts at reading blocks and blasting through small holes for big gains. He also was regarded as one of the greatest short yardage backs, especially when near the goal line. When the final tallies were in on the professional career of Marcus Allen, they were breathtaking. He became the first to break both the 10,000-yard rushing and the 5,000-yard receiving barriers. He rushed for 12,243 yards and 123 touchdowns, and caught 587 passes for 5,411 yards and 21 touchdowns.[3]

## *Jon Arnett*

To strive and work hard is the driving force behind someone who toils at the task they perform. Many of those who passed through Manual Arts High School in Los Angeles lived up to their moniker of "the Toilers." From Medal of Honor recipients, to Academy Award winners, and many other success stories from all walks of life, Manual Arts' proud history is hard to match.

One who helped elevate the Purple & Gray to stellar accolades in the field of athletics was Jon Arnett from the class of 1952. "Jaguar Jon" was a 5-11, 197-pound natural athlete that possessed all the physical tools needed to be a successful running back. Balance, breakaway speed, and elusive moves, all made Arnett an easy choice when the voting for the 1951 Los Angeles High School Player of the Year Award was being decided.

When it came to continuing his education and football career, Arnett stayed in the neighborhood, and his fellow residents of the City of Angels were happy to see the local product dazzle and awe on Saturday afternoons. While at USC, Arnett's abilities on the LA Coliseum turf, and those across the college football landscape, allowed him to still be regarded as one of the greatest to ever don the Cardinal and Gold of the Trojans.

From 1954 through 1956, "Jaguar Jon" was the team's premier go-to man. In 1954, he led the Trojans in rushing (601 yards), scoring (55 points), pass interceptions (3), and punt return yardage (129). The following year, he once again topped the Trojans in most team categories while tallying a conference-leading 108 points on 15 touchdowns and 18 extra points.

One blemish that hurt Arnett in his time at USC occurred before his senior year. At the time, he was a heavy favorite to win the Heisman Trophy, but an illegal payment scandal thwarted any hopes of that ever happening. The Pacific Coast Conference commissioner, Victor O. Schmidt, presented allegations that Arnett and other senior players from four other PCC teams had accepted cash from boosters to pay for schooling, books, and rent. It was ruled that the players mentioned would be limited to playing in only five games throughout the 1956 season.[1]

Despite the harsh blow to his Heisman chances, it still came as no surprise when Arnett once again dominated USC's offensive categories in his senior season of 1956. He played in the first five games of the season, and was leading the nation with 150 yards rushing per game before having to forfeit the remainder of the year. However, his efforts in the first half of the season did not go in vain. His talents in those five games were too great to ignore, and Arnett was chosen as an All-American and winner of the Voit Trophy, given to most outstanding player on the Pacific Coast, in both 1955 and 1956. He also added the 1956 Pop Warner Award to his credit, which signified him as the most valuable senior on the Pacific Coast. Arnett was a three-year letterman (1954–56), a two-time all-conference selection (1955–56), and elected team captain for the '56 campaign. In three years as a Trojan running back, Arnett amassed 1,898 yards in 336 carries for a 5.7 average, and scored an overall total of 30 touchdowns. If his football skills were not enough, Arnett took to the track in the spring, and did not disappoint in that endeavor. In 1954, he placed second in the long jump at the NCAA track meet to help USC win the team championship. The Trojans then defended their team title the following year.

When the 1957 NFL draft came up, it came as no surprise when Jon Arnett's name was announced near the top. He remained in his native Los Angeles, as the Rams selected him in the first round, and second overall pick of that year's draft. From 1957 through 1963, Arnett continued to dazzle on a football field, and was selected to five straight Pro Bowls (1957–61). He then finished out his professional career with the Chicago Bears from 1964 through the 1966 season. While with the Bears, Arnett played for the legendary coach George "Papa Bear" Halas, who was one of the founders of the NFL, and a man who saw every player from the 1920s to the early 1980s perform. With his eyes cast upon all the talent over those 60-plus years, Halas honored Jon Arnett by stating that he was the best running back he ever saw. In 1994 Arnett was honored with induction into the USC Athletic Hall of Fame, and seven years later, he was enshrined into the College Football Hall of Fame.[2]

## *Johnny Baker*

In front of every great running team are the trench warriors that open holes for backs on their trek to glory and headlines. The "Thundering Herd" of USC fame gained their fair share of media attention in the national dailies, in addition to everlasting lore in the Land of Troy, thanks in large part to the blocking prowess of 5-10, 185 pound guard John "Bake" Baker, the pride of Denison, Iowa.

The future Trojan lineman was a product of the Hawkeye State, and attended part of his scholastic days in Iowa at Greenfield High School. He then finished up his time at Kingsburg High School, located in the city of Kingsburg, California, which is part of Fresno County. After walking onto the USC campus to further his education and football career, it did not take Baker long to establish himself as a competent lineman under legendary Trojan mentor Howard Jones. He was also considered one of the fastest linemen to ever play on the collegiate level. Playing along side the likes of Tay Brown, Ernie Smith, and Aaron Rosenberg, Baker helped this Trojan wall of blockers become one of the best to grace the history of college game days. During the time span of 1929 through 1931, this collection of linemen helped the Trojans compile a 37.5-point per game average and capture the 1931 national championship. En route to that title, Baker's services were not just limited to blowing open holes for others to gain major time in the newspapers. Against

Notre Dame in 1931, it was Baker who earned the biggest headlines, when he kicked a last minute field goal to put the Trojans on top in a 16–14 win that snapped the Fighting Irish's 26-game winning streak.

The Trojans had a 28–5 record while Baker was a main part of the squad, and won two conference titles in addition to the national crown. He earned three letters in football, and was a consensus All-American in 1931. After hanging up his #30 USC jersey, Baker went into coaching, predominately on the college level. Much of his post-USC career centered around the Sacramento, California area, where he died at age 72 on February 6, 1979. He was inducted posthumously into the College Football Hall of Fame in 1983.[1]

## *Roy Baker*

America in 1920s has been dubbed "the Jazz Age," "the Decade of Decadence," and "the Lawless Decade," and all have come to represent a wild, free wheeling existence consisting of good times and bootleg liquor. The decade also came to be known as "the Golden Age of Sports," with athletes from all types of competitions earning accolades and the admiration from the American public.

It was during this time that the emergence of USC football captured the attention of the college gridiron scene, thanks in large part to the dynamic talents of Roy "Bullet" Baker.

The town of Casper, Wyoming, is located near the Laramie Mountain Range along the North Platte River. It was in this surrounding that Roy Marion Baker was born on November 4, 1900.

Baker eventually migrated to California, and attended Long Beach Poly High School, where he won the 1918 California High School Football Player of the Year Award. The school has long earned a reputation as a hotbed for future Trojan football players, and Baker's talents as a prep star got the Poly pipeline to the Land of Troy started in the early stages of the Roaring Twenties. The 5-8, 180-pounder, originally from "the Cowboy State," then went on to become one of USC's first standout performers. Along with Howard "Hobo" Kincaid, Baker made up a running tandem that became USC's first explosive backfield. Baker's speed left many opponents dazed, and it earned him the nickname of "Bullet."

With Baker dazzling the opposition with his quickness, the Trojans used that weapon to carry themselves into their first bowl appearance following the 1922 season. In the 1923 Rose Bowl against Penn State, Baker ran for 123 yards and a touchdown to help propel the Trojans to a 14–3 victory in their inaugural post season experience.

Following his days as a collegiate star, Baker took a shot in the professional ranks. He played with the New York Yankees of the upstart American Football League in 1926, and then played in the NFL with the Green Bay Packers, Chicago Cardinals, Staten Island Stapletons, and the St. Louis Gunners, where he also served as coach in 1932. He was a member of the Packers' NFL championship team in 1929, and he passed away on June 18, 1961 at age 60 in Long Beach, California.[1]

## *Damon Bame*

It only seemed fitting that Damon Bame played on a high school team nicknamed the Dynamiters. Throughout the history of USC football, there have been many linebackers whose exploits were nothing short of magnificent. Damon Bame was one of those linebackers that hammered his way to illustrious heights, while patrolling the defense waiting to inflict punishment on opposing ballcarriers. At 5-11, 192-pounds, Bame might not have appeared to match up physically with other All-American linebackers that have added to USC's legacy, however, one would be hard pressed to find amongst them a linebacker that hit harder.

A native of Oklahoma, Bame moved to California and attended Glendale High School, the home of the red and black-clad Dynamiters. Glendale's colors might have been red and black, but over the course of a game, the opposition left the field black and blue after coming in contact with Bame. For his efforts on the prep level, he was honored with selection onto the All-California Interscholastic Federation (CIF) team.[1]

Bame remained in the area of his high school by attending Glendale Junior College. As a member of the Vaqueros under the coaching reins of Mike Giddings and Don Bennett, Bame earned Junior College All-America honors in 1960 and 1961. Regarded as one of the greatest defenders to suit up for Glendale, he helped the program improve from a dismal 1–8 in 1959 to a combined 16–3 record during his All-American seasons.[2]

His solid reputation earned Bame an opportunity with the Trojans starting in 1962. It was a perfect time to join the USC football program, as they were about to embark on a journey to a spotless record that was culminated by being 1962 national champions. With Bame at linebacker, the defense shut out three opponents and allowed a mere 55 points overall during the regular season.[3]

From his middle linebacker position, Bame had incredible instincts when it came to seeking out the ball carrier. He would get to wherever the action was, and when he arrived, it was to deliver a bone-jarring tackle.[4] His two seasons at USC were met with awesome results, as he earned All-Conference and All-American recognition in 1962 and 1963. He was also a two-time winner of the USC Lineman of the Year Award. In addition to his stellar play at linebacker, Bame also served the Trojans as an offensive guard.

It was hard to fathom, but this talented keg of dynamite wearing #64 for the Trojans went undrafted by the professional ranks. Instead of playing, Bame took his football knowledge and went into a coaching career. Bame's coaching career included stops at USC, where he worked with the freshman team before becoming the youngest defensive coordinator in the college ranks at age 22 for San Jose State. He also coached on the college level at Long Beach State and New Mexico before getting a chance in the pros with the Hawaiians of the World Football League, a team based in Honolulu in the mid–1970s. He then returned to the high school level in California, serving as head coach at El Segundo High School, and assisting at two others.[5]

## *Chip Banks*

From the 1950s through the mid–1980s, the presence of tough disciplinarian, David Dupree, was felt by all of those who fastened on a chinstrap. As football coach at Lucy C. Laney High School in Augusta, Georgia, Dupree led the red and grey Wildcats to a 209–60–13 record spanning 26 years. Regional and state championships added to Dupree's legacy, as did having eight of his charges make it into the professional ranks. One of them, William (Chip) Banks, stopped off at USC on his way to the National Football League, and while there, added to the proud tradition of Trojans' football.[1]

Born on September 18, 1959, in the city of Lawton, Oklahoma, Banks established himself as a top-rated performer in Georgia. His impact on the field was so great, that it was felt clear across the country in Los Angeles. During John Robinson's tenure as head coach of the Trojans, Georgia had been extremely kind to him. Multiple players from the "Peach State," such as Joey and Keith Browner, Walt Underwood, and August Curley, had performed for the Cardinal & Gold at a high level.[2] Banks not only added his name to that roll call of honor, but also set a standard of excellence all for himself.

During his time as a star linebacker at USC, Banks earned four letters in football, played on the national championship team in 1978, was selected as a two-time All-Pac-10 linebacker (1980–81), and capped off his college career by being named to the 1981 All-America Team. The Trojans posted a 40–6–2 record during his time as a fierce tackler. In 1980, Banks led the conference-best Trojans' defense in tackles and tackles for losses. The following year, he topped the team in interceptions with four. In his four seasons as a Trojan, Banks recorded 365 tackles, 33 of which were for a loss of 197 yards, and picked off eight passes.[3]

The 6-5, 230-pound defensive menace did not have to wait long to find out what his post-college days were going to entail. The Cleveland Browns made that decision an easy one for Banks, as they selected him in the first round, and the third overall pick, of the 1982 college draft. He then went on to have a solid professional career that lasted from 1982 through 1993. He earned the 1982 NFL Defensive Rookie of the Year Award, and four trips to the Pro Bowl. He played with the Browns (1982–86), San Diego Chargers (1987), and Indianapolis Colts (1989–93).

## *Matt Barkley*

Matt Barkley had a tremendous interest in history. Ironically, the quarterback not only loved history, but had the opportunity to claim his place among the elite in the long and proud heritage of Trojan football.

The path that took Barkley to prominence in the annals of USC football history began with his birth on September 8, 1990 in the high-end, ocean community of Newport Beach, some 45 miles south of the USC campus. It was among these beautiful Orange County surroundings that made Newport Beach one of the most idyllic cities in California, where Barkley displayed traits of athleticism from early on. At a mere eight months, he was already walking. By the age of one, he was capable of riding on a boogie board, and at three years old, he could ride a bicycle without the assistance of training wheels.[1] After conquering the physical side of life, Barkley switched to the other side of the spectrum, teaching himself to read by age five. His incredible display of intelligence gained him entry into Huntington Beach's Pegasus School for gifted students.[2]

Barkley began playing football in the sixth grade, and like other successful ventures throughout his young existence, he quickly dominated the sport. He assumed the starting quarterback position, and never relinquished that status whenever he was able to suit up for a game.[3]

California's Orange County earned a solid reputation as being a satellite for the USC football program and a breeding ground for quarterbacks. It almost seemed that it was Barkley's destiny to lead the Trojans' offense. In addition to being a talented quarterback from an early age on, and coming from Orange County, he had cardinal and gold running through his veins, as his father attended USC and was an All-American water polo player during his time there.[4]

Mater Dei High School is also one of the reasons for Orange County's distinction of being a football hotbed. It has been dubbed "Quarterback High" for its lineage of prep signal callers that have gone on to great heights, including Heisman Trophy winners John Haurte and Matt Leinart. The Scarlet & Gray Monarchs have enjoyed decades of success, with a great deal of the victories piled up under the leadership of long-time head coach Bruce Rollinson, whose collegiate pedigree was that of a defensive back and receiver for USC under John McKay in the late 1960s and early 70s.[5]

Two of Mater Dei's signal callers went on to lead the Trojans following their prep careers. Todd Marinovich and Matt Leinart each established themselves as top-level quarterbacks while at USC, and Barkley took his first step toward achieving the same success of his predecessors as a 14-year old starter on the varsity. By the time his four seasons of quarterbacking the Monarchs was complete, he not only surpassed all those before him at Mater Dei in the school's record books for all-time passing yards, but conquered the entire Orange County one as well.

As a freshman, Barkley quickly set the tone for what his abilities could achieve by throwing a 48-yard touchdown pass on his first-ever high school pass attempt.[6] By the end of the 2005 season, the freshman golden boy compiled 1,685 yards through the air and 10 touchdowns. In 2006, Barkley showed no ill effects from a broken collarbone suffered in the playoffs during the previous season. He made the Cal-Hi Sports All-State Sophomore Team after recording 1,349 passing yards and 11 touchdowns. He then unleashed the furry that was his right arm in his junior year of 2007, ringing up a whopping 3,576 yards, which set an Orange County record, and 35 touchdowns against a mere nine interceptions. He was named the Male Gatorade High School Athlete of the Year, and became the first junior to win the Gatorade National Football Player of the Year Award. He also received the first-ever Joe Montana Quarterback of the Year Award, the Glenn Davis Award (best high school football player in Southern California), and made the Junior All-America second team.[7]

Barkley's talented right was gaining momentum with college recruiters, but it appeared that USC had a lock on the Mater Dei student. The Trojans' offensive coordinator at the time was Lane Kiffin, and he came to see Barkley practice during spring drills. Kiffin came away totally impressed, and took his findings back to USC's head coach Pete Carroll. It did not take long after that to offer Barkley a scholarship. He verbally accepted USC's offer on January 23, 2008 without ever making an official visit to any other university.[8]

With his future education and football career mapped out, Barkley proceeded to lead the Monarchs through one final campaign. In the beginning of his senior year, Barkley started off slowly, but by the conclusion of the year, he rallied to complete 177 of his 325 pass attempts for 2,877 yards and 23 touchdowns. He was honored with numerous national All-America selections, including Super Prep All-American, Prep Star All-American, and Super Prep Elite 50. He was the 2008 All-Trinity League Co-MVP, and was rated as the number one overall high school prospect in the United States.[9]

Barkley graduated from Mater Dei in December 2008, which enabled him to enroll at USC a month later and be able to attend spring drills. For most of its history, USC had built a reputation as a program rich in running back tradition. The dawn of the new millennium changed that when the quarterback position rose in status. Carson Palmer and Matt Leinart each won the Heisman Trophy, and Mark Sanchez proved to be very successful as the decade of the 2000's forged ahead. Freshman Matt Barkley was up next, looking to add his name to the stellar lineage that came before him. By the time he was through leading the Trojans, Matt Barkley's name definitely could be found among the all-time great signal callers to ever wear cardinal and gold.

After Mark Sanchez left for the NFL following the 2008 season, the Trojan signal caller job was up for grabs. During spring drills, like so many times in his life, Barkley impressed coaches with his abilities. By the end of August 2009, USC head coach Pete Carroll announced that Barkley would be his starting quarterbacking. With the announcement, he became the first true freshman to open a season as the starting signal caller. He then went out and completed 15 of 19 pass attempts for 233 yards and one scoring strike. By season's end, the freshman was a solid team leader, hitting on nearly 60 percent of his passes for 2,735 yards and 15 touchdowns and getting honorable mention Freshman All-American recognition.

In 2010, his leadership was so impressive that he became USC's first sophomore to be named a team captain. He would go on to serve the team in that capacity for his final two seasons, thus becoming the first three-time captain in USC's history. He connected on 62.6 percent of his passes for 2,791 yards and 26 touchdowns. He also had a streak of 140 straight pass attempts throwing an interception.

Barkley's 2011 season was one that saw him establish new school records on multiple occasions, and he finished sixth in the Heisman Trophy voting, and placed high in other national award voting. He led the Trojans to a 10–2 record while connecting on 69.1 percent of his passes. He threw for 3,528 yards and 39 touchdowns against only seven interceptions, and earned the 2011 College Football Performance Awards National Performer of the Year Award, and made the Associated Press' All-American third team. In addition, he was selected All-Pac-12 first team by College football News and CBS Sports.com. On a team level, he was presented with the 2011 USC Most Valuable Player Award.[10]

The 6-2, 230-pound Barkley was definitely a hot commodity following his junior year. He was looked at as a solid NFL prospect if he decided to forgo his senior season and enter the pro draft. He put the question of his future plans to rest on December 22, 2011 by announcing that he would remain a Trojan for his senior year.[11] With that commitment, Barkley and the Trojans rose to the top of the pre-season college football world. He was considered the Heisman Trophy favorite, and USC was ranked number one going into the 2012 season. Unfortunately, things did not pan out on the field for Barkley or the Trojans like they did on paper. A week three loss to Stanford knocked the Trojans out of national championship contention, and Barkley suffered a shoulder injury against UCLA that ended his USC career. Even though the year did not climax with championships or a Heisman Trophy, Barkley still performed as a true competitor. He hit on 64.8 percent of his passes for 2,972 yards and 33 touchdowns. For his USC career, he compiled 1,001 completions for 12,327 yards, both of which established new Pac-12 career records. He was selected by the Philadelphia Eagles in the 4th round and 98th overall player chosen, in the 2013 NFL draft.

## *Mike Battle*

Mike Battle was a native Californian who earned a reputation as a tough football player despite being only 6-1, and 175 pounds. However, he showed no signs of fear when roaming the secondary as a defensive back or returning punts for the Trojans in the late 1960s.

Battle was born in South Gate, California, seven miles southeast of downtown Los Angeles, on July 9, 1946. His prep career consisted of being a roll out style quarterback for the Lawndale Cardinals before attending Long Beach Community College. It was after that he went from being a Cardinal at Lawndale, to wearing cardinal and gold for the USC Trojans from 1966 through 1968.

He was looked at as being on the thin side for a football player, but once opponents played against him, it was quickly realized that he was a fierce competitor. Nicknamed "Razor," Battle sliced his way across college gridirons, returning punts with reckless abandon. In 1967, he set a USC and conference record with 49 returns in a season, and also established a new school record with 608 yards gained on those returns. He also returned two punts for touchdowns that year. In the same season, Battle led the team with five interceptions and made first team All-Conference. The following year, he earned All-American status.[1]

At the conclusion of his three seasons, he received three letters, was a part of three conference championship teams, a national championship in 1967, and left the USC campus as the all-time team leader with 99 punt returns, came in second in punt return yardage with 1,014, and his 13 career interceptions ranked him sixth all-time in that category.

In 1969, he was selected in the 13th round of the draft by the New York Jets, and played with them through 1970. While in the Big Apple, Battle's reputation as a fearless return specialist followed him clear across the country.

It was once claimed that Battle rode his motorcycle off a pier in California.[2] This ride on the wild side apparently prepared him for a brief movie appearance with fellow New York Jet, Broadway Joe Namath. In 1970, Namath was the star of an outlaw biker film *C.C. and Company*, and Battle enjoyed a small role as a character named "Rabbit."[3]

## *Hal Bedsole*

The greatness of USC football has long been revered, with players and coaches alike having had many accolades bestowed upon them. As of 2012, the College Football Hall of Fame reflected the proud legacy of Trojans' football by making the selection of at least one individual with USC ties a common practice 10 out of 13 years leading up to 2012. The twelfth year of the new millennium was no exception, as Hal Bedsole was selected to take his place among 37 previously elected Trojan alumni in the hallowed shrine dedicated to the collegiate gridiron heroes of yesteryear.

The Hal Bedsole saga began on December 21, 1941, in Chicago, Illinois. When he was a youngster, his family moved to Northridge, California, in the San Fernando Valley.[1] He attended Reseda High School, where he quarterbacked the football team, served as a catcher on the baseball team, and in his spare time, tossed the shot put 54 feet in track. The gifted schoolboy athlete won an award for being the best player on the high school level in 1959, and was sought after by USC. However, Bedsole's grades were not up to standard for USC at the time. In an attempt to work on his studies, Bedsole spent a year at Pierce Junior College, where he was honored with Junior College All-American status as a quarterback.

It was then time for Bedsole to enter USC, but quarterback was not the position head coach John McKay wanted him. Pete Beathard and Bill Nelson were the signal callers playing in front of Bedsole. With very little chance of taking a job away from these two quarterbacks, he would have been reduced to sitting the bench and have his athleticism go to waste. Standing at six-foot-five-inches tall, and weighing 221 pounds, Bedsole made for the perfect target in passing situations. He was regarded as the first big wide receiver in the college ranks, and was a main weapon in USC's first national championship of the John McKay era in 1962.

Nicknamed "Prince Hal," Bedsole was not afraid to speak his mind or display what was thought to be cockiness. However, he backed up his demeanor on the field, and when his days as a Trojan were complete, Bedsole left behind a stellar body of work. He was a three-time letterman (1961–63), two-time All-Conference selection (1961–62), and a consensus All-American in 1962. He became the first Trojan to surpass 200 yards receiving in a game, set numerous school receiving records, and finished his college career with 82 receptions for 1,717 yards for a 20.9 yards-per-catch-average, and 20 touchdowns in an era when throwing the ball was still not a common thing in the college game. His greatest season at USC came during the team's run at the 1962 national championship. He caught 33 passes for 827 yards for 11 touchdowns, and had recorded two touchdown receptions in the 1963 Rose Bowl win over Wisconsin.

It was apparent that Bedsole had the talent to perform at the next level of competition, and the Minnesota Vikings though the same thing, making him their second round selection of the 1964 college draft. Bedsole then played three seasons (1964–66) for the Vikings as a tight end. In addition to his College Football Hall of Fame enshrinement in 2012, "Prince Hal" also is a member of the USC Athletic Hall of Fame since 2001.[2]

## *Ricky Bell*

It only seemed fitting that Ricky Bell played for a high school team that had a mascot named Pathfinder. For over the course of his football career, Bell blazed a path over a great deal of real estate en route to opposing end zones.

The native of Houston, Texas, was born on April 8, 1955, and when he was nine years old, his family moved to Los Angeles. It was while in these new surroundings that Bell decided to pursue athletics. Football and basketball were the ones that Bell gravitated toward, and this future All-American never looked back after that. He never wanted to be just an average player, and his desire to rise above the rest paid off.

At Fremont High School in Los Angeles, Bell received All-City honors, and the big 6-2, 218-pound running back quickly gained the attention of USC head coach John McKay. The powerful running back then decided to make his address change, not far away, traveling a mere five north of Fremont's South San Pedro Street location, to the campus of USC and everlasting fame as a Trojan.

It was at fullback that Bell first gained the attention of USC faithful and opponents alike. He became a bone-crushing fullback who earned a reputation as an effective and devastating blocker out of the backfield for tailback Anthony Davis. He also could pound the ball between the tackles for the tough yardage. In 1974, Bell carried the ball 45 times for 299 yards and one touchdown on the Trojans' national championship team.

Upon Anthony Davis' departure from USC in the spring of 1975, coach John McKay looked to Bell to fill the void at tailback. At first Bell looked at the promotion to one of the most coveted positions in all of college football with apprehension. He knew that the tradition of the USC tailback carried a huge responsibility, and Bell had initial doubts about carrying that burden. Before his debut as a USC tailback on September 12, 1975, Bell's nerves prevented him from sleeping the night prior to the game. His stomach then acted up due to nerves right before the team was ready to take the field. However, all the emotions and burden that Bell brought into the game were soon extinguished. In his first experience as a USC tailback, Bell carried the ball 34 times for 256 yards, which set the single-game school rushing record that stood for 19 years.[1] From that point on, Bell's junior campaign in 1975 was one that quickly earned him the right to be billed as one of the greatest Trojan runners of all time. He finished with 1,875 yards on the ground during the regular season to lead the nation in rushing, was named All-Conference and a unanimous All-American. He was the MVP of the Liberty Bowl in coach John McKay's final game as coach of the Trojans, and came in third in the Heisman Trophy voting.

Bell worked extremely hard at his craft, starting off each day with 150 pushups before hitting the weight room, where he was capable of bench-pressing 365 pounds.[2] He was nicknamed "Bulldog" by his teammates due to his tough and fierce running style.[3] Unlike other USC tailbacks, Bell did not attempt to avoid collisions. He wanted to dish out the same amount of punishment on would-be tacklers by crashing into them. With his size and power, the results proved badly for opposing defenses on a consistent basis.

As an encore for his incredible debut at tailback, Bell had to expand his trophy case due to all the awards he garnered at season's end. Despite missing some games with injuries, Bell managed to rush for 1,433 yards and 14 touchdowns on his way to another All-Conference and All-American selection. He finished second in the 1976 Heisman Trophy voting, but took home numerous other awards including the Voit Trophy, presented to the outstanding player on the Pacific Coast, the Pop Warner Award (most valuable senior on the Pacific Coast), Pac-10 Player of the Year, and USC's MVP for the second straight year. He also broke his own school single-game rushing record by gaining 347 yards on 51 carries against Washington State on October 9, 1976.[4]

Bell earned four football letters (1973–76), and helped the Trojans compile a 38–8–2 record during his college career, which included a national title in 1974 and a second place finish in the polls in 1976 after the team ended the season at 11–1.

In 1976, John McKay departed USC for the National Football League to serve as coach for the expansion Tampa Bay Buccaneers. McKay wasted little time in getting Bell to join him in Tampa, as he selected his former USC tailback number one overall in the 1977 college draft. He was signed to a five-year contract worth an estimated $1.2 million, making it the most lucrative deal given to an NFL rookie up to that time.[5]

At first the Buccaneers suffered dearly as fodder for the rest of the league, losing every game of their initial season in 1976. Bell's arrival did not stop the losing, as the team lost their first 12 games of the '77 campaign to set an NFL record 26 straight defeats. By 1979, McKay had worked out the problems, and Tampa Bay and Bell exploded to bring home the NFC Central Division crown. The Bucs came one game away from earning a spot in the Super Bowl, but lost to the Los Angeles Rams, 9–0, in the NFC title game. This also marked Bell's greatest season as a pro when he rushed for 1,263 yards. He played with Tampa Bay through the 1981 season, and then finished his career with the San Diego Chargers in 1982. Unfortunately, Bell's time on Earth was a short one. He suffered from dermatomyositis, an inflammation of the muscles or skin. Despite it being prevalent in the muscles or skin, it can occur in the heart in rare cases, which was what happened to Bell.[6] The disease forced him to retire in 1983, and one year later, on November 28, 1984, Ricky Bell died of heart failure at age 29. However, his presence in the Land of Troy and the college football world will never fade. In 1997, Bell was enshrined into the USC Athletic Hall of Fame, and in 2003, he was inducted in to the College Football Hall of Fame.

## *Duane Bickett*

Coming across something unexpectedly that would provide success and huge dividends is the dream of countless individuals. In the case of USC's football program, the experience came while viewing the game film of a player they were interested in pursuing. However, their attention quickly shifted to a two-way performer from Glendale High School named Duane Bickett. The native of Los Angeles, who one day would rise to the heights of All-American on a 6-5, 235-pound linebacker, came to the Trojans as a lightly recruited tight end/defensive end that never saw action at the linebacker position until his days at USC.

Glendale High School was one of the first schools in Southern California to offer sports to its students, and their athletic heritage is one of continued pride.[1] Bickett helped the proud legacy of the Glendale Dynamiters growing u in the late 1970s and into the decade of the 1980s as a three-sport star. Besides football, Bickett played basketball and baseball at Glendale.[2]

As a sophomore, he played tight end, and earned a starting job halfway through the year. The next season, he was performing on both sides of the ball, remaining at tight end and adding defensive end to his duties. Despite his apparent athletic skills, not many college programs expressed interest. It was then that fate stepped in, taking his life on the road to Troy.[3]

The Trojans were looking to get a player that Bickett and his Glendale teammates played against, and while reviewing game film, they came away impressed with a tough-nosed performer that once caught 14 passes in a playoff game despite a painful bicep injury. He also scored a pair of touchdowns and played on defense. Even though he was a talented athlete, Bickett himself was very surprised when the Trojans wanted to give him a scholarship offer.

Upon his 1981 graduation from Glendale, Bickett followed the same path to USC that a former Dynamiter did nearly sixty years before him. Back in the 1920s, a star lineman named Marion Morrison left Glendale and headed off to USC. However, an injury cut his time with the team short, and he went off to pursue a career in motion pictures under the name of John Wayne, one of Hollywood's most prolific screen icons of all-time.

Bickett might not have reached the status on the silver screen as Wayne achieved, but he did obtain stardom in something the film could not, being a legend among Trojan football players. In four seasons at linebacker, Bickett was a dominant force that recorded 291 tackles and six interceptions from 1981 through 1984. He earned three letters (1982–84), All-Conference and All-American honors both in 1984, and was presented with the 1984 USC Defensive Player of the Year Award. He also helped the Trojans win the 1984 Pac-10 championship, which was followed up with a win over Ohio State in the Rose Bowl.

In addition to being a powerful force on the football field,

Bickett proved to be the same in the classroom. In 1984 he was bestowed with Academic All-American honors, the National Football Foundation Scholar-Athlete Award, the USC Football Alumni Award (for highest grade point average), and earned a NCAA Post-Graduate Scholarship in 1984.

Bickett chose to continue his football career when the Indianapolis Colts made him their first round selection, and fifth overall pick, in the 1985 NFL draft. He remained with the Colts from 1985 through 1993 moving on to the Seattle Seahawks (1994–95), and then finishing off his professional career with the expansion Carolina Panthers in 1996.[4]

## *Tony Boselli*

Boulder, Colorado's Fairview High School has a majestic view of the beautiful landscape that has captivated countless individuals over many years. Fairview was also a mini pipeline to USC football, sending three of its gridiron alumni from the 1970s and 80s to the Land of Troy, with Tony Boselli being one of them.

In his first experience at Fairview, Boselli was a quarterback, and by the time he was donning USC's Cardinal & Gold, his job became that of a protector of signal callers. By his senior year of high school, he was the trench warrior coach Sam Pagano called upon to open holes for runners to get the yardage needed at crucial times.

Despite becoming one of the best Trojan linemen ever, Boselli's dream was to play for Notre Dame. After very minimal interest from the "Fighting Irish," the massive 6-7, 285-pound offensive lineman sought out other offers at Michigan State and Colorado. However, after visiting USC, he decided to stop searching for his institution of higher learning. The Trojans' reputation as "Tailback U" is legendary, but the backs who rack up the yardage could not get anywhere without the blockers up front. It was this opportunity to be a part of a great tradition that sold the Colorado product on attending college in the City of Angels.

Boselli then established himself a Trojan legend almost from the very beginning of his arrival on the USC campus. He came in his freshman year, tabbed as the top-rated newcomer into college football by a national publication, and was regarded as a player who had the capability to dominate an opponent.[1]

All the expectations on Boselli's success was proven correct, as the offensive tackle was a dominant factor on the line of scrimmage. He was a four-time letterman (1991–94), three-time All-American (1992–94), and three-time All-Conference selection (1992–94). In 1991 he logged the most minutes played on the team and was awarded USC's Most Valuable Offensive Player of the Year Award for his efforts. He won the 1994 USC MVP award, in addition to being honored with the 1994 Morris Trophy, presented to the top lineman in the Pac-10. He was a true testament to the concept of brains and brawn by earning a high grade point average and getting to be a 1994 National Football Foundation Scholar-Athlete.

Boselli's talents were ready to be taken to the next level by the spring of 1995, and his abilities were well respected by NFL scouts. For that reason, he was the second overall pick of that year's college draft, and the first-ever player chosen by the expansion Jacksonville Jaguars. His pro career in the state of Florida lasted through the 2001 season, until he was selected as the Houston Texans first pick in the expansion draft in 2002. By the time he was selected by the Texans, multiple injuries had begun to take their toll. He was placed in injured reserve and never got a chance to play for Houston, and retired following the 2002 season. When he was healthy, Boselli was respected as one of the best left tackles of his time, and earned five trips to the Pro Bowl.[2]

## *Tay Brown*

Success in athletics followed Raymond "Tay" Brown throughout his time at USC and during his coaching career. The "Hub City" of Compton, California, southeast of downtown Los Angeles, was the place Brown called home and where he was born on December 29, 1911.

Upon completion of his scholastic years at Compton High School, Brown stayed in the vicinity by enrolling at USC. The 6-0, 204-pound tackle wearing #29, proved to be a force on the line from 1930 through 1932. This was at a time when players of Brown's physical stature were considered big men, unlike in the modern game where his height and weight would not allow him any chance to play on the line. His three seasons of varsity football earned Brown All-American honors in 1932, and the acknowledgement of his teammates, who elected him captain for the '32 campaign. He was a member of two national championship teams (1931–1932), and blocked four kicks in one game.

Brown enjoyed major success as a player, and continued on a winning path in his post-USC days. He began his coaching career at the University of Cincinnati as head basketball coach and assisted on the football team. He remained in the "Queen City" from 1934 to 1937, and the returned to his native Los Angeles, gaining an incredible legacy at Compton Junior College. In 17 years at Compton, Brown guided the football team to a record of 140–33–9, which included five national championships and three wins out of four appearances in the Junior Rose Bowl. His was also Compton's athletic director. Brown was inducted into the College Football Hall of Fame in 1980, and died on July 16, 1994 at age 82.[1]

## *Willie Brown*

Long Beach Poly High School has a long-standing reputation as a football power. It also has been a pipeline for USC, with many of Poly's players becoming Trojans. Willie Brown was one of the former Poly Jackrabbits that was fortunate enough to don the Cardinal & Gold after completing his prep days at the "Home of Scholars and Champions." In addition to being a part of the pipeline from Poly to USC, Brown was also the torchbearer for another type of pipeline. One of the monikers associated with the Trojans' football program during the John McKay era in the early 1960s and beyond is "the USC Tailback Pipeline," of which Brown became the first to excel at that position under McKay.

Born on March 21, 1942, in Tuscaloosa, Alabama, Brown made a name for himself at Poly High School. Sports had been a huge part of Brown's life, and he made the most of the opportunities presented to him, regardless of the playing surface. In Brown's three years on the football team, the Jackrabbits only lost one game, and won back-to-back CIF championships in 1958 and 1959. During the 1959 season, Brown averaged 13.5 yards each time he carried the ball. He then earned the honor of being a three-sport star, excelling in basketball and baseball as well.

At USC, Brown earned three letters in football (1961–63), and was the first tailback used in what became the famed USC I-Formation. He was not considered a big, power back like those that followed him such as Mike Garrett, O.J. Simpson, Anthony Davis, or Ricky Bell, but he was the original and his skills began the continued tradition of excellence. His fine athletic abilities allowed Brown to not only run the ball well on sweeps, but cut across the middle to catch passes. In 1962, Brown helped the Trojans achieve perfection with an 11–0 record, which allowed them to win the national title. During that championship run, Brown ran for a team-high 574 yards and a 6.5 average per carry. He also led the team in kickoff and punt returns, interceptions, and was voted USC's Back of the Year for his exploits. The following year he was elected team captain, led the USC receiving corps with 33 receptions for a 13.2 average, and led the team in scoring with 44 points, punt returns, and interceptions.[1] He was honored in 1963 by being chosen USC's Most Inspirational Player. Over his three impressive seasons, Brown was considered a clutch performer, ran for 1,294 yards, and earned two All-Conference selections (1962–1963).

When spring rolled around, Brown replaced his helmet and shoulder pads for a bat and glove to serve the Trojans as an outfielder and shortstop on the baseball team. The season and sport might have been different, but Brown's athletic prowess remained the same. He lettered three times in baseball (1962–1964), and led the 1963 Trojans in batting average (.352) and runs (39). In 1963 he also earned All-Conference honors while helping the Trojans capture the College World Series Championship.[2]

After winning national titles in both football and baseball as a collegiate, Brown got the chance to test his skills on the professional level. The 5-11, 172-pounder was selected in the third round, and the 32nd overall pick, of the 1964 NFL draft by the Los Angeles Rams. He remained with the Rams from 1964 through 1965, and finished his pro career with the Philadelphia Eagles in 1966 after seeing playing time in 37 total games.[3]

Brown returned to the Land of Troy as an assistant under his old coach John McKay from 1968 through 1975, helping a new group of Trojans capture two national championships in 1972 and 1974, and also assisted on the baseball team. He later became an academic monitor for the university. In 2005, Brown joined many former USC football greats into the USC Athletic Hall of Fame.[4]

## *Brad Budde*

Throughout the long history of Kansas City's Rockhurst High School, dating back to 1914, the Blue & White Hawklets have produced many stellar moments in athletic endeavors. In the mid–1970s, the name Brad Budde was added to Rockhurst's legacy. Upon his high school graduation, the 6-5, 253-pound guard took his talents to the Land of Troy, where over a varsity career that spanned four seasons, he was the standout blocker for USC's famed "Student Body Right" running attack. He was also the first freshman to start a season opening game since World War II.[1] Budde's #71 was seen blowing open holes for four seasons as a starter from 1976 through 1979. His blocks helped the Trojans capture the 1978 national championship, and for Charles White to run his way to the 1979 Heisman Trophy.

During Budde's time in the trenches at USC, the team posted an impressive 42–6–1 record, and he was awarded the 1979 Lombardi Award as the nation's top college lineman. He was tough, intense, and intelligent, earning All-American honors for his performance on the field and in the classroom as well. In addition to his selection as a football All-American in 1979, Budde was a three-time All-Conference guard (1977–79), USC's Offensive Player of the Year (1979), and recipient of the USC's Davis-Teschke Award in 1979, given to the team's most inspirational player. Budde's father Ed was a standout offensive lineman for the Kansas City Chiefs from 1963 though 1976, and history repeated itself in 1980, when the Chiefs made Brad their first round selection of the 1980 college draft, and the 11th player picked overall. He played with the Chiefs from 1980 to 1986, and was inducted into the USC Athletic Hall of Fame in 2001 and the College Football Hall of Fame in 1998.[2]

## *Reggie Bush*

In the long, illustrious history of college football, there were those that stood out with electrifying feats that still make gridiron aficionados gasp long after their exploits are reduced to memories.

In the early to mid–2000's, the University of Southern California had Reggie Bush, who was that type of performer, as he carried on the proud tradition of "Tailback U." More often than not, whenever #5 in cardinal and gold touched the ball, something magical happened. Whether running, receiving, or returning kickoffs or punts, Bush was a scoring threat with the ball in his hands.

This multi-talented offensive juggernaut was born Reginald Alfred Bush II on March 2, 1985, in San Diego, California. When he was eight years old, his desire to play little league football engulfed him, but the dream was thwarted when his mother vetoed the request. The youngster's passion to play did not diminish with the passing of time. Refusing to waver in his desire, Bush pressed on, and one year later, he got his stepfather to talk his mother into approving the idea.[1] Needless to say, Reggie Bush finally won out in his quest, and at nine years of age, the merger of football and extreme talent became a union that spelled success at every level of competition for the San Diego native.

In his first game of little league football, the nine-year-old Bush was positioned at tailback. On the initial carry of what would amount to thousands of carries throughout his playing days, Bush took a pitchout and amazed the spectators by taking off on a scoring jaunt. After that, his ultimate conquest of the little league circuit was on, as Bush racked up incredible yardage and six-pointers. He definitely had a talent for running the ball, and within four or five years after his debut, it was becoming obvious that football as a career was not out of the realm of possibility.[2]

Bush's next stop was Helix High School, in LaMesa, California, and by his senior year, he was one of the most highly toted college recruits in the America. In 2000, Bush began to create a buzz among those close to the California prep scene when he was named to the Cal-Hi All-State Sophomore Team. His junior year was nothing short of spectacular, as he rushed for over 2,200 yards and 26 touchdowns, averaging an incredible 36.4 yards per scoring jaunt. He also scored six receiving touchdowns and two on punt returns for a total of 204 points and 3,135 all-purpose yards. He was an easy choice when awards were handed out at the conclusion of the 2001 season. He was selected to the Cal-Hi All-State first team, the All-State Underclass first team, and took home the All-CIF San Diego Section Offensive Most Valuable Player Award.[3]

As his final year of donning the green and gray of the Helix Highlanders came upon the horizon, Bush was in the upper echelon of prep players in the country. A broken wrist caused him to miss four games, but he rallied to once again produce a magnificent campaign that saw him rack up eye-popping statistics. He rushed for 1,691 yards, averaged 12.1 yards a carry, scored 27 touchdowns, and earned All-State and All-American honors. Bush also gathered in numerous MVP awards, and was regarded as the top prep running back in the country. For his high school career, Bush gained 4,995 yards and scored 450 points. He was also a track star, finishing third at the 2002 California state meet with a time of 10.4 in the 100 meters. His blazing speed over 100 meters allowed him to gain status as the fastest senior prep football player in 2002.[4]

Bush could have virtually punched his ticket for any big college football program in the nation after his incredible years at Helix. However, the Trojans of USC had a legacy of great tailbacks, and one passionate head coach in Pete Carroll. Carroll's enthusiasm sparked a stagnant program after his hiring in 2001, and within one season, he had the Trojans back on top of conference standings and looking for higher goals. Carroll's zest for the game was real, and it allowed him the opportunity to recruit many of the top players from the prep ranks. He saw in Reggie Bush the kind of player whose talents could be used in every offensive category. He envisioned the Helix High product as one who could run, pass, catch, and return kickoffs and punts.[5] With Carroll's passion and vision, coupled with the proud heritage of USC football, Bush signed his name on the dotted line. With Bush now ready to don the Cardinal & Gold, the Trojans were about to embark on one of the greatest periods in team history.

All the hype surrounding Bush's arrival on the USC campus culminated on his initial day of practice. Regarded as the nation's premier high school running back, Bush's reputation now had to be backed up by his talents. He definitely did not disappoint, as he used speed, elusive moves, and grit, to perform whatever task was presented to him. It did not take long for observers to realize that in Bush the Trojans had the makings of the ultimate offensive weapon.[6]

In his freshman season of 2003, Carroll started Bush off as a reserve, but that did not mean he sat on the bench. To the contrary, Bush saw action in all of USC's 13 games, and produced up to the standard that was expected of him as a multi-talented performer. He rushed for 521 yards on 90 carries for a 5.8-yard average and scored three touchdowns. He caught 15 passes for an additional 314 yards and four touchdowns. Despite the impressive stats by a freshman, Bush was not done, as he led the conference with 18 kickoff returns for 492 yards (27.3 average) and one six-pointer. In topping the Pac-10 in kickoff returns, Bush became the first Trojan since Anthony Davis in 1974 to possess that honor. When he was done running over and around the opposition, Bush set a USC freshman record with 1,331 all-purpose yards, earned Freshman All-American status, won the 2003 ESPN Pac-10 Newcomer of the Year Award, and helped USC win the Associated Press national championship with a 12–1 record.

Reggie Bush had definitely lived up to his billing as a blue chip recruit, but resting on his laurels was not in his repertoire. On both a team and individual basis, Bush and the Trojans conquered all the opposition in 2004. From the opening game through a convincing 55–19 victory over Oklahoma in the BCS Championship Game, the Trojans remained #1 in the polls, and claimed a second straight national championship with a spotless 13–0 record. Bush was a main reason why the Trojans were so dominant. He rushed for 908 yards on 143 carries for a 6.3 average and six touchdowns. He added 43 receptions for 509 yards and seven touchdowns, and threw one pass, which resulted in a 52-yard scoring strike. When not providing the Trojans with offensive firepower, he lent his talents to the special teams unit by returning 21 kickoffs for 537 yards (25.6 average), and 24 punts for 376 yards (15.7 average) and two touchdowns. His all-purpose yardage added up to 2,330 yards, and earned him the distinction of leading the conference in that category.

Bush's amazing sophomore season did not go unnoticed, as the awards piled up for one of the most exciting players in USC history. He was selected as player of the year from the Touchdown Club of Columbus, the Pac-10, and the University of Southern California. He also earned All-American and All-Conference honors, and finished fifth in the Heisman Trophy voting.[7]

The 2005 college football season could have been dubbed, "the year of Reggie Bush," as he turned in one of the greatest single seasons in history. He ran for 1,740 yards on 200 carries (8.7 average) and 16 touchdowns. He added another 478 yards on 37 receptions and added another two six-pointers to his total. On special teams, Bush gained 493 yards on 28 kickoff returns and 179 yards on 18 punt returns and a touchdown. He led the entire college ranks with 222.3 all-purpose yards per game, and came in fourth in rushing with a 133.8 yards per game average. For his three seasons of college football, Bush compiled 6,541 all-purpose yards to rank tenth all-time in that category.[8]

He once again earned All-American and All-Conference recognition, in addition to bringing home many awards. Among them were the Walter Camp Award, the Doak Walker Award, presented to the top college running back, The Sporting News Player of the Year Award, the Pigskin Club of Washington, D.C. Offensive Player of the Year Award, and the AP Player of the

Year Award. He repeated as winner of the Touchdown Club of Columbus Player of the Year Award, the Pac-10 Offensive Player of the Year Award, and USC MVP. However, it was the prize from the Downtown Athletic Club that rose above all others. With a whopping 784 first place votes, Reggie Bush easily won the 2005 Heisman Trophy, long regarded as one of the ultimate sports awards. Bush also helped the Trojans to another perfect regular season, but the quest for a third straight national title ended in a close loss to Texas in the BCS Championship Game.[9]

On January 12, 2006, Bush decided not to return for his senior season and declared himself eligible for the NFL draft. It was understood that he would go extremely high in the draft, some experts even predicted number one. The experts were close, but Bush was selected second overall by the New Orleans Saints. He continued to play a key role on offense and special teams once in the pros. In his rookie year of 2006, Bush ran for 565 yards and six touchdowns, caught 88 passes for 742 yards and two scores, and added 28 punt returns for 216 yards to his impressive inaugural NFL season. In 2008, he entered the NFL record books by tying two records. The one came when he returned two punts for touchdowns in one half against Minnesota on October 6, 2008. One week later, against the Oakland Raiders, he tied the record for fastest player to reach 200 career receptions, a feat he accomplished in only 34 games. His efforts were rewarded with his selection to the All-Pro team. Bush was also on hand when the Saints overcame years of frustration and failure with a victory in Super Bowl XLIV. Despite missing 11 games due to knee surgery, he came back strong in the playoffs leading up to the Super Bowl. He remained with the Saints through the 2010 season, and then went to the Miami Dolphins in 2011.[10] On March 13, 2013, Bush signed a free agent contract with the Detroit Lions.

The legacy of Reggie Bush is one filled with amazing and exciting athletic prowess, and his exploits on the field will forever be remembered when discussing the all-time greats of USC football. Unfortunately, along with great moments there were dark ones, and in the case of Bush, his came prior to the 2006 NFL draft.

On April 23, 2006, news that Bush and his family allegedly received upwards of $300,000 in cash and gifts from sports agents Lloyd Lake and Michael Michaels, who were attempting to build an agency called New Era Sports & Entertainment with Bush as the main attraction. The apparent gifts were given to Bush and his family while the superstar was still in college, which was in direct violation of NCAA policies of a student athlete accepting such items while still in college.[11]

Problems arose when Bush decided to sign with another agency, which left New Era without its star, and that loss eventually led to Lake suing the Bush family for loss of funds, the demise of the business venture, and Bush's legacy as a Trojan. After a four-year investigation into the affair, on June 10, 2010, the NCAA ruled on sacking the USC football program with a four-year probation, and forced the university to vacate the final two games from the 2004 season and the entire 2005 season. They were also prohibited from appearing in any post-season bowl games in 2010 and 2011, and lost 30 scholarship opportunities within a three-year time period. The NCAA also made the University of Southern California break ties with Bush in every way possible. One month later, USC announced that it would take away any reminders of Bush's incredible career that were on display. Included in this sweep was Bush's 2005 Heisman Trophy, which the university returned to the Heisman Trophy Trust.[12]

The governing body of the Heisman Trophy then got involved, claiming that they would strip Bush of his award. In September 2010, Bush decided to return his cherished prize back to the Heisman Trust, and his place among fellow winners is now vacated.[13] However, memories cannot be erased as easily, and the image of Reggie Bush with the ball in hands while donning the Cardinal & Gold, and leading the program to restored greatness in the mid–2000's, will never fade.

## *Mark Carrier*

Mark Carrier has run the gamut of football, first as a player and then a mentor in both the college and professional ranks. Along the way from student to teacher, Carrier paved out a football career full of stellar acknowledgements.

Born on April 28, 1968, in Lake Charles, Louisiana, Carrier earned his way into USC after making a name for himself at Long Beach Polytechnic High School. The home of the green and gold Jackrabbits has a long-standing reputation for excellence in both academics and athletics, definitely living up to its motto of "Home of Scholars and Champions." Long Beach Poly can also boast of sending over 60 former football players into the National Football League, which is more than any other high school in history.[1]

Mark Carrier was one of those who helped Poly earn that status, as his scholastic playing days were an indicator that he had the abilities to make it to the ultimate level of competition. He was a three-year starter at free safety on one of the top-rated teams in the country, and was rated as one of the nation's best defensive backs. He was named High School All-American for the 1985 season, and received many scholarship offers from big name schools.

Deciding on USC, Carrier became one of the greatest defensive backs in Trojan history. Nicknamed "Aircraft," he destroyed anyone coming in his direction whether by land or air. He recorded 336 tackles over three varsity seasons, and 13 interceptions, which ranked him near the top of USC's all-time list in that category. His seven thefts in 1989 led the Pac-10. He was a three-year letterman (1987–1989), two-time All-Conference selection (1988–1989), and was selected All-American in those same years. He also became the first USC player to receive the Jim Thorpe Award (1989), presented to the nation's top college defensive back.

The Chicago Bears made Carrier the sixth overall pick of the 1990 NFL draft, and he did not disappoint. His 10 interceptions in his first season led the league, and he received the 1990 Defensive Rookie of the Year Award for his efforts. Those 10 interceptions proved to be the most by a Chicago Bear in a single season throughout the team's long history. He played in Chicago through the 1996 season, and then made stops in Detroit (1997–1999) and Washington (2000) before embarking on a coaching career. As of 2012, Carrier served on coaching staffs with Arizona State University (2004–2005), the Baltimore Ravens (2006–2009), the New York Jets (2010–2011), and the Cincinnati Bengals (2012). He was inducted into the USC Athletic Hall of Fame in 2007.[2]

## *Chris Claiborne*

Sixty miles east of Los Angeles, John W. North High School in Riverside, provided a catalyst that eventually led Chris Claiborne to All-American status, and a career in the National Football League. If Claiborne's high school career was any indication of his future gridiron plans, then it came a surprise to no one when he reached the pro ranks a few short years after graduating in 1996.

Donned in the blue and gold of the Huskies, Claiborne achieved an almost inconceivable feat of earning All-State honors at two positions. However, Claiborne did the near impossible under coach Mark Paredes, as he was selected All-State at fullback and linebacker while helping to lead John W. North High School to the 1995 Division 4 CIF championship. To top off his high school football career, Claiborne was the recipient of the 1995 Glenn Davis Award, presented to the best player in the Los Angeles area.

Claiborne decided to stay in the Los Angeles area by accepting a scholarship to USC. He then continued on his way to earning more honors for his solid performance as a linebacker. A starter from his freshman year, he won three letters, recorded 312 tackles and intercepted eight passes. The 6-3, 250-pounder was selected as an All-American in 1998, and won the Dick Butkus Award the same year, which is presented to college football's top linebacker. The awards continued to pile up, as he was a two-time All-Conference selection (1997–1998), the 1998 Pac-10 Defensive Player of the Year, and the 1998 USC MVP.

Deciding to pass up his senior season, Claiborne made himself eligible for the NFL draft in 1999. The Detroit Lions made him their first round selection, and ninth player picked overall, in the draft. He remained with the Lions through the 2002 season, and then played for Minnesota (2003–2004), St. Louis (2005), the New York Giants (2006), and finished up his NFL career with the Jacksonville Jaguars in 2007.[1]

## *Paul Cleary*

By the time Paul Cleary arrived in the Land of Troy in 1946, he already had a large dose of life experience. At five years old, he stepped on a rusty nail and got lockjaw. With no antibiotics available at the time to fight off the effects, most individuals died from it.[1] Cleary was one of the lucky few to survive, and grew into a force on the football field at Santa Ana High School.

Upon high school graduation in 1940, Cleary's next stop was Santa Ana Junior College, where he was elected team co-captain of the 1942 squad that won a national championship. In Cleary's two seasons at Santa Ana, the team posted an almost spotless record of 18–1.[2]

World War II was raging at the time Cleary played at Santa Ana Junior College. He joined the majority of able-bodied young men in the fight. However, by the time he was set to partake in the invasion of Japan in August, 1945, the war ended, and Cleary escaped the conflict without ever having to use his rifle.[3]

Following his three years of military service as a first lieutenant, Cleary looked to continue his education and football career. At first he looked to attend Stanford, but it was USC that won out and started him on his way toward a solid two seasons with the Trojans. His performance as an end was so impressive that his head coach Jeff Cravath boasted that he was the best to ever play the position at USC. It appeared that others thought highly of him as well when he was All-Conference and All-American in 1947.

Cleary was selected by the Detroit Lions in the 10th round of the 1948 NFL draft, but wound up playing for the New York Yankees of the All-America Football Conference instead. He spent one year in New York and one with the AAFC Chicago Hornets before going on to a successful career in business. He was inducted into the College Football Hall of Fame in 1989, and the USC Athletic Hall of Fame in 2003. He died one month shy of his 74th birthday on January 9, 1996.[4]

## *Shaun Cody*

The game of football on any level is won in the battle up front. It is up to the offensive line to prevent the defense from creating havoc on a game plan. On the opposite side of the spectrum, it is the job of the defensive line to penetrate into the opposing backfield and disrupt and destroy anyone wearing a different colored jersey.

In the Land of Troy at the start of the new millennium, the Trojans' offense rolled and the defensive line caused opponents to stall more often than succeed. The results produced two national championships in 2003 and 2004 with Shaun Cody being responsible for much of the damage caused to opposing offenses.

Cody's success as an All-American and champion at USC was not a surprise for anyone who saw him perform at the scholastic level. In 2000, he turned in one of the best single-season performances in the nation as a senior at Los Altos High School in Hacienda, California. On defense, he recorded 105 tackles and 22 sacks, which earned him first-team high school All-America honors. However, he did not rest on his stellar defensive laurels. On the offensive side, he played tight end and running back, where he caught 50 passes for 850 yards and 15 touchdowns. He then added 327 rushing yards and 10 more touchdowns to his incredible 2000 senior season. Cody's yeoman effort helped greatly in Los Altos go 14–0 and clinch their second straight CIF Division VII championships.

College offers poured in for the 6-5, 255-pound scholastic powerhouse, but thankfully for Trojan faithful, Cody chose to don the Cardinal & Gold on Saturday afternoons. He then proceeded to carry on with his winning ways and excellent abilities by helping the USC program re-build its reputation as a dominant force. The highly recruited freshman did not sit all that long, as he earned the starting right defensive tackle after the fourth game of the 2001 season. He went on to record 39 tackles and five sacks on his way to Freshman All-America honors.[1]

After starting off the 2002 season in fine fashion, Cody tore ligaments in his right knee during the sixth game that caused him to miss the remainder of the year. He came back strong in 2003, earning All-Pac 10 honors on a Trojans team that captured a share of the national championship. In 2004, the Trojans rolled to a perfect record and their second straight national championship with Cody as the leader of the defensive line and team captain. He registered 45 tackles and 10 sacks while All-America honors in addition to being named Pac-10 Co-Defensive Player of Year and USC Co-Defensive Lineman of the Year.[2]

Cody was selected by the Detroit Lions in the second round of the 2005 NFL draft, and remained with the team through 2008. He then went to the Houston Texans in 2009.

## *Sam Cunningham*

A trek north of the USC campus on U.S. Highway 101 that covers roughly over 100 miles will bring upon the "American Riviera," an impressive moniker used to describe the city of Santa Barbara. Wedged between the Santa Ynez Mountains and the shores of the Pacific Ocean, Santa Barbara can boast of a Mediterranean-like climate, and owns the rights of having one of the oldest and most respected high schools in California.

Santa Barbara High School, the olive and gold-clad "Home of the Dons," has alumnus consisting of Academy Award winners, Pulitzer Prize recipients, Olympic gold medalists, All-Americans in various sports, and professional athletes.

One such All-American and professional football player, Sam Cunningham, was a bruising, battering ram-like fullback that provided a punishing ground attack for the USC Trojans in the early 1970s. The 6-3, 212-pound Cunningham came onto the USC campus at the end of the 1960s after winning the California state shot put championship in track. He was also a sprinter on the track team, which showed evidence of both speed and power.[1] By the time he finished his collegiate career, "Sam the Bam" garnered top accolades and was team captain on the 1972 Trojans, regarded as one of the greatest squads ever assembled.

Cunningham came to "Tailback U" under the legendary coach John McKay, and quickly established himself as a powerful force with or without the ball in his hands. As a sophomore in 1970, he tore through a solid Alabama team for 135 yards and two six-pointers on 12 carries, and finished the season with 488 yards on just 76 carries for a 6.4 yards-per-carry average. Following a junior year that produced 742 yards, Cunningham assumed the position of being what then-assistant coach John Robinson claimed to be the best blocker out of the backfield he had ever witnessed.[2]

Cunningham showed no selfishness when taking on his new role as a blocking fullback. As team captain, he led by example, doing whatever was needed to take the '72 Trojans to a spotless 12–0 record and a national championship. With "Sam the Bam" lined up in the famous USC I-Formation behind the quarterback, and in front of tailback Anthony Davis, the ground attack was one to be reckoned with. With Cunningham leading the way out of the backfield, Davis was able to tear off huge chunks of real estate across the football landscape. In addition to his devastating blocks, Cunningham utilized his power in short yardage situations, especially near the goal line. It was in those situations that the moniker of "Sam the Bam" came into play, as he smashed his powerful frame into the end zone 13 times in 1972. He capped off his USC career, and added to his reputation as a short yardage weapon by scoring four touchdowns against Ohio State in the 1973 Rose Bowl, earning the game's Most Valuable Player Award in the process.

He also walked away from that great '72 season with All-American honors and received USC's Back of the Year Award. He averaged 4.6 yards-per-carry over his USC career, allowing him the distinction of being called the greatest rushing fullback in school history.

Cunningham's accomplishments did not go unnoticed by the National Football League. The New England Patriots made him their first round selection, and 11th player selected overall, in the 1973 draft. He played his entire professional career with the Patriots, compiling 5,543 rushing yards, to leave the organization as its all-time leading ground gainer. His accomplishments on the gridiron were honored with induction into many halls of fame. Cunningham is a member of the Rose Bowl Hall of Fame, the USC Athletic Hall of Fame, the College Football Hall of Fame, and the New England Patriots Hall of Fame.[3]

## *Anthony Davis*

The definition of win is to be successful or victorious. Many can claim the right to that definition, but in the mid–1970s, USC's Anthony Davis was the embodiment of it. His ticket to immortality in the Land of Troy was punched by leaving USC with more accolades than most could only dream of achieving.

One of the most prolific tailbacks, in a program known for excellence at that position, was born in Huntsville, Texas, on September 8, 1952. Davis would eventually leave Texas at an early age, and the Lone Star State's loss was a huge gain for the Golden Coast. In preparation for his days as a Trojan, Davis was a multi-talented scholastic sports star at San Fernando High School. While a member of the Tigers' football team, Davis was honored as Co-Los Angeles Player of the Year, in wrestling, he captured the city crown at his weight class, and on the baseball diamond in the spring, Davis received the City Player of the Year Award.[1]

Upon graduation from high school, Davis left behind the black and gold of the "Mighty Tigers" on O'Melveny Avenue in San Fernando, and headed 25 miles south to the USC campus. It was there that he would dazzle the throngs of Trojan faithful on Saturday afternoons clad in cardinal and gold with #28 on his jersey from 1972 through 1974.

The flashy, 5-9, 183-pound keg of dynamite in cleats that fought and clawed his way for every yard, came to be known as "AD," and gained headlines as a sophomore during USC's incredible 1972 run at a perfect record and a national title. After a slow beginning, that did not see Davis start until the eighth game of the season, he more than made up for lost time. He finished the year with 1,191 rushing yards, and established himself as a Trojan legend in just his first season on the varsity by singlehandedly dismantling Notre Dame. The sports section in the *Los Angeles Times* on the day following the Notre Dame game said it, as in bold print across the top of the page was DAVIS! DAVIS! DAVIS! DAVIS! DAVIS! That said it all, as the sophomore juggernaut scored six touchdowns and amassed 368 yards of total offense against the Fighting Irish. It was that game that earned Davis the nickname of "Notre Dame Killer," and his exploits against one of USC's top rivals will never be forgotten. Two years later, Davis once again lived up to his moniker by helping to bring the Trojans back from a 24–6 halftime deficit against the defending national champion Fighting Irish, who also boasted in having the number one ranked defense in 1974. Davis returned the second half kickoff for a touchdown, and over the next sixteen minutes, the Trojans ran up 49 points, with Davis added two more six-pointers, and USC shocked the college football world by prevailing, 55–24, en route to a second national championship with Davis at tailback.

In his three seasons as a Trojan tailback, Davis became the first player in Pac-8 history to top the 1,000-yard rushing mark each season. His running style was to attack a defense and keep them off balance, and he did his job very well. He left the Land of Troy with 5,400 all-purpose yards and 52 touchdowns. He received two First Team All-Pac-8 honors (1973–1974), was a 1974 All-American, won the Voit Trophy (presented to the most outstanding player on the west coast) in 1972 and 1974, the 1974 Pop Warner Award (for most valuable senior on the Pacific Coast), USC's Back of the Year Award in 1974, and was runner-up for the 1974 Heisman Trophy. He led the Trojans in rushing, scoring, and kick returns in all three of his varsity seasons, and was a major contributor in USC going 31–3–2, and making three trips to the Rose Bowl, from 1972 through 1974.[2]

If Davis' presence on the football field was not enough to make him a legend, he achieved even more status in the spring. As an outfielder on the USC baseball team, Davis received two more national championships to his credit in 1973 and 1974, which allowed him the opportunity to become the only athlete in USC history to start for national champions in both football and baseball. His prowess on the diamond was so impressive that the Minnesota Twins selected him in the 1975 amateur baseball draft. However, he decided to stay with football as a post-USC athletic career, and was selected in the second round of the 1975 NFL draft by the New York Jets.

Davis did not go to the Jets, instead opting to play in the World Football League, in its second year of existence. His impact on the new league was great, as he led the WFL in rushing with 1,200 yards for the Southern California Sun. He also scored 16 touchdowns. Unfortunately, the WFL folded after 12 games during the 1975 season, and Davis had to seek work carrying the football elsewhere.

His next stop was north of the border, playing for the Toronto Argonauts of the Canadian Football League in 1976. His talents were so impressive to the Toronto ownership that they made Davis the CFL's first-ever "Million Dollar Man." Despite all the hype, Davis ran into a conflict with Toronto's head coach, and he was gone after rushing for 417 yards.

Davis was then re-united with John McKay in Tampa Bay, but he never reached the level of play that he enjoyed as a Trojan or in the WFL. He rushed for 297 yards in 11 games for Tampa Bay in 1977, and made stops with the Houston Oilers in 1978 and the Los Angeles Rams in 1979, where his NFL career ended with seven rushing yards in two games. He attempted a comeback in 1983 with the Los Angeles Express of the United States Football League, but fizzled out after carrying the ball 12 times for 32 yards. He then went into the real estate business and also acted. He was inducted in the USC Athletic Hall of Fame in 1999, and the College Football Hall of Fame in 2006.[3]

## *Clarence Davis*

The tailback tradition at USC is represented by different running styles. However, for all those who had the honor of playing tailback in the Cardinal & Gold uniform, one common factor was that they were all tough. In the case of Clarence Davis, his style was that of a brawler, not willing to back away from anyone. An example of his toughness came when he once had four front teeth knocked loose in the first half of a junior college game, had his gums stitched up, and returned to action.

Davis was born in Birmingham, Alabama, on June 28, 1949. He moved to the Bronx in New York City before settling in Los Angeles at age 15.[1] While at Los Angeles Washington High School, Davis developed into a quick, powerful runner at 5-10, and under 200 pounds. In addition to his running back duties, he also proved his toughness as a member of the defensive line. When not blasting his way across gridirons throughout the Los Angeles area, Davis showed his prowess as a track star by winning the city shot put championship.[2]

After ending his scholastic career, Davis went to East Los Angeles Junior College in 1968. He made the most of his opportunity on the junior college level by breaking O.J. Simpson's national junior college records. Simpson proved to be the one who helped USC get Davis after he was offered scholarships from the University of Washington and Kansas.[3] At first, Davis was nervous to carry on the proud tradition of USC tailback, having to follow Heisman Trophy winners Garrett and Simpson. However, after running for 80 yards in his first game as a Trojan, he calmed down and finished the 1969 season with 1,351 yards on the ground and earned All-American honors. He led the Pac-8 in rushing in 1969, was a two-time All-Conference selection (1969–1970), and won USC's Back of the Year Award in 1969 and 1970. He rushed for 972 yards in his senior season of 1970, and was ranked in the upper echelon among USC all-time leaders in career rushing yards (2,323 yards to rank 13th) and kickoff return yardage (477 yards to rank 20th). He also had nine 100-yard rushing games over his two seasons as a Trojan.

On draft day in 1971, Davis went from USC's famed Student Body formations to the skull and crossbones of the Oakland Raiders, as the Silver & Black made the durable back their fourth round selection. He then went on to have a solid pro career that lasted until 1978. He gained a reputation as an excellent kickoff return man in the first three years of his time with the Raiders, and was instrumental in two of the team's greatest moments. In a 1974 AFC Playoff Game against the two-time defending Super Bowl champion Miami Dolphins, Davis caught a touchdown pass in the closing seconds to pull out a victory in what became known as the "Sea of Hands Game." Two years later, he rushed for 137 yards against the Minnesota Vikings in Super Bowl XI to help the Raiders win their first world championship.[4]

## *Charley Dean*

It was during the coaching reign of Elmer "Gloomy Gus" Henderson that the Trojan football program began its rise to national prominence. When Henderson took over as head coach in 1919, he had the opportunity to have the services of left halfback Charley Dean for the first three years of his coaching tenure.

Dean came into the Cardinal & Gold fold on the heels of Frank Malette's exit after reigning as USC's first in a long line of backfield icons. Dean came to the USC from Calexico, California, a city located approximately 122 miles east of San Diego, and 62 miles west of Yuma, Arizona.[1] Dean's exploits at the dawn of the Roaring Twenties allowed him to become one of the Trojans' all-time stellar performers, and one of the best in the nation during his time.

At 174 pounds, Dean was a powerful runner that was capable of pounding the ball through the line with hard charges that wore a defense down. His abilities allowed him to shift from a power runner into an elusive one once he got past the line of scrimmage. He was also an outstanding tackler on defense, and his all around tremendous play earned him honorable mention on Walter Camp's All-American team. His teammates also appreciated his talents so much that they elected him captain of the 1921 USC team.[2]

## *Jack Del Rio*

From his days at Hayward High School, to the ranks of NFL head coach, Jack Del Rio has had his share of accolades. The gifted athlete that would one day add his name to those of other USC greats, was born on April 4, 1963, in Castro Valley, California.

From an early age, Del Rio had an interest in sports, and by the time he was a student at Haywood High School, his athletic prowess earned him a solid reputation as a three-sport star. Haywood had an excellent history in sports, as the football program can boast as having the most all-time wins in their conference. The baseball team has deep roots of success, and the basketball team was responsible for adding many trophies to the school's trophy case.

On many of these occasions, Del Rio helped Haywood add to their proud heritage, and it came as no surprise when he was offered a chance to play college football at USC. He also had an opportunity to sign a pro baseball contract with the Toronto Blue Jays straight out of high school.

Deciding on going the college route, Del Rio arrived on the USC campus in 1981, and left three years later as an All-American and Trojan legend. The 6-4, 235-pound linebacker earned four letters in football, was selected All-Pac-10 twice (1982–83), won USC's Defensive Player of the Year award in 1983, the 1984 Pop Warner Award, which is presented to the most valuable player on the Pacific Coast, was an All-American in 1984, and co-MVP of the 1985 Rose Bowl game. In addition, he was runner-up for the 1984 Lombardi Award, and was chosen to play in two post-season college All-Star games. In his four seasons as a starter, Del Rio recorded 340 tackles for the Trojans. Ironically, he batted .340 on the USC baseball team as a catcher in 1983 and 1984.[1]

The National Football League proved to be an obvious choice for Del Rio's next venture. The New Orleans Saints made the talented linebacker their third round selection in the 1985 draft, and the 68th player selected overall. His impact on the professional ranks came quickly, as he was named to the NFL All-Rookie Team, and won the Saints' Most Valuable Rookie award. After two seasons in the "Big Easy," Del Rio moved on to the Kansas City Chiefs (1987–88), the Dallas Cowboys (1989–91), and finished out his playing career with the Minnesota Vikings from 1992 through 1995.[2]

Del Rio took all of the knowledge he learned over the course of his playing days and entered the coaching profession in 1997 with the New Orleans Saints. He won a Super Bowl ring in 2000 as an assistant with the Baltimore Ravens, served as head coach with the Jacksonville Jaguars from 2003 to 2011, and as of 2012, is an assistant with the Denver Broncos.[3]

## *Morley Drury*

The Roaring Twenties in America has long been linked to wild times, bootleg alcohol, and jazz. It was also referred to as the golden age of sports, with many now-iconic sports figures mesmerizing spectators from coast to coast. College football was one of the most popular spectator sports during the decade of decadence. Each region of the United States had an individual that stood out above all others on the football field, and will forever be ranked among the elite.

The University of Southern California had such a revered figure in Morley Drury, co-patriarch, along with teammate Mort Kaer, of the famed USC tailback tradition. Drury's exploits on the gridiron were so great that *Los Angeles Examiner* reporter Mark Kelly crowned him "the Noblest Trojan of Them All."[1]

The man who came to be honored with such high praise was born on February 5, 1903, in Midland, Ontario, Canada. His father passed away when Morley was seven, and eight years later, his mother moved the family consisting of two boys to Long Beach, California. Before heading to high school, Drury worked in shipyards for two years, and played football for the Keel Club against other work teams throughout the Long Beach area. At the age of 17, he entered Long Beach Poly High School where he established himself as a force on the football field. His previous experience with the Keel Club helped Drury land a varsity spot on the high school team in his freshman year. In

1920 he was a part of a Poly team that finished the season with a spotless 7–0 mark, and two years later, he helped the team win the CIF championship over Glendale.

After a great scholastic career, it was then time for Drury to enter the University of Southern California and immortality among Trojan legends. He came into the football program as a 21-year old, 6-0, 185-pounder. He was older than his teammates upon arriving, and one of the biggest players on Howard Jones' squad. He was also multi-talented and tough, doing whatever was asked of him, and doing it well.[2] He earned a reputation as a power runner that played every backfield position during his Trojan days, as well as safety on defense. He could run, pass, punt, and it was not rare to see him perform all of those tasks for the full 60 minutes of a game.[3]

Drury was definitely a workhorse and the power behind USC's famous "Thundering Herd" teams of the late 1920s. He was also a great team leader and excellent under pressure.[4] He once carried the ball 45 times in a game during his senior year, and that record stood for 41 years until O.J. Simpson broke it in 1968.[5] Another record that Drury set and it was not surpassed until the 1960s also came in his senior season of 1927. He rambled for 1,163 yards in the course of a nine-game schedule, thus earning the distinction of being the first USC running back to surpass one thousand yards rushing in a single season. That record was Drury's until Mike Garrett topped it in 1965. His exploits were so impressive during his time in the Cardinal & Gold, that following his final college game appearance, a crowd of 60,000-plus rose in the Los Angeles Memorial Coliseum to give him a thunderous ovation as he walked off the field.[6]

Accolades became commonplace for Drury during his Trojan days. He was a three-year letterman (1925, 1926, 1927), team captain (1927), and consensus All-American (1927). He was voted as the winner of USC's Davis-Teschke Award in 1927, given to the most inspirational player on the team, as well as being named the Amateur Athletic Foundation Southern California Athlete of the Year, also in 1927. He was the first USC player to be inducted into the College Football Hall of Fame (1954), and entered the USC Athletic Hall of Fame in its second year of existence in 1995. In addition to lettering in football, Drury also lettered in water polo, hockey, and basketball at USC.

Following his days of dazzling the Trojan fateful, Drury worked as an investment broker, real estate agent, in the advertising business, and served as an executive in the building materials industry.[7] He also had the opportunity to hear the roar of the crowd display gratitude to him one more time nearly sixty years after his final game. In August 1988, USC celebrated its football centennial, and Drury, though confined to a wheelchair, was once again on the field for the festivities, and received an ovation worthy of his greatness by the crowd inside the LA Coliseum.[8] Five months later, two weeks shy of his 86th birthday, Morley Drury died of a stoke at a Santa Monica hospital.

## *Sedrick Ellis*

In the first few years of the new millennium, both USC football and Sedrick Ellis were becoming forces to be reckoned with. While Pete Carroll was rebuilding the Trojans into a powerhouse, some forty miles east of the USC campus, at Chino High School, Ellis was earning a reputation as one of the premier defensive lineman in the nation. As a standout scholastic trench warrior for the Chino Cowboys, Ellis began creating a buzz during the 2000 season when he earned a spot on the Cal-Hi Sports All-State Sophomore Team. The following year he recorded 108 tackles and found his name attached to numerous All-Conference or All-State teams. He also helped Chino earn back-to-back berths in the California Interscholastic Federation (CIF) title game in 2000 and 2001. His senior season of 2002 allowed Ellis to showcase his abilities at an even higher level. By season's end, he had 122 tackles, and once again dominated the lists of the best players in not only California, but in the entire United States. The prep All-American was considered one of the top 50 players in the country, and looked at as a top college prospect.[1]

The Chino native decided to trust his 6-1, 285-pound frame with USC head coach Pete Carroll, and together, they both rose to championship heights. After a fractured left ankle took away his 2003 freshman season, Ellis was redshirted. He returned to action the following fall, and backing up All-American Mike Patterson at nose tackle, Ellis appeared in 11 games in the Trojans' run to the 2004 national championship. In 2005, Ellis earned the starting nose tackle job. He played in all 13 games, recorded 50 tackles, and earned honorable mention on the 2005 All-Pac-10 team.[2]

In 2006 Ellis had 34 tackles and was selected All-Pac-10, named to the *College Football News* All-American team, and was winner of the 2006 Morris Trophy, awarded to the top offensive and defensive linemen in the Pac-10. The following year, Ellis decided to play his senior season instead of entering the NFL draft. The 2007 season proved to be very productive for Ellis, as he had 58 tackles and once again earned him All-Pac-10, All-American honors, and another Morris Trophy. He also served as a co-captain in 2007, won the Pac-10 Defensive Player of the Year Award and the USC Co-Defensive Lineman of the Year Award. Ellis was also a powerful weight lifter, able to bench-press over 500 pounds. This feat allowed Ellis to take home another award, this one being USC Co-Lifter of the Year.[3]

The National Football League was Ellis' obvious future endeavor, and the New Orleans Saints made the standout nose tackle the seventh overall pick in the 2008 draft. With the Saints, Ellis had the opportunity to have his former assistant coach, and the man who recruited him for USC, Ed Orgeron, on the New Orleans' staff. Ellis came out strong during his rookie year, starting 13 games. In 2009, he once again started, and helped the Saints march to a Super Bowl XLIV victory. As of the 2012 season, Ellis is still with the Saints, and creating havoc on opposing offenses with his 6-1, 307-pound frame.[4]

## *John Ferraro*

The City of Angels saw the legacy of John Ferraro grow from his scholastic days at Bell High School to his public service career as police commissioner and city councilman in Los Angeles. Ferraro's journey through life took him on many paths, and it all began with his birth on May 14, 1924, in the town of Cudahy, California, some 11 miles southeast of Los Angeles.

The last of eight children born to his parents, Ferraro graduated from Bell High School in the winter of 1942 after succeeding on both the football field and inside the classroom. Going by the nickname of "Jakes" at Bell High, he was an overwhelming choice when it came to handing out All-City honors. Standing at six-foot four-inches tall, and weighing in at 245 pounds, the All-City tackle accepted a football scholarship to USC, which allowed him the opportunity to continue on with his athletic and academic pursuits close to his hometown.[1]

Trading in the moniker of "Jakes" for "Big John," Ferraro carried on with his reputation as a dominant trench warrior. With the manpower shortage caused by World War II, the eligibility rules at the time preventing freshman from playing on the varsity were lifted. This gave Ferraro the chance to earn four letters in football (1943–44, 1946–47).[2] His impact was felt immediately, as he pounded away on opposing lineman and ball carriers, earning All-American status following his sophomore season in 1944. He then went off to serve in the U.S. Navy, missing the 1945 season.

Following his return, Ferraro once again fastened his chinstrap for two more seasons as a Trojan. In 1946, he suffered a back injury that forced him to perform below his expectations. Despite the injury, he played well enough to gain recognition on the All-Pacific Coast Conference team, and as a second team All-American.[3] By his senior year in 1947, Ferraro once again returned to top form, and at season's end, had his name grace the first team All-American squad. He also became the first Trojan to ever be selected first team All-Conference three times (1944, 1946–47), and helped lead the Trojans to three PCC championships.[4] His dominance as a tackle was such that Braven Dyer of the *Los Angeles Times* proclaimed that the only way a tackle in the college game could be better than Ferraro was if he had the abilities of both Superman and Hercules.[5]

Despite being drafted by the Green Bay Packers, Ferraro chose to skip the chance to play professionally. He took his degree in Business Administration earned in 1948, and plunged into what turned out to be a highly successful insurance company. He then entered Los Angeles politics, and served as a City Council member for 35 years, which is the longest tenure in LA history.[6] He was also instrumental in helping Los Angeles get the bid to host the 1984 Summer Olympics. Regarded as a stellar athlete and for his public service, John Ferraro died at age 76 in Los Angeles on April 17, 2001.[7]

## *Roy Foster*

Anonymity is usually commonplace in the world of offensive line play. However, when a lineman is blocking for All-Americans and Heisman Trophy-winning tailbacks, recognition is plentiful for the massive men up front who battle for control of the trenches.

Such was the case for offensive linemen in the Land of Troy since the 1920s. A fine example of this yeoman's effort that allowed USC tailbacks to garner the bold headlines in morning newspapers is guard Roy Foster, who earned the distinction of opening up holes for Heisman Trophy winners Charles White and Marcus Allen.

Foster was born on May 24, 1960, in Los Angeles, and prepped at William Howard Taft High School in his native Southland before finishing up his scholastic days in Overland Park, Kansas. After leaving behind his days as a Taft Toreador, Foster wore the Black & Gold of the Shawnee Mission West High Vikings, who were runner-ups for the state football title in 1977.

Upon high school graduation, Foster returned to Los Angeles as a USC Trojan, earning four letters in football (1978–81), any many other accolades. The dominant 6-4, 265-pound lineman quickly gained attention, as his #64 was constantly spotted opening up alleys for Charles White and Marcus Allen to dash to glory through. When his USC days were complete, Foster left the campus as a three-year All-Pac10 selection, and a two-time All-American (1980–81). He was a two-time recipient of the Morris Trophy (1980–81), awarded to the top offensive and defensive linemen in the Pac-10, and helped the Trojans gain two Pac-10 titles and a share of the 1978 national championship. In 1981, his abilities were also honored with his selection as the USC Offensive Player of the Year.

The professional ranks seemed like a sure thing for this talented guard, and the Miami Dolphins made his rise to the next level of competition a reality by selecting Foster in the first round of the 1982 draft. He then played with the Dolphins from 1982 through 1990, appearing in Super Bowls XVII and XIX following the 1982 and 1984 seasons. He then completed his NFL career with the San Francisco 49ers from 1991 through 1993. During his NFL career, Foster became the only lineman to have the privilege of blocking for quarterback greats Dan Marino, Joe Montana, and Steve Young.[1]

## *Mike Garrett*

The 26th President of the United States was Theodore Roosevelt. His political career was one considered to be very successful, and earned him the respect of those who lived during his time and many future historians. Roosevelt was also a huge sports enthusiast. It would have made this grandiose leader of the free world proud to know that a high school bearing his name produced such an athletic marvel as Mike "Iron Mike" Garrett.

The forerunner of John McKay's I-Formation tailbacks was born on April 12, 1944, in Los Angeles. He grew up in Boyle Heights, a tough, low-income area of East Los Angeles, where gang violence was highly prevalent. In an attempt to avoid the pitfalls of gangs, Garrett immersed himself in sports, establishing himself on Boyle Heights' Evergreen Playground as a touch football dynamo.[1]

Garrett's progress as a student/athlete eventually got him to the doors of Roosevelt High School. At first his high school coach, Ray McLean, inserted Garrett at quarterback, but his future at handing the ball off instead of receiving handoffs was short-lived.[2] Halfway through the season, injuries depleted Roosevelt's inventory of running backs, and coach McLean made a decision that changed the course of Garrett's life. He moved his young charge over to fill the void at running back, and "Iron Mike" responded by dashing for over fifty yards on his carry, and ended the game with multiple touchdowns. Despite his incredible debut, unbeknownst to many was the fact that Garrett was terrified and just ran out of fear.[3]

In time the fear was replaced by confidence, and the young scholastic five-foot nine-inch running back was well on his way to stardom at every level of competition. In his senior season at Roosevelt, Garrett earned All-City and All-American honors in addition to being named league most valuable player. All these accolades turned into offers from colleges. However, he decided to keep his talents in the neighborhood at USC.

Going into his sophomore year as a Trojan, it was apparent to the coaching staff that they had something special in Garrett. Head coach John McKay had big plans for Garrett, but before installing him at tailback, he wanted to see how tough the Boyle Heights product was. In a spring practice, McKay kept calling for Garrett to carry the ball, and the sophomore running back showed more than enough grit to allow the coach to come away convinced that he had the right man to serve as the first of many star I-Formation tailbacks at USC.[4]

In McKay's I-Formation, the tailback was called upon to carry the bulk of the ground attack, which meant that the runner had to not only be extremely talented, but tough as well to absorb all the pounding. Garrett quickly established himself as the man for the job, and thus, the great USC legacy was born. Even though Garrett was not very tall, he was fast, elusive, tough, and possessed and the ability to cut quickly in midstride without slowing down. He also was one of the hardest workers during practice and on game day.[5] This combination was good for USC, and bad for their opponents.

During the 1963 season, Garrett ran for 833 yards, and then improved to 948 in 1964. It was then time for his senior season, and the college football world would be turned upside down by what he accomplished. This was at a time when rushing for 1,000 yards in a single season was not an ordinary feat. In fact, no USC running back since 1927 was able to crack the plateau despite having many talented players carrying the ball. In 1965, not only did Garrett make it to the 1,000-yard barrier, he shattered it. He ran the ball an unheard of 267 times, which was a lot for this time period, and amassed an NCAA-leading 1,440 yards in just ten games. He averaged 5.4 yards per carry, and scored 13 touchdowns.

When Garrett finally hung up his famed #20 jersey for the last time, he had compiled 3,221 rushing yards to become college football's all-time career leader in that category, erasing the old record set by the University of San Francisco's Ollie Matson 15 years earlier. He set 14 NCAA, conference, and USC records along the way to earning All-American status twice (1964–65), three All-Conference selections (1963–65), and virtually every award possible. He had 14 100-yard rushing games during his college career, and was the first Trojan to lead the conference in rushing three straight years.[6]

While growing up, Garrett idolized Ohio State running back, and 1955 Heisman Trophy winner, Howard "Hopalong" Cassady.[7] Ten years after his idol received college football's ultimate prize, the name of Mike Garrett was added to the Heisman Trophy list of honor on November 23, 1965, becoming the first Trojan to receive the prestigious award. He also was a standout outfielder on the USC baseball team, receiving All-Conference recognition on two occasions.[8]

Despite being drafted by the Los Angeles Dodgers and Pittsburgh Pirates of Major League Baseball, Garrett decided that his future was as a football player. Both the NFL's Los Angeles Rams and the AFL's Kansas City Chiefs drafted Garrett in 1966, and he chose to go with the Chiefs. This was prior to the NFL and AFL merger in 1970, so both leagues competed for talent. Garrett played with Kansas City from 1966 through 1970, and earned two Pro Bowl selections in his first two years. He also got the opportunity to play in the first-ever Super Bowl in January 1967, which the Chiefs lost to the Green Bay Packers, 35–10, at the Los Angeles Memorial Coliseum, the same site where Garrett dazzled so many as a Trojan. Three years later, Garrett and the Chiefs were once again back in the Super Bowl, and this time they redeemed themselves with a stunning, 23–7, upset victory over the highly favored Minnesota Vikings in what was the final Super Bowl encounter between the AFL and NFL. In that game, Garrett scored the Chiefs' first touchdown. He then finished up his playing days with the San Diego Chargers (1970–73). Throughout his professional career, Garrett recorded 8,049 all-purpose yards and 49 touchdowns. He was enshrined into the College Football Hall of Fame in 1985 and into the USC Athletic Hall of Fame in 1994.

Upon his retirement, Garrett was appointed director of business development for the Great Western Forum from 1988 to 1990, and served as USC's associate athletic director from 1990 to 1992. In January 1993 Garrett was elevated to athletic director. He held the post until August 2010 when USC President Max Nikias decided to make changes in the athletic department after the football and basketball programs came under fire for NCAA violations.[9]

Throughout all the success enjoyed by famed USC tailbacks since the 1960s, there is only one original, and Mike Garrett is the proud holder of that honor.

## *Frank Gifford*

From hall of fame football player, on both the collegiate and professional levels, to award-winning sportscaster, Frank Gifford carved out a solid reputation at every endeavor he attempted. Born on August 16, 1930, in Santa Monica, California, Gifford's first opportunity to play football came on the beach with an older brother. From then on, the son of an oil driller father struck black gold many times with his gridiron exploits, winning countless accolades at every level of competition.

At first, the future for Gifford as a football icon looked bleak due to his physical stature. He was a 5-7, 120-pound quarterback in high school, which was not the type of frame needed to absorb the crushing hits that football delivered. However, in time, he sprouted into a 6-1, 197-pound specimen, and was well on his way to attracting attention for his prowess on the football field as a member of the Bakersfield High School Drillers, which saw Gifford star on a team that captured the 1947 Central Section championship. Unfortunately, in the classroom, Gifford stumbled a bit, and had to work extremely hard to keep himself at a respectable level.[1]

Despite his abilities on the field, which were up to the athletic standards needed to enter the University of Southern California, his academic status did not fare as well. This setback did not prevent Gifford from focusing on his desire to attend USC. If his grades improved, then it was just a matter of time before a Trojans jersey would be draped over his torso. In an attempt to make that possible, Gifford enrolled at Bakersfield Junior College for a semester to work on his studies. During that short span, incredible things happened for the soon-to-be-Trojan. His grades rose enough to gain admittance into USC, and on the football field, he tore up the junior college circuit by earning All-Metropolitan Conference as a halfback in 1948 and Junior College All-American honors.[2]

It was now time for the Santa Monica product to show the major college world what he could accomplish. With a coveted scholarship to the university of his choice, Gifford was now a member of the USC Trojans as of 1949. At first, he was recruited as a quarterback. When an injury to a safety occurred, plans for the new arrival took a different route. Gifford was inserted into the game against Navy to replace the fallen defensive back, and he quickly established himself as a multi-talented player who was capable of adapting to another position. He intercepted two passes, and it appeared that he would earn his place as a defender. Over his sophomore and junior seasons, he was used almost exclusively as a defensive back. His fortunes changed in 1951 when Jess Hill replaced Jeff Cravath as head coach and looked to move Gifford over to tailback for his senior year. The young charge once again took to the switch with exceptional results. He compiled 1,144 yards of total offense, 841 of which were gained running out of the tailback position. He scored seven touchdowns and completed 32 of 61 pass attempts for 303 yards and an additional pair of six-pointers. In addition to showing remarkable talent on both offense and defense over three varsity seasons, Gifford also handled the punting and place kicking duties. However, it was as a running back that Gifford gained accolades during his senior year. He was named to the All-Pacific Coast Conference team, as well as becoming an All-American in 1951.[3]

Following his days as a Trojan, Gifford packed his bags and headed clear across the United States to showcase his talents on the next level. In 1952, the New York Giants selected him in the first round of the college draft, and the 11th player picked overall. Over the course of a professional career that lasted until 1964, Gifford earned six All-Pro selections, made eight trips to the Pro Bowl, was a member of the NFL's All-Decade Team for the 1950s, won the NFL Most Valuable Player award in 1956, and helped the Giants win the league title that same season. He rushed for 3,609 yards and 34 touchdowns, and caught 367 passes for another 5,434 yards and 43 additional touchdowns. In 1977, he was enshrined into the Professional Football Hall of Fame, is also a member of the College Football Hall Fame (1975), the USC Athletic Hall of Fame since 1994, and had his #16 retired by the New York Giants.[4]

Despite his greatness as a player at every level, Gifford will probably best be remembered as an announcer on Monday Night Football from 1971 to 1997. He also covered other major sporting events for ABC television. His work in the medium of television was also recognized for its excellence in 1995 when he was the recipient of the Pete Rozelle Award given to him by the Pro Football Hall of Fame.[5]

## *Marv Goux*

No volume dedicated to the outstanding heritage that is USC football can be documented without mention of "Mr. Trojan," Marv Goux. Over the course of a playing career, and 26 years of coaching dedication, mixed with undying passion for all things cardinal and gold, the likes of Goux are seldom witnessed. Along the way through a three- decade relationship with the Trojans, Goux played in two Rose Bowls, coached in 11 of them, and was part of five national championship teams.

Like so many individuals that went on to establish stellar careers in all walks of life after prepping at Santa Barbara High School, Goux left "the Home of the Dons" in search of success. As a 5-10, 185-pounder, his first stop after Santa Barbara was Ventura Junior College, where he earned status as a JC All-American linebacker in 1951. It was then on to the place where his passion never waivered. Donning his cardinal and gold #52 jersey, Goux became a three-year varsity starter in 1952, but missed the '53 season due to injury. In his final two campaigns of 1954 and 1955, Goux performed on both sides of the ball as a center and linebacker. His dedication to the Trojans earned him the respect of coaches and teammates alike, as he was elected captain for the 1955 season, and was the proud recipient of the Davis-Teschke Award twice, which is presented to USC's most inspirational player.[1]

Goux made the transformation from passionate player to passionate mentor upon graduating from USC with a bachelor's degree in physical education in 1956. His time away from the campus was not a lengthy one, and by 1957, Goux was back in the Trojans' fold as a member of Don Clark's coaching staff. In the interim, before making his way back to USC, Goux became head coach at California's Carpinteria High School, and led the Warriors' football team to a 9–1 record and the 1956 Tri-Valley League championship.[2]

From 1957 to 1982, Goux served as an assistant under Clark, John McKay, and John Robinson. He was a tough, very competitive coach, able to pass on his extreme desire to his charges. He would shout, swear, and work his players like a military drill instructor. In the end, his work ethic, coupled with the team's high success rate, allowed his men to love him. They played their hearts out for him, and the results were 11 of them earning First Team All-America honors. Despite his rough demeanor, Goux truly cared for his players, and helped them get jobs, or whatever else he could do to assist them. Unfortunately, in 1982, the NCAA found out that Goux had helped his players sell their game tickets to provide them with extra money. The NCAA then slapped USC with a three-year probation, which Goux took full responsibility for.

In 1983, Goux followed John Robinson into the pro ranks, serving on Robinson's staff with the Los Angeles Rams until 1990. He then worked in the team's front office until he retired in 1994. He continued to be a part of the Trojans' family until his death on July 27, 2002, at age 69. Goux was honored by the university in 1994 when he was inducted into the USC Athletic Hall of Fame's first class in 1994. The university also established the Marv Goux Award, presented to the USC player of the game in their cross-town rivalry clash with UCLA, the Marv Goux "Trojan For Life" Award, given each year to an alumnus that gives back to the football program, and the entrance to the USC practice field is known as "Goux's Gate."[3]

## *Jimmy Gunn*

Screen legend William Holden's character of Pike Bishop was the leader of a formidable gang in the 1969 western film classic, *The Wild Bunch*. At the same time that Holden was leading his cinematic band of outlaws in 1913 Texas, Jimmy Gunn was leading a group of defenders into opposing backfields for the USC Trojans. Taking the same name from the popular motion picture of the time, Gunn and fellow defensive linemen Charlie Weaver, Tody Smith, Al Cowlings, Willard "Bubba" Scott, and reserves Tony Terry and Gary McArthur, were dubbed the "Wild Bunch." Made up of players with size and quickness, this group created havoc and nightmares for opposing offenses.

Jimmy Gunn was considered the best of the "Wild Bunch," and while leading this band of defensive marauders, Gunn helped the Trojans to an almost spotless 29–2–2 record from 1967 through 1969, which included three conference titles and a national championship.

Born on November 27, 1948, in Augusta, Arkansas, Gunn prepped at San Diego's Lincoln High School before coming to USC.[1] His physical stature of 6-1, 210 pounds more suited that of a receiver than a defensive end. However, he was strong and extremely quick, with his speed making it difficult for opposing linemen to block him.[2] At the snap, his speed, mixed with power, would propel him into backfields to either crush a ball carrier or quarterback. The results were lethal, as Gunn's #83 was the last thing that the person with the ball saw before being slammed to the ground. His abilities did not go unnoticed by the national media, as he was selected a consensus All-American in 1969. The three-year letterman was also elected team captain in 1969, and was the recipient of USC's Lineman of the Year award in that same season.

When it came time to hang up his jersey, Gunn moved on to new football apparel as the 13th round selection of the Chicago Bears in the 1970 NFL draft. He played with the Bears from 1970 to 1975, the New York Giants, also in 1975, and then ended his professional career with the expansion Tampa Bay Buccaneers in 1976, where he was reunited with his college coach John McKay. His greatness as a Trojan was immortalized in 2001 when Gunn was enshrined into the USC Athletic Hall of Fame.[3]

## *Pat Haden*

Brains and brawn are common bonds that many hope to possess. In the case of Pat Haden, he truly succeeded in both capacities. He used his brilliant academic and athletic skills to emerge as one of the greatest high school quarterbacks in California history, was the field leader of a national championship team at USC, and earned the prestigious Rhodes Scholarship that entitled him to travel to England to do his postgraduate work at Oxford University.

This highly gifted individual was born on January 23, 1953, in Westbury, New York. A strong work ethic was instilled in Haden from an early age on, as he worked multiple jobs as a youth for extra money. This character trait followed him through his playing career, in the classroom, and into his post-college life.

The Haden family relocated to California, and it was there that Pat made a name for himself on the football field. He attended Bishop Amat Memorial High School in LaPuente, which was 20 miles east of downtown Los Angeles. While donning the royal blue and gold of the Lancers, Haden became a legend at the quarterback position. In his three-year varsity career, he connected on 537 out of 850 pass attempts and 82 touchdowns. His efforts were rewarded by being named co-CIF 4A Player of the Year in 1970. The prep star he shared the prestigious hardware with was his receiver, J.K. McKay, who caught 48 of the 82 six-pointers tossed by Haden. McKay and Haden were good friends, and the star receiver was also the son of USC's legendary coach John McKay. When Haden's parents had to move, the quarterback decided to remain in California and live with the McKays during his senior year.[1]

With this talented quarterback living under his roof, and his offspring being Haden's friend and top receiver, this had to prove to be the easiest recruiting job throughout McKay's coaching career. Despite a great deal of attention being shown to Haden and McKay from other universities, the duo signed on with USC. Over the course of his three varsity seasons, Haden did not disappoint the Trojan faithful. After serving as a backup to Mike Rae on the 1972 national championship team, Haden assumed the starting quarterback responsibilities for the next two. He led the Trojans to a pair of PAC-8 titles and another national title in 1974. In a dramatic 18–17 win over Ohio State in the 1975 Rose Bowl that clinched USC's second national crown in three seasons, Haden earned co-MVP honors along with his friend J.K. McKay. In three varsity seasons under center for the Trojans, Haden completed 241 out of 468 pass attempts for 3,288 yards and 33 touchdowns. His career numbers still allow him the privilege to be ranked among the upper echelon of all-time USC quarterbacks.

His success at USC was not limited to the football field. In the classroom, Haden excelled to heights that earned him a Rhodes Scholarship, and the opportunity to study at the prestigious Oxford University in England. From 1975 to 1978, Haden studied at Oxford University, where he received a degree in economics. In addition to his studies abroad, he also holds a bachelor's degree magna cum laude from USC, and a degree from Loyola Law School.

Haden also found the time to play in the professional ranks. He was a seventh round selection of the Los Angeles Rams in 1975, but opted to play in the World Football League with the Southern California Sun. He returned to the Rams after the WFL folded, and remained with the team from 1976 to 1981. He led the Rams to NFC title game appearances in 1976 and 1978, along with earning a trip to the 1977 Pro Bowl. He suffered a broken finger during the 1979 season, which was the year that the Rams made it to the Super Bowl. While recovering from knee surgery following the 1981 season, Haden was offered a broadcasting job with CBS, and he retired from the Rams. He covered football action for Fox Sports and TNT in addition to CBS for over a decade.

In addition to his broadcasting career, Haden also was a partner in a private equity firm in Los Angeles. On August 3, 2010, Pat Haden was appointed USC's athletic director, replacing fellow Trojan football alumni Mike Garrett. His incredible talent as an athlete and student not only paid off in his professions, but will carry on for future generations to witness. For his prowess on the football field, Haden was honored with induction into both the Rose Bowl Hall of Fame and National High School Hall of Fame in 1995. Seven years prior to those dual honors, he was enshrined into the GTE Academic All-American Hall of Fame.[2]

## *Jesse Hibbs*

Jesse Hibbs might have been a native of Normal, Illinois, but there was nothing normal about his life. Just the opposite was true, as Hibbs went on to star as a tackle on USC's "Thundering Herd" teams of the late 1920s, and then proceeded to work with stars as a long-time director in Hollywood.

Hibbs' life began on January 11, 1906 in Normal, Illinois. When it was time to attend high school, Hibbs enrolled at Lake Forest Academy. This was one of the most prestigious preparatory schools in America, with students coming from many states and foreign countries. The home of the black and orange Caxys has long been the starting point for successful careers, including many actors and actresses, one of them being the legendary sex symbol Jean Harlow.

Following graduation from Lake Forest, Hibbs set out to add his name to the institution's roll of honor. The 6-0, 183-pound tackle donning #10 at USC, did not disappoint in his first quest for stardom. While blocking for the likes of Trojan legends Mort Kaer, Morley Drury, and Don Williams, Hibbs earned three letters (1926–28), and became USC's first-ever two-time All-American (1927–28). With Hibbs winning the battle of the trenches, the Trojans ran up a near-perfect record of 25–3–2 during his college career, and won two conference championships and the program's first national title in 1928, a year in which Hibbs served as team captain. In addition to his excellence on the football field, he also played basketball for USC in 1927.

With his successful college days behind him, Hibbs returned to Illinois to play with professional football with the Chicago Bears in 1931. This allowed him the privilege of playing for two of football's all-time great coaches in Howard Jones, and then George "Papa Bear" Halas in the pro circuit. It was then back to the Golden Coast for Hibbs, who began a long career in the film industry.[1]

While still a student at USC, Hibbs, like many of his fellow Trojans, found work in the motion picture business. He played himself in 1927's *The College Widow*, and then performed in unaccredited appearances in three films with college life themes, from 1931 to 1933. From 1937 to 1953, Hibbs served as an assistant director on 51 motion pictures, including the sports classic, *Knute Rockne All-American*, in 1940. In 1953 he directed his first film, *The All-American*, a football drama starring Tony Curtis, and over the course of the next five years, he was credited with 10 more directing duties in motion pictures. He then shifted over to television, and directed on some of that mediums greatest shows. Included on his television directing resume from 1958 to 1970 were *Gunsmoke, Bonanza, Rawhide, Perry Mason, The Fugitive, The Wild Wild West, and The F.B.I.* On February 4, 1985, at age 79, Jesse Hibbs passed away in Ojai, California, and was inducted into the USC Athletic Hall of Fame in 1999.[2]

## *Dwayne Jarrett*

Countless youths throughout the decades have tossed footballs with friends and relatives, and Dwayne Jarrett was no exception to the rule. However, Jarrett separated himself from the bulk of the masses when he took the skill of catching a football all the way to stardom on multiple levels.

The New Jersey native made great strides in gaining the highest honors a prep performer can obtain as a member of the New Brunswick High School Zebras. At the end of his junior season in 2002, Jarrett caught 40 passes for 956 yards, which averaged out to an incredible 23.9 yards per reception. He scored 17 touchdowns, and on the defensive side, had 24 tackles and six interceptions. The following year saw Jarrett rule not only the New Jersey scholastic scene, but was one of the premier players in the nation. He earned that type of praise after scoring 26 touchdowns, five coming on punt returns, where he averaged an eye-popping 48.0 yards per return. He was a one-man wrecking crew in the 2003 New Jersey state championship game when he scored three touchdowns in New Brunswick's 21–14 win. He received the New Jersey Offensive Player of the Year award, the Super Prep All-Northeast Offensive MVP award, was selected as one of the top 50 players in the United States, and named to the 2003 Parade All-American Team, in addition to being on the Super Prep All-American and Prep Star All-American squads. Jarrett also found time after his illustrious football seasons to play basketball.[1]

The 6-5, 215-pound receiver was naturally on the wish lists of countless college programs. However, the star receiver decided to head out clear across the country to be among the stars of Hollywood. At the time of Jarrett's arrival on the USC campus, the Trojans had just seen top receiver Mike Williams depart for the NFL. However, Jarrett's impact was immediate, as the freshman clad in the Cardinal & Gold with #8 on his jersey, filled the void left by Williams. In 2004, he used his weapons of speed, size, and a great pair of hands, to haul in 55 passes for 849 yards and 13 touchdowns to earn Freshman All-American honors. His stellar freshman effort helped the Trojans to a spotless 13–0 record and the national championship. This allowed Jarrett to go right from a state championship in high school to a national title in college in back-to-back seasons.

The following year Jarrett and the Trojans cruised to another spotless regular season record and a return to the national championship game, but this time, USC lost to Texas in a very close game. On an individual level, Jarrett's sophomore season was nothing short of spectacular, as he caught 91 passes for 1,274 yards and 16 touchdowns on his way to All-American status. He received another All-American selection in 2006, and with it, became the first-ever USC receiver to earn All-American twice. For the 2006 season, the junior superstar hauled in 70 receptions for 1,015 yards and 12 touchdowns.

Jarrett was a two-time All-Conference selection (2005–06), won the Touchdown Club of Columbus' Wide Receiver of the Year Award, and was the MVP of the 2007 Rose Bowl. After three seasons, Jarrett was the all-time career reception leader for USC, and decided to pass on his senior year and go into the National Football League. He was more than ready for the next phase of competition, and the Carolina Panthers also thought so, making him their second round pick of the 2007 NFL draft. He played with the Panthers until 2010 and then went to the Saskatchewan Roughriders of the Canadian Football League for the 2011 season.[2]

## *Gary Jeter*

Cathedral Latin High School in Cleveland, Ohio, produced one of the greatest athletic legacies that the Buckeye State ever had. From 1916 to 1979, the Catholic preparatory school on Cleveland's east side stood as a symbol of excellence in both academia and athletics. The purple and gold colors of the school proved to be the envy of many and for good reason. In its history of athletic competition, the Lions accounted for numerous city and state championships, all thanks to some of the greatest talent the city had ever witnessed.

One such individual that helped Cathedral Latin achieve ever-lasting status was Gary Jeter, a 6-4, 255-pound defensive force whose abilities drew the attention of college football coaches from coast to coast, including that of USC's John McKay some 2,400 miles from Cleveland. However, this talented athlete, who McKay once tabbed as the best to play the tackle position in the country, almost never came to be.[1]

When Jeter was 14 years old, he was stabbed in the chest, with the knife missing his heart by a mere six inches.[2] After rebounding from this near-fatal assault through a steady weight-training program, Jeter became one of the greatest prep defensive linemen in the nation throughout the early 1970s. In his senior season of 1972, Jeter collected prep All-American honors and received the Ohio High School Lineman of the Year award. After narrowing down the countless college offers bestowed upon him to Notre Dame, Ohio State, and USC, Jeter decided to join the program of the reigning national champion Trojans.

It did not take the powerful freshman long to establish himself as a force at the next level of competition. Jeter impressed the coaching staff so much that he was given a starting job at defensive tackle by the third game of his freshman season. At the time, such a promotion for a freshman was virtually unheard of, especially on a team swarming with talent.

Jeter had incredible physical ability, and he used his size and strength to dominate the opposition. Teammate and powerhouse running back Ricky Bell once proclaimed that the hardest defense he ran against was in practice and opposing Jeter. If he was tough against his own teammates, one can only imagine the pounding that opponents took every week over the course of four seasons.

Jeter earned four letters in football (1973–76), along with three All-Conference selections (1974–76), and All-American status in 1976. He played in three Rose Bowls, and was a key member of the Trojans 1974 national championship team. He received the 1975 USC Defensive Player of the Year Award and the 1976 USC Special General Excellence Award.

Following his illustrious college career, that saw him record 234 tackles, it came as no surprise when the National Football League came beckoning. The New York Giants quickly selected Jeter in the first round, and made him the fifth overall player taken in the 1977 NFL draft. He then performed at the highest level a football player can for 12 years. He was a member of the Giants from 1976 through 1982, the Los Angeles Rams (1983–88), and ended his pro career with the New England Patriots in 1989.[3]

## *Keyshawn Johnson*

From the home of the LA Dorsey Dons on Farmdale Avenue, to wearing the Blue & Gold of the West Los Angeles College Wildcats, and completing his football journey through the City of Angels at the Memorial Coliseum, Keyshawn Johnson was an exciting performer that became a Trojan legend.

Johnson was born on July 22, 1972, in Los Angeles. As a youth, things could have seriously gone wrong for him due to problems with the law that led to Johnson serving time at a reformatory camp. He was also injured in a drive-by shooting. However, the saving grace in his young life was football. Due to this passion and talent for the game, he was able to elevate himself from a life of despair to that of a highly successful individual.

It was at USC, and through the help of head coach John Robinson, that allowed Johnson to make a turn down the right path in life. Robinson brought him in to help the team out by doing jobs for the USC football team. Whether it was bringing footballs or equipment, the opportunity to be a part of the Cardinal & Gold culture served as a springboard to his own greatness.

In his senior season at Dorsey, Johnson caught 33 passes for 668 yards and six touchdowns, which earned him First Team All-State honors. He also lettered in track. His grades were not stellar, so he went to West Los Angeles College to improve his studies. Eventually, he focused on the classroom and received an associate's degree. On the football field, Johnson continued to marvel all with his talents, as he became one of the top junior college players in the country. After being honored with Junior College All-America status, Johnson was ready for the big time.[1]

The Trojans have had a long-standing, solid reputation of taking in players from the junior college ranks and guiding them to heights of greatness. Keyshawn Johnson lived up to that billing by becoming one of the most prolific pass receivers in USC history. His 6-4, 210-pound frame was the main target for Trojan signal callers and the nightmare for defenders covering him. Whether diving for passes, or earning a reputation for making tough catches across the middle, Johnson used a competitive drive, speed, and strength, to elevate himself to a superstar level.[2]

In his first year as a Trojan in 1994, Johnson snagged 66 passes for 1,362 yards, nine touchdowns, and was named the MVP of the 1995 Cotton Bowl. If that impact was not enough, for an encore, he set the college football world on fire in 1995 by gathering in 102 receptions for 1,434 yards and seven touchdowns. By season's end, he was a unanimous selection for All-American, two-time All-Conference receiver, rewrote the USC record books for receiving on numerous occasions, was the Pac-10's Offensive Player of the Year, brought home the Pop Warner Award, given to the Pacific coast's most valuable senior, and finished off his college days with the MVP award being presented to him at the conclusion of the 1996 Rose Bowl.

Upon hanging up his #3 jersey for the final time, the buzz about Johnson was at a fever pitch throughout the professional circuit. The New York Jets ended any hopes that the other NFL teams might have had about selecting him in the 1996 draft. They quickly made the star receiver the first overall pick that year, and Johnson lived up to that sterling honor. Over the course of an 11-year professional career, Johnson caught 814 passes for 10,571 yards and 64 touchdowns, to rank among the highest of all-time receivers. He played with the Jets from 1996 to 1999, the Tampa Bay Buccaneers (2000–03), the Dallas Cowboys (2004–05), and the Carolina Panthers in 2006. While in Tampa, he was a member of the 2002 team that reigned victorious in Super Bowl XXXVII. He was inducted into the Cotton Bowl Hall of Fame in 2007 and USC's Athletic Hall of Fame in 2012.[3]

## *Mort Kaer*

There have been many who graced the hollowed halls of the USC campus that exhibited incredible athletic prowess. In the 1920s, the presence of Mort Kaer on the campus was a reminder of how lucky the Trojan faithful were to have this Red Bluff product on their side.

The 5-11, 167-pound backfield star of the Trojans was born Morton Kaer on September 7, 1902, in Omaha, Nebraska. He eventually settled in Red Bluff, California, some 200 miles north of San Francisco, and that was where the legend began. By the mid–1920s Kaer would be the toast of the campus for his skills on both grass and cinder surfaces. He also earned the distinction of being mentored by three of the greatest coaches in USC history. He played under Elmer "Gloomy Gus" Henderson and Howard Jones on the football team, and then was a standout trackman for the legendary "Maker of Champions," Dean Cromwell in the spring.

The Trojans had headline-grabbing running backs in the likes of Frank "Rabbit" Malette, Charley Dean, and Roy "Bullet" Butler prior to Kaer's arrival, but they never matched the national attention that was bestowed on the Red Bluff product. The term Devil-may-care is a phrase that can mean reckless. In a play on words with his last name, his moniker appropriately became "Devil May" Kaer, and he lived up to it by attacking opponents with reckless abandon, en route to earning the title of first-ever Trojan to be named a consensus All-American in 1926. He was a three-year letterman (1924–26), led the Trojans in rushing and scoring in 1925 and 1926, and was the leading scorer and in the entire nation in 1925. He also led the nation in touchdowns with 19. He set the since broken USC all-time scoring record with 216 points, with all of them coming by running the ball, and his 1,588 career rushing yards still ranks among the top 30 of all-time in school history. Besides All-American status, Kaer was also named the 1925 Amateur Athletic Foundation Southern California Athlete of the Year.[1]

When spring came upon the scene in Southern California, the cinder track was the place for Kaer to be found. Instead of using cleats, he laced up track spikes and proceeded to dominate in the same manner that he did in the fall on football fields. In 1924, he represented the United States at the Summer Olympics in Paris, coming in fifth in the pentathlon. Two years later, Kaer helped USC win the 1926 national collegiate track championship.

Five years after playing his final college football game, Kaer entered the National Football League for one season in 1931 with the Frankford Yellow Jackets. It was then on to Weed, California, which was made famous as a town mentioned in literary giant John Steinbeck's 1937 classic novel, *Of Mice and Men*. Weed is 617 miles north of Los Angeles, and approximately 100 miles north of Kaer's old stomping grounds of Red Bluff. It was there at Weed High School that Kaer spent 28 years as a teacher and coach, guiding the Weed Cougars to an impressive 187–47–7 record that included 17 conference championships.[2]

In 1972, Mort Kaer was rightfully honored to reside alongside other immortals when he was inducted into the College Football Hall of Fame. In 1997, the institution that he helped bring to athletic prominence bestowed him with enshrinement into the USC Athletic Hall of Fame. The legend that was Mort "Devil May" Kaer lived until January 12, 1991, passing away at age 88 in Mt. Shasta, California.[3]

## *Ryan Kalil*

Every offensive play begins with the snap from center. In the case of USC in the early 2000's Ryan Kalil was the center that ignited the high-powered Trojan offensive juggernauts that captured two national championships, and he was an excellent one.

Servite High School in Anaheim, California, prides itself in preparing students for success and leadership qualities through an extremely challenging academic program, and can also boast of a solid reputation in athletics.[1] Servite's lessons in life skills and athletics served Kalil well, as he not only became one of USC's best offensive linemen of all-time, but a team leader who anchored a group of trench warriors that allowed quarterback Matt Leinart and running back Reggie Bush to bring home Heisman Trophies in 2004 and 2005.

Before donning the Cardinal & Gold at USC, Kalil was busy earning accolades as one of the top prep linemen in the country. As a member of the Servite Friars, he was bestowed with Prep All-American honors in 2002, along with many other awards. Kalil's blocking skills were so solid that he never gave up a sack in both his junior and senior seasons.[2]

It was then on to USC at a time when Pete Carroll was about to unleash an offensive attack that was virtually unstoppable. Kalil was a physical marvel at 6-3, 285 pounds, who could bench press 225 pounds 34 times and run a 4.9 in the 40-yard dash. With strength, quickness, and great blocking technique, Kalil became a four-year letterman (2003–06), All-Pac-10 twice (2005–06), and All-American in 2006. He also won the 2006 Pac-10 Morris Trophy, awarded to the outstanding lineman in the conference.[3]

After helping the Trojans to a 48–4 record during his stay in the Land of Troy, Kalil was selected by the Carolina Panthers in the second round of the 2007 NFL draft. He continued to excel on the professional level, being selected to three Pro Bowls (2009–11), earned All-Pro honors in 2011, and is regarded as one of the top offensive linemen in the NFL.[4]

## *Desmond Koch*

On May 10, 1932, Desmond Koch was born in Lincoln County, Tennessee. Over the course of the next 24 years, he would first become the most prolific punter in USC history, and earn a spot on the medal stand at the Summer Olympics. As a prep track star at Reed High School in Shelton, Washington, Koch emerged as the nation's top high school discus thrower.[1]

While a member of the USC Trojans under coach Jess Hill, Koch led the nation with a 43.4 yards-per-punt average in 1952 as a junior. In the 1953 Rose Bowl Game, won by USC, 7–0, Koch nailed a record-setting 72-yard punt. He then booted the ball for a 43.5 average as a senior. Despite his excellent talent for punting, it was as a track star that he reached international fame. After winning the national discus championship in 1955, Koch secured a place for himself on the 1956 United States Olympic team as a substitute. However, when Ron Drummond was forced to pass on representing the United States due to other commitments, Koch filled in.[2] In those Games, held in Melbourne, Australia, Koch proved to be a worthy addition to the team, winning a bronze medal, which allowed the United States to sweep in that event. Al Oerter won the gold, and Fortune Gordien the silver. Standing six-foot tall and weighing 209 pounds, Koch's all-time personal bests in the shot put was 52' and 180–8 in the discus. He lived until age 58, passing away on January 26, 1991 in Los Angeles, California.[3]

## *Grenville Lansdell*

Great Barrington, Massachusetts, has the distinction of being a small town with an energetic feel to it. Its history was helped by the advent of the railroad, which turned the area into a resort town for rich families to build massive dwellings to escape the daily grinds of city life.

It was in this quaint setting, 135 miles west of Boston, that the world was introduced to Grenville "Grenny"Archer Lansdell, Jr., on July 16, 1918. In time, this product of "the Bay State" would make a name for himself clear across the country in the sunny climes of Los Angeles, as one of the greatest multi-threat college football players of his generation.[1]

Sportswriter Braven Dyer, who had the privilege of witnessing the majority of USC football talent through the 1930s, once dubbed Lansdell as the best all-around performer in the history of the program. The Los Angeles scribe made this assumption in 1939 while Grenny was leading the Trojans to much success in the final years of the Howard Jones era.

In the days before substitution, and the two-platoon system came into the game of football, a player had to perform on both sides of the ball. The ability to achieve success in both capacities was reserved for a select few, and Lansdell was one of the true standouts.

The University of Southern California had the ability throughout their history to take junior college transfers and make All-Americans out of them, with Lansdell being the first to accomplish the prestigious honor. Coming to the Land of Troy after attending Pasadena Junior College, Lansdell established himself as a threat every time he touched the ball on offense, was a sure tackler on defense, a devastating kick returner, and also handled the kicking chores. The 6-0, 190-pounder was listed as a quarterback, but his real position was that of a single-wing tailback who took every snap. It was then that Lansdell had the option to either run or pass, both of which he did exceptionally well. He had the ability to be a punishing power runner or loft a pass with ease.

In three varsity seasons from 1937 through 1939, Lansdell was USC's offensive weapon. With incredible talent at running in the open field, and delivering a ferocious straight-arm blow to anyone attempting to bring him down, he led the team in passing all three seasons, and twice in rushing, with 462 yards on the ground in 1938 and 742 throughout the following campaign. He also topped the Trojans in virtually every other offensive category during his time wearing the Cardinal & Gold. His #78 was the focal point for followers of USC football to cheer for on a consistent basis and the one that gave opponents nightmares on how to stop the Trojan juggernaut in cleats. Accolades have a way of gravitating toward those who display incredible effort, and Lansdell definitely collected his fair share of honors. He was a main reason why the Trojans won two conference titles and the national championship in 1939. He earned three letters, and in 1939, he received All-Conference and All-American recognition.

After guiding USC to a 21–6–4 record in the late 1930s, Lansdell opened the decade of the 1940s as the first round draft pick of the New York Giants. After seeing limited action during his rookie year, Lansdell, like most of the young men in America at the time, went off to serve in the military while World War II was raging on. As Captain Lansdell, the former USC star was a pilot in the Army Air Corps, where he flew missions in the Pacific Campaign.

When the war ended in 1945, Lansdell opted not to continue his professional football career. He settled in Newport Beach, California, and used his piloting skills to fly for Trans World Airlines for 30 years. He died on May 14, 1984 at age 65, and was inducted into the USC Athletic Hall of Fame in 2003. A part of the former Trojan great lived on when his grandson, Morgan Craig, was a walk-on for USC in 2002–03 as a quarterback and fullback.[2]

## *Matt Leinart*

Matt Leinart is the embodiment of what the fighting spirit of USC is all about. Overcoming childhood adversity, he conquered all detractors on his way to the summit of the college football world. In doing so, Leinart became one of the greatest to ever wear the Cardinal & Gold in a program deep in spectacular heritage.

This future Trojan quarterback was a native Californian from birth, coming into the world in Santa Ana on May 11, 1983. He was born with strabismus (crossed eyes) that had his left eye not in the same position as the right one.[1] When he was three years old, surgery was performed to correct the problem, but he needed to wear thick glasses up to the time he was ready for high school. A weight problem, coupled with the thick glasses, only added to his grief, as he became the brunt of many cruel jokes from his peers. His weight problem was eventually solved by a growth spurt during his teenage years.

Despite his woes, Leinart possessed athletic skills, which proved to be his solace and eventual redemption against all of those that mocked him. He showed prowess in basketball and flag football, but was passionate about baseball. He was also exceptional at the sport, capable of hitting the 80's on a radar gun as a 14-year old left-handed pitcher.[2] His days as a pitcher came to an end when he suffered a torn labrum and damage to his rotator cuff of his throwing arm. Despite the setback that saw baseball now a faded memory, Leinart remained steadfast in his athletic pursuits, turning his attention to football at Mater Dei High School.

West Edinger Avenue in Santa Ana, California, has an iconic structure on it that boasts of being one of the largest private Catholic schools in the country. Shortly after opening in 1950, it also earned the distinction of possessing a football history rich in success and tradition. As of 2012, the program has close to 500 all-time victories, numerous championships, and is only one of two high schools that can boast of having two future Heisman Trophy winners as part of its heritage. John Haurte (class of 1961), was the first in 1964 while playing for Notre Dame. Forty years later, it was Matt Leinart's turn to hoist college football's grandest individual prize at the Downtown Athletic Club in New York City. However, before his crowning moment with the Heisman, Leinart honed his talents as a scarlet & gray-clad Monarch for Mater Dei under legendary coach Bruce Rollinson.[3]

His 1998 sophomore season was lost due to a rotator cuff injury in his left shoulder. Unlike in his baseball career, this time the injury only proved to be a minor setback. Leinart came back strong in 1999, throwing for 2,400 yards and 15 touchdowns while completing close to 65 percent of his pass attempts. His efforts helped him to be selected the All-Serra League MVP after guiding the Monarchs to an 11–2–1 record, a league title, and a Division I California Interscholastic Federation (CIF) championship.[4]

In his senior season of 2000, Leinart hit on 62 percent of his pass attempts for 2,870 yards and 28 touchdowns, as the Monarchs finished at 9–3. One of his highlights from this season came when he threw for 447 yards and four six-pointers against national champion De La Salle High School. Top-rated national awards were bestowed on the left-handed prep star, including *Parade* All-American, Super Prep All-American, Student Sports Senior All-American, and the Prep Star Dream Team. He was also honored as the Gatorade California Player of the Year, the All-CIF Division I Co-Offensive MVP, the Los Angeles Times All-Orange County Back of the Year. He also made numerous All-Star Team lists, and was toted as one of the top college prospects in the nation.[5]

After setting many passing records at Mater Dei in his #7 jersey, Leinart traveled 40 miles north of his alma mater to become a USC Trojan. The heavily recruited signal caller came to USC in the fall of 2001, the same year in which Pete Carroll began his coaching stint at the university. In time, this duo would dominate the college football universe. However, at first, Leinart's time as a Trojan was anything but spectacular. In 2001, he was redshirted, and the following year he served as Carson Palmer's backup, learning all he could from the player who went on to win the 2002 Heisman Trophy.[6]

It was at this time that Leinart contemplated leaving USC for more opportunities elsewhere. His spirit seemed gone while watching from the sideline, and the USC coaches did not have much confidence in him taking over the quarterback reins in 2003. Once again, like when he was a child, Leinart reached deep down inside himself for the missing passion. He beat out Matt Cassel and Brandon Hance for the starting job during spring practice. Pete Carroll displayed confidence in Leinart, and after learning he won the starting job, he told the coaches that they would not regret their decision. Leinart stuck to his promise by guiding the Trojans and Pete Carroll to great heights over the next three seasons.[7]

From 2003 through 2005, the Trojans under Leinart ran up an almost perfect record of 37–2, winning two national championships (2003- 2004) and playing for a third in 2005. He started off his incredible run as the all-time top quarterback in USC history by throwing for a touchdown on his first-ever pass as a Trojan. The team ran off three straight wins to open the season before losing in triple-overtime to California. The

Trojans bounced back, won eight straight, and finished at 11–1 to claim the Associated Press national title with Leinart ending his first season as the starter, with 3,556 yards and a whopping 38 touchdowns against a mere nine interceptions. He captured the 2003 Pac-10 Offensive Player of the Year, becoming only the second sophomore, joining Stanford's John Elway, in the history of the conference to win the award. This breakout season also ended with Leinart winning the Touchdown Club of Columbus' Archie Griffin Award, an honor that he repeated in 2004, earned All-American status, and finished sixth in the 2003 Heisman Trophy voting.[8]

In 2004, Leinart and the Trojans left nothing to chance, as USC assumed the #1 position in the ranking from the first to the final game. They capped off the year with a resounding 55–19 mauling over Oklahoma in the BCS Championship Game to win the national title with a spotless 13–0 record. Throughout the season, Leinart was virtually flawless at the controls of Pete Carroll's high-powered offense. He threw for 3,322 yards and 33 touchdowns en route to becoming USC's sixth Heisman Trophy winner, in 2004. Other top prestigious honors to come his way following the season were the Pac-10 Co-Offensive Player of the Year Award, the Walter Camp Player of the Year Award, Associated Press Player of the Year, the Manning Award, and the Victor Award. The Manning Award is presented to the nation's top college quarterback, and Leinart was the first-ever recipient. The Victor Award is presented to both professional and amateur athletes of the year. He was also a consensus All-American in 2004.[9]

Leinart did not rest on his laurels after his incredible junior year. He passed for 3,815 yards and 28 touchdowns while once again leading the Trojans to a perfect 12–0 regular season in 2005. However, the quest for a third straight national title ended in a close, 41–38 loss to Texas in the BCS Championship Game. Seeing that he was a former Heisman Trophy winner, Leinart had a vote in helping to nominate future recipients. As a true team leader, he cast his first place vote for eventual winner and teammate Reggie Bush, while finishing third in the final voting. Despite missing out on a second Heisman, Leinart still received many of the sport's top awards. He won the Johnny Unitas Golden Arm Award (top senior quarterback), the Touchdown Club of Columbus' Quarterback of the Year, the Pop Warner Award (top senior on the West Coast), *The Sporting News* Sportsman of the Year Award, and the Southern California Sportsman of the Year Award. He also became USC's second player in history to earn All-American honors three times, joining Richard Woods, in that category.[10]

Leinart finished his incredible run as USC's signal caller par-excellence with 10,693 career yards and 99 touchdown passes. He was a four-time letterman (2002–05), team captain in 2004 and 2005, and a three-time All-Pac-10 first team selection. He also set numerous USC, Pac-10 marks, and NCAA records.[11]

The 6-5, 225-pound Leinart was a first round selection of the Arizona Cardinals in the 2006 NFL draft, and played with them from 2006 through 2009. While with the Cardinals, he was a member of their Super Bowl XLIII team. He then went to the Houston Texans (2010–11) and the Oakland Raiders (2012). He was an easy choice for enshrinement into the USC Athletic Hall of Fame in 2007, and had his #11 USC jersey retired by the university.[12]

## *Ronnie Lott*

Rialto, California, located between San Bernardino and Fontana, is the site of Dwight D. Eisenhower High School, although Lott's drive to be a winner started at Bradley Elementary School in Maryland. By the time he crossed the threshold of Eisenhower High School in the mid–1970s, Lott was ready to use his scholastic football career as a springboard to elite status among the greats of the game.[1]

Under the guidance of coach Bill Christopher, Lott started off as a wide receiver in his sophomore year. By his senior season, he started at both quarterback and safety, and ended the year as winner of the Ken Hubbs Award, presented to the top ranked high school athlete from San Bernardino, California.

During his years at USC, Ronnie Lott received a degree in public administration, and administered a great deal of pain on opposing offenses from his safety position. He patrolled the Trojans' secondary from 1977 through 1980, and earned a stellar reputation as a fierce, hard-hitting tackler and excellent pass defender. Lott was truly the complete package, and reaped the rewards of his hard work. He was honored as an All-American in 1980, received All-Pac-10 status in 1979 and 1980, was USC's team captain in 1980, and the Trojans' MVP in the same season. As a starter since his sophomore season, Lott recorded 14 interceptions and 250 tackles in three seasons. His eight thefts of enemy passes led the nation in his senior year. He helped the Trojans earn a national championship in 1978, two Rose Bowl victories after the 1978 and 1979 seasons, and was part of a 28-game unbeaten streak.[2]

In 1981, it came as no surprise when the name Ronnie Lott appeared on top of the NFL draft board. The San Francisco 49ers quickly snatched up the player regarded as one of the most complete defensive backs to ever roam the secondary. Lott came to the "City by the Bay" as their first round pick, and eighth overall player taken in the '81 draft.

It did not take Lott long to show that he belonged in the professional ranks, as he earned a starting job at left cornerback in his rookie season. The 6-0, 203-pounder then proceeded to destroy anyone in an opposing jersey carrying the ball, and his solid play helped the 49ers win four Super Bowls (1981, 1984, 1988, 1989), and earn the distinction of being the "Team of the Decade." His reputation as a tough-nosed hitter and pass defender allowed Lott the opportunity to be selected to ten Pro Bowls and eight All-Pro teams over a professional career that lasted from 1981 to 1995. Lott was also elected to the All-Decade Team in both the 1980s and 90s, the NFL's 75th Anniversary All-Time Team, had his #42 retired by San Francisco, and made himself an easy choice for voters in 2000 when he was enshrined into the Professional Football Hall of Fame. In addition to playing with San Francisco from 1981 to 1990, Lott also patrolled the secondary for the Los Angeles Raiders (1991–92), the New York Jets (1993–94), and the Kansas City Chiefs (1995). In the same year the saw Lott's illustrious football career come to a conclusion, he was also honored with induction into the 1995 class of the USC Athletic Hall of Fame.[3]

## *Frank Malette*

A running back is considered one of the most glamorous positions in football. He is a main force on the offensive side of the ball, mixing the abilities to run, receive, block, and at times, pass. At USC, the running back position has earned national recognition and iconic status in college football history. The trophy cases at USC are filled with awards won by backfield stars, and their exploits have been told countless times. Tailback U. has long been a revered moniker associated with Trojan football, and the forefather of USC's proud backfield tradition can be traced to one Frank "Rabbit" Malette.

The San Diego product's all-around gridiron talents at USC could best be compared to those of Reggie Bush, a multi-purpose weapon that was the main focal point of the offense, and a threat to score anytime the ball was in his possession. What made Malette's feats even greater was the fact that he played at a time when it was required to perform on both offense and defense. After dazzling the crowd, and frustrating the defense with his offensive prowess, Malette shifted over to defense and played with the same spectacular skills. He was also an accomplished kicker, who connected on field goals and conversions on a consistent basis.

Malette was a three-year letterman for USC from 1915 through 1917 under coaches Ralph Glaze and Dean Cromwell. He was elected team captain in 1917, and easily earned All-Southern honors during his time in a Trojan uniform.[1]

## *Bruce Matthews*

The Matthews family earned a reputation of possessing excellent athletic ability, and the youngest of five children, Bruce, helped solidify that legacy with induction into the Pro Football Hall of Fame. The path that took Matthews to having his bust forever on display in Canton, Ohio, in 2007, began 517 miles south of the front door of pro football's ultimate shrine, on August 8, 1961, with his birth in Raleigh, North Carolina.

Football was in the Matthews' blood, as Bruce's father, Clay, Sr., played professionally with the San Francisco 49ers in the 1950s. His brother, Clay, J., also an All-American at USC, played 16 seasons at linebacker for the Cleveland Browns and three with the Atlanta Falcons.[1] Bruce's springboard to the professional ranks began at Aracadia High School, located 13 miles northeast of Downtown Los Angeles in the San Gabriel Valley. Under head coach Dick Salter, Matthews was a standout offensive and defensive lineman on two Aracadia Apaches Pacific League title teams in 1977 and 1978, both of which resulted in the team's appearance in the CIF championship games. He also showed talent on the wrestling mat, earning All-league honors in that sport.[2]

The University of Southern California was the next stop for the star lineman, and he did not even have to change school colors, as Aracadia's were the same cardinal and gold as USC's. The 6-5, 265-pound Matthews then went on to gain All-American status as a guard for the Trojans in 1982. In addition to that honor, he won three football letters (1980–82), was voted team captain (1982), selected All-Pac-10 twice (1981–82), and won the 1982 Pac-10 Morris Trophy, presented to the conference's top lineman. His abilities to open holes allowed Marcus Allen to surpass 2,000 yards rushing in 1981 on his way to winning that season's Heisman Trophy.[3]

This talented guard did not last long come draft day in 1983. The Houston Oilers used their first round pick to make Matthews the ninth overall player picked in the NFL draft. He then paid the organization back with solid play that brought him countless honors. From 1983 through 2001, Matthews slugged it out in the trenches, first in Houston and then after the franchise moved to Tennessee following the 1996 season, and he proved durable in his way through almost twenty seasons in the NFL. When he retired, with the exception of kickers and punters, he established a record of playing in 296 games. The record was since broken by Jerry Rice and Brett Favre, but still remains the all-time leader among offensive linemen. Along the way to setting the record, Matthews started in 229 straight games. He was selected to 10 All-Pro teams, received 14 invitations to the Pro Bowl, was the 2000 NFL Alumni Offensive Lineman of the Year, and the 2000 Bart Starr Man of the Year Award winner, which acknowledges an NFL player each year for his outstanding character and leadership at home, on the field, and in the community. He was also a member of the NFL's All-Decade Team for the 1990s, and on the 1999 AFC champion Tennessee Titans. The Titans' retired Matthews' famous #74 jersey, and in 2007, in his first year of eligibility, he was enshrined into the Pro Football Hall of Fame. He then went into coaching in the NFL, first with the Houston Texans in 2009, and he then returned to the Titans in 2011 to serve as offensive line coach.[4]

## *Clay Matthews*

The McKeever brothers played a dominant role in USC's football program in the late 1950s. Twenty years later, it was the Matthews brothers that earned their place among the legends of Troy. Unlike the McKeever twins, Clay and his brother Bruce helped the Trojans at separate times, but each left the USC campus as All-Americans and future top- level professionals.

Clay paved the way for the Matthews legacy at USC from 1974 through 1977. He was born in Palo Alto, California, on March 15, 1956, and received his high school education in Illinois. New Trier High School had reached an all-time high enrollment of 6,558 students in 1972, and Clay Matthews, Jr. was one of them.[1]However, it was not long until Matthews rose above the crowd to establish himself as a star athlete. Playing fullback and linebacker, Matthews earned All-State honors at both positions, and All-American status at linebacker. As a senior, he rushed for 1,000 yards and averaged nearly nine yards per carry. He was a guard in basketball, and also a member of the tennis team.[2]

Matthews returned to his native California upon high school graduation to embark on a journey that brought him championships and national recognition. His #60 became a focal point of the USC defense, and his 6-2, 232-pound frame provided workhorse effort from his middle linebacker position. He was a four-year letterman (1974–77), and the Trojans compiled a 37–10–1 record with Matthews leading the defense. He was a member of two conference championship teams (1974, 1976), two victorious Rose Bowl squads, and one national championship team (1974). Besides playing in two Rose Bowls, Matthews also served the Trojans in the Liberty Bowl (1975), and the Bluebonnet Bowl (1977). His hard-working effort was respected so much by his teammates and coaches that Matthews was elected team captain in 1977. He was a two-time All-Conference selection (1976–77), and an All-American in 1977. Over his USC career, Matthews recorded 266 tackles and two interceptions.[3]

With such an impressive college career behind him, it did not take the pros long to realize that Clay Matthews was a solid player. The Cleveland Browns wasted no time pondering his value, making Matthews their first round selection, and 12th overall player taken, in the 1978 draft.

The Browns got even more than they could have bargained for with Matthews on the team. He proved to be outstanding at rushing the quarterback or defending against the pass. He was the complete middle linebacker, and was regarded as one of the NFL's top-rated performers at his position. In addition to performing his job extremely well, Matthews was also one of the most durable players in league history. This gridiron warrior played for 19 seasons at one of the most demanding positions, and suited up for 278 games, which ranked him 17th all-time in that category in NFL history through 2012. He played with Cleveland (1978 through 1993), and Atlanta (1994–96). Throughout that long run in the professional ranks, Matthews recorded 69.5 sacks, 16 interceptions, and one touchdown. He also set an NFL record by being the oldest player to have a quarterback sack, which he achieved at age 40 years and 282 days.[4] In honor of his outstanding college and professional career, Matthews was enshrined into the Cleveland Browns Legends in 2002, and the USC Athletic Hall of Fame in 2005. Not only was he a great player, but he also produced one in his son, Clay Matthews III, who followed his father to USC and professional fame.

## *Rey Maualuga*

Sporting Polynesian warrior tattoos on massive arms, a wild mane of hair, and a look of absolute passion for the game in his eyes, Rey Maualuga blasted his 6-2, 260-pound frame into anything with an opposing jersey. He patrolled the turf of stadiums from coast to coast, performing with reckless abandon, causing Trojan faithful jubilation and opposition desperation and fear. Born on January 20, 1987, this future Cardinal & Gold-clad wrecking machine began life on January 20, 1987 to American Samoan parents at a U.S. Army hospital in Fort Sill, Oklahoma while his father was in the military. The family settled in Hawaii close to Honolulu. It was amidst the paradise of America's 50th state that the football career of Rey Maualuga began.[1]

His initial experience in the sport happened when Maualuga was in the sixth grade, and passion he brought to his days at USC was apparent from his pre-teen years on. Following the sixth grade, his family relocated to Oxnard, California, in Ventura County, some 35 miles west of Los Angeles. However, it was not Maualuga's final stop during his pre-college schooling. Eureka is in the upper region of northern California, approximately 100 miles south of the Oregon boarder. It was this location that Maualuga's father served the community as a minister and Rey continued on his path to greatness in the game of football.[2]

While in Oxnard, Maualuga attended St. Bonaventure High School in Ventura, and then at Eureka High School from his sophomore year up to graduation. Throughout his junior year, Maualuga had 146 tackles, 11 sacks, and one interception en route to leading Eureka to a 13–0 record and the North Coast Section championship. His more-than-impressive junior year earned him All-American, and All-State recognition, and set the tone for the greatness to come from this incredible talent.[3]

In a senior season that saw him dominate the prep All-American rosters, Maualuga once again dominated on the field. He had 96 tackles, four interceptions, two of which went for touchdowns, and two fumble recoveries. In his final two high school seasons as a Eureka Logger, the team posted a 20–2–1 record, and the fierce linebacker was now ready to elevate his skill level to the college ranks.[4]

Maualuga had proved that he was a winner, and that success continued in his four years at USC under head coach Pete Carroll. As a four-year letterman (2005–08), the Trojans recorded a 46–6 record with Maualuga hunting down the opposition all over the field at a steady pace. In four seasons, he had 273 tackles and five interceptions. Along with fellow All-Americans Keith Rivers and Brian Cushing, plus Clay Matthews III, Maualuga was part of one of the greatest linebacking corps in college football history. In 2005, he earned Freshman All-American honors, in addition to winning the John McKay Award (presented to the USC underclassman with the most competitive spirit). He received Sophomore All-American honors in 2006, unanimous All-American in 2008, and was a first team All-Pac-10 selection three times (2006–08). In 2008, he won the Pac-10 Defensive Player of the Year Award, the USC MVP Award, the CBSSports.com National Defensive Player of the Year Award, and the Bednarik Award, presented annually to college football's top defensive player. His football future was secured following his college playing days when the Cincinnati Bengals selected him in the second round of the 2009 draft.

## *Taylor Mays*

Taylor Mays was tailor made to be a football player. Born on February 7, 1988, he is the son of Stafford Mays, who was a defensive lineman at the University of Washington, and in the NFL with the St. Louis Cardinals (1980–86) and Minnesota

Vikings (1987–88). Taylor looked to follow in his father's line of work, displaying a passion for the game of football from an early age on. He was so engrossed with the idea of being a football player that he even did his homework with a helmet on at age 14. However, he almost did not see his dream turn into reality, as his parents did not want him to play football. Instead he turned to soccer, but in time he grew bigger than his contemporaries, and was a very physical player. By the time seventh grade came around, his parents gave permission for Taylor to unleash his football talent on the rest of the world.[1]

With the chance to play the game he yearned for, Taylor's passion and talent took him to All-American honors and the National Football League as a standout defensive back. The Maroon & Gold Fighting Irish of Washington's O'Dea High School served as the location where Mays earned a great deal of attention for his athletic endeavors. In order to work more on his speed, Mays went out for track during his sophomore year. In the spring of 2004, he achieved his goal by winning the 100 and 200-meter state championships.[2]

It was then on to football, where he continued on a path to stardom. During his junior season in the fall of 2004, Mays had 124 tackles and five interceptions on defense, earning Junior All-American status, and caught 25 passes for 700 yards as a wide receiver on offense. In 2005, Mays had 166 tackles and five interceptions while playing safety on defense. He gathered in 36 receptions for 765 yards and 15 touchdowns as a receiver, and was bestowed with All-State honors. He also was selected as the 2005 All-Metro League Mountain Division Offensive MVP and the Defensive Co-MVP.[3]

At 6-3, 218-pounds, with strength and speed (4.43 in the 40-yard dash), Mays was sought by many top college programs besides USC, including UCLA, Miami, and his father's alma mater, Washington. He claimed that USC's head coach Pete Carroll won him over with a passion and coaching technique that Mays could not turn down. Therefore, on August 14, 2005, prior to his senior season at O'Dea, he made his decision to attend USC.[4]

His #2 Cardinal & Gold jersey quickly became a focal point, and nightmare, for opposing offenses. He established himself quickly as a hard-hitting force in the USC secondary from his freshman year through his final game as a senior. In his freshman season of 2006, Mays recorded 62 tackles and three interceptions. His excellent work earned him selection onto the Freshman All-American first team and he also received the Pac-10 Co-Freshman of the Year Award.[5]

By the time his days as a Trojan were complete, Mays compiled three All-American selections (2007–2009), two All-Pac-10 selections (2008–2009) and won the 2008 Bob Chandler Award, presented to the underclassman that excelled on and off the field and in the classroom. Over the course of his USC career, the four-year letterman had 276 tackles and five interceptions while helping the Trojans to a 43–9 overall record. Like his father, Taylor succeeded in making it all the way to NFL. Taylor's quest for a spot in the professional ranks began when the San Francisco 49ers made him their second round pick, and 49th overall player chosen, in the 2010 NFL draft. He remained with the 49ers for one season, and was then traded to the Cincinnati Bengals on August 22, 2011.[6]

## *Paul McDonald*

Located some 20 miles east of downtown Los Angeles is Bishop Amat Memorial High School in the city of La Puente. Rich in football tradition, the battle cry of "Go Big Blue!" was shouted out loud and proud, and attracted the attention of USC football recruiters. The Royal Blue & Gold Lancers had a reputation of being a talent pipeline for the Trojans, as some quality players have advanced their academic and athletic careers at USC after their prep days at Bishop Amat were complete.[1]

In the 1970s, the Lancers possessed two future Trojan signal callers that were both brilliant and championship-caliber leaders. Pat Haden started the decade off as one of the most prolific high school quarterbacks of his time. In the mid–1970s, while Haden was leading the Trojans to their second national championship in three seasons, and then embark on a professional career, a Montebello, California quarterback was making a name for himself at Bishop Amat. His name was Paul McDonald, and in time, his left arm would rain passes down across the college football world, and allowed him the opportunity to set USC passing records, gain All-American notoriety, lead the Trojans to a 31–5–1 record during his tenure, and win a national championship in 1978.

McDonald was born on February 23, 1958, in Montebello, a city located in the southwestern part of the San Gabriel Valley, east of Los Angeles. It was while in these surroundings that McDonald first became a gifted athlete, and he then honed his skills at Bishop Amat, where he became a part of that program's stellar lineage. His abilities as a field general allowed McDonald to become a top-notch high school quarterback, which helped him make honorable mention on California's All-Time Prep Football Team. During his days as a high school quarterback, McDonald worked hard throughout the summer to perfect his talent, and that strong effort paid off with a scholarship offer to USC.

The amazing thing about McDonald's college career was the fact that he compiled impressive passing yardage, and earned All-American honors at a school known for running the ball with excellent results. With Heisman Trophy winner, and teammate, Charles White racking up record after record from the famed USC tailback position, McDonald still had the opportunity to rely on his arm to balance the offensive attack.

With a brilliant mind and cool demeanor on the field, the 6-2, 180-pound left-handed signal caller was a three-year letterman (1977–79), and guided the Trojans to a pair of Pac-10 titles (1978–1979), two Rose Bowl victories, a national championship (1978), a 13th place in the final polls in 1977, and a second place finish in 1979.[2]

In his freshman year of 1976, McDonald saw very little playing time behind Vince Evans, but still managed to take a few snaps en route to completing three of seven pass attempts for 34 yards. He got a bit more experience in 1977, completing 17 of 27 pass attempts for 191 yards. When his junior season of 1978 came upon the scene, he was ready to take the controls of the offense on a regular basis. He connected on 115 passes out of 203 attempts for 1,690 yards and 19 touchdowns. He led the Pac-10 in passing (151.5 yards per game average), and won the

USC Football Alumni Club Award (highest grade point average).[3]

In his senior year of 1979, McDonald completed 164 passes out of 264 attempts for 2,223 yards and 18 touchdowns. He was USC's total offense leader (2,149 yards), selected All-Pac-10 first team, All-American, sixth in the Heisman Trophy voting, and received the USC MVP Award, the USC Gloomy Gus Henderson Award (most minutes played), and the NCAA Today's Top Six Award. McDonald was also an exceptional student, and was honored for his stellar work in the classroom with Academic All-American honors in 1979, and received a 1979 Football Foundation Scholar-Athlete Award, and an NCAA Post-Graduate Scholarship.[4]

The Cleveland Browns selected McDonald in the fourth round of the 1980 NFL draft, and he played for them from 1980 through 1985. He then finished up his playing career with the Dallas Cowboys (1986–87). Following his professional career, McDonald worked as an investment banker and owned a business marketing company. In 1998, he returned to football as a radio analyst for USC games, where his work across the airwaves earned him awards for his excellence.[5]

## *Tim McDonald*

The lineage of great defensive backs in USC history is filled with hard hitters and All-Americans. The pride of Fresno, California, Tim McDonald, is an example of both these qualities. Born on January 6, 1965, this future bone-jarring defensive back was an award winning prep star for the Edison High School Tigers in Fresno. In the early 1980s, McDonald was a multi-talented football player that ended his high school career with many honors. He was selected as a Prep All-American, All-California, All-Northern California, and the most valuable player of his league. He played quarterback, where he completed nearly 60 percent of his passes en route to compiling 2,739 yards through the air and 30 touchdowns. He ran the ball for 400 yards and six more touchdowns, and picked off five passes and made 123 tackles on defense.[1]

At 6-3, 205 pounds, McDonald's talents were well received by the Trojans. He was a four-year letterman, two-time All-Pac-10 selection at safety (1985–86), and two-time All-American (1985–86). He was a team captain in 1986, USC's most valuable player in 1985 and 1986, and left the Land of Troy ranked high on the all-time interception list. He finished his college career with 339 tackles and 11 interceptions.[2]

He was drafted into the NFL as a sixth round selection of the Arizona Cardinals in 1987, and played with them until 1992. He finished off his professional career with the San Francisco 49ers from 1993 through 1999, winning a Super Bowl ring with them in 1994.[3]

## *Marlin and Mike McKeever*

On the first day of the 1940s, the city of Cheyenne, Wyoming, saw the dawn of not only a new decade, but also the birth of two future USC Trojans, and the greatest brother tandem in the history of the football program. Marlin and Mike McKeever were born on January 1, 1940, and left the "Cowboy State" of Wyoming with their parents for the Golden Coast, settling in an area associated with West Los Angeles named Sawtelle.

When it came time for the twins to enter high school, many of the Catholic school programs expressed interest in having Marlin and Mike on their sports teams. The gifted athletes decided on Mt. Carmel High School in Los Angeles. At first the duo received scholarships for basketball. At this time period, both were 5'5" and weighed 135 pounds as freshmen. A growth spurt hit both of them prior to their sophomore year, and now at close to six feet and 180 pounds, they were advised to focus on football.[1]

The decision proved to be highly successful, as the McKeever's ruled the prep gridiron fields throughout the City of Angels. In 1957, Marlin was selected as an All-American Lineman of the Year, the Los Angeles Examiner Scholastic Association Athlete of the Year, and found his way onto the All-Catholic League Team. Mike did not lack attention when it came time for the awards to be pressed out, as he received the California Interscholastic Federation Player of the Year Award, All-C.I.F. League honors, and joined Marlin as a prep All-American. Besides football, the twins excelled in baseball and track. At one time, Mike owned the California state record in the shot put. They easily won the Mt. Carmel Crusader Athletes of the Year Award and were both crowned as the school's Most Valuable Players. To top off all these stellar accomplishments was the fact that the McKeever twins also were extremely gifted in the classroom, earning spots on the Honor Roll in all four years of high school.[2]

By the time their high school careers were concluding, the 6'1,' 230-pound student/athletes were ready to advance to the next level of competition. Over twenty big school programs expressed interest in the twin wrecking machines. Notre Dame pressed hard for their services, but the twins had a devout affection for Los Angeles, and the University of Southern California won out.[3]

Marlin became a three-year letterman (1958–60) as a fullback and end. He caught 30 passes over his varsity career, which was a lot at this time, seeing that most teams ran the ball more than throwing it. He led the team in receptions twice (1959–60), handled the punting chores, and was a bone-jarring blocker. His skills were honored with three All-Conference selections (1958–60), was a two-time All-American (1959–60) in football, and an Academic All-American in 1959, and received the 1960 USC Lineman of the Year Award. He also performed on the USC track team in 1959 as a shot putter and discus thrower.[4]

He was selected by the Los Angeles Rams in the first round of the 1961 NFL draft and by the San Diego Chargers in the third round of the AFL draft. He decided to play for the Rams, and had two stints with them from 1961 through 1966, and again in 1971 and 1972. In between his times with the Rams, Marlin played for the Minnesota Vikings (1967), the Washington Redskins (1968–70), and the Philadelphia Eagles (1973).[5]

While Marlin was excelling on offense, Mike was terrorizing opponents from his linebacker position, and also played guard.

He led the Trojans in most defensive statistics during his sophomore and junior seasons, recording 199 tackles during that time. He was known for his rough style of play that consisted of making bone-crushing tackles, and on one occasion, he broke the jaw of an opposing halfback while tackling him. He received All-Conference and All-American honors in 1959, and was the recipient of the 1959 USC Davis-Teschke Award, presented to the most inspirational player. He won three letters in football (1958–60), was a two-time Academic All-American (1959–60), and the winner of the USC Football Alumni Club Award in 1960, presented to the senior player with the highest grade point average. In addition to his football prowess, Mike joined brother Marlin on the 1959 USC track team, where he competed in the shot put and discus. The twins also found time to add work in the film industry to their bulging list of accomplishments. In the 1962 film, *The Three Stooges Meet Hercules*, they played Siamese twin Cyclops Ajax and Argo, and also served as slave rowers and centurion guards in the same film.[6]

On October 29, 1960, during the sixth game of the season against Stanford, Mike suffered a head injury that resulted in two blood clots. He went through surgery to remove the clots, but his USC career was over. Prior to his injury, Mike was regarded as one of the top professional prospects in the country. Despite his serious season-ending injury, he was selected by the Los Angeles Rams in the 13th round of the 1961 NFL draft, and by the San Diego Chargers of the AFL in the 30th round. He attempted to take a shot at the pros with San Diego, but could not pass a physical exam because of his head injury.[7]

After graduation, his dreams of playing football might have been gone, but his desire to compete still remained. Mike decided to work toward making the U.S. Olympic team in track and field as a hammer thrower while working in the construction business. On December 3, 1965, all of his dreams came to an end when he was involved in a car accident that left him in a coma for 22 months. He never regained consciousness, and died on August 24, 1967 at age 27.[8]

Mike was inducted into the College Football Hall of Fame in 1987, and the USC Athletic Hall of Fame along with Marlin in 1995. Marlin lived until age 66, passing away on October 27, 2006, in Long Beach, California.[9]

## *Dan McMillan*

There is not one major college football program that has not suffered from losing out on a talented player, whether in the recruiting process or by transfer. In the case of USC, one of those occurrences happened prior to the Trojans rise to power in the 1920s. Lineman Dan McMillan has long been regarded as one of the best performers in USC's early history.

A native of Los Angeles born on June 29, 1898, McMillan prepped at famed Manual Arts High School. Upon graduation, he decided to remain in the Los Angeles area by enrolling at USC and looked to continue his football career in 1917. At 6-1, 190 pounds, McMillan was considered big for his time, and he utilized his powerful frame for the good of the Trojans. On both sides of the ball, he was a devastating force. As a blocker, he plowed through opposing linemen to create openings for his backfield. On defense, there was no better, as he crushed anyone with the ball.

After giving USC two incredible seasons, McMillan entered military service at the time of World War I. He was sent to flight school close to the University of California in Berkeley, and that was where USC's fortunes took a bad turn in the case of their talented two-way lineman.[1] He became friends with some members of the Cal football team, and through this bond, McMillan decided that Berkeley was the place where he wanted to continue his studies and football career.

Upon his release from the military, McMillan joined the Golden Bears just as the team was about to embark on becoming one of the greatest of all time. Under head coach Andy Smith, McMillan was part of Cal's "Wonder Teams" that eventually went on a 50-game unbeaten streak in the early 1920s. In both 1920 and 1921, McMillan received All-American recognition and helped the Golden Bears to an 18–0–1 record. He was elected to the College Football Hall of Fame in 1971, and died on October 22, 1975 at age 77.

## *Ron Mix*

"The Intellectual Assassin" was the perfect nickname for the man who came into the world as Ronald Jack Mix on March 10, 1938 in Los Angeles, California. Mix was extremely well spoken, and used the power of his brain to earn a law degree and study the game of football. In regards to the latter, Mix took what he learned about football and became a devastating offensive tackle that earned All-American and All-Pro honors, plus eventual enshrinement into the Pro Football Hall of Fame. The incredible thing about Mix's gridiron journey was the fact that he truly did not care to pursue the sport initially. Luckily, he did, and the sport of football got itself one great performer.

The route that one day led Mix to the hallowed shrine of pro football immortals on George Halas Drive in Canton, Ohio, began thousands of miles west at Hawthorne High School on El Segundo Boulevard. However, while attending the home of the scarlet and gold Cougars, Mix could never have envisioned the accolades he would achieve over the next quarter century. In regards to athletics, Mix had a desire to play baseball, and was good in track. Football was not on his desired list of extra curricular activities, but he somehow managed to gravitate toward the team.

Hal Chauncey became a coaching legend at the high school level while mentoring his charges at Hawthorne, and Mix was in one of the school's first classes under his guidance. It might be hard to fathom now, but the man who became one of the greatest professional offensive linemen in history, hardly gained any notoriety in high school. As a senior, he was a 6-2, 168-pound end that only mustered up honorable mention for all-league.[1] It was at this time that Mix had decided to retire his shoulder pads and cleats when he was playing in his final high school game.[2] Fate then interceded, as he was selected to play in a prep all-star game. Despite his disdain for football, Mix played in the game, and impressed the hierarchy of USC football enough that he was offered a scholarship four months later.[3]

Upon his arrival at USC, Mix was placed at the end position on the freshman team, and remained there during his sophomore season of 1957.[4] The following year was when he made the switch to offensive tackle, and it was then that the legend began, but not right away. The 1958 season saw him playing backup to starter Monte Clark. Finally, as a senior in 1959, Mix was a starting tackle, elected co-captain, made All-Conference, and All-American. He capped his incredible year off by winning the 1959 USC Lineman of the Year Award. His development was swift, as he used weight training to bulk up to 250 ponds and emerge as the top offensive tackle in the college ranks.[5]

Mix was regarded as one of the biggest linemen of his time at 6-4, 255 pounds when he was selected by the two-time defending NFL champion Baltimore Colts in the first round of the 1960 draft. The American Football League was just beginning in the same year, and the Boston Patriots also drafted Mix. Neither team won out for his services, as he was offered a better contract to play in his hometown with the Los Angeles Chargers.

By this time of his career, Mix was extremely dedicated to his craft, and the rest of the pro football world soon figured this out. The Chargers moved south to San Diego the following year, but the new address did nothing to slow Mix down. He was big, fast, and able to block a defensive end away from running lanes or lead power sweeps. The AFL lasted the entire decade of the 1960s prior to merging with the NFL in 1970, and Mix earned eight All-Star Game selections and was a nine-time All-Pro.[6]

The Chargers and Paul Lowe were the AFL's dream team and premier running back during the first half of the 1960s. The team appeared in five of the league's first six championship games, winning the title in 1963. Lowe was the AFL's elite running back during this time, but he was very aware that the men up front in the trenches were the reason for his success, especially Mix. Lowe once gave a great analogy by comparing Mix to a big brother protecting a younger sibling against fierce opposition.[7] Mix finished up his pro career in 1971 with the Oakland Raiders, was elected to the Pro Football Hall of Fame in 1979, and the USC Athletic Hall of Fame in 1997.

## *Orv Mohler*

Over a six-year span from 1926 through 1932, Orv Mohler compiled enough accolades that most people earn over a complete lifetime. Beginning as a high school star in the San Gabriel Valley, and then eight miles away at USC, his abilities in athletics are what legends were made of.

Football was king at Alhambra High School for a long period of time, and Mohler was a major reason for the program's success in the late 1920s. He was a team captain in his senior season of 1928, and led by example. He earned All-Coast League honors and won the All-Southern California Most Valuable Player Award while helping the Moors capture the state championship. His talents were so great on the football field that he was named to the *Pasadena Star News* 1920s "Team of the Decade," and on the same paper's All-Century Team as a back.[1]

His accolades as a high school athlete were not just limited to football. He was an outstanding baseball player who earned All-Coast League honors three times (1926–1928). Upon his high school graduation in 1929, Mohler looked to the next level of competition, and once in a Trojan uniform, the awards kept coming for the San Gabriel Valley product. In his sophomore year at USC, he rushed for 983 yards, averaged 6.8 yards a carry, and scored 17 touchdowns. His impressive numbers earned Mohler All-American status in 1930. He ran for 778 yards the following season and despite a neck injury that took him out of action for some of the 1932 season, he still managed to gain 264 yards on 74 carries and earn All-Conference honors. Over his three years on the varsity team, Mohler compiled 2,025 rushing yards, which still ranks him in the top 20 all-time in USC history as of 2012. The Trojans had an almost spotless record with Mohler on the team, posting a 28–3 record along the way to two national championships (1931–1932), and two conference titles. Besides being a three-year letterman in football, he also accomplished the same feat in baseball.[2]

Following his playing career Mohler was employed as an aviation department executive for an oil company and an Air Force colonel. On November 26, 1949, Mohler was piloting a B-25 bomber in Dixiana, Alabama, when trouble with an engine occurred. Two others were on board when the problem started, and they both bailed out. One crewman parachuted to safety, but the other's parachute failed to open. Mohler decided to attempt a landing with the power still coming from one engine. Unfortunately, the bomber did not cooperate, and it crashed, killing the former USC All-American.[3] Mohler was inducted into the USC Athletic Hall of Fame in 1995.

## *Johnnie Morton*

Johnnie Morton's career at USC was one that saw him progress from a freshman seeing action at receiver, to a pass-catching wizard that destroyed secondaries by the time he was an All-American after his senior year.

Morton was born on October 7, 1971, in Inglewood, California, a mere eight miles northeast of where he would emerge as a premier collegiate receiver by the early 1990s. Before arriving on the USC campus, Morton attended South High School in Torrance, California. As a member of the Spartans' football team, he displayed talent at tailback before switching back over to split end, where he felt he truly belonged.[1] The change worked out perfectly for him, as his abilities earned the opportunity to enroll at USC.

Morton's impact in the classic cross-town rivalry with UCLA in his freshman campaign of 1990, allowed him the impressive moniker of "Johnnie Hero," given to him by USC's broadcaster Pete Arbogast. Morton hauled in a 23-yard game-winning pass from quarterback Todd Marinovich with just 16 seconds left in what ended a high-scoring affair in USC's favor, 45–42.[2] Throughout that first season as a Trojan, Morton caught 15 passes, and then increased his total to 49 in each of the following two seasons. It was in 1993 that the 6-0, 190-pound receiver exploded. He caught 88 passes for 1,520 yards and 14 touchdowns on his way to earning All-American honors. He also received the 1993 Pop Warner Award (given to the most valuable senior on the Pacific Coast), the 1993 USC MVP Award, and All-Pac-10 recognition. He set numerous USC receiving records, led the team in receptions three times (1991–93), and his 201 career catches as a Trojan ranked Morton near the top of the university's all-time list.[3]

Morton's talents were far too great for the professional teams to pass up. The Detroit Lions agreed, selecting him in the first round of the 1994 NFL draft. He played with Detroit from 1994 through 2001, the Kansas City Chiefs (2002–04), and finished his pro career with the San Francisco 49ers in 2005. Throughout his 12 seasons in the NFL, Morton caught 624 passes for 8,719 yards and 43 touchdowns. He also had a part in the movie *Jerry Maguire*, and is involved with Mixed Martial Arts.[4]

## *Anthony Munoz*

On August 1, 1998, Anthony Munoz stood before a throng of thousands in Canton, Ohio, to give his enshrinement speech at the Pro Football Hall of Fame. It served as a culmination of many years in the trenches as an offensive tackle par excellence. On that day in August, a stellar career came full circle for Munoz, a journey that began on August 19, 1958 in Ontario, California, some 35 miles east of downtown Los Angeles.

When he was a youngster, Munoz wanted to play Pop Warner football, but was declared ineligible to take part in the sport on the little league level due to surpassing the maximum height restrictions. Having to wait until he could play football on the junior high and high school level, Munoz shifted his interest to baseball. This time his size did not hamper him from playing, and he used it to his benefit as a power pitcher and slugger.[1]

Munoz attended Chaffey High School, which was the same one that Ernie Smith graduated from in the 1930s. Smith then went on to a stellar career at USC as a two-way lineman. As a freshman, Munoz was over six feet tall, powerfully built, and displayed talent in football, basketball, and baseball. He became Chaffey's star athlete in the mid–1970s, and gained national attention as a prep All-American tackle. Recruiting letters from many colleges stated their interest in the massive lineman. The University of Southern California allowed Munoz the opportunity to miss spring football drills in order to play baseball for the Trojans.[2]

At 6-7, 278-pounds, and blessed with agility, quickness, strength, and incredible foot speed, Munoz had all the tools needed for greatness. USC head coach John Robinson claimed that he was the most sensational offensive lineman he had ever witnessed. Unfortunately, knee problems would hamper his college career, but when healthy, Robinson's claim held true.[3]

In his freshman year, Munoz's right knee was damaged when he tore ligaments in it during the ninth game of the year. He came back strong in his sophomore year, proving that all the praise regarding his talents were no fluke. He completely dominated opponents during that season, as he was able to single-handedly cave in his side of the line, leaving defenders scattered on the turf wondering what just plowed them over. His sophomore year also was the only one in which Munoz was healthy enough to play baseball, and as a pitcher, he helped lead the Trojans to the 1978 NCAA baseball championship.[4] His junior year came to an end in the seventh game when he once again suffered ligament damage in the right knee.

There was no doubt that All-America honors would be his for the taking in his senior year of 1979. However, this time his right knee remained intact, but the left one did not. In the season opener, another bout of torn ligaments looked like his USC career was over.[5] However, he was determined to make it back before USC's trip to the 1980 Rose Bowl. He worked hard hitting the weights even before his cast was removed, and as soon as it came off, he was running. Come game time, he was ready to lead Heisman Trophy winner Charles White through holes, and protect quarterback Paul McDonald from enemy forces. In a 17–16 victory over #1 ranked Ohio State, Munoz did what he did best, totally dominant anyone not in a cardinal and gold jersey. Throughout the game, he controlled the left side of the offensive line, and nailed a Buckeye defender with a bone-jarring block that opened the hole for Charles White to run through for the winning touchdown. It was a fitting way for this gifted offensive lineman to end his collegiate career.

Despite three knee operations, the 22-year old trench warrior was still considered a force to be reckoned with. His abilities were never in question, but pro scouts were leery about investing in someone who already had three knee surgeries. Munoz's knees went through extensive exams by pro scouts before they were considered worth investing in. The Cincinnati Bengals made him and his knees the number three overall pick of the 1980 NFL draft.

In a professional career that spanned 13 seasons from 1980 through 1992, Munoz lived up to his reputation as a force unlike no other. The master of straight-on blocking used a rigorous training program of weight lifting and running to constantly stay in top physical condition. This allowed him to miss a mere three games over his entire pro career. There were not many offensive tackles so honored throughout their careers as Munoz was. He made the All-Rookie Team in 1980, and then 11 straight selections onto the All-Pro Team, and the same number of trips to the Pro Bowl. He was honored with the NFL Lineman of the Year Award in 1981, 1987, and 1988, and received the NFL Players Association Lineman of the Year Award four times (1981, 1985, 1988, 1989). He appeared in two Super Bowls following the 1981 and 1988 seasons, and was named to the NFL's 75th Anniversary Team. In addition to his incredible blocking prowess, Munoz also caught seven passes for four touchdowns on the tackle eligible play throughout his 13 seasons. After becoming one of the greatest offensive linemen in the history of the NFL, it came as no surprise when Anthony Munoz was selected for induction into the Pro Football Hall of Fame in his first year of eligibly.[6]

## *Carson Palmer*

Until 2002, the University of Southern California had four Heisman Trophy winners, all tailbacks, which allowed the Trojans' football program to earn an everlasting legacy as the premier school for running backs. Carson Palmer changed all that when he proudly accepted the coveted 13 ½" tall, 25-pound symbol of excellence at the Downtown Athletic Club in New York City on December 14, 2002.

Twenty-three years earlier, Palmer was born in Fresno, California, on December 27, 1979. It should come as no surprise that athletics were prevalent in the future Trojans' life from an early age. While honing his skills as an adolescent, it became clear to coaches and spectators alike that Palmer's ability to throw a football or baseball harder and farther, easily made him stand out from the rest of his peers.[1]

In football, he wanted to be a quarterback, and that became the only position where he saw action. With a strong, accurate passing arm, no one doubted why he was a signal caller. When spring rolled around, and attention shifted to baseball, Palmer's golden right arm was put to good use as a pitcher and outfielder.[2] At age 12, Palmer attended a football camp run by Bob Johnson, who was regarded as one of the best prep coaches in Orange County, California. Johnson was considered to be very astute when assessing the talent levels of quarterbacks. The abilities that the pre-teen Palmer displayed impressed Johnson, and by the time the young signal caller was of high school age, his reputation was already a stellar one.[3]

Orange County's Santa Margarita High School won out for Palmer's services during his prep career. The home of the Blue & Gold Eagles established itself as an athletic powerhouse, winning well over 100 league titles, 40-plus California Interscholastic Federation crowns, regional, and state championships since opening in September 1987.[4] In the mid-to-late 1990s, Palmer's strong right arm helped add championship hardware to the school's trophy case, garner individual awards, and made him the nation's top scholastic quarterback recruit.

In his junior year of 1996, Palmer passed for 2,089 yards and 24 touchdowns en route to leading the Eagles to a 13–1 record, a third-place ranking among Orange County schools, a league title, and the CIF-SS Division V Championship. He made the Cal-Hi Sports Junior All-State second team, All-Seaview League first team, and was Santa Margarita's Offensive Most Valuable Player. His senior year in 1997, once again produced excellent results for Palmer and the team. He threw for 2,685 yards and 31 touchdowns against only four interceptions for the undefeated Eagles. The team once again captured the CIF-SS Division V Championship with Palmer throwing for 419 yards and five six-pointers in the title game. He set 27 school records, made virtually every All-America team that can be presented to a high school football player, in addition to receiving numerous All-League, All-State, and All-Region honors. He was also the winner of the All-Seaview League Offensive MVP Award, and the All-CIF Division V Offensive Co-MVP Award. What made his accomplishments so great was that he achieved them while suffering from a stress fracture in his right foot. He also helped the basketball team post a 32–2 record and capture the 1998 CIF and State Division II championships.[5]

After contemplating offers from Notre Dame, Colorado, and Miami, Palmer decided on USC. In the fall of 1998, Palmer strolled onto the USC campus, and at first, the positive hype surrounding this quarterback wizard held up. The strong, powerful arm of the freshman quickly captured the attention of then coach Paul Hackett and his staff. They knew that they had something special in the 6-6, 230-pound Palmer, and by the season opener, it was clear that the freshman had the tools needed to take over the starting job. On August 30, 1998, USC opened the season in the Pigskin Classic IX against Purdue. With the team stagnant against the Boilermakers, Hackett turned to his freshman signal caller to help the offense out. Palmer then led the Trojans to a 27–17 victory in his debut. The Trojans finished the year at 8–5, and Palmer threw for 1,755 yards and seven touchdowns. The future seemed as bright as a Southern California summer day for Palmer going into his sophomore campaign.

In the third game of the 1999 season, Palmer suffered a broken collarbone and was lost for the year. With the injury coming so early in the year, Palmer was able to petition for an extra season of eligibility and received it. After his redshirt sophomore year, Palmer came back ready to resume his rise to the top of the college ranks at the dawn of the new millennium. Unfortunately, Hackett's reign as USC's coach was coming to an end. The offensive line was not panning out, and the lack of obtaining a standout running back to help take pressure off the passing game, stymied the offense. Palmer did throw for 2,914 yards and 16 touchdowns, but he was not at his best, as he was forced to come back from being down on the scoreboard many times during the dismal season that ended with the Trojans posting a 5–7 record.[6]

Following the poor showing in 2000, Paul Hackett was fired and Pete Carroll was hired to replace him. It was feared that Palmer might lose his confidence after playing behind a sub-par offensive line and his second head coach and a multiple offensive coordinators. After meeting with Carroll and new offensive coordinator Norm Chow, Palmer came away with renewed vigor.[7] Things did not turn around quickly for the new regime, as the Trojans finished at 6-6, and Palmer threw for 2,717 yards and 13 touchdowns, but also tossed 12 interceptions.

As his senior season of 2002 came around, Palmer was not living up to the star billing that he had in his debut as a freshman four years earlier. It just appeared that he would finish his USC career as an average quarterback, whose exploits would quickly fade into history. It was then, amidst this bleak prediction, that Palmer rose like the Phoenix from the ashes, and secured his place among Trojan immortals with the guidance of offensive coordinator Norm Chow, who rejuvenated the offensive attack.[8] Under Chow's direction, Palmer led USC to an 11–2 record, a share of the Pac-10 championship, and threw for 3,942 yards and 33 touchdowns, while serving as a team captain.[9]

When all the voting was in for the 2002 college football awards, Palmer's name was inscribed on many of them. Besides becoming USC's fifth Heisman Trophy winner, he won the Johnny Unitas Golden Arm Award (nation's top senior quarterback), the Pop Warner Award (most valuable senior on the West Coast), *The Sporting News* National Player of the Year Award, the Pac-10 Co-Offensive Player of the Year Award, and the USC Most Valuable Player Award. He capped off this incredible turnaround year with All-American and All-Pac-10 recognition. He threw for a USC career total of 11,818 yards and 72 touchdowns. His all-time passing yardage and total offense figure of 11,621 yards set Pac-10 records. His 31 games of 200-plus passing yards also established a Pac-10 record. In all, Palmer owned or shared 33 Pac-10 and USC records.[10]

Despite some roadblocks over the course of three seasons, Palmer redeemed himself in 2002 by proving that he truly was the top blue chip recruit that the Trojans thought he was back in his high school days. The Cincinnati Bengals believed in what Palmer could do by making him the number one overall pick in the 2003 NFL draft. He played with the Bengals from 2003 through 2010 and the Oakland Raiders from 2011 through 2012. In 2005, Palmer guided the Bengals to an AFC North title, passed for league-high 32 touchdowns, and received the NFL Alumni Quarterback of the Year Award, the FedEx Air Player of the Year Award, and the AFC Player of the Year Award following the 2005 season. He was selected for two Pro Bowls (2005–06), and was the MVP of the 2006 contest.[11] He was elected into the USC Athletic Hall of Fame in 2003.[12]

## Rodney Peete

Despite narrowly missing out on becoming the first quarterback for USC to bring another Heisman Trophy back to the Land of Troy, Rodney Peete was able to become the first Trojan signal caller to earn the Johnny Unitas Award, presented to the top senior college quarterback.

Peete was originally from Mesa, Arizona. Born in the "Grand Canyon State" on March 16, 1966, he became Arizona's top prep football player following his junior year at Tucson's Sahuaro High School, home of the scarlet and navy Cougars. He also excelled in basketball and baseball. After winning the Arizona High School Player of the Year Award in football, Peete moved to Kansas to complete his scholastic career where "Rocky the Raider" resides, Shawnee Mission South High School in Overland Park, Kansas. After his lone year of donning the green and gold of Shawnee, Peete returned out west for his collegiate career in cardinal and gold.[1]

In four years as the Trojans' field general, Peete threw for 8,225 yards and 54 touchdowns, setting two USC career-passing records and one single game passing record. He had 19 games in which he threw for over 200 yards, and compiled 8,640 yards of total offense, to rank near the top of Trojan greats in that category. He received four letters in football (1985–88), was elected team captain in 1988, and led USC to four bowl game appearances, including two Rose Bowls in 1988 and 1989. The Trojans posted a 31–17 record with Peete at quarterback, and earned a share of the Pac-10 title in 1987, and won it outright the following season. In 1988, he was runner-up for the Heisman Trophy, but collected many other top honors. In addition to the 1988 Johnny Unitas Award, he received in the same year, the Pop Warner Award (most valuable senior on the Pacific Coast), the Pac-10 Offensive Player of the Year Award, and USC's MVP Award, which he also won in 1987. Added to his bulging trophy case were two USC Offensive Player of the Year awards won in 1986 and 1987. He topped his accolades off with All-Conference and All-American recognition, both in 1988. His athletic skills were not just limited to the football field, as Peete played baseball for USC (1985, 1987, 1988).[2]

The Detroit Lions selected Peete in the sixth round of the 1989 NFL draft, and he played with them from 1989 through 1993. Throughout a long NFL career, he made stops with the Dallas Cowboys (1994), Philadelphia Eagles (1995–98), Washington Redskins (1999), Oakland Raiders (2000–01), and Carolina Panthers (2002–04), where he was part of that team's 2003 NFC championship season. In 2009, Peete received the well-deserved honor of being inducted into the USC Athletic Hall of Fame, and will always be regarded as one of the greatest Trojans to ever play the quarterback position.[3]

## Erny Pinckert

Erny Pinckert earned the distinction of becoming the first USC football player to achieve All-American status twice. The native of Wisconsin became a running back that coaches can only dream of, and Howard Jones was the one that had Pinckert in Cardinal & Gold at the dawn of the 1930s. Blessed with speed and the ability to block, Pinckert was the complete offensive weapon.

Born on May 1, 1908 in Medford, Wisconsin, located in the north-central area of the Badger State, Pinckert migrated to California, and attended San Bernardino High School, one of the oldest schools in Southern California. As a member of the Cardinals' football team, Pinckert's talents as a running back earned him the 1926 California High School Football Player of the Year Award.

It was then on to USC as one of head coach Howard Jones' charges. Going from San Bernardino Cardinal to donning the Cardinal & Gold of the Trojans, the transition was an easy one for the talented, multi-threat running back. His reputation as a blocker out of the backfield earned him the greatest praise. He relished the responsibility, and found pride in his skill of knocking defenders to the ground with punishing blocks, to allow his fellow backfield mates the opportunity to advance the ball.[1] Howard Jones was one of the best college coaches in the game's history, and was well aware of Pinckert's abilities. Even though Jones used him mainly for his blocking prowess, the coach also knew that Pinckert was a swift runner that proved to be a menacing force to opponents. Jones utilized Pinckert's speed by designing a double reverse for him that was very successful. On that play alone, the speedster from San Bernardino recorded two long touchdown runs of 75 yards against Stanford in 1930, and one from 80 yards in a 1931 clash with Montana. In the 1932 edition of the "Granddaddy of Them all," the Rose Bowl, Pinckert's speed on the double reverse accounted for two touchdowns from 27 and 30 yards out in a 21–12 victory over Tulane, in which he was voted the game's MVP award. Added to his stellar running abilities, he was also a solid receiver and played defense.[2]

The hard-working Trojan's efforts did not go unnoticed, as Pinckert became the first USC player to grace the All-America team twice (1930–1931). He earned two All-Conference selections (1930–1931), three football letters (1929–31), and was the winner of the 1931 USC Davis-Teschke Award, given to the Trojan who is regarded as the most inspirational football player.

During his tenure as a Trojan, the team posted a 28–5 record, won two conference titles, and the 1931 national championship.[3]

Pinckert decided to play professionally, and spent his entire nine pro seasons with the Washington Redskins. However, when he first started playing in 1932, the team was known as the Boston Braves. From 1933 through 1936, they were the Redskins, and the following year the franchise moved to the nation's capital and captured the 1937 NFL championship. He retired from pro football after the 1940 season and then owned a business that designed clothes. Pinckert passed away at age 69 in Los Angeles on August 30, 1977. He is a member of both the College Football Hall of Fame (1957), and the USC Athletic Hall of Fame (1995).[4]

## *Troy Polamalu*

Following in the footsteps of former USC great Ronnie Lott, Troy Polamalu has solidified his place among the all-time great defensive backs in professional football history. Also just like Lott, Polamalu established himself as a premier player leading up to his status in the pro ranks.

Troy Polamalu's quest at becoming a dominant force in football began with his birth on April 19, 1981 in Garden Grove, a town in northern Orange County, California. At age nine, he left California to go live with relatives in Tenmile, Oregon, some 200 miles from Portland in the southwestern portion of "the Beaver State." This move from his native California was meant to protect him from swaying toward street gang affiliation. Instead of getting into serious trouble on the streets of California, Polamalu found interest in woodworking and studying the Bible.

It was also in this environment of the Great Northwest that he gravitated toward football, which appeared to be in his blood. His brother, uncles, and cousins all played the sport in college, and some even had professional experience. However, Polamalu not only followed in his relatives footsteps, he blazed new trails on his way to creating a legacy of his own.

Winston, Oregon, is home to the Wildlife Safari, and Douglas High School proved to be the catalyst that ignited what would turn out to be an illustrious gridiron career.[1] Polamalu made an instant splash into Oregon's talent pool as a sophomore in 1996 by rushing for 1,003 yards, added 340 more via receiving, and 20 touchdowns. On defense he intercepted six passes for the crimson and gray Trojans, and was rewarded for his effort by garnering All-Far West League first team honors for his running back prowess, and made the second team as a defensive back. He never suffered from the sophomore jinx, and his junior year was just as spectacular. He rushed for 1,040 yards, had an additional 310 yards receiving, scored 22 six-pointers, and recorded 65 tackles and eight interceptions on the defensive side of the ball. Douglas posted a 9–1 record and Polamalu earned All-State recognition and was chosen as the All-Far West League Offensive Most Valuable Player. His senior season of 1998 was reduced to four games due to a bruised kidney, shoulder problems, and torn muscles in his back. In the games he did suit up for, he was able to compile 671 rushing yards, nine touchdowns, and three interceptions. Despite his limited action, Polamalu impressed the experts enough to receive a place on the 1998 Super Prep All-Northwest team, the Tacoma News Tribune Western 100, and made second team All-Far West League.[2]

When it came time to suit up in the college ranks, his initial passion was to play running back at USC. However, the coaching staff had other ideas for this football warrior, and their vision turned out to be perfect. He was moved over to defense, and saw action in eight games as a freshman, playing safety and linebacker. After seeing playing time as a backup in 1999, and doing well when called upon, Polamalu earned a starting position at strong safety. He was in on the action for all 12 games during the 2000 season. He recorded 83 tackles, and shared the team lead with two interceptions and seven deflected passes. His solid performance allowed him to receive All-Pac-10 honorable mention.[3]

In Pete Carroll's first year as head catch in 2001, Polamalu was selected as a team captain, and responded to the responsibility by starting in all 12 games once again, and leading the team with 118 tackles and three interceptions. He was named to numerous All-American teams, becoming the first USC safety to gain that honor since Mark Carrier in 1989. He made All-Pac-10 and received the USC Most Valuable Player Award.[4]

Even though Polamalu was a solid performer gaining national attention, he never stopped working hard to perfect his game. On the field he played hard, leaving everything he had on the turf. At practice sessions, he stayed after drills were over, to work more on ways to improve. He was the total team player and leader that a coach can only dream of having on his roster. He came into his senior season of 2002 as a three-year starter at safety and was once a team captain. Even though a troublesome ankle injury hampered him during the second half of the year, he fought through it, ending the season as USC's first two-time All-American since Tony Boselli achieved the dual honors in 1992 and 1994. He was an All-Pac-10 first team honoree, and won the 2002 Most Inspirational Player Award, after making 68 tackles and snagging one interception.[5]

It was then time to hang up his famed #43 cardinal and gold jersey, replacing it with a black and gold one for the Pittsburgh Steelers. The Steelers selected Polamalu in the first round, and the 16th overall pick, of the 2003 NFL draft. He retained his #43, and then made it one of the most noticed jerseys in the league. Playing with reckless abandon from his strong safety position, Polamalu carved out a career that will land him in the Pro Football Hall of Fame within the minimum allotted time upon his retirement. He has received multiple All-Pro honors, was selected to Pro Bowls, and in 2010, received the AP NFL Defensive Player of the Year Award, the NFL Alumni Player of the Year Award, and was the Pittsburgh Steelers' MVP. He also received recognition as a member of the NFL 2000's All-Decade Team. Through the 2012 season, Polamalu has been the defensive leader of a team that won three AFC Championships (2005, 2008, 2010), and two Super Bowls following the 2005 and 2008 seasons.[6]

## *Marvin Powell*

Marvin Powell was a scholar, writer, and eventually received a law degree. He was also a devastating offensive tackle that laid down the law in the battle for the trenches while blocking for All-American tailbacks. This highly talented student/athlete was born on August 30, 1955, growing up around Fort Bragg, where both his father and stepfather were soldiers.

Powell was big for his age, and by age ten, was already in a size 10 shoe. He was not only big and bulky, but awkward as well. It was a challenge proposed by a junior high coach that eventually led him to go out for football. Initially, Powell did not know offense from defense, but no doubts came into play by the time he was a senior at Fayetteville's 71st High School. Any awkwardness that he had a few years earlier were obliterated, just as many of the opponents who crossed paths with the Prep All-American linebacker for a state championship team. When a player gains All-American status in high school, there is no doubt that college programs will come calling. In the case of the 6-5, 265-pound Powell, he received so many offers that he had them crammed into garbage bags to keep some order.[1]

The University of Southern California won out, and Powell was on his way to helping add to the proud lineage of devastating Trojan linemen. He used his mass to create an ominous presence that led to crushing blocks. He was a three-year letterman (1974–76), blocked for Trojan tailback legends Anthony Davis, Ricky Bell, and Charles White, and was a member of USC's 1974 national championship team. He was a three-time All-Conference selection at tackle (1974–76), and a two-time All-American (1975–76).

Following his dominant college days in the City of Angels, it was on to the Big Apple for Powell after the New York Jets made him their first round selection, and fourth overall pick, of the 1977 NFL draft. He played with the Jets (1977–85), and Tampa Bay Buccaneers (1986–87) before becoming an attorney and getting enshrined into the College Football Hall of Fame (1994).[2]

## *Aaron Rosenberg*

Needlework is a term most associated with sewing or embroidery. However, during USC's run to dominance in the early 1930s, Aaron Rosenberg gave the term a whole new meaning. From 1931 through 1933, the Brooklyn, New York native used to torment opposing linemen with chatter that was dubbed "Needle Work," which was designed to frustrate and take away their concentration.

Born on August 26, 1912, in Brooklyn, New York, Rosenberg prepped at Fairfax High School in Los Angeles. His talents on the football field allowed him to earn four straight All-City nominations for the Fairfax Lions and gain a chance to play for USC. He took the motto from Fairfax of "Say and Do," and applied it to his college football career. He was known to constantly talk to opponents on the field, and backed up his words with incredible blocking and tackling.

At 6-0, 210 pounds, Rosenberg was big at the time he entered USC in 1930. Not only was he big, but was also one of the fastest players on the team, and tough. He proved his toughness by playing with sprains and broken bones while never wavering from giving a solid performance.[1] He was a complete two-way player that could open holes with ferocious blocks for backs to run through, and on defense, his bone-jarring tackles left many opponents dazed on the ground. His play on defense helped the Trojans hold opponents to a mere 13 points, and no rushing touchdowns, throughout the entire 1932 season.[2] Rosenberg was a three-year letterman (1931–33), two-time All-Conference selection at guard (1932–33), and a two-time All-American (1932–33). During Rosenberg's time on the team, the Trojans were 30–2–1, won the national championship in 1931 and 1932, and had a perfect 3–0 record against the mighty Notre Dame Fighting Irish.[3]

Rosenberg majored in journalism at USC, but declined to go into that profession, nor that of professional football. Instead, he opted for the motion picture industry, starting off as a second-assistant director at 20th Century–Fox right after graduation.[4] His old Alma Mater, Fairfax High School, had a long-standing reputation for producing many influential figures associated with the entertainment field.[5] In time, Rosenberg became one of them, as he directed 70 films and also worked on television projects until his retirement in 1974. Rosenberg died on September 1, 1979 at age 67 in Los Angeles, the city where his dreams truly came true in both athletics and the entertainment industry.

## *Tim Rossovich*

Virtually every football program, regardless of the level or era, can boast of having at least one individual that will be remembered for possessing a touch of quirkiness. In the case of the Trojans, Tim Rossovich's name could possibly be at the top of the quirky list. It was claimed that this massive 6-5, 235-pound lineman ate glass, streaked on campus, and did other "interesting" things.[1]

Rossovich's actions truly did gain him a place among the all-time quirky football players, but his actions on the field also allowed him the right to be placed along with the greats from USC. Positioned at defensive end, Rossovich's #88 went on constant seek-and-destroy missions that left opposing ball carriers and quarterbacks flat on their backs. He was regarded as one of the most dominant defensive linemen of his time, and an exceptional pass rusher.

He was a three-year letterman (1965–67), played on two conference championship teams, and was a member of USC's 1967 national championship squad. He served as co-captain of the 1967 team, earned All-Conference and All-American honors that same year, as well as being bestowed with the USC Lineman of the Year Award.[2]

The Philadelphia Eagles made Rossovich their first round selection of the 1968 NFL draft, and he played in the "City of Brotherly Love" from 1968 to 1971. He then returned to the west coast for a two-season stint with the San Diego Chargers (1972–73), before wrapping up his professional career with the Houston Oilers in 1976. He then went on to pursue an acting career and also worked as a stuntman.[3]

## *Tim Ryan*

On Blossom Hill Road in San Jose, California, is the "Home of the Eagles," Oak Grove High School. The school opened in

1967, and over time, established a successful athletic history.[1] The football program has enjoyed much of the school's proud history, and future Trojan Tim Ryan helped add to Oak Grove's status. In addition to his football skills, Ryan was an accomplished boxer as a youngster, winning five Junior Olympic championships.[2]

Ryan was born on September 8, 1967, in Memphis, Tennessee, in the same year that Oak Grove first opened its doors. After his prep career was complete, the 6-5, 260-pound defensive tackle looked to take on the college ranks. He had no problem adapting to the next level of competition, as he became a four-year letterman at USC (1986–89), and earned many accolades during his tenure wearing the cardinal and gold.[3]

Three times during his USC career, Ryan recorded over 100 tackles (1986, 1987, 1989), and finished with 389 over four years. He was an All-Pac-10 selection in 1988 and 1989, earned All-American honors (1988–1989), and won the 1989 Pop Warner Award (most valuable senior on the Pacific Coast), and was runner-up for the Lombardi Award in 1989.

The Chicago Bears made Ryan their third round selection of the 1990 NFL draft, and he remained with the team from 1990 through 1993. Following his retirement from professional football, Ryan owned a company dealing with building maintenance, and also served as a radio announcer for USC (1998–2001), and was an NFL analyst on television.[4]

## Jim Sears

In each decade since the 1920s, the University of Southern California has boasted of possessing star running backs. In the 1950s, it was Frank Gifford who garnered headlines at the dawn of the decade. A few years later, Jon Arnett was the focal point of the offense. Wedged in between this duo of California born and raised natives was another residence of the Golden Coast, Jim Sears.

When Sears first arrived at USC in 1950, his first two seasons overlapped that of Gifford's. However, when Gifford went off to start what would become a Hall of Fame career in New York, Sears assumed the role as heart and soul of the Trojans' offensive weaponry. Before wearing his #32 cardinal and gold jersey at USC, Sears honed his gridiron skills at Inglewood High School and El Camino Junior College in Torrance, California.[1]

The 5-9, 164-pound halfback earned a reputation as being capable of performing any skill exceptionally well,[2] but was especially valuable as a tailback in the single-wing offense.[3] His devotion and talent impressed USC's head coach Jess Hill so much that the coach proclaimed him the most dedicated player he had ever witnessed.[4]

As a senior in 1952, Sears proved that Hill's praise held true by embarking on a season that ended with his name being attached to many of college football's most prestigious honors. He led the Trojans in passing (712 yards), total offense (1,030 yards), scoring (36 points), and punt returns (478 yards) en route to gaining accolades such as All-Conference and consensus All-American selection. He also finished seventh in the 1952 Heisman Trophy voting. Other awards that Sears added to his collection following the '52 season were the Pop Warner Award (most valuable senior on the Pacific Coast), the Voit Trophy (outstanding player on the Pacific Coast), and the Davis-Teschke Award (USC's most inspirational player).[5]

Sears was selected in the sixth round of the 1953 NFL draft by the Baltimore Colts, but never played for the team. Instead, he found his way to the Windy City, and played with the Chicago Cardinals (1954, 1957–58). He then returned to USC in 1959 to be an assistant on Don Clark's staff that included John McKay and the future coach and owner of the Oakland Raiders, Al Davis. He gave pro football another try in 1960 with the Los Angeles Chargers in the newly established American Football League, and ended his playing days with the Denver Broncos in 1961. Sears is a member of both the El Camino College and USC Athletic Halls of Fame, and he died at age 70 on January 4, 2002.[6]

## Junior Seau

American Samoa is part of the Samoan Island chain, located in the South Pacific, and consisting of an area covering 76.1 square miles. Despite being a rather small piece of real estate approximately 5,000 miles from the west coast of the United States, the worlds of American college and professional football draw many players from this region into their ranks. Numbering in the hundreds, football players of American Samoa heritage have recently competed on the Division I level in college, with many finding their way onto NFL rosters. They are tough warrior-like performers that play the game hard. Of all those football players with American Samoa in their heritage, two of the all-time greatest to have conquered the college and pro game, are former USC Trojans, Troy Polamalu and Junior Seau.[1]

Born Tiaina Baul Seau, Jr., on January 19, 1969, in San Diego, California, this future Trojan went on to become the first famous American Samoan to ever grace the playing surfaces of the National Football League. Before reaching the status of a professional football legend, Seau made a name for himself in the third largest city in San Diego, Oceanside. This coastal city on California's south coast is the home of the Oceanside High School Pirates, and in the mid-to-late 1980s, Junior Seau was the school's athletic alpha dog.[2]

While donning the green and white of Oceanside, Seau was a multi-sport star that excelled at football, basketball, and track. In football, he played linebacker and tight end. Following his senior season, he was bestowed with the Avocado League Offensive Most Valuable Player Award and Prep All-American honors after helping the Pirates capture the San Diego 2A championship. After hitting the hardwood in the winter months, Seau emerged from the prep basketball season as the California Interscholastic Federation San Diego Section Player of the Year. Rounding off his accomplishments in high school, Seau was crowned the Avocado League shot put champion.[3]

After dominating three sports on the high school level, it was time for this San Diego product to take on new challenges. He had no trouble doing just that, as he became one of the best linebackers to ever play at USC. Throughout the 1988 and 1989 seasons, the Trojans compiled a 19–4–1 with the 6-3, 245-pound wrecking machine wearing #55 patrolling the defense. Seau was blessed with incredible athletic ability mixed with speed and strength, which enabled him to become an excellent pass rusher and tackler.[4] He was like a keg of dynamite ready to explode into anyone with the ball in an opposing jersey.

During the 1989 season, he turned in one of the finest performances by a Trojan linebacker, making 72 tackles, 27 of which went for lost yardage. In his two seasons at USC, he had 107 tackles, 33 of them accounting for a loss of 188 total yards. He played on two Pac-10 championship teams and in the Rose Bowl following both years. When it was time to hand out awards, Seau's name found its way onto many of them. He earned All-American and All-Pac-10 honors in 1989, was the 1989 Pac-10 Defensive Player of the Year, the 1989 USC MVP, and the 1989 USC Defensive Player of the Year.[5]

Following his incredible junior year of 1989, Seau made himself eligible for the NFL draft. His hometown San Diego Chargers brought him back to the place of his birth by selecting him in the first round, and fifth overall pick, of the 1990 draft.[6] He then did not disappoint on the professional level, and dominated it just like he did during his high school and USC days.

From 1990 through 2002, Seau became the face of the San Diego Chargers. He not only was one of the most popular players on the team, but a leader as well. He rose to legendary status by becoming a 12-time Pro Bowler and eight-time All-Pro First Team selection. He won the 1992 NEA NFL Defensive Player of the Year Award and the 1992 UPI AFC Defensive Player of the Year Award. In 1994, he helped the Chargers reach their first-ever Super Bowl berth, and in the process, took home the 1994 AFC Player of the Year Award, and the 1994 NFL Man of the Year Award, presented to the player for his accomplishments on the field, and for his efforts as a volunteer and in charity work. This is one of the most treasured awards given out to a player, and in 1999 was re-named the Walter Payton Man of the Year Award in honor of the late, great Chicago Bears running back. While as a member of the Chargers, Seau was honored as one of the players selected to the NFL 1990s All-Decade Team. He also had his famous #55 San Diego jersey retired by the team, is a member of the Chargers' Hall of Fame, and was selected for the Chargers 50th Anniversary Team.[7]

On April 16, 2003, Seau was traded to the Miami Dolphins, where he remained through the 2005 season. While with the Dolphins, he continued to be a standout performer, winning the 2003 NFL Alumni Linebacker of the Year Award. An Achilles tendon injury forced him to miss the second half of the 2005 season, and on March 6, 2006, the Dolphins released him. However, the pro career of Junior Seau was not over. He signed with the New England Patriots, and started 10 of the team's first 11 games before a broken arm sidelined him for the rest of the season. He returned the following year, and was a part of New England's run at a perfect 16–0 regular season in 2007. Once again he was a member of an AFC championship team, but the Patriots lost their bid for an undefeated season, including the playoffs, when they lost to the New York Giants in Super Bowl XLII.[8]

Seau remained with the Patriots through the 2009 season before announcing his retirement from pro football on January 13, 2010, six days shy of his 41st birthday. Following football, he was active in different ventures, including his long-standing community service activities, of which the Junior Seau Foundation was a major part of since 1992. The purpose of the foundation is to help young people overcome all types of roadblocks on their way to a better life.

The world was shocked on May 2, 2012, when this man who gave so much of himself in every endeavor he pursued, was found dead from a self-inflicted gunshot wound to the chest at his residence in Oceanside, the community where the legend of Junior Seau began as a high school star.[9] It was later learned through studies on his brain following his death, that Seau had chronic traumatic encephalopathy (CTE), caused by repeated head injuries.[10] It was also learned that due to the trauma suffered from years of collisions, Seau had bouts of wild mood swings, forgetfulness, insomnia, and depression. In public he was able to hide his condition, but those close to him saw the effects first hand.[11] Eventually the condition worsened and more than likely led to his suicide.

## *Gus Shaver*

The city of Los Angeles was where Gaius "Gus" Shaver shined in the national spotlight during the early 1930s. The area was also where this future Trojan made his debut into the world on August 14, 1910, some 20 miles east of downtown Los Angeles in the city of Covina. Despite being a small city, Covina can boast of its fair share of many prominent citizens from athletics and the world of entertainment.[1]

Gus Shaver was well on his way to establishing himself among his hometown's elite while a student-athlete at Covina High School. The football and track teams have enjoyed much success over the decades, and Shaver's exploits back in the 1920s helped add to the legacy of the cardinal and white Colts. At the time of Shaver's stay at Covina, the school was barely thirty years old, and its acclaim in California prep sports was just getting started. Shaver helped the Colts on their way to prestige by playing a major role in the school capturing state football championships in 1925 and 1926. In 1927, he was selected as winner of the California Football Player of Year Award. He also owned the school's pole vault record of 12'-6," which at the time was an extremely impressive height for the high school level.[2]

Upon graduation, Shaver entered USC at a time when the Trojans were in their early stages of creating a legacy as a college football powerhouse. Just like at Covina, where he helped that school on its way to earning a solid reputation in athletics, Shaver assisted USC in that same capacity.

At the time he came onto the campus, USC was about to embark on their first national championship in football in 1928. Shaver was then on the varsity under legendary coach Howard Jones from 1929 through 1931, where his days as a Trojan culminated with being a major contributor to the program's second national championship team in 1931. His 1931 season not only included a national title, but earned him All-America status as well after leading the team in rushing (936 yards) and scoring (100 points). He also gained everlasting fame during that '31 season by scoring a pair of touchdowns in USC's 16–14 comeback victory over #1 ranked Notre Dame, which was the first time that the Trojans left South Bend with a win over the powerful Fighting Irish.[3]

The 1932 Summer Olympic Games were held in Los Angeles, and the Olympic committee looked to introduce American football to the world as a demonstration sport. It was basically a college All-Star game pitting the top-ranked players from the east against the best from the west, with the Los Angeles Memorial Coliseum serving as the venue. The west prevailed by a 7–6 final count with 60,000 in attendance. On this stage, right in his own neighborhood, Gus Shaver topped all rushers with 145 yards on 16 carries while serving as the west's team captain. This was the first and only time that American football was part of the Olympic experience, and the event also proved to be the swan song for Shaver's playing days. He did return to USC as an assistant coach from 1940 to 1945 before going into the business world. He was elected into the USC Athletic Hall of Fame in 1995, and passed away three years later on October 11, 1998 at age 88 in Fallbrook, California.[4]

## *O.J. Simpson*

John McKay once proclaimed that O.J. Simpson had the most ability of any running back that he had ever seen.[1] This impressive statement came from a coach that saw his share of talented backs in USC uniforms, but his observation on Simpson cannot be denied. He was big, fast, and the perfect specimen to play the position. He was able to shoot through the smallest hole created for him and accelerate into the clear. It seemed that he never allowed defenders to get a solid shot at him, as he had the ability to sidestep, cut back, and change stride while going downfield.[2] He was also durable, carrying the ball 35 times a game as a senior in 1968 en route to All-American honors and the Heisman Trophy. Tough was also a word used to describe Simpson, as he once ran for 220 yards on a damaged ankle. Put all the accolades together, and the result was that Simpson possessed all the qualifications to be a supreme running back.[3]

Despite the greatness that any athlete possesses, the path to gridiron stardom is filled with pain, blood, sweat, and extreme highs and lows. In the end, for an elite fraternity, the journey concludes with enshrinement among the game's immortals. In the case of Orenthal James Simpson, his road to stardom began in the "City by the Bay," San Francisco, California, on July 9, 1947.

While growing up in housing projects of the Potrero Hill area of San Francisco, Simpson was associated with a tough crowd, and trouble was a common bond shared by the group. He eventually became a member of a street gang called the Persian Warriors. The only thing that accomplished for the teenaged Simpson was getting him to serve a week at a youth correctional facility.

Athletic ability allowed him an opportunity to shift focus to other things rather than juvenile delinquency. With Galileo High School serving as his springboard, he catapulted to heights of success on the prep level. Galileo's motto is *"eppure si muove,"* translated from Italian to mean "and yet it moves," and Simpson definitely accomplished that by darting across football fields on his way to earning All-San Francisco honors as a running back for the purple and gold Lions of Galileo.

He also possessed talent as a catcher on the baseball team until a broken hand in his sophomore year ended his days on the diamond.[4] Another very important athletic skill that Simpson possessed was blazing speed, clocking in at an eye-popping 9.4 seconds in the 100-yard dash.

Despite his high level of athletic skills, the classroom was where O.J.'s performance went stagnant up to this time of his life. His desire was to attend USC and play for John McKay. However, with subpar grades, the star running back had to first enroll in junior college to improve his studies.

San Francisco City College was Simpson's next stop in the fall of 1965, and after two seasons, his grades were up to USC's standards, and junior college football records fell. Wearing what would become his trademark #32 jersey, Simpson performed as receiver and running back for the Rams out of the Split T formation.[5] Using his toughness and blazing speed, he rushed for a national junior college career record of 2,552 yards over two seasons, a mark that stood for 27 years. He averaged 9.2 yards every time he ran the ball, scored 54 touchdowns, earned conference player of the year twice, as well as Junior College All-American honors in 1965 and 1966.

Even though the University of Southern California was his desired destination, Arizona State and Utah made a play for the running back after his freshman year at City College. It was then that USC assistant Marv Goux talked Simpson into remaining at City College for one more year, and then USC would be there waiting for him. To seal the deal, Goux displayed his 1962 national championship ring he earned as a USC assistant, and felt that Simpson was the caliber of player that could help the Trojans gain another one. The star running back decided to remain at City College for the 1966 season and then go to USC to finish his studies and college football career.[6]

In the spring of 1967, O.J. Simpson was on his way to the campus that he originally yearned to attend while at Galileo High School. Being a part of the USC Trojans carried a certain amount of prestige, but in order to carry that honor, a player had to work hard to achieve it, even a talented athlete like Simpson.

His right of passage into Trojan immortality began on a cool April day during spring drills. At 6-1, 207 pounds, and possessing world-class speed, Simpson had all the tools needed to be a tailback. However, in John McKay's world, that was not enough. McKay needed to witness Simpson's toughness before handing him one of the most prestigious assignments in college football history, with that being an I-Formation USC tailback.

On that cool day in April, Simpson was placed at the tailback position with the third string offense supporting him. His next task was to perform against the team's starting defensive unit. McKay then called for Simpson to carry the ball on eight straight occasions to see how O.J. would handle the pounding. This exercise in measuring one's grit was called "gut check." On one of Simpson's final carries in this drill, he bolted up the middle and headed toward All-American Tim Rossovich. Simpson gained speed and slammed right into Rossovich and sent him to the turf. After seeing that display of speed, power, and toughness, McKay knew he had something special in Simpson. The coach then proceeded to the locker room to inform the media that the Trojans had their tailback, and thus was born another USC legend.[7]

The O. J. Simpson era at USC lasted only two seasons, but he managed to produce more in that time span than anyone could imagine of over the course of four seasons of college football. In 1967, he finished first in the nation with 1,451 yards on 266 carries and 11 touchdowns en route to being runner-up for the Heisman Trophy to UCLA's Gary Beban. Among other numerous honors, he won The United Press International Back of the Year Award, was the Amateur Athletic Foundation Southern California Athlete of the Year, earned All-Conference and All-American honors, was Rose Bowl MVP, and helped the Trojans win the national championship. It seemed that USC assistant Marv Goux's prediction was right when he showed Simpson his 1962 championship ring and told him that he might get one for himself someday as a Trojan.

Up to this point in his collegiate career, Simpson was regarded as the college football world's premier runner. In 1968, he was elected co-captain, and took his game up even higher. At the conclusion of another magnificent year, Simpson took home the college game's most coveted individual honor, the Heisman Trophy, in the biggest landslide in the award's history. He finished with 2,853 votes to 1,103 given to runner-up Leroy Keyes of Purdue. He completely dominated the voting by receiving 855 first place votes, while Keyes had only 49. In walking away with the award, he joined Mike Garrett (1965 winner) in becoming USC's second I-Formation tailback in four seasons to bring Mr. Heisman to Los Angeles. In all, O.J. collected 21 post-season awards, including the Maxwell Award (1968 national player of the year), repeated as winner of USC's Back of the Year Award and USC's Most Valuable Player Award, received his second Walter Camp award in recognition of being the nation's top player, the Pop Warner Award (most valuable senior on the Pacific Coast), and the Voit Trophy (outstanding player on the Pacific Coast), in addition to the Heisman. On his way to expanding his trophy case, Simpson easily was once again named All-Conference and All-American after rushing for 1,709 yards on 355 carries and scoring 22 touchdowns. With his second All-American selection, he became USC's first player to ever receive the honor with back-to-back unanimous voting. USC was 19–2–1 during Simpson's two illustrious seasons, were two-time conference champs, national champs, and finished Simpson's senior season at #4 in the final polls. He finished his career with 17 100-yard or better rushing games, and tied or owned outright 19 NCAA, conference or USC records. In addition to his legendary status among the all-time college football greats, Simpson also found the time to lend his world-class speed to the USC track team. In that capacity, he was part of USC's world record-setting 440-yard relay in 1967. As a team, the Trojans captured the NCAA track championship with Simpson as a member in 1967 and 1968.[8]

When the 1969 NFL draft came along, the Buffalo Bills made Simpson the number one overall selection. Despite the Bills struggling for most of Simpson's stay in Buffalo, his #32 was the one focal point that fans could embrace during many dismal seasons. He was the NFL's rushing champion four times, made All-Pro five times, and was selected to play in six Pro Bowls. In 1973, he became the first running back in pro football history to eclipse 2,000 rushing yards, and in doing so, earned the NFL Most Valuable Player Award among many other honors at the conclusion of that record-setting season.

Simpson played with the Bills through the 1977 season, and then returned to his native San Francisco to finish out his professional career with the 49ers from 1978 through 1979. He retired as the NFL's second leading rusher of all-time with 11,236 yards, and was selected to the 1970s All-NFL Decade Team and the NFL's 75th Anniversary All-Time Team. His incredible talents on the football field will always amaze, and recognition of those skills were immortalized with induction into the Pro Football Hall of Fame in his first year of eligibility in 1985. He is also a member of the Rose Bowl Hall of Fame (Class of 1993), and the USC Athletic Hall of Fame (class of 1994).[9]

With his first and middle initials being O.J., his nickname became "the Juice," as a play on words meaning orange juice. However, juice can also mean something that electrifies or is powerful.[10] In the case of Simpson, the latter meanings best suit this legend.

## *Tony Slaton*

Hudson Houck is regarded as one of the best offensive line coaches of his time. He was a member of USC's 1962 national championship team, and later returned to his Alma Mater as an assistant coach in 1976. Between the years of 1976 to 1983, Houck passed his knowledge onto a new generation of trench warriors, and came away from the Trojans as the mentor to some of the greatest offensive linemen to ever serve USC.[1] Near the end of Houck's tenure at USC, he had the opportunity to guide center Tony Slaton, who emerged as one of the best to ever open holes for running backs or protect the signal caller.

Born on April 12, 1961, in Merced, California, Slaton came to the Trojans as a 6-4, 260-pounder, and left as one of the school's most revered linemen. He was a three-year letterman (1981–83), elected team captain in 1983, was an All-Conference selection three times (1981–83), and All-American in 1983. His talents in the trenches were so great, that he was bestowed with the honor of being named the 1983 USC Offensive Player of the Year Award.[2] He also had the chance to be a part of an offensive line that assisted Marcus Allen in winning the 1981 Heisman Trophy after becoming the first college running back to surpass the 2,000-yard barrier in a single season.

Slaton was the Buffalo Bills' sixth round selection of the 1984 NFL draft, but he never played for that team. Instead, he was able to remain in the Los Angeles area, playing for the Rams from 1984 through 1989, where he was able to once again be tutored by Hudson Houck, who served as an assistant for the Rams during Slaton's entire stay. Slaton then finished up his professional career with the Dallas Cowboys in 1990. He played in 74 NFL games, started in 25 of them, and had the privilege of blocking for two of the greatest running back in league history, Eric Dickerson in LA, and Emmitt Smith in Dallas.

## Ernie Smith

A devastating two-way tackle on back-to-back national championship teams, Smith opened holes for four All-American running backs, and his defensive play helped the Trojans earn the moniker of "Whispering Herd," which stemmed from the way the USC defense silenced the opposition.[1]

Born on November 26, 1909, in Spearfish, South Dakota, Smith came to USC at the end of the Roaring Twenties, and left four years later as a Trojan legend. Big for his time at 6-2, 215 pounds, he proved to be a multi-talented, hard-hitting tackle and kicker for two of coach Howard Jones' championship teams in 1931 and 1932. Jones would praise his trench warrior for always giving everything he had, and one opposing coach claimed that Smith was the best at his position in the entire country. If that was not enough, Smith also played the trombone in the marching band.

In his days as a devastating college lineman, Ernie Smith received three football letters (1930–32), two All-Conference selections, and was USC's first-ever unanimous All-American, gaining that status in 1931. After he helped the Trojans to a 28–3 record during his time on the line, Smith played professionally with the Green Bay Packers from 1935 to 1937, and in 1939, earning two NFL championships in 1936 and 1939. He was inducted into the College Football Hall of Fame in 1970, and the USC Athletic Hall of Fame in 1997. He died at age 75 on April 25, 1985 in Los Angeles.[2]

## Harry Smith

Countless individuals have sat in darkened movie theaters dreaming of one day becoming a star on the silver screen. However, one young man in Ontario, California, also had a dream while in a theater, but his did not involve the motion picture industry.

A teenager named Harry Smith was watching a news reel about USC's exciting 16–14 win over Notre Dame in 1931, and he immediately became smitten with the idea of playing for the Trojans. Five years later, Smith's dream came true when he enrolled at USC as a freshman in 1936. Three years later, Smith emerged from the Land of Troy with his dream fulfilled and his legacy in Cardinal & Gold solidified for the ages.

Born on August 26, 1918, in Russellville, Missouri, Smith eventually settled in "the Gateway to Southern California," Ontario, a city 35 miles east of Los Angeles, in San Bernardino County. After his days as an Ontario High School Tiger were complete, Smith entered USC ready to play football for the "Headman," coach par-excellence, Howard Jones. Like most of Jones' charges, Harry Smith highly respected his coach, and gave everything he had to make the program a success.[1]

For his time, Smith was big in stature at 5-11, 218 pounds, and used his powerful frame to become a dominant two-way lineman. His toughness and solid play allowed him to be the anchor of USC's trench warriors on two conference championship teams (1938–1939), a pair of Rose Bowl victories, and Jones' final national championship team in 1939. He earned three letters (1937–39), All-Conference honors, and was a two-time All-American (1938–39).[2]

He earned the nickname "Blackjack" while slugging it out on the line. A myth went around that the name was given to him after he used a cast on his right hand to blast opponents into oblivion. In reality, a scribe for the *Los Angeles Times* wrote something to the fact that Smith was hammering opponents throughout a game with his blackjack. It seemed like a good description of how Smith dominated the opposition, and the word became part of Smith's identity.[3]

Following college, Smith was drafted by the Detroit Lions in 1940 and played with them for that lone season. He then went into coaching, serving as an assistant at the University of Missouri and USC under Jeff Cravath before taking over as head coach of the Canadian Football League's Saskatchewan Roughriders, who he led to a division title in 1951, and the team's first appearance in the CFL championship game (Grey Cup), in 17 years.[4]

## Lynn Swann

The athleticism that began at College Park Junior High School, and was honed along that way at Serra High School, eventually earned Lynn Swann a scholarship to play for John McKay at USC. His skills as a wide receiver helped the Trojans to a national championship in 1972, and later four Super Bowl crowns with the Pittsburgh Steelers. When Swann's body of work on the gridiron was complete, there was no doubt that his career would be immortalized in both the College and Pro Football Halls of Fame.

Born on March 7, 1952, in Alcoa, Tennessee, Swann's athletic prowess was established 2,500 miles to the west while a resident of San Mateo, California, some 20 miles to the south of San Francisco. Serra High School is a private Roman Catholic institution that provided the stepping-stone for Swann to become a college and pro football legend. In the late 1960s, Swann's skills as an athlete were on display, and they left opponents and spectators awestruck. It was not a far-reaching conclusion after witnessing Swann as a multi-sport prep star that a future in athletics was not out of the realm of possibility.

He had grace, incredible body control, leaping ability, grit, concentration, toughness, and speed. He then applied all these skills to the football field, basketball court, and track. In autumn, he played quarterback, and dominated the northern section of California, winning the 1969 Northern California Player of the Year Award, and the WCAL Player of the Year Award.[1] When he took to the hardwood, Swann as an All-League selection, and in the spring, he won the California state long jump championship over future Olympic gold medalist Randy Williams. He also clocked in at 9.8 in the 100-yard dash.[2]

Upon his graduation from Serra High School in 1970, Swann went from the blue and gold Padres to the cardinal and gold Trojans. USC coaching legend John McKay was so impressed with Swann's talents that he looked to use him as much as possible.[3] At 6-0, 180 pounds, he moved over to receiver and punt returner, and it came as no surprise that he excelled in both.

With the USC offensive attack focused mainly on the tailback position, passing the ball was not as common of a practice back when Swann played. However, with so much talent, he was not ignored. Over three varsity seasons, he caught 95 passes for 1,562 yards and 11 touchdowns, averaging 16.4 yards per catch. He added 49 punt returns to his resume, covering 599 yards for a 12.2 average, and scored three six-pointers. His 253 return yards in 1972 led the Pac-8, and he is ranked fourth all-time in career punt return yardage.[4] His days as a high school quarterback and basketball player allowed Swann to develop tremendous hand-eye coordination. Applying that ability to the receiver position made Swann one of the best to ever play the position.

At the end of his college career, Swann received three letters in football (1971–73), the 1973 USC Most Valuable Player of the Year Award, the 1973 Pop Warner Award (most valuable senior on the Pacific Coast), All-Conference first team honors (1973), was a consensus All-American in 1973, and also served as team captain during his senior season of 1973. The Trojans were 27–6–2 during Swann's three varsity seasons, and he was a member of the 1972 national championship team, regarded by many as the greatest college team of all-time.

Swann went from individual and team success on the college level, and right into the same in the professional circuit. He was selected in the first round of the 1974 NFL draft by the Pittsburgh Steelers, who were about to become one of the greatest dynasties in American sports history.

As a rookie in 1974, Swann was used primarily in the early part of the season as a punt returner. He quickly established himself as the best by leading the entire league with 577 yards on 41 returns. It also set a Pittsburgh team record. Toward the end of his rookie year, he saw more time at receiver, and proved his worth by scoring what turned out to be the game-winning touchdown in the AFC Championship Game over the Oakland Raiders. That win catapulted the Steelers into their first Super Bowl, which they won over Minnesota, 16–6.

The following year saw Swann as a full time receiver. His speed, graceful moves, and ability to leap, was a thing of beauty to witness. At the end of the season, he led the league with 11 receiving touchdowns and the Steelers repeated as world champions. In a 21–17 victory over the Dallas Cowboys in Super Bowl X, Swann caught four passes for 161 yards and the eventual game-winning touchdown from 64 yards out. For his efforts, he was selected as the game's MVP.

Swann continued to perform up to his elite level until the end of 1982, playing all his nine seasons with the Steelers. He finished his NFL career with 336 receptions for 5,462 yards, and 51 touchdowns. He added two more Super Bowl rings to his collection following the 1978 and 1979 seasons, was an All-Pro three times (1975, 1977, 1978), and elected to three Pro Bowls. His performances on the sport's biggest stage earned him the distinction of being the Super Bowl's all-time leader in receiving yards upon his retirement, as he amassed 364 yards in four games.

The accolades continued for Swann long after his retirement, as his body of work was honored with enshrinement into the College Football Hall of Fame (1993), the Pro Football Hall of Fame (2001), and the USC Athletic Hall of Fame (2005). In addition to his hall of fame honors, Swann was also presented with the NCAA Silver Anniversary Award in 1999.[5]

## *Brice Taylor*

Brice Taylor's resume is the stuff legends are made of. His life's journey spanned the course of nearly three quarters of the 20th century, and produced many incredible accolades, any of which would have made numerous individuals have a fulfilled existence.

This future USC legend, and the first to ever garner All-American honors in football at the university, was born on America's 126th birthday, July 4, 1902, in the Emerald City of Seattle, Washington, as a descendant of Native American chief Tecumseh. He was born without a left hand, and orphaned at age five, but despite these setbacks, Taylor persevered and became an amazing athlete, competing in football, baseball, and track, at Franklin High School. He marveled people with his ability to throw and catch even without a hand.[1]

The University of Southern California was Taylor's next stop, a trip that took him into Trojan history. He played guard under two of USC's greatest coaches in Elmer "Gloomy Gus" Henderson and Howard Jones from 1924 through 1926. As a blocker he was quick and strong on a compact 5-9, 185-pound frame, and earned a stellar reputation by obliterating defenders with powerful thrusts.[2] He was so fast that his speed was comparable to that of a running back. The Trojans went 28–6 with Taylor on the varsity, and he earned three football letters and became the first-ever Trojan on the gridiron to receive All-American status. In 1925 Taylor also competed in track at USC for another legendary Trojan coach, Dean "Maker of Champions" Cromwell. In that regard, he helped add to Cromwell's moniker as a sprinter, hurdler, and member of USC's world record-setting mile relay team.[3]

Part of Franklin High School's mission statement is for graduates to share their expertise with others. Taylor undoubtedly lived up to that mission statement by becoming an educator after leaving USC. He coached at four colleges throughout the south, served as a teacher, coach, and administrator in the Los Angeles City School District, and was president of Guadalupe College in Texas. In addition to his full life, Taylor also invested well in Los Angeles real estate and became a pastor. He lived until age 72, passing away on September 18, 1974, in Downey, California, 21 years before being inducted into the USC Athletic Hall of Fame in 1995.[4] A plaque honoring him is in Heritage Hall on the USC campus, which reads, "Aim High," "Believe in Yourself," "Capable of Great Things," and "You Will Succeed." No better words can describe the legend that was Brice Taylor.

## *Dennis Thurman*

Santa Monica High School on Pico Boulevard is right in the heart of some of the city's most treasured points of interests. Within walking distance of the historic high school is the Third

Street Promenade, an excellent venue for great food, shopping, and entertainment. The famous Santa Monica Pier is nearby, as is the majestic Pacific Ocean. The school itself is also famous for having many world-renowned stars of television and film as alumni, and was the sight used to film some of the scenes for the classic 1955 motion picture, *Rebel Without a Cause*, starring James Dean.[1]

Samohi, as it is called, can also boast of an impressive collection of athletes that went on to fame on both the college and professional levels, and Dennis Thurman is one the alum that gained success on both levels after his days as a blue and gold Viking were complete.

Born on April 13, 1956, in Los Angeles, Thurman gained a stellar reputation as a prep quarterback and defensive back at Santa Monica High School. In the early 1970s, Thurman helped fill the school's trophy case with championship hardware as a member of three CIF Division I football championship teams. While Thurman was playing, the Vikings posted a near-perfect 39–1–1 record.[2]

Upon graduation, Thurman said goodbye to the blue and gold Vikings and hello to the cardinal and gold Trojans. His abilities allowed Thurman the opportunity to play on the varsity all four years, earning letters each season. In his first year of 1974, the Trojans captured a national title, and went 37–10–1 during Thurman's tenure of patrolling the secondary as a defensive back. He also saw some time as a receiver, catching three passes in 1975, and as a kick returner. As a safety, he had 13 career interceptions, which ranked him sixth all-time in USC history in that category, and in 1976 he led the Pac-8 with eight thefts. He recorded 169 career tackles, returned 38 punts and five kickoffs.[3]

The many talents of this Trojan did not go unnoticed, as he earned All-Conference and All-America honors as a defensive back in 1976 and 1977. He also was presented with the USC Most Valuable Player Award, and USC's Defensive Player of the Year Award, both after his senior season of 1977.[4]

Thurman was selected in the 11th round of the 1978 NFL draft by the reigning world champion Dallas Cowboys, and played with them from 1978 through 1985. He finished his pro career with the St. Louis (later Arizona) Cardinals in 1986. He then decided to teach future generations of players by becoming a coach. In that capacity, Thurman has held positions in the NFL with the Cardinals, Baltimore Ravens, and New York Jets. He also coached in the World Football League with the Ohio Glory, and USC from 1993 though 2000.[5]

## *Kenechi Udeze*

"The School That Works for the 21st Century!" This mantra is associated with Verbum Dei High School in Los Angeles, the home of the blue and gold Eagles.[1] It was also the home of Kenechi Udeze, who would live up to his school's slogan by working his way to giving nightmares to college opponents from 2001 through 2003.

The Los Angeles native was born on March 5, 1983, and while at Verbum Dei High School, Udeze came away with numerous honors including All-State and Prep All-American status. The powerful 6-4, 285-pound defensive lineman also threw the shot put 56'7" as a member of the track team.

Following his graduation, Udeze came to USC just as the Pete Carroll era was beginning. Nicknamed "BKU," the defensive end helped Carroll renovate the Trojans to national prominence as one of college football's top-rated defensive linemen. On his way to earning All-Pac-10 and All-American honors in 2003, Udeze was a member of USC's 2003 national championship team, shares the NCAA career record for forced fumbles, led the country in sacks in 2003 with 16.5, had 42 tackles for loss, and 51 overall in three years.[2] He earned three letters (2001–03), was named the 2003 National Defensive Player of the Year by the Pigskin Club of Washington, D.C., and was a two-time recipient of the USC Defensive Lineman of the Year in 2002 and 2003.[3]

The Minnesota Vikings were impressed enough in Udeze's abilities to make him their first round selection, and 20th overall pick, of the 2004 NFL draft. He played with the Vikings from 2004 through 2007. In February 2008, Udeze was diagnosed with acute lymphoblastic leukemia. He rallied from the illness, and attempted a comeback in 2009. However, effects from chemotherapy caused him to suffer from peripheral neuropathy in his feet, which led to numbness that would not allow him to plant his feet and fire off the line. He decided to retire on July 29, 2009, but he stayed in football, serving as an assistant strength and conditioning coach with the Washington Huskies under head coach, and former USC assistant, Steve Sarkisian.[4]

## *Keith Van Horne*

Notre Dame and UCLA decided to pass on Keith Van Horne when it came time for the Fullerton High School product to advance to the next level of football competition. With their fiercest rivals rejecting Van Horne, USC assistant coach Hudson Houck felt that the Trojans could put the 6'7" lineman's stature to good use.[1] Houck had built a solid reputation through the years as one of the best molders and shapers of offensive line talent. Many of his players at USC went on to great status as trench warriors in college and the professional level.

Van Horne was one lineman who made Houck a star maker. He added about 40 pounds of bulk to his frame by hitting the weights, and tipped the scales at 265 pounds. With that extra weight added to his height, Van Horne became a force to be reckoned with. His blocking prowess as a tackle helped open holes for Charles White to run his way to the 1979 Heisman Trophy, and allowed quarterback Paul McDonald time to find open receivers. En route to becoming one of the greatest offensive linemen in USC history, Van Horne received four letters (1977–80), served as team captain (1980), earned All-Conference honors twice (1979–80), was an All-American once (1980), and won the 1980 USC Offensive Player of the Year Award. Also in 1980, Van Horne got revenge on UCLA for not wanting him by receiving USC's Offensive Player of the Game Award in that season's annual cross-town battle with the Bruins.[2]

It was inevitable that the NFL was in Van Horne's future when draft day arrived in 1981. The only question was where the talented tackle would go. The Chicago Bears quickly solved that mystery by selecting him in the first round, and the 11th overall pick. He did not disappoint the team from the Windy City, as he played with the Bears from 1981 through 1993, starting in 169 of the 186 games he was in. He was also a member of the 1985 world champions Chicago Bears, regarded by many to be one of the greatest Super Bowl teams of all-time. In his football career, Van Horne had the privilege of blocking for one of the best all-time running backs in college (Charles White), and on the professional level (Walter Payton).

## *Irvine "Cotton" Warburton*

Many athletes have been able to make the transition from the playing field to acting. However, the list of those who conquer both venues with the ultimate accolades gets extremely slim. In the world of college football, Irvine "Cotton" Warburton not only was honored with All-American status as a quarterback, but with an Academy Award as well. He also received the lifelong nickname of "Cotton" due to his crop of blond hair.[1]

The life of this talented football player and film editor began on October 8, 1911 in San Diego, California. "The Old Grey Castle" was a classic name given to the oldest high school in San Diego during the time period of 1907 to 1973.[2] It was in this historic building that the legacy of Irvine Warburton began. In his time at San Diego High School, this future Trojan showcased his ability as a three-sport star that used his swift legs to claim the 1930 California state championship in the 440-yard dash.[3]

It was then time to display his athleticism on the college level, and as a member of the USC football team under Howard Jones, Warburton utilized his talents of speed and elusiveness to become the best open-field runner of the early 1930s, and one of the forefathers of the brilliant lineage of USC running backs. The amazing thing about Warburton was he devastated defenses while standing a mere 5-7, and weighing in at 145 pounds.[4]

Howard Jones was one of the all-time great college coaches, and demanded the absolute effort of his charges. In that regard, Warburton succeeded up to his coach's expectations. However, just as elusive as he was on the field, the swift backfield star had to be just as elusive in the training room. One of Jones' rules was that all of his players had to weigh in at no less than 175 pounds. There was no was way that Warburton could come close to that requirement, but his talents were too great to pass up on. Jones was very diligent about making sure that the players were weighed before and after practice sessions. When Warburton hit the scale, despite not even coming close to the required goal, the team manager would write down 175 pounds. If Jones did know about the fake readings, he never confronted either the manager or Warburton. In return, the speedster helped Jones carry on with his outstanding legacy as a mentor.[5]

During his time as USC's premier backfield man, the team rolled to a 24–7–2 record and captured the 1932 national championship. There was nothing that Warburton could not do on the field. He led the team in rushing in 1932 (420 yards) and in 1933 (885 yards). He was the team's leading scorer in 1933 (72 points), and punted, returned kicks, passed, caught, and played on defense.[6] In 1933 he received All-Conference and All-American honors before hanging up his famed #13 USC jersey and heading off to Hollywood.

The Chicago Bears offered Warburton a chance to play professionally, but he passed up the opportunity. After his college graduation in 1934, he went to work for Metro-Goldwyn Mayer Studios, and stayed there for 19 years. It took about eight years of honing his skills at MGM before he received his initial credit as a film editor on the Laurel & Hardy motion picture *Air Raid Wardens* in 1943.[7] In 1953, he worked on *Crazylegs,* a screen adaptation of the life of Elroy Hirsch, who was one of pro football's top receivers of the 1950s for the Los Angeles Rams. This merger of football and film editing proved successful for Warburton, who received an Academy Award nomination for his work.[8]

Not long after working on *Crazylegs*, Warburton left MGM and gravitated to Walt Disney Studios. On the night of April 5, 1965, at the Santa Monica Civic Auditorium, the Academy Awards were given out for excellence from films produced throughout 1964. It was on this night that Warburton achieved the crowning achievement of the film industry when he received an Academy Award for film editing on the classic *Mary Poppins.* He continued to work in Hollywood until retiring after working on Disney's *The Cat From Outer Space* in 1978. Warburton died on June 21, 1982 in Culver City, California, at age 70.[9] He was inducted into the College Football Hall of Fame in 1975, the USC Athletic Hall of Fame (1995), and the U.S. Softball Hall of Fame.[10]

## *Charles White*

While Anthony Davis was earning his place among USC's immortal tailbacks in the early and mid–1970s, Charles White was making a name for himself on the scholastic scene some 25 miles north of the campus. While Davis' exploits at San Fernando High School were still fresh in the memories of that area, White was creating his own legacy for the same "Mighty Tigers."

The high school on O'Melveny Avenue was the football showcase of the area when White attended there. Operating out of a wishbone formation, the future USC star and his teammates led the Tigers to Los Angeles city championships in 1974 and 1975. They were also the #1 ranked team in the country, and one of the most explosive. White gained 1,118 yards on the ground during his senior year, averaged 9.4 yards a carry, and scored 14 touchdowns.[1]

The amazing thing was that White was not even the leading rusher for San Fernando in 1975. That honor went to fellow running back Kevin Williams with 1,402 yards. Along with White and Williams, quarterback Kenny Moore and running back Raymond Williams also dazzled opponents and spectators alike. As a whole, this quartet earned the impressive moniker of "the Dream Backfield." When it came time to hand out awards, this backfield garnered so much attention that White, Moore, and Kevin Williams all were bestowed with the 1975 Los Angeles City Player of the Year Awards.[2] Charles White's talents were not just limited to the gridiron. When spring rolled around, he blazed his way to stardom on the track. In the spring of 1976, White produced a national prep record in the 330-yard low hurdles with a time of 36.0 seconds.[3]

John Robinson had just assumed the head coaching duties at USC at the time White was set to embark on a college career. Robinson had the task of replacing the legendary John McKay as head coach, and looked to carry on the tremendous tradition set by his predecessor. Charles White helped to make that transition go a lot smoother by making Robinson's recruiting of him very simple. Fellow San Fernando alum and recent Trojan legend Anthony Davis had already convinced White to sign up with the Cardinal & Gold. White wanted to go to USC after watching Davis tear through opponents on his way to All-American status.

With White easily committed to play for USC, Robinson's future over the next four seasons would allow him to create his own stellar legacy among all-time Trojan coaches. Those four seasons would also make a legend of Charles White in the Land of Troy.

When he first came onto the campus, White was listed as a fourth or fifth string running back. However, that was just a formality, and he did not remain there long. After a few weeks, he worked his way up the depth chart to position himself right behind All-American senior Ricky Bell.[4] White's rise came from a tireless work ethic. This mentality allowed him to take hit after hit, eventually wearing an opposing defense down.[5] He was an elusive runner who also possessed power, exceptional balance and vision, in addition to having a ferocious competitive streak.[6] He was also virtually indestructible, missing only one of 49 games over his USC career, and finished up with 31 games of 100-plus yards while in his famed #12 Trojan jersey. After being around this incredible talent for four seasons, John Robinson came away from the experience feeling that White was the toughest player he was ever associated with.[7] One more impressive statistic on White was the fact that he had a mere 1.94 percent body fat.

Stardom as a Trojan seemed to engulf White right from the beginning of his time on the USC campus. In his freshman year, White was seen in Heritage Hall, where the Heisman Trophies of Mike Garrett and O.J. Simpson were on display. Witnessing the presence of college football's ultimate individual award, White proclaimed that he could win two of them.[8] For most people, making a statement like that would be considered a case of wishful thinking that had no chance of becoming reality. In the case of Charles White, the idea was not that farfetched.

Boasting about winning the Heisman is one thing, but then setting your sights on obtaining it are two different things. White quickly began on a path that gave him a very legitimate chance at hoisting the 25-pound symbol of excellence at the Downtown Athletic Club before his days as a Trojan were over.

He made great strides in his quest right from his freshman year. Ricky Bell missed some games due to injuries in 1976, and White rose to the challenge, setting a USC freshman rushing record for most yards gained in a single season. During the regular season, he ran for 744 yards and nine touchdowns. He then gained national attention in the 1977 Rose Bowl. Once again filling in for the injured Bell, White ran for 122 yards and a touchdown in a 14–6 win over Michigan, and the Trojans finished the year at 11–1 and second in the national rankings.

With Ricky Bell off to the NFL in 1977, the starting tailback position belonged to White, and he made the most out of performing one of the most coveted jobs in college football. He finished the regular season with 1,291 rushing yards and seven touchdowns, led the Pac-10 with a 117.4 yards per game average, was selected All-Conference, and then capped off the year with 187 yards in a wild 47–28 Bluebonnet Bowl victory over Texas A&M. In 1978, White rushed for 1,760 yards and 12 touchdowns during the regular season. He then ran for 99 yards in a 17–10 Rose Bowl victory over Michigan and earned Co-MVP honors at the conclusion of the game. The Trojans finished the year at 12–1, and won a piece of the 1978 national championship. White repeated as an All-Conference selection and Pac-10 rushing champion, this year with a 146.7 average, added the Pac-10 scoring title (6.7 average) to his impressive resume, and also earned the Voit Trophy (outstanding player on the Pacific Coast), the Pac-10 Player of the Year Award, USC Most Valuable Player Award, All-American status, and came in fourth in the 1978 Heisman Trophy voting.

After coming in among the top vote getters for the Heisman after his junior year, White was considered a top candidate for the trophy in 1979 along with the previous winner, Billy Sims of Oklahoma. White left nothing to chance, and in the end, he lived up to his prediction of winning the Heisman Trophy, albeit one and not the two he predicted. With a runaway victory in the voting, White amassed 1,695 votes to 773 for runner-up Billy Sims.

The route that got White the privilege of having his name engraved on the 1979 Heisman Trophy saw the Trojan team captain gain 1,803 yards and 18 touchdowns in regular season competition. He led the entire nation with a 180.3 yards per game average, and was the Pac-10 scoring champion (12.5 points per game). In addition to his Heisman, White was the top award winner for the 1979 season. He won the Walter Camp Award (national player of the year), Pop Warner Award (most valuable senior on the Pacific Coast), Maxwell Award (nation's top player), the Amateur Athletic Foundation Southern California Athlete of the Year, repeated as the Pac-10 Player of the Year and USC Most Valuable Player, and easily received All-Conference and All-American honors. In his four seasons at USC, White ran for 5,598 regular season yards to become the NCAA's second all-time leading rusher and USC's all-time leader in that category. Counting bowl game appearances, White ran for 6,245 yards. He also set or tied 22 NCAA, Pac-10, USC, or Rose Bowl records.[9]

He always seemed to rise above all others in the Rose Bowl, and in the 1980 contest against #1 ranked Ohio State, White provided Trojan faithful and a world-wide audience with possibly the greatest swan song ever. In his final game in the Cardinal & Gold, White ran for a Rose Bowl record 247 yards, with 71 of them coming on an eight-play, 83-yard march in the closing minutes. He then capped the drive off with 1:32 remaining by scoring from the 1-yard line to give USC a narrow 17–16 victory, an 11–0–1 record, and second place in the final rankings. He easily won his second Rose Bowl MVP trophy after a performance for the ages. This was also a true testament to his toughness, as he was battered and beaten, but refused to give up. He just kept coming back for more, eventually wore the Ohio State defense down, and once again left the field as the supreme conqueror.

The Cleveland Browns made White their first round selection in the 1980 draft, and he remained with the team through the 1984 season. He was then reunited with his USC coach John Robinson, who took over the reins of the Los Angeles Rams in 1983. White played for the Rams from 1985 through 1988. In 1987, he led the NFL with 1,387 rushing yards. When his days as a player were over, White returned to USC as an assistant in the athletic department, and was also a member of the coaching staff from 1993 to 1997. He was inducted into the Rose Bowl Hall of Fame in 1979, the USC Athletic Hall of Fame in 1995, and the College Football Hall of Fame in 1996.[10]

## *Lendale White*

Thunder and lightning are powerful forces sent from the heavens. This intimidating combination can quickly strike fear and an ominous presence to many in their paths. College football had a rendition of thunder and lightning in the mid–2000's in the form of backfield tandem Reggie Bush and LenDale White. They brought speed and power each week en route to making the USC Trojans college football's elite program during their time together.

Prior to earning success as a Trojan, White began on his way to football glory in Denver, Colorado. Located on the south side of the Mile High City, in the Washington Park area, is South High School. Even though his time at South High was limited to two seasons (1999–2000), White made the most of that experience. He was named to the Rocky Mountain News All-Colorado first team in 2000, and received Rocky Mountain News Class 5-A All-State honors following both seasons.[1]

White then transferred to Chatfield High School in Littleton, Colorado, some 15 miles southwest of South High. It was there as a running back for the Chatfield Chargers that White carved out his remaining path to becoming a high school legend. While donning the maroon, silver, white, and black uniform of Chatfield, LenDale rushed for 1,850 yards and 30 touchdowns as a junior in 2001. He also had 185 yards receiving, and an additional two touchdowns. He played a major role in Chatfield finishing the season with a spotless 14–0 record and the Class 5-A championship. He was named to the Rocky Mountain News All-Colorado first team, and the Rocky Mountain News Class 5-A All-State team.[2]

For his high school swan song, White rushed for 1,683 yards and 21 touchdowns as a senior in 2002. He was once again named to the Rocky Mountain News All-Colorado first team, and for the fourth straight year, the Rocky Mountain News Class 5-A All-State Team. He also received the 2002 Gatorade Colorado Player of the Year Award. As a four-year starter, White compiled 7,803 rushing yards, which set a new Colorado state record. In addition to those state accolades, White earned selection onto numerous All-America teams.[3]

White carried over his success into the college game, as he quickly became a powerful force in the Trojans' offensive attack. With his 6-2, 235-pound frame smashing mostly inside the tackles, White played in all 13 games, gained a team-high 754 yards on 141 carries, and scored 13 touchdowns. He also had six receptions for 15 yards and a touchdown. What was so impressive about his accomplishments was the fact that he gained his yards coming off the bench. His rushing total was the second best for a USC freshman, only behind Charles White's 858 yards in 1976. His 13 rushing touchdowns set a USC freshman record, and his 14 total six-pointers tied a USC freshman record first set by Mike Williams in 2002. White was also the first freshman in USC's history to gain 100 yards rushing or more in back-to-back games. He received Freshman All-American second team honors from Collegefootballnews.com, and was that media outlet's Pac-10 Freshman of the Year Award winner. He also gathered in the 2003 ESPN.com All-Pac-10 Newcomer of the Year Award, the Sporting News Offensive Freshman of the Year Award, as well as being named to that publication's Pac-10 All-Freshman first team, and received honorable mention All-Pac-10 selection. On top of all this, White capped off this incredible freshman season by helping the Trojans gain a share of the 2003 national championship.[4]

The 2004 season saw the Trojans ranked number one in the country from wire to wire, and LenDale White was right there to make things happen. With Reggie Bush slashing his way on sweeps, earning his moniker of USC's version of "Lightning," White did pounded the ball between the tackles to produce the "Thunder" of the vaunted Trojan juggernaut. White started in 11 games, and played in all 13 en route to USC's perfect 13–0 record that culminated into a second straight national championship. However, this time, the Trojans did not have to share the crown with anyone, as they totally dominated the Oklahoma Sooners in the BCS Championship Game, 55-19. In that championship rout, White rushed for 118 yards on 15 carries and two touchdowns.[5]

Along the way on the Trojans' quest to dominance of the college football world, White ran for 1,103 yards on 203 carries and 15 touchdowns despite being hampered by an ankle sprain suffered in the seventh game of the season against Washington, which gave him problems throughout the remainder of the year. To prove his toughness, the battering ram runner gained 676 of his rushing yards after being hit. He added 11 receptions for 97 yards and two touchdowns to his season total. His team-high total of 17 touchdowns was the most since Marcus Allen's 23 in 1981. It was also the first time since Allen's feat that a USC player led the Pac-10 in total touchdowns scored. He was named to the 2004 All-Pac-10 second team, the Collegefootballnews.com All-American second team, and the ESPN.com All-Pac-10 first team.[6]

In his junior season of 2005, White once again helped the Trojans to a spotless regular season record of 12–0, that included another year of USC being ranked number one from the first game all the way through to the BSC Championship Game. This time the Trojans came up three points short of another national title, losing to Texas, 41–38. However, White's performance throughout this great season produced 1,302 rushing yards on 197 carries and a nation-leading 24 touchdowns. He added 14 receptions for 219 yards and two touchdowns to his impressive college statistics. After three seasons as the Trojans' power back, White rushed for 3,159 yards for a 5.8 yards per carry average, and a USC record 52 rushing touchdowns. He had 31 receptions for 331 yards and five additional six-pointers.[7]

Upon the completion of his junior season, White decided to bypass his final year of college eligibility and declare himself available for the 2006 NFL draft. Unfortunately, he did not impress many pro scouts that felt White had gained too much weight before the NFL scouting combine. White claimed a hamstring injury had hampered his working out. Despite his incredible college career, White appeared out of shape when the pros came calling, and it caused his value to slip. Regardless of how many scouts felt about White's physical condition, the Tennessee Titans selected him in the second round, and 45th overall player taken.[8]

Once in the pros, White could not seem to find the magic that got him to this point in his rookie year. He played in 13 games, gained 244 yards on 61 carries, and caught 14 passes for 60 yards. However, the following season saw White show signs of his old self, as he rushed for 1,110 yards and seven touchdowns. After the season he had arthroscopic surgery on his knee, and by the start of the 2008 season, he was ready to go. Along with rookie Chris Johnson, White formed the "Smash and Dash" backfield, and ran for 773 yards and 15 touchdowns. His touchdown total was tops in the AFC that season. In 2009, White went through a tough training regiment that saw him cut down to 229 pounds, but his playing time was not as great. Chris Johnson had become the featured running back in Tennessee's arsenal, and White only carried the 64 times for 222 yards and two touchdowns.[9]

White was traded to the Seattle Seahawks in 2010, which allowed him the opportunity to reunite with his college coach Pete Carroll. This time around with Carroll as his coach did not go as well as his USC days. White failed an NFL drug test and faced a four-game suspension at the beginning of the season. Without ever playing a down for Carroll in Seattle, White was released on May 28, 2010. He next stop was with the Denver Broncos, but in the final pre-season game, he tore an Achilles tendon, and never played during the regular season. The Broncos then released him on August 16, 2011. For his pro career, White carried the ball 628 times for 2,349 yards and scored 24 touchdowns.[10]

## *Mike Williams*

"Strength Through Unity" is the motto of Henry B. Plant High School in Tampa, Florida. It can also apply to the game of football, and for Mike Williams, the two create one common bond. With the support of teammates and his own talent, Williams rose to All-American status on both the prep and college levels while playing on a national championship team at USC.

The future Trojan receiver, who grew into a 6-5, 241-pound pass catching demon with 4.5 speed in the 40-yard dash, was born on January 4, 1984, in the city dubbed, "the Lightning Capital of the World," Tampa, Florida. The Black & Gold Panthers of Henry B. Plant had a winning tradition in football, and Williams helped to build on that reputation from 1999 through 2001. Over the course of those three seasons, Williams caught 101 passes for 2,223 yards and 24 touchdowns, gaining 24 yards per reception. As a junior he made All-State Second Team, and as a senior, he received many accolades, including prestigious All-American honors. He also played basketball, where he averaged 16.9 points-per-game, and was selected All-County in his junior year.[1]

After graduation, Williams set his sights on the City of Angels, and played under Pete Carroll at USC. His career as a Trojan was brief, but legendary. Right from the moment he fastened his chinstrap for the first time as a USC receiver, Williams dominated secondaries with his skills. He was proficient at breaking tackles and no one was better than him at running with the ball after a catch.[2] As a freshman in 2002, he caught 81 passes for 1,265 yards and 14 touchdowns, averaging 15.6 yards per reception. His staggering output set both USC and Pac-10 freshman records. His yards and touchdowns were also NCAA records for a freshman.[3]

When awards were given out following the 2002 season, Williams found his name attached to many of them. He was an easy choice for Freshman All-American, won the Pac-10 Freshman of the Year Award, and the Pac-10 Freshman Offensive Player of the Year. His efforts also helped USC quarterback Carson Palmer win the 2002 Heisman Trophy.

To prove that he suffered no sophomore jinx, Williams went out and hauled in 95 passes for 1,314 yards and 16 touchdowns for a 13.8 average in 2003. En route to assisting the Trojans obtain a share of the national championship, Williams earned All-Pac-10 and All-American honors, in addition to being named CBS Sportsline.com National Player of the Year. In two seasons, Williams recorded 12 games of 100 or more receiving yards, and 10 games where he caught eight passes. After two seasons he was ranked sixth all-time in USC history with 176 receptions, and had the distinction of being the receiver for two Heisman Trophy winners in Palmer (2002) and Matt Leinart, who was Trojans quarterback in 2003 and won the award in 2004. There was no telling the heights that Williams could have reached. Undoubtedly, he would have shattered many USC receiving records if he stayed on pace, however, after the 2003 season, Williams' future accolades as a Trojan would remain strictly speculative.[4]

Following his incredible sophomore season, he decided to forgo his remaining college eligibility and enter the NFL. A rule established by the NFL prohibited a player two years removed from high school to be able to enter the league. Ohio State running back Maurice Clarett challenged the rule after he was suspended by Ohio State following his freshman season of 2002. A federal judge ruled that the NFL could not ban Clarett from attempting to play in the league, which opened the door for Williams to pursue a pro career after only two years of college football. Many felt that Williams was an easy first round pick. He hired an agent and signed the proper paperwork needed to declare himself eligible for the 2004 draft, which officially prevented Williams from reinstatement back into college football.

Everything appeared to be in order, but right before the draft, the United States Court of Appeals for the Second Circuit, decided against the original federal judge's ruling. With this turn of events, the new ruling made it impossible for Clarett and Williams to enter the 2004 draft. Unable to progress into the pro ranks, and now ineligible to return to college football, Williams was forced to miss the entire 2004 season, regardless of the level of competition.[5]

Williams' stock did not diminish with the passing of a calendar year, as the Detroit Lions made him their first round selection and 10th overall pick of the 2005 draft. He played with the Lions (2005–2006), Oakland and Tennessee in 2007, and Seattle (2010–11).[6]

## *Richard Wood*

Bill Kane's crime fighting superhero Batman debuted in *Detective Comics #27* in May 1931. As protector of Gotham City, Batman donned his famous mask and cape in a quest to keep his fair metropolis safe from evil forces. Forty years later, the USC Trojans had their own version of the Capped Crusader in the form of Richard "Batman" Wood. Instead of a mask and cape, Wood used his helmet and shoulder pads to lead the defensive unit from his middle linebacker position against enemy forces. Along the way, Wood emerged victorious more often than not, much like his superhero counterpart.

The future Trojan defender was born on May 31, 1953, in Elizabeth, New Jersey. Athletic prowess was in his blood, as one of his brothers played major league baseball for several seasons with the Detroit Tigers. Wood did not follow in his brother's footsteps when it came to baseball, more than likely because he was busy excelling at other sports. While at Thomas Jefferson High School, Wood starred in football, wrestling, basketball, and track.[1]

Wood's hometown of Elizabeth is some 120 miles north of the gambling Mecca Atlantic City, however, no one could have bet against him succeeding on the next level of competition. He elected to go clear across the country to pursue a college football career, and the USC was happy to have him.

Upon arriving at USC, Wood received the nickname that stuck with him from that time on. As a freshman, the new arrivals to the team had to tell a joke before stating their name. Wood was unable to come up with one, and appeared too serious. It looked to those gathered in the room that Wood might inflict bodily harm due to his serious look. In an attempt to come up with something to say, he claimed to be Batman from Gotham City, which might not have been a knee-slapping joke that was expected, but it made the room break up with laughter. That simple statement taking all of a few seconds to blurt out, created the defensive wrecking machine known forever as Richard "Batman" Wood.[2]

He was a dominant presence capable of covering the entire field. With 4.6 speed in the 40-yard dash, the 6-2, 213-pound Wood was fast enough to hunt down running backs, and his strength allowed him to hit with the impact of a hammer, as his coach John McKay once described his ability to tackle.[3] His debut on the varsity in 1972 was nothing short of amazing. He recorded 18 tackles and an interception against Arkansas, and at the conclusion of that season, he had 30 more tackles than anyone else on the team.

In the entire history of USC, and all the incredible talent that played football there, Wood stood out above others when he became the school's first to earn All-American status three times. He was also a three-time All-Pac-8 selection, team captain in 1974, and USC had a record of 31–2–2 during his tenure patrolling the field. In the three seasons that Wood played, the Trojans captured three Pac-8 titles, and two national championships in 1972 and 1974.[4]

Wood was selected by the New York Jets in the third round of the 1975 NFL draft and played that one season for the Jets. He then went to Tampa Bay, where he was reunited with his college mentor John McKay from 1976 through 1984. Following his playing career, Wood coached in the NFL, Europe, and on the high school level, where he was selected as the 2002 Florida Coach of the Year. His stellar USC career was recognized with enshrinement into the USC Athletic Hall of Fame in 2003 and the College Football Hall of Fame in 2007.[5]

## *Robert Woods*

Exciting, imposing, a threat to score whenever he possesses the football. This observation can apply to many of those in Cardinal & Gold since the days of Frank "Rabbit" Malette in the 1910s. Picking up the torch from iconic offensive weapons of Trojan past as the new millennium entered its second decade was Robert Woods. This electrifying ball carrier wasted little time earning a place among USC's all-time greats shortly after fastening his chinstrap as a freshman.

Born on April 10, 1992, in Gardena, California, located in the southwestern part of Los Angeles County, Woods grew into a 6-1, 190-pound force of speed and power. Gardena's motto is "the City of Opportunity," and Woods is living proof of it. He took his incredible talents, honed them in his hometown, and then travelled 11 miles north. The home of the royal blue and scarlet-clad Cavaliers of Gardena's Junipero High School have had the structure on South Van Ness Avenue become a focal point of stellar athletic achievement since the dawn of Reaganomics in the 1980s. The Cavaliers have compiled state championship hardware at a steady pace beginning in 1980, and while Woods was a student/athlete there, the tradition continued thanks to his skills in football and track.[1]

At the time of his high school graduation in 2010, Woods was considered the nation's top wide receiver prospect and number one overall prep athlete. The legacy that Woods created for himself at Junipero began in his sophomore season of 2007. He had 45 receptions for 801 yards, which was 17.8 yards per catch average, and 12 touchdowns. He also rushed for 273 yards and recorded 81 tackles and nine interceptions while on defense. He earned Sophomore All-State honors, All-CIF Northwest Division first team selection, and was presented with the 2007 All-Del Rey League Defensive MVP Award.[2]

His junior season of 2008 was nothing short of spectacular.

He caught 81 passes for 1,378 yards and 19 touchdowns. When he wasn't catching passes and scoring touchdowns, he was preventing them by recording 87 tackles and seven interceptions, two of which he returned for six-pointers. He was an easy choice for many honors, and took home the All-CIF Northwest Division Co-Defensive MVP Award, the South Bay daily Breeze All-South Bay Player of the Year, the All-Del Rey League MVP Award, and was named to the All-State team from numerous media outlets.[3]

By his senior year of 2009, Woods was a bona fide superstar prep football player. He lived up to earning a place on virtually every All-American team possible, and received the All-CIF Northwest Division Defensive MVP Award, the Los Angeles Time All-Star Back of the Year Award, the South Bat Daily Breeze Player of the Year Award, and the All-Del Rey League MVP Award. His accolades were earned after a season that saw him catch 66 passes for 1,112 yards and 15 touchdowns, make 96 tackles, and intercept eight passes, returning two of scores. Woods' skills helped Junipero Serra to a perfect 15–0 record that included the CIF Northwest Division championship and the California Division III title. In the state championship game, Woods compiled 226 yards of total offense.[4]

The athletic gifts that Woods possessed were not limited to the football field. He was also an incredible sprinter, gaining national recognition on the *USA Today's* 2010 All-USA track & field team. In the spring of 2009, Woods took third place in the 400 meters at the state meet, and anchored Serra's 2009 state championship 400-meter relay team. In 2010, he took second in the state meet in the 400 meters, third in the 200 meters, and anchored the state championship-winning 1,600-meter relay team. He was also crowned the 2008–09 Cal-Hi Sports Division IV Boys State Athlete of the Year, and the 2009–10 Cal-Hi Sports Boys State Athlete of the Year.[5]

It was then on to USC for this exceptional talent, and he never missed a beat. In his freshman year of 2010, Woods started 13 games, and hauled in a team high 65 receptions for 792 yards and six touchdowns. In addition to his receiving skills, Woods also returned kickoffs and punts, accumulating 1,817 all-purpose yards that set a USC freshman record. His 38 kickoffs returns, and 971 yards gained on those returns, both established new USC single-season records. He was named to many Freshman All-America teams, earned All-Conference first team honors, and won the 2010 Pac-10 Offensive Freshman of the Year Award. He also was presented as winner of both the Bob Chandler Award (presented to the USC underclassman who displays excellence on and off the field, and in the classroom) and the John McKay Award (presented to the USC underclassman with the most competitive spirit).[6]

Resting on his laurels was not an option for the 6-1, 190-pound athletic phenomenon. In the Trojans' opening game of the 2011 season against Minnesota, Woods caught 17 passes to set a new USC single-game record previously held by Johnnie Morton (15 receptions in 1993). Woods gained 177 yards on those receptions, and tied a school record with three touchdown catches, with all of them coming in the first half. By season's end, Woods compiled numbers that some do not even get over a full college career. He had 111 receptions for 1,292 yards and 15 touchdowns. His 111 catches set both conference and USC single-season records. He was an easy selection for All-Pac-12 first team honors, consensus All-American, won the 2011 USC Offensive Perimeter Player of the Year Award, and was a finalist for the Biletnikoff Award, presented annually to college football's top receiver.[7]

In 2012, Woods had to share the offensive spotlight with former high school teammate Marqise Lee. The offense looked to make the sophomore Lee more of a focal point, but Woods still managed to emerge with impressive numbers. He caught 76 receptions for 846 yards and 11 touchdowns. The Buffalo Bills made Woods their 2nd round selection, and 41st overall player taken, in the 2013 NFL draft.[8]

## *Ron Yary*

Despite all the great USC offensive linemen that fought off charging defenders over the decades, Ron Yary is the only Trojan to ever be honored with the Outland Trophy, presented annually to college football's best interior lineman.

Before dominating opponents from his tackle position in Los Angeles, Yary's time on Earth began in Chicago, Illinois on July 16, 1946. His origins were in the Windy City, but his skills as a football player were honed in the Los Angeles suburb of Bellflower, California. It only seemed fitting that the future USC Trojan would be a member of a high school whose colors were cardinal and gold. As a member of the Bellflower Buccaneers, Yary was an All-San Gabriel Valley selection at tackle in his junior year before switching over to fullback as a senior.[1]

When it came time for college, Yary did not yearn for any particular program to play for. He just loved the sport of football, and wanted to be a part of a team somewhere. He initially settled on Cerritos Junior College in Norwalk, California, just under four miles northeast of Bellflower. Cerritos had its fair share of future professional baseball and football players pass through on their way to the big time, including Hall of Fame coach of the Washington Redskins, Joe Gibbs.[2]

Yary would someday join Gibbs in pro football's hallowed shrine in Canton, Ohio, but many years and battles in the trenches would have to ensue before that honor. His first step on to greatness on the collegiate level was when he received All-Metropolitan Conference honors as a tackle.

After one season in the junior college ranks, Yary enrolled at USC, and a Trojan legend was born. Yary started his USC career as a defensive tackle, where he won All-Conference honors. He then switched back over to offensive tackle, and that was where he would become a hall of famer multiple times.

At 6-5, 245 pounds, Yary was big, fast, and so strong that he was almost immovable. The position of lineman calls for players to be big, but at times they may not be able to handle the growth and become cumbersome as a result. Yary did have that problem, and handled his size with exceptional athleticism, was durable, and never projected any weakness. After mixing up all these stellar qualities, the complete offensive tackle emerged in the form of Ron Yary, and the USC coaching staff was glad to have him on their side.[3]

In his final two seasons at USC playing offensive tackle,

Yary earned All-Conference and All-American honors (1966–67), and was USC's first, and the first offensive tackle from the west coast, to win the Outland Trophy. He was also a key member of two conference titles and one national championship in 1967.[4]

Another first came for Yary when the Minnesota Vikings selected him as the number one overall pick of the 1968 draft, and in doing so, made him the first USC football player to be selected that high. He did not disappoint the Vikings for thinking so highly of his skills. Over the course of the next 14 seasons, Yary was the anchor of Minnesota's offensive line. He played with the Vikings from 1968 through 1981, and then ended his pro career with the Los Angeles Rams in 1982.

On his way through a long NFL career, Yary was regarded as one of the greatest offensive linemen in the history of the game. He was a six-time First Team All-Pro (1971–76), two-time Second Team All-Pro (1970, 1977), eight-time All-NFC (1970–77), seven-time Pro Bowl selection (1971–77), NFC Offensive Lineman of the Year three times (1973, 1974, 1975), on the NFL's All-Decade Team for the 1970s, was selected as one of the 50 greatest Minnesota Vikings, is in the Minnesota Vikings Ring of Honor, and played in four Super Bowls following the 1969, 1973, 1974, and 1976 seasons. When it came time for induction into halls of fame, Yary hit the trifecta. He was enshrined into the College Football Hall of Fame in 1987, the USC Athletic Hall of Fame in 1997, and the Pro Football Hall of Fame in 2001.[5]

## *Adrian Young*

Back in 1912, Chauncey Olcott and George Graff, Jr. wrote the lyrics, and Ernest Ball set their words to music for what became the beloved all-time classic, "When Irish Eyes are Smiling."[1] However, 55 years after its release, on October 14, 1967, the song had the sentiment of a double-edged sword. For on that date, a legend was created at USC with roots firmly set in Ireland, and who sent Notre Dame faithful into despair with a game for the ages.

Matthew Adrian Young was born on January 31, 1946, in Dublin, Ireland. After spending a good portion of his youth in "the Land of Saints and Scholars," Young and his family moved clear across the globe, settling in California. It only seemed fitting that the Young's new residence on the Golden Coast would be in La Mirada, a city located in southeast Los Angeles County, and founded by fellow Irishman Andrew McNally, in the late 1880s.[2]

The sport of football soon became of interest to Adrian, and by high school age, he was a member of the Bishop Amat High School Lancers. As a sophomore, he was a 150-pound defensive back, but through growth and weight training, Young built himself up into a 6-1, 210-pound linebacker ready to take on the next level of competition.[3]

Some 20 miles east from where he prepped as a schoolboy athlete, was USC. It was there, under the guidance of another Irishman, coach John McKay, that Young solidified his place among Trojan immortals. The Fighting Irish of Notre Dame had just come off another national championship season as the Trojans were set to invade South Bend for the 39th meeting between these fierce rivals. It had been 28 years since USC left South Bend victorious, and the Fighting Irish looked to keep that impressive streak going. However, when the game clock hit 0:00 on that October day in 1967, the Dublin native and his Irish coach McKay were definitely smiling while hoards of Notre Dame diehards wept. Over the course of sixty minutes, which culminated in a 24–7 USC victory, Young intercepted four Notre Dame passes to tie a conference record for most thefts in a single game.

By the end of that 1967 season, Young and Trojans replaced Notre Dame as national champions, and the linebacker donning the #50 on his jersey, walked away with many accolades to go with his record-setting performance against Notre Dame. He was a three-year letterman (1965–67), defensive captain for the '67 team, was selected All-Conference and All-American in 1967, and was the winner of the 1967 Davis-Teschke Award, given to USC's most inspirational player. He was selected by the Philadelphia Eagles in the third round of the 1968 NFL draft, and played with them from 1968 to 1972, a year in which he also saw time with the Detroit Lions. He then finished up his professional career with the Chicago Bears in 1973.[4]

## *Charles Young*

Unanimous All-American, three-year letterman, and a vital part in the 1972 Trojans' drive to becoming one of the greatest teams of all time, were only a few accolades that could describe Charles "Tree" Young.

Born on February 5, 1951, in Fresno, California, Young grew into a 6-4, 228 pound gifted football player. Before he went in USC history as the school's best tight end, he attended the "home of the Tigers," Fresno's Edison High School. In addition to his skills on the football field, Young also marveled crowds on the hardwood, leading the Tigers in to the valley playoffs in basketball.[1]

Upon graduation from Edison in 1969, Young enrolled at USC, and over the course of three varsity seasons, he emerged as the all-time record holder in receptions for a tight end. He was powerful, had fluid moves like a halfback, and was an exceptional blocker.[2] He was indeed the complete package when looking for a tight end. From 1970 through 1972, Young caught 68 passes for 1,090 yards and 10 touchdowns, averaging 16.1 yards per reception. He earned All-Pac-8 and All-American honors in 1972, and was voted the 1972 co-winner of the USC Lineman of the Year Award, which he shared with John Grant.[3]

The Philadelphia Eagles selected the premier college tight end in the first round, and sixth overall pick, of the 1973 NFL draft. He played with the Eagles from 1973 through 1976 before returning to the Los Angeles area with the Rams from 1977 through 1979. He also made stops in San Francisco (1980–82) and Seattle (1983–85). He appeared in two Super Bowls (XIV with Los Angeles following the 1979 season, and XVI with San Francisco following the 1981 season). He was enshrined into the College Football Hall of Fame in 2004 and the USC Athletic Hall of Fame in 2007.[4]

*Three*

# All-Time Rosters (1888–2012)

All-Time Rosters (1888–2012) is as complete an alphabetical listing of all USC players as possible. (In the early years of the program, much of the information was never recorded.) Every effort to give the most detailed account was expended.

The following information will be provided for each player (when available): First then last name; Years played; Position

Jim Abbott: 2004–07; Defensive Back
Sultan Abdul-Malik: 1997–2000; Defensive End/Linebacker
Shamsud-Din Abdul-Shaheed: 1998–2000; Defensive End/Defensive Tackle
Steve Aboytes: 1993; Halfback
Fabian Abram: 1955–56; Tackle
Adam Abrams: 1996–98; Kicker
Andre Abrams: 1992, 1994–95; Offensive Tackle/Offensive Guard
George Achica: 1979–82; Nose Guard
Frank Acker: 1904–05
Bill Adams: 1966–68; Center
Dave Adams: 1979–80; Running Back
Gene Adams: 1904–05
Gordon Adams: 1979–80; Quarterback
Halley Adams: 1922–24; Center
Hobbs Adams: 1923–25; End
Holly Adams: 1922–24; Center
Pete Adams: 1970–72; Offensive Tackle
Harry Adelman: 1941–42; Guard
Jody Adewale: 2003–07; Running Back
Rob Adolph: 1973–74; Quarterback
Erik Affholter: 1985–88; Kicker/Split End
Joe Agapay: 1955; Halfback
Nelson Agholor: 2012; Wide Receiver
John Aguirre: 1941, 1945–46; Tackle
John Akiba: 2012; Running Back
Kris Albarado: 2011–12; Punter
Rikki Aldridge: 1967; Kicker/Flanker
Madden Alefosio: 1992; Defensive End/Inside Linebacker
Joe Alekski: 1925, 1927; Guard
DelVaughn Alexander: 1993–94; Wide Receiver
Harold Alexander: 1923
Roy Allan: 1908–10; Center
Marcus Allen: 1978–81; Running Back
Chris Allen: 1987
Javorious Allen: 2011–12; Tailback
Dick Allmon: 1966–68; Defensive End
Marcell Allmond: 1999–2003; Wide Receiver/Cornerback
John Allred: 1993–96; Tight End
Augusto Alonso: 2010–11; Linebacker
Michael Amico: 1983, 1985–86; Inside Linebacker
J. Almy: 1907; Quarterback
Dick Ambrosi: 1957; Fullback
Brad Anderson: 1981; Wide Receiver
Chuck Anderson: 1960–61; Guard
Harry Anderson: 1948–49; Fullback
Heath Anderson: 1993; Middle Linebacker
Mickey Anderson: 1938, 1940–41; Quarterback
Mickey Anderson: 1983; Quarterback
Norm Anderson: 1922–24; Tackle
Otto Anderson: 1922–24; Halfback
Will Andrew: 2009–12; Linebacker
Charlie Ane: 1951–52; Quarterback/Tackle
Sam Anno: 1983–86; Linebacker
Charles Anthony: 1971–73; Middle Linebacker
Frank Anthony: 1927–29; Tackle
Ken Antle: 1956–58; Center
Russell Antles: 1944–46; Center
David Apolskis: 1990, 1992–93; Center/Offensive Guard
Marger Apsit: 1928–30; Halfback
Michael Arakelian: 2012; Defensive End
Garrett Arbelbide: 1929–31; End/Halfback
Kevin Arbet: 1999–2001, 2003–04; Safety/Cornerback
Bobby Archuleta: 1987; Safety
Bud Ardanaz: 1957; Guard
Armond Armstead: 2008–11; Defensive End
Hal Arnest: 1961; End
Bob Arnett: 1957–58; Halfback
Jon Arnett: 1954–56; Halfback
James Arnold: 1918
Paul Arnold: 1889; Quarterback
Gene Arrington: 1985–88; Flanker
Jim Arrivey: 1980–81; Quarterback
Chuck Arrobio: 1963–65; Tackle
Mickey Artenian: 1952–53; Guard
Walt Ashcraft: 1948–49, 1952; Tackle
Walker Lee Ashley: 2006; Defensive Line
Collin Ashton: 2001–05; Linebacker
Taylor Ashton: 2010–11; Cornerback
Alex Atanasoff: 1937; Center
John Aubrey: 1996–97; Linebacker
Earl Audet: 1943
John Auran: 2011–12; Safety
David Ausberry: 2006–10; Wide Receiver
Don Avery: 1941–42; Offensive Lineman
Ralph Avery: 1896; Back
R.W. Avery: 1897; Tackle
Yonatan Aviv: 2012; Defensive Tackle
Fred Axe: 1919–21; Guard
Ron Ayala: 1968–70; Kicker/Safety
Blake Ayles: 2008–10; Tight End
John Baccitich: 1966; Center
Morris Badgro: 1924–26; End
Dion Bailey: 2010–12; Free Safety
Harvey Bailey: 1888; Back
Burt Bailie: 1903–05
Bill Bain: 1973–74; Offensive Tackle
Marv Bain: 1964–65; Linebacker
John Bain: 1969; Linebacker
John Baker: 1929–31; Guard
Roy Baker: 1922–23; Halfback
Sam Baker: 2004–07; Offensive Tackle
Al Baldock: 1949–50, 1953; End
Lyle Baldridge: 1925–26, 1928; Guard
Damon Bame: 1962–63; Guard/Linebacker

Chip Banks: 1978–81; Outside Linebacker
Zach Banner: 2012; Offensive Tackle
Al Bansavage: 1959: Guard
Brad Banta: 1989–93; Tight End
Jack Banta: 1938–40; Fullback
Kurt Barber: 1988–91; Outside Linebacker
Richard Barber: 1931–32; Fullback
Oliver Bardin: 1932–33; Guard
Matt Barkley: 2009–12; Quarterback
Dan Barnes: 1986–89; Defensive Tackle
Mercer Barnes: 1948–50; Center
Terry Barnum: 1992–95; Running Back
Andy Baroncelli: 1983; Center
Nate Barragar: 1927–29; Center
Chris Barrett: 2003–06; Defensive Line
Allan Barry: 1952; Tackle/Guard
Joe Barry: 1992–93; Inside Linebacker
Nelson Barry: 1930; Quarterback
Steve Barry: 1965–66; Guard
Bob Bastian: 1946–48; Guard
Mike Bastianelli: 1995–98; Wide Receiver
Jim Bates: 1960–61; Halfback
Louis Batinski: 1940; Halfback
Art Battle: 1946, 1948–49; Halfback
Mike Battle: 1966–68; Cornerback
Brian Baucham: 2008–12; Cornerback
Dillon Baxter: 2010–11; Tailback
Eugene Bayley: 1914; Tackle
Francis Beard: 1932–34; Fullback
Greg Beard: 1975; Offensive Guard
Pete Beathard: 1961–63; Quarterback
Eugene Beatie: 1926–27; Tackle
Richard Beatie: 1995; Offensive Tackle
Blanchard Beatty: 1930–31; Quarterback
Homer Beatty: 1934–36; Halfback
Gene Beck: 1948–50; Center
Harry Beck: 1948; Halfback
Henry Becker: 1929; Halfback
Hal Bedsole: 1961–63; End
Bob Beeson: 1940; Halfback
Allen Behrendt: 1924–26; End
Max Belko: 1934–36; Tackle
Bobby Bell: 1955; End
David Bell: 1996, 1998–2000; Punter
Howard Bell: 1926; Guard/Tackle
Joseph Bell: 1943; Quarterback
Ricky Bell: 1973–76; Tailback
Jack Belloni: 1940; Fullback
George Belotti: 1954–56; Tackle
Brett Beloud: 1993; Tailback
Wes Bender: 1991–92; Fullback
Frank Bennett: 1939–40; Tackle
Carl Benson: 1938–40; Guard/Tackle
Jeff Benson: 1985; Offensive Tackle
George Berg: 1968; Linebacker
Ryan Bernstein: 2012; Defensive End
John Berry: 1981, 1983; Inside Linebacker
Lorne Berry: 1985; Cornerback
Mike Berry: 1969–70; Tailback
Richard Berryman: 1936; Fullback
Robert Berryman: 1939–40; Quarterback
Julius Bescos: 1932–34; End
Oliver Best: 1904; Quarterback
Gary Bethel: 1975–77; Center
George Bettinger: 1935; End
Bill Betz: 1946–48; Quarterback
Steve Bianchi: 1941–42, 1946; Center
Duane Bickett: 1982–84; Defensive Tackle/Linebacker
Keith Biggers: 1983–84; Inside Linebacker
Henry Biggs: 1930–32; End
Darnell Bing: 2003–05; Safety
Henry Binkley: 1941; Halfback
Jim Bird: 1947–49; Tackle
Richard Bird: 1919–20
Rupert Black: 1930; Guard
Steve Blackhart: 2009; Wide Receiver
Victor Blackwell: 2011–12; Flanker
Horace Blair: 1922; Tackle
John Blanche: 1966–68; Linebacker/Guard
Ed Blecksmith: 1964–65; Safety
Leo Bledsoe: 1941–42; Halfback
William Bledsoe: 1940–42; Halfback
Melvin Bleeker: 1940–42; Fullback
Gene Blodgett: 1955; Guard
Chris Bocage: 2002–04; Defensive Back
Grant Boelter: 1996; Offensive Tackle
Tom Bohlinger: 1972–73; Defensive End/Linebacker
Winchell Boice: 1922; End
Herb Boies: 1949; Guard
Larry Boies: 1957–58; End
Joe Bok: 1985; Inside Linebacker
David Boler: 2001; Wide Receiver
Ward Bond: 1928–30; Tackle
Marcus Bonds: 1994–95; Defensive End
Herschel Bonham: 1926–28; Fullback
John David Booty: 2004–07; Quarterback
Bing Bordier: 1954–55; End
Dennis Born: 1966–67; Tackle
William Bosbyshell: 1906
Tony Boselli: 1990, 1992–94; Offensive Tackle
Joe Boskovich: 2000–03; Tight End/Center
Martin Boskovich: 1993; Punter
Rod Botelho: 1957–58; Guard
Clyde Bott: 1896–97; Guard
Alex Bottom: 1999–2002; Long Snapper
Jay Bottom: 2001–03; Defensive End
Dave Boulware: 1971–73; Punter/Flanker
Ken Bowen: 1995–98; Offensive Tackle
Bill Bowers: 1949–50; Halfback
Wilson Bowie: 1965–68; Flanker
Brandon Bowlin: 1986–88; Safety
Charles Bowman: 1939; Quarterback
Gerald Bowman: 2012; Safety
Jerry Bowman: 1940; Punter/Quarterback
James Boyd: 2009–10; Tight End
Mark Boyer: 1982–84; Tight End
Robbie Boyer: 2008–11; Wide Receiver
Johnny Boyle: 1920–22; Tackle
George Bozanic: 1950–53; Quarterback
Allen Bradford: 2006–10; Fullback/Tailback/Safety
Joe Bradford: 1945; Center
Joe Bradley: 1895; Fullback
Mario Bradley: 1994–95; Cornerback
Otha Bradley: 1973–74; Nose Guard
Greg Brady: 1981; Wide Receiver/Kick Returner
John Brame: 1949; Quarterback
Mark Bratonia: 1971; Tailback
Danny Bravo: 1998, 2000; Safety
Larry Braziel: 1977–78; Cornerback
Garrett Breeland: 1983, 1985; Outside Linebacker
Jeff Bregel: 1983–86; Offensive Guard
Scott Brennan: 1985–88; Center
Hoby Brenner: 1978–80; Tight End
Morgan Breslin: 2012; Defensive End
Tony Brewer: 1982–83; Safety
Walter Bridewell: 1907; Halfback
Kenneth Bright: 1932–33; Center
Greg Briner: 1969; Quarterback
Mike Brittingham: 2003–06; Running Back
Louis Brock: 1983, 1985–86; Cornerback
Kenneth Brockman: 1918
Charles Broderson: 1898, 1902–04; End
Bill Brodie: 1957; Quarterback
Richard Bronson: 1955, 1957; Guard
Bruce Brooks: 1977; Offensive Guard
Willard Brouse: 1931; Quarterback
Raphael Brousseau: 1935–37; Guard
Anthony Brown: 2010–12; Cornerback
Bob Brown: 1967; Fullback
Booker Brown: 1972–73; Offensive Guard
Charles Brown: 2006–09; Offensive Tackle
Dave Brown: 1970–72; Center
Everett Brown: 1928–30; Quarterback
Fredrick Brown: 1906, 1908
George Brown: 1889; Tackle
Justin Brown: 2001–02; Offensive Tackle
Luthur Brown: 2005–09; Linebacker
Marcel Brown: 1990; Cornerback
Raymond Brown: 1930–32; Tackle
Rocky Brown: 1999; Wide Receiver

Ron Brown: 1954–55; Halfback
Ron Brown: 1985–86; Outside Linebacker
Rory Brown: 1990, 1992–93; Fullback
Van Brown: 2002–03; Defensive End
Willie Brown: 1961–63; Halfback
Dick Brownell: 1964
Joey Browner: 1979–82; Safety/ Cornerback
Keith Browner: 1981–83; Outside Linebacker
Richard Browning: 1941; Quarterback
Ward Browning: 1932–34; End
John Brownwood: 1962–64; End
Kevin Bruce: 1973–75; Inside Linebacker
Mike Brummett: 1983; Offensive Guard
T.J. Bryant: 2008–11; Cornerback
Chris Brymer: 1994, 1996–97; Offensive Guard
William Buchanon: 2001–05; Wide Receiver
Bob Buckley: 1951–53; Halfback
Brad Budde: 1976–79; Offensive Guard
David Buehler: 2006–08; Kicker/Fullback/Safety
Don Buford: 1957–58; Defensive Back/ Halfback
Rudy Bukich: 1951–52; Tailback
Frank Buncom: 1960–61; End
Mike Bundra: 1959–61; Tackle
Bill Bundy: 1939–41; Halfback
Frank Bunker: 1907, 1909; Center
Gerald Burchard: 1933–35
Stanley Burek: 1905–08; Fullback
Don Burke: 1948–49; Fullback
Red Burkett: 1916
Charles Burks: 2011–12; Defensive End/ Fullback
C.W. Burnett: 1893, 1895; Guard
Tony Burnett: 2010–12; Cornerback
Dan Burns: 1976–77; Tight End
DeChon Burns: 1989; Cornerback
Mike Burns: 1975–76; Cornerback
Ross Burruel: 2004–05; Offensive Line
Stuart Busby: 1961; Tackle
Ernie Busch: 1947; Center
Reggie Bush: 2003–05; Running Back
Ron Bush: 1974–76; Cornerback
Steve Busick: 1978–80; Inside Linebacker
Ron Butcher: 1961–62; Tackle
Matt Butkus: 1993; Nose Tackle
Brice Butler: 2008–11; Wide Receiver
Doyal Butler: 2000–02; Tight End
Ray Butler: 1978–79; Wide Receiver
Clarence Butterfield: 1917, 1919–20
Tracy Butts: 1985–88; Cornerback
Jeff Byers: 2004, 2007–09; Center/ Offensive Line
Dominique Byrd: 2002–05; Defensive End/Tight End
Glenn Byrd: 1972–73; Defensive Tackle
Lou Byrd: 1957–58; Guard
Mac Byrd: 1962–64; Guard/Tackle
Sunny Byrd: 2001–02; Fullback
Dave Cadigan: 1985–87; Offensive Tackle
Ray Cahill: 1965–66; Split End
Lynn Cain: 1977–78; Fullback
Ron Calabria: 1954
Sean Calcagnie: 2006–09; Wide Receiver
Dan Caley: 1902–03; Halfback
Elwin Caley: 1902–03; Halfback
George Callanan: 1943–44; Halfback
Howard Callanan: 1942; Halfback
Jim Callanan: 1943–44, 1946; End
Leo B. Calland: 1920–22; Guard
Don Cameron: 1923
Jordan Cameron: 2008–10; Wide Receiver
Rodney Cameron: 1933–35; Quarterback
Gordon Campbell: 1921–23; Halfback
Jack Campbell: 1978; Offensive Tackle
Jim Campbell: 1917; Guard
Jordan Campbell: 2007–09; Running Back
Frank Candela: 2001; Wide Receiver
Pat Cannamela: 1950–51; Guard/Linebacker
Al Cantor: 1948–49; Halfback
John Cantwell: 1973–74; Flanker
Phil Cantwell: 1973; Wide Receiver
Robert Cardona: 1940; Guard
Troy Cardona: 2011–12; Safety
Mike Carey: 1974–77; Rover
Amir Carlisle: 2011; Tailback
Greig Carlson: 2001–05; Wide Receiver
Al Carmichael: 1950–52; Halfback
C.C. Carpenter: 1888; End
Kenneth Carpenter: 1934, 1937
Roy Carpenter: 1905–06
Mark Carrier: 1987–89; Safety
Arthur Carroll: 1888; Back
Brandon Carswell: 2007–11; Wide Receiver
Red Carten: 1894; Back
Allen Carter: 1972–74; Tailback
Frank Carter: 1996–99; Safety
Kent Carter: 1970–71; Defensive End/ Linebacker
Greg Caruso: 2010; Safety
Gerald Caruthers: 1993–94; Outside Linebacker
Thomas Nixon Carver: 1888 -89; Back
Frank Case: 1905; Tackle
Jurrell Casey: 2008–10; Defensive Tackle
Chris Cash: 2000–01; Cornerback
Pat Cashman: 1966–67; Cornerback
Tyler Cashman: 1993–95; Tight End
Matt Cassel: 2001–04; Quarterback
Curtis Cassell: 1920–21; Center
Al Casten: 1950; Tackle
Ed Catoe: 1976–77; Defensive Tackle
Reese Cave: 1946; End
Preston Cavignac: 2008; Wide Receiver
Mario Celotto: 1974–77; Outside Linebacker
Mahlon Chambers: 1927–29; Quarterback
Jay Champlain: 1981; Wide Receiver
Bob Chandler: 1968–70; Flanker
Chris Chaney: 1970–72; Flanker
Tom Chantilles: 1939–41; Guard
Ben Charles: 1958–61; Quarterback
Marco Chavez: 2003–04; Linebacker
Sal Chavez: 1988; Nose Guard
Delmar Chesley: 1986–89; Inside Linebacker
J.R. Chesley: 1990; Outside Linebacker
Martin Chesley: 1985–88; Tight End
Bob Chestnut: 1917, 1919
Matt Childers: 1999–2000; Defensive End
Eric Childs: 2010–11; Tight End
Howard Christianson: 1919; End
Charles Christy: 1896–97; Center
Joe Chuha: 1957; Center
John Churchill: 1969; Linebacker
Chris Claiborne: 1996–98; Linebacker
Travis Claridge: 1996–99; Offensive Guard
Avery Clark: 1971; Outside Linebacker
Don Clark: 1942, 1946–47; Guard
Gordon Clark: 1931–33; Halfback
Jack Clark: 1935
Jay Clark: 1962–63; Halfback
Kevin Clark: 1993; Fullback
Lyle Clark: 1955, 1957; Tackle
Monte Clark: 1956–58; Tackle
Ray Clark: 1916–17
Roger Clark: 1959–61; Tackle
Ron Clark: 1969; Defensive Tackle
Stephen Clark: 1905–08
Tanqueray Clark: 1998–99; Cornerback
Eugene Clarke: 1930–31; End
Leon Clarke: 1953–55; End
Frank Clayton: 1952–54; Halfback
Paul Cleary: 1946–47; End
Cal Clemens: 1932; Halfback
Jerry Clemens: 1919
David Clinco: 2007; Offensive Tackle
Greg Coauette: 1984–87; Outside Linebacker
Gary Cobb: 1976–78; Linebacker/Defensive End
Marvin Cobb: 1972–74; Defensive Back
Ernest Cochran: 1909

Marcus Cockrell: 1991; Kicker/Cornerback
Shaun Cody: 2001–04; Defensive End
Thomas Cohn: 1910; Quarterback
Angelo Coia: 1958–59; Halfback
Keary Colbert: 2000–03; Wide Receiver
John Coleman: 1967; Center
Julian Coleman: 2012; Linebacker
Martin Coleman: 2007–11; Offensive Line
Michael Coleman: 2005–06; Running Back/Tailback
Neil Colgrove: 1950; Quarterback
Tom Colley: 1948–49; Guard
Thearon Collier: 2010; Wide Receiver
Pat Collins: 1971–73; Defensive Back
Will Collins: 2003–07; Offensive Line
Tony Colorito: 1983–85; Nose Guard
Cleveland Colter: 1986–89; Safety
Craig Combs: 1981; Inside Linebacker
John Conde: 1949–51; Tackle
Dan Conforti: 1946; Center
Jordan Congdon: 2007–09; Kicker
Rod Connors: 1977; Tailback
James Joseph Conroy: 1956–57, 1959; Quarterback/Fullback
Jerry Conroy: 1965; Guard
Jim Contratto: 1953–55; Quarterback
Curtis Conway: 1990–92; Quarterback/Flanker
Brian Cook: 1982; Cornerback
Chad Cook: 2001; Tight End
Rashard Cook: 1995–98; Safety
Ken Coones: 1958–59; Guard
Jalen Cope-Fitzpatrick: 2012; Tight End
Mike Cordell: 1973–75; Offensive Guard
Joe Cormier: 1983–85; Tight End
Fred Cornwell: 1981–83; Tight End
Aaron Corp: 2007–09; Quarterback
Dave Corsinotti: 1981; Nose Guard
Marcus Cotton: 1983, 1985–87; Outside Linebacker
Cole Cottrell: 2012; Wide Receiver
Alvie Coughlin: 1932–34; Tackle
John Cousins: 2000–01
Humphrey Covington: 1968–69; Fullback
Al Cowlings: 1968–69; Defensive Tackle
Bob Cox: 1951–52; Guard
Kenneth Cox: 1924–26; Tackle
Michael Cox: 2011; Tight End
Morgan Cox: 1918–19–20; Center
Tom Cox: 1981–85; Center
Leslie Coyle: 1927; Halfback
Gerald Craig: 1914–16; End
Morgan Craig: 2003; Running Back
Rod Craig: 1948; Halfback
Stanley Cramer: 1947–49; End
Dennis Crane: 1966–67; Defensive Tackle
Bob Crane: 1989–91; Tight End
Jeff Cravath: 1924–26; Center
Willie Crawford: 1977–78; Safety
Estrus Crayton: 1991–92; Tailback
Joel Crisman: 1990–93; Offensive Guard
Muir Crittenden: 1941–42; Halfback
Omari Crittenden: 2007–10; Defensive Back
Wallace Crittenden: 1944; Guard
Bob Crosbie: 1949; Tackle
Lindon Crow: 1952–54; Halfback
Jim Crowther: 1941; Tackle
Donald Cruickshank: 1924–26; Tackle
Fred Crutcher: 1981, 1983–85; Tailback
Cliff Culbreath: 1969, 1971–72; Linebacker/Offensive Guard
William Culler: 1940; Center
Ross Cumming: 2008–11; Linebacker
Ralph Cummings: 1921–23; Tackle
Bill Cunerty: 1965; Kicker
Samuel Cunningham: 1970–72; Fullback
August Curley: 1980–82; Inside Linebacker
Edsel Curry: 1943, 1946–47
Nic Curry: 2010–11; Wide Receiver
Willard Curry: 1915–16
Louis Bud Curtis: 1944; Guard
Mike Curtis: 1965, 1967; Defensive End
Mark Cusano: 1995–98; Linebacker
Brian Cushing: 2005–08; Linebacker
George Custin: 1906
Cosmino Cutri: 1950–51; Halfback
Joe Cziguth: 1949–50; Tackle
Tom Dabasinskas: 1987–89; Center/Offensive Tackle
Ron Dale: 1988–91; Punter
Steve Dale: 1966–67; Halfback
Jeff Daley: 1997; Tight End
Matt Dalton: 1999–2000; Wide Receiver/Quarterback
Jasper D'Ambrosi: 1948; Guard
Aramis Dandoy: 1952–54; Halfback
Richard Danehe: 1940–41; Center
Mario Danelo: 2003–06; Kicker
Byron Darby: 1979–82; Defensive Tackle/Linebacker
Mario DaRe: 1952–54; Tackle
Spencer Darlin: 2012; Wide Receiver
Anthony Davis: 1972–74; Tailback
Clarence Davis: 1969–70; Tailback
David Davis: 1934–36; Quarterback
David Davis: 2001–02; Kicker
Ennis Davis: 1997–2000; Defensive Tackle
Frank Davis: 1888; Tackle
Fred Davis: 2004–07; Tight End
George Davis: 1934; Guard
George Davis: 1944, 1947–49; Center
Jesse Davis: 1994–95; Safety
Joe Davis: 1940–42; End
Joe Davis: 1973–75; Offensive Guard
Keith Davis: 1984–87; Inside Linebacker
Michael Davis: 1981; Cornerback
Mike Davis: 2005–06; Defensive Line
Robert Davis: 1922; End
Steve Davis: 1998; Defensive Tackle
Thomas Davis: 1914
Tyler Davis: 2006; Quarterback
William Davis: 1940; Quarterback
Lamar Dawson: 2011–12; Middle Linebacker
Oliver Day: 1937–38; Quarterback
Anthony Daye: 2001–02; Defensive End
Zolo DeArmand: 1917; Guard
David De Beyer: 1956
Benji DeBord: 1995; Wide Receiver
Phil Debovsky: 1955, 1957; Guard
Courtney Decius: 1906–07, 1909
Dan Deckas: 2006–09; Linebacker
George Decker: 1929–30; Tackle
Jim Decker: 1953–54, 1956; Fullback
Derrick Deese: 1990–91; Offensive Guard
Clarke DeGroot: 1924–26; Tackle
John DeHetre: 1934, 1937; Center
Terry DeKraai: 1968–69; Split End
Gary Delaney: 1960; Guard
J.P. DeLappe: 1904
Bob deLauer: 1940–41; Tackle
Bruce Del Conte: 1962; Halfback
Jack Del Rio: 1981–84; Linebacker
Bobby Demars: 2001; Defensive End
Ed Demirjian: 1950; Quarterback
Edward Dempsey: 1938–40; Center
Eric Denmon: 1998–2000; Center
Hershel Dennis: 2002–07; Tailback
John Denvir: 1985; Offensive Guard
Vaughn Deranian: 1928–30; Guard
Gurjot Dhaliwal: 1998; Tight End
Rigo Diaz: 1988; Split End
Kori Dickerson: 1998–2001; Defensive End/Tight End/Linebacker
Sam Dickerson: 1968–70; Split End
Shelton Diggs: 1973–76; Flanker
Lawrence Dihel: 1926–27; End
Dean Dill: 1947–48; Quarterback
Ryan Dillard: 2012; Cornerback
Jeff Diltz: 1994–96; Tight End
Paul DiLulo: 1978–80; Fullback
Rich Dimler: 1975–78; Defensive Tackle/Nose Guard
Giovanni Di Poalo: 2010–12; Center
Art Dittberner: 1933–35
Joe Dixon: 1984; Middle Linebacker
Don Doll: 1944, 1946–48; Offensive Back/Defensive Back

Chet Dolley: 1922–24; Quarterback
John Dominis: 1941, 1943; Halfback/End
Dan Donahue: 1967–68
Rob Dooley: 2012; Safety
Monte Doris: 1971–73; Defensive End/Nose Guard
Dick Dorsey: 1957; End
Gene Dorsey: 1923–26; End
David Dotson: 1993–94; Tailback
Harold Dougher: 1922; Guard
Morton Dougherty: 1902; End
Don Douglas: 1957–58; End
Rome Douglas: 1996–98; Offensive Tackle
Kevin Downey, Jr.: 2012; Tight End
Bob Downs: 1948–50; Guard
Chris Doyle: 2002; Offensive Line
Don Doyle: 1940; Guard
John Drake: 2003–04; Offensive Tackle/Offensive Line/Offensive Guard
Ronald Drake: 1966–67; Split End
Travis Draper: 2004–06; Offensive Line/Defensive Line
Milford Dreblow: 1943–46; Defensive Back/Running Back
Morley Drury: 1925–27; Halfback
Phillip Duboski: 1936–39; Halfback
J.J. Dudum: 1991; Kicker
Pat Duff: 1949–51; Halfback
Marshall Duffield: 1928–30; Quarterback
Warren Dunaway: 1934; Guard
Brodie Dunn: 1967; Center
Coye Dunn: 1936
Corwin Dunning: 1932; Center
Reginald Dupuy: 1922–24; Guard
Alex Duran: 1991–92; Defensive Tackle/Offensive Guard
Harvey Durkee: 1928–29, 1931; End
Sandy Durko: 1967–69; Safety
Gordon Duvall: 1953–55; Fullback
George Dye: 1929; Center
John Dye: 1931–33; Guard
William Dye: 1933–34; Guard
Bruce Dyer: 1969–71; Split End
Daniel Anthony DyQuisto: 1988–89; Defensive Back
Raymond Earle: 1923–25; Halfback
Phillip Eaves: 2001–02; Offensive Tackle
Chuck Ebertin: 1985–88; Offensive Tackle
Andy Eddy: 1985; Fullback
Harry Edelson: 1927–29; Halfback
E.O. Edgarton: 1896; Fullback
Bob Edwards: 1958–59; Center
Dennis Edwards: 1978–81; Defensive Tackle
Hugh Edwards: 1925; End
Mel Edwards: 1957, 1959; Fullback
Dirk Eldredge: 1955; Center
Carl Elliot: 1904–06
Dick Elliott: 1965; Quarterback
E. Elliot: 1893; Halfback
Earl Elliot: 1904; Fullback
Howard Elliott: 1925–27; Quarterback
Ian Elliott: 1941; Halfback
Sedrick Ellis: 2004–07; Defensive Tackle
Kevin Ellison: 2005–08; Defensive Back/Safety
Rhett Ellison: 2007–11; Defensive Back
Riki Ellison: 1978–82; Linebacker
John Elmore, Jr.: 1914; Fullback
Aaron Emanuel: 1985–89; Tailback
Albert Embree: 1889; Guard
Richard Emmons: 1922; End
Roy Engle: 1937–39; Halfback
Dick Enright: 1954–56; Guard/Tackle
Robert Erickson: 2006–09; Defensive Back
Bob Eriksen: 1969–71; Defensive End
Robert Erskine: 1931–33; Tackle
Anthony Ervin: 1985; Defensive Tackle
Ricky Ervins: 1987–90; Tailback
Douglas Essick: 1941–42, 1946; End/Halfback
Charlie Evans: 1969–70; Fullback
John Evans: 1943
R. Evans: 1917
Vince Evans: 1974–76; Quarterback
Rod Everling: 1967; Defensive Tackle
Landon Exley: 1953; Quarterback
Walt Failor: 1968–70; Split End
Hebron Fangupo: 2009–10; Defensive Tackle
Salo Faraimo: 2003; Linebacker
Justin Fargus: 2002; Tailback
Mark Farlin: 1994, 1996; Fullback
Dave Farmer: 1973–76; Wide Receiver
George Farmer: 2011–12; Split End
Greg Farr: 2002–04; Defensive Back
Jim Fassel: 1969–70; Quarterback
Steve Fate: 1971–72; Rover/Defensive Back
Kenneth Fay: 1931–33; Halfback
Claude Ferguson: 1902; Quarterback
James Ferguson: 1972; Cornerback
Jim Ferguson: 1966–67; Linebacker/Center
Orlando Ferrante: 1953–55; Guard
John Ferraro: 1943–44, 1946–47; Tackle
Lou Ferrigno, Jr.: 2006; Linebacker
Craig Fertig: 1961–64; Quarterback
Dan Ficca: 1958–60; Tackle
Alfred Fidel: 1959
Reg Fielder: 1967; Middle Guard
Scott Fields: 1992–95; Safety
Gary Finneran: 1957–59; Tackle
Hal Finney: 1942
Frank Fiorentino: 1956–58; Guard
Jeff Fisher: 1977–80; Cornerback
Bill Fisk: 1937–39; End
Gary Fite: 1965; Fullback
James FitzPatrick: 1983–85; Offensive Tackle
Tom Fitzpatrick: 1969; Fullback
Miguel Fletcher: 2001; Tailback
Oliver Fletcher: 1948; End
Paul Fletcher: 1905–06
Ron Fletcher: 1954–56; Tackle
Sandy Fletcher: 2000–03; Wide Receiver/Safety
Fay Flint: 1903; End
Jeff Flood: 1973, 1975; Center
Bob Floro: 1959–60; Tackle
De'Von Flournoy: 2009–12; Wide Receiver
W. Floyd: 1897; Holder
Dennis Fluet: 1965; Center
Shane Foley: 1989–90; Quarterback
George Follett: 1971–72; Defensive Tackle/Defensive Guard
Chris Foote: 1977–79; Center
Cole Ford: 1991–94; Kicker
Dwight Ford: 1974–76, 1978; Tailback
Lonnie Ford: 1998–2001; Defensive End/Tight End
William Ford: 1926, 1928; Quarterback/Fullback
Chris Fornataro: 2008; Running Back
Roy Foster: 1978–81; Offensive Guard
Ed Fouch: 1952–54; Tackle
John Fouch: 1949–50; Halfback
Jack Fox: 1926–27; Center
John Fox: 1915–16, 1919; Tackle
John Fox: 1997, 1999; Linebacker/Tight End/Quarterback
Herman Franklin: 1969; Cornerback
Scott Fraser: 1977, 1979; Offensive Guard
George Freeman: 1921–23; Tackle
Luke Freeman: 2010–12; Linebacker
Scott Freier: 1987–89; Tight End/Center/Offensive Guard
Martin French: 1985; Cornerback
Bill Friend: 1924–26; Tackle
Gene Fruge: 1987–90; Defensive Guard/Nose Guard
Bill Fudge: 1972–73; Fullback
Bob Fuhrer: 1932–34; End
Seymour Fuhrman: 1941–42; Tackle
J.B. Funk: 1894; Back
Lou Futrell: 1948; Halfback
C.J. Gable: 2006–10; Tailback
Derrick Gachett: 1985–88; Fullback
Stuart Gage: 1993–95; Defensive Tackle
Bill Gaisford: 1935–36

Scott Galbraith: 1986–89; Tight End
Michael Gale: 1961–62; Tackle
Charles Galindo: 1925; Fullback
Chris Galippo: 2007–11; Linebacker
Allen Gallaher: 1970–72; Offensive Tackle/Offensive Guard
Ron Gallaher: 1969; Tight End
Darren Gallaway: 1991–93; Defensive End/Offensive Guard
George Galli: 1953–55; Guard
Amor Galloway: 1921–22; Quarterback
Clark Galloway: 1927–29; Guard
Harold Galloway: 1918, 1922; Fullback
Jeremy Galten: 2011–12; Offensive Tackle/Offensive Guard
Glen Galvin: 1936–39
Dan Garcia: 1978–79; Wide Receiver
Cal Garland: 1966–67; Guard
Donald Garlin: 1944, 1946–48; Halfback
Dwayne Garner: 1986–89; Cornerback
Troy Garner: 1997; Wide Receiver
David Garness: 2011–12; Offensive Tackle
Nick Garratt: 2005–09; Linebacker
Mike Garrett: 1963–65; Tailback
Norberto Garrido: 1992–95; Offensive Tackle
Edesel Garrison: 1969, 1971–72; Split End
Mike Garzoni: 1943–46; Guard
Lynn Gaskill: 1959–61; Halfback
Phil Gaspar: 1937–39; Tackle
Chris Gatena: 2008; Tight End/Center/Offensive Tackle
William Gay: 1975–77; Tight End
Michael Gaytan: 1991; Offensive Tackle/Offensive Guard
Doug Gee: 1945; Fullback
Matt Gee: 1988–91; Inside Linebacker
Roscoe Geller: 1908–09
Dick Genther: 1950; Fullback
Byron Gentry: 1930–32; Guard
Greg George: 1967, 1969–70; Linebacker
Raymond George: 1936–38; Tackle
Kamaron Germany: 2011; Tailback
Ben Gerpheide: 1923; End
Louis Gerpheide: 1923; Halfback
Bob Getz: 1932; Fullback
Anthony Gibson: 1979–80, 1982; Tailback
Craig Gibson: 1990–93; Center
David Gibson: 1996–99; Defensive Back
Don Gibson: 1987–90; Defensive Guard/Nose Guard
Mike Giers: 1963–64; Tackle
Cody Gifford: 2011; Wide Receiver
Frank Gifford: 1949–51; Halfback/Quarterback
Al Giguette: 1904–05
Robert Girogetti: 1969; Flanker
James Givehand: 1972; Defensive End
William Glenn: 1922; End
John Gobel: 1949–50; End
Winston Goller: 1949–51; End
Alex Gomez: 2002–05; Defensive Back
Jesse Gomez: 1995; Center
Mark Gomez: 2001; Tailback
Stan Gonta: 1962; Guard
Harold Goodenow: 1906–08
Adam Goodman: 2007–09; Running Back
Rashaad Goodrum: 2004–06; Defensive Line
Nathan Goodson: 2001; Defensive End
Clifford Gordon: 1920–21; End
Len Gorecki: 1992; Offensive Tackle
Walt Gorrell: 1955–56; Center
Marv Goux: 1952, 1954–55; Linebacker/Center
Robert Gowder: 1927–29; Guard
Ken Grace: 1993–94; Wide Receiver
Jerry Gracin: 1934
Steve Grady: 1965–67; Defensive Back
Tyler Grady: 2010–11; Defensive Tackle
Allan Graf: 1970–72; Offensive Guard
Derek Graf: 2001–02; Center/Offensive Guard
Kevin Graf: 2009–12; Offensive Tackle
Aaron Graham: 1999–2002; Linebacker
Jason Grain: 1997–99; Offensive Guard
Hank Gramberg: 1950; Tackle
John Grant: 1970–72; Defensive Tackle
Jermyah Graves: 2005; Defensive Line
Bill Gray: 1943; Linebacker/Offensive Line
Gordon Gray: 1943–44, 1946–47; End
John Gray: 1889, 1893; Fullback
Ken Gray: 1972–74; Fullback
William Gray: 1943; Center
Brad Green: 1979; Center
Broderick Green: 2007–08; Running Back
Edward Green: 1923–24; Halfback
Garrett Green: 2006–09; Quarterback/Safety
J.B. Green: 2009; Wide Receiver
Leonard Green: 1994–95; Tailback
Max Green: 1939–41; Halfback
Paul Green: 1985–88; Tight End
Tim Green: 1983–84; Quarterback
Kevin Greene: 2009–12; Outside Linebacker
Paul Greene: 1920–21
Chuck Greenwood: 1953–54; End
Mike Gregg: 1967; Defensive Tackle
Everson Griffen: 2007–09; Defensive Line
Frank Griffin: 1988–90; Tight End
John Griffin: 2003–06; Running Back
Chuck Griffith: 1954–55; End
Homer Griffith: 1931–33; Quarterback
Xavier Grimble: 2010–12; Tight End
Jim Grissum: 1968, 1970; Defensive End/Outside Linebacker
Matt Grootegoed: 2001–04; Linebacker
Dan Gueguett: 1903
Greg Guenther: 2001–03; Tight End
John Guerrero: 1985–88; Offensive Guard
Nathan Guertler: 2010–12; Offensive Tackle
Jimmy Gunn: 1967–69; Defensive End
Walt Gurasich: 1955–57; Tackle
Ed Gutierrez: 1976–77; Outside Linebacker
Brian Haas: 1992–95; Linebacker
Boyd Hachten: 1948–49; Center
Pat Haden: 1972–74; Quarterback
H. Haddock: 1895
Jerry Hagy: 1957; Tackle
Charles Haigler: 1905–08
Chester Haigler: 1905–06
Richard Halderman: 1927; Center
Chris Hale: 1987–88; Cornerback
D. Hale: 2001–03; Wide Receiver
Elmer Hall: 1888; Back
Frank Hall: 1954–56; Quarterback
Patrick Hall: 2010–11; Safety
Travis Hall: 1996; Tight End
Willie Hall: 1970–71; Defensive End
Tom Hallock: 1983–85; Offensive Guard
Clayton Halloway: 1914–15; Quarterback
Mike Haluchak: 1968–70; Linebacker
Ray Halvorsen: 1936; Guard
Tom Hamilton: 1948; Center
William Hamilton: 1904–05
Wright Hamilton: 1917; End
Harold Hammack: 1929–31; Halfback
Clint Hampton: 1981–82; Defensive Tackle/Nose Guard
Harold Han: 1952–53; Fullback
Brandon Hance: 2003–04; Quarterback
Brandon Hancock: 2002–06; Fullback
Mike Hancock: 1972–73; Defensive Tackle/Nose Guard
Simeon Hanes: 1914; Guard
Travis Hannah: 1989–92; Flanker
H.J. Hansch: 1924
Ellis Hansell: 1981; Cornerback
Owen Hanson: 2003–04; Tight End
James Harbin: 2010–11; Cornerback
Donald Hardy: 1943–44, 1946; End
Jim Hardy: 1942–44; Quarterback
Jacob Harfman: 2009–10; Punter/Kicker
David Harlan: 1932–33; Tackle
Pat Harlow: 1987–90; Defensive Tackle
Daniel Harper: 2007–10; Defensive Back/Cornerback

Hueston Harper: 1932–34; Guard
Michael Harper: 1979–80, 1982–83; Tailback
Andy Harrah: 1983
Antoine Harris: 1997–2000; Tight End
Antoinne Harris: 1999; Cornerback
Cary Harris: 2005–08; Defensive Back/Cornerback
DaJohn Harris: 2007–11; Defensive Line
Lou Harris: 1969–71; Tailback
Torin Harris: 2009–12; Cornerback
Will Harris: 2005–09; Defensive Back/Safety/Cornerback
Quincy Harrison: 1994–95; Cornerback
Billy Hart: 2001–04; Quarterback
Justin Hart: 2005–09; Defensive Back
Speedy Hart: 1980; Wide Receiver
T.J. Jake Hart: 1964–65; Guard
Craig Hartsuyker: 1987–90; Outside Linebacker
Carter Hartwig: 1976–78; Cornerback
Clarence Harvey: 1945
John Harvey: 1981–82; Defensive Tackle
Tom Harwood: 2005; Quarterback
H. Hasen: 1902; Back
David Haskell: 1940; End
R. Haslam: 1896; Back
Ken Haslip: 1995–98; Cornerback
William Hatch: 1908; Tackle
Hal Hatfield: 1948–50; End
Clay Hattabaugh: 1991–92, 1994–95; Center/Offensive Guard
Bill Hattig: 1950–52; End
Stanley Havili: 2006–10; Running Back/Fullback
John Hawkins: 1922–24; Tackle
William Hawkins: 1930; Center
Addison Hawthorne: 1952–53; Fullback
Jim Hayes: 1952–53; End
Luther Hayes: 1958–60; End
Michael Hayes: 1977, 1979; Wide Receiver
Norm Hayes: 1949; Guard
Windrell Hayes: 1998–99; Wide Receiver
Bill Hayhoe: 1965–68; Split End
Jerry Hayhoe: 1964–66; Tackle
Tommy Haynes: 1983–84; Cornerback
Matt Hayward: 2001–03; Linebacker/Long Snapper
Vidal Hazelton: 2006–08; Wide Receiver
Blake Headley: 1944
Zack Heberer: 2006–10; Offensive Line
Zuri Hector: 1989–92; Safety
Andre Heidari: 2011–12; Kicker
Ed Heidental: 1949; Tackle
Sylvester Heinberg: 1945
Michael Helfrich: 2009; Safety
Ron Heller: 1962–64; Fullback
Deryl Henderson: 1985–86; Defensive Tackle
James Henderson: 1935–36; End
Ryan Henderson: 2011–12; Cornerback
Trey Henderson: 2007–08; Defensive Line
Robert Hendren: 1946–48; Tackle
Ed Henke: 1948; Tackle/Center
Jerald Henry: 1991–94; Cornerback
Ken Henry: 1985–87; Split End
Mike Henry: 1956–58; Tackle
John Herpin: 1992–94; Cornerback
Errick Herrin: 1994–95; Linebacker
Thomas Herring: 2005–08; Offensive Line
Lloyd Hershberger: 1924–26; Guard
Rob Hertel: 1974–77; Quarterback
Edward Hervey: 1993–94; Wide Receiver
Orie Hester: 1917, 1919,1921; Guard
John Heydenreich: 1950; Guard
Christian Heyward: 2011–12; Defensive Tackle
Ralph Heywood: 1941–43; Punter/End
Gene Hibbs: 1935–37
Jesse Hibbs: 1926–28; Tackle
Don Hickman: 1955–56; Halfback
Donnie Hickman: 1974–76; Offensive Guard
Harry Hicks: 1923; Guard
Clark Higgins: 1944; Tackle/Guard
Arthur Hill: 1909–10
DeShaun Hill: 2000–02; Defensive Back/Safety/Cornerback
Fred Hill: 1962–64; Defensive Back/ End
Gary Hill: 1962–64; Defensive Back/Halfback
Hillard Hill: 1956, 1958
Jeffery Hill: 2001; Fullback
Jess T. Hill: 1928–29; Halfback
Prentice Hill: 1995–98; Cornerback
Matt Hillier: 2008; Fullback
Jonathan Himebauch: 1994–97; Center
Lew Hindley: 1939–41; End
Rocky Hinds: 2004; Quarterback
C.J. Hinman: 1893, 1896–97; Tackle
Charles Hinton: 1971–72; Tailback/Cornerback
Mike Hinz: 1990–93; Nose Tackle
Eric Hipp: 1979–80; Kicker
Cyrus Hobbi: 2011–12; Center
Bryce Hodges: 1941–42; Tackle
Bob Hoffman: 1937–39; Halfback
John Hoffman: 1965; Tight End
Doug Hogan: 1973–75; Defensive Back
Jeremy Hogue: 1992–95; Offensive Guard
Clark Holden: 1957–59; Halfback
Dave Holden: 1984; Offensive Tackle
Jess Holguin: 1995; Running Back
Bill Holland: 1969–71; Fullback
Chas Holland: 1897; Guard
Jamere Holland: 2006; Wide Receiver
Thomas Holland: 1991–93; Defensive Tackle/Nose Guard
Lamont Hollinquest: 1988–89, 1991–92; Strong Safety
William Holman: 1902; Back
Alex Holmes: 2000–04; Tight End
Calvin Holmes: 1988–91; Tailback/Cornerback
Khaled Holmes: 2008–12; Offensive Guard
Mike Holmgren: 1967–69; Quarterback
Leroy Holt: 1986–89; Fullback
Jim Homan: 1965–66; Guard
Bob Hooks: 1951–52; End
Roger Hooks: 1954; Quarterback
Phil Hoover: 1961–62/ End
Neil Hope: 1981–84; Inside Linebacker
Marcus Hopkins: 1988–90; Safety
Darrel Hopper: 1982–84; Cornerback
Tarriel Hopper: 1993–95; Linebacker
Randy Hord: 1988–89; Defensive Guard/Nose Guard
Shane Horton: 2008–11; Safety
Wes Horton: 2008–12; Defensive End
Hudson Houck: 1962–64; Center
Dick Hough: 1966; Quarterback
Joe Houston: 2007–10; Kicker
Bill Howard: 1957; Halfback
Chris Howard: 2001; Tailback
Mike Howell: 1973–75; Tight End
Nick Howell: 2005–09; Offensive Line
Pat Howell: 1976–78; Offensive Guard
Lindsay Hubby: 1953, 1956–57; End
Scott Huber: 1999–2002; Tight End/Fullback
Tyrone Hudson: 1969–70; Cornerback/Safety
Tommy Huff: 2001–03; Punter
Jack Hughes: 1904–05
John Hughes: 1923
Mike Hull: 1965–67; Fullback
Rod Humenuik: 1956–57; Tackle
Edward Hummell: 1910; End
Loran Hunt: 1961–63; Halfback
Paul Hunt: 1917
Herbert Hunter: 1917–18; Fullback
James Hunter: 1978–80; Tight End
Keith Hunter: 1921
Mike Hunter: 1965–66; Safety
Joe Hurst: 1933–34; End
Harold Huyck: 1916
Ted Iacenda: 1997; Fullback
Sydney Ickes: 1908–09; Quarterback
Israel Ifeanyi: 1994–95; Defensive End/Outside Linebacker

Bob Isaacson: 1954–56; Fullback
Bill Isenhouer: 1919–20
Ed Isherwood: 1956–57; Fullback
Austin Jackson: 2001; Linebacker
Duaine Jackson: 1981–84; Cornerback
Jabari Jackson: 1998–99; Tailback
James Jackson: 1990–92; Cornerback
John Jackson: 1986–89; Flanker
Lawrence Jackson: 2004–07; Defensive End
Malik Jackson: 2008–09; Defensive End
Melvin Jackson: 1973–75; Linebacker
Sean Jackson: 2011; Cornerback
Vic Jackson: 1976; Fullback
Yonnie Jackson: 1989–92; Tight End
Walter Jacobsmeyer: 1942; End
Alec Jaffe: 2011–12; Tailback
George James: 1914
Dick Jamison: 1941–42; Halfback
Jim Jansen: 1946; Center
Bill Jaroncyk: 1966–67; Cornerback
Dwayne Jarrett: 2004–06; Wide Receiver
Cedric Jefferson: 1994–97; Defensive Tackle
Bill Jenkins: 1969; Cornerback
Bob Jensen: 1967–69; Linebacker
Robert Jensen: 1930; Guard
Erick Jepsen: 2011–12; Center
Bill Jessup: 1948–50; End
Gary Jeter: 1973–76; Defensive Tackle
Charley Johnson: 1916
Dennis Johnson: 1977–79; Linebacker
Eddie Johnson: 1971–72; Cornerback
Jahi Johnson: 1997; Tailback
Kendrick Johnson: 1916
Keyshawn Johnson: 1994–95; Wide Receiver
Marcus Johnson: 2001–02; Cornerback
Matt Johnson: 1982–85; Cornerback
Paul Johnson: 1964–65; Center
Ricky Johnson: 1977, 1979; Fullback
Rob Johnson: 1991–94; Quarterback
Ron Johnson: 1973; Defensive Back
Ronald Johnson: 2007–10; Wide Receiver
Skip Johnson: 1960–61; Center
Stafon Johnson: 2006–09; Running Back
Tom Johnson: 1962–63; Guard
C.J. Johnston: 1904
E. Johnston: 1918
Rex Johnston: 1956–58; Halfback
A.E. Jones: 1889; End
Bob Jones: 1939–41; End
Derrick Jones: 2004; Wide Receiver
Don Jones: 1980; Cornerback
Ernie Jones: 1961–63; Fullback
Herbert Jones: 1915
James Jones: 1936–38; Halfback
Jarvis Jones: 2009; Outside Linebacker
Jimmy Jones: 1969–71; Quarterback
Marshall Jones: 2007–11; Running Back
Michael Jones: 1991–92; Fullback
Philo Jones: 1895–96
Randy Jones: 1962; Tackle
Robert Jones: 1897
Shannon Jones: 1990, 1992–93; Defensive End/Inside Linebacker
Frank Jordan: 1977–78; Kicker
Matthew Jordan: 2005–08; Defensive Back
Steve Jordan: 1981–84; Kicker
Ellwood Jorgenson: 1932, 1934–35; Center/Tackle
Vincent Joseph: 2006–07; Defensive Back/Cornerback
Clarence Joslin: 1917
Martin Juhnke: 1946; Center
Anthony Jurich: 1929, 1932
Winston Justice: 2002–03, 2005; Offensive Tackle
Morton (Mort) Kaer: 1924–26; Halfback
Bob Kaiser: 1965–66; Defensive Back
Ryan Kaiser: 2000–01; Wide Receiver
Matt Kalil: 2008–11; Offensive Tackle
Ryan Kalil: 2003–06; Center
Pete Kalinich: 1939
John Kamana: 1980–83; Wide Receiver/Fullback
Brett Kan: 2010; Quarterback
Kolomona Kapanui: 2001; Tight End
Michael Kaprillian: 1910; Tackle
Don Kasten: 1955, 1957–58; Fullback
John Katnik: 1986–87; Center
John Katnik: 2011–12; Center/Offensive Guard
Kurt Katnik: 2002–04; Offensive Line
Norm Katnik: 2001–03; Offensive Line
George Katrib: 2012; Wide Receiver
Uona Kaveinga: 2008–09; Linebacker
Ludwig Keehn: 1955–56; End
Jason Keiderling: 1993; Offensive Tackle
Stewart Kellar: 1909–10
Dallas Kelley: 2011–12; Middle Linebacker
Brian Kelly: 1994–97; Defensive Back
Fred Kelly: 1914–16; Fullback
Kareem Kelly: 1999–2002; Wide Receiver
Robert Kelly: 1957; Tackle
Sean Kelly: 2003–05; Wide Receiver
Rockwell Kemp: 1927–29; Quarterback
Donta Kendrick: 1998–99; Offensive Guard
Matt Keneley: 1993–96; Defensive Tackle
Todd Keneley: 1999; Defensive Tackle
Devon Kennard: 2009–12; Defensive End/Outside Linebacker
Hubie Kerns: 1946; Halfback
J.T. Kerr: 2012; Tight End
Rob Kerr: 1977–79; Kicker
Cody Kessler: 2011–12; Quarterback
Eddie Keyes: 1980; Cornerback
Fred Khasigian: 1967–69; Guard
Allen Kidder: 1934–35
Ryan Killeen: 2002–04; Kicker
Patrick Kim: 2010–11; Offensive Guard
Arthur King: 1921
Eddie King: 1963, 1965–66; Linebacker
Harold King: 1967; Defensive Tackle
Marty King: 1977–78; Punter
Jack Kirby: 1946–48; Halfback
Al Kirkland: 1952; Halfback
Gary Kirner: 1962–63; Tackle
David Kirtman: 2001–05; Fullback/Tailback
Ellsworth Kissinger: 1954–56; Quarterback
Bob Klein: 1966–68; Tight End
Gary Klein: 1984–85; Safety
Quentin Klenk: 1939–40; Tackle
Darryl Knight: 1998–2000; Linebacker
Ryan Knight: 1984–87; Tailback
Sammy Knight: 1993–96; Strong Safety
Tully Knoles: 1901–02; Quarterback
Steve Knutson: 1973–74; Offensive Tackle
Matt Koart: 1982–85; Defensive Tackle
Desmond Koch: 1951–53; Fullback/Punter
Tony Kochinas: 1965–66; Safety
Matt Koffler: 1994–96; Quarterback
Dong Koo: 1995; Offensive Guard
Jeff Kopp: 1991–94; Outside Linebacker/Inside Linebacker
John Kordich: 1948; Halfback
Pete Kovac: 1934
Rudy Kraintz: 1934; Fullback
Doug Kranz: 1955–56; Halfback
Darrell Kroll: 1942; Fullback
Al Krueger: 1938–40; End
Gaylord Kuamoo: 1984–85; Offensive Tackle
John Kubas: 1957; End
Gil Kuhn: 1934–36; Center
Chuck Kunsaitis: 1985; Offensive Tackle
Wayne Kurlak: 1954–56; Quarterback/Fullback
Alfred Kurle: 1910; Guard/Center
Zach Kusnir: 2010–12; Defensive End
Theodore Kutchel: 1921; Center
Darnell Lacy: 1996–98; Safety
George Lady: 1932–34; Tackle
Eugene Laisne: 1927–28; Halfback
Matt Lamb: 1983; Offensive Tackle/Offensive Guard

Grant LaMont: 1925
Charlie Landrigan: 1999–2001; Fullback
R.C. Lane: 1904–05
Lawrence Langley: 1935–36
Dave Langlois: 1982; Safety
Grenville Lansdell, Jr.: 1937–39; Quarterback
John Lanza: 2003–05; Offensive Line
Frank Lapham: 1888; Tackle
Myron Lapka: 1977–79; Defensive Tackle
Manuel Laraneta: 1924–26; Fullback
Ben Lardizabel: 1945, 1955–57; Guard
Duane Larrabee: 1933–34; End
Lawrence Larry: 1995–98; Defensive End/Linebacker
Chandler Larsen: 2011–12; Fullback
Tom Larsen: 1996
David LaVelle: 1943–44; Guard
Leslie LaVelle: 1926–27; End
Tim Lavender: 1978; Cornerback
Tim Lavin: 1990–91; Fullback
Jim Lawrence: 1965–68; Flanker
Gene Lawryk: 1976; Center
Aubey Layno-Moses: 2007; Wide Receiver
Jason Leach: 2001–04; Safety
John Leadingham: 1918–21; Fullback
Ed Leahy: 1920–22; Halfback
Bob Lee: 1924–26; Fullback
Devin Lee: 1983; Running Back
Jim Lee: 1971–72; Offensive Tackle/Defensive Tackle
Junior Lee: 1974–75; Split End
Larry Lee: 1980; Offensive Guard
Marqise Lee: 2011–12; Flanker/Kick Returner
Philip Lee: 1964–66; Defensive Back
Zephrini Lee: 1982–85; Tailback
Henry Lefebvre: 1923–25; Fullback
Brad Leggett: 1986–89; Offensive Guard
Steven Lehmer: 1967–69; Guard
Chuck Leimbach: 1954–56: End
Joe Leimbach: 1980–83; Center
Matt Leinart: 2002–05; Quarterback
Matt Lemos: 2001–03; Cornerback
Ryan Lenderman: 1993–94; Wide Receiver
Walter Lennox: 1904; Quarterback
Rich Leon: 1966; Split End
Steve Levario: 2003; Wide Receiver
Robert Levingston: 1959–60; Halfback
Dexter Levy: 1985–86; Cornerback
Butch Lewis: 2006–10; Offensive Line
Dave R. Lewis: 1974–76; Outside Linebacker
Mike Lewis: 1958
Whitney Lewis: 2003, 2005; Wide Receiver/Tailback
Harry Lillie: 1888; End
Verl Lillywhite: 1945–47; Fullback
Chris Limahelu: 1973–74; Kicker
Sean Limahelu: 2005; Punter
Irwin Lincoln: 1992–93; Cornerback
Logan Lindley: 1918–21; Guard
Lowell Lindley: 1920–22; Center
Tony Linehan: 1946–49; End
Dean Lingenfelter: 1971–73; Tight End
Leroy Littlejohn: 1942; Guard
Leonard Livernash: 1914–15
Scott Livingston: 1981; Punter/Kicker
Bryson Lloyd: 2009, 2012; Tight End
David Lloyd: 1944, 1947–48; End
William Lloyd: 1896; Halfback
Frank Lockett: 1919–21; Fullback
John Lockwood: 1964–65; Defensive End
Scott Lockwood: 1987–88, 1990–91; Fullback/Tailback
Dale Logie: 1974–75; Inside Linebacker
Frank Lopez: 1964–65: Guard
Karl Lorch: 1972; Defensive Tackle
Ray Lorentzon: 1907; End
Ronnie Lott: 1977–80; Safety
John Loustalot: 1923; Quarterback
Robert Love: 1932–33; End
Russ Lowell: 1947–48; Guard
Willie Lowery: 1993–96; Defensive End
Robert Loya: 1992–95; Center/Offensive Guard
Oscar Lua: 2002–06; Linebacker
Pete Lubisich: 1961–63; Guard
Al Lucas: 1920–21; Center
Jim Lucas: 1973–74; Defensive Back/Punter
Lawrence Lucas: 1914
Pete Lucas: 1917
Rick Luce: 1999; Safety
Brian Luft: 1981–84; Defensive Tackle/Nose Guard
Bruce Luizzi: 1989–92; Safety/Outside Linebacker
Le Valley Lund: 1914; Halfback
Tom Lupo: 1962–64; Defensive End/Kicker
Taitusi Lutui: 2004–05; Offensive Line
Ford Lynch: 1934–36; Fullback
Mike MacGillivray: 1998–2001; Punter
Doug MacKenzie: 1979–81; Fullback
Malaefou MacKenzie: 1997–2000, 2002; Fullback/Tailback
Doug MacLachlan: 1944; End
Robert MacMoore: 1935
Peter MacPhail: 1941–43; End
Tre Madden: 2011–12; Outside Linebacker
Gary Magner: 1965–67; Defensive Tackle
Elic Mahone: 1990–92, 1994; Defensive End/Tight End
Kaluka Maiava: 2005–08; Linebacker
Faaesea Mailo: 1996, 1999–2001; Offensive Tackle/Offensive Guard
John Malcolm: 1908–10; Guard
Duane Maley: 1940–41; Guard
Thomas Mallory: 1929–31; Halfback
Tom Malone: 2002–05; Punter
Al Maloney: 1930; Quarterback
Alatini Malu: 2004–07; Offensive Line
Robert Manker: 1923; Halfback
Ferdinand Manlove: 1925
Dick Manning: 1941–42, 1946; Fullback
John Manoogian: 2009–12; Quarterback
Lee Mantel: 1948; Tackle
Jim Maples: 1959–61
Greg Marderian: 1971, 1973–74; Defensive End
Jeff Maree: 1985–87; Safety
Andrew Marincovich: 1943
Marv Marinovich: 1959, 1961–62; Tackle
Todd Marinovich: 1988–90; Quarterback
Abe Markowitz: 2008–12; Center
Theodore Marks: 1915–16
Derrell Marshall: 1988; Offensive Tackle
George Marshall: 1915
Bill Martin: 1948–49; Fullback
G. Martin: 1895
Harry Lee Martin: 1893; Quarterback
Marcus Martin: 2011–12; Offensive Guard
Rod Martin: 1975–76; Outside Linebacker
John Martinez: 2009–12; Center
Edward Marxen: 1915
Marc Matock: 1996–98; Defensive Tackle
Eric Matranga: 2012; Wide Receiver
Bruce Matthews: 1979–82; Offensive Guard
Clay Matthews: 1974–77; Inside Linebacker
Clay Matthews: 2004–08; Linebacker
Garland Matthews: 1932–34; Quarterback
Kyle Matthews: 2001–03; Linebacker/Safety
Robert Matthews: 1938–40, 1942
Grant Mattos: 2001–02; Wide Receiver
Don Mattson: 1957; Tackle
Fred Matua: 2002–05; Center/Offensive Line/Offensive Guard
Rey Maualuga: 2005–08; Linebacker
Tom Maudlin: 1957–58; Quarterback
Ray May: 1965–66; Defensive End
Taylor Mays: 2006–09; Safety
John Mazur: 1981; Quarterback
Drew McAllister: 2008–12; Safety
Gary McArthur: 1967–69; Defensive Tackle
Mike McAuley: 1970; Defensive Back

Peter McBride: 2011–12; Long Snapper
Hilton McCabe: 1926–28; Center
Chris McCaffery: 2008; Quarterback
Bob McCaffrey: 1972–74; Center
Brent McCaffrey: 1998–2000; Offensive Tackle
Don McCall: 1965–66; Halfback
Fred McCall: 1941–42, 1946–47; Tackle
Mickey McCardle: 1942–43, 1946–47; Quarterback
Lawrence McCaslin: 1926–28; End
Bob McClanahan: 1980–81; Fullback
Rich McCombs: 1967; Split End
Steve McConnell: 1967–68; Guard
Pat McCool: 1980–82; Tight End
Walter McCormick: 1945–47; Center
Howard McCowan: 1990; Safety
Anthony McCoy: 2006–09; Tight End
Earl McCullouch: 1966–67; Safety/Receiver
Sultan McCullough: 1999–2002; Tailback
Mozique McCurtis: 2005–07; Cornerback
Daylon McCutcheon: 1995–98; Cornerback
Jack McDade: 1985–86; Inside Linebacker
Terry McDaniels: 1990–93; Defensive Tackle
Michael McDonald: 2004–07; Quarterback
Mike McDonald: 1976–79; Inside Linebacker
Paul McDonald: 1977–79; Quarterback
Tim McDonald: 1983–86; Safety
T.J. McDonald: 2009–12; Strong Safety
Dwight McFadden: 1992–93; Tailback
Don McFarland: 1954–55: End
Chris McFoy: 2002–06; Wide Receiver
Tom McGarvin: 1940; End
Bob McGee: 1949–50; Tackle
Willie McGinest: 1990–93; Defensive End/Outside Linebacker
Francis McGinley: 1931–32, 1934; Guard
John McGinn: 1944–45; Guard
Mike McGirr: 1970–71, 1973; Offensive Tackle/Defensive Tackle
Larry McGrew: 1976–79; Outside Linebacker
Tim McGuigan: 2010; Wide Receiver
Joe McGuire: 2001–02; Offensive Tackle/Offensive Guard
J.K. McKay: 1972–74; Wide Receiver
Erik McKee: 1984–86; Tight End
Marlin McKeever: 1958–60; Tight End
Mike McKeever: 1958–60; Guard
Harry McKinney: 1944–47; End
Joe McKnight: 2007–09; Running Back/Punt Returner
Kevin McLaughlin: 1997; Wide Receiver
Kevin McLean: 1984–87; Quarterback
Craig McMahon: 2010–12; Kicker
Rich McMahon: 1961–63; Fullback
Ryan McMahon: 2008–09; Safety
Dan McMillan: 1917, 1919
Paul McMurtry: 1948–50; Guard
Curtis McNeal: 2008–12; Tailback
Don McNeil: 1936–38; Center
Rod McNeill: 1970, 1972–73; Tailback
George McNeish: 1934–36; Center
Robert McNeish: 1931–33; Defensive Back/Halfback
Kevin McPartland: 1976; Defensive Tackle
Matt McShane: 1998–99; Center
Chase McWhorter: 2005–07; Defensive Back
Johnny McWilliams: 1993–95; Tight End
Matt Meikle: 1990; Cornerback
Jim Melillo: 1967; Tackle
Phil Mellinger: 2005; Kicker
Pete Mellos: 1957; Fullback
Salvador Mena: 1938–40; End
Bob Mendenhall: 1948; Guard
Ernie Merk: 1954–55; Halfback
Matt Meyer: 2008; Guard
John Michels: 1994–95; Offensive Tackle
Roger Mietz: 1957–60; Guard
Lawrence Miles: 2004–06; Defensive Line
Claude Millard: 1973; Offensive Tackle
Billy Miller: 1995–98; Wide Receiver
Bob Miller: 1965–68; Tight End
Bob Miller: 1973; Linebacker
Chris Miller: 1995–96; Wide Receiver
Jeff Miller: 2012; Defensive End
Jimmy Miller: 2004–08; Tight End
John Miller: 1953–55; Guard
Lloyd Miller: 1967; Cornerback
Reed Miller: 1902–05; Guard
Rick Miller: 1976; Offensive Tackle/Offensive Guard
Robert Miller: 1917; Halfback
Ron Miller: 1951–53; End
Pat Mills: 1965; Quarterback
Johnny Milton: 1921–22; End
Cliff Minkoff: 1991; Cornerback
Dale Mitchell: 1972–74; Defensive End/Outside Linebacker
Jason Mitchell: 2002–04; Wide Receiver
Marc Mitchell: 1980; Defensive Tackle
Sheppard Mitchell: 1903
Ron Mix: 1957–59; End/Tackle
Fili Moala: 2005–08; Defensive Tackle/Defensive Line
Orville Mohler: 1930–32; Quarterback
Junior Moi: 1991–92; Defensive End/Outside Linebacker
Robert Mojica: 2012; Running Back
Ahmed Mokhtar: 2009; Fullback/Tailback
Jerry Mollett: 1959–60; Fullback
Jerry Moloney: 1949–50; Halfback
Jim Monson: 1948–49; Guard
Marv Montgomery: 1969–70; Offensive Tackle
Emmanuel Moody: 2006; Running Back/Tailback
Michael Moody: 1988–91; Offensive Tackle
Mike Mooney: 1990, 1992; Fullback
Brent Moore: 1983–85; Defensive Tackle
Byron Moore: 2009; Cornerback
Darryl Moore: 1981–82; Offensive Tackle, Offensive Guard
Denis Moore: 1965–66; Defensive End
Jim Moore: 1949; Guard
Kenney Moore: 1978–80; Safety
Kyle Moore: 2005–08; Defensive End/Defensive Line
Malcolm Moore: 1979–81, 1983; Split End
Manfred Moore: 1971–73; Tailback
Rex Moore: 1984–87; Inside Linebacker
Zeke Moreno: 1997–2000; Linebacker
Boyd Morgan: 1936–38; Halfback
Dave Morgan: 1959–61; Center
D.J. Morgan: 2010–12; Tailback
John Morgan: 1999; Safety
Michael Morgan: 2006–10; Linebacker
Mike Morgan: 1969–71; Flanker
Daniel Morovick: 1976–79; Safety
Charles Morrill: 1938–40; Center
Pat Morris: 1975; Offensive Guard
Robert Morris: 1944; Halfback
Marion Morrison: 1926; Tackle
Robert Morrison: 1932; Fullback
Alex Morrow: 2003–07; Defensive Line
C.E. Mort: 1894–96; End/Tackle
Jesse Mortensen: 1928–29; Halfback
A.O. Morton: 1895, 1897; End
Chad Morton: 1996–99; Tailback/Safety/Cornerback
Johnnie Morton: 1990–93; Wide Receiver
Don Mosebar: 1979–82; Offensive Tackle
James Moser: 1925–27; Tackle
Charlie Moses: 1978; Outside Linebacker
Don Moses: 1927–29; Fullback
Greg Moses: 1971; Split End
Jonathan Mosley: 1997; Linebacker
Bob Moss: 1965; Fullback
Marv Motley: 1966; Halfback
Dave Moton: 1963–65; End
Steve Moyer: 1980; Offensive Tackle
Forrest Mozart: 2001–03; Wide Receiver

Will Mullen: 2007; Offensive Tackle
Ryan Muller: 2011; Linebacker
Gerry Mullins: 1968–70; Tackle/Tight End
Anthony Munoz: 1976–79; Offensive Tackle
George Murphy: 1944, 1946–48; Quarterback
Joe Murray: 1982; Offensive Guard
Philip Murray: 1915–16; Quarterback
Thomas Murray: 1934
Gidion Murrell: 1990–93; Inside Linebacker
Bill Musick: 1939–41; Fullback
Bob Musick: 1941–42, 1945–46; Quarterback/Fullback
Jackie Musick: 1944; Tackle/Guard
Jackie Musick: 1946; Guard
Jim Musick: 1929–31; Fullback
Mitch Mustain: 2008–10; Quarterback
Russ Nash: 1940–42; End
Craig Nason: 1923; Fullback
Johnny Naumu: 1946–47; Halfback
Sol Naumu: 1950–51; Fullback
Doyle Nave: 1938–39; Quarterback
Omar Nazel: 2000–03; Defensive End
Kyle Negrete: 2010–12; Punter/Linebacker
David Neidhardt: 1929; Center
Sid Neighbors: 1910; Fullback
Caleb Nelan: 2007; Wide Receiver
Bill Nelsen: 1960–62; Quarterback
Robert Nelson: 1940; Halfback
Drew Ness: 2008–09; Wide Receiver
Luis Nevarez: 2011–12; Safety
David Newbury: 1999–2001; Kicker
Kenneth Newert: 1923; Guard
P.H. Newman: 1893–95; Offensive Line
Wallace Newman: 1922–24; Guard
Anthoney Neyer: 2010–11; Quarterback
Hugh Nicholson: 1905–06; End
Matt Nickels: 1999–2000; Wide Receiver
Tom Nickoloff: 1951–53; End
Carl Nielsen: 1969; Tackle
Ryan Nielsen: 1998–2001; Defensive End/Defensive Tackle
Jack Nix: 1948–49; End
Lloyd Nix: 1915–16
Allen Noble: 2009–11; Cornerback
Bill Noble: 1941–42; Guard
Kevin Noble: 2010; Wide Receiver
Garrett Nolan: 2008–09; Offensive Line
Dennis Noor: 1936–37
Ron Nordstrom: 1951; Tackle
George Norene: 1930–31; Center
Hank Norman: 1982–85; Split End
Ash Norris: 1940; Tackle
Neil Norris: 1930–32; End
Francis Norton: 1928; Halfback
John Norton: 1888; Guard
Kendall Nungesser: 1966–67; Defensive Back
Dick Nunis: 1951–52; Halfback
Ronald Nunn: 2002–04; Cornerback
Larry Nunnally: 1975; Defensive Tackle
Paul Nyquist: 1965; Safety
Joe Obbema: 1967–69; Defensive End
Mike Ober: 1967; Linebacker
Rich Oberreuter: 1967, 1969; Guard
Jim Obradovich: 1973–74, 1976; Tight End
Bill O'Brien: 1973; Defensive Back
Nick O'Brovac: 1950; Guard
Juan Ochoa: 1905; Fullback
Brennan Ochs: 1997–2000; Fullback
Taylor Odegard: 2004–06; Punter
Ricky Odom: 1976–77; Cornerback
Kristopher O'Dowd: 2007–10; Offensive Line
Bernard Oertley: 1915
George Oertly: 1917–18
Newell Oestreich: 1946; Fullback
Steve O'Grady: 1977; Outside Linebacker
Ifeanyi Ohalete: 1997–2000; Linebacker/Safety
Pat O'Hara: 1988, 1990; Quarterback
Tony Olivarria: 1979; Fullback
Jason Oliver: 1990–93; Safety/Cornerback
Ralph Oliver: 1966–67; Middle Guard
Sherm Olmstead: 1971; Linebacker
Bill O'Malley: 2007–09; Punter
Jack O'Malley: 1965–68; Defensive Tackle
Gary Orcutt: 1968–69; Flanker
Aaron Orndorff: 2001; Linebacker
Vic Orsatti: 1925–26; Quarterback
Tony Ortega: 1956–58; Halfback
Gerald Ostling: 1933–34; End
Bobby Otani: 2001–03; Linebacker
Brad Otton: 1994–96; Quarterback
Henry Oudermeulen: 1924–25
Dan Owens: 1986–89; Nose Guard
James Owens: 1931, 1933; Quarterback
Stephon Pace: 1989–92; Safety
David Packard: 1932; Tackle
Holmes Packer: 1919
Whitey Packman: 1918
John Page: 1986–87; Offensive Tackle
Mike Page: 1957; Fullback
Otis Page: 1976–78; Offensive Tackle
Toby Page: 1965–67; Quarterback
Carson Palmer: 1999–2002; Quarterback
Ford Palmer: 1930–33; End
Fred Palmer: 1932; End
John Papadakis: 1969–71; Linebacker
Petros Papadakis: 1997–98, 2000; Tailback
Taso Papadakis: 1994, 1996; Fullback/Inside Linebacker
Bill Papanikolas: 1967; Cornerback
Nick Pappas: 1935–37; Quarterback
Artimus Parker: 1971–73; Safety
Larry Parker: 1994–96, 1998; Wide Receiver
Brent Parkinson: 1986–89; Offensive Guard
Bruce Parks: 1985–86; Center/Offensive Guard
Alex Parsons: 2006–09; Defensive Tackle
Charles Parsons: 1903–04; Tackle
Earle Parsons: 1942–43; Halfback
William Patapoff: 1943
Doug Patrick: 1964–65; Defensive Tackle
Bill Patten: 1955; Guard
Mike Patterson: 2001–04; Defensive Tackle
Travon Patterson: 2006–09; Wide Receiver
Marty Patton: 1973; Center
Harold Paulin: 1908–10
Frank Pavich: 1952–54; Guard/Tackle
Crawford Peake: 1925
Grant Pearsall: 1994–96, 1998; Safety
Angelo Peccianti: 1936, 1938; Fullback
Rodney Peete: 1985–88; Quarterback
John Pehar: 1944; Tackle
Al Pekarcik: 1971–72; Defensive Back
Robert Peoples: 1938–40; Fullback
Antwine Perez: 2006; Defensive Back/Safety
Chuck Perpich: 1955; End
Jay Perrin: 1946–47; Tackle
George Perry: 1994–97; Defensive End
John Perry: 1980; Punter
Nick Perry: 2008–11; Defensive End
Reggie Perry: 1992–93; Quarterback/Safety
Jerry Persinger: 1957–58; Fullback
Ray Peters: 1978; Center/Nose Guard
Volney Peters: 1948–50; Tackle
Chuck Peterson: 1948–49; Tackle
Larry Petrill: 1965–66; Middle Guard
Dick Petty: 1950, 1952–53; End/Center
Bob Peviani: 1950–52; Tackle/Guard
Ron Pharris: 1969; Tailback
Arthur Phelps: 1923
Charles Phillips: 1972–74; Defensive Back
Floyd Phillips: 1938–40; Guard
Jim Phillips: 1983; Defensive Back
Micah Phillips: 1992–95; Safety
Victor Phillips: 1925
Hayden Phythian: 1922–24; End
Fred Pierce: 1955; Halfback
Chad Pierson: 1999–2002; Fullback

Mel Pierson: 1946–47; Guard
Erny Pinckert: 1929–31; Halfback
Josh Pinkard: 2004–09; Defensive Back/Safety/Cornerback
Jahleel Pinner: 2012; Fullback
George Pitman: 1894; Tackle
Devin Pitts: 2001; Wide Receiver
Ivan Pivaroff: 1960–61; End
Alfred Plaehn: 1930–32; Tackle
K.C. Pola: 2010; Fullback
Kennedy Pola: 1982–85; Linebacker/Fullback
Troy Polamalu: 1999–2002; Linebacker/Safety
Kris Pollack: 1991–94; Offensive Guard
Marvin Pollard: 1988–91; Cornerback
Mike Pollard: 1998, 2000–02; Linebacker
Junior Pomee: 2011–12; Tight End
Steve Ponder: 1967; Defensive Tackle
Will Poole: 2003; Cornerback
John Porter: 1927–28; Guard
Vincent Porter: 1942, 1946; Fullback
Darryl Poston: 2001–02; Tailback
Gary Potter: 1962; End
Alfred Poulsen: 1933; Center
Phalen Pounds: 1994–95, 1997; Offensive Tackle/Offensive Guard
Ray Pourchot: 1946; End
Chris Pousson: 2008–11; Long Snapper
Ryan Powdrell: 2004–06; Linebacker
Ed Powell: 1972–74; Defensive End/Outside Linebacker
Marvin Powell: 1973–76; Tight End
Jim Powers: 1947–49; Quarterback
John Pranevicius: 1940–41; Guard
David Pratchard: 1996–98; Center/Offensive Guard
Kyle Prater: 2010–11; Wide Receiver
Pernel Pratt: 1897; Fullback
William Premo: 1895
Marc Preston: 1988–89; Punter
Rob Preston: 1978–79; Quarterback
Ron Preston: 1970; Linebacker
Bill Prindle: 1985; Safety
Cliff Propst: 1933–35; Fullback
Chris Prosser: 2000–02; Linebacker
Al Prukop: 1958–60; Quarterback
Dave Pryor: 1979–82; Punter
Jim Psaltis: 1951–52; Fullback
Ed Pucci: 1951–53; Guard
Ralph Pucci: 1948–50; Linebacker/Halfback
Allen Pugh: 1977–78, 1980; Defensive Tackle/Center/Offensive Guard
Hayes Pullard: 2010–12; Linebacker
Steve Pultorak: 1970; Defensive Tackle
Dave Purling: 1982–84; Defensive Tackle/Nose Guard
James Pursell: 1921–23; Guard
Christian Putnam: 2007–08; Offensive Line
Ernie Pye: 1962–64; Fullback
Marc Raab: 1990–91; Center
Chilo Rachal: 2004–07; Offensive Line
Drew Radovich: 2003–07; Offensive Line
Mike Rae: 1970–72; Quarterback
Terry Ragan: 1946; Halfback
Vic Rakhshani: 1978–80; Tight End/Flanker/Back
Theron Ramey: 1930; Guard
Kian Ramsay: 1989; Offensive Guard
Kyle Ramsay: 1992–95; Offensive Tackle/Offensive Guard
LaJuan Ramsey: 2002–05; Defensive End/Defensive Tackle/Defensive Line
Ken Randle: 1973, 1975–76; Split End
Walt Ransom: 1977–78; Quarterback
Vivian Rapp: 1914, 1916; Guard
John Ratliff: 1961–63; Guard
Sherman Ratliff: 1983–84; Inside Linebacker
Terrel Ray: 1967–68; Split End
Gordon Rayburn: 1924
John Rea: 1945–47; Guard
Lynn Reade: 1962; Guard
Pat Reagan: 1956–57; Guard
Michael Reardon: 2007–10; Defensive Line
Al Reboin: 1932–34; Quarterback
Silas Redd: 2012; Running Back
Bill Redding: 1967–69; Middle Guard
Clarence Reece: 1973; Split End
Danny Reece: 1973–75; Cornerback
Desmond Reed: 2003–07; Defensive Line
Dick Reed: 1945
Edgar Reed: 1888; Center
Eric Reese: 1999–2001; Tailback/Cornerback
Adam Rendon: 1995, 1997; Kicker
Bill Renison: 1964
Tim Rhames: 1973–75; Nose Guard
Brad Rice: 1973; Split End
Paul Rice: 1975; Halfback
Kris Richard: 1998–2001; Cornerback
Troy Richardson: 1983–85; Punter
Jonathan Richert: 2005–06; Offensive Line
Denis Richman: 1964; Tackle
Junior Rickman: 1994, 1996–97; Tight End/Offensive Guard
Bill Riddle: 1951–53; Quarterback
John Riddle: 1922–24; Halfback
Darrell Rideaux: 1999–2002; Cornerback
Gene Ridings: 1931–33; Fullback
Leo Riggs: 1946; Quarterback
Harold Rightmire: 1918; End
Art Riley: 1973–74; Defensive Tackle
Bernard Riley: 1999–2002; Defensive Tackle
Steve Riley: 1971–73; Offensive Tackle
Robert Rimes: 1902; Back
Bob Rippen: 1965; Center
Bert Ritchey: 1928, 1930; Fullback
Autin Rittenour: 2010; Linebacker
Keith Rivers: 2004–07; Linebacker
Ted Roberson: 1973–75; Cornerback
C.R. Roberts: 1955–56; Fullback
Gene Roberts: 1935; Guard
Trevor Roberts: 1999–2000; Offensive Tackle/Offensive Guard
Robert Robertson: 1939–41; Halfback
Wilbur Robertson: 1948–50; Quarterback
Nickell Robey: 2010–12; Cornerback
John Robinson: 1919–21; Tackle
Mike Robinson: 1976; Split End
Skip Robinson: 1967; Flanker
Thomas Robinson: 1888–89; Back
Don Rodeen: 1934–35
Marc Rodgers: 1988–90; Flanker/Split End
Francis Rodriguez: 1983; Split End
Quin Rodriguez: 1987–90; Kicker
Ray Rodriguez: 1972–73; Inside Linebacker
Boomer Roepke: 2009–11; Punter/Cornerback
Don Rogers: 1948–49; Halfback
Ed Rogers: 1934; Center
Jacob Rogers: 2000–03; Offensive Tackle
William Rojas: 2010; Cornerback
Bruce Rollinson: 1969–71; Safety/Cornerback
Alvin Romer: 1946; Tackle
Marshall Romer: 1943–44, 1946; Tackle
Cody Romness: 2010–11; Safety
Russell Roquet: 1940; Tackle
James Rorison: 1934–36; Tackle
Mason Rose: 1935
Aaron Rosenberg: 1931–33; Guard
Bob Rosendahl: 1955–56; End
Ben Rosin: 1959–61; End
Mike Ross: 2002–03; Defensive Back/Safety
Scott Ross: 1987–90; Inside Linebacker
Taylor Ross: 2011–12; Tailback
John Rossetto: 1946; Fullback
Tim Rossovich: 1965–67; Defensive End
Mike Roth: 1982; Center
Jay Roundy: 1947–49; Halfback
Alfred Rowe: 2006–07; Defensive Back
Mazio Royster: 1990–91; Tailback
Karl Rubke: 1955–56; Center
Frosty Rucker: 2003–05; Defensive End

Ken Ruettgers: 1982–84; Offensive Tackle
Jabari Ruffin: 2012; Linebacker
Grant Runnerstrum: 1989–90; Kicker
George Runyon: 1902; Guard
John Runyon: 1902–04; Back
Dick Ruppert: 1969–70; Offensive Tackle
Theodore Rusenhhaupt: 1908; Guard
Darrell Russell: 1994–96; Defensive Tackle
Sam Russo: 1923; Halfback
Mike Ryan: 1970–72; Offensive Guard
Richard Ryan: 1927; Halfback
Tim Ryan: 1986–89; Defensive Tackle
H.D. Ryus: 1899; Halfback
Jarrod Sabourin: 1983
Emon Saee: 2010–12; Quarterback
Eddie Saenz: 1943; Halfback
Mark Sager: 1985–88; Offensive Tackle
Larry Sagouspe: 1962–63; Linebacker/Center
Ted Sahiberg: 1925; Center
Paul Salata: 1944, 1946–47; End
Sean Salisbury: 1982–85; Quarterback
Mike Salmon: 1990–93; Safety/Cornerback
Ty Salness: 1964–67; Defensive End
Bill Samarin: 1948; Guard
Brett Sampiri: 1996; Offensive Tackle/Offensive Guard
Ben Sampson: 1950, 1952; Linebacker/Center
Vern Sampson: 1953–55; Center
Jim Samuel: 1960; Guard
Al Sanbrano: 1949–51; Guard
Armando Sanchez: 1962–63; Defensive Back/ Center
Mark Sanchez: 2005–08; Quarterback
Pete Sanchez: 1967; Quarterback
Anthony Sanford: 1995–96; Defensive Tackle
Mike Sanford: 1973–75; Quarterback/Free Safety
William Sangster: 1937–39; Fullback
Anthony Sarao: 2011–12; Outside Linebacker
Hugh Sargent: 1940–41, 1949; Guard
Dallas Sartz: 2002–06; Outside Linebacker
Russ Saunders: 1927–29; Fullback
Bill Savoy: 1940; Halfback
Mike Scarpace: 1965–67; Guard/Tackle
Gus Schabre: 1922; Guard
Alvin Schaub: 1926–28; Halfback
Teddy Schell: 1983
Albert Scheving: 1925–27; Tackle
Bob Schildmeyer: 1941; End
Ambrose Schindler: 1936–39; Quarterback
Nick Schlossberg: 2012; Linebacker
Denny Schmidt: 1962; Center
Henry Schmidt: 1955; Tackle
Dean Schneider: 1949–51; Quarterback
John Schuhmacher: 1976–77; Offensive Tackle
William Schultz: 1989; Offensive Tackle
George Schutte: 1946–48; Tackle
Jeff Schweiger: 2004–06; Defensive End/Defensive Line
Eric Scoggins: 1977–80; Outside Linebacker
Dan Scott: 1966–68; Fullback
Doug Scott: 2011–12; Linebacker
Joe Scott: 1945, 1949–50; Halfback
Joel Scott: 1989–92; Split End
Walter Scott: 1923–25
Willard Scott: 1967–69; Defensive Tackle
Jesse Scroggins: 2010–11; Quarterback
Jim Sears: 1950–52; Halfback
Wes Seastrom: 1948; End
Junior Seau: 1988–89; Linebacker
Jason Sehorn: 1992–93; Safety/Cornerback
William Seitz: 1928–29; Tackle
John Seixas: 1932–33; End
William Seixas: 1940–42; Guard
Leon Sellers: 1951–53; Fullback
Ewald Selph: 1909
Walter Semeniuk: 1946; Guard
Frank Sentous: 1918; Halfback
Rodney Sermons: 1994–97; Fullback/Tailback
Mike Serpa: 1985–88; Inside Linebacker
Jeff Serrano: 2010; Defensive End/Long Snapper
Rocky Seto: 1997–98; Linebacker
Joseph Seymour: 1902–03; End
Kevon Seymour: 2012; Cornerback
Don Shafer: 1985–86; Kicker
Kenneth Shannon: 1932–33; Halfback
Tim Shannon: 1980; Safety
Ryan Shapiro: 1999–2000; Linebacker
Bob Shaputis: 1971–73; Offensive Tackle
Gaius Shaver: 1929–31; Quarterback/Tailback/Fullback
Gerry Shaw: 1967–69; Rover/Safety
Jesse Shaw: 1928–30; Tackle
Josh Shaw: 2012; Safety
Nate Shaw: 1964–66; Defensive Back/Halfback
Pat Shea: 1960–61; Tackle
Joe Shell: 1937–39; Halfback
Devian Shelton: 2012; Cornerback
Arthur Sheppard: 1916
Rod Sherman: 1964–66; Halfback
Zach Sherwood: 2001–03; Punter
Alan Shields: 1959–60
George Shindler: 1921
Joe Shipp: 1977; Tight End
D.J. Shoemate: 2008–09; Wide Receiver
Pete Shubin: 1957; End
Edward Shuey: 1935; Guard
Eugene Shute: 1905–07
John Sigler: 1916; Guard
Antuan Simmons: 1997–99, 2001; Linebacker/Safety/Cornerback
Derek Simmons: 2006–10; Defensive Line
Hunter Simmons: 2009–12; Fullback
Jeff Simmons: 1979–82; Wide Receiver
Jordan Simmons: 2012; Offensive Tackle
Marquis Simmons: 2009–12; Outside Linebacker
Melvin Simmons: 2002–03; Linebacker
Vaughn Simmons: 1983–84
Randy Simmrin: 1975–77; Wide Receiver
Edward Simpson: 1915–16, 1919; Center
O.J. Simpson: 1967–68; Tailback
Jim Sims: 1972–73; Defensive End
Leonard Sims: 1965–66; Defensive Back
A.J. Single: 2001–02; Center
Forrest Single: 1910
Ken Skarg: 1966; Fullback
Cody Skene: 2011–12; Wide Receiver
John Skiles: 1970–71; Defensive Tackle
J. Skinner: 1907
Carl Skvarna: 1960–61; Kicker
Hank Slade: 1955; Guard
Tony Slaton: 1981–83; Center
James Slatter: 1937–39; Halfback
Greg Slough: 1969–70; Linebacker
Erroll Small: 1993–94; Outside Linebacker
Ron Smedley: 1961–62; Guard
Ben Smith: 1893; End
Brad Smith: 2007; Kicker
C.E. Smith: 1895
Charles Smith: 1889; Guard
Corby Smith: 1992; Quarterback/Holder
Ernie Smith: 1930–32; Tackle
Dennis Smith: 1977–80; Safety
George Smith: 1925; Center
Harry Smith: 1937–39; Guard
Herbert Smith: 1917
James Smith: 1918–21; End
Jeff Smith: 1964–65; Defensive End/Offensive Tackle
Larry Smith: 1983
Malcolm Smith: 2007–10; Linebacker
Martin Smith: 1969; Linebacker
Mike Smith: 1973–74; Offensive Guard
Pat Smith: 1996; Center
R. Smith: 1910
Robert Smith: 1934; Fullback
Roy Smith: 1954–55; Tackle
S. Smith: 1918; Halfback

Sid Smith: 1967–69; Tackle
Stanley Smith: 1932; Guard
Steve Smith: 2003–06; Wide Receiver
Tody Smith: 1969–70; Defensive Tackle
Tyron Smith: 2008–10; Offensive Tackle
Wil Smith: 2004–05; Wide Receiver
Huber Smutz: 1923; Center
Jim Snow: 1965–68; Linebacker
Frank Snyder: 1946; End
Jim Snyder: 1946–48; Guard
Steve Sogge: 1966–68; Quarterback
Ben Sohn: 1938–40; Guard
Art Sorce: 1977; Kicker
Glenn Souers: 1950; Fullback
R. Jay Soward: 1996–99; Wide Receiver
Matt Spanos: 2003–07; Defensive Line
Raymond Sparling: 1930–32; End
Ernest Spears: 1986–89; Cornerback
Raoul Spears: 1990–91; Fullback
Irwin Spector: 1953–54
Carl Speer: 1916
Todd Spencer: 1980–83; Tailback
Chris Sperle: 1985–88; Punter
Ty Sperling: 1977–79; Defensive Tackle/Nose Guard
Averell Spicer: 2005–09; Defensive Line
Spencer Spiegel: 2008–09; Safety
Edward Spraggins: 1934
Marc Springer: 1971; Linebacker
C.W. Sprott: 1914
Dallas Stahr: 1967; Linebacker
Ralph Stanley: 1936–38; End
Jim Stare: 1904
Jawanza Starling: 2009–12; Strong Safety
Scott Starr: 2012; Linebacker
Markus Steele: 1999–2000; Linebacker
Elijah Steen: 2012; Safety
Jason Steen: 1997; Defensive End/Linebacker
Barry Stephens: 1929–31; Halfback
Scott Stephens: 2006–09; Wide Receiver
Cooper Stephenson: 2006–09; Tight End
Warren Stephenson: 1960–61; Fullback
Tony Steponovich: 1927–29; End
Joseph Stall: 1946; Tackle
Harold Steele: 1975–76; Nose Guard
Todd Steele: 1983–86; Fullback
Jason Steen: 1998; Defensive End/Linebacker
Nate Steinbacher: 2000–03; Offensive Tackle
Lawrence Stevens: 1931–33; Guard
Edward Stevenson: 1936
Steve Stevenson: 1999–2001; Wide Receiver
Bill Stever: 1924
George Stewart: 1973–74; Defensive Tackle
Bob Stillwell: 1947–49; End
Don Stillwell: 1949–52; End
Bob Stirling: 1969–71; Center/Offensive Guard
Howard Stoecker: 1937–39; Tackle
Bill Stokes: 1986–87; Outside Linebacker
Jim Stone: 1970; Defensive End
Nicki Stone: 1983
Howard Stonebraker: 1938–39; End
John Stonehouse: 1992–95; Punter
Byron Stookey: 1906–07, 1909–10; Tackle
Jim Strangeland: 1942; End
Brad Streelman: 1978–79; Defensive Tackle/Nose Guard
Frank Strong: 1998–2001; Linebacker/Tailback/Safety
Deon Strother: 1990–93; Fullback/Tailback
Clint Strozier: 1975–76; Safety
Melvin Stuart: 1919
Michael Stuart: 2004; Linebacker
R. Stuart: 1916
Howard Studdard: 1977; Wide Receiver
Conner Sullivan: 2012; Quarterback
J.P. Sullivan: 1986–89; Defensive Tackle
Tim Sullivan: 1981–82; Inside Linebacker
James Sutherland: 1934–36
Bob Svihus: 1962–64; Guard/Tackle
Adam Swaney: 1989–90; Defensive Line
Lynn Swann: 1971–73; Flanker
Pat Swanson: 1997–99; Tight End
Steve Swanson: 1966–67; Linebacker
Calvin Sweeney: 1977–78; Wide Receiver/Flanker/Split End
Cordell Sweeney: 1986–89; Outside Linebacker
Frank Swirles: 1939–40; Quarterback
Jess Swope: 1948–49; Tackle
Duron Sylvester: 2006–08; Quarterback
Tom Tancredy: 1949–50
Ted Tannehill: 1945–47
Randy Tanner: 1984–87; Flanker
Francis Tappaan: 1927–29; End
Bernard Tarver: 1976; Fullback/Tailback
Herbert Tatsch: 1931, 1933–34; Tackle
Joshua Tatum: 2006; Linebacker
Lofa Tatupu: 2003–04; Linebacker
Mosi Tatupu: 1974–77; Fullback
J.R. Tavai: 2011–12; Defensive Tackle
Conrad Tavarez: 2010; Defensive Tackle
Art Taylor: 1917
Arthur Taylor: 1914; End
Brice Taylor: 1924–26; Guard
Mike Taylor: 1966–67; Defensive Tackle
Paul Taylor: 1941–42; Quarterback
Randall Telfer: 2010–12; Tight End
Greg Tellam: 1994, 1996; Defensive End
Cody Temple: 2011–12; Offensive Guard
George Templeton: 1927–29; Center
Tony Terry: 1967–69; Defensive Tackle
Cliff Thiede: 1929; Quarterback
Hal Thienes: 1957; End
Alonzo Thomas: 1970–71; Defensive Back
Christian Thomas: 2010–12; Defensive End/Tight End
Fay Thomas: 1923–24; Tackle
John Thomas: 1963–65; End
Kelly Thomas: 1981–82; Offensive Tackle
Kevin Thomas: 2005–09; Defensive Back/Cornerback
Lloyd Thomas: 1926–28; Halfback
Max Thomas: 1926–27; Fullback
Ronald Thomas: 1940–42; Guard
Terrell Thomas: 2003–07; Defensive Back
John Thomassin: 1937–39; Tackle
A.P. Thompson: 1893–95, 1897; Quarterback
Dale Thompson: 2004–07; Tight End
Ed Thompson: 1904; Center
Field Thompson: 1924–26; Halfback
Gordon Thompson: 1923; Guard
Ken Thompson: 1951–53; Tackle
Roderick Thompson: 1930–31; Tackle
Leavitt Thurlow: 1934–36; Tackle
Toby Thurlow: 1962; End
Dennis Thurman: 1974–77; Safety
Junior Thurman: 1985–86; Safety
Phillip Tiernan: 1920–22; Fullback
George Timberlake: 1952–53; Center
Curt Timmons: 1970–71; Cornerback
Brandon Ting: 2003–05; Defensive Back/Safety/Cornerback
Ryan Ting: 2003–05; Defensive Back/Safety/Cornerback
Scott Tinsley: 1979–82; Quarterback
Howard Tipton: 1930–32; Halfback
Joe Tisdale: 1955; Fullback
Christian Tober: 2012; Wide Receiver
William Tober: 2012; Cornerback
Hal Tobin: 1960–61; Fullback
Travis Tofi: 2003–06; Defensive Tackle/Defensive Line
Jeff Tola: 2004–05; Defensive Line
Dennis Tolbert: 1997; Defensive Tackle
Justin Tolliver: 2001–05; Cornerback
Ernie Tolman: 1946–48; End
Amerigo Tonelli: 1936–38; Guard
Andy Toolen: 1919–21
Spencer Torgan: 2001–03; Offensive Guard
Eric Torres: 2000–03; Offensive Tackle/Offensive Guard
Greg Townsend, Jr.: 2011–12; Defensive End

Ken Townsend: 1918–20
Tommie Townsend: 1998
Jerry Traynham: 1958–60; Halfback
Jack Treier: 1958–60; Center
Guy Troisi: 1955; Fullback
James Truher: 1928–29; End/Tackle
Phil Truman: 1965; Split End
Sam Tsagalakis: 1952–54; Halfback
Mark Tucker: 1987–90; Offensive Guard
Sam Tucker: 1893; End
Max Tuerk: 2012; Offensive Tackle
Ray Tufs: 1904
Titus Tuiasosopo: 1990–92; Offensive Guard
Brian Tuliau: 1987–90; Inside Linebacker
Christian Tupou: 2007–11; Defensive Line
Joe Turner: 1980–81; Cornerback
Patrick Turner: 2005–08; Wide Receiver
Ryan Tyiska: 1994–97; Linebacker
Jerome Tyler: 1982–85; Safety
Marc Tyler: 2008–11; Running Back
Cyril Typton: 1919
Kenechi Udeze: 2001–03; Defensive Line
Jason Uhl: 1990–91, 1993; Nose Tackle/Defensive Guard
George Uko: 2010–12; Defensive Tackle
Butch Underwood: 1973; Linebacker
Walt Underwood: 1975–77; Defensive Tackle
Brian Unsworth: 1987; Wide Receiver
Mickey Upton: 1965; Defensive Back/Wide Receiver
Daniel Urquhart: 2002–03; Defensive Line
Charles Ussery: 1980–81; Defensive Tackle
Vic Vaca: 1983; Inside Linebacker
Soma Vainuku: 2011–12; Fullback
Troy Van Blarcom: 2005–06; Kicker
Nick Vanderboom: 2003–06; Tight End/Quarterback
Lenny Vandermade: 2000–03; Center/Offensive Guard
Bob Van Doren: 1950–52; Tackle
Vinny Van Dyke: 1976–77; Defensive End
Keith Van Horne: 1978–80; Offensive Tackle
Brook Van Muijen: 2007; Kicker
Mike Van Raaphorst: 2000; Quarterback
Victor F. Vasicek: 1945; Guard
Simione Vehikite: 2009–12; Fullback
Chris Vella: 1970–72; Tight End/Center
John Vella: 1969–771; Offensive Tackle
Jim Vellone: 1964–65; Tackle
Norm Verry: 1940–41; Guard
Spencer Vigoren: 2006–09; Wide Receiver
Theo Viltz: 1963–65; Defensive Back
Robert Voiles: 1955, 1957; End
Anthony Volsan: 1994–97; Cornerback
Wolfgang Von Aspe: 1994; Fullback
Don Voyne: 1957; End
Ned Vukovich: 1949; Fullback
Kyle Wachholz: 1992–93, 1995; Quarterback
Don Waddell: 1945
Lowell Wagner: 1941–42; Fullback
Aundrey Walker: 2011–12; Offensive Guard
Brad Walker: 2004–07; Wide Receiver
Glen Walker: 1975–76; Punter
Jim Walker: 1964–65; Guard/Linebacker
John Walker: 2001–05; Safety/Cornerback
Tommy Walker: 1947
John Wall: 2000–01; Kicker
Willard Wall: 1943–44; Guard
Henry Wallace: 1998–2000; Linebacker
Kenneth Wallace: 1907–10
Larry Wallace: 1989–92; Flanker/Split End
Jim Walsh: 1969; Rover; #36
Joe Walshe: 1985–88; Nose Guard
Shawn Walters: 1993–96; Tailback
Ian Wandler: 2009; Tight End
Irvine (Cotton) Warburton: 1932–34; Quarterback
Herb Ward: 1978–79; Cornerback
John Ward: 1927–29; Tackle
Jason Wardlow: 2001; Defensive End
Scott Ware: 2004–05; Defensive Back/Safety
Timmie Ware: 1982–84; Flanker
Al Washington: 1985; Flanker
Chauncey Washington: 2003, 2005–07; Running Back/Tailback
Dave Washington: 1959–60; End
Delon Washington: 1994–97; Running Back/Tailback
Gerald Washington: 2006–08; Defensive Line
Marlon Washington: 1986–89; Flanker
Ray Washmera: 1971–73; Fullback
Travis Watkins: 2001–04; Offensive Guard
Ryan Watson: 2003; Defensive Line
Elbert Watts: 1985; Cornerback
Elmer Wayahn: 1918, 1922–23; Fullback
Charlie Weaver: 1969–70; Defensive End
David Webb: 1989–92; Defensive Tackle/Outside Linebacker
James Webb: 1932–34; Halfback
John Webb: 1904
Lee Webb: 2001–04; Linebacker
Scott Weber: 1969–71; Defensive End
Tom Weber: 1952–53; Tackle
Steven Webster: 1985–88; Tailback
L.V. Weddle: 1924
Chuck Weeks: 1951–52; Tackle
Ray Wehba: 1936–38; End
Andrew Weiss: 2008; Defensive End
Benjamin Weiss: 1916–17
Harry Welch: 1951–52; Halfback
Matt Welch: 1998–99; Tight End/Offensive Tackle
Gary Wellman: 1987–90; Flanker
Harry Wells: 1966; Defensive Tackle
Lou Welsh: 1950–52; Linebacker/Center
Richie Wessman: 2001; Quarterback
Pat West: 1944; Fullback
Troy West: 1981–82; Safety/Cornerback
Clem Westcott: 1925; Center
Jack Westcott: 1925; Tackle
Charles Westover: 1905
Dick Westphal: 1954–55; Tackle
Mike Westphal: 1965; Defensive Tackle
Pop Wheatley: 1902–03; Fullback
Chad Wheeler: 2012; Offensive Tackle
Harold Wheeler: 1926; Halfback
Ed Whitcomb: 1919
Will C. Whitcomb: 1888; Back
Charles White: 1976–79; Tailback
Jack White: 1904
Kenneth White: 1921; End
LenDale White: 2003–05; Running Back/Tailback
Lonny White: 1985–86; Flanker
Oliver White: 1926; Guard
Timmy White: 1980–82; Wide Receiver
Duane Whitehead: 1943–46; Fullback
Scott Whitehouse: 1990–94
Julian Whittier: 1929; Guard
Bruce Wiker: 1950; Guard
Robert Wilbur: 1934; Guard
Paul Wilcox: 1919; End
Thomas Wilcox: 1927–29; Fullback
Glenn Wilder: 1959; End
Joe Wilensky: 1934–36; Guard
Isiah Wiley: 2011: Cornerback
Dennis Wilkerson: 1955; Center
John Wilkins: 1959–60; Tackle
Morton Wilkins: 1932; Tackle
Don Willer: 1940–42; Tackle
Elmer Willhoite: 1950–52; Guard
Aaron Williams: 1996–99; Defensive End/Defensive Tackle
Brian Williams: 1991–94; Linebacker
Britt Williams: 1959–61; Defensive Lineman
Carl Williams: 1897–01; Fullback
Charles Williams: 1935–37; End
Chris Williams: 1982
Damian Williams: 2008–09; Wide Receiver

Don Williams: 1926–28; Quarterback
Eric Williams: 1975–76; Inside Linebacker
Hal Williams: 1940–41; End
Homer Williams: 1964, 1966; Fullback
Jamaal Williams: 2001; Defensive End
Jamel Williams: 2005–06; Defensive Back
Jerry Williams: 2005–06; Defensive Back
Jim Williams: 1949; Halfback
Johnny Williams: 1949–51; Halfback
Kevin Williams: 1977–80; Wide Receiver
Kyle Williams: 2002–06; Offensive Line
Leonard Williams: 2012; Defensive End
Marv Williams: 1981, 1983; Safety
Michael Williams: 1986–89; Outside Linebacker
Mike Williams: 2002–03; Wide Receiver
Rod Williams: 1982–83; Cornerback
Thomas Williams: 2003–07; Linebacker
Frank Williamson: 1931–33; Guard
Jack Williamson: 1932–34; Guard
Stanley Williamson: 1929–31; Center
Matt Willig: 1988–91; Defensive Tackle/Defensive Guard
Jack Willis: 1957; Halfback
Gary Willison: 1985–86; Defensive Tackle
Laird Willott: 1954–56; Guard
Don Willumson: 1945, 1948; End
Alan Wilson: 1990–91; Outside Linebacker/Defensive Guard
Ben Wilson: 1960–62; Fullback
Charles Wilson: 1902–03; End
DeVante Wilson: 2012; Defensive End
W. Wilson: 1916; Center
Zack Wilson: 1999–2002; Offensive Tackle/Offensive Guard
Jeff Winans: 1971–72; Defensive End
Paul Wing: 1934–35; Fullback
Bob Winslow: 1937–39; End
Gary Winslow: 1962–63; Halfback
Troy Winslow: 1963, 1965–66; Quarterback
Lloyd Winston: 1959–61; Halfback
Carl Wirching: 1909; End
Dominique Wise: 2005–06; Offensive Line
Max Wittek: 2011–12; Quarterback
Greg Woidneck: 2006–08; Punter
Greg Wojcik: 1965–66; Center
Joe Wolf: 1942–43; Center
Alex Wood: 2012; Kicker
Don Wood: 1965; Guard
Richard Wood: 1972–74; Linebacker
Willie Wood: 1957–59; Quarterback
Andre Woodert: 2001–05; Wide Receiver
Antwaun Woods: 2011–12; Nose Tackle
John Woods: 1920; Guard
Lavale Woods: 1994–97; Running Back/Fullback/Tailback
Quincy Woods: 1997; Quarterback
Ray Woods: 1940–42; Quarterback
Robert Woods: 2010–12; Wide Receiver/Punt Returner/Kick Returner
Roy Woods: 1940; Guard
Malcom Wooldridge: 2001; Defensive Tackle
Telford Work: 1916
Harry Worsley: 1924–25
Haskell Wotkyns: 1932; Quarterback
Dana Woudenberg: 1965–66; Guard; #68
Jim Wren: 1996–97; Punter
Demetrius Wright: 2010–12; Cornerback/Strong Safety
Dudley Wright: 1946; End
Eric Wright: 2003–04; Defensive Back
Foster Wright: 1895–97; Quarterback
James Wright: 2010; Wide Receiver
Manuel Wright: 2003–04; Defensive Tackle/Defensive Line
Shareece Wright: 2006–10; Defensive Back/Cornerback
Justin Wyatt: 2002–05; Defensive Back/Wide Receiver/Cornerback
Teruo Yamamoto: 1963; Halfback
Ron Yary: 1965–67; Defensive Tackle/Offensive Tackle
Wayne Yary: 1969–70; Offensive Guard
Kyle Yatabe: 2011–12; Outside Linebacker
Peter Yobo: 2010–11; Defensive End/Tight End
Sam Yocum: 1925–26
Brent Yoshida: 2007; Wide Receiver
Curtis Youel: 1931–33; Center
Adrian Young: 1965–67; Linebacker
Charles Young: 1970–72; Tight End
J. Edward Young: 1888–89; Guard
John Young: 1968–69; Cornerback
Pat Youngworth: 1889; Center
Don Zachik: 1959–60
Pierre Zado: 1997–99; Safety
Ernie Zampese: 1955–58; Tailback
John Ziegler: 1916
John Zilka: 2002–06; Wide Receiver
Dan Zimmerman: 1949–51; End

*Four*

# All-Time Head Coaches

Some of USC's head coaches were not only master tacticians, but in the university's formative years, they were intellectuals who earned life-long reputations for endeavors away from the gridiron. This is a chronological listing of these sideline generals from the 1880s through 2012.

## *Henry H. Goddard*

In the world of collegiate athletics, one of the most coveted positions is that of head football coach at the University of Southern California. The status that permeates from owning that title has been honed by the success created by coaching forefathers who led the Cardinal & Gold to the top of the college football world on a consistent basis for many decades. However, despite all the accolades laid on USC's gridiron mentors, and all those who have dreamt of holding the elite position, the man that began this proud heritage took the job on a whim after traveling to "the Golden Coast" to visit one of his four sisters.

The patriarch of USC football coaches came into the world as Henry Herbert Goddard on August 14, 1866 in East Vassalboro, Maine, as the fifth and final child, and only son, to Quaker parents. Before travelling clear across the country to guide USC's inaugural football team, Goddard suffered the loss of his father at age nine. His father, Henry Clay Goddard, was speared by a bull, lost his farm, and after finding work as a farmhand, succumbed to the persistent effects of the bull attack. Upon his father's passing, Goddard went to live with one of his married sisters for a short time before going off to Vassalboro's Oak Grove Seminary in 1877. Following one year at Oak Grove, Goddard attended the Friends School in Providence, Rhode Island.[1]

In 1883 it was on to the Keystone State of Pennsylvania for Goddard's next academic challenge and his debut into the world of college football. Staying close to his religious roots, Goddard studied at Haverford College, located in a suburb of Philadelphia, and known for its strong Quaker values. He played football and graduated in 1887, after which he decided to travel across the country to visit a sister in California. It was then that the name of Henry Goddard forever became linked to the glorious heritage of USC football, even though at the time, the prestige of leading the men of Troy onto the gridiron did not carry the same reverence as it would in the future.

While on his trek throughout the "Golden State," Goddard decided to introduce himself to the University of Southern California, which was still in its infant stages as a place of higher learning. Goddard then made a 400-mile journey north of Los Angeles to apply for teaching positions in the Oakland area, but within a few weeks he was contacted by the University of Southern California. After reviewing his letter of introduction, USC decided to offer Goddard a position of teaching Latin, History, and Botany.[2]

Seeing that Goddard had some experience in football from his playing days at Haverford College, USC approached him about coaching a group of students that banded together to form a football team. Goddard accepted the offer, and along with co-coach Frank Suffel, he guided the upstart Methodists (name used prior to Trojans). The first-ever USC football team posted a perfect 2–0 record, and did not give up a point, under the mentoring of Goddard. However, that inaugural campaign in the City of Angels was all Goddard had time for. Upon completion of the spotless 1888 season, Goddard said his goodbyes to USC and returned to his alma mater of Haverford to pursue a Master's degree in Mathematics in 1889. Despite his brief run at USC, Goddard remains the only head coach to leave the university with a perfect career record, and never see his players give up a single point during his tenure. The University of Southern California would not have a head football coach for the next nine years.[3]

Academia was the driving force behind Goddard's existence, and he dedicated his life to the cause of educating the next generation and beyond. Upon completion of his master's degree in 1889, Goddard travelled to Ohio to take a principal position at Damascus Academy until 1891, where he also taught and oversaw Quaker church services.

In 1891, Goddard went back to Oak Grove Seminary in his hometown, and took over as principal after two years. Three years later, Goddard entered Clark University, and in 1899, he received his doctorate in Psychology. In the first six years of the 20th century, Goddard worked as a teacher at State Normal School in West Chester, Pennsylvania.[4]

Over the course of the next 12 years, from 1906 to 1918, Goddard headed up the research department at Vineyard Training School in New Jersey, which helped mentally challenged children. His research included designing IQ tests, and he became a successful author, with his most well known work being *The Kallikak Family*, in 1912. The premise of this work detailed how a man's affair with a mentally challenged woman created criminals spanning multiple generations. This provided Goddard's firm belief in the field of Eugenics, which claimed that through controlled breeding, only the most desirable traits of two people would be passed on to offspring. His work in Eugenics allowed Goddard to create IQ testing for immigrants on Ellis Island in 1913, which eventually helped in bringing the Immigration Act of 1924 into law. The Act, signed by President Calvin Coolidge, allowed the United States to limit the number of new arrivals from Europe that were considered to be from ethnic backgrounds that were found to be undesirable according to IQ testing.[5]

Goddard continued with his work dealing with the human mental state, and earned two honorary degrees along the way. The first one came in 1943 from Ohio State University, and three years later from the University of Pennsylvania. In 1947, the 81-year old Goddard returned to California, living out the remaining decade of his life in Santa Barbara. He died on June 18, 1957, two months shy of his 91st birthday.[6]

## *Lewis R. Freeman*

No one could ever argue that Lewis Freeman did not lead an adventurous life. His resume consisted of being an explorer, journalist, war correspondent, and author. If these stellar accomplishments were not enough, Freeman was also an outstanding multi-talented athlete. While studying at Stanford University, he managed to find the time to add his name to the list of all-time head coaches in USC football history.

The man who would one day travel the globe came into the world on October 4, 1878, in Genoa Junction, Wisconsin, a quaint village of three hundred people at the time of his birth, and located 43 miles southwest of Milwaukee. Genoa Junction was later renamed Genoa City, which is the name used as the setting for the highly popular daytime drama, *The Young and the Restless,* that is filmed at CBS Television City on Beverly Boulevard, only a short distance from the USC campus.

The Freeman family left Wisconsin for Pasadena, California, when Lewis was a youngster. His athletic prowess allowed him the opportunity to play many different sports on the collegiate level at Stanford University, earning letters in football, baseball, tennis, and track. Freeman somehow simultaneously served as USC's football coach for the 1897 season, while completing his studies at Stanford nearly 400 miles north of Los Angeles.

In 1897, Freeman guided USC to a 5–1 record, and also introduced new uniforms with "USC" embossed on the front, which helped to make the players seem more united as a team.

Freeman graduated from Stanford University in 1898, and was off on his life's adventures. This once again left a coaching void for the Methodists, who would have to perform without a mentor for another four years. As for Freeman, his journeys after coaching USC for six games became that of dreams for many. From 1899 to 1912, he trekked his way through North and South America, Asia, Africa, and islands throughout the Pacific. Amazingly, he still found time to pursue his passion for athletic competition. In 1903, Freeman came back to Pasadena and claimed the men's singles and doubles championships at the Ojai Tennis Tournament.[1]

In 1905 Freeman was employed as a war correspondent during the Russo-Japanese War, a year-and-a-half long military clash involving Russia and Japan over the rights to control Manchuria and Korea. This quest for Imperialism was said to be the first prominent war of the 20th century. Following the war, Freeman served as a representative for the Pacific Coast Chambers of Commerce in China before once again finding himself involved in war journalism.[2]

He wrote about the struggles going on during World War I as a correspondent along with British, French, and Italian military forces from 1915 to 1917. He then served in the Royal Naval Volunteer Reserve as a lieutenant at the end of the "Great War" from 1917 to 1918. At war's end, Freeman was appointed a staff member to the Inter-Allied Naval Armistice Commission that went to Germany in 1918.[3]

With the conclusion of World War I, Freeman decided to continue is pursuit of writing, and had the first of 21 books, *Many Fronts*, published in 1918. Over the next four years, he produced eight more books, and then had one book per year published from 1923 to 1928. Six more works with Lewis Freeman's name on them were released between 1928 and 1942, with *Brazil, Land of Tomorrow*, being his final one in 1942.[4]

In addition to his books, Freeman found the time to serve as a correspondent assigned to the U.S. Navy's Pacific Fleet that travelled to Australasia, an area that includes Australia, New Zealand, New Guinea, and other islands in the Pacific, in 1925. He also went along with the U.S. Navy on ventures in 1929, 1932, and 1935, and became a boatman and photographer in addition to his many other interests.

Other journeys that Freeman was a part of included expeditions through the Grand Canyon, Central and South America, the Juan Fernandez Islands, the Amazon, Ecuador, southern Mexico, Guatemala, the Galapagos islands, Columbia, Bolivia, Peru, and Brazil.

Despite his many worldwide jaunts and adventures, Freeman still found the time to visit Pasadena, where he eventually settled down into retirement in 1955. Lewis Freeman's incredible, adventurous existence came to an end on November 6, 1960, when he passed away at the age of 82 in Pasadena.[5]

## *Clair S. Tappaan*

One game allowed Clair Tappaan to gain entry onto the prestigious USC coaching lineage. Tappaan's road to the Land of Troy began clear across the United States on May 14, 1878, in Baldwinsville, New York, a village on the Seneca River, and part of the Syracuse area known for farming and small industrial work at the time Tappaan was born.[1]

His formative years were spent at Baldwinsville Free Academy, and then it was on to Ann Arbor, Michigan, to advance his education. Following two years at the University of Michigan, Tappaan returned to the Empire State to continue his college career. He enrolled at Cornell University of the prestigious Ivy League in Ithaca, New York, some 70 miles south of his native Baldwinsville. While working his way toward a Bachelor of Laws degree in 1900, Tappaan was a member of the football team.[2]

Upon graduation, Tappaan applied his Ivy League knowledge to practicing law in the Syracuse area until he decided to relocate to Los Angeles in 1901. While working in a law office for his brother-in-law, Tappaan decided to put his football playing days to use by joining up with the Los Angeles Athletic Club team. The year 1901 proved to be a very busy one for the young 23-year old New Yorker. He moved clear across the country, played football, and earned his place on the proud roll call of coaches that served the University of Southern California, despite the briefest tenure of any mentor the team ever had. Like his predecessors at USC, Tappaan's focus was not to make football his life's work. He had another agenda, but before heading out to continue on what turned out to be a highly distinguished law career, Tappaan took the time to guide the Methodists during the 1901 season, which consisted of a one-game schedule. His lone experience as head coach went into the history books as a 6–0 loss to Pomona on December 7, 1901. However, his days at USC were not over, as he was on the initial faculty of the University's Law School in 1904. He also provided the USC football program with an All-American and three-year letterman in his son Francis, who earned national recognition as an end in 1929.[3]

By the late 1920s Tappaan was well on his way to establishing an everlasting legacy in the court system. He served the state of California on the Superior Court and Court of Appeals. He also continued as a faculty member with the USC Law School until 1928, but still found time to give lectures there, as well as at Loyola Law School. On November 30, 1932, Tappaan attended a luncheon held by the Los Angeles Bar Association. He then began walking back to his office in downtown Los Angeles when he suffered a fatal heart attack at the age of 54.[4]

## *John Walker*

Despite the best efforts, sometimes information is lost to history. Such was the case for John Walker, who went down in USC history as the football program's third head coach. He was credited with a final record of 4–2 in his only season at the helm of the team. According to the USC Sports Information Office, the only known piece of biographical information pertaining to John Walker was that he was also the "head of the voice department" at the university. It was also claimed by the same source that a conflicting report had the team captain, Dan Caley, serving as a player/coach for the 1903 squad.[1]

## *Harvey R. Holmes*

Harvey Holmes had the distinction of being the first in USC history to earn a salary as head football coach. His tenure was also the longest of any of his predecessors. Holmes was born on January 16, 1873, in Geneva, Minnesota. He then travelled 250 miles away from his hometown to continue his education and football career at the University of Wisconsin-Madison, which is the oldest of any institutions of higher learning in "the Badger State."

Established in 1848 right after Wisconsin became a state in 1848, the University fielded its first football team in 1889. During Holmes' days on the field as a tackle during the 1897 and 1898 seasons, the Badgers were in the midst of their first experience as a winning program. Under head coach Phillip King, Wisconsin finished 9–1 in both years Holmes was on the team. They won the Western Conference Championship in 1897, which was the name for what eventually became the Big Ten Conference.[1]

Holmes decided to pursue a coaching career after leaving Wisconsin. He accepted an offer from the University of Utah in 1900, and became the first coach in their history to guide the football team throughout multiple campaigns. He posted a 16–9–1 record over the course of four seasons, and is also remembered as the individual who composed the lyrics to the school's fight song "Utah Man" in 1904. Holmes also coached the Utah baseball team from 1901 through 1904.

After leaving his mark on "the Beehive State," Holmes travelled to the warm climes of Southern California to take on the head coaching position of the USC Methodists beginning in the 1904 season. In the four seasons under Holmes, the Methodists posted a 19–5–3 record for a .759 winning percentage. The team also travelled outside of the Southern California area for the first time with Holmes as coach for the historic event. Holmes took his footballers up north to face the tough, well-established Stanford team on November 4, 1905, in which USC lost, 16–0.[2]

Holmes decided to multi-task like he did at Utah, and took on the responsibility of coaching the USC baseball team in 1908, and added four seasons of mentoring the University's track team to his impressive resume. With his acceptance of guiding the baseball team, Holmes became the first official coach of that sport in USC history. He led the Methodists to a 17–2 record during the 1908 baseball season before leaving USC for Idaho.[3]

At the time of Holmes' coaching tenure at USC, there was much concern about the state of college football. It was deemed too violent by various interest groups, as many players died due to football related injuries in the early days of the sport. With the fear of serious injury or death looming over the sport like an ominous shroud, numerous colleges and universities decided to partake in rugby as a substitute for football. Some considered rugby to be safer, although just as physical as football. Many colleges dropped football during this time, and USC was reduced to scheduling opponents from high schools, small colleges, athletic club teams, and military bases. USC eventually dropped their own football program from 1911 through 1913, replacing it with a rugby team. Due to the weaker opposition, USC could not justify keeping a coach of Holmes' status on payroll, so the parties decided to end their union at the climax of the first decade of the twentieth century.[4]

The next stop on the coaching carousel for Holmes was at the Academy of Idaho, which later became Idaho State. From 1909 through 1914, Holmes led the team to a 28–10 overall record, with a perfect 5–0 slate in his first season.

At every athletic endeavor Holmes was associated with going back to his playing days at Wisconsin, the Minnesota native emerged as a winner. Holmes eventually returned to Utah, where he died at age 75 in Salt Lake City on May 10, 1948.[5]

## *William I. Traeger*

The path of William Traeger and the University of Southern California seemed destined to merge from birth, as both came to be in California during the same year. The man who guided the USC football team in the early years of the 20th century was born on February 26, 1880, in Porterville, California, a city in the San Joaquin Valley, 165 miles to the north of the USC campus.[1] Porterville was also the city in which future USC alumnus and legendary basketball player and coach Bill Sharman grew up fifty years after Traeger's birth.

While working on his academics as a youth, Traeger helped his father in the blacksmith profession. By the time he was 18, the young man saw his country involved in a conflict, and he answered the call to duty. During the Spanish-American War, Traeger was assigned to the 6th California Volunteer Infantry, moving up to the rank of corporal, during seven months of duty that ended on December 15, 1898.[2]

With military life now behind him, Traeger enrolled at Stanford University with a mere $1.25 in his possession. He knew that a solid education would be the best way to place more money in pockets than the amount he had upon arrival at Stanford. He studied law, and worked any job he could get to help pay for college. In addition, Traeger found his way onto the Cardinal football team. He not only was a member of the team, but also earned enough respect from his teammates, that they elected him team captain in 1901 under first-year head coach Charles Fickert. With Traeger leading by example, the Cardinal earned a spot in the first-ever Rose Bowl Game on January 1, 1902.[3]

The task of winning the inaugural Rose Bowl appeared to be an insurmountable one, as Stanford would have to take the field against one of the greatest collegiate football teams ever assembled. The 1901 Michigan Wolverines were coached by the legendary Fielding Yost, who coached Stanford in 1900 before taking over at Michigan. The Wolverines had a spotless 10–0 record coming into their clash with Stanford, and outscored the opposition by an astounding 501–0. The team scored so often, that it was dubbed "Point-a-Minute," and did not rest on their laurels against Stanford, dominating them, 49–0. Despite the beating Stanford took, William Traeger showed the grit of a champion. During the game, Traeger tore a ligament in his shoulder, but refused to come out of the game.[4]

With his days at Stanford complete, Traeger relocated to Los Angeles in 1902, and decided to remain close to athletics while pursuing other ventures. His first head-coaching job was leading Pomona College to a 3–2 slate in 1902. It was then on to the city of Eagle Rock in the northeastern section of Los Angeles to guide the Occidental College Tigers to a 2–1 record in 1903. He also began a three-year stint as a deputy United States Marshal in 1903, and remained in that capacity until 1906.[5]

After one season at Occidental, Traeger remained away from head coaching while continuing on his career in law enforcement. In January 1907, Traeger was hired as a deputy sheriff in Los Angeles County, and stayed with that job until 1911. In addition to his law enforcement duties, he also made extra income by working with a general contractor.

Since his early days, Traeger was no stranger to hard work, and he continued on with that quality while studying law at USC and coaching the football team at the same time. He guided USC to a 3–1 record in 1908, which was his lone season as coach at the university. This also proved to be his final job as a head football coach.[6]

In 1909, Traeger became a lawyer and went into private practice. Two years later, he was appointed deputy clerk for California's Supreme Court, and stayed at that job for 10 years. He then served as Sheriff of Los Angeles County starting in 1921, winning re-election on three occasions, and held the post until December 1932. During his time as Sheriff, Traeger also served as the first-ever president of the Los Angeles County Peace Officers' Association in 1929.

After his time as Sheriff ended in 1932, it was on to the world of politics, when Traeger ran as a Republican for a seat in Congress. He won the election, and served with the 73rd United States Congress from March 4, 1933 until January 3, 1935. Seventeen days after giving up his seat in the Congress following a loss in the 1934 election, William Traeger suffered problems with his liver, and passed away at age 54 on January 20, 1935 at Wadsworth Hospital in Los Angeles.[7]

## *Dean B. Cromwell*

Monikers have long been a staple in the world of athletic competition, with most being extremely flattering to one's prowess. Dean Cromwell's coaching skills allowed many of his charges to earn nicknames reflecting stellar accomplishments. In the process, Cromwell was also bestowed with the ultimate praise that any coach would want, being dubbed, "Maker of Champions."

Turner, Oregon, "The Good Neighbor Town," is located on the banks of Mill Creek, and earned its place in USC history as the birthplace of legendary coach Dean Bartlett Cromwell on September 20, 1879. When he was a youngster, Cromwell's father died, and the family relocated to Southern California. It was in the Los Angeles area that Cromwell gained ever-lasting fame, first as an athlete, and more importantly, as a mentor.[1]

His own personal athletic accomplishments were achieved at Occidental Prep School, and then at Occidental College, where he graduated from in 1902. He rose above the rest of the competition in football, baseball, track, and cycling, and his stellar reputation earned him the 1901 Helms Athletic Foundation Award as the top athlete in the Southern California area.

Cromwell stayed close to the world of sports upon his college graduation by competing on a local amateur level while employed with the telephone company for seven years. In 1909, Cromwell was given the positions of head football and track coach at USC. He did a fine job as mentor of the Trojan footballers, but it was on the cinder oval over the course of 40 years that he blazed a path of greatness that will never be surpassed.[2]

His link to USC athletics went back to 1903 when he officiated football games for the university. He even played against USC in 1905 for Harvard School, along with coaches from both teams, in an attempt to bolster a very outmanned Harvard squad. As the head coach of USC, Cromwell served two tenures, with the first from 1909 to 1910, and the second from 1916 to 1918. In his first two seasons, he recorded a 10–1–3 record, and went

11–7–3 in his second, which saw his ranks drained, due to players going off to fight overseas during World War I.[3]

His overall football record at USC was a very respectable 21–8–6, but it was his guidance in the area of track and field that made him a legend in the Land of Troy. From 1909 through 1948, with a break in coaching track coming in 1914 and 1915, Cromwell produced a 128–47–1 dual meet record. Starting in 1930 and going through his final season as coach, the Trojan trackmen only lost four dual meets. He led USC to 12 NCAA titles and five second-place finishes. Of those dozen titles under Cromwell, the Trojans brought home nine straight, beginning in 1935 and running through 1943. Cromwell's mark of nine consecutive NCAA titles has never been surpassed, and it is highly unlikely that it ever will be. He also saw 34 of his charges win individual NCAA championships and set 17 world records. Each year from 1912 through 1948, Cromwell produced at least one Olympic champion. In all, 12 of his track and field athletes came back from Olympic competition with 12 gold medals in their possession. He served as assistant coach for the United States Olympic Team at the Berlin Games in 1936, and head coach for the team at the London Games in 1948.[4]

Cromwell was famous for donning a trademark bow tie, and calling every one of his athletes "champ," regardless of their status as a performer. It was an outstanding psychological tool that made even the average athlete feel like a winner, especially with praise coming from such a revered figure as Cromwell.

In 1949, Cromwell retired from coaching, but his talents were still used in an advisory role, and he also worked for the Los Angeles Rams as a field announcer. On August 3, 1962, the 82-year old "Maker of Champions" succumbed to a fatal heart attack at his home in Los Angeles. He was an easy selection to the National Track & Field Hall Fame's first class in 1974, and was elected to the USC Athletic Hall of Fame in 1995. As an everlasting tribute to the man who played a major role in making the University of Southern California's athletic legacy one to be revered, the university named its track Cromwell Field.[5]

## *Ralph Glaze*

From the Mile-High City of Denver, to the prestigious Ivy League, and many points in between, Daniel Ralph Glaze displayed his athletic talents at every stop. The world was introduced to this multi-talented sports star on March 13, 1882, in Denver, Colorado. Glaze developed a reputation as a highly skilled athlete in football and baseball during his formative years in Denver. It was that dual prowess which garnered him an opportunity to perform at the next level of competition in his native state. In 1901, Glaze entered the University of Colorado, and played football under head coach Fred Folsom for one season. After being a part of a 5–1–1 team at Colorado, Glaze decided to travel to Hanover, New Hampshire, to continue his athletic and educational pursuits at the prestigious Ivy League institution, Dartmouth College, in 1902.[1]

In 1903, Glaze was reunited with his coach from Colorado, Fred Folsom, who was a Dartmouth graduate, when he came back east to take over as head coach of the "Big Green." The reunion between player and coach proved successful, as Dartmouth rolled up a 23–2–3 record on the tough Ivy League gridiron trail over the time period from 1903 through 1905. During those three seasons, one of the highlights came in 1903 when Dartmouth defeated the perennial alpha dog of the Ivy League, Harvard University, for the first time in their history. Despite being the smallest player on Dartmouth's roster at 5'8" and 153-pounds, Glaze showed his grit by capping off his college football career with his selection onto the prestigious Walter Camp All-American team in 1905.[2]

When springtime rolled around in Hanover during the early years of the 20th Century, one thing was commonplace at Dartmouth. The great American pastime of baseball was upon the scene, and the "Big Green" were certain of having a successful campaign on the diamond, which is a tradition long enjoyed throughout the years at Dartmouth. The abilities of Ralph Glaze helped to build the foundation for Dartmouth's long-standing status in baseball. He pitched a no-hitter, and his career Earned Run Average of 1.78 still ranks near the top of the school's all-time best in that category.[3]

Following his graduation from Dartmouth in 1906, Glaze signed a professional contract with the Boston Americans. The team became known as the Red Sox beginning with the 1908 season. Glaze made his Major League debut on June 1, 1906, and over the course of three seasons in the American League, the right-handed pitcher posted a 15–21 record, 137 strikeouts, and an ERA of 2.89 in a total of 61 games and 340 innings on the mound. His final game in the Major Leagues was on June 15, 1908. On November 9, 1908, the Red Sox sold Glaze to the Indianapolis Indians of the American Association, and he played out the remainder of his baseball career in the minor leagues with the Beaumont Oilers (1913) and the Topeka Jayhawks (1914), before embarking on a coaching career.[4]

Glaze's interest in coaching began while he was with the Boston Red Sox during the offseason. Beginning in 1906, he served as an assistant football coach at Dartmouth and worked with the baseball team in 1908 prior to his final stint in the Majors.

In 1910, Glaze was given the opportunity to serve as a head coach for the first time at Baylor University. His football team at Baylor gave Glaze a solid reason to remain in the business by producing a stellar 6–1–1 record in 1910. In the three seasons Glaze served as Baylor's football coach, he compiled a 12–10–3 record. He also served as the university's basketball and baseball coach from 1910 through 1913.[5]

Following his final stints as a player in the minor leagues in 1913 and 1914, Glaze returned to the coaching profession on a permanent basis. In 1914, Glaze was hired to lead the USC football team after the university did away with football from 1911 through 1913 in exchange for rugby. He also coached the baseball, basketball, and track teams during the time period from 1914 to 1916. In doing so, Glaze became the first and only coach in the university's history to guide four different sports teams. He was also the first to coach the USC football team under their nickname of the Trojans.

On the football field, Glaze took a program that was just starting over after an absence of three seasons and produced a winning 4–3 record. He was also the first coach in USC history to lead the team against an opponent outside of California. That historic game was played on November 26, 1914, against Oregon. However, things ended badly for the Trojans on that day, as they suffered a brutal 38–6 defeat. After a 3–4 record in 1915, Glaze stepped away from coaching football at USC after posting a 7–7 career record at the university.

In 1916, Glaze left USC to coach football and basketball at Drake University in Des Moines, Iowa. After one year at Drake, Glaze returned to his native Colorado to coach at Colorado State Teachers College (later renamed University of Northern Colorado), the Colorado School of Mines, and Lake Forest College in Illinois.

In 1927, his wife of 20 years passed away, and he retired from coaching around the same time. He then went into business in Denver before returning east to supervise a railroad terminal in Charlestown, Massachusetts. Glaze remarried and eventually settled in Cambria, California, a seaside village located between San Francisco and Los Angeles. Glaze stayed physically fit into his 80's, and passed away on October 31, 1968, at age 87.[6]

## *Elmer C. Henderson*

There were eight head coaches in the Land of Troy prior to the arrival of Ohio native Elmer C. Henderson. However, Henderson's tenure at USC allowed the university to emerge from the dark ages to that of national prominence.

Elmer Clinton Henderson was born on March 10, 1889, in Oberlin, Ohio, 35 miles southwest of Cleveland. Upon his graduation from Oberlin College, Henderson took off for the Great Northwest, landing a coaching position at Broadway High School in Seattle, Washington. Broadway had the distinction of being the first building dedicated solely for use as a high school in Seattle. It also earned a solid reputation as a football power thanks to innovative concepts created by Henderson. During a four-year span at Broadway, Henderson compiled a 24–2–1 record and outscored the opposition by an incredible 586 to 84 point margin. He also served his country during World War I as a lieutenant in the United States Navy.[1]

Henderson was one of the first to use what is known today as a "spread offense," which is highly successful against more sophisticated defenses. Back when Henderson was using early versions of it, defenses were not as astute to stopping it, and that allowed the "spread" to be used with devastating results. This formation calls for the use of three to five receivers to go into the defense and force openings for the running or passing game. This hampers the defense due to the fact that the unit has to spread itself across the field in order to cover the receivers. With areas left open, the offense can attack those spots for excellent gains.

Henderson was also a top-notch recruiter that relied on his players to help obtain talent. Whatever location a current player came from was his so-called scouting territory.[2] This system appeared to work very well for Henderson, as it produced All-Americans and laid the foundation for USC's successful run at national recognition that exists to this day. Henderson was also a very kind man who cared about his players, and they returned the favor by compiling a 45–7 record during the coaches reign at USC for an .865 winning percentage that still stands as the best in the program's history.[3] Henderson also served as coach of the USC baseball team in 1920 and 1921, and also guided the basketball squad from 1919 to 1921. Henderson also had the ability to never swear, which can be difficult for coaches at times. In order to work his way around using foul language himself, Henderson hired an assistant coach that had no problem cursing. When the time came for such jargon to be used to prove a point, Henderson unleashed the assistant on his players.[4]

This legendary mentor entered the Land of Troy in 1919, and served as head coach through the 1924 season. In his first outing at the helm of the Trojans, they finished at 4–1. He then improved on that in the first year of the Roaring Twenties by guiding USC to its first perfect season, of more than three games, with a 6–0 record. In their final year without any conference affiliation, the Trojans entered a 10–1 season into their record books in 1921, which was the first time in the history of the program that the team produced double-digit wins.

Henderson's concept of a "spread offense" was working its magic on opponents, as he suffered only two losses out of his 22 games at USC. Despite his obvious success, Henderson always found a way to predict the worst possible outlook for his team. This might have been a psychological tool he used to downplay the juggernaut in cleats that he had built to possibly keep the players attentive to the fact that no team should be taken lightly. This has been a coaching tool for many decades, and will continue to be used at all levels of competition as a means to keep a team humble and not allow an opponent to feel that they were being taken as an easy win. Overconfidence could spell disaster, and then sloppy play against a slightly inferior team could end up causing a major upset. Regardless of Henderson's beliefs, *Los Angeles Times* writer Paul Lowry attached a moniker to the coach that would be forever linked to him. At the time, a comic strip character created by Fredrick Burr Opper named Happy Hooligan was extremely popular. One of Hooligan's friends was a consummate pessimist by the name of "Gloomy Gus," who never saw the silver lining in anything. Lowry immediately jumped on the comparison between Opper's character and the leader of USC's gridiron program. Thus, the Southland scribe presented his readers with "Gloomy Gus" Henderson, and the rest is history.

"Gloomy Gus" continued to downplay his team, and they kept on proving him wrong, as USC rang up a 25–5 over the next three seasons. Under Henderson's watch, the Trojans also joined the Pacific Coast Conference in 1922, went to their first Rose Bowl, and moved into the newly constructed Los Angeles Memorial Coliseum in 1923. The behemoth Coliseum had a capacity of 75,144 at the time of its opening, and with the success enjoyed by the team under Henderson, the excitement over Trojans' football grew, and spectators came out in droves. This allowed USC football to quickly grow in popularity, and that passion continued to increase with the passing of the years. The large crowds also brought in solid revenue for the university, which assisted in the construction of new buildings on the campus.[5]

Despite Henderson's incredible dominance of most opponents, the albatross that tormented him resided nearly 400 miles north of the USC campus. The University of California at Berkeley enjoyed their greatest football success during the first half of the 1920s. California coach Andy Smith had built an absolute powerhouse, and during the span from September 25, 1920 through October 10, 1925, Smith's "Wonder Teams" ran up a record of 46–0–4.[6] Henderson went against Cal on five occasions, only to lose every time.

At this same time, Cal and Stanford began to question USC's scholastic policies, claiming that they were not up to standard. Allegations into offering cash to players to come to USC were also brought up.[7] Things escalated in 1924 when Cal stated that they were going to end athletic competition with USC at the conclusion of the football season. Word quickly spread throughout the USC campus as Stanford was coming to town for a game in November. It was felt by USC that if they were considered below the standards of Stanford and Cal, then why not break off relations right away instead of waiting until the end of the season. The game against Stanford was called off, and a replacement contest against St. Mary's was substituted.[8]

It was understood by the "powers that be" at USC that their games with Stanford and Cal were huge moneymakers. They needed those rivalry games, and it appeared that something had to be done to improve relations. Seeing that Henderson had such a dismal slate against Cal, and controversy was brewing during his tenure as head coach, whether real or imagined, the university relieved Henderson of his duties following the 1924 season.[9]

Henderson's coaching career was far from over after leaving the Southland. The following year, he was back on the sidelines, this time as mentor at the University of Tulsa. His impact on the Golden Hurricane was immediate, as Tulsa captured the Oklahoma Intercollegiate Conference Championship in 1925. Tulsa earned four more conference crowns under Henderson in 1929, 1930, 1932, and in his final season at the university in 1935. He left Tulsa with a 70–25–5 record, and his victory total still stands as the most by a football coach in school history.

After 11 years away from Los Angeles, Henderson returned in 1936 to try his hand in the professional ranks. Once again, despite the venue, Henderson provided instant success. The Bulldogs were formed with the intent to join the National Football League in 1937. They played nine games in their inaugural season, with six of their opponents being NFL teams. The Bulldogs recorded a 3–2–1 record against NFL opposition and finished 6–3–1 overall. The Bulldogs' hopes of joining the NFL were thwarted in 1937 when the league decided to add the Cleveland Rams instead of the Bulldogs.

A new league called the American Football League began play in 1936, and the Los Angeles Bulldogs were brought into the fold. This was the second attempt to start an AFL, with the first one lasting only one season in 1926. This is not to be confused with the American Football League that was formed in 1960 and eventually merged with the NFL in 1970.

The 1937 Bulldogs took the new league by storm, completely dominating all comers. With Henderson's guidance, Los Angeles finished with a perfect 8–0 record and captured the only league championship. This version of the AFL folded in 1938, and Henderson then found himself coaching the Detroit Lions of the NFL. Henderson led the Lions to a 6–5 record in 1939. However, Henderson's days in the Motor City were numbered. Prior to the 1940 season, the team was sold and then new owner decided to part ways with Henderson. A return to Los Angeles took Henderson to Occidental College as head coach from 1940 to 1942. During that run, Henderson had an overall record 11–10–2, but Occidental postponed their football program during World War II, and that was the final coaching stint of Henderson's long and successful career.[10] Henderson passed away on December 16, 1965 at the age of 76 from pneumonia in Desert Hot Springs, California. Forty years after his death, the legendary coach, who brought the USC football program into the national spotlight, was enshrined into the USC Athletic Hall of Fame in 2005.[11]

## *Howard H. Jones*

From the Buckeye State to the Ivy League, and eventually as head master of the Trojans, Howard Jones was a winner that continued on with fellow Ohio native and predecessor Elmer Henderson's quest to make the USC football program a perennial powerhouse.

Excello, Ohio, now a part of Middletown, which is located in the southwestern part of Ohio, is known for the Miami & Erie Canal, the Harding-Jones Paper Company, and on August 23, 1885, the birthplace of future coaching legend, Howard Harding Jones. Upon completing his high school studies, his credentials were impressive enough to allow Jones acceptance into prestigious Yale University. While an Ivy Leaguer, Jones made the most of the experience of his time in college, both in the classroom and on the football field. Despite playing for three different head coaches during his time there, Jones and the Bulldogs never lost a game from 1905 through 1908. With a combined 28–0–2 record during Jones' days as a star end, Yale also claimed three national championships. Yale was so dominant at this time that they won 26 of 38 national titles from 1872 through 1909.[1] Jones was also a pitcher on the baseball team.

Upon graduating from Yale in 1908, Jones was hired as head football coach at Syracuse that same year. Under Jones' guidance, Syracuse finished at 6–3–1 in newly constructed Archbold Stadium, which was considered a "state of the art," multi-purpose facility. Jones' lone campaign at Syracuse also marked the school's ninth straight winning football season.

The allure to go back and coach at one's alma mater is a common dream for many in the coaching profession. Jones was allowed that opportunity in 1909 when he returned to New Haven, Connecticut, to hopefully continue the success enjoyed there for so long. He also became the first head football coach in Yale history to draw a salary for his service. Another first that included Jones was when he opposed his brother Tad's Syracuse team, in which Howard won, 15–0. It marked the first time that two brothers faced each other as head coaches. Not only did Jones carry on the proud tradition of Yale football, but wrote his own chapter of it by leading the Bulldogs to a spotless 10–0 season that saw his team never give up one single point, and claim yet another national championship.

In 1910, after successfully leading his alma mater, Jones decided to return to his native state as head coach of Ohio State University, where he guided the Scarlet & Gray to a very respectable 6–1–3 record. He then took some time off from coaching to pursue a career in private business. However, football was in his blood, and he found time to return to the sidelines for one season as head coach at Yale. In 1913, Jones led the Bulldogs to a record of 5–2–3 before heading back to work outside of the gridiron. Finally, by 1916, Jones realized that it was the world of X's and O's for him, and the allure of mentoring up-and-coming football players proved too great to pass up.

Reed Lane was a former Yale student along with Jones. He was also a member of the Iowa Athletic Board at a time when the University of Iowa was looking to hire a replacement for head football coach Jesse Hawley following the 1915 season. Lane knew the abilities of his fellow New Haven alum Howard Jones, and with his recommendation, the Hawkeyes landed Jones as the university's 11th head football coach.

Iowa offered Jones a five-year contract worth $4,500 a year, which was considered a very hefty salary at the time. It was also the largest sum and longest contract ever offered a head football coach at Iowa up to that time. In his first two campaigns at the helm in the Hawkeye State, Jones suffered through the worst defeats of his illustrious coaching career. While leading Iowa to a 4–3 record in 1916, Jones' charges lost to Minnesota, 67–0, and then 47–0 to Nebraska the following year during a 3–5 finish, which was the first losing season in his career.[2]

Over the course of the next six seasons at Iowa, Jones produced a solid 35–9–1 record and lived up to the worth of his contract. During that stretch from 1918 to 1923, Jones led Iowa to two straight undefeated seasons in 1921 and '22. Those two 7–0 finishes also resulted in back-to-back Big Ten championships, with the 1921 crown being the first in 21 years for the Hawkeyes. During a 20-game winning streak from 1920 to 1923, Jones beat Notre Dame's coaching icon Knute Rockne in the first-ever clash between these legendary gridiron mentors. In the 1921 game, Iowa snapped a 20-game Notre Dame winning streak, and the longest of Rockne's stellar career.[3]

Despite his success at Iowa, Jones ran into a disagreement with the chairman of athletics. Jones' wife was not all that receptive about dwelling in Iowa City. In an attempt to please his better half, Jones insisted on a new contract that would allow his family the opportunity to reside in Iowa City only throughout the football season and then head to another location for the rest of the time. Things did not pan out for Jones, and with tensions running high between the coach and his bosses, a parting of the ways loomed on the near horizon. In the end, it was the coach that packed up his belongings and headed to a new future.[4]

Duke University is nearly one thousand miles southeast of Iowa City, and it served as the next stop for Jones, whose reputation as a football coach did not force him to seek employment for very long. It was now time to depart the cornfields of Iowa for the tobacco fields of North Carolina to further his career. In 1924, Jones took over as head coach at Duke University, known at the time of Jones' stay as Trinity College. In his lone campaign at Duke, the team finished at 4–5, thus giving Jones only his second losing season in 13 attempts up to this time. This was also the only time that he left a program with a career losing mark.

After making his coaching trek through the east, north and south, there was only one unchartered region remaining to be conquered for Jones. It would also prove to be his greatest accomplishment, and provided him with everlasting recognition.

By 1925, stability was the standard in regards to the USC football program thanks to Elmer "Gloomy Gus" Henderson's efforts at the dawn of the 1920s. When the Trojans were looking for a new man to lead them, the program had taken a major hit in their reputation due to rumors regarding less-than-sufficient academic credibility brought to the forefront by rivals Stanford and the University of California.[5] When Jones was hired prior to the 1925 season, he provided two important factors. First off, he was a proven winner that could keep the Trojans going in the right direction toward greatest, and second he brought an Ivy League education with him. It would be hard for any other school to complain about academic standards when the man guiding the football program had a sheepskin from Yale, one of the most revered institutions of higher learning in the world.

Even though Jones would lead the Trojans to incredible heights that allowed the program to continue on a quest of greatness seldom matched by peers over the decades that followed his tenure, he was not USC's first desire. At this time in American sports, one college coach, and one alone, stood out above all others, and that was Knute Rockne. From 1918 through 1924, Rockne coached 65 games at Notre Dame, winning 58 of them and just clinched the 1924 national championship with his third undefeated season during his reign. He would go on to produce a 105–12–5 career record that ended with the 1930 season, which was good for an incredible .881 winning percentage.

Following the end of the 1924 regular season, Rockne and his legendary backfield of the Four Horsemen and the Seven Mules, who consisted of the linemen that opened the holes for runs of glory, were playing in the Rose Bowl against Stanford. With the close proximity of the Rose Bowl to Los Angeles, and the Trojans in need of a new coach, it seemed like the perfect time to plant the seed that USC wanted Rockne on their sideline at the Los Angeles Memorial Coliseum come the 1925 campaign. Rockne was a master at public relations, and when approached by USC, he used it as a bargaining tool to get more of a monetary gain out of Notre Dame. Rockne met with USC officials, but no one will ever know for sure if the coaching legend wanted to really coach the Trojans, or any other team for that matter. What was known was the fact that once a Los Angeles-based newspaper reporter got a scoop on the possibility of Rockne coming to USC, the story hit the wire services and the merger between the coach and USC was no longer a secret. Once the news reached Notre Dame, it was then that the chances of Rockne leaving South Bend were finally laid to rest. It appeared that the coach was in the midst of a ten-year contract with Notre Dame, and when the university's president, the Rev. Walsh, explained to Rockne that there would be severe legal woes for the coach if the contract was broken, the idea of leaving South Bend suddenly did not appeal to Rockne any longer, if it ever did in the first place.[6]

After the Rockne story had been extinguished, the university set out to land a new coach, and on February 3, 1925, Howard Jones was placed in charge of USC's football future. Shortly after Jones arrived on the USC campus, Al Wesson, the director of USC's athletic news service, gave him the moniker of "Headman," due to his approach to delegating authority upon his assistants, and to be available for any problems or guidance that he could offer.[7] Jones was a true football man with a vast passion and understanding for the game, and his knowledge was invaluable. It would also help lead the Trojans to their first great run as a consistent championship-caliber team.

Many college football coaches throughout the history of the game had personalities that allowed them to not only become great leaders, but beloved by the media for their humor and jovial demeanor. Howard Jones was not one of those. Despite his incredible skills as a coach, Jones did not possess a feel good personality, at least not among those involved with his profession.

He was regarded as a man so absorbed with the game of football, that he found it hard to relate to matters outside of the sport. Both assistants and players alike could not get close to him on a personal level due to an invisible barrier created by the "Headman." This allowed for him to be described as aloof, absent-minded, and very intimidating. He was also horrific at speaking in public, had no sense of humor what so ever, and very rarely cracked a smile. His thoughts regarding football were so great that at times he would get into thinking about the game that he drove right past the USC campus on his way to work, forget where his car was parked, and even forget to pick up his paycheck.[8] He did not have an office at the university, and after the season was complete, Jones would depart the campus until spring drills and then leave until workouts began in the summer.[9] He was a man of few words off the field, but once in command of his charges, he was tough, had unlimited energy, and when he spoke, he got immediate respect. Jones was also not fond of the recruiting process, and put that task into the hands of his assistants. He did, however, allow himself to enjoy a game of bridge or round of golf, both of which he played with the same intensity and desire to win that he possessed in the gridiron world.

Despite personality traits that made Jones the type of person he is remembered for being, he will also be forever embraced as one of the greatest coaches of his time. The college football world at the time of Jones' tenure called for predominant usage of a running attack. The USC Trojans were no exception to the rule, and with Jones' mind constantly on the X's and O's, the Land of Troy became a powerhouse, ground-pounding juggernaut.

From 1925 through 1940, the Trojans under the "Headman" compiled 121 wins against 36 losses and 13 ties. Along the way, Jones produced 23 All-Americans, nine of which were running backs. He also led USC to five conference titles, shared two others, won five Rose Bowls in just as many appearances, and four national championships in 1928, 1931, 1932, and 1939.

On the sweltering morning of July 27, 1941, shortly before another USC squad under Jones was about ready to partake in training camp for the new season, the coach was washing his car at his Toluca Lake residence, some 14 miles away from the USC campus, when he suddenly did not feel well. He contacted his physician, but by the time help arrived, Howard Jones was dead of a heart attack at the age of 55.[10] The loss shocked the football world, and left the University of Southern California without their legendary sideline general. However, the legacy of the "Headman" allowed the program to carry on a glorious tradition that would have made Jones proud.

## *Justin M. (Sam) Barry*

Sam Barry's name is synonymous with success in the Southland, not only while he coached, but half a century after his death as well. He was one of only three men to coach programs to the NCAA basketball Final Four and the College World Series, and his "Triangle Offense" on the hardwood was a big influence on the Los Angeles Lakers' quest to become the NBA's premier team of the new millennium.[1]

The man who provided so much to the Los Angeles sports scene began his life in Aberdeen, South Dakota, on December 17, 1892 as Justin McCarthy Barry. He earned his initial prowess in the athletic world as a triple-sport star at Wisconsin's Madison High School. Football, basketball, and baseball were the sports in which Barry excelled, and he continued with his elite skills at Lawrence University in Appleton, Wisconsin, upon his high school graduation.[2]

Barry eventually completed his college education at the University of Wisconsin in Madison. He then set out to pursue athletics as his chosen profession. His beginnings at mentoring future generations were at his alma mater, Madison High School in the 1910s. That was the first and only coaching experience Barry ever had at the high school level, as the remaining 32 years of his career were spent guiding college athletes in football, basketball, and baseball.

In 1918, Barry left Wisconsin for Knox College in Galesburg, Illinois, some 200 miles west of downtown Chicago. He had a full workload guiding the purple and gold-clad Prairie Fire, coaching football, basketball, baseball, and track, while also serving as Knox's athletic director. During his time coaching the football team, Knox College compiled a 15–12–4 record, which consisted of a spotless 8–0 record in 1919. After gaining his status at a small school, Barry earned his chance at coaching in the upper echelon of college sports in 1922 when he was named head basketball coach at the University of Iowa, a position he held through the 1929 season.[3]

From 1908 to 1922, the University of Iowa basketball fortunes were dismal, as the Hawkeyes finished no better than fifth place in the Big Ten. Barry changed all that, as Iowa did a complete turnaround in his first season at the helm. The team ended the 1922–23 season with a 13–2 record, which included Iowa's first Big Ten championship. Barry also guided the Hawkeyes to a share of a Big Ten title in 1926, while ringing up a career record of 62–54 at the school. In addition to his hardwood duties, Barry was appointed as an assistant on Howard Jones' football staff in 1922, and served the university in that capacity until 1928. During his time on Jones' staff, the Hawkeyes registered a perfect 7–0 finish in 1922.[4]

By the time the 1920s were coming to a climax, Howard Jones was already entrenched as one of the top-rated football men in the country at USC, and his opinion was highly regarded. When the University of Southern California found the need to find a replacement for basketball coach Leo Calland, Jones recommended his old friend and Iowa colleague Sam Barry. Barry got the job, and going into it, it appeared that he would have a big task ahead of him, as he was taking over for a coach that established a high standard of excellence over the previous two seasons. Calland left USC to take over as head football coach and athletic director at the University of Idaho in 1929 after posting a 38–10 record over two seasons, which included a conference title and a school best .792 winning percentage.[5]

Calland had definitely set the mark high on the USC hardwood program, but Barry was more than capable of carrying on the success, as well as establishing a legacy of his own. In his first season at the helm of the Trojans' basketball squad, Barry's team finished with a 15–5 record, which included winning the 1930 PCC championship. However, Barry's initial success was no fluke, as his Trojans dominated the PCC throughout the 1930s. He won eight PCC southern division titles, and two more outright conference championships in 1935 and 1940. In all, Barry posted a career record at USC of 260–138, which still stands as the most victories compiled buy one coach in the university's basketball history.[6]

Barry was also regarded throughout the basketball community as an innovator that changed the game. He helped to do away with the center jump after a free throw or successful basket, which allowed for the game to be sped up and exciting to watch. He was responsible for the center line and 10-second rule, in addition to creating the "Triangle Offense."[7] It was this offensive attack that was perfected by one of Barry's players at USC, Tex Winter, who later taught it to NBA coaching icon Phil Jackson. In turn, Jackson took what Barry initially started, and Winters perfected, and then established himself as the greatest NBA mentor in the history of the game. He won six NBA titles in the 1990s with the Michael Jordan-led Chicago Bulls, and five more with Shaquille O'Neal and Kobe Bryant leading the Los Angeles Lakers in the 2000's.

The legacy of Barry at the University of Southern California was not just restricted to the basketball court. He also guided the Trojans' baseball team for nearly twenty seasons, winning nine PCC championships along the way, the 1948 NCAA championship, and compiled an outstanding 219–89–3 record on the college diamond circuit.

In the fall, Barry did not let up on his workload, as he served on Howard Jones' football staff from 1929 through 1940. His work as head scout and defensive strategist helped the Trojans win two national championships and establish the program as one of the best in the country.

On a sweltering July 27, 1941 day in Los Angeles, Barry's duties abruptly changed, as his friend and colleague of close to twenty years, Howard Jones, died suddenly of a heart attack. However, the heartbeat of the USC football program had to continue, so that all of Jones' hard work would not go to waste. The university looked to former Trojans' player and assistant coach Jeff Cravath to take over for Jones. However, Cravath had recently signed on with the University of San Francisco as head football coach, and could not wiggle free from his contract.[8]

The fortunes of the Trojans were then offered to Barry, who already had a full workload as head basketball and baseball coach. Barry was a true company man, and his devotion to USC, and Howard Jones' memory, more-than-likely guided him to accept the role as head coach of the football program.

The dawn of the 1940s did not prove to be kind to the Trojans, as they posted a rare sub-par season, finishing at 3–4–2 and seventh place in the Pacific Coast Conference in the final year under Jones.[9] Barry attempted to steady the ship, but it continued to sink, as the Trojans ended the '41 campaign at 2–6–1. Besieged by injuries and sickness, Barry's squad was reduced to 28 players.[10] In the true fighting spirit of Troy, Barry forged ahead, and as the season progressed, his work with the offense allowed USC to be more competitive in the final three weeks. They almost upset fourth ranked Notre Dame, losing a close 20–18 decision, and managed to come out of their other rival game with a 7–7 deadlock against UCLA.

One day after USC's finale against UCLA, the entire world changed for the United States, as the Japanese attack on Pearl Harbor brought America into World War II. Like so many college athletes and coaches, Barry answered the call of his country, joining the Navy in 1942. Serving as a lieutenant commander in the South Pacific, Barry was put in charge of physical and military training programs for Navy personnel.

At the end of the war in 1945, Barry returned to USC as head coach of the basketball and baseball teams, and as an assistant on the football staff under Jeff Cravath. Despite Barry's incredible success, it came with a price. The stress created by his long tenure at multi-tasking caused wear and tear on his health. Even when he was warned to cut his workload back to help ease the burden on him physically, Barry kept forging ahead. On September 23, 1950, while scouting an upcoming USC foe at the University of California, Berkeley, Barry was stricken with a heart attack as he was walking up a hill toward the stadium, and expired before he could get help at a hospital.[11]

Despite being taken from this Earth at age 57, Sam Barry's accomplishments and devotion at USC could never be duplicated as long as there is a game of some type to be played in the Land of Troy. His 19 years of service to the football program ranks him second all-time behind Marv Goux, many of his former basketball players went on to stellar coaching careers, including Bill Sharman, Alex Hannum, and Tex Winter, and he mentored 14 baseball players that eventually found their way into the major leagues.[12]

## *Newell J. Cravath*

In a classic case of the student becoming the teacher, Jeff Cravath first played for USC coaching legends Elmer Henderson and Howard Jones before adding his name to the Trojans coaching lineage himself.

Breckenridge, Colorado, is a historic town with slightly over 4,500 residents. Despite its small populous, the area is a hotbed for skiing enthusiasts in the winter. Other activities such as hiking and fly-fishing, to name a few, keep Breckenridge busy with lovers of the great outdoors.

Long before this quaint community became a tourist destination, it provided the birthplace for future USC player and coach, Newell Cravath, on February 3, 1903. Cravath had the odds stacked against him immediately upon drawing his first breath. His mother died during childbirth and his father passed away when he was six years old, leaving him an orphan. Despite the devastating circumstances surrounding the youth, he persevered like a champion, thanks to support from both sets of grandparents and an uncle, Clifford Carlton "Gavvy" Cravath, a major league outfielder from 1908 to 1920, who was regarded as one of the best power hitters of his time.[1]

The future Trojan was even given a nickname of a champion that stuck with him throughout life. At the time of Cravath's birth, James Jeffries was boxing's heavyweight champion of the world, and is regarded as one of the greatest to ever hold the title. During his adolescence, he was called "Little Jeffries," and then it was shortened to "Jeff."[2]

Cravath's formative years were spent in Santa Ana, California, with his paternal grandparents, Augustus and Kate Cravath. He attended Santa Ana High School, which later earned the reputation of being the oldest and largest high school in California's Orange County. Following graduation, Cravath chose the University of Southern California to pursue a higher education. He also became a member of the football team, starting out on the varsity in 1924 under "Gloomy Gus" Henderson and ending his collegiate career as a center on Howard Jones' first two seasons as coach of the Trojans in 1925 and 1926. He served as team captain in 1926, and had a teammate that season named Marion Morrison, a reserve tackle, who would soon go on to become motion picture icon John Wayne.[3]

After a solid college career that ended with his appearance in the 1927 East-West Shrine All-Star Game played in January 1927, Cravath decided to embark on a coaching career. Howard Jones knew the qualities that Cravath possessed, and made his former team captain a part of his coaching staff starting in 1927. Following USC's national championship in 1928, Cravath decided to attempt his first head coaching opportunity. The University of Denver allowed Cravath his initial chance at running a football program, and he succeeded by leading the Pioneers to an 11–9–1 record from 1929 to 1931. One of school's football milestones came during Cravath's stay, as they defeated Regis, 40–0, in the first-ever night game played at Denver's stadium.[4]

In 1932, Cravath said goodbye to the oldest university in the Rocky Mountain region, giving up his coaching reins at Denver to successor Percy Locey. He returned to California to take an assistant coaching position with the Chaffey College Panthers, a junior college located in San Bernardino County. After one season at Chaffey, Cravath took a 40-mile trek west to return to his roots at USC for another tenure on Howard Jones' staff. His second stint as a USC assistant lasted from 1933 through 1940, and he once again helped in guiding the Trojans to another national title in 1939 as a line coach. That title was USC's fourth under Jones, and second with Cravath on his staff.[5]

Howard Jones died suddenly of a heart attack in July 1941, thus creating a major void in the football program. Cravath appeared to be the likely candidate that USC wanted to take over the fortunes of the program. However, Cravath had already committed to a head coaching job with the University of San Francisco and could not free himself from his contractual obligation.[6]

The task of guiding the Trojans following Jones' death was laid upon assistant Sam Barry's shoulders, at least for one season. The United States was then thrust into World War II at the conclusion of USC's final game of the 1941 season, and Barry joined the Navy, while Cravath's opportunity to enter the military was rejected due to poor vision. By this time, Cravath had completed a 6–4 record at the University of San Francisco, and upon Barry's departure, he recommended Cravath for the USC job. Barry already had a major workload at the university, serving as head basketball and baseball coach, in addition to his football duties. He basically took the head position with the football team out of obligation to the program. His recommendation of Cravath came with the thought of him carrying on as coach, not solely on an interim basis until Barry's return, but for as long as Cravath and the university were content with each other.

On March 18, 1942, USC's president Rufus B. von KleinSmid announced that the future of the football program was Jeff Cravath's responsibility.[7] With his hiring, he became the first former Trojan student/athlete to be hired as head football coach.

Cravath was able to breathe new life into the program, taking the Trojans to seven straight winning seasons after posting a 5–5–1 record in his first outing as head coach in 1942. From 1943 through 1949, Cravath's teams returned USC to the upper ranks of respectability. Three straight Pacific Coast Conference titles were added to the proud heritage that is Trojan football from 1943 through 1945, with the '43 squad finishing unbeaten at 8–0–2 that included a 29–0 Rose Bowl victory over Washington. The following season saw the Trojans return to the Rose Bowl, with the results being the same, as USC once again emerged from the New Year's Day classic with a shutout victory, this time over Tennessee, 25–0.

Cravath went down in the annals of USC gridiron history as a hard-driving mentor, who believed the game of football was one of major significance. His beliefs were similar to those of Howard Jones, and just like his former coach, Cravath insisted on absolute dedication from his team both physically and mentally. He instilled an offensive attack based on speed and passing, and brought the Trojans into the age of using the T-Formation.[8]

The Trojans under Cravath's guidance had some excellent talent, but also had a big advantage in obtaining some stellar players during World War II. This occurred when USC offered officer training on the campus, and many football players came to the university for that purpose and played for the Trojans. This helped keep USC successful for the duration of the war when virtually every other college program was depleted of talent due to the military draft.[9]

At the conclusion of the war in 1945, Cravath's tenure was still in the midst of a successful run. However, despite winning their third straight PCC championship in 1945, the season was climaxed by Cravath's first Rose Bowl defeat, with Alabama walking on the Trojans by a 34–14 final count. This was the first time the Trojans lost in Rose Bowl competition after eight straight victories in the post-season classic.

After a 6–4 finish in 1946, that ended USC's three-year reign as kings of the PCC, the Trojans returned top the top of the conference with a 7–2–1 record in 1947. Cravath's fourth trip to the Rose Bowl was the prize for winning the PCC, but once again the result proved to be dismal for the Trojans. A powerhouse Michigan team awaited USC in Pasadena, and the Wolverines showed why they were the #2 ranked team in the nation by pounding USC, 49–0, to produce their fifth shutout victory en route to a spotless 10–0 record.

The lopsided defeat at the hands of Michigan began a slow decline for Cravath as coach of the Trojans. Between 1947 and 1949, his teams compiled a 13–11–5 record. Even though the program still had a winning record during that time, it was not up to the standards that USC was known for. The USC alumni also expressed displeasure in the fact that fierce rival Cal had become the alpha dogs of the Pacific Coast Conference during the late 1940s.

A 2–5–2 finish in 1950 all but sealed Cravath's fate, but he still managed to muster up some of that championship spirit that served him well as a player and coach. Against rival Notre Dame, the Cravath-led Trojans scored a major upset on USC's homecoming by knocking off the defending national champion Fighting Irish, 9–7, for USC's 300th all-time football victory. Notre Dame was riding a four-game unbeaten streak coming into this game, and following the historic win, Cravath's players hoisted their coach up on their shoulders for a victory ride.[10] This proved to be the final such ride for Cravath, as he was relieved of his duties on December 20, 1950 after compiling a record of 54–28–8 in his nine years at the helm of the Trojans.[11]

For the first time in many decades, Cravath was not a part of the college football world, and at age 48, he looked to embark on new ventures. After working as a race official at Santa Anita Park for two winters, Cravath relocated to El Centro, California, some 210 miles southeast of Los Angeles and bordering Mexico and Arizona. It was in El Centro that Cravath decided to try his hand at ranching. A USC connection from nearly thirty years earlier allowed Cravath to also partake in the making of a motion picture from October to December 1952. John Wayne, his former teammate from the 1926 squad, which Cravath captained, was signed on to do *Trouble Along the Way*, and Cravath was called on to help out as a technical advisor.[12] This was not Cravath's first time working in the film industry. While an assistant under Howard Jones, he was cast as a coach in the films *Fighting Youth* (1935) and *Life Begins in College* (1937).

Cravath's life was cut short one year after working on the John Wayne film. While driving his pickup truck in Calexico, California, Cravath's vehicle crashed into a dump truck, causing the former Trojan to sustain multiple life threatening injuries. An emergency tracheotomy was performed in an attempt to save him, but he remained unconscious and died a day after the accident on December 10, 1953 at age 50.[13]

## *Jesse T. (Jess) Hill*

Like his predecessor Jeff Cravath, Jess Hill played football for USC before guiding future Trojans from the sidelines. His dedication to the Land of Troy began in the Roaring Twenties, and ended in the 1970s. In between that vast time span, Hill played, coached, oversaw numerous championships as athletic director, and performed on the professional baseball circuit.

This multi-talented Trojan legend was born on January 20, 1907, in Yates, Missouri. As a youngster, the Hill family relocated to Corona, California, 47 miles east of Los Angeles.[1] Once on the golden coast in a town dubbed, "the Lemon Capital of the World," Hill's athletic future was honed at Corona High School and Riverside City College. His athletic prowess performing five sports at Corona, and four at Riverside, made Hill a well-respected legend. It was then on to USC in 1927, thus beginning an association with the university that spanned nearly half a century and earned him the moniker of "Mr. Trojan."

As a running back under Howard Jones in 1928 and 1929, Hill was a member of USC's famed "Thundering Herd" that claimed the national championship in 1928. The following year, he used his exceptional speed to average 8.2 yards per carry, which led the Pacific Coast Conference, and helped the Trojans claim a third straight PCC championship and a blowout victory over Pitt in the 1930 Rose Bowl.

Despite being a very talented running back, it was during the spring that Hill truly excelled. The Trojans had two coaching legends that graced the USC campus during Hill's college career, and he had the good fortune of being mentored by both. After his season in cleats and shoulder pads under Jones was complete, Hill slipped on track spikes for Dean "the Maker of Champions" Cromwell. Adding three letters in track to his collection, Hill established a record of 25 feet, 7/8 inches to capture the 1929 intercollegiate national broad jump championship during his junior year. In 1930, he capped off his outstanding college athletic career by winning the PCC batting title with a .389 average en route to earning his sixth varsity letter at USC.[2]

As a multi-talented athlete on the college level, it was apparent that Hill had the skills to compete as a professional, either in football or baseball. If track and field had a pro league in the United States, he could have conquered that venue as well. It was summer's green cathedrals that eventually beckoned the USC outfielder, and upon college graduation, Hill placed his name on a professional baseball contract with the Hollywood Stars of the Pacific Coast League.[3]

Up to this time in his athletic pursuits, Hill rose to the challenge of every level of competition with stellar results. His introduction to the highest level of competition proved to be no different. In Los Angeles' Wrigley Field, he blasted a home run in his first at-bat against the Los Angeles Angels. The New York Yankees were the elite team in major league baseball at this time, and the club's scouting department knew a good thing when they saw it. They purchased Hill's contract from the Stars, and the 5–9, 165-pound outfielder with speed was sent to play in Newark, New Jersey, in 1932. He then spent time in St. Paul, Minnesota, in 1933, and went back to Newark the following season.[4]

In 1935, he proved himself enough to be brought up to "the Show," meaning he was about to embark on the making the dreams of many, but the reality of only a few, come true. At age 28, Hill made his big league debut in the famed pinstripes of the Yankees, in 1935. He played in 107 games, had a .293 batting average that included 115 hits, four home runs, and 33 RBI. He also had the opportunity to play on the same team with such Yankee legends as Lou Gehrig, Bill Dickey, and Tony Lazzeri.[5]

After one season in the Big Apple, Hill was traded to the Washington Senators, where he hit for a .305 average while playing in 85 games. During his time in the nation's capital, Hill's speed earned him the distinction of being named the fastest man in the American Association. He remained with the Senators until 33 games into the 1937 season. On July 13, 1937, he was purchased by the Philadelphia A's, where he saw action in 70 games and hit for a .293 average. While with the A's, Hill had the privilege to play under one the game's greatest managers in

Connie Mack. Up to this time in his life, he performed for and with some of the most iconic individuals in their prospective fields of athletic endeavor. From Howard Jones, the Thundering Herd, and Dean Cromwell, at USC, to Lou Gehrig, Bill Dickey, and Tony Lazzeri, with the Yankees, and finally to Mack in Philadelphia, Hill's personal experience with such individuals could have filled hours of gripping conversation or volumes of books.[6]

On November 5, 1937, Hill was sent back to the Pacific Coast League to play for Oakland, and thus came full circle as a baseball player. He played in Oakland during the 1938 and 1939 seasons before retiring from the game at age 32. In his time playing professional baseball, Hill amassed close to or over $25,000 as a reserve, which was a good amount of money while the country was still in the grips of the Great Depression, and a few dollars in one's pocket was considered a healthy sum to possess.

Hill remained close to sports during his off-seasons in baseball by returning to California and coaching on the high school and junior college levels. Upon his retirement from baseball, Hill pursued a coaching career, passing along his knowledge to up and coming athletes at Corona High School, Riverside Junior College, and Long Beach City College.

Three months after Japanese forces attacked Pearl Harbor and brought the United States into World War II, Hill answered his country's call to arms by enlisting in the Navy in March 1942. He served in the Navy until his discharge in February 1946, leaving military life with the rank of lieutenant—commander. During his time in the service to his country, Hill was assigned to the Navy's V-5 aviation cadet program, where he had the opportunity to work along with USC's athletic director Willis O. Hunter. This association would lead to Hill's future career, which took him back to his alma mater for the next quarter century.[7]

Upon his return to civilian life, Hill was hired by Hunter to coach freshman football and work with the track team. His freshman football team was a talented group that only succumbed to defeat one time, and that was to USC's junior varsity charges. He remained coach of the freshman team through the 1948 season, and then moved up the ranks to replace a legend.

In 1949, after forty years and 12 NCAA championships, Dean Cromwell retired as USC's track coach. The "Maker of Champions" passed the coaching torch over to one of his former star pupils, Jess Hill, and he did not disappoint his legendary mentor. The Trojan track program remained the elite of the college world, as Hill guided them to Pacific Coast Conference titles and NCAA championships in 1949 and 1950 while compiling a 12–0–1 dual meet record.[8]

On December 20, 1950, Jeff Cravath was relieved of his duties as head football coach of the Trojans. Initially, the university looked to obtain Notre Dame's Frank Leahy to replace Cravath. Leahy had guided the Fighting Irish to a record of 64–7–6 over the course of eight seasons up to this time that USC expressed interest in his services. Included in his stellar body of work were five unbeaten seasons and three national championships. He was definitely the elite college football coach at this time, and looked at in high regards. This appeared to be very similar to USC's pursuit of Knute Rockne in the 1920s when they looked to replace Elmer Henderson as coach in 1925. However, just like Rockne, Leahy did not budge from his South Bend residence. He remained with Notre Dame through the 1953 season, finishing his career with a record of 87–11–9, good for an incredible .855 winning percentage over 11 seasons.[9]

After a month of the USC coaching position still vacant, buzz in the Los Angeles dailies surfaced about Hill possibly taking over. Speculation became reality on January 31, 1951, when Hill was named head coach of the Trojans.[10] He handed over his track position to Jess Mortensen, who continued to guide that program to success over the next decade.

When Hill assumed the head coaching responsibilities of the football program, he brought an even-keel approach to the job. He had a gentle demeanor, and was a soft-spoken man that was looked at in high regard by his players.[11] Despite his passive makeup, Hill would explode with a joyous display of emotion after a victory, much to the amazement of all those around him. Victories were indeed important to Hill. There is no coach that ever went into the business without wanting to win. However, in Hill's case, winning did not consume his every thought, very unlike his USC coach Howard Jones, or his predecessor Jeff Cravath. Hill's philosophy was to make sure the team was as prepared for a game as possible, and then give everything a player can on the field. If the concepts of preparedness and all-out effort were given, then win or lose, Hill was satisfied with the result. He felt that even a loss could not take away from the hard work his players and coaches achieved to get ready to take the field.[12]

In Hill's case, this philosophy worked out well, as the Trojans finished with a 45–17–1 record during his six seasons as head coach. Included in Hill's body of work was a 10–1 finish in 1952 that saw the Trojans capture the Pacific Coast Conference title, and a Rose Bowl victory over Wisconsin. The victory was the first time that a PCC team won the Rose Bowl over a Big Ten opponent since the two conferences started competing exclusively against each other in the game beginning in 1947.

During Hill's tenure, two incidents occurred that gained major attention, with both coming in his final season at the helm. The Trojans were scheduled to play the Texas Longhorns on September 22, 1956 in the Lone Star State. At the time, USC had three African-American players on the team, and they were not allowed to stay in the team's hotel in Austin. This was a time when many states were still practicing segregation, and African-Americans had to stay in separate hotels, among other establishments. Hill quickly informed the management of the hotel that if his three players could not join the rest of the team, then the entire USC squad would not use the hotel as well.[13] It seemed that Hill had an idea of what would happen in Austin and planned ahead. He called a USC alumnus in Austin, who had no problem arranging for every member of the team to stay at a different hotel in town.[14] It was a move that proved no matter what color a person's skin is, unity among the team meant everything.

During that same season, Hill saw his beloved USC caught up in the middle of a scandal pertaining to illegal funds given out to athletes from programs in the Pacific Coast Conference. In addition to USC, the other universities hit by this scandal were UCLA, Washington, and California.[15] The PCC issued penalties to these programs for athletes getting more monetary assistance than allowed by the conference for tuition, books, and other miscellaneous things. Two of USC's star performers, running backs C.R. Roberts and Jon Arnett, were affected by the scandal, and had to forfeit playing in five games during the 1956 season. Despite the distraction, Hill managed to guide the Trojans to a successful 8–2 finish, which was good for a second place in the PCC.

When athletic director Willis O. Hunter retired in 1957, Hill replaced him, and held that position until 1972. Throughout his 15 years of guiding USC's sports programs, the Trojans compiled a United States college record of 29 NCAA championships. That incredible amount of titles won by one athletic director will more than likely never be surpassed. His stellar work was rewarded in 1969 when the Columbus (Ohio) Touchdown Club selected Hill as The Athletic Director of the Decade. He also received the Corbett Award, presented by the National Association of Coaches and Athletic Directors, in 1972.[16] He did return to coaching at USC in 1962 when track coach Jess Mortensen died suddenly. Under Hill, the USC track team posted a 9–1 dual meet record, won the conference championship, and placed third at the NCAA meet.

After retiring from USC in 1972, Hill took over as commissioner of the Pacific Coast Athletic Association until 1978. The man who gave so much of himself to USC as an athlete and administrator, passed away on August 31, 1993 at age 86 from complications of Alzheimer's disease in Pasadena, California. Two years after his passing, "Mr. Trojan" was honored with induction into the USC Athletic Hall of Fame.[17]

## *Don R. Clark*

The pride of Shurdan, Iowa, Don Clark, came to USC in the late 1950s. With a coaching staff that boasted two future legendary figures, Clark rebuilt a program that briefly fell on hard times.

The journey that took Donald Rex Clark from the Hawkeye State to the Land of Troy began three days before Christmas in 1923. While growing up on a farm in Iowa, Clark had his first experience with USC football thanks to the wonder of the radio. It was while doing his chore of milking cows in a barn that he heard the Trojans play in the Rose Bowl. In 1939, when Clark was a teenager, his family moved to Los Angeles, where he attended the home of the red and blue-clad Generals, Washington High School, earning All-City honors for his talents on the football field.[1]

After leaving the hallowed halls of Washington on South Denker Avenue, Clark had the opportunity to turn his gridiron dreams he envisioned in an Iowa barn, some 1,700 miles east of Los Angeles, into reality. An easy eight-mile trip north of Washington High School was where Clark embarked on his next academic and athletic adventure. In 1942, he was officially made a member of the Cardinal & Gold fold, playing guard for the USC Trojans under Jeff Cravath, who was in his first year as head coach.

While Clark was striving for success in both the classroom and on the football field, allied servicemen across the globe were also striving to keep the axis powers of Germany and Japan from advancing on their conquests throughout Europe and the Pacific in the early stages of World War II. Like millions of others in his age bracket, Clark answered his country's call to duty, putting his civilian existence on hold in exchange for military life.

Enlisting in the Army, Clark saw heavy combat over the course of 18 months. Included in the action he participated in was the famous Battle of the Bulge that was fought from December 16, 1944 to January 25, 1945. Clark was one of 610,000 American soldiers committed to the battle that became a fierce struggle waged in the Ardennes Mountain region of Belgium, France, and Luxembourg on the Western Front against tough German opposition. This was one of the hardest battles fought in American history, with U.S. forces suffering 89,000 casualties, including 19,000 killed. While in the Army, Clark received a battlefield commission, which meant he was promoted in rank while in the midst of combat.[2]

Army life also presented Clark with the opportunity to meet one of America's all-time greatest military leaders. At the conclusion of the war in Europe in May 1945, Clark was able to display his athletic skills in military track meets as a shot putter. It was during this competition that he received the highlight of the experience when he was presented an award from "Old Blood & Guts," General George S. Patton, regarded as one of the most colorful, feared, and respected military men in United States military history.[3]

Following his discharge from the Army, Clark returned to Los Angeles to resume his college education and football career. He played with the Trojans in 1946 and 1947, earning the honor of being selected USC's team captain in 1947, a year that saw the Trojans capture the Pacific Coast Conference title.[4]

Upon the end of his college career, Clark traveled up to northern California to test his skills as a professional with the San Francisco 49ers of the All-America Football Conference. This was a league that competed with the National Football League from 1946 through 1949. Clark played with the 49ers in 1948 and 1949 as a linebacker and guard before putting his playing days behind him.[5] During Clark's time with San Francisco, the team had an impressive 21–5 record, and considered the second-best team in the four seasons that the AAFC was in existence. The Cleveland Browns ruled the AAFC, winning every league title, and in 1949, they defeated the 49ers with Clark on the team, for the championship. Clark's playing career might have been over at the dawn of the 1950s, but the game would continue to be the focal point of his professional career throughout the decade, taking him from Annapolis, Maryland, and back to USC.

In 1950, Clark began his coaching tenure as an assistant at the United States Naval Academy under Eddie Erdelatz, who would go on to become the first head coach of the Oakland Raiders in 1960. When Clark joined Erdelatz's staff in 1950, the Naval Academy's football program was a disaster. Over the previous five seasons, the Midshipmen only produced four victories. A major rebuilding job was needed, and it took a toll on Erdelatz physically, as he lost fifty pounds during the season. Navy only mustered three wins in 1950, but the one that mattered most was a 14–2 win over rival Army, that came into the game riding a 28-game unbeaten streak.[6]

Following that season, Clark departed Annapolis, and headed back to Los Angeles to serve on Jess Hill's USC staff in 1951. Clark remained an assistant at his alma mater until Hill stepped down as head coach following the 1956 season. Clark had earned a reputation as a well-respected football man that possessed a passion for athletic competition. Sporting a crew cut and solid built, he had the perfect appearance for a coach at this time period. He was thought of in such high regard, that upon Hill's departure as head coach, the Trojan football players were ready to circulate a petition to the university in order to get him promoted to the vacant head coaching position.[7]

On February 7, 1957, minus the petition, the university granted the wishes of its players by naming Don Clark head coach of the Cardinal & Gold. Now, armed with a four-year deal, Clark looked to guide the Trojans to continued success. Unfortunately, he assumed the head-coaching job at one of the most trying times in the football program's long and proud saga.

Payments to athletes that were over the limits set by the Pacific Coast Conference brought sanctions down on USC, UCLA, California, and Washington, affecting the 1956 and 57 seasons. The seniors caught up in the incident were allowed to suit up for only half the games during the 1956 season. The juniors involved were forced to forgo the 1957 season, which put a serious handicap on Clark going into his initial year at the helm. He lost 11 players to graduation and eight more due to the PCC sanctions.[8]

Adding to the already shaky situation was the fact that recruiting was scarce for two years due to harsh restrictions placed on the program that made it difficult to get top performers. A few months into his tenure as head coach, Clark's prospects for the upcoming 1957 season were reduced to walk-ons and little talent at the quarterback and receiver positions. Regardless of the obstacles he inherited, Clark forged through a 1–9 season, which was the worst finish record-wise in USC history.

With his ravenous passion for sports, Clark was able to rebuild the lethargic program from rubble back up to respectability. He managed to recruit players that turned out to be stellar performers, and the team improved to 4–5–1 in 1958. However, the third time was the charm, as the 1959 season would prove.

In his third year at the controls, Clark brought USC's football program back full circle, and once again placed championship hardware in the university's trophy case. The Trojans ran off eight straight wins and finished at 8–2, winning the first-ever Athletic Association of Western Universities championship in the process. The AAWU was formed after the scandal of 1956 caused much animosity and eventually led to the disbandment of the Pacific Coast Conference.[9] Unfortunately, the only losses on the year were to their ultimate rivals, UCLA and Notre Dame. The fallout of losing to the rivals caused all the negative remarks to land right on Clark despite all that he did to accomplish a successful turnaround after such a disastrous beginning two years earlier.[10]

In addition to rebuilding the program, Clark also assembled one of the greatest coaching staffs in college history. On his staff in 1959 were John McKay, Al Davis, Marv Goux, and Mel Hein. McKay would go on to succeed Clark at USC and he became a legend. Davis took his incredible football mind into the professional ranks, and eventually emerged as the Managing General Partner of the Oakland Raiders, which under his guidance compiled the best winning percentage in professional football from 1963 to 2003, amassing three Super Bowl titles along the way. Goux was a former Trojan as a player, and displayed a passion for the program that was unmatched in its history. He then passed that passion onto his charges, with the results being highly successful for many seasons as an assistant. Hein was regarded as one of the greatest professional football players in NFL history as a linebacker and center for the New York Giants in the 1930s and 40s. His reputation as an outstanding player was solidified with induction into the Pro Football Hall of Fame's first class in 1963.

If assembling this incredible staff, and rebuilding the program within three seasons was not enough, during Clark's reign, USC produced 20 players that went on to the professional ranks, including hall of famers Willie Wood and Ron Mix, who both served as captains on the 1959 team.[11]

Regardless of all the positive aspects of his character and coaching abilities, Clark decided to resign as head coach on December 15, 1959. He entered the business world, first serving as vice president of his family's business, the Prudential Overall Supply Company in Costa Mesa, California. He later became president of the company. On August 6, 1989, while jogging in Huntington Beach, California, Clark suffered a heart attack and died at age 65.[12]

## *John McKay*

Throughout USC's one hundred-plus years of football, a handful of men rose up the ranks of elite status among the college game's all-time great mentors. Elmer "Gloomy Gus" Henderson and Howard Jones paved the way for the Trojans initial prominence as a national power on a consistent basis from the 1920s through the early 40s. Twenty years later, another future legend signed his name on a contract, thus becoming the 15th head coach to lead the men of Troy.

John McKay was his name, and during most of his 16-season tenure as head coach, the University of Southern California created a reputation as a dominant force seen year after year. McKay's quest for greatness in the Southland began in wild and wonderful West Virginia on July 5, 1923 in the small mining town of Everettsville, which no longer exists.[1] When the coal dried up, the people moved on and that brought an end to the town of McKay's birth.

John Harvey McKay was the third of five children born into a Catholic family of Scotch and Irish heritage. He was close to both of his parents, but very much so to his father, who was a hard working mine superintendent. When athletics began to interest McKay, he originally gravitated toward baseball, a sport that his father was very good at.[2] The McKay family enjoyed a relatively comfortable lifestyle during John's adolescence, made possible by his father's position in the mining industry. However, when McKay was 13 years old, his world changed tragically and drastically, when his father died from pneumonia at age 45.[3]

The family was crippled financially from the loss, and McKay looked to help his mother and siblings out through hard work. He delivered newspapers, did janitorial work in restaurants and schools, delivered concrete, and was an electrician's assistant in a coal mine.[4] In between working long hours, he continued on with his education and athletic pursuits.

After relocating several times, the McKays settled down in Shinnston, West Virginia, in 1938, where local athletes were idolized.[5] While at Shinnston High School, McKay was one of those revered athletes in football in basketball. In football, he was a breakaway runner that earned All-State honors as a running back, and led Shinnston to a pair of league championships.[6] When it was time to take to the hardwood during the winter months, McKay excelled at that sport. Shinnston's coach was Mickey McClung, and he possessed fervor for coaching that captivated the teenage McKay.

There were two types of young men in the town of Shinnston. On the one side, working in the coal mines like their ancestors was commonplace. The other option was to excel at sports and use that ability to get to college and earn an education so that the long, grueling work in the mines would not be a lifetime job.[7] It was during this time of his young life that McKay realized what path he wanted to pursue for his future. Coaching was what he wanted as a profession, and looked to someday return to Shinnston and work with McClung as his assistant and eventually replace his mentor.[8]

After receiving his high school diploma in 1941, McKay set his sights on putting the coal mines of West Virginia out of his future plans by accepting a football scholarship to Wake Forest. However, when he went down to North Carolina to enroll at Wake Forest in August, his mother became ill.[9] Without ever getting an opportunity to sit in a classroom at Wake Forest, McKay hurried home to help his family out financially. His mother did recover from her illness, but McKay opted to remain near her and went to work on a substation that provided electrical power.[10]

Around the same time, Japanese military forces bombed Pearl Harbor on December 7, 1941, which brought the United States into World War II. Like millions of other young men, McKay went off to fight overseas. He was called up for duty in the summer of 1942, serving in the Army Air Corps as a tail gunner aboard a B-29 Superfortress in the South Pacific. While in the military, one of McKay's superiors was a former All-American at Purdue University. He persuaded the young tail gunner to continue his academic and athletic quests at Purdue in West Lafayette, Indiana.[11] Initially, Purdue's interest in McKay was for his basketball skills, but his discharge from the Army Air Corps in January 1946 did not come in time for him to compete for a full basketball season.[12] It was then that he took his first step toward what would make him a legend in the Southland and beyond. Instead of sitting idly by waiting for almost a complete year to pass before a new basketball season would begin, McKay decided to test his skills as a football player during Purdue's spring drills.

His former All-State abilities as a running back impressed the coaching staff enough to offer him a spot on the varsity as a 23-year-old freshman. McKay became a starting defensive back for the 1946 season, and also saw time at running back. Cecil Isbell, a former star halfback at Purdue and the NFL's Green Bay Packers, was in his third and final year as head coach of the Boilermakers at the time of McKay's arrival. Following the 1946 season, Isbell decided to try his hand at coaching in the pros, and departed for the Baltimore Colts of the All-America Football Conference in 1947, thus leaving Purdue without a mentor.

What occurred next in McKay's life proved that the old adage regarding what a small world it really is held true. Purdue's trainer also left at about the time of Isbell's departure to serve the University of Oregon in the same capacity as he did the Boilermakers. Once in the Emerald State, the trainer informed Oregon's football coach, Jim Aiken, about McKay's abilities. It just so happened that Aiken was a good friend of McKay's old high school coach Mickey McClung, who then got in touch with his former All-State running back from Shinnston, West Virginia, convincing him to transfer to Oregon.[13]

McClung's words of advice paid off, as McKay travelled to the Great Northwest in 1947, and remained at Oregon until 1959. In 1948 and 1949 he played halfback, and helped the Ducks earn a 9–1 record and a share of the Pacific Coast Conference championship in 1948. Following graduation in 1950, McKay looked to pursue his dream of coaching. However, instead of returning to West Virginia, he remained in Oregon as an assistant on Aiken's staff.

After McKay's first season as an assistant, Aiken left Oregon. At this point, McKay thought his future with the Ducks was in jeopardy. He sought a job with the Federal Bureau of Investigation, but that idea was thwarted when Oregon's new head coach, Len Casanova, retained him after the school's athletic director, who was a friend of McKay's, put in a good word for him with Casanova.[14]

As the decade of the Fabulous Fifties rolled along, McKay established a friendship with USC assistant Nick Pappas while on scouting trips. Pappas was a former running back for the Trojans in the 1930s, and he came away highly respectful of McKay's football knowledge.[15] In the early portion of 1959, McKay went to Los Angeles to speak at a coaching clinic and to do some recruiting. Pappas and USC's head coach Don Clark were also there at the clinic, and the Trojans had an opening for an assistant position that they needed to fill. Pappas threw McKay's name out to Clark, who agreed and approached McKay about the job.[16] McKay's initial reaction to the opportunity was to contemplate the offer for a couple of weeks before giving an answer either way. His hesitation stemmed from his thinking that staying in Oregon would increase the chances of him eventually getting the head-coaching job there.[17]

At this time, the football program at USC found itself in an unfamiliar position. A descent toward the bottom of the rankings brought on by NCAA violations in 1956 reduced the perennial powerhouse to one win in 1957 and four the following year. The sanctions were about to be lifted at the time McKay was offered an assistant job. The general consensus from those close to the situation felt that McKay knew his opportunities would be better for advancement at a more highly acclaimed football school like USC.[18] Not hurting his decision was the fact that McKay's wife was a native Californian that wanted to return to the golden coast.[19] Meanwhile, Nick Pappas continued to apply pressure on McKay to take the USC job. After everything was compiled in the 36-year old McKay's cranium, he was packed and ready to head down Pacific Coast Highway some 900 miles and become one of Don Clark's assistants.

Upon his arrival, McKay's responsibilities were those of coaching the offensive backfield, running the offense, and also working with the defensive backs. His acceptance to be on Clark's staff in 1959 also allowed McKay the opportunity to be part of an incredible collection of coaches. Included in this stellar collection was future Oakland Raiders coach and eventual owner Al Davis, who possessed one of the game's greatest minds. In addition to Davis, the staff included Marv Goux, regarded as Mr. Trojan for his long-standing devotion and passion for the University of Southern California, and Mel Hein, one of the NFL's greatest linemen for the New York Giants during the 1930s.

McKay truly enjoyed working for Don Clark, and the team rolled to eight straight wins to go into their final two contests undefeated.[20] However, unbeknownst to all at the time, was that the future of USC football was established due to the results of those final games. The last two opponents on the 1959 USC schedule were their top rivals, UCLA and Notre Dame. Going into them, the Trojans were possibly in contention for a national title, but losses to both the Bruins and the Fighting Irish brought the proverbial journalistic hammer down hard on Don Clark. The scribes in the Southland lambasted Clark in the local dailies for the team's failure against their ultimate rivals, which might have cost the Trojans a championship.

McKay saw the treatment Clark was receiving from many media outlets, and was highly displeased with it. It became such a mess, that he looked to exit the college ranks and try using his expertise with the pros. He proceeded in that direction by contacting ex–Oregon teammate and star NFL quarterback Norm Van Brocklin, who was looking to take over the head coaching position of the Philadelphia Eagles, if their current mentor Buck Shaw retired in 1960. He had no problem offering McKay a position, but a turn of events stopped McKay from relocating to the City of Brotherly Love. Shaw decided to stay on one final season, and Van Brocklin played for him one more year, with the results adding up to an NFL championship for the Eagles. Van Brocklin did enter coaching following his retirement with the expansion Minnesota Vikings, but by then McKay was committed to USC.[21]

With the pressure adding up day after day, Don Clark decided to resign on December 15, 1959, thus leaving the Trojans with a void. At first, USC president Norman Topping looked to promote assistant Ray George, who had past head coaching experience at Texas A&M from 1951 to 1953. The job was George's for the taking, but he turned it down, claiming that McKay would serve the university better. Whether or not Ray George was a visionary, his thoughts about McKay's future turned out to be true, but in December 1959, the iconic coaching career that McKay carved out for himself could only be a distant dream. After George's words of praise, Topping called McKay, and he accepted the job on the same day Clark resigned.[22]

The success that McKay would pave out for himself over 16 seasons did not start off looking good. In fact, if the first two seasons of the John McKay era were any type of indicator as to his future leading the team, bleak would have been a perfect word to describe it. After coming off an 8–2 finish in 1959, the Trojans slumped to 4–6 in 1960 and 4–5–1 the following year. However, despite only eight wins over the course of two seasons, something happened in USC's third game of the 1961 season that proved to be a precursor for great things to come with McKay at the helm.

In his first two seasons at USC, McKay used the Wing "T" and sprint-out offense, but began putting together a game plan using the I-Formation. The I-Formation's maturation is traced back to Tom Nugent in 1950 while he coached at Virginia Military Institute. It was created as a substitute for the single-wing formation and another alterative to the T-Formation. It is mostly used in running situations, with the tailback being the focal point to the attack. It is set up with the fullback lined up directly behind the quarterback and the tailback positioned behind the fullback some six to eight yards from the line of scrimmage. The tailback stands in an upright position with his hands on his knees, thus allowing him more visibility to scan for weak spots to attack once the ball is placed in his hands. With the fullback used mostly as an extra blocker, the tailback, using speed and power, can do serious damage to a defense. Don Coryell, a coach that would one day go on to become a passing game specialist in the NFL, used the I-Formation while coaching high school in Hawaii, and on the college level in the mid-to-late 1950s. He then served one year on McKay's staff in 1960, and brought the I-Formation concept with him.[23]

On October 7, 1961, Iowa came into their game with USC as the top-ranked team in the nation. McKay's work with the I-Formation up to this time in the young season was anything but successful. The media looking down from the press box often enjoyed defining the "I" as incompetent, intolerable, and ineffective.[24] As the press corps was probably gearing up for more insulting monikers to incorporate into their sagas, the Trojans, after being down 21–0, came back to score 34 points and lost by a mere point, 35–34, in the closing minute. With the I-Formation as the Trojans' offensive weapon, the ground forces ate up the Hawkeye defense for 220 yards. This showing quickly took the USC I-Formation from incompetent, intolerable, and ineffective, to invincible.

Despite his I-Formation being on the cusp of possibly something great, his two-year record was no indicator that McKay's future in Los Angeles would be a long-standing one. He felt that his first two squads were the slowest he was ever around, and that his days as head coach were numbered. The university president, Norm Topping, decided against firing him, even though pressure was coming from alumni to end McKay's tenure quickly. Topping wanted to give McKay an extra year to showcase the players that he personally had a hand in recruiting, and that decision would pay off with huge dividends.[25]

In 1962, the Trojans and the I-Formation merged into what became an iconic union and one of the most revered in the history of college football, all with John McKay serving as the grand master. In time, McKay had 32 versions of the I-Formation in the USC playbook, and he never stopped finding ways to improve on it. Running the ball out of what became the famed Student Body Left and Right formations was without a doubt the focal point of McKay's reign at USC. He had immense confidence in his running attack, but liked to mix things up with a solid passing game to keep a defense off balance.[26]

He was also a staunch believer in recurrent substitution,

and practiced that belief by dividing the team into three groupings dubbed Red, Green, and Gold units. The Red unit took the field for the first five minutes of every quarter, followed by the Gold for the next four minutes, and the Green came in for the next three minutes. It was then back to the Red unit for the final three minutes of the quarter, and they remained on the field to start off the first five minutes of the new quarter.[27] This allowed every player to get on the field, produced no egomaniac attitudes, and made for a close-knit atmosphere.[28] At times, McKay might have had regrets about not taking one of the units off the field if it was moving the ball well. However, he remained steadfast in his plan, not wanting to have tired players on the field when the opposition was still full of vigor.[29]

With his philosophy, and many of the players he recruited all coming together as one, McKay's 1962 Trojans took on all comers and defeated each of them en route to an 11–0 record and a national championship. Following this incredible turnaround, McKay's future in Los Angeles was safe and as bright as a Southern California summer day. With his Red, Green, and Gold units working their way across the college football landscape throughout the 1960s and half of the 1970s, McKay produced a 127–40–8 record for a .749 winning percentage. His victory total still stands as the all-time best in USC history, and will not likely be toppled for a long time to come. Along the way to amassing those 127 wins, McKay guided the Trojans to eight outright conference titles, tied for a ninth, brought four national championships to USC, had 25 of his players reach All-American status, 89 achieve All-Conference honors, and saw two of his famed I-Formation tailbacks receive college football's ultimate award, the Heisman Trophy, with Mike Garrett and O.J. Simpson winning the coveted prize in 1965 and 1968 respectively.

Like every human being that has walked this Earth, John McKay was a person of many characteristics. He cast an imposing presence, was aloof at times, moody, quick to have his temper flared, cocky, and yet could possess a humorous, quick-witted personality, and an insecurity, if that was all possible considering all of his accolades.[30] His ability at quick humor allowed him to become known as "the Quipper," and left many laughing with hilarious one-liners. He was also highly intelligent, and a great judge of talent. He was a master at the recruiting process, which proved itself with the way he rang up victories at a steady clip for many years. He had the ability to move a player to another position and make All-America candidates out of them.[31] He might have been known for his offensive prowess, but McKay had his fare share of incredible defensive players. He loved the game of football, and thought about it constantly. Always looking for ways to improve, he would design plays on whatever was available when the inspiration struck. Sometimes he would scrawl plays on a cocktail napkin or a tablecloth.[32] Regardless of the surface it was written on, the odds were good that the play helped the Trojans continue on the path of greatness under McKay.

His persona struck fear in his players, but his assistants idolized him, as did the fans and media.[33] He was the alpha dog among football coaches, both college and professional, throughout Los Angeles during most of his time at USC. He virtually owned the City of Angels.

During his successful run in the college ranks, the National Football League saw the brilliance that McKay produced in the Southland. Looking to get him to join the NFL was not an uncommon practice, as the Cleveland Browns, New England Patriots, and Los Angeles Rams, all attempted to lure him away from the Trojans. Each time he refused, but the challenge of building a team from the ground up proved too great an opportunity to decline.

In 1976, the Tampa Buccaneers came in to the NFL as an expansion team, and McKay was there from the beginning to guide the infant franchise to success. However, in the beginning, things were brutal for McKay. The team lost every one of their games in their first season, and the first 12 in 1977. It was in the midst of this horrific 26-game losing streak that McKay delivered a classic one-liner that truly made his moniker of "the Quipper" stand up. When asked about his team's execution following a loss, McKay quickly responded that he was all for it.[34]

The Buccaneers were awful, but McKay persevered, and by 1979, he had the team at the doorstep of a Super Bowl. The Bucs finished at 10–6, won the NFC Central Division title, and beat the Philadelphia Eagles in a divisional playoff game. That victory allowed McKay and his upstarts the chance to play for the NFC championship. Unfortunately, the city that McKay owned, and where he achieved his fame, ended Tampa Bay's dream season. The Los Angeles Rams defeated Tampa Bay 9–0 to advance to Super Bowl XIV against the Pittsburgh Steelers.

After a dismal 5–10–1 finish in 1980, McKay led the Buccaneers to another division title in 1981, but the team suffered a loss to the Dallas Cowboys in the first round of the playoffs. In a strike-shortened 1982 season, Tampa Bay finished with a 5–4 record in 1982, made the playoffs, but once again fell victim to Dallas in the opening round of the playoffs. The team under McKay then reverted back to their old ways, finishing with a 2–14 record in 1983, and 6–10 in 1984.

Following the 1984 season, McKay stepped down as coach of the Buccaneers after posting a 44–88–1 record. Four years after his departure from Tampa Bay, the college football world recognized his incredible impact by inducting McKay into the College Football Hall of Fame in 1988.

On June 10, 2001, John McKay passed away in Tampa, Florida, from complications caused by diabetes at age 77. He returned to the Los Angeles Memorial Coliseum one final time following his death, as his ashes were scattered on the football field that saw his charges carve out an everlasting legacy for him. For his tireless efforts to make the Trojans a powerhouse, and the envy of many, the Los Angeles Coliseum commissioners honored him with a plaque in the Coliseum's "Court of Honor."[35]

His contributions to the Buccaneers also did not go unnoticed, as his guidance in getting the franchise get off the ground allowed McKay the honor of being inducted into Tampa Bay's "Ring of Honor" on December 5, 2010.[36] The name John McKay will always stand as the mark of excellence that all future USC head coaches can aspire. As a lasting tribute to this dedicated mentor, the University of Southern California opened the John McKay Center on the campus in 2012. Costing $70 million to build, and covering 110,000 square feet, the complex is an athletic and academic site that houses the USC football department, and includes everything to help make a player better both on the field and in the classroom.

Since his days under coach Mickey McClung at Shinnston High School, McKay dreamt of putting his athletic and academic skills to use in an attempt to avoid the drudgery of working in coal mines. He definitely was successful, and with college football as his stage in the same neighborhood as the Hollywood dream factories, the world was surely entertained and enriched by "the Quipper."

## *John Robinson*

The thought of replacing a legend can seem like a harrowing experience. In some incidents, that type of pressure is commonplace, but not in the case of John Robinson. For upon assuming the USC head coaching reins from John McKay, Robinson not only continued on with the "Quipper's" winning tradition, but he created his own lasting place among the best of his profession.

Shortly after a year-and-a-half following the repeal of the Noble Experiment known as Prohibition, the city of Chicago, forever to be remembered as the Mecca of that era's lawlessness, saw the future mentor of the Trojans draw his initial breath. Born on July 25, 1935, John Alexander Robinson remained a resident of the Windy City until his family moved to Provo, Utah, when he was six years old. Three years later, it was off to California for the nine-year old Robinson, where his family settled in Daly City. Named after California businessman John Daly, Robinson's new residence was the largest city in San Mateo County, which is just south of San Francisco.

Daly City was also the site where Robinson met not only a life-long friend, but one of the top professional head coaches of all-time. His name was John Madden, and together with Robinson, this duo became disciples of the school of sports obsession. Their young lives were totally consumed with all things sports, which is a common practice for many youngsters. However, this dynamic duo actually looked toward the future and how to turn their dreams into reality.

Initially, their plans consisted of playing for the New York Yankees in the summer and the San Francisco 49ers in the fall. As time passed and juvenile dreams met the harsh roadblocks of reality, the pair shifted direction, but were still on course for careers in sports. Coaching replaced actual performing as a profession for their future plans. However, both were still dedicated to participating in sports for as long as possible, and each became very accomplished athletes long before patrolling the sidelines as mentors.

The coaching aspect hit them early, as they would go to 49ers practice sessions and dissect what was going on.[1] While watching training camp at St. Mary's College in Moraga, California, the pair not only knew the players and their positions, but attempted to guess what coverages would be used, and discuss all other aspects of what occurred on the field.

When it came time to attend high school, Madden went to Jefferson High School, where he excelled in football and baseball. Robinson decided to enroll at Junipero Serra High School in San Mateo, located in the San Francisco Bay Area. The private Catholic school was established ten years before Robinson entered the Blue & Gold fold of the Padres. This was also the same high school that produced star athletes Lynn Swann, Barry Bonds, and Tom Brady. Robinson might not have reached the legendary status as an athlete like that trio, but he did achieve his fair share of accolades. He was a talented lineman that earned national recognition by being named to the Catholic All-America team as a senior. On the state level, Robinson was bestowed with All-Cal and All-Northern California honors.

Upon high school graduation in 1954, Robinson headed up to the University of Oregon to play football for head coach Len Casanova. It was at Oregon that childhood friends were reunited, as John Madden joined Robinson during their freshman year. Madden then transferred to California Polytechnic State University in San Luis Obispo. Robinson remained, and was a member of Oregon's Rose Bowl team following his senior season.[2] The 1957 Oregon team was picked to end the year in seventh place in the Pacific Coast Conference. However, with the PCC's top-rated scoring defense, a solid offensive running game, and a group of hard-fighting players that refused to give up, the Ducks finished the season at 7–4, and shocked the college football community by winning the conference and making their first Rose Bowl appearance in 38 years. Despite losing the Rose Bowl, 10–7, to Ohio State, Oregon fought hard even though they were 20-point underdogs going into the game.

It was under these great conditions that Robinson ended his playing career, and looked to the future, with football about to become his life's work. After serving in the Army, Robinson was ready to delve into the world of coaching, and Len Casanova gave his former player an opportunity to test his skill level at his old alma mater. Robinson served under Casanova as an assistant offensive coach until the coach left his position following the 1966 season to become Oregon's athletic director. Even though Robinson was more than capable of being elevated to fill Casanova's job, another assistant, Jerry Frei, took over at the helm of the program from 1967 through 1971.

During his 12 seasons as an offensive assistant, Robinson helped the Ducks compile a winning 61–58–6 record, with most of the victories coming during the Casanova years. Despite the team's fortunes, Robinson was a proverbial ball of energy with overwhelming enthusiasm, regardless of the amount of wins or losses. His passionate approach for the game resembled that of his friend John Madden, who had no trouble expressing his emotions on the sidelines. Despite Oregon not being in the upper echelon of the conference standings on many occasions, Robinson's positive belief in the team always brought out the bold prediction that the Ducks would be Rose Bowl bound by the end of the regular season. However, when the opposite occurred, the alumni did not have any problems displaying their unhappiness for the passionate assistant. Even though disapproval was commonplace when Robinson's predictions failed to become reality, he always remained steadfast with his belief year in and year out.

Robinson also had the ability to absorb information related to the game of football and convey it to his players. He could get the most out of his players, and made them believe in themselves. Two of his charges at Oregon in the late 1960s and early 70s were quarterback Dan Fouts and running back/receiver Bobby Moore, who changed his name to Ahmad Rashad after converting to Islam in 1972. Under Robinson's guidance, Fouts set 19 Oregon passing records, and Rashad earned All-American honors. Both then went on to have excellent professional careers, with Fouts eventually earning enshrinement into the Pro Football Hall of Fame.

Following the season finale against Oregon State in 1971, Robinson received a phone call from former Oregon assistant, and now firmly entrenched USC legend, John McKay. He sought Robinson out to come to Los Angeles and serve as USC's offensive coordinator. While McKay was an assistant under Len Casanova at Oregon, he was Robinson's favorite coach on the staff. McKay saw Robinson's passion for the game, and always took time to discuss football with him.[3] When McKay went off to create a legendary coaching career in the Southland, and Robinson was an Oregon assistant, the two still stayed in contact.

The change of scenery was drastic for Robinson when he accepted McKay's offer. He departed from his alma mater after nearly two decades of association with the Ducks as a player and coach, with many seasons hovering near or below the .500 mark. At USC, Robinson was thrust into a new world, where winning records were a yearly occurrence.

After years of knowing what Robinson was capable of achieving, McKay felt that he perfect for the job of rejuvenating the Trojans' offense after two straight seasons of finishing at 6–4–1, which was not bad for some schools, but at USC it was looked at as being sub-par. Robinson did not waste time upon his arrival in Los Angeles. His belief was to play hard, and execute on both sides of the ball, and grind out a solid running attack. This no doubt had been the plan of countless coaches throughout football history, but it took a special kind of person to bring it out of players. Robinson was that type since his Oregon days, and accomplished the same with the Trojans. After studying film over countless hours, and evaluating the talent presented to him, Robinson and McKay discussed all the material, and what they accomplished was history making.[4]

In Robinson's first year on McKay's staff, the 1972 Trojans took on all comers and emerged victorious each time. They won the national championship with a spotless 12–0 record, and are regarded as one of college football's greatest teams. Robinson was part of two more Pac-8 title teams (1973, 1974), and helped bring USC a second national championship in 1974.

With three Pac-8 titles and two national championships added to his resume, Robinson looked to expand his coaching experience by departing the college game after 15 years for an opportunity to serve as an assistant on John Madden's Oakland Raiders staff in 1975. By this time, Madden was one of the NFL's premier head coaches. This allowed the duo a chance to put in motion what they fantasized about decades earlier while watching San Francisco 49ers practice sessions to good use.

While Robinson was assisting his old friend in Oakland, his previous boss, John McKay, had announced that the 1975 season would be his swan song at USC. For just like Robinson, McKay looked to head off to the NFL to help mold and shape the expansion Tampa Bay Buccaneers. Halfway through the 1975 season, McKay contacted Robinson in an effort to get him to come to Tampa with him starting in 1976. However, Robinson declined his old mentor's offer, possibly on the whim that he might get the USC job. It was a big gamble, but it eventually paid off.[5]

At the same time as McKay's announcement at USC, another coaching legend from the same neighborhood stated that he was retiring. The "Wizard of Westwood," UCLA basketball coaching legend John Wooden informed the media that he was stepping down as coach of the Bruins after bringing 10 NCAA championships to the university. With the departure of one of the most revered coaches in basketball history, and USC's all-time greatest football coach leaving the Southland at the same time, the city's sports scene was left with a feeling of emptiness.

The exodus of Wooden and McKay created what was dubbed "the Big Turnover" in Los Angeles.[6] Despite the emptiness created by McKay's announcement, the position of head coach had to be addressed and filled. Initially, USC alumni felt that Dave Levy would be appointed the new coach. He was McKay's top assistant, serving on USC's staff since 1960, and was regarded as one of college football's elite assistants. Also in the running was Marv Goux, whose passion for Trojan football was second to none. Both of these men were very well respected by all USC faithful, and it seemed apparent that one of them would be crowned as the successor to McKay's throne.[7]

Even though the buzz around the City of Angels might have been about Levy and Goux, a big hush hovered over the USC campus. It seemed that USC's chancellor, Dr. John Hubbard, who was a big football fan, already had his man in mind. Hubbard's passion for the gridiron took him to the practice field on a regular basis, and he had many discussions with Robinson while he was an assistant at USC. It was through those conversations that Hubbard came away impressed with Robinson's expertise. During McKay's final season at USC, Hubbard contacted Robinson while he was assisting friend John Madden in Oakland, and offered him the soon-to-be-vacant head coaching position at USC.[8]

Needless to say, Robinson jumped at the offer. However, despite his excitement for the opportunity, those close to the university, the alumni and media, were not bursting with joy over the decision. It was assumed that a big name would be announced to fill one of the most prestigious jobs in college football within the confines of the glitz and glamour of Hollywood. On November 10, 1975, the Land of Troy was presented with the Trojans' new football coach, John Robinson. Puzzled looks were commonplace when the new coach was announced, but in time, his name would be spoken with reverence.[9]

After taking over the throne following the reign of a legend, Robinson was very cautious not to take away any of the traditions that McKay started and successful with. He kept the vaunted "Student Body Left and Right" running attack, and would continue to use it with incredible results that produced All-Americans in Ricky Bell, Charles White, and Marcus Allen, with the latter two winning the Heisman Trophy. He did some minor tweaking, and hired some new assistants to breathe new life into the program. In an effort to boost a passing attack that had trouble recently, Robinson brought in a well-respected offensive coach in Paul Hackett to work with the quarterbacks. He also gave some young assistants an opportunity, bringing into the Trojan fold Hudson Houck, Norv Turner, and Bob Toledo, all of which would go on to earn impressive careers in coaching.[10] Rounding out his first coaching staff at USC, Robinson retained Foster Andersen, Marv Goux, Skip Husbands, and Don Lindsay from McKay.

With all the new pieces in place, the 1976 Trojans were now ready to display what Robinson had honed to take on the college football world, with supporters and detractors alike awaiting the outcome. However, it appeared that the detractors won the first round of the Robinson era after USC's opening game on September 11, 1976. With an opening day crowd of 49,535 on hand at the Los Angeles Memorial Coliseum, the Trojans burst onto the field led by a new mentor for the first time in 16 years. Robinson was so pumped up with emotion as he proceeded to lead the team out of the Coliseum tunnel and onto the field for the dawn of a new era in USC football. However, an omen of things to come on that day occurred when Robinson stumbled and a good portion of the team kept going, running over their coach in the process.[11] Despite the mishap getting out to the sideline, the day got worse for Robinson, as the Trojans were outclassed by Missouri, 46–25. Robinson felt the team was ready for the game, but some big mistakes proved costly. Things got so bad, that when quarterback Vince Evans went down with an injury, the crowd booed him as he was walking off the field.[12]

This was not the beginning that Robinson had hoped and dreamed of. The next phase following the embarrassment on the field was when he had to face the media, and also personal appearances with alumni as the week wore on. Even though both outlets were not too pleased with Robinson, the coach only blamed himself, and stated that what happened against Missouri would not be seen again. This was the same attitude that he showed as an assistant at Oregon, when he predicted Rose Bowl appearances every year despite the team not being up to that quality of competition. The only difference from his passionate predictions in Oregon, to those as USC's head coach, was that his words held true. The Trojans went out the following week and destroyed Robinson's alma mater Oregon, 53–0, and ran the table the rest of the way, finishing the regular season at 10–1. It was then on to the Rose Bowl, and with a 14–6 victory over Michigan, USC finished the year at 11–1 and in second place in the national polls. An interesting footnote to Robinson's first year, was eight days following the Rose Bowl, he saw his old friend John Madden's Oakland Raiders capture the organization's first Super Bowl victory on the same field. Both men dreamt of this day back in Daly City, and in the first week of 1977, reality saw them as champions.

The following year saw USC finish at 8–4 and with a victory in the Bluebonnet Bowl. During that season, which was considered sub-par under USC standards, it became apparent to Robinson that opposing defenses were learning how to play against the powerful I-Formation that made USC Tailback U. Teams were lining up eight players in the box, meaning that a defensive back would come in closer to the line of scrimmage to help out the defensive linemen and linebackers stop the run. Robinson counterbalanced this move by being one of the first college coaches to have a player in motion, then stop, turn around, and then shoot through the targeted point of attack that the offense was looking to strike. This plan, along with a solid passer in junior quarterback Paul McDonald and the running of another junior, Charles White, helped the 1978 Trojans create a well-balanced attack. Mixed into the group were talented players throughout the roster, and the result was a 12–1 finish that included a Robinson's second conference title in three seasons, plus a national championship.[13]

In 1979, Robinson's Trojans once against won a conference championship, and contended for a repeat national title, but a 21–21 tie with Stanford was considered the one blemish that more-than-likely cost them that opportunity. The Trojans finished the 1979 season at 11–0–1, beat the previously undefeated Ohio State Buckeyes in the Rose Bowl, and added another Heisman Trophy winner, Charles White, to the university's proud football legacy.

By this time in Robinson's tenure as head coach at USC, he had compiled a 42–6–1 record, three conference titles, three Rose Bowl victories, and a national championship. His smooth and congenial approach with media, coupled with an impressive run as coach, solidified his legacy as one of USC's top-rated mentors of all-time. He also had the ability to put the blame for losses on his own shoulders, never throwing it at his team. This allowed his players to respect him, and they were willing to give everything they had for him.[14]

With his place firmly entrenched as leader of the Cardinal & Gold, Robinson looked to keep the good times rolling as the 1980s came upon the horizon. However, the magic from the late 1970s did not carry over, as the Trojans finished at 8–2–1 in 1980, followed by 9–3 and 8–3 finishes in 1981 and 1982. Robinson also suffered his lone bowl defeat while coach of the Trojans, with that coming in the Fiesta Bowl after the 1981 season against Penn State. In 1982, the Trojans were hit with an NCAA penalty due to players selling their tickets, and the team was prohibited from appearing in any bowl game following the season. Marcus Allen provided excitement for the program at this time by becoming the first running back in college football history to surpass 2,000 yards on the ground, and for his efforts, he was awarded the 1981 Heisman Trophy.

After compiling a 67–14–2 record over seven seasons, Robinson resigned as head coach of the Trojans on November 23, 1982 at age 46, much to the surprise of many. He felt like he needed a change, and went in a completely different direction. He was appointed vice president of USC in charge of fundraising. After his stellar career, coupled with his passionate personality, it seemed like a perfect fit. However, a few months into his new career, Robinson yearned to get back to the sidelines.[15]

In 1983, the Los Angeles Rams gave Robinson the opportunity to get back into the sometimes-frenzied world of coaching. He responded to the challenge with the same type of passion that he exhibited at USC, and his results were successful. From 1983 through 1991, the Rams under Robinson had a record of 75–68, won two division titles (1985 and tied for it in 1988), went to the playoffs six times out of eight seasons, and played in two NFC championship games, losing both times to the eventual Super Bowl champs.

After two losing seasons in 1990 and 1991, in which the Rams won a combined eight games, Robinson was released as coach. This dismal time could have been blamed on bad decisions from the team hierarchy, mixed with poor draft selections. These two negatives never produce positive results, and Robinson was on his way out. He then went to work in broadcasting until 1993, when the glory of his past was needed in the worst way.

The Trojans' football program was headed downward by

the end of the 1992 season. The tenures of Ted Tollner and Larry Smith, despite some good times, was not up to the standards that USC fans, alumni, and university leaders, had come to expect since the days of Elmer Henderson back in the 1920s. The program needed to be rejuvenated, and John Robinson was looked to as the person who could bring back the glory. On January 3, 1993, Robinson took over for a highly disgruntled Larry Smith, who was fired two days earlier.

His second term as head coach lasted for six seasons, and he did manage to produce five winning records, coupled with one at .500. Robinson also took the Trojans to three straight bowl games in his first three seasons back at the helm, and won all of them. However, Robinson saw that things were not looking up for the program, and it appeared that it was once again heading downward. Relations with athletic director Mike Garrett were stagnant at best, and his second tenure ended on December 17, 1997, although he was never spoken to about it. The action bordered on theater of the absurd, as the university hired Paul Hackett without the new coach present at the news conference, and USC officials did not understand why Robinson was not on hand during the announcement. However, while the news conference was going on at USC, the 62-year old Robinson held a conference of his own a few miles off campus. He handled the situation with style and class. He felt that USC was a special place to be, and was thankful for the opportunity he was presented with to lead the Cardinal & Gold for a combined 12 seasons, which saw him produce an incredible all-time record of 104–35–4.[16]

Two years after his farewell to USC, Robinson resurfaced on the sidelines in Sin City as head coach at the University of Nevada Las Vegas. He also served as UNLV's athletic director for one year in 2002. Robinson managed to work some of his old magic after posting a 3–8 record in his first year leading the Rebels. In 2000, he guided UNLV to an 8–5 record and a victory in the Las Vegas Bowl while earning Mountain Coach of the Year honors fort himself. Unfortunately, that season proved to be the only successful one during the six he spent in Las Vegas. Following a 2–9 record in 2004, and a combined 28–42 slate, Robinson left the program. In 2009, Robinson was inducted into the College Football Hall of Fame. With that everlasting honor, he matched his old friend John Madden, who is enshrined in the Pro Football Hall of Fame, in obtaining immortality among the heroes of the game. Not bad for two Daly City products that dared to dream big and made the most of the opportunities presented to them on their way down life's path.

## *Ted Tollner*

Ted Tollner carried on the proud tradition of Rose Bowl conquests first established by sideline generals of Trojans past. In four seasons at the helm of the Trojans, Tollner captured victory in the "Granddaddy" of all bowl games, when tenth ranked USC knocked off fifth ranked Ohio State in the 1985 Rose Bowl. However, that was only a small tidbit of the complete story of Tollner's existence.

The 17th head coach in USC football history was born on May 29, 1940. The native Californian, whose hometown was San Francisco, established himself as a solid athlete in football and baseball. His abilities led him to California Polytechnic University (San Luis Obispo) to continue his athletic pursuits and education in the late 1950s. He became the Mustangs starting quarterback for two seasons, was elected team captain, and used his stellar throwing arm in the spring as a pitcher in baseball for four campaigns. In addition to earning All-Conference honors in football and baseball, Tollner also played for the USA baseball team at the 1962 Pan American games. His prowess on the gridiron and diamond garnered Tollner permanent honor in 1989 when he was enshrined into the Cal Poly Athletic Hall of Fame.

In life there is a saying that along with the good comes the bad. In the case of Ted Tollner, while his college days were filled with exceptional moments of athletic achievement, they will be remembered for a horrific incident that drastically changed the lives of 48 people on October 29, 1960.[1]

The Mustangs were attempting to build on a winning tradition created under coach LeRoy Hughes in the late 1950s, which saw Cal Poly compile a 59–18 record from 1952 through 1959. The great Hall of Fame coach for the Oakland Raiders, John Madden, was an All-Conference two-way tackle for Cal Poly toward the end of the Mustangs' dominance in the decade. With many of the stars graduated, the future of the program rested in the hands of a team led by a large group of underclassmen, with Tollner being one of them. This group, led by Tollner, rebounded from a season opening 34–14 loss to Brigham Young University, with a commanding 34–6 victory over San Diego State. Three straight losses to Montana State, Fresno State, and California State-Long Beach followed, as the team set out to travel to Bowling Green University in Ohio for a matchup on October 29th.[2]

Cal Poly was totally outclassed on that day, losing by the worst margin of the year, 50–6. The game was over by the middle of the day, but the team was not scheduled to fly out of Toledo until 8:00pm. When time arrived to takeoff, a heavy fog engulfed the area. Despite much apprehension, and two hours of discussions between pilots on whether to fly or wait until the fog cleared, the decision was made to leave the Buckeye State. It was then that the C-46 twin-engine airliner took off into the air and its ill-fated place in aviation history.[3]

Within a few minutes after takeoff, with Ted Tollner sitting by the left wing, one of the engines made a sputtering noise and then fell silent. It was estimated that the plane was 100 feet off the ground when that engine shut down. The plane began to shake wildly, and then the other engine shut down. It was then a plunge to Earth that concluded with the plane landing on its nose on a runway of the airport. The plane split into two halves with fire and explosions occurring. Some of the passengers were thrown from the plane, with Tollner being one of them. He was still strapped in his seat and was temporarily knocked unconscious. Once he awoke amidst the burning carnage, he attempted to help anyone he could, but he could not stand up due to an injured foot. Some of his teammates found him and dragged their captain to safety. In all, 22 passengers died, including 16 Cal Poly football players.[4]

After healing from his injury, Tollner completed his athletic career and earned a Bachelor's Degree from Cal Poly in 1962. He later completed work on a Master's Degree in Physical Education. Armed with a college education, a strong athletic background, and a powerful life experience, despite the terrible circumstances, Tollner decided to pursue a career as a teacher and coach.

From 1963 to 1967, he served in both capacities at Woodside High School in San Mateo County, California.[5] Woodside gained a reputation since opening its doors in 1958 as the alma mater of pro football player Julian Edelman of the New England Patriots, NBA player Rich Kelly, and Olympic gold medal-winning swimmer John Naber.[6] Tollner began his time with the Woodside Wildcats as an offensive coordinator and then was promoted to head coach before his departure to the college ranks.

Eleven miles north of Woodside High School is the campus of San Mateo College. It was there that Tollner traded in the Wildcats for the Bulldogs, serving the latter as an assistant and head coach from 1968 to 1972. The ever-changing life of a coach next saw Tollner travel to the southern area of California to be a member of Claude Gilbert's coaching staff at San Diego State, serving as offensive coordinator from 1973 to 1980. In 1981, Tollner served one season in Utah, coaching quarterbacks at Brigham Young University, where two of his charges, Jim McMahon and Steve Young, would go on to lead teams to Super Bowl glory.[7]

In March of 1982, Tollner was summoned back to his native California by USC head coach John Robinson, who looked to the 42-year old long-time assistant to boost the Trojan offense. Nine months following his hiring as offensive coordinator, Tollner was cast into the role of head coach. On November 23, 1982, John Robinson resigned as head coach, but not before singing the praises of his offensive coordinator. It was felt that Tollner was a low profile, astute type of football man that was shocked by the promotion. Not only was this his first opportunity to be the head coach at a Division I school, but it was one of the most high profile jobs in his profession.[8]

When all the euphoria that the announcement brought with it quickly faded, the realization of guiding such a storied program sunk in. It was claimed that Tollner might not have been absolutely primed for the task, in most part due to upcoming sanctions put on the football program by the NCAA, which included bowl game and recruiting restrictions.[9] However, Tollner was a football man with a long-standing resume behind him, and looked to delve into the job with his confidence high.

Despite the natural feeling that all coaches have about succeeding, Tollner learned early on that handling the responsibilities of a powerhouse program like USC's could be overwhelming. The football aspect was the easy part for him. It was something that he did for many years, and he had confidence in himself when dealing with that part of the job.[10] It was the other items on his itinerary down the coaching path at USC where time seemed lost, with so much of it dedicated to handling media and alumni outlets.[11]

The pros and cons of the USC job fought against each other in his initial season as head coach in 1983, as the Trojans finished well below their normal standard at 4–6 and fourth place in the Pac-10. Things appeared to be on the upswing for Tollner in his second year, as he adapted to his surroundings and developed a more calm approach to the high-powered position he held.[12] As a result, the Trojans were back in familiar territory. They finished at 9–3, won the Pac-10 championship and conquered Ohio State, 20–17, in their first Rose Bowl trip in five years. For his efforts, Tollner was awarded with the 1984 Pac-10 Coach of the Year Award.

That victorious 1984 season proved to be the end of a joyous alliance with the Trojans. An effort to keep the team growing after another Rose Bowl conquest fell extremely short over the next two seasons. In 1985 the team broke even at 6–6, followed by a 7–5 record in 1986, with both years ending in fourth place finishes in the Pac-10. In Tollner's time with the Trojans, he had won 21 Pac-10 games, which was only second to UCLA's 22, and posted a 6–1 record against teams ranked in the top ten nationally. In that regard, he was doing well, but against USC's most intense rivals, UCLA and Notre Dame, he had a paltry 1–7 combined record. Added to this albatross was the fact that Athletic Director Dick Perry, who hired Tollner as head coach, was no longer his boss. Dr. Mike McGee had assumed the AD role, and his relationship with Tollner was not the best. Personalities clashed and trust issues arose, and the outcome of the final two games on the 1986 schedule eventually led to separation between Tollner and USC.[13]

After UCLA romped to a 45–25 victory, headlines in Los Angeles screamed out that the team was going to be playing for Tollner's job in the season finale against Notre Dame.[14] That is indeed what happened, as the Trojans fell to Notre Dame by a mere point, 38–37, on November 29th. One week to the day later, on December 6, 1986, Tollner was relieved of his duties as head coach of the Trojans after four seasons and a record of 26–20–1.

Following his time at USC, Tollner initially went to the National Football League to serve as receiver coach with the Buffalo Bills from 1987 through 1988. He then went to the San Diego Chargers (1989–91 as quarterback coach and offensive coordinator), and the Los Angeles Rams (1992–93 as quarterback coach), before finding his way back into the college game. From 1994 through 2001, Tollner was head coach at San Diego State. His sterling season leading the Aztecs came in 1998, when San Diego State finished in a tie with Brigham Young for the Pacific Division title in the Western Athletic Conference. For his work, Tollner received the 1998 Western Athletic Conference Coach of the Year Award. After a 43–48 record at San Diego State, and a combined 69–68–1 record as a head coach in college, Tollner headed back to the NFL. He worked for the San Francisco 49ers (2002–04, 2007–08), Detroit Lions (2005), and the Oakland Raiders (2009–10).[15]

## *Larry Smith*

Within a span of 25 years, Larry Smith went from being an assistant coach at Shawnee High School to the bright lights of Los Angeles as a mentor in the Land of Troy. The trek that took Smith to mentor of the Trojans began 2,200 miles east of the USC campus in Van Wert, Ohio, located in the northwestern part of the Buckeye State. It was there that Smith was born on September 12, 1939.

While attending Van Wert High School, Smith was a three-sport star before graduating in 1957. During his time at the school, the Cougars won three straight league championships in football. He then set his sights on attending the United States Military Academy at West Point. His dream was achieved when he earned acceptance, but only remained there until 1958. It seemed his priorities changed, and the realization that he wanted to become a coach took him in a different direction.[1]

It was the calling to pursue the world of coaching that brought Smith back home to Ohio. Some 80 miles north of his birthplace, Smith enrolled at Bowling Green State University, and it was there that he took the first step toward his life's profession. Smith became a three-year letterman (1959–61) as a two-way end under head coach Doyt Perry. Smith helped the Falcons ride a wave of success that produced a combined 25–3 record. The team captured two Mid-American Conference championships (1959, 1961), and finished in second place in 1960.[2] The 1959 team posted an undefeated season and was named the best small college in the nation. Smith's efforts in getting the Falcons to one of the greatest time periods in the football program's history, was rewarded by him earning All-Mid-American Conference honors. He also served as team captain in 1961. In addition to his successful college football career, Smith earned a Bachelor's degree in Mathematics in 1962. Five years later, he completed work on his Master's degree in Education.

Armed with a solid football background and a college education, Smith set out to conquer his desired profession. His first stop on the coaching carousel was at Lima Shawnee High School, located approximately 70 miles north of Dayton, Ohio. He began his career as an assistant in 1962, and served in that capacity until 1964, when he was promoted to head coach. Smith proved to be a defense-minded coach and tolerated no nonsense. Under his leadership, the Shawnee Indians captured the Western Buckeye League championship in 1964 and 1966.

After four years on the high school level. Smith had proven himself enough that the college ranks beckoned, and it was Bo Schembechler that allowed him an opportunity starting in 1967. At the time, Schembechler was head coach at Miami University in Ohio. Long regarded as the "Cradle of Coaches," Miami was responsible for getting many stellar mentors on their way toward legendary status. Woody Hayes, Ara Parseghian, and in the late 1960s, Bo Schembechler, were just some of the coaches that established themselves there. Smith had the opportunity to be a part of this tradition as assistant coach in charge of defensive ends for two seasons, and help the team obtain a 13–7 record during his stay. When Schembechler left Miami to carve out his place among coaching immortals at the University of Michigan, Smith went along, serving as the Wolverines' offensive line coach from 1969 through 1972. With Smith on the staff, the Maize and Blue posted a 38–7 record that included one outright Big Ten title in 1971, and a share of two more in 1969 and 1972.

Also on Michigan's staff at this time was fellow Van Wert native Jim Young, who also was a high school teammate of Smith's. In 1973 Young was hired as head football coach at the University of Arizona, and he recruited Smith to come along. From 1973 through the 1975 season, Smith served on Young's staff as linebacker coach, defensive coordinator, and assistant head coach. Prior to the Young and Smith tandem coming to the Grand Canyon State, the Arizona football program was in disarray, suffering through four straight losing seasons before Young took over. In 1973, the program was turned completely around, as the Wildcats finished at 8–3 and tied for the Western Athletic Conference championship. Over Smith's time with Arizona, the team put together a 26–7 record, and by 1976, he had earned enough success and experience as an assistant that he was ready to guide a team of his own.

Bourbon Street and the French Quarter are hot destinations in New Orleans. Six miles from those locations is the home of the Tulane University Green Wave. Unlike the popular attractions in the French Quarter, the Tulane football program was suffering through extremely hard times as America's bicentennial came upon the scene in 1976. For over the previous 25 seasons, the Green Wave finished with a losing record on 19 occasions. The university looked to Larry Smith in an effort to build their football program into something other than a mockery.

Taking on a program with such little success for over a quarter of a century is a difficult task, but it was also an opportunity to test his skills as the man in charge. It first appeared that Smith's journey to the Big Easy was going to be a bumpy one. In his first year as a head coach, Tulane only mustered two wins against nine losses. However, Smith's guidance seemed to be leading the team in the right direction. The following two seasons saw Tulane improve by one win over the previous year, finishing with three victories in 1977 and four in 1978. By 1979, the Green Wave was ready to bust out of the football doldrums that plagued the program for so long. They started off the season by defeating 13th ranked Stanford, and used that uplifting victory to carry them on the way to an impressive 9–2 regular season finish. It seemed that interest in Tulane football was at an all-time high thanks to Smith's coaching ability. A testament to Smith's leadership occurred when 73,496 fans turned out to watch the Green Wave play Louisiana State University in the final game of the regular season. This marked the largest crowd to ever witness a Tulane football game in the New Orleans Superdome, and Smith's charges did not disappoint the throng, as they defeated their Big Easy rivals, 24–13. They were ranked 15th in the national polls, and earned a trip to the program's first bowl game in six years. They met Penn State in the Liberty Bowl, but lost a close 9–6 battle with the Nittany Lions.[3]

Despite Smith's overall record at Tulane being 18–27, he rebuilt the program, with half of those victories coming in the 1979 campaign. He also produced ten All-Americans in his four seasons at Tulane. The turnaround he accomplished at Tulane garnered him much attention. He was wooed by Arizona University, and accepted the offer to return to the Wildcats, this time replacing Tony Mason as head coach beginning in 1980.[4]

The dawn of the 1980s saw Arizona entering their third season in the Pac-10, and just coming off a Fiesta Bowl loss. As leader of the Wildcats, Smith was a staunch proponent of in-state recruiting, heightened the intensity of the rivalry with Arizona State University, and drove his team through the philosophy of running and hitting. His first season ended at 5–6, but the best was yet to come. That was Smith's lone season under

.500 while at Arizona. In 1981, the Wildcats improved to 6–5, and recorded a major upset by knocking off the top ranked USC Trojans. Another six wins followed in 1982, and over the course of the next four seasons, Arizona never ended the year with fewer than seven victories. Smith finished seven seasons at Arizona with a 48–28–3 record that included seven All-Americans and two bowl games appearances. He tied Georgia in the 1985 Sun Bowl, and then ended his tenure at Arizona with a victory over North Carolina in the 1986 Aloha Bowl.[5]

While Smith was basking in the success he accomplished at Arizona, the University of Southern California was headed down a stagnant road. A team used to continued success for many years, the Trojans were hanging on at the .500 mark over the two previous years. When USC's athletic director Dick Perry left, Dr. Mike McGee took over the position in 1984. His relationship with football coach Ted Tollner was slightly less than congenial, and he looked to install his own man at the helm of the team. Following Tollner's combined 1–7 record against USC's top rivals, Notre Dame and UCLA, McGee felt he had a legitimate reason to do out with the old and in with the new.[6] Tollner was relieved of his duties on December 6, 1986, and the team was without a football coach throughout the rest of the year. It was felt by many insiders that the team needed the new coach to come from within the Trojan fold, but McGee already had his good friend Larry Smith in mind. McGee felt that Smith would bring his tough discipline to the program and steer it in the right direction upward. Smith also had a reputation for being hard on his players' academic pursuits, and molding them into becoming solid individuals character-wise.[7]

On January 2, 1987, it became official, as Smith took over the USC Trojans. With his hiring, Smith became the first head football coach without any previous links to USC since Howard Jones in 1925.[8] His knack of taking over programs stuck in limbo and building them back up was once again apparent with the Trojans. McGee looked like a genius when his friend Larry Smith took the Trojans to a combined 27–8–1 record over his first three seasons from 1987 through 1989. During that time, USC won three straight Pac-10 championships, made three trips to the Rose Bowl, and won a then-USC record 19 straight conference games.

The 1988 team proved to be Smith's best. With Heisman Trophy hopeful Rodney Peete at quarterback, the Trojans got out to a 10–0 start and were the 2nd ranked team in the country. Unfortunately, the Trojans then lost to eventual national champion Notre Dame, and a few weeks later, suffered a 22–14 defeat to Michigan in the Rose Bowl. The team came back strong in 1989, posting a 9–2–1 record and got revenge over Michigan in the Rose Bowl with a 17–10 victory.

It appeared that at this stage of his USC tenure, Smith was going to make the Rose Bowl a second home, much like it was for the Trojans under John McKay and John Robinson. However, by the beginning of the 1990s, the love fest between coach and those involved with the football program, began to unravel. Like most human beings, Smith was talked about in positive ways, but in other circles, he was not too well received.

Jon Arnett, a Trojan star in the 1950s, along with a business associate, wrote a lengthy letter calling for major changes at the top of the helm. The letter's contents were not meant to reach the public sector, but like so many times in history, the written word has a way of leaking out to the masses. Such was the case of Arnett's rant, which stated that Smith had an insufficient philosophy, and not a very creative play calling selection.[9] An apology was sent to Smith from Arnett about the story leaking out, but not in regards to its content.[10]

Smith did little to help his cause. His relationship with the media and alumni was sour, despite both outlets being extremely important factors within the workings of the program. A congenial working relationship with both was also a large part of a coach's job.[11] Another major dose of negativity surrounding Smith was his tampering with the USC tailback philosophy, which was looked at as sacrilegious in the Land of Troy. From the McKay and Robinson eras, tailbacks at USC were the focal points of the offense. They were big, tough runners that were capable of carrying the ball 30 to 40 times a game and either blast between the tackles or quickly get to the outside on a sweep around the end. In Smith's system, he wanted his tailbacks to be smaller, at 5–10 or so, and not as muscular.[12] With this physical stature, Smith's idea of a tailback would be one that could wiggle through a defense with a cut-back style of running and not power. It appeared that he was looking for a pony to replace a thoroughbred. Initially, Smith's concept on the tailback position worked out somewhat, but then it began to fail.

Smith also began to have an extremely strained relationship with his quarterback sensation, Todd Marinovich. Marinovich had been programmed since birth by his father to become the perfect quarterback. With a regimented upbringing that saw Marinovich on a strict diet of health foods and exercise, that included quarterbacking drills, he became a perfect physical specimen at the quarterback position.

The coach and quarterback union is an important one. When the dynamics of the relationship click, success and admiration are abundant from both parties. However, when the opposite is true, a volatile situation occurs that can tear a team apart. The latter was the case with Smith and Marinovich, who was an excellent passer but had trouble adapting to Smith's not so creative offensive schemes.[13] A strained co-existence between the two totally ruptured on December 31, 1990 in a 17–16 loss to Michigan State in the John Hancock Bowl. In front of a national television audience, Marinovich and Smith engaged in a heated verbal conflict that consisted of swearing and rants of anger from both participants. Within a month following this loss, Marinovich was arrested on cocaine possession charges. A short time after that, he left USC to play for the then–Los Angeles Raiders in the NFL. Marinovich's arrest was not the only legal woe suffered by the Trojans, as three players were brought up on sexual assault charges, but were later acquitted. Two other players were then found guilty of kidnapping-robbery.

It seemed that Smith's strong discipline and character-building skills were not working at this stage of his USC career. Neither was his rebuilding of a program. In other stops prior to USC, Smith was able to take a team from the cellar to the penthouse. However, the opposite was true with the Trojans. After his incredible first three seasons, the team began to crumble. In 1991, the team fell to 3–8 for USC's third losing season over the previous thirty years.[14]

In 1992, the team improved to 6–5–1, which was still below the norm for such a storied program. They did qualify for a bowl game, but it proved to be another disaster for the team with Smith in charge. Their opponent for the Freedom Bowl was Fresno State, who came into this game with the 98th ranked defense. This bottom feeding defensive unit then rose to the top over sixty minutes of play against USC. They picked off three passes, held the Trojans to 183 yards of total offense, and won convincingly, 24–7.

Following the game, Smith arrived at the press conference in an angry mood. This was not uncommon for a losing coach, but the words Smith spewed out proved to be the final act of his tenure at USC. He claimed that there were no alpha dogs in college football, and that names and logos meant nothing. Boy, was he wrong. The names and logos did mean everything to a school, especially one like USC, with such a long and proud tradition. Needless to say, alumni and boosters were not pleased by the coach's choice of words.[15] With his friend and supporter athletic director Dr. Mike McGee ready to take over as AD at South Carolina, coupled with the Freedom Bowl loss and his negative comments, it was highly unlikely that Smith was looking to return as coach of the Cardinal and Gold. The decision was made easier three days following the Freedom Bowl, when on January 1, 1993, Smith was relieved of his duties as head coach. He still had three years left on his contract, and received $750,000 in a buyout, but still remained very bitter about what transpired at USC.[16] Despite the way he left, Smith did produce a winning overall record of 44–25–3, saw 13 of his players earn All-American status, and 33 make the NFL. However, in the last three seasons he was at USC, the team broke even at 17–17–2.

After one year away from coaching, Smith became head coach at the University of Missouri in 1994. He remained with the school until November 18, 2000 when he was let go after suffering a 66–0 defeat to Kansas State. Smith managed to once again rebuild a program after a slow start. In his first two seasons at Missouri, he had a combined 6–16–1 record. He then finished at 5–6, and in 1997, Smith took the Tigers to a bowl game following a 7–5 finish. The team then finished with their best record under Smith in 1998. They went 8–4 and once again were invited to a bowl game. The team then slipped to 4–7 and 3–8 in 2000.

Smith left the coaching business after his stint at Missouri with a career record of 143–126–7. He moved to Tucson, Arizona, where he worked as an announcer for Arizona football games for the Fox Sports Network. Larry Smith lived out the rest of his life in Arizona. He battled lymphocytic leukemia since 1999, and succumbed to the disease on January 28, 2008 at age 68.[17]

## *Paul Hackett*

Paul Hackett had the distinction of coaching some of the greatest players, and working with some of the best minds in football. Through a long career, Hackett earned championship rings on the college and professional levels.

Much of Hackett's football career saw him as a resident of California, but his life began clear across the country on July 5, 1947 in Burlington, Vermont, the largest city in the Green Mountain State, and approximately 45 miles south of the Canadian border. Right from birth Hackett appeared to have a bond with USC, as he shared the same birthday with legendary USC football coach John McKay.

The future leader of the Trojans left Vermont, and relocated to California, where he attended the home of the green and black Matadors, Miramonte High School, in Orinda, a town situated in the Bay Area of northern California. It was there that Hackett established himself as a triple threat athlete. Besides football, he also played basketball and baseball.

When it came time to test his body and mind on the college level, Hackett decided on the University of California Davis, some 70 miles north of Orinda near the state capital of Sacramento. Later in his professional life, he was able to achieve status as a highly respected offensive coach, and to convey his knowledge, stemmed from the experience he received as a three-year starting quarterback for the U.C. Davis Aggies from 1966 through 1968, a year that saw him emerge as the Far Western Conference passing leader. While managing to conquer the competition on the college level, he did the same in the classroom, graduating with a Bachelor's degree in History in 1969.[1]

The coaching profession would eventually take Paul Hackett to many locales, but the genesis of his mentoring some of the game's biggest names was at his alma mater, U.C. Davis, in 1969. He struck instant success in his initial coaching job as an assistant by helping the freshman team achieve a perfect 13–0 record over the course of two seasons.[2]

An opportunity to coach at Cal arose for the young assistant, and he left U.C. Davis following the 1971 season to pursue it. Returning to an area just eight miles west of where he played high school football, Hackett began his career at Cal as a graduate assistant under head coach Mike White. From 1972 through 1975, Hackett was the Golden Bears' receivers coach (1973), and quarterback coach (1974–75), all the while being a part of a staff that helped the team rise from a 3–8 record in 1972 to an 8–3 mark in 1975 and a share of the Pac-8 championship.[3]

Up to this time in his young career, Hackett already had compiled an exceptional resume. After helping to guide the Aggie freshman team at U.C. Davis to a spotless record, he then assisted in the rise of the Golden Bears at Cal in the mid–1970s. To top things off, he also mentored two All-American quarterbacks at Cal. In 1974, under Hackett's guidance, Steve Bartkowski led the nation in passing yardage, became an All-American, and then went on to being the first overall selection in the 1975 NFL draft.[4]

Hackett's success with signal callers at Cal continued with Bartkowski's successor, Joe Roth, who topped the Pac-8 in passing while leading Cal to a Pac-8 co-championship in 1975 and earning All-American status in the process. As a team, the Golden Bears led the nation in total offensive production by averaging 458.6 yards per game.[5] Sadly, Joe Roth's life was cut short when he passed away at age 21 from cancer on February 19, 1977.[6]

After his work produced excellent results in the northern half of California, Hackett took his expertise to the southern part of the state, and once again achieved success. When John Robinson replaced John McKay as head coach at USC before the 1976 season, Hackett was hired on as an assistant in charge of quarterbacks and receivers for the first two of five seasons he spent at USC as an assistant. The final three seasons in this stint were spent as quarterbacks coach and passing game assistant.

In Hackett's time with the Trojans under Robinson from 1976 through 1980, the team produced a highly impressive 50–8–2 record that included four bowl game appearances, a national championship (1978), and a Heisman Trophy winner in Charles White (1979). Hackett had gained a reputation as a coach that paid great attention to every detail, regardless of how minor. He then worked with his charges until perfection was commonplace. He also had the reputation of taking college quarterbacks and turning them into All-Americans and future professionals. At USC, he guided quarterback Paul McDonald to All-American status in 1979, and prepared him for an NFL career with the Cleveland Browns and Dallas Cowboys.[7]

With championships and All-Americans to his credit, Hackett seized the chance to try his hand in the National Football League. In 1981 he was given the opportunity to advance to the upper level of football competition with the Cleveland Browns, serving the team as a quarterback assistant coach on head coach Sam Rutigliano's staff. He had the opportunity to work with the 1980 NFL Most Valuable Player, quarterback Brian Sipe, and was reunited with his former USC signal caller Paul McDonald, who served as a backup to Sipe during Hackett's two seasons with the team.[8]

In 1983, Hackett returned to northern California to coach quarterbacks and receivers for the San Francisco 49ers. While there, he had the distinct pleasure to work under one of the game's greatest head coaches in Bill Walsh. As a member of Walsh's staff, he also had the chance to work with future Hall of Fame quarterback Joe Montana. In his second season with the 49ers, the team produced a near-perfect 18–1 record that included a resounding victory over the Miami Dolphins in Super Bowl XIX.[9]

Following the 1985 season, Hackett was off once again, this time relocating to the Lone Star State as a member of another coaching icon's staff. This time he worked for Tom Landry as pass offense coordinator for the Dallas Cowboys. After three seasons in Dallas, Hackett returned to the college game for the first time in nine years. He served as offensive coordinator under Mike Gottfried at the University of Pittsburgh in 1989, and then assumed his first-ever opportunity to be a head coach in 1990. His tenure really started with the 1989 John Hancock Bowl, which Pitt won, 31–28, over Texas A&M. He led the Panthers for three seasons, compiling a 13–20–1 record. In 1992, despite a 3–8 finish, Hackett had Pitt ranked eighth in the nation in total offense and passing offense. Once again he also worked his magic with a quarterback. He guided Pitt's quarterback Alex Van Pelt to a Top 10 ranking in total offense during both the 1991 and 1992 seasons.[10]

Hackett then went back to the NFL, this time as offensive coordinator for the Kansas City Chiefs from 1993 through 1997 under head coach Marty Schottenheimer. This was a glorious time in Chiefs history, as the team won 57 games and advanced to the post-season in four out of his five seasons there. The 1997 team produced the best record in the AFC at 13–3. While with the Chiefs, Hackett once again had the chance to work with quarterback Joe Montana and record-setting Hall of Fame running back Marcus Allen, who was one the players on the 1978 USC championship team that Hackett served on.

On December 17, 1997, John Robinson's second tenure as head coach at USC came to an end, and with it, the Paul Hackett era was christened on January 8, 1998 when he signed a five-year contract to lead the Trojans. At the time of his hire at USC, Hackett brought 29 seasons of coaching experience to the job, serving as an assistant to legendary coaches and working with some of the all-time great performers.

At first, it appeared that USC was hot on the trail of another former Notre Dame coach. Just like back in 1925 when the university pursued Knute Rockne, or in 1951 when Frank Leahy was on their wish list. This time around it was Lou Holtz, who guided the Fighting Irish to a national championship in 1988. Everything appeared to be heading in the right direction with Holtz, but as the appointment was getting closer, he decided not to take the job.[11] Many other top names were considered after Holtz turned the offer down. Jeff Fisher, the head coach of the Tennessee Titans, and former USC player, was thought about until the owner of the Titans stepped in to stop the pursuit. Denny Green, Norv Turner, Gary Barnett, and Dave Wannstedt, were all talked about until Hackett's name was added to the list.[12] What helped Hackett's case was the fact that he had been a part of the USC program earlier, and helped the team win the 1978 national championship.

The Paul Hackett tenure began on a high note, as the Trojans scored 17 points in the final two minutes against Purdue to win, 27–17. This marked the first time since 1951 that a USC head coach won his debut game. The momentum from that thrilling victory allowed the team to finish with a more-than-respectable 8–4 regular season record. They then lost in the Sun Bowl to Texas Christian University.

The magic that Hackett had as a top-notch assistant could not be transferred into his head coaching duties. The team slipped to 6–6 and 5–7 over the next two seasons, and many games were filled with turnovers.[13] His final two seasons of 1999 and 2000 were the first time since 1960–61 that the Trojans had back-to-back non-winning years. His 2000 team also found the Trojans in an unpredictable position, with that being in last place in the conference. It seemed that the team was going backward fast, and fans that filled the Coliseum began to cry out, "Goodbye Hackett."[14] After a loss to Notre Dame in 2000, in which the Trojans had punts blocked and passes picked off by a fighting Irish team that was not a powerhouse, it appeared that Hackett's tenure as head coach was about to end.[15] The university wasted little time making a decision on Hackett's future. Two days following the loss to Notre Dame, on November 27, 2000, he was fired three years into his five-year contract. A buy out agreement of $800,000 was paid to him, and he was sent on his way despite feeling that he was not given the right amount of time to nurture the prospects he recruited.[16]

After USC, Hackett travelled clear across the country to serve as the offensive coordinator with the New York Jets from 2001 to 2004. He then was a quarterback coach for the Tampa Bay Buccaneers (2005–07), and from 2008 to 2010, he worked in the same capacity with the Oakland Raiders.[17]

## *Pete Carroll*

Elmer Henderson, Howard Jones, John McKay, and John Robinson. These names serve as a roll call of USC's elite group of mentors during the 20th century. In the first decade of the new millennium, the accolades of California native Pete Carroll allowed him the distinct honor of being mentioned amongst the coaching legends in the Land of Troy.

Irish and Austrian heritage became one with the birth of Peter Clay Carroll on September 15, 1951 in San Francisco. Like every other future coach, the world of athletics engulfed the adolescent, who would one day become the top college coach in the first decade of the 21st century. He had no trouble performing in sports, but he hit a snag right before his freshman year of high school.[1]

The physical transformation between adolescence and teenage years can be awkward for many young people. In Carroll's case, that time period saw his weight hover at a mere 110 pounds for a brief time. His athletic skills were never in question, but coming in as a freshman football player weighing so little was a cause for concern. So much so in fact that he needed to have permission from a doctor to try out for the team. This incident could have proved to be a challenge that many would forgo and just give up on the quest. However, Carroll was not that type. He was determined to succeed regardless of obstacles thrown at him. This characteristic not only proved successful throughout his high school years from 1965 to 1969, but carried over into his chosen profession as well. It appeared to be a blazing eternal flame inside of him that will not allow defeat to get the best of him.[2] Due to this unwavering spirit, Carroll rose up to become an excellent athlete on the prep and college levels, and earned the same stellar acknowledgement that linked him with the all-time great coaches in college football history.

Redwood High School in Larkspur, California was the alma mater of Pete Carroll. In the late 1960s, the future Trojan mentor overcame his early stunt in growth, worked hard, and came away a winner. Under long-time coach Bob Troppmann, Carroll excelled as a quarterback, receiver, and defensive back for the Redwood Giants. His talents were not just limited to the football field. He considered his favorite sport to be the one in season at the time. He backed this up by performing extremely well in basketball and baseball, earning a reputation as a three-sport star. His abilities were so impressive that he was honored with Redwood's 1969 Athlete of the Year Award.[3] Forty years after his graduation, he became a member of Redwood High School's first Athletic Hall of Fame class in 2009. Even long after Carroll's high school days were reduced to distance memories, his relationship with coach Troppmann remained strong. Troppmann was a major influence on Carroll in high school, and that admiration continued well in to his USC days. Even when Carroll was ringing up victories at a steady pace in the Southland, he would call his old mentor from the sideline prior to kickoff of every game to go over strategy.[4]

Carroll's next step after his Redwood days took him to the junior college level. Looking to continue his education and football career, he enrolled at College of Marin, located in the north San Francisco bay area, across the Golden Gate Bridge from San Francisco County. After two years at Marin, he transferred to the University of the Pacific in Stockton, California. While with the orange and black Tigers, Carroll played free safety for two seasons, gaining All-Pacific Coast Athletic Conference recognition in 1971 and 72. He also worked his way to earning a Bachelor's degree in Business Administration in 1973.[5]

With his college playing days now complete, Carroll took a chance in the professional ranks. The World Football League started up in 1974 and lasted only one complete season, but it gave Carroll an opportunity to try out with the Honolulu Hawaiians. However, problems with his shoulder hampered his chances and the dream of drawing a paycheck as a professional football player was over. In an effort to make money, he sold roofing supplies in the San Francisco area. This form of employment did not last long, and the call of the gridiron beckoned.[6]

Chester Caddas, the head football coach at the University of the Pacific, came away very impressed from the experience of knowing Carroll. He admired his former player's upbeat, congenial personality, and his desire to work hard. These traits, coupled with his football knowledge, allowed Carroll to be brought into the coaching fold for the first time. Caddas caught word that his former charge was looking to get on the coaching carousel, and presented an opportunity to test his abilities as a graduate assistant at Pacific.[7]

After accepting the offer, Carroll returned to the classroom while serving on Caddas' staff for three years coaching wide receivers and defensive backs. The end results were all positive, as Carroll walked away with a Masters degree in Physical Education in 1976 and multiple seasons of coaching experience.[8]

Upon securing his Masters degree, Carroll was offered a position on Lou Holtz's staff at Arkansas in 1977. He was given this opportunity when fellow Pacific assistant Bob Cope went to Arkansas and recommended Carroll to Holtz. In his lone season coaching the Arkansas defensive backfield, the Razorbacks won the 1978 Orange Bowl. While with Arkansas, Carroll worked with defensive coordinator Monte Kiffin, whom he and his wife would help babysit for. The child in question was Kiffin's two-year old son Lane, who would go on to grow up and become Carroll's offensive coordinator and eventual successor as head coach of the Trojans.[9]

Following his short stay in Arkansas, Carroll headed to Iowa State University to coach the defensive backfield under Earle Bruce. After Iowa State played in the Hall of Fame Bowl following the regular season, Bruce went off to replace the legendary Woody Hayes at Ohio State, and took Carroll with him to guide the defensive backfield of the scarlet and gray Buckeyes. This proved to be an excellent time to be at Ohio State, as the Buckeyes went undefeated in the regular season, captured the 1979 Big Ten title, and gained a Rose Bowl berth as the top-ranked team in the nation. Unfortunately, the Buckeyes fell one point short of claiming the national championship, thanks to a 17–16 USC victory in the 1980 Rose Bowl.[10]

Once again, following one season, Carroll was off to explore another region of the country. This time he made his way to North Carolina State, but this time he remained longer than one year. From 1980 through 1982, Carroll was the defensive coordinator and defensive backfield coach of the Wolfpack under his former Arkansas colleague Monte Kiffin. In 1983 Bob Cope, who got Carroll to come to Arkansas from the University of the Pacific six years earlier, was hired as head coach at Pacific. He then got Carroll to return to his alma mater as assistant head coach and offensive coordinator for one season.[11]

After ten years of his attempt to get into professional football as a player, Carroll returned to the upper echelon of football competition as a coach. In 1984 he entered the National Football League by shuffling off to Buffalo with an appointment as the Bills' defensive backs coach. Following his first season in the pro ranks, Carroll left Buffalo for the Minnesota Vikings, serving that team in the same capacity from 1985 to 1989. He gained a solid reputation as an assistant coach while first working under legendary Hall of Fame head coach Bud Grant, who was in his final year of guiding the Minnesota Vikings when Carroll joined the staff. He then worked under Jerry Burns for the rest of his stay in Minnesota, helping the Vikings reach the NFC Championship Game in 1987, and mentored a unit that led the league in pass defense in 1989.[12]

Carroll's name began to surface in head coaching circles. In 1989, he was a contender for the head coaching vacancy at Stanford University, but that position went to Dennis Green. For the time being, he continued on in the NFL as the defensive coordinator of the New York Jets from 1990 to 1993. During his stay with the Jets, Carroll's name once again rose to the top of vacant coaching speculations. This time he was a strong candidate for the head-coaching job with the Minnesota Vikings. However, once again it was Dennis Green that thwarted Carroll's opportunity when he was named head coach in 1992.[13]

In 1994, Carroll received his first chance to be a head coach, as the New York Jets promoted him after the team fired Bruce Coslet. Carroll's fortunes in the Big Apple matched those of his predecessor. The Jets started out 6–5, but then spiraled out of control, losing their five remaining games to finish at 6–10. Not willing to continue on with the Pete Carroll era, the Jets released him after one season.

His experience, knowledge, and passion for the game did not leave Carroll unemployed for very long. He returned to his old stomping grounds in northern California as defensive coordinator for the San Francisco 49ers for the 1995 and 1996 seasons. The 49ers won the NFC Western Division in both of Carroll's seasons, and he once again gained attention for vacant head coaching positions.[14]

In 1997, one year removed from winning the AFC championship, Bill Parcells resigned as coach of the New England Patriots after problems with ownership. Carroll was offered the job, accepted, and made the cross country trek to try his hand as an NFL head coach for the second time in three years. This time around, he finished at 10–6 in his first season, which was good enough to win the AFC Eastern Division title. The Patriots then lost in a divisional playoff game against Pittsburgh. In 1998, Carroll had the Patriots back in the playoffs, this time, complements of a 9–7 record. However, the team made an early exit from the post-season, losing to Jacksonville in the AFC Wild Card Game. The following year saw the Patriots break even at 8–8 and miss the playoffs. This cost Carroll his job, but unbeknownst to him, was an opportunity that would take him to heights of unequaled success throughout most of the 2000's.

After his release from the Patriots following the 1999 season, Carroll was sought by some teams in the NFL to work as a defensive coordinator. He decided to pass on the offers, and concentrated his time on doing consultant work for both the NFL and college programs. He also delved into charity work for the NFL, and became a columnist for CNNSI.com, dealing with the world of professional football.[15]

On December 15, 2000, Pete Carroll began a journey that would forever link him as one of the greatest football coaches in the proud history of USC. It also allowed him the prestige of becoming one of the college football world's most revered coaches of his time.

However, despite the fame, fanfare, and accolades that Carroll would amass as mentor of the Trojans, he was not the university's initial choice to replace Paul Hackett. In an attempt to bring back the luster to this glamorous football program, athletic director Mike Garrett set his sights on a high-profile individual with experience and success in the college ranks.

At this time, Dennis Erickson was one of the game's top figures, and appeared to fit all that USC was looking for. His experience in the college game went back to 1969 when he began his coaching career as a graduate assistant at Montana State. In 1982, he received his first head coaching opportunity, and remained in the profession at that position over the course of career, with numerous stops along the way going into the new millennium. His greatest work occurred at Florida's University of Miami from 1989 through 1994. In those six seasons with the Hurricanes, Erickson posted a 63–9 record for a school-best .875 winning percentage, and guided the team to national championships in 1989 and 1991. Following a stint in the NFL with the Seattle Seahawks, Erickson returned to the college ranks with a big project ahead of him. The Oregon State University Beavers had earned the reputation as permanent residents at the bottom of the Pac-10 standings for many years. Erickson accepted the challenge, and in his first with the program, he lead the Beavers to a 7–5 finish for the school's first winning football season in 29 years. This was the type of coach the Trojans needed at such a critical time in their history. It appeared that USC was close to 100 percent sure that Erickson was going to come to the rescue, but in the end, he chose to sign a contract extension with Oregon State.

When Erickson's name went off the table, things changed for the Trojans. Oregon coach Mike Bellotti was interviewed, but according to Mike Garrett, was never offered the job despite what the media claimed.[16] Bellotti in turn signed a contract extension with Oregon. Mike Riley, who Erickson followed at Oregon State, and was felt to be responsible for starting the Beavers back up to respectability, was the head coach with the San Diego Chargers when the USC job opened up. He was also a former USC assistant under John Robinson during his second term as head coach in the 1990s. Riley was considered to have excellent prowess when it came to the offensive side of the game, and was a popular coach with the players.[17] Riley came off well in the interview with USC, and was possibly close to signing on to be the next coach of the Trojans when fate stepped in. The president of the Chargers, Dean Spanos, informed Riley that if he went up to Los Angeles to continue talks with USC, then his job in San Diego was over. With nothing absolutely solid regarding the USC job, Riley did not want to take the chance and lose his job in San Diego.[18]

It was at this time that the name of Pete Carroll began to create interest. However, it seemed, according to Garrett, that it was Carroll whom he wanted throughout this hunt.[19] The genesis of the Pete Carroll hiring could be traced back to words of wisdom from Garrett's assistant Darryl Gross. Gross was a former scout for the New York Jets while Carroll was the team's defensive coordinator there in the early 1990s. Gross used to tell Garrett about Carroll's strong work ethic, his magnetic personality, astute football mind, and the ability to communicate with players.[20] It seemed that Carroll's enthusiasm for life and the game quickly was absorbed into all those under him, and there was nothing they would not try to do for him. All these traits had the makings of a perfect leader, and Garrett came away impressed with Carroll. As a matter of fact, before Paul Hackett was hired as head coach in 1998, Carroll's name came up in discussions regarding the USC job. However, he was head coach of the New England Patriots at the time, and apparently not interested in going back to the college game.[21]

Once again fate reared up to change things, and the USC football program would be returned to days of glory. By the time Hackett was relieved of his duties at USC, Carroll was also out of coaching, after being let go by the Patriots following the 1999 season. Unemployed from the business of football for over a year, Carroll's name did not seem to have the right amount of flash needed to reboot the sluggish Trojan football program.[22] That was why Dennis Erickson rose to the top of the list of candidates. After his name was removed from the list, and the others, Pete Carroll's was at the top of Mike Garrett's wish list.

At the time that the USC job was looming on the horizon for Carroll, he was back in Massachusetts pondering what he wanted to pursue as a new career. He was part of a group that was attempting to get a football network going on television, among other ideas.[23] It was then that the union between USC and Carroll took place. Garrett informed Darryl Gross to contact Carroll, and the rest is history.

Even though the Pete Carroll era at USC would become one of the greatest reigns in college football history, it appeared to have an ominous shroud hovering over it when his name was announced on December 15, 2000 after an 18-day search to find Paul Hackett's replacement. The media outlets had a field day dispelling the hiring as another ill-fated move. They felt that Carroll was another coaching retread that might have been a good coordinator, but twice failed as a head coach in the NFL. Also, he was removed from the college game for close to twenty years at the time of his hiring. The displeasure got so great that the USC Athletic Department was flooded with thousands of e-mails, calls, and faxes from alumni, expressing their negativity toward the hiring. Many individuals that gave donations to the program informed the university that not another penny would come from them, unless Carroll was released from his position.[24]

Regardless of the initial disappointment surrounding the announcement of his hiring by media and the USC faithful, Carroll stood before the microphones and flashing cameras to greet the doubting masses. He quickly used his high energy, congenial, passionate personality to diffuse the less-than-jovial gathering. His jargon was upbeat as he moved about the room selling himself to the audience, and Garrett was looking on, totally sold on his new hire.[25] Positive remarks also came from former USC players who thought that Carroll was the perfect fit for the college game due to his personality.

With all the remarks towards Carroll, negative or positive, the bottom line was that he would be leading the Trojans out of the Coliseum tunnel for at least the 2001 season. For the time being, the Trojans under Carroll held off the doubters by winning their opener over San Jose State. Unfortunately, interest in USC football had fallen low, as a sparse crowd of only 45,568 was on hand in the vast confines of the Coliseum. To make matters worse, the doubters once again sang out loud and clear, as USC dropped their next four games, three of which were in the conference. Even though negative remarks were rampant, Carroll remained his usual upbeat self. He saw things in his team that gave him hope for a brighter future, and then went out and convinced his players of the same thing. They responded by winning five of the next six games, one of which was a 27–0 victory over UCLA. With a team comprised of leftovers from the Paul Hackett tenure, Carroll took the Trojans to a 6–6 finish.[26]

Starting in 2002 through the rest of the decade, Pete Carroll not only built on the hopes of a better future for the Trojans, but became the contractor of a dynasty in the process. When he took over the Trojans, it was claimed that the balance of power in the Pac-10 had leveled out, and schools from Washington and Oregon were obtaining players that USC had no problem getting in the past. Carroll was ready to change all that.

He was a master recruiter, possibly the best of his time as a college coach at USC. He stressed academics, and with his incredible vibrant personality, and ability to relate to high school players, he was able to rebuild the program. He first looked to get the top players from California, and then had no trouble going anywhere in the country to pursue talent, regardless of whom he competing against. His recruiting skills allowed the Trojans to rank #12 in *Super Prep Magazine* in 2002, which was the highest USC finished since 1996.[27] From 2003 through the 2006 recruiting class, USC finished as the top-rated program three times according to the Scout.com rankings.

Carroll's enthusiasm allowed him to perpetually be 18 years old despite being trapped in a 50-year old body. He never stopped running around on the field, displaying energy that people half his age could not exhibit. He was a pat-on-the-back type of coach that made players feel like they were the ultimate performers. His philosophy stemmed from a never-ending pursuit to find the competitive advantage, and summed his commitment up in two words, "win forever." The concepts behind those words were to keep making improvements on things accomplished in order to stay on top year after year. Also, never stop competing, even in practice. The Trojans under Carroll might have had fun with such a vibrant coach, but they worked hard at practice. He wanted his players to complete whatever task was presented, whether it was plays, drills, or practice, never give up. He instilled the belief to create more turnovers than you give up, and to respect everyone, teammates, the university, and opponents.

What Carroll accomplished quickly turned his tormentors into allies. After his 6–6 start in 2001, he guided the Trojans to an 82–9 record from 2002 through 2008. Included in that stretch were four outright Pac-10 championships (2003–2005, 2008), three ties (2002,2006–2007), two national championships, and three Heisman Trophy winners. His teams had seven straight Top–4 finishes in the AP, six BCS bowl victories out of seven attempts, 33 straight weeks at the AP's top-ranked team, an NCAA record of 63 consecutive games of scoring 20 or more points, a 34-game winning streak from 2003 to 2004, 25 first team All-Americans, 53 players drafted into the NFL, a home game winning streak of 21, and a home game wining streak of 17 against Pac-10 teams. Carroll also had a 14–2 record against USC's long-standing rivals, UCLA and Notre Dame, and compiled an overall record at USC from 2001 through 2009 of 97–19 for an 83.6 winning percentage. He reached the 50-win plateau quicker than any other head football coach in USC's history. On a personal level, Carroll was presented with 14 Coach of the Year honors from different organizations. Included in those honors were four Pac-10 Coach of the Year awards (2003, 2004, 2005, 2006).[28]

Following a 9–4 finish in 2009, the Trojan football program was hit with NCAA violations stemming from 2005 Heisman Trophy winner Reggie Bush receiving improper gifts while still at the university. On June 10, 2010, the NCAA ruled that USC would have a two-year bowl ban, elimination of thirty football scholarships, and were forced to forfeit wins from the 2004–05 season, including the 2004 BCS championship, and all the victories from the 2005–06 season.[29]

Carroll was obviously upset by the findings, but did not have to be around for the aftermath. He had accepted an offer to return to the NFL as head coach of the Seattle Seahawks starting in 2010. He stated that the decision to leave USC had nothing to do with the sanctions.[30]

Just like when he came to USC, there were those critics that pounced on Carroll for leaving amidst the NCAA's ruling, but people have the right to say what they want. In the final analysis of the Pete Carroll era at USC, he restored the program to the luster that was eroding at the start of the new millennium. He brought excitement and incredible highs for all those whose passions run deep for the Cardinal & Gold. Unfortunately, he was the focal point of the team at a rough time at the end of the decade, however, he was not the first, nor will he be the last, to endure problems stemming from NCAA investigations. Pete Carroll was a winner, and his reign at USC will never be questioned regarding his commitment to "win forever."

## *Lane Kiffin*

Lane Kiffin seemed groomed for the coaching profession due to both his pedigree and association with one of college football's most storied programs. On a personal level, his father is Monte Kiffin, one of the most respected defensive coaches, with many years of experience in the National Football League behind him. On a professional level, he had the opportunity to serve as an assistant under Pete Carroll at USC during one of that program's greatest eras.[1]

The man who appeared destined to make a career out of coaching was born on May 9, 1975, in Bloomington, Minnesota. Upon his high school graduation from Jefferson High School in 1994, Kiffin decided to head for warmer climes to continue on with his education. He went to Fresno State, where he served as a backup quarterback through his junior year, and played on the basketball team. By the time he was a senior, Kiffin decided to give up the rest of his college eligibility to set his sights on a coaching career. He got his first chance to prove himself in the profession as a student assistant at Fresno State in 1998. The next year saw him coaching the offensive line as a graduate assistant at Colorado State University.[2]

At the age of 25, Kiffin chose to test his skills in the professional game, going to work for the Jacksonville Jaguars as a quality control assistant in 2000. The following year saw Kiffin back in the college game after accepting an offer from Pete Carroll at the beginning of what would be one of USC's greatest dynasties. With the Trojans, Kiffin was on a coaching staff that produced two national championships in 2003 and 2004, played for a third in 2005, and saw USC ranked near the top of the national polls in other seasons.[3]

After starting off as tight end coach in 2001, and receiver coach in 2002, Kiffin had the passing game added to his responsibilities as well. Under Kiffin's guidance, quarterback Matt Leinart led USC to an undefeated season, back-to-back national championships, and on an individual level, he earned All-American status and the 2004 Heisman Trophy. In 2005, Kiffin was elevated to offensive coordinator, and the Trojans' were an offensive juggernaut that went undefeated through the regular season and produced another Heisman Trophy winner in Reggie Bush. In addition to his coordinator duties, Kiffin also handled the job of recruiting coordinator and still worked with the wide receivers.[4]

While serving Pete Carroll in many capacities, his mentoring helped send many USC players into the National Football League. It only seemed fitting that before too long, Kiffin himself would join many of his USC charges into the professional ranks. On January 23, 2007, that opportunity came when the Oakland Raiders announced that Kiffin would become the sixteenth head coach in the organization's history. At the time of his hiring, he was 31 years old, thus becoming the youngest head coach in Raiders history, and the youngest in the modern era of the NFL (1946 to present).[5]

When Kiffin assumed the reigns of the Raiders, the once dominant franchise had fallen on extremely hard times, winning a mere 15 games in their 64 previous outings. Oakland became a destination where players dreaded going as the 2000's neared their conclusion. However, there was one young 31-year old man looking for his first chance at a head coaching position who hoped of bringing the Silver & Black back to their glory days of the 1960s, 70s, and 80s.

The union between Kiffin and the Raiders' late maverick owner Al Davis was not one that ended with warm feelings. In fact, right from the start, it appeared that things were not copacetic. Davis referred to his new coach as Lance instead of Lane, and things soured from there over the course of twenty months. A few months after his hiring, the Raiders used the number one overall draft selection on quarterback JaMarcus Russell, despite Kiffin's wishes. Davis then relayed his thoughts about the incident to Kiffin by letter, telling him to get over the pick and just focus on coaching the team.[6]

When Kiffin was coaching the team, he realized during training camp that the Raiders lacked depth, and blasted some of the team's high-profiled performers. Once again, Davis was less than pleased with the way his new coach was leading his beloved Raiders, and more animosity arose. Winning has a way of making animosity disappear, but in the case of the 2007 Raiders, the team finished with another horrific finish at 4–12 and friction between owner and coach grew to ugly proportions. Stories surfaced that Kiffin wanted to get rid of defensive coordinator Rob Ryan. Davis then stated that Kiffin wanted Ryan gone so that his father, Monte, could be hired. Two days later, once again in a letter, Davis informed Kiffin that would have no say in managing the assistant coaches, deciding on what players the team would take in the draft, or any moves dealing with roster changes. It was alleged that at this time, Kiffin was given a letter of resignation, but he refused to sign it. In the end, both of these stories were swiftly denied by the organization.[7]

As the 2008 training camp opened, the feud between Davis and Kiffin continued to grow due to constant verbal jabs coming from both parties. When the regular season began with a 41–14 loss to the Denver Broncos, Kiffin refused to confront the problems surrounding the defense, allowing Rob Ryan to deal with the unit. On September 12, 2008, Davis gave Kiffin a warning via a letter that his negative actions were getting him close to being terminated. Two days after seeing a 15-point lead disappear en route to another loss on September 28, 2008, Kiffin received a phone call stating that Davis had fired him.[8]

With his first taste of head coaching experience not going well at all, Kiffin still remained determined to forge ahead. Two months after his turbulent tenure in Raider Nation was terminated, Kiffin returned to the college ranks, signing on as head coach at the University of Tennessee on November 28, 2008. At 33 years of age, he became the youngest active head coach in Division I college football.[9] Kiffin's impact on the Volunteers was swift, as he turned a 5–7 finish from the previous year to a winning 7–6 record in 2009. All appeared headed in the right direction for Kiffin and the Vols until the University of Southern California had an opening for a head coach after the departure of Pete Carroll to the Seattle Seahawks.

Kiffin jumped at the chance to return to the place where he enjoyed so much success. Despite his pleasure in coming back to the Southland, his departure from Knoxville after one lone season caused many students to be perturbed. Some students even took to rioting to show their resentment, to which police and fire units had to be brought in when students blocked the exit of Neyland Thompson Sports Complex Center and began to start small fires.[10]

Regardless of how those passionate fans of the Volunteers felt, Kiffin was 2,000 miles west of Knoxville, ready to lead the Trojans after signing a contract on January 12, 2010. Six months after his hiring, the USC football program was hit with sanctions by the NCAA following a four-year investigation into reports that 2005 Heisman Trophy winner Reggie Bush accepted vast monetary gifts, in addition to other things, from two sports agents while he was still at USC as a student/athlete.[11]

Kiffin's initial season at the helm of the Trojans saw the program banned from post-season bowl games, and the loss of 30 scholarships over the course of three years. Even in the midst of controversy, Kiffin steadied the ship enough, and guided the Trojans to an 8–5 finish. In 2011, the Trojans enjoyed a very successful season, finishing at 10–2, with the year being climaxed by victories over rivals California, Oregon, Notre Dame, and a 50–0 blowout over UCLA in their finale.[12]

In his two years at USC, Kiffin posted an 18–7 record, which was good for a .750 winning percentage. His 18 victories in his first two seasons is second only to USC coaching legends Howard Jones and John Robinson, who each had 19 after their first two outings leading the Trojans.[13] Things looked bright for the Trojans as they headed into the 2012 season. The bowl ban was finally lifted, and USC received the #1 ranking by many media outlets in their pre-season polls. Unfortunately, the team did not live up to their huge expectations. After starting the season off with two straight wins, a loss to Stanford in week three stymied their quest for a national championship. They rebounded by winning four straight, but then lost five of their final six games, including a Sun Bowl defeat at the hands of Georgia Tech. Adding to the team's woes was a late season shoulder injury to quarterback Matt Barkley.

Lane Kiffin's self-professed "dream job" of coaching the Trojans would not last another full season. Following a dismal 62–41 beating at the hands of the Arizona State Sun Devils, USC fell to 0–2 in the Pac-12 for the first time since 2001. Despite still having a winning overall record of 3–2, the offense was stagnant. Athletic director Pat Haden, a former star quarterback for the Trojans in the 1970's, decided that it was time to part ways with Kiffin at the helm of the program.

Following that terrible loss to Arizona State, Haden relieved Kiffin of his duties at the Los Angeles International Airport following the team's return home at 3:00 a.m. on Sunday morning, September 29, 2013. Kiffin finished his days as USC's mentor with a 28–15 overall record. Assistant head coach Ed Orgeron assumed Kiffin's vacant position on an interim basis through the remainder of the 2013 season.[14]

*Five*

# Trojan Traditions

## *Giles "Super Fan" Pellerin*

Debates over the greatest all-time player or coach in USC football history will always persist. The world of sports is filled with interesting, and sometimes hotly contested, conversation. However, when it comes to the University of Southern California football, no argument will ever take place over the identity of the number one all-time fan. For that title will always belong to Giles Pellerin.

Imagine the thought of witnessing first hand the rise to power of USC football from its infant stages under coach Elmer "Gloomy Gus" Henderson, to being one of college football's juggernauts created over the span of eight decades. In the case of Giles "Super Fan" Pellerin, no imagination was necessary. He was in the stands for ever USC game, home and away, from 1926 to the annual cross-town matchup with UCLA in 1998, watching the majority of the greatest players work their cardinal and gold magic on 100-yard pieces of real estate across the college football landscape.

On January 1, 1923, Pellerin was in the midst of his high school years at Huntington High School in California. On that first day of 1923, he was a part of the 43,000 that witnessed USC's first-ever bowl appearance. "Gloomy Gus" Henderson's charges from the Land of Troy showed no signs of being novices to post-season play, and came away with a 14–3 victory over Penn State.[1]

After graduating from high school, Pellerin enrolled at USC, and returned to the stands for the Trojans opening game in his sophomore year. On September 25, 1926, Pellerin watched USC roll over Whittier, 74–0, and he then decided to return for the next game, and the one after that, and so on until he personally saw the Trojans compile a 532–225–40 record over 797 straight games. It was estimated that from September 25, 1926 to November 21, 1998, the greatest USC football fan in history travelled over 650,000 miles, and spent close to $100,000 doing what he loved. He also earned a degree in electrical engineering from USC, and eventually retired as an executive from the telephone company.[2]

Even though he never played the sport, his devotion to USC football was truly amazing. However, his incredible streak almost ended on multiple occasions, but through a yeoman's effort each time, Pellerin remained steadfast in his quest. In 1949, his appendix had to be removed five days prior to a game at the LA Coliseum. With the effects from the operation still being very painful, he found a way to "fight on" and achieve "conquest," to coin a pair of classic phrases forever linked to the Trojans. He informed the nurses that he was going for a stroll around the hospital. What he failed to tell the angels of mercy watching over him was that his stroll took him to the Coliseum. Following a 40–13 victory, Pellerin made it back to his hospital room without the nurses knowing he was gone for several hours.[3]

On two other occasions, medical problems almost thwarted the streak, but like the true Trojan he was, Pellerin fought through his woes. He also refused to listen to the medical community. In 1969, a few weeks prior to the season opener, he had a tumor removed from his stomach. Doctors told him to remain in bed for a recuperation period of six weeks. That schedule did not work well with the patient, and he went against specific orders, and was on hand to watch the Trojans beat Nebraska. Nearly a quarter century later, he fell victim to an abdominal aneurysm at his hotel following a narrow one-point loss to Penn State on September 11, 1993. He was admitted to a Harrisburg, Pennsylvania, hospital for 12 days. Good fortune might not have shined on him physically, but the Trojans had a bye week coming up, so their number one fan was able to get out of his Pennsylvania sick bed after he signed a waiver that released the hospital from any liabilities. He then made it back to the Golden Coast in time to watch USC at home against Washington State on September 25, 1993.[4]

In addition to his health problems coming between him and his beloved team, one time a water pump on the car he was driving blew up near Oklahoma City a day-and-a-half prior to USC's clash with Notre Dame in South Bend. There were also times when he had to scurry about looking for misplaced tickets. Not even the love of a good woman prevented Pellerin from a 1935 game in Hawaii. In order to make it to the Aloha State, he delayed his honeymoon by eight months.[5]

As the decades passed by, and countless memories were gathered in this living encyclopedia of Trojan lore, Pellerin's story was often the focus of major media outlets seeking interviews, including *Sports Illustrated* and *USA Today*. He was also called upon for speeches to share his devotion and knowledge. He became such a fixture that he was greeted by players and coaches, and was able to travel with the team on their chartered plane.[6] Pellerin and his wife never had children of their own, but he always felt that the football team was like a family to him, consisting of over 120 All-Americans, Heisman Trophy winners, legendary coaches, and eight national championship teams, and he looked forward to each new season with excitement, regardless of his age.[7] In 1994, he was inducted into the USC Athletic Hall of Fame. Two years later, he received the first-ever Sears DieHard Fan Award as the nation's ultimate NCAA Division I college sports fan.[8]

Pellerin was in attendance for eight decades of football games in more than 50 cities, 75 stadiums, and through all types of weather conditions. He also made sure he took in other USC sporting events, in particular making himself a regular at basketball games. Giles and his wife also donated $1 million over the years to help with sports scholarships at USC. The passion for the Trojans ran deep in the Pellerin family, as his brother Oliver ran his own streak up to 637 games from 1945 to 2001, and another brother, Max, ran up over 300 straight games.[9]

On November 21, 1998, Giles was with his brother Oliver at the Rose Bowl watching the annual USC-UCLA game. During the game, he began to feel ill and wanted his brother to take him home to his townhouse in Pasadena. When he was outside of the Rose Bowl, the 91-year old died of cardiac arrest in the parking lot.[10] He passed away doing what he loved, and at the same stadium in which he first saw the Trojans play back in 1923. His devotion to USC was felt even after this incredible man left this world. In addition to donating $1 million to help with sports scholarships throughout his life, he left another $2 million he accumulated from investments to the USC athletic department upon his death.[11]

The number one Trojan of all-time once claimed that divine intervention had to allow his incredible streak to continue for as long as it did. Pellerin felt that God must have been a Trojan fan to give him the chance to compile such a record despite some close calls.[12] If his feelings are true, then rest assured that on USC game days, God is looking down upon the Trojans with Giles Pellerin watching right next to him.

## *The Trojan Nickname*

Larry Bird, Admiral Richard Byrd, and the Birdman of Alcatraz, have long been made famous. Larry Bird's basketball abilities allowed him to rise to the heights of immortality for the Boston Celtics. Admiral Byrd (despite the different spelling of his surname) was a legendary explorer. Robert Stroud, who was not only famous but infamous as well, resided in prison for the last 54 of his 73 years. He was a violent individual incarcerated for murder, but earned the moniker of "Birdman of Alcatraz" for his work with birds during his long stay behind bars.

In the Land of Troy, another individual with the surname of Bird, typed seven letters on a piece of paper that created a moniker forever synonymous with success. However, unlike Larry Bird, Admiral Byrd, or "the Birdman of Alcatraz," Owen R. Bird's legacy was lost to history.

Owen Bird displayed excellent athletic ability as a collegian at Occidental College. He never received a degree, but found a way to make his mark as a scribe for L.A.'s premier newspaper over the span of three years as an editor and writer of close to 800 articles. His affiliation with *The Los Angeles Times* began five months prior to coining one of the most popular nicknames in college athletics.[1]

As 1911 gave way to a new year, USC's athletic director, Warren Bovard, was seeking help to give the university a more intimidating nickname. Since USC's first football season in 1888, the sports teams were dubbed the Wesleyans and the Methodists until 1912. Bird had a special place in his heart for underdogs, and at the time, USC definitely fit the description of one. Both players and coaches alike at the university were faced with incredible odds stacked against them, opposing much more high-powered programs than USC's. Still, despite the huge disadvantages they faced, USC athletes gave everything they had to be competitive. This fighting spirit reminded Bird of the gallant forces of Troy, who fought hard in battle regardless of the incredible odds they faced.[2]

On February 24, 1912, at age 25, Bird wrote a preview for an upcoming USC track meet, and compared the team's will to that of a Trojan soldier. This was the first time the moniker was used to represent USC, and over a century later, Bird's usage of one word made the USC Trojans one of the most-revered nicknames on a universal scale. At the time of coining "Trojans," the football program was non-existent. From 1911 through 1913, USC opted for rugby instead of football. In 1914, the football program was returned, and it was the first season that "Trojans" was linked to USC football.

Despite the incredible fame that Bird brought to the university with seven letters, his life never reached the heights of USC's. He fought in war, was married three times, held many jobs, resided in numerous dwellings, and constantly looked to find greater ways to achieve rushes of adrenaline.[3]

With life apparently spinning out of control, Bird ultimately hit rock bottom on a winter evening in 1929. He came home to find his wife, Laura, in conversation with his best friend Percival Watson. There had been no signs of Watson coveting Mrs. Bird upon her husband's arrival. All they were doing was talking, but Bird apparently did not see it that way. He got a pistol and shot Watson in the face, arm, and stomach, and he died as a result of his wounds. Bird was found guilty of manslaughter, and served two years in prison. He continued to drift through the remaining years of his life, once again holding down numerous jobs and living at multiple addresses. He was alienated from his children, and his last known employment was that of a security guard. He died at the age of 78 due to the effects of emphysema.[4]

## *Team Colors*

From USC's beginning to 1895, gold served as the school color. The College of Liberal Arts adopted cardinal as its color. Even though the College of Liberal Arts was part of USC, it was the largest educational subdivision within the university's makeup. For that reason, it was able to create its own separate hue. All that changed in 1895 when the cardinal and gold merged into a union that will forever represent one of the most respected institutions of higher learning.[1]

## *Tailback U*

Off Ehukai Beach in Pupukea, on Oahu's North Shore, there is one of Hawaii's most popular destinations. The Banzai Pipeline is the attraction, and it is regarded as surfing's most famous wave. Over many years, it has drawn those willing to challenge it, with spectators looking on in amazement as surfers and the majestic Pacific Ocean merge into one.

Nearly four thousand miles away from Ehukai Beach in Los Angeles, another pipeline was created in the 1960s, making the word synonymous with greatness. However, instead of shouting the classic surfing term, COWABUNGA!, it was Student Body Left and Student Body Right that fed the mystique inside the Los Angeles Memorial Coliseum and college gridiron venues across the United States.

The legacy of great runners donned in the Cardinal & Gold of USC have dazzled the football scene since the days of Prohibition in the 1920s. Mort Kaer and Morley Drury started the proud lineage, with Erny Pinckert, Gus Shaver, Cotton Warburton, and Grenny Lansdell continuing the tradition throughout the 1930s. Frank Gifford, Jim Sears, and Jon Arnett showcased their talents during the Fabulous Fifties, and then the John McKay era came at the dawn of what became President Kennedy's New Frontier. McKay also established a new frontier of his own with the emergence of the USC tailback running out of the I-Formation, which by the latter stages of the 1960s, became the college football world's most glamorous position.

The I-Formation had been in use for a decade when McKay took over the USC program in 1960. With the tailback lining up six to eight yards behind the line of scrimmage, in an upright stance behind the quarterback and fullback, the tailback in the I-Formation can glance over the defensive alignment and spot weak areas to attack. With the fullback adding extra blocking support, the tailback can be a threat anytime he touches the ball.[1]

The pioneer that paved a path through McKay's frontier came in the form of Willie Brown, a 5-11, 172-pound tailback from Long Beach. When McKay incorporated the I-Formation into USC's offensive scheme, Brown was his man to make it go, and the Trojans prospered by winning the national championship in 1962. However, it was not until the following year that the Trojans received the player many felt was the quintessential torchbearer for the USC tailback position. This was Los Angeles native Mike Garrett, a 5-9, 180-pound tailback parexcellence. The Roosevelt High School alumnus possessed the skills needed to be a top-notch runner. Quickness, elusive moves, and a tough-as-nails body were the three ingredients that paid off in huge dividends. In 1965 Garrett brought USC's first Heisman Trophy home, but it would not be the last earned by Trojan tailbacks. O.J. Simpson, Charles White, Marcus Allen, and Reggie Bush all ran their way to college football's ultimate prize, while Anthony Davis and Ricky Bell came close during their spectacular tenures in the backfield.

The USC tailback might be regarded as the most coveted and glamorous position in college football, but the work that goes into earning those accolades is filled with grueling punishment and high expectations. The natural athletic abilities of these young men are what allowed them the chance to be a part of the greatness created at USC. However, many hours of hard work at practice is what allowed these icons to emerge supreme. McKay taught those tailbacks under his watch at USC to run hard, challenge defenses, and be tougher than they ever thought they could be.[2] With legs churning, and their bodies battered, the USC tailback forged ahead, sometimes carrying the ball 35 to 40 times a game.[3] In the end, all the hard work paid off, as conference and national championships were won with these young men plowing through defenses. Also, individual honors piled up in droves, paid for with determination, sweat, and blood. Being a USC tailback is indeed an elite fraternity. Despite the different personalities and running styles that each possessed, every one of them left USC with a lasting legacy that will never diminish, but only grow with the passing of each autumn.

## *USC–Notre Dame Rivalry*

The ingredients needed for a revered college football rivalry is a mixture of two long-storied programs with many of the game's greatest performances exhibited in the clashes that date back to the 1920s. Add some of the most legendary coaches and players, national championships at stake, and heart-stopping climaxes during their games together, and the end result is the greatest college football rivalry with no conference affiliation. Between them, USC and Notre Dame have compiled the most national titles and Heisman Trophy winners, and each year they wage a gridiron battle that started back in 1926 when iconic coaches Knute Rockne patrolled the sidelines for the Fighting Irish and Howard Jones for the Trojans.

Notre Dame already possessed the most celebrated pedigree in college football leading up to the initial time that the ball left the tee to kickoff their first matchup with USC. Nestled in South Bend, Indiana, the Notre Dame football program had its debut in 1887. The team enjoyed moderate success until the mid 1910s when coach Jesse Harper guided the Fighting Irish to national recognition with an overwhelming 35–13 win over a powerful Army team. This game, played on November 1, 1913, is often looked at as the one that started Notre Dame on its path to legendary status. It was also regarded as the first time the forward pass was used regularly in a game, with quarterback Charlie "Gus" Dorais and All-American end Knute Rockne, getting the credit for its success. That team finished the season at 7–0, and Harper posted an impressive 34–5–1 record over five seasons. However, the best was still to come.[1]

In 1918, Rockne took over for his mentor Jesse Harper, and at the conclusion of his 13 seasons at the helm, the legacy of both the university and Rockne were well entrenched in the annals of college football history. From 1918 through the 1930 season, Rockne compiled an almost spotless 105–12–5 record that included five undefeated teams without a tie and three national championships. His .881 winning percentage over Division I competition will not likely be overtaken.[2]

It was during the height of Rockne's fame, and the emergence of USC as a football power, that the conception of a yearly clash with the Trojans grew into a phenomenon that never diminishes. There is no doubt about the intensity that permeates from players, alumni, and fans, past and present, when these two titans of the college football world meet.

There are, however, multiple theories as to just how this rivalry came to be. Possibly the most interesting one did not even focus on football, but weather and wives. This account had the wives of Knute Rockne and USC Athletic Director Gwynn Wilson conversing on how wonderful it would be for Mrs. Rockne to visit the near-perfect climes offered by the Los Angeles area when her husband's team travelled west to play USC. The meeting of the wives apparently took place when the Wilsons were sent by USC to scout for a national rival. The mission saw the couple travel to Lincoln, Nebraska to watch the Cornhuskers and Rockne's Fighting Irish play on Thanksgiving Day, November 26, 1925. It was claimed that Mrs. Wilson sold Mrs. Rockne on the fact that travelling to sunny and warm Los Angeles every other year would be much better than freezing and snowy conditions in Nebraska. The sales job applied by Mrs. Wilson seemed to be an easy one, as Mrs. Rockne relayed the prospect of an annual meeting with the Trojans to her husband. This great piece of USC–Notre Dame lore then ended with Knute Rockne agreeing to place USC on their schedule every year, and on December 4, 1926, the legendary clash between these two powers began.[3]

The next explanation, and the one that has driven the human race for centuries, was for monetary gains. Notre Dame's popularity was so great by the mid 1920s that the team travelled all over the country looking for big paydays for the university. The University of Southern California was on the cusp of creating a successful heritage at this time, and wanted to test their mettle among some of the nation's top talent. In order to be the best, one had to beat the best, and there was no one better at the time than Rockne's Fighting Irish. The demand to see Notre Dame was strong among west coast Notre Dame faithful. The Rose Bowl committee was well aware of the allure to get Notre Dame out to the coast, and offered a concept that a team from the Pacific Coast Conference (modern day Pac-12) would play against Rockne's team in the Rose Bowl in Notre Dame's season finale each year. All looked good, but not every member of the PCC was overjoyed by the prospect of a Rockne road show.[4]

Stanford and California felt that Notre Dame had low academic standards and declined to take the field. It was then that Elmer "Gloomy Gus" Henderson offered up his Trojans for an annual meeting. However, before the USC and Notre Dame annual bash would kick off its classic meetings, Stanford jumped into the foray. They won the PCC title in 1924, and because of this recognition, Stanford was allowed first crack at the Fighting Irish in a Rose Bowl meeting on New Year's Day in 1925. Once again, the power of the wallet spoke louder to Stanford than its initial beliefs of opposing such a below standard academic institution.[5]

Elmer Henderson might have offered up his Trojans, but he never got the opportunity to square off against Rockne. He was dismissed following the 1924 season, and replaced by Howard Jones, thus bringing another theory into the USC–Notre Dame saga. After Rockne's incredible "Four Horsemen" rolled over every opponent en route to the national championship, the University of Southern California desired to have Rockne guide the Trojans. The great coach might have flirted with the idea, but eventually turned the offer down. He did offer another solution to USC's quest, with that being his friend Howard Jones, who looked to turn the Trojans into a national powerhouse. The two great football men knew each other from Jones' days coaching at Iowa. This relationship, once again coupled with big paydays, might have been a major factor in starting the annual event.[6]

From the lawless decade of the Roaring Twenties, through the Great Depression, military conflicts, political assassinations, Reaganomics, and the dawn of the new millennium, turbulent and exuberant times. Through all these circumstances, the USC–Notre Dame matchups marched along, bringing cheers and tears to all those passionate followers of the "Glamour Game." The Trojans and Fighting Irish have staged some of the greatest moments witnessed in the history of college football. The struggles over 100 yards of turf, whether in South Bend or Los Angeles, were no doubt incredible. However, possibly the most compelling saga to emerge from this classic rivalry did not occur on a football field staged over sixty minutes of controlled violence. It unfolded on a remote piece of real estate unknown to the majority of Americans until one of the darkest times in United States military history engulfed the masses from Maine to California like an ominous shroud.

The place was 530 square miles called the Bataan Peninsula, but to American servicemen and their Filipino allies, the horror they faced made Hell look like a vacation spot. The Japanese war machine was at the height of its power right after attacking Pearl Harbor on December 7, 1941. The momentum of dominance created by this military juggernaut appeared to be unstoppable. In January, 1942, Bataan was invaded by Japanese forces against American and Filipino resistance. The allied forces held out as long as they could, but on April 9, 1942, they were forced to surrender after being seriously outmanned and ravaged by sickness and lack of food and medical supplies. What transpired next was one of the worst displays of cruelty to ever unfold in American military history. It was also during this dark time amidst this human conflict that humanity shined through, all due to roots deep in USC–Notre Dame tradition.[7]

Mario "Motts" Tonelli was a tough running back for Notre Dame from 1936 through 1938. After playing for the Chicago Cardinals of the NFL in 1940, Tonelli entered the Army. The 26-year old was a Sergeant with the U.S. Army 200th Coast Artillery at the time he was one of the 60,000 to 80,000 combined American and Filipino defenders that surrendered on Bataan.[8] The huge throng of battle-weary allies then embarked on a seven-day, 62-mile trek from Bataan to a prisoner of war camp. They were denied food and water for the first three days, and when finally allowed to rehydrate, they had to drink from dirty water along the side of the road. The heat, coupled with fatigue and lack of food or clean water, quickly sapped the men that were forced to keep moving. Those that began to get weary and lag behind were usually killed along the way. Others were beaten and forced to keep walking. It was estimated that 2,500 soldiers died on the road before reaching the POW camp.[9]

As Tonelli carried on through this grueling journey, he had in his possession a Notre Dame graduation ring with a diamond and the words *Notre Dame* engraved on the sides. On the initial day of what became known as the Bataan Death March, Japanese soldiers went through the lines taking personal belongings from the prisoners. One Japanese soldier noticed Tonelli's ring and pointed at it with his bayonet. The proud Notre Dame graduate and football star now faced a crossroad. Either hand over his prized possession or die. A fellow American soldier whispered to him to give it up or he would be killed right where he stood. With a heavy heart, Tonelli took off the ring and handed it over.[10]

It was then, moments later, through all the horrendous circumstances unfolding before him, that Tonelli received a sliver of human kindness from an unlikely source. It was a Japanese officer who engaged the Notre Dame alumnus in perfect English. He wanted to know if one of his soldiers took the ring from him, to which Tonelli replied that he had. The officer reached down into his pocket and emerged with the Notre Dame ring. It was then that the Japanese officer said that he went to the University of Southern California and graduated in the same year as Tonelli. He added that he was at the Notre Dame-USC game when Tonelli broke free for a long run that beat the Trojans in 1937. He told Tonelli he was one hell of football player, returned the ring, and wished him luck. Despite the global conflict that saw these two soldiers on opposite sides of the spectrum, the common bond thousands of miles away from the United States was the Notre Dame-USC rivalry and the intense devotion that it permeates worldwide.[11]

Tonelli made it through the terrible experience with his ring hidden deep in a soap dish under his barracks at the POW camp he was assigned to so that it could not be stolen from him. It served as a good luck token, and gave him hope of returning to the States one day to get on with his life. And that is what he did. Despite suffering from malaria, dysentery, scurvy, and beriberi over his 42 months of brutal torment in three POW camps, Tonelli made it out alive at barely 100 pounds.[12] After time in the hospital, he regained his strength and took the field for the Chicago Cardinals as a 140-pound running back in 1945.[13] Ironically, his #58 was the same one he wore at Notre Dame and also the one assigned to him in his last stay at a POW camp. He played on more season of professional football with the Chicago Rockets of the All-America Football Conference in 1946 before going into politics in Illinois.[14] Tonelli passed away on January 7, 2003 at age 86. The whereabouts of the Japanese officer from USC were never known. He might have faded into legend, but his act of kindness during such a savage and cruel moment in time will never wane.

## *USC-UCLA Rivalry*

The world of college football is filled with intense rivalries that have existed for generations, and only grow with the passage of time. This is one of the main reasons for the public's passion for the college game. Rivals from different states lock horns once a year in the hope of securing bragging rights until the calendar shows that another clash with the same school is on the horizon. However, no other rivalry in major college football battles for the rights of one city, with the exception of the USC—UCLA conflict that has been going on since the latter stages of the Roaring Twenties. With a mere 13 miles separating these two excellent institutions of higher learning, passions run deep.

The genesis of this great rivalry began on an autumn afternoon in 1917 at the Jonathan Club in Los Angeles. It was there that a 38-year old Sheboygan, Wisconsin, native named Edward Dickson, and 46-year old Ernest Carroll Moore, discussed the embryonic stages of what would one day be The University of California Los Angeles. Dickson was the political editor of the *Los Angeles Express*, and was on the governing board of the University of California, Berkeley. He graduated from Cal in 1901, and was the lone member of the board living in Southern California. Moore was the president of the Los Angeles State Normal School.[1]

These two stellar members of the education community had a shared desire to establish a branch of Cal Berkeley in Los Angeles. At first, regardless of the excellent idea, the leaders of the main campus in Berkeley refused to approach the concept congenially. The regents from the northern part of the Golden State felt that a new college would take away faculty, students, and funding. After much political struggle, Dickson had a force that came into play that pushed the Berkeley delegation into siding with him. Threatening to invade the City of Angels was a new group of regents that determined to set up a college not affiliated with Cal-Berkeley. If that happened, it meant Cal-Berkeley would have to share monetary growth with the new institution. The ultimatum was heard loud and clear. Taking a major hit to one's wallet can constitute a rapid change of heart. Such was the case with Cal-Berkeley expanding its influence to Los Angeles.[2]

In 1919, Dickson and Moore had their dream reach maturation when the University of California, Southern Branch opened for business with 1,338 students. The new university also began its football program that same year, and over the course of their first six seasons, the results were brutal. With the trio of coaches Fred Cozens, Harry Trotter, and James Cline, the team managed only six wins from 1919 through 1924.[3]

In 1925, both UCLA and USC had a reversal of fortune with the arrival of new coaches that help guide their respective teams to greater heights. In regards to USC, they were on the rise to national prominence under Elmer "Gloomy Gus" Henderson in the first half of the 1920s, and Howard Jones escalated what his predecessor began by taking the Trojans to powerhouse status. Thirteen miles away, the University of California Southern Branch hired William Henry Spaulding. He was a firm believer in conditioning, and ran his players ragged.[4] The results were the 1925 team finishing with the university's first winning football season. At 5-3, Spaulding's efforts allowed the team to win almost as many games in one season than the program was able to accomplish in six previous ones. This was also the year that the school moved from its original 25-acre spot on Vermont Avenue to a new one slightly west of the famous Beverly Hills.

The football program continued to grow under Spaulding's guidance. In 1926 the nickname was changed to the Bruins after starting off as the Cubs and Grizzlies. The following year saw the name of the entire university change from the University of California Southern Branch to the University of California at Los Angeles. In 1958, the "at" was dropped and was then called what it is known by worldwide, the University of California Los Angeles.[5] Then, in 1928, the Bruins were admitted to the Pacific Coast Conference along with the mighty USC Trojans, who would go on to win the national championship that year under Howard Jones and his "Thundering Herd."

In slightly under ten years, UCLA had grown, and looked to continue to on a steady rise. Gwynn Wilson, the graduate manager (modern day athletic director) at USC was one who was following the progress going on across town, and came away highly impressed. So much so in fact, that he jumped on a streetcar in early 1929 and traveled west until he got to the UCLA campus. What he had on his mind would some day become one of the greatest college football rivalries in history.

Wilson went to converse with UCLA's athletic director, Steve Cunningham, about the prospect of starting up a series pitting the Bruins against Wilson's alpha dogs in Cardinal & Gold. Cunningham was stunned at the offer. He did not feel that the Bruins were ready to face off against the powerful Trojans. Wilson convinced his peer that the two programs would eventually play each other in the future, so why prolong the inevitable. The odds might have been stacked against the upstart Bruins at the beginning of this series, but in time, UCLA would have the chance to be on equal ground with their powerhouse neighbors. Obviously, Wilson emerged victorious in his quest, and his vision allowed this classic series to get underway starting in 1929.[6]

In addition to Wilson's belief in this matchup, *Los Angeles Times* sportswriter Braven Dyer expressed his prediction that in the years to come, this rivalry had the chance to grow into one of college football's truly great spectacles in the western region of the United States. However, when the teams met for the first time on September 28, 1929, the Trojans lived up to their status as a national powerhouse, mauling the Bruins, 76-0. The Bruins took such a beating in the first two meetings that UCLA decided to cancel the game from 1931 through 1935 in an attempt to build up their program so that they could be more competitive against the Trojans.

By the latter part of the 1930s UCLA did just that, and over the years, not only rose up to equal ground with USC, but surpassed them on many occasions. This passion of this rivalry was also heated by the fact that the conference championship was usually at stake when these two slugged it out. One of the greatest quotes regarding this series came from UCLA head coach Henry "Red" Sanders, who took the Bruins to championship glory during the 1950s. He felt that beating USC was not a matter of life and death, but was much more important than that.[7]

## *Conference Affiliation*

Affiliation with a conference has garnered a great deal of athletes the opportunity to boast of rising to the top of the conference and hoisting not only championship hardware, but also the right to be the alpha dog for at least one year. Through the years, there have been, and continue to be, some conferences that rule above all others, whether it be in prestige or athletic dominance. The Ivy League, Big Ten, and Southeastern Conference, all come to mind when prestige and long bouts of dominance are discussed.

The Pac-12 is also considered to be among the elite in college sports, and USC's long-time successful affiliation with the conference, has added to its status. However, prior to joining what became the Pac-12, USC belonged to the Southern California Intercollegiate Conference for a few seasons in the early 20th century. When USC returned to playing football in 1914, they were a member of the SCIC along with Occidental, Pomona, Whittier, and Redlands. The Trojans then left the conference the following season in an attempt to elevate the program into greater status in the college football ranks.[1]

The origin of what came to be known as the Pac-12 was formed on December 2, 1915, as the Pacific Coast Conference, with charter members consisting of the University of California, Berkeley, the University of Oregon, the University of Washington, and Oregon Agricultural College (now Oregon State). Washington State College came into the fold in 1917, and Stanford joined the next year.[2]

The PCC remained as a six-team conference until 1922, when the University of Idaho and USC joined. The University of Montana became a member in 1924, and stayed until 1950, and UCLA was added in 1928. The conference had a reputation for strictness regarding high standards, a paid commissioner, a complex constitution, a solid code of conduct, and a network in place that reported eligibility issues.

Just like any business affiliation, there are times when things do not always go well. The PCC might have been a stellar group on both the playing fields and in the classroom, but animosity still came into play. The California universities and those of the Northwest had growing tensions that could have put an end to the PCC. A regent of the University of California, Edwin Pauley, did not have any warm feelings for the universities of the Great Northwest, and suggested that the California-based schools leave the PCC and start up a "California Conference." One of Pauley's dislikes stemmed from the Northwest schools not having the same high level of education as those in California, and wanted to compete with programs from universities with a higher academic standard. Even the California-based schools had a falling out over academics. In 1924, Stanford and Cal felt that USC was not maintaining high enough academic standards, and not enforcing eligibility rules.[3] The schools look to break off relations with USC, but by 1925, problems were ironed out after realizing that profits would be hurt if the rivalries were not continued.

Despite the harsh feelings, the PCC did not break up at that time, but a quarter of a century later, allegations surfaced that eventually led to its demise. In 1951, charges were brought against the University of Oregon's football coach, Jim Aiken, in regards to violation of financial aid and athletic subsidies. Aiken resigned from his position, and Oregon persuaded the governing body of the PCC to investigate UCLA as well. After five years, the scandal left the confines of the PCC and reached the masses. In January 1956, a few Washington players looked to revolt against their coach. When the coach was relieved of his duties, the PCC pursued their search of allegations regarding a slush fund, which meant that there was a reserve of money used primarily for illicit purposes such as bribery. The PCC's investigation found proof of illegal goings on by an organization called the Greater Washington Advertising Fund, and set forth to bring sanctions down.

In March 1956, charges of illegal payments by two booster clubs affiliated with UCLA hit the news. In no time, like a domino effect, USC and Cal were dragged into the proceedings. In 1957,the PCC was in shambles, and two years later, it disbanded after 42 years of operation. Over their time in the PCC, the USC Trojans won 12 football championships.[4]

After the PCC was dissolved, the Athletic Association of Western Universities was formed on July 1, 1959. This new grouping consisted of Cal, Stanford, UCLA, USC, and Washington. From 1960 to 1962, the AAWU was also called "the Big Five." When Washington State joined in 1962, it was dubbed "the Big Six." In 1964, Oregon and Oregon State became members, and the AAWU changed its name to the Pac-8 starting in 1968. Ten years later, Arizona and Arizona State joined the conference, and from 1978 until 2011, it was called the Pac-10. On July 1, 2011, the name was changed to the Pac-12 after the University of Colorado and Utah came on board. The Pac-12 proclaimed itself the "Conference of Champions." This bravado stemmed from the fact that its members recorded the most NCAA national championships over all other conferences. As of 2011, the Pac-12, which includes going back to its forefather, the PCC, has produced 400 NCAA team titles in all sports, with UCLA, Stanford, and USC leading the way.[5]

## *USC Bowl Appearances*

Simply put, with 33 trips and 24 victories at the Rose Bowl, USC stands alone as the most successful descendant in the long lineage of the "Granddaddy of Them All." Those 33 victories in the Rose Bowl allow the Trojans the privilege of owning the all-time record for most wins by a school in one bowl game. As of the 2012 season, the Trojans have also made appearances in 12 other bowl games, consisting of the Christmas Festival, Liberty Bowl, Bluebonnet Bowl, Fiesta Bowl, Aloha Bowl, Florida Citrus Bowl, Sun (John Hancock) Bowl, Freedom Bowl, Cotton Bowl, Las Vegas Bowl, Orange Bowl, and Emerald Bowl. Throughout their many travels for bowl game competition, the Trojans have posted the third all-time highest winning percentage (.667) in college football history. During the first decade of the 2000's under Pete Carroll, the Trojans appeared in an exceptional streak of seven straight BCS bowl games (2003–2009).[1]

## *The Hollywood Connection to USC*

With the motion picture industry being right in the neighborhood, it comes as no surprise that there is a strong link to USC and the Hollywood dream factories. Many stars of the silver screen and television have attended the University of Southern California, with some also starring for the Trojans on the football field.

When Howard Jones arrived at USC in 1925 to take over as head coach, he quickly realized the potential of having one of the most appealing industries just a few miles away. He saw a perfect union emerge between his players and the film studios in regards to helping members of the USC football team obtain jobs that could help out monetarily. In the 1920s, a film extra had the opportunity to earn eight to 25 dollars a day, which was a hefty amount for that time period. Hollywood also produced a fair share of films with a college theme, and Howard Jones and his players had the chance to perform small roles in them.[1] Many players took the opportunity to perform as extras, and some of them went on to more pursuits in Hollywood.

The biggest name in Hollywood history to grace the gridiron before rising to iconic cinematic status is John Wayne. Icon, legend, and treasure are a trio of exemplary words from the English language that can best describe the status that John "the Duke" Wayne garnered. For over half a century, Wayne worked in the film industry, eventually earning recognition as one of the greatest celebrities in American cinema. However, long before storming the beaches as Sgt. Stryker in *"The Sands of Iwo Jima,"* or winning an Academy Award with his portrayal of the cantankerous Rooster Cogburn in the western classic *True Grit*, Wayne was a very good football player.

The town of Winterset, Iowa, was the place that laid claim to calling Wayne a native son. Born Marion Robert Morrison on May 26, 1907, his family moved to California, first to Pasadena, and then Glendale, when Morrison was six years old. As a youngster, he had an Airedale terrier named Duke, and the two were inseparable. A fireman used to see the pair regularly, and he began calling Marion "Little Duke." In time, he became "Duke" Morrison, and the moniker forever became synonymous with him.

Morrison was a standout guard for Glendale High School, playing a major role in obtaining both the 1924 Central League and Southern California championship. The team was so talent-laden that seven of its members were offered football scholarships to USC. In addition to his football prowess, Morrison excelled in the classroom, performed in plays, and was the president of his senior class in 1925.

The big, 6'4" talented guard accepted the offer to attend USC after being declined by the Naval Academy. He took to the football field under Howard Jones as a pre-law student. Scholarships were not what they became, and at the time of Morrison's entrance into USC, they covered $280 a year to help with tuition, and one meal a day. To gain extra money, Morrison served food at sorority houses and worked for a phone company on movie lots. He also joined the Sigma Chi fraternity.

Like many in the USC fold, Morrison was able to get work with the film studios thanks to head coach Howard Jones. Jones got him work helping out in the conditioning of western silent movie star Tom Mix for the film, *The Great K and A Train Robbery*. He also found work as an extra in two football-related films, *Brown of Harvard* and *Drop Kick*. Unbeknownst at the time was the fact that as John Wayne, the young USC tackle "Duke" Morrison, would surpass Mix and many others as the king of western film stars. Until that time, however, he was still a student/athlete looking toward his future.

By the end of his sophomore year, Morrison was on pace to earn a possible starting job at right tackle on USC's immortal "Thundering Herd" team of the late 1920s. One day, three weeks after the beginning of training camp in 1927, Morrison decided to head for Balboa Beach in Newport, California, to try his hand at body surfing on big waves that were dubbed "Wedge," and the cause of many injuries to those willing to challenge the power of the waves. By the end of this adventure, Morrison was one of the many who suffered from the powerful surf, as he dislocated his right shoulder.

In Howard Jones' system, the person playing right tackle had to use his right shoulder to block all the time. The USC power game relied on it, and Morrison was having trouble during drills due to his injured shoulder. Howard Jones was a no nonsense type of coach, who demanded absolute commitment to the game of football, and was so consumed by the sport, that it was all he thought about every day of the year. It was this kind of a coach that Morrison would have had to confront about how he sustained an injury. Allegedly, the story goes that Morrison was so intimidated by Jones, as every player was, that he decided not to tell the coach about his injury. Without the knowledge of the injury, Jones just assumed that Morrison did not have what it took to perform for him. Instead of explaining why he could not perform up to standard, Morrison saw his status slip to the fourth and fifth team. Jones also apparently took away his training table privileges, which meant that Morrison would have to support himself if he wanted to eat. In addition to that, he owed his fraternity money, and was asked to leave the house until he could make payment.

Faced with dire straits, Morrison left USC to look for work at Fox Studios. It was then that Morrison met director John Ford, who came away impressed with the strong work ethic of the young, strong, and athletic former Trojan. Ford started him off as a prop man, and saw something in Morrison's appearance that made the director feel compelled to place him in front of the camera. In 1928, Morrison was featured in the film *Hangman's House,* and two years later, he received a starring role in the 1930 western, *The Big Trail.* It was at this time that the director on the film, Raoul Walsh, apparently was a major influence in Morrison changing his name to John Wayne. Throughout the 1930s Wayne starred in many low-budget films, predominately westerns, for most of the studios. After appearing in 82 films through 1938, Wayne hit the big time, shedding the low-budget roles. In 1939, Wayne's old friend, director John Ford, got him to star in the 1939 western classic *Stagecoach*, as "the Ringo Kid." The year 1939 was considered one of the greatest in Hollywood history, with many cinematic classics coming out during that time, and *Stagecoach* was near the top of the list. It shot Wayne up the ranks of Hollywood royalty, of which he never slipped. Upon his death on June 11, 1979, Wayne had appeared in 184 films, mostly of the western or war genres. Despite the fact that he never got the chance to finish his football career or college education at USC, Wayne remained loyal to the Cardinal & Gold. He helped Howard Jones get work for players on films, and even received an honorary doctorate from USC.[2]

## Ward Bond

From a small town in Nebraska, to a member of a national championship football team, to appearing in over 200 motion pictures, Ward Bond got a lot of living out of his 57 years on Earth. Born Wardell Edwin "Ward" Bond, on April 9, 1903, in Benkelman, Nebraska, Bond graduated from East High School in Denver, Colorado. It was then time for the strapping 6'2," 195-pound lineman to head off to the bright lights and success that awaited him in Los Angeles.

While playing for the legendary Howard Jones at USC, Bond became a starting lineman on the famous "Thundering Herd" teams of the late 1920s, helping the Trojans obtain their first national title in 1928. He developed a life-long friendship with John Wayne, starting from their days at USC. In 1929, Wayne, Bond, and the entire USC football team were selected to appear in the football drama *Salute*, starring George O'Brien and Helen Chandler. Wayne and Bond were unbilled performers, but they established a solid relationship with the film's director, John Ford.

Ford, like John Wayne, would go on to become revered Hollywood icons in their chosen professions, and Bond's relationship with both men allowed him the opportunity to carve out a much-respected film career of his own. After his appearance in *Salute*, Bond remained in the film business until 1960. He performed in *The Big Trail* in 1930, which was John Wayne's first leading role, and got to star with his friend a total of 23 times. Of the 200-plus films Bond eventually appeared in, predominately in supporting roles, he also had the chance to work with director John Ford on 25 occasions, among them the Hollywood classics, *The Searchers, Drums Along the Mohawk, The Quiet Man,* and *Fort Apache.*

Over the course of his long career, Bond had the opportunity to star in many other motion pictures considered to be among the all-time greatest. They included *It Happened One Night, You Can't Take it With You, Gone With the Wind, The Grapes of Wrath, The Maltese Falcon, Sergeant York, They Were Expendable, It's a Wonderful Life, Joan of Arc, Mister Roberts,* and *Rio Bravo.* Eleven times with Bond appearing on screen, the film received an Academy Award nomination for best picture of the year, and three of them won Hollywood's grand prize *(It Happened One Night* in 1934, *You Can't Take it With You* in 1938, and *Gone With the Wind* in 1939).

In 1957, Bond was selected to star in the television series *Wagon Train*, and the show went on to become a very popular staple among viewers. On November 5, 1960, while in Dallas, Texas, to attend a football game, Bond suffered a fatal heart attack at age 57. John Wayne gave the eulogy at his funeral, and for his lengthy film career, Bond was presented with a star on the Hollywood Walk of Fame, located at 6933 Hollywood Blvd. In 2001, he was inducted to the Western Performers Hall of Fame at the National Cowboy & Western Heritage Museum in Oklahoma City.[3]

## Bobby Robertson

Robertson worked as an extra for the top film studios while at USC, and had the distinction of appearing in the 1939 Academy Award-winning classic, *Gone With the Wind*, as one of the dead bodies at the Atlanta railroad station.[4]

## Ambrose Schindler

Schindler gained football fame as the Player of the Game in the 1940 Rose Bowl, and on the silver screen, he subbed for the Tin Man in a scene during the filming of *The Wizard of Oz* in 1939.[5]

## Julie Bescos

The captain of the 1934 USC team, Bescos first distinguished himself as a three-sport star at USC, earning eight letters in football, basketball, and baseball. He had the opportunity to do occasional film work, with the crowning glory of his Hollywood career being a stunt double for Clark Gable on the 1935 Academy Award-winning film *Mutiny on the Bounty*. He also worked as an unaccredited actor in three other films from 1934 to 1937.[6]

## Cotton Warburton

Following his All-American football career at USC, Warburton became a film editor, and worked in the film industry until 1978. He received an Academy Award for film editing on the 1964 motion picture *Mary Poppins*.[7]

## Nate Barragar

Barragar was an All-American lineman at USC in 1929, and then received All-Pro honors in the NFL with the Green Bay Packers (1931–32, 1934–35). His football abilities awarded him with induction into the USC Athletic Hall of Fame (2003), and the Green Bay Packers Hall of Fame (1979). Barragar's second career brought him back to Los Angeles following his professional football days. He became a second unit director and assistant director for many motion pictures and television shows from 1946 to 1965. He had the chance to work with former Trojan John Wayne on the films, *Sands of Iwo Jima* and *Hondo*, both as an assistant director. His television work saw his name appear as assistant director on such classic western shows as *Gunsmoke*, *The Rifleman*, and *Bonanza*, plus many other series.[8]

## Jesse Hibbs

Hibbs' life took him from All-American status as a tackle at USC to the director's chair down the street from the campus in Hollywood, with a one-season stop in the NFL with the Chicago Bears in 1931 in between. Hibbs worked predominately in television, with 36 titles to his credit. His involvement with television series began in 1958 with *Zane Grey Theater,* and continued through 1970. During that time period, Hibbs was a director for some of the most-renowned series, including *Hawaiian Eye, The Rifleman, Gunsmoke, Bonanza, Rawhide, Perry Mason, Wagon Train, Death Valley Days, The Fugitive, The Wild, Wild West, The Invaders, The Rat Patrol,* and *The F.B.I.*[9]

## Aaron Rosenberg

After earning All-American honors at USC as one of the Trojans' greatest linemen in school history, Rosenberg entered a long and respected career as a Hollywood producer. From 1948 to 1974, he was a producer of 61 projects.[10]

## Marshall Duffield

Duffield led the Trojans to a Rose Bowl victory in 1930, and served as team captain in 1930. While a member of head coach Howard Jones' teams, Duffield helped the Trojans post a 27–4–1 record. He briefly worked as an assistant director before marrying a Hollywood starlet named Dorothy Lee in 1933. The couple divorced two years later, and Duffield went off to start an import-export business that became highly successful.[11]

## Frank Gifford

Gifford's personal appearance and athletic prowess seemed to make him the perfect fit for a life in front of the camera. He was handsome, an All-American, and an All-Pro with the New York Giants of the NFL. His resume appeared to make him destined to be a star of some sort. It did not take those in Hollywood long to recognize Gifford's attributes, and while still at USC, he made his film debut with the top comedy team of the time, Dean Martin and Jerry Lewis in 1951's *That's My Boy*. Gifford was a stand-in for Lewis when kicking the football was required. The part was unaccredited, and so were his appearances in *The Unknown Man* (1951), *Sally and Saint Anne* (1952), and *Bonzo Goes to College* (1952). In 1953, while with the New York Giants, Gifford received a credited role as Stan Pomeroy in the film *The All-American* starring Tony Curtis and Mamie Van Doren. Also included in the film was USC All-American Jim Sears. Over the next seven years, Gifford made appearances in *Walking My Baby Back Home* (1953), *Sign of the Pagan* (1954), *Darby's Rangers* (1958), *Up Periscope* (1959), and *Turnpike Cop* (1960). Near the end of his pro career, Gifford appeared in an episode of the television comedy, *Hazel*, starring Shirley Booth, in 1963, and in *The Reporter* in 1964.

Following his retirement from professional football following the 1964 season, Gifford worked as a commentator for NFL games on the CBS network. In 1971, he launched a career as a play-by-play announcer on *Monday Night Football*, and was revered for his work on that broadcast until he left in 1997. Gifford also worked on ABC's *Wide World of Sports*, and commentated during the Olympics through the years. He was twice nominated for an Emmy Award in the category of Outstanding Sports Personality (1974, 1976), and received a Lifetime Achievement Emmy Award in 1997.[12]

## Ron Miller

Miller played left end for the Trojans (1951–53), and while at USC, he went on a date with Diane Disney, the daughter of legendary Hollywood icon Walt Disney. The relationship blossomed into marriage and four children. After serving in the United States Army, Miller played one season as a tight end for the Los Angeles Rams in 1956. In one game that his father-in-law Walt saw from the stands, Miller was knocked unconscious. Following the conclusion of the season, Disney approached his son-in-law with a less violent way to make a living. It was then that Miller was brought into the Disney fold as a second assistant, following seven games as a professional football player. He eventually worked his way up the corporate ladder to produce and direct. In time, Miller became president of Walt Disney Productions in 1980, and CEO in 1983. Under his leadership, Disney continued to grow into one of the all-time greatest media outlets.[13]

## Russ Saunders

Saunders had a busy life even before his career as a second unit director and assistant director in Hollywood. Nicknamed "Racehorse," Saunders ran over and around the opposition on many occasions in football. He earned the Most Valuable Player award of the 1930 Rose Bowl, and was one of the models used for the famed Tommy Trojan statue. He then went on to play a year of professional football with the Green Bay Packers in 1931. It was then on to a long career in the film industry from 1931 to 1976. He was nominated for an Academy Award in 1938 in the best assistant director category for his work on *The Life of Emile Zola.*[14]

## Mike Henry

Henry was a tackle for the Trojans in the late 1950s. In the 1958 NFL draft, he was selected by the Pittsburgh Steelers in the 9th round, and was the 100th overall pick of that year's draft. He played in 76 professional games as a middle linebacker, first with Pittsburgh from 1958 to 1961, and finished off his career with the Los Angeles Rams from 1962 to 1964. While still playing professional football, Henry was under contract with Warner Brothers Studios, and appeared in the television shows *Surfside 6, Hawaiian Eye,* and *Cheyenne,* and in the motion picture *Spencer's Mountain* in 1963. When the classic series Batman was going through the development stages, Henry was considered to play the title character. The part eventually went to Adam West. Henry played Tarzan in three films, starred opposite John Wayne in *The Green Berets* (1968), and was the character Junior Justice in the three *Smokey and the Bandit* motion pictures.[15]

## O.J. Simpson

While still a professional, record-setting running back, for the Buffalo Bills, Simpson set out to pursue an acting career. He appeared in the block buster television mini-series *Roots* in 1977, and the motion pictures *The Klansman* (1974, *The Towering Inferno* (1974), *The Cassandra Crossing* (1976), and *Capricorn One* (1978), all while still in the NFL. He tested his comedic talent in *Back to the Beach* (1987), and in *The Naked Gun* films (1988, 1991, 1994). At the end of his professional career, Simpson started a film production company called Orenthal Productions, which predominately created projects for television. In addition to his work in television and films, Simpson was a commentator on *Monday Night Football* (1983–85) and the *NFL on NBC.*[16]

## Tim Rossovich

While at USC, Rossovich had the future Hollywood star Tom Selleck as a roommate. Following their USC days, Selleck went on to pursue his acting career, while Rossovich played professional football as a middle linebacker with the Philadelphia Eagles (1968–71), San Diego Chargers (1972–73), and the Houston Oilers (1976), of the NFL. He also played for the Philadelphia franchise of the defunct World Football League (1974–75). Rossovich then set out to join his college roommate in the acting profession. He landed an unaccredited role as a bodyguard on the television series *Soap* for three episodes in 1978. From there, he worked at a steady pace on television, appearing 47 times in many television series and several motion pictures from 1978 to 1998. His credits included guest roles on television's *Charlie's Angels, Turnaround, Wonder Woman, The A-Team,* and *Magnum, P.I.,* on which Tom Selleck portrayed the main character.[17]

## Allen Graf

Graf went from an All-American high school football player at San Fernando High School, to a college career at USC, which was culminated by being an offensive guard on the 1972 national championship team. After graduating from USC, Graf tried out with the Los Angeles Rams as a free agent before playing with the Portland Storm of the obsolete World Football League in 1974. When the WFL folded, Graf switched career paths, and the decision paid off well. He received a chance to be a stunt double for former Chicago Bears Hall of Famer Dick Butkus in the 1976 film *Gus.* From there, Graf was employed as a stunt man on television and in films. In time, his expertise allowed Graf to serve the industry as a second unit director and stunt coordinator on many motion pictures. Graf also earned the recognition of being the first stuntman to cannon role a bus at 60 miles-per-hour.[18]

## Lynn Swann

After a Hall of Fame career as a receiver on four Super Bowl winning teams with the Pittsburgh Steelers, Swann retired from professional football in 1983. While still with the Steelers, Swann began a broadcasting career on ABC's *Wide World of Sports* in 1976. His affiliation with ABC lasted until 2006, and he was involved in covering many of the top sporting events throughout that time. His acting credits came on the television series *The Paper Chase* (1984), *Hotel* (1985), *Family Matters* (1991), and *Built to Last* (1997). He appeared in the Adam Sandler comedy *The Waterboy* in 1998, and also tried his hand at hosting the television series *To Tell the Truth* from 1990 to 1991. His stint on the show lasted just 14 weeks, and he was replaced by Alex Trebek, who is long regarded as one of the all-time greats in game show hosting.[19]

## Anthony Davis

The player dubbed "the Notre Dame Killer," for his incredible performances against the Irish from 1972 through 1974, took his football skills into the pro ranks for six seasons. The All-American tailback also dabbled in the acting profession from 1978 to 1985. His appearances included work on the television series *Roots: The Next Generation* (1979), *The Incredible Hulk, Buck Rogers in the 25th Century, Hotel,* and *Police Woman.*[20]

## Rodney Peete

The All-American quarterback from the late 1980s had a lengthy professional football career from 1989 through 2002, and has appeared on game shows, talk shows, and reality series, plus a few episodes of television series as himself. Among his credits are appearances on *Celebrity Blackjack* (2004), *Dancing With the Stars* (2006), *The Oprah Winfrey Show* (1996, 2004, 2007), *The Apprentice* (2010), *The Wendy Williams Show* (2012), and *Entertainment Tonight* (2008, 2010). Peete is also married to actress Holly Robinson.[21]

### Lou Ferrigno, Jr.

The Santa Monica native is the son of bodybuilding legend Lou Ferrigno. In 2006, he was a walk on at USC as a linebacker. However, a knee injury prevented him from continuing on with a football career. The old adage of when one door closes another one opens held true for Ferrigno. While going through rehabilitation on his knee, his dedication to pursuing artistic talents came into play. His artwork, described as "Pop-Surrealist," has gained attention, along with his acting pursuits. He has appeared on the daytime drama *Days of Our Lives* (2013), and the popular sitcom *How I Met Your Mother* (2013).[22]

### Clara Bow

Obviously, Clara Bow was not a member of the Trojans football team. However, she was a devoted fan like so many other Hollywood stars. She led an extremely colorful life, and her passion for USC football during the days of the "Thundering Herd," are worth mentioning.

The Brooklyn, New York native was 21 years old when she attended her first USC game. Despite her young age, Bow was already a superstar on the silver screen during the silent era. Her film persona, as well as her personal life, was that of a devil-may-care, Roaring Twenties flapper. She was the first Hollywood female sex symbol, and dubbed "the It Girl." Whatever "It" was, Bow surely had an overabundance of it. She was very sexy, with a fantastic figure and looks that would attract attention no matter what the decade was. It was also alleged that Bow had a voracious sexual desire that became legendary, and her conquests many.

This quintessential wild child of the Hollywood set went to see the Trojans play for the first time in 1926 as part of a promotion centered around one of her films. This was a time before professional sports invaded the Los Angeles area, and the USC Trojans were immensely popular. They were also very good and Bow was hooked on the Cardinal & Gold. This passion for the men of Troy, mixed with her sexual prowess, started the rumor mills churning out stories of wild activities involving Clara and the 1927 Trojans. Tales were told of drunken orgies that had Bow engaging in sex with the entire team of alcohol-swigging football players.

Through the decades, the story continued to be a staple in conversation when Clara Bow and the Trojans came up. However, the old adage of not letting the truth get in the way of a good story, truly came into play on this occasion. Years later, it was revealed by All-American Morley Drury, who was the star of the "Thundering Herd," and even went on a double date with Bow, that nothing happened at those parties as reported. Drury claimed that Bow did indeed invite the team over, but dancing and swimming were the activities, and that alcohol was apparently never served.[23] In addition to Bow's passion for the Trojans, there were countless other Hollywood stars that loved the team and enjoyed conversing with the players and attending games.[24]

## *The Spirit of Troy (USC Marching Band)*

The perception of when music began can be traced to the beat of the human heart. From there it grew into sounds that created musical genres of all types. Despite a person's musical taste, one thing is certain, and it might help to theorize the concept of the heartbeat, acting as the catalyst that began this wonderful feeling of expression. Listening to a song can bring on the whole gamut of emotions that moves people to their soul. Mix this concept with the heart-pumping excitement of a football game, and you have the makings of a marching band. In the case of the University of Southern California, you have "the Spirit of Troy," an iconic group of musicians that has been linked to USC since the university's first year in 1880.

Over the many years of playing music, the band had incredible opportunities to perform with some of the most respected musicians of their time, including John Phillip Souza, recognized as "the March King," Henry Mancini, Quincy Jones, and Leonard Bernstein. It has performed for seven United States presidents, and appeared at the Academy Awards, the Grammy Awards, on various television shows, commercials, and was featured in magazines. It also earned two platinum albums for work on Fleetwood Mac's *Tusk* in 1979, and the group's 1997 reunion album, *The Dance.*

The Spirit of Troy consists of over 300 members, with 20 percent working toward a degree in music. The work is tough, as the band performs a new halftime show at each home game, and it takes over 100 hours of practice for the shows. By the end of the year, it is estimated that the band marches 90 miles in their travels around the country playing at USC football games. It has not missed a game, home or on the road, since 1987, and performs at 350 events every year. The band is so popular, that it has been invited to perform in international venues as well. In addition to supporting the football team, the band has performed at some of the greatest spectacles in sports. Two Summer Olympic Games hosted by Los Angeles in 1932 and 1984, four Super Bowls, one World Series (1988), and Rose Bowls, are on the bands stellar resume. In 2009, ESPN.com ranked the "Spirit of Troy" as the best college band in the nation. There are many other accolades that have been bestowed on the band over the decades, and the stories surrounding them could fill a volume all its own.[1]

## *Fight On*

A contest was proposed by USC in 1922 with the concept being to come up with a spirited song that would be linked to the university. Like many other hopefuls, dental student Milo Sweet and co-creator Glen Grant scrawled down some words in an attempt to be the ones that rose to the forefront of the competition. What they eventually unleashed was a classic fight song that has been rousing USC competitors and fans alike since the Roaring Twenties.

"Fight On" was the song that made it thanks to Sweet and

Grant, and is played mostly after first downs and touchdowns. It has also been afforded those in the entertainment business the chance to use it in musical recordings and motion pictures. One interesting claim on the lore of "Fight On" occurred during World War II. From June 3, 1942 to August 15, 1943, the United States Army and Navy, along with their Canadian allies, were engaged in a battle against Japanese forces for control of the Aleutian Islands. It was claimed that while American forces invaded the beaches, one of the transport ships off shore blared "Fight On." Once the soldiers heard it, they let out a thunderous bellow and charged ahead to eventual victory in the campaign.[1]

"FIGHT ON"

Fight on for ol' SC
Our men Fight On to victory.
Our Alma Mater dear,
looks up to you
Fight On and win
For ol' SC
Fight On to victory
Fight On!

## *Conquest*

Alfred Newman is one of the most prestigious composers to work in Hollywood. Over a career of forty years, Newman composed music for over 200 motion pictures, and received nine Academy Awards for his magnificent work, which is the most for a composer in the history of Hollywood's most coveted statuette.[1] He is also known as the genius behind USC's "Conquest." The song was first heard in Newman's score for the 1947 film *Captain from Castile.* In 1954 it was played at a USC basketball game against Oregon State, and the rest is history. It can be heard during football games after the Trojans score and after a win.[2]

## *Song Girls*

The Trojans have had many moments of being the top-ranked football team in the country. However, this honor did not just apply to the action on the field, but on the sideline as well. The USC Song Girls earned the top ranking at being the best at what they do by *Sports Illustrated* magazine. In addition to that recognition, ESPN.com gave the group, along with "the Spirit of Troy Marching Band," the top award as the best in the country.

Glitz and glamour has long come to symbolize Hollywood and its surrounding area since the first motion picture cameras rolled in the Southland back in the early 1900's. Those same two words, glitz and glamour, have been linked to many things in the City of Angels. In the case of USC, the Song Girls have personified glitz and glamour inside the LA Coliseum and other college football stadiums since their birth in 1967.

The timing could not have been more perfect for this dance squad of Southern California beauties to begin, seeing that the Trojans won the national championship in the Song Girls first year of existence. Back in 1967, the troupe consisted of seven young beautiful women, and over the course of time, the names and faces might have changed, but not the popularity. The group eventually expanded to twelve women dressed in white uniforms with cardinal and gold trim.

The Song Girls work hard to perfect their routines, practicing five days a week while performing for the sports teams and other events. They perform three dozen new dance routines during the year, and can be seen at football, basketball, volleyball games, pep rallies, and different types of university functions. They work with the "Spirit of Troy Marching Band," and during the football season, the Song Girls have to learn new choreography for the many halftime shows the band puts on. They have also entertained on a worldwide scale, traveling to many countries around the globe.

Becoming one of these hard-working goodwill ambassadors donned in the Cardinal and Gold, is just as hard as the actual job itself. To even be considered for the elite group, a candidate has to possess a solid background in dance training in both jazz and ballet. A shining personality and appeal is also a must. The Song Girls are a true testament to the Beach Boys singing the praise of California girls, and are an integral, memorable, and mesmerizing part of the Trojan tradition.[1]

## *Yell Leaders*

Much like on the field of play, the offense and defense help the other unit out, and when successful, victory is almost always assured. Unfortunately, a football team cannot win every game. However, in the case of USC's Yell Leaders assisting the Song Girls and the Spirit of Troy Marching Band, the outcome of their performances is always top notch.

With the Song Girls duties as primarily a dance squad, the Yell Leaders' duties are all about cheerleading. Back in 1919, a first-year student at USC named Lindley Bothwell started the tradition of the Yell Leaders. With the help of some friends, Bothwell looked to get the crowd going with rousing cheers for the Trojan football team. They created their own cheers, with the most popular being the "Floating T," which entailed those in the stands to take a cardinal or gold colored balloon attached to their seat and let it go airborne when told to. Bothwell also came up with the idea to use colored cards in place of balloons. The first time this occurred was on October 21, 1922 during the halftime show against Nevada. The cards spelled out TROJANS, and the crowd roared with enthusiasm at the site of the word. The card routine was eventually incorporated at other universities, but Bothwell was the torchbearer to the great tradition. Not only was USC the first school to do the card routine, but they are also in the Guinness Book of World Records for getting 8,000 students to participate in it at USC's 1978 homecoming game.[1]

The Yell Leaders have worn white, long sleeve sweaters since their beginning. They perform amazing physical stunts, which require them to stay in condition throughout the year. It is a major commitment to be a part of this cheerleading squad, and the devotion for the task is only second to the squad's academic performance. When not drumming up team spirit during football season, the Yell Leaders can be found doing the same job at basketball and volleyball games.[2]

## *Spirit Leaders*

In addition to the Song Girls and Yell Leaders, the Spirit Leaders are also a member of the USC sideline entertainment. The Spirit Leaders are one of the newest traditions at USC, but their presence is well received by the thousands of Trojan faithful in the stands. The Spirit Leaders are a co-ed group whose duty it is to lead the crowd in rousing chants that they hope will shake the foundation of the LA Coliseum or any other venue they are in. They are busy all year long. When not cheering for the Trojan football team, the squad is a vital part of the spirit at basketball, volleyball, water polo, soccer, and baseball games. Their involvement in charities and rallies on campus is also a part of who the Spirit Leaders are.[1]

## *Los Angeles Memorial Coliseum*

One of America's grandest structures dedicated to athletic competition is located at 3911 South Figueroa Street in Los Angeles. Its official name is the Los Angeles Memorial Coliseum, and since 1923, the massive venue has been the site for championships in professional sports, and two Summer Olympic Games.

With the architectural tandem of John and Donald Parkinson serving as designers, ground was broken for the Coliseum on December 21, 1921. Within 17 months, the behemoth structure was completed on May 1, 1923, at a cost of $954,873. The concept behind the design of this magnificent athletic venue was for it to serve as a memorial to World War I veterans. In 1968, it was re-dedicated to honor veterans of all wars. When it first opened its turnstiles to the masses, the seating capacity was 76,000. The number of seats was later expanded to 101,574 in time for Los Angeles to host the 1932 Summer Olympics. This was also when the Olympic torch was constructed above one of the main entrances. The Olympic rings are also there right below the torch. This combination of torch and rings serves as the most common photograph when looking at imagers of the Coliseum. In addition to those reminders of the Olympics are two life-sized male and female bronze statues that were constructed for the 1984 Summer Olympics, also hosted by the city of Los Angeles.

Despite all the great sporting events held in the Coliseum, the USC Trojans own the bragging rights as the first to use the facility. On October 6, 1923, the Coliseum hosted the USC freshman football team in a 30–0 win over Santa Ana High School. It was followed by the first-ever varsity game held at the Coliseum, which saw the Trojans christen the venue in fine fashion, beating Pomona College, 23–7. The University of California Los Angeles (UCLA), also called the Coliseum home from 1928 through the 1981 football season.

Through the decades since then, the Coliseum became the only American stadium to play host to Olympic Games, pre–Super Bowl NFL Championship Games, a World Series (1959), two Super Bowls (1967, 1973), NFC and AFC title games, and various Pro Bowls. Legendary performers from all athletic endeavors have left their mark on the field, with many more incredible moments to come for as long as the structure remains a part of the Los Angeles landscape.[1]

Before the Coliseum became their home, the USC Trojans played football at the following locations:

**USC Campus**—Before 1893, the football team played on a field next to Jefferson. In 1893, the students petitioned the university to built a new athletic field. In time, their wish became reality, as the university gave them a field located on the northwest section of the USC campus. This field seemed to be suitable for practice sessions, but was not up to standard for big games. Looking to grow as a football program, the university rented out Athletic Park, Fiesta Park, Washington Park, and Prager Park, for major games until 1904.[2]

**Bovard Field**—During the summer of 1904, the football field got a facelift. Bleachers were added, and at the start of the season, it was called "College Campus," but as the season went on, the name was changed to Bovard Field. At its peak toward the end of the 1910s, Bovard expanded its seating capacity to 12,000 after bleachers were brought over from Fiesta Park. However, with the growing popularity for the Trojan football team as the 1920s emerged, Bovard Field was just not big enough to accommodate the many who wanted to see the team. It was then that the Los Angeles Memorial Coliseum was built, and USC moved there in 1923. In all, the Trojans played 73 football games on the campus between 1888 and 1923.[3] A plaque dedicated to Bovard Field is located on the USC campus between Annenberg School of Communication and Bing Theatre, east of Heritage Hall.

**Athletic Park**—Located on the northeast corner of Seventh and Alameda, it opened on Thanksgiving Day in 1891. The first major college football program to use the field was Stanford on December 29, 1894. The Trojans used the field as their home for four games between 1895 and 1898.[4]

**Fiesta Park**—Located on the northwest corner of Grand and Pico, this site served as USC's home field for 22 games from 1897 to 1916.[5]

**Washington Park**—Located at the corner of Washington and Grand, the Trojans played two games there in 1900. It served better as a baseball stadium, and in 1911, a bigger Washington Park was built at Washington and Hill. It was in that new facility that the Trojans played three games from 1915 to 1917.[6]

**Tournament Park**—located on the southeast corner of California and Wilson in Pasadena, the Trojans played four games there between 1918 and 1921.[7]

**Sportsman's Park**—Located at North Los Robles and Colorado, this site served for many firsts in USC football history. In 1889, this marked USC's first game played in Pasadena, their first Thanksgiving Day game, and the first time the varsity team ventured outside of the Los Angeles area.[8]

**Prager Park**—Located on Washington Avenue across from Chutes Park, the Trojans used it for six games in 1903.[9]

## *George Tirebiter*

A vagabond mongrel wandering in front of an ice cream parlor appears to have all the ingredients needed for the making of a feel-good song or motion picture. In the case of Trojan lore, however, this was the beginning of the legend that came to be known as George Tirebiter.

Spotted roaming near Curry's Ice Cream Parlor by some USC students in the 1940s, this little mutt soon won the hearts of Trojan faithful. It was claimed that a student saw a likeness in the dog to a Navy V-12 student named George Kuhns, thus giving birth to the dog's first name. His surname was given after witnessing his true passion in life. George enjoyed chasing cars near the USC campus and biting the tires. In no time flat, he was christened George Tirebiter.

He had a spirited personality that quickly won over the campus, and he was the school's unofficial mascot for a time during the 1940s. In true Hollywood fashion, George was transported to games in a limousine, and then escorted the USC Marching Band onto the field. His place as part of USC history was cemented when he bit UCLA's mascot, Joe Bruin, on the nose, and ran after another rival mascot, Oski the Golden Bear of Cal-Berkeley fame, at the LA Coliseum.

George's fame ended via his passion. One day in 1950, while doing what he loved, he was struck by a car and killed while attempting to live up to his moniker. He was given a grand sendoff that included a public funeral at USC, and in 2006, a statue commemorating his existence was dedicated on the campus. The statue is a life-size likeness of George with a shredded piece of tire. After the original George, USC had several other Georges serve as mascots until 1957.[1]

## *Traveler*

Imagine one of the most storied structures dedicated to athletic competition, filled with a throng donned in Cardinal and Gold with a usually sun-drenched afternoon serving as the backdrop. College game day in the City of Angels personified. Then suddenly a majestic mascot comes onto the field through a tunnel and onto the field amidst a frenzy permeating from the stands. Even though all in attendance are there to witness the mighty men of Troy wage battle for 100 yards of real estate, prior to the game, it is Traveler's time to shine in the spotlight.

Since the September 22, 1961 home opener against Georgia Tech, Traveler has served as the mascot for the USC Trojans. The tradition of the magnificent white horse with a Trojan warrior mounted on it has become one of college football's most famous mascots. The saga of Traveler was born when Bob Jani, USC's director of events, saw Richard Saukko riding a white horse in the 1961 Rose Parade. The horse's name was Traveler, and Jani had the idea of bringing Saukko and his horse into the USC fold during football games.

Initially, Saukko was mounted on Traveler wearing the outfit used by actor Charlton Heston in his Academy Award-winning performance in 1959's *Ben Hur*. In 1962, Saukko designed and made his own leather rendition of an outfit befitting a Trojan warrior, and used the statue of Tommy Trojan as his inspiration. Saukko's design is still used by those aboard Traveler. Saukko rode Traveler until 1988, when health problems prohibited him from the activity. Saukko died in 1992, but the proud tradition of riding the majestic mascot was carried on by a handful of riders since 1988.

There have been seven Travelers as of the 2012 season, and despite being of different breeds, the horses used were always white. The breeds used were Arabian/Tennessee Walker, purebred Tennessee Walker, purebred Arabian, and Andalusian. In addition to being at USC home games, and some road games as well, Traveler makes public appearances at charity events, parades, has been in motion pictures, on stage, in commercials, *Vogue Magazine*, and accompanied numerous musical and Hollywood figures at public events.

Even though Traveler is a major factor in the Trojan tradition, it was not the first time a horse was used as a mascot for the university. In 1927, a person by the name of Louis Shields rode a white horse at Trojan football games for a four-year period. In 1948, a palomino was ridden by a person dressed as a Trojan and carrying the team colors of cardinal and gold. In 1954 prior to the USC—Pittsburgh game, a member of the spirit group, the Trojans Knights, rode a white and gray horse, but was not a very accomplished rider. The next game a USC alumnus, who knew more about riding, came out with his white horse named Rockazar, and continued to perform until 1959.[1]

## *Tommy Trojan*

Artist Roger Noble Burnham created a legacy of work that still captivates the eyes of all who observe his statues. The Hingham, Massachusetts native was in his early 50s, and already well established in his chosen profession, when he was commissioned to sculpt a life size bronze statue of a Trojan for the University of Southern California.[1]

Burnham was born on August 10, 1876, and graduated from Harvard University in 1899. After living in Rome, Italy, and Hawaii, he set permanent roots down in the City of Angels in 1925. Throughout Los Angeles, Burnham's work is highly prevalent. His "Aspiration," was dedicated to the memory of silent screen legend Rudolph Valentino in DeLongpre Park, the MacArthur Monument, and the United Spanish War Veterans statue, are some of the creations that serve as Burnham's legacy.

Despite his lasting stamp on the Southland's culture, his best work resides in the center of the USC campus, and goes by the name of Tommy Trojan. Burnham was commissioned in the spring of 1929 to create the statue after Harry Lee Martin and Dr. James McCoy came up with the concept. Upon getting the job to bring the concept to life, Burnham produced many paintings of football players from the USC roster. After sorting through the images, he decided that the statue would be a combination of the physical characteristics of Russ Saunders, Erny Pinckert, Henry Becker, Larry Stevens, and John Ward.[2]

On June 6, 1930, at 2:45 p.m. Dr. McCoy's daughter Janet, the vice president of the student body, unveiled the statue in celebration of the university's 50th anniversary.[3] It took $10,000 to bring the statue to completion, and a $1 surcharge was tacked onto the tickets for football games to assist in helping with the cost. The original name was to be The Spirit of Troy, but that name already applied to USC's marching band, and for that reason, at the statue's base in inscribed "THE TROJAN," along with the university's seal, and the Latin motto of *"Palmam qui meruit ferat,"* which translates into "let him who deserves it bear away the palm." Listed below the university seal are inscribed the qualities of the ultimate Trojan warrior, "Faithful, Scholarly, Skillful, Courageous, and Ambitious."[4]

The life-size bronze symbol of USC appears to stand ready for battle, and has the distinction of showing every muscle of the body flexed at the same time.[5] Through the changing times that occurred since its unveiling, Tommy Trojan still remains a proud focal point of the campus grounds, and is a common meeting place for students and visitors to USC. It also serves as a popular photo opportunity to countless visitors.

In addition to being a symbol of pride, Tommy Trojan has become a target for pranks through the years from cross-town rival UCLA. The first known incident of an attack on the statue came in October 1941, when it was painted UCLA colors of blue and gold. To stop having the statue donned in Bruins colors, it is protected with a covering. To avoid other attacks on it, an all-night watch group consisting of members from the Trojan Knights, guard against UCLA invasions during the week leading up to the annual clash with the Bruins. The sword in his hand has also become a target for thievery. Instead of replacing it with a costly new brass sword, he now holds a wooden one.[6] Its creator, Roger Noble Burnham, lived a long life, dying at age 85 on March 15, 1962.[7]

Despite all the trivia that surrounds the tradition of this testament to the fighting spirit of the Trojans, one unsolved mystery cannot be explained, and that is how the statue got the name of Tommy.[8]

## *Shillelagh*

Despite the intense rivalry between USC and Notre Dame, which makes this intersectional clash one of college football's greatest matchups, respect for each other, and the proud traditions of both universities is also present. As a symbol of those qualities, the Notre Dame Alumni Club of Los Angeles conceived the idea of having an award given to the annual winner of the game based on the suggestion by an individual named Vern Rickard.

The concept became reality after John Groen designed what became the symbol of victory in "the Glamour Game." A shillelagh is a Gaelic war club made of oak or blackthorn saplings, and it was this weapon that served as the inspiration, and then the treasured prize of this storied rivalry. When completed in 1952, Groen's work was a foot-long shillelagh consisting of Trojan heads made of rubies, and shamrocks made of emeralds. The Trojan heads are placed next to USC victories along with the year and score, and the emerald shamrocks serve the same purpose in regards to a Notre Dame win. Each year since the series began in 1926 is represented. The Shillelagh resides for one year with the winner. Prior to regular season games going into overtime, if a tie occurred, the Trojan head and shamrock are combined into one piece. Engraved on the end of the club are the words, "From the Emerald Isle."

When Groen's masterpiece was completed in 1952, it was brought from Ireland to the United States by business mogul Howard Hughes' pilot. The original trophy was filled up after the 1989 contest, and is on permanent display at Notre Dame. The task of getting a new shillelagh was assigned to Jim Gillis, who was affiliated with both universities. He played baseball for both USC and Notre Dame, and once held the presidency of the Notre Dame Club of Los Angeles. With such a solid background at both institutions, the job of getting a new shillelagh fell into very capable hands. The replacement shillelagh was crafted by hand in County Leitrim, Ireland, is a bit longer than its predecessor, and has game results beginning in 1990 represented on it.[1]

## *Victory Bell*

In the last quarter of the 19th century, the Southern Pacific Railroad was a dominant force in the western region of the United States. The locomotive that powered its freight across miles of track had a bell sitting on top, clanging along the route.

One such 295-pound bell came to represent the spoils that go to the victor of the annual USC-UCLA football game. The story that accompanies how the bell became one of college football's most treasured gems is an interesting one, with its origins going back to 1939. The bell started off as a gift presented to UCLA by the university's alumni association. For two seasons, the bell resided in Westwood, serving strictly as a part of UCLA's football program. The Bruin cheerleaders would ring the bell after the team scored, and this practice was a ritual until UCLA's opening game of the 1941 season.[1]

In an attempt to pull off a prank against their cross town rivals, six members from USC's Sigma Phi Epsilon fraternity managed to blend in with UCLA rooters during the Bruins September 26, 1941 game against Washington State. Spirits were high after head coach Edwin Horrell's charges won by a slim 7–6 margin. Joyous UCLA revelers were loading the bell onto a truck that was ready to take it back to the Westwood campus. However, unbeknownst to the UCLA students was the fact that those six fraternity members from USC were among the 20 or so who assisted in placing the bell on its transport. One of the USC students slipped over and snatched the truck's keys, and the infiltrators then suggested that the UCLA delegation go get help while some of the others call the Automobile Club. The advice seemed like a good idea, but it was strictly used as a ruse to clear the path for the USC students to make a clean getaway.[2]

The fraternity members drove off with their rivals' coveted bell, whose whereabouts were unknown, except to those involved, for over a year. The bell's hiding spots have ranged from the basement of the fraternity house to the Hollywood Hills, among other places, including a haystack. The Bruin supporters gave a yeoman's effort to find their cherished piece of tradition, but each time they came up empty in their quest.

Things reached a fever pitch when a photograph of the stolen bell made the pages of a USC college magazine. This sparked a great deal of rage in the student body from Westwood's institution of higher learning, and they set out to get even. Tommy Trojan served as a beacon to UCLA students, and that storied piece of USC tradition was painted in UCLA's blue and gold colors, and its sword was stolen. Numerous volleys were sent by the warring parties, including dumping paint in the UCLA offices, and burning USC on the lawns of residences known to have UCLA students dwelling inside. On many occasion, Los Angeles' finest had to be called to restore order in the midst of this college high jinx.[3]

With things reaching out-of-controlled proportions, the president of USC, Dr. Rufus B. von KleinSmid, stepped to the forefront of this issue, proposing to cancel the annual clash between the rivals if these incidents did not stop. This threat called for the action of cooler heads to prevail, and thus, on November 12, 1942, the student body presidents from both universities met on the USC campus with the Victory Bell perched in front of Tommy Trojan. On this date, USC's student body president Bill McKay signed an agreement with his peer from UCLA, Bill Farrer, that the Victory Bell would become the property of the winner of the annual USC-UCLA football game for one full year. In the case of a tie, the bell would go to the school that won the previous meeting between the teams. The first time the Victory Bell was officially used in this great rivalry was on December 12, 1942, when the Bruins defeated the Trojans for the first time in their history.[4]

Despite it being one of college football's most cherished prizes, the Victory Bell resides in recluse fashion for most of the time. It is only on display for the first three quarters of the annual game, and then it makes its way to the winning university. Following that brief appearance, it is then stored in a warehouse or vault.[5]

*Six*

# Awards and Honors

## All-Americans

| Year | Name, Position |
|---|---|
| 1925 | Brice Taylor, G |
| 1926 | Mort Kaer, B |
| 1927 | Morley Drury, B |
| 1927 | Jesse Hibbs, T |
| 1928 | Jesse Hibbs, T |
| 1928 | Don Williams, B |
| 1929 | Nate Barragar, G-C |
| 1929 | Francis Tappaan, E |
| 1930 | Garrett Arbelbide, E |
| 1930 | Orv Mohler, B |
| 1930 | Erny Pinckert, B |
| 1931 | Johnny Baker, G |
| 1931 | Erny Pinckert, B |
| 1931 | Gus Shaver, B |
| 1931 | Stan Williamson, C |
| 1932 | Tay Brown, T |
| 1932 | Aaron Rosenberg, G |
| 1932 | Ernie Smith, T |
| 1933 | Aaron Rosenberg, G |
| 1933 | Larry Stevens, G |
| 1933 | Cotton Warburton, B |
| 1938 | Harry Smith, G |
| 1939 | Grenny Landsdell, B |
| 1939 | Harry Smith, G |
| 1943 | Ralph Heywood, E |
| 1944 | John Ferraro, T |
| 1947 | Paul Cleary, E |
| 1947 | John Ferraro, T |
| 1951 | Pat Cannamela, LB |
| 1951 | Frank Gifford, B |
| 1952 | Jim Sears, DB |
| 1952 | Elmer Wilhoite, G |
| 1955 | Jon Arnett, B |
| 1959 | Ron Mix, T |
| 1959 | Marlin McKeever, E |
| 1959 | Mike McKeever, G |
| 1960 | Marlin McKeever, E |
| 1962 | Hal Bedsole, E |
| 1962 | Damon Bame, LB |
| 1963 | Damon Bame, LB |
| 1964 | Bill Fisk, OG |
| 1964 | Mike Garrett, TB |
| 1965 | Mike Garrett, TB |
| 1966 | Nate Shaw, DB |
| 1966 | Ron Yary, OT |
| 1967 | O.J. Simpson, TB |
| 1967 | Ron Yary, OT |
| 1967 | Adrian Young, LB |
| 1967 | Tim Rossovich, DE |
| 1968 | O.J. Simpson, TB |
| 1968 | Mike Battle, DB |
| 1969 | Jimmy Gunn, DE |
| 1969 | Al Cowlings, DT |
| 1969 | Sid Smith, OT |
| 1969 | Clarence Davis, TB |
| 1970 | Charles Weaver, DE |
| 1970 | Marv Montgomery, OT |
| 1971 | John Vella, OT |
| 1971 | Willie Hall, LB |
| 1972 | Charles Young, TE |
| 1972 | Richard Wood, LB |
| 1972 | Sam Cunningham, FB |
| 1972 | Pete Adams, OT |
| 1972 | John Grant, DT |
| 1973 | Lynn Swann, FL |
| 1973 | Richard Wood, LB |
| 1973 | Booker Brown, OT |
| 1973 | Artimus Parker, DB |
| 1973 | Steve Riley, OT |
| 1974 | Anthony Davis, TB |
| 1974 | Richard Wood, LB |
| 1974 | Charles Phillips, DB |
| 1974 | Bill Bain, OG |
| 1974 | Jim Obradovich, TE |
| 1975 | Ricky Bell, TB |
| 1975 | Marvin Powell, OT |
| 1976 | Ricky Bell, TB |
| 1976 | Dennis Thurman, DB |
| 1976 | Gary Jeter, DT |
| 1976 | Marvin Powell, OT |
| 1977 | Dennis Thurman, DG |
| 1977 | Clay Matthews, LB |
| 1978 | Pat Howell, OG |
| 1978 | Charles White, TB |
| 1979 | Charles White, TB |
| 1979 | Brad Budde, OG |
| 1979 | Dennis Johnson, LB |
| 1979 | Paul McDonald, QB |
| 1980 | Ronnie Lott, DG |
| 1980 | Keith Van Horne, OT |
| 1980 | Roy Foster, OG |
| 1981 | Marcus Allen, TB |
| 1981 | Roy Foster, OG |
| 1981 | Chip Banks, LB |
| 1982 | Don Mosebar, OT |
| 1982 | Bruce Matthews, OG |
| 1982 | George Achica, NG |
| 1983 | Tony Slaton, C |
| 1984 | Jack Del Rio, LB |
| 1984 | Duane Bickett, LB |
| 1985 | Jeff Bregel, OG |
| 1985 | Tim McDonald, DB |
| 1986 | Jeff Bregel, OG |
| 1986 | Tim McDonald, DB |
| 1987 | Dave Cadigan, OT |
| 1988 | Erik Affholter, SE |
| 1988 | Mark Carrier, DG |
| 1988 | Rodney Peete, QB |
| 1988 | Tim Ryan, DT |
| 1988 | Cleveland Colter, DB |
| 1989 | Mark Carrier, DB |
| 1989 | Tim Ryan, DT |
| 1989 | Junior Seau, OLB |
| 1989 | Mark Tucker, OG |
| 1990 | Scott Ross, ILB |
| 1992 | Curtis Conway, FL-RS |
| 1992 | Tony Boselli, OT |
| 1993 | Johnnie Morton, WR |
| 1994 | Tony Boselli, OT |
| 1995 | Keyshawn Johnson, WR |
| 1998 | Chris Claiborne, LB |
| 2001 | Troy Polamalu, DB |
| 2002 | Carson Palmer, QB |
| 2002 | Troy Polamalu, DB |
| 2003 | Mike Williams, WR |
| 2003 | Jacob Rogers, OT |
| 2003 | Kenechi Udeze, DE |
| 2003 | Tom Malone, P |
| 2003 | Matt Leinart, QB |
| 2004 | Reggie Bush, TB |
| 2004 | Matt Leinart, QB |
| 2004 | Shaun Cody, DT |
| 2004 | Matt Grootegoed, LB |
| 2004 | Mike Patterson, DT |
| 2004 | Lofa Tatupu, LB |
| 2005 | Reggie Bush, TB |
| 2005 | Dwayne Jarrett, WR |
| 2005 | Taitusi Lutui, OG |
| 2005 | Matt Leinart, QB |
| 2005 | Darnell Bing, S |
| 2005 | Sam Baker, OT |
| 2006 | Dwayne Jarrett, WR |
| 2006 | Sam Baker, OT |
| 2006 | Ryan Kalil, C |
| 2006 | Sedrick Ellis, DT |
| 2006 | Steve Smith, WR |
| 2007 | Sedrick Ellis, DT |
| 2007 | Sam Baker, OT |
| 2007 | Fred Davis, TE |
| 2007 | Keith Rivers, LB |
| 2007 | Taylor Mays, S |
| 2008 | Rey Maualuga, LB |
| 2008 | Taylor Mays, S |
| 2008 | Brian Cushing, LB |
| 2009 | Taylor Mays, S |
| 2009 | Charles Brown, OT |
| 2011 | Robert Woods, WR |
| 2011 | Matt Kalil, OT |
| 2011 | T.J. McDonald, S |
| 2012 | Marqise Lee, WR |

## All-Conference First Team Selections

| Year | Name, Position |
|---|---|
| 1928 | Nate Barragar, C |
| 1928 | Lloyd Thomas, B |
| 1929 | Francis Tappaan, E |
| 1929 | Nate Barragar, G |
| 1929 | Marsh Duffield, B |
| 1930 | Garrett Arbelbide, E |
| 1930 | Johnny Baker, G |
| 1930 | Marsh Duffield, B |
| 1930 | Erny Pinckert, B |
| 1931 | Ray Sparling, E |
| 1931 | Johnny Baker, G |
| 1931 | Stan Williamson, C |
| 1931 | Gus Shaver, B |
| 1931 | Erny Pinckert, B |
| 1931 | Ernie Smith, T |
| 1932 | Ernie Smith, T |
| 1932 | Tay Brown, T |
| 1932 | Aaron Rosenberg, G |
| 1932 | Homer Griffith, B |
| 1932 | Orv Mohler, Q |
| 1933 | Aaron Rosenberg, G |
| 1933 | Cotton Warburton, B |
| 1934 | No USC Selections |
| 1935 | No USC Selections |
| 1936 | Gene Hibbs, E |
| 1937 | Amby Schindler, B |
| 1938 | Not Available |
| 1939 | Phil Gaspar, T |
| 1939 | Harry Smith, G |
| 1939 | Grenny Lansdell, B |
| 1939 | Bob Hoffman, B |
| 1939 | Howard Stoecker, T |
| 1940 | Al Krueger, E |
| 1941 | Bob Robertson, B |
| 1942 | Mickey McCardle, B |
| 1943 | Ralph Heywood, E |
| 1943 | Bill Gray, C |
| 1943 | Mickey McCardle, B |

| Year | Name, Position |
|---|---|
| 1944 | Jim Callahan, E |
| 1944 | Don Hardy, E |
| 1944 | John Ferraro, T |
| 1944 | Jim Hardy, B |
| 1944 | Gordon Gray, B |
| 1945 | Not Available |
| 1946 | John Ferraro, T |
| 1947 | Paul Cleary, E |
| 1947 | John Ferraro, T |
| 1947 | Bob Hendren, T |
| 1947 | Don Doll, B |
| 1948 | Don Doll, B |
| 1949 | Bill Martin, B |
| 1950 | Volney Peters, T |
| 1951 | Frank Gifford, B |
| 1951 | Pat Cannamela, G |
| 1951 | Johnny Williams, B |
| 1952 | Elmer Wilhoite, G |
| 1952 | Jim Sears, B |
| 1952 | Lou Welsh, C |
| 1952 | Bob Hooks, E |
| 1952 | Bob Van Doren, T |
| 1952 | George Timberlake, LB |
| 1952 | Jim Psaltis, HB |
| 1952 | Lindon Crow, B |
| 1953 | George Timberlake, LB |
| 1953 | Aramis Dandoy, B |
| 1953 | Ed Fouch, T |
| 1954 | Ed Fouch, T |
| 1954 | Lindon Crow, B |
| 1955 | Leon Clarke, E |
| 1955 | Orlando Ferrante, G |
| 1955 | Jon Arnett, B |
| 1956 | Jon Arnett, B |
| 1956 | C.R. Roberts, B |
| 1957 | No USC Selections |
| 1958 | Marlin McKeever, E |
| 1958 | Frank Fiorentino, G |
| 1959 | Marlin McKeever, E |
| 1959 | Ron Mix, T |
| 1959 | Mike McKeever, G |
| 1959 | Jerry Traynham, B |
| 1960 | Marlin McKeever, E |
| 1961 | Hal Bedsole, E |
| 1961 | Frank Buncom, T |
| 1961 | Britt Williams, G |
| 1961 | Pete Beathard, QB |
| 1961 | Ben Wilson, FB |
| 1962 | Hal Bedsole, E |
| 1962 | Gary Kirner, T |
| 1962 | Damon Bame, G |
| 1962 | Pete Beathard, QB |
| 1962 | Willie Brown, HB |
| 1963 | Gary Kirner, T |
| 1963 | Damon Bame, G |
| 1963 | Willie Brown, HB |
| 1963 | Mike Garrett, HB |
| 1964 | Bob Svihus, OT |
| 1964 | Bill Fisk, OG |
| 1964 | Mike Garrett, HB |
| 1964 | Jeff Smith, DE |
| 1964 | Gary Hill, DB |
| 1965 | Chuck Arrobio, OT |
| 1965 | Frank Lopez, OG |
| 1965 | Paul Johnson, C |
| 1965 | Mike Garrett, HB |
| 1965 | Jim Walker, DE |
| 1965 | Ron Yary, DT |
| 1965 | Jeff Smith, LB |

| Year | Name, Position |
|---|---|
| 1965 | Nate Shaw, DB |
| 1966 | Ron Drake, E |
| 1966 | Ron Yary, OT |
| 1966 | Jim Homan, OG |
| 1966 | Rod Sherman, HB |
| 1966 | Ray May, DE |
| 1966 | Larry Petrill, NG |
| 1966 | Nate Shaw, DB |
| 1967 | Earl McCullouch, E |
| 1967 | Ron Yary, OT |
| 1967 | O.J. Simpson, RB |
| 1967 | Tim Rossovich, DE |
| 1967 | Adrian Young, LB |
| 1967 | Mike Battle, DB |
| 1968 | Bob Klein, E |
| 1968 | Sid Smith, OT |
| 1968 | Fred Khasigian, OG |
| 1968 | Steve Sogge, QB |
| 1968 | O.J. Simpson, RB |
| 1968 | Jim Gunn, DE |
| 1969 | Sid Smith, OT |
| 1969 | Fred Khasigian, OG |
| 1969 | Clarence Davis, RB |
| 1969 | Jim Gunn, DE |
| 1969 | Al Cowlings, DL |
| 1969 | Tyrone Hudson, DB |
| 1970 | Clarence Davis, RB |
| 1970 | Charles Weaver, DE |
| 1971 | John Vella, OT |
| 1971 | John Grant, DE |
| 1971 | Willie Hall, LB |
| 1972 | Charles Young, E |
| 1972 | Pete Adams, OT |
| 1972 | Dave Brown, C |
| 1972 | John Grant, C |
| 1972 | James Sims, DL |
| 1972 | Richard Wood, LB |
| 1973 | Jim Obradovich, E |
| 1973 | Booker Brown, OT |
| 1973 | Anthony Davis, RB |
| 1973 | Lynn Swann, WR |
| 1973 | Monte Doris, DL |
| 1973 | Richard Wood, LB |
| 1973 | James Sims, LB |
| 1973 | Artimus Parker, DB |
| 1974 | Jim Obradovich, E |
| 1974 | Marvin Powell, OT |
| 1974 | Bill Bain, OG |
| 1974 | Anthony Davis, RB |
| 1974 | Chris Limahelu, PK |
| 1974 | Gary Jeter, DL |
| 1974 | Art Riley, DL |
| 1974 | Richard Wood, LB |
| 1974 | Ed Powell, LB |
| 1974 | Charles Phillips, DB |
| 1974 | Danny Reece, DB |
| 1974 | Marvin Cobb, DB |
| 1975 | Marvin Powell, OT |
| 1975 | Ricky Bell, RB |
| 1975 | Gary Jeter, DL |
| 1975 | Kevin Bruce, LB |
| 1975 | Danny Reece, DB |
| 1976 | Marvin Powell, OT |
| 1976 | Donnie Hickman, OG |
| 1976 | Ricky Bell, RB |
| 1976 | Gary Jeter, DL |
| 1976 | David Lewis, OLB |
| 1976 | Rod Martin, OLB |
| 1976 | Clay Matthews, ILB |

| Year | Name, Position |
|---|---|
| 1976 | Dennis Thurman, DB |
| 1977 | Pat Howell, OG |
| 1977 | Brad Budde, OG |
| 1977 | Charles White, RB |
| 1977 | Walt Underwood, DL |
| 1977 | Clay Matthews, LB |
| 1977 | Dennis Thurman, DB |
| 1978 | Charles White, RB |
| 1978 | Kevin Williams, WR |
| 1978 | Pat Howell, OG |
| 1978 | Brad Budde, OG |
| 1978 | Anthony Munoz, OT |
| 1978 | Rich Dimler, DL |
| 1978 | Dennis Johnson, LB |
| 1978 | Marty King, P |
| 1979 | Paul McDonald, QB |
| 1979 | Charles White, RB |
| 1979 | Hoby Brenner, TE |
| 1979 | Roy Foster, OL |
| 1979 | Keith Van Horne, OL |
| 1979 | Brad Budde, OL |
| 1979 | Dennis Johnson, LB |
| 1979 | Riki Gray, LB |
| 1979 | Ronnie Lott, DB |
| 1979 | Dennis Smith, DB |
| 1980 | Marcus Allen, RB |
| 1980 | Roy Foster, OG |
| 1980 | Keith Van Horne, OT |
| 1980 | Dennis Edwards, DL |
| 1980 | George Achica, DL |
| 1980 | Chip Banks, LB |
| 1980 | Ronnie Lott, DB |
| 1980 | Dennis Smith, DB |
| 1981 | Marcus Allen, RB |
| 1981 | Tony Slaton, OL |
| 1981 | Bruce Matthews, OL |
| 1981 | George Achica, DL |
| 1981 | Dennis Edwards, DL |
| 1981 | Chip Banks, DL |
| 1982 | Tony Slaton, OL |
| 1982 | Bruce Matthews, OL |
| 1982 | Don Mosebar, OL |
| 1982 | George Achica, DL |
| 1982 | Jack Del Rio, LB |
| 1982 | Joey Browner, DB |
| 1983 | Tony Slaton, OL |
| 1983 | Jack Del Rio, LB |
| 1984 | Fred Crutcher, RB |
| 1984 | Ken Ruettgers, OL |
| 1984 | Tony Colorito, DL |
| 1984 | Duane Bickett, LB |
| 1984 | Tommy Haynes, DB |
| 1985 | Jeff Bregel, OL |
| 1985 | James FitzPatrick, OL |
| 1985 | Tim McDonald, DB |
| 1986 | Jeff Bregel, OL |
| 1986 | Marcus Cotton, LB |
| 1986 | Tim McDonald, DB |
| 1987 | Steven Webster, RB |
| 1987 | Dave Cadigan, OL |
| 1987 | Paul Green, TE |
| 1988 | Rodney Peete, QB |
| 1988 | Leroy Holt, RB |
| 1988 | Erik Affholter, WR |
| 1988 | Scott Galbraith, TE |
| 1988 | Mark Tucker, OL |
| 1988 | Tim Ryan, DL |
| 1988 | Dan Owens, DL |
| 1988 | Scott Ross, ILB |

| Year | Name, Position |
|---|---|
| 1988 | Mark Carrier, S |
| 1988 | Cleveland Colter, S |
| 1989 | Todd Marinovich, QB |
| 1989 | Ricky Ervins, RB |
| 1989 | Leroy Holt, RB |
| 1989 | John Jackson, WR |
| 1989 | Scott Galbraith, TE |
| 1989 | Brad Leggett, OL |
| 1989 | Brent Parkinson, OL |
| 1989 | Tim Ryan, DL |
| 1989 | Dan Owens, DL |
| 1989 | Junior Seau, OLB |
| 1989 | Scott Ross, ILB |
| 1989 | Mark Carrier, S |
| 1990 | Gary Wellman, FL |
| 1990 | Mark Tucker, OL |
| 1990 | Pat Harlow, OL |
| 1990 | Don Gibson, DL |
| 1990 | Scott Ross, ILB |
| 1991 | Tony Boselli, OL |
| 1991 | Curtis Conway, RET SP |
| 1992 | Curtis Conway, RET SP |
| 1992 | Tony Boselli, OL |
| 1992 | Willie McGinest, DL |
| 1993 | Rob Johnson, QB |
| 1993 | Johnnie Morton, WR |
| 1993 | Willie McGinest, DL |
| 1994 | Keyshawn Johnson, WR |
| 1994 | Tony Boselli, OL |
| 1995 | Keyshawn Johnson, WR |
| 1995 | John Michels, OL |
| 1995 | Darrell Russell, DL |
| 1995 | John Stonehouse, P |
| 1996 | Darrell Russell, DL |
| 1996 | Sammy Knight, LB |
| 1996 | Daylon McCutcheon, DB |
| 1997 | Chris Claiborne, LB |
| 1997 | Brian Kelly, DB |
| 1998 | Travis Claridge, OL |
| 1998 | Ennis Davis, DL |
| 1998 | Chris Claiborne, LB |
| 1998 | Daylon McCutcheon, DB |
| 1998 | Rashard Cook, DB |
| 1999 | Travis Claridge, OL |
| 1999 | David Gibson, DB |
| 2000 | No USC Selections |
| 2001 | Troy Polamalu, DB |
| 2001 | Kevin Arbet, SPT |
| 2002 | Carson Palmer, QB |
| 2002 | Jacob Rogers, OL |
| 2002 | Matt Grootegoed, LB |
| 2002 | Troy Polamalu, DB |
| 2003 | Matt Leinart, QB |
| 2003 | Mike Williams, WR |
| 2003 | Jacob Rogers, OL |
| 2003 | Norm Katnik, OL |
| 2003 | Kenechi Udeze, DL |
| 2003 | Shaun Cody, DL |
| 2003 | Mike Patterson, DL |
| 2003 | Will Poole, DB |
| 2003 | Tom Malone, P |
| 2004 | Matt Leinart, QB |
| 2004 | Reggie Bush, TB, PR |
| 2004 | Shaun Cody, DL |
| 2004 | Mike Patterson, DL |
| 2004 | Matt Grootegoed, LB |
| 2004 | Lofa Tatupu, LB |
| 2004 | Tom Malone, P |
| 2005 | Matt Leinart, QB |

| Year | Name, Position |
|---|---|
| 2005 | Reggie Bush, TB |
| 2005 | Dwayne Jarrett, WR |
| 2005 | Ryan Kalil, OL |
| 2005 | Taitusi Lutui, OL |
| 2005 | Sam Baker, OL |
| 2005 | Frostee Rucker, DL |
| 2005 | Lawrence Jackson, DL |
| 2005 | Darnell Bing, S |
| 2006 | Dwayne Jarrett, WR |
| 2006 | Sam Baker, OT |
| 2006 | Ryan Kalil, C |
| 2006 | John David Booty, QB |
| 2006 | Steve Smith, WR |
| 2006 | Sedrick Ellis, DT |
| 2006 | Keith Rivers, LB |
| 2006 | Rey Maualuga, LB |
| 2007 | Fred Davis, TE |
| 2007 | Chilo Rachal, OG |
| 2007 | Sam Baker, OT |
| 2007 | Sedrick Ellis, DT |
| 2007 | Lawrence Jackson, DE |
| 2007 | Keith Rivers, LB |
| 2007 | Rey Maualuga, LB |
| 2007 | Kevin Ellison, S |
| 2008 | Mark Sanchez, QB |
| 2008 | Kristofer O'Dowd, C |
| 2008 | Fili Moala, DT |
| 2008 | Brian Cushing, LB |
| 2008 | Rey Maualuga, LB |
| 2008 | Kevin Ellison, S |
| 2008 | Taylor Mays, S |
| 2008 | David Buehler, PK |
| 2009 | Damian Williams, WR |
| 2009 | Jeff Byers, OL |
| 2009 | Charles Brown, OT |
| 2009 | Taylor Mays, S |
| 2010 | Tyron Smith, OT |
| 2010 | Jurrell Casey, DT |
| 2010 | Robert Woods, KOR |
| 2011 | Robert Woods, WR |
| 2011 | Matt Kalil, OT |
| 2011 | Nick Perry, DE |
| 2011 | T.J. McDonald, S |
| 2011 | Nickell Robey, CB |
| 2011 | Andre Heidari, PK |
| 2011 | Rhett Ellison, SPT |
| 2012 | Marqise Lee, WR |
| 2012 | Khaled Holmes, C |

# *USC Players Who Won National Awards*

## Heisman Trophy

Awarded annually by the Downtown Athletic Club in New York City to the person considered the most outstanding player in college football.

1965—Mike Garrett—Tailback
1968—O.J. Simpson—Tailback
1979—Charles White—Tailback
1981—Marcus Allen—Tailback
2002—Carson Palmer—Quarterback
2004—Matt Leinart—Quarterback
2005—Reggie Bush—Tailback

Bush's Heisman Trophy win was later vacated due to an NCAA penalty

## Outland Trophy

Awarded annually since 1946 to the most outstanding interior lineman in the nation by the Football Writers Association of America.

1967—Ron Yary—Offensive Tackle

## Lombardi Award

Awarded annually since 1970 to the nation's top college lineman who also 'best exemplifies the discipline of Vince Lombardi.

1979—Brad Budde—Offensive Guard

## Thorpe Award

Awarded annually since 1986 to the nation's top defensive back

1989—Mark Carrier—Free Safety

## Butkus Award

Awarded annually since 1985 to the nation's top linebacker

1998—Chris Claiborne

## Mackey Award

Awarded annually since 2000 to the nation's top tight end

2007—Fred Davis

## Walter Camp Award

Awarded since 1967 to the top player in college football by the Walter Camp Football Foundation.

1967—O.J. Simpson—Tailback
1968—O.J. Simpson—Tailback
1979—Charles White—Tailback
1981—Marcus Allen—Tailback
2004—Matt Leinart—Quarterback
2005—Reggie Bush—Tailback

## Maxwell Award

Awarded since 1937 to the nation's top college player by the Maxwell Club of Philadelphia, Pennsylvania.

1968—O. J. Simpson—Tailback
1979—Charles White—Tailback
1981—Marcus Allen—Tailback

## Johnny Unitas Golden Arm Award

Awarded since 1987 by the Kentucky Chapter of the National Football Foundation Hall of Fame to the nation's top senior quarterback

1988—Rodney Peete
2002—Carson Palmer
2005—Matt Leinart

## Doak Walker Award

Awarded since 1990 by the SMU Forum to the nation's top running back

2005—Reggie Bush

## Chuck Bednarik Award

Awarded since 1995 by the Maxwell Football Club to the nation's top defensive player

2008—Rey Maualuga

## American Football Coaches Association Coach of the Year

Awarded since 1935 to the nation's top coach
1962—John McKay
1972—John McKay
2003—Pete Carroll

## Football Writers Association of America Coach of the Year

Awarded since 1957

1962—John McKay
1972—John McKay

## Voit Trophy

From 1951 to 1978, the Voit Trophy was presented to the outstanding football player on the Pacific Coast by the West Coast football writers.

1952—Jim Sears—Running Back
1955—Jon Arnett—Running Back
1956—Jon Arnett—Running Back
1965—Mike Garrett—Tailback
1968—O.J. Simpson—Tailback
1972—Anthony Davis—Tailback
1974—Anthony Davis—Tailback
1976—Ricky Bell—Tailback
1978—Charles White—Tailback

## Glenn "Pop" Warner Award

Awarded since 1949 by the Palo Club to the most valuable senior college football player on the Pacific Coast.

1952—Jim Sears—Running Back
1956—Jon Arnett—Running Back
1965—Mike Garrett—Tailback
1968—O.J. Simpson—Tailback
1972—Mike Rae—Quarterback
1973—Lynn Swann—Wide Receiver
1974—Anthony Davis—Tailback
1976—Ricky Bell—Tailback
1979—Charles White—Tailback
1981—Marcus Allen—Tailback
1984—Jack Del Rio—Linebacker
1988—Rodney Peete—Quarterback
1989—Tim Ryan—Defensive Tackle
1993—Johnnie Morton—Wide Receiver
1995—Keyshawn Johnson—Wide Receiver
2002—Carson Palmer—Quarterback
2005—Matt Leinart—Quarterback

## Pac-12 Conference Player of the Year

Awarded since 1975 by the Pac-12 Conference

1976—Ricky Bell—Tailback
1978—Charles White—Tailback
1979—Charles White—Tailback
1981—Marcus Allen—Tailback
1984—Duane Bickett (Defense)—Linebacker
1988—Rodney Peete (Offense)—Quarterback
1989—Junior Seau (Defense)—Linebacker
1995—Keyshawn Johnson (Offense)—Wide Receiver
1998—Chris Claiborne (Defense)—Linebacker
1999—Kareem Kelly (Freshman)—Wide Receiver
2002—Carson Palmer (Co-Offense)—Quarterback
2002—Mike Williams (Freshman)—Wide Receiver
2003—Matt Leinart (Offense)—Quarterback
2004—Matt Leinart (Co-Offense)—Quarterback
2004—Reggie Bush (Co-Offense)—Tailback
2004—Shaun Cody (Co-Defense)—Tackle
2005—Reggie Bush (Offense)—Tailback
2006—Taylor Mays (Freshman)—Safety
2007—Sedrick Ellis (Defense)—Tackle
2008—Rey Maualuga (Defense)—Linebacker
2010—Robert Woods (Freshman Offense)—Wide Receiver
2012—Marqise Lee (Offense)—Wide Receiver
2012—Leonard Williams (Freshman Defense)—Tackle

## Pac-12 Conference Coach of the Year

Awarded since 1975 by the Pac-12 Conference

1976—John Robinson
1978—John Robinson
1984—Ted Tollner
1987—Larry Smith
1988—Larry Smith
2003—Pete Carroll
2005—Pete Carroll
2006—Pete Carroll

## Morris Trophy

Awarded since 1980 to the Pac-12's outstanding offensive and defensive linemen.

1980—Roy Foster (Offense)—Guard
1981—Roy Foster (Offense)—Guard
1982—George Achica (Defense)—Nose Guard
1982—Bruce Matthews (Offense)—Guard
1985—Jeff Bregel (Offense)—Guard
1990—Pat Harlow (Offense)—Tackle
1994—Tony Boselli (Offense)—Tackle
1996—Darrell Russell (Defense)—Tackle
1999—Travis Claridge (Offense)—Tackle
2003—Jacob Rogers (Offense)—Tackle
2006—Ryan Kalil (Offense)—Center
2006—Sedrick Ellis (Defense)—Tackle
2007—Sedrick Ellis (Defense)—Tackle
2009—Charles Brown (Offense)—Tackle
2010—Tyron Smith (Offense)—Tackle
2011—Matt Kalil (Offense)—Tackle

# *Trojan Team Awards*

## Mike Mckeever Memorial Award

Awarded to the Most Valuable Player of season annually. The Award is selected by the football coaches.

1967—O.J. Simpson
1968—O.J. Simpson
1969—Jimmy Jones
1970—Jimmy Jones
1971—Willie Hall
1972—Mike Rae
1973—Lynn Swann
1974—Pat Haden
1975—Ricky Bell
1976—Ricky Bell
1977—Dennis Thurman
1978—Charles White
1979—Paul McDonald, Charles White
1980—Ronnie Lott
1981—Marcus Allen
1982—Joey Browner
1983—Jeff Brown
1984—Neil Hope
1985—Tim McDonald
1986—Tim McDonald
1987—Rodney Peete
1988—Rodney Peete
1989—Junior Seau
1990—Scott Ross
1991—Curtis Conway
1992—Curtis Conway
1993—Johnnie Morton
1994—Tony Boselli
1995—Keyshawn Johnson
1996—Sammy Knight
1997—Cedric Jefferson
1998—Chris Claiborne
1999—Chad Morton
2000—Zeke Moreno
2001—Troy Polamalu
2002—Carson Palmer
2003—Matt Leinart
2004—Reggie Bush
2005—Reggie Bush
2006—Steve Smith
2007—Sedrick Ellis, Fred Davis
2008—Rey Maualuga
2009—Damiam Williams
2010—Jurrell Casey
2011—Matt Barkley
2012—Marqise Lee

## Bob Chandler Award

Awarded to the underclassman football player, based on his athletic ability, academic scholarship, and character on and off the playing field—including the individual's leadership, courage, tenacity, discipline, loyalty, and high standards of morals and values.

1995—Sammy Knight
1996—Jonathan Himebauch
1997—Chad Morton
1998—Aaron Williams
1999—Mike Van Raaphorst
2000—Charlie Landrigan
2001—Darrell Rideaux
2002—Keary Colbert
2003—Jason Leach
2004—Lofa Tatupu
2005—Ryan Kalil
2006—Keith Rivers
2007—Kevin Ellison
2008—Taylor Mays
2009—Christian Tupou
2010—Robert Woods
2011—Hayes Pullard
2012—Randall Telfer

## Brice Taylor Memorial Award

Awarded through 1992 to the Offensive Player of the Year in memory of USC's first All-American.

1976—Donnie Hickman
1977—Mosi Tatupu
1978—Lynn Cain
1979—Brad Budde
1980—Keith Van Horne
1981—Roy Foster
1982—Jeff Simmons
1983—Tony Slaton
1984—Ken Ruettgers
1985—James FitzPatrick
1986—Rodney Peete
1987—Rodney Peete
1988—Erik Affholter
1989—Ricky Ervins
1990—Gary Wellman
1991—Tony Boselli
1992—Curtis Conway
1993—Discontinued

## Roy Baker Memorial Award

Awarded through 1975 to the player chosen as the Back of the Year by the coaching staff.

1961—Ben Wilson
1962—Willie Brown
1963—Mike Garrett
1964—Mike Garrett
1965—Mike Garrett
1966—Mike Hull
1967—O.J. Simpson
1968—O.J. Simpson

1969—Clarence Davis
1970—Clarence Davis
1971—Jimmy Jones
1972—Sam Cunningham
1973—Pat Haden
1974—Anthony Davis
1975—Ricky Bell
1976—Discontinued

## Sid Cherniss Memorial Award

Awarded through 1992 to the Defensive Player of the Year and donated by Judge Sid Cherniss, Jr. In 1974–75 it was given to the outstanding defensive lineman.

1974—Dale Mitchell
1975—Gary Jeter
1976—Eric Williams
1977—Dennis Thurman
1978—Rich Dimler
1979—Larry McGrew
1980—Ronnie Lott, Dennis Smith
1981—Dennis Edwards
1982—Riki Gray
1983—Jack Del Rio
1984—Duane Bickett
1985—Matt Johnson
1986—Marcus Cotton
1987—Greg Coauette
1988—Scott Ross
1989—Junior Seau
1990—Scott Ross
1991—Matt Gee, David Webb
1992—Willie McGinest
1993—Discontinued

## Service Team Players of the Year Award

Awarded from 1998 to the top scout team player. Originally called the Black Shirt Players of the Year Award from 1998 to 2000.

1998—Zach Wilson (off)
Rocky Seto (def)
1999—Sandy Fletcher (off)
Rick Luce (def)
2000—Ryan Kaiser (off)
Aaron Orndorff (def)
2001—Billy Hart (off)
Jay Bottom (def)
2002—Kurt Katnik (off)
Travis Tofi (def)
2003—Andre Woodert (off)
Lawrence Jackson (def)
2004—Chris Bocage (off)
Fili Moala (def)
2005—Mark Sanchez (off)
Kaluka Maiava (def)
2006—David Ausberry (off)
Alex Parsons (def)
2007—Mitch Mustani (off)
Christian Tupou (def)
2008—Steve Gatena (off)
Jurrell Casey (def)
2009—Michael Reardon (off)
Marquis Simmons (def)
2010—D.J. Morgon (off)
George Uko (def)
2011—Cyrus Hobbi (off)
Anthony Sarao (def)
2012—Jordan Simmons (off)
Jabari Ruffin (def)

## John Dye Memorial Award

Awarded to the varsity football player chosen as the Lineman of the Year by vote of the coaching staff.

1946—Jim Callahan
1947—Walt McCormick
1948—Bob Stillwell
1949—Jack Nix
1950—Volney Peters
1951—Al Sanbrano
1952—Bob Peviani
1953—Ed Pucci
1954—Ed Fouch
1955—Orlando Ferrante
1956—Mike Henry
1957—Mike Henry
1958—Hillard Hill
1959—Ron Mix
1960—Marlin McKeever
1961—Mike Bundra
1962—Damon Bame
1963—Damon Bame
1964—Bill Fisk
1965—Paul Johnson
1966—Larry Petrill
1967—Tim Rossovich
1968—Bob Klein
1969—Jim Gunn
1970—Gerry Mullins
1971—John Vella
1972—John Grant
Charles Young
1973—Booker Brown
1974—Bob McCaffrey
1975—Melvin Jackson
1976—97—Not Given
1998—Travis Claridge (off)
Ennis Davis (def)
1999—Travis Claridge (off)
Ryan Nielsen (def)
2000—Brent McCaffrey (off)
Ennis Davis (def)
2001—Jacob Rogers (off)
Lonnie Ford (def)

2002—Zach Wilson (off)
Keneche Udeze (def)
2003—Jacob Rogers (off)
Kenechi Udeze (def)
2004—Sam Baker (off)
Shaun Cody (def)
Mike Patterson (def)
2005—Taitusi Lutui (off)
Lawrence Jackson (def)
2006—Ryan Kalil, Sam Baker (off)
Lawrence Jackson (def)
2007—Sam Baker, Matt Spanos (off)
Sedrick Ellis, Lawrence Jackson (def)
2008—Kristofer O'Dowd (off)
Fili Moala (def)
2009—Jeff Byers (off)
Christian Tupou, Jurrell Casey (def)
2010—Tyron Smith (off)
Jurrell Casey (def)
2011—Matt Kalil (off)
Nick Perry (def)
2012—Khaled Holmes (off)
Morgan Breslin (def)

## Perimeter Player of the Year Award

2011—Robert Woods (off)
T.J. McDonald (def)
2012—Marqise Lee (off)
T.J. McDonald (def)

## Mario Danelo Special Teams Player of the Year

1987—Greg Coauette
1988—Chris Hale
1989—Kurt Barber
1990—Quin Rodrigues
1991—Bruce Luizzi
1992—Bruce Luizzi
1993–97 Not Given
1998—Ifeanyi Ohalete
1999—Frank Carter
2000—Kori Dickerson
2001—Kevin Arbet
2002—Darrell Rideaux
2003—Will Poole
Marcell Allmond
2004—Desmond Reed
2005—Mario Danelo
Kaluka Maiava
2006—Kaluka Maiava
Clay Matthews
2007—Thomas Williams
Clay Matthews
2008—David Buehler
Clay Matthews
2009—Garrett Green
2010—Chris Galippo
2011—Ross Cumming
2012—Tony Burnett

## Trojan Club Award

Awarded through 1975 to the player chosen as the most improved man on the varsity football team. Chosen by vote of the coaching staff.

1960—Bill Nelson
1961—Jim Maples
1962—Gary Potter
1963—John Thomas
1964—Mac Byrd
1965—Jim Walker
1966—Steve Barry
1967—Earl McCullouch
1968—Steve Barry
1969—Willard Scott
1970—John Grant
1971—Bob Eriksen
1972—Charles Hinton (back)
Jeff Winans (lineman)
1973—Rod McNeill (back)
Steve Riley (lineman)
1974—Marvin Cobb (back)
Art Riley (lineman)
1975—Mosi Tatupu (back)
Walt Underwood (lineman)
1976—Discontinued

## Special General Excellence Award

1976—Gary Jeter (only year given)

## Joe Collins Walk-On Award

Awarded to the team's top non-scholarship player.

2010—Tony Burnett
2011—Kyle Negrete
2012—Nathan Guertler and Ryan Dillard

## Davis-Teschke Award

Awarded annually to the most inspirational player on the varsity football squad. Chosen by vote of the varsity lettermen at the end of the season.

1919—John Fox
1920—Jimmy Smith
Ken Townsend
1921—Orrie Hester
1922—Leo Colland
1923—Chet Dolley
1924—John Hawkins
1925—Jeff Cravath
1926—Ted Gorrell

1927—Morley Drury
1928—Lloyd Thomas
1929—Russ Saunders
1930—Ralph Wilcox
1931—Erny Pinckert
1932—Tay Brown
1933—Larry Stevens
1934—Herb Tatsch
1935—Max Belko
1936—David Davis
1937—Owen Hanson
1938—Ray George
1939—Bill Fisk
1940—Ed Dempsey
1941—Ben Sohn
Bobby Robertson
1942—Bill Seixas
1943—Bill Gray
1944—Duane Whitehead
1945—Jackie Musick
1946—Bob Musick
1947—Don Clark
1948—Don Doll
1949—Bill Martin
1950—Pat Cannamela
Ralph Pucci
1951—Lou Welsh
1952—Jim Sears
1953—Dick Petty
1954—Marv Goux
1955—Marv Goux
1956—Don Hickman
1957—Ken Antle
1958—Ken Antle
1959—Mike McKeever
1960—Roger Mietz
1961—Warren Stephenson
1962—Marv Marinovich
1963—Willie Brown
1964—Craig Fertig
1965—Mike Garrett
1966—Ray May
1967—Adrian Young
1968—Steve Sogge
1969—Al Cowlings
1970—Charlie Weaver
1971—John Papadakis
1972—Dave Brown
1973—Manny Moore
1974—Pat Haden
1975—Joe Davis
1976—Vince Evans
1977—Mosi Tatupu
1978—Otis Page
1979—Brad Budde
1980—Ronnie Lott
1981—Dennis Edwards
1982—George Achica
1983—Jeff Brown
1984—Neil Hope
1985—Matt Johnson
1986—Rex Moore
1987—Leroy Holt
1988—Leroy Holt
1989—Leroy Holt
1990—Scott Ross
1991—Matt Willig
1992—Mike Mooney
1993—Willie McGinest
Deon Strother
1994—Jeff Kopp
1995—Terry Barnum
1996—Sammy Knight
1997—Brian Kelly
1998—Marc Matock
1999—John Fox
2000—Petros Papadakis
2001—Antuan Simmons
Charlie Landrigan
2002—Troy Polamalu
2003—Keary Colbert
2004—Matt Grootegoed
Lofa Tatupu
2005—Taitusi Lutui
Frostee Rucker
2006—Ryan Kalil
2007—Thomas Williams
2008—Kyle Moore
2009—Stafon Johnson
2010—Stanley Havili
2011—Christian Tupou
2012—T.J. McDonald

## Theodore Gabrielson Award

Awarded annually to the outstanding player in the USC–Notre Dame game

1969—Greg Slough
1970—Willie Hall
1971—Edesel Garrison
1972—Anthony Davis
1973—Charles Anthony
1974—Pat Haden (off)
Charles Phillips (def)
1975—Ricky Bell
1976—Ron Bush
1977—Walt Underwood
1978—Paul McDonald
1979—Danny Garcia
1980—Chip Banks
1981—George Achica
1982—Jeff Simmons
1983—Duane Bickett
1984—Brian Luft
1985—Jeff Bregel
1986—Todd Steele

1987—Erik Affholter (off)
Tim Ryan (def)
1988—Erik Affholter (off)
Scott Ross (def)
1989—John Jackson (off)
Mark Carrier (def)
1990—Mazio Royster (off)
Todd Marinovich (off)
Scott Ross (def)
Gidion Murrell (def)
1991—Bradford Banta (off)
Yonnie Jackson (off)
Stephon Pace (def)
1992—Rob Johnson (off)
Willie McGinest (def)
1993—Thomas Holland
1994—John Stonehouse
1995—Not given
1996—Sammy Knight
1997—Mark Cusano
1998—Rashard Cook
1999—Not given
2000—Zeke Moreno
2001—Lonnie Ford
2002—Justin Fargas
2003—Matt Leinart
2004—Matt Leinart
2005—Reggie Bush
2006—Dwayne Jarrett
2007—Mark Sanchez
2008—Kaluka Maiava
2009—Anthony McCoy
2010—Not given
2011—Nickell Robey
2012—Not given

## Marv Goux Award

Awarded annually to the varsity football team member chosen by the team as having contributed the most during the USC-UCLA game of that season.

1952—Bill Hattig
1953—Dick Petty
1954—Orlando Ferrante
1955—Gordon Duvall
1956—Bob Voiles
1957—Bob Voiles
1958—Lou Byrd
1959—Al Bansavage
1960—Marlin McKeever
1961—Frank Buncom
1962—Marv Marinovich
1963—Pete Beathard
1964—Mike Garrett
1965—Mike Garrett
1966—Mike Hull
1967—O.J. Simpson
1968—O.J. Simpson
1969—Al Cowlings
1970—Sam Dickerson
1971—Lou Harris
1972—Richard Wood
1973—Monte Doris
1974—Anthony Davis
1975—Ricky Bell (off)
Walt Underwood (def)
1976—Ricky Bell
1977—Bob Hertel
1978—Charles White (off)
Ty Sperling (def)
1979—Charles White (off)
Ronnie Lott (def)
1980—Keith Van Horne (off)
Ronnie Lott (def)
1981—Marcus Allen (off)
George Achica
1982—Scott Tinsley (off)
Joey Browner (def)
1983—Michael Harper (off)
Tommy Haynes (def)
1984—Hank Norman (off)
Jack Del Rio (def)
1985—Joe Cormier (off)
Matt Koart (def)
1986—Rodney Peete (off)
Rex Moore (def)
1987—Rodney Peete (off)
Erik Affholter (off)
Mark Carrier (def)
1988—Rodney Peete (off)
Aaron Emanuel (off)
John Guerrero (off)
Tim Ryan (def)
Don Gibon (def)
1989—Ricky Ervins (off)
Mark Carrier (def)
1990—Mazio Royster (off)
Stephon Pace (def)
1991—Estrus Crayton (off)
Calvin Holmes (def)
1992—Rob Johnson (off)
Stephon Pace (def)
1993—Rob Johnson
1994—Keyshawn Johnson
1995—Delon Washington
1996—R. Jay Soward
1997—R. Jay Soward
1998—Not given
1999—David Gibson
2000—Carson Palmer
2001—Antuan Simmons
2002—Carson Palmer
2003—Mike Williams
2004—Reggie Bush
Ryan Killeen

2005—Reggie Bush
Lawrence Jackson
2006—Not given
2007—Terrell Thomas
2008—Patrick Turner
2009—Allen Bradford
2010—Allen Bradford
2011—Marqise Lee
2012—Not given

## Elmer C. "Gloomy Gus" Henderson Award

Awarded through 1992 to the varsity football player who plays the greatest number of minutes during the season.

1966—Mike Scarpace
1967—Dick Allmon
1968—Gerry Shaw
1969—Gerry Mullins
1970—Ron Ayala
1971—Willie Hall
1972—Dave Brown
1973—Bob McCaffrey
1974—Jim Obradovich
1975—Joe Davis
1976—William Gay
1977—William Gay
1978—Pat Howell
1979—Paul McDonald
1980—Steve Busick
1981—Roy Foster
1982—Don Mosebar
1983—Keith Browner
1984—Mark Boyer
1985—Jerome Tyler
1986—Junior Thurman
1987—Greg Coauette
1988—John Guerrero
1989—Brad Leggett
1990—Pat Harlow
1991—Tony Boselli
1992—Craig Gibson
Len Gorecki
1993—Discontinued

## Jack Oakie "Rise and Shine" Award

Awarded through 1992, from 1998 to 2000, from 2002 to 2005 and from 2007 to the player with the longest run from scrimmage of the season, in 2003 for the player with the longest run, and from 1993 to 1997 and in 2001, 2006 and 2009 to the player making the biggest hit of the year.

1985—Kennedy Pola (37 yards)
1986—Rodney Peete (32)
1987—Scott Lockwood (38)
1988—Calvin Holmes (60)
1989—Ricky Ervins (78)
1990—Scott Lockwood (66)
1991—Deon Strother (92)
1992—Estrus Crayton
Dwight McFadden (32)
1993—Jason Oliver
1994—Donn Cunnigan
1995—Sammy Knight
1996—Grant Pearsall
1997—Anthony Volsan
1998—Frank Strong (73 yards)
1999—Sultan McCullough (48)
2000—Malaefou MacKenzie (69)
2001—Mike Pollard
2002—Sultan McCullough (62)
2003—Reggie Bush (96)
2004—Reggie Bush (84)
2005—Reggie Bush (84)
2006—Kevin Ellison
2007—Joe McKnight (59)
2008—Joe McKnight (55)
2009—Taylor Mays
2010—Allen Bradford (73)
2011—Curtis McNeal (79)
2012—Robert Woods (76)

## Howard Jones/Football Alumni Club Award

Originally the Football Alumni Club Award, awarded annually to the senior varsity football letterman who has achieved the highest accumulative grade point average

1959—Gary Finneran
1960—Mike McKeever
1961—Warren Stephenson
1962—Ken Del Conte
1963—Tom Johnson
1964—Bill Fisk
1965—Chuck Arrobio
1966—Phil Lee
1967—Toby Page
1968—Steve Sogge
1969—Fred Khasigian
1970—Tyrone Hudson
1971—John Papadakis
1972—Dave Brown
1973—Monte Doris
1974—Pat Haden
1975—Melvin Jackson
1976—Eugene Lawryk
1977—Gary Bethel
1978—Paul McDonald
1979—Gordon Adams
1980—Gordon Adams
1981—Jay Champlain
1982—Jim Arrivey
1983—Rod Williams
1984—Duane Bickett
1985—Matt Koart
1986—Jeff Bregel
1987—Keith Davis
John Page

1988—Chuck Ebertin
1989—Tom Dabasinskas
1990—Shane Foley
1991—Marc Raab
1992—Bruce Luizzi
Mike Mooney
1993—Rory Brown
1994—Tony Boselli
1995—Jeremy Hogue
1996—Matt Keneley
1997—Jonathan Himebauch
1998—Adam Abrams
1999—Todd Keneley
2000—Mike Van Raaphorst
2001—Mike MacGillivray
2002—Scott Huber
2003—Matt Cassel
2004—Ryan Ting
2005—Brandon Hancock
2006—Nick Vanderboom
2007—Garrett Green
2008—Garrett Green
Jordan Congdon
2009—Garrett Green
2010—Augusto Alonso
2011—Augusto Alonso
2012—Khaled Holmes

## Chris Carlisle Courage Award

2002—Malaefou MacKenzie
Justin Fargas
2003—Melvin Simmons
2004—Ryan Kalil
2005—Scott Ware
2006—Desmond Reed
2007—Matt Spanos
2008—Jeff Byers
2009—Josh Pinkard
2010—Christian Tupou
2011—Curtis McNeal
2012—Robert Woods

## Howard Jones Incentive Award

Awarded annually through 1992 to the varsity player who has the greatest increase in his grade point average in the previous academic year.

1979—Danny Garcia
1980—Roy Foster
1981—Don Mosebar
1982—Darryl Moore
1983—Tony Brewer
1984—Timmie Ware
1985—Brent Moore
1986—Bruce Parks
1987—Ken Henry
1988—Erik Affholter
1989—Dan Barnes
1990—Shannon Jones
1991—Alan Wilson
1992—Travis Hannah
1993—Combined with Football Alumni Club Award

## John Wayne Memorial Scholarship

Awarded to the senior with aspirations of continuing in higher education who chooses not to participate in professional football.

1980—Ty Sperling
1981—Jay Champlain
1982—Jim Arrivey
1983—Rod Williams
1984—Mark Boyer
1985—John Denvir
1986—Lonnie White
1987—John Page
1988—Chuck Ebertin
1989—Tom Dabasinskas
1990—Shane Foley
1991—Marc Raab
1992—Bruce Luizzi
Mike Mooney
1993—Martin Boskovich
Rory Brown
1994—Jeremy Hogue
1995—Terry Barnum
1996—Matt Keneley
1997—LaVale Woods
1998—Adam Abrams
1999—John Fox
2000—Mike Van Raaphorst
2001—Bobby DeMars
2002—Not given
2003—Scott Huber
2004—Matt Cassel
2005—Travis Watkins
2006—Brandon Hancock
2007—Nick Vanderboom
Brandon Hancock
2008—Jody Adewale
2009—Garrett Green
2010—Not given
2011—Not given
2012—Kyle Negrete

## Champion of the Year Award

Awarded through 1992 to the player who "performed like a champion."

1987—Marcus Cotton
Ryan Knight
1988—Tracy Butts
Jeff Brown
1989—Aaron Emanuel
Marlon Washington

1990—Shane Foley
Brian Tuliau
1991—Michael Gaytan
Alan Wilson
1992—Travis Hannah
Zuri Hector
1993—Discontinued

## Sam Barry Spartan Award

After 1952, this award went to the Spartan team member selected by the coaching staff who contributed the most to the development of the varsity squad during the season. Prior to 1952 the award was known as the Richard Barrett Award for the most cooperative member of the varsity squad.

1940—Carl Benson
1941—Max Green
1942—Mel Bleeker
1943—Bill Gray
1944—Duane Whitehead
1945—Jack Musick
1947—Johnny Naumu
1948—Bill Martin
1949—Bob Stillwell
1950—Lou Welsh
1951—Don Zimmerman
1952—Jim Smith
1953—Hank Green
1954—Dennis Wilkerson
1955—Bill Howard
1956—Larry Snyder
1957—Hank Slade
1958—Larry Gilhooly
1959—Bill O'Brien
1960—Marv Marinovich
1961—Gary Winslow
1962—Vern Vihlene
1963—Jerry Hayhoe
1964—Gary Magner
1965—Leonard Sims
1966—Dick Elliott
1967—Cal Garland
1968—Kendall Nungesser
1969—Curtis Timmons
1970—Manfred Moore
1971—Bob McCaffrey
1972—John Racanelli
1973—Joe Shipp
1974—Bill O'Brien
1975—Bernard Tarver
1976–81—Not given
1982—Andrew Jackson
1983—Discontinued

## Lifters Award

2001—Matt Cassel
Kenechi Udeze
2002—Grant Mattos
Troy Polamalu
2003—Lenny Vandermade
Mike Patterson
2004—Mike Patterson
Lofa Tatupu
2005—Reggie Bush
Taitusi Lutui
Sam Baker
2006—Sam Baker
Oscar Lua
2007—Sedrick Ellis
Keith Rivers
Kevin Ellison
2008—Brian Cushing
Kevin Ellison
Clay Matthews
2009—Jeff Byers
Will Harris
Taylor Mays
2010—Christian Tupou
Stanley Havili
2011—Rhett Ellison
Jawanza Starling
2012—Kevin Graf
Nickell Robey

## John McKay Award

Given to the underclassman with the most competitive spirit.

2002—Mike Ross
2003—Lofa Tatupu
2004—Thomas Williams
2005—Rey Maualuga
2006—Brian Cushing
2007—Christian Tupou
2008—Damian Williams
2009—Devon Kennard
2010—Robert Woods
2011—Nickell Robey
2012—Marqise Lee

## Leadership Award

2011—Rhett Ellison
2012—Khaled Holmes

# Chapter Notes

## *Introduction*

1. Leonard Pitt and Dale Pitt, *Los Angeles A to Z: An Encyclopedia of the City and County,* p. 272.
2. Wikipedia, Founding of Los Angeles.
3. Pitt and Pitt, p. 297.
4. Jim Heimann, *Sins of the City, The Real Los Angeles Noir*, p. 5.
5. Pitt and Pitt, pp. 271–272.
6. Wikipedia, Phineas Banning.
7. Pitt and Pitt, p. 416.
8. Wikipedia, Robert Widney.
9. Wikipedia, Ozro Childs.
10. Ibid.
11. Wikipedia, Isaias Hellman.
12. Ibid.
13. Wikipedia, Potato Famine.
14. Wikipedia, John Downey.
15. Wikipedia, Widney Hall.
16. Wikipedia, Marion Bovard.
17. Wikipedia, History of American Football.
18. Ibid.

## *Chapter One*

1888–1907, 1909—All information is from 2013 USC Football Media Guide, pp. 80–81.

### 1908

1. 1910 El Rodeo Yearbook, p. 126.
2. Ibid.

### 1910

1. 1912 El Rodeo Yearbook, p. 155.
2. Ibid.
3. Ibid.
4. Ibid., p. 156.
5. Ibid.
6. Ibid.
7. Ibid., p. 157.
8. Ibid., p. 158.

1911–1913—No football was played at USC.

### 1914

1. *Daily Trojan*, September 29, 1914, p. 1.
2. Ibid., Oct. 13, p. 1.
3. Ibid., Oct. 27, p. 1.
4. Ibid., Nov. 4, p. 1.
5. Ibid., Nov. 10, p. 1.
6. Ibid., Nov. 17, p. 1.
7. Ibid., Dec. 1, p. 1.

### 1915

1. *Los Angeles Times*, October 3, 1915, p. VII.
2. Ibid., Oct. 17, p. VII.
3. *Daily Trojan*, Oct. 26, p. 1.
4. Ibid., Nov. 9, p. 1.
5. Ibid., Nov. 23, p. 1.
6. Ibid., Nov. 30, p. 1.
7. Ibid., Dec. 14, p. 1.

### 1916

1. *Daily Trojan*, Oct. 10, 1916, p. 1.
2. Ibid., Oct. 17, p. 1.
3. Ibid., Oct. 24, p. 1.
4. Ibid., Nov. 9, p. 4.
5. Ibid., Nov. 14, p. 1.
6. Ibid., Nov. 27, p. 1.
7. Ibid., Dec. 5, p. 1.
8. Ibid., Dec. 12, p. 1.

### 1917

1. *Daily Trojan*, Oct. 23, 1917, p. 1.
2. Ibid., Oct. 30, p. 1.
3. Ibid., Nov. 6, p. 1.
4. Ibid., Nov. 13, p. 1.
5. Ibid., Nov. 20, p. 1.
6. Ibid., Nov. 27, p. 1.
7. Ibid., Dec. 4, p. 1.

### 1918

1. 1920 El Rodeo Yearbook, p. 182.
2. Ibid., p. 184.
3. Ibid.
4. Ibid.
5. Ibid.
6. Ibid.

### 1919

1. 1921 El Rodeo Yearbook, p. 230.
2. Ibid., p. 231.
3. Ibid., p. 232.
4. Ibid., p. 231.
5. Ibid., p. 230.

### 1920

1. 1922 El Rodeo Yearbook, p. 104.
2. Ibid., p. 105.
3. Ibid., p. 107.
4. Ibid., p. 104.
5. Ibid., p. 107.
6. Ibid., p. 111.

### 1921

1. *Daily Trojan*, Oct. 5, 1921, p. 1.
2. Ibid.
3. Ibid., Oct. 12, p. 1.
4. Ibid., Oct. 14, p. 1.
5. Ibid., Oct. 18, p. 1.
6. Ibid., Oct. 20, p. 1.
7. Ibid., Nov. 1, p. 1.
8. Ibid., Nov. 9, p. 1.
9. Ibid., Nov. 22, p. 1.
10. Ibid., Dec. 2, p. 1.
11. Ibid., Dec. 6, p. 1.

### 1922

1. 1924 El Rodeo Yearbook, p. 45.
2. Ibid.
3. Ibid.
4. Ibid., p. 47.
5. Ibid., p. 48.
6. Ibid.
7. Ibid., p. 52.
8. Ibid., p. 53.
9. Ibid., p. 55.
10. Ibid., p. 56.
11. *Daily Trojan*, Jan. 5, 1923, p. 1.

### 1923

1. *Daily Trojan*, Oct. 2, 1923, p. 3.
2. Ibid., Oct. 9, p. 1.
3. Ibid., Oct. 16, p. 3.
4. Ibid., Oct. 23, p. 1.
5. Ibid., Oct. 30, p. 1.
6. Ibid., Nov. 13, p. 1.
7. Ibid., Nov. 20, p. 1.
8. Ibid., Nov. 28. p. 3.

### 1924

1. *Daily Trojan*, Sept. 30, 1924, p. 1.
2. Ibid., Oct. 7, p. 1.
3. Ibid., Oct. 14, p. 1.
4. Ibid., Oct. 21, p. 1.
5. Ibid., Oct. 28, p. 1.
6. Ibid., Nov. 5, p. 3.
7. Ibid., Nov. 11, p. 3.
8. Ibid., Nov. 18, p.1.
9. Ibid., Nov. 26. p. 1.
10. Ibid., Dec. 9, p. 1.
11. Ibid., Jan. 6, 1925, p. 3.

### 1925

1. *Daily Trojan*, Sept. 28, 1925, p. 1.
2. Ibid.
3. Ibid., Oct. 5, p. 1.
4. Ibid., Oct. 12, p. 1.
5. Ibid., Oct. 19, p. 1.
6. Ibid., Oct. 26, p. 1.
7. Ibid., Nov. 2, p. 1.
8. Ibid., Nov. 9, p. 1.
9. Ibid., Nov. 16, p. 1.
10. Ibid., Nov. 23, p. 1.
11. Ibid., Dec. 1, p. 3.
12. Ibid., Dec. 7, p. 1.
13. Ibid., Dec. 14, p. 1.

### 1926

1. *Daily Trojan*, Sept. 27, 1926, p. 3.
2. Ibid., Oct. 4, p. 4.
3. Ibid., Oct. 11, p. 4.
4. Ibid., Oct. 18, p. 4.
5. Ibid., Oct. 26, p. 1.
6. Ibid., Nov. 1, p. 1.
7. Ibid., Nov. 12, p. 3.
8. Ibid., Nov. 22, p. 3.
9. Ibid., Nov. 29, p. 3.
10. John Robinson and Joe Jares, *Conquest: A Cavalcade of USC Football*, p. 73.
11. Bill Cromartie and Jody H. Brown, *The Glamor Game*, pp. 11–16.

### 1927

1. *Daily Trojan*, Sept. 26, 1927, p. 1.
2. Ibid., Oct. 3, p. 1.
3. Ibid., Oct. 9, p. 1.
4. Ibid., Oct. 17, p. 1.
5. Ibid., Oct. 24, p. 1.
6. Ibid., Oct. 31, p. 1.
7. Ibid., Nov. 15, p. 3.
8. Ibid., Nov. 21, p. 1.
9. Bill Cromartie and Jody H. Brown, *The Glamor Game*, pp. 20–23.
10. *Daily Trojan*, Dec. 5, p. 1.

### 1928

1. *Daily Trojan*, Oct. 1, 1928, p. 1.
2. Ibid., Oct. 8, p. 1.
3. Ibid., Oct. 15, p. 1.
4. Ibid., Oct. 22, p. 1.
5. Ibid., Oct. 29, p. 1.
6. Ibid., Nov. 5, p. 1.
7. Ibid., Nov. 13, p. 1.
8. Ibid., Nov. 19, p. 1.
9. Ibid., Nov. 26, p. 1.
10. Bill Cromartie and Jody H. Brown, *The Glamor Game*, pp. 28–29.

### 1929

1. *Daily Trojan*, Sept. 30, 1929, p. 1.
2. Ibid., Oct. 7, p. 1.
3. Ibid., Oct. 14, p. 1.
4. Ibid., Oct. 21, p. 1.
5. Ibid., Oct. 28, p. 1.
6. Ibid., Nov. 4, p. 1.
7. Ibid., Nov. 12, p. 1.

8. Bill Cromartie and Jody H. Brown, *The Glamor Game*, pp. 34–37.
9. *Daily Trojan*, Nov. 25, p. 1.
10. Ibid., Dec. 3, p. 1.
11. 1930 El Rodeo Yearbook, p. 148.
12. *Daily Trojan*, Jan. 3, 1930, p. 3.

## 1930

1. 1931 El Rodeo Yearbook, p. 39.
2. Ibid., p. 40.
3. Ibid., p. 41.
4. Ibid., p. 42.
5. Ibid., p. 45.
6. Ibid., p. 46.
7. Ibid., p. 51.
8. *Daily Trojan*, Nov. 17, 1930, p. 3.
9. 1931 El Rodeo Yearbook, p. 56.
10. Bill Cromartie and Jody H. Brown, *The Glamor Game*, pp. 44–45.

## 1931

1. *Daily Trojan*, Sept. 29, 1931, p. 1.
2. Ibid., Oct. 6, p. 1.
3. Ibid., Oct. 13, p. 1.
4. Ibid., Oct. 20, p. 1.
5. Ibid., Oct. 27, p. 1.
6. Ibid., Nov. 10, p. 1.
7. Ibid., Nov. 17, p. 1.
8. Bill Cromartie and Jody H. Brown, *The Glamor Game*, pp. 53–59.
9. *Daily Trojan*, Dec. 8, p. 1.
10. Ibid., Dec. 15, p.1.
11. Ibid., Jan. 4, 1932, p. 1.

## 1932

1. *Daily Trojan*, Sept. 26, 1932, p. 1.
2. Ibid., Oct. 3, p. 1.
3. Ibid., Oct. 10, p. 1.
4. Ibid., Oct. 17, p. 1.
5. Ibid., Oct. 24, p. 1.
6. Ibid., Nov. 7, p. 1.
7. Ibid., Nov. 14, p. 1.
8. Ibid., Nov. 28, p. 1.
9. Bill Cromartie and Jody H. Brown, *The Glamor Game*, pp. 63–65.
10. *Daily Trojan*, Jan. 3, 1933, p. 1.

## 1933

1. 1934 El Rodeo Yearbook, p. 252.
2. Ibid.
3. Ibid., p. 253.
4. Ibid., p. 256.
5. Ibid., p. 255.
6. Ibid., p. 257.
7. Ibid., p. 258.
8. Ibid., p. 260.
9. Ibid., p. 262.
10. Bill Cromartie and Jody H. Brown, *The Glamor Game*, pp. 63–65.
11. *Daily Trojan*, Dec. 4, 1933, p. 3.
12. 1934 El Rodeo Yearbook, p. 264.

## 1934

1. 1935 El Rodeo Yearbook, p. 131.
2. Ibid.
3. Ibid.
4. Ibid., p. 132.
5. Ibid., p. 133.
6. Ibid., p. 136.
7. Ibid., p. 135.
8. Ibid., p. 137.
9. *Daily Trojan*, Nov. 19, 1934, p. 1.
10. 1935 El Rodeo Yearbook, p. 139.
11. Bill Cromartie and Jody H. Brown, *The Glamor Game*, pp. 73–74.

## 1935

1. 1936 El Rodeo Yearbook, p. 218.
2. *Daily Trojan*, Oct. 7, 1935, p. 3.
3. 1936 El Rodeo Yearbook, p. 219.
4. Ibid., p. 220.
5. Ibid., p. 221.
6. Ibid., p. 222.
7. *Daily Trojan*, Nov. 18, 1935, p. 3.
8. Bill Cromartie and Jody H. Brown, *The Glamor Game*, pp. 79–82.
9. 1936 El Rodeo Yearbook, p. 226.
10. Ibid., p. 227.
11. Ibid., p. 228.
12. *Daily Trojan*, Jan. 2, 1936, p. 1.

## 1936

1. *Daily Trojan*, Sept. 28, 1936, p. 1.
2. Ibid., Oct. 5, p. 3.
3. Ibid., Oct. 12, p. 3.
4. 1937 El Rodeo Yearbook, p. 230.
5. Ibid., p. 234.
6. *Daily Trojan*, Nov. 9, 1936, p. 3.
7. Ibid., Nov. 16, p. 3.
8. Ibid., Nov. 30, p. 3.
9. Bill Cromartie and Jody H. Brown, *The Glamor Game*, pp. 85–87.

## 1937

1. *Daily Trojan*, Sept. 27, 1937, p. 3.
2. 1938 El Rodeo Yearbook, p. 195.
3. Ibid., p. 196.
4. Ibid., p. 201.
5. Ibid.
6. Ibid., p. 203.
7. Ibid., p. 204.
8. *Daily Trojan*, Nov. 15, 1937, p. 3.
9. Bill Cromartie and Jody H. Brown, *The Glamor Game*, pp. 93–94.
10. *Daily Trojan*, Dec. 6, 1937, p. 1.

## 1938

1. *Daily Trojan*, Sept. 26, 1938, p. 3.
2. Ibid., Oct. 3, p. 3.
3. Ibid., Oct. 10, p. 3.
4. Ibid., Oct. 17, p. 3.
5. Ibid., Oct. 24, p. 3.
6. Ibid., Oct. 31, p. 3.
7. Ibid., Nov. 7, p. 3.
8. Ibid., Nov. 14, p. 3.
9. Ibid., Nov. 28, p. 3.
10. Bill Cromartie and Jody H. Brown, *The Glamor Game*, pp. 98–99.
11. Steve Bisheff and Loel Schrader, *Fight On! The Colorful Story of USC Football*, pp. 299–300, and Mal Florence, *The Trojan Heritage: A Pictorial History*, p. 172.

## 1939

1. *Daily Trojan*, Oct. 2, 1939, p. 3.
2. Ibid., Oct. 9, p. 3.
3. Ibid., Oct. 16, p. 3.
4. Ibid., Oct. 30, p. 3.
5. Ibid., Nov. 6, p. 3.
6. Ibid., Nov. 13, p. 3.
7. Bill Cromartie and Jody H. Brown, *The Glamor Game*, pp. 103–105.
8. *Daily Trojan*, Dec. 4, p. 3.
9. Ibid., Dec. 11, p. 3.
10. Ibid., Jan. 2, 1940, p. 1.

## 1940

1. 1941 El Rodeo Yearbook, p. 202.
2. Ibid., p. 204.
3. Ibid., p. 206.
4. Ibid., p. 208.
5. Ibid., p. 211.
6. Ibid., p. 212.
7. Ibid., p. 214.
8. *Daily Trojan*, Dec. 2, 1940, p. 1.
9. Bill Cromartie and Jody H. Brown, *The Glamor Game*, pp. 109–111.

## 1941

1. 1942 El Rodeo Yearbook, p. 226.
2. Richard Cohen, Jordan Deutsch and David Neft, *Ohio State Scrapbook*, p. 108.
3. 1942 El Rodeo Yearbook, p. 229.
4. Ibid., p. 230.
5. Ibid., p. 232.
6. Ibid., p. 233.
7. Bill Cromartie and Jody H. Brown, *The Glamor Game*, pp. 116–118.
8. 1942 El Rodeo Yearbook, p. 235.
9. Ibid., p. 239.

## 1942

1. 1943 El Rodeo Yearbook, p. 230.
2. Ibid., p. 232.
3. Ibid., p. 234.
4. Ibid., p. 236.
5. Ibid., p. 238.
6. Ibid., p. 240.
7. Ibid., p. 242.
8. Bill Cromartie and Jody H. Brown, *The Glamor Game*, pp. 122–126.
9. 1943 El Rodeo Yearbook, p. 246.
10. Ibid., p. 248.
11. 2011 USC Football Media Guide, p. 83.

## 1943

1. 1944 El Rodeo Yearbook, p. 170.
2. Ibid., p. 171.
3. Ibid., p. 172.
4. Ibid., p. 173.
5. Ibid., p. 174.
6. Ibid., p. 175.
7. Ibid., p. 176.
8. Ibid., p. 177.
9. Ibid., p. 178.
10. Ibid., p. 168.

## 1944

1. 1945 El Rodeo Yearbook, p. 170.
2. Ibid., p. 171.
3. Ibid., p. 172.
4. Ibid., p. 173.
5. Ibid., p. 174.
6. Ibid., p. 175.
7. Ibid., p. 176.
8. Ibid., p. 177.
9. *Daily Trojan*, Nov. 27, 1944, p. 1.
10. 1945 El Rodeo Yearbook, p. 169.

## 1945

1. *Daily Trojan*, Sept. 24, 1945, p. 1.
2. Ibid., Oct. 1, p. 1.
3. Ibid., Oct. 8, p. 1.
4. 1946 El Rodeo Yearbook, p. 248.
5. Ibid., p. 250.
6. Ibid., p. 252.
7. Ibid., p. 254.
8. Ibid., p. 256.
9. Ibid., p. 258.
10. Ibid., p. 260.
11. Ibid., p. 262.

## 1946

1. 1947 El Rodeo Yearbook, p. 213.
2. Ibid., p. 215.
3. Ibid., p. 217.
4. Ibid., p. 219.
5. Ibid., p. 221.
6. Ibid., p. 223.
7. Ibid., p. 225.
8. Ibid., p. 227.
9. Bill Cromartie and Jody H. Brown, *The Glamor Game*, pp. 129–131.
10. 1947 El Rodeo Yearbook, p. 231.

## 1947

1. 1948 El Rodeo Yearbook, p. 212.
2. *Daily Trojan*, Oct. 6, 1947, p. 1.
3. 1948 El Rodeo Yearbook, p. 216.
4. *Daily Trojan*, Oct. 20, 1947, p. 1.
5. Ibid., Oct. 27, p. 1.
6. Ibid., Nov. 3, p. 1.
7. Ibid., Nov. 10, p. 1.
8. Ibid., Nov. 24, p. 1.
9. Bill Cromartie and Jody H. Brown, *The Glamor Game*, pp. 134–146.
10. *Daily Trojan*, Jan. 5, 1948, p. 1.

## 1948

1. *Daily Trojan*, Sept. 20, 1948, p. 3.
2. 1949 El Rodeo Yearbook, p. 222.
3. *Daily Trojan*, Oct. 4, 1948, p. 1.
4. 1949 El Rodeo Yearbook, p. 224.
5. Ibid., p. 226.
6. Ibid., p. 228.
7. Ibid., p. 230.
8. Ibid., p. 232.
9. Ibid., p. 234.
10. Bill Cromartie and Jody H. Brown, *The Glamor Game*, pp. 140–144.

## 1949

1. 1950 El Rodeo Yearbook, p. 238.
2. Ibid., p. 240.
3. Ibid., p. 243.
4. Ibid., p. 244.
5. Ibid., p. 247.
6. Ibid., p. 249.
7. Ibid., p. 251.
8. Ibid., p. 252.
9. Bill Cromartie and Jody H. Brown, *The Glamor Game*, pp. 146–149.

## 1950

1. 1951 El Rodeo Yearbook, p. 171.
2. Ibid., p. 172.
3. Ibid., p. 175.
4. Ibid., p. 177.
5. Ibid., p. 178.
6. Ibid., p. 181.
7. Ibid., p. 182.
8. Ibid., p. 185.
9. Bill Cromartie and Jody H. Brown, *The Glamor Game*, pp. 151–156.

### 1951

1. 1952 El Rodeo Yearbook, p. 71.
2. Ibid., p. 73.
3. Ibid., p. 75.
4. Ibid., p. 77.
5. Ibid., p. 78.
6. Ibid., p. 81.
7. Ibid., p. 82.
8. Ibid., p. 85.
9. Ibid., p. 87.
10. Bill Cromartie and Jody H. Brown, *The Glamor Game*, pp. 159–162.

### 1952

1. *Daily Trojan*, Sept. 22, 1952, p. 1.
2. Ibid., Sept. 29, p. 1.
3. Ibid., Oct. 6, p. 1.
4. Ibid., Oct. 13, p. 1.
5. Ibid., Oct. 20, p. 3.
6. Ibid., Oct. 27, p. 1.
7. Ibid., Nov. 10, p. 1.
8. Ibid., Nov. 17, p. 1.
9. Ibid., Nov. 24, p. 1.
10. Bill Cromartie and Jody H. Brown, *The Glamor Game*, pp. 159–162.
11. *Daily Trojan*, Jan. 5, 1953, p. 1.

### 1953

1. 1953 El Rodeo Yearbook, p. 220.
2. Ibid., p. 222.
3. Ibid., p. 224.
4. Ibid., p. 226.
5. Ibid., p. 228.
6. Ibid., p. 230.
7. Ibid., p. 232.
8. Ibid., p. 235.
9. Ibid., p. 236.
10. Bill Cromartie and Jody H. Brown, *The Glamor Game*, pp. 169–174.

### 1954

1. 1955 El Rodeo Yearbook, p. 189.
2. Ibid., p. 190.
3. Ibid., p. 192.
4. Ibid., p. 195.
5. Ibid., p. 197.
6. Ibid., p. 199.
7. Ibid., p. 201.
8. Ibid., p. 202.
9. Ibid., p. 205.
10. *Daily Trojan*, Nov. 22, 1954, p. 1.
11. Bill Cromartie and Jody H. Brown, *The Glamor Game*, pp. 175–178.
12. *Daily Trojan*, Jan. 3, 1955, p. 1.

### 1955

1. 1956 El Rodeo Yearbook, p. 168.
2. Ibid., p. 170.
3. Ibid., p. 173.
4. Ibid., p. 174.
5. Ibid., p. 176.
6. Ibid., p. 178.
7. Ibid., p. 181.
8. Ibid., p. 183.
9. *Daily Trojan*, Nov. 21, 1955, p. 1.
10. Bill Cromartie and Jody H. Brown, *The Glamor Game*, pp. 181–184.

### 1956

1. 1957 El Rodeo Yearbook, p. 254.
2. Ibid., p. 255.
3. Ibid., p. 256.
4. Ibid., p. 257.
5. Ibid., p. 258.
6. Ibid., p. 259.
7. Ibid., p. 260.
8. Ibid., p. 261.
9. *Daily Trojan*, Nov. 26, 1956, p. 1.
10. Bill Cromartie and Jody H. Brown, *The Glamor Game*, pp. 191–192.

### 1957

1. 1958 El Rodeo Yearbook, p. 276.
2. Ibid., p. 277.
3. Ibid., p. 278.
4. Ibid., p. 280.
5. Ibid., p. 282.
6. Ibid., p. 283.
7. Ibid., p. 284.
8. Ibid., p. 286.
9. Ibid., p. 287.
10. Bill Cromartie and Jody H. Brown, *The Glamor Game*, pp. 196–197.

### 1958

1. 1959 El Rodeo Yearbook, p. 300.
2. Ibid., p. 301.
3. Ibid., p. 302.
4. Ibid., p. 304.
5. Ibid., p. 305.
6. Ibid., p. 306.
7. Ibid., p. 308.
8. Ibid., p. 310.
9. *Daily Trojan*, Nov. 24, 1958, p. 4.
10. Bill Cromartie and Jody H. Brown, *The Glamor Game*, pp. 200–203.

### 1959

1. *Daily Trojan*, Sept. 22, 1959, p. 4.
2. Ibid., Sept. 28, p. 8.
3. Ibid., Oct. 5, p. 4.
4. Ibid., Oct. 19, p. 4.
5. Ibid., Oct. 26, p. 4.
6. Ibid., Nov. 3, p. 4.
7. Ibid., Nov. 9, p. 4.
8. Ibid., Nov. 16, p. 4.
9. Ibid., Nov. 23, p. 4.
10. Bill Cromartie and Jody H. Brown, *The Glamor Game*, pp. 206–208.

### 1960

1. 1961 El Rodeo Yearbook, p. 270.
2. Ibid., p. 272.
3. Ibid., p. 274.
4. Ibid., p. 275.
5. Ibid., p. 277.
6. Ibid., p. 278.
7. Ibid., p. 279.
8. Ibid., p. 280.
9. *Los Angeles Times*, Nov. 20, 1960, p. G-1.
10. Bill Cromartie and Jody H. Brown, *The Glamor Game*, pp. 209–212.

### 1961

1. 1962 El Rodeo Yearbook, p. 269.
2. Ibid., p. 271.
3. Ibid., p. 272.
4. Bill Cromartie and Jody H. Brown, *The Glamor Game*, pp. 215–217.
5. 1962 El Rodeo Yearbook, p. 276.
6. Ibid., p. 278.
7. *Daily Trojan*, Nov. 6, 1961, p. 4.
8. 1962 El Rodeo Yearbook, p. 283.
9. Ibid., p. 284.
10. *Los Angeles Times*, Nov. 26, 1961, p. L-1.

### 1962

1. *Los Angeles Times*, Sept. 23, 1962, p. C-1.
2. Ibid., Sept. 30, p. C-1.
3. 1963 El Rodeo Yearbook, p. 217.
4. Ibid., p. 218.
5. Ibid., p. 220.
6. Ibid., p. 222.
7. Ibid., p. 225.
8. Ibid., p. 226.
9. Ibid., p. 228.
10. Bill Cromartie and Jody H. Brown, *The Glamor Game*, pp. 220–222.
11. *Los Angeles Times*, Jan. 2, 1963, p. B-1.

### 1963

1. *Daily Trojan*, Sept. 24, 1963, p. 4.
2. Ibid., Sept. 30, p. 4.
3. 1964 El Rodeo Yearbook, p. 250.
4. Bill Cromartie and Jody H. Brown, *The Glamor Game*, pp. 227–229.
5. 1964 El Rodeo Yearbook, 253.
6. *Daily Trojan*, Sept. 29, p. 4.
7. Ibid., Nov. 4, p. 4.
8. Ibid., Nov. 11, p. 4.
9. Ibid., Nov. 18, p. 4.
10. *Los Angeles Times*, Dec. 1, 1963, p. J-1.

### 1964

1. *Daily Trojan*, Sept. 22, 1964, p. 5.
2. Ibid., Sept. 28, p. 4.
3. Ibid., Oct. 5, p. 4.
4. Ibid., Oct. 12, p. 4.
5. Ibid., Oct. 19, p. 4.
6. 1965 El Rodeo Yearbook, p. 217.
7. Ibid.
8. *Daily Trojan*, Nov. 10, 1964, p. 4.
9. 1965 El Rodeo Yearbook, p. 219.
10. Bill Cromartie and Jody H. Brown, *The Glamor Game*, pp. 233–238.

### 1965

1. 1966 El Rodeo Yearbook, p. 383.
2. Ibid., p. 385.
3. Ibid., p. 386.
4. Ibid., p. 389.
5. Ibid., p. 391.
6. Bill Cromartie and Jody H. Brown, *The Glamor Game*, pp. 240–245.
7. 1966 El Rodeo Yearbook, p. 392.
8. Ibid., p. 396.
9. *Los Angeles Times*, Nov. 21, 1965, p. H-1.
10. 1966 El Rodeo Yearbook, p. 400.

### 1966

1. 1967 El Rodeo Yearbook, p. 38.
2. Ibid., p. 42.
3. *Daily Trojan*, Oct. 3, 1966, p. 4.
4. 1967 El Rodeo Yearbook, p. 61.
5. Ibid., p. 73.
6. Ibid., p. 78.
7. Ibid., p. 87.
8. Ibid., pp. 92–94.
9. *Los Angeles Times*, Nov. 20, 1966, p. C-1.
10. Bill Cromartie and Jody H. Brown, *The Glamor Game*, pp. 249–251.
11. *Los Angeles Times*, Jan. 3, 1967, p. 1.

### 1967

1. 1968 El Rodeo Yearbook, p. 56.
2. *Daily Trojan*, Sept. 25, 1967, p. 4.
3. Ibid., Oct. 2, p. 4.
4. Ibid., Oct. 9, p. 4.
5. Bill Cromartie and Jody H. Brown, *The Glamor Game*, pp. 256–257.
6. 1968 El Rodeo Yearbook, p. 59.
7. *Daily Trojan*, Oct. 30, 1967, p. 4.
8. 1968 El Rodeo Yearbook, p. 60.
9. Ibid., pp. 60–61.
10. *Daily Trojan*, Nov. 20, 1967, p. 1.
11. Ibid., Jan. 3, 1968, p. 1.

### 1968

1. *Daily Trojan*, Sept. 23, 1968, p. 4.
2. 1969 El Rodeo Yearbook, p. 225.
3. *Daily Trojan*, Oct. 8, 1968, p. 4.
4. 1969 El Rodeo Yearbook, p. 227.
5. Ibid., p. 228.
6. *Daily Trojan*, Nov. 5, 1968, p. 7.
7. Ibid., Nov. 11, p. 4.
8. Ibid., Nov. 18, p. 4.
9. Ibid., Nov. 25, p. 4.
10. Bill Cromartie and Jody H. Brown, *The Glamor Game*, pp. 262–264.
11. *Daily Trojan*, Jan. 7, 1969, p. 4.

### 1969

1. 1970 El Rodeo Yearbook, p. 248.
2. *Daily Trojan*, Sept. 29, 1969, p. 13.
3. Ibid., Oct. 6, p. 22.
4. 1970 El Rodeo Yearbook, pp. 252–254.
5. Bill Cromartie and Jody H. Brown, *The Glamor Game*, pp. 268–270.

6. *Daily Trojan*, Oct. 27, p. 21.
7. Ibid., Nov. 4, p. 8.
8. Ibid., Nov. 10, p. 20.
9. Ibid., Nov. 17, p. 21.
10. *Los Angeles Times*, Nov. 23, 1969, p. G-1.
11. Ibid., Jan. 2, 1970, p. B-1.

## 1970

1. *Los Angeles Times*, Sept. 13, 1970, p. C-1.
2. Ibid., Sept. 20, p. C-1.
3. *Daily Trojan*, Sept. 28, p. 20.
4. Ibid., Oct. 5, p. 29.
5. *Los Angeles Times*, Oct. 11, 1970, p. B-1.
6. Ibid., Oct. 18, p. B-1.
7. *Daily Trojan*, Oct. 26, p. 20.
8. Ibid., Nov. 3, p. 21.
9. Ibid., Nov. 9, p. 16.
10. *Los Angeles Times*, Nov. 22, 1970, p. B-1.
11. Bill Cromartie and Jody H. Brown, *The Glamor Game*, pp. 272–277.

## 1971

1. *Daily Trojan*, Sept. 15, 1971, p. 29.
2. Ibid., Sept. 20, p. 8.
3. Ibid., Sept. 27, p. 4.
4. Ibid., Oct. 5, p. 8.
5. Ibid., Oct. 12, p. 8.
6. Ibid., Oct. 18, p. 20.
7. Bill Cromartie and Jody H. Brown, *The Glamor Game*, pp. 281–285.
8. *Daily Trojan*, Nov. 1, 1971, p. 29.
9. Ibid., Nov. 8, p. 4.
10. Ibid., Nov. 15, p. 28.
11. Ibid., Nov. 22, p. 4.

## 1972

1. *Daily Trojan*, Sept. 13, 1972, p. 72.
2. Ibid., Sept. 19, p. 8.
3. Ibid., Sept. 25, p. 11.
4. Ibid., Oct. 2, p. 11.
5. Ibid., Oct. 10, p. 8.
6. Ibid., Oct. 16, p. 12.
7. Ibid., Oct. 21, p. 8.
8. Ibid., Oct. 30, p. 11.
9. Ibid., Nov. 4, p. 12.
10. Ibid., Nov. 20, p. 10.
11. Bill Cromartie and Jody H. Brown, *The Glamor Game*, pp. 288–291.
12. *Los Angeles Times*, Jan. 2, 1973, p. A-1.

## 1973

1. *Daily Trojan*, Sept. 18, 1973, p. 12.
2. Ibid., Sept. 25, p. 8.
3. Ibid., Oct. 1, p. 8.
4. Ibid., Oct. 9, p. 8.
5. Ibid., Oct. 16, p. 8.
6. Ibid., Oct. 23, p. 8.
7. Bill Cromartie and Jody H. Brown, *The Glamor Game*, pp. 294–300.
8. *Daily Trojan*, Nov. 6, p. 8.
9. Ibid., Nov. 12, p. 8.
10. Ibid., Nov. 20, p. 9.
11. Ibid., Nov. 27, p. 8.
12. Ibid., Jan. 8, 1974, p. 8.

## 1974

1. *Daily Trojan*, Sept. 17, 1974, p. 12.
2. Ibid., Oct. 1, p. 11.
3. Ibid., Oct. 8, p. 12.
4. Ibid., Oct. 15, p. 15.
5. Ibid., Oct. 22, p. 8.
6. Ibid., Oct. 29, p. 12.
7. Ibid., Nov. 5, p. 11.
8. Ibid., Nov. 12, p. 12.
9. Ibid., Nov. 19, p. 12.
10. Ibid., Nov. 26, p. 11.
11. Bill Cromartie and Jody H. Brown, *The Glamor Game*, pp. 304–309.
12. *Daily Trojan*, Jan. 7, 1975, p. 11.

## 1975

1. *Daily Trojan*, Sept. 17, 1975, p. 16.
2. Ibid., Sept. 23, p. 8.
3. Ibid., Sept. 30, p. 8.
4. Ibid., Oct. 7, p. 8.
5. Ibid., Oct. 14, p. 8.
6. Ibid., Oct. 21, p. 8.
7. Bill Cromartie and Jody H. Brown, *The Glamor Game*, pp. 311–314.
8. *Daily Trojan*, Nov. 4, p. 8.
9. Ibid., Nov. 11, p. 8.
10. Ibid., Nov. 18, p. 8.
11. Ibid., Dec. 2, p. 1.
12. *Los Angeles Times*, Dec. 22, 1975, p. E-1.

## 1976

1. *Daily Trojan*, Sept. 14, 1976, p. 45.
2. Ibid., Sept. 21, p. 16.
3. *Los Angeles Times*, Sept. 26, p. D-1.
4. *Daily Trojan*, Oct. 5, p. 16.
5. Ibid., Oct. 12, p. 1.
6. Ibid., Oct. 25, p. 8.
7. *Los Angeles Times*, Oct. 31, 1976, p. D-1.
8. *Daily Trojan*, Nov. 9, p. 16.
9. Ibid., Nov. 15, p. 12.
10. *Los Angeles Times*, Nov. 21, p. D-1.
11. Bill Cromartie and Jody H. Brown, *The Glamor Game*, pp. 320–322.
12. *Los Angeles Times*, Jan. 2, 1977, p. A-1.

## 1977

1. 1978 El Rodeo Yearbook, p. 220.
2. *Daily Trojan*, Sept. 20, 1977, p. 24.
3. Ibid., Sept. 26, p. 8.
4. 1978 El Rodeo Yearbook, p. 225.
5. *Daily Trojan*, Oct. 11, p. 16.
6. 1978 El Rodeo Yearbook, p. 228.
7. Bill Cromartie and Jody H. Brown, *The Glamor Game*, pp. 324–329.
8. *Daily Trojan*, Nov. 1, p. 16.
9. Ibid., Nov. 7, p. 11.
10. 1978 El Rodeo Yearbook, p. 229.
11. *Los Angeles Times*, Nov. 26, 1977, p. C-1.
12. Ibid., Jan. 2, 1978, p. D-1.

## 1978

1. *Los Angeles Times*, Sept. 10, 1978, Part III, p. 1.
2. Ibid., Sept. 17, Part III, p. 1.
3. Ibid., Sept. 24, Part III, p. 1.
4. Ibid., Sept. 30, Part III, p. 1.
5. Ibid., Oct. 15, Part III, p. 1.
6. Ibid., Oct. 22, Part III, p. 1.
7. Ibid., Oct. 29, Part III, p. 1.
8. Ibid., Nov. 5, Part III, p. 1.
9. Ibid., Nov. 12, Part III, p. 1.
10. Ibid., Nov. 19, Part III, p. 1.
11. Bill Cromartie and Jody H. Brown, *The Glamor Game*, pp. 334–337.
12. *Los Angeles Times*, Dec. 3, Part III, p. 1.
13. Ibid., Jan. 2, 1979, p. 1.

## 1979

1. *Los Angeles Times*, Sept. 9, 1979, Part III, p. 1.
2. Ibid., Sept. 16, Part III, p. 1.
3. Ibid., Sept. 23, Part III, p. 1.
4. Ibid., Sept. 30, Part III, p. 1.
5. Ibid., Oct. 7, Part III, p. 1.
6. Ibid., Oct. 14, Part III, p. 1.
7. Ibid., Oct. 21, Part III, p. 1.
8. Ibid., Oct. 28, Part III, p. 1.
9. 1980 El Rodeo Yearbook, p. 155.
10. *Los Angeles Times*, Nov. 11, 1979, Part III, p. 1.
11. Ibid., Nov. 25, Part III, p. 1.
12. Ibid., Jan. 2, 1980, p. 1.

## 1980

1. 1981 El Rodeo Yearbook, p. 145.
2. Ibid.
3. Ibid., p. 148.
4. Ibid., p. 147.
5. Ibid., p. 148.
6. Ibid., p. 153.
7. Ibid., p. 151.
8. *Daily Trojan*, Nov. 11, 1980, p. 16.
9. 1981 El Rodeo Yearbook, p. 153.
10. *Daily Trojan*, Nov. 24, 1980, p. 12.
11. Bill Cromartie and Jody H. Brown, *The Glamor Game*, pp. 346–351.

## 1981

1. 1982 El Rodeo Yearbook, p. 212.
2. Ibid., p. 213.
3. Ibid., p. 214.
4. *Sports Illustrated*, Oct. 12, 1981, p. 62.
5. Ibid., Oct. 19, p. 91.
6. *Daily Trojan*, Oct. 19, p. 12.
7. Bill Cromartie and Jody H. Brown, *The Glamor Game*, pp. 352–356.
8. 1982 El Rodeo Yearbook, p. 216.
9. Ibid., p. 218.
10. Ibid., p. 224.
11. *Daily Trojan*, Nov. 23, p. 16.
12. *Los Angeles Times*, Jan. 2, 1982, p. C-1.

## 1982

1. *Daily Trojan*, Sept. 13, 1982, p. 16.
2. Ibid., Sept. 20, p. 12.
3. Ibid., Sept. 27, p. 12.
4. 1983 El Rodeo Yearbook, p. 261.
5. *Daily Trojan*, Oct. 19, p. 20.
6. Ibid., Oct. 25, p. 12.
7. 1983 El Rodeo Yearbook, p. 265.
8. Ibid., p. 266.
9. Ibid., p. 269.
10. *Daily Trojan*, Nov. 22, p. 12.
11. Bill Cromartie and Jody H. Brown, *The Glamor Game*, pp. 359–363.

## 1983

1. 1984 El Rodeo Yearbook, p. 188.
2. Ibid., p. 189.
3. Ibid. p. 190.
4. Ibid., p. 192.
5. Ibid., p. 193.
6. Ibid., p. 195.
7. Bill Cromartie and Jody H. Brown, *The Glamor Game*, pp. 364–368.
8. 1984 El Rodeo Yearbook, p. 201.
9. Ibid., p. 198.
10. Ibid., p. 204.
11. *Daily Trojan*, Nov. 21, 1983, p. 12.

## 1984

1. 1981 El Rodeo Yearbook, p. 314.
2. Ibid., p. 312.
3. Ibid., p. 314.
4. Ibid., p. 316.
5. Ibid., p. 317.
6. Ibid., p. 318.
7. Ibid., p. 320.
8. Ibid., p. 322.
9. Ibid., p. 324.
10. *Daily Trojan*, Nov. 19, 1984, p. 8.
11. Bill Cromartie and Jody H. Brown, *The Glamor Game*, pp. 369–372.
12. *Daily Trojan*, Jan. 11, 1985, p. 32.

## 1985

1. 1986 El Rodeo Yearbook, p. 312.
2. Ibid., p. 314.
3. Ibid., p. 316.
4. *Daily Trojan*, Oct. 7, 1985, p. 16.
5. 1986 El Rodeo Yearbook, p. 318.
6. Bill Cromartie and Jody H. Brown, *The Glamor Game*, pp. 374–378.
7. 1986 El Rodeo Yearbook, p. 320.
8. Ibid., p. 330.
9. Ibid., p. 324.
10. *Daily Trojan*, Nov. 25, 1985, p. 15.
11. 1986 El Rodeo Yearbook, p. 332.
12. *Los Angeles Times*, Dec. 29, 1985, p. 1.

### 1986

1. 1987 El Rodeo Yearbook, p. 146.
2. Ibid., p. 148.
3. Ibid., p. 152.
4. Ibid., p. 156.
5. Ibid.
6. Ibid., p. 150.
7. Ibid., p. 154.
8. Ibid., p. 164.
9. Ibid., p. 160.
10. *Los Angeles Times*, Nov. 23, 1986, p. 1.
11. Bill Cromartie and Jody H. Brown, *The Glamor Game*, pp. 384–390.
12. *Los Angeles Times*, Jan. 2, 1987, p. 10.

### 1987

1. 1988 El Rodeo Yearbook, p. 246.
2. *Los Angeles Times*, Sept. 20, 1987, Part III, p. 1.
3. Ibid., Sept. 27, Part III, p. 1.
4. Ibid., Oct. 4, Part III, p. 1.
5. Ibid., Oct. 11, Part III, p. 1.
6. Ibid., Oct. 18, Part III, p. 1.
7. Bill Cromartie and Jody H. Brown, *The Glamor Game*, pp. 391–395.
8. *Los Angeles Times*, Nov. 1, 1987, Part III, p. 1.
9. Ibid., Nov. 8, Part III, p. 1.
10. Ibid., Nov. 15, Part III, p. 1.
11. Ibid., Nov. 22, Part III, p. 1.
12. Ibid., Jan 2, 1988, p. 1.

### 1988

1. *Los Angeles Times*, Sept. 2, 1988, Part III, p. 1.
2. Ibid., Sept. 11, Part III, p. 1.
3. Ibid., Sept. 25, Part III, p. 1.
4. Ibid., Oct. 2, Part III, p. 1.
5. Ibid., Oct. 9, Part III, p. 1.
6. Ibid., Oct. 16, Part III, p. 1.
7. Ibid., Oct. 30, Part III, p. 1.
8. Ibid., Nov. 6, Part III, p. 1.
9. Ibid., Nov. 13, Part III, p. 1.
10. Ibid., Nov. 20, Part III, p. 1.
11. Bill Cromartie and Jody H. Brown, *The Glamor Game*, pp. 396–401.
12. *Los Angeles Times*, Jan. 3, 1989, Sports Section p. 1.

### 1989

1. *Los Angeles Times*, Sept. 5, 1989, Part III, p. 1.
2. Ibid., Sept. 17, Part III, p. 1.
3. Ibid., Sept. 24, Part III, p. 1.
4. Ibid., Oct. 1, Part III, p. 1.
5. Ibid., Oct. 8, Part III, p. 1.
6. Ibid., Oct. 15, Part III, p. 1.
7. *Los Angeles Times*, Oct. 22, 1989, p. C-1.
8. Ibid., Oct. 29, Part III, p. 1.
9. Ibid., Nov. 5, Part III, p. 1.
10. Ibid., Nov. 12, Part III, p. 1.
11. Ibid., Nov. 19, Part III, p. 1.
12. 2011 USC Football Media Guide, p. 102.

### 1990

1. *Daily Trojan*, Sept. 5, 1990, p. 44.
2. 1991 El Rodeo Yearbook, p. 179.
3. Ibid., p. 182.
4. Ibid., p. 179.
5. Ibid., p. 183.
6. Ibid., p. 181.
7. Ibid., p. 186.
8. Ibid., p. 187.
9. Ibid., p. 190.
10. Ibid., p. 191.
11. *Los Angeles Times*, Nov. 18, 1990, p. C-1.
12. Ibid., Nov. 25, 1990, p. 1.
13. 2011 USC Football Media Guide, p. 102.
14. Wikipedia, Todd Marinovich.

### 1991

1. 1992 El Rodeo Yearbook, p. 164.
2. Ibid., p. 168.
3. Ibid., p. 173.
4. Ibid., p. 165.
5. Ibid., p. 176.
6. Ibid., p. 162.
7. *Daily Trojan*, Oct. 28, 1991, p. 14.
8. 1992 El Rodeo Yearbook, p. 170.
9. Ibid., p. 179.
10. Ibid., p. 177.
11. *Los Angeles Times*, Nov. 24, 1991, p. C-1.

### 1992

1. *Los Angeles Times*, Sept. 6, 1992, p. 1.
2. 1993 El Rodeo Yearbook, p. 74.
3. Ibid., p. 77.
4. Ibid., p. 78.
5. Ibid., p. 80.
6. Ibid., p. 82.
7. Ibid., p. 84.
8. Ibid., p. 86.
9. Ibid., p. 88.
10. *Los Angeles Times*, Nov. 22, 1992, p. C-1.
11. Ibid., Nov. 29, p. C-1.
12. Ibid., Dec. 30, p. C-1.

### 1993

1. 1994 El Rodeo Yearbook, p. 76.
2. Ibid., p. 77.
3. Ibid., p. 78.
4. Ibid., p. 79.
5. Ibid., p. 80.
6. Ibid., p. 81.
7. Ibid., p. 82.
8. *Los Angeles Times*, Oct. 24, 1993, p. C-1.
9. 1994 El Rodeo Yearbook, p. 86.
10. *Daily Trojan*, Nov. 8, 1993, p. 15.
11. 1994 El Rodeo Yearbook, p. 90.
12. *Los Angeles Times*, Nov. 21, 1993, p. C-1.
13. 2011 USC Football Media Guide, p. 103.

### 1994

1. 1995 El Rodeo Yearbook, p. 76.
2. Ibid., p. 78.
3. Ibid.
4. Ibid., p. 81.
5. Ibid.
6. Ibid., p. 82.
7. *Daily Trojan*, Oct. 24, 1994, p. 20.
8. 1995 El Rodeo Yearbook, p. 87.
9. Ibid.
10. *Los Angeles Times*, Nov. 20, 1994, p. C-1.
11. *Daily Trojan*, Nov. 29, 1994, p. 20.
12. 2011 USC Football Media Guide, p. 103.

### 1995

1. 1996 El Rodeo Yearbook, p. 52.
2. *Daily Trojan*, Sept. 18, 1995, p. 12.
3. Ibid., Sept. 25, p. 15.
4. 1996 El Rodeo Yearbook, p. 56.
5. Ibid., p. 58.
6. Ibid., p. 60.
7. *Los Angeles Times*, Oct. 22, 1995, Sports Section p. 1.
8. 1996 El Rodeo Yearbook, p. 64.
9. *Daily Trojan*, Nov. 6, 1995, p. 20.
10. 1996 El Rodeo Yearbook, p. 68.
11. *Los Angeles Times*, Nov. 19, 1995, p. C-1.
12. Ibid., Jan. 2, 1996, p. 1.

### 1996

1. *Daily Trojan*, Aug. 28, 1996, p. 22.
2. Ibid., Sept. 9, p. 15.
3. Ibid., Sept. 16, p. 16.
4. Ibid., Sept. 23, p. 14.
5. Ibid., Oct. 7, p. 14.
6. Ibid., Oct. 14, p. 11.
7. Ibid., Oct. 21, p. 16.
8. Ibid., Oct. 28, p. 14.
9. Ibid., Nov. 4, p. 21.
10. Ibid., Nov. 12, p. 14.
11. *Los Angeles Times*, Nov. 24, 1996, p. C-1.
12. Ibid., Dec. 1, Sports Section, p. 1.

### 1997

1. 1998 El Rodeo Yearbook, p. 64.
2. Ibid., p. 66.
3. Ibid., p. 70.
4. Ibid., p. 64.
5. Ibid., p. 68.
6. *Los Angeles Times*, Oct. 19, 1997, Sports Section p. 1.
7. 1998 El Rodeo Yearbook, p. 68.
8. Ibid., p. 72.
9. Ibid., p. 76.
10. Ibid
11. *Los Angeles Times*, Nov. 22, 1997, p. C-1.

### 1998

1. *Los Angeles Times*, Aug. 31, 1998, p. 1.
2. Ibid., Sept. 13, p. 1.
3. Ibid., Sept. 20, p. 1.
4. Ibid., Sept. 27, p. 1.
5. Ibid., Oct. 4, p. 1.
6. Ibid., Oct. 11, p. 1.
7. *Daily Trojan*, Oct. 19, 1998, p. 16.
8. Ibid., Oct. 26, p. 28.
9. *Los Angeles Times*, Nov. 1, 1998, p. 1.
10. *Daily Trojan*, Nov. 10, 1998, p. 16.
11. *Los Angeles Times*, Nov. 22, 1998, p. 1.
12. Ibid., Nov. 29, p. 1.
13. Ibid., Jan. 1, 1999, p. 1.

### 1999

1. *Los Angeles Times*, Sept. 5, 1999, p. 1.
2. Ibid., Sept. 19, p. 1.
3. Ibid., Sept. 26, p. 1.
4. Ibid., Oct. 3, p. 1.
5. Ibid., Oct. 10, p. 1.
6. Ibid., Oct. 17, p. 1.
7. *Daily Trojan*, Oct. 25, 1999, p. 20.
8. *Los Angeles Times*, Oct. 31, 1999, p. 1.
9. Ibid., Nov. 7, p. 1.
10. *Daily Trojan*, Nov. 15, 1999, p. 16.
11. *Los Angeles Times*, Nov. 21, 1999, p. 1.
12. *Daily Trojan*, Nov. 30, 1999, p. 10.

### 2000

1. *Los Angeles Times*, Aug. 8, 2000, p. 1.
2. Ibid., Sept. 10, p. 1.
3. Ibid., Sept. 24, p. 1.
4. Ibid., Oct. 1, p. 1.
5. Ibid., Oct. 8, p. 1.
6. Ibid., Oct. 15, p. 1.
7. Ibid., Oct. 22, p. D-1.
8. Ibid., Oct. 29, p. D-1.
9. Ibid., Nov. 5, p. D-1.
10. Ibid., Nov. 12, p. D-1.
11. Ibid., Nov. 19, p. D-1.
12. Ibid., Nov. 26, p. D-1.

### 2001

1. *Los Angeles Times*, Sept. 2, 2001, p. S-1.
2. Ibid., Sept. 9, p. S-1.
3. Ibid., Sept. 23, p. S-1.
4. Ibid., Sept. 30, p. S-1.
5. Ibid., Oct. 7, p. S-1.
6. Ibid., Oct. 14, p. S-1.
7. Ibid., Oct. 21, p. S-1.
8. Ibid., Oct. 28, p. S-1.
9. Ibid., Nov. 4, p. S-1.
10. Ibid., Nov. 11, p. S-1.
11. Ibid., Nov. 18, p. S-1.
12. Ibid., Dec. 26, p. D-1.

### 2002

1. 2013 USC Football Media Guide, p. 119.
2. Ibid., p. 120.
3. Ibid., p. 121.
4. Ibid., p. 122.
5. Ibid., p. 123.
6. Ibid., p. 124.
7. Ibid., p.125.
8. Ibid., p. 126.
9. Ibid., p. 127.
10. Ibid., p. 128.
11. Ibid., p. 129.
12. Ibid., p. 130.
13. Ibid., p. 131.

### 2003

1. 2004 USC Football Media Guide, p. 126.
2. Ibid.
3. Ibid., p. 127.
4. Ibid., pp. 127–128.
5. Ibid., p. 128.

6. Ibid., pp. 128–129.
7. Ibid., p. 129.
8. Ibid., p. 130.
9. Ibid., pp. 130–131.
10. Ibid., p. 131.
11. Ibid., pp. 131–132.
12. Ibid., p. 132.
13. Ibid., p. 133.

### 2004

1. 2005 USC Football Media Guide, p. 65.
2. Ibid.
3. Ibid., p. 66.
4. Ibid.
5. Ibid., p. 67.
6. Ibid.
7. Ibid., p. 68.
8. Ibid.
9. Ibid., p. 69.
10. Ibid.
11. Ibid., p. 70.
12. Ibid.
13. Ibid., p. 71.

### 2005

1. 2006 USC Football Media Guide, p. 62.
2. Ibid.
3. Ibid., p. 63.
4. Ibid.
5. Ibid., p. 64.
6. Ibid.
7. Ibid., p. 65.
8. Ibid.
9. Ibid., p. 66.
10. Ibid.
11. Ibid., p. 67.
12. Ibid.
13. Ibid., p. 68.

### 2006

1. 2007 USC Football Media Guide, p. 64.
2. Ibid.
3. Ibid., p. 65.
4. Ibid.
5. Ibid., p. 66.
6. Ibid.
7. Ibid., p. 67.
8. Ibid.
9. Ibid., p. 68.
10. Ibid.
11. Ibid., p. 69.
12. Ibid.
13. Ibid., p. 70.

### 2007

1. 2008 USC Football Media Guide, p. 64.
2. Ibid.
3. Ibid., p. 65.
4. Ibid.
5. Ibid., p. 66.
6. Ibid.
7. Ibid., p. 67.
8. Ibid.
9. Ibid., p. 68.
10. Ibid.
11. Ibid., p. 69.
12. Ibid.
13. Ibid., p. 70.

### 2008

1. 2009 USC Football Media Guide, p. 64.
2. Ibid.
3. Ibid., p. 65.
4. Ibid.
5. Ibid., p. 66.
6. Ibid.
7. Ibid., p. 67.
8. Ibid.
9. Ibid., p. 68.
10. Ibid.
11. Ibid., p. 69.
12. Ibid.
13. Ibid., p. 70.

### 2009

1. *Los Angeles Times*, Sept. 6, 2009, p. C-1.
2. Ibid., Sept. 13, p. C-1.
3. Ibid., Sept. 20, p. C-1.
4. Ibid., Sept. 27, p. C-1.
5. Ibid., Oct. 4, p. C-1.
6. Ibid., Oct. 18, p. C-1.
7. Ibid., Oct. 25, p. C-1.
8. Ibid., Nov. 1, p. C-1.
9. Ibid., Nov. 8, p. C-1.
10. Ibid., Nov. 15, p. C-1.
11. Ibid., Nov. 29, p. C-1.
12. Ibid., Dec. 6, p. C-1.
13. Ibid., Dec. 27, p. C-1.

### 2010

1. 2011 USC Football Media Guide, p. 58.
2. Ibid.
3. Ibid., p. 59.
4. Ibid.
5. Ibid., p. 60.
6. Ibid., pp. 60–61.
7. Ibid., p. 61.
8. Ibid., pp. 61–62.
9. Ibid., p. 62.
10. Ibid., pp. 62–63.
11. Ibid., p. 63.
12. Ibid., pp. 63–64.
13. Ibid., p. 64.

### 2011

1. 2012 USC Football Media Guide, p. 59.
2. Ibid.
3. Ibid., p. 60.
4. Ibid.
5. Ibid., p. 61.
6. Ibid.
7. Ibid., p. 62.
8. Ibid.
9. Ibid., p. 63.
10. Ibid.
11. Ibid., p. 64.
12. Ibid.

### 2012

1. 2013 USC Football Media Guide, p. 59.
2. Ibid.
3. Ibid., p. 60.
4. Ibid.
5. Ibid., p. 61.
6. Ibid.
7. Ibid., p. 62.
8. Ibid.
9. Ibid., p. 63.
10. Ibid., p. 64.
11. Ibid.
12. Ibid.
13. *Cleveland Plain Dealer*, Jan. 1, 2013, p. D-3.

## *Chapter Two*

### Marcus Allen

1. *Sports Illustrated*, September 1, 1986, p. 28.
2. Richard J. Shmelter, *Raiders Encyclopedia*, p. 273.
3. Ibid.

### Jon Arnett

1. Steve Bisheff and Loel Schrader, *Fight On! The Colorful Story of USC Football*, p. 107.
2. 2013 USC Football Media Guide, p. 130.

### Johnny Baker

1. 2013 USC Football Media Guide, p. 128.

### Roy Baker

1. David Wharton, *USC Football: Yesterday & Today*, p. 21.

### Damon Bame

1. www.glendale.edu/index.aspx?page=637.
2. Ibid.
3. Ibid.
4. Steve Bisheff and Loel Schrader, *Fight On! The Colorful Story of USC Football*, pp. 331–332.
5. www.glendale.edu/index.aspx?page=637.

### Chip Banks

1. *The Augusta Chronicle*, August 25, 2000, "Laney's Glory Days."
2. John Robinson and Joe Jares, *Conquest: A Cavalcade of USC Football*, p. 68.
3. 2010 USC Football Media Guide, p. 137.

### Matt Barkley

1. *Sports Illustrated*, August 20, 2012, p. 71.
2. Ibid.
3. Ibid.
4. Ibid.
5. Ibid., p. 72.
6. Ibid.
7. Wikipedia, Matt Barkley.
8. *Sports Illustrated*, August 20, 2012, p. 72.
9. Wikipedia, Matt Barkley.
10. www.usctrojans.com/sports/m-footbl/mtt/barkley_matt00.html.
11. Wikipedia, Matt Barkley.

### Mike Battle

1. 2012 USC Football Media Guide, p. 130.
2. Steve Bisheff and Loel Schrader, *Fight On! The Colorful Story of USC Football*, p. 329.
3. IMDB, *C.C. and Company*.

### Hal Bedsole

1. *Sports Illustrated*, October 21, 1963.
2. 2013 USC Football Media Guide, p. 130.

### Ricky Bell

1. *Orlando Sentinel*, December 28, 1986.
2. *People Magazine*, October 20, 1975.
3. www.usctrojans.com/sports/m-footbl/spec-rel/091201aab.html.
4. 2010 USC Football Media Guide, p. 135.
5. Wikipedia, Ricky Bell.
6. Wikipedia, Dermatomyositis.

### Duane Bickett

1. Wikipedia, Glendale High School.
2. *Los Angeles Times*, May 9, 1985, p.10.
3. Ibid.
4. 2012 USC Football Media Guide.

### Tony Boselli

1. *Los Angeles Times*, October 11, 1991, p. C-4.
2. 2013 USC Football Media Guide, p. 138.

### Tay Brown

1. 2013 USC Football Media Guide, p. 128.

### Willie Brown

1. Steve Bisheff and Loel Schrader, *Fight On! The Colorful Story of USC Football,* pp. 327–328.
2. saas.usc.edu/about/staff/willie-brown/.
3. Ibid.
4. Ibid.

### Brad Budde

1. 2010 USC Football Media Guide, p. 136.
2. Ibid.

### Reggie Bush

1. Steve Bisheff and Loel Schrader, *Fight On! The Colorful Story of USC Football*, p. 287.
2. Ibid., p. 288.
3. www.usctrojans.com/sports/m-footbl/mtt/bush_reggie00.html.
4. Ibid.
5. Wikipedia, Reggie Bush.
6. Bisheff and Schrader, p. 289.
7. 2012 USC Football Media Guide, pp. 137–138.
8. Wikipedia, Reggie Bush.
9. 2012 USC Football Media Guide, pp. 137–138.
10. Wikipedia, Reggie Bush.
11. Ibid.
12. Ibid.
13. Ibid.

### Mark Carrier

1. Wikipedia, Long Beach Polytechnic High School.
2. 2013 USC Football Media Guide, p. 137.

### Chris Claiborne

1. 2013 USC Football Media Guide, p. 138.

### Paul Cleary

1. *Los Angeles Times*, July 14, 1990, p. 1.
2. Ibid.
3. Ibid.
4. 2013 USC Football Media Guide, p. 129.

### Shaun Cody

1. www.usclegends.org/shauncody.php.
2. Ibid.

### Sam Cunningham

1. John Robinson and Joe Jares, *Conquest: A Cavalcade of USC Football*, p. 55.
2. Ibid.
3. 2013 USC Football Media Guide, p. 133.

### Anthony Davis

1. Wikipedia, Anthony Davis.
2. 2013 USC Football Media Guide, p. 133.
3. Ibid.

### Clarence Davis

1. John Lombardo, *Raiders Forever*, p. 132.
2. Ibid.
3. Ibid., p. 131.
4. Richard J. Shmelter, *Raiders Encyclopedia*, p. 283.

### Charley Dean

1. Wikipedia, Calexico, California .
2. 1923 El Rodeo Yearbook, p. 143.

### Jack Del Rio

1. 2013 USC Football Media Guide, p. 136.
2. Ibid.
3. Ibid.

### Morley Drury

1. *Los Angeles Times*, January 24, 1989, Sports Section p. 3.
2. John Robinson and Joe Jares, *Conquest: A Cavalcade of USC Football*, p. 35.
3. *Los Angeles Times*, January 24, 1989, Sports Section p. 3.
4. Robinson and Jares, *Conquest: A Cavalcade of USC Football*, p. 35.
5. Ibid.
6. Ibid.
7. 2013 USC Football Media Guide, p. 127.
8. *Los Angeles Times*, January 24, 1989, Sports Section p. 3.

### Sedrick Ellis

1. www.usctrojans.com/sports/m-footbl/mtt/ellis_sedrick00.html.
2. Ibid.
3. Wikipedia, Sedrick Ellis.
4. Ibid.

### John Ferraro

1. Wikipedia, John Ferraro.
2. John Robinson and Joe Jares, *Conquest: A Cavalcade of USC Football*, p. 38.
3. Wikipedia, John Ferraro.
4. 2013 USC Football Media Guide, p. 129.
5. John Robinson and Joe Jares, *Conquest: A Cavalcade of USC Football*, p. 38.
6. Wikipedia, John Ferraro.
7. Ibid.

### Roy Foster

1. 2013 USC Football Media Guide, p. 136.

### Mike Garrett

1. Steve Bisheff and Loel Schrader, *Fight On! The Colorful Story of USC Football*, p. 151.
2. Ibid., p. 152.
3. Ibid.
4. Ibid., p. 153.
5. *Pro Magazine*, December 1982, pp. 68–69.
6. 2010 USC Football Media Guide, p. 132.
7. Bisheff and Schrader, p. 152.
8. 2010 USC Football Media Guide, p. 132.
9. Wikipedia, Mike Garrett.

### Frank Gifford

1. www.espn.go.com/classic/biography/s/Gifford_Frank.html.
2. Ibid.
3. Steve Bisheff and Loel Schrader, *Fight On! The Colorful Story of USC Football*, pp. 100–101.
4. 2013 USC Football Media Guide, p. 129.
5. Wikipedia, Frank Gifford.

### Marv Goux

1. John Robinson and Joe Jares, *Conquest: A Cavalcade of USC Football*, p. 40.
2. *Los Angeles Times*, July 28, 2002, p. B-15.
3. Steve Bisheff and Loel Schrader, *Fight On! The Colorful Story of USC Football*, pp. 160–162.

### Jimmy Gunn

1. 2012 USC Football Media Guide, p. 130.
2. Steve Bisheff and Loel Schrader, *Fight On! The Colorful Story of USC Football*, p. 335.
3. 2012 USC Football Media Guide, p. 130.

### Pat Haden

1. Wikipedia, Pat Haden.
2. Ibid.

### Jesse Hibbs

1. 2013 USC Football Media Guide, p. 127.
2. Wikipedia, Jess Hibbs.

### Dwayne Jarrett

1. Wikipedia, Dwayne Jarrett.
2. 2013 USC Football Media Guide, p. 140.

### Gary Jeter

1. John Robinson and Joe Jares, *Conquest: A Cavalcade of USC Football*, p. 59.
2. Ibid.
3. 2012 USC Football Media Guide, p. 132.

### Keyshawn Johnson

1. Wikipedia, Keyshawn Johnson.
2. Steve Bisheff and Loel Schrader, *Fight On! The Colorful Story of USC Football*, p. 343.
3. 2013 USC Football Media Guide, p. 138.

### Mort Kaer

1. 2013 USC Football Media Guide, p. 127.
2. Wikipedia, Mort Kaer.
3. 2013 USC Football Media Guide, p. 127.

### Ryan Kalil

1. Wikipedia, Servite High School.
2. Wikipedia, Ryan Kalil.
3. Ibid.
4. 2012 USC Football Media Guide, p. 138.

### Desmond Koch

1. www.sports-reference.com/olympics/athletes/ko/des-koch-1.html.
2. Ibid.
3. Ibid.

### Grenville Lansdell

1. Wikipedia, Grenville Lansdell.
2. 2013 USC Football Media Guide, p. 129.

### Matt Leinart

1. Steve Bisheff and Loel Schrader, *Fight On! The Colorful Story of USC Football*, p. 281.
2. Ibid.
3. Wikipedia, Mater Dei High School.
4. Wikipedia, Matt Leinart.
5. Ibid.
6. Bisheff and Schrader, p. 281.
7. Wikipedia, Matt Leinart.
8. 2012 USC Football Media Guide, p. 137.
9. Ibid.
10. Ibid.
11. Ibid.
12. Ibid.

### Ronnie Lott

1. Wikipedia, Ronnie Lott.
2. Ibid.
3. 2013 USC Football Media Guide, p. 135.

### Frank Malette

1. 1918 El Rodeo Yearbook, p.62.

### Bruce Matthews

1. Wikipedia, Bruce Matthews.
2. Wikipedia, Aracadia High School.
3. 2012 USC Football Media Guide, p. 134.
4. Wikipedia, Bruce Matthews.

### Clay Matthews

1. Wikipedia, New Tier High School.
2. 1990 Cleveland Browns Media Guide, Clay Matthews .
3. 2012 USC Football Media Guide, p. 132.
4. Wikipedia, Clay Matthews.

### Rey Maualuga

1. Wikipedia, Rey Maualuga.
2. Ibid.
3. Ibid.
4. Ibid.

### Taylor Mays

1. Wikipedia, Taylor Mays.
2. Ibid.
3. Ibid.
4. Ibid.
5. Ibid.
6. Ibid.

### Paul McDonald

1. Wikipedia, Bishop Amat High School.
2. 2012 USC Football Media Guide, p. 133.
3. Ibid.
4. Ibid.
5. Ibid.

### Tim McDonald

1. Wikipedia, Tim McDonald.
2. 2012 USC Football Media Guide, p. 135.
3. Ibid.

### Marlin and Mike McKeever

1. Mt. Carmel Crusaders newsletter 19, no. 1 (October 2011).
2. Ibid.
3. Ibid.
4. 2012 USC Football Media Guide, p. 128.
5. Ibid.
6. Mt. Carmel Crusaders newsletter.
7. Ibid.
8. Ibid.
9. 2012 USC Football Media Guide, p. 128.

### Dan McMillan

1. David Wharton, *USC Football Yesterday & Today*, p. 21.

### Ron Mix

1. John Robinson and Joe Jares, *Conquest: A Cavalcade of USC Football*, p. 43.
2. *Sports Illustrated*, September 16, 1963.
3. *Los Angeles Times*, July 11, 1990, p.7A.
4. Robinson and Jares, p. 43.
5. *Los Angeles Times*, July 11, 1990, p.7A.
6. Ron Smith, *Pro Football's Heroes of the Hall*, p. 249.
7. Ibid.

### Orv Mohler

1. Wikipedia, Alhambra High School.
2. 2012 USC Football Media Guide, p. 125.
3. www.3.gendisasters.com/alabama/dixianabombercrashnov.1949.

### Johnnie Morton

1. *Los Angeles Times*, October 21, 1988.
2. Wikipedia, Johnnie Morton.
3. 2012 USC Football Media Guide, p. 136.
4. Wikipedia, Johnnie Morton.

### Anthony Munoz

1. Joe Horrigan, "Anthony Munoz," *The Coffin Corner*, 20, no. 4 (1998).
2. Ibid.
3. Ibid.
4. Steve Bisheff and Loel Schrader, *Fight On! The Colorful Story of USC Football*, pp. 346–347.
5. Ibid.
6. Wikipedia, Anthony Munoz.

### Carson Palmer

1. Steve Bisheff and Loel Schrader, *Fight On! The Colorful Story of USC Football*, p. 246.
2. Ibid.
3. Ibid., p. 247.
4. Wikipedia, Santa Margarita .
5. www.eaglesfootball.com/alumni/palmer/palmer.php.
6. Bisheff and Schrader, p. 251.
7. Ibid.
8. Wikipedia, Carson Palmer.
9. 2012 USC Football Media Guide, p. 137.
10. Ibid.
11. Wikipedia, Carson Palmer.
12. 2012 USC Football Media Guide, p. 137.

### Rodney Peete

1. Wikipedia, Rodney Peete.
2. 2012 USC Football Media Guide, p. 135.
3. Ibid.

### Erny Pinckert

1. John Robinson and Joe Jares, *Conquest: A Cavalcade of USC Football*, p. 35.
2. www.hickoksports.com/biograph/pinckerternie.shtml.
3. 2012 USC Football Media Guide, p. 126.
4. Ibid.

### Troy Polamalu

1. Wikipedia, Winston, Oregon.
2. www.usctrojans.com/sports/m-footbl/mtt/polamalu_troy00.html.
3. Ibid.
4. Ibid.
5. Ibid.
6. Wikipedia, Troy Polamalu.

### Marvin Powell

1. *Pro Magazine*, October 1981, p. 47.
2. 2012 USC Football Media Guide, p. 132.

### Aaron Rosenberg

1. John Robinson and Joe Jares, *Conquest: A Cavalcade of USC Football*, p. 37.
2. Mal Florence, *The Trojan Heritage: A Pictorial History*, p. 45.
3. 2012 USC Football Media Guide, p. 126.
4. Robinson and Jares, p. 37.
5. Wikipedia, Fairfax High School.

### Tim Rossovich

1. Steve Bisheff and Loel Schrader, *Fight On! The Colorful Story of USC Football*, p. 329.
2. 2012 USC Football Media Guide, p. 130.
3. Ibid.

### Tim Ryan

1. Wikipedia, Oak Grove.
2. 2012 USC Football Media Guide, p. 135.
3. Ibid.
4. Ibid.

### Jim Sears

1. 2012 USC Football Media Guide, p. 127.
2. Steve Bisheff and Loel Schrader, *Fight On! The Colorful Story of USC Football*, pp. 326–327.
3. Jack Clary, *College Football's Greatest Dynasties USC*, p. 50.
4. John Robinson and Joe Jares, *Conquest: A Cavalcade of USC Football*, p. 33.
5. 2013 USC Football Media Guide, p. 129.
6. Ibid.

### Junior Seau

1. Wikipedia, American Samoa.
2. Wikipedia, Junior Seau.
3. Ibid.
4. Steve Bisheff and Loel Schrader, *Fight On! The Colorful Story of USC Football*, p. 342.
5. 2012 USC Football Media Guide, p. 135.
6. Ibid.
7. Wikipedia, Junior Seau.
8. Ibid.
9. Ibid.
10. *The Plain Dealer*, January 11, 2013, p. D-3.
11. Ibid.

### Gus Shaver

1. Wikipedia, Covina.
2. Wikipedia, Gus Shaver.
3. Ibid.
4. Ibid.

### O.J. Simpson

1. Editorial Staff at USC, *A Century of Troy 1888–1988: A Salute to USC Football*, p. 20.
2. Jack Clary, *College Football's Greatest Dynasties USC*, p.36.
3. Editorial Staff at USC, *A Century of Troy 1888–1988: A Salute to USC Football*, p. 20.
4. George Sullivan, Great Running Backs, p. 220.
5. Steve Bisheff and Loel Schrader, *Fight On! The Colorful Story of USC Football*, p. 167.
6. Ibid., pp. 169–170.
7. Ibid., p. 165.
8. 2012 USC Football Media Guide, p. 129.
9. Ibid.
10. Wikipedia, O.J. Simpson.

### Tony Slaton

1. Wikipedia, Hudson Houck.
2. 2012 USC Football Media Guide, p. 134.

### Ernie Smith

1. Mal Florence, *The Trojan Heritage: A Pictorial History*, p. 46.
2. 2012 USC Football Media Guide, p. 126.

### Harry Smith

1. Smithusc.247sports.com/Article/Yesterdays-Trojans-Blackjack-Harry-Smith-671.
2. 2012 USC Football Media Guide, p. 127.
3. Smithusc.247sports.com/Article/Yesterdays-Trojans-Blackjack-Harry-Smith-671.
4. Ibid.

### Lynn Swan

1. www.serrahs.com/page.cfm?p=2541.
2. John Robinson and Joe Jares, *Conquest: A Cavalcade of USC Football*, p. 56.
3. Ibid.
4. 2012 USC Football Media Guide, p. 131.
5. Ibid.

### Brice Taylor

1. http://blackathlete.net/2006/01/trojan-trail-blazer/.
2. Ibid.
3. 2012 USC Football Media Guide, p. 125.
4. Ibid.

### Dennis Thurman

1. Wikipedia, Santa Monica High School.
2. Wikipedia, Dennis Thurman.
3. 2012 USC Football Media Guide, p. 132.
4. Ibid.
5. Ibid.

### Kenechi Udeze

1. Wikipedia, Verbum High School.
2. Wikipedia, Kenechi Udeze.
3. 2012 USC Football Media Guide, p. 137.
4. Wikipedia, Kenechi Udeze.

### Keith Van Horne

1. John Robinson and Joe Jares, *Conquest: A Cavalcade of USC Football*, p. 64.
2. Ibid.

### Irvine "Cotton" Warburton

1. 2012 USC Football Media Guide, p. 126.
2. Wikipedia, San Diego High School.
3. Wikipedia, Cotton Warburton.
4. Ibid.
5. Jack Clary, *College Football's Greatest Dynasties USC*, p.21.
6. 2012 USC Football Media Guide, p. 126.
7. Wikipedia, Cotton Warburton.
8. Ibid.
9. Ibid.
10. 2012 USC Football Media Guide, p. 126.

### Charles White

1. *Los Angeles Times*, December 22, 1999.
2. Ibid.
3. John Robinson and Joe Jares, *Conquest: A Cavalcade of USC Football*, p. 66.
4. Steve Bisheff and Loel Schrader, *Fight On! The Colorful Story of USC Football*, p. 202.
5. David Wharton, *USC Football Yesterday & Today*, p. 76.
6. Bisheff and Schrader, p. 203.
7. Ibid., p. 202.
8. *Sports Illustrated*, September 10, 1979, p. 39.
9. 2012 USC Football Media Guide, p. 133.
10. Ibid.

### LenDale White

1. Wikipedia, LenDale White.
2. Ibid.
3. http://www.usctrojans.com/sports/m-footbl/mtt/white_lendale00.html.
4. Ibid.
5. Ibid.
6. Ibid.
7. Ibid.
8. Wikipedia, LenDale White.
9. Ibid.
10. Ibid.

### Mike Williams

1. Wikipedia, Mike Williams.
2. Steve Bisheff and Loel Schrader, *Fight On! The Colorful Story of USC Football*, p. 341.
3. Ibid.
4. Ibid.
5. Ibid.
6. Ibid.

### Richard Wood

1. www.collegefootballhalloffame/richardwood.
2. Ibid.
3. Ibid.
4. 2012 USC Football Media Guide, p. 131.
5. Ibid.

### Robert Woods

1. http://www.usctrojans.com/sports/m-footbl/mtt/woods_robert00.html.

2. Ibid.
3. Ibid.
4. Ibid.
5. Ibid.
6. Ibid.
7. Ibid.
8. Wikipedia, Robert Woods.

### Ron Yary

1. www.profootballhof.com/history/release.aspx?release_id=345.
2. Wikipedia, Cerritos Junior College.
3. www.profootballhof.com/history/release.aspx?release_id=345.
4. 2012 USC Football Media Guide, p. 129.
5. Ibid.

### Adrian Young

1. Wikipedia, "When Irish Eyes Are Smiling."
2. Wikipedia, Andrew McNally.
3. John Robinson and Joe Jares, *Conquest: A Cavalcade of USC Football*, p. 48.
4. 2012 USC Football Media Guide, p. 129.

### Charles Young

1. Wikipedia, Charles Young.
2. Steve Bisheff and Loel Schrader, *Fight On! The Colorful Story of USC Football*, p. 349.
3. 2012 USC Football Media Guide, p. 130.
4. Ibid.

## *Chapter Three*

All information for this section is from www.fanbase.com and 2013 USC Football Media Guide pp. 156–167.

## *Chapter Four*

### Henry H. Goddard

1. Wikipedia, Henry H. Goddard.
2. Ibid.
3. Ibid.
4. Ibid.
5. Ibid.
6. Ibid.

### Lewis Freeman

1. Wikipedia, Lewis Freeman.
2. Ibid.
3. Ibid.
4. Ibid.
5. Ibid.

### Clair S. Tappaan

1. Wikipedia, Baldwinsville, NY.
2. Wikipedia, Clair S. Tappaan.
3. Ibid.
4. Ibid.

### John Walker

1. Information gathered in email correspondence with Tim Tessalone of USC's Sports Information Office.

### Harvey R. Holmes

1. Wikipedia, Wisconsin Badgers Football History.
2. Wikipedia, Harvey R. Holmes.
3. Ibid.
4. Ibid.
5. Ibid.

### William I. Traeger

1. Wikipedia, Porterville, California .
2. Wikipedia, William I. Traeger.
3. Ibid.
4. Ibid.
5. Ibid.
6. Ibid.
7. Ibid.

### Dean Cromwell

1. Wikipedia, Dean Cromwell.
2. Ibid.
3. Ibid.
4. Ibid.
5. Ibid.

### Ralph Glaze

1. Wikipedia, Ralph Glaze.
2. Ibid.
3. Ibid.
4. Ibid.
5. Ibid.
6. Ibid.

### Elmer C. Henderson

1. Wikipedia, Elmer C. Henderson.
2. Editorial Staff at USC, *A Century of Troy 1888–1988: A Salute to USC Football*, p. 65.
3. Steve Bisheff and Loel Schrader, *Fight On! The Colorful Story of USC Football*, p. 28.
4. John Robinson and Joe Jares, *Conquest: A Cavalcade of USC Football*, p. 18.
5. Bisheff and Schrader, p. 30.
6. Ibid., p. 31.
7. Wikipedia, Elmer C. Henderson.
8. Bisheff and Schrader, p. 31.
9. Wikipedia, Elmer C. Henderson.
10. Ibid.
11. Ibid.

### Howard Jones

1. Wikipedia, Yale Football History Page.
2. Wikipedia, Howard Jones.
3. Ibid.
4. Ibid.
5. Steve Bisheff and Loel Schrader, *Fight On! The Colorful Story of USC Football*, p. 33.
6. Ibid., p. 38.
7. Ibid., p. 34.
8. Ibid.
9. Ibid.
10. Wikipedia, Howard Jones.

### Justin M. "Sam" Barry

1. Wikipedia, Justin "Sam" Barry.
2. Ibid.
3. Ibid.
4. Ibid.
5. Wikipedia, USC Basketball History.
6. 2011–12 USC Basketball Media Guide, History Section.
7. Wikipedia, Justin "Sam" Barry.
8. Steve Bisheff and Loel Schrader, *Fight On! The Colorful Story of USC Football*, p. 95.
9. Ibid., p. 96.
10. Wikipedia, Justin "Sam" Barry.
11. Ibid.
12. Ibid.

### Newell Jeff Cravath

1. Wikipedia, Gavvy Cravath.
2. Wikipedia, Jeff Cravath.
3. Ibid.
4. Ibid.
5. Ibid.
6. Steve Bisheff and Loel Schrader, *Fight On! The Colorful Story of USC Football*, p. 95.
7. *Los Angeles Times*, March 19, 1942, p. 19.
8. Jack Clary, *College Football's Greatest Dynasties USC*, p. 24.
9. John Robinson and Joe Jares, *Conquest: A Cavalcade of USC Football*, p. 24.
10. Ibid.
11. *Los Angeles Times*, December 21, 1950, p. C-1.
12. Wikipedia, Jeff Cravath.
13. Ibid.

### Jesse T. Hill

1. Wikipedia, Corona, California.
2. Wikipedia, Jess Hill.
3. Ibid.
4. Ibid.
5. Ibid.
6. Ibid.
7. Ibid.
8. Wikipedia, Dean Cromwell.
9. Steve Bisheff and Loel Schrader, *Fight On! The Colorful Story of USC Football*, p. 100.
10. *Los Angeles Times*, February 1, 1951, p. C-1.
11. Jack Clary, *College Football's Greatest Dynasties USC*, p. 28.
12. Ibid.
13. Bisheff and Schrader, p. 102.
14. Ibid.
15. Ibid., pp. 102–103.
16. http://www.riversidesporthalloffame.com/jess-hill/.
17. Wikipedia, Jess Hill.

### Don R. Clark

1. *Los Angeles Times*, August 8, 1989, p. 8.
2. Wikipedia, Don R. Clark.
3. Ibid.
4. Ibid.
5. Ibid.
6. Richard J. Shmelter, *Raiders Encyclopedia*, p. 228.
7. *Los Angeles Times*, February 5, 1957, p. C-1.
8. Ibid., August 8, 1989, p. 8.
9. Wikipedia, Pac-12 page.
10. John McKay with Jim Perry, *McKay: A Coach's Story*, p. 72.
11. *Los Angeles Times*, August 8, 1989, p. 8.
12. Ibid.

### John McKay

1. John McKay with Jim Perry, *McKay: A Coach's Story*, p. 28.
2. Ibid.
3. Ibid., p. 37.
4. Ibid., p. 27.
5. Ibid., p. 38.
6. Ibid., p. 39.
7. Ibid., p. 28.
8. Ibid.
9. Ibid., p. 40.
10. Ibid., p. 41.
11. Ibid., pp. 44–45.
12. Ibid., p. 46.
13. Ibid., p. 47.
14. Ibid., pp. 59–60.
15. Ibid., p. 63.
16. Ibid., p. 69.
17. Ibid., p. 70.
18. Ibid.
19. Ibid.
20. Ibid., p. 71.
21. Ibid., p. 72.
22. Steve Bisheff and Loel Schrader, *Fight On! The Colorful Story of USC Football*, p. 128.
23. Wikipedia, I-Formation.
24. 2010 USC Football Media Guide, p. 124.
25. Wikipedia, John McKay.
26. Jack Clary, *Great College Football Coaches*, p. 91.
27. Ibid., p. 90.
28. Bisheff and Schrader, p. 131.
29. Clary, p. 90.
30. Bisheff and Schrader, p. 127.
31. Ibid., p. 136.
32. Ibid., p. 135.
33. Ibid., p. 127.
34. Wikipedia, John McKay.
35. Ibid.
36. Ibid.

### John Robinson

1. *Sports Illustrated*, October 26, 1987.
2. Ibid.
3. Steve Bisheff and Loel Schrader, *Fight On! The Colorful Story of USC Football*, p. 189.
4. Ibid., p. 190.
5. Ibid., p. 191.
6. Ibid., p. 187.
7. Ibid., p. 188.
8. Ibid.
9. Ibid., p. 187.
10. Ibid., p. 189.
11. Ibid., p. 191.
12. Ibid., p. 192.
13. Ibid., p. 193.
14. Ibid., p. 196.
15. Ibid., p. 198.
16. *Los Angeles Times*, December 18, 1997, p. 1.

### Ted Tollner

1. http://mustangdaily.net/remember-the-mustangs-the-story-of-the-1960-football-team/.
2. Ibid.
3. Ibid.
4. Ibid.
5. http://goaztecs.cstv.com/sports/m-footbl/mtt/tollner_ted00.html.
6. Wikipedia, Woodside High School.

7. http://goaztecs.cstv.com/sports/m-footbl/mtt/tollner_ted00.html.
8. Steve Bisheff and Loel Schrader, *Fight On! The Colorful Story of USC Football*, p. 223.
9. Ibid., p. 224.
10. Ibid.
11. Ibid.
12. Ibid.
13. Ibid., p. 225.
14. *Los Angeles Times*, November 26, 1986, p. 4.
15. Wikipedia, Ted Tollner.

### Larry Smith

1. Wikipedia, Larry Smith.
2. Wikipedia, Bowling Green Football History.
3. Wikipedia, Larry Smith.
4. Ibid.
5. Ibid.
6. Steve Bisheff and Loel Schrader, *Fight On! The Colorful Story of USC Football*, p. 225.
7. Ibid., p. 226.
8. Wikipedia, Larry Smith.
9. Bisheff and Schrader, pp. 226–227.
10. Ibid.
11. Ibid., p. 227.
12. Ibid.
13. Ibid.
14. Wikipedia, Larry Smith.
15. Bisheff and Schrader, p. 228.
16. Ibid.
17. Wikipedia, Larry Smith.

### Paul Hackett

1. http://www.usctrojans.com/sports/m-footbl/mtt/hackett_paul00.html.
2. Ibid.
3. Ibid.
4. Ibid.
5. Ibid.
6. Wikipedia, Joe Roth.
7. http://www.usctrojans.com/sports/m-footbl/mtt/hackett_paul00.html.
8. Ibid.
9. Ibid.
10. Ibid.
11. Steve Bisheff and Loel Schrader, *Fight On! The Colorful Story of USC Football*, p. 231.
12. Ibid.
13. Ibid.
14. Ibid., p. 232.
15. Ibid.
16. Wikipedia, Paul Hackett.
17. Ibid.

### Pete Carroll

1. Wikipedia, Pete Carroll.
2. Ibid.
3. http://www.usctrojans.com/sports/m-footbl/mtt/carroll_pete00.html.
4. *Los Angeles Times*, April 9, 2009, p. C-7.
5. Wikipedia, Pete Carroll.
6. Ibid.
7. Ibid.
8. Ibid.
9. Ibid.
10. Ibid.
11. Ibid.
12. Ibid.
13. Ibid.
14. Ibid.
15. Ibid.
16. Steve Bisheff and Loel Schrader, *Fight On! The Colorful Story of USC Football*, p. 238.
17. Ibid.
18. Ibid., p. 239.
19. Ibid., p. 237.
20. Ibid., p. 239.
21. Ibid.
22. Ibid.
23. Ibid., p. 241.
24. Wikipedia, Pete Carroll.
25. Bisheff and Schrader, p. 242.
26. Ibid., p. 243.
27. Ibid., p. 268.
28. Wikipedia, Pete Carroll.
29. Ibid.
30. Ibid.

### Lane Kiffin

1. Richard J. Shmelter, *Raiders Encyclopedia*, p. 249.
2. Ibid.
3. Ibid.
4. Ibid.
5. Ibid.
6. Ibid.
7. Ibid.
8. Ibid.
9. Wikipedia, Lane Kiffin.
10. Ibid.
11. Ibid.
12. Ibid.
13. http://www.usctrojans.com/sports/m-footbl/mtt/kiffin_lane01.html.
14. *Los Angeles Times*, Sept. 30, 2013, p. A-1.

## *Chapter Five*

### Giles "Super Fan" Pellerin

1. http://www.usctrojans.com/trads/usc-superfan.html.
2. Steve Bisheff and Loel Schrader, *Fight On! The Colorful Story of USC Football*, p. 235.
3. http://www.usctrojans.com/trads/usc-superfan.html.
4. Ibid.
5. Ibid.
6. Bisheff and Schrader, p. 234.
7. Ibid.
8. Ibid., p. 235.
9. http://www.usctrojans.com/trads/usc-superfan.html.
10. Wikipedia, Giles Pellerin.
11. Bisheff and Schrader, p. 235.
12. http://www.usctrojans.com/trads/usc-superfan.html.

### The Trojan Nickname

1. *Los Angeles Times*, February 24, 2012, p. C-1.
2. Ibid.
3. Ibid.
4. Ibid.

### Team Colors

1. 2010 USC Football Media Guide, p. 200.

### Tailback U

1. Wikipedia, I-Formation.
2. John McKay with Jim Perry, *McKay: A Coach's Story*, p. 171.
3. Steve Bisheff and Loel Schrader, *Fight On! The Colorful Story of USC Football*, p. 137.

### USC–Notre Dame Rivalry

1. Wikipedia, Notre Dame Football History.
2. Ibid.
3. Wikipedia, USC–Notre Dame Football Rivalry.
4. Ibid.
5. Ibid.
6. Ibid.
7. Wikipedia, Battle of Bataan.
8. Wikipedia, Mario Tonelli.
9. Wikipedia, Battle of Bataan.
10. http://news.nd.edu/news/6448-mario-g-motts-tonelli-1916-2003-ex-irish-star-survived-bataan/.
11. Ibid.
12. Ibid.
13. Ibid.
14. Ibid.

### USC-UCLA Rivalry

1. http://www.spotlight.ucla.edu/special-guests/ed-dickson_founder/.
2. Ibid.
3. Wikipedia, UCLA Football History.
4. Wikipedia, William Henry Spaulding.
5. Wikipedia, UCLA History.
6. Steve Springer and Mike Arkush, *60 Years of USC-UCLA Football*, p. 40.
7. Wikipedia, Henry "Red" Sanders.

### Conference Affiliation

1. Steve Bisheff and Loel Schrader, *Fight On! The Colorful Story of USC Football*, p. 28.
2. Wikipedia, Pacific Coast Conference.
3. Bisheff and Schrader, p. 31.
4. Wikipedia, Pacific Coast Conference.
5. Wikipedia, Pac-12 Conference.

### USC Bowl Game Appearances

1. http://www.usctrojans.com/trads/usc-rose.html.

### The Hollywood Connection to USC

1. Steve Bisheff and Loel Schrader, *Fight On! The Colorful Story of USC Football*, p. 83.
2. Steven Travers, *The USC Trojans College Football's All-Time Greatest Dynasty*, pp. 28–34.
3. Wikipedia, Ward Bond.
4. Bisheff and Schrader, p. 82.
5. Ibid., p. 86.
6. http://www.legacy.com/obituaries/lbpresstelegram/obituary.aspx?pid=127791413#fbLoggedOut.
7. IMDB—Cotton Warburton.
8. IMDB—Nate Barragar.
9. IMDB—Jesse Hibbs.
10. IMDB—Aaron Rosenberg.
11. *Los Angeles Times*, July 8, 1990.
12. IMDB—Frank Gifford.
13. Wikipedia, Ron Miller Disney Productions.
14. IMDB—Russ Saunders.
15. IMDB—Mike Henry.
16. Wikipedia, O.J. Simpson.
17. IMDB—Tim Rossovich.
18. IMDB—Allan Graf.
19. Wikipedia, Lynn Swann.
20. IMDB—Anthony Davis.
21. IMDB—Rodney Peete.
22. http://louferrignojr.com/.
23. Bisheff and Schrader, pp. 85–86.
24. Ibid., p. 86.

### The Spirit of Troy (USC Marching Band)

1. 2010 USC Football Media Guide, p. 201.

### Fight On

1. http://www.usctrojans.com/trads/usc-songs.html.

### Conquest

1. Wikipedia, Alfred Newman—Composer.
2. 2010 USC Football Media Guide, p. 201.

### Song Girls

1. http://sait.usc.edu/recsports/spirit/song/.

### Yell Leaders

1. http://sait.usc.edu/recsports/spirit/yell/about/history.html.
2. Ibid.

### Spirit Leaders

1. http://sait.usc.edu/recsports/spirit/leaders/.

### Los Angeles Memorial Coliseum (and other stadiums in USC football history)

1. Richard J. Shmelter, *Raiders Encyclopedia*, p. 307.
2. 2010 USC Football Media Guide, p. 97.
3. Ibid.
4. Ibid.
5. Ibid.
6. Ibid.
7. Ibid.
8. Ibid.
9. Ibid.

### George Tirebiter

1. Wikipedia, George Tirebiter.

### Traveler

1. 2010 USC Football Media Guide, p. 199.

### Tommy Trojan

1. *Daily Trojan*, March 16, 1962, p. 1.
2. Wikipedia, Tommy Trojan.
3. *Daily Trojan*, March 16, 1962, p. 1.
4. 2010 USC Football Media Guide, p. 199.
5. Wikipedia, Tommy Trojan.
6. 2010 USC Football Media Guide, p. 199.
7. *Daily Trojan*, March 16, 1962, p. 1.
8. 2010 USC Football Media Guide, p. 199.

### Shillelagh

1. 2010 USC Football Media Guide, p. 200.

### Victory Bell

1. 2010 USC Football Media Guide, p. 200.
2. Steve Springer and Mike Arkush, *60 Years of USC-UCLA Football*, p. 72.
3. 2010 USC Football Media Guide, p. 200.
4. Ibid.
5. Ibid.

## *Chapter Six*

All information from this section came from 2013 USC Football Media Guide, pp. 127–153.

# Bibliography


## *Books*

Bisheff, Steve, and Loel Schrader. *Fight On! The Colorful Story of USC Football*. Nashville: Cumberland House, 2006.
Clary, Jack. *College Football's Great Dynasties USC*. New York: Smithmark, 1991.
_____. *Great College Football Coaches*. New York: Gallery Books, 1990.
Cromartie, Bill, and Jody Brown. *Notre Dame vs. USC: The Glamor Game*. Nashville: Ritledge Hill Press, 1989.
Florence, Mal. *The Trojan Heritage: A Pictorial History of USC Football*. Virginia Beach: JCP Corp. of Virginia, 1980.
Heimann, Jim. *Sins of the City: The Real Los Angeles Noir*. San Francisco: Chronicle Books, 1999.
Lombardo, John. *Raiders Forever*. Lincolnwood, IL: Contemporary Books, 2001.
McKay, John, with Jim Perry. *McKay: A Coach's Story*. New York: Atheneum, 1974.
Pitt, Leonard, and Dale Pitt. *Los Angeles A to Z: An Encyclopedia of the City and County*. Berkeley: University of California Press, 1997.
Robinson, John, and Joe Jares. *Conquest: A Cavalcade of USC Football*. Santa Monica: Arthur Neff, 1981.
Shmelter, Richard, J. *The Raiders Encyclopedia*. Jefferson, NC: McFarland, 2011.
Smith, Ron. *Pro Football's Heroes of the Hall*. St. Louis: The Sporting News, 2003.
Springer, Steve, and Michael Arkush. *60 Years of USC-UCLA Football*. Stamford, CT: Longmeadow, 1991.
Travers, Steven. *The USC Trojans: College Football's All-Time Greatest Dynasty*. Lanham, MD: Taylor Trade, 2006.
University of Southern California Department of Athletics. *A Century of Troy 1888–1988: A Salute to USC Football*. Chapel Hill: Four Corners Press, 1988.
Wharton, David. *USC Football: Yesterday & Today*. Lincolnwood, IL: Publications International, 2009.

## *Newspapers & Periodicals*

*Cleveland Plain Dealer*
*Daily Trojan* (newspaper for the University of Southern California)
*Los Angeles Times*
*Sports Illustrated*

## *Yearbooks*

El Rodeo Yearbook (USC) 1908 to 1997

## *Web Sites*

www.trojans.com
Wikipedia

# INDEX


Affholter, Erik 125, 127, 129, 130
Allen, Marcus 107, 109, 110, 112, 113, 114, 115, 116, 193–194
Aloha Bowl 124
Arizona State University 107, 112–113, 117, 119, 120, 122, 125, 130, 135, 138, 140, 148, 151, 153, 155, 157, 158, 159, 161, 163, 165, 168, 170, 174, 178, 179, 183, 185, 187, 191
Arnett, Jon 62, 63, 64, 65, 66, 194
Athletic Association of Western Universities (AAWU) 298
Auburn University 126, 162, 165

Badgro, Morris 23, 24
Baker, Johnny 31, 194–195
Baker, Roy 19, 20, 195
Bame, Damon 195
Banks, Chip 196
Barkley, Matt 181, 182, 183, 184, 185, 186, 187, 188, 189, 190, 191, 192, 196, 197
Barragar, Nate 300
Barry, Justin "Sam" 44, 268–269
Battle, Mike 197–198
Baylor University 70–71, 122, 124, 145
Beathard, Pete 72, 73, 74, 75, 76
Bedsole, Hal 73, 75, 76, 198
Bell, Ricky 99, 100, 101, 102, 103, 198–199
Bescos, Julie 300
Bickett, Duane 199–200
Bird, Owen 293
Bluebonnet Bowl 106
Bond, Ward 299
Booty, John David 173, 174, 175, 176, 177, 178
Boselli, Tony 200
Boston College 127, 129, 183–184
Bovard Field 304
Bow, Clara 302
Bradford, Allen 173, 174, 177, 183, 185
Brigham Young University 165, 167
Brown, Tay 200
Brown, Willie 73, 74, 75, 76, 200–201
Bryant, Paul "Bear" 89, 90
Budde, Brad 201
Bush, Reggie 165, 166, 167, 168, 169, 170, 171, 172, 173, 201–203

Cal Tech 8, 10, 18, 20, 21, 23, 26
Caley, Elwin 10
Callanan, George 46, 47, 48
Carmichael, Al 57, 58, 59, 60
Carrier, Mark 203
Carroll, Pete 161, 163, 171, 184, 197, 202, 217, 286–290
Chandler, Bob 84, 85, 86, 88, 89, 90
Christmas Festival Bowl 22–23
Citrus Bowl 126
Claiborne, Chris 204
Clark, Don 273–274
Cleary, Paul 204
Clemson University 80
Cody, Shaun 204–205
Colbert, Keary 163, 165, 167
College of the Pacific 34, 35, 38, 46, 47, 49
Colorado State University 167
*Conquest* 303
Conway, Curtis 135, 138, 140, 142
Cotton Bowl 146–147
Craig, Gerald 13, 14
Cravath, Newell "Jeff" 24, 25, 26, 57, 269–271
Cromwell, Dean 12, 14, 263–264
Crutcher, Fred 116, 118, 120, 122, 123
Cunningham, Sam 89, 90, 91, 93, 94, 205

Dandoy, Aramis 59, 61, 62, 63
Danelo, Mario 170, 171, 172, 173, 174, 175, 176
Davis, Anthony 92, 93, 94, 95, 96, 97, 98, 99, 205–206, 301
Davis, Clarence 86, 87, 89, 90, 206–207
Davis, David 35, 36, 37
Dean, Charley 16, 17, 18, 19, 207
Del Rio, Jack 207
Diggs, Shelton 98, 102
Dorsey, Gene 21
Drury, Morley 23, 24, 25, 26, 27, 207–208
Duffield, Marshall 27, 28, 29, 30, 300
Duke University 40, 73, 99
Elliott, Howard 23, 24, 25, 26
Ellis, Sedrick 208
Emerald Bowl 183–184
Ervins, Ricky 129, 130, 132, 133, 134, 135
Evans, Vince 97, 99, 100, 101, 102, 103

Ferraro, John 208–209
Ferrigno, Lou, Jr. 302
Fertig, Craig 74, 75, 76, 77, 78
Fiesta Bowl 116
*Fight On* 302–303
Florida State University 153, 155
Ford, Cole 138, 139, 141, 142, 147
Foster, Ray 209
Freedom Bowl 141–142, 144–145
Freeman, Lewis 261
Fresno State University 141–142, 172

Gable, C.J. 173, 174, 175, 176, 180
Garrett, Mike 75, 76, 77, 78, 79, 209–210
George Tirebiter 305
Georgia Tech 72, 87, 95, 192
Gifford, Frank 54, 56, 57, 58, 210–211, 300
Glaze, Ralph 14, 264–265
Goddard, Henry 260–261
Goux, Marv 211–212
Graf, Allen 301
Gunn, Jimmy 212

Hackett, Paul 285–286
Haden, Pat 92, 93, 94, 95, 97, 98, 99, 212–213
Halas, George 194
Hardy, Jim 46, 47, 48, 55
Henderson, Elmer "Gloomy Gus" 16, 17, 18, 20, 21, 22, 265–266
Henry, Mike 301
Hertel, Rob 102, 103, 104, 105, 106
Heywood, Ralph 44, 46
Hibbs, Jess 213, 300
Hill, Jesse "Jess" 28, 57, 70, 211, 271–273
Holmes, Harvey 262

Jarrett, Dwayne 168, 169, 170, 171, 172, 173, 174, 175, 176, 213–214
Jeter, Gary 214
John Hancock Bowl 137
Johnson, Keyshawn 145, 146, 147, 148, 150, 214–215
Johnson, Rob 140, 141, 142, 143, 144, 145, 146, 147
Johnson, Stafon 176, 178, 179, 180, 181, 182
Jones, Howard 23, 24, 25, 26, 27, 30, 38, 42, 43, 100, 266–268, 295, 298, 299
Jones, Jimmy 86, 87, 88, 89, 90, 91, 92
Jordan, Frank 104, 105, 106, 107, 108

Kaer, Mort 21, 23, 24, 25, 26, 215
Kalil, Ryan 215–216
Kansas State University 161, 162–163
Kelly, Kareem 157, 158, 159, 161
Kiffin, Lane 184, 188, 197, 290–291
Knight, Ryan 120, 121, 122, 123, 124, 125
Koch, Desmond 216
Krueger, Al 39, 40, 41, 42, 43

Langley, Laurence 38
Lansdell, Grenville 38, 39, 40, 41, 42, 216–217
Laraneta, Manuel 24, 25
Las Vegas Bowl 162
Lee, Marqise 187, 188, 190, 191
Leinart, Matt 165, 166, 167, 168, 169, 170, 171, 172, 173, 217–218
Liberty Bowl 101
Limahelu, Chris 95, 96, 97, 98, 99
Livernash, Leonard 13, 14
Long Beach Poly High School 200, 203
Los Angeles Memorial Coliseum 304
Lott, Ronnie 218–219
Louisiana State University 109–110, 120
Louisiana Tech University 158

MacKenzie, Malaefou 153, 162
Malette, Frank 13, 14, 15, 16, 19, 219
Marinovich, Todd 132, 133, 134, 135, 136, 137

Mater Dei High School 196, 217
Matthews, Bruce 219
Matthews, Clay 219–220
Maualuga, Rey 220
Mays, Taylor 220–221
McCardle, Mickey 45, 46, 50, 51
McCullough, Sultan 159, 160, 161, 162
McDonald, Paul 107, 108, 109, 110, 111, 221–222
McDonald, Tim 222
McKay, J.K. 92, 95, 96, 98, 99, 212
McKay, John 71, 72, 74, 77, 81, 82, 86, 91, 100, 101, 198, 199, 200, 210, 212, 274–278
McKeever, Marlin 222–223
McKeever, Mike 222–223
McKnight, Joe 177, 179, 181, 182
McMillan, Dan 223
Memphis State University 138
Michigan State University 75, 77, 82, 92, 107, 127, 128–129, 137
Miller, Ron 300–301
Mix, Ron 223–224
Mohler, Orv 29, 30, 31, 32, 224
Morton, Chad 154, 155, 156, 157, 158
Morton, Johnnie 136, 139, 140, 141, 142, 143, 144, 224–225
Munoz, Anthony 225

Nave, Doyle 38, 40, 41, 42
Nelsen, Bill 71, 72, 73, 74
Northwestern University 59, 62, 84, 86, 149–150

Occidental College 8, 11, 12, 13, 16, 17, 18, 19, 24, 27, 28, 33, 34
Ohio State University 38, 39, 44, 45, 50, 51, 53, 54, 63, 69–70, 71, 76, 77, 85–86, 94, 96–97, 98–99, 111–112, 121–122, 132, 135, 179, 182
Orange Bowl 169–170
Oregon State University 13, 15, 19, 22, 24, 25, 26, 27, 28, 29, 31, 32, 33, 34, 35, 36, 38, 39, 41, 43, 44, 49, 50, 51, 53, 57, 59, 61, 63, 65, 67, 68, 69, 71, 76, 78, 80, 83, 85, 86–87, 92, 95, 97, 99, 102, 103, 107, 109, 114, 117, 118, 122, 127, 130, 133, 135–136, 143, 145, 148, 150, 154, 155, 157, 159, 161, 163, 166, 168, 174, 177–178, 179, 182, 185
Otton, Brad 146, 147, 148, 149, 150, 151, 152, 153

Pacific Athletic Conference (Pac-8) 298
Pacific Athletic Conference (Pac-10) 298
Pacific Athletic Conference (Pac-12) 297, 298
Pacific Coast Conference (PCC) 297–298
Palmer, Carson 156, 157, 159, 160, 161, 163, 164, 225–227
Peete, Rodney 123, 124, 125, 126, 127, 128, 129, 130, 131, 227, 301–302
Pellerin, Giles "Super Fan" 156, 292–293
Penn State University 20, 116, 135, 138, 142, 145, 150, 159, 181
Pinckert, Erny 29, 30, 31, 227–228
Poi Bowl 36
Polamalu, Troy 228
Pomona College 9, 10, 11, 12, 13, 15, 16, 17, 18, 19, 20, 21, 23
Powell, Marvin 228–229
Powers, Jim 51, 52, 53, 54, 55
Purdue University 81, 99, 101, 155

Redlands College 12, 13, 16
Rice University 51, 53, 90
Roberts, C.R. 64, 65, 66
Robertson, Bobby 299–300
Robinson, John 101, 102, 103, 104, 118, 142, 149, 153, 193, 214, 278–281
Rockne, Knute 25, 29, 30, 31, 32, 294, 295
Rose Bowl Game 20, 29, 31–32, 33, 40–41, 42–43, 47, 48, 49, 52, 60, 63, 75, 81, 83–84, 85–86, 88, 94, 96–7, 98–99, 103, 108–109, 111–112, 121–122, 128–129, 131, 134, 149–150, 164, 166–167, 172–173, 175–176, 178–179, 181
Rosenberg, Aaron 229, 300
Rossovich, Tim 229, 301
Royster, Mazio 132, 135, 136, 138
Rucker, Drean 165
Ryan, Tim 229–230

St. Mary's College 14, 15, 22, 24, 27, 33, 48, 49
Salisbury, Sean 116, 117, 118, 119, 120, 122
Sanchez, Mark 177, 179, 180, 181
Sanders, Henry "Red" 297
San Diego State University 140, 155, 157
San Jose State University 147, 159, 161, 181
Santa Clara University 23, 23, 26
Saunders, Russ 27, 28, 29, 51, 65, 301
Schindler, Ambrose 37, 38, 39, 41, 42, 300
Sears, Jim 56, 57, 59, 60, 230
Seau, Junior 230–231
Shaver, Gus 28, 29, 30, 31, 32, 231–232
Sherman, Rod 77, 78, 80, 81
Shillelagh 306
Simmons, Jeff 116, 117, 118
Simmrin, Randy 99, 101, 103, 104, 105, 106
Simpson, O.J. 82, 83, 84, 85, 86, 232–233, 301
Slaton, Tony 233
Smith, Ernie 234
Smith, Harry 234
Smith, Larry 127, 282–285
Song Girls 303
Southern Methodist University 72, 73
Soward, R. Jay 150, 151, 153, 154, 155, 156, 157
Spirit Leaders 304
Spirit of Troy Marching Band 302
Stanford University 11, 16, 17, 19, 21, 23, 25, 26, 27, 28, 30, 31, 32, 33, 34, 35, 37, 38, 40, 42, 43, 44, 45, 50, 52, 53, 54, 56, 58, 59, 61, 63, 64, 66, 67, 68–69, 70, 71, 73, 74, 76, 77, 78, 80, 82, 84, 87, 91, 92, 96, 98, 100, 102, 105, 107, 110, 113, 114–115, 117, 119, 120, 122, 125, 127–128, 129, 133, 135, 138, 140, 143–144, 145, 148, 151, 154, 156, 158, 159, 161, 163, 165, 168, 171–172, 174–175, 177, 180, 183, 185, 188, 189–190
Strother, Deon 138, 139, 140, 142
Sun Bowl 156–157, 192
Swann, Lynn 91, 92, 94, 95, 234–235, 301
Syracuse University 22, 135, 187, 189

Tailback U 294
Tappaan, Clair 261–262
Tatupu, Mosi 101, 105
Taylor, Brice 235
Team Colors (USC) 293
Texas A&M 77, 101, 106
Texas Christian University 57, 58, 62, 71, 103–104, 156–157
Texas Tech University 106, 109, 146–147
Thurman, Dennis 235–236
Tollner, Ted 118, 281–282
Tommy Trojan 305–306
Tonelli, Mario "Motts" 295–296
Traeger, William 263
Traveler (USC mascot) 305
Trojan nickname 293
Tulane University 31, 45, 51
Turner, Patrick 173, 177, 178, 179, 180
Tyler, Marc 184, 185, 187

Udeze, Kenechi 236
United States Military Academy at West Point (Army) 58, 59
United States Naval Academy 54, 56, 74
University of Alabama 39, 49, 88, 89, 90, 104, 106, 124
University of Arizona 15, 19, 21, 22, 23, 27, 110, 113, 114, 117, 120, 125, 128, 129, 133, 135, 139, 140, 143, 146, 147, 151, 159, 161, 166, 168, 170–171, 174, 177, 180, 183, 185, 187, 190–191
University of Arkansas 92, 95, 97, 170, 173
University of California–Berkeley 14, 15, 16, 17, 18, 19, 21, 22, 25, 26, 27, 28, 30, 31, 32, 33, 34, 35, 37, 38, 40, 41, 43, 44, 45, 46, 48, 49, 50, 51, 53, 54, 56, 57, 59, 61, 62–63, 64, 66, 67, 68, 70, 71, 73, 74, 76, 77, 79, 80–81, 83, 85, 87, 91, 93, 96, 97–98, 100, 102, 105, 107, 110, 113, 115, 117, 119, 120, 123, 125, 127, 130, 132–133, 135, 139, 140, 143, 145, 148, 150–151, 153, 155, 158, 159, 161, 163, 165, 168, 172, 175, 178, 180, 182, 185, 187, 190
University of California–Los Angeles (UCLA) 28, 29, 37, 39, 40, 42, 43, 44, 46, 47, 48, 49, 50, 52, 53, 54, 56, 58, 59–60, 61, 63, 64, 66, 67, 69, 70, 71, 73, 74, 76, 77, 79, 81, 83, 85, 87–88, 89, 92, 93, 96, 98, 100, 101, 102, 105–106, 107–108, 111, 113–114, 115–116, 117, 119, 120–121, 123–124, 125, 128, 130, 133–134, 136, 139, 140–141, 144, 146, 148, 151–152, 154–155, 156, 158, 159–160, 161, 163–164, 166, 169, 172, 175, 178, 180–181, 183, 186, 188–189, 191–192
University of Colorado 26, 75, 76, 77, 159, 162, 188, 190
University of Florida 116, 118
University of Georgia 31, 34, 71
University of Hawaii 30, 36, 108, 157, 165, 170, 184, 189
University of Houston 142, 147, 150
University of Idaho 20, 21, 22, 23, 25, 28, 29, 176
University of Illinois 35, 37, 41, 43, 73, 74, 90–92, 122, 124, 132, 150, 178–179
University of Indiana 61, 83, 84, 114, 116
University of Iowa 24, 56, 72, 74, 97, 99, 101–102, 164
University of Kansas 118
University of Miami, Florida 80, 84
University of Michigan 52, 67, 68, 88, 103, 108–109, 131, 134, 166, 167, 175–176
University of Minnesota 61, 64, 78, 84, 109, 112, 184, 186–187
University of Missouri 22, 101, 103
University of Montana 23, 25, 31, 35, 45
University of Nebraska 86, 173, 176–177
University of Nevada–Las Vegas (UNLV) 153
University of Nevada (Reno) 17, 19, 21, 22, 29
University of North Carolina 68, 142
University of Notre Dame 25, 26, 28, 29, 33, 35, 36, 37, 39, 40, 42, 43, 44, 45, 50, 51, 52, 53–54, 55, 56–57, 58, 60, 61–62, 63, 64–65, 66, 67–68, 69, 70, 72, 73, 74, 75–76, 77–78, 79, 81, 82–83, 85, 87, 89–90, 91, 93–94, 95–96, 98, 100, 102–103, 104–105, 108, 110, 114, 115, 118, 119, 121, 123, 125–126, 127, 130–131, 133, 136–137, 138–139, 141, 143, 146, 148, 152–153, 153–154, 156, 157–158, 160, 161, 164, 165–166, 168–169, 171, 175, 177, 180, 182, 185–186, 187–188, 192
University of Oklahoma 75, 77, 90–95, 114, 116, 129, 140, 169, 170
University of Oregon 14, 31, 32,

33, 35, 37, 38, 40, 41, 43, 44, 45, 50, 53, 54–55, 56, 61, 62, 64, 66, 67, 68, 83, 84–85, 90–91, 93, 95, 97, 100, 101, 104, 106, 113, 116–117, 120, 124, 125, 127, 129, 138, 140, 143, 145, 154, 155–156, 157, 159, 161, 163, 170, 175, 177, 179, 182–183, 185, 188, 191
University of Pittsburgh (Pitt) 29, 32, 34, 36, 62, 67, 69, 73, 79, 97
University of South Carolina 112, 118
University of Southern California Bowl Game Appearances 298
University of Tennessee 42, 48, 112, 114
University of Texas 64, 65, 80, 82, 172–173
University of Utah 14, 16, 17, 23, 32, 53, 144–145, 162, 187, 190
University of Virginia 179, 184
University of Washington 21, 27, 28, 30, 31, 32, 34, 35, 36, 37, 38, 40, 42, 43, 44, 45, 47, 48, 49, 50, 51, 53, 54, 56, 57, 59, 61, 63, 64, 65, 67, 69, 70, 71, 73, 74, 76, 77, 78, 80, 83, 84, 87, 91–92, 93, 96, 98, 100, 102, 105, 107, 111, 113, 115, 119, 120, 123, 124, 127, 130, 132, 135, 139, 140, 144, 145, 148, 151, 154, 156, 161, 163, 166, 168, 171, 174, 177, 180, 182, 184–185, 188, 190
University of Wisconsin 60, 64, 65, 75, 78, 80
University of Wyoming 79
USC–Notre Dame rivalry 294–296
USC–UCLA rivalry 296–297
Utah State University 15, 27, 30, 120, 132

Van Horne, Keith 236–237
Victory Bell 306–307
Virginia Tech University 167

Walker, John 262
Warburton, Irvine "Cotton" 32, 33, 34, 237, 300
Washington, Chauncey 173, 174, 175, 177, 178
Washington, Delon 145, 148, 151, 153, 154
Washington State University 19, 20, 24, 26, 27, 29, 30, 31, 32, 33, 34, 35, 37, 38, 39, 43, 44, 45, 50, 51, 54, 56, 57, 59, 60, 62, 64, 66, 67, 68, 82, 87, 91, 93, 95, 97, 99–100, 102, 104, 110, 115, 118–119, 120, 123, 125, 127, 132, 135, 138, 140, 142–143, 145–146, 148, 151, 153, 155, 158, 159, 163, 166, 168, 171, 174, 177, 179–180, 182, 184
Wayne, John 298–299
Wellman, Gary 132, 134, 135, 136
West Virginia University 70
White, Charles 102, 103, 104, 105, 106, 107, 108, 109, 110, 111, 112, 237–239
White, LenDale 165, 166, 167, 168, 170, 171, 172, 173, 239–240
Whittier College 8, 10, 11, 12, 13, 14, 16, 19, 22, 23, 24, 33, 34
Williams, Damian 182, 183, 184
Williams, Don 25, 26, 27, 28
Williams, Mike 163, 164, 165, 166, 240–241
Wittek, Max 192
Wood, Richard 92, 241
Woods, Robert 184, 185, 186, 187, 188, 189, 190, 191, 192, 241–242

Yary, Ron 242–243
Yell Leaders 303–304
Young, Adrian 243
Young, Charles 243